•Lovebirds, •Cockatiels, •Budgerigars:

Behavior and Evolution

To Marisa T. Garcia,
Florence Kaplan,
Betty Kappe

•Lovebirds, •Cockatiels, •Budgerigars:

Behavior and Evolution

J. Lee Kavanau
University of California at Los Angeles

Science Software Systems, Inc.
Los Angeles, California

ISBN #0-937292-03-6

Library of Congress Catalogue Card Number 85-062124

Published in the United States of America by Science Software Systems, Inc.

INTRODUCTION

BIRDS

Throughout the ages birds have attracted Man's keenest attention. Aves has become both the best-known class of organisms and the one for which our knowledge of distribution is most extensive (103, 486). Man also has been more susceptible to the charms of birds than to those of any other creature. "Professional ornithologists usually have been captivated by birds long before they thought of themselves as biologists, in this respect they differ from their colleagues, few of whom, for example, came to science through their love of fruit flies or rats" (1,256).

Even Old Stone Age Man found birds to be fascinating, as cave decorations near Montignac in France abundantly testify (1,287). Prehistoric inhabitants of the Sahara frequently depicted Ostriches (*Struthio camelus*) on rocks, and the Egyptians and Romans raised the huge birds in captivity. Birds' vivid colors, beauty of form and plumage, grace of flight, melody of voice, lovely songs, and lively, varied behavior, have been extolled by poets and other writers ever since the times of the Greeks (155, 174, 189). Both Chaucer's and Shakespeare's works have numerous references to avian lore. The first printed book on birds in 1544 by William Turner was a commentary on the birds of Aristotle and Pliny (see 1,287). The Rock Dove or Rock Pigeon (*Columba livia*) might possibly be the oldest of domestic animals, having been selectively bred and employed to convey messages by the Egyptians more than 4,000 years ago (439, 998, 1,380), and Indians in New Mexico domesticated the Turkey (*Meleagris gallopavo*) thousands of years ago (481).

Birds are the primary agents of insect control throughout the world. Without their contributions, Earth would become virtually uninhabitable to us (174). The ill effects of a diet of polished rice on domestic fowl in 1896 led to the discovery of vitamins, and Louis Pasteur's development of the first vaccine for cattle anthrax originated from his investigation of fowl cholera. The pioneer of modern domestic fowl breeding, the British biologist William Bateson, discovered the basic principles of inheritance in chickens even before Mendel's genetic experiments with plants were generally known (481).

Darwin's studies of the Galápagos finches (Geospizinae) played an important role in the development of his thoughts about natural selection, and the remarkable complexity and sophistication of his thinking are revealed particularly well in his discussions of sexual dimorphism and sexual selection in birds (1,227, 1,231). Many recent refinements in evolutionary theory derive from field studies of birds. The analysis of fossil avifaunal remains promises to be an important tool for paleoenvironmental reconstructions. Such analyses of Early Oligocene deposits in Egypt suggest that the earliest stages of hominoid primate (ancestors of Man and apes) evolution occurred in an environment of equable, tropical swampland bordered by forest and open woodland or grassland (1,398). Nut dispersal by Blue Jays (*Cyanocitta cristata*) is believed to have been the facilitating mechanism for the phenomenally rapid North American, postglacial northward advance of oak trees (at the rate of about 350 m per annum; 1,399).

Because they frequently appear to be more sensitive or vulnerable than other vertebrates to environmental contaminants, birds often are regarded as key indicators of subtle changes in the ecosystem. Certainly they are the most commonly used vertebrates for this purpose. In 1894, G.B. Grinnell documented cases of waterfowl mortality following their ingestion of spent lead shot (1,324). Birds gave the first alert to the dangers of DDT, have been used to monitor the level of heavy metals polluting air in urban areas, including lead emitted from motor vehicles, and continue to expand our understanding of how environmental changes affect many forms of life (189, 1,324). "Birds provide a 'window' through which both laymen and scientists can learn of their kinship to the rest of the animal kingdom" (174). With each question answered concerning the behavior of these delightful, intriguing creatures--how and why they do what they do--we achieve a better understanding of ourselves (16, 189).

Birds also offer therapeutic relief from the travail of today's hectic existence and to many they provide one of life's great pleasures. In Augusta's words (92), "The song of birds, from the simplest twittering to the full-throated trills and melodies, gladdens the heart of all who hear it. It gives new strength and comfort to the sad and encouragement to those who labor in the fields." The evolution of Man's music appreciation may have been influenced by hearing and imitating birds' songs (109); it is said of the antiphonal songs (duetting) of Bell Shrikes (*Laniarius aethiopicus*) that "....it is the kind of harmony to which man aspired and which probably reached its peak in Mozart" (see 479). There is no doubt that some of Man's dancing is of avian origin; members of many primitive tribes throughout the world perform dances clearly copied from those of courting or fighting birds; some even dress as birds (28).

Many biologists long have regarded birds as "the best natural vehicle for the exploration of process and form in the biological realm" (103). Ornithologists and other students of birds have made significant and, often, pioneering contributions to nearly all aspects of biology: to embryology; to immunology--without the study of the dual immune systems of birds, modern immunology would have shifted more slowly to a recognition of the major effectors in specific immunity, the B and T lymphocytes; to the study of visual mechanisms, which, because of the high degree of development of the avian visual system, may lead to a better understanding than is now possible from studies in mammals; to behavioral and population endocrinology; to island biogeography, producing ideas of potentially great importance in conservation; to behavioral ecology or ecoethology, including theories about competition and niche partitioning, which have had a great impact on evolutionary thought; to community ecology, which concerns the patterns that characterize natural assemblages of species; to studies of long-distance migration; to theories of sexual selection and speciation, and to modern systematic concepts, such as the polytypic species; to the adaptive significance and evolution of mating systems and their relationship to sexual dimorphism; to evolutionary morphology, for which studies of the avian skeletomuscular system have set the pace; to the neural basis of learning, for which imprinting and song learning have proved to be most useful vertebrate models; and to social behavior, the basic principles of social organization, and ecological sociobiology (189, 310, 421, 488, 654, 725, 762, 1,389). It would not be an exaggeration to say that birds have been the principal subjects for studies in most of these areas.

Birds have been the greatest favorites in studies of ethology, the discipline dealing with animal behavior as shaped by natural selection, and they continue to be studied intensively by a great many workers. In fact, these studies made such rapid progress that most of our knowledge of animal behavior derives from work with birds. The principal exception has been our knowledge of the genetic foundations of behavior, in which studies of fruit flies, some piscene species, and rodents have led the way.

The are many reasons for favoring birds: they are numerous and widespread; they are of small size and are easy to observe in confinement and in the field; they are easy to handle, manipulate experimentally, and care for; they are in the main diurnal, their sensory capacities bear similarities to those of Man, and their social behavior depends primarily on visual and auditory signals; their moods are more readily preceptible than those of any other organism; many species possess large repertoires of striking, easily recognizable "instinctive" movement patterns or displays (351, 419); and they have developed some of the most spectacular adaptations to changing environmental conditions, so that many types of life histories and many variations on behavioral themes are found among them.

In addition: many birds exhibit extensive physical and behavioral sexual dimorphism; birds have developed some highly advanced forms of reproductive behavior and provide a fine and varied array of materials for analytical and comparative study, for example, their flexibility in the division of parental investment between the sexes and their richness in the extent and variety of parental care patterns (488, 646); the longevity of most species is optimal for the study of many aspects of their behavior by humans; many of the social institutions related to marriage and familial behavior in Man find their counterparts in the behavior of birds (488), by far the most monogamous of organisms; avian social systems, even among related species, show enough variation to afford illuminating comparisons (583); and birds have a great learning ability and respond in a highly intelligent (see definitions on p. 344) manner in many types of tests. Not only are many aspects of their learning capabilities comparable with those of most mammals (351, 419), they surpass many mammals in some respects (19, 88, 143, 476). For example, Canaries (*Serinus canaria*) outperformed domestic cats in solving an oddity problem, and a Raven (*Corvus corax*) outperformed an elephant in a switched-symbols discrimination (see 476).

PARROTS

Just as birds have attracted the greatest general interest and are the most popular pets, members of the "wondrous parrot family" (2)--330 or more species--have long been the most popular birds. More species of parrots (members of the order Psittaciformes) probably have been habituated and reared in captivity than those of any other avian group (24).

In the Chronicles of Alexandria, Kallixenus describes how the Greeks carried parrots in processions as long ago as 284 B.C. Alexander the Great had the distinction of being the first to import Indian Ring-necked Parakeets (genus *Psittacula*) to Greece (138). Parrots also were highly valued as pets by the Romans many years before Christ, and the Romans were the first to introduce parrots into Europe. From then on, every caravan returning from the east and every ship from the west brought home its quota of parrots. Primitive South American peoples have domesticated parrots and taught them to talk from time immemorial (24, 109, 1,056). Practically all explorers (for example, Columbus), on discovering a new tropical country, found that the natives kept parrots as household pets (137).

The principal basis for the popularity of parrots, of course, is their outstanding vocal mimicry (see p. 269 *et seq.*). Taken in combination with their manipulative versatility, their beauty of plumage, their exceptional intelligence among birds (see pp. 345-350), the fascinations of their complex, varied, and challenging behavior, and the "uplifting experiences" and "joyous company" that they afford (1,056), it is easy to understand the well nigh irresistible attractions that parrots have for most people who become closely acquainted with them.

On the other hand, parrots have not enjoyed a comparable favoritism with ornithologists. Despite their exceptional vocal mimicry, their syringes and song are comparatively simple. Not only is their courtship behavior also simple, it is difficult to observe in the wild. Little of their brooding behavior has been studied (as they are hole-nesters), their phylogenetic affinities (with other groups and with each other) are obscure and often a matter of guesswork, and the fossil record (pp. 1-2) is poor. Even in confinement there have been few intensive studies of their behavior, most notably those of Dilger (3, 4) with lovebirds (genus *Agapornis*) and Brockway (67) with Budgerigars (*Melopsittacus undulatus*).

LABORATORY STUDIES AND "WHAT CAN HAPPEN"

Not long ago many students of behavior and ecology were inclined to regard results obtained with confined animals as artificial and distorted. They tended toward the "puristic view" that the study of animals in the wild was the only worthwhile approach, scorned though it was by "....myopic laboratory scientists whose experience goes no farther than the grossly oversimplified and narrowly categorized environments of their laboratories" (554). Thus one heard: only under free, natural conditions can one observe "normal behavior in its full complexity and significance" (22); "do the processes shown in the laboratory relate in any way to what goes on in the field?" (358); "all behavior, including learned behavior, must be studied under normal conditions, for only in this way can its adaptive value presumably be assessed" (106); and "we do not want to depend on museum-bound theorists and interpreters who are not in touch with the living organism in its natural setting. Ornithology is a field science in large measure ...." (485). Some field workers in avian sociobiology even oppose controlled field experiments and find "the idea....quite unsettling" (see 584).

This bias against the study of confined animals and captive breeding was not limited to segments of the scientific establishment. It extended even to conservation organizations, which, at one time, were reluctant "to consider birds in captivity as possessing the same precious genes as their conspecific species-members in the wild" (124). Even in recent years there have been adherents to the "rather-dead-than-bred" philosophy (see 644). Twenty-five years ago there was general doubt among biologists as well as conservationists about the potential of captive breeding of endangered species. Now, results in the field of "manipulative aviculture" are most encouraging, as captive propagation becomes more predictable.

Well-known avicultural techniques, including the induction of additional clutches, artificial insemination and incubation, foster parenting, hand rearing, and supportive feeding already have given rise to important programs for wild birds of prey, cranes, pheasants, and waterfowl (644).

Although it is recognized that manipulative management techniques do not provide a final solution, and perhaps should be reserved as a last resort, there is little doubt that they can save a species from extinction (566). Thus, the Nene (Hawaiian Goose, *Branta sandvicensis*) has been rescued from this fate (560), wild Peregrine Falcons (*Falco peregrinus*) have been re-established successfully by releases of captive-reared birds at several sites (663), and captive-raised Andean Condor (*Vultur gryphus*) chicks have been introduced to Condor habitat in Peru with encouraging, if preliminary, success (644).

However, only 28 (11%) of the world's endangered species are being bred in captivity as part of an organized conservation effort and only 6 of these are being reintroduced regularly to the wild. An innovative alternative that has proved to be successful for a few endangered endemic birds living on small islands around New Zealand has involved a transfer of a threatened population from an island on which an exotic predator was present to nearby predator-free but unoccupied islands (see 1,325).

On the other hand, some workers took the attitude that only theoretical and experimental approaches were valid (see 206). "If you're not doing an experiment every moment, you're wasting time" (see 1,392). These workers were inclined to ignore and wave aside the contributions of field ecologists as "old fashioned natural history" (see 488), which "....is too descriptive to contribute much any longer" (see 553), is "boring, muddled, uninspiring....and of no value in itself," provides information that "is so incomplete as to be of little value for broader purposes," and is "a 'contemplative and reflective activity,' sometimes deeply satisfying but always of value solely to the individual observer" (see 1,392).

Natural history courses are conspicuously absent in some quarters and viewed as pointless anachronisms in others (1,392). Indeed "natural history" recently "seemed headed for oblivion until restored to respectability in the name of ecology....From the point of view of controlled conditions in the laboratory, the outside world is decidedly untidy" (1,256). Some workers have disdained careful descriptive fieldwork "as an activity for pseudo-scientists and amateurs, which can only provide fodder for the real scientists, the theoreticians" (see 553). Others claimed that natural selection theory was untestable and, therefore, unscientific, and that sociobiology was just "story telling" (203, 204). Still others wrote off the museum tradition as "anacronistic and obsolete" (see 206).

Many gaps in our knowledge of the biological role of structural features of birds stemmed from the failure to combine field and laboratory work (113). Fortunately, there were those who took the enlightened view that now prevails: "the modern student of birds, whatever his specialized interest, realizes that his workroom includes the field, the museum and the laboratory" (29); "....ornithology progresses when those who are efficient in gathering data employ their efforts in testing predictions proposed by theoreticians and when theoreticians employ their efforts explaining the data gathered by field workers or modeling the explanations offered by others" (556). "All techniques must be applied in such a way that they are complementary; we can afford to neglect none" (725); "field and laboratory complement one another and each gives rise to new questions for the other" (727). "....natural history provides an interpretive context for addressing both broader and narrower questions....it is the 'idea and induction' part of 'the' scientific method, the essential prelude to formulating hypotheses as well as the raw material for testing them" (1,392).

It now is amply recognized that there frequently is a need to alternate repeatedly between field observations and laboratory work, or engage in joint undertakings, to check the findings made in each phase of a study (421, 727). Such correlated studies appear to be crucial for a better understanding of various aspects of avian song learning, of the ecological and evolutionary significance of physiology-behavior interrelationships, of the control of numerous population processes (reproduction, recruitment, social status, aggression, nutrition), etc. (656, 727). It was the availability of both field and aviary observations that permitted a many-faceted approach to the classification of the Anatidae (ducks, geese, and swans) and that helped to correct many errors in earlier systems (486).

Although neither the field, laboratory, nor museum worker need any longer defend his approach (nonetheless, some workers feel that museum science is ebbing; 645), I believe it is appropriate to discuss further the comparative strengths of laboratory and field studies. I take this view principally because one of the chief merits of laboratory studies seems not yet to have been aired adequately in the literature; many of the findings presented here have precisely this merit.

The comparative aspect that I would emphasize is that the most one hopes to ascertain from studies in the wild is **what does happen**; in the laboratory, one can aspire to learn much more. One is able to explore in detail **what can happen**. In the wild, one merely gets "snapshots" in time --one finds out how animals behave over relatively brief periods in the conditions that prevail today. In the laboratory, one can examine the potentials of the animals to adapt to other conditions and see how they respond to conditions that might be encountered in the future or were in the past.

One also can explore variations in the ways different individuals respond in identical circumstances. The survival of a species may depend on the breadth of these differences. The greater the breadth, the greater the probability that a population will include individuals (genotypes) that will survive unfavorable conditions, particularly those of an extreme nature. In the arena of studies relating to learning and intelligence it has been asserted, I feel with good reason, that "passive observations of animals in the wild do not necessarily reveal the full extent of their capacities....efforts to determine the limitations of the animal's capacities would have to be made in 'unnatural' situations, to see how far novel demands might be met" (1,091).

Overtones of the "puristic view" even can be detected among sympathetic ornithologists. For example, it sometimes is claimed that the striking individual differences in nesting behavior of confined parrots must be due in part to the artificial conditions that they encounter (1). In other words, some workers feel that it is necessary to account for, or excuse, the lack of uniformity of behavior in confined birds. Even in our laboratories and classrooms there has been "a tendency to regard variability as a nuisance--as noise in the system--to be compensated for by appropriate experimental design, sampling techniques and statistical analysis" (739).

I would suggest that we need not decry, nor excuse, any lack of uniformity of behavior of confined birds, nor even necessarily look upon it as being "unnatural." "....animals are individuals, each with its personal developmental history, its personal relationships to places and other individuals" (739). As Beer points out, "....there are aspects of social and reproductive behavior in birds that demand this viewpoint if they are to be discerned at all" (739). The amount of food delivered to nestlings by a non-breeding helper, for example, depends on circumstances related to the helper's social and ecological environment, such as its age, sex, and position within the flock or social unit (see 780).

Variation is the rule among individuals in natural populations (578)--"huge individual variation in wild birds" (727). Walkinshaw goes so far as to say of the nesting behavior of Sora Rails (*Porzana carolina*) that "there is always a marked difference in the behavior of individual birds ...." (216). And variability of behavior is evident even among organisms with the most rigid of stereotyped behavior, such as the hunting wasps (297). "As no ethologist is prepared to abandon the view of species-specificity of behavior and its survival value for the species as a result of natural selection, it would be a contradiction in terms were he to stress the extreme variability of behavior and environment" (1,272). "Biological variability is the raw material of natural selection....Variation, both within and between species, is one of the most fundamental attributes of organisms. Analysis of this variation can offer insights....just as surely as can the delineation of the central tendencies" (1,275). Since many field studies of behavior and ecology are made at a single locality or on a single local population, they usually are unlikely to detect even the existence of geographic variability.

The information obtained in the laboratory often is more conclusive than even the most accurate record of what occurs in the wild. In fact, it is not unusual for interpretations of well-documented field studies to be inconclusive or controversial (80, 81). For example, equivocal results often are obtained in studies of community ecology, particularly analyses of community structure and organization (see 568, 654). This remains a controversial subject area in which it is seldom possible to perform experiments to test theories (837), and ecologists today are sharply divided in a controversy over the importance of interspecific competition in natural communities (1,157).

There have, of course, been some striking field successes. It is unnecessary to elaborate on the critical need for long-term, even lifetime, field studies of individually recognizable birds (583), and field studies in such disciplines as evolutionary ecology and ecological morphology (421, 424). One such success has been the prediction of prey choices from optimal-foraging theory (see 555, 614, 649). Another has been the detection of the regularities in avian distribution and abundance. In general, avian ecologists have sought to define avian communities by the plant communities that they inhabit (1,324); it now is possible to predict the number and, sometimes, even the identity of avian species to be found in given forests (see 307, 315). This has come to be the test of being a "good bird-watcher."

But despite the ease with which birds can be studied--because of their conspicuousness and predominantly diurnal habit--avian population problems, such as the regulation of rates of reproduction--even only the determination of clutch size (549, 1,051)--have proved to be very difficult to solve. And, although food supply and weather very likely are the two dominant environmental factors controlling avian populations, no definitive population theory either exists or appears to be in the offing (46, 313).

Thus, a feature that some workers consider to be the most remarkable avian attribute (352)--the comparative stability of populations over long periods--remains incompletely understood. There are practical problems, of course, including the absence of a feasible method of measuring a variable such as food-harvesting effectiveness (307) or genetic fitness (646), difficulties in obtaining reliable census data across a wide spectrum of species in the tropics (654), a paucity of reliable information on sex ratios (1,231), and the frequent need to rely on single-year population surveys in the absence of knowledge of the temporal and spatial variability to which they are subject (594). The main problem, however, was that field studies typically relied almost completely on observational data and consequently did not benefit from a proper experimental design or the use of careful controls. This *modus operandi* made it difficult or impossible to distinguish between causes, consequences, and mere accompaniments.

In the absence of experiments, the ecologist tended to rely heavily on the results of comparative studies. Although these can provide useful insights when they are interpreted within a sufficiently broad context, the comparative approach has the weakness that the correlations that are found may be explained equally well by several alternative hypotheses (220). "Many adaptive 'explanations' are more a reflection of an observer's ingenuity rather than a description of what is going on in nature" (836). It is difficult to draw strong inferences even from the "natural experiments" that island communities seem to present (195). Accordingly, it has become increasingly imperative that field studies expand their use of experimental approaches--which already have come to be a powerful tool--and place a greater emphasis on the formulation of falsifiable hypotheses (205). In this connection, Marshall was one of the first to recognize that field studies often pay "the best....dividends" by "opportunist methods in which the environment can sometimes be used as a natural laboratory" (350).

It will be evident in the following that most of the relict responses in the repertoire of Cockatielian behavior (some of which also are characteristic of lovebirds and Budgerigars) could scarcely have been detected by studies other than experimental ones under controlled conditions. The circumstances that activated these responses in the wild may have ceased to occur with any significant frequency tens of millions of years ago, at the time the ancestors of the birds became hole-nesters.

ORIGIN OF THE STUDIES

The observations of previously unknown and little-known behavior of parrots that are reported here were partly fortuitous. Birds of the order Psittaciformes were of particular interest to me because they are among the most intelligent of birds. My initial objective was to ascertain how parrots would compare with mammals in their learning abilities and other aspects of their behavior, as assessed in light-preference tests. In these tests, the animals themselves perform the manipulations that directly control the levels of ambient illumination to which they are exposed during activity and rest.

With this objective in mind I acquired 3 pairs of Budgerigars (*Melopsittacus undulatus*), a pair of Cockatiels (*Nymphicus hollandicus*), and a pair of Peach-faced Lovebirds (*Agapornis roseicollis*). These became the founders of my colony. It soon became evident that the Peach-faced Lovebirds were by far the most suitable birds with which to begin. They are miniature "dynamos" of activity--in all their ways of moving about, manipulating objects with their feet and bills, and interacting among themselves. They also are bold, exceptionally inquisitive, and are of ideal size for learning and preference studies in experimental enclosures.

One of my initial projects was to breed the birds to obtain a sufficient working stock of individuals of known origin and experience. In these endeavors, I was most successful, at first, with the lovebirds and Cockatiels. They reproduce very readily in single pairs. Budgerigar pairs require the stimulation provided by the company of 1 or 2 other pairs, though it is said that a lone pair sometimes can be stimulated to breed in the presence of a mirror (67, 138, 439).

The course of much of my research quickly was channeled into an unexpected direction, following observations of unprecedented new facets of parrot breeding behavior. From the time of these initial observations, it became evident that a wealth of new information could be obtained about the behavior of these birds merely through detailed observations and simple experimental manipulations. The findings appear to have significant implications for the past evolution of avian reproductive practices, as well as indirect bearings on other aspects of avian evolution.

LENGTHY, CONTINUOUS, CLOSE, OBSERVATIONS

Avian studies most frequently focus attention on readily-approachable questions that give promise of yielding quick answers, and they usually are pursued with relatively large numbers of birds, most often in the breeding season. Data about the activities and strategies of birds during the non-breeding season are meager, probably on the theory that anything done then by a bird beyond surviving has little influence on its reproductive success in the spring. In Schreiber's words, "Would that more studies of birds could last long enough with enough marked individuals so that we could get reasonably close to the truth... and would that ornithologists were not 'forced' to publish their data prematurely!" (306). "In order to evaluate the adaptive nature of social structures, it is necessary to follow individuals throughout their lives such that lifetime reproductive success may be determined, and to follow the 'behavior' of populations long enough to witness circumstances under varying environmental and demographic regimes" (1,323; see also 725).

Only relatively infrequently have observers followed the behavior and interactions of individuals over long periods. For example, it took 20 years of study to find that a sea-faring gull shows differential sex- and age-specific mortality, a sample of 234 dispersers over 11 years was required to show a strong heritable component to dispersal distances in the Great Tit (*Parus major*; see 583), and it took the perspective of continuous 30-year studies of Bobwhite Quail (*Colinus virginianus*) to evaluate their responses to land-use changes, management practices, and hunting. The latter showed, for example, that continuous harvesting stimulated productivity (612).

Since I practically lived with my birds, I was able to observe virtually every noteworthy occurrence from hatching on, sometimes in great detail, 9-12 hours per day, 7 days a week, for over 5 years. From the results of these observations, it became clear that the usual views of parrots that one obtains from mere time schedules of their development and care, and enumeration of their habits, are almost as drab and unrepresentative of their lives and interactions as are views of their skeletons for their living appearance.

In contrast to what is known about the nesting and breeding habits of most other groups of birds, information on parrots has been relatively unsystematic and generalized, even for the common species (1). Because of their hole-nesting habits and consequent relative inaccessibility, most of what is known about parrots has had to be obtained from studies of confined birds. Since I sometimes was observing closely 2, or even 3, family groups over the same period, I had to be selective, concentrating my attention in areas where the least was known, and the behavior was least likely to be altered by confinement. These included early breeding activities, care of eggs and chicks, chick behavior, and interactions among family members.

When I was able to observe the care of eggs and young continuously in the nestbox or open nests, often from within a few cm, it became evident that much of the past literature dealing with the behavior of these birds within the nestbox has bordered on mere guesswork. Rather than the mundane events that have been assumed from the piecing together of bits of unsystematic observations, much of what actually occurs is extraordinary, sometimes involving behavior that was previously unknown in birds.

RELICT RESPONSES

Through my close association with parrots and some very simple experimental manipulations, I discovered an ensemble of relict responses that were unobserved before in any bird, as well as some other remarkable and previously unknown behavior. Certainly the least expected of these findings was what is perhaps the first experimentally elicited evidence with implications for the nesting and egg care of ancestral birds and their forerunners. This evidence appears to bridge a gap of well over 150 million yr, even extending back to the times of birds' early post-reptilian ancestors. Some of these findings emerged as a result of observing the influences of changes in light conditions.

These studies call attention to the fact that neural circuits or motor programs for archaic responses have been preserved in the central nervous systems of some vertebrates. Only the appropriate long-absent stimuli are needed to call these responses "back to life." The secret to activating them lies not only in "where to look," as suggested recently (132), but also in "how to look." The best known of these responses until now were the protective superficial reflexes and spinal automatisms of Man (see pp. 523-526), most of which are vestigial and are little-known outside the disciplines of neurology and neurosurgery.

In the light of the existence of a mosaic of essentially unambiguous relict responses in Cockatiels, one may be unduly pessimistic to conclude that fossils provide the only evidence from which we can learn of "adaptations....of birds in former geological periods...." (590). Even the view that the conclusions of evolutionary studies of behavior "....can never be defended by anything better than indirect evidence and can never be tested by experiment" (see 739) may not be entirely unassailable.

Not only may vertebrate central nervous systems be the richest repositories of tangible records of past behavior, the records retained there would appear to be in a much better state of preservation than any others. Using clues provided by the order in which relict responses and other egg-care behavior appear or become accessible during Cockatielian breeding, I have been led to postulate that successive stages in the egg care of Cockatiels recapitulate the equivalents of successive evolutionary stages of the egg care of their ancestors.

Similarly, I would postulate that the number of maturing follicles that exist in the ovary during the 3 discrete developmental follicular maturational stages of Budgerigars may tend to recapitulate the number of maturing follicles and the number of eggs in the clutches of the ancestors of Budgerigars during 3 major evolutionary stages. There also are discrete follicular maturational stages in other birds, as well as in many reptiles, and these also may tend to recapitulate the equivalents of ancestral reproductive states. More generally, I would suggest that the phenomenon of follicular atresia during maturation of the ovaries themselves is the major evolutionary adaptation by means of which clutch and litter size have been reduced progressively in the course of evolution from distant, ancestral marine vertebrates.

When one considers: that the relict responses were detected merely by making close observations of normal behavior, and of the reactions of the birds to very simple experimental manipulations; that follicular maturation stages may give clues to ancestral evolutionary stages; that the flightless avian fossils discovered recently in Hawaii have been said to be anomalous beyond the ornithologist's wildest imagination (175); that it is predicted that "....future successes expected in the study of avian morphology.... will be spectacular and will eclipse those achieved during the golden age of vertebrate morphology" (421); and that, until recently, much of "the phylogeny and relationships of birds....have been misinterpreted and misunderstood to an astonishing degree" (194); then one may be justified in assuming that many rich veins of avian evolution remain to be probed.

To hazard an impression gained in the course of the present studies, I would suggest that many of the clues needed to reconstruct the evolution of birds and their behavior still are accessible to us. They may be preserved both overtly and covertly in avian relict responses and central nervous systems, cycles of maturation of avian reproduction in all of its aspects, the spectrum of avian reproductive habits, avian ontogeny and fossils, and certain of the like categories for reptiles, particularly cycles of maturation of reproduction, reproductive habits, and fossils. Though fleshed-out avian ancestors are inaccessible, knowledge of their behavior and life styles may not be, and some of the latter well may find their equivalents among various living forms.

The present reconstruction of avian evolution finds the most important channeling factors to have been the invasion of arboreal and aerial habitats by reptilian ancestors, onset and eventual waning of the warm, equable Mesozoic climatic regimes, transition from the employment of unattended nests buried at a depth to attended eggs and young in near-surface and surface nests, and the ready susceptibility of ovarian function to modulation. The value of this reconstruction lies not so much in its details, as in expanding our perspectives by bringing new considerations to bear on problems of avian evolution.

ANTHROPOMORPHISMS

In interpreting the behavior of animals, I often feel justified to draw parallels with human behavior and emotions. Nevertheless, I customarily describe and interpret behavior with guarded objectivity. To facilitate the detailed descriptions of social interactions that are given here I sometimes relax this caution. However, I indicate each such relaxation by setting off the concerned expression with apostrophes. The parallels with human behavior that are implied but not qualified in this way are intentional. In fact, there will be many occasions in the treatments of the social interactions of Peach-faced Lovebirds in Chapters 3, 5, and 7 when the reader will be impelled to see our own behavior mirrored in the actions of the birds, and I do not hesitate to draw such parallels.

FOR THE GENERAL BIOLOGIST, AVICULTURIST, AND STUDENTS OF AVIAN EVOLUTION

By ranging in great breadth over the available pertinent information and bringing together in one copiously indexed sourcebook material scattered in the literature, the present treatment aspires to provide extensive factual bases that will facilitate the progress, not only of other students of avian evolution, but also of workers interested in other aspects of avian biology. In pursuit of this goal, the text and topics are abundantly cross referenced by titles and page numbers. Nor do I overlook general biologists or aviculturists. For their benefit I have included up-to-date, extensive general treatments of those aspects of ornithology that either are most pertinent to avian evolution or that I feel are of the greatest general or ancillary interest. For the benefit of the latter readers I have employed frequent parenthetical expressions to clarify the meanings of technical and specialized terms.

The copious references often favor accessible sources, and not infrequently are given primarily for the benefit of non-specialists as guides to further reading. Both general and technical references to a topic often are included. My objectives in making this work accessible to aviculturists are to make known to them the potentially rich field of avian relict responses and to emphasize the value and relative ease of taking part, themselves, in studies of avian behavior. Discoveries still are possible without profound knowledge or elaborate equipment. "The very complexity of biology has left unsolved mysteries within the reach of any imaginative person" (1,256). Furthermore, "It would appear that in some circumstances the untrammelled mind of the talented amateur may be more productive with striking break-throughs in knowledge...." (1,287). Broadened cultivation of interests in birds is more desirable now than ever before, with a major portion of the world's avifauna severely threatened.

J. Lee Kavanau,

Los Angeles, California,
February, 1987

FOREWORD

In the present work I have departed from customary practice in two principal ways. The capital-letter leads or titles to paragraphs serve several purposes. They pinpoint the locations of material cross referenced in the text, they assist generally in finding and indexing specific topics, and they give an introductory synopsis of the subject matter treated.

The use of non-alphabetized references--numbered, but not serialized in order of occurrence--had two advantages. It gave greater freedom in dealing with references in the course of preparing the work, and it greatly reduced the volume of main text required for citing references. The Reference Number Index gives the page numbers on which each numbered reference is cited. Reference numbers for a given author are obtained by referring to the pages listed for the author in the Author Index.

Numbers enclosed in parentheses and not otherwise identified are references. When preceded by the word, "see," the references are secondary, otherwise they are primary. The use of many secondary references, in which several primary references often are cited, has made it possible to keep the Reference Index within manageable size, else its length would have been at least doubled.

Available and widely accepted common names of species usually are used at every specification or identification, but the scientific name is included only at the first occurrence (with the exception of names in the Introduction). Otherwise only scientific names are used. To obtain an existing common name, given only the scientific name, one refers to the pages given under the entry in the Scientific Name Index.

Individual birds and mated pairs were studied over periods of many months, in some cases for 4 or 5 years, including numerous successive clutches and broods, and stages of development from hatchlings through adulthood. Accordingly, for purposes of reference, correlation, and easy identification, and to make it possible to follow readily the sequential order of the studies, most times of occurrence are specified by calendar dates, and names are employed for individual birds.

Since the work is intended primarily as a reference text and for the use of researchers, diagrams are restricted to those concerned with the research program itself. Diagrams related to the topics reviewed are to be found in the cited references. Similarly, the treatments of topics in avian biology are not inclusive. Rather, as mentioned above, the topics selected are those most pertinent to the research program or to the biology of small parrots, or they are those that have been subjects of recent intensive studies or advances in knowledge.

Abbreviations have been held to a minimum. Aside from those that are conventional, such as **sec, min, h, yr, mya, cm, m, k, k.p.h., C.N.S., AMP, LH,** and **FSH**, I have employed only **NB** (nestbox), **NBs** (nestboxes), and **IA** (incubative area). Times of day are given on a 24-h basis, such as **08:30 h** and **22:27 h**. All confidence limits are standard errors.

For his many helpful editorial suggestions and corrections, I am very much indebted to Mr. A.E. Whitehorn. For primarily scientific reviewing, I am greatly indebted to many individuals. Early versions of the Introduction and/or limited sections of Chapter 1 were reviewed by Drs. T.L. Bucher, M.L. Cody, N.E. Collias, R. Gibson, T.R. Howell, and D. Perry, and Mr. Ove Hoegh-Guldberg. The Introduction and the General Discussion of Chapter 3 were reviewed by Drs. A.D. Grinnell and P. Narins. Limited sections of Chapter 4, Part 3 were reviewed by Dr. D. Perry, Dr. L. Vitt, and an anonymous colleague. Various versions of all material through Chapter 5 were reviewed by Drs. F. Crescitelly and W.M. Hamner. The entire final text was reviewed by Dr. E.C. Olson, my student, Michael Cornish, and his wife, Gail. Shortcomings that remain are my responsibility. I am indebted to Mr. Daryoush Jamal for participating in the compilation of the Author and Common Name Indices.

J. Lee Kavanau

Los Angeles, California
February, 1987

CONTENTS

CHAPTER 1. THE BIRDS AND THE CONTINENTS

PART 1. GENERAL ORIGINS, AUSTRALIA, ORIGINS IN AUSTRALIA

THE ORIGIN AND DISTRIBUTION OF PARROTS

DISTRIBUTION. Parrots (birds of the order Psittaciformes) are pantropical in distribution, occurring throughout the Neotropical, Ethiopian, Oriental, and Australian regions, eastward in the Pacific Ocean to Tahiti and southward to Macquarie Island on the edge of the Antarctic Ocean (308). None of the roughly 330 neospecies (modern-day species) crosses the Himalayas. There is no obvious close relationship between parrots and birds of other groups. Despite many differences, parrots are widely regarded as being most closely related to the Columbiformes (composed of the sandgrouse and pigeon families, the Pteroclidae and Columbidae, respectively). Similarities to birds of prey are thought to have resulted from evolutionary convergences (106, 1,285).

Nearly half of the species are inhabitants of Australia, New Guinea, and the Pacific Islands (56 species in Australia and 42 species in New Guinea, falling into a total of 38 genera). Approximately 140 species are found in Central and South America and the Caribbean islands. The remainder inhabit Africa and southern Asia (31, 815). Eight of the 19 species occurring in Africa are lovebirds, genus *Agapornis*. Countrywise, Brazil has the most species, numbering 70. Only the recently exterminated Carolina Parakeet (*Conuropsis carolinensis*) occurred regularly in the U.S. (308). Two of the species being treated here--the Budgerigars and the Cockatiels--are endemic (native or indigenous) to Australia; the Peach-faced Lovebirds are endemic to southwest Africa.

In general, parrots have a relatively narrow habitat tolerance, combined with relatively limited powers of sustained flight. Comparatively narrow barriers of unfavorable territory seem to be sufficient to constrain populations. For example, the Lombok Straits determine the natural range of members of both of the tribes Cacatuini and Loriini, and no member of the Platycercini is found in New Guinea, whereas the tribe has more representative species than any other in Australia and New Zealand. The geographical features that limit the southern margin of the Holarctic region--the "Mexican," Saharan, and Arabian deserts, and the Himalayan chain --seem largely to have prevented a post-glacial expansion northward, except in northeastern Indochina, where several species have penetrated into southeastern China. By contrast, because there is no substantial barrier to post-glacial dispersal in the southern hemisphere, 70 species in 35 genera now live south of the tropic of Capricorn (819).

FOSSIL RECORD. Because parrots are not waterfowl, their chances of fossil preservation are slight and their record on a world-wide scale (like that of passerines) is poor (see 290, 487). The earliest known fossil remains are from Lower Eocene (Early or Ypresian; see Table 1) strata of London Clay at Walton-on-the-Naze in Essex, and Medial Eocene strata of the Elmor Formation from Gosport, Hampshire in Britain (293). These are of small birds (*Palaeopsittacus georgei* sp. nov.) comparable in size with the extant Senegal Parrot (*Poicephalus senegalus*). They lack most of the salient features that distinguish modern parrots. [The wing of *Palaeopsittacus* was more generalized than that of recent parrots; it was longer and perhaps less vigorously beaten in flight, a conclusion supported by the structure of the pectoral girdle (293).]

Only 3 other pre-Quaternary finds are known, *Psittacus (Archaeopsittacus) verreauxi* a small species of parrot from the early Miocene epoch (Aquitanian; see Table 1) of France, probably closely related to members of the modern genus, *Psittacus*, a medium-small parrot, *Conuropsis* fratercula, from the early Miocene (late Hemingfordian) of Nebraska, and several recoveries from the Medial Miocene Nördlinger Ries in southern Germany and at Sansan, France (see 106, 294, 308, 574). These finds are zoogeographically important in that they suggest a more widespread distribution of parrots in the Cenozoic era, during those times when climates were warmer and more equable than in the late Tertiary period (106). Many contemporary species apparently have evolved since Pleistocene times, over the past million yr (31).

ORIGIN AND DISPERSAL. Parrots probably originated in the Southern Hemisphere (106, 308). The "amoropsittinine" ("forpinine") parrots of South America may be advanced forms within the Australian Platycercinae and an example of a transarctic dispersal in the Cretaceous or early Tertiary period, facilitated by the interconnections between the Southern Continents. The presence of peculiar groups in Australasia, such as the Strigopinae and Nestorinae in New Zealand, and the Cacatuinae, Loriinae, and Micropsittinae (see Table 2) in Australia and the islands to the north, and the high level of generic endemicity, indicate a long period of differentiation that probably began sometime in the Cretaceous period (106, 1,086). The considerable amount of evolution that has taken place in Australia and South America suggests that the early history of the order was Gondwanan (even the primary radiation of birds; see p. 25) and that the paleogeography of the Southern Continents probably was important (106, 308).

CLASSIFICATION. Like their phylogenetic relationships with other groups, the classification of parrots (reviewed in 1,285) presents a difficult problem concerning which there is as yet no general agreement. The classification based almost entirely on external morphology, which Salvadori proposed in 1891, has been the main source for almost all subsequent arrangements (see 819). Peters (301) divided the order into a single family and 6 subfamilies, as in Table 2a (see, also, 309, 334, 587). This was modified by Forshaw (1), as in Table 2b. A more recent, more broadly-based proposal by Smith (27, 819) is followed here (Table 2c).

EXTINCTIONS. Relatively speaking, losses through recent extinctions have been greater for parrots than for any other group. There have been 24 extinctions since 1960, plus several others, if the losses of the Antillean and Mascarene (of Madagascar and associated islands) parrots, known only from questionable verbal descriptions, are valid. Even though less than 20% of all avian species are insular, 93% of all species that became extinct between 1600 and 1980 were of these species. Insular species are particularly vulnerable because they usually have a small population size, even under the most favorable circumstances. It has been calculated that 32% of the avian extinctions since 1600 involved habitat modification, 91% involved the impacts of introduced species, and 25% involved excessive destruction by Man (123).

Table 1. Timetable of the Phanerozoic Eon

0*--**Cenozoic era**--65

- 0--**Quaternary period**--2
  - 0--Holocene (Recent) epoch--0--Pleistocene epoch--2
- 2--**Tertiary period**--65
  - 2--Neogene subdivision--38½
    - 2--Pliocene--5 epoch
    - 5--Miocene--24 epoch [5--Late--11--Middle--15½--Early (15½--Langhian-Burdigalian--18½ --Aquitanian--24)--24]
    - 24--Oligocene--38½ epoch [24--Late--33--Early--38½]
  - 38½--Paleogene subdivision--65
    - 38½--Eocene--55 epoch [38½--Late--44--Middle--55½--Early (Ypresian)--55]
    - 55--Paleocene--65 epoch [55--Late--66--Early--65]

65--**Mesozoic era**--245

- 65--**Cretaceous period**--129
  - 65--Late--95 [65--Maastrichtian--73--Campanian--84--(Santonian-Coniacian-Turonian)--90--Cenomanian--95]
  - 95--Early--129 [95--Albian--107--Aptian--110--Barremian--112--Hauterivian--117--Valanginian--125--Berriasian--129]
- 129--**Jurassic period**--200
  - 129--Late--158 [129--Tithonian--134--Kimmeridgian--138--] Oxfordian--150]
  - 158--Middle--175 [150--Callovian--160--Bathonian--169--(Bajocian-Aalenian)--175]
  - 175--Early--200 [175--Toarcian--189--Pliensbachian--195--Sinemurian--198--Hettangian--200]
- 200--**Triassic period**--245
  - 200--Late--225 [200--Rhaetic--209--Norian--215--Carnian--225]
  - 225--Middle--248 [225--Ladinian--235--Anisian--240]
  - 248--Early--245 [240--Scythian--245]

245--**Paleozoic era**--575

- **Periods** [245--Permian--290--Carboniferous (Pennsylvanian--320--Mississippian)--360--Devonian--410--Silurian--435--Ordovician--500--Cambrian--575]

*Millions of years since beginning or end of interval

According to present knowledge, continental Africa has not lost a single species of bird in the last 300 yr. In this respect Africa is unique, because on all the other continents many birds have been exterminated. Even if one includes Madagascar and other nearby islands but excludes the remote, isolated islands and archipelagos in the Indian Ocean, Africa still has lost far fewer birds than other continents. Four birds have become extinct since the 17th century. They are the Great Elephant Bird (*Aepyornis maxima*), the Principé Island Olive Ibis (*Lampribis olivacea* rotschildi), the Madagascar Coucal (*Coua delalandre*), and the Sao Thomé Island Grosbeak Weaver (*Neospiza concolor*; 1,155).

The best documented prehistorical extinctions indubitably attributable to Man appear to be those of the moas in New Zealand about 500 yr ago (see 286). Lending emphasis to the severity of such losses is the recently discovered fact that 45 or more species of Hawaii's endemic birds vanished in the prehistoric Polynesian period, including 17 flightless ones. The existence of these unusual birds was unknown prior to the last decade (190).

On the other hand, massive extinctions of small passerines appear to be correlated with the destruction of lowland habitats by Polynesians (206). The avifauna of other Pacific islands probably also suffered extensive extinctions at the hands of Man (206). Since 1680, the year in which the Dodo (*Raphus cucullatus*) became extinct, extinction of an avian species has occurred about once every 4 yr; at least 92 species have been lost during this period. The rate is likely to increase to 1 extinction every 6 months by the yr 2000 (123).

The present study of the breeding habits, particularly the egg care, of Cockatiels, Budgerigars, and Peach-faced Lovebirds, and their responses to simple experimental manipulations suggest that the birds retain many very primitive behavioral responses. Some of these responses give possible clues to the habits of ancestral birds, others to those of more distant predecessors, and still others to those of the earliest post-reptilian ancestors of birds. The times of the earliest of these predecessors extend back into the Mesozoic era, possibly even into the Triassic period. Since the phylogeny of parrots--always enigmatic--now takes on more than usual interest, inasmuch their origin in the southern hemisphere is very likely, and since paleoclimates loom large as factors that influenced avian evolution, it is desirable to include reviews of pertinent aspects of both the paleohistory and present of the Australian and African continents, where the birds of this study are endemic.

AUSTRALIA AND ITS BIOTA

Australia is a continent of generally low, subdued relief, a vast peneplain with 99% of its area below 1,000 m. Even the highest summits barely exceed 2,000 m and the tree line reaches to within 300 m of them. None of them is permanently snow-capped (287, 1,060, 1,074). Australia has very few natural barriers and, consequently, very little orographic precipitation (precipitation induced by the presence of mountains). It is the smallest (7,614,500 sq. km, 1/40th of the Earth's surface and 1/16th of the

Table 2. Outlines of Parrot Classification

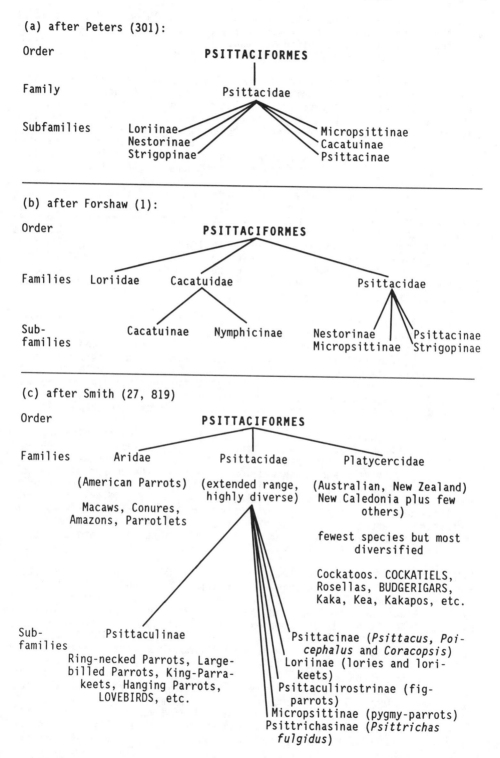

(a) after Peters (301):

- **Order:** **PSITTACIFORMES**
  - **Family:** Psittacidae
    - **Subfamilies:** Loriinae, Nestorinae, Strigopinae, Micropsittinae, Cacatuinae, Psittacinae

---

(b) after Forshaw (1):

- **Order:** **PSITTACIFORMES**
  - **Families:**
    - Loriidae
    - Cacatuidae
      - **Subfamilies:** Cacatuinae, Nymphicinae
    - Psittacidae
      - **Subfamilies:** Nestorinae, Micropsittinae, Psittacinae, Strigopinae

---

(c) after Smith (27, 819)

- **Order:** **PSITTACIFORMES**
  - **Families:**
    - Aridae
      - (American Parrots)
      - Macaws, Conures, Amazons, Parrotlets
    - Psittacidae
      - (extended range, highly diverse)
      - **Subfamilies:**
        - Psittaculinae — Ring-necked Parrots, Large-billed Parrots, King-Parrakeets, Hanging Parrots, LOVEBIRDS, etc.
        - Psittacinae (*Psittacus*, *Poicephalus* and *Coracopsis*)
        - Loriinae (lories and lorikeets)
        - Psittaculirostrinae (fig-parrots)
        - Micropsittinae (pygmy-parrots)
        - Psittrichasinae (*Psittrichas fulgidus*)
    - Platycercidae
      - (Australian, New Zealand) New Caledonia plus few others)
      - fewest species but most diversified
      - Cockatoos. COCKATIELS, Rosellas, BUDGERIGARS, Kaka, Kea, Kakapos, etc.

continental lithosphere), most compact, most isolated, and most arid of all the inhabited continents, with the greatest percentage of evaporation and the lowest percentage of runoff (nearby New Guinea, on the other hand, ranks with the wettest environments on Earth; 1,061).

Continentality is not extreme, and influences of the surrounding maritime environment extend into the innermost regions of the Continent. Nowhere does the Continent experience either the high degree of seasonal contrast found, for instance, in the landlocked deserts of Asia, or the altitudinal gradients of South America. In contrast to Saharan Africa, Australia lacks hyperarid environments, even in its driest regions near Lake Eyre and the Simpson Desert, where rainfall, though highly irregular, is sufficient to maintain a vegetational cover on most dunes (1,061, 1,328).

More than half the land area of Australia is continuously or seasonally arid (the Eremian Zone or Province). More than 2/3rds of continental Australia receives an annual rainfall of less than 500 mm, and 1/3rd receives less than 250 mm. The latter precipitation level defines the "arid zone," except for a possible extension to 350 mm in the north, where temperatures are higher. Rainfall increases with elevation in eastern Australia, so that the lowland areas in the rainshadow of uplands are prone to drought (1,060, 1,072, 1,081, 1,213). The only continent to receive less precipitation is Antarctica.

THE AUSTRALIAN BIOTA is rich and highly diversified, and all the major adaptive zones are filled. There is no reason to believe that the flora and most faunal groups are not as rich, area for area, as those of other continents, although until now this has been demonstrated only for mammalian and avian faunas. Centers of high biotic diversity vary with the group. Overall, tropical New Queensland is the most species-rich part of the Continent; for agamid lizards and some other groups, it is the western desert, and for most endemic plant genera, it is the southwest corner.

Among the continents, Australia possesses the fewest avian species, numbering around 745, of which about 600 are resident and 383 endemic (300). The plant species that exist today in Australia possess remarkable powers of survival and regeneration, which must have served them well during the fluctuating climates of the late Tertiary and Quaternary periods. Associated with it's long isolation, large series of primitive forms persist, or have persisted, in Australia. These include early types of angiosperms, archaic conifers, the monotremes, the ant, *Nothomyrmecia*, archaic shrimps, and others. But no common distribution pattern characterizes these types (1,076, 1,089).

INFLUENCES OF PLATE MOVEMENTS. From its equatorial border with southeast Asia in Timor and New Guinea, Australia extends 50° southward between the Indian and Pacific Oceans. Its structure reflects convergence of the Pacific Plate on the northeast and east, convergence with the Sundaland salient (the Sunda Island Complex of Java, Sumatra, and Borneo, formerly connected to each other and to the southeastern arm of the Asian Continent) of Southeast Asia on the northwest, and divergence from the rest of Gondwana on the south and west, consequences of the growth of the eastern part of the Indo-Australian Plate out of Eastern Gondwana. Plate divergence along the southern margin is reflected in the latter's simple, low-lying morphology. Its convergent boundary is marked by high relief, intense earth movement, seismicity, and scattered volcanism. South of this boundary, as befits its intra-plate position, Australia is low-lying and quiescent, except for diffuse seismicity in the southwest, in the central-west at 22°S, 127°E, in the south about longitude 138°, and in the southeast, and two areas of volcanism. Outside of these areas, earth movement presumably is very slow (1,213).

STRUCTURAL SUBDIVISIONS. In the broadest sense, Australia consists of 3 major physiographic and structural subdivisions. The half of the Continent west of the Tasman Line is covered by the Great Plateau or Great Western Shield. This consists of exposed Precambrian blocks and fold belts overlain by thin Phanerozoic (Paleozoic, Mesozoic, plus Cenozoic; see Table 1) basins, mostly now eroded to sand and stony desert. It has an average height of 400-500 m. Low ranges, such as Macdonnell, Petermanns, and Rawlinsons, and massive areas of rock outcrop rise to heights of 500-750 m above the plateau, and constitute striking local features. The Cambrian ridges and terraces of the Davenport province of the Tennant Creek region (20°S x 134°E) may have existed as subaerial landforms for some 500 million yr and might be the oldest persisting, virtually undenuded landforms in the world (the porous, siliceous conglomerate and sandstone are incapable of substantial alteration). Though they provide little relief from the generally arid surroundings, a few permanent rockholes support freshwater fishes and other aquatic forms.

The 2nd major subdivision, the Central or Great Artesian Basin, lying to the east of the Tasman Line, consists of exposed Phanerozoic fold belts overlain by younger basins. It has never been elevated to any extent. Most of Australia's Jurassic and Cretaceous dinosauran fossils are found in this area. Southward-moving subterranean waters, derived mainly from precipitation over the western watershed of the Great Dividing Range in Queensland, give this section its identity as the Great Artesian Basin. Lesser sedimentary basins (Murray-Darling, Eucla, Coastal Plains, Northwest, Desert, and Gulf) around the Continental periphery owe their origins to marine inroads at different times in the Mesozoic era and Tertiary period; these can be identified edaphically (based on soil types). The 3rd major subdivision, the Eastern Highlands, the backbone of which is the so-called Great Dividing Range, have had a diversified history since their major elevation in the late Miocene, having been subject to successive phases of folding, elevation, warping, and erosion (1,089, 1,213, 1,387).

THE DRAINAGE SYSTEMS of Australia are of 3 types. Drainage over the Western Shield is uncoordinated, with scant and ephemeral surface waters (arheic). The drainage system of the arid zone, with the significant exception of the Murray-Darling Basin, is internal. Thus, drainage of the Macdonnell Range and the Lake Eyre Basin terminates in inland salt lakes or saline pans (endorheic), some less than 1 km in diameter. The drainage system of the remaining 30% of the Continent consists of rivers flowing into the sea (exorheic). At the distal ends of the major seasonal rivers, that ferry quartz sand from their headwaters to the arid depressions, there are well-defined concentrations of linear dunes.

Only the peripheral section of the Continent has deep and permanent waters that support diversified aquatic ecosystems. The low drainage divide that runs the length of the east coast diverts streams inland, contributing to the Continent's major drainage basin, the extensive Murray-Darling system in the southeast. This supports extensive inland riverine plains and savannas. It is traversed by the Lachlan, Murrumbidgee, Murray, and Goulburn Rivers, draining the southestern montane slopes, with the Darling River, a small sinuous channel that rises in the Queensland summer rainfall zone, entering from the north to join the Murray in the center of the Mallee country. Although the central areas of the Continent formerly were much better watered, Australia today lacks a major central drainage system comparable to the Mississippi or Amazon (1,089, 1,213, 1,328).

WATERS. Thus, Australia is characterized by a paucity of freshwater permanent lakes and rivers, an abundance of temporary waters, both standing and flowing, and the occurrence of a great number of permanent or temporary salt lakes. Despite a 6-8 month dry season, the northern rivers, with their high seasonal runoff, discharge more water into the sea than all but a few of the southern watercourses. As a general rule, the upland rivers and streams are fresher than the lowland ones (1,081).

The groundwaters are fresh in typical desert areas, and salt-tolerance problems probably rarely arise for the arid-country fauna. The presence of shrubs and trees and these fresh groundwaters are vitally important in the ecology of the avifauna, and the nonadaptability of some desert inhabitants to salt intake probably traces to the occurrence of the fresh groundwaters. The piscene freshwater fauna is dull compared with the rich counterparts that evolved in tropical Africa and South America.

Saltlakes are common over much of the southern half of the Continent. Even in Victoria, the best-watered of the mainland states, most natural bodies of standing water, have salinities in excess of 3% (311, 1,081, 1,213). [The Rock Parrot (*Neophema petrophila*), which inhabits the often waterless islets of the west and south coasts, can maintain its weight drinking seawater (see 311).]

AUSTRALIA'S VAST, DRY INLAND PLAINS (the half arid and half semi-arid Eremean Zone with unreliable rainfall) occupy 70% of its area and lie between the northern and northeastern Tropical zones with a summer monsoonal rain system that extends down from the north, and the southern Temperate Zone, with a winter Antarctic rain system that comes up from the south. The center of the Continent lies at, or toward, the limits of penetration of both systems, either or both of which may fail in a particular year. Even much of the better-watered fringes have long dry seasons. The eastern coast of Australia shows a more general distribution of rainfall throughout the year (311, 1,060, 1,061, 1,074, 1,089, 1,328).

In the virgin condition, almost the whole of the arid zone was covered by vegetation, there having been no extensive area of soil exposed to the elements. Some bare areas did exist, including some rock exposures on hills, the salt-covered surfaces of dry lakes (playas) and some sand dunes in driest regions. Structurally, the main arid-region plant communities are classified as woodlands, shrublands, and grasslands. In each of these, floristically-determined alliances can be recognized (1,072).

DUNES---DESERT FLORA. About 40% of the present land area of Australia is mantled by wind-blown sand, as opposed to only 20% of the much drier Saharan Desert (1,213). The 3 largest deserts, the Great Sandy, the Great Victoria, and the Simpson (Arunta) consist of parallel sand ridges, sometimes more than 150 km long. The stony desert areas include the Gibson Desert in Western Australia, the desert area west of Lake Eyre in South Australia, and the Sturt Desert in the northeast corner of South Australia, extending into Queensland (1,307).

Extensive fields of longitudinal "fossil" dunes and sand sheets cover immense areas. Except for aeolian sand movement on dune crests, they are currently stable but have been evolving for at least 250,000 yr. Dunes or sand ridges also fringe more than half of the coast (287, 1,060). Dunes farthest from the arid core are vegetated by eucalypt scrub in the southeast and *Acacia* scrub in the tropical northwest (1,329). In the past, in conditions of severe water stress on plants and the strong winds of glacial ages, these dunes moved toward the east in the southern part of the Continent, essentially toward the north in the Simpson and Strzelecki duneforms, and toward the west in the northern part of the whorl. In general, these directions agree with the present prevailing winds: easterly in the trades, northerly in the interzone, and westerly in the zone of traveling anticyclones (1,328). The arid-core dunes have seen aeolian activity on more than one occasion during the Holocene epoch, with the last major phase of construction having been 25,000-13,000 yr ago (1,329, 1,330).

Even in the most arid region, the Simpson Desert, north of Lake Eyre, the dunes are fixed by spinifex tussocks (*Triodia*)--"an ocean of Spinifex covered waves" (see 1,329)--with only summit crests of "live" sand (see 311, 1,060). Interior distances seem unlimited; to the traveler, the horizon is just as far ahead one day as it was the day before. "The country comes in large pieces, miles of woodland, then days of saltbush and mulga; the spinifex seems to extend forever". The same kinds of birds and shrubby habitat are found distributed for nearly 3,000 km (139, 1,085).

Although these vast Australian plains comprise the most extensive desert area in the Southern Hemisphere, no part of them falls in the category "extreme desert" in the sense of Meigs (see 311). They are characterized by a hot summer and a cold winter, and the presence, even in very dry areas (mean annual rainfall of 200 mm), of woody shrubs, or even trees, such as mulga (*Acacia aneura*), several species of desert eucalypts, desert oak (*Casuarina decaisneana*), succulents (e.g., *Atriplex*), and others (311), all in a climatic zone where elsewhere one would expect only a treeless semi-desert (1,298).

A MAJOR FEATURE OF THE ARID COUNTRY FLORA is an abundance of annuals, a life-history strategy favored by erratic rainfall. But the sclerophylly (xeromorphy--structure adapted to arid conditions--that includes a reduction in leaf size and plant size) is more an adaptation to soils of low fertility than to erratic rainfall (1,068). The low rainfall is associated with generally clear skies, allowing large net radiant heat influxes by day and large losses by night (when the color temperature of the sky may approximate -10°C; 1,087), particularly in the summer. These fluxes result in large changes in, and extreme values of, ambient temperatures, particularly within the latitude range 22-27°S. Daytime temperatures may range above 55°C and nighttime temperatures drop to 10°C or less, frequently falling below freezing in the winter, but the combination of low relief, low altitude, and relatively high humidity prevents the development of very low temperature extremes (830, 1,328).

The total angiospermous flora of the arid zone amounts to 102 families, 503 genera, and about 2,600 species, with the Myrtaceae having 362 species, Compositae 253, Gramineae 190, Papilionaceae 183, Mimosaceae 165, and Chenopodiaceae 136 (1,068). Some life forms that are typical of desert flora elsewhere are inconspicuous or lacking, for example deciduousness and spinescense. The plains support an extraordinarily rich, highly habitat-specific, lacertilian (of or relating to lizards) fauna, very probably the richest in the world (see 408, 1,085, 1,089).

VEGETATIONAL ZONES. As a consequence of the subdued relief and the vast land area, Australian vegetational zones are determined mainly by the prevailing climate, though in certain areas the geology and soil types play considerable roles. Thus, since the inland plains are surrounded by belts of progressively wetter country, this has led to a broad semi-concentric zonation of vegetation and, to a lesser extent, of soils, which are of great biogeographical and ecological significance (68, 73, 1,061, 1,074). The seasonality of the precipitation also has a major influence on biogeographic patterns and modes of adaptation. More than 80% of the Continent has at least 3 months each year that are without effective precipitation (1,061).

Because of its high rate of endemism at the species level (with many examples of parallel evolution), the Southwestern Province generally is considered to be a floral "ecological island." Thus, the persisting arid regimes in central and northwestern Australia isolate southwestern Australia from the rest of the Continent by 2,000 km of arid terrain. The Nullarbor region should perhaps be regarded as an edaphic and, probably, periodic climatic barrier to transcontinental plant dispersal, though it may not have been effective throughout its existence (1,074). In having only 66 species of forest-woodland passerines, southwestern Australia shows the same kind of avifaunal impoverishment as Tasmania (see pp. 36, 37; 1,086).

INFERTILE SOILS---EDAPHIC CLIMAXES. Many of the soils seen over Australia are of ancient origin. They have been leached for many millions of yr (probably in a tropical-subtropical environment) and, more recently, have been subjected to considerable increments of cyclic salt, and possibly of calcareous loess, blown inland from exposed coastal areas. These pedogenic processes have led to vast areas of soils with marked deficiencies in many essential major and minor vegetational nutrient elements or to soils that may induce calcium toxicity or salinity problems for plant growth. From an ecological and evolutionary standpoint, these are the most outstanding characteristics of the edaphic mantle of Australia (and of New Guinea and Tasmania; 287, 1,060; 1,064).

Saline edaphic landscapes are developed most extensively in arid inland Australia, particularly on the Western Plateau and in the Central Lowlands, where they are associated with former drainage patterns and saline lake systems. But quite apart from these, very extensive areas of salt-affected soils occur, covering about 1/3rd of the Continent. Most of these salt-affected soils are of low to very low fertility (1,061). The sclerophyllous (heath) flora of Australia typically is found on infertile soils derived from sandstone or acidic granitic rocks or on wind-blown sands, whereas the flora of savannas is well developed on more fertile soils derived from argillaceous (clayey) rocks or alluvial deposits (1,064).

Certain edaphic types--such as heavy gray and brown cracking clays, highly calcareous soils, saline soils, and soils of low nutrient status--may induce marked changes in the vegetation to produce an edaphic climax vegetation within the climatic climax. Such edaphic climaxes are characteristic of large areas of the Australian landscape. The upper stratum of the vegetational formation may be modified or even absent on these soils; the understory may be distinctly different, varying from a savanna of grasses and herbs, to sclerophyllous (heath-*Triodia*), to a chenopodous understorey of *Atriplex*, *Maireana*, etc. Minor edaphic barriers are particularly important in the speciation of plants, for example in the strikingly floristically-rich, southwest of Australia (1,062, 1,089).

Oligotrophic (nutrient poor) soils have favored the heathland elements; calcareous and solonized soils have led to the expansion of chenopodous shrublands and some mallee species of eucalyptus across southern Australia, and contributed to the disjunctions of heathland elements on oligotrophic soils across southwestern Australia; the cracking clays and young basaltic soils have favored the development of grasslands; the deep red volcanic loams trap most of the rain and have enabled the tropical-subtropical rainforests to survive in a series of refugia along the eastern coast (1,076).

FIRE-TOLERANT FLORA. At the present time, the Continent is under a dry climatic regime, comparable to what it was on several other occasions in the Pleistocene and Sub-Recent (164; see pp. 37, 38). This combination of low soil fertility and a dry climatic regime has favored the dominance of such plants as eucalypts with an associated flora of sclerophyllous, fire-tolerant shrubs that possess long-lived, small sclerotinous leaves and heavily-armored, serotinous fruits, that are comparatively resistant to predation. The shrub layer may be continuous or broken with a ground vegetation of grasses and low sclerophyllous plants. Much of this associated flora survives even intense burns. On good soils not exposed to drought, the eucalypt associations are replaced by rainforests. In dry regions, the eucalypts give way to grasslands or desert, and on poor soils near the coast, heath and shrub communities prevail (641, 1,062).

THERMAL ADAPTATIONS OF PLANTS. In terms of thermal adaptations of the flora, it is possible to recognize 3 broad groups, the megatherms (tropical), mesotherms (warm temperate), and microtherms (cool temperate), with their thermal optima at 28°, 18-22°, and 10-12°C, and lower threshold temperatures of 10°, 5°, and at or below 0°C, respectively. Under the present climatic regime these are concentrated in zones where the mean annual temperatures exceed 25°, 15-20°, and 10-15°C, respectively (20-25°C for the subtropical macrotherms). Prominent members of the microthermal element are the austral conifers and *Nothofagus* (1,061). The critical air-temperature thresholds for seasonal shoot growth of *Nothofagus* is 10°C, for most southern species of *Eucalyptus* it is 16-18°C, and for subtropical to warm temperate species of arid-zone *Acacia* it is 24-26°C; for tropical species of *Eucalyptus* it probably is about 25°C. Understorey species may have temperature thresholds a few degrees lower than species in the upper stratum (1,064).

GENERAL CLIMATIC CHARACTERISTICS OF AUSTRALIA, New Guinea, and Tasmania are dictated by their latitudinal positions astride the mid-latitude, high-pressure belt. Spanning the range of 10° to 44°S, Australia, like southern Africa straddles climatic zones from the tropic of Capricorn through the subtropical high pressure belt to the zone of southern westerlies. The effects of this range of climatic zones is imprinted on the landscape--on its sediments and soils--finding expression through the diversity of its various land forms.

The absence of high orographic barriers in Australia reduces the components of circulation patterns that are caused by local geographical variability. The prevailing wind patterns and general aridity over continental Australia reflect the dominant control by eastward-moving anticyclonic cells that track between 37-38°S latitude in the summer and between 29-32°S in the winter. Seasonal changes are linked with these solar-controlled shifts in the paths of the anticyclonic cells and associated movements of the south-easterlies in the inter-tropical convergence zone, which influence the climate of eastern and northern Australia and New Guinea, and the westerlies, which influence the climate of southern Australia and Tasmania (1,061, 1,328).

DIRECT EFFECTS OF GLACIATION on the Continent have been almost insignificant, with the exception of Tasmania, which experienced substantial glaciation, but the indirect effects have been substantial. The latter were expressed in changes in water balance and variations in intensity and frequency of aeolian events in the dry interior. The diversity and extent of these effects in the legacy of rivers, lakes, and sand dunes, was such that few elements of the Australian landscape can be said to have escaped the influence of changes that accompanied the last glacial to post-glacial cycle, spanning the past 120,000 yr. Notwithstanding this legacy, the contribution of glacial processes to our knowledge of Quaternary Australian environments is subordinate to reconstructions that are based on sedimentation sequences, which often are far-removed from glacial or peri-glacial areas.

THE PROBLEM OF CATEGORIZING DESERT ENVIRONMENTS is a complex one. Although the vegetation of a region generally may indicate its climate with much greater accuracy and sensitivity than meteorological data (1,298), it does not always suffice merely to describe a habitat as being composed of, say, mulga, spinifex, sand dune, or salt lake (160). A variety of land forms and vegetation types can occur even in relatively small areas, and this diversity is reflected in the distribution of fauna. In the case of inland areas of Australia, the rainfall usually has been described as erratic. But detailed recent studies have shown that only a small area of the arid inland does not receive at least 50 mm of summer and 25 mm of winter rain in 8 out of every 10 yr (see 160).

Because microtopographical features occur in the arid zone, these tiny but regular rainfalls are concentrated in small areas, sometimes as much as 10-12-fold. As a result, precipitation is concentrated in small areas of perhaps only 5% of the arid land surface, producing favorable edaphic moisture conditions for vegetational growth, even after falls of as little as 1 cm at a time. These "mesic areas" are the sites of most of the annual growth of plants in the arid zone, where most of the birds occur. Accordingly, the extreme conditions that often have been cited as typical of the arid Australian inland, may not be typical of the areas used or relied upon by the fauna (see 160). In fact, it can be asserted generally that local relief in Australia has particular significance for the creation of microhabitats and refugia (1,061).

Accordingly, rather than rely on the amount of precipitation and its seasonal distribution as measures of the aqueous regimes that influence biotic responses, it generally is mandatory to adopt a water-balance approach. This should take into account the nature of the vegetative surface, the buffering effects of soil water storage and losses due to runoffs, deep drainage, and evapotranspiration (1,061). For example, speaking of the Kalahari Desert, "Even in the worst parts of it there is a cover of bushes and small trees which survive one or two-year droughts" (1,297), presumably because of the presence of underground water supplies.

THE HIGHLANDS. There is little high land in Australia. The Great Dividing Range (Eastern Divide or Highlands) that separates the narrow coastal plains from the dry interior is a relic of an early phase of interaction with the Pacific Plate--the ridges and oceanic basins of the adjacent southwest Pacific are the more modern relics. The Great Dividing Range is by far the greatest highland area and probably was the first considerable topographical barrier. It is a dynamic boundary that splits the pan-Australian fauna into two great assemblages--the distinctive southern Bassian and central and western Eyrean faunal provinces or ecologically distinct areas of W. Baldwin Spencer--which, accordingly, evolved independently (164). It sweeps down the Continent from north to south, forming a great boomerang-shaped arc of mountains, gullies, and high plains paralleling the eastern coastline.

In the far north, at the base of Cape York, The Divide consists merely of a series of low hills, whereas in the southeast it rises to over 2,000 m, culminating in Mt. Kosciusko in the Snowy Mountains at 2,340 m, the highest point on the Continent; it never has been more than several 100 m higher. Apart from this Divide, the only areas over 600 m in altitude are small parts of the Hamersley Range (up to 1,230 m) in the arid northwest and the Macdonnell and Musgrave Ranges (up to 1,520 and 1,440 m, respectively) in the center. These highlands constitute the Continent's major watershed, forming an important divide between the shorter eastward-flowing rivers that mostly flow directly to the sea, and the extensive westward-flowing meandering streams of low gradient of the Murray-Darling and Carpenteria basins to the west (139, 1,061, 1,073, 1,089 1,292).

THE TECTONIC MOVEMENTS that gave rise to the Great Dividing Range commenced in the Mesozoic era (see Table 1) and continued into the Tertiary period and are broadly coincident in time with the break-up of Gondwana and the eventual rifting and separation of Australia-Antarctica. Various lines of evidence suggest that upland areas and drainage patterns of much the same configuration as today existed by early to mid-Tertiary time. While further elevation occurred in the Pliocene epoch, the Great Dividing Range did not experience the very strong late Pliocene and Pleistocene upthrusts that brought the Andes to their present height. As mentioned above, not all of the Great Dividing Range, though elevated, is mountainous. There are some relatively flat plains, such as those around Canberra, as well as remnants of a flat landscape that existed in past geological time. The latter has been uplifted, dissected, and eroded, leaving characteristic high plateaux.

Moreover, Australian ranges and mountains are not craggy pinnacles. Although some are steep, most are in the form of plateaux, often defined by relatively abrupt scarps, or are merely large, rounded masses of granite. Mt. Kosciusko is not a peak, but the highest point of a gently rising ridge system. Little of the Divide is below 600 m and much is above 900 m. The climate is generally harsh throughout the highlands, though there are many differences from place to place. The yearly temperature range is considerable, frosts are common, as are sleet and snow in the higher mountains, even sufficient for skiing. Because of its situation in the belt of westerly wind regime and associated sub-antarctic low-pressure influences, this plateau terrain intercepts heavy precipitations, from about 760 mm in some of the relatively dry subalpine areas (from climatic treeline to 300-450 m below it) up to more than 2,540 mm in leeward alpine sites (above climatic treeline). Consequently, stream flow is highly reliable compared with that in most other parts of Australia (139, 1,073, 1,292).

THE GEOLOGY AND CLIMATE OF THESE HIGHLANDS have produced a highly varied topography and multifarious avian habitats. There are rich tropical rainforests on the lava plateaux of the Atherton Tablelands and the Lamington plateau, the largest of these not much more than about 2,600 sq. km; there are the bleak plains and eucalypt forests of the igneous hills of New England; there are the sandstone plateaux of the Blue Mountains and the granite mountains of the southeastern highlands; there are the fluted dolerite ramparts of the Tasmanian highlands; and there are some small glacial lakes. At the southwestern extremity of the highlands in western

Victoria is the Grampian Range, which has a rich flora, including about 20 endemic species. This range probably acted as a refugium for plants during epochs when there were marine incursions into the Murray-Darling Basin.

Compared with that of other Australian habitats and New Guinean rainforests, the Australian rainforest fauna has a low diversity (see 1,088). Though appearing physically insignificant throughout their length, the highlands presently form the barrier between the coastal eastern and southern fauna, and the inland and western fauna, including distinct coastal and inland avifaunal assemblages. On the whole, the two faunal groups remain quite well separated, providing support for distinguishing between Bassian and Eyrean faunal subdivisions (see 139, 1,074, 1,089, 1,292).

PALEOBOTANY AND PALEOCLIMATOLOGY

Generally speaking, the Australian angiospermous flora usually is regarded as unusual, chiefly in the presence of a high proportion of endemic, xeromorphic species, and partly because two genera, *Eucalyptus* and *Acacia*, dominate the vegetation of much of the Continent. At the level of families (but not of species or genera), the rainforest flora of the Australian region appears to have the widest array of primitive angiosperms (flowering plants) in the world, suggesting that the rainforest refugia of Australasia are of great antiquity. It seems probable that the Australian angiospermous flora has evolved from a segment of a ancient world flora that contained several dozen and perhaps more than 100 families. Having become isolated in Australia, the various taxa of this segment developed independently to produce a host of endemic groups in response to the ever-changing and peculiar environmental conditions (1,068, 1,071). [Some of the world's smaller families have their highest representation of genera and/or species in Australia, and it is possible that most or all of these families originated there (1,068).]

THE HISTORY OF THE ANGIOSPERMOUS FLORA OF AUSTRALIA can be divided into 3 main phases: (a) the ancient Gondwanan flora; (b) the xeromorphic flora, which evolved from certain Gondwanan lineages; and (c) the arid-zone flora, which was derived from some modified Gondwanan lineages, some xeromorphic taxa, and some littoral taxa. In addition, throughout the ages, dispersal from distant sites (probably mostly by birds) must be invoked to explain the presence on the Continent of numerous other taxa, including many from southeastern Asia, a number from South America and the subantarctic islands, and many littoral taxa (1,068).

The closed forests and sclerophyllous communities of Australia contain a very high proportion of angiosperms that have retained primitive floral and/or morphological characters, an indication that the flora developed early in the evolutionary history of angiosperms. It is suggested that the environmental gradients seen today in tropical New Guinea hold all the clues needed to elucidate the evolutionary development of the Australian angiospermous flora. Although the fossil evidence is not conclusive, the indications are that all of the major groups found in New Guinea today, both taxonomic and physiological, were widespread across southern Australia early in the Tertiary period. The important difference between Australia and New Guinea is that, whereas New Guinea has maintained its climatic characteristics relatively intact through the Tertiary to the present, southern Australia has become 5-10°C cooler since the late Tertiary; in addition, annual rainfall over much of the Continent has decreased considerably and become more seasonal (see 1,064).

THE ANGIOSPERMS apparently colonized Australia (probably via Antarctica) from the northerly regions of Gondwana in Albian times (see Table 1). This was considerably later than the inception of angiosperms in southern South America (Barremian-Aptian times)--also a possible source--and in northern Gondwana and southern Laurasia (in the Barremian). An equally important feature of Australian Cretaceous flora was the proliferation of podocarpacean gymnosperms (plants that produce naked seeds, for example conifers). Angiosperms did not become pre-emptive of the gymnosperms until the succeeding Paleogene subdivision of the Tertiary period, when many Gondwanan families and genera occupied the Continent (1,065, 1,071).

The phytogeographical evidence suggests that many genera and families of angiosperms evolved in the early Cretaceous period or earlier, before Australia and East Antarctica drifted apart. They may have arisen in, or first pioneered, ecotonal situations near pre-angiospermous rainforests or adjacent transitional regions, perhaps as shrubs rather than long-lived trees. Those lineages that adapted to the rainforest environment very probably became long-lived trees and thereby embraced the least restrictive conservative device (long life) available to the genetic systems of plants. (1,071, 1,075, 1,076). [see also p. 613 *et seq.*, **Phylogeny of Angiosperms**]

DISJUNCT FLORISTIC DISTRIBUTIONS within Australia indicate that the flora was formerly much more widespread from north to south and east to west. The incursion of seas, depositing great depths of limestone sediments over large areas of the southern coastline of Australia during the Miocene epoch, would have caused east-west disjunctions in the original calciphobic, tropical-subtropical, sclerophyllous flora of the south, which had been able to extend over large areas of lateritic soils. An example of these is the Nullarbor karst region, which emerged in the mid-Pliocene and undoubtedly has remained dry land since then. As mentioned above, this region probably has been and continues to be an edaphic barrier to the interchange of plants between the southwest and southeast since the late Tertiary period.

Disjunctions also are found between the south and the north on both the eastern and western coastlines, as well as across northern Australia. Remnants of the flora also have been stranded in central Australia. Vegetational fragmentation appears to have resulted from the marked change in climate over the last 10 million yr, as arid conditions developed over much of the Continent; at the same time the climate of the southern part of the Continent became cooler, stranding a sub-tropical flora in a warm-temperate to cool-temperate environment (1,063-1,065, 1,068).

THE FOSSIL RECORD OF PLANTS IN AUSTRALIA is inadequate to pinpoint the geographic origins of its plant taxa, but it does show the continual evolution of the flora under the influence of changing climate. Given the overriding control of climate, the phytogeographic zones are likely to have been in existence for no more than 2 million yr (282), and the present distribution of the biota must be regarded as a very recent, temporary phenomenon. Inasmuch as rapid changes are apparent from the Quaternary record, accurate chronology is essential. It now is apparent that Quaternary climatic changes were as rapid and profound in Australia as they were in the better-known continents of the Northern Hemisphere (287).

LATEST JURASSIC THROUGH MIDDLE MIOCENE. As gauged from the mega- and microfossil records, the Australian flora during the latest Jurassic and earliest Cretaceous times contained prolific gymnosperms in which podocarpaceous conifers and cycadeoidalean plants were strongly represented. Cryptograms were diverse. The evidence argues strongly in favor of a pan-Australian gymnospermous flora during the Neocomian and Aptian. This vegetation was dominantly podocarpacean, although araucariacean, ginkoalean, and cycadeoidalean plants were represented significantly. The cryptogamous element underwent major modification, though not always synchronously in different areas.

The vegetational assemblages suggest a temperate climate with moderately high rainfall and seasonally dry periods. The medial portion of the Cretaceous period (Albian to Turonian) was a time of major vegetational change; it was marked especially by the introduction of angiosperms and by qualitative changes in both gymnospermous and cryptogamous elements. Thus, gymnospermous elements underwent progressive alteration. In the southeast, the Cycadeoidales declined in importance during the Albian and were virtually absent by the Cenomanian. The conifers, which were abundant throughout the Albian, assumed increasing dominance in Cenomanian megafloras. Cryptogamous floras were strongly diversified. The Ginkoales persisted, with some modification, throughout the Albian. The cool, temperate climatic regime possibly persisted, but with some warming into the Cenomanian, when schizaeaceous ferns displayed an increased diversity. The rapid decline of the latter and the introduction of *Dacrydium franklinii*-type pollen implies cool Turonian conditions (1,065).

The warm-temperate equable-climate and rainforest vegetation of late-Cretaceous times continued with few changes into the Tertiary. By the time the Continent broke free from East Antarctica and began drifting northward in the Eocene epoch, Proteacea (including *Banksia*-, *Dryandra*-, and *Grevillea*-like types) and a range of other elements characteristic of the present day (*Casuarina*, cycads close to the modern genera *Bowenia* and *Lepidozamia*) had already been acquired. Direct overland dispersal into Australia via the South Tasman Rise may have been possible until the close of the Eocene epoch.

In general, it is fairly well documented that there was a subtropical-tropical climate over the entire Continent, with conditions varying locally with time and latitude (see 106, 816). Many taxa that would be considered as tropical on present-day distributions have been in Australia for most of the Tertiary period. Many were present in southeastern Australia when it was adjacent to Antarctica.

GRASSES have been a component of the Australian flora since early in the Tertiary period. A large number of genera of these appear to have been on the Continent since the time of its association with other parts of Gondwana, and so represent an ancient element of the flora (1,070). The major changes in pollen assemblages coincide with paleoclimatic changes (1,067). For example, grass pollen becomes increasingly prominent in fossil material collected from the center of the Continent after the increasingly frequent periods of aridity began in the middle Miocene epoch, and fossil pollen of *Acacia* appears for the first time in widespread localities (1,076).

Large parts of the present Continental area--across southern and into central Australia--were vegetated by a broad-leafed, lush, mesophytic flora (vegetation requiring a moderate water supply). This was characterized by mixed forests of austral gymnosperms and evergreen angiosperms. Floral diversity was high, 200 taxa occurring in one assemblage. Such types as the southern beeches (*Nothofagus*), podocarps, and araucarias, that now are restricted to pockets of subtropical and temperate rainforests, were well represented (173). The wide distribution of *N. brassi* pollen suggests very high precipitation levels; present requirements of the group are in the vicinity of 1,500-1,800 mm/yr (1,060). [Fossil plant data are lacking from central and northern Australia for the Eocene epoch and for the Tertiary period in general (1,089).]

The Paleogene fossil floras of southern Australia also contain spores and pollen types that appear to represent present-day genera that occur in areas that have seasonal climates (e.g., Mediterranean-type areas) and on nutrient-deficient soils. The presence of contrasting types in the pollen assemblages probably indicates that a diversity of habitats existed in southern Australia at that time, rather than a mixture of diverse elements in a single uniform habitat. It also indicates that the Gondwanan-derived elements had diversified to include plants that were able to tolerate seasonal or semi-arid environments and soils of low nutrient status (1,074). In this connection, the finding of considerable amounts of trees in Australian climatic zones where, elsewhere, one would expect only a treeless semi-desert, may indicate that tall, woody species had a much longer time to adapt to arid conditions than was the case on other continents (1,298).

Concerning the composition of the southern Australian flora prior to and during the period of separation of Australia and Antarctica in the late Eocene, it appears that a diversity of geographically distinct floras existed before the Continental break, and that the flora after the break is physiognomically very little different and no more diverse taxonomically. The rainforests covering the southern region in those times may have been populated in the majority by genera that are now extinct. What is certain is that the *Nothofagus* Proteaceae-Myrtaceae forest that left its pollen signature across Australia existed in the Eocene (1,066).

A substantial drop in Continental temperatures occurred in the late Eocene epoch as Australia moved northward (1,089). An abundant rainfall supported extensive freshwater lakes into the Miocene and Pliocene epochs. The climate was humid and remained equable but temperatures fell in the medial Miocene, dropped markedly in the latest Miocene (5-6 mya), and warmed markedly (judging from sea-water temperatures) in the early Pliocene (3.9-4.3 mya; 164, 287, 1,089). The Pliocene Myrtaceous assemblages of the southeast are thought to represent mostly closed forest with some open areas (1,067). Molds and casts of fruits resembling *Eucalyptus*, *Angophora*, and other eucalypts are found in Tertiary deposits of either Miocene or Eocene-Oligocene age (68; see also p. 55, **Trees of the Genus *Eucalyptus***). There is no evidence of the existence of arid zones in Australia prior to about 20 mya. The vast arid to subhumid stretches that now characterize most of the continent are of relatively recent origin in late Pliocene-Pleistocene time, about 2½ mya, though localized areas of desert probably have existed in inland Australia for much longer (172, 282). Open savanna, woodland-forests and grasslands, now typical of the Australian landscape, did not become widespread until the Pleistocene epoch (1,067).

LATE MIOCENE THROUGH PLIOCENE. A deterioration from tropical-like conditions to strongly marked seasonal climates with increasingly frequent periods of aridity took place in the medial-to-late Miocene epoch, and deep sea cores south of Australia strongly indicate that sea surface temperatures were highly variable (106, 287, 816). The invariable responses to increasing aridity were reduction in the foliage canopy, survival of the more xerophytic species, extinction of many taxa, and decrease in the number of taxa. There was a drastic geographical "withdrawal" of mesophytic and rainforest elements to the east coast and New Guinea. Other species that previously were found in the southwest "withdrew" to the northern regions, and still others became restricted to Tasmania.

Thus, the cool, temperate *Nothofagus* forests containing the *fusca-menziesii* sections survived in eastern Victoria and Tasmania and in small areas in the highlands on the border of New South Wales and Queensland. Subtropical-warm temperate heathland taxa that were widespread across Australia during much of the Tertiary period now are markedly reduced in number and diversity in the lowland, monsoonal north of the Continent; a limited number of genera and families survive in montane habitats of north Queensland and New Guinea. At the same time there was a diversification and a rise in dominance of xeric (arid-thriving) genera like *Eucalyptus*, *Casuarina*, and *Acacia*, and of the grasses and Compositae that characterize Australia today (281 1,060, 1,076).

The faunal evidence also indicates changes in humidity and temperature in much of Australia during the Cenozoic. For example, there occur in Mid-Cenozoic sediments of interior Australia a high diversity of medium-sized to large mammals, including Koalas from the Simpson Desert and porpoises in the Lake Frome area. Taken together, these finds suggest more humid, more heavily vegetated conditions supporting long-lasting inland bodies of water and perennial rivers, which are atypical of these regions today (173). [Perennial rivers and streams are restricted essentially to those waterways with substantial catchments in areas with runoff exceeding 250 mm/yr (1,060).] The changes in these faunas through the remainder of the Cenozoic suggests progressive climatic deterioration and cooling to the present time (106, 280).

PLEISTOCENE. Extensive mountain building that began in the late Tertiary and was most extensive in the late Miocene and Pliocene continued into the Pleistocene and gave rise to the Great Dividing Range and the Mt. Lofty and Flinders Ranges. Combined with broad warping and desiccation, these changes isolated the Lake Eyre region from the sea. Cenozoic volcanism extended through eastern Australia from Cape York Peninsula to Tasmania. A large number of lakes of volcanic origin occur in western Victoria, as well as elsewhere. Lakes resulting from Pleistocene glacial action are confined almost entirely to Tasmania. There are only 5 lakes of this type on the mainland, namely those near Mt. Kosciusko (287, 1,081).

Having occurred in relatively restricted area and in brief spasms separated by long quiescent intervals, volcanism would not *per se* have greatly affected the Australian biota (287). Indirectly, though, volcanism significantly affected edaphic conditions and vegetation by providing substantial islands with favorable soil-water conditions or relatively high nutrient status on a generally dry and infertile continent (287, 1,060). An archipelago of "islands" of soil landscapes with high nutrient status stretches from New Guinea down through the Great Dividing Range into Tasmania. At these localities, uplift and dissection together with volcanism have provided base-rich materials for soil development, of which basaltic volcanic rocks of Tertiary to Quaternary age and derived alluvium are the primary sources. The dominant soils in this class in Australia are black, self-mulching clays usually developed on basalt, which show no response to added nutrients (1,061).

It was during the Pleistocene ice ages that the greatest climatic oscillations took place, and these were as rapid and profound in Australia as they were in the continents of the Northern Hemisphere (287). For example, from 25,000 to 15,000 yr ago, which includes the last glacial period, it is estimated that the mean annual temperature was lowered by 6-10°C. Though there is considerable evidence of a dominantly drier climate throughout the whole period, lakes in southern Australia filled at the time when temperatures were lowest (282). Though there was no extensive glaciation, there were marked pluvial (prolonged periods of wet climate) and arid periods, with the formation of the great inland arid regions. These still dominate fuanal distribution patterns and influence the speciation process (164).

The great central Lake Diere covered an area of 100,000 sq. km at its maximum during the Pleistocene pluvial peaks. This created a formidable barrier dividing dry-adapted terrestrial organisms into eastern and western populations. Lake Diere now is represented by the remnant salt Lakes Eyre, Frome, and Torrens; the major cause of the salinity of these lakes is atmospheric transport of oceanic salts (311). Lake Diere's barrier effects in those times would have been reinforced by the Flinders range and the sea bight to the south (which existed during heightened sea levels at pre- and interglacial maxima). It has been suggested that this barrier complex allowed many members of the Eyrean (see below) avifauna to differentiate into eastern and western forms, some so markedly different that they now form valid species (see 164).

Where the Quaternary paleobotanical record extends back far enough, it shows periods in which 2 types of vegetation alternate. One example of these 2 types is comprised of 2 periods of eucalypt forest or woodland with a shrub understorey, alternating with open woodland, 50,000-11,000 yr ago in southeastern Australia. Another example is comprised of 5 wooded periods (wet sclerophyll in the oldest to dry sclerophyll in the youngest and at present) alternating with non-wooded periods over a time span of 350,000 yr at Lake George in the eastern highlands (282). These periods are linked with the glacial-interglacial cycles and marked climatic variations.

INFLUENCES OF FIRE ON THE FLORA. Except in rainforests, fire is a frequent and predictable, although irregular event throughout Australia. The long association with fire--at least since the onset of aridity in the late Tertiary period, and possibly long before--has led to the evolution of a wide range of adaptations by plants to particular regimes of fire, with the result that even intense fires are followed by a rapid renewal of the vegetation. The adaptations that enable Australian plants to survive fire include thick, insulating layers of bark, woody fruits that open after being heated, epicormic buds, subterranean woody structures with numerous dormant buds, such as the lignotuber of eucalypts and other species that grow in regions of frequent fire, and hard seeds that accumulate in the soil and germinate after being heated.

Of 93 species studied in sclerophyllous woodland, 43% regenerated vegetatively and from seed, 27% were killed by fire and regenerated from seed, 22% regenerated by vegetative means, and 7% regenerated by means unknown (1,062, 1,064). It should be borne in mind, however, that many features of Australian plants that have been described as adaptations to fire may be considered more broadly as traits that are adaptive to recovery after stress. The plants are not adapted simply to fire, but to a particular climatic regime, of which fire is a part (see 1,062).

There is some evidence that aboriginal Man could have played a very prominent role in shaping the natural vegetational history of Australia through the use of fire, as reconstructed from the abundance of charcoal particles. The oldest confirmed date for Man's presence is 32,000 yr ago, but he may have been present at least 8,000 yr earlier (see 282, 1,061).

THE PARROTS AND OTHER AVIFAUNA

DIVERSITY. The avifauna of Australia is diversified and well-balanced, and is characterized by a major nectarivorous component. It is of "world" type, with widespread and cosmopolitan families well represented (see below for a discussion of its unbalanced aspects). Australia shares with Asia 8 of the 24 groups of accipiters and falcons, 7 of the 13 groups of herons, and many genera of ducks and rallids, but these are exceptions among the Australian avifauna. Endemism is clearly higher at the generic level than in Africa. All the Australian owls, apart from the tytonids, most of the genera of kingfishers and pigeons, and the genera of parrots (except for some that extend to Indonesia), are endemic (815). Some 18 families (28% of the total number), most of them passerines, also are endemic, as compared to 30 families in South America and only 7 in Africa (1,255). For comparison of diversity, the number of families per 250,000 sq. km is 1.87 for Australia, 1.17 for Neotropica, and 0.87 for Africa. The corresponding figures for species are 16.6 (27.4 if New Guinea is included), 39.7, and 20.0, respectively (292, 815, 1,086).

Although the greatest number of parrot species in any country are found in Brazil, the greatest diversity of types in the world are found in Australia and New Guinea (Australia also has a much higher diversity of terrestrial predatory lizards than any other land mass; 408, 1,085, 1,089). Australia is inhabited by the world's smallest and largest parrot species (the 10-cm-long pygmy parrots, *Micropsitta*, and the up-to-45-50-cm-long Palm Cockatoos, *Probosciger aterrimus*). All 6 subfamilies (Table 2a) occur there, 3 of which extend into the Oriental Region (335). Diversity in Africa and Asia is surprisingly low (173). The extent to which adaptive radiations of Australian parrots (and meliphagids) have capitalized on prominent ecological "opportunities" provides parallels to the radiations of the marsupials (153). The parrots, for example, occupy a far wider range of roles or adaptive zones than elsewhere, including some roles for which, at first sight, they would seem to be ill-fitted structurally (292; see also below). Allopatry is marked in many genera (815).

In both Australia and Africa, aquatic niches are dominated by wide-ranging or cosmopolitan avifaunal groups. A lower proportion of Australian terrestrial birds belong to widespread groups of superspecies than is the case for African avifauna. This reflects the greater isolation of Australia than Africa, today and in the past (815; see below and pp. 239-244, **Paleogeography and Paleoclimatology of Africa, Influences on Avifauna**).

HABITATS---FEEDING ADAPTATIONS. The major factor that governs avian distribution is vegetation. There are distinct assemblages of rainforest, eucalypt, woodland, and spinifex desert species. It is suggested that the Australian desert birds and ants play the granivorous trophic role at the expense of mammalian (rodent) granivores, and members of the Meliphagidae and Psittaciformes occupy the adaptive zones of southwestern avian families elsewhere (see 1,089). The variety of habitats penetrated by Australian parrots range from the coastal, tropical rainforests to the rocky, offshore islets and the arid deserts of the interior. The species that inhabit open country also show a strong attachment to trees (1). Of 53 species, no less than 38 forage for the larger amount of their food from low herbage or on the ground (127). The cockatoos and lorikeets are restricted to Australasia and only 5 of the genera of parrots found in Australia are not endemic to the Continent (139).

Although the restricted bodily morphology and very specialized kind of bill structure (for nipping and cutting, or crushing) of Australian parrots scarcely seem amenable to such novel adaptations, they have produced nectarivorous, berry, fruit, flower-petal, and fungus-eating forms, forms that dig for roots and corms, powerful nut-crackers, and terrestrial and arboreal species with specializations for feeding on seeds ranging from those of the smallest grasses to the 2-cm-long seeds of eucalypts. There are large black cockatoos that even get at wood-boring grubs by tearing the bark from trees, much like a woodpecker (153, 292).

Thus, Australian parrots have, in essence, entered the adaptive zones of finches, sparrows, and weavers, grosbeaks and barbets, bulbuls and tanagers, meliphagids (honey-eaters), sunbirds, bananaquits and conebills, woodpeckers, and even terrestrial rodents (166, 1,086). Their abilities to diversify so far morphologically and to "capture" a wide range of adaptive zones, find their bases in their adaptive versatility, the isolation of potentially competing groups, and their long history on the Continent. Presumably, they preceded potential competitors in their roles and could readily diversify into empty or under-utilized niches.

Given time, they became well-established and well-adapted. Isolation has played a major role in maintaining them. On the other hand, the nectarivorous, frugivorous, and granivorous forms, though having managed to extend as far as Wallace's Line, seem not to have been able to gain a toehold in the rainforests of Borneo, which has a diverse avifauna of ecologically equivalent barbets, sunbirds, hornbills, and others (292).

GENERALIZED DESERT BIRDS. There is no distinctive montane avifauna in Australia, probably because the altitudes involved are not very great. In sharp contrast to what has happened in Africa during the Pleistocene, only 17 species--3% of the total Australian avifauna--have evolved into a characteristic Australian desert or Eyrean avifauna restricted to its deserts and semi-deserts (73). Instead of desert forms persisting and often evolving spectacular adaptations as in Africa, most of the avian inhabitants of Australian deserts have tended to be more generalized and, as a result of a low premium on the evolution of terrestriality (166), have not lost their arboreal habits. Species of generalized avifauna from the neighboring grass steppe, savanna woodland, and sclerophyll forest penetrate widely into the desert areas (311).

In a survey in 1961, it was found that of the 531 species of terrestrial and freshwater birds covered, 16% were purely or predominantly inhabitants of rainforests, 16% were inhabitants of sclerophyllous forest, 28% inhabited woodland, 11½% savanna grassland, 2% mallee, 4½% mulga, 3% mangroves, and 14% were swamp-marsh dwellers. The combined sclerophyllous forest and woodland avifaunas account for no less than 44% of all species. The richness of this endemic "eucalypt-inhabiting" component, which is expected from the area covered by these formations, greatly exceeds the component found in the rainforests which, by contrast, cover only a very small area of the Australian mainland (1,086).

REPRODUCTIVE ADAPTATIONS--NOMADISM. Since periods of shrinking of the desert environment in Australia would tend to cause extinctions (see pp. 35, 36), the selective pressures for surviving forms have been for adaptability, rather than speciation (164, 311). These pressures have produced an avifauna remarkably well adapted to the very special climatic conditions that prevail in the vast inland deserts. The co-adaptations found in these Australian dry-country birds are: (a) a tendency for breeding to be linked to rainfall, whether irregular or protracted, rather than to an annual periodicity; (b) maintenance of breeding condition throughout the year (as a result of continuous hypophysial and gonadal activity); (c) early sexual maturity; (d) a tendency toward maintaining pair bonds for as long as both birds survive; (e) a tendency toward communal breeding; (f) helping to allofeed the young by members of the previous brood; (g) molting does not seem to inhibit reproduction; and, of course, (h) nomadism.

"The whole secret of life in arid regions is movement, a readiness and a freedom to migrate" (1,297) without regard to season or direction, and to concentrate wherever the best living conditions are offered in the particular year or season. No overseas region appears to compare with Australia in the extent to which nomadism has developed to so high a degree in so many species of birds. This reflects chiefly the variability of the climate over much of the Continent and the wide year-to-year and place-to-place variations in rainfall occasioned by the erratic paths of cyclonic disturbances through interior regions (311), but it also is influenced by the patchy distribution of regularly occurring fires and burnt-out areas (641). It has been estimated that 26-30% of the land birds that breed in Australia, and up to 60% of the interior birds undertake nomadic movements, with true south-north migrants comprising only about 8% (68, 84, 153). These comprise no less than 30% of all the nomadic birds in the world (155).

INSECTS HARVESTED PRIMARILY BY LIZARDS. Australian desert areas support fewer species of ground-foraging insectivorous birds than do comparable sites in the Kalahari. The scant insect resources of Australian deserts, are harvested mostly by lizards, whereas it is the birds who are the main insect consumers in North American deserts. Probably this is partly because the ectothermic lizards are able to capitalize better than the endothermic birds on the scant, variable insect crop supported by the comparatively predation-resistant sclerotinous-leaved and serotinous-fruited flora of Australian deserts (356, 641, 1,085).

In addition, reptiles tolerate changes in amounts of body fluids and in the osmotic concentrations of these fluids to a much greater extent than do birds, again probably because of their ectothermic metabolism (360, 872). The latter allows them to estivate over the long periods that may transpire between uncertain rains, a strategy not open to birds. It also is suggested that the high air temperatures and abundant solar radiation of the arid central regions of Australia allow lizards to maintain high, fairly-constant body temperatures more easily than can species that inhabit more heavily vegetated regions with greater rainfall (408).

The fact that insectivory also is very low among the birds of southern Africa (except, perhaps, in the Kalahari Desert; 356), in the absence of any spectacular lacertilian radiation, speaks against competition with lizards playing a major role in the low insectivory of Australian desert birds (641). Direct competition for arthropodan prey by anoles and insectivorous birds does appear to occur in sclerophyllous scrub habitats on West Indian islands (767). Anoles present in high densities may exclude small insectivorous birds from the lower, more connected portions of habitats; the latter have a competitive advantage over lizards only in forest outer canopy (884).

THE ORIGINS OF AUSTRALIA'S TERRESTRIAL AVIFAUNA

A SEPARATE BIOGEOGRAPHICAL UNIT. As early as the mid-19th century, the peculiarity of Australia's avifauna led to recognition of the Continent as a separate biogeographical unit, faunally distinct from the Asian mainland and complexly intermingling with the mainland fauna in the Indonesian archipelago (173). The origins of Australia's terrestrial birds, and their nearest relatives elsewhere, remain enigmatical to this day, although phylogenies based on DNA homologies are providing promising leads (see 188, 196 and pp. 33, 34, **Oscines Seemingly Resolved into Two Major Groups**).

The solution to this puzzle is important to ornithologists and biogeographers, because the avifauna of Australia is, area for area, if not among the richest, certainly among the most colorful in the world, with many unique groups and species (see 106). For example, nowhere else in the world do parrots display such variations of form as in Australasia (Australia, New Guinea, and New Zealand), while birds of paradise, bower birds, lyrebirds, cockatoos, Cockatiels, the nectarivorous lories, and the ground-feeding broad-tailed parrots are found only in Australasia. The present outline of the origins of Australia's terrestrial birds draws heavily on the treatments by Keast (153, 292, 1,086), Schodde (84), and Serventy (164), to which readers are referred for further details.

ENDEMIC FORMS DOMINANT. The relationships of other, less colorful, yet familiar, Australasian birds with their "look-alikes" outside of the region were, until recently, uncertain (see below). The distinctive nature of the Australian avifauna is further emphasized by the fact that endemic groups and species (comprising 49% of the total--as opposed to only 28% for the families) are the dominant ones. Yet few of the dominant avian families of Asia and Africa are represented here, and those few by only 1 or 2 members.

A good proportion of these families have apparently colonized Australia only in comparatively recent Miocene or Early Pliocene times (see p. 29, **Impaction of Australia upon Southeastern Asia** and pp. 32, 33, **Colonization from Indomalaysia**) and have yet to make a significant impact on the endemic families (152, 153). In their prior absence, the endemic families radiated, particularly in their adaptations to diverse feeding habitats. They now fill niches in all corners of the Continent and all sections have their share.

COCKATIELS AS BEHAVIORAL LINKS TO AVIAN ANCESTORS. Our particular interest in the origins and evolution of Australian land birds resides in the following. Insofar as repertoires of egg-care responses are concerned, the present studies suggest that Cockatiels possess close behavioral links to both ancestral birds and their pro-avian and pre-avian forerunners, possibly more so than any other living bird. This topic is treated detailedly in Chapter 4.

ABSENCE OF INTERMEDIATE AND LINKING FORMS. The very fact that Australian terrestrial birds include many apparently old endemic groups of uncertain origin makes it difficult to reconstruct their sources and their evolutionary relationships. The missing clues that are needed to form a coherent picture are the intermediate and linking forms that would serve to establish the ties of these birds to groups living on other continents. Unfortunately, the seabirds, shorebirds, and freshwater birds of Australia shed little light on these questions, since they are of widespread distribution elsewhere. And the fossil record--the only source of potentially complete answers--is scattered, imperfect, and very little studied. Virtually all of the known fossils are non-passeriforms (630).

TRADITIONAL VIEW. The traditional, and formerly widely accepted, view of the origins of Australian terrestrial birds, whose relatives clearly are Palearctic and Oriental, saw Asia as their only feasible source. The early avian colonists were thought to have moved in a series of 5 major waves, island-hopping down through the Indonesian (Malay) archipelago and New Guinea to northern Australia (see 151, 152). Guided by the expected rates of evolution in birds, the first arrivals were believed to have put in their appearance at least 20 mya. These would have been the ancestors of the main groups of endemic birds, including parrots. The last, and very recent, arrivals would have been the representatives of species that are widespread elsewhere (Asia, Africa, etc.) today and can only be subspecifically separated from their old world derivatives.

AUSTRALIAN GROUPS MORE CLOSELY RELATED TO EACH OTHER. Except for the dispersal of this last group, the traditional scenario now has been altered radically. Recent research on the structure of the syrinx (voicebox), the morphology of the columella (bony stapes; 120), and DNA homologies (see 188, 196, and pp. 33, 34), have called into serious doubt the existence of close affinities between Australian groups and their apparent counterparts elsewhere. The Australian groups are more closely related to each other than to any groups outside the Continent.

[An argument against the traditional view was the fact of an absence or marginal occurrence in Australia of representatives of many widespread families. Among these are the Old World vultures, pheasants, skimmers, sandgrouse, trogons, barbets, babblers, woodpeckers, broadbills, bulbuls, thrushes, tits, orioles, buntings, jays, sylvid warblers, the true finches, and hornbills. These absences point to a comparatively unbalanced composition of the existing Australian avifauna that was not easily reconciled with the traditional colonization view (164, 335).]

ADAPTIVE CONVERGENCE. Specific examples of these close relationships could be given. Should such close relationships between groups of Australian birds prove to be general, it would mean that species of typical Australian songbirds have evolved from a few obscure ancestors, probably dating from a colonization route via Africa and Antarctica. [More or less direct dispersal between Africa and Australia via Madagascar, India, and East Antarctica was possible into the middle Cretaceous period (184).]

The similarities in appearance and ways of life between these groups and extant Asian birds appear to have resulted entirely from similar adaptations to similar environmental situations (parallel evolution or adaptive convergence), not from common ancestry (see pp. 33, 34). The Australian birds (particularly the parrots and meliphagids) bear all the earmarks of a fauna that has undergone a long period of evolution in isolation.

GONDWANAN ORIGINS OF SOME AUSTRALIAN TERRESTRIAL BIRDS. In the light of present knowledge of the process of continental drift, it has become evident that at a time 30-20 mya, when the first Australian terrestrial birds were thought to have begun to make their appearance, according to the traditional scheme, the water barriers to invasion from Asia were much wider than envisioned. In fact, these barriers would have been much more difficult, and even impossible, for birds of many groups to cross.

Although present fossil evidence provides no confirmation, the primary radiation of birds may well have occurred in West Gondwana. The latter also is the probable site of early differentiation of angiosperms in the Barremian subdivision of the very early Cretaceous period, from an undetermined gymnospermous ancestor (1,065; see also pp. 613-618, **The Transition to Herbivory**). This would have been followed by colonization of the Northern Hemisphere from Africa to Europe by the late Jurassic period, by which time, or earlier, birds had a worldwide distribution (652). An origin of birds in Antarctica might help to explain the scarcity of reptilian-avian transition forms in the fossil record of the more accessible continents (659). Many workers now strongly support the view that many Australian avian groups, including parrots and galliforms, are of Gondwanan origin (though until a good fossil record is at hand, the origin of many of them will remain controversial; 106, 290, 1,098). [An origin of the order Passeriformes in the Southern Hemisphere, with dispersal in the mid-Tertiary era, has been hypothesized by Feduccia and Olson (see 574).]

In other words, Australia almost certainly inherited some of its terrestrial birds from the huge Southern-Hemisphere supercontinent called Gondwana, of which it was a part about 130-125 mya (together with Africa, India, Madagascar, Antarctica, New Zealand, and South America). Among others, many members of the Psittaciformes and Columbidae (of which Australia has 5 endemic genera and New Guinea 6) are good candidates for having colonized along a Gondwanan route, entering Australia from the south (62, 164). Thus, they are highly endemic, near relatives may be present in South America, and relationships to extra-Australian taxa are at suprageneric taxonomic levels (290). Despite shared Gondwanan origins, the contemporary avifauna of South America and Australia have little in common (1,086). An unusually broad range of adaptive radiations of Australian terrestrial birds occurred during the long period of isolation from other land masses during the Tertiary period. Many of the resulting major adaptive zones (ways of life) are quite differently partitioned among the various taxonomic groups compared to their mode of partitioning on other continents (153). [It is unlikely that any portion of Southeast Asia or Indonesia was once a part of Gondwana and moved northward. Both paleontological and geological evidence speak against such a pattern of drift (184).]

PLATE TECTONICS----SEPARATION OF GONDWANAN COMPONENTS. An understanding of past environments and their geological contexts is essential for the study of Australian and Southwest Pacific biogeography. Dynamic changes in the Earth since 150 mya have contributed significantly to environmental changes in these regions, principally through: (1) the break-up of Gondwana with concomitant development of volcanic island chains or archipelagos along the interfaces between the dispersing fragments and the Pacific Ocean basin; (2) The northward movement of Australia, New Zealand, and other Southwest Pacific coastal blocks into lower latitudes and away from the south pole which, itself, was moving; (3) world-wide climatic changes, of which the late Cenozoic glaciation is an example, and which perhaps are attributable to changes in the obliquity of the Earth's axis of rotation or to variations in solar luminosity (see 1,057).

[Rifting of Gondwanan components involved the entire lithosphere, not just the crust. A plate does not rupture instantaneously; rather it apparently is stretched and thinned over a period of millions of years (1,395).]

Although one would not wish to minimize the influences of contraction of the tropics and the development of high-latitude "environmental filters," on the distribution of contemporary birds (652), the impressive changes in paleogeography and paleoclimatology that occurred in the late Mesozoic and early Cenozoic eras significantly influenced the evolution of present-day vertebrate families, which were originating or differentiating then (106). By Jurassic to early Cretaceous times, perhaps in the Valanginian age (see Table 1), Greater India already had begun to leave Antarctica and southwestern Australia, resulting in the isolation of India from all the other Gondwanan continents (284, 1,058, 1,343). By the early-to-late Cretaceous period (at the latest ca. 132 mya), southeastern Africa and West Antarctica had broken apart and were separated by a widening ocean, the onset of drift commencing significantly earlier than rifting between South America and Africa (see immediately below). Break-up of the Australian-Antarctic segment, lying in high southern latitudes, also was delayed.

The initial opening of the South Atlantic basin was scissors-like, as the southern part of the basin opened more rapidly than the northern part (rotation pole at 46.75°N, 32.65°W). Africa and South America remained broadly connected in the early and probably middle Cretaceous period. A land bridge between Brazil and a stretch running from Western Nigeria to the Ivory Coast seems likely, but it may have been subject to a series of marine transgressions and regressions (see 106). The establishment of marine conditions on the Agulhas Bank, which can be dated as late Valanginian, occurred at a time approximately coeval with that accepted for the initiation of continental drift (i.e., at the time of formation of the earliest oceanic crust) in the southeastern Atlantic Ocean and the Natal Valley. [Much of the floors of the oceans are only of Cenozoic age (see 106).] In contrast, the final separation of the two continental blocks, i.e., the clearing of the Falkland Plateau from the southern tip of the Agulhas Bank does not appear to have coincided with any particular crustal movement-related episode; it is dated variously at 104.3-98.3 mya (172, 284, 1,343, 1,382).

Direct terrestrial vertebrate exchange between Africa and Antarctica would have had to be across a major seaway from the Valanginian age onward. At the end of the Cretaceous period, about 65 mya, about 580 km separated Africa and South America at their closest points. They remained partially linked by numerous islands along the Mid-Atlantic Ridge and its flanks. New Zealand had a long and independent history from Australia, having separated from Antarctica about 80 mya, with the formation of the Tasman Sea and New Caledonian Trough. Gondwana in the Cretaceous period consisted only of South America, Antarctica, and Australia, and lay in very high southern latitudes (see 285, 1,090, 1,343).

Connections between South America and Australasia persisted even longer. Sixty mya and earlier, Australia was firmly attached to East Antarctica (which may have been separated from West Antarctica--along the Weddell Sea-Transantarctic Mountains-Ross Sea lineament) along their eastern boundary There is good evidence, however, for believing that rifting had begun as early as 110-90 mya along the western part of the boundary between Australia and Antarctica (see 284). [In another view, the two continents were separated by a narrow seaway at the time, with fully marine conditions not being established until the Eocene epoch (see 287).]

South America was connected to West Antarctica via an archipelago across what at present is the Strait of Magellan. The Gondwanan climate at that time supported cool, temperate rainforests in at least southeastern and south central areas of Australia. The Asia complex of crustal plates (Southern Asia) may have been as much as 40-50° of latitude to the north at that time. The opening of the Drake Passage between South America and Antarctica occurred sometime in the Oligocene epoch, 30-37 mya (see 972). However, very shallow flanking ridges obstructed significant water movement through the Drake Passage until 23½ mya, when oceanic depths were achieved. Only then, at the beginning of the Miocene epoch, could the circum-Antarctic current develop, with its profound significance for climates in the Southern Hemisphere (1,057).

AUSTRALIA DRIFTS NORTHWARD. Although some initial rifting may have begun as early as 95 mya, by the middle-to-late Eocene epoch, some 46 mya, Australia began to sever from its cool, temperate southern position adjacent to East Antarctica (with southern Australia adjacent to Wilkes Land), as the South Indian Oceanic Ridge became more active. Australia was about 30°S of its present position and northern Australia would have been at about the latitude of Bass Strait today (see 1,089, 1,213). Australia maintained contact with East Antarctica until post-Eocene times only through the South Tasman Rise, a periodically-flooded, linear, incipient rift corridor (106, 285, 972). This bridge was covered by shallow seas in the late Eocene, but remained as a barrier to effective circum-Antarctic oceanic circulation (1,059). Relative drift between Australia and India ceased during the Eocene, though this did not affect Australia's northward motion throughout the remainder of the Cenozoic (see 1,213).

For the first time the Continent acquired a Mediterranean-type southern climate by virtue of its new southern ocean boundary (288). Rainforests were spreading across Australia from the east to the southwest and inland to central Australia (284), and the overall pollen spectrum is compatible with a cool, moist climate (see 1,059). The moisture to support these cool, temperate rainforests would have derived from a westerly airflow. Within this stream, semi-permanent anticyclonic systems over land and sea may have drawn in moisture from the warm seas to the southeast of the Continent (1,059). A final separation between Australia and East Antarctica did not occur until about 37 mya at the Eocene-Oligocene boundary (see 972). The post-Eocene disintegration of the drainage network in the western half of Australia was one outcome of Australia's equatorward drift, as was the inception and expansion of the arid zone throughout inland Australia (1,213).

Late Paleocene mean annual sea surface temperatures had been at the very high values of 18-20°C for such high latitudes. Normal oceanic crust began to form between Australia and the Antarctic Continent as it started its roughly 27° northward drift to its present latitude, a drift that carried it through a range of climatic belts, some wetter and warmer, whose width and nature were changing at the same time. The growth of the Southeastern Indian Ocean between Antarctica and Australia occurred in two phases of spreading: the 1st at a very slow rate, from breakup (95 mya) to 44 mya, and the 2nd at a rapid rate (about 6 cm/year) from 44 mya to the present (285, 287, 288, 1,213).

[Australia is the only continent to show such a large latitudinal change--some 800 km north since the mid-Miocene epoch. Tertiary movements of the other continents have been in an east-westerly direction with relatively little change in latitude, while most of India's northward movement occurred earlier, in the Cretaceous (see 282, 1,213).]

The Eocene epoch was a time of major marine incursions across Southern Australia, with shallow, relatively warm seas (20°C in the early Eocene) penetrating into the Eucla Basin in the middle Eocene, followed by a more widespread incursive phase in the late Eocene and again in the early Miocene epoch. Warm, shallow seas then extended across much of Southern Australia. Viewed as a whole, the Eocene paleobotanical data suggest a high humidity throughout the epoch and closed-canopy rainforest appears to have been widespread. Neither the climate nor the vegetational types of these forests appears to have a contemporary counterpart (285, 1,059).

The surface water temperatures for the open ocean were around 20°C in the early Eocene epoch, but declined in a series of fluctuations throughout the epoch, to a low of about 10°C by the late Eocene. This probably was accompanied by a gradual decline in precipitation, and an associated increase in the intensity and northward movement of westerly wind belts. It seems unlikely that ice cover on the Antarctic was extensive during the Eocene epoch (1,059).

INTO A LOW RAINFALL BELT---GENERALLY INCREASING ARIDITY. By 38 mya, the Tasmania-Antarctic corridor was a seaway and there was ice-rafting near Antarctica. Australia continued to move northward during the Oligocene epoch. The nature and extent of the ice cover at the time remain unknown. But all evidence available indicates that there was a significant cooling in the high latitudes. Over Australia as a whole it seems likely that precipitation would have been lower than it was in the Eocene epoch and the north and northwest seem likely to have been relatively arid.

Surface waters near Australia seem to have remained relatively warm in the early Miocene epoch. In the Tasman Sea, a temperature rise of about 3°C over Oligocene times is evident. The early Miocene also saw a major transgression of shallow seas across the Australian continent, as reflected by limestones in the Eucla, Murray-Darling, and Otway Basins. The diversity of Australia's vegetation fell during these times as the Continent's northward movement brought it into a low rainfall belt. Aridity began to develop in some regions but much of the Continent continued to have wet, and perhaps relatively warm climates, as indicated by paleontological data and evidence of widespread deep weathering profiles and laterized surfaces (1,059). In fact, by that time the deeply weathered landscape so typical of present-day Australia was widely developed (1,060).

Temperate rainforest communities were widespread, dominating in much of southeastern Australia, and forests with a high proportion of *Nothofagus brassi* and abundant gymnosperms and broadleaf Lauraceae and Myrtaceae suggest high precipitation levels along a very broad coastal belt. In addition, middle Miocene palynological data indicate that there were at least localized populations of rainforests in regions close to Alice Springs (24°S x 134°E) and in the Lake Eyre and Lake Frome drainage basins, suggesting deep inland penetration by rain-bearing winds (287).

Australia then lay far from New Zealand and Antarctica and an extensive sea separated it from the island arc forming proto-New Guinea (284, 287). Australia's southern coast lay in latitudes ranging from 42°S to 50°S, and only the northernmost edge of the Continent extended north of 20°S. Shallow shelf waters off of the southern coast experienced temperatures (15-20°C) which could be described as subtropical (287). The climate was about 5°C warmer than at present (1,076).

VAST LOWLAND---DEEP-WEATHERED REGOLITH--EDAPHIC UNIFORMITY. By late early Miocene times, temperatures fell as ice accumulation intensified in Antarctica, and there was a shallowing and retreat of the seas from most of the southern coastal regions. By about middle Miocene times, central Australia was dry enough, at least periodically, for areas of grassland to develop locally between wetter regions (284, 285, 1,059). At the time, Australia was a vast lowland covered by a deep weathered regolith. Continued deep weathering in places into the later Cenozoic tended to create edaphic uniformity. Still later, extensive dissection of the regolith, especially in the Great Dividing Range, around the Continental margin, and in the Lake Eyre basin greatly increased the edaphic diversity by exposing different horizons of the deep-weathered profile (287).

IMPACTION OF AUSTRALIA UPON SOUTHEASTERN ASIA. By the late Miocene epoch (10 mya) much of the northern edge of Australia had collided with the Southeastern Asian area and the present land mass of New Guinea had been created. The evidence indicates that by the Miocene epoch the present Torres Straits (a land-link between Australia and New Guinea for much of the Quaternary) had already reached the paleolatitude of 14°S, and in the last 25 million yr its latitude decreased only a further 4°. The vigorous tectonism continued to cause folding and uplift in central New Guinea and fragmented plates, creating the Indonesian islands. These islands might have connected the continents of Asia and Australia, which came close together in the late Miocene, and permitted the first wave of Asian migrants to enter the Australian region. By the Pliocene, most of New Guinea had emerged from the sea. Uplifting of the central ranges continued until the Holocene, creating peri-orogenic troughs parallel to the ranges. The island did not reach its present size until the Pleistocene (see 1,088, 1,090).

By the end of the Miocene epoch, extensive intermingling of Australian and Asian faunas should have occurred. Between 10 mya and the present, the Australian Continent has moved further north, and the nucleus of Southeast Asia further west, so that there could have been some increase in the distance between the large continental blocks. [Weber's Line (the line of faunal balance between interacting Southeastern Asian and Australian faunas) may have migrated in the sinistrally-rotating island arc system, but Wallace's Line (the boundary between a rich, diverse, oriental, Southeastern Asian fauna and an impoverished Australian fauna) and its Australian counterpart (separating the diverse Australo-Papuan mainland fauna from the limited insular fauna of the Banda Islands), should have remained approximately along the edges of their respective continental margins (1,058).]

ANTARCTIC ICE-SHEET EXPANSION---SPREAD OF CENTRAL DESERTS. In the very late Miocene epoch, there was a sudden, marked drop in ocean temperatures to less than 5°C, accompanied by a major rapid expansion of the Antarctic ice sheet (and followed by a marked warming of early Pliocene seas and renewed cooling; 287). This expansion would have had a major impact on Australia; the subtropical belt of dry anticyclonic circulation would have moved north (from about 50°S) over Australia and increased in frequency. This doubtless was accompanied by a decrease in rainfall, possibly an abrupt one, a lowering of temperatures, an increase in seasonality, and seasonally different precipitation regimes in northern and southern Australia (288). Indeed, relatively rapid retreats of rainforest vegetational types show up at that time in the pollen counts. Throughout the epoch, Australia seems likely to have lain in latitudes influenced by westerly wind systems (1,059).

The remainder of the Tertiary and Quaternary records is one of generally increasing aridity, development of markedly different subregions within Australia, and (by 2½ mya) the eventual spread of the central Australian deserts, with aridity such as occurs today. This trend was accompanied by complex perturbations during the Pleistocene, including repeated fluctuations in sea level through a range exceeding 200 m in response to the growth and decay of continental ice sheets (284, 285, 1,060).

CIRCUM-ANTARCTIC CURRENT---STEEP POLAR-EQUATORIAL TEMPERATURE GRADIENT. Continental movements have had a major effect on climate through the initiation of the circum-Antarctic current, now the most voluminous of all the ocean currents. Cool water apparently began to flow through the newly developed Southeastern Indian Ocean between Australia and East Antarctica about 41-36 mya (see 172), But it was not until about the mid-Oligocene epoch, several million yr later, that the South Tasman Rise cleared Antarctica (285). The gap between Antarctica and South America, however, may have been too shallow to permit establishment of the circum-Antarctic current until the opening of the Drake Passage about 23 mya, but possibly as late as 5 mya. The trans-Antarctic land dispersal route between Australia and South America (see pp. 31, 32) had ceased to have practical significance some time before, and perhaps long before, pronounced separation of South America and West Antarctica had taken place (284, 285, 1,213).

As the Antarctic continent became refrigerated and climatically and topographically isolated from warmer northern seas by the development of a circumpolar deepwater circulation between it and Tasmania, there resulted an intensification of global cooling and a sharpening of the polar-equatorial temperature gradient (166). The latter owed its origin to the fact that the circum-Antarctic current effectively blocked the equatorial currents from traveling into and effecting heat transfer to the higher latitudes (282). Mountain glaciers on Antarctica formed, coalesced, and eventually grew into major icecaps. With the completion of the development of the West Antarctic icecap during the mid-Miocene epoch and peaking of the Antarctic ice sheet at the end of the Miocene, Antarctica became the land one knows today: the coldest and driest continent in the world (1,213, 1,326). [During these same times there is no definite sign of large-scale glaciations in the Northern Hemisphere, except for Alaskan mountain glaciers about 9 mya; the Arctic probably was essentially ice-free (1,326).]

From the late Eocene epoch onward, sea-surface temperatures on the Southern Ocean fell by 10-15°C, and the decline may have been global in extent. Surface water temperatures on the Campbell Plateau attained 6-7°C. By maintaining a steep temperature gradient between the equator and pole via the effects of the circum-Antarctic current and meltwater, the Antarctic icecap (see p. 242, **Influences of Antarctic Glaciations** for its development) exerts a powerful influence on Australia's climate. Oceanic patterns and intensities of circulation resembling contemporary ones were discernible by the late Miocene or early Pliocene, and it seems reasonable to suggest that atmospheric circulation followed a similar pattern of development (285, 1,059, 1,213). In this connection, it is noteworthy that the atmosphere above the Antarctic is much colder than that above the Arctic, resulting from the different heat budgets, so that the tropospheric circulation of the Southern Hemisphere is stronger and expands across the equator, shifting the "meteorological equator" an annual average of about 6°N (averaging as much as 12°N in July; 1,326).

From about 3 mya onward, and particularly after continental Arctic ice sheets developed suddenly about 2½ mya, the northern ice became a decisive factor modulating global climates. As icecaps waxed and waned, sea levels fell and rose. The high pressure belt (see above) would have moved still further north and essentially modern patterns of circulation would have been established. During the past 1.8 million yr of Quaternary time, there have been at least 17 distinct glacial-interglacial cycles, each of about 100,000 yr duration, with interglacials occupying about 10% of each cycle. Throughout the Quaternary, these interglacials were times when global ice volumes were low, sea levels were at or even slightly above present levels, and world climates were warm and wet relative to glacial maxima--broadly similar to those of today. Desert dunes in Australia became vegetated, montane forests encroached on alpine grasslands, tropical rainforests expanded again, and lake levels rose in the wetter parts of southern Australia.

It seems that at least the last 7 glacial maxima were broadly similar in terms of global ice volume, sea-level lowering (as much as 150-200 m lower than at present), and intertropical aridity. The contrast between the 30 million yr involved in the 10°C cooling of the Southern Ocean and the 10,000 yr involved in the 5-10°C postglacial warming of Australia and New Guinea, suggests that the rate of Quaternary climatic change may have been up to 1,000 times faster than Tertiary climatic oscillations of broadly comparable magnitude (287, 1,213).

DISPERSAL VIA AUSTRALIAN-ANTARCTIC-SOUTH AMERICAN ROUTE--ISOLATION FOR PART OF THE TERTIARY---CONTINENTAL IMPACTING. Excellent opportunities for dispersal between South America and Australia, both across archipelagos and via Antarctica, probably existed from the late Mesozoic era until the mid-to-late Eocene epoch (292). A dramatic change in conditions commenced about 47 mya in the medial Eocene, when truly oceanic influence became apparent, spreading eastward diachronously. This has been associated with the onset of active separation of Australia and Antarctica. Biotic exchanges between these Continents may have terminated at that time, but it seems more likely that dispersal between the two continental blocks was maintained via the South Tasman Rise until perhaps as recently as 37 mya in the early Oligocene epoch--as long as the two continental blocks were sliding past each other along a transform.

Many plants and animals certainly followed the Antarctic route. For part of the Tertiary period, however (for 22-32 million yr, between about 47-37 to 15 mya), terrestrial birds would have been isolated in Australia. By the end of this period they had become fairly modernized. They must have remained isolated until the water gaps between Australia and the Indonesian archipelago decreased significantly by the medial Miocene and the relatively direct exchange of avifauna along a chain of volcanic islands between these two areas began (184).

[There is evidence for the persistence of land connections or virtual connections between Australia, Antarctica, and South America well into the Cenozoic, and for marsupials, plants, insects, ratites, and parrots probably having dispersed along the Antarctic route. But despite the apparent existence of such routes, no ancient placental group already present in the Paleocene of South America got through the "filter system" to Australia, presumably because of persistent water gaps and/or profound climatic barriers having developed before the end of the Cretaceous period.]

With the mid-Miocene impacting of the Australian plate into the Asian area (see p. 29), the New Guinean highlands began to rise, and the Great Divide probably became elevated further, creating a more severe rainshadow across its interior (288). The effect of the latter, together with other climatic changes caused by Australia's more northerly position (such as the loss of its major northern oceanic circulation as water gaps closed), and the progressive drop in global temperature and global precipitation, was a changeover of the vegetation across Australia from rainforest to open forests to grasslands and savanna woodlands, as described above (280).

DISPERSAL ROUTES. Much evidence, most conclusively of paleobotanical origin suggests that different climates characterized the dispersal routes through the Antarctic in the late Mesozoic era and early Tertiary period (reconstruction of which is difficult) and by way of Indomalaysia in the medial-to-late Cenozoic and Recent times. The Antarctic route apparently was warm-temperate to cool-temperate, depending on the location, and capable of supporting forests of sizable deciduous and coniferous trees--probably dominated by southern beech trees of the genus, *Nothofagus*--and diverse plants (106). Although extensive ice sheets may have existed by the late Miocene, there may have been nothing more than local glaciation between the early Eocene epoch and a time 6-3.4 mya.

In marked contrast, the Indomalaysian dispersal route was essentially tropical. Both, however, though archipelagos at best, were certainly amenable to occupation by birds. Accordingly, since many modern families of birds had differentiated by the early Tertiary period, both dispersal routes may have figured importantly in shaping Australia's terrestrial birds (see 173).

COLONIZATION FROM INDOMALASIA. Throughout most of the Tertiary period, the rich biota of Australia's lush forests would have offered considerable resistance to invaders. Some of the endemic suprageneric taxa, however, may represent the earliest colonizers, when Australia was farther south and much more isolated (107). Later in the Tertiary, however, and particularly in the Pleistocene, the disturbed environments, together with the extreme climatic variations and rapidly altering topography would have offered excellent opportunities for colonizers from southeast Asia, particularly after Australia approached the Asiatic block.

It probably was at that time that the majority of the northern island-hoppers established a bridgehead. Upon their successful entry, many members of the archaic fauna, particularly those that had lost ecological flexibility by becoming irreversibly adapted to the equable pre-Oligocene conditions, must have been eliminated (see below). Active speciation of the more adaptable pan-Australian avifauna (both the endemic forms and the newer immigrants from Asia) could only have become general after the varied effects of climatic, topographic, and vegetational changes introduced the first barriers and disrupted the continuity of distribution of populations from the Pliocene onward (164). [The previously existing uniform and mild conditions and low relief would not have provided much in the way of isolating mechanisms to facilitate speciation.]

The first considerable barrier was The Great Dividing Range. After it split the pan-Australian fauna into two great assemblages, independent evolution could have occurred within each of them. The development of the central arid area was equally important in shaping the later Tertiary, Pleistocene, and Recent faunal distribution patterns. The interior history of the later Tertiary period and Pleistocene epoch was one of extensive river systems and lakes, although terminally these largely dried up. The central arid area fluctuated in both size and position during the Pleistocene and segregated a northern tropical fauna from most of the rest of Australia.

It was the periodic expansion of the arid center, with an intensification into desert conditions during Pleistocene and Recent time, bringing about the isolation of fragments of formerly continuous populations into humidity refugia, that perhaps was the major causative factor in recent speciation. Vegetational belts must have migrated up and down, expanded and contracted, their species compositions gradually being modified. These changes created an "archipelago effect" within the Continent, allowing pockets of isolated populations to differentiate from each other at all levels, from subspecies to full species. They also provided opportunities for differentiation through double and multiple east-west invasions (164).

BIRDS OF GONDWANAN ORIGIN---FOSSIL REMAINS. The birds of Gondwanan origin are among the most primitive living forms. These include the cassowaries and emus, the mound-builders, the plains wanderers, the parrots, the pigeons, the cuckoos, and the rails. Most of them have relatives on other southern continents, either exclusively or in greater abundance than in North America or Eurasia. Dromornithids and emus (Casuariidae) appear in the Australian fossil record concomitantly in the Miocene epoch, the former ranging over most of the Continent and reaching their greatest known diversity in the Miocene (617).

Birds or their forerunners have been placed in Australia as early as 135 mya, nearly contemporaneous with *Archaeopteryx*, by the discovery of four fossil feathers, the first 3 in 1966. The latter were found in Lower Cretaceous (Neocomian; perhaps even Upper Jurassic according to Prof. J. Warren of Monash University) claystones in the Strezlecki Group from ancient lacustrine sediments (those of a freshwater lake) in a roadcut 4 km east of Koonwarra in southern Gippsland, Victoria (see 151, 169, 290, 308, 1,383). Otherwise, the Australian fossil record of birds is not good until the Miocene epoch and is highly biased toward waterfowl (290).

ORIGINS OF PRIMITIVE FAMILIES OF PASSERIFORMS. The primitive families of passeriforms (such as the pittas and broadbills in Africa and Southeastern Asia, the ovenbirds, the ant thrushes, and the tyrant flycatchers in South America, and the New Zealand wrens) are centered in the southern continents and may have arisen there. It seems rather doubtful, though, that they had a common Gondwanan origin. The beginning of the Gondwanan breakup probably occurred long before the ancestors of these passeriforms had evolved.

OSCINES SEEMINGLY RESOLVED INTO TWO MAJOR GROUPS. The recent findings of Sibley and Ahlquist (188, 194, 803) appear to have answered some of the outstanding questions. These workers have found, by DNA homologies (which reflect degrees of genetic similarity), that the suborder Passeres (Oscines) apparently falls into two major parvorders (see below), that diverged some 60-58 mya in the Paleocene, when Australia was far south of its present position and connected to Antarctica.

One of these is the parvorder **Corvi** (3 superfamilies, 10 families), which now would include crows, ravens, magpies, jays, cuckoo-shrikes, true shrikes, vireos, and orioles, as well as the most prominent songbirds of the Australian region (lyrebirds, bowerbirds, scrub-birds, treecreepers, fairy-wrens, honeyeaters, fantails, drongos, and birds-of-paradise). This group "must have originated in Australia because its oldest elements, the Menuroidea and Meliphagoidea obviously evolved there and the Corvi radiated during the Tertiary when Australia was isolated from other large land masses" (803). When Australia drifted closer to Asia in the late Oligocene-Miocene (30-20 mya), representatives of some of the groups of Corvi dispersed to Asia, and radiated in Asia and Europe.

AUSTRALIAN "LOOK-ALIKE" SPECIES PROBABLY RESULT OF CONVERGENCE. The other group, the parvorder **Muscicapae** (3 superfamilies), includes all the Oscine groups that are not members of the Corvi, such as starlings, thrushes, bulbuls, finches, flycatchers, pipits, wagtails, weaverbirds, waxbills, sparrows, larks, swallows, mockingbirds, sunbirds, and warblers. This group apparently originated in Africa and dispersed throughout Eurasia and the Americas, although an origin from an Asian ancestor is not ruled out. The paradoxical Muscicapae "look-alike species" of Australia--the "wrens," "warblers," "robins," "nuthatches," "chats," "songlarks," "creepers," and "flycatchers" would have evolved in Australia. They would not be members of the Muscicapae, but would belong to the Corvi. In this view, the strikingly morphologically similar ecological counterparts are not homologous. They would be merely analogous, and have resulted from rampant convergence between members of the Australo-Papuan species with groups based upon European, Asian, and African types, obscuring the true relationships of the old endemic Australian taxa (188, 194, 803).

RECENT HISTORY OF AUSTRAL-ASIAN AVIFAUNA

NEW ZEALAND. The history of the terrestrial and freshwater avifauna of Australasia is rather better understood after its establishment than before. New Zealand has an impoverished avifauna characterized by a series of distinctive, archaic elements and more modern forms. Its extreme geographical isolation limited its original avifauna to those few species that were able to cross considerable stretches of open water, probably including an early archipelagic dispersal route from West Antarctica (819, 1,098). However, New Zealand's separation from Australia and West Antarctica clearly occurred too early for it to be reached by members (apart from members of the Chiroptera) of many characteristically Australian biotic groups (1,213). The complete absence of competitive mammals and the few terrestrial birds reduced selective pressure on the parrots, allowing them to radiate into extreme forms (819).

New Zealand clearly has received much, if not most, of its present-day terrestrial and freshwater birds by dispersal by flight across the Tasman Sea from Australia and the nearby islands (see R.A. Falla, 1953, 1955, in 335), a process that still is occurring. Almost certainly the meliphagids, sylviids, parakeets (*Cyanoramphus*), some rails, pigeons, and one endemic owl (*Sceloglaux*) have their closest relatives in Australia. The New Zealand fossil record shows that the process of colonization has been going on for a long time. Insular influences on the evolution of New Zealand birds are seen in the development of flightlessness in various groups, in the loss of sexual dimorphism, and in the occurrence of melanistic forms (106, 1,086).

[Moas and kiwis (the smallest of the ratites) are known only from New Zealand, the earliest record of the former apparently is from the Pliocene (but see 574), and of the latter from the Pleistocene epochs (308). Most ornithologists are of the opinion that they differentiated from a flying ancestor after it reached New Zealand (see 106). The Australian ratites appear to be decidedly distinct from moas and kiwis (which form a close-knit osteological group) and apparently are the most primitive of all the ratite groups. The ancestral form may have been advanced over that which gave rise to the moas and kiwis (and elephant birds). If the radiation took place during the early to mid-Cretaceous, the stem stock could have walked or flown between Australia and the remaining southern land masses, inasmuch as connections still existed between them (see above and 617).]

Dispersal, in fact, has accelerated in post-European times, with the clearing of the land and creation of open conditions more characteristic of Australia. A classic example is the colonization of New Zealand by the Australian Silvereye (White-eye; *Zosterops lateralis*) in the middle of the 19th century (335). A dispersal of exceptional magnitude occurred in 1951-1952 when the fertile peripheral areas of Australia were invaded by unusual species and unusually large numbers of nomads, some of the latter of which crossed the Tasman Sea to New Zealand (311). The ancestors of the Owl Parrot (*Strigops habroptilus*; Strigopinae), allied to the Australian Night Parrot (*Geopsittacus occidentalis*), may have originated from the ancient terrestrial connection with Australia, or Owl Parrots may be the descendants of later colonizers that crossed the Tasman Sea.

THE AVIFAUNA OF NEW GUINEA (785,000 sq. km; 1,061) is larger than that of Australia proper and is adapted to life in tropical rainforests, whereas most of the Australian avifauna is adapted to life in drier eucalypt forest and woodland. For example, New Guinea has a great diversity of arboreal, frugivorous, and nectarivorous fruit doves and lories. The Australian parallels are an array of ground-feeding granivorous bronzewing pigeons and broad-tailed parrots. For these reasons, it had been thought that a good number of rainforest species of Australia had trickled across from New Guinea (which only had its origin in the Eocene) over terrestrial bridges that were exposed during the ice ages up to 1 mya or more, as the continental shelf connecting Australia and New Guinea was flooded and exposed alternately some 8 or 9 times. It now is realized that the opposite movements probably took place. Australia is the likely source of the New Guinean avifauna. Thus, as noted earlier, 40-30 mya, Australia was extensively rainforested. The kinds of Antarctic beech and flesh-fruited conifers that now are confined to the distant ranges of New Guinea and New Caledonia then spread as far westward as western Australia.

The last terrestrial link between Australia and New Guinea was severed about 8,000-6,500 yr ago. Flooding of the Sahul Shelf was accomplished by an influx of warm sea water into the Gulf of Carpentaria as the equatorial ocean current resumed its flow westward through the Torres Strait (long after the first Aborigines settled in Australia), by which time the Bassian Plain that once joined Tasmania to the mainland also was submerged (see 816, 1,060, 1,086, 1,213).

[This flooding appears to have stranded some birds on land-bridge islands in the Strait, which now apparently represents a barrier to the movements of 28% of the islands' terrestrial birds, including 38% of the terrestrial birds that are shared by Australia and New Guinea. Thus, many populations of Australian birds cannot be replenished from New Guinea (817).]

ICE AGES AND ISOLATING MECHANISMS. From then on, as Australia drifted from temperate into Earth's desert latitudes (the "Horse Latitudes" of cool descending upper atmospheric air that takes up moisture as it warms during descent) in the late Miocene epoch, its climate gradually became cooler and drier. Although Pliocene climatic data from the Australian Continent are more sparse than for any other Cenozoic interval, marine data suggest that sea-surface temperatures were fluctuating rapidly, with an overall cooling trend after a brief warm and relatively wet interval (287). This trend culminated in the sequences of extreme cold and dry periods, and warm and semi-arid periods, of the 4 major glaciations and superimposed minor cycles of the last million or more yr.

The effects of these formidable climatic and topographic changes on the rich and distinctive avifauna of Australia were severe but not as drastic as was believed previously (290). Much of the older avifauna disappeared, though fossil evidence is limited to the flamingos (164). The present-day relict ranges of the primitive passerines, *Atrichornis* and *Menura* in Australia and *Xenicus* in New Zealand suggest that others may have vanished earlier. But as mentioned above, these formidable conditions provided isolating mechanisms that would have favored speciation. No pre-Pleistocene record of a parrot is known as yet in Australia, probably because of a lack of record rather than an absence from the mid-Tertiary avifauna (the Quaternary material appears to be indistinguishable from that of extant species; 290).

While the Cape York Peninsula has been and continues to be a major zone of biotic interchange between Australia and New Guinea, it is also a strong filter that varies in its selectivity according to the adaptations or habitat specializations of the concerned groups. Recent avian immigrants from New Guinea are primarily adapted to humid tropics and are found mostly in the rainforests of Cape York Peninsula. Recent emigrants to New Guinea from Australia, on the other hand, are sclerophyllous habitat species with a wide distribution in Australia. They have been able to colonize the savanna areas of southwestern New Guinea better than the New Guinean rainforest forms have been able to colonize Australia.

These two groups form the shared avifauna of the two land masses. The difference in environments between the Cape York Peninsula and the New Guinean lowlands is reflected in the proportion of rainforest avifauna in the total fauna of each region (more non-rainforest species in Cape York Peninsula and more rainforest species in New Guinea). The recency and paucity of the avifauna in the minor habitat within each region (rainforest in the western Peninsula and non-rainforest in southern New Guinea) are indicated by the colonization of each habitat by only a portion of the species of the other region. Rainforest species form 75-86% of those birds that are shared with New Guinea and are distributed in northeastern or eastern Australia (1,088).

TASMANIA (67,800 sq. km; 1,060) and New Guinea are separated from Australia by shallow seas. They have been joined and separated from the Continent repeatedly during the 4 Pleistocene glaciations of the Northern Hemisphere, when Pacific sea levels were perhaps 40-60 m lower (166, 184, 282). In fact, it has been the rule rather than the exception for them to form one landmass, Terra Australis, during the last few million yr. The annual rate of change in sea level easily could have exceeded 25 mm, causing shoreline shifts of 10-30 m/yr on typical continental shelves. Three major glaciations of early Pleistocene, penultimate glacial, and last glacial ages are known in Tasmania but they represent only a fraction of the

Pleistocene cold phases that are likely to have affected the Island (287, 1,060).

Tasmania is analogous to southwestern Australia in the sense of being an outlier of the Bassinian fauna (see below). In this case, it is the intermittent existence of Bass Strait, which is wider, deeper, and stormier than Torres Strait, that separates the fauna instead of a desert land barrier. It would have been open for thousands of yr longer than Torres Strait during each glaciation, and it may not have closed during many interstadials. The last severing of the land bridge occurred about 13,500-12,000 yr ago (164, 1,060). There is a strong possibility that several of Tasmania's 14 endemic species evolved in the last 18,000 yr, and at least 19 endemic subspecies appear to have evolved in this period. Tasmania has one monotypic genus now confined to the Island (*Tribonyx*) and 3 cases of speciation by double invasion (in *Acanthiza*, *Pardalotus*, and *Sericornis*) (310, 1,087).

An interesting consequence of the avifaunal impoverishment of Tasmania (43 breeding passerines compared to 89 in southern Victoria) is that some species show changes in feeding zones that apparently can be linked directly to their broader ecological opportunities. For example, in the absence of trunk-feeding tree-creepers and nuthatches, a shrike-thrush, 2 meliphagids, and a warbler have become trunk feeders in part; and in the absence of the foliage-gleaning warblers, *Acanthiza lineata* and *A. nana*, their cogener, *A. pusilla*, has extended its feeding zone to the tops of the eucalypts. A similar phenomenon is seen in the ecologically-isolated, southwestern Australia, where both *A. pusilla* and *A. inornata* respond to the absence of the arboreal foliage gleaners by becoming more arboreal in their feeding. But whereas vacant niches in Tasmania could become occupied by adapted forms only by colonization from over the sea, "deficiencies" in the southwestern avifauna have been made up, in part, by dry-country forms invading the forest (1,086).

SPECIATION---AUSTRALIAN "HUMIDITY REFUGIA" BUT NOT "ARIDITY REFUGIA." The expansion and contraction of arid areas during the Pleistocene (3 glacial and 3 interglacial periods are recognized; see 1,288) and post-Pleistocene climatic fluctuations have stimulated speciation processes in neighboring humid habitats, rather than in the arid regions themselves. Desert encroachment frequently fragmented formerly continuous humid habitat into "humidity refugia," where the isolated animal populations evolved, in turn, into recognizable races, species, and new genera, as beautifully illustrated in Australia (see 311).

On the other hand, "aridity refugia" could scarcely exist in Australia in the glacial climatic phases that led to the shrinking of the desert environment, "apart from a probable single one in the centre of the continent, which by itself would provide no opportunity for speciation among dry-country birds" (see 165, Introduction). In contrast, because of the geographical patterns of various types of forest regions in Africa, it has been possible for aridity refugia to exist at the height of the wet eras, as well as humidity refugia in the dry ones. This provided opportunities for both arid- and humid-country species to undergo active speciation (165; see also p. 243, **Radiations**).

The most recent periods of aridity, tied to advancing and retreating Antarctic, Pleistocene glaciations, and alternating with periods of higher rainfall over the last several 100,000 yr (with declines of as much as 200 m in sea level), shaped present Australian landforms and seem to have been the main force in effectuating the present distribution of Australian birds. Populations repeatedly have been joined in rings around the drier interior and then become broken, isolated, and fragmented in peripheral refugia. Many of these dispersed populations began to evolve into the species and subspecies of today. A striking example of a fragmented and intergrading ring is to be seen in the several species of pale-cheeked rosellas (84, 281, 1,089).

[It has been postulated that during glacial-age regimes, the combination of low humidity, high wind speeds, increased pressure gradients, and high radiant summer energy would have produced evaporative losses by up to 20% greater than occur today, even at current precipitation levels (1,328).]

THE EXTREME OF THE LAST GLACIATION was attained at about 26,000-22,000 yr ago (as compared to about 18,000-17,000 yr ago in the Northern Hemisphere), when the Continental dunes moved for the last time and lunettes formed on the leeside of playa lakes (287, 1,327). [The maximum Holocene warming around 9,000 yr ago is 3,000 yr before maximum warmth is observed in Europe and North America (1,327); see also pp. 242, 243, **Influences of Antarctic Glaciations**.] Sea level was at its lowest, having dropped about 130 m, and climatic deterioration reached a peak. Temperatures are believed to have been about 5-10°C lower than at present and precipitation was perhaps 50% less. At that time, Australia, New Guinea, and Tasmania coalesced to form a single land mass (Terra Australis) of about 10½ million sq. km (286, 287, 1,089). Probably correlated with this change and/or Man's arrival, the whole fauna of central Australia became the arid-adapted one of the present. At about the same time, many of the contemporary desert features--the salt lakes, sand dunes, etc.--became the dominant features of the distinctive area now called the Eyrean Subregion. The climate has been relatively stable for the last 10,000 yr, including generally moister regimes in the southeast (1,074).

EXTINCTIONS---MOUNTAIN REFUGIA. Toward the end of the last ice age, the last of the giant running birds, the giant flightless mound-builders, at least 4 Australian flamingos, a penguin, a pelican, a darter, at least 2 eagles, possibly a vulture, and a host of other birds became extinct. Most of these birds were affected by gigantism (290). Under the arid conditions, the originally rich and varied Tertiary rainforests and their avifauna contracted to the moister north and east periphery of the Australian-New Guinean continent.

The Great Dividing Range, as far north as Cairns, and the rising mountain ranges of New Guinea became the haven for the species more adapted to temperate conditions (816). In a sense, the whole distribution of Australian rainforests is refugial, and nowhere else in the world can large ecological islands of closed forest be seen with such clarity as among the open sclerophyllous vegetation of Australia. Each type of rainforest refugium has biogeographical implications (1,071).

[The vegetation of the Australian rainforests is conveniently regarded as composed of 4 main floristic elements which roughly approximate the geographical regions; hot and dry monsoonal forests in the north, hot and moist vine forests in the northeast, and warm forests and cool, moist fern and mossy forests in the southeast (1,071).]

There are relatively vast New Guinean refugia, such as the moist multiform highlands, where independent vegetational development subsequently took place but where close floristic relationships in structurally equivalent rainforest types are still preserved (1,071). These form the main refugium for what is left of the older Australian rainforest avifauna of the Tertiary period. Other remnants are found in Australia's southerly rainforests along the east coast, in the Mt. Lofty and Flinders Ranges in South Australia, in the Musgrave, Macdonnell, and Everard Ranges in central Australia, and in the rainforest pockets in the Kimberleys and Arnhem Land. Similar relationships exist in the structure and floristics of the rainforests and their mammalian faunas. The more primitive species in more widespread endemic or near endemic avian families are believed to occur in these areas (the "Tumbunan division;" see 816).

The poverty of the rainforest avifauna of Australia compared to those of New Guinea and the southwestern Pacific islands is attributed to the facts that the amount of rainforest habitat in Australia is very low. Because of the lack of fragmentation, the rainforest habitat does not readily enable isolates to form, and about half of the genera entering Australia do not have rainforest species and never invade the rainforest habitat. Horton (1,288) asserts that rainforest forms of Australia "definitely do not go extinct," so that it is not high rates of extinction that account for the low number of rainforest species in Australia, but, rather, the lack of fragmentation of their habitat sufficiently to form species (though it is fragmented sufficiently to form subspecies and varieties).

The Australian rainforest seems to act as a "pool," with one species per genus remaining in it and continually expanding outwards to other parts of the Continent. Only 17% of all extinctions in the 3 interglacial periods and Recent epoch in Australia were rainforest species, as compared to 56% in the southwestern Pacific islands and 69% in New Guinea (the glacial periods are seen as periods of movement of species, the interglacials as periods of speciation; 1,288).

MODERATE TECTONISM. Throughout the past 22 million yr in Australia, tectonism has been moderate and there has been no very high mountain range. Tectonic stability has been marked in much of northern Australia (including the Davenport province referred to on page 7) since 1,500 mya, particularly since 500 mya. Episodic uplift in the broad highland belt that parallels the east coast began in the Paleocene epoch or earlier but the major elevation occurred in the late Miocene and Pliocene epochs (287, 1,387). The uplift of the New Guinean Highlands and the Great Dividing Range into cooler altitudes, with retention of the precipitation regime, preserved a fauna and flora of essentially mid-Miocene character (280, 282). It is asserted that in climbing the mountains of the lush highlands of the "Tumbunan division" one, in effect, climbs back into the medial-Miocene past (see 288).

PART 2. BUDGERIGARS

Introduction

Budgerigars or Budgerygahs (*Melopsittacus undulatus*), also called Undulated, Warbling, or Green Grass Parakeets, Shell Parakeets, and Shell Parrots, are the most widely known cage and exhibition birds in the world (137, 1,056). Since much more is known of their biology than that of any other parrot, they receive the most thorough general treatment (excepting the general behavior of adults, for which the reader is referred to 67). As with Cockatiels (see p. 231), their affinities are obscure although Forshaw suggests that the genus is transitional between *Neophema* and *Pezoporus* (1).

This section also is used to introduce some properties of all parrots, of birds in general, of bats, of certain other mammals, and of reptiles, particularly crocodilians, birds' closest living relatives, and to introduce the Australian habitats to which Budgerigars and Cockatiels are endemic. The other parrot, general avian, chiropteran, and other mammalian data are useful for comparative purposes, and the comparisons with reptiles are crucial for considerations of avian evolution, as treated in Chapter 4.

OCCURRENCES---INTRODUCTORY DESCRIPTIONS---EXPORT. Budgerigars probably are the most abundant of all Australia's parrots. They are small, hardy, adaptable, streamlined birds, extremely easy to feed, house, and breed. They are among the most charming and attractive of all exotic birds (138). "The beauty in color, form and stance of the budgie is hard to equal...." (185). They become extremely tame with careful handling. As an aviary bird they have no rival, and, all things considered, are by far the best exotic birds for the avicultural novice to keep (138, 1,056). Females are said to be more prone to bite, and to bite hard, than males (137, 138), a property that some workers find useful in tentative sexing of the young (67).

Budgerigars were introduced to England by the noted British ornithologist and gifted painter of birds, John Gould, in 1840, on his return from an expedition to Australasia. The great appeal of their lively mannerisms, bright coloring, and soft, chattering voices, led to immediate and spectacular popularity among aviculturists. In 1879, about 50,000 birds arrived in England in the first few months, and hundreds of thousands were imported every year (5, 138). France also imported the birds in great numbers (about 100,000 pairs per year). [The first live parrot imported into Europe from Australia seems to have been a Rainbow Lorikeet (*Trichoglossus moluccanus*) brought back by Sir Joseph Banks in 1771 (1,056). Exports of Australian parrots were banned in 1939.]

[Gould also is known for incisive and expert analyses of the avian species brought back on the Beagle by Darwin in 1836. It was he, not Darwin, who recognized that the bill of the Galapagos finches "appears to form only a secondary character," that is, that the bills had to be abandoned as a key character (192). The diversity of bill types and feeding behavior now are believed to have been achieved without apparent significant genetic change (580). Gould's accomplishments in the field of natural history "....are truly monumental. No other ornithologist has ever exceeded (or will ever exceed) the number of Gould's bird discoveries...." (210).]

THE "PERFECT" BUDGERIGAR---THE BUDGERIGAR CLUB AND SOCIETY. Domestication of Budgerigars has such a long history that a universally recognized standard of qualities has been drawn up for deportment, shape, markings, color, etc. Efforts to breed the "perfect" Budgerigar reached their greatest heights in the United Kingdom. The aim was to bring the recognized colors to a peak of perfection (104). Today's magnificent exhibition birds are said to have been bred to "almost unbelievable strata of perfection" (185). Along another avenue, the "English Budgerigar," selected for maximum weight, has achieved thrice the weight of its wild conspecifics, but is much less graceful in shape (434, 787). A Budgerigar Club was formed at the Crystal Palace Exhibition in London in 1925. Five yr later, it became The Budgerigar Society, under the patronage of His Majesty King George V; many local societies now exist.

THE FIRST CAPTIVE BREEDING of Budgerigars is credited to Gould's brother-in-law, Charles Coxon (136), but it was not long before breeding was achieved by others. The Antwerp Zoological Garden was the first to breed them on a very large scale, and they have been bred in Europe on a grand scale ever since. After the large commercial breeding flocks had been built up and had flourished for years (l'Etablissement Bastide at Toulouse always kept 80,000-100,000 birds in stock), precipitous price declines left breeders barely showing a profit (104).

At no time in history has a pet so endeared itself or been in greater demand throughout the civilized world (5). Breeding in the U.S. began early in this century, leading to the 'budgie craze,' during which it was common to find one or more Budgerigars in American homes, frequently with the freedom of the house. Their popularity as cage birds in their native Australia began with the appearance of the yellow variety (see pp. 58, 59), a few such pairs having been introduced from abroad in about 1900 (1,056).

The Birds in the Wild

THE NOMADIC STRATEGY. Budgerigars are spectacular practitioners of the nomadic strategy. Gould noted of them, "...the beautiful little warbling Grass Parrakeet (*M. undulatus*), which prior to 1838 was so rare in southern parts of Australia that only a single example had been sent to Europe, arrived in that year in such countless multitudes on the Liverpool Plains, that I could have procured any number of specimens...." (317). They are wandering inhabitants of the dry inland plains of Australia, and highly successful exploiters of food and water resources whenever and wherever they become available (311, 312). When food is in short supply, Budgerigars start to move; experienced birds move toward traditional locations; naive birds either follow experienced birds or move at random. When ample food is found the birds settle. If the food is sufficiently abundant and nest holes and water are available, breeding occurs (171).

RANGE. Budgerigars are nearly ubiquitous in Australia. They range throughout the interior and, at certain places in the mid-south and northwest, to the coast; otherwise there are only occasional coastal irruptions (116, 1,056). They only occasionally visit the sparsely-timbered grasslands in the southeastern highlands (139). They occur in enormous numbers in the interior plains. Since they fill the air with their melodious, prolonged, warbling chatter, they generally are heard before being seen. [One Budgerigar is stimulated to vocalize by hearing another one (67, 109).]

FOOD AND FORAGING. Energy-rich seeds (80% energy availability, a caloric value approximately equal to that of animal tissue; 975, 1,338) of grasses and herbaceous plants, on or near the ground, in various degrees of ripeness, form the principal diet of Budgerigars and mainly govern their migrations (5). Though seeds contain the most concentrated food of plant origin, they usually are deficient in proteins and other essential nutrients. As a consequence, rather large quantities are required to satisfy the nutritional needs of individual birds. The seeds of herbaceous plants, however, tend to be richer in proteins than other seeds (968). Based on wet weight, the protein content of seeds is 10.9%, compared to 1-1.4% for fruits, 17.7% for insects and 18.1-22.9% for the flesh of various vertebrates (975).

[In an annual rainfall of, say, 200 mm, much of the total productivity of plants consists of fast-growing annuals that are able to take full advantage of occasional years of relatively high rainfall. These plants typically have small root systems and thin stemmy upper parts, but produce abundant flowers and seed very quickly. Seed then lies dormant until, in the next year of a high rainfall, the desert "blossoms like a rose" (259).]

The seeds are dehulled and swallowed whole or broken. Seeds of spinifex (Triodia) and tall tussock grasses (Mitchell grass; *Astrebla* spp.) are important items in the diet (139). The birds climb up the tillers of the latter and extract seeds from the seedheads. They rise in flocks to the nearest trees when flushed. Feeding typically is accompanied by a subdued (but sometimes sharp), constant chattering, which is one of the Budgerigars delightful traits. When alarmed, they utter a subdued, disyllabic screech. Eight discrete calls have been recognized (see p. 87, **Vocalization by Budgerigars**; 171, 1,055).

Large feeding congregations, sometimes of several thousand birds, occur in open grasslands in early morning and late afternoon; at other times the flocks are smaller. The composition of large feeding congregations changes frequently as attracted flocks descend to the ground from flight and others fly off. Directions of movements change constantly, large congregations drift about, and flock leaders change frequently (171).

SOCIALITY---PAUCITY OF AGGRESSIVE DISPLAYS. Budgerigars, Cockatiels and Peach-faced Lovebirds conform to the general correlation (573) between flock foraging and colonial breeding or roosting (of those species that forage in flocks, 26% breed in colonies; 34). These habits lend credence to Lack's conclusion (34) that colonial breeding and roosting by many terrestrial birds with nidicolous young (see pp. 193-195) and some aquatic birds result from a combination of particular foraging habits (ground and low-level foraging) and use of inaccessible nesting or roosting sites.

Members of all 3 species are strongly social (colonial) the year around and normally aggregate into small parties or large flocks. This practice provides the opportunity for frequent social contacts and doubtless promotes feeding success and leads to increased protection from predators. In keeping with their sociality, Budgerigars possess few agonistic displays (displays accompanying aggressive acts) and usually do not injure one another; females tend to be more aggressive than males. Judging from studies of their aggressive behavior, Brockway concluded that an individual Budgerigar "says what he feels" (67). There appears to be little social stratification, because birds of different ages and sex mix in flocks without obvious hierarchical construction and with few agonistic encounters. At times, though, juveniles separate from their parents' flocks and form large congregations composed mostly of young birds; at times, flocks are composed predominantly of members of one sex or the other, for example, of males when females are ovipositing or incubating (171).

THE FLIGHT of large flocks of Budgerigars usually is swift and somewhat erratic but remarkably cohesive, as an entire flock twists and turns as one. Smaller groups fly more slowly, with even turns and more apparent purpose (84, 1,056). Flying birds that remain together as a cohesive unit typically comprise less than 100 individuals; on some occasions, particularly before roosting, several hundred birds congregate in flight (171). Both screeching call notes and the color and pattern of the tail feathers serve in flock coordination signalling (3, 67, 1,055).

Studies of Budgerigars flying in wind tunnels have revealed a maximum range and economy at a flight speed of 42 k.p.h. At that speed, the birds consume (lose) 1/1,250th of their body weight per km travelled, with 72% of the energy being derived from fat metabolism. Budgerigars can fly for short periods and gain altitude at a simulated height of 6,100 m (330). Their respiratory rate in flight varies from about 3.33 to 4½ Hz, and they may require as much as 21 times more oxygen than when at rest (19, 23, 330), as compared to a mere 8.3-11.2-fold increase in free-flying Rock Pigeons (see E.A. LeFebvre, 1964, in 1,001). The energy expenditure in sustained flight is independent of ambient temperature, since the flight muscles generate excess heat that must be dissipated, eliminating the need for additional thermoregulation (see 967 and the Discussion in 976). Flight temperatures also appear to be independent of the ambient temperature in cool and moderate environments.

Body temperatures of some birds in flight rise 1.5-2.6°C; in others they may be as much as 4°C higher than at rest (perhaps linked to the tolerance for hyperthermia--i.e., an increase in body temperature to above the normal value--when not in flight; 1,087). Budgerigars could not be made to continue flying in a wind tunnel after their body temperature had reached 44°C (330). They overheat, even flying at 33.8-34.8°F (see V. A. Tucker, 1969, in 157). The major role of flight hyperthermia may be to provide tissue temperatures that enhance metabolic capacities for sustained, vigorous activity (see 37, 829). More or less continuous fliers, such as swallows and swifts, have special flight adaptations of wings and body structures that reduce the amount of energy required per unit of time. For example, longer-winged species, often with pointed wings, have high aspect ratios that decrease induced drag and the energetic cost of powered flight (see 425 and D.S. Lyuleeva, 1970, in 967).

KINEMATIC-AERODYNAMIC studies of the mechanical power output of 6 species in straight and level flight in wind tunnels showed that the power required per unit weight was correlated with speed but not with average weight. At optimum speeds, all species, large and small, fast and slow-flying, required almost the same amount of energy per unit weight to cover the same distance in still air (636). Average air speeds of free-flying gulls, terns, and skimmers flying in the vicinity of colonies under various wind conditions were such as to achieve primarily a minimum cost of transport relative to the ground but the minimizing of metabolic rate also was a factor "....air speeds can be increased or decreased considerably with only a relatively small increase in metabolic rate or cost of transport" (690). Heat transfer in flight generally is 3-6 times as great as during rest, owing to the exposure of more-poorly insulated parts of the body and to external and internal forced convection (422, 518).

[Many birds customarily fly at airspeeds of 32-48 k.p.h. The normal flight speed of geese and starlings, however, is 80 k.p.h., for sandgrouse it is 72 k.p.h., while Peregrine Falcons (*Falco peregrinus*) dive on prey at speeds of 252-324 k.p.h. (380, 469, 470, 1,206). Migrating flocks of Canada Geese (*Branta canadensis interior*) travel at airspeeds of 57-77 k.p.h., of Lesser Snow Geese (*Anser c. caerulescens*) at 71-81 k.p.h., and of Mallards (*Anas platyrhynchos* var. *domesticus*) at 91 k.p.h., but a large proportion of migrant species do not exceed 40 k.p.h. (1,052).

It appears that birds decrease their air speed as that of favorable winds increases and increase it as the speed of headwinds increases (711). Before embarking on long flights, the bodies of many migratory birds consist of 25-50% of stored fat by weight in the form of triglycerides (for fuel; structural body fats are chiefly phospholipids, the higher the body temperature, the greater the degree to which the latter are unsaturated; 28, 1,099). The available evidence, including field observations, suggests that the longest, non-stop flights of birds are possible, physiologically speaking, only if the birds are aided, or at least not hindered, by winds (976). Winds of the northeast monsoon are absolutely vital to even the most powerful fliers among palaearctic migrants crossing some 4,000 km of the Indian Ocean (1,052).]

ACTIVITY TIMES---SEEK SHADE FROM HOT SUN---MAINLY ARBOREAL. Activity in the morning starts shortly before sunrise, with preening, soft calls, and movements within the trees. Within a few min of sunrise the birds fly from their roosts to foraging areas, at times as a single flock, at other times as several flocks that leave in quick succession (171). Budgerigars are most noticeable and most intensely active in the cooler early morning and late afternoon hours, when they repair to their watering grounds, scurry through the grass in search of seeds, or fly from tree to tree. During the hottest, most stressful afternoon hours, Budgerigars are likely to be overlooked, as they seek shelter in the shade, usually in green trees, where they are well camouflaged. Sometimes 1,000 or more birds gather and spread over 2 or more trees (33, 171).

During these hottest hours they habitually keep silently hidden, with a minimum of movement, sometimes remaining almost motionless for hours at a time in trees and tall bushes bordering watercourses, in sparsely-timbered grasslands, in mallee scrub (sparse eucalypt woodland of stunted and multi-stemmed trees), in mulga scrub (*Acacia aneura*), and in saltbush plains (5, 531). A tendency toward midday inactivity, at least insofar as vocalizations are concerned, also is noted in confined Budgerigars (529). Like most parrots, Budgerigars are mainly arboreal (tree-dwellers), climbing about among the branches and trunks, and making considerable use of their hooked bills. Not being shy, they usually allow a close approach.

As sunset approaches, foraging Budgerigars move back into timbered country and forage in small flocks or perch and preen on exposed branches, often in dead trees. At sunset the flocks rise in spectacular display flights, calling loudly and swirling at high speed above the trees. Afterwards, they fly off on a fairly straight course for the roosting site and drop into the foliage. Sometimes they settle down quickly, at other times they move and fly about within the roosting tree and neighboring trees, occasionally dropping to the ground briefly in small groups and foraging. They change from active and noisy to silent and still on an average of 21 min after sunset. After going to roost at night the birds remain still and silent and stay in the same tree unless disturbed; if disturbed they abandon the roost as a cohesive unit. Roosting occurs in various trees, for example, *Eucalyptus microtheca* (Coolibah), *Acacia longifolia*, *Bauhina cunninghamii*, and *Santalum acuminatum*, most commonly in *E. microtheca* (171).

BATHING---DRINKING AND WATER NEEDS. Budgerigars are fond of bathing by rolling in dew-wet grass (136). Like Cockatiels and lovebirds, they sometimes bathe in a dish of water by head-ducking (67; see p. 284). This is thought to be relatively infrequent behavior among Budgerigars, but my flighted birds sometimes engaged in it when a large bowl of water was available. As with most birds, Budgerigars tend to be very regular in both the manner and the time scheduling of their drinking, with a daily intake of about 5½% of their body weight for adults--about 2-5 ml for confined birds (15, 331, 443, 520; amounting to 18-20% of body weight in young birds).

As mentioned above, Budgerigars visit waterholes in early-to-mid morning and mid-to-late afternoon (or between mid-morning and mid-afternoon; 171), but birds perching in trees over water during midday frequently descend in relays of small groups to drink (171, 1,056); there are few more spectacular sights in the Australian bush than those of Budgerigars coming in to drink (311; see also 171). When large flocks do so, many individuals land on the surface of the water with outstretched wings, drink hurredly, and take flight (1,056).

[On the other hand, some other Australian birds have different drinking habits; 7 species of estrildine finches in the Kimberly, northern Australia, drink only in the early morning and interrupt the act periodically to scan for predators, while the desert-dwelling Zebra Finches (*Poephila guttata*) typically drink in the middle of the day, and Galahs (*Eolophus roseicapillus*) drink in the evening (811). Sandgrouse in the Kalahari Desert drink either 1-2½ h after sunrise or 1½ h before sunset, sometimes both, sometimes at night. Before flying to the water, they usually gather in large flocks. Members of mated pairs arrive and depart together (1,206).]

In the absence of temperature stress, the relative water consumption of terrestrial birds is inversely related to body size (331). Like a few small songbirds (some Fringillidae, Estrildidae, Ploceidae, and Alaudidae; 161, 621) and some other small desert birds and non-passerines, Budgerigars that are not under stress can go for long periods without drinking. In some of these birds, including Budgerigars, the amount of pulmocutaneous water loss becomes reduced relative to metabolism (see 1,087). As with many animals, they obtain "metabolic water" as a by-product of digesting seeds, an ability that, in times of need, may allow them the mobility to reach areas where conditions are favorable (829). Thus, Budgerigars can remain in good health for as long as 150 days on dry seeds, about 7-10% of the dry weight of which can be metabolized to water (28, 157).

However, this probably is a reserve capacity made use of primarily in foraging at relatively great distances from surface water and in nomadic or migratory movements and droughts (157, 1,087). Budgerigars doubtless drink every day in the wild (15), as field evidence indicates that they are tied rigidly to their water sources (311). [Wyndham, however, suggests that Budgerigars in the field drink infrequently, except when it is very hot (171).] Nor are Budgerigars found to exist under drought conditions or where no surface water occurs. Water deficits probably develop regularly in some Australian birds as they forage widely in hot weather, and then are eliminated by drinking during periodic visits to water holes (1,087).

[Angiotensin II (a final product of the renin-angiotensin system) induces drinking in most avian species. However, birds that originate in arid areas and/or can survive without water for extended periods, such as carnivores, are exceptional in that angiotensin II usually does not induce drinking. In responding vertebrates, angiotensin II seems to transfer information of dehydration to the adrenal gland, neurosecretory cells, kidney, subfornical organ, and preoptic area of the hypothalamus (926, 1,122).]

SUCTION MECHANISM OF IMBIBITION. Budgerigars and hanging parrots or parakeets (genus *Loriculus*) drink like members of the Columbidae, hummingbirds and some finches, by putting the bill into water and then rapidly ingesting by means of piston-like movements of the tongue, creating cycles of low pressure regions, first in the mouth and then in the pharynx. This causes suction of water into the mouth and then transports it over the glottis and the ventral pharyngeal valves into the esophagus (67, 79, 998). This method of drinking is thought to have multiple origins. In inhabitants of arid regions it may be an adaptation that allows a bird to exploit small accumulations of water effectively and rapidly and may make possible a reduction of the time spent at risk while drinking. This can be a very important consideration, since risks of predation are thought to be severe at water holes (see 828, 1,087).

EVAPORATIVE WATER LOSS---WATER CONSERVATION. Resting birds under normal conditions (20-30°C) usually lose more water by evaporation than they gain by the production of metabolic water (829). The disparity increases with decreasing body weight, with the evaporative loss being 5 times greater than the production gain in the smallest birds (161, 423). At low temperatures, however, evaporative loss is reduced and the production of metabolic water increases, the effect again being greatest in small species; water loss at these temperatures apparently is of minor importance (423). In Budgerigars, evaporative water loss can be balanced by metabolic water production at temperatures below 14°C (1,244); the evaporative water loss increases greatly with temperature, being 16 times at great at 45°C as at 25°C (see 171).

Virtually all birds and reptiles conserve water by excreting nitrogen in the form of colloidal solutions of uric acid and urates rather than urea (28, 161, 442, 522, 999). Birds, however, are the only vertebrates other than mammals that can produce a urine that is more concentrated in solutes than is the plasma (usually by a factor of 2-3; 2.33 in Budgerigars; 933, 999, 1,087). Ordinarily a Budgerigar would excrete 1 g of water per day (15). Additional water conservation can be achieved during periods of limited access by reducing evaporative loss by behavioral means, by tolerance of hyperthermia, and by voiding drier-than-normal excreta. Budgerigars with normal access to water void excreta containing 75-80% water, as opposed to only 60% when they have but limited access (311, 1,087).

During dehydration, consequent upon limited access to water, Budgerigars reduce the amount of water lost from the skin (normally 63% of the total evaporative loss at 30°C; see 1,087) and respiratory system per "unit of metabolism" (157). With fluid deprivation, their plasma chloride concentration increases 13% after 2 weeks and then begins to decline slowly to original levels by the 5th week. At the same time, food consumed either remains normal or declines briefly and then returns to normal (see 1,087).

The remarkable powers of water conservation of Budgerigars may be judged from the fact that they do not lose weight until the water on which they are maintained exceeds a salinity of about 0.20 M NaCl (15). [For comparison, domestic fowl chicks accept NaCl solutions only up to a concentration of 0.9% (0.15 M); when no alternative is available, many die of thirst rather than consume a toxic 2% solution (513).] On the other hand, the members of the Columbiformes that inhabit arid environments appear to have no exceptional potential for water conservation, but are strong fliers capable of reaching available water sources (see 999).

KIDNEYS AND URINE. For various reasons, including the lability of the total-kidney glomerular filtration rate, it is infeasible to make a general statement that would describe the role of the avian kidney in the maintenance of salt and water balance (933). However, water conservation capabilities of Budgerigars very likely are made possible by the ability of their kidneys to excrete a concentrated urine; the same is true of the kidneys of some of the songbirds that can go for long periods without drinking (161). From 67% to as much as 99% of the filtered water load is resorbed in various species (1,087). Savanna Sparrows (*Passerculus sandwichensis*) produce the most concentrated avian urine known (180-195 cones/kidney; see 999). Despite the capability of birds to vary greatly their rates of urine production in meeting varying demands, and the fact that urine production, as in mammals, is achieved via tubular water resorption, the avian kidney, with few exceptions, appears to be inferior to the mammalian kidney in the excretion of salts. This traces primarily to the smaller numbers of tubules with loops of Henle (311, 325, 933, 999).

[The avian nephrons of the "reptilian" type, which are located in the cortex of the kidney, lack loops of Henle, whereas those of the "mammalian" type, which occur in the medulla, possess loops of Henle of varying lengths, some very long (442, 522, 621). The nephrons of the reptilian type, at least, are "shut down" (glomerular intermittence) during periods of stress, apparently largely or partly by the action of arginine vasotocin, the avian antidiuretic hormone, but alterations in the filtration rate of individual nephrons also may be involved in changes in total kidney filtration rates (933, 999; see below). The same hormone also aids in water conservation by increasing water reabsorption in the collecting ducts and tubules (134, 832, 999). Adrenal corticosteroid hormones are involved in the control of the excretion of salts and water (522).]

Many birds that excrete a concentrated urine generally are found to have overcome this limitation through the acquisition of larger numbers of loops of Henle, that is, a greater proportion of tubules with medullary loops (see 323, 442, 621). This is achieved through the medium of a greater number of medullary cones with a relatively small volume of cortex and a higher proportion of mammalian-type nephrons (621). Although the medullary lengths of these cones show some correlation with urine-concentrating ability, the correlation is not as close as is that for the number of cones per kidney. Highly effective water conservers have kidneys with only 33-50% as much cortex per medullary cone as is possessed by the kidneys of less effective water conservers (see 999). Although the relation between renal function and morphology is a complex one, it appears that birds that are adapted for an existence in xeric (dry) environments have smaller kidneys with fewer nephrons; the large kidneys of passerines with large numbers of small nephrons may be a legacy of their having evolved in moist tropical habitats (933).

[In general, avian kidneys comprise different percentages of body weight in species of different size ranges (1% in the Rock Pigeon, 0.6-0.8% in various species of doves) and are proportionately larger than mammalian kidneys. Avian kidneys have several apparent adaptations that facilitate the elimination of precipitated urates: (1) an arboreal branching system of medullary collecting ducts and uretal branches; (2) spherically shaped urate precipitates, which presumably facilitates their flow like balls; (3) peristaltic milking activity by the ureters; and (4) renal mucoid materials that act as "protective colloids" and physical lubricants (see 999).]

THE COPRODEUM AND RECTUM (large intestine) also appear to play roles in water resorption, as indicated by the fact that the material in the rectal lumen has a lower moisture content than the material in the ileum, and the presence of a resorptive type of epithelial lining and a wealth of villi in both regions. The mucosal organization in these regions in Australian birds varies in a manner that appears to be functionally significant. In the dehydrated state, significant amounts of cations and water are absorbed by solute-linked (NaCl) water transport and then recycled to the kidneys, permitting continued excretion of urates. It has been estimated that cloacal absorption from uretal urine in dehydrated or salt-depleted birds may result in conservation of 10-15% of the water and 67% of the NaCl excreted by the kidney (134, 322, 521, 621, 626, 829, 832, 999, 1,087).

Thus, more efficient resorption of water from urine in the coprodeum and large intestine also could play a prominent role in the exceptional water conservation capabilities of some species (see also pp. 110, 111, **Water Resorption**). In fact, post-renal water conservation in the Galah, a xerophilic (thriving in a dry environment) Australian parrot, is substantially more effective than in the domestic fowl (*G. gallus* var. *domesticus*; see 621). On the other hand, in the cases of fructivorous and nectarivorous birds in the deserts of southern Arizona, the supply of preformed water in the diet is so great as to require the output of dilute urine even in conditions of heat stress that require evaporative cooling (829).

[It has been suggested that osmotic stress in avian species stimulates the hypothalamic neurosecretory system, with a resulting increased secretion, release, and depletion of the antidiuretic hormone, arginine vasotocin, from the neurohypophysis (920; see pp. 127, 128). The effectiveness of water extraction and conservation devices is shown by the fact that 71 of 118 species of birds inhabiting arid portions of Australia either visited water sources on less than half of the days when the temperature exceeded 30.6°C or were not observed to drink at all. The birds that were dependent upon drinking usually drank at times when they were not exposed to high temperatures and intense sunlight. Being most dependent upon surface water, seed-eaters were most numerous at water sources (157, 1,057).]

THE TOLLS OF HEAT WAVES. Birds are predisposed or preadapted to a desert existence, with a tolerance for weight loss during dehydration of perhaps 30-50% and a tolerance for hyperthermia that conveys distinct advantages in connection with temperature regulation and water economy. Hyperthermia permits them to store an amount of heat that raises the body temperature about 4°C (37, 64, 157, 311). Despite this, Budgerigars are "cut down mercilessly" by the tens of thousands, perhaps even millions in excessively hot weather (5, 66, 68, 311). Such was the case in the record heat wave of 1932, when the January average in the shade was 44.2°C at the Rumbala rail station near Oodnadatta (28°S x 136°E) in the interior of South

Australia (117 mm avg. annual rainfall) and reached 52.2°C on some days (66).

NORTH-SOUTH MIGRATIONS AND BREEDING---SHORT BREEDING CYCLES. There is a tendency for nomadic birds living in the so-called "wooded-deserts" of the Australian interior to move north in the Autumn, where they get the benefits of conditions created by the summer monsoonal rain system, and to come south of latitude 30-33° in the spring to the area of Mediterranean-type climate, with winter rains that originate in dominant winter westerlies (71, 1,328). Budgerigars follow this pattern; their movements and breeding broadly follow patterns of maximum seasonal growth of pasture land (171). Male Budgerigars arrive at breeding grounds with the cycle of spermatogenesis well advanced, but females arrive with undeveloped ovarian follicles (see 171). Migrating flocks sometimes merge into one huge concourse, so vast as to obscure the light of the sun. One north-bound flight of untold millions, during the 1932 heat wave, took from 05:00 h to 09:00 h to pass over Paratoo (65). At no time do the birds lay down fat deposits; they apparently stop to feed each day (171).

Budgerigars arrive in their far southern breeding grounds (250 mm avg. winter rain) at the end of winter (Aug.) or in the early spring (Sept.-Dec). After breeding there, they travel to the north (625 mm avg. summer rain) in the summer or autumn (Feb. or March), following the wet season, and breed yet again (June-Sept.), sometimes residing there for extended periods. There is no record of the species remaining in the south throughout the year. In medial latitudes, with rains at any time of the year, they usually are present and breed during the hot months (mostly Feb.-May.), but follow an underlying seasonal pattern (116, 171, 1,056). Because of the nomadic existence of Budgerigars, and the premium placed on time, selection has favored very short breeding cycles (see 127).

RAIN AND BREEDING. A large-scale monsoonal system develops in the tropical latitudes of both hemispheres during their respective summers, but it is weakest by far and least regular in the Southern Hemisphere (1,326). In the hot summer (about Dec.-Apr.) of northern Australia, the monsoonal tropic rains and heavy electric storms are followed, with impressive rapidity, by growth of the life-supporting grasses. [In this connection, it is known that grass growth is linearly related to rainfall of up to 500 mm/yr in both southwestern Australia and southwestern Africa (see 830, 960).] The birds appear "suddenly in parts where the magic of heavy rains has turned the desert into one vast, luxurious meadow" (5). By the time the grasses are bearing seeds, Budgerigars are hatching (67).

[The rate at which the Australian bush "greens up" after a fire also is quite remarkable. Within days of the fire there is a green "haze" over the ground as grass and ferns shoot up and seeds germinate (the primary response of seedlings on or near deep ashbeds is to nutrients). Trees and shrubs are equally quick to sprout new leaves (1,062).]

But the birds also are opportunistic; any good rain will set them to nesting, even when they are in the energetically very costly process of molting (see pp. 64, 65, **Molting**). The latter requires 6-8 months and is as erratic as their breeding (5, 116, 311, 312). [In fact, active molt in breeding birds has been reported for more than 100 species (see 319).] There is, however, a notable lack of quantitative data as to the effectiveness of these opportunistic or erratic breedings in terms of the survival of the young to maturity; it has been suggested that the biologically significant breeding follows the seasonal pattern (160).

THE "ZEITGEBER" AND TEMPERATURE. The proximate factor in inducing breeding in Budgerigars and many other arid-country species, that is, the breeding stimulus or "Zeitgeber," appears to be the sight of rain itself, or of clouds. Another possibility, suggested by the results of studies of confined Zebra Finches, is that rain and increased humidity quickly relieve the effects of dehydration, particularly on the testis (381; perhaps mediated via increased plasma levels of FSH, i.e., follicle stimulating hormone). [Masked Bobwhite Quail (*Colinus virginianus ridgwayi*) require the combination of long daylength, warm temperatures, and relative humidity of at least 25% (732).] Following several months of drought, the first nuptial displays of many Australian nomads take place within a few min of the beginning of the first rain. This adaptation is an extremely important one, since it allows the birds to commence breeding as soon as favorable conditions can be anticipated (23, 63, 101, 125, 155, 312).

To give an example: after the very first showers of drought-breaking rains, Zebra Finches may copulate within 10 min, begin building nests within 4 h, and start laying eggs within 1 week (see 63, 233, 311, 381, 895). Some birds even may begin to build nests while rain still is falling (730). The Bush Chat (*Ashbyia lovensis*) built a nest 3 days after rains that broke an almost year's drought and oviposited in it 6 days later (see J.N. McGilp, 1919, in 311). Several passerine species in the Kalahari ovulate within 6-10 days of the onset of rainfall (see 730). Courtship of Black-faced Woodswallows (*Artamus cinereus*) began several min after rain began to fall, breaking several months of drought, the first copulation occurred 2 h later, and a nest was being built the next day. In fact, it was a common remark among observers in these areas long before Immelmann published his remarkable findings (63) that, "when a cloud passes over the sky, Black-faced Woodswallows begin to pick up nesting sticks" (311).

Although the precise triggering mechanism remains to be established, a retinal response to the sight of rain presumably stimulates the hypothalamus (see pp. 124-134). It is possible, however, that there is a threshold temperature below which breeding does not occur, and breeding rarely occurs in extremely hot weather (5, 116, 312, 928, 1,123). Moreover, the onset of unfavorable environmental conditions may halt ovulation reflexly, even after oviposition has commenced (348, 350). The more seasonal the climate and the more severe the dry season, the smaller, in general, is the amount of rain required to initiate breeding in different species and populations (311).

RISE IN WATER LEVEL. In the case of the nomadic ducks of interior Australia, an increase in water level caused by distant rainfall at the headwaters is followed closely by intensified sexual displays. These synchronize all individuals in a population of the most opportunistic species. The Gray Teal (*Anas gibberifrons*), a complete nomad, begins increased sexual displays as soon as a water rise becomes evident and can oviposit within 12 days. At the same time there is a vast increase in the populations of the insect, *Corixa*, the principal food of the ducklings. The Australian Black Duck (*A. superciliosa*; which also has a regular breeding season) and some others need deeper water than the Gray Teal and delay breeding until the billabongs (blind channels or stagnant pools) are full and some permanence of deep water is ensured. The Pink-eared Duck (*Malacorhynchus membranaceus*), which feeds on plankton and breeds in shallow drying floodwaters, delays ovulation until the floodwaters actually flow across the plains (731). In the most opportunistic of these nomads there is continuous spermatogenesis, even in times unsuitable for breeding (see 731).

[Breeding flexibility of Australian birds and a dependence on rainfall characterize mainly the inhabitants of the western and central parts. There appears to be far more regularity of breeding in temperate southeastern Australia and in the humid southwest corner, while in Northern Australia, breeding periods occur on a regular timetable (311). Natural selection generally has favored the establishment of annual breeding cycles, particularly in the avifauna of subarctic and temperate zones (414).

The most dependable Zeitgeber for most species in these regions, of course, is the seasonal appearance of a specific and appropriate daylength when the light coincides with a restricted photosensitive phase of a circadian-based rhythm in the course of the increasing daylengths in the spring. The response is mediated primarily extra-retinally, via stimulation of the hypothalamo-hypophysial system, and adjusted or fine-tuned by "local" information, principally temperature (350, 724, 734, 927); in some cases the modulating influences of weather, particularly temperature, influence the final reproductive effort only indirectly, by influencing the abundance of food (1,123).

Several avian species (White-crowned Sparrows, *Zonotrichia leucophrys*, and quail) show very rapid responses to an altered photoperiod (see 1,028). For example, FSH and LH secretion by Japanese Quail (*C. coturnix japonica*) males increase manyfold (followed by testicular recrudescence) after abrupt transformation from short-day to long-day photoperiods, with an increase often being noted by the end of the first long day. Reversal of the photostimulation suppresses LH and FSH secretion and leads to gonadal regression, but only after a lag period of 10-14 days (the "carry-over" phenomenon), suggesting the occurrence of a semi-permanent alteration of the nervous system (see 1,045).

Both the eyes and extra-retinal photoreceptors are involved in the regulation of circadian activity in the House Sparrow and male Japanese Quail. In the latter case, stimulation of the hypothalamic photoreceptors at the proper time is crucial for a massive release of gonadotropin but visual input seems obligatory in setting the hypothalamic rhythm. These findings and the existence of a retino-hypothalamic tract strongly support the view that the eyes play a role in mediating gonadal recrudescence (1,045, 1,118).

The magnitude of the photoperiodic response is a function of the duration of the coincidence of the photosensitive phase with the environmental photophase (the "external coincidence" model; 927, 1,045). The Zeitgeber signals the imminence of optimum weather and consequent favorable ecological conditions for raising young. For discussions of the "internal coincidence" model and refs., see 989, 1,045.

In temperate latitudes of Eurasia and America, the vast majority of species start laying in the spring and brood young in late spring and early summer. A few temperate-zone species, however, regularly breed in autumn or begin to oviposit before or around the winter solstice (730). At the northern and southern boundaries of the range of a temperate-zone species, temperature may be equally as important as photoperiod in regulating the time of nesting. The breeding season in the House Wren (*Troglodytes aëdon*), for example, may well be determined and regulated by the proper synchronization of photoperiod and temperature (723).]

"ANTICIPATING" RAIN---EXCEPTIONALLY ERRATIC RAINFALL. Australian ornithologists were long under the impression that Budgerigars could anticipate rain (5). It would appear, rather, that the birds are able to "home in" on areas with recent rainfall by following the pressure gradients toward the centers of cyclonic depressions (see 63). In this connection, birds are known to be able to detect changes in barometric pressure and approaching weather fronts (12, 112, 118).

For example, the general consensus is that the movements of north-temperate-zone birds in eastern Canada are intimately related to the eastward-advancing high and low-barometric pressure centers. The most dense spring flights are likely to be just behind the warm front to the west of a high-pressure center and ahead of an advancing low pressure cell with its associated cold front. This marks the northward advancing edge of warm, moist winds. Autumnal movements are likeliest on the east side of a high pressure cell behind an advancing cold front to the west of a low-pressure center (377, 671). Other possible cues are the cloud banks associated with heavy cyclonic rain--visible from 300-400 km at ground level, the noise of thunder--also perceptible at distances of hundreds of km, and storm-associated lightning (831, 960).

[The opportunistic desert-nesting Afro-Asian sandgrouse (Pteroclidae) also occupy low rainfall habitats with diel temperature extremes. It is suggested that, since much desert rainfall derives from thunderstorms whose associated cloud systems rise 10-15 km above the ground and are easily visible from a distance of 100 km, these birds might be attracted by this cue. In this way sandgrouse may exploit relatively tiny areas of improved conditions within great tracts which may have had droughts lasting for years (830).]

One can understand the evolution of the ability to "home in" on areas with recent rainfall in terms of the intenseness of the selective pressure for it in Australia. Even though rainfall typically is erratic in all deserts, "Nowhere else in the world is there such a huge area of pastoral land of such erratic rainfall as the pastoral country of Australia....the rainfall tends to be least reliable in the central section...." where the cyclonic disturbances take erratic paths (see 68, 311). These climatic conditions may date back to the late Pleistocene, which ended 11,000-10,000 yr ago.

COLONIAL BREEDING---MONOGAMY---PROMISCUITY. In regard to breeding, Budgergars are obligatorily colonial (67, see p. 121, **Need for Interactions with Other Birds**). They customarily breed in large, loose colonies. Breeding records suggest that they breed throughout their range (116). Like most parrots, Budgerigars are monogamous and pair for very long periods, perhaps as long as both birds survive. Some sexual promiscuity occurs in confined birds, particularly by males, but only in the absence of the mate (and it is terminated by the appearance and interfering actions of the mate; 67, 104, 137). Pairs may raise several broods in succession.

Courtship, copulation, and selection of nest holes occur when flocks are in timbered areas. Selection and defense of the nest site are carried out primarily by the female (859) and this also is true of confined birds (see 844 and pp. 777, 778). During periods of oviposition and incubation and while nestlings are young, the hens remain in and near their nests and are allofed by their mates. Only the hens incubate. The males spend most of the daylight hours foraging and allofeeding the females in their nests. They are more likely to enter and spend time in the nest hole near the end of the nestling period than earlier. Females leave the nests briefly and join males in nearby trees, where they court, preen, and rest. During incubation and when the chicks are young the female also spends the night in the nest hole. It had been thought that only she feeds the hatchlings and young chicks, but this seems unlikely as a general rule in view of recent studies (843, 844) and the present findings (see p. 783 *et seq.*). As the chicks get older, the females leave the nest with increasing frequency and join the foraging males. Chicks then appear at the nest entrance and are allofed there by both parents. Neither parent is apt to allofeed the young after they have fledged (171, 843).

LOCATION OF NESTS. As is the habit of almost all parrots, Budgerigars are secondary cavity nesters, that is, they make their nests in pre-existing cavities. Since these usually are reached through entrances that are too small (3-6 cm minimum width) to admit sympatric (inhabiting the same region) hole-nesting birds, including avian predators, nest holes are not necessarily limiting. [The principal exceptions to hole-nesting in Australia are the secondarily open-nesting Swamp, Night, Rock, Golden-shouldered, Hooded, and Paradise Parrots (1).] A few parrots excavate fresh cavities; for example, *Cyanoliseus patagonus* and *Psilopsiagon aurifrons* nest in tunnels dug into the vertical faces of cliffs (see 819), and some New World parrots routinely excavate cavities in arboreal or terrestrial termitaria (termite nests; 1). The Gang-Gang Cockatoo (*Callocephalon fimbriatum*) and the Thick-billed Parrot (*Rhynchopsitta pachyrhyncha*) enlarge and extend hollows and entrances by chewing at the sides and either scraping out the chips or using them as a bedding for the nest (139, 484).

Budgerigars nest in any available wood hollows--even between roots or in a fencepost or a log lying on the ground--but favor those in eucalypt trees (see pp. 55-56), particularly Coolibahs. Suitable holes usually are found only in dead trees or old live ones (171; see also pp. 229, 230, beginning with **Eucalypts Sensitive to Microhabitat Changes**). Several nests have been found, not only in the same tree, but even in the same branch, though usually 3-5 m apart (139, 171). [Thick-billed Parrots are known to nest as close as 2 m apart (484).] The holes used by Budgerigars usually are not modified, nor is a nest constructed inside; the chicks and eggs usually are found from 25 cm to several meters inside the hollow, on the bottom. Breeding pairs defend a small space near the entrance to their nest. Unlike the situation with confined birds (see below), the presence or position of a perch near the nest hole is unimportant (171).

THE NEST BEDDING OF HOLE-NESTING PARROTS usually is very frugal. For Budgerigars, it is said to be a soft mat of decaying wood dust and droppings (171). For Thick-billed Parrots, it is described as wood chips and feathers (484), for Vernal Hanging Parrots (*Loriculus vernalis*), one nest had some soft, black earthy-looking powder which evidently had fallen from the tops and sides of the cavity, another nest had a very few dry leaves at the bottom of the cavity, and a 3rd nest had a few fragments of chipped wood. In a 4th nest, however, a 45-cm-deep cavity was filled to about 15 cm of the entrance hole with pieces of green leaves and fronds of bracken, torn into pieces roughly 2½ cm sq.

The bedding in one Ceylon Hanging Parrot (*L. beryllinus*) nest cavity was a 2½-cm-thick pad of green leaves (1,261); another observer described the bedding of these birds as generally a large mass of strips of green leaves about ½ cm wide and 2½-5 cm long (1,263). The sympatric Crimson and Eastern Rosellas (*Platycercus elegans* and *P. eximus*) and Red-rumped Parrot (*Psephotus haematonotus*) are said to deposit their eggs on a lining of decayed wood, in the former case just inside the nest hollow or at the terminus of the entrance passageway (1,264).

Eucalypts

TREES OF THE GENUS *EUCALYPTUS* (about 600 species in the genus, mostly trees and most of them found in Australia), also called "gum" trees, are extraordinarily prevalent in the Australian woody vegetation, making up 90% of the forest and woodland trees over much of northern and tropical Australia. They have come to occupy many sites throughout the Continent, particularly those with frequent water stress during seasonal or periodic drought, or where soil moisture is low (1,069). On the other hand, they are sensitive to frost (1,328).

Inasmuch as no eucalypt can grow under heavy rainforest cover--they are almost all "light-demanders"--they are absent from rainforests. Only a few species have been successful on the margins of rainforests or have penetrated into subalpine habitats up to the limit of tree growth. They dominate the open forest and woodland formations, including tropical savannas, arid mallee communities, watercourse communities, and mallee communities fringing the arid zone in the south. Species of *Acacia* predominate in the upper stratum of arid and semiarid areas. In many such areas, however, at least one eucalypt species is within sight. Not more than a dozen or two eucalypt species occur within the arid zone, either confined to rocky out-crops, along seasonal water courses, along specialized habitats, or on particular substrates (68, 1,063, 1,069, 1,072).

Nearly all eucalypt species are evergreen. A syndrome of features lead to easy recognition of most species of the *Eucalyptus* alliance as "eucalypts" rather than members of any other genus. Members of the genus are relatively uniform in their structure--similarly-shaped leaves that hang vertically on slender flexible or somewhat stiff petioles, generally similar flowers, broadly similar inflorescences, and the same kind of fruit. Physical maturity for a great many species is at 200-400 yr (68). One species, *E. regnans*, is the tallest hardwood in the world, not infrequently topping 92 m, with a record of 115 m (some claim 150 m; 1,376). A large number of *Eucalyptus* species, even some of the tall, forest eucalypts (in extreme habitats), may develop the "mallee habit," in which several stout woody stems sprout from an underground lignotuber.

The taxonomic evidence strongly suggests that Australia was the center of origin and of primary diversification of eucalypts; a site of origin somewhere in southern-central Australia has been suggested. The Tertiary fossil record of eucalypts within Australia is meager and possibly extends back into the Eocene. Thus, molds and casts of fruits resembling *Eucalyptus*, *Angophora*, and other eucalypts are found in Tertiary deposits of either Miocene or Eocene-Oligocene age. Eucalypts became prominent in the Australian flora in Oligocene times and later. Their radiation and rise to dominance seems to have involved the parallel evolution (doubtless begun earlier) of features that enabled them to survive and to become established on newly available sites, under circumstances of some water stress and under light or open canopy conditions (68, 282, 1,069).

A possible factor in the long-term and broad success of eucalypts is their apparent fire dependency; in fact, some eucalypts, such as *E. regnans*, do not regenerate in the absence of fire, and many other Australian plants require fire for successful reproduction (1,062). It has been suggested that eucalypts compete successfully against alternative vegetation because they have evolved adaptations that have enabled them to flourish after being burnt and to survive for long periods between fires. Eucalypts generally are among the most resistant of trees to intense fires, most species having the capacity to sprout again from proventitious buds on the trunk, producing "epicormic shoots," even after fires in which limbs as much as 10-15 cm in diameter have been burned from the crown. The usually-very-thick bark is evidently an effective insulator, which assists the process (1,069). "Without fire there would be no forest eucalypts. Without the eucalypts there would be fewer or smaller forest fires" (see A. Mount, 1969, in 1,062).

Flexibility and twisting of the slender branchlets and the petioles of eucalypts allow the leaves to hang in such a way as to reduce the heating and drying effects of insolation. This has a profound effect on the undergrowth by allowing light to pass through the canopy, even in quite dense stands, resulting in a clear vertical layering (though lacking a lianoid-epiphytic layer). The enhanced drying of the litter facilitates fires in the grassy or shrubby undergrowth (1,069). Apart from the canopy, there is a diversified small tree-tall shrubby layer, a well-developed low shrubby layer, and a great diversity of ground plants, which presumably accounts for the considerable avian species diversity in eucalypt forests.

Morphology and Characteristics

Birds have tended to be ignored by classical anatomists, largely because of their small size and relative morphological uniformity. But precisely those characteristics of birds that were responsible for this ill favor suit them ideally for studies of evolutionary morphology. The wealth of species that are well known biologically and taxonomically, and that exhibit a wide range of morphological diversity, make birds excellent material with which to formulate general principles of biological comparison and evolutionary mechanisms (421). Nevertheless, our knowledge of avian anatomy remains incomplete, in the sense that findings have not been checked and rechecked by independent researchers (533).

RACES. Rogers recognizes 3 races or subspecies of Budgerigars in Australia. The principal type is *M. u. undulatus*, which is found in most Australian states. A race that is paler in color on the neck and back, and darker on the head (*M. u. intermedius*) inhabits the northern areas, while a generally paler race (*M. u. pallidiceps*), especially on the head, comes from the western region. The ranges of the 3 races overlap peripherally, and members of all 3 have been noted together in migrating flocks. It is assumed that interbreeding occurs. The admixture of the 3 races, together with the natural variations in patterns of their markings, have contributed to the expression of the numerous and varied domesticated strains now in existence (136). On the other hand, other observers recognize no geographical variation in the species (1,056).

SIZE---SLIGHTLY SEXUALLY DIMORPHIC---GENERAL APPEARANCE---WEIGHT. Budgerigars are 17-19 cm in length from the bill to the tip of the long, wedge-shaped tail, with its pointed feathers. Whereas most parrots are sexually indistinguishable (monomorphic), mature Budgerigars are slightly sexually dimorphic (occurring in two forms), as described below. All 3 species of parrots of this study conform to the correlation that, though many granivorous species are sexually dimorphic for plumage features, relatively few are dimorphic for characteristics such as bodily size or bill dimensions (it seems likely that the highly selective forces favoring size divergence are associated with increasing the attractiveness of males to females; 968).

[There appears to be no great general need for sexual dimorphism in parrots, as a means of identifying potential mates. In those species in which it occurs, it is suggested that it: functions primarily as an isolating mechanism; is a consequence of some aspect of behavior that makes the species more reliant on sexual selection than are the monomorphic species; or makes possible quick sexual identification in desert and semi-desert dwellers with opportunistic breeding habits (see 819). The existence of the W chromosome in female birds was demonstrated cytologically for the first time in Budgerigars (see 440).]

The body is short and broad, with a straight back line and a deep breast. The skin over most parts of the body is thin, loosely attached, dry, and highly pliable, particularly where the wings join the body and in the neck. In effect, the entire epidermis is a sebaceous gland (440, 795). [The structure of the crocodilian epidermis closely resembles that of birds and mammals (880).] Adults vary in weight from 35-60 g or more, averaging 45-50 g (137), roughly the same as for Peach-faced Lovebirds. Birds in the wild, however, weigh only about 27-31 g (29.2 ± 1.92 g for males and 28.8 ± 2.09 g for females; 842). [The weight of individuals of some avian species may vary by as much as 12% during the day (see 487).] As in all parrots, Budgerigars have a large head (judged by some to be larger and more domed in the males), a relatively short neck, and a short, broad, strongly-down-curved, sharply-pointed, olive-gray bill.

METABOLIC PARAMETERS. The standard metabolic rate (as a function of T°C) of Budgerigars that averaged 25.2 g in weight and were studied at night by Gavrilov and Dol'nik (see 967) is 19.1 - 0.478T kcal/bird/day [1 kcal/day = 0.0484 watts; 1 kcal = 4,184 Joules]. This is the minimum rate of heat production of the resting (psychic and muscular repose) bird at a given temperature while not digesting or absorbing food, molting, or reproducing. The corresponding lower critical temperature for the birds is 27°C (or, according to another source, 29°C; 1,244); the latter is the temperature below which the maximum insulative capacity of a bird under standard conditions is exceeded and body temperature cannot be maintained without an increase in heat production over basic metabolic levels. The birds of Gavrilov and Dol'nik had a surplus of food and water always available, and there was a limited amount of activity permitted within the confines of the 40 x 30 x 25-cm enclosures.

The corresponding basal metabolic rate of Budgerigars is 6.2 kcal/bird /day; this is the standard metabolic rate in the zone of thermoneutrality (29-41°C; 1,244), in which body temperature (about 41.7°C; 1,244) is regulated primarily by changing the effectiveness of the bodily insulation, in this case at the value of the lower critical temperature. [The metabolic rate of fasting birds sitting quietly in the dark during their normal activity period generally is about 1.25 x basal metabolic rate (967); at night it is 30% lower than during the day (1,244). It has been suggested that free-living birds function at 3-4 times the standard metabolic rate (729).] The corresponding existence metabolic rate (as a function of temperature) in summer photoperiods is 28.8 - 0.68T kcal/bird/day; this is the rate at which energy is used by confined birds at a given temperature in maintaining a constant weight (± 1-2%) over a period of days when not reproducing, molting, in migratory unrest, growing, nor depositing fat. Oxygen consumption (ml/g/h) within the thermal neutral zone is 6.29 - 0.105T(body), whereas at ambient temperatures less than 29°C it is 5.65 - 0.127T(amb.) (1,244). In essence, the existence metabolism amounts to a summation of the energy requirements of basal metabolism and temperature regulation, the heat increment of feeding (specific dynamic action or heat generated in all phases of the assimilation of food), and the energy expended in enclosures and in locomotor activity (and the accumulation of energy during the daytime and its loss from the body at night; 967).

COLOR. The plumage of the majority of parrots is basically green. The upper parts of wild-type Budgerigars are a pale earth-brown, with barrings of black and yellow. The stripes are narrow on the head and mantle but coarse on the wings, where the feathers are fringed with white. Budgerigars are unusual among parrots in possessing pale stripes on the undersurface of each wing, formed by patches on the underside web on contiguous flight feathers (31, 819). The lower back, rump, upper tail coverts, and underparts usually are grass green. As in many birds (for example, the Catbird, Dumetella carolinenesis), but not in Peach-faced Lovebirds or Cockatiels, the crissum (see p. 63) is differentially colored from the remainder of the ventral plumage; in this case it is yellow. Females generally are slightly duller in overall color than are males (185).

The face, throat, "bib," and forehead are yellow, and differ distinctly from the surrounding green plumage. Some feathers of the cheeks are tipped with blue. Six black, round, "necklace" spots ("cheek patches") are arranged in a row across the throat, each on a single yellow feather. The 2 outer spots generally are smaller than the others (but not in exhibition birds) and lead to a purplish-black stripe extending in the direction of the cere (67). The black necklace spots and purplish-black stripe generally are smaller in the female (1,056). The forehead is finely barred in immature birds and the general color above and below is much duller than the plumage of the adult (429, 1,056).

COLOR VARIETIES---COLOR---SCHIZOCHROISM. Budgerigars exist in more color varieties than any other species of bird or other animal (787). The distinctive color and marking of their crown and throat feathers correlate with the great importance of these feathers for purposes of signalling (67). The blue and yellow (lutino) strains of the common green Budgerigar are the results of melanin-carotenoid schizochroism, the absence of one of the pigments normally present in the plumage. In the blue strain the yellow carotenoid pigment is lacking (23, 440). The yellow strain lacks melanins, while albinos lack both melanins and carotenoids.

Though these color varieties generally are rare in wild birds, they occur regularly in wild Budgerigar populations (see R.A. Stamm and U. Blum, 1971, in 440). The delicate blue-green color of Budgerigars results from a non-iridescent blue color (see 795 and p. 59), coupled with a greenish-yellow pigment in the barbs (441). Budgerigars also possess fluorescent pigments (23). Unlike the situation in the Canary (*Serinus canaria*), the general shape of Budgerigars of all colors is the same, but the birds vary somewhat in size, weight, and other qualities (136).

[Carotenoid (lipochromes) pigments are fat-soluble and absorbed from the diet. They consist of carotenes and xanthophylls, which give yellow through orange to red hues and occur dissolved in fat globules in the feather cells. Occasionally a red pigmentation is present--the bright red remiges and head feathers in certain turacos (Musophagidae)--which is not due to carotenoids but to a copper-containing pigment, porphyrin. Melanins (eumelanin and phaeomelanin) are rather insoluble and are synthesized in melanocytes by the bird. They give all shades from palest gray, yellow, and brown, to jet black; 23, 28, 414, 440, 443, 795).]

The non-iridescent blue color--Tyndall blue--is the result of a structural effect--scattering of light on particles less than 0.6 micron in diameter--whose source is the unusually fine, canal-like pores that perforate the walls of the colorless "box cells" in the cortical region of the barbs of the blue feathers ("Dyck-texture" or "Tyndall-texture"). The innumerable air-filled spaces present an extraordinary number of reflecting surfaces for scattering blue light (Tyndall or Rayleigh scattering; 337). This is the basis for the blue plumage in most or all birds (28).

In the case of white plumage (in the absence of pigment), all incident light is scattered equally. Whiteness may be of either a structural or translucent type. The former type is most prevalent and usually is seen in flight feathers; the latter type contributes most to the color of down feathers, contour feathers, and semiplumes (440). Iridescent structural colors are produced by diffraction and interference phenomena, vary with the angle of viewing, and are almost ubiquitous in birds (440, 441).

THE GENETICS OF PLUMAGE CHARACTERS in wild birds has been studied very little. It is only through plumage aberrations that it is known that: when melanins are absent the red face of Nyasa Lovebirds (*Agapornis personata lilianae*) is unaffected, while the maroon wing patches of Rose-necked Parakeets (*Psittacula krameri*) become brick red; the heads of schizochroic Plum-headed Parakeets (*P. cyanocephala*) remain rose-pinkish but lack the exquisite plum bloom of normal birds; the dorsal black neck ring in *P. krameri* is retained in a schizochroic lutino that has lost some of its melanins; and the color of the body and the tail probably are inherited separately in African Gray Parrots (*Psittacus e. erithacus*), since one form of lutino is all white except for a brilliant scarlet tail (see 440 and C.J.O. Harrison, 1963a, therein). Much remains to be learned about the mechanisms of color production involving scattering, interference, and various kinds of pigments.

FLIGHT FEATHERS AND FLIGHT

AVIAN WINGS generally are characterized by reduction and fusion of the distal bones (as compared to, say, mammals), and are covered by a thin skin. Those of Budgerigars are relatively long. When folded, the tips of the primary feathers of Budgerigars are held over the rump. The humerus, radius, and ulna are held parallel to the line of the back in normal perching. The remiges (large flight feathers) originate at the distal (outermost) portion of the wing on the trailing edge and are directed caudo-dorsally, crossing the line of the back at a 45° angle. There are 10 primary feathers (numbered 1 to 10) attached to the manus (hand) or pinion (carpometacarpus and digits), and 11 secondary feathers (numbered 1 to 12, with #5 missing = diastataxic or aquincubital) overlying the ulna. The tertiaries lie over the humerus (elbow), the scapulars above the shoulder, and the interscapulars between the shoulders (441).

There are about 30 intrinsic muscles of the wing and 15 extrinsic ones. Those controlling the movements of the tip of the wing make up a complicated system: some move the bones of the wrist and the digits while others act directly on the primary feathers (1,003). Both the primary and the secondary flight feathers are rather free to rotate in their sockets around their longitudinal axis through an angle of about 90° from the normal orientation with the feather in the plane of the wing, allowing the passage of air through the wing (1,202 and below).

THE THRUST FORCE necessary for the forward motion of a bird in flight is generated by beating and pitching oscillations of the wings. The aerodynamically relevant parameters of the form and movements of the wing of a House Sparrow (*Passer domesticus*) during a single wingbeat recently have been measured using high-frequency stereo-photogrammetry during free flight in a wind tunnel. These measurements confirm that the wing twists like a propeller blade in the downstroke, during which the primaries become slightly separated and are rotated upwards and backwards.

In a general way it could be stated in the past that in the first part of the downstroke the contracting pectorals mainly accelerated the wings to give them sufficient speed; in the 2nd phase the wings were rotated in order to increase the angle of attack and thereby the air loads on them (see C.J. Pennycuick, 1968, in 1,003). In the new analysis, the changes in the geometrical twisting of the wing depend on the speed of beating in a way similar to that in an automatically adjusting propeller. The fully-extended wing during downstroke always is presented in such a way that the airflow attacks it at aerodynamically useful, small-to-medium angles along its full length during the entire period of the stroke (635), which occupies about 1/3rd of a cycle (see 1,003). As the shape of the wing changes, patagial muscles tense and relax the patagium so as to resist the deforming effects of air pressure and maintain the wing's surface area (796). As in bats, the arm wing (the secondaries and coverts) supplies most of the lift, and the hand-wing (the primaries) most of the thrust (769). The wing tips move with a beat shaped like a figure 8 in relation to the body (see 1,003).

THE UPSTROKE DURING TAKEOFF is a much more complicated maneuver than the downstroke. First the humerus is adducted (pulled backward) and simultaneously is rotated in such a way that the radius and ulna are brought into a vertical position, Then, suddenly (occupying 36 msec in the Rock Pigeon), the wings are pulled backward and upward violently and at the same time are extended. This latter flick of the wing is lacking in fast flight (1,003), during the entire measured upstroke of which the arm-wing moves upward only slightly and always is held positively against the airflow, producing vertical lift throughout the stroke. On the other hand, the hand-wing is rotated at the wrist and the primaries are rotated around their longitudinal axis and twisted, opening like a venetian blind. As a result of its rotating movements, the hand-wing receives airflow from above and behind during the upstroke, producing a strong thrust (635). The automatic adjustments of the angles of attack of the feathers throughout the cycle of wing beating, despite the continually varying direction and speed of the relative wind, are accounted for by a recent mechanical and aerodynamical theory (1,202).

The negative vertical lift produced by the hand-wing is exceeded by the positive vertical lift of the arm-wing, while the negative thrust of the latter is exceeded by the positive thrust of the former. Thus, there is net thrust and vertical lift during the entire upstroke (see 635). The body of the swooping Zebra Finch, with its wings folded completely and held more or less close to the body, not only produces drag, but also lift (637). [Some lift also is produced during the upstroke in bats but this stroke is less efficient and probably requires only a fraction of the power required by the downstroke (769).] Analyzing flight in terms of a vortex-ring model, the vorticity shed by the wings in the course of each powered stroke deforms into a small-cored elliptical vortex ring. A chain of such rings makes up the wake. Reaction to the process of imparting momentum to each ring sustains and propels the bird (1,015).

HOVERING in Hummingbirds (Trochilidae), a foraging mode that is dictated primarily by floral architecture (1,105), is achieved with pointed, uncambered wings with slots, that move mainly in the horizontal plane, where they function like variable-pitch propellers. The power required for such flight is considerable, requiring pectoral musculature that makes up 30% of the body weight (795). [The wing slots found in many birds provide increased lift through allowing each primary feather tip to work as an independent aerofoil, allow the anterior primary feathers to bend up more than the posterior ones, thereby reducing the propensity for wing-tip stall, and may reduce the aeroelastic deformation of the wingtip (839).]

Mechanoreceptors associated with the breast feathers of siskins (Fringillidae), and perhaps other birds, function as an air current sense organ in the control of flight behavior. Thus, when suspended freely in a harness, siskins initiate flight movements when air is blown against their breast feathers, and even adjust the thrust and direction of the flight movements according to the strength and direction of the airstream. This is one of several instances in which one can suggest a relationship between a distinct behavior and the properties of cutaneous receptors (see 801). A wingbeat reflex may be responsible for the basic rhythm of the wingbeats during normal flight (1,003).

FLIGHT MUSCULATURE, COMPARISONS WITH BATS. Birds have tended to concentrate all of the power for wing beating in the pectoral muscles. These are the largest and most powerful of avian muscles; they account for 15-39% of adult body weight in most groups (1,003, 1,150). The M. pectoralis is broadly attached on the sternum and keel at one end and inserts on the strong deltoid crest of the humerus at the other. It accomplishes the downstroke, carrying the wings downward and backward, with minor assistance from the much smaller posterior M. coracobrachialis and perhaps also from the M. subcoracoideus. The concerted action of these muscles allows the adjustment of the angle of attack in the control of flight.

In the Rock Pigeon the pectorals are activated several times per wingbeat, performing short, tetanic contractions to achieve sufficiently long contraction times to complete each downstroke. In Budgerigars and finches, on the other hand, they are activated only once per wingbeat and thereby perform twitch contractions during the downstroke of normal flight. In strenuous flight, however, Budgerigars exhibit the tetanic contraction pattern seen in the Rock Pigeon (1,003).

By having only a short lever arm to work on, the pectoralis is able to move the humerus through a large angle with minimum shortening. In order to transfer the force from the M. pectoralis to the wing, it is essential that the shoulder joint be fixed. Therefore the pectoral girdle in birds is built very strongly and braced rigidly against the axial skeleton, serving as a rigid base for the wings. The flattening of the rib cage by the contraction of the powerful paired pectoralis is prevented by bracing of the shoulder against the sternum by the coracoids, which are firmly spread and immobilize the shoulder socket, and by a rigid sternum (155, 769, 1,019).

The largest elevator muscle, which, acting antagonistically, accomplishes the upstroke, is the ventral M. supracoracoideus. It is far smaller than the pectoralis, usually only 10% or less of the latter's volume (except in hummingbirds, where it is as much as 60% of the size of the pectoralis). It also originates on the sternum, but has a long tendon that runs up to and passes through the foramen triosseum and inserts on the medial surface of the head of the humerus near the deltoid crest. Thus, though the M. supracoracoideus lies in the same position as the M. pectoralis, a contraction of it lifts the humerus and the wing, with the triosseal canal acting as a pulley (see 1,003). The M. supracoracoideus acts with the aid of several dorsal muscles, including the deltoids, whose main action is the retraction of the humerus (155, 796, 1,003). [An absence of the foramen triosseum in *Archaeopteryx* indicates that the latter, relatively weak, dorsal muscles, alone, powered the upstroke (1,019).]

The flight musculature situation in bats is almost the reverse of that in birds. In bats, a division of labor has evolved between a number of muscles that control the wingbeat. Bats retain a large, broad scapula and a pectoral girdle that is nowhere attached immovably to the axial skeleton, retaining considerable mobility. The downstroke of the wings is controlled by the M. pectoralis, the posterior division of the M. serratus anterior, and the M. subscapularis. The coracoid head of the M. biceps brachii also helps to varying degrees in the downstroke, depending upon the species. The division of labor is achievable because the scapula is movable, faceted, and has a large surface area, making it possible to provide origins for the large flight muscles.

The upstroke is powered by dorsally situated muscles, including the trapezius group, the deltoideus group, and the large M. infraspinatus. Since the major flight muscles in bats are not all situated ventrally, their weight distribution in flight is not as stable as that in birds. The division of labor in the bat flight muscles tends to create a broad moderately flat body, which allows bats to fit into crevices and other narrow spaces. It seems likely that the basic chiropteran muscular and osteological adaptations for flight are the result of bats having been crevice dwellers during the period of their early evolution, and that selective pressures operated against the development of a deep-chested bodily form, such as that of birds (769).

[The flight musculature is only one of many differences and functional similarities in the ways that bats and birds solved similar problems of aerodynamics and associated needs, and became volant (see 782). For example, as opposed to birds, all or almost all bats have: hair, teeth, non-nucleated erythrocytes, no air sac, no reduction of tarsal bones, parts of all 5 fingers present, a urinary bladder, small, weak feet, big external ears, a small keel on the sternum, a flat head, no renewable flight structure, dull colors, wings that can work independently of each other in flight, fairly long gestation periods, mechanisms for lengthy sperm storage, delayed implantation or delayed development, no alula, red pectoral muscles, comparatively low rates of reproduction, smaller ranges of ambient temperature tolerance, a smaller range of size, and a small range of wingbeat frequency.

In addition all (or almost all) bats are viviparous, very maneuverable in flight, use the hindlimbs in flight and the forelimbs in terrestrial and arboreal locomotion, feed during nocturnal flight, live in crevices and caves, do not build nests, hibernate, and lactate. Some bats, like some birds, apparently have strong terrestrial affiliations, have widely varied food habits and food-procuring structures, have hollow bones, and are powerful vocalizers. "Apparently no other grade of mammal has ever had so many eccentric and extremely specialized characters combined into such a highly 'successful' organism," as bats (782).]

THE TAIL AND ITS SPREADING. In all but a single genus of parrots, the tail is composed of 6 pairs of rectrices. The latter are interconnected basally by fibrous tissue and dermal muscles (61, 441). The central tail feathers of Budgerigars are greenish-blue, whereas the outer ones are green, with a yellow band across the centers. The tail feathers are supported by the uropygium, a shortened, swollen, pointed, movable, terminal portion of the longitudinal axis of the body, containing 6 articulated caudal vertebrae and the blade-or keel-like pygostyle. The latter is the embryonic fusion of several caudal vertebrae at the base of the tail, to which the rectrices are anchored firmly. The tail is capable of considerable movement, owing to the freely articulating caudal vertebrae and their associated muscles (441). There is a superficial and deep dorsal series of levators, a lateral series of abductors, and a ventral series of depressors.

The tail appears not to be the primary means of longitudinal (pitch) or directional control in modern birds. Its primary function seems to be to help maintain lift at very low speeds (425). It also acts as an air brake or flap while landing (as the rectrices simultaneously are directed downward), is used for balance when climbing, is used for signalling in flocking, and may be used by some birds for minor adjustments of pitch and yaw (425, 441, 796). [The long, dorso-ventrally flattened tail of *Archaeopteryx* may, however, have played a major role in pitch control.] Most birds can vary the tail area by a factor of 3-4 by fanwise spreading of the rectrices, and the tail normally is spread in low-speed flight (particularly when landing and taking off) and furled in fast flight. In slow flight the spread tail influences airflow in such a way as to increase the lift coefficient of the wings (425). In slow flapping flight the tail is moved up and down in synchrony with the wingbeat.

ALULAR DIGIT---SCRATCHING THE CRISSUM. Four contour feathers are attached to the most mobile of the 3 digits of the manus, the alular digit (rudimentary pollex or pollicis), constituting the alula (ala spuria; the spurious or bastard wing), which protrudes from the leading edge of the main wing. The alula can be elevated with the aid of a small muscle, for defense or to obtain purchase on the ground for escape (135). As with all other feathers except filoplumes (see p. 64), even the individual feathers of the alula can be controlled, by an elaborate system of at least 4 small muscles intrinsic to the manus (28, 624, 796). The alula forms a leading edge slot that acts as an auxiliary airfoil that is important in controlling lift during slow flight (635) and is essential to reduce the danger of crashing when taking off and alighting (470). Extending or flexing the major and minor digits has the effect of spreading or folding the primary feathers (796).

Budgerigars are the only birds known to use their feet to scratch the sides of the crissum (constituting the plumage about the vent together with the undertail coverts). They accomplish this feat by scratching with the tarso-metatarsal-phalangial joint together with the surfaces of the anterior toes, whereas they scratch their heads with the claw of the longest (3rd) front toe (67).

PILOERECTION. Birds have elaborate control systems for regulating feather movements and positions. For example, the insulating properties of the plumage can be varied by the activity of the ptilomotor nerves, which innervate the arrectores plumorum muscles, contraction of which (as a result of impulses from sympathetic nerve fibers) orients feather shafts more nearly perpendicular to the skin surface (518, 1,004). This piloerection increases the volume of air trapped around the bird, essentially doubling the thermal resistance, as compared to a sleeked feather posture. The energetic cost of the pilomotor responses is small in comparison with their effectiveness (1,004).

POWDER DOWN---AFTERFEATHERS---FILOPLUMES. As in other parrots, the powder down feathers of Budgerigars are scattered throughout the plumage (their distribution generally is useful in taxonomy). The barbs at the tips of these feathers, which never are molted, constantly disintegrate into a very fine, talc-like, water-resistant powder that coats the plumage (28). Many, if not all, parrots have feathers with aftershafts or afterfeathers, usually with very feeble rachises (23, 174, 441). These are secondary inner feathers that arise from the superior umbilici (small openings on the ventral surfaces of feathers) and may be as large as the main feather. Their presence is regarded as a primitive condition, namely, a relic of a device in primitive birds that provided a thicker layer of insulation (23, 28).

Filoplumes have a long, hair-like rachis with a bunch of flexible barbs at the tip; they grow in circles of from 1 to 10 around the bases of contour and down feathers. They are the only feathers that do not have muscles attached to the follicles, and are thought to be concerned with the sensory input for controlling the positions of the larger feathers (795).

MOLTING in birds is a type of growth that is characterized primarily by the accretion of protein in the form of feathers, and secondarily by the regeneration of other epidermal structures. It can entail a deposition of an amount of protein approximating to or even exceeding ¼th the total content of the body. Feathers over the head, body, and tail frequently are replaced in the first basic molt, but loss of the wing feathers is often offset in time, so that a 2nd and even a 3rd molt may occur in other sites before the flight feathers are lost (795, 973). Molting birds usually have increased metabolic rates, increased thyroid activity (519, 929; perhaps the inducing factor, particularly when combined with low levels of androgens, which exert a protective effort on mature feathers), and their body temperature may be elevated by ½-1°C. The activity of confined birds often is reduced greatly during molt (257), free-living birds are more secretive and less active during the postnuptial molt than at other times, and the productive energy of some birds is known to increase (519, 973).

It has been suggested that molting has a large energetic cost because it entrains a general acceleration of protein metabolism and other processes, including physiological modifications, beyond those associated directly with the synthesis of keratin (see 243, 257, 973). The increase usually is greatest during the regeneration of the flight feathers and usually is less in young birds than in adults (519). Though substantial efforts have been devoted to the topic of molt energetics, and the major techniques employed give generally similar results, the subject remains in a confused state (257). Unlike egg formation, in which part of the calcium requirement is met by mobilization from body reserves, molting birds typically are able to meet the protein requirements of feather synthesis (most notably, the sulfur-containing amino acids) through their food, alone (244).

[The energetic cost of molting has been estimated at averaging 20-40% of standard metabolic rate in White-crowned Sparrows (*Zonotrichia leucophrys gambelii*), 14-26% in the Ortolan Bunting (*Emberiza hortulana*), 45% in the domestic fowl, 15-30% in the Chaffinch (*Fringilla coelebs*), and 15-45% in the domestic fowl (see 257, 442, 519, 648, 973).]

In its timing and rate of occurrence, molting is possibly the most extraordinarily plastic and adaptable aspect of avian growth. In small birds with nidicolous young, adults usually undergo a complete molt following, but not overlapping with, the breeding season (except in tropical species with long breeding seasons). Molt lasts anywhere from 2-4 months in temperate-region species and up to 5 months or longer in the tropics (see 975). Most confined parrots molt continually throughout the year (448).

Confined Budgerigars, molt twice or thrice a year, at any time (445), although they molt continually in the wild (818; also true of Zebra Finches; 809). New feathers come in as old ones fall out, and the process usually takes several months. Some trophic action of nerves may ensure the synchrony of feather growth on the two wings (795), but very little is known of how the rate and sequence of feather replacements are regulated, or how the actual stimuli act at the level of the feather follicles. However, the chief mechanism of control of both loss and replacement is indubitably endocrinological (260, 318, 319, 795), for example, molt in the adult domestic fowl is triggered by the levels of thyroxine and estrogen in the circulation (795). The endocrinological control of molt varies among avian groups and differs in adult and immature birds, but the role of the hypophysial gonadotropins is largely indirect (319, 795). Progesterone is known to induce molting in domesticated and semi-domesticated species that breed the year around, including Budgerigars, but not in wild species that have a restricted breeding season (see 1,176).

The temporal relationships among migration, molt, and reproduction, and the selective forces that have produced the array of patterns of occurrence of these events in contemporary avian species, comprise one of the most fascinating aspects of modern ornithology. This is true particularly among small migratory species that breed at high latitudes (551). These temporal relationships apparently reflect the independent evolution of mechanisms that enhance fitness by controlling annual cycles and ensuring the temporal separation of functions that have high energetic requirements (see 551). If there is a common scheme for the physiological control of avian molt, it still eludes us (319). Regarding its dynamics, however, one may state the generalities that the process is relatively slow (see above), that feather growth in many species proceeds at the same rate by day and by night (257), that in other species it varies in rate in a diurnal rhythm (318), and that the rate of feather growth changes during the entire period of regeneration (see F.R. Lillie, 1940, in 318).

Except in the case of many Australian and neotropical avian species, molting and breeding tend to be mutually exclusive (311, 551). For example, of 190 African species, only about 4% showed any overlap in molting and breeding (28, 319). In temperate regions, the main molt normally follows the breeding season, but much variability may exist (503). Presumably the endocrine activity of the gonads delays the onset of the postnuptial molt (551). In at least some species, this molt has an endogenous circannual periodicity, the phasing of which can be modified by photostimulation (550). [Under the influence of estrogens, birds generally develop a female-type plumage, whereas in the absence of this hormonal stimulus, a male-type develops, i.e., the male-type plumage is "anhormonal" (260).]

LEGS--CLAWS---SCALES---OBLIGATE ZYGODACTYLS. All parrots have short legs covered with small, granular scales, and stout, grasping feet, with 4 sharp-clawed toes. Like the rhamphotheca (horny bill), the claws grow continuously, are strongly keratinized, and contain hydroxyapatite crystals. In a few groups, claws also occur on the digits of the manus. In its formation, the avian claw is like the reptilian claw, in that it fits like a pointed thimble over the germinal epidermis at the tip of the digit (795). The legs and feet of male Budgerigars are bluish-gray; those of females are pink-hued (67, 439). In normal flight, the feet either are carried horizontally beneath the tail or are tucked up under the flank feathers, with the ankle joint fully flexed (425). [The prospective skin of the embryonic foot appears to be capable of giving rise to either, or both, feathers and scales (see M.E. Rawles, 1963, in 441).]

Parrots are obligately zygodactylous, a condition in which the foot is adapted for grasping, especially in perching. The 4th toe is reversed permanently and has an enlarged accessory articulating process, the "sehnenhalter" (276). Parrots possess one of the 4 distinct types of tarsometatarsal morphology that occurs among obligate zygodactyls (see 276). In perching, the 2nd and 3rd toes grasp the front of the perch, opposing the 1st and 4th toes to the rear. The 4th toe is the principal caudally-directed one; the 1st toe usually is short. One muscle provides simultaneous flexion of opposing toes, giving a coordinated grasping movement (796).

[The earliest known parrots (genus *Palaeopsittacus*, from the Eocene) also were zygodactylous but their foot and leg structure suggests that, though they could grasp objects with the foot, their ability to climb and clamber among branches may not have been well developed (293). As is most common in contemporary birds, occurring in a wide variety of forms of many adaptive types, *Archaeopteryx* had an anisodactylous foot (hallux directed caudally, 2nd, 3rd, and 4th toes directed cranially; 796) and probably climbed mostly upward in trees. It is suggested that the reversed 4th toe in zygodactyls evolved in compensation for a primitively weak hallux (see W.J. Bock and W.DeW. Miller, 1959, in 796).]

UROPYGIAL GLAND. The cutaneous glands of birds include the small wax-secreting auricular glands in the external wall of the auditory meatus (see below), the small mucous-secreting vent glands, and the large uropygial (or oil or preen) gland. The uropygium bears the uropygial gland above and the vent below. The gland, always visible to the naked eye (795), is covered by a dense connective tissue capsule and lies embedded in a cushion of fat between the dorsal skin and muscles, usually immediately rostral to the pygostyle, above its levator muscles and the posterior free caudal vertebrae.

The uropygial gland is a holocrine, compound-alveolar, bilobed glandular complex of uncertain function (see below) and only vaguely conjectural phylogeny. It is absent entirely in some parrots, though present in their embryos (337), and also is absent in the Ostrich (*Struthio camelus*) and other ratites, and some strains of domesticated doves (Columbidae; 795). The glandular body usually can be recognized as an eminence, from the caudal end of which the uropygial papilla protrudes (433).

Eighty species of the Psittaciformes recently served as a model to test the variability of the uropygial gland within the higher and lower taxa (433). This account is based on that analysis. The only certain generalization regarding the size of the uropygial gland is that, without exception, it is large in birds that swim and dive. In some taxa, including the

Oscines, the relative weight of the gland is inversely proportional to bodily weight--a smaller body, having a relatively larger surface, requires a relatively larger amount of secretion. The uropygial gland is the only well-developed, generally relatively large, sebaceous gland possessed by birds; the functions of its secretions probably are much more complex than previously believed.

With rare exceptions the glandular organ proper consists of two lobes separated by a connective tissue septum continuous with the gland's capsule. The lobes, which are very variable in shape and position among the Psittaciformes, contain the active secretory tubules and a duct system. The ducts drain the central cavities of the lobes of the breakdown products of the glandular cells, and lead through the papilla, at the apex (tip) of which they reach the surface of the body via two or more orifices, whence the secretions leave the body. Obstruction of the ducts by abscessing (uropygitis or "pip") is fairly common in Budgerigars (185, 445). In many birds the orifices are surrounded by a circlet of downy feathers--8 in Budgerigars--that form a tuft. In Budgerigars, this acts as a wick that receives the secretions (441). Many parrots have very long tufts, and the number of feathers in the tufts can vary by as much as 30%. The papilla usually is separated clearly from the lobes by an isthmus.

Besides the internal smooth musculature of the gland, all striated muscles of the tail region can have an indirect mechanical effect on the uropygial gland by a movement of the tail or the individual rectrices. A pair of muscles that flank the gland on both sides (M. lateralis caudae) usually have no direct connection with the capsule, but in some parrots, including Cockatiels and Peach-faced Lovebirds, portions of the muscle penetrate the side of the capsule to the areas between the tubules. In Finsche's Pygmy-Parrot (*Micropsitta finschii*), a specialized tree-climber that uses its tail like a woodpecker does, large bundles of smooth muscle fibers (M. levator recticium) enter the gland from the side and reach the interlobular septum.

The uropygial gland produces a greasy material, which is induced to flow by contact of the bill with the uropygial papilla (an infrequent action in Rock Pigeons; 1,011). After being coated onto the bill, the bird smears this material into the plumage from time to time in preening. The tail usually is flexed laterally each time the bird reaches over the gland when preening. Plumage oiling is said to be performed frequently by hanging parrots, genus *Loriculus* (79), but only after bathing by lovebirds (3). Except perhaps for certain scent organs, the uropygial gland appears to be the only secretory organ in the vertebrate skin whose secretion is distributed actively over the body by the animal itself.

The functions of the uropygial gland secretion still are uncertain but it seems likely that birds obtain some waterproofing--the secretion appears to be more water-repellent in aquatic birds (795)--and certain that they obtain flexibility of the feathers by impregnating them with the unusual lipids, especially monoester waxes of which it is composed. [Of the two types of waxes found in parrots, Budgerigars possess both.] The secretions probably also serves other functions in plumage hygiene, such as regulating the microflora through its anti-microbial properties and acting against parasites; the gland also appears to produce a pheromone of importance in inducing sexual behavior (see 1,149). The gland in adult male ducks is known to possess highly specific cytosolic receptors for estradiol and to be androgen responsive; for example, testosterone, induces processes of cellular differentiation, and castration is depressive (1,141).

Jacob and Ziswiler (433) suggest that the uropygial gland has evolved only once in avian phylogeny, at the very latest in the early Cretaceous. It possibly already existed in *Archaeopteryx*, but has been lost secondarily in some species. They also deduce that the higher differentiation of feathers in the course of evolution paralleled the development of the uropygial gland, and that the existence of this gland is an important prerequisite for such differentiation.

There are some avian orders and families in which the gland is very uniform--not including parrots--and has significant diagnostic value. Membership in the Passeriformes, for example, can be deduced from the morphology of the papilla. Members of the Sphenisciformes, Procellariiformes, and Pelecaniformes, considered to be phylogenetically older orders, possess very complex preen waxes, whereas phylogenetically more recent groups have comparatively simple waxes, suggesting secondary simplifications. The two chemically different groups possessed by members of the Psittaciformes bear no recognizable relationship to those of the other orders. On the other hand, a qualitative differentiation of these parrot waxes is said to occur at the family level.

THE VERTEBRATE PINEAL BODY AND PARIETAL EYE are central-nervous-system components that are involved in both ectothermic behavioral thermoregulation and endothermic temperature control. In the past, at least, they appear to have been more elaborate and to have had relatively greater significance, functioning as sensory systems for monitoring environmental thermal extremes (413, 879). As such, they may have guided the taxic responses of early endothermic vertebrates to environmental temperatures, perhaps tracing back at least to small theropods. With the phylogenetically gradual involution of photoreceptive cells of ectotherms into secretory rudimentary photoreceptor cells and, subsequently, into classical secretory pinealocytes, pineal bodies assumed a more important role in thermoregulation, as endothermy became established and the parietal eye was lost. Pineal sense organs represent only one component of vertebrate photo-neuroendocrine systems, and their interaction with the deep encephalic photoreceptor(s) and the retino-hypothalamic link is understood only poorly (413, 1,171).

THE AVIAN PINEAL BODY (epiphysis cerebri) is a median dorsal outgrowth of the posterior diencephalon. It consists of a narrow, approximately conical distal vesicle that exhibits a glandular appearance, located in the narrow triangular space between the cerebral hemispheres and the cerebellum. Its dorsal side is exposed at the surface of the brain and is attached tightly to the meninges and the large meningeal vessels. A relatively slender stalk containing abundant nerve fibers extends from the distal area or apex to the systems of the habenular and posterior commissures. The dorsal surface of the pineal body forms a triangle with its base adjacent to the cerebellum. Sinuses run along the edges and join each other at the body's antero-dorsal side. Blood vessels penetrate densely into the antero-lateral wall of the vesicle. In Budgerigars and *Nycticorax*, the distal end of the pineal vesicle develops anteriorly along the central sulcus between the telencephalic hemispheres (917, 1,113).

The neuroepithelial matrix of the diencephalon, from which the avian pineal develops, is a rather unique region of the vertebrate central nervous system, capable of giving rise to both photosensory elements (lateral eyes, pineal complex in ectotherms, and the encephalic photoreceptor system) and secretory neurones. The rapid decrease in the number of ganglion cells (afferent nerves) in the avian pineal after hatching is specific to the organ, greatly exceeding the decrease that occurs in other nervous tissues (917, 1,113).

The overall shape, size, structure, and neuronal apparatus of the gland are remarkably diverse among species and taxonomic groups, probably reflecting the plasticity of the organ in the process of adaptation to different functional needs. Occasionally, rather regular outer segments and synaptoid structures with vesicle-crowned ribbons are observed. From the point of view of the development of its afferent innervation and functional capacities, the avian pineal body can be said to be transitional in character between the corresponding organs of amphibians and mammals.

[In amphibians, the pinealocyte is a photoreceptor (labile photopigment with an absorption peak at 502 ± 3 nm) connected synaptically with an afferent nerve. Its outer segment (and those of many other less advanced vertebrates) is a centriolar derivative that protrudes into the pineal lumen, which connects with the 3rd ventricle. As a result, the outer segments of amphibian (and avian; see below, **Avian Pinealocytes**) pineal photoreceptor cells are bathed in the circulating cerebrospinal fluid, which may serve for the release and uptake of metabolites (1,171).

In mammals, the receptor portion is lost completely and the cell is of closed type; its connection with the afferent nerve is lost and its secretions are released into blood capillaries. The direct response of pinealocytes to light is replaced by a mediation of the photic information via the lateral eyes and the sympathetic afferents. However, transitional stages may exist in a given pineal organ, and even the pinealocytes of neonate mammals still may have some sensory properties (1,164, 1,171).]

AVIAN PINEALOCYTES are either "rudimentary photoreceptor cells"--with outer segments having irregular shapes or only simple cilia--or, most typically, "recepto-secretory cells." In young birds, at least, they are photosensitive and transmit impulses to the brain via the pineal neural tracts. The N-acetyltransferase activity of pinealocytes exhibits a circadian rhythm; the activity probably is controlled by the nucleus, which also probably is the site of direct photoreception. The function of the pinealocytes is influenced by the neural inputs of central and sympathetic fibers, by humoral factors borne by the blood, and probably by the same factors borne by cerebrospinal fluid. In response to these stimuli a pineal hormone is released into the blood and/or into the pineal lumen, which connects to the 3rd ventricle (1,113, 1,120).

There is no clear association between the size and structure of the avian pineal body and any physiological characteristic, nor to brain or bodily size. But the structure and cytology (elaboration of dense-core vesicles in the Golgi fields) of the pineal body suggest a predominantly secretory function and, as in lizards, its secretory activity is very intense (see 629, 917, 1,171). Serotonin has been demonstrated in pinealocytes by fluorescence histochemistry, and the passeriform pineal is rich in acetyl cholinesterase-positive neurons, synaptoid contacts, and axon bundles that form a tract directed toward the brain (736, 1,113). The pineal stalk of the House Sparrow contains approximately 1,000 axons of unknown origin (1,171). Additionally, neurons projecting to the pineal body have been detected in the habenular complex (see 917).

[In the frog, a tract of about 60-70 myelinated amd 200 unmyelinated fibers project from the pineal complex to the pretectal area and the reticular gray of the mesencephalic tegmentum; efferent fibers originate in preoptic hypothalamic, limbic, and visual centers (1,171).]

The number of gangliocytes varies widely, depending upon the species and age (see 1,120). Afferent nerves are more densely distributed in the posterior wall of the stalk--probably more sensory in nature--whereas sympathetic nerves are developed better in the anterior region of the vesicle --probably more secretory in nature. The developmental replacement of the rapidly degenerating afferent neurons by sympathetic nerves in some birds begins in the vesicles and advances toward the stalks, probably reflecting the direction of the evolutionary functional transition from sensory to secretory roles (1,113). Though the indoleamine, melatonin, currently is the favored and most studied pineal hormone in birds, it may not be the only one of several indoleamines produced by the pineal body that acts as a hormone, and the character of the peptidic products of the pineal body still is unknown. Melatonin synthesis exhibits a strict circadian rhythmicity, as also do the reciprocal changes between serotonin and melanin in the pineal body (918, 1,028, 1,120, 1,164, 1,171).

PINEAL BODIES should be "understood as simple modulators of the central nervous system, exhibiting circadian and seasonal organization..." (see C.L. Ralph, 1978, in 917). The avian pineal body apparently plays roles directly or indirectly, through melatonin secretion, in the processes of photoreception, reproduction, the circadian rhythmicity of activities (e.g., locomotor activity), and the coupling of such rhythms, that is, in the integration of several aspects of the bird's response to its photic environment (420, 917, 1,028; see also pp. 536, 537, **Pineal Body of Coelurosaurs**). There is ample evidence that even isolated pineal bodies of passerine and gallinaceous birds still respond to light (1,120).

PINEALECTOMY generally seems to have only transitory effects on avian breeding cycles, but notable responses are known in adult male ducks and male Indian Weaver Finches (*Ploceus philippinus*; 1,045). At present, a discrepancy exists between the experimental results that demonstrate the avian pinealocyte to be a self-sustained oscillator and the different kinds of inputs that are demonstrated morphologically. A fine-tuning of the hormonally-driven mechanism may occur by a neuronal feedback mechanism from certain components of the circadian system located in the brain (1,119).

THE NASAL CAVITY of birds is both the organ of smell and the passageway of entry into the respiratory system (see below), and it has shown remarkable adaptability in subserving these two vital functions (797). It follows the same plan as in reptiles. As in the latter, birds possess 3 nasal choanae and lack a vomeronasal (Jacobsen's) organ, although such an organ is present in the early embryo (see 513). Two elongated nasal ducts or chambers leave the external nares (nostrils) at the base of the upper mandible and run across the palate to 2 large internal apertures or choanae in the buccal cavity (only a single, slit-like median choana exists in Budgerigars; 441). These are separated from one another by the thin bony or cartilaginous nasal septum (solid in most birds but pierced in some; 797). In general, each such duct or chamber swells into 3 regions in antero-posterior sequence, in each of which regions the cartilaginous walls form either a fold or a spiral scroll (turbinal or concha). An infraorbital sinus on each side is in communication with the nasal chamber.

The conchae fill the antrum but allow inspired air to pass around and between them, greatly increasing the surface over which this air passes.

The first chamber, the vestibular region, is structurally the most variable region of the nasal cavity and the primary determinant of intranasal airflow. It is critical for warming the inspired air to body temperature, for saturating it with water vapor, and for vaporizing substances therein. It is lined almost entirely with keratinized and non-keratinized squamous epithelium that overlies a rich vascular bed (797).

[Heat is removed from the nasal mucosa in the vaporization of water, and the mucosal temperature falls, in some cases to a level cooler than that of the inspired air. Expired air, essentially saturated with water vapor, leaves the parabronchi at body temperature. Passage over the cool nasal surfaces during exhalation cools this air and a quantitatively important portion of its water content condenses on the mucosa. For example, at 15°C and 25% relative humidity, Cactus Wrens (*Campylorhynchus brunneicapillus*) recover 75% of both the heat and water added to the inspired air, conserving 16% of their metabolic heat. The mechanism is partially effective at lower temperatures. Respiratory water loss and heat conservation are much less restricted under heat stress, when the temperature of the nasal mucosa is higher and there ultimately is a shift to breathing through the mouth (see 829, 1,087, 1,099).]

The 2nd or main chamber contains the principal concha (homologous with that always present in reptiles and with the maxilloturbinal of mammals), the nasal valve, when present, the opening of the nasolacrimal duct, and the aperture of the infraorbital sinus, all of which are lined by muco-ciliated epithelium (797). The 3rd chamber (posterio-superior)--the olfactory chamber--which connects with the buccal cavity through the paired choanae (or single median choana), is usually the one that has true olfactory receptors in its lining epithelium (neuroepithelium) or mucosa. It contains either a prominent tubercle or a more highly developed variously-shaped conchal system. The size of the surface area of the latter is expected to give an indication of a bird's spectrum of olfactory discrimination (28, 343, 417, 513, 797).

In some species, true olfactory neuroepithelium (mucosa) also may lie along the roof and on the posterior, ventrolateral, and upper portions of the nasal septum of the olfactory chamber (see 398). As in other vertebrates, this epithelium consists of receptor cells, supporting sustentacular cells, and basal cells. The receptor cells, typical of vertebrates, are bipolar neurons with their cell bodies embedded in the mucosa, and their dendrites extending through the overlying mucosa. The active points of stimulus transduction are believed to be the cilia at the unmyelinated terminal swellings of most dendrites. Neural information originating in the olfactory mucosa eventually reaches many areas in the forebrain of the Rock Pigeon (*Columba livia*; 417, 797, 801, 1,005). It is of interest in this connection that the olfactory sensory neurons are the only elements of the adult vertebrate nervous system known to undergo turnover and to be replaced after experimental degeneration (see 1,386).

Fluid secretions produced by the lacrimal glands and the nasal gland are discharged into the nasal cavity by way of their ducts, whereas secretions of the olfactory glands and the mucous glands of the respiratory membrane are produced *in situ* and removed continually by mucociliary traction (797). The tips of the unmyelinated nerve endings of the receptor neurons are covered by a mucoserous secretion of these olfactory glands, in which odorous molecules must dissolve in order to stimulate the receptor cells. Continuous removal of the secretion by the surrounding respiratory cilia allows the continued reception of new olfactory information (797).

The unmyelinated axons of individual neuroreceptor cells are gathered into two compact, sheathed bundles that constitute the left and right olfactory nerves. The latter project to the first relay station in the central olfactory pathway, the olfactory bulb at the anterior pole of the forebrain, but by a course and through patterns of connections that vary in different species. There is no firm evidence for an anterior olfactory nucleus, suggesting that certain projection sites may receive information in the form in which it leaves the bulb without further processing. No direct projection has been found between the two olfactory bulbs.

Bulb size is positively correlated with the number of receptor cells in the mucosa and of their axons in the olfactory nerve. The anatomy of the avian olfactory bulb is similar to that of mammalian forms in all species studied; there is a glomerular layer, a mitral cell layer with axons connecting to a variety of structures both ipsilateral and contralateral, and an internal granule cell layer. Detailed anatomical examinations reveal no unique feature of the internal organization of the bulb that would suggest a functional difference from that in other advanced vertebrates and the same is true of the results of electrophysiological studies. Little is known of the neural projections from the olfactory bulb. These are so extensive in some species, for example in the Rock Pigeon, as to suggest a considerable involvement of olfaction in their behavior (see 42, 797, 1,005).]

OLFACTION consists of two physiological processes: the more primitive one is specific and provides the basis for discrete discriminations, associations, and orientation; the other process is a diffuse, non-specific arousal system that activates other sensorimotor systems, which, in their simplest forms, guide the animal toward or away from the stimulus. In ancestral vertebrates, the center for this olfactory arousal mechanism was the telencephalon, from which impulses were projected downward to the diencephalon, midbrain, and lower centers. This formed the basis of the primitive limbic system. The olfactory arousal function gradually enlarged, and eventually became independent of olfaction. This independence is established clearly in teleosts (bony fishes), in which the non-olfactory arousal mechanism of the telencephalon seems to influence almost every kind of behavior that has been investigated (1,270).

With regard to the olfaction of birds, the picture is far from complete, though it is clear that birds generally have been emancipated from the dominance of this sense. The importance of olfaction increasingly is being recognized, and the morphological facts argue strongly for widespread olfactory capabilities (343). "....it is perfectly clear that some birds, if not all, show the same kind of activity in the olfactory system that is seen in other vertebrates whose olfactory ability has never been questioned" (42). Thus, in the absence of stimulation, bulbar intrinsic activity shows the same synchronized bursts of high-amplitude activity at 15-20 Hz that is linked to inspiration in other vertebrate species. Presentation of odors alters the pattern in different ways, usually either desynchronizing the background activity or markedly increasing spindle bursts at lower frequencies. The magnitude of such effects usually varies in parallel with changes in odor concentration, etc.

The Rock Pigeon's olfactory system responds in a typical way to appropriate olfactory stimulation and this information can be used to regulate responses by either skeletal or smooth muscles. Different odors can be distinguished but with a sensitivity that may be relatively poor (1,005). Members of other species selectively discriminate among only those odors relevant to their own habits (see E.D. Adrian, 1951, in 797). The main unanswered question concerns how much use birds make of their olfactory and gustatory senses in ongoing behavior (417).

There is little doubt that some birds are able to detect odors with considerable sensitivity (28, 42, 398). The Turkey Vulture (*Cathartes aura*), for example, is able to locate carcasses by scent, and also is attracted to the scent of chemicals that are present in putrifying flesh (155). Its olfactory bulbs are the largest found in any vulture. Members of the Procellariiformes have comparatively impressive nasal architecture and olfactory bulbs and have been shown to be attracted consistently to sources of food-related cues under natural conditions (541). Similarly, experimental studies with the Brown Kiwi (*Apteryx australis*) have shown it to be a macrosmat (see 797). Black-billed Magpies (*P. pica*) use both memory and visual or olfactory cues to recover and "steal" cached food (238). Employed along another avenue, olfactory cues sometimes are used in navigation by several species of marine birds and perhaps by Rock Pigeons (117, 657, 1010; see also T.C. Grubb, Jr., 1971, 1972, in 417). A number of experiments on both Rock Pigeons and rats have provided evidence for a tonic influence of the olfactory system on behavior (such as reactivity to handling, aggression, and visial discrimination learning) that is distinct from its phasic, or cue, function (see 1,020).

In connection with the above, fibers from the olfactory bulbs of the Rock Pigeon project ipsilaterally (on the same side) to the prepiriform complex, the hyperstriatum ventrale (of which the corresponding structure in reptiles receives no olfactory input), and the lobus parolfactorius; fibers project contralaterally via the anterior commissure to terminate primarily in the paleostriatum primitivum and, to lesser extent, in the paleostriatum augmentatum and the caudate lobus parolfactorius. Whereas stimulation of the contralateral bulb appears to activate neurons in the paleostriatum primitivum, stimulation of the ipsilateral bulb inhibits these neurons. It is suggested that if the paleostriatum primitivum is, indeed, involved in motor activities (based on its homology with the mammalian globus pallidus, which receives no olfactory input), its olfactory input may be concerned with the use of olfactory information in homing or navigation (1,092).

[An avian species in which the length of the olfactory bulb is greater than 25% of the longest diameter of the ipsilateral cerebral hemisphere is likely to be a ground-nesting, water-associated, colonially-breeding, carnivorous or piscivorous bird, whereas if the length is less than 10% the species is likely to be mainly tree-nesting, terrestrial, solitarily-breeding, and granivorous or omnivorous (see 797).]

[Since a pair of prominent olfactory nerves enter the telencephalon of reptiles, it seems evident that their cerebral hemispheres must have an olfactory function, and, in fact, the classical picture of the reptilian telencephalon was as a largely olfactory correlation center. There is, however, only minimal olfactory representation in the hippocampus, where optic, auditory, and cutaneous discharges converge. As in teleosts, the olfactory mechanism seems confined to a limited portion of the telencephalon, mostly in the subpallium (1,270).]

THE CERE. The sex of the mature Budgerigar also can be distinguished by the color of its cere, an enlarged, fleshy covering at the base of the upper mandible, through which the external nares (nostrils) open. The cere consists of a soft, thickened portion of the rhamphotheca or horny bill (318), the same modified type of integument (skin) that invests the bill. The cere is present in all parrots but is partly feathered in many species, for example, in lovebirds.

The soft, thickened, tumescent cere of Budgerigars is a rich blue color in the adult male, and whittish-tan, pink, light blue, or brown to dark-brown in the female. Changes in the color of the cere in mature birds may accompany altered states of health and breeding condition, those occurring in the female during breeding being induced by estrogens (135, 136, 171, 442). Thus, the ceres of males in peak breeding condition are a bright, shiny blue (purplish-pink in the red-eyed and pied birds), those of similarly-conditioned hens are of deep chocolate color (136; not confirmed by Brockway; 67). A drastic change in cere color in adults often is a sign of degeneration of the ovary or testes (185). The nostrils of immature females tend to be rimmed with white (67, 439). The importance of cere color in preliminary sex recognition is shown by the fact that male Budgerigars will attack a female whose cere is painted blue but court a male whose cere is painted brown (see 441).

[In general, the plumage, plumage color, and integumentary derivatives and skin appendages of birds, such as the horny bill, comb, and wattles are under hormonal control (260); controls of the sexual accessories by testicular secretions are believed to represent relationships as old as the Vertebrata (295).]

NASAL GLANDS. The pale-yellow, ovoid, nasal (salt) glands of Budgerigars lie within the orbits dorsomedial to the eyeballs and are comparatively large, considering the usual low salt diet of the bird. Each gland sends its duct forward through a foramen in the frontal bone, beneath the frontonasal suture, across the hinge of the upper mandible, to open into the ipsilateral nasal chamber. It is here that the hypertonic salt solutions apparently are excreted; in some species these excretions have nearly twice the total salt concentration of seawater (473). The osmoreceptors that control nasal salt gland secretion are located in or near the heart, the brain, and possibly in the salt-gland ganglion (see 934). An adrenocortical response to hypersalinity or dehydration involves corticosterone secretion and probably is of major importance in the maintenance of salt-gland excretion (934). The ability of certain avian nasal glands to concentrate NaCl is greater, and the corresponding expenditure of water is less, than that of any other organ in higher vertebrates, with the possible exception of the mammalian kidney (630). [The sublingual glands of the crocodile, *Crocodylus porosus*, are capable of producing a secretion with an osmotic pressure 2-3 times greater than that of the blood (see 1,312).]

In birds with functional nasal glands (associated with increased weight of the kidneys of nonpasserines), 60-85% of the salt intake is excreted via that route (522). It has been postulated, but not demonstrated, that the glands function in conjunction with resorptive processes in the coprodeum and rectum (see 829). Whether the the glands can function for the secretion of salt in any parrot (or passerine) is unknown. Budgerigars do, however, have comparatively large nasal glands and a remarkable ability to cope with salt water (see p. 48), suggesting that they may imbibe from the inland salt lakes of Australia (441, 442). The nestlings of the Australian Pratincole (*Stiltia isabella*) have well developed salt secreting glands; these probably assist them in retaining water from their insect diet for use in the extensive evaporative cooling required in the very hot surroundings of the nests (see 1,087).

THE RESPIRATORY SYSTEM

The basic structural principles of the lungs and coelomic subdivisions of reptiles have been inherited by birds (619). But the avian respiratory system is unique and the most elaborately constructed of any found among vertebrates (see also pp. 83-87, **Vocal Apparatus and Vocalization**). At least 12 different muscles are involved in its performance at rest. The system differs markedly in its basic structure from that of mammals, including a substantial heterogeneity, in that it possesses morphologically distinct subunits (the paleopulmo and neopulmo; 687). It consists of:

(a) generally 4 paired, relatively-large, pulmonary air sacs and one median unpaired sac with numerous and extensive diverticulae; [These act primarily as bellows for receiving and then delivering a flow of air through the respiratory passageways. They connect through several ostia to the bronchi (air passages of the lungs) and offer a means of increasing ventilation without incurring a change in the blood gases and pH, because very little gaseous exchange takes place between the blood and the air in the air sacs (see p. 78).]

(b) relatively small, rigid, somewhat-flattened parabronchial lungs, within the dorsal portion of the thorax, extensively fused to the horizontal septum and to the outer wall of the pleural cavity;

(c) the trachea and bronchi, which lead outside air from the external nares and nasal cavities into the lungs and airsacs;

(d) the associated blood vessels and nerves.

This system provides a completely different pattern of respiratory air circulation from that found in mammals. Respiratory gas flow is unidirectional in the paleopulmo, from the caudal dorsobronchi through secondary parabronchi to the cranial ventrobronchi. This contrasts with the non-unidirectional "neopulmonic" gas exchange pathway that involves parabronchi connecting the caudal air sacs with the main bronchus and the dorsobronchi (435, 687, 699, 702). The latter neopulmonic parabronchi anastomose repeatedly with one another and with paleopulmonic parabronchi (1,001).

An outstanding characteristic of the avian respiratory region is the ceaseless movement of a sheet of secreted mucus along genetically-determined pathways (mostly into the pharynx in the domestic fowl), transported by cilia that beat irreversibly in a given direction. In all terrestrial vertebrates, including birds, this function is crucial to both olfaction and respiration, and is the primary means of defense against infectious diseases of the lower respiratory tract (see 797 and p. 212).

The gas-exchanging lungs are located dorsally in the body cavity and are supported ventrally and caudally by septae. They are relatively rigid and small (generally about 10% of the respiratory tract volume but achieving 16.6% in the Rock Pigeon; 435, 446, 1,001); they present an exceedingly compact gas exchanging surface; they are not expanded and contracted by a diaphragm; airway resistance is higher in inspiration, rather than in expiration (see 698); and there normally is no pause between inspiration and expiration, both of which are active processes and depend on contraction of respiratory muscles (see below). Although the costoseptales muscles tend to oppose volume changes, in most medium-sized and small birds there is a passive change in the volume of the parabronchi imposed by the movements of the ribs. Though this change in the volume of the lungs is essential for ventilation, there apparently is no recoil to aid the expiratory muscles during expiration. (see 442, 1,001). The respiratory center appears to be in the region of the pons and rostral part of the medulla oblongata (517, 1,001).

BRONCHI---AIR AND BLOOD CAPILLARIES. The paired primary bronchi proceed laterally and caudally from the syrinx into the lungs. Gas exchange occurs after only 3 orders of bronchial branching along the open-ended tube-like parabronchi. After entering the hilus (indented region) of the lung on the ventromedial surface, an intrapulmonary primary bronchus (mesobronchus) gives rise on its medial surface to several large secondary bronchi (ento-, ecto-, latero-, and dorsobronchi), comprising an anterior group, both dorsal and ventral, and a similar posterior group. From the secondary bronchi arise the tertiary bronchi (parabronchi), which connect the interior and posterior groups of secondary bronchi. No tertiary bronchus ends blindly and many join to form long curved circuits. The interconnections between the primary, secondary, and tertiary bronchi are labyrinthine and differ greatly from the tree-like branching found in mammalian respiratory passages (321).

The walls of the tertiary bronchi are lined by a mesh of smooth muscle and pierced by numerous openings that lead, in turn, to the atria, which then branch into infundibula and a complex network of anastomosing, microscopic air capillaries (3-10 micra in diameter; 692)--the respiratory exchanging sites, which are in intimate contact with the blood capillaries. The long, poorly-connected blood capillaries arise from arterioles at the outer surfaces of the tertiary bronchi and are collected mainly by venules on the luminal side (692). Each blood capillary is about 6 micra in diameter and anastomoses with adjacent blood capillaries to form a homogeneous 3-dimensional lattice (696). The air capillaries issuing from the walls of the tertiary bronchi lie in close apposition to and occupy the interstices between these blood capillaries, forming an identical lattice which is the 3-dimensional mirror-image of the blood capillary network. The two interdigitating latticeworks together form the so-called "parabronchial mantle" (692, 696).

Among vertebrates, the arrangement of the vascular system has attained its most complex development in the avian lung. The avian pulmonary circulation perfuses all points along a tertiary parabronchus with mixed venous blood. Hence there is a cross-current flow of blood and air in these interdigitating lattices, with a diffusion barrier only 0.1-0.2 micra thick (441, 446, 517, 696, 1,001). Because of the unusual arrangement of the blood capillaries, gas exchange is not evenly allocated along the length of the tertiary parabronchi, leading to complicated profiles of both oxygen and carbon dioxide concentrations in the contained gas (see 695, 698). The "overlap" of arterial and expired oxygen and carbon dioxide partial pressures suggests enhanced gas exchange in cross-current lungs compared to that in alveolar lungs, in which expired and arterial blood gases can, at best, come to equilibrium (1,001). The combination of rigid air capillaries and a constant-volume lung makes possible an extremely thin avian gas-blood barrier. In birds with high activity rates and oxygen consumption it is less than half the width of the least mammalian barrier (702).

The air and blood capillaries occupy from 35 to 50% of the total lung volume in several avian species. A large area of each air capillary is exposed to blood, making the size of the exchanging surface per unit volume of the avian lung at least 10 times that of the lung of Man (517). In the

Budgerigar and small songbirds, the air capillaries of adjacent tertiary bronchi interconnect freely (see H.R. Duncker, 1971, in 441). The abundantly present smooth muscles in the avian lung appear to be involved mainly in controlling the diameter and resistance of the lumina of tertiary bronchi and their tubular subdivisions, partly via respiratory gas concentrations, particularly that of carbon dioxide (517).

AIR SACS. Despite its small size, the Budgerigar (and most other birds of comparable dimensions) has many comparatively huge, effectively ventilated, air sacs (normally numbering 9 but Stone claims 11 for Budgerigars, adding an axillary pair to the 9 listed by Evans and by Gandal; 441, 445, 446), as well as air spaces distributed throughout the body (441). The Rock Pigeon has an abdominal sac that is relatively larger, and a caudal thoracic sac that is relatively smaller than in most birds. Rock Pigeons also have a slightly developed cervicocephalic air-sac that is generally not connected to the pulmonary air-sac system, but pneumatizes the head region (see 1,001). The air sacs usually do not reach a functional state of development in young birds until some days into the nestling period, for example, between 5 and 9 days in the House Wren (see 1,150). [There normally are 8 or 9 air sacs in most birds: the median (or paired) cervical sac(s), the median clavicular, and the paired cranial thoracic, caudal thoracic, and abdominal sacs (1,053).]

The total volume of the avian respiratory system occupies 5-20%, averaging about 15%, of the bodily volume; of this volume, the major portion is contributed by the pulmonary air sacs, while all the air sacs together constitute about 80% of the total respiratory volume. Because of the contributions of the voluminous air-sac system, the total volume of the avian respiratory tract is roughly 3 times as great as in a mammal of similar size (321).

Each air sac is composed of a thin connective tissue layer containing elastic fibers and is only very lightly vascularized (446). The walls of the air sacs always are attached to the walls of the subpulmonary cavity, except for those sites where the sacs surround passing structures or are adjoined to one another (619). It is unlikely that the stretching of the thin-walled air sacs requires a significant amount of work during inspiration or that a subsequent recoil aids expiration (517).

The ciliated, cuboidal epithelial lining of a sac near the openings to the lung (ostia) is replaced in the more remote portions by a squamous (flattened) epithelium (340). The sacs are in direct communication with the tracheal and bronchial respiratory passages and the air spaces in the pneumatic bones (most vertebrae and ribs, the humerus, coracoid, sternum, ilium, ischium, and pubis; 441). Diverticulae from the air sacs extend outside the coelom into subcutaneous regions of the neck and proximal parts of the limbs (340, 517). [A fowl with its trachea ligatured can breath through its cut humerus (see 338, 517).] A variety of relatively simple to highly complicated diverticulae arise from the main chambers of the interclavicular, cervical, and abdominal air sacs. Generally, the individual sacs have one direct connection to a primary or secondary bronchus and may have several indirect connections to other secondary or tertiary bronchi (321).

Normally the respiratory movements of the abdominal musculature of the sternum and rib cage act principally to compress and expand the air sacs, all of which are effectively ventilated (340, 396, 435). For example, when the coracoid and sternum are thrust (pivoted) cranially and ventrally around the shoulder joint, and the ribs are moved laterally by contraction of the inspiratory muscles, the thoraco-abdominal cavity becomes enlarged dorsoventrally and air is drawn into the air sacs and the bronchial tubes (441, 442). Pressure changes attain a magnitude of only a few cm of water and are fairly evenly distributed in the thoraco-abdominal cavity as it expands and contracts with ventilatory movement. The great effectiveness of small pressure changes in inducing volume changes in the avian respiratory system probably traces mainly to the ready "unfolding" of the air sacs and stretching of the abdominal wall. This may explain the generally lower respiratory frequency in birds as compared to mammals (see 1,001 and below, **Ventilatory Rate**).

One role of the air sacs is the provision of unidirectional, continuous ventilatory air flow through the parabronchial lungs. Although aerodynamic effects appear to be involved in flow rectifications, the exact mechanisms and functional significance of unidirectional flow are not yet understood fully (435). It is well established, however, that much of the gas from the posterior thoracic sacs is directed to the lungs during expiration, and there appears to be a preferential shunting of the respiratory dead space to the posterior thoracic sacs prior to filling of the lungs during inspiration (697). The pectoralis muscle is not activated during either inspiration or expiration in the resting bird (1,001).

In addition to their purely ventilatory role in breathing and panting, the air sacs provide buoyancy in flight and are believed to help cool the body during vigorous activity or climatic thermal stress, through the internal evaporation of water (340, 446, 450). A few percent of the respiratory exchange also occurs across their surfaces (see 699 and J. Makowski, 1938, in 442). It also is suggested that the changes of volume and pressure exerted by the air sacs profoundly influence the venous return of blood to the heart (450). In support of this suggestion is the fact that when blood pressure is measured directly, waves with the frequency of the respiratory movements are seen in the trace; these are influenced by the gradient for venous return and by the pulmonary vascular volume. It is concluded that they are caused by gas pressure changes within the lungs (515).

VENTILATORY RATE. The mechanisms involved in the regulation of ventilatory rate (and tidal volume) in birds still are understood poorly (442), though some believe that the reflex control is similar, if not identical, to that in mammals (340). Intrapulmonary chemoreceptors, particularly those activated by carbon-dioxide, probably play an important role but these receptors have no mechanical sensitivity (693).

The resting ventilatory rate at thermoneutrality is inversely proportional to bodily size. It is very labile but generally varies from 0.3-2.0 Hz (1.3-1.66 Hz in Budgerigars and 0.47 Hz in Rock Pigeons; 445, 449, 1,001). In flight it increases to 2.91-5.0 Hz (3.34-4½ Hz for Budgerigars; 340, 471). Berger and Hart quote an increase in ventilatory rate by a factor of 3-19 from rest to flight, with the increase being greatest in large birds (423; see also 518). The respiratory minute volume increases by an even greater factor (see p. 80, **Flight Metabolism**) because of a concomitant increase in the respiratory tidal volume (518). Resting ventilatory rates, which range from 0.05 to 0.80 Hz in a variety of species, of weights between 50 g and 10 kg (see 1,289), generally are lower than those of mammals, weight for weight, but this disparity is partially offset by higher avian tidal volumes (321).

THE SKELETON is involved as a whole in the rhythmic respiratory movements of expansion and contraction. It is composed of very hard, thin-walled, highly mineralized, porcelain-like bones comprising only about 7% of total bodily weight (135, 290), and its component bones have been more plastic in evolution than the components of any other bodily system (28). The furcula--the ventral fusion of the collar bones or clavicles (forming the "wishbone")--of Budgerigars, however, is composed of cartilage (31). Pneumatization of the bones gives the avian skeleton greater strength for a given amount of bone than if the bones were solid. However, the weight savings in the long, pneumatized wing bones are offset by the robustness of the leg bones, with the result that avian skeletons are not relatively lighter than those of mammals (691). [Congenital bone dislocations are not uncommon in Budgerigars (135).]

OXYGEN FOR FLIGHT. Although birds apparently possess greater flexibility in varying the affinity of the blood for oxygen, the oxygen-transport characteristics of avian blood are similar to those of mammals in general (see 618). Increased oxygen for flight is provided by a massively augmented depth and rate of respiration, an increase in cardiac output, and a probable increase in the diffusing capacity of the lungs (23). In Sooty Terns (*Sterna fusca*), the metabolic rate during flight increases to 4.8 times the standard value (197).

RESPIRATORY PATTERNS IN FLIGHT. For anatomical reasons, the respiratory and wing-movement systems would appear to be essentially independent, since they are controlled by different factors (423). In many cases, though, the changeover from inspiration to expiration is associated with a phase of the wing-beat cycle that markedly reduces inspiratory flow. In this limited sense, wing action may be thought of as controlling expiration, even though this rhythm does not dominate the respiratory cycle. Rather, coordination appears to be brought about by a central control center (see 423).

In any event, the respiratory patterns in flight usually are coordinated with wing beats, and an analogous situation probably obtains in bats (769). But respiratory patterns are known to be synchronized with wingbeat at a ratio of 1:1 only in Rock Pigeons (wingbeat frequency of 5.4 Hz; 1,003) and Common Crows (*Corvus brachyrhynchos*; 320, 321, 1,001). In most species the coordination ratio is at 1:5 to 1:2, with 1:3 being most common (423). However, there is no fixed relation between these variables in Budgerigars flying in a wind tunnel. In that situation, wing-beat frequency remains constant at 14 Hz at all flight speeds, whereas the coordination ratio varies from 1:4.2 to 1:3.1 (330).

Furthermore, there is no single value or narrow range of values for the "resting" respiratory rate within the thermoneutral zone, analogous to the situation that usually obtains for the basal metabolic rate. Rather, respiratory function, including the resting respiratory rate, are likely to vary considerably with temperature in the thermoneutral zone, just as do other physiological, postural, and behavioral parameters. In fact, the lability of respiratory patterns in birds is one of their most striking characteristics. Rigorous comparative analysis of avian respiratory function is possible only if careful attention is paid to the effects of ambient temperature on response patterns and if "resting" values are reported as standard values (by specifying the temperature; 1,289).

[In insects and hummingbirds, at least, wingbeat frequencies can be accounted for fully by the theory of driven damped mechanical oscillators. The wingbeat frequencies of the Ruby-throated Hummingbird (*Archilochus colubris*) is 53 ± 3 Hz under a great variety of flight conditions, including hovering (788).]

FLIGHT METABOLISM. The most reliable estimates of the level of flight metabolism indicate a 7-15-fold increase over standard metabolic levels (37, 321, 1,001, 1,004). Measurements of gas composition in the cannulated air sacs and the rate of carbon-dioxide production during wind-tunnel flight of wild European or Common Starlings (*Sturnus vulgaris*) yielded increases in metabolic rate and minute volume by factors of 8.9 and 8.2, respectively, over resting values (694). It is unknown as yet whether gas exchange in the lung becomes rate-limiting for tissue oxygenation in flight, or whether the limiting link in the oxygen transport chain is the circulatory system (435). A large part of respiratory evaporation takes place in the air sacs, particularly the anterior ones, which lie just under the flight muscles (340). It has been suggested that the upper limit of flight speed is determined by the maximum safe rate of heat loss (see 487).

THE RESPIRATORY SYSTEM AND TEMPERATURE CONTROL

HEAT EXCHANGE. Respiratory evaporative cooling is an extremely important mechanism in birds. As ambient temperature increases to very high values, evaporation from surfaces of the respiratory system becomes progressively more important for the dissipation of heat and the maintenance of normal body temperature. When the upper critical temperature is exceeded (when ambient temperature exceeds the skin temperature), heat losses across the feathered and unfeathered regions of the integument cease. Up until this point there is a good correlation between cutaneous evaporation and the difference between ambient and mean body temperatures (1,004). Beyond this point, evaporation from respiratory surfaces becomes the sole method of heat dissipation (349). Rock Pigeons in stable flight dissipate 17% of flight heat production as evaporative heat loss via exhaled air (324). In Budgerigars flying at moderate temperatures the corresponding figure is 13-22% (28, 330).

Such mechanisms for evaporative cooling, together with thermal dissipation through feathered regions of the integument and the naked feet, are crucial, since birds do not have sweat glands. Although it does not have a particularly low metabolic rate, under hot conditions in a suitably low humidity, the Budgerigar can dissipate 56% more heat by evaporative cooling than is produced in metabolism (see 1,087). The pneumatic bones also must be effective heat exchangers, lying as they do at the centers of large muscle masses and having air regularly circulated through them (193). In most avian species, not much more than 20% of the calories resulting from metabolism (at an air temperature of 40°C) are lost by non-evaporative routes; herons and gulls, however, can dissipate, almost their entire metabolic heat production (at an air temperature of 35°C) through the legs, in which there are profuse, flow-facilitating A-V anastomoses (37, 320, 630).]

WATER LOSS. Except in the Ostrich, avian respiratory evaporative water loss at rest in approximate thermoneutrality accounts for only 16-58% of the total evaporation; this is 4-8-fold greater than in lizards (422). Respiratory water loss of the Budgerigar during moderate activity is 250 mg/h, whereas the sleeping bird loses only 44 mg/h (15). At moderate temperatures, flying Budgerigars and Rock Pigeons lose about 13-22% of their heat production by respiratory evaporation, with the remainder being lost over the entire bodily surface, particularly the legs and the poorly-insulated sides of the thorax, via convection, radiation, and evaporation (330; see also 37, 321, 324, 423, 630, 829). The diffusion barrier appears to be situated in the striatum corneum of the epidermis and to involve an unidentified lipid in close association with keratin fibers (see 1,099).

The heat transfer coefficient of these birds in flight increases 5-fold or more, while their evaporative water loss during horizontal, non-soaring flight exceeds resting values by at least 400% in moderate and warm ambient temperatures (330; see also 37, 829). The extent of evaporative water loss through the skin during flight has not been measured but doubtless increases over that at rest (418, 423). In studies of these phenomena, there clearly is a need to partition total evaporative water loss during flight into its respiratory and cutaneous components (518). [Under certain conditions cutaneous evaporative water loss in birds when not in flight can exceed that from the respiratory tract (see 518).]

The respiratory evaporative component of water loss increases with temperature in flying Budgerigars, attaining 40-47% at 36-37°C (330). At these temperatures the Budgerigars also extend the naked portions of their legs into the slip stream. It is unknown to what extent respiratory heat loss in flight can be regulated, or if it has a more or less fixed value determined only by external temperature, pressure, humidity, etc. (423).

PANTING and/or gular flutter are engaged in by birds when not in flight to combat hyperthermia. Panting (thermal polypnea) involves an increase in respiratory minute volume brought about by vigorous movements of the thoracic cage. The frequency of such movements increases to about 0.67-1.17 Hz, depending on the species, while the tidal volume decreases (37, 518).

The manner in which heat stress induces panting varies. Commonly, breathing rate increases steadily with heat load, until body temperature exceeds some characteristic value between 40 and 44°C (no bird appears to tolerate a body temperature above 47°C, and survival between 46 and 47°C is of very limited duration in desert and non-desert species alike). At that point, open-mouthed panting commences, as in the domestic fowl and passerines. In others, the changeover is abrupt, from a relatively low breathing rate to a high one, as in the Ostrich and Barn Owl (*Tyto alba*; 37, 422). The rate of panting movements ranges from 15.7-26.5 times the resting respiratory rate and may attain 5 Hz in the domestic fowl hen and 11 Hz in the Rock Pigeon (311, 422, 829).

Panting causes increased evaporation from the nasal, buccal, and upper pharyngeal regions, and from the trachea and bronchi and the walls of the air sacs in the Ostrich but apparently not in other birds; see 829, 1,099). The latent heat of evaporation of water from the saliva cools blood circulating in the mucosa of these regions (795). It is believed that much of the increased ventilation accompanying the increase in respiratory rate, is limited to the respiratory dead space, in which gas exchange between blood and air does not occur (518). Air is shunted directly between the trachea and the air sacs without passing through the lungs. Thus, an increase in evaporative cooling is achieved by hyperventilation with lessened risk of apnea consequent upon a development of respiratory alkalosis, although the latter commonly occurs (see 349, 442, 1,099). Both Budgerigars and Monk Parakeets (*Myiopsitta monachus*) may employ lingual flutter to augment evaporative cooling by panting; in the latter species it was noted that the thick, moist tongue is raised and lowered in synchrony with the movements of the thorax (1,243, 1,244).

Panting appears to be mediated by a pacemaker center in the anterior dorsal mesencephalon (the nucleus mesencephalicus lateralis pars dorsalis, which may possibly be homologous with the pneumotaxic center in the mammalian pons; 517) and by neurons in the anterior hypothalamus and preoptic areas (321, 340, 422, 518). The latter area is assumed to represent a center of integration of temperature signals in the thermoregulatory system (see 700). The panting center acts by stimulating the respiratory center to produce an increase in respiratory rate (340). Skin temperature changes are relatively unimportant in the control of panting (1,099).

Panting is an important and effective mechanism. Many birds are quite capable of dissipating all of the heat that they produce by respiratory evaporation in a hot environment (518). It often is of limited value alone, however, and it is ineffective in hot environments that also are humid (349). In some cases its energetic cost is substantial; for example, about 40% of the heat dissipated by panting in the Cardinal (*Richmondena cardinalis*) merely offsets the concomitant heat production of respiratory muscles (518). [The effectiveness of increased ventilation in thermoregulation is an inverse function of the relative humidity of the environmental air (442).]

GULAR FLUTTER (not practiced by parrots) consists of a rapid vibration of the membranous gular region (the mucosa of the pharynx, anterior esophagus, and buccal cavity) actuated by flexure of the hyoid apparatus and requiring relatively little energy for its maintenance. Its movement rate can reach 9.17-11.5 Hz. It permits evaporation from areas that are not involved in normal respiratory ventilation, because it moves air across the moist mucosa of the buccal cavity and esophagus, which become conspicuously suffused with blood during heat stress (37, 54, 518). Three patterns of enhanced evaporation are known: panting alone, panting with synchronous gular flutter, and panting with independent gular flutter (422).

Gular fluttering has two advantages over panting. First, the air movement is restricted to surfaces that do not participate in respiratory gas exchange, circumventing any danger of hyperventilation. Second, the energetic cost of moving the gular area is considerably less than that of moving the larger thoracic cavity. Consequently, the heat loss mediated by gular flutter is not offset to any great extent by heat production in the musculature of the hyoid apparatus (518). In some birds that employ both mechanisms, the frequencies of the two movements are the same, in most birds they are not.

The frequency of gular flutter usually is higher than that of panting, consistent with the smaller weight of the gular-hyoid structure. In a few species, the rate increases with increasing heat load, but more generally remains constant, in which case its contribution to evaporative cooling is adjusted by intermittent operation and by varying the amplitude of flutter and the area mobilized (see 37). Gular flutter commences before panting in several species and probably occurs at the resonant frequency of the gular region (54).

Evaporative cooling of most birds at highest temperatures produces dissipation of amounts of heat representing 100-200% of heat production, though some birds, such as the Poor-will (*Phalaenoptilus nuttallii*) and Spotted Nightjar (*Eurostopodus guttatus*) achieve even greater amounts of dissipation (829). The latter bird can prevent overheating during exposure to an ambient temperature of 5?°C (1,087). Passerines, with their relatively high level of metabolism ... st evaporate water at more rapid rates than non-passerines of simila... to dissipate the same proportion of their heat production. Birds ... low metabolic levels, such as caprimulgids (Poor-wills, ni... awks) can dissipate their metabolic heat with a far lo... ater than other birds of comparable size that have h... 37). Some birds with a well-developed gular flut... during exposure to ambient temperatures 4°C ... lethal body temperatures (37, 829).

THE SP... resent a thermosensitive area ... respiratory rate changes ... t loss can be elicit... Pigeon spinal cord. ... lts in shivering, ... rature, whereas ... panting, vasodi...

It ... signals are generated by ther... hermal susceptibility of the synap... rature signals, i.e., by a modificatio... nsors located outside of the central nerv... retation is favored by results with deafferent...

[It has been sugge... atory system is a very promising one for future phylogen... ry) and systematic investigations: the patterns of the seve... the systems of communication of the air sacs, and the developmen... parabronchial network, would appear to offer possibilities for r... ing new systems of radiation among birds (156).]

VOCAL APPARATUS AND VOCALIZATION

THE LARYNX of birds, unlike that of mammals, does not possess vocal chords and is not known to generate vocal sounds. It is a valvular structure that chiefly regulates the flow of air--providing sharp onset and termination of flow--between the buccal and anterior pharyngeal cavities and the trachea, via an opening and closing of the glottis. It also aids in preventing the aspiration of foreign material into the lower part of the respiratory tract. It is too near the mouth and insufficiently provided with adequately large resonating chambers to amplify sounds appreciably at medium frequencies; at most, it has an effect on resonance and on the harmonic spectrum. Thus, variations in the condition of the glottal aperture could alter the tracheal resonances from those of a tube closed at one end to those of a tube closed at both ends. Such resonances would be superimposed on the amplitude spectrum produced at the syrinx (155, 426, 1,284; see also below).

THE TRACHEA or windpipe is a flexible tube, kept open by calcified cartilaginous rings in its walls. It connects the larynx with the syrinx and lies to the left of the esophagus. Since the average cross-sectional area of the syringeal passage is much less than that of the cross-sectional area of the trachea, the tracheal tube essentially is closed at the syringeal end (1,284). The tracheal rings in Budgerigars are complete (closed) for the most part but occasionally are open with overlapping ends (441).

THE SYRINX is the major sound-producing organ in most birds. It is formed by modified cartilages of the trachea or bronchi, or by a combination of both, with associated membranes and muscles. The muscles are capable of changing the shape of the cavity or the tension on the membranous parts of the organ. The syrinx is not bilaterally divided in parrots, and is suspended within the interclavicular air sac deep in the thorax; both syringeal halves contribute equally to the control and production of the vocal repertoire in the Orange-winged Amazon (*Amazona amazonica*), which, like Peach-faced Lovebirds is vocally monomorphic (1,284). In owls, the syringes of females are smaller than those of males (see 497).

As in other parrots, Budgerigars have a dorso-ventrally compressed trachea and a basically tracheal rather than bronchial syrinx. [According to Evans (441) and Nottebohm (1,284), the syrinx can be categorized as tracheo-bronchial, which is the type possessed by all Oscines (961) and believed to have been ancestral.] A single set of very thin, elastic, internal tympaniform membranes occur as modifications of the lateral walls of the region rostral to the junction of the two bronchi with the syrinx--stretched across the open ends of the bronchial rings (207, 396, 1,250). The structural simplifications represented by the possession of an undivided syrinx and but one pair of tympaniform membranes (which are external in *A. amazonica*; 1,284), though not unique to parrots, are rare. Few of the other species that show them are noted for vocal virtuosity (258). Syringeal sexual dimorphism has been noticed in some songbirds but its relation to the nature of the sounds produced is unclear (426).

THE BUDGERIGAR SYRINX consists of a bony and membranous chamber formed by an expansion of the trachea where it bifurcates into the two extrapulmonary primary bronchi, followed by paired, free, cartilaginous or partially ossified semi-rings (incomplete medially; 340), each of which connects with a bronchus by means of membranes (441). In *A. amazonica*, the bronchial semi-rings #2, #3, and #4 are ossified partially and are heavier than the rings that follow caudally. The 4 caudal tracheal rings are fused dorsally and ventrally, but not laterally. The last tracheal ring has a caudal process on which the two halves of the tympanum abut (1,284).

THREE PAIRS OF TRACHEO-BRONCHIAL (SYRINGEAL) MUSCLES, one extrinsic (having one attachment to a nontracheal structure) and two intrinsic (arising and inserting in some part of the tracheal system) are used in vocalizations. In *A. amazonica*, the latter muscles control the positions of the external tympaniform membranes and of the first bronchial semi-ring (1,284). Each group of muscles inserts only onto the ipsilateral bronchial rings, and the left and right muscles appear to receive separate innervations. Among other things, these muscles serve to modulate the fundamental frequency of vocalizations, probably determining the amount of air flowing past each tympaniform membrane by modifying the bore of each bronchus. They also may play an important role in respiration (426). Since these muscles are under direct central control via motor axons of the tracheosyringeal branches of the hypoglossal nerve, rather than being controlled by way of spinal neurons, the hypoglossal nucleus provides both a controlling motor output and a starting point into central processing.

THE BASIC OSCINE PATTERN, in contrast, consists of 6 pairs of tracheo-bronchial muscles, from which no deviation has been observed. Each pair of muscles seems to affect the membranous portions of the syrinx by adjusting the positions of bronchial bars in a different manner from the others. The functional relationships between the number, shape, and position of syringeal muscles and the functional significance of the "turdine thumb" (a thumb-like extension of the dorsolateral muscles) to the characteristics of the vocal repertoire are as yet entirely unknown. The pattern of the syringeal muscles should, however, prove to be useful for establishing taxonomic relationships (961). [The numerous reports of from 4 to 9 pairs of oscine tracheo-bronchial muscles appear to have resulted from nomenclatural confusion. The main form of variation that exists is in the points of insertion (rarely, of origin) of the muscles (961).]

The weight, and probably the power of some of these muscles and the weight of the syrinx are affected by steroidal hormones, which thus can influence the quality of vocalization (260). However, the most effective hormonal treatment, in terms of restoring singing behavior in the Zebra Finch, is not most effective for restoring syringeal muscle mass (745). The intrinsic muscles are perhaps the key innovation in permitting vocal plasticity and typically can affect the syringeal configuration by some means other than adjusting the position of the caudal end of the trachea (258).

One of these intrinsic muscle pairs, the tracheobronchialis, spans the tympaniform membrane. Its contraction rotates a set of fused bronchial bars to constrict the syringeal lumen, regardless of the position of the trachea. The other pair arises and inserts in such a manner that its action opposes that of the first pair, allowing an extremely precise regulation of both the bore of the syrinx and the tension on the medial ends of the rotating bronchial bars (258).

SOUND PRODUCTION is initiated when the expiratory ventilator musculature of the body wall compresses the interclavicular air sac, the integrity of which is indispensable for vocalization (426). This compression creates a pressure head that drives air through the trachea. The airflow induces a pressure deficit (Bernoulli effect) on the inside of the internal tympaniform membranes as the air passes the membranes and draws them into the syringeal lumen. [Studies of vocalizations in domestic fowl chicks give an indication that different types of muscle fibers, and thus of motoneurons, may be involved in ventilatory as opposed to vocal exhalations (581).]

There are 3 major mechanisms for sound production in the syrinx. The 1st involves vibrations of the tympaniform membranes at the fundamental frequency of the sound produced (perhaps responsible for complex tones such as harsh and broadband calls). The 2nd does not involve vibrations of these membranes. Rather, a series of air vortices or periodic disturbances are produced by shearing forces, as the airstream is forced through slots produced by the initial changes in syringeal configuration, involving similar actions to those of lip-whistling by Man. These vortices usually are responsible for pure-tone whistles, the most common kind of avian phonation. The latter can be very loud, even with the flow of only small volumes of air. The 3rd mechanism involves both effects together (258, 426).

In all of these mechanisms, the sound appears to be modulated at its source. The frequency of sounds is thought to be modified when the syringeal muscles contract, changing the relative positions of the bronchial and tracheal rings, and hence altering the tension on, and conformation of, the tympaniform membranes (1,250). The extent to which the trachea and syringeal membranes interact in sound production remains controversial; rather than there being a rigid coupling between the sound source and the properties of the tracheal cavity, the influence of tracheal length on the fundamental frequency may reflect changes in resistance to air flow or changes in turbulence patterns (258, 426). [In domestic ducks, the pitch of vocalizations produced by ducklings is said to be determined by the resonant frequency of the trachea: as this lengthens with growth, it supports longer wavelengths, i.e., sounds of increasingly lower pitch (1,150).] In Greenewalt's view, "the primary vibrations produced in the syrinx traverse the trachea without attenuation, amplification, or change of any kind" (480). In this connection, it is noteworthy that the frequency range of sound produced by the isolated syrinx of the Rock Pigeon equals that of the bird's natural vocalizations (1,012).

Many interactions between syringeal components influence vocal frequencies and other aspects of sound production. Among these are the average diameter of the bore of the lumen opposite the flexible portions of the syrinx and the elastic properties of these flexible portions, the rate of airflow through the syrinx, and the pressure in the interclavicular airsac. There also is the possibility of utilization of various combinations of mechanical and aerodynamic vibrations. The duration of sounds and the intervals between them, for example, can be adjusted by varying the airflow.

AMPLITUDE AND FREQUENCY MODULATION are intimately linked (see 498, 581) but uncertainties remain over the method of achieving modulation of freqquency and generating harmonics; the latter are source generated, however, arising and perhaps being selectively emphasized in the syrinx itself (see 1,284). In this connection, the majority of members of the Passeriformes sing only in the frequency range that gives rise to phrases free of harmonics, whereas birds of other groups sing only in the range that gives rise to harmonic phrases (480, 498). It is unlikely that different patterns of sound modulation in closely related cogeners are determined by differences in syringeal anatomy. It is more likely that these differences are attributable to differences in their neural substrate. (207, 258).

DUAL SYRINX. Many birds, including members of the suborder Oscines, possess a dual syrinx and can activate sound sources in both the right and left bronchi simultaneously, a phenomenon associated with left hypoglossal dominance. Those that have the appropriate musculature can produce completely different sounds, independently-modulated, from the two sides, an ability termed the "two-voice" phenomenon (see 258, 426, 480, 498, 1,284). [However, in parrots, neither hypoglossal nerve has become dominant, and both tympaniform membranes are driven by a single column of air and by its turbulence patterns (1,284; see p. 273, **Vocal Control in Parrots**).]

Some findings with unilateral innervation suggest that one side of the syrinx occasionally can produce two well-modulated and harmonically unrelated sounds, but an alternative explanation is that the expiratory air pulses on the denervated side produce a sound that adventitiously mimics a natural sound (see 1,250). The two syringeal sources also can be coupled to interact in a nonlinear fashion, as in the Black-capped Chickadee (*Parus atricapillus*), producing a sound with multiple frequency components that are heterodyne products resulting from cross modulation (1,211).

THREE DISTINCT PATTERNS CORRELATING SOUND PRODUCTION and respiration have been described (321). Some birds produce sounds during continuous expiration, others during rapid, shallow respiratory movements, also producing the sounds during expiration, still others produce sounds during both expiration and inspiration (see, for example, 537). Although falling primarily in the second category, some parrots produce occasional sounds during inspiration, and the latter vocalizations may be included in their repertoires (207).

THE NEURAL CONTROL OF VOCALIZATION is intimately related with respiratory circuits and, in view of the highly conservative nature of the evolution of the nervous system (see pp. 379-386), probably has been derived from them (396). Production of song by the electrical stimulation of discrete brain areas is most effective in the midbrain area spoken of as the torus semicircularis. Most experimenters find the points of lowest threshold to lie in the nucleus intercollicularis, areas of which may coordinate breathing and vocalization. This nucleus is situated medial and adjacent to the nucleus mesencephalicus lateralis pars dorsalis, which is known to be an ascending auditory relay nucleus. Other song regions have been found in the hypothalamus, septum, and archistriatum (512, 1,012; see also pp. 269-277, **Vocal Mimicry and Manipulation**).

VOCALIZATION BY BUDGERIGARS. Eight discrete calls of Budgerigars in the field have been identified by Wyndham (171). A *chirp* call is most common, being given frequently throughout the day, singly or in quick repetition. It may correspond to the Whedelee call of Brockway (67; 1964, Non-reproductive behavior) and it apparently serves partly or largely to signal location or merely presence. A *pre-flight zit* call is given at the start of flight or as a signal of intention of flight and is thought to correspond to the "squaaaaaak" call of Brockway. It also is given frequently during feeding and drinking. An *alarm zit* call is given by individuals that are in danger and cannot escape. An *aggressive ehh* call is an individual call given during agonistic encounters.

A *roosting ehh* call is similar in sound to an *aggressive ehh* but is a flock call given when the birds are settling to an evening roost. *Warbling* and *tuk-tuk* calls are given frequently by breeding pairs, usually by the males, and often during courtship. The *warbling* call is composed of *chirps, zits, tuk-tuk*, and many other elements. *Tuk-tuk* calls, although also occurring during *warbling* sequences, always occur when males are either face-to-face with females or nudging females. *Food-begging* calls are given by nestlings and juveniles for a short time after they leave the nest, in association with other food soliciting behavior. In my experience with 3 broods from one breeding pair, the food-solicitng calls are given during allofeeding (feeding of one individual by another) from the time of hatching and merely gain steadily in amplitude, frequency of repetition of individual notes, and frequency of repetition of the calls, giving the distinct impression of ever greater urgency and emphasis of ‘demand’ for food.

HEARING

THE APPARATUS FOR HEARING consists of three regions, the external auditory meatus, the middle ear, and the inner ear. Airborne sound waves are transmitted by the external auditory meatus and the middle-ear structures to the inner ear fluids, which are forced to oscillate. The induced movements of the basilar membrane, acting as a mechanical stimulus, result in an excitation of the secondary sensory cells, the hair cells. From the cochlea, the auditory information is transmitted to the central nervous system, where the further processing that occurs results in audition and behavioral responses (1,007).

THE EXTERNAL AUDITORY MEATUS OR CANAL begins at the external ear opening and ends bluntly at the cone-shaped tympanic membrane, which is pushed outward by the scapus of the columella. The tympanic cavity (middle ear) is a generally spacious, air-filled cavity in the skull. It is bounded by bone, except for the tympanic membrane, communications with air spaces in the surrounding bone (and thence with the contralateral tympanic cavity, acoustically coupling them), and the opening into the pharyngo-tympanic (Eustacean) tube that leads to the pharynx (air pressure in the two cavities thus is equilibrated).

THE TYMPANIC CAVITY contains a bony ossicle, the columella, which consists of a scapus (shaft or extra columella) fused to an expanded proximal base or footplate. The columella transmits acoustically-induced vibrations of the tympanic membrane to the basilar membrane of the vestibular (oval) window in the lateral wall of the inner ear and thence to its fluids. The tympanic cavity is lined by a mucosa that also covers the inner surface of the tympanic membrane and is reflected to envelop the entire columellar complex (798).

THE EXTERNAL AUDITORY MEATUS generally is a short, often-curved tube, caudal and ventral to the eye at the level of, or a little dorsal to, the gape. It is relatively large in Oscines and parrots, and its main function may be to remove the tympanic membrane from the head surface to a more protected location, allowing it to be larger, thinner, and more delicate (798). The opening to the meatus is oval in shape in Budgerigars, Cockatiels, and lovebirds, and is surrounded and hidden from view by specialized, protective, filamentous, auricular feathers that minimize impedance to the penetration of sound waves and reduce drag caused by turbulence (345, 513, 798). Its diameter is only of the order of a few mm in most birds and its size, like that of the tympanic membrane and the external auditory meatus, is correlated with hearing ability or ecological specializations, rather than only with body or head size (798).

The skin surrounding the opening to the meatus can be drawn forward by a special muscle (the dermo-osseus), whereupon the oval-shaped opening narrows to a perpendicular slit that limits access to the canal (441). The meatus is lined with skin that differs little from the outer epidermis, except for the lack of feathers and the occurrence of more glands (798). [A bird's skin generally is much looser and less elastic than that of a mammal (135).]

THE APPARATUS OF THE TYMPANIC CAVITY, acting as an impedance transformer, makes possible the transformation of a much greater fraction of impinging sound than would occur if the signal were to be transmitted directly from air to cochlear fluids (798). In accomplishing this, the large amplitude, high-speed vibrations of the tympanic membrane are converted into vibrations of small amplitude but great force at the vestibular window. Up to a frequency of 3 kHz, the range of communication and best sensitivity for most birds, the frequency response of the tympanic cavity is within 6dB of that of the 3-ossicle chain of the mammalian ear.

The transfer function of the tympanic cavity of the Ring Dove (*Streptopelia roseogrisea* var. *risoria*) limits high-frequency hearing to about 10 kHz (roll-off rate of 27 dB/octave at 10 kHz), which is the cutoff value for most birds (see 1,007). The very general occurrence of communicating tympanic cavities via connecting air cavities suggests that pressure differentials may be in general use for avian sound localization (798). [The insertion, innervation, and action of the columellar muscle (which, among other functions, acts as a bandpass filter) show a number of similarities to those of the tympanic muscle of crocodiles and of the stapedius muscle of mammals (see 798).]

THE INNER EAR functions both in hearing and equilibration. Hearing occurs in the cochlear organ and equilibration in the vestibular organ. The cochlear organ is of particular interest, inasmuch as it contains some structural features that appear to be common to all birds but also others that differ among species. It also is the site of the greatest histological differences between the inner ears of birds and mammals. The inner ear is composed of two parts, the membranous labyrinth and the bony labyrinth, the latter enclosing the former. The membranous labyrinth is filled with the fluid endolymph, while the spaces between the membranes and bony labyrinths contain the fluid perilymph (799).

THE BONY LABYRINTH protects the delicate structures within the inner ear from physical trauma and acts as a barrier of low permeability that retains in place the large liquid pool of perilymph. It consists of 3 divisions: the bony semicircular canals caudally, the cochlea rostrally, and the connecting vestibule. The latter contains the utricle and saccule of the membranous labyrinth, while the bony semicircular canals contain its semicircular ducts.

THE COCHLEA OF BIRDS does not possess the coiled configuration found in mammals. It is a flattened tube, almost straight in very small birds (including many passerines) but slightly curved in medium-sized ones, such as the Rock Pigeon and domestic fowl. There are two fibrous membranes within the cochlea, the basilar membrane and the tectorial membrane, the movements of both of which activate the sensory (hair) cells. The two sensory structures of the cochlea are the macula of the lagena and the basilar papilla. The latter is composed of the basilar membrane that supports the neuroepithelium, consisting of sensory hair cells and supporting cells. The hair cells are provided with many stereocilia, which protrude from a cuticular plate that reaches deep into the cytoplasm, and one intact kinocilium located outside the cuticular plate (1,007).

THE COCHLEAR DUCT is closed off above the papilla by the well-vascularized tegmentum vasculosum (which probably maintains the high potassium concentration of the endolymph). There are two openings in the lateral wall of the bony labyrinth, the vestibular window, closed off by the footplate or base of the columella, and the cochlear (round) window, closed off by the secondary tympanic membrane. Both windows are located at the base of the cochlea and both open onto the tympanic cavity.

THE MEMBRANOUS LABYRINTH contains the saccule, the utricle, the sacculocochlear duct, the utriculosaccular duct, the endolymphatic duct, and the vestibular end of the cochlear duct. It resembles the membranous labyrinth of mammals in being a closed epithelial tube filled with endolymph and divided into compartments containing the neuroepithelia and other highly-specialized cell groups.

THE PERILYMPH surrounds the membranous labyrinth and fills the space between it and the bony labyrinth. It conducts the vibrations set up by airborne sound in the tympanic membrane and columella to the endolymph and basilar membrane, the maximum displacement of which depends upon the vibrational frequency. The perilymph appears to be a blood ultrafiltrate. The endolymph, which fills the cavity of the membranous labyrinth, on the other hand, is not a blood ultrafiltrate. A positive resting potential of

10-15 mV exists between the cochlear endolymph and the perilymph. Though this (endocochlear) potential is closely related to the function of the sensory hair cells, its precise role has not been established. On the other hand, the cochlear microphonic potential, which is an image of the sound waves and is responsive to both tone frequency and intensity, generally is considered to be the receptor potential of the hair cells; there is depolarization for an upward movement (rarefaction phase of a sound wave) of the basilar membrane, and hyperpolarization for a downward movement (799, 1,007). The avian ear is said to be almost inaccessible to bone-conducted sound because of the air spaces that largely surround the inner bone structure (500, 513).

TONOTOPIC PROJECTION---COCHLEAR NUCLEI. The overall organization of the auditory pathways is the same in all reptiles and birds, and the avian telencephalic auditory pathways appear to be organized in a manner similar to that of their visual ectostriatal system (1,236; see pp. 355-361, **Avian Visual Pathways**). Although the basic construction of the external and middle ears in birds is more like that of their reptilian ancestors than is that of mammals, the design has evolved to the extent that the inner ear and central nervous system can perform recognition and localization to a very high degree (798). While recognition of a unique and stereotyped signal, even if acoustically complex, is a relatively trivial task for a specialized network, recognition of multiplicity and variability is not trivial, particularly if there is partial overlap of ranges of parameters among different sounds.

The evolutionary solution to the problem of acoustic signal recognition is to represent and analyze a multiplicity of variable signals in neuronal maps. These are organized in such a way that neurons representing a continuum of important stimulus variables are laid out along spatial dimensions within the anatomical structure. All available data from birds and mammals favor the view that a basic organizational feature of auditory maps is tonotopy, which is projected from the cochlea onto most of the central auditory structures in the brain. This tonotopy is a simple means of monitoring and comparing frequencies systematically.

The evolution of the particular mechanisms in the central auditory system that relate to this tonotopic organization may have been a basic need for recognition of wide-band sounds. There are, however, significant constraints on the analysis of vocal sounds by this method, once the specific maps have been formed in the course of evolution. Inasmuch as learned vocalizations are shaped by audition, including self feedback, these auditory analytical constraints also may impose constraints on the design of species-specific vocal sounds (1,205).

The primary auditory fibers preserve the orderly sequence of innervation on the basilar membrane of the cochlea as they travel from the inner ear to the acoustic ganglion and project ipsilaterally to two nuclei in the medulla, the nucleus magnocellularis and the nucleus angularis; this projection is tonotopic and the projection pattern suggests that the nucleus magnocellularis and part of the nucleus angularis correspond to the mammalian ventral cochlear nucleus, with the remainder of the nucleus angularis corresponding to the mammalian dorsal cochlear nucleus (see 1,091).

The medullary projection also is tonotopic in mammals (and crocodilians; 1,048), and the method of frequency analysis also is the same (387, 441). Not only is a tonotopic organization preserved through the relays of the avian auditory system up to the telencephalic level, but some cells in the system respond selectively to complex properties of sound stimuli (see 1,091). In fact, there are two functionally distinct regions in the mid-brain auditory area of the Barn Owl. In addition to a tonotopically organized region, there is a space-mapped region. In the latter, limited-field units that respond to frequencies at the high end of the owl's auditory range (5.0-8.7 kHz) are located exclusively along the lateral and anterior borders of the auditory area. These units are arranged according to the azimuths and elevations of their receptive fields, in essence producing a physiological map of auditory space (1,214).

Representations are taken even a step further in the Mustache Bat (*Pteronotus parnellii ribiginosus*), in which neurons tuned to different target ranges are arranged systematically along the rostrocaudal axis of the area that processes frequency-modulated signals according to the delays to which they respond best. Target range then is represented in terms of cortical organization--an odotopic representation (1,224).

The avian nucleus angularis and the nucleus magnocellularis project bilaterally to the nucleus laminaris which projects, in turn, to the superior olive, the nucleus of the lateral lemniscus, and the nucleus mesencephalicus lateralis dorsalis, the homologue of the mammalian inferior colliculus. The nucleus laminaris may be the homologue of the mammalian medial superior olive, for in birds that rely on acoustic localization of prey, such as owls, the nucleus laminaris is particularly large. Fibers from the nucleus mesencephalicus lateralis dorsalis project bilaterally to the nucleus ovoidalis of the thalamus and thence, still tonotopically organized, ipsilaterally to Field L (see below, **Field L**, and pp. 270, 351) of the caudal medial neostriatum. In one view, this appears to be the only telencephalic region that receives a direct auditory thalamic projection, which suggests a difference between birds and reptiles (and mammals), since the latter have both pallial and striatal auditory projection areas (see 1,091); in another view, the avian nucleus ovoidalis also projects to the paleostriatum (1,236), which is striatal, in which case such a difference would not exist.

[Within the nucleus angularis, basal fibers terminate most caudal and dorsal, apical fibers most rostral and ventral, and middle fibers in intermediate positions. Within the nucleus magnocellularis, basal fibers terminate most rostral and medial, and apical fibers most caudal and lateral (1,007).]

FIELD L consists of at least 3 congruent tonotopic subdivisions that appear to be organized in a manner similar to higher order auditory cortices in mammals. Many units in Field L of European Starlings are highly selective in their response to a restricted subset of sounds in conspecific calls and song, as opposed to broad tuning curves in a restricted area of the frontal neostriatum (see 1,269). Field L, in turn, projects to the hyperstriatum ventrale and to part of the archistriatum. The hyperstriatum ventrale, in turn, projects to a portion of the parolfactory lobe (nucleus x) and to the nucleus robustus of the archistriatum. Both nucleus x and the nucleus robustus give rise to long descending pathways to the thalamus and midbrain, and fibers from the nucleus robustus terminate directly on the hypoglossal motor nucleus, which innervates the syrinx. Additional pathways interconnect Field L with other regions of the telencephalon (see 1,048, 1,236).

[Little is known of the auditory capacities of reptiles but the basic organization of the reptilian auditory system is not dissimilar from that of mammals. Primary auditory fibers with cell bodies in the intraotic ganglion project to two medullary nuclei, the nucleus angularis and the nucleus magnocellularis, which form part of a medullary nuclear complex--the auditory tubercle. Thence, fibers from the nucleus angularis project to 4 sites: to the ipsilateral superior olive, to the contralateral nuclei of the trapezoid body, to the lateral lemniscus, and to the central nucleus of the torus semicircularis. The latter nucleus projects, in turn, to a region of the dorsal thalamus known as the nucleus medialis in lizards and as the reuniens in crocodilians. Finally, thalamic auditory projections ascend to the telencephalon, terminating principally in a medial region of the dorsal ventricular ridge (see pp. 350, 351, **The Dorsal Ventricular Ridge of the Telencephalon**) but also elsewhere in it. There is a degree of tonotopic organization of the torus semicircularis in *Caiman* (see 1,048, 1,091). The nucleus angularis of crocodilians is highly differentiated, and similar subdivisions are recognizable in a laminar region of the cochlear nucleus of birds (see 890).]

THE VESTIBULAR LABYRINTH consists of the saccule, utricle, and semicircular ducts; both of the former contain statoconal organs. This labyrinth contains 6 separate sensory structures, one in the saccule, 2 in the utricle, and one in each of the 3 ampullae of the semicircular ducts. The function of the vestibular organ as a whole is that of equilibration, and the sensory structures are responsive to angular and linear accelerations and positional changes. It generally is accepted that the semicircular ducts are sensitive to angular accelerations, whereas the statoconial organs are responsive to linear accelerations and to gravity, but these functions are not separated *in toto*. No information is available regarding the composition of the vestibular endolymph of birds, but it is expected to be similar to that of the Guinea Pig (*Cavia cobaya*), with a high concentration of potassium (799).

THE MACULA OF THE LAGENA, the neuroepithelium at the slightly-expanded blind end of the cochlear duct, seems to be primarily a vestibular organ. Like the basilar papilla, it is composed of a group of sensory hair cells and supporting cells. The majority of fibers of the lagenar nerve project to vestibular nuclei but some project to cerebellar and auditory nuclei (799). The possession of an auditory function, however, is not established by physiological evidence (1,007).

THE HEARING OF BUDGERIGARS ranges from 40 to 14,000 Hz. Parrots, in general, have unusually long cochleae and hear considerably higher sound frequencies than almost all other birds (155, 345). The frequency discrimination of Budgerigars surpasses ours and is greatest in the range of 2-4 kHz. That also is the range in which the Budgerigar's hearing is most sensitive and in which most of the energy of its vocalizations is concentrated (109, 119). It generally is true that the area of best auditory performance of birds usually is closely matched to the range of sound frequencies that the birds themselves produce (494).

Budgerigars can distinguish clearly between sounds differing in frequency by only 0.3-0.7% (see S. Knecht, 1940, in 345 and R.J. Dooling and J.C. Saunders, 1973, in 513). Barn Owls, which show good sensitivity over a wide frequency range, are almost equally perceptive, and have good frequency discrimination over the range 3½-10 kHz (see 799 and D.G. Quine and M. Konishi, 1974, in 513). The frequency range in which single avian species can receive and process auditory signals generally is narrower than in mammals. Most birds do not hear ultrasonic vibrations and they are less sensitive than Man to tones in the upper and lower extremes of their hearing range (418).

VISION

THE EYES AND ORBITS. The eyes of the Budgerigar, and birds in general, have reached a state of perfection found in no other animal (28; see also pp. 355-367, beginning with **Avian Visual Pathways**). Their large size necessitates large orbits, with a consequent caudal displacement of the brain. Typically avian eyes are so large relative to the skull that they almost meet in the middle of the head and usually are separated only by a thin body septum. In all species they are placed laterally within the skull. Even in species frequently described as having frontally-directed eyes, such as owls (Strigiformes), the optical axes may diverge by 55° (800).

In the great majority of birds, for example, Columbiformes, Psittaciformes, and Galliformes, the eye is flattened, as in lizards, with an antero-posterior axis that is much shorter than the diameter. Birds that require greater visual acuity, including some of the passerines and most members of the Falconiformes, have "globular" eyes, with more nearly equal vertical and horizontal axes (416). Some eagles have eyes with axial lengths that are so great that the eye is almost tubular in shape (405). The posterior segment of the eye, however, always is hemispherical. In all birds, the globe of the eye fits tightly into the orbit and the eye muscles are reduced to thin ribbons. In many, if not all, birds there typically is a marked nasal-temporal asymmetry which may serve to maximize the width of the panoramic field. The pupil generally is spherical but there are reports of slightly ellipsoidal pupils and slit pupils (441, 800).

In the Budgerigar, Cockatiel, and members of the genus *Cyanoramphus* the zygomatic processes (cheekbones) join to a closed orbital or sclerotic ring, which may be a primitive feature, inasmuch as scleral ossicles also occur in reptiles (the ring is open in lovebirds and most other parrots). The sclerotic ring consists of 12 overlapping scleral ossicles (compact, bony plates) in front of each eyeball, surrounding the thin cornea (31, 441). These rings stiffen the concavity of the eyeball at the corneoscleral junction and presumably strengthen the skull across the orbit, which is important when biting hard (819). They thereby reduce or prevent deformation of the cornea as the eye accommodates (177, 339).

The avian eye, like that of all vertebrates, has just two principal refractive components: the relatively simple convexo-concavo cornea, and the more complex biconvex lens. The total refractive power of the eye of the Tawny Owl (*Strix aluco*) is divided approximately equally between the lens and the cornea, whereas in the Rock Pigeon the refractive power of the cornea is over twice that of the lens (800). It is not yet possible to discern any general rule that would account for the comparative refractive powers of these two structures.

The central part of the avian lens is surrounded by an annular pad of disputed function, the "Ringwulst," a feature otherwise found only in reptiles (405, 800). Both the size and shape of the lens show marked interspecific differences, and this presumably is related to differences in the refractive powers, accommodation ranges, and visual fields of the eyes (800).

A distinct prefrontal bone, which is so prominent in many birds, does not exist above the eye of the Budgerigar (441). The outer layer of the eye, the sclera, contains cartilage, as it also does in reptiles. It is opaque in all regions except at its transparent exposed surface, where it unites with other tissues to form the cornea (513). For a description of the retina and retinal topography, see reference 800.

THE EYELIDS---LACRIMAL APPARATUS---PUPIL---LENS---BINOCULAR FIELD. There are 3 functional eyelids in birds, as in many reptiles. The upper and lower lids move vertically and close only during sleep. When open, they typically cover the whole of the anterior portion of the eye except the cornea, giving the impression that the eyes are smaller than they actually are (800). In general, closure of the eye is brought about mainly by the movement of the lower lid. Though feathered in many birds, the lids are unfeathered in parrots (800). The nictitating membrane moves mediolaterally. It covers the eye in flight while, at the same time, allowing the bird full vision (513, 800). Both the upper and lower lids of the Budgerigar bear setae or cilia. These are short, bristle-like lashes made up of specialized contour feathers with a stiff rachis on which the barbs generally are restricted to the proximal end (23, 441, 795).

The lacrimal glands provide lubricant for the eyelids and nourishment for the cornea, while the lacrimal ducts drain the tears from the conjunctival sac into the lacrimal sac, lacrimal canal, and nasal chamber. The pupil of the iris, a pigmented, continuous extension of the choroid, is controlled by circular constrictor muscle fibers and radial dilator fibers. The lenses of parrots are almost flat in front and highly convex behind (155). Budgerigars and other parrots have the smallest binocular fields yet found in birds (usually between 6° and 10°). The only exception to this generalization is the Owl Parrot or Kakapo of New Zealand (23).

HEART AND HEART RATE

Avian hearts are 4-chambered, as in mammals, but the atria are relatively small and somewhat indistinct from each other externally (441). The left ventricle is 2-3 times thicker than the right one but the left atrium is smaller than that on the right. Avian hearts are proportionately larger (1.4-2 times as large, weight for weight), more elongate, and more powerful than those of mammals. In addition, the anatomical pathways by which the excitatory impulses spread to different parts of the avian heart are more specialized than in mammals (516).

The relative size of the avian heart and its rate of beating vary inversely with size: the smaller birds with higher metabolic rates have the largest and fastest beating hearts (339, 515). Thus, hummingbirds have the largest hearts of all birds, weight for weight. For example, the relatively very large heart of the Scintillant Hummingbird (*Selasphorus scintilla*) comprises 2.4% of total body weight (see 320), whereas the value in the Rock Pigeon is 1.02-1.38% (1,002) and in the Ostrich only 0.098% (28). Avian cardiac muscle cells (3-5 micra in diameter) are only 10-20% of the size of those of mammals and have no transverse (T) tubules (see 1,002).

There appears to be little correlation between avian heart rate and arterial blood pressure (515). But since the avian arterial system is relatively non-compliant, and cardiac output is high, arterial blood pressure also is high; kinetic energy of flow may raise arterial root pressure 6 mm of Hg above left ventricular pressure. Birds have powerful pressor reflexes; these regulate arterial pressures at normal levels by decreasing the heart rate and thereby the cardiac output when arterial pressure is too high, or induce tachycardia during hypotension. The arterial pulse pressure--the difference between peak systolic and minimum diastolic pressure--is 30-46 mm Hg in the Rock Pigeon (see 515, 1,002).

As a rule, the "resting" heart beats less rapidly (but see 442) in birds than in mammals of comparable weight (320, 321, 423). Avian cardiac outputs tend to be higher when compared on the same basis (630). In the case of Budgerigars, the relative cardiac output appears to be more than 7 times the maximum value for Man and the dog (330). Examination of the distribution of blood suggests that this higher cardiac output in birds reflects adaptations to flight, with very large volumes (approximately 75% in the anesthetized duck) going to the wings, the flight muscles, and the head. A large number of anastomoses play a vital role in providing an adequate level of cerebral perfusion (630).

A slightly lower peripheral resistance in birds compared to mammals does not compensate entirely for the high cardiac output, with the consequence that an elevated arterial pressure is required to drive the high rates of flow. On the other hand, high pressures are not seen in the pulmonary circulation, suggesting a low vascular resistance of the avian lung (630).

When related to cardiac weight, rather than bodily weight there may be very little difference in the cardiac rates of birds and mammals (423). The resting cardiac rate in Budgerigars is 5.0-8.33 Hz. The domestic fowl cardiac rate is lowest at night and increases with exposure to light and exercise (516). The cardiac rate of the flying bat is comparable to that of a flying bird of similar size; the bat's smaller cardiac output is compensated for by its higher hematocrit (60%, compared to about 48% in the House Sparrow; 642).

The cardiac rate is synchronized with wingbeat during flight, the ratio in different species apparently being either 1:1 or 1:2 (320). The increase during short flights is by a factor of 2-4, with the lower values tending to be for the smaller species (320, 423). In Rock Pigeons the increase is from 2.75 Hz at rest to 9.4-11.1 Hz during stable flight (324; 339, 1,002). [Both cardiac and respiratory rates are of only limited diagnostic value for illnesses (135).]

MANDIBLES, ORAL CAVITY, TONGUE, AND FOOD MANIPULATION

JAW APPARATUS. By definition, the upper jaw of vertebrates is the maxilla and the lower jaw, the mandible. However, because of the absence of teeth and other specializations in birds, both the upper and lower jaws traditionally are referred to as "mandibles" (28). The jaw apparatus consists of the horny bill or rhamphotheca (see p. 97), the bony parts of the mandibles and skull, the system of binding ligaments and articulations, and the jaw muscles and their innervation. This apparatus in birds is highly developed and mechanically refined. In many other vertebrates, including Man, the mobility of the whole jaw apparatus operates with only one paired joint between both mandibles and the braincase, whereas in birds, a complicated system of bony bars, joints, and flexion zones have developed (627).

The generalized type of adult avian jaw apparatus consists of 4 bony units, namely the lower mandible, the upper jaw-braincase-palatine complex, a pair of pterygoid bones, and a pair of quadrate bones. It is formed by the fusion of over 40 embryonic bones of the upper mandible, the braincase and interorbital region, the ethmoid-prefrontal-frontal region, the palatine bones, the vomer, and the pair of jugal bars.

THE UPPER MANDIBLE is a rigid, more or less triangular block that is moved as a whole. It consists of a fusion of: a pair of processes of the premaxillary and nasal bones and, in some birds, the rostral part of the nasal-interorbital septum (designated collectively as the median dorsal bar); the main part of the maxillary bone and processes of both the nasal bone and the premaxillary bone (designated collectively as paired ventral bars); the maxillary process of the nasal bone, the tip of which is fused with the maxillary bone (designated collectively as paired nasal bars); and the bony tip. The upper mandible forms the anterior portion of the palate, the so-called "horny palate," which is particularly well developed among groups of graminivorous (grass-eating) birds (322). In nearly all birds, the skeleton of the lower mandible has evolved as a single bony unit derived from the fusion of 12 embryonic bony primordia (627).

ARTICULATION OF MANDIBLES----POWERFUL LEVERAGE IN PARROTS. The upper mandible of parrots is massive and closes over the small lower mandible. It is attached to the cranium by a flexible naso-frontal or transverse craniofacial hinge and the palatines. These allow it to move up and down freely (kinesis), permitting very wide gapes, as in yawning and biting. The flexible attachment of the upper jaw with the cranium is little noticeable when eating, but when climbing (see p. 98) the bill is said to open with a simultaneous parting of both mandibles (819). As a consequence of the hinging of the upper mandible in medium-sized parrots (*Charmosyna*, *Poicephalus*), the original flexion zones between the upper mandibles and the braincase, jugal bars, and palatine bones have been transformed into syndesmotic (firmly-bound ligamentous contacts) or synovial joints with cartilaginous enclosures (see 627). Flexion zones have been retained, however, in the Budgerigar and possibly in other small parrots.

The articulation (hinging) of the lower, horseshoe-shaped mandible is like that of reptiles. Its rather loose articulation to the mobile quadrate bone of the skull in parrots allows opening widely, with considerable freedom of rostral (forward) and caudal (backward) movement. The articulating surfaces are not visible beneath the feathers (441). Some portion, at least, of the upper mandible is movable or kinetic in almost all birds (237, 338, 421). When the lower mandible is depressed, opening the mouth, the lower end of the quadrate bone moves forward and this movement is imparted to the zygomatic arch (the maxilla, jugal, and quatratojugal bones), on the one hand, and the pterygopalatal (pterygoid and palatine) bones, on the other. The result is to raise the upper mandible in the cranium. In addition, the dorsum of the upper mandible is attached to the cranium only by the slender ascending processes of the premaxillae, and these are sufficiently flexible to allow the upper mandible to bend upward. [A few carinate birds are virtually akinetic, the upper mandible being quite rigid, and the ratites also show a marked reduction in kinesis (338).]

Freely flexible hinging of the upper mandible of parrots makes possible a leverage greater than that achieved in any other bird, and enables the birds to crush extremely hard seeds and nuts, the sizes of which in the diet appear to be correlated with the size of the bill (see 443). In addition, the independent movements of the mandibles allow a very precise manipulation of food (see p. 98). In this connection, it is speculated that among North American birds, only Evening Grosbeaks (*Coccothraustes vespertinus*) and Carolina Parakeets have or had the ability to crack open cypress cones and other very hard food items (215).

RHAMPHOTHECA. The rhamphotheca or "horny bill" of raptors, granivores, and graminivores is the hard, tough, keratinized and mineralized, olive-gray, epidermal surface covering of both mandibles. It is a modified horny layer that consists of sheets of flattened, keratin-filled cells held together firmly by cell junctions that do not break down. Its shape is basically that of the underlying bone, from which it is separated by thin, fibrous (collagenous) dermis, modified by local thickenings. The presence of the rhamphotheca is vital for seed hulling, since complete removal of it would leave the mandibles incongruent and incapable of interfacing for this action (441, 795). The rhamphotheca grows continually toward the tips and tomia (cutting edges of the mandibles), where it gets worn down (318). The keratin at the tips of Budgerigar mandibles is thicker than elsewhere (441). [It often remains even after skeletal preparation by dermestid beetles has eliminated other non-mineralized tissues (441).]

In Budgerigars, the rhamphotheca is very deeply grooved on the underside of the hook of the upper mandible, producing a corrugated effect (31). Such grooves are arranged in many different patterns in different parrot groups. Furthermore, papillae and ridges of dermis that invade the epidermis commonly are found in the rhamphotheca, palate, and tongue, particularly in lightly cornified regions (318).

The color of the rhamphotheca of many birds, in addition to changes during maturation, is subject to hormonally controlled sexual and seasonal variations, often including "eclipse" seasons. Pigmentation is of two main kinds: that produced by melanins and melanophores that become injected into rhamphothecal cells moving out from areas of proliferation; and yellow, red, and orange carotenoids absorbed from the diet (414, 747). Because of the presence of tactile receptors (see pp. 100-103), the rhamphotheca must be regarded not merely as a covering for the bill but as a true tactile organ (318). In this connection, a definitive topographical representation of the bill region is present in the nucleus prosencephali trigeminalis of the telencephalon of the Rock Pigeon (306, 388).

JAW MUSCLES. Seven pairs of muscles act together on the mandibles of most birds. These are relatively well-developed in Budgerigars and other parrots. Inasmuch as the lower mandibular joint of parrots allows a gliding movement (see above), the pterygoid muscle, the largest muscle complex of the entire jaw apparatus, also can effect a rostral translation of the lower mandible. Moreover, since the upper mandible is used in climbing (see p. 98), and as a powerful counterpart of the lower mandible in chewing, a large part of the pterygoid muscle is not attached to the lower mandible but inserts on the ventral surface of the braincase; it is specialized to hold or lower the upper mandible. In addition, the ethmomandibularis muscle, which is characteristic of the parrots, has an insertion on the medial surface of the lower mandible, far from its fulcrum. This is a prerequisite for powerful biting forces, and it allows special rostral movements of the lower jaw, which are important in parrot chewing (627).

CLIMBING. As is typical of all parrots, Budgerigars use the bill to assist in climbing upward and downward, and it may be that the short neck and markedly hinged upper mandible are adaptations for tripodal progression (819; crossbills, *Loxia*, which are food specialists on the seeds of spruce, *Picea*, also use this method; 309). In climbing upward, the upper mandible is hooked repeatedly over higher supports. The bill having taken purchase, the muscular neck than "strides" in coordination with the leg movements (3, 819). To climb downward, a support below and to one side is grasped. Then the bird lets go with its feet and lets its body fall until it hangs vertically below its head. The feet then regrasp some support and the performance is repeated (3). Lateral movements along vertical surfaces are achieved in a similar manner.

ORAL CAVITY---SALIVARY GLANDS---TONGUE, AND FOOD MANIPULATION. The oral cavity and pharynx are lined by a stratified squamous epithelium, which is keratinized in areas that are subject to abrasion. An almost continuous layer of salivary glands, which have numerous openings into the oral and pharyngeal cavities, lie in the connective tissue beneath the epithelium. Each gland consists of a variable number of lobules, each lobule being composed of many secretory tubules that open into a common cavity (620).

Avian lingual adaptations fall into three main categories; adaptations for collecting food, manipulating food, and swallowing food. In any species, it usually is possible to identify one of these adaptations as being responsible primarily for the form of the tongue, although several adaptations exist side-by-side in most instances (see 620). Whereas most birds do not have lingual muscles, the bulk of the parrot tongue consists of intrinsic muscles (441), though fat and cavernous vascular tissues also are present (620). The tip of the tongue of Budgerigars is smooth, except for several radiating shallow grooves (31, 441).

As with many other parrots that feed on fruits and seeds, Budgerigars have a short, thick (only slightly protrusible), muscular, prehensile tongue. As in most parrots, it ends rostrally in a dilated tip supported on a narrower neck. Within the tip are the entoglossal bones with their associated muscles. The parrot tongue allows the manipulation of foods with great dexterity, with a range of movements encompassing rolling a seed into any position to investigate or crack it (135, 442). The tip referred to above is used much like a human finger tip to hold an object against the upper mandible or its palatal notch, while the knife-sharp edge of the lower mandible is free to bite into it (see also p. 99, **Dehusking Seeds**, and A.H. Garrod, 1874, in 441).

When the bill is shut, the dorsal surface of the tongue is applied to the palate; its form consequently is complementary to that of the palate (620). The surface of the tongue is covered with a particularly strong cornified epithelium that is developed maximally on the upper side. The club-shaped tongues of many parrots are adapted for testing special foods (322). Parrots are distinguished from all other birds by the shapes of their hyoid bones (the bones that provide support for the tongue, anchorage for its muscles, and an attachment for the larynx) and an elaborate musculature suspension of the hyoid apparatus. In Budgerigars, in particular, there also is an inseparable fusion of the basihyal and urohyal bones, such that they function as a single bone (441). The short, gently-curved hyoid horns are consistent with the limited ability of Budgerigars to protrude the tongue.

TONGUE AND PALATE STRUCTURE AND PHYLOGENY. Tongue structure may be useful in elucidating phylogenetic relationships between parrots, because it is conservative among closely related species but differs between higher taxa (larger groups). These differences allow one to deduce the sequences in which the changes in structure are likely to have occurred (31). The structure of the lower part of the skull, particularly of the palate, also preserves ancestral traits of some phylogenetic validity, as they are little affected by the environment and, therefore, little acted upon by selective forces (155). The floor of the cranium also is suggested as a fertile area for study in this regard (487).

Caution may be in order, though, in drawing conclusions about affinities based on the common possession of a paleognathous palate. If this were merely a result of the embryonic condition being retained into adulthood (neoteny), in derivation from a neognathous ancestor, it could theoretically develop in many kinds of birds. The possession of a paleognathous palate by the ratites, for example, might be of this origin (190, 504, 575; see also T. Edinger, 1942, in 487). For detailed discussions of this complex issue, see references 574, 587, and 617.

DEHUSKING SEEDS. Removal of the husks from seeds involves special kinds of manipulations that have developed in many graminivores (322). Thus, the tip of the parrot tongue generally steadies the seed against the broad, ridged underside of the upper mandible, much like a finger tip. Meanwhile, the front cutting edge of the lower mandible peels away the seed coat (1), a process that requires the independent movement of the upper and lower jaws, along with the coordination of the tongue (441). The palate bears two prominent, well-vascularized, fleshy pads, forming a palatal notch against which the tongue can hold an object (441).

MECHANICAL EVENTS OF FEEDING during pecking in the Rock Pigeon consist in principle of 8 phases: a preparatory phase consisting of visually-guided search behavior (arousal phase) resulting in approach and fixation of the seed (orienting phase); a final approach or peck phase characterized by head descent and eye closure; a grasp phase in which the seed actually is seized between the tips of the mandibles; a repositioning or stationing phase which occurs when particularly large seeds are not exactly in the preferred position to elicit the next throw phase for transport; a transport or mandibulation phase in which seeds are transported through the mouth; a first collection phase in which food stays on the base of the tongue; a swallowing phase; and a 2nd collection phase in which food stays in the rostral esophagus (see 802).

NEURAL CONTROL OF FEEDING. Some aspects of the neural control of seed manipulation have been elucidated by a neurobehavioral analysis of the temporal organization of feeding in Rock Pigeons. These studies indicate that mandibulation requires about 100-150 msec and is initiated and maintained by contact of the grain with the tip of the bill. From comparisons of the sensory control and time course of mandibulation with the receptive field characteristics and adaptive properties of tactile units of the trigeminal system, it could be suggested that the nucleus basalis and the main sensory trigeminal nucleus contain neurons that signal the presence of a kernel of grain at the tip of the bill, provide complementary information about its positions and movements within the buccal cavity, and monitor the displacements of the mandibles (388).

There apparently is no trigeminal sensory innervation of the avian tongue, only of the mandibles and pharyngeal cavity (388). The lingual nerve is the sensory nerve of the avian tongue, supplying afferent fibers to the entire organ. The laryngolingual ramus of the hypoglossal nerve innervates the extrinsic (via fibers from the spinal elements) and intrinsic (via fibers from the brainstem) muscles of the tongue (632).

MECHANORECEPTORS AND THERMORECEPTORS

Cells that are sensitive to pressure, touch, and deep touch or vibration (Herbst, Merkel, and Grandry corpuscles or bodies; 343, 418) are referred to as "mechanoreceptors." These occur widely in the avian body, including the buccal and pharyngeal cavities (322; 343). In the latter locations, they enhance the ability of parrots to feel the seed parts as they manipulate them. The palatal pads on the roof of the mouth (see p. 99) appear to aid in these maneuvers (most birds have no soft palate; 520). Some avian mechanoreceptors referred to as "Merkel's corpuscles," are smaller in general than those of the Grandry type (see below) and are located more superficially. They are widespread in various regions of the skin, tongue, and bill of all species (418).

[Gottschaldt and Kräft (801) have proposed to call all variants of specialized cells that occur in vertebrate mechanoreceptors "terminal cells," indicative of their location at the sensory nerve terminals. The traditional name "Merkel cell," commonly is employed to refer to slowly-adapting mechanoreceptors in the dermis of the bill just below the epithelium (1,006). Following the proposal of Gottschaldt and Kräft, the term, "Merkel cell," should be used only for their mammalian intra-epidermal variants in secondary, slowly-adapting mechanoreceptors, and the term "Grandry cell" only for the particular variant that occurs in the classical Grandry corpuscle, as done in the following (see 801).]

On the other hand, Grandry's corpuscles appear to occur only in ducks, geese, some granivorous songbirds, and owls, principally in the dermis of the rhamphotheca. They seem to be topographically associated with Herbst corpuscles but generally are smaller and lie at more superficial locations in the dermis, close underneath the epithelium (28, 343, 386, 418, 801). They function in detecting the speed components of mechanical stimuli (801).

The most significant morphological criterion for determining the functional properties of a mechanoreceptor appears not to be its size, shape, or location, but the manner in which the sensory nerve endings are connected directly to specific, non-nervous receptor structures that are derived from the nervous sheath cells and connective tissue elements (801). Comparative observations on tissue receptors in amphibians, reptiles (in which 4 types have been distinguished), birds, and mammals have shown that such structures appear to be necessary for the transfer of mechanical stimuli to the mechanoreceptor and are lacking in thermoreceptors (880). With respect to function, the presence or absence of a capsule is perhaps the least significant aspect, structurally, of an avian mechanoreceptor. Thus, both Herbst corpuscles and, say, muscle spindles have a well-developed capsule, but very different response properties. Conversely, Ruffini endings (see p. 102) in the dermis of the bill of geese lack a distinct capsular structure, yet have similar response properties to the Golgi tendon organs, which are encapsulated (801).

HERBST LAMELLATED CORPUSCLES are mechanoreceptors that respond to acceleration components in vibratory stimuli in the frequency range of at least

50-2,000 Hz. They are perhaps the most widely-distributed mechanoreceptors in the avian body, occurring everywhere in the glabrous and feathered integument, between muscles and connective tissue surrounding the bones of the leg, in lacunae (small cavities) in bones, in tendons, along blood vessels, in the basal portion of the touch papillae of the bill tip, in the rhamphothecal dermis, and in joint capsules. They tend to be most numerous at the tip of the bill and tongue.

Herbst corpuscles are involved in many control functions, such as arranging and cleaning the plumage and adapting it to the varying requirements of thermoregulation, breeding behavior, and the aerodynamics in flight. They are incapable of coding either the speed or the amplitude of mechanical displacements, because these components are attenuated by high-pass filter functions of the auxiliary receptor structures; the latter transmit only acceleration components (801, 1,006).

The Herbst corpuscles in the bill appear to be the most functionally versatile array, their number and locations apparently being related to the manner in which the bill is used in tactile exploration during feeding. Thus, they are found in lacunae in the premaxillary and dental bones of charadriiforms and the distal parts of the bones of the bill of anseriforms. In feathered skin they are present primarily at the base of contour feather follicles. The Herbst corpuscles present in the interosseus membrane between the tibiotarsus and fibula provide sensitivity to vibrations transmitted through the air and the ground independently of hearing (318, 322; 343, 345, 386, 418, 801).

Herbst corpuscles differ only slightly from mammalian Vater-Pacinian corpuscles, with which they conform functionally and share many physiological properties (386, 418). They always possess a characteristic arrangement of neural and non-neural structural components, the sensory nerve ending in the center of the corpuscle being enclosed by cells that form a lamellar system around it. In addition, this lamellar system usually is surrounded by a wide space, which in turn is demarcated externally by a distinct capsule and contains a circularly-arranged system of collagen fibers.

The sensory nerve terminal usually is oval in transverse section and is embedded completely in an inner core or bulb of two opposing rows of 8-30 pairs of Schwann cells of specialized structure and unusual orientation of polarity. The myelinated axon of Herbst corpuscles often parallels the skin surface and loses its myelin sheath before entering the inner bulb. As in all mechano-receptive nerve endings, the receptor axon in the Herbst corpuscle typically contains many mitochondria, lysosomes, multivesicular bodies, etc. The morphology of the transducer sites suggests that axon processes are deflected by displacements of their specialized Schwann-cell lamellae, which stretch the receptor membrane, and are returned to their original position by the inherent elasticity of their microfilaments (801, 1,006).

RECEPTORS THAT DETECT SPEED COMPONENTS OF MECHANICAL STIMULI include those in feathered skin, Grandry corpuscles, and structurally related "terminal cell" receptors. Such receptors adapt rapidly to stimuli and their responses always are restricted to the movement or displacement part of mechanical stimuli. Although rapidly-adapting mechanoreceptors have been reported in electrophysiological studies on the bill and feathered skin of several domesticated avian species, there is considerable uncertainty over how many types of such receptors exist in avian feathered skin and particularly about the morphology of these receptors. In fact, birds are unique among vertebrates in the morphological variety of the cutaneous receptors that incorporate specialized terminal cells (801).

Two types of rapidly-adapting mechano-sensitive receptors have been found in the dermis of both domestic fowl and ducks. About 50% of all mechano-sensitive units of the bills of geese, including about 2/3rds of the rapidly-adapting units, were found to be speed-sensitive (these are referred to as "Grandry units") and distinct from the speed-insensitive but vibration-sensitive Herbst corpuscle afferents. Differences in the threshold and speed sensitivity were accounted for by the varying size of individual Grandry corpuscles. The latter consist of orderly stacks of 2-12 specialized cells (10-40 micra in diameter), between which are sandwiched the disc-like terminals of an afferent nerve fiber, the entire complex being enclosed by Schwann cells, and innervated by a single (shared or unshared) myelinated fiber.

Electron-optical studies have revealed that Grandry cells, as well as the terminal cells occurring in other receptor associations, share a number of cytological features with mammalian Merkel cells. However, Grandry cells, and almost certainly all other kinds of cells associated with mechanoreceptors, are auxiliary receptor structures that do not generate receptor potentials; the mechano-electric transduction must take place directly at the sensory nerve endings themselves. This probably takes place by mechanical deformation of the axon processes, with the generation of a receptor potential essentially as in Herbst corpuscles.

[In contrast to the situation in other vertebrates, most of the intra-epithelial nerves of reptile mechanoreceptors terminate, not as free tapered nerve endings, but as relatively large terminal expansions. The very compact lamellations of the Schwann cells of sheathed lizard mechanoreceptors have no interposition of connective tissue elements comparable to the inner core lamellations of avian Herbst corpuscles; the looser lamellation of caimans with interlamellar neural tissue is comparable to the inner core lamellation of the Vater-Pacinian corpuscles in the skin of mammals (see 880).]

Other terminal cell receptors with presumed rapidly-adapting response properties found in the bills of anseriform birds are the "terminal cell column receptors" (first called "Merkel cell column receptors") and the "diffuse" (diffusely organized) terminal cell receptors (also called "subepithelial Merkel cell receptors") found in the palatine mucosa and the skin of domestic fowl (801).

RECEPTORS THAT DETECT AMPLITUDE COMPONENTS IN MECHANICAL STIMULI include Ruffini nerve endings, "branched" terminal cell receptors, Golgi tendon organs, and muscle spindles. These must be able to respond to static stimulus conditions, that is, they must have slowly-adapting response properties. These are found in small numbers in feathered skin, perhaps in the bills of domestic ducks, and in the tips of the bills of geese, either underneath the horny plates at the tips of the mandibles or directly within the touch papillae of the bill-tip organ (see paragraph immediately below). As in mammalian skin, slowly-adapting receptors in avian skin may show a marked sensitivity to temperature; most of them have temperature responses that resemble those of the specific cold receptors in mammalian skin and mammalian slowly-adapting cutaneous receptors (see 801).

BILL-TIP ORGAN. In many avian species, the horny substance of the bill tip shelters a unique sense organ, one that may be the most sophisticated of the complex sensory structures that occur in vertebrate skin or its derivatives. In its functional significance, this bill-tip organ--first described in parrots--may be considered as an avian equivalent of the mammalian sinus hair system, Eimer's organ in the mole, or the touch papillae of lizards and the caiman (these papillae contain a wide variety of nerve terminals; 801, 880). The general structure of the bill-tip organ appears to be similar in all avian species in which it is known, namely, in those in which the bill is used to search for, catch, select, or manipulate food, as in parrots and waterfowl.

As described in members of the Anatidae (geese, ducks, and swans), the bill-tip organ consists of arrays of cylindrical "touch papillae" that protrude from the deep dermis underneath the hard, outer, horny tissue at the tips of the mandibles (the "nails"). Their tips reach the free surface at the rostral rims of the mandibles. Each touch papilla consists of a dermal core covered by an epidermal, relatively soft, tubular, horny coat--the papillary horn. Each touch papilla is innervated by a bundle of 30-100 myelinated axons as well as some non-myelinated fibers, about 80% of the former of which terminate on several different kinds of mechanoreceptors (including Herbst and Grandry corpuscles) within each papilla. A very high density of papillae in the bill of the goose, with at least 40 receptors in each, is reflected by a disproportionately large representation area of the bill-tip organ in the forebrain of geese and ducks. [Jerison suggests that maps of the sensory and motor surfaces of the bodies of all vertebrates are repeated again and again in different parts of their brains, enlarged in larger species, following the enlargement of the bodily surfaces that are represented (1,102).]

THERMORECEPTORS are characterized by a spontaneous activity that depends on epidermal temperature over a wide thermal range. Additionally, a phasic response usually is elicited by rapid temperature changes. "Cold receptors" are excited by cooling and inhibited by warming. They have been found in the Rock Pigeon tongue and borders of the bill and less numerously in feathered areas. "Warmth receptors" are excited by warming and inhibited by cooling. They have been found only within the buccal cavity (1,006). It has been suggested that the evolution of thermally sensitive neurons probably has occurred by way of an effect of temperature on the permeability of the cell membranes to cations (1,099).

ASCENDING SOMATOSENSORY PATHWAYS. There is little information on ascending somatosensory pathways to the avian telencephalon. Both the anterior hypostriatum and medial neostriatum caudale are known to be responsive to somatosensory stimuli and the anterior Wulst (see pp. 357, 358, **The Smaller Thalamofugal Visual Pathway**) of owls is characterized by a somatosensory map of the contralateral toes. This information reaches the Wulst via projections from the nucleus dorsalis intermedius ventralis anterior, a thalamic relay nucleus that receives its input from nuclei in the dorsal spinal column. Although there appear to be primarily sensory areas within various portions of the Wulst and dorsal ventricular ridge (DVR; see pp. 350, 351), these areas are widely separated from the neuronal populations that give rise to long descending pathways by complex neuronal populations that are described best as higher order integrative areas of the dorsal cortex and DVR (see 1,236).

THE SENSE OF TASTE

There is much experimental evidence that birds have an acute sense of taste. Presumably this encourages the ingestion of nutrients, allows discrimination between available foods, and possibly enables those that are toxic to be avoided (see 802). However, no chemical, physical, nutritional, or physiological pattern correlates consistently with avian taste behavior. A bird's response can be influenced by the behavioral, ecological, or chemical context of the taste stimulant. Individual differences between birds also exist and there are absolute differences between some species. Some responses suggest that birds do not share human taste experiences (513; see also pp. 289, 290, **Treats and Flavor Preferences**).

In the case of food straining by Mallards, it is evident that taste discrimination is hierarchically organized and that food intake behavior may be modified and interrupted at different levels. There are 5 possible positions in which taste may influence intake behavior in the Rock Pigeon: during positioning of the seed in the preferred position in the bill; during contact with the rostral palate (in the transfer of small seeds); during contact with the base of the tongue; during contact with the laryngeal mound; and/or during contact with the caudal palate. Certain experiments show that screening of the taste of a food particle works as a safety mechanism or warning device; in the case of unwanted food items this results in a learned aversive reaction that can be acquired through a few exposures. Oropharyngeal factors not only play a role in food selection, but also provide an important positive reinforcement for the maintenance of feeding and drinking (see 802).

As in all vertebrates, taste impulses in birds are generated in taste buds. Although the number of taste buds reportedly present in birds is low in comparison with other vertebrates, their number appears to have been underestimated (802). Budgerigars and parrots, in general, have more, and more variable, taste buds than most other birds (numbering 300-400, with about 40 sensory cells per bud; 343, 802). Thus, they have 5-15 times as many taste buds as do Rock Pigeons (27-59), but only 1/26th as many as does Man (45, 397, 1,005). Parrot taste perception may, indeed, be comparable to that of some mammals. This finding is consistent with many other aspects in which parrots are judged to be an ancient avian group (see pp. 388-390). [Although taste also is reduced in amphibians and reptiles, it achieves by far its greatest reduction in birds (58).]

In shape, avian taste buds resemble those of reptiles, being intermediate between those of fishes and mammals (513). They consist of flask- or barrel-shaped groups of elongated fusiform sensory cells that lie perpendicular to the mucosal surface and differ markedly from the other epithelial cells of the surrounding mucosa (see 802). Many of them are distributed free in the oral mucosa. They tend to be scattered over the posterior part, at the base of the tongue and on the floor of the oropharynx, most abundantly in the soft part of the palate and around the glottis. None apparently is present on the free portion of the Budgerigar tongue (441). They also may occur beneath the tongue--particularly in species with small tongues (155, 322, 397, 417)--in the bill and bill-tip region, just caudal to the bill-tip organ in the Mallard (see 802), and in close association with the openings of the salivary glands and their ducts (see 513, 620, 802).

A duct communicates between the oral cavity and the lumen of a taste bud, through which dissolved nutrients reach the receptor (sensory) cells (417). In mammals, the initial interaction of a taste stimulus and a receptor cell appears to occur on the latter's microvilli (513) but the situation in birds remains uninvestigated.

The buds are variously innervated by the laryngo-lingual portion of the lingual branch of the glossopharyngeal nerve, the palatine branch of the facial nerve, and fibers of the chorda tympani nerve, depending upon their location. Individual axons typically enter each taste bud from a small plexus just beneath it, and 20-30 axons supply each bud. The central representation of the chorda tympani nerve in the Mallard and Rock Pigeon is in 2 distinct subnuclei of the nucleus of the solitary tract (the nucleus sensorius nervi facialis and the nucleus ventrolateralis rostralis). The main terminal fields for the glossopharyngeal nerve are restricted to the rostral pole of the central rostral component of the nucleus of the solitary tract and to the nucleus ventrolateralis rostralis (see 802, 1,005).

THE POST-BUCCAL DIGESTIVE SYSTEM AND ASSOCIATED STRUCTURES

THE GASTRIC APPARATUS is functionally and morphologically the most widely varied of all the internal organs of birds (322). It usually consists of an elongated, thin-walled anterior "glandular stomach" or proventriculus and a posterior, rounded, thick-walled "muscular stomach," also known as the ventriculus or gizzard. The transition from the surface relief of the esophagus to that of the proventriculus usually is abrupt and the inner wall of the proventriculus generally is without the huge folds or ridges that characterize the esophagus (620). The glandular stomach, or in a number of species, the muscular stomach, is suspended by an attachment to the left lateral peritoneal wall (619).

The size of the muscular stomach as compared to that of the glandular stomach is greatest in granivores, herbivores, omnivores, and insectivores, in which the diet consists primarily of tough food requiring mechanical treatment before being acted upon by gastric juice (620). Some parrots, however, may have even larger glandular than muscular stomachs (441). The glandular stomach is lined by mucous membrane and characterized by an abundance of compound and simple tubular gastric glands that lie embedded in its walls. In many graminivores, parrots, and pigeons, the compound glands principally secrete the acid gastric juice, including HCl and pepsin, while the simple tubular glands probably are involved only in the production of mucus (442).

THE PROVENTRICULUS also may serve as a storage chamber as in carnivorous and piscivorous species (341, 442). Its secretory functions vary according to requirements for digesting the amount and type of food present. They are regulated through both neural and hormonal mechanisms. The passage of food to the glandular stomach from the crop and thence to the muscular stomach is influenced by movements in both the crop and the muscular stomach. Normally food remains in the glandular stomach for only a relatively brief time (520).

THE MUSCULAR STOMACH is characterized by the great enlargement and massive muscular development of its walls and its thick, resilient, ridged, keratinoid-like lining, traversed by simple tubular glands. It is lined by a thick, continuous, glycoprotein layer of the secretion of these glands--the cuticle--the surface of which usually is being worn away and replaced continuously; in some birds, however, it is shed periodically (441, 620). The muscular stomach serves as an organ of mechanical or physical digestion (trituration) in many species and it both refluxes the semi-liquid digesta orad into the proventriculus and propels it aborally into the duodenum (925). It also serves as a chamber for preliminary acid proteolytic digestion (at pH 2.0-3.5 in domestic fowl but 0.9-1.1 in Rock Pigeons; 998) and, in numerous species, as an organ of storage. Its activity is characterized by regular rhythmic contractions of variable frequency and amplitude (about 0.033-0.05 Hz in the domestic fowl hen; 520).

RETENTION OF FOOD IN THE MUSCULAR STOMACH is for highly variable periods--from a few min to a few hours--from species to species and also depends upon the functional state of the digestive tract. Furthermore, the space between the openings of the glandular stomach and duodenum (curvatura minor) is narrow, permitting food that does not require grinding to be passed directly into the duodenum (441). Thus, in certain nectarivorous species that feed on both nectar and insects, the proventricular and pyloric openings in the muscular stomach are so close together that the easily digestible nectar can pass directly to the duodenum, even when the muscular stomach is filled with insects (620). A neural ring in the muscular stomach controls the automatic movements of the proventriculus and the duodenum (341).

The musculature of the ventriculus is most highly developed in granivorous, herbivorous, and omnivorous birds. In these, the main body of a biconvex muscular stomach is made up of two thick, opposed, lateral muscles, the ends of which are attached to a central aponeurosis (flattened tendinous expansion), and two thin anterior and posterior intermediary muscles (520). The structure of these muscles allows for a rapid spread of impulses throughout the organ and an unusually powerful form of contraction, which is under exceedingly complex neural control (620).

The muscular stomach is relatively poorly developed in some parrots, particularly the frugivores and nectarivores (322), and may be long, saccular, and distensible (520). In some frugivores it is strikingly reduced to a narrow transparent zone (620). In the nectarivorous and pollen-feeding Loriidae, such as the Red-flanked Lorikeet (*Charmosyna placentis*), a large intermediate zone immediately caudal to the glandular stomach replaces the relatively small muscular stomach as the site of gastric proteolysis. In many birds, however, particularly those in which an isthmus separates the glandular and muscular stomachs, the intermediate zone probably functions mainly as a contractile barrier between the two chambers (620).

THE SMALL INTESTINE receives the secretions of the pancreas and liver, and is the principal avian organ for the hydrolytic reactions that reduce foods to absorbable entities (except for cellulose; 341). Absorption generally occurs very quickly, with amino acids appearing in the bloodstream within 10 min of eating protein (see 925). Within the small intestine the acidic chyme from the muscular stomach is neutralized, so that the proton concentration, especially in the ileum, is between pH 6 and 8.

THE DUODENUM is the initial loop, beginning at the pylorus; most of the pancreas, an avian gland of both exocrine and endocrine functions, lies within its proximal descending and distal ascending limbs. Part of the pancreas in the Budgerigar lies along the outside of the duodenal loop (620). Opening into the duodenum are the pancreatic and bile ducts. [Avian pancreatic exocrine secretion begins almost immediately upon feeding, suggesting a neural component in its release (925).] The duodenum usually extends caudally to about the level of the interpubic space before turning back on itself, with the ascending loop returning approximately to the level of the muscular stomach. Secretions of the embryonic adrenal and thyroid glands, or perhaps the adrenal alone, are believed to be involved in the differentiation and maturation of the duodenum in the last few days before hatching in the domestic fowl embryo (see 1,053).

The junction between the duodenum and jejunum usually is defined to be the point where the distal limb of the duodenal loop crosses the abdominal cavity from left to right. The boundary between the jejunum and ileum is placed arbitrarily at the point of origin of the vitelline (Meckel's) diverticulum (see p. 192, **Residual Yolk**). The arrangement of the jejunum and ileum shows more interspecific variation than any other part of the intestinal tract (620).

Avian intestines undergo peristaltic and segmental (local food-particle breakup and mixing) movements (520), the rhythmicity being modified by extrinsic excitatory and inhibitory innervations (620). The ileum, in which most absorption takes place, tends to have its own rhythm of movements and shows many typical adaptations to the type of nutritional intake (341, 442, 925). The anterior quarter is most active in carbohydrate, amino acid, and lipid transport, the distal half in the reabsorption of endogenous metabolites of protein and bile salts (925).

THE ILEUM in Budgerigars and several other birds consists of 4 loops (jejunal, axial, ileal, and supraduodenal) tightly packed on the right side of the muscular stomach (441). It is relatively long (as is the food retention time) in herbivores and graminivores. The distal portion of one or more of the intestinal loops of parrots forms a spiral. The simplest form of avian intestines (in ratites and galliforms) is strikingly similar to that of crocodilians (620).

The surface area of the small and large intestines of all birds is increased by being thrown variously into a series of projections, the folds and villi, which vary in length in different regions. In some parrots the villi of the small intestine grade over into a simple network of folds in the rectum (large intestine; 620). The mucosa of the small intestine is characterized by crypts (of Lieberkühn) of varying degrees of development that extend down into the mucous membrane between the villi. The villi are well-developed and finger-like in carnivores but flattened and leaf-like in herbivores. The epithelium usually consists of simple columnar cells with many goblet cells. Lymphocytes, which are present in large numbers in the lamina propria, are distributed diffusely or in isolated lymph follicles or in Peyer's patches (520). The small intestine harbors a vast microbial flora, that may have a role in making nutrients available for absorption (341).

GASTROINTESTINAL ENDOCRINE CELLS are scattered within the epithelia throughout the entire gastrointestinal tract but there are remarkable accumulations in the pyloric region (1,114). The cells are oval, pyramidal, or pear-shaped in the surface epithelium of the proventriculus, muscular stomach, pyloric region, and intestinal crypts, and columnar or spindle-shaped in the intestinal villi. Those that reach the lumina seem to act as chemoreceptors that receive chemical information therefrom; those with cytoplasmic processes that run along the basement membrane of the proventricular glands and never reach a lumen may serve as mechanoreceptors of the proventriculus. Ten kinds of cells have been identified by immunocytochemistry--gastrin, somatostatin, glucagon, glicentin, motilin, pancreatic polypeptide, bombesin, secretin, and substance P-immunoreactive cells--but their physiological significance remains to be elucidated (1,114).

DIGESTIVE SYSTEM PECULIARITIES---THE CROP. Parrots and some other birds possess a permanent, highly-differentiated, sac-like diverticulum or dilatation of the caudal part of the cervical esophagus, the crop. It lies nestled in the thoracic inlet, lightly bound to the surrounding structures and served by several arteries and veins (441, 620). It is expansible and lined by a mucous membrane that possesses mucous glands in some species (441, 442). The presence of enzymes in the crop and their role in digestion have been subjects of controversy (521).

THE CHIEF FUNCTION OF THE CROP seems to be the storage of quantities of seed for efficient transport. In some species, however, it serves for overnight food storage to augment and/or substitute for lipid storage (973), and nectar storage in the crop is important on an hour-by-hour time scale in the time-energy economy of hummingbirds. The evolution of a storage organ is more or less essential for a species with nidicolous young (see pp. 193-195, **Nidicoles**), the adults of which feed on large quantities of food of relatively low nutritive value and make long flights between feeding grounds and the nest to feed developing young.

In addition, the possession of a crop may allow individuals to internalize seeds rapidly and thereby maximize both the time available for foraging for patchily distributed seeds and the exploitation of localized food sources before competitors discover and exhaust it (see 968). In adult parrots, in addition to serving for temporary storage, the crop functions in the softening and swelling of food for the young, primarily via hydration. This appears to be an important preliminary digestive process (442).

In hawks and parrots, the crop extends ventrally, whereas in many passerines it protrudes laterally or dorsally (322). The very large cervical crop of the Owl Parrot is superficially very similar to the remarkably large and complex crop of the Hoatzin (*Opisthocomus hoatzin*), the latter's primary organ of physical digestion, but with a much thinner circular muscle layer and poorly developed internal ridges (620). In the Budgerigar, the crop is a fusiform widening that narrows at the pectoral portion, contains circular muscle fibers, and normally undergoes some peristalsis (445).

PERISTALTIC CONTRACTION begins in the esophagus and spreads down the crop to the muscular stomach, with the grouping and speed of the waves depending on the state of hunger, the amount of food in the crop, and other factors. When the muscular stomach is empty, the entrance to the crop is closed by contraction of the longitudinal muscle layer of the esophagus, and food travels directly to the stomach. With relaxation of the muscle, food is diverted into the crop and stored. In species that lack a crop, food may be stored throughout the entire length of the esophagus (620). Food traveling to the stomachs may not enter if the latter are contracting, but may move back to the crop by retroperistalsis (520, 620). In most species the crop is susceptible to impaction (446). This is not uncommon in young male Budgerigars, and usually is attributed to overeating (see 451).

Like most parrots, Budgerigars lack a gall bladder (an organ that primarily stores bile, the exocrine secretion of the liver), which is possessed only by cockatoos and the Cockatiel (819). They also lack mucous glands in the cervical esophagus, where they are present in large numbers in most birds (620). Nor is there an indication of the boundary between the small intestine and the large intestine in either adult or embryonic Budgerigars, because adult parrots do not have a pair of caeca (see below) at this location (nor do crocodilians; 322, 441, 442; 659). Two vestigial caeca are present in the Rock Pigeon (998). The disposition of the intestinal loops is much more constant in birds than in mammals, as the demands of flight require that the intestine (and other organs) be held in place more firmly (155).

CAECA are sac-like extensions or "blind guts," most extensively developed in grouse (Tetraoninae) and very large and well-developed in sandgrouse (Pteroclidae), of which many adult birds have a pair. Although they generally are of uncertain function, they undergo peristalsis and possess villi and other forms of surface elaborations (520, 620). A role of caeca in the fermentative microbial digestion of crude fiber (cellulose) and significant microbial synthesis of vitamins seems almost certain in some avian species (341, 521, 925). Their usually chocolate-colored droppings can be distinguished readily from rectal excreta (521). When wild Red Grouse (*L. lagopus scoticus*) were confined, the caeca and small intestine became shorter with each generation removed from the wild (as a consequence of a less fibrous diet). Over a period of only a few yr the lengths of these organs were reduced to 50% and 72%, respectively, of their initial values (see 727). [However, there appears to be no correlation between diet and occurrence and size of the caeca in lizards (876).]

THE RECTUM or large intestine is a relatively short (about 3% of the total intestinal length in granivorous birds; 998), straight, slightly-enlarged, posterior extension of the small intestine from the level of the caeca (where present). Histologically, the rectum is similar to the small intestine except for differences in the size of the villi (520). It has little function as a digestive organ but it has an important role in the absorption of water from both feces and urine (134). This function is shared with the cloaca, a chamber that is common to the digestive, reproductive and excretory systems, and is regarded as a primitive vertebrate character (442, 626).

THE CLOACA is a very mobile and complicated region divided into 3 chambers by annular ridges that are extremely-variable between species (626). The rectum empties mid-ventrally into the first of these, the coprodeum, which possesses sphincters on each side (624). This region temporarily stores the semi-solid feces and usually is of greater caliber than the rectum. The coprodeum also tends to be the largest of the 3 chambers. [A true rectocoprodeal fold is known only in some ratites and an immature *Falco tinnunculus* (626).]

THE COPRODEUM is continuous with and separated by a fold from a dorsal area, the urodeum, which holds the semi-solid, white "urine," and generally is the smallest of the three chambers.The proctodeum stores the excrement and is closed at its end by the muscular vent, the opening to the exterior of the body. The urodeum is demarcated from the proctodeum by a definite uroproctodeal fold. Both the urodeum and the coprodeum are in open communication with the proctodeum, which possesses powerful ejection muscles. Many Herbst corpuscles lie immediately beneath the epithelium of some regions of the urodeum. They are relatively less numerous and more deeply situated in the wall of the proctodeum (626). The urodeal region can be everted for the purpose of sexual union. Normally urine and feces (together comprising the excreta or egesta) are voided simultaneously from the cloaca.

THE BURSA OF FABRICIUS is a tubular or pear-shaped dorsal diverticulum of the cloaca. It frequently contains more or less hard feces, but it may be empty (626). The bursa is a paracloacal derivative, typically at the junction of the rectum and the cloaca, with its orifice very close to the uroproctodeal fold (322, 622). It reaches its maximum development before 4 months of age in domestic fowl (4-5 months in the Rock Pigeon; see 997) and then diminishes rapidly in size with the approach of sexual maturity. The steroids secreted by the testes appear to contribute to this regression, which is inversely related to the development of the adrenal gland. The latter gland appears to exert the primary endocrine influence on bursal growth (924).

Long of enigmatic significance, the bursa now is known to function importantly in physiological homeostasis. It plays a central role in conferring immunological competence (responsible for controlling the first stage in the differentiation of B lymphocytes from multipotent stem cells to fully mature humoral-antibody-secreting plasma cells), it responds to and possibly influences the actions of certain hormones, it possesses a number of special cell types, and it synthesizes numerous humoral substances (379, 630).

In domestic fowl, lymphocytes derived from the bursa and the thymus can be divided functionally into bursa-dependent and thymus-dependent lines. The latter appear as early as the 11th day of embryonic development, the former not until after 12 days (924). The bursa-dependent line is represented morphologically by the larger lymphocytes of the germinal centers and by the plasma cells. These cells bear surface immunoglobulins or immunoglobulin receptors that appear to function as antibody receptors for various antigens. Experimental extirpation of the bursa-dependent line results in agammaglobulinaemia and an inability to produce detectible antibody when stimulated in various ways (623). Bursectomy and thymectomy of Rock Pigeon hatchlings, however, does not seem to affect significantly the capacity to produce antibodies (997).

RECEPTION OF URINE AND SEX CELLS---WATER RESORPTION. The urodeum receives the urine from the kidneys by way of the ureters. These are capable of peristaltic movement and generally enter the cloaca dorsally, medial to the vasa deferentia in the male and dorsal to the oviduct in the female (441, 626). The presence of a functional sphincter, or even of a sphincter-like action, at these orifices is not established (621).

From the urodeum the urine commences a retrograde movement into the coprodeum and rectum (even into the caeca in the Roadrunner, *Geococcyx californiana*, and various galliforms). Within these structures, the water content of the combined urinary and fecal components can be reduced by solute-linked transport of water, generally involving NaCl. This solute-linked transport prevents hyperosmotic uretal urine from producing any net withdrawal of water from the coprodeum and rectum, even in such species as the Budgerigar and Galah, which can attain urine/plasma osmotic ratios approximating 2½ (134, 621, 626, 829, 830, 832; see also p. 47). This operation is very important in water metabolism, since it results in a saving of water, which is particularly valuable for desert birds, many of which do not have an enhanced renal capacity for water resorption (see

621, 829, 832). Cloacal water loss can be adjusted in response to the state of water economy (832; see also pp. 47-49, **Water Conservation** ***et seq.***).

The urodeum also receives the gametes (sex cells) from the ovary or testes, by way of lateral or ventrolateral openings of the oviduct or the vasa deferentia. In members of the Anatidae, the opening of the oviduct is closed by a membrane that generally is not eliminated until the attainment of sexual maturity (626). "Ripening" or maturation of spermatozoa occurs in the vasa deferentia of the domestic fowl male. (135, 511). In several species of birds, not including Budgerigars, there is a "knot" or enlargement of convoluted deferent duct close to the cloacal wall, in which spermatozoa possibly are stored (441, 511). [As noted above, the terminal portion of the oviduct is the vagina. Its mucous glands and muscular walls aid in oviposition (see pp. 162-164, **Vagina and Oviposition** ***et seq.***).]

THE VENT. The vent is the opening of the proctodeum to the exterior of the body. When resting, it is guarded by dorsal and ventral lips that meet laterally in the left and right commissures of the vent. When the cloaca is partly everted during the normal evacuation of excreta, the vent orifice is circular. Radial furrows on vent lips probably are typical of birds generally. Large numbers of Herbst corpuscles occur immediately beneath the stratified squamous epithelium of the lips of the vent and in the proctodeal mucosa, and may be involved in the coordination cloacal functions, such as oviposition, copulation, and voiding. In many species, the lips of the vent also possess simple tubular mucous glands of unknown function that open on the surface of the stratified squamous epithelium (626).

SEMEN TRANSFER---EVERSION AND RETRACTION OF CLOACAL LIPS. The vasa deferentia pass through the wall of the urodeum as the ejaculatory ducts, which consist of erectile tissue. When an ejaculatory duct is forced against the cloacal wall by eversion of the proctodeum, it forms a slightly raised papilla. This facilitates the transfer of semen to the everted, apposed orifice of the vagina of the female by muscular contractions during cloacal contact (441), which also is the mode of semen transfer in many urodeles and the Tuatara (*Sphenodon punctatus*; 628). Adjacent specialized lymph folds and vascular bodies also may be involved in sperm discharge, since they are erected with the ejaculatory ducts during sexual excitement of the domestic fowl male (see 348). The cloacal lips of the female are known to evert and retract rapidly during copulation (1,011) and I noted on one occasion, when I had a favorable view, that these eversions and retractions continued for 1 or 2 sec after the male Cockatiel, Cosimo, dismounted from his mate Carmen.

Avian semen is extremely viscous, due mainly to its high concentration of spermatozoa. Depending on the species, it is minute to small in volume, since it lacks the secretory products of accessory genital glands, which are absent in birds (625). After deposition in the female urodeum, the spermatozoa find their way through the genital papilla into the left oviduct and move up toward its expanded, open, ciliated end, the infundibulum, whose contractile folds envelop the ovum as it breaks out of the ovarian follicle (see p. 152, **Infundibulum and Fertilization**).

GENITAL TUBERCLE--CLOACAL PROTUBERANCE--PROCTODEAL GLAND. During embryogenesis a "genital tubercle," a rudimentary copulatory organ, arises in the ectoderm of the ventral wall of the cloaca. Though this becomes vestigial in most species, it persists long enough in male domestic fowl hatchlings to allow sexing with an accuracy of 95%. This tubercle develops into a functional, sizable, twisted intromittent structure, capable of protruding from the cloaca, in members of the Anseriformes and in the ratites, in which the female homologue, the clitoris, also persists. The structural basis of the avian phallus is to be found in the phallus of crocodiles and turtles, (348, 628, 1,027). The only substantial difference between the phallus in the Brown Kiwi and the Tinamidae as opposed to the chelonian and crocodilian phallus is the asymmetry of the avian phallus, which curves to the left (628).

In most, if not all, passerines the seasonal hypertrophy of male seminal sacs forces out the posterior wall of the cloaca into a nodular "cloacal protuberance" caused by the terminal convolutions of the vasa deferentia, the caudal ends of the ureters, and the caudal end of the alimentary tract. It can be used to sex various species. Its presence is a reliable indication of reproductive capability. Since the temperature in the ends of the vasa deferentia is several degrees below body temperature, they may be a site for the maturation of spermatozoa (see 348, 626). [The vasa deferentia are the principal sites of temporary (non-seasonal) storage of spermatozoa in crocodilians (759).]

An externally visible proctodeal (cloacal or foam) gland, embedded in the dorsal lip of the proctodeum, has been described in Eurasian Quail (C. coturnix) and Japanese Quail and is known to be androgen dependent. The gland is larger in males than in females, in which it generally is rudimentary. Inasmuch as the males also have a small penis, the secretions of the gland may serve as a lubricant during copulation (see 23, 743). A marked sexual dimorphism in the testosterone metabolism of the gland--the male glands produce more 5-alpha-reduced metabolites--contributes to the dimorphism in gland size in intact adults (743).

WARBLING. To me, the most delightful trait of Budgerigars is their soothing, subdued, melodious warbling. One of my birds sings virtually continually, even when "napping," with his bill amongst the feathers of the shoulder--"under the wing". He is silent only during sleep. [The practice of tucking the bill amongst the feathers reduces the rate of loss of heat, by as much as 12% in domestic fowl (97, 349). In this manner the birds provide themselves with pre-warmed air to breath and reduce their exposed bodily surface area (28). Heat loss through the integument of the head is high because the feathers covering it are short (see 967). Rock Pigeons, however, are not known to tuck the head under the wing (1,101).]

INTELLIGENCE. Some workers believe that Budgerigars are the most intelligent of domesticated birds. Indeed, some experiments have shown that Budgerigars and Ravens (*Corvus corax*) can "count" up to 7 or 8, with a good likelihood that they can form a concept of number; the limit is 5 or 6 in Rock Pigeons and 6 in Jackdaws (*C. monedula*; see 28, 174, 351, 419, 476, 1,091). Budgerigars also can remember complicated sets of incidents in correct sequence (other parrots were not tested in these experiments). Along other lines, Budgerigars can be trained to distinguish between short sequences of notes, and they retain the ability to make the distinctions after changes of tempo, pitch, and timbre (see 419). A Budgerigar learning to take the lid off of a pot by watching an experienced bird, tended to use the same movements that it saw the experienced bird employ (419; see the further treatments of avian intelligence on pp. 344-348).

Reproductive Behavior

HORMONAL CONTROL

STEROIDAL SEX-HORMONES secreted during a critical period of ontogeny play crucial roles in avian behavioral and brain development--transforming irreversibly the brain and several other steroid-dependent structures--and are a major determinant of adult sexual differences in behavior and in hormonal responsiveness (741, 743, 747, 1,030). In galliforms, for example, female differentiation is a demasculinization induced by embryonic ovarian estrogen secretion; the male appears to be the neutral or anhormonal sex (741, 743). Although members of both sexes produce androgens and estrogens, males generally produce more androgens and are more sensitive to them, whereas females produce more estrogens and are more sensitive to estrogens (1,027). Peptidic hormones also appear to affect behavior, presumably by actions on the central nervous system (1,030).

STEROIDAL HORMONES are derived from the precursor, pregnenolone, and the latter from cholesterol (1,025). They have roles in regulating voice and temperament, bodily growth, feather growth, structure, and molting, and, in some species, bill and cere color, comb size, and plumage pigmentation. Their functioning and that of thyroid hormone depend on passive diffusion across the target cell membrane and binding to protein-molecule receptors within the cytoplasm of the target cells. Alternatively, some steroids activate surface membrane receptors causing a coupled G-protein subunit to bind guanosine triphosphate. The bound subunit complex then dissociates from the membrane and activates or inhibits adenylate cyclase, which catalyzes cyclic AMP synthesis. In the case of nerve cells, e.g., both excitatory and inhibitory effects may be produced, depending upon the type and/or manner of G-protein coupling that is affected (see 40, 1,304).

Cytoplasmic steroid-receptor complexes, in which the size and shape of the receptor are altered, are transported to and penetrate the nucleus where the steroids bind to intra-nuclear proteinaceous receptor molecules that are weakly associated with nuclear components in the absence of ligand (or the steroid may bind directly to the intranuclear receptor without prior binding in the cytoplasm). [However, a high affinity for binding sites, as identified by radioligand techniques, does not necessarily imply a potency in physiological action. Evidently, it is possible for a hormone to interact with a particular binding site without having a subsequent physiological effect (1,174).]

Binding of the hormone to its intranuclear receptor results in conversion of the receptor-steroid complex to a form that associates with high affinity with the chromatin and/or other nuclear components, after which selected sets of responsive genes are activated. As a result, DNA (desoxyribonucleic acid) and mRNA (messenger ribonucleic acid) syntheses in the target cells are altered, and there are changes in the syntheses of specific mRNA's and proteins involved in the regulation of cellular proliferation, differentiation, and physiological function. For example, in the oviduct, estradiol increases the production of the mRNA for ovalbumin, and progesterone accomplishes the same end for avidin (916, 1,022, 1,030). In the liver, glucocorticoids increase mRNA production for tryptophane oxygenase, etc. [Steroid-receptor genes of Man and the avian erythroblastosis viral oncogene may be derived from a common primordial gene (1,022).]

Steroidal hormones circulate mostly in a bound form with plasma proteins. The latter fall into 3 major groups. Albumins bind most steroids, including conjugated metabolites, with low affinity and very high capacity. Corticosteroid-binding globulin is present in virtually all advanced vertebrates and binds glucocorticosteroids and progesterone with high affinity, whereas aldosterone and sex steroids are bound less strongly. A 3rd protein, often termed SHBG, also may be present but is dispensible in homeothermic endotherms and, accordingly, is absent in birds and many mammals; it binds sex steroids with an affinity and specificity that varies with the species. This protein binding decreases the metabolic clearance rate, allows the maintenance of higher steroidal concentration in the blood circulation, and inactivates the steroids. Thus, only unbound steroid can diffuse into cells and encounter cytoplasmic receptors (1,172).

AMINO ACID-DERIVATIVE, PEPTIDIC, AND PROTEINACEOUS HORMONES, on the other hand, first combine with a specific receptor on the cell membrane and most of them act, at least in part, via the adenylate cyclase system situated on the inner surface of the cell membrane. After combining with the membrane-bound receptor and activating adenylate cyclase, the latter converts ATP (adenosine triphosphate) into cyclic AMP (adenosine monophosphate), an intracellular "second messenger" (possibly an antagonistic "second messenger" to GMP--guanosine monophosphate). In most tissues cyclic AMP then activates a protein kinase that mediates most of the effects of the cyclic nucleotide. In the case of the hypophysis, for example, it has been suggested that a protein kinase is activated and that this then dephosphorylates certain membrane constituents, promoting exocytosis of cytoplasmic hormone-secreting granules. The latter migrate to, and fuse with, the cell membrane, extruding their granular core to the extracellular space, particularly at the vascular pole of the cell (1,029, 1,030, 1,042; see, for example, pp. 127, 128, **Hypothalamic Neurohypophysial Hormones**).

Unlike steroidal hormones, which are the product of complex sequences of biochemical reactions, and far removed from the genes that determine these reactions, peptidic and proteinaceous hormones are the direct expression of the transcription and translation of structural genes. "They bring us to the 'grass roots' of the evolutionary process; at the level of primary molecular structure, where genetic variation is first expressed, and at the level of tertiary structure which, because of its functional implications, is where natural selection must act" (1,162).

These hormones often are synthesized as larger precursor molecules which then are fragmented by post-translational enzymatic action. Moreover, the duplication of structural genes permits the production of two initially identical molecules which then can undergo structural and functional divergences. Such divergences have led to the evolution of new hormones, and it commonly is assumed that this has been effected by the natural selection of advantageous substitutions. Thus, peptidic and proteinaceous hormones may have provided a continuing pool from which new hormonal relationships were established to meet new needs. At least some of the hormonal molecules that have been thought of as characteristic vertebrate products may have long pre-vertebrate evolutionary histories and a great diversity of functions (1,162).

All peptidic hormones are synthesized in endocrine cells and stored *in situ* in the form of secretory granules that are produced by the rough endoplasmic reticulum and Golgi system. Formation of the thyroidal hormones, triiodothyronine and thyroxine (amino acid derivatives), on the other hand, requires more complex steps. These hormones are not synthesized directly from their constituents, tyrosine and iodine, in the cell; a part of the synthetic process occurs in the extracellular lumen (1,177).

HORMONAL INTERACTIONS WITH THE CENTRAL NERVOUS SYSTEM, principally hypothalamic loci and the adenohypophysis (anterior pituitary), regulate and synchronize all aspects of avian reproduction, from the maturation of spermatozoa and eggs to the expression of species-specific behavior patterns. Different neurons have different affinities for different steroidal metabolites, which find their bases in the binding of the steroids with receptors (916, 935).

If an affected brain center is wired directly with the efferents (outwardly conducting nerves) of a certain behavior pattern, a direct hormonal influence on behavior results. In most cases, however, several brain areas will respond to a change in concentration of steroidal sex-hormones in the plasma, and the direct hormonal influence will be masked by several indirect effects. Thus, the sensitivity of sensory inputs might be changed, neurosecretory activity might alter thresholds in specific brain areas and transmitter systems, the general responsiveness of the central nervous system might be affected, the persistence of attention might be altered, etc. (see 935). In addition, steroidal sex-hormones seem to have a permanent effect on behavior. In embryos or in very young birds, they affect the differentiation of some brain centers; for example, they determine whether an individual will react subsequently to circulating testosterone as a male or a female. To what extent such an effect reduces the general bisexual potential in adults not only varies with the species but with the category of behavioral pattern (see 935).

AROMATIZATION---ANDROGENS VERSUS ESTROGENS. Such endocrine control of reproductive behavior is complex and often highly specific. In some species, aromatization of testosterone to estradiol, or indeed, estradiol itself is critically involved in the activation of reproductive behavior in males. In other cases it is the reduction to the 5-alpha-androgens, particularly 5-alpha-dihyrotestosterone, that is important for biological action within the central nervous system, hypophysis, and peripheral target tissues, including the proctodeal gland of quail, the comb of domestic fowl, and the songbird syrinx (see 611, 742, 745). Although the 5-beta-reduction of testosterone is very extensive in the hypophysis and hypothalamus of 1-day-old domestic fowl chicks, it seems unlikely that this process plays a direct role in the regulation of LH (luteinizing hormone) secretion, although it may play a role in behavioral regulation (1,134). Androgens, apparently of ovarian origin, are involved in oviductal maturation in domestic fowl (951). [Progesterone is converted to both 5-alpha- and 5-beta-pregnane-3,20-dione, and, as in mammals, the former effects a slight positive feedback on LH release (1,134).]

In some species, androgens activate some behaviors, estrogens activate others, and both are required to activate the normal repertoire of male courtship behaviors. In other species, estrogens alone have no effect on courtship behavior, which depends on androgens alone or a combination of androgen and estrogen. In contrast to the hormonal activation of courtship behavior, activation of avian copulation appears to be largely sensitive to estrogenic metabolites. It has been suggested that the activation of full male behavior in most avian and mammalian species depends upon interactions at the neural level between both androgens and estrogens (745).

[In mammals, a combination of androgen and estrogen appears to be necessary to activate the full pattern of the male social behavior, but in many species the neural mechanisms that control copulation and high-intensity aggressive behaviors appear to be activated by estrogen alone (745).]

In Japanese Quail, either testosterone (or other aromatizable androgen) or estrogen activates male copulatory behavior; a non-aromatizable (reduced) derivative of testosterone stimulates crowing, strutting, and proctodeal gland growth, whereas estrogen activates none of these (741). Cooing in Ring Doves can be activated by either androgen or estrogen, depending upon the context, with androgen activating Bowing-cooing and estrogen activating Nest-cooing (see 745 and section below).

[The Japanese Quail is a species in which the members of the sexes differ primarily with respect to the potential for male-typical characteristics; female-typical characteristics are accessible to the male upon appropriate hormone treatment. Females, by contrast, almost never show male copulatory behavior, even when ovariectomized and injected or implanted with large amounts of testosterone (741, 743).]

KEY ROLES OF ANDROGEN-METABOLIZING ENZYMES. It now appears that changes in the activity of the enzymes that regulate the conversion of testosterone to active metabolites in the various target tissues have an important role during both development and the behavioral transitions that occur within individual reproductive cycles. Testosterone is metabolized to a variety of 5-alpha- and 5-beta-reduced androgens in peripheral tissues, and to these hormones and various estrogens in the brain (see 745). A sexual difference in testosterone metabolism thus could explain sex-related behavioral dimorphism (see 611, 742, 743).

An example of such a mechanism has been formulated for the male Ring Dove. Aggressive male Hop-charging and Bow-cooing, inducing the female to "shy" away and take shelter, lead, within hours, to a surge in circulating male testosterone. Acting in the preoptic and posterior hypothalamic areas (see pp. 438, 439, **Activational effects**), the testosterone induces a 3-5-fold increase in aromatase activity in these areas by a presumed positive-feedback mechanism. Activation of aromatase probably is the crucial rate-limiting step that converts the testosterone to estradiol-17-beta. Increased levels of the latter metabolite in the preoptic-hypothalamic area lead to a behavioral transition from predominantly aggressive courtship to predominantly nest-oriented behavior in the male, mostly Nest-cooing and Wing-flipping (744, 750). The latter acts lure the female toward him. Male androgen levels decline to baseline values during incubation (752).

The course of events in the female appears to be as follows. As a result of the male's courtship activities, the female's hypothalamo-hypophysial-ovarian system is stimulated and follicles develop. The thecal cells of the largest of these secrete estrogen that induces the female to Nest-coo. The latter behavior, by positive "self-feedback," stimulates further follicular development and increased estrogen secretion. The granulosal cells of the largest follicle appear to synthesize progesterone (under the influence of gonadotropin) and the combined action of estrogen and progesterone activates nest building (750, 753). When nest building reaches a certain stage, it modulates the pre-ovulatory gonadotropin secretions [causing an LH surge and depressing FSH (follicle-stimulating hormone)] that trigger ovulation, followed by oviposition. Sexual crouching is activated by the secretion of estrogen and gonadotropin releasing hormone (750). The species specificity of the action of peptidic hormones (somatostatin, mesotocin, oxytocin, etc.) appears to be primarily a consequence of species specificity of the hormone-receptor interaction (915).

HORMONES INCREASE OR DECREASE RESPONSE PROBABILITIES. Hormones do not, in general, release specific individual responses. Rather, by their actions on the central nervous system, directly and indirectly through influences on peripheral structures, they make possible a whole range of responses and even facilitate them (346, 419). In Beach's words (715), the action of a hormone on the behavior of an animal is to "increase or decrease the probability that a given response will occur under carefully specified conditions of external stimulation and previous history of the individual." Thus, whatever their mode of action, the effects of hormones on behavior may be affected by experience, by the presence of a mate, and by other situational factors (419).

Behavioral patterns affected by hormones include those that are employed to defend a territory, court a mate and form a pair bond, copulate, care for eggs and young, etc. The importance of testosterone for the occurrence of male song and other territorial calls, for example, is established firmly for some birds (426, 655). The activities of the hypophysis and the gonads, which produce the most important hormones that regulate these behavioral patterns, are themselves controlled indirectly by the environment (see below) and usually also by endogenous circadian and circannual rhythms (260, 390).

HORMONES STIMULATE TARGET-TISSUE DIFFERENTIATION, NOT GROWTH. Classical studies involving endocrine gland removal and replacement therapy with specific hormones have established the concept that many hormones are involved in the regulation of cell proliferation and/or differentiation and product synthesis by their target tissues. For example, ACTH (adrenocorticotropic hormone) and thyrotropic hormone (see pp. 129-131, **The Adenohypophysiotropic Regulating and Inhibiting Factors** *et seq.*) are thought to be responsible for both growth and functioning of the adrenal cortex and thyroid glands, respectively. Recent studies indicate that, whereas the classical hormones may, indeed, be involved in target-tissue differentiation at both the morphological and physiological levels, they are not responsible for the stimulation of target-cell growth. Rather, the latter is stimulated by more or less ubiquitous (mitogenic) growth factors, with the classical hormones merely regulating ancillary growth-related effects, such as cell shape, spreading, and vascularity (1,173).

ADRENAL FUNCTION AND REPRODUCTION. Studies of the last decades increasingly support the hypothesis that complex interactions link the hypophysial-adrenal axis to the avian reproductive system. Seasonal fluctuations in the weight, as well as histological alterations of the adrenal gland are widespread in birds but the patterns of change do not appear to bear any general relationship to gonadal cycles.

A number of lines of evidence suggest that adrenal steroids play a role in terminating the reproductive period in some photosensitive species. In passerines, it has been proposed that these steroids participate in controlling the induction and maintenance of the photo-refractory period that terminates the breeding season. Changes in corticosterone during the ovulatory cycle in domestic fowl appear to reflect both the external 24-h light-dark cycle and the 26-h cycle of ovulation and oviposition. In some species, changes in corticosterone can synchronize the diurnal rhythm of response of the reproductive system to other hormones, such as prolactin and FSH, and also affect the timing of fat storage, molt, and migratory behavior. In domestic fowl photoperiod may act via the hypophysial-adrenal axis in regulating the timing of the periods in which pre-ovulatory surges in LH occur. These effects probably derive from a direct influence of the hormone on the central nervous system (1,121, 1,140).

It is likely that hypophysial-adrenal hormones are responsible in part for the short- and long-term depression of the hypophysial-gonadal axis that is observed in conditions of stress, such as confinement and crowding. The mode of action of adrenal hormones on the avian reproductive system probably is very complex and is largely unknown, particularly in the male. However, there is evidence that adrenal steroids can by themselves inhibit the male reproductive system and recent studies suggest that corticosterone acts by favoring the transformation of testosterone into biologically inactive androgens in the male hypophysis (see 1,121).

CIRCADIAN AND CIRCANNUAL ENDOCRINE RHYTHMS. There is abundant evidence of diurnal cycles in the circulating concentrations of a number of hormones in birds (and mammals). These daily variations probably reflect changes in rates of secretion from the glands of origin, although the possibility that there are diurnal changes in the rates of disappearance from the circulation cannot be excluded (1,125). Of particular importance are the adenocortical rhythm and the melatonin rhythm, both of which are driven by endogenous oscillators. The basic components of the machinery of the former rhythm are located within the hypothalamic-limbic system. The adenocortical rhythm is an essential fuel producer to the phase-related diurnal activity rhythm and also may drive the diurnal sexual cycle. In addition, pro-opiocorticotropin, the common precursor of ACTH and endorphins, might also drive the circadian prolactin rhythm.

The diurnal rhythm of the thyrotropin releasing hormone-thyroid stimulating hormone would appear, in birds, as in mammals, to be closely related to the corticotropin releasing factor-ACTH rhythm. The thyrotropin releasing hormone could be considered tentatively as the driver of the circadian rhythm in growth hormone (somatotropin). The diurnal melatonin rhythm may be another primary endocrine rhythm whose role is essential to basic circadian behavioral and metabolic rhythms (929). A definite diurnal pattern of plasma LH concentration with elevated nocturnal levels is observed in the domestic fowl. [In another view, growth hormone shows no discernible pattern of diurnal change but is secreted episodically (1,125).

Much less is known about circannual endocrine rhythms. In some species the sexual cycle is driven by an endogenous circannual oscillator, in others it may depend on a circannual cycle in the photosensitivity of the gonadotropic machinery. The annual thyroidal hormone cycle appears, in conjunction with the annual gonadal, adenocortical and growth-hormone cycles, to have considerable adaptive value in a great variety of avian species. By providing a powerful intrinsic phase-locking mechanism between the sexual and thyroidal cycles, the thyroid-gonadal interactions are crucial for the programming of the sequence of circannual seasonal events, leading from prenuptial migration to brooding, to postnuptial molt, and, finally, to postnuptial migration (929, 1,169).

The annual pattern of concentration changes in growth hormone in the plasma of adult migratory Canada Geese and Peking Ducks (*Anas platyrhynchos* var. *domesticus*) in large, outdoor aviaries is relatively simple; there is a midsummer maximum and a winter minimum. Similar patterns are observed in teal and Red Grouse in outdoor aviaries, but there is no clear-cut relationship between the growth hormone concentration and any single environmental factor. Elevated plasma concentrations of LH during spring breeding of these species is well established (1,125).

MATING OR PAIR-BOND FORMATION. Courtship, copulation, and selection of nest holes occur when flocks are in timbered areas, either perching or foraging in small groups between trees (171). The reproductive cycle of the female Budgerigar is characterized by a sequence of somatic, behavioral, and hormonal changes. Confined Budgerigar females choose the males to whom they are most attracted on the basis of number and size of throat spots, color, pattern, voice, and "energy" (see 3, 67); blue birds prefer blue mates, and green birds, green mates (see 440). Males in breeding condition are bright-eyed, energetic in their movements, inclined to be quarrelsome among themselves, and generally lively--"constantly calling, strutting, displaying the bloom of excellent condition, the cocks with shiny, deep-blue ceres, their beaks beating a tattoo against any solid partition in amorous eagerness" (185). Like the males, females in readiness also are inclined to squabble; they are restless, continually call loudly to any nearby males (185), and generally search about for nesting sites in aviary corners (136). According to Trillmich, pair bonds are maintained in flocks of confined Budgerigars and reformed with partners after separations of as long as 70 days (1,229).

THE MALE ASSUMES THE MORE ACTIVE ROLE in courtship; the female performs few sexual displays. The courting male ruffles his feathers and hops up and down on the female's perch, while bobbing his head, chirping, and shrieking. His jerky, hesitant approach indicates his conflict between advancing and fleeing. He performs for one female after another until he finds one who is receptive (see 67). Typical pair formation begins after the male commences Loud Warble (a component of the delightful "chatter" so commonly associated with Budgerigars), and requires an average of about 30 min to be consummated (ranging between 5 min and 2 h). In the wild, these activities and copulation occur at nest entrances, on nearby branches, or in trees near nests (171).

REINFORCING THE PAIR BOND----MOST BEHAVIOR AVAILABLE TO BOTH SEXES. Pairing birds must come into close proximity, after which either or both birds jerk or flick their heads from side to side, while oriented toward the other. These activities vary greatly, depending upon prior contacts, the presence of other birds, etc. The pair bond is reinforced or "cemented" by mutual allogrooming of the head, courtship feeding, and, perhaps, Loud Warble. Males often courtship-feed females (who commonly solicit), but the latter sometimes feed the males. In fact, except for sperm emission and oviposition, members of both sexes can perform all precopulatory and copulatory behaviors of either sex. Members of homosexual female pairs, court and perform all other actions, except sperm emission, that typically are performed by the males of heterosexual pairs (67).

PRECOPULATORY ACTIVITY. A sequence of precopulatory acts begin when the male turns to or approaches the female. He then performs any combination of various movements, including head-bobbing, Nudging, Pumping (of the head and neck), vocalizations (particularly Soft Warble), courtship feeding (for 'reward' or 'appeasement'), and even mounting (stimulated by both estrogen and testosterone). Many such sequences are performed, including sidling toward and away from the female (reflecting tendencies both to approach and flee), before ceasing and initiating another act (perching, warbling, grooming; 67).

Meanwhile the females may or may not perform various aggressive acts or movements. But as they become sufficiently stimulated, they are less aggressive and evasive, and signal their readiness for or permit copulation. During precopulatory behavior, the crown and throat feathers of the male typically are ruffled, and he often Loud Warbles, while those of the female usually are normal or sleeked. These postures of the crown and throat feathers may represent the degree of conflict between agonistic (of or relating to aggressive or defensive acts) and sexual drives. The male ruffling also may serve to appease the female. His feathers are sleeked during courtship feeding, but not before or after (67). [In this connection, birds generally sleek the feathers when warm, and fluff them when cold.]

A courting male may follow his departing mate into the NB (nestbox) and continue his previously initiated courtship behavior. Hearing the vocalizations of other pairs stimulates extensive precopulatory behavior in males. It has been shown that activities of the Budgerigar female in the NB, full ovarian development, and oviposition, also can occur in the absence of these precopulatory interactions, provided that the hens can see and/or hear (particularly hear) other pairs. [In general, precopulatory behavior is the most conservative sexual behavior and sometimes can serve as a guide in phylogenetic analyses at the higher taxonomic levels (155).]

COPULATION. A male shows intention movements for mounting by facing at right angles to the female and raising his foot nearest her, or by placing it briefly on her back. After climbing on the female's back, the male grasps her inner secondary feathers and those of the upper flank with his toes. After orienting his body parallel to hers, he lowers his rump region along one side of her elevated tail, bringing their vent regions into contact. Then he extends and drapes a wing over her opposite shoulder and begins the typical copulatory movements (67). [To facilitate breeding, no more than 2 securely fastened perches are recommended for the breeding enclosure (185).]

After a sequence of these movements, he may rise and repeat them on the same or other side, or he may fly off. The female occasionally turns her head during copulation, so that her bill touches or is in close proximity to the male's. Following successful coitus, the female remains motionless for a few sec while her mate rejoins her. Then she shakes her body, rearranges the disrupted feathers, and typically gets allofed by the male (67).

BARE NEST-HOLES---WHITE EGGS ARE ADAPTIVE. As mentioned above, Budgerigars, like most parrots, do not bring lining material to the nest, but oviposit on decayed wood dust or bare wood in the hollow. The whiteness of the eggs of hole-nesters may be adaptively advantageous, because it increases egg visibility, so that the eggs are less likely to be broken or left uncovered by the incubating bird (101). In this connection, hole-nesting birds lay more eggs than those that construct nests in trees, and their incubatory and nestling periods tend to be longer (97, 105).

IMPORTANCE OF A NESTBOX. Confined females first show an interest in the NB about 1-4 weeks before oviposition (67, 847, 860). They typically examine its outside many times per hour in the first 1 or 2 days. Subsequently, they venture to enter it in gradual stages. Occupancy is induced by estradiol (see 928). The females enter more frequently and remain longer during the following days, and spend half their time in it during the last few days before oviposition. The stimuli provided by the NB, particularly its dark interior, are essential for initiating the physiological changes leading to oviposition (see 842, 849, 850). The females also show a diurnal reproductive sensitivity to light, as assessed by oviposition, being most sensitive when a test light is presented 12-14 h after "lights-on" (1,047). [Rock Pigeons prefer nest sites in semi-darkness, and eggs or chicks provided in a warm, dark or dimly-lit room will induce domestic fowl hens with regressed ovaries to incubate or brood (see 989, 1,011).]

Behavior patterns of females in the NB include walking about, looking out of the entrance hole, preening, pecking the floor, and sitting or standing in the future IA (incubative area; 860). Even under otherwise suitable aviary conditions, ovarian development does not occur unless the females have opportunities to engage extensively in such activities. Significant development of both the ovary and oviduct occurs in most females after about 3-6 days of NB-related activities (860). Correspondingly, in many nest-building birds, the onset of nest building is coincident with follicular growth of the ovary and oviductal development (718, 845). The distance of the perch from the entrance hole has an influence on the suitability of a NB for confined birds (67). Males are said to enter the NB about a week before the females oviposit and to spend considerably less time there than do the females (860).

[Although the temporal sequence of nesting, nest building, ovarian, and oviductal development is relatively similar in domestic Canaries, Ring Doves, and Budgerigars, there appear to be differences in the hormonal factors underlying nesting in Budgerigars and nest building in other species. It would appear that the sequences of hormonal events can be traced in the female Budgerigar and Ring Dove, and that they involve the action of estrogen followed by progesterone or prolactin. For example, injections of estradiol in combination with prolactin stimulate normal nest behavior (of the type seen in the 3 days before oviposition) in female Budgerigars, whereas estrogen alone induces only the initial phases of nesting behavior. Ovariectomized birds do not enter NB's (see 860). Estrogen also induces nesting behavior in males, but to a lesser extent (67).]

NEED FOR INTERACTIONS WITH OTHER BIRDS. Interactions with birds other than her mate are necessary if a Budgerigar hen is to attain the final stages in her reproductive development. Two or 3 pairs usually are needed before breeding will occur, but group housing somewhat inhibits experienced females (67, 439). The stimuli from other pairs may primarily affect the males, stimulating their Warble vocalizations to the females; the males of isolated pairs usually Warble very little (67, 529). It apparently is the Loud Warble of other males that stimulates a male to Loud Warble himself (but not to Soft Warble). The vocalizations of other breeding females also stimulate ovarian activity and oviposition (849). There is a bimodal, diurnal rhythmicity in the total vocalization of confined birds, with the main peak occurring in the 5 h after "lights-on" and a lesser peak occurring in the 4 h preceding "lights-off" (light regime, 14L:10D). Most Warbling is confined to the first 1 or 2 early morning hours, when the hypophysis apparently is most sensitive to light, but a small amount of Warbling also occurs after "lights-off" (529).

Indeed, Brockway suggests that these external factors probably play a more important role in the immediate or specific induction of courtship behavior than do sexual-identity or hormonal factors (67). Of the Budgerigar vocal repertoire, only Loud Warble, Soft Warble, Tuks, and Whedelees appear to be associated with activity of the gonads (the ovary or testes).

MALE SINGING STIMULATES OVARIAN ACTIVITY---ALSO SELF STIMULATORY. The Soft Warble and Loud Warble, almost exclusively the province of the male, are associated with male precopulatory behavior and are the functional equivalent of passerine song. These Warbles greatly stimulate the activity of the ovary (which is a hormonally bisexual gland), oviposition, and all levels of NB activity of the female (67, 440), particularly during the first half of the light period (on 14L:10D cycles; 1,047) and during the first few days of NB occupancy (849, 860). In fact, singing is required for their full expression.

Similar circumstances have been quantified for Canaries; large song repertoires of males have been shown to be more effective than small ones in inducing nest-building and ovulation by females (see D.E. Kroodsma, 1976, in 241). [Ovarian recrudescence in the Green Anole (*Anolis carolinensis*) also is stimulated by male behavior (see refs. to D. Crews in 874).] In addition to hearing the singing of male Budgerigars, interacting with them, as opposed to their mere presence, is even more effective. Auditory stimuli also have a stimulatory effect on reproductive behavior by Ring Doves, particularly in the female (see 989; and next paragraph). The maximum daily caloric costs of ovarian and oviductal recrudescence probably do not exceed 10% of standard metabolic rate (729).

Male singing also greatly stimulates the male's own and other males' testicular activity (via secretion of gonadotropins; 442), i.e., continued sperm production and heavier testes and vasa deferentia (sperm ducts; 67, 97, 109). [According to Witschi (347) seasonal changes in the size and histology of the male gonaducts occur only in birds that have distinct breeding cycles.] But the performance of the singing, particularly Loud Warble, by each male, himself, is essential for maintaining his own full testicular activity. Thus, the testes of surgically devocalized male Budgerigars regress, even when the birds can hear other males singing (67). [This was the first direct evidence that auditory self-stimulation played a role in regulating the maturation of species-typical neuroendocrine or reproductive physiological activity (1,278). In this connection, if the hypoglossal nerves of a female Ring Dove are severed, which prevents her from vocalizing, the ovary will not grow in response to the courting of an intact male (see 989).] Under conditions in which males and females in the wild hear one another's vocalizations continually, they enjoy the selective advantage of always being able to proceed directly to breeding activities (67).

TESTICULAR ACTIVITY. Confined Budgerigar males retain some testicular activity at all times, and testicular recrudescence appears to be independent of photoperiodic regimes (see 842). A high individual variability in gonadal regression of confined birds of both sexes under uniform conditions may reflect the diverse genetic origins of domestic stocks (842). In the field some observers find distinct cycles in both the testes and ovary, and inactivity in non-breeding birds (116), while others observe that "there is the greatest difficulty in collecting birds with completely non-active gonads" (311). There is greater unanimity concerning Zebra Finches; birds with completely inactive gonads hardly ever are found. Males maintain spermatogenically active testes, and females have ovaries containing follicles in an advanced resting stage until appropriate conditions are encountered (311). Lack of food would appear to be the proximate factor that initiates gonadal regression in members of both sexes of wild Budgerigars (842); the same factor is responsible for testicular atrophy and a considerable reduction in circulating levels of testosterone in the males of many other species (928).

In most birds, the left testis is larger than the right one (348, 625) and contains a germinal epithelium that is capable of developing into an ovarian cortex (792). However, the right testis of young Budgerigars, some pigeons (Columbidae), and the domestic Broad-breasted Bronze Turkey

(*Meleagris gallopavo* var. *domesticus*) usually is slightly larger than the left one (453, 625), and this also is true in crocodilians (759). Such size differences between the testes in most birds is attributable to a deficiency of cortex and germ cells in the smaller gonad, at least in the embryo, but the differences tend to disappear in older birds (625). Unlike the condition in most mammals, the testes of birds are intra-abdominal, loosely suspended by short mesorchia (peritoneal folds).

Numerous experiments have shown that the males of many avian species react to a real or simulated lengthening of the day by development of the testes, and to a shortening thereof by testicular regression (155). Budgerigar males respond differently; if they are kept in almost total darkness with warmth and adequate sustenance, they will produce bunches of spermatozoa within 60 days (350). The sex glands may increase by a factor of several 100 to a 1,000 times or more in conversion from the inactive to the breeding condition (23, 28, 348, 414). This is attributable mainly to (a) increases in the length and diameter of the seminiferous tubules, within which the germinal cells propagate and steroid biosynthesis occurs (possibly including estrogenic steroids), and (b) an increase in the number of interstitial cells, which produce the steroidal sex-hormones, leading to a greater capacity to produce both semen and androgens (625, 734). The extremely rapid growth of which the testis is capable appears to be facilitated by a positive feedback mechanism (self-potentiation) of FSH acting synergistically with testosterone on the chromatin of Sertoli cells, inducing an increase in the number of FSH receptors (915).

Avian spermatozoa, though varying tremendously in appearance, are of typical vertebrate male-germ-cell morphology (414). Two general types can be recognized. The 1st type shows a remarkable similarity to that of some reptiles, being relatively short with a smooth tapering head, as in galliforms. The 2nd type is longer and has a spiral shape, as in passeriforms (625). See references 28, 414, 625, 930 for treatments of spermatogenesis and other aspects of male reproduction, and reference 643 for an account of the ultrastructural changes in the testis of the Budgerigar during a photoperiodically-induced cycle. It may be stated as a generality that the neuroendocrine mechanisms that regulate testicular function are similar in all vertebrates (734).

STORAGE AND TRANSPORT OF SPERMATOZOA. Once inside the oviduct, the spermatozoa of parrots are relatively long-lived compared to those of mammals. In some birds the spermatozoa are stored in the shell gland-vaginal region in branched, tubular crypts ("sperm-host glands") in the lamina propria of the mucosal folds (270, 441, 622). They are released thence slowly and continually over a period of about 10 days following normal copulation (see 944, 989). Little is known of the manner in which spermatozoa gain entrance to the crypts, how they survive in them, or how and at what times they are released. Hatch suggests that such sperm-storing structures may occur throughout the Class Aves (270).

In the domestic fowl hen, at least, spermatozoa also are stored in specialized tubular infoldings ("glands") in the infundibulum (see p. 152, **Infundibulum and Fertilization**), and it is in that site that long-term survival occurs (see 510, 511). Spermatozoa can survive there for 35 days and for as long as 10 weeks in Turkeys (511). Release of the spermatozoa may occur with the passage of the yolk (see 989). Spermatozoa can survive in Cockatiels for over a month (127) but, of course, they must reach the infundibulum to fertilize an egg. Sperm aged excessively *in vivo* lead both to a decreased incidence of fertile domestic fowl and Turkey eggs and to a decreased hatchability of fertile eggs (see 989).

Some spermatozoa in domestic fowl hens reach the site of fertilization in the infundibulum within 15 min after insemination. Unless they are stored subsequently in the infundibular glands, they may be lost for the purpose of fertilization. The mechanism of transport to the infundibulum probably is a combination of passive transport by oviductal contractions and ciliary movement, and by swimming movements of the spermatozoa (989).

[In chelonians, spermatozoa are found to be stored in glands (the normal glands at the respective regions) at the junction of the oviductal magnum and aglandular zone and at the junction of the shell-forming zone and the vagina (770; see pp. 149-165 for treatments of avian and chelonian oviducts). Female chelonians of some species can store spermatozoa for multiple seasons, but stepwise reduction in fertility has been observed in each successive year (see 771). In most squamates, spermatozoa are retained in "seminal vesicles," which are specialized alveolar glands at the base of the infundibulum, whence ducts lead into the oviductal lumen. In iguanids, the "seminal vesicles" are in the anterior segment of the vagina and project like the fingers of a glove, whereas gekkonids have such structures between the shell-forming zone and the infundibulum (989). Marsupials are known to store sperm in the fallopian tubes for days and there is indirect evidence that this also occurs in the oviducts of monotremes (see 1,308).]

BREEDING AND THE HYPOTHALAMUS. Because of its unique dual role as an organ of both the endocrine and the nervous systems, the hypothalamus occupies a central position in the mechanism that controls reproductive activity (442). In birds, for example, the hypothalamus is crucial in the regulation of the ovulatory cycle. Lesions in the hypothalamus prevent both spontaneous ovulation and progesterone-induced ovulation, while electrical stimulation in the hypothalamus of laying hens delays ovulation. Injections of progesterone into the hypothalamus induce premature ovulations, and injections of progesterone into the 3rd ventricle of the brain result in LH release, progesterone and testosterone secretion, and premature ovulation. The hypothalamus contains material, presumably LH-releasing factor (see pp. 129, 130) which, upon infusion into the adenohypophysis, results in premature ovulation. Two, and possibly 3 hypothalamic regions are essential for photo-induced testicular recrudescence and several types of experiments suggest the presence of photoreceptive regions in the anterior hypothalamus (see 989, 1,045, 1,117).

The hypothalamus forms only a small portion of the avian brain, comprising the floor of the diencephalon, bounded dorsally by the hypothalamic sulcus and ventrally by the neurohypophysis. One can distinguish anterior or rostral (preoptic, supraoptic, suprachiasmatic, and pretuberal) and posterior or caudal (tuberal) areas. The nuclei of the anterior area contain numerous secretory neurons arranged in a cluster-like pattern which may enable a "laminar flow" of ascending and descending neuronal communications. The neurons in some of these nuclei contain secretory granules 100-200 nm in diameter. The posterior tuberal area shows a mosaic-like arrangement of clusters composed of small and larger nerve cells and has proved to be hypophysiotropic in all vertebrates that have been studied (919, 1,165).

The hypothalamus also is heavily innervated with aminergic and cholinergic tracts (1,045). Though the hypothalamus acts as an endocrine organ in its regulation of the hypophysis, it remains an integral part of the brain. This is reflected in its structure. As in mammals, one can distinguish between a medial region that adjoins the 3rd ventricle and contains many cell bodies that are involved in endocrine functions, and a lateral region characterized by the fiber tracts that traverse it and connect extrinsically with other brain centers (735).

THE HYPOPHYSIS or pituitary gland probably has dominated the process of reproduction since the Ordovician period, 500 mya, and is indispensible to the maturation of gonads in all vertebrates that are more advanced than the cyclostomes (940). In keeping with its function as "the master endocrine gland," the hypophysis has an extremely complex blood supply (630). The avian hypophysis is suspended from the ventral surface of the hypothalamus by an infundibular stalk. It consists of an anterior lobe or adenohypophysis and a posterior lobe or neurohypophysis. In Budgerigars the gland is relatively large (1.75-2.0 mm in diameter). Its anterior lobe is located on the ventral surface of the brain between the optic chiasm and the medulla, tightly lodged in a saddle-like depression (the sella turcica or hypophysial fossa) of the sphenoid bone of the skull by a diaphragma sellae (fold of dura mater; 441, 455).

THE ADENOHYPOPHYSIS is derived from Rathke's pouch, an upward-extending outpocketing of the stomodeal ectoderm, and consists of the pars distalis and pars tuberalis (birds and hagfishes lack a morphologically distinct pars intermedia and some reptiles lack a pars tuberalis). The pars distalis usually is subdivided into cephalic and caudal lobes. These lobes correspond closely to the parts derived from the oral and part of the aboral divisions of Rathke's pouch, respectively. They develop independently and differently, beginning at an early stage in ontogeny, and are distinct in both their morphology (cellular constituents) and physiological functions.

The pars tuberalis derives from the lateral lobe of the original Rathke's pouch and forms the only adenohypophysial contact with the brain, usually covering part of the diencephalon and encircling the infundibular stem. The pars tuberalis of adults consists mostly of chromophobic cells arranged in a sheath 1-4 cells thick, through which the portal vessels pass from the surface of the median eminence to the pars distalis. Although the pars tuberalis contains cells that appear to be secretory, its function is unknown (1,112, 1,149, 1,166, 1,168).

THE NEUROHYPOPHYSIS is derived from a concurrently expanding infundibular outgrowth from the post-optic portion of the floor of the diencephalon, and usually remains distinct from the adenohypophysis, separated from it by a sheath of connective tissue. It is composed of the neural lobe or pars nervosa, the infundibular stem, and the median eminence or pars eminens. The neural lobe is the distal part of the neurohypophysis, formed by proliferation from the top of the succus infundibuli; in many reptiles and birds it is a thin-walled, lobulated, hollow organ.

The neurohypophysis proper contains two cellular types: axon terminals and pituicytes. The latter are regarded as homologues of neuroglia that may play a role in modulating the activity of the axons. The axon terminals form a part of the magnocellular system of the hypothalamus, with cell bodies in the supraoptic and paraventricular nuclei. These nuclei are the sites of synthesis and granular packaging of the neurohypophysial hormones, the former nuclei primarily synthesizing arginine vasotocin and the latter primarily mesotocin (see below; 1,024, 1,166).

[In early stages, the embryonic hypophysis appears to be formed primarily in a passive manner, not as commonly described, "formed in two separate parts that unite secondarily," attributing to the adenohypophysial anlage an active role in reaching the infundibular process. In this ontogeny, birds are distinguished by the early separation of the adenohypophysial anlage from the neural epithelium and the consequent lack of differentiation of the pars intermedia. The restricted development of the anterior pars distalis is the distinctive feature of hypophysial ontogeny in mammals. In reptiles, as in birds, the anterior pars distalis proliferates (developed from tissues originally anterior to the hypophysial stalk) and constitutes a major portion of the tissue of the pars distalis.

Histological sections of early stages of hypophysial development in crocodilians appear to be very similar to those of birds: the hypophysial stalk forms at the anterior end of the anlage, and the lateral lobes, described as "string-like" in both groups, develop in a similar manner. In birds and in crocodilians, cell cords of the pars distalis grow dorsoventrally, as opposed to antero-posteriorly in many reptiles (762).

It has been proposed that the original adaptive value of the organized relationship between the brain and the hypophysis in primitive vertebrates was to facilitate alterations of integumentary pigments in response to environmental cues. Following this hypothesis, the pars intermedia may have been the first adenohypophysial structure to evolve in vertebrates. The pars distalis may have evolved from the epithelial stalk tissue that carried the anlage of the pars intermedia toward the neurohypophysis. The lamprey may represent a stage of evolution in which there is inefficient, if any, regulation of adenohypophysial function by the adjacent anterior neurohypophysis. Three primitive piscine groups, the Holocephali, Selachii, and the Coelacanthini appear to typify a condition in which the median eminence is only developed partially and part of the pars distalis is not yet vascularized by the hypophysial portal system. If this were to be the case, the absence of a median eminence in lampreys would represent a primitive evolutionary phase rather than a degenerate condition (1,168).]

THE MEDIAN EMINENCE is defined as that portion of the neurohypophysis in which hypothalamic neurosecretory axons terminate upon a vascular capillary network; this capillary network drains into a series of venules, the hypophysial portal vessels and often is covered by the juxta-neural part of the pars tuberalis. It has neurohistologically distinct anterior and posterior divisions, each with its characteristic and essentially separate hypothalamo-hypophysial portal capillary bed. These beds are drained by the anterior and posterior groups of portal vessels that supply, respectively, the essentially separate sinus systems of the cephalic and caudal lobes of the pars distalis. This organization suggests the possibility of a morphological basis for the action of single neurohormones in the control of 2 different hypophysial hormones, for example, LH releasing factor controlling the release of both LH and FSH (1,149; see also pp. 129, 130, **The Adenohypophysiotropic Releasing and Inhibiting Factors** *et seq.*).

[LH-releasing factor from the preoptic area might be transported axonically to the median eminence, released there and carried to the cephalic lobe of the pars distalis by anterior hypophysial portal vessels, causing release of LH. Similarly, LH-releasing factor from the infundibular nucleus might be transported largely to the posterior median eminence by the tuberoinfundibular tract and thence by the posterior hypophysial portal vessels to the caudal lobe of the pars distalis, and there effect the release of LH (1,175).]

CONTROL OF REPRODUCTIVE ACTIVITY AND THE AUTONOMIC NERVOUS SYSTEM. The hypothalamus not only plays a central role in the internal mechanisms that control avian reproductive activity and migration, it also is involved in the ultimate control and coordination of the autonomic nervous system. Thus, it possesses centers for temperature regulation (control of the mechanisms of endothermy; 422, 518), for control of ptilomotor activity (518), for taste (397), for feelings of hunger (lateral nucleus), thirst (lateral nucleus), satiety (ventromedial nucleus), etc. (520). On the basis of the most recent concepts of hypothalamic structure, it appears that functionally different systems may exist within minutely circumscribed hypothalamic regions (919).

The determinants of hypothalamic hormone secretion are humoral feedback from the ovary and possibly the adrenal gland, neurochemical signals, environmental stimuli, and input from extra-hypothalamic central nervous structures. In the control of ovulation, the latter are, particularly, the amygdala, the hippocampus, and the mesencephalon (see 1,039). [In the present accounts of the hypothalamo-hypophysial-ovarian axis, I include some reasonable generalizations based largely on mammalian studies.]

It is perhaps a primitive chordate feature to possess secretory neurons in the brain that control the functions of structures outside of the brain, that is, to employ neurohormones (1,165). It is the critical influence of the avian hypothalamus on the secretory activity of the neighboring hypophysis, and, consequently, on nearly all of the other endocrine glands that is of concern here (23, 28, 295, 414). This includes absolute control over hypophysial gonadotropic glycoproteinaceous secretions, upon which gonadal steroidogenesis is dependent in all vertebrate species, with the possible exception of members of the Myxiniformes. Hypothalamic influence is achieved via two routes.

HYPOTHALAMIC NEUROHYPOPHYSIAL HORMONES. First, there is a synthesis of the peptidic neurohormones, mesotocin and the ubiquitous diuretic arginine vasotocin (which also acts on the oviduct during oviposition and influences various processes related to learning or memory, and can exert powerful effects on behavior in mammals)--apparent carry-over functions from the time when endocrine function originated in the nervous system (455, 523, 930, 1,031, 1,367, 1,368). Vasotocin consists of a 20-membered, disulfide-linked, macrocyclic ring system (pressinoic acid), to which is attached a COOH-terminal tripeptide (Pro-Arg-Gly-NH_2; 1,305). These hormones are synthesized by separate neurosecretory cells of different size classes concentrated together in preoptic, supraoptic, and paraventricular nuclei, and to lesser extent in the tubero-infundibular hypothalamus (vasotocin also is synthesized in the suprachiasmatic nucleus of Japanese Quail). This distribution of neurons that secrete vasotocin and mesotocin within certain nuclei may be an indication of homologies of these nuclei among various vertebrate groups. There is no evidence for the presence of oxytocin in birds (see 919, 920, 1,166).

The neurohormones are conducted in granules--probably bound chemically to a neurophysin--via axonal flow in the neurosecretory cells through the supraoptico-neurohypophysial tract to axon terminals in the glandular layer of the neurohypophysis. They also are conducted in some species to the vascular organ of the lamina terminalis. An additional vasotocinergic tract terminates in contact with the capillaries of the neurohemal zone of the anterior median eminence, presumably to regulate adenohypophysial corticotropic cells. At these destinations, the neurohormones are secreted from the nerve terminals, still in granular form, for storage and subsequent release into the systemic circulation (with prior cleavage from the neurophysins; 920, 1,023, 1,111). The hypothalamus is extraordinarily rich in secretory neurons that do not belong to any of the immunocytochemically identified groups (1,110).

[The same neurohypophysial hormones occur in lungfishes, amphibians, and reptiles. Arginine vasotocin is found in the neurohypophysis of all vertebrate classes, and is considered to be the ancestral neurohypophysial peptide (see 920, 1,023, 1,167). In the ontogeny of the rat, the hormone appears to recapitulate an evolutionary progression, being present in the hypophysis of the early fetus, declining during the latter part of gestation, and apparently being absent in the adult (1,167). Although several neurohypophysial peptidic hormones are known, only two of them usually are produced in the adult of any given species (1,023).]

ADENOHYPOPHYSIOTROPIC NEUROHORMONES AND ADENOHYPOPHYSIAL HORMONES. Second, there is a release of neurohumoral releasing and inhibiting factors from specific neurosecretory neurons whose cell bodies lie in the basal hypothalamus (see p. 126, note at bottom) and whose axons form an extensive tuberoinfundibular tract. These releasing and inhibiting factor-producing neurons appear to be in synaptic contact in the hypothalamus with a host of secretory neurons containing putative synaptic transmitters. The axons of the tuberoinfundibular tract terminate in anterior and posterior portions of the median eminence of the neurohypophysis in juxtaposition to the primary capillary plexus in the palisade layer (736, 919 1,029). [As compared with mammals, the avian tuberoinfundibular tract carries a much lesser population of dopaminergic fibers (see 1,045).]

The anterior median eminence receives a rich supply of Gomori-positive fibers from the anterior hypothalamus and some fibers from the tuberal complex, whereas the posterior median eminence receives very few Gomori-positive terminals but a dense tract of fibers from the infundibular nuclei. In many avian species the fiber tracts to the anterior median eminence contain at least 5 types of fibers with clear vesicles and dense granules. The variety of sizes and densities of the granules may reflect the different chemical natures of the neurohormones, and granules of the same size may be of similar chemical composition throughout the Tetrapoda (1,166).

The tuberoinfundibular tract of neurons plays the key role in transforming incoming neural information into the secretion of neurohormones, apparently different ones from each of its separate neurosecretory fiber systems. There appear to be two populations of neurons for LH-releasing factor, one population located in the preoptic anterior hypothalamic region and the other in the arcuate nucleus of the infundibular region, the former terminating in the anterior and the latter in the posterior median eminence (736, 920, 921, 1,131, and p. 126, **The Median Eminence**). There also are peptidergic projections directed toward the organum vasculosum of the lamina terminalis, which may serve as a functionally significant neurohumoral area.

Still other secretory neurons display projections that establish contacts with "ordinary" nerve cells located in different intra-hypothalamic and extra-hypothalamic sites. The neuropeptidic systems are incorporated into numerous hormonal and non-hormonal mechanisms and are open to the influence of exogenous and endogenous, intra- and extracerebral stimuli. Little is known of the pattern of their very complex circuitries. For example, numerous factors, such as hormones, stress, and food deprivation are capable of altering the release of LH in the domestic fowl, and most of them probably do so via the hypothalamus and LH-releasing factor (1,132).

As a postsynaptic element, the peptidergic neuron transmits the received signal. It accomplishes this either neurohormonally, by secreting its peptide into blood capillaries, the intracellular space, or the cerebrospinal fluid, or by a non-neurohormonal action. For example, the peptide may remain in the intracellular space and modulate the process of transmission of another chemical messenger. A synaptic contact between a peptidergic terminal and either a conventional or a peptidergic neuronal structure is an unequivocal indication of a non-neurohormonal function of the neuropeptide. All peptidic systems except mesotocin (vasotocin, somatostatin, methionine-enkephalin, corticotropin, neurotensin, gonadoliberin, etc.) are connected to various neuronal entities, for example, nuclei of branchial nerves, of the olfactory system, etc. (919, 1,111).

Since, compared to less advanced vertebrates, there has been a reduction in the number of peptidergic neurons that come into contact with the cerebrospinal fluid in birds, the most conspicuous colonies of neurons that make such contacts are aminergic. These accumulate most notably in the paraventricular organ. The significance of the persistence of large numbers of phylogenetically ancient senso-neuroendocrine neurons in the avian brain is unknown. In contrast, there has been a spectacular regression of such elements in mammalian brains (1,110).

THE ADENOHYPOPHYSIOTROPIC RELEASING AND INHIBITING FACTORS are transported to, and reach, the adenohypophysis in high concentrations by means of the hypothalamo-hypophysial portal system of veins. The basic pattern of this portal system is similar throughout the tetrapods, strongly suggesting its great significance as a functional link between the hypothalamus and adenohypophysis. The peculiar arrangement of the portal vessels may be related to the cytological and functional differentiation of the cephalic and caudal lobes of the pars distalis. The anatomical relationship between these lobes and the median eminence suggests that the functions of the cephalic lobe are controlled by blood from the anterior part of the median eminence, whereas those of the caudal lobe are controlled by blood from the posterior part (1,112, 1,166).

In the domestic fowl embryo, the first membrane-bounded secretory granules appear in the cytoplasm of occasional cells in the cephalic lobe of the pars distalis on the 7th day, while by the 8th day most of the cells in both the cephalic and caudal lobes contain secretory granules (1,166). There is evidence for FSH- and LH-releasing factors, a prolactin-releasing factor, an adenocorticotropin-releasing factor, growth hormone-releasing and inhibiting factors (the inhibiting factor, somatostatin, can inhibit a variety of secretory processes, and may have remained evolutionarily stable in both its structure and roles; 1,165), melatropin-releasing and inhibiting factors, and a thyrotropin-releasing factor (TRF). These factors stimulate or inhibit the secretion of one or another of at least 7 adenohypophysial hormones: the peptides, ACTH and melatropin, the proteins, prolactin and somatotropin or growth hormone (GH), the double-chained glycoproteins, LH, FSH, and thyrotropin or TSH.

The hormonal state of the bird is very important in determining the responsiveness of the adenohypophysis to these various factors (415, 442, 455, 1,023, 1,029). The gonadotropins (LH and FSH) are secreted in a discontinuous and episodic fashion, with the amplitudes and pulses being influenced by the gonadal steroids (1,038; see also p. 145, **Ovulation** *et* *seq.*). In Japanese Quail, the cephalic lobe of the pars distalis contains separate cell populations that secrete ACTH, prolactin, thyrotropin, gonadotropins (FSH and LH), while those in the caudal lobe secrete somatotropin and gonadotropins. The cells that secrete the gonadotropins are distributed throughout both lobes, with a few in the pars tuberalis (1,112).

ALL THE RELEASING AND INHIBITING FACTORS PROBABLY ARE PEPTIDES of very unusual structure, but this has as yet been confirmed only for somatostatin (a tetradecapeptide), LH-releasing factor (a decapeptide), and TRF (a cyclic tripeptide), and even the existence of the FSH-releasing factor remains controversial (1,029). Prolactin-releasing factor and growth hormone-releasing factor are of unknown structure but widespread in occurrence and seemingly structurally conservative, judging from their biological activity (1,165). The overall configuration of the releasing factors appears to be important for their biological activity, probably for binding to the receptors in target tissues (1,023).

A number of exceptions to an absolute specificity of releasing factors are known in mammals. For example, LH-releasing factor stimulates the release of FSH as well as LH, and TRF can stimulate release of prolactin as well as TSH. In addition, TRF has been found in the spinal cord, raising the possibility that it may be capable of addressing neurons in the central nervous system, besides stimulating TSH release by the glandular cells of the adenohypophysis. From additional studies in mammals, including the distribution of releasing factors in the brain, the concept is emerging that other releasing factors also may have important extra-hypophysial actions, possibly even serving as peptide neurotransmitters. The latter role conceivably could be even more important than that of governing the release of adenohypophysial hormones (1,029-1,031).

PROLACTIN appears to have assumed more different functions during the course of vertebrate evolution than has any other hypophysial hormone. In birds, prolactin influences the gonads, accessory sex structures (brood patch, crop gland in columbids), bodily growth, feather growth, behavior (incubatory, migratory timing and restlessness), metabolism, and osmoregulation (increases calcium concentration in the plasma of Japanese Quail), and stimulates the renal conversion of 25-hydroxyvitamin D_3 to the active hormone, but, except in some migratory species, its precise role in the reproductive cycle is not established firmly (1,023, 1,024). In one view, its role in the regulation of migration, gonadal growth and other functions in avian species that breed at mid-to-high latitudes depends on the phase angle between the circadian rhythms of the circulating levels of prolactin and corticosterone. The changing phase angles of these internal oscillations may have a circannual rhythm that is entrained by daylength and modulated by other factors, such as ambient temperature (see 1,123).

[Prolactin is the growth-promoting hormone in larval amphibians and also may be the hormone that promotes bodily growth in neonatal rats. It is becoming recognized increasingly as a major hypercalcemic factor in teleosts, in which it usually is controlled by a prolactin-inhibiting factor, probably dopamine. In amphibians, it appears to be controlled both by releasing and inhibiting factors. In Man, it may play a role in regulating amniotic fluid volume and composition by effects on the amnion itself (see 1,163, 1,165, 1,170). In domestic fowl embryos incubated at 33.8°C (instead of the normal 37.8°C) in the late pre-hatching period, prolactin and triiodothyronine (the active form of the thyroidal hormone in chicks) are involved in stimulating the increased relative growth rate, beginning in the 2nd week after hatching (see 1,136).]

Prolactin concentration varies inversely with that of LH in the laying domestic fowl hen, being low at the time of the preovulatory LH peak (see pp. 146-148, **Oviposition** *et seq.*) and high at 4 h after ovulation (see 989). The role of prolactin in the activity of the crop glands of columbids is well established, it having been shown recently that the growth and regression of the crop in the natural breeding cycle are paralleled by synchronous changes in endogenous prolactin secretion (922). A compelling postulate, adopted in the following as a working hypothesis, is the Mead-Morton paradigm of dual prolactinic control, according to which a surge of prolactin generally both terminates ovulation and induces the onset of incubation (see 1,106 and p. 148), with far-reaching consequences for the practice of egg care, past and present.

Not only does prolactinic activity have a fair degree of autonomy in some species, with respect to its hypothalamic control, but a dual facilitating and/or inhibiting prolactin-release pathway appears to exist in the avian hypothalamus. Thyrotropin (thyroid-stimulating hormone) acts on the thyroid gland. Adrenocorticotropic hormone acts on the adrenal glands; etc. (23, 28, 295, 348, 733, 748, 921). A well-defined adrenocorticotropic area of the hypothalamus is located in the dorsal part of the infundibular complex (see 921).

SYNAPTIC TRANSMITTERS AND RELEASING FACTORS. Putative synaptic transmitters involved in controlling the release of adenohypophysiotropic neurohormones are as follows. Norepinephrin, which seems to act mainly at the higher hypothalamic levels, appears to be implicated in triggering the surge of LH and also can stimulate the release of FSH. Dopamine plays a minor role in both the stimulation (dependent on prior estrogen priming; 1,030) and inhibition of LH release. Serotonin, which probably also has its primary impact on higher hypothalamic circuits, plays an inhibitory role in LH release and is mainly concerned with the regulation of rhythmic circadian inputs to neurosecretory systems. In contrast with mammals, birds seem to lack serotonin-containing elements in the suprachiasmatic nucleus (see 1,045).

[The monoamines (norepinephrine, dopamine, serotonin) are the secretions of the sympathetic nervous system, of which the adrenal medulla is a part. While sympathetic nerve cells have long axons and secrete the monoamines locally at the surfaces of the innervated cells, the adrenal medullary cells lack neurones and secrete the hormones into the circulation, thereby causing general reactions throughout the body (1,053).]

The precise role of cholinergic synapses in LH release remains to be established. ACTH release appears to be under inhibitory norepinephric control and possibly under stimulatory cholinergic and serotoninergic control. Serotonin acts to depress growth hormonal secretion, while norepinephrine stimulates it, both presumably acting in the hypothalamus. Thyrotropin appears to be under epinephric control. Prolactin definitely is under inhibitory control of tuberoinfundibular dopamine, which can reach the hypophysis directly through the portal system. Dopamine can be viewed as mainly involved in direct actions on the neurosecretory neurons or on the hypophysis itself and is perhaps a stable element in the evolution of prolactinic control systems. A peptidic prolactin-inhibiting factor also appears to exist (released from terminals in the median eminence). Norepinephrin may have an excitatory role in prolactin release (acting on neurons whose cell bodies lie in the suprachiasmatic nuclei; 1,029, 1,040, 1,125). Monoaminergic and cholinergic neurons are multipolar, that is, numerous processes emerge from their cell bodies. These processes contain swellings or varicosities that are thought to be the active terminals from which the transmitters are released (1,049).

LH AND FSH PROBABLY ARE OF EXTREMELY ANCIENT ORIGIN, with a dual gonadotropic system being a primitive feature of tetrapods, and FSH and LH molecules being structurally homologous among all tetrapod classes. Both hormones seem to be present in amphibians and reptiles, though squamates apparently have lost the LH analogue secondarily (1,165, 1,174; see also note on pp. 147, 148). LH probably stimulates steroidogenesis by thecal and granulosal cells, while FSH probably stimulates follicular growth and possibly synthesis and secretion of estrogen (905; see also pp. 133, 137).

In any given species, the alpha chains of these gonadotropins and TSH (produced in different types of basophilic cells) are very similar or identical to one another. The beta chains are different and mainly responsible for establishing the specificity of biological action in fishes and mammals, whereas it is the alpha chains that are mainly responsible for determining specificity in reptiles and birds. But even the beta chains may show considerable similarity, and similarities also have been noticed between the alpha and beta chains. Thus, all these subunits appear to be homologous. This is further evidence of evolutionary relationships, even of the existence of a single primordial glycoproteinaceous hypophysial hormone that subserved both gonadotropic and thyrotropic functions. It appears that both the proteinaceous and carbohydrate moieties of these glycoproteinaceous hormones are important for biological function (see 1,023, 1,024, 1,178).

It is suggested that somatostatin assists in the regulation of nutrient absorption and ultimate distribution within vertebrates. It may play a role in adjusting the secretion of glucagon and insulin, both by bloodborne and intra-pancreatic paracrine messages (925). Growth hormone and prolactin (both produced by acidophilic cells) share a number of amino acid sequences in common, which suggests a close evolutionary relationship. In some instances, a certain amount of overlap has been detected in their biological activities. Much more work is required, and upon a more diversified species sampling, before firm conclusions can be reached about the interrelationships between the androgenic metabolites of the neuroendocrinological tissues of the male and their possible regulatory role on gonadotropic secretions (930).

AN INTACT HYPOTHALAMO-HYPOPHYSIAL LIAISON, including the hypothalamo-hypophysial portal system and several kinds of specific nerve terminals in the median eminence, is an absolute prerequisite for any gonadotropic function (733). All of the nervous stimuli by which the gonadotropic function is controlled by the environment lead eventually to a modulation of the synthesis and transfer of hypothalamic hormones within the portal system. From an evolutionary standpoint it appears that once the modulating role of the central nervous system on all hypophysial functions became extensive and "delicately tuned," there evolved a special topographical distribution of all cell types of the adenohypophysis in relation to the portal vessels from different origins (733).

A PATHWAY FROM THE RETINA TO THE HYPOTHALAMUS is one of the basic neural projections of vertebrates, and direct retinal-hypothalamic neural junctions have been described in several avian species. Moreover, photosensitive neurons lying in the infundibular complex of the hypothalamus of some species, for example Japanese Quail, possess the ability to cause the secretion of gonadotropin-releasing factors when they are subjected to either local or environmental photostimulation. In the White-crowned Sparrow such extra-retinal photoreceptors are located in the ventromedial region of the hypothalamus and/or in the tuberal complex, and perhaps also in or near the nucleus rotundus in the thalamus.

There is little doubt that retinal signals play a role in the photosexual response of birds whose breeding is controlled by photoperiod, although some questions are raised by studies that suggest that, with extra-retinal receptors blocked, the information about the photoperiod that is received by the eyes is ignored (see 921, 989, 1,028 and K. Yokoyama *et al.*, 1978, in 989). More generally, it appears that, depending on the circumstances, the central nervous system may exploit any convenient and appropriate signal from the internal or external environments to trigger reproductive behavior, though its responses probably are organized neonatally by steroidal sex-hormones (895).

Without implying that the hormonal control of reproduction in rain-breeding birds, such as the Budgerigar and Zebra Finch, is entirely understood, the following relationships appear to have been established. Under the influence of the behavioral factors discussed above (requirements with respect to nesting sites, mates, interactions with other individuals, etc.), as mediated through vision, audition, touch, temperature, and other external stimuli, nerve impulses are transmitted ultimately to neurosecretory cells in the hypothalamus (in no species is it known precisely how the information is integrated and passed to the neurosecretory system).

These cells of the hypothalamus then transform the afferent (incoming) neural signals into neurohormonal information, mediated by neurohypophysial hormones and adenohypophysial releasing factors (415), provided that they are not inhibited by the effects of unfavorable environmental conditions, such as low temperature or lack of water. These rain-breeding species remain reproductively active as long as environmental conditions are favorable (442). The adenohypophysial hormones have various targets. Thus, two gonadotropins, FSH and LH, act on the gonads and control their production of sexual cells (by FSH) and steroidal hormones (by LH).

This particular type of control of reproductive activity contributes to the relative ease with which confined Budgerigars can be induced to breed (442). In addition, many studies have implicated the release of neurohypophysial hormones (principally mesotocin and arginine vasopressin) as the initial acts that trigger a chain of events in the migratory process (see 920). Not only would the release of these hormones into the general circulation be expected to elicit metabolic responses in target organs, but release of arginine vasotocin from the anterior median eminence into the adenohypophysis through the portal vessels could influence the release of certain of the above-mentioned adenohypophysial hormones, leading to significant metabolic effects (920).

In addition, there is increasing evidence that steroidal sex-hormones can modify gonadotropic secretion and influence reproductive behavior by direct actions on discrete areas of the brain, the anterior hypothalamic-preoptic complex being one of the major binding regions (260, 391, 735, 916; see also pp. 438-441, **Hormones and the Nervous System**). Calls can be evoked by electrical stimulation at sites within this complex (396) and progesterone stimulates the preoptic area of the forebrain to induce ovulation in domestic fowl hens (415). The action of progesterone on the hypothalamus and hypophysis of the laying hen may occur at 6-8 and 14-18 h before ovulation (916). [The anterior hypothalamic-preoptic complex also seems to regulate behavioral thermoregulatory responses (518).]

Germ Cell Formation, Fertilization, Embryogenesis

THE AVIAN OVARY AND OOCYTE DEVELOPMENT

SIZE AND COLOR OF EGGS. Egg size varies among species from 2-27% of bodily weight (5.6% in ducks, 6.5% in hawks and owls, 10.3% in passerines, 17.2% in shorebirds, and up to 27% in kiwis) and generally is inversely related to bodily weight (34, 430). There also are intraspecific and intra-individual variations (see 314). The value for Budgerigars ranges from 7-11% of bodily weight. Parrot eggs are dull white and tend to have rather thin shells. [Unless otherwise specified, the following descriptions of oocyte development, folliculogenesis, fertilization, oviposition, embryogenesis, hatching, etc., generally apply to domestic fowl.]

PRIMORDIAL GERM CELLS. It generally is believed that all of the definitive oocytes in birds (about 8,000,000 at birth and 5,500 at 15 days of age) are derived from 20-100 primordial germ cells (Urkeimzellen). These are thought to originate in embryonic areas, probably posteriorly in the deep layers of the blastoderm and vitelline wall during the blastular stage, remote from the site of the genital ridges (the future ovaries). [In chelonians and lizards they are formed from blastomeres of the vegetal pole of the morula (989).] They migrate to these sites--partly under the influence of chemotactic factors--by a combination of active ameboid activity and passive transport in the vascular network, aided by morphogenetic movements of the embryonic tissues.

It is thought that no primordial germ cell arises from a proliferation of the germinal epithelium during embryonic development (852, 901). Primordial germ cells can be recognized at very early embryonic stages by their large size (10-18 micra in birds and reptiles), well-defined cell outlines, vesicular nucleus, high glycogen content, and (during migration) abundant lipid droplets and yolk platelets. About 21 days after hatching, they start to regress and finally disappear (901).

OOGONIA (diploid) arise by division of the primordial germ cells and are smaller than the latter but larger than somatic cells. Oogonia in mitosis become numerous in the 9-13-day-old chick ovary, and the total population of germ cells, as a net result of oogonial proliferation in the left ovarian cortex of the chick, increases about 25-fold between the 9th and 17th days of incubation. Proliferation is completed in almost all avian species by the time of hatching. Once multiplication ceases, the germ cells are referred to as "primary oocytes." Oogonia do not persist in the adult ovary of most birds, mammals, elasmobranchs, and cyclostomes, and all follicles are formed by the time of puberty (913).

Almost nothing is known of the endocrinological control of oogonial proliferation in birds. Gonadotropins and, perhaps, gonadal steroids may stimulate oogonial division in some adult fishes, amphibians, and reptiles, but no influence has been shown in avian embryos (903). Oogonial degeneration has been identified in almost all vertebrates but appears to be more prevalent in birds--which produce a single pool of germ cells during embryogenesis--than in amphibia and reptiles, which continue to produce germ cells in the adult during some phase of their reproductive cycles.

INTER-OOGONIAL BRIDGES. The most striking aspect of oogonial organization in fishes, amphibians, reptiles, birds, and mammals is the existence of intercellular bridges containing bundles of microfilaments that connect oogonia. This phylogenetically widespread distribution of intercellular bridges supports the suggestion that such structures are of basic importance in early germ-cell development. By functionally connecting oogonia, intercellular bridges may be a structural means of determining: synchrony of oogenesis, selective oogonial atresia (degeneration), and the extent of oogonial proliferation (756, 903). Synchronous oocyte development ceases when the intercellular bridges are disrupted by the investing follicular cells during folliculogenesis (903).

PRIMARY OOCYTES---GERMINAL DISC. The primary oocytes derived by oogonial multipication are arrested in the prophase of the 1st meiotic division. The plane of the 1st cleavage division in domestic fowl and quail is at an angle of 90° to the chalazal axis (see p. 154), whereas in the Rock Pigeon the angle is about 45° (997). The cell nucleus of the primary oocyte is contained in the germinal disc, a thickening of the surface cytoplasm about 3 mm in diameter that comes to float on a cone-shaped mass of "white yolk" and identifies the animal pole (622, 949). The embryo eventually develops from this disc (referred to as the blastodisc before fertilization and the blastoderm afterward). The entire stock of oocytes are produced during a brief embryonic period and they are recognizable first in the 16-day-old embryo (see 903).

VITELLOGENESIS---YOLK PRECURSORS. The primary oocyte possesses a large yolk, the central yolk mass of the oviposited egg. The yolk precursors are formed almost entirely in the liver, under the stimulation of estradiol (also the case in lizards), often in synergy with testosterone (904, 906, 928, 997, see also pp. 137, 140), or with growth hormone (in the Rock Pigeon; 997). The synthesis of these precursors (vitellenin, a low-density lipoprotein, the water-soluble livetins, and the granular lipovitellins and phosvitin; see p. 138) is associated with dramatic changes in the liver (see 906). Some intact livetins may be utilized directly by the embryo (see 950). The yolk precursors enter the oocyte via the follicular blood vessels (756), but the precise mechanisms involved in yolk deposition are not understood. Some oocytes in meiotic prophase in the chick ovary have been observed to be connected by intercellular bridges--at most 2 (see 903).

[Changes in blood composition during ovipositional phases usually parallel increased requirements for nutrients for egg formation. Thus, at that time blood lipids increase 35% in Rock Pigeons, about 50% in the domestic fowl, and about 500-600% in the Ring-necked Pheasant (*Phasianus colchicus*) and doves. Blood sugar increases by about 20% during ovulation in Rock Pigeons and its level is twice as great during oviposition and brooding as during nest building and burrowing in Bank Swallows (*R. riparia*; 975; see pp. 157-160, **Medullary Bone**, for blood calcium levels).]

YOLK STRUCTURE AND OUTER COVERING. Structurally, the yolk consists primarily of large, osmotically-active, membrane-limited "yolk spheres" (25-150 micra in diameter) which generally contain numerous osmophilic "subdroplets" (up to 2 micra in diameter). Though the latter contain closely packed particles about 30-60 Å in diameter, they do not have a crystalline matrix (see 906, 942). The yolk is enclosed in a cellular cytolemma of flattened granulosal cells, probably derived from the surface (coelomic) epithelium (903) and a perivitelline layer. The former contain prominent nuclei, mitochondria, dense granules, lipidic droplets, and some other organelles (1,115). The perivitelline layer is composed of a coarse network of long collagenous fibers formed from the similar material that lines the inner surface of the follicular epithelium, and is produced by the investing granulosal cells (336, 622). The fibers are arranged parallel to the surface of the oocyte and have pore spaces about 2 micra in diameter that are filled with an amorphous ground substance (622).

[Oogonial mitoses have been observed in the embryonic ovaries of numerous reptiles, and oogonia and oocytes in various stages of development are found in the ovaries of possibly all adult reptiles. The oogonia are located in one or more germinal beds, the number of which may be one factor that determines clutch size (see 903). As in birds, the oocytes are arrested in prophase (diplotene) of the first meiotic division and do not enter following meiotic stages until immediately before ovulation (852).]

THE ZONA RADIATA of light microscopy is formed of ultrastructural elevations or microvilli of the perivitelline layer, along with the follicle-cell processes that extend toward the oocyte. These may facilitate the entrance of the yolk materials during vitellogenesis (yolk deposition; 414, 904). Such elevations also are seen in the oocytes of the Pond Slider (*Pseudemys scripta*; see 771). They doubtless are an expression of micropinocytotic activity, the mechanism known to be involved in yolk and yolk-precursor uptake in, for example, lizards and teleosts (756, 866).

MEMBRANOUS JUNCTIONS---SPACES BETWEEN FOLLICULAR CELLS. Birds possess unique, specialized, membranous junctions ("lining bodies") between oocytes and their investing follicular cells. These increase greatly in number just before yolk deposition and may play a role in the formation or transfer of the large amount of yolk in avian oocytes (see 903, 904). In addition, the cells in the investing follicular epithelium of large vitellogenic follicles become stretched, and the resulting intercellular spaces are thought to provide a pathway for nutrients from the also-increased thecal vasculature to the oocyte (904). [An outstanding feature of the mammalian membrana granulosa is the presence of a large number of specialized intercellular connections, mostly gap junctions, that are believed to play an important role in intercellular communication (1,042).] A period of slow growth by the deposition of yolk, apparently consisting mainly of fine lipidic droplets of neutral fat and "yolk spindles," begins in the embryo and continues for several months or even years, depending on the species. During this period the follicle forms around the perivitelline layer. Primary follicles form 10-15 days after hatching in the Rock Pigeon and some of them undergo atresia 10 days later (997).

GROWTH PHASES---WHITE YOLK---WHITE FOLLICLES. The avian ovarian follicle is one of the most rapidly growing structures found in advanced vertebrates. Before sexual maturity (at 18-20 weeks of age), some follicles switch from the phase of slow growth to an intermediate growth stage, during which transparent vacuoles appear and yolk is formed within them. This phase lasts about 60 days (oocyte size, about 2-6 mm in diameter). During this phase the nucleus comes to lie eccentrically and a large number of yolk spheres or vacuoles form throughout the cytoplasm. As the population of yolk spheres increases, they become filled with granular subdroplets containing densely osmophilic material, and large glycogen granules appear in the cortical zone. The yolk at this stage is characterized by a relatively high content of protein relative to lipid and usually is referred to as "white yolk." It represents no more than 2% of the total yolk and surrounds the blastodisc, eventually extending down through the yellow yolk to its center (see 851, 900, 941, 949).

The rapid phase of vitellogenesis involves a 25-fold increase in the rate of growth of the oocytes, and lasts for a period of 4-11 days, depending on the species (931). It begins about 7-11 days before ovulation and culminates in ovulation (or atresia) in large birds, and 3-4 days beforehand in small birds. The rapid phase of vitellogenesis begins about 7-8 days before ovulation in the domestic fowl hen, in which the oocyte acquires 99% of its ovulatory size (about 2 mm/day radial increase) in the last 6 days, increasing in weight on successive days by roughly 2, 6, 10, 14, 18, 22, and 26% of its ovulatory weight (718, 729, 975).

The follicular wall of growing follicles secretes estradiol during the vitellogenic phase, and this, in turn, stimulates the production of yolk precursors to be deposited in the follicle. In this connection, the white follicles and the ovarian stroma contain much higher concentrations of estrogens than do the yellow follicles (see 1,145). Estradiol is essential for yolk production and oocyte maturation in all oviparous vertebrates (915; see also p. 140). Moreover, changes in plasma testosterone appear to mirror those of estradiol during the ovulatory cycle, as they also do in the Painted Turtle (*Chrysemys picta*; see 905).

YELLOW YOLK---YELLOW FOLLICLES. During the rapid phase of vitellogenesis, yellow yolk is formed and deposited in a relatively small number of follicles. Yellow yolk has a relatively high lipidic content and has been described as an oil-water emulsion with the continuous phase an aqueous protein. Floating in this are the fluid-filled yolk spheres, containing subdroplets of more electron-dense material. The subdroplets of yellow yolk differ from those of white yolk in being less refractive, smaller, and more numerous. Unlike the spheres in white yolk, no sphere of yellow yolk is membrane limited (949). The thyroidal status of the embryo appears to affect the rate at which yolk material is absorbed by the embryo during the latter stages of incubation (see 1,053).

FOLLICULAR SIZE HIERARCHY. One follicle enters the rapid growth phase on each successive day. As a result, 4-6 follicles usually are undergoing rapid growth immediately before the 1st ovulation, and exist in a size hierarchy. Some of these undergo atresia, but a larger, growing follicle never is overtaken by a smaller one (1,116). After the 1st ovulation (when the follicle is about 40 mm in diameter), a new white follicle enters the hierarchy from the pool of smaller, previtellogenic follicles, and another is recruited after each ovulation (or after a large follicle becomes atretic). The recruitment and growth of a white follicle to a yellow follicle occurs exclusively within the period of 8-14 h after the last ovulation, at a time when plasma FSH levels are high, suggesting that the action of FSH may be the major factor in bringing about both recruitment and growth (1,116). In hens that are incubating a clutch, the large follicles that remain after the final ovulation undergo atresia (see 900). There is some evidence which suggests that atretic follicles may be reactivated and subsequently be ovulated (943).

Yolk formation accounts almost entirely for the enormous gain in weight of the ovary during the last 10-12 days before ovulation begins, and is terminated only by actual ovulation (at least, in domestic fowl). A single follicle may increase in weight from 0.5 to 19 gm in 9 days, and in size by about 4 mm per day (622, 851, 853). The daily energy expense of egg production peaks on the 7th day after activation of the 1st follicle. The peak cost varies from 39-239% of standard metabolic rate in various non-passeriform species (257, 648, 729, 975, and below).

[As yolk matures there is a general increase in alpha- and beta-livetins and a decrease in the gamma-livetins (the water soluble yolk proteins); phosvitin (the major phosphoprotein of yolk) tends to increase, and the lipovitellins (the high-density lipoproteins of yolk) to decrease with the age of the follicle and oocyte. The proportion of alpha-lipovitellin relative to beta-lipovitellin also increases. In addition, increases occur in the ratio of lipid to non-lipid during follicular growth and maturation. Control of the chemical composition of yolk almost certainly is brought about within the follicle itself (941, 942).]

Vitellogenesis ceases or declines in rate in the last 24 h preceding ovulation (see 510). Most of the energy stored in the yolk, the main source of energy for the developing embryo, is in the form of lipids (519). [Chelonian yolk, on the contrary, has a relatively high proteinaceous and low lipidic content, suggesting that chelonian embryos are not as well prepared as birds to generate water by yolk catabolism (757).] Both the lipidic and proteinaceous levels in the yolk are relatively uniform between avian taxa but the aqueous content varies considerably (838).

THE AVIAN OVARY differentiates earlier than the testes (792). It lies in the cranial part of the body cavity, ventral to the aorta at the cephalic extremity of the left kidney, suspended from the dorsal body wall by the mesovarian ligament, and attached to the vena cava by an "ovarian stalk." It consists of an outer, comparatively dense cortex composed of a stroma of connective tissue fibers, fibroblasts, cells of epithelial origin, and spindle-shaped cells, among which follicles containing primary oocytes are distributed, and an inner, highly vascularized, core or medulla containing an extensive network of lacunae (also the case in reptiles; 853). The ovary is covered by a cuboidal superficial epithelium that is continuous with the peritoneal epithelium lining the body cavity. The blood vessels, nerves, and lymphatics that supply the ovary pass into the medulla along its region of attachment to the bodily wall (the ovarian stalk; see pp. 143, 144). [In the mature ovary (40-60 g) in the breeding season the distinction between the cortex and the medulla is almost obliterated (622).]

FOLLICLES AND FOLLICULOGENESIS. The basic hormonal patterns involved in follicular growth, ovulation, and vitellogenesis seemingly were established very early in vertebrate evolution, even prior to the appearance of reptiles, and the patterns of progesterone secretion in reptiles appear to antedate the major patterns of progesterone secretion of extant birds and mammals (1,318). The avian medulla generally contains large numbers of follicles in various stages of sigmoid growth in a hierarchical sequence (see 729). Their development and ovulation involve neuroendocrinological control mechanisms that are peculiar to the female (931), including feedback effects of ovarian steroidal hormones on the secretion of FSH and LH by the adenohypophysis (see p. 129). However, the precise means by which the hierarchy of developing follicles is established is not well understood. An atretic follicle in the follicular hierarchy is equivalent to a gap, since subsequent development and ovulation then fail to occur at the normal time. But if the atresia occurs toward the end of follicular maturation, normal nesting takes place, just as if ovulation had occurred (948). [In mammals, a water-soluble, non-steroidal protein, inhibin, of gonadal origin, also inhibits the release of FSH (1,401)]

Although there is little doubt that the growth of the large, vitellogenic follicles is controlled directly or indirectly by hypophysial gonadotropins, the role of hormones in the growth and maintenance of smaller follicles is controversial (911). The situation is complicated further by evidence that suggests the existence of a hierarchical structure even in the small "resting" follicles (941). There is an indication that the extensive and complex innervation of the ovary is involved in the later stages of preferential selection of follicles (622, 941).

[The mechanism proposed for the control of selective growth of only one follicle at a time to preovulatory size in the Green Anole (see p. 540, 541), is pertinent to the above discussion, although it does not account for the establishment of the size hierarchy. Jones (937) suggests that when a follicle reaches a critical diameter of about 2 mm, circulating gonadotropin (similar in activity to mammalian FSH) stimulates estrogenic secretion from the follicular granulosal cells. This estrogen then stimulates the local release of histamine and resulting hyperemia, and also increases the permeability of the blood vessels of the secreting follicle. As a result, circulating gonadotropin and yolk protein gain even greater access to the follicle, setting up a positive feedback loop that leads to biased growth and ovulation of the follicle.

This type of mechanism was proposed first by A.V. Nalbandov in 1959 and 1961 for the maintenance of the follicular size hierarchy in avian and mammalian ovaries (see 937); following Nalbandov's scheme, the number of follicles that mature to ovulatory size is controlled by endogenous gonadotropic levels and follicular vascularity, the most vascular follicles receiving more gonadotropin and growing at a greater rate.]

Folliculogenesis begins after hatching, characteristically when most oocytes are in the diplotene stage of meiotic prophase (of long duration in birds and characterized by lampbrush chromosomes). Investment of the primary oocyte with prefollicular cells, derived from the coelombic epithelium, is initiated 4-5 days after hatching (903). The follicular cells flatten and overlap as they extend along the oocyte surface, producing a pseudostratified epithelium. As the oocyte grows, these cells become stretched and form a single, flattened layer throughout subsequent follicular growth (it becomes multilayered at some stages of follicular maturation in squamates and mammals).

The cytology and histochemistry of follicular cells suggest that they have either steroidogenic activity or the potential for it during maturation of the follicular epithelium (see 904, 906). [In mammals, the granulosal cells have an ultrastructure characteristic of protein-synthesizing cells and the theca interna (see below) of the pre-ovulatory follicle is a major source of steroids (1,042).] Studies on the post-ovulatory follicle suggest that the granulosal tissue is composed of more than one cellular type (941). The primordial follicles of all vertebrates are remarkably similar in appearance; only growing follicles differ markedly in form and function (903, 913).

Interdigitation of processes from the oocyte and follicular cells is a common feature of primary oocytes in the diplotene stage. The visible functions of the follicular cells appear to be to provide lipids, glycogen, proteins, RNA, and possibly DNA, and then to facilitate their transfer along the follicular cell processes into the oocyte. They also may help to prepare the oocyte for the final phase of yolk formation and early embryogenesis. In addition, some follicular cells are taken into the ooplasm of rapidly growing previtellogenic oocytes, where they degenerate, yielding products that apparently serve to nourish the growing oocyte. Several other follicular cells degenerate *in situ* in growing previtellogenic and early vitellogenic follicles, and also contribute in this manner (similar phenomena occur in many reptiles; 904). As the follicle grows and the stalk develops, the arterial and venous systems (see pp. 143, 144, beginning with **Follicular Vascularization**) are drawn into this stalk (941).

THECA INTERNA AND STEROIDAL SYNTHESIS. A thick, well-defined basement membrane of amorphous ground substance separates the granulosal cells from the theca (941). The theca consists of stromal cells, smooth muscle cells, collagenous fibers, and blood vessels; the latter two components progressively increase in numbers with growth of the follicle. The thecal wall of large follicles can be subdivided into the theca interna and the theca externa. The former is a compact cellular capsule containing a narrow inner layer of collagenous fibers, a middle layer of fibroblasts, and an outer layer of vacuolated cells. The latter is wider and looser than the theca interna and consists of rows of fibroblasts interspersed with collagenous fibers. The follicle is covered by a loose connective tissue containing smooth muscle derived from the ovarian stroma. Some cells of the theca interna become glandular during follicular growth and most steroidogenic activity in many non-mammalian vertebrates apparently is concentrated in this layer.

[Estrogen appears to be the major hormone of the follicular phase of the reproductive cycle in reptiles, and is involved in the synthesis of yolk proteins by the liver. There is evidence for a regulatory estrogen feedback at the level of the hypothalamus and the hypophysis, and some data also implicate this hormone in the development of female reproductive behavior (1,318). However, in the Green Anole, and many other reptiles, the granulosal cells seem to be the major site of ovarian steroidogenesis. Squamates appear to secrete only one gonadotropin, similar to that of the beta-subunit of mammalian FSH (see 908, 913, 937 and below). Dispersed follicular cells from the ovary of the Painted Turtle, produce estradiol, progesterone, and testosterone *in vitro*. Addition of FSH leads to an increase in the production of all 3 hormones, whereas LH addition increases the production only of progesterone and testosterone (989).]

Since, in birds, the glandular cells of the theca interna present all the histochemical and ultrastructural details of steroid-secreting cells, they undoubtedly are a site of avian steroidogenesis, and the probable site of testosterone and estradiol production. The latter is stimulated by gonadotropins, probably via a cell-membrane linked adenylate cyclase. In the Turkey hen this stimulation is blocked by the injection of large doses of prolactin, which thus may play a regulatory role in ovarian steroidal secretion. Estradiol secretion must occur prior to the final phase of follicular maturation, since vitellogenesis is dependent on this hormone (see 904, 905, 939, 941).

An essential involvement of avian granulosal cells in follicular steroidogenesis is indicated by the studies of Huang and Hammond and their coworkers. Thus, the major steroidogenic product of the granulosal cells is progesterone, which presumably diffuses to the thecal cells. There it acts as the precursor of testosterone, which then can be aromatized to estrogens by the thecal cells. Progesterone release from granulosal cells can be promoted by LH or FSH, mediated in the former case, at least, by cyclic AMP (see refs. in 989, 1,145).

ESTRADIOL AND ANDROGENIC PRODUCTION and concentration, under the steroidogenic influence of LH, appear to be greater in the smaller follicles in the hierarchy, as determined by follicular wall analyses. However, since the concentration of estradiol in the venous plasma from the various follicles in the hierarchy is the same, its secretion may be constant, with only its deposition and storage in the follicular wall being greater in the smaller members of the hierarchy (1,137). After the follicle becomes the 2nd-largest in the hierarchy, aromatase activity (see above) declines, and progesterone and testosterone syntheses increase. The main steroid synthesized in the mature pre-ovulatory follicle is progesterone, whose concentration in the plasm increases when the follicle is fully developed. The ability of the mature follicle to respond to LH by producing progesterone is aquired only during the last 24 h before ovulation, when the steroidogenic response increases markedly; progesterone production increases dramatically during the last 6 h and relatively very large quantities are being produced by 3 h before ovulation (see 907, 931, 1,137).

[In the regulation of granulosal-thecal cell proliferation, differentiation, and function of developing ovarian follicles in hypophysectomized rats, steroidal and proteinaceous hormones can act as follows: (a) estradiol acting on the granulosal cells increases the number of receptors for estradiol; (b) FSH increases the number of receptors for FSH and, following estradiol priming, acts on large pre-antral follicles to increase the number of receptors for LH; (c) LH, acting on pre-ovulatory follicles effects a luteinization-related decrease in the number of receptors for estradiol, FSH, and LH, but an increase in the number for prolactin; (d) prolactin, in turn, increases the number of luteal cell receptors for LH. In considerations of mechanisms (b) and (d), it would appear that different hormones, presumably acting via different mechanisms, can regulate the synthesis of a single protein. In a final analysis, steroidal as well as proteinaceous hormonal regulation of ovarian cellular function appears to be essential for follicular and luteal cellular differentiation (1,043).]

THE SIZES OF THE PRIMARY OOCYTES within the graded sequence of follicular sizes appear to be random, since follicular size alone does not always reflect other characteristics, such as degree of yolk deposition and vascularity (see 510, 848). At this time the ovary in many species takes on the characteristic avian "bunch of grapes" appearance (crocodilian follicles and those of many other reptiles also protrude from the surface of the ovary and are pedunculated; 759, 853).

FOLLICULAR GROWTH AND ATRESIA--FINAL MATURATIONAL PROCESS. In almost all vertebrates, the number of germ cells in ovarian tissue greatly exceeds the number ovulated in each breeding cycle. Large numbers of germ cells do not ovulate and instead remain dormant or degenerate in a given cycle. The process of female germ cell selection follows consistent and often characteristic patterns within a species. After birth and in adulthood it is partially or totally a process of follicular selection (911). A prominent feature of the avian ovary is that the number of small follicles decreases rapidly after hatching and large numbers of follicles continue to undergo atresia-"negative selection"--during a bird’s life, particularly in species that have a short breeding season (853).

[Several kinds of germ cell selection occur within the vertebrate ovary: (1) most oogonia degenerate, with only a small percentage of germ cells initiating meiosis and becoming primary oocytes; (2) many primary oocytes degenerate, with only a small proportion becoming incorporated into primordial follicles; (3) only a selected proportion of primordial follicles begin to grow (stimulated by FSH in mice) at any given time--many others do not grow or become atretic; (4) many growing follicles (rate of growth stimulated by LH in mice) eventually undergo atresia--only a few mature and ovulate. These processes can occur concurrently or at separate times, depending upon the species. In all species studied, an increase in circulating gonadotropins increases the number of follicles in (at least) more advanced stages (911).]

In the case of the female chick, all the oocytes present enlarge between the 4th and 21st day after hatching. Thereafter, only some continue to grow, while others remain essentially constant in size for considerable periods, even until after the onset of sexual maturity (852). About 300,000 oocytes disappear per day during the 1st 2 weeks (908). Between the 3rd and 6th weeks, a majority of the enlarged oocytes become atretic when they reach 400 micra in diameter, a high incidence that corresponds to the mammalian situation. Some of the remaining follicles then grow to a larger size in the 11th week, but these also become atretic (see 900, 908).

Accordingly, follicular growth followed by mass atresia is characteristic of the ovary of the immature female, and because the number of germ cells is fixed after hatching, this number becomes greatly reduced before sexual maturity is reached (see above). Although a group of follicles enters a rapid phase of growth at each wave of follicular maturation in higher vertebrates, the final maturation process affects only the much smaller number of follicles that are destined to ovulate, and frequently only a single one (855).

FOLLICULAR DEVELOPMENTAL STAGES IN BUDGERIGARS. Follicles in the undeveloped ovary of domesticated Budgerigars are approximately 1 mm in diameter (860). In breeding adults, developing ovarian follicles pass through 3 stages: (1) there are 10-20 follicles that are 1.0-1.5 mm in diameter and larger than the others; (2) there are 2-5 follicles that are 2.0-2.5 mm in diameter and larger than the others; and (3) there is one follicle larger than the rest, and 5-8 smaller follicles, forming a graded series 4-12 mm in diameter (860).

In the Ring Dove, before courtship and nest building, the ovary contains only small resting follicles and 5-10 larger follicles, 1-5 mm in diameter. During courtship and nest building, 2 of the latter follicles enter the rapid growth phase (these apparently secrete estrogen and then progesterone in response to LH). One of the 2 eggs derived from these follicles is oviposited at about 18:00 h and the other at about 6:00 h the following day (see 900). For Canaries and many other species, there is a stage in which 5-6 follicles 1-2.2 mm in diameter and filled with yolk are larger than the rest, and a stage in which there is only one follicle 2.0-8.0 mm in diameter and larger than the rest (845, 851).

[The iguanid Desert Night Lizard (*Xantusia vigilis*) like all xantusiids, is nocturnal and viviparous (868). Follicular maturation takes 3 yr. Each year one of the germinal beds (1-5 layers of oogonia, naked primary oocytes, and primordial follicles in various stages of development, 10-60 micra thick) in each ovary gives rise to 20-40 new oocytes, all but one or 2 of which are destined to undergo atresia. By the spring and summer, the 20-40 original oocytes in each ovary have given rise to about half as many follicles, and these have reached a diameter of about 0.1 mm.

By the end of the year, about half of these follicles have attained a size of 0.5-0.6 mm. During the next year, these follicles undergo further attrition and again only about half survive. By May or June of the following year, each ovary contains 2 or 3 surviving follicles of 1.5 mm in diameter, only one of which matures; the others become atretic. The final growth of the surviving follicle to a diameter of 6.5 mm is very rapid. Accordingly, one ovum (exceptionally 2) is ovulated from each ovary each year from the 3rd onward. The gestational period is about 92 days (857).

A similar situation is said to occur in the tropical Australian lizard, *Leiolopisma rhomboidalis*, which ovulates a single egg concurrently from each ovary (monoautochronic ovulation), with a clutch size of 2 (see 911). In the Green Anole, which has one germinal bed per ovary and ovulates a single egg alternately from each ovary (monoallochronic ovulation) at 10-11-day intervals, about 11 growing follicles are present in each breeding ovary, 1 or 2 of which are atretic. Pharmacological dosages of mammalian gonadotropins disrupt the orderly, stepwise, follicular size hierarchy and more than one large, vitellogenic follicle appear in each ovary, creating a polyautochronic-like condition (more than one follicle ovulated concurrently from each ovary). If large gonadotropic dosages are administered to polyautochronically ovulating species, their ovaries become hyperstimulated to ovulate more than the normal number of follicles. The monoautochronically ovulating gecko, *Lepidodactylus lugubris*, also possesses one germinal bed per ovary, but only 5 growing and 2 atretic follicles (see 911).

Reptilian oocytes may become atretic at any stage of development, but, as is true of other vertebrates with yolky eggs, atresia is more frequent in the larger vitellogenic follicles. Atresia of small and medium-sized follicles in the Garden Lizard (*Calotes versicolor*) is most common after ovulation (see 903). Follicular atresia is a common occurrence in the lacertan ovary. It occurs at all months of the year in the Desert Night Lizard, but does not become extensive until after the rapid deposition of yolk begins, preceding ovulation (see 857). In the Johnny Darter (*Etheostoman nigrum*), only about a 1/3rd of the developing oocytes (class I) are oviposited, the smaller class II and III oocytes are resorbed (912).]

FOLLICULAR VASCULARIZATION. The ovary is one of the most highly vascularized organs of the body (it has 7 times the blood flow to the brain or liver and nearly as much as that to the kidneys, on a weight for weight basis) and makes tremendous demands on its vasculature as it oscillates through several different stages, sizes, and shapes while carrying out its diverse functions. It also is endowed with a surprisingly rich lymphatic system. In the clearance of extravascular proteins and fluids, these are indispensible to normal ovarian function. The arterial supply is variable: usually it arises from the left gonado-renal artery via its own ovario-oviductal branch. In some cases the ovarian branch from the gonado-renal artery is missing and the ovarian artery itself branches directly from the aorta (see 941). It has been suggested that prostaglandins (see p. 146) are involved in the regulation of ovarian blood flow, in that manner exerting their influence on ovarian function (1,045).

AN EXTENSIVE VASCULAR PLEXUS OF SPIRAL ARTERIES nourishes each primary oocyte. This plexus develops within the thin-walled, multi-layered, follicular sac and is derived from the 2-4 arteries entering the follicular stalk. These spiral arteries constrict when the ruptured follicle collapses and, thus, little if any bleeding occurs at the time of ovulation (909). In mammals, large, growing antral or vitellogenic follicles are hypervascular and their thecal vessels increase in permeability, resulting in ever increasing hyperemia.

A resulting great rate of delivery of gonadotropins and other bloodborne substances from the vascular plexus to these follicles, or from thecal vessels to the follicular wall and into the oocyte, may be one of the factors that influences follicular selection. Thus, it seems likely that large follicles become very susceptible to the withdrawal of gonadotropin and yolk-protein, and that peaks of atresia of growing follicles occur during periods of rapid growth of larger follicles (as is known to occur in some lizards). In addition, there is evidence of differential permeability of the vessels of follicles of similar stage. Ovulation presumably leads to shunting of blood to the next-largest follicles in the size hierarchy (see 911).

[Mast-cell histamine secretion, through vasodilatation of the thecal vessels, may play an important role in ovarian follicular vasodynamics in the Green Anole, with an influence on follicular growth and maturation. Some evidence suggests that histamine and antihistamines also can influence follicular growth in mammals, and mast cells occur in the ovaries of at least some mammalian species (see 913, 937).]

THE OVARIAN VENOUS DRAINAGE SYSTEM consists of intercommunicating layers of veins surrounding the growing follicle and is even much more extensively developed and complex than the arterial system. The first layer, a series of short venules penetrating the theca interna and derived from the capillary bed adjacent to the basement membrane, gives rise to two progressively larger venous networks that finally unite to form two main ovarian veins: the cranial ovarian vein joins with the left suprarenal vein which empties into the left side of the vena cava, and the caudal ovarian vein empties directly into the ventral part of the vena cava at about the level of the external iliac veins (see 941). Circular arrangements of smooth muscles at arteriole-capillary junctions in Man are thought to control flow in individual capillaries, which are extremely permeable, and most arteriole-venule shunts also contain smooth muscle; both of these regions of the microvasculature thus are under nervous and chemical control (909).

FOLLICULAR INNERVATION. The adrenal, renal, and aortic neural plexuses, branches from the sympathetic chains, and, perhaps, some fibers from the pelvic plexus form a meshwork of nerve fibers that envelop the ovarian blood vessels, enter with them via the ovarian stalk, and innervate the avian ovary (910). The nervous supply is so complex, however, that the above subdivisions may not be physiologically meaningful; the neural network probably acts as a coordinated single unit. Many of the nerves are associated with blood vessels and smooth muscles of the ovarian medulla and cortex but others run directly to the developing and mature follicles (941).

FOLLICULAR WALLS AND THECAL LAYERS ARE INTENSELY INNERVATED with varicose plexuses of both adrenergic (sympathetic) and cholinergic (parasympathetic) fibers, particularly when the follicles are mature. Ten or more large bundles of axons, each containing 50-100 single fibers, pass through the follicular stalk and break up into a network in the thecal regions. A high density of adrenergic axon terminals and possible cholinergic terminals are in membranous contact with steroid-producing cells and smooth muscle cells and around blood vessels in the theca interna; myelinated fibers are found in the peripheral layers while unmyelinated fibers make specialized direct contacts with steroidogenic cells. The stroma and theca interna of both small and large follicles are extremely well innervated, whereas the granulosa receives very little innervation (see 910, 939).

The function of the nerves is uncertain. They may: (a) regulate the distribution of blood-borne gonadotropins (perhaps causing differential access to different follicles), (b) control the secretion rate of steroids by the glandular cells of the theca interna by regulating the blood flow to them, (c) regulate the supply of yolk precursors--again by regulating blood flow, and (d) be involved in ovulation (as in the domestic cat and rabbit), either directly by affecting smooth muscle and producing tension at the stigma or indirectly by occluding blood vessels or releasing neural secretory products.

FOLLICULAR GROWTH AND OVULATION IN DENERVATED OVARIAN TRANSPLANTS. Neural involvement in ovulation has been indicated by an increasing amount of experimental pharmacological data (414, 622, 851, 907, 910, 939). Some evidence suggests that autonomic neural control of ovulation is only modulatory or regulatory, rather than essential, since ovulation also occurs in transplanted ovarian tissue. Although the common findings of re-establishment of neural connection to transplanted ovarian tissue (even in the anterior chamber of the eye) rendered most of the latter studies inconclusive (see 907, 939), excessive follicular growth and multiple ovulations apparently also occur in ovarian transplants in which denervation is not in doubt (see 948), supporting the modulatory view.

OVULATION. Rupture of a mature follicle (about 40 mm in diameter) quickly follows the completion of vitellogenesis. This occurs about 24 h after the breakdown of the oocyte nucleus in preparation for the 1st maturation division (reductional), which is completed a few hours before ovulation in the domestic fowl and Turkey. Rupture occurs at the outward-bulging stigma or cicatrix, a clear streak, 2-3 mm wide, in the long axis of the follicular wall at the apical pole, supplied with but a few veins and arteries and having an extremely thin (or almost lacking a) connective tissue coat.

A few min before ovulation, a little bleeding occurs at the stigma, which gradually becomes wider in a transverse direction and translucent along its mid-portion. At the time, the mid-portion where the rupture is expected to occur becomes thinner and the stratum granulosum and theca interna no longer can be seen. Rupture begins as a tiny opening at one end and spreads as a slit-like tear, with the release of a secondary oocyte from the surface epithelium and stimulation of the activity of the left oviduct (salpinx).

Usually, before the tear has extended along more than 10 mm of the stigma, the secondary oocyte has been squeezed out of the follicle, mainly by intra-follicular pressure produced by the latter's rapidly contracting wall, which contains smooth muscle fibers. After rupture, only the theca externa of the stigma remains, tapering off to the point of rupture. The disappearance of the stratum granulosum and the theca interna in the stigmal region is caused by degeneration and detachment of the cells of these tissues from one another to form a wide gap as the overlying theca externa and its collagen fibers also disintegrate (856, 941, 1,115).

[Ovulation from the ovarian surface epithelium is a conservative characteristic of all vertebrate ovaries (913). In mice, the preovulatory degradation of the follicle starts at the outside with the surface (peritoneal) epithelium of the ovary and successively progresses to the interior of the follicular wall, with the granulosa being the last layer to remain intact before ovulation (see 907).]

The extrusion of the secondary oocyte through an opening of only half its own diameter testifies to the elasticity of its cytolemma and perivitelline layer (856). The nuclear changes in the primary oocyte leading to extrusion of the 1st polar body and formation of the secondary oocyte apparently are under the control of LH (851). Direct application of proteolytic enzymes to the surface of the follicular wall can induce ovulation (see 907), and it was suggested some time ago that local ischaemia of the follicular wall is a prerequisite for stigmatic rupture (see 943).

THE PROSTAGLANDINS generally are regarded as primarily local tissue hormones that are not stored in significant amounts in cells but are synthesized rapidly from phospholipids, and that are rapidly degraded in the pulmonary circulation (95% loss per passage). The triggering event for synthesis, which may be a neural, physical, or endocrine stimulus, is believed to cause an alteration of the cell membrane that facilitates splitting off precursor fatty acids (see 1,042, 1,147). Prostaglandins have been implicated in the processes of corpus luteal regression, estrus, and follicular rupture (LH-induced ovulation) in some mammals (932, 1,044, 1,145).

The theca of the largest follicle in the hen produces prostaglandins during (and after) ovulation, releases them immediately before the preovulatory peak of shell-gland contraction, and plays an important role in the induction and timing of oviposition (see also below). It apparently does not synthesize prostaglandins in response to stimulation by LH. Another possible physiological relationship in birds could be between ovarian prostaglandins and steroidogenesis in the largest follicle, such as is known to exist in mammals, since there is an inverse relationship between prostaglandin and steroidal hormonal content, and the prostaglandin and progesterone contents of the largest follicle increase simultaneously. Whether prostaglandins are involved in the process of follicular rupture remains to be established (1,144-1,147).

OVIPOSITION occurs roughly 24 h after ovulation. While LH peaks sharply in the serum at 4-6 h (8 h in the Turkey) before ovulation and some threshold level of this hormone undoubtedly is the inducing stimulus for ovulation (1,138), little is known of the details of ovulatory control. There is evidence, however, that important pre-ovulatory changes within the follicle already have begun a few hours before ovulation (943). The LH peak is accompanied by a sharp peak in progesterone and is preceded by peaks in estrogen and testosterone. The latter may be involved in some regulatory function of the hypothalamo-hypophysial-ovarian axis (989). [Although the 2nd-, 3rd-, and 4th-largest follicles appear to provide relatively more testosterone per unit of producing tissue than the largest follicle, particularly the 3rd- and 4th-largest follicles 15 h before oviposition, their contribution to the total plasma content of testosterone may be very small (1,137).]

Estrogen injections never stimulate LH release but prime the hypothalamo-hypophysial system for such release, thus facilitating the effect of progesterone, the major source of which is the largest follicle. Progesterone stimulates LH secretion through a positive feedback mechanism, apparently when given at any stage of the ovulatory cycle, except when preovulatory LH levels are falling. When administered just prior to the occurrence of the preovulatory LH surge, it induces premature ovulation and oviposition of the oviductal egg, so that both processes occur nearly simultaneously. Treatment with a corticosterone depressant (dexamethasone) inhibits the LH surge and ovulation, an effect that can be reversed with an injection of ACTH (see 1,140).

In inducing LH release, progesterone acts not only on the hypothalamus but also on the adenohypophysis itself, and progesterone receptors and acceptors are present in the cytosols and nuclei, respectively, of both organs. Those in the cytoplasm peak in concentration 18 and 8 h before ovulation, whereas the number of nuclear binding sites peaks at 14 and 6 h (see 931, 989, 1,117, 1,133, 1,137). Lesions in the ventral preoptic area of the hypothalamus block both spontaneous and progesterone-induced ovulation, whereas electrical stimulation of the same area induces ovulation (see 1,027). Work on the gonadotropin content of the hypophysis suggests that LH release occurs twice, once about 14-16 h before ovulation and once within the last 8 h (943). [Although injected testosterone induces ovulation, the hormone may play no physiological role during the ovulatory cycle (1,117).]

It appears that the preovulatory release of LH is facilitated by the combined actions of estrogen and progesterone in a 2-phase process; the priming phase depends upon the activity of both hormones, as provided by a fully-developed hierarchy of yellow, yolky follicles, whereas the inductive phase depends only upon the increase in plasma progesterone, probably acting through an increase in the concentration of LH-releasing factor in the hypothalamus. In this connection, injection of progesterone into specific regions of the hypothalamus and caudal neostriatum induce premature ovulation, as do also intraventricular (3rd ventricle) injections of LH-releasing factor, and anti-progesterone serum (but not anti-estriol serum) blocks ovulation (see 1,138, 1,145). LH-releasing factor may cause an increase in the production and release of both LH and FSH (931, 1,133). Plasma FSH exhibits a major peak at 11-14 h before ovulation and a minor peak at ovulation, and is thought to augment the action of LH in inducing ovulation (see 900, 905, 1,117). At the end of the ovipositional period, plasma LH levels decline in a number of species (see 1,106).

A neural stimulus evoked by oviposition may control follicular rupture (854), and a pending ovulation is inhibited by the mechanical stimulation provided by the egg or other object (even a thread) in the oviduct (1,035). After ovulation, a ruptured follicle contracts to a cup-shaped structure, becomes filled with granulosal cells, invaded by erythrocytes, lymphocytes, and a very large number of fibroblasts, regresses rapidly, disintegrates, and becomes cleared by phagocytosis within days or weeks (414, 622). Those of the pheasant or Mallard Duck may persist for months.

[Two different molecules, chemically similar to mammalian FSH and LH, have been identified in 2 species of turtle and the American Alligator. The LH of the latter is "reasonably close" in amino acid composition to that of the Turkey and domestic fowl (see 905). In Green Sea Turtles (*Chelonia mydas*), once ovulation is initiated in the "membranous-curtain-like" ovary, it proceeds rapidly on both surfaces until all of the upwards of 120 adequately-developed follicles have ruptured and passed into the paired oviducts (770). It appears likely that ovulation of all mature follicles is an essentially simultaneous process in response to a surge in LH, probably "primed" by a surge in FSH (771).

There also appears to be a preovulatory surge of gonadotropin in squamates that probably initiates ovulation. However, there may be no LH homologue in squamates (nor in fishes). The role of FSH in ovarian function in this group may encompass that normally attributable to LH in, say, mammals (908, 913, 937), and both the testes and ovaries of members of these species generally are nonspecific in their response to FSH and LH (1,174). Some workers regard the FSH homologue as possibly representing the ancestral gonadotropin, from which the separate FSH and LH molecules of more advanced vertebrates have evolved (1,041). Others see LH as the more likely primitive form, with FSH appearing later and assuming some of the former's functions (1,178). There is a pre-ovulatory rise in progesterone in many oviparous squamates and chelonians (and a declining level of secretion associated with corpus luteal formation and regression). There also is continued luteal secretion in viviparous squamates that peaks after the corpus luteum is fully developed. These actions may depress further ovarian development until the onset of the next cycle (905, 1,318).]

THE MEAD-MORTON PARADIGM OF DUAL PROLACTINIC CONTROL. Several lines of evidence suggest that prolactin is involved in the termination of ovulation. Thus, it causes a decrease in ovarian size in domestic fowl and inhibits the response of the ovaries and oviducts to FSH and LH in White-throated Sparrows (*Zonotrichia albicollis*), though not in White-crowned sparrows. [The discordant results may hinge on species-specific differences in hormonal sensitivity during the 24-h cycle.] Injection of prolactin also prevents the pre-ovulatory surge of estradiol and progesterone in domestic Turkeys *in vivo* and in domestic fowl *in vitro* (granulosal cells; 1,135) and prevents ovulation as well if presented at the proper time (see 1,106). [Injection of prolactin in lizards inhibits both follicular growth in response to exogenous gonadotropin and ovarian recrudescence (1,318).]

A significant increase in serum prolactin levels precedes the onset of incubatory behavior of Turkeys and the levels continue to climb after the onset, reaching 1,000 ng/ml on the 7th day after the onset, compared to 83.4 ng/ml in ovipositing flockmates. Generally the hens with consistently elevated prolactin levels (above 300-400 ng/ml) cease oviposition and show manifestations of incubatory behavior (1,139). Moreover, an injection of an antiserum to prolactin leads to an increase in LH levels in incubating domestic fowl hens, suggesting that increased levels of prolactin are the basis for the decrease in LH secretion that marks the termination of oviposition (see 1,106). It is strongly supportive of this paradigm that, in Wilson's Phalarope (*Steganopus tricolor*), in which only the males incubate the eggs and brood the young, the hypophyses of males during the incubatory period contain 3½ times as much prolactin as those of females, even though the level in females doubles between early reproductive stages (undetectible in males at that time) and the time of incubation. Moreover, though only the males possess brood patches, these can be induced in females by injections of prolactin plus androgen (see 1,176).

In view of findings such as those cited above, the fact that complementary physiological effects often are regulated by the same endocrinological mechanism, and the known association of prolactin with incubatory behavior (see pp. 130, 131), Mead and Morton (1,106) have proposed that changes in prolactin levels are responsible for both the inhibition of ovulation and the initiation of incubation. Modulatory control over clutch size might then be exerted by the rate of prolactinic synthesis and release. This paradigm is adopted as a working hypothesis in Chapter 4 (Part 3) in the treatment of evolutionary transitions in egg care from avian ancestors that did not incubate to ancestors that did (see pp. 569-571, **Within an Endocrinological Framework**).

POST-OVULATORY FOLLICLE. There is no corpus luteum in birds, but as in the case of the mammalian corpus luteum, the post-ovulatory follicle has a direct or indirect effect on oviductal function, though only for 24 h. The granulosal cells actively synthesize steroids, including progesterone, through an LH-promoted adenylate cyclase-cyclic AMP system (see 951, 1,145). Excision of the post-ovulatory follicle an hour after ovulation results in delayed oviposition and affects the associated, seemingly endocrine-controlled, nesting behavior, which may be entirely absent (622, 753). Ovulation of the next follicle in the hierarchical sequence does not occur until about 15-75 min after oviposition (510).

[With the exception of birds, luteal bodies occur in every class of vertebrates, both oviparous and viviparous (855). Thus, most or all reptiles form postovulatory corpora lutea (regardless of the presence or absence of a placenta), and it appears that regression of these structures occurs around the time of parturition or oviposition (759, 913). They are derived, at least in part, from the thecal layer that surrounds the follicle (852). They synthesize progesterone, a surge in which, after ovulation and during nesting, is believed to stimulate a rapid release of albumen in the oviductal magnum as the oocytes traverse it. The rapidity of the albumen release is suggested by the fact that pre-calcified oviductal chelonian eggs have not been described (759, 771, 905, 915). In at least one viviparous lizard and in viviparous snakes, corpus luteal secretions (e.g., progesterone) may influence the timing of oviposition or parturition, probably by influencing oviductal contractility, and this may be a primitive function of the corpus luteum (see 913).]

OVIDUCTS AND FEMALE GONADS

THE LEFT OVIDUCT is a tortuous tube some 80 cm long, derived from the embryonic Müllerian ducts. It extends from the left ovary to the cloaca and occupies a large part of the abdominal cavity. It is suspended in the coelom from the dorsal abdominal wall by a double-layered sheet of peritoneum that divides to dorsal and ventral ligaments, both of which contain smooth muscles. The left dorsal oviductal ligament, the left abdominal air sac, and the body wall together form the "ovarian pocket" which guides the oocyte into the infundibulum after ovulation (851, 944; see p. 152). Lymphatic aggregates may occur in the lamina propria at any level and are unrelated in either size or number to the segment of the oviduct in which they occur. Scattered lymphocytes also are present, apparently migrating through the epithelium; plasma cells are similarly distributed and usually abundant (see 944).

The left oviduct and its relationship with the left ovary are singularly uniform throughout the Class Aves; they present none of the considerable variations found in members of the classes Mammalia and Reptilia. Where they exist, differences are of a minor nature and their functional significance is largely unknown. [Indeed, the diversity of oogenesis and of the reproductive system in reptiles is unique among amniotes (see 756). For example, in squamates, either sex may retain both Müllerian and Wolffian ducts (1,027).] The fact that the gonaducts of various vertebrates "follow rules of their own" probably is related to the fact that in the evolutionary past they had excretory (i.e., nonsexual) functions and commonly were retained in both sexes (see 1,027).

There is a gradient of spontaneous motility in the oviduct, with highest motility in the fimbriated region and lowest in the vaginal region, particularly at the shell gland-vaginal junction (see 510). Transport of the developing egg may be affected by estrogen and progesterone (951). Like the left ovary, the left oviduct has an extensive blood supply and drainage with a closely correlated cyclic development (845). In Budgerigars, during reproductive development, there is a 50-fold increase in oviductal weight and a 4-fold increase in the diameter of the magnum (to 2.5-2.75 mm), both of which are estrogen-dependent effects (860, 904). The left oviduct probably can synthesize estrone, estradiol, and dehydro-epiandrosterone (see 951). Both the left ovary and oviduct undergo complete regression in the laying hen within 6 days after hypophysectomy (see 733).

[In a brood parasite, the Brown-headed Cowbird (*Molothrus ater*), the left ovary and oviduct do not regress between separate sets or clutches of eggs, which makes it possible for them to resume laying after only 1 or 2 days (the average female lays about 40 eggs in 56 days), whereas at least 5 days usually intervene in non-parasitic passerines between the loss of a nest and the 1st egg of a replacement clutch (1,356).]

RIGHT FEMALE GONAD. With comparatively few exceptions, for example, Accipitrinae, Falconinae, Buteoninae, Cathartidae, and occasionally Ring Doves, Rock Pigeons, Herring Gulls, and domestic fowl, only the left ovary is functional in birds (see 718, 1,027). The surface epithelium of the avian right female gonad, which appears similar to that of the left one in earlier embryonic stages, loses its cuboidal arrangement and becomes a thin layer of flat cells separated from the inner epithelial cords (see 902), probably under the influence of early estrogenic secretion from the left ovary (940). It generally remains in an ambisexual state.

[The failure of one ovary to develop fully also is typical of some reptiles and certain rodents (for example, *Lagidium peruanum*) and bats (e.g., members of the Vespertilionidae; see 852), some monotremes (1,308), some elasmobranchs (865), and even some myxinoid cyclostomes (hagfishes; 863, 989), in which there is no gonoduct. The right ovary of the Duck-billed Platypus (*Ornithorhynchus anatinus*) contains oocytes that never mature (1,308).]

THE RIGHT OVIDUCT in most avian species regresses to nothing more than a minute vestige, though its development can be induced by treating the embryo with estrogen (28, 414, 622, 851). In some 81% of adults examined, the vestiges vary from cysts ranging in size from 0.5-20 cm in diameter, to tubes ranging from about 1-cm long to fully developed oviducts; in one case a fully formed and functional right oviduct was present (956). Elements of right oviducts have been reported in over 30 species belonging to many orders, including Psittaciformes (1,407). [Wolffian ducts persist as rudiments in normal adult females and may enlarge during the breeding season in some species (see 1,027).]

There is evidence for the presence of 2 fully-formed oviducts in at least 23 species belonging to 12 orders (348, 1,407). Flocks are known with a high incidence of persistent right oviduct (see 956) and the incidence appears to be higher in inbred strains (see 944, 989). In one view the regression of the right oviduct is a consequence of a less firm attachment of its ostial junction to the pleuroperitoneal septum, leading to breakage on stretching (see J. Thiebold, 1975, in 989).

[Certain snakes, for example blind worm-snakes (Typhlopidae), possess only the right oviduct, or have the left oviduct reduced to a non-functional vestige, though they ovulate several oocytes concurrently from both ovaries (see 953, 989). In the ovoviviparous ray, *Dasyatis*, both the right ovary and the right oviduct are absent (989). The right oviduct of the Duck-billed Platypus is never as well developed as the left one but its terminal portion (the "uterus") hypertrophies and shows a luxuriant growth of glands during the breeding season (1,308).]

THE LEFT FEMALE GONAD, in contradistinction to the gonad on the right, undergoes further growth of both inner and surface epithelial tissues accompanied by an increase in stromal tissue and vascularization, until an ovary with two well-developed topographical regions, the cortex and the medulla, is formed (902). If the ovary is removed by surgery or is diseased, the right gonad in some groups (such as ducks and songbirds) hypertrophies and usually develops into a testis or ovotestis; spermatogenesis may take place if ovariectomy is performed within a month of hatching. Later removal results in a great incidence of ovotestes and ovaries, some of the latter of which have follicles that can be ovulated (see 792, 851). Complete, permanent, functional sex reversal has not yet been produced in birds (1,027).

[In a number of reptilian embryos a lower initial number of germ cells were found in the left gonad. In some squamatan genera, the left oviduct is vestigial or non-functional, although both ovaries are present and functional and normal clutches are produced (914). Much more commonly the left lacertilian ovary is reduced in size (e.g., *Crotaphytus* and *Plestiodon*). Though the number of germ cells is distinctly higher in the right side of the chelonian blastoderm, the gonads of the adult are very nearly symmetrical (see 861).]

TWO OVARIES. Although the right ovaries of domestic fowl and ducks usually lack a cortex, and at most contain only scattered cortical traces (see 792, 853), cases are known where 2 functional ovaries and oviducts were present and 2 eggs were laid each day (monoautochronic ovulation; see 941, 1,407), and there is evidence for 2 ovaries in 86 species belonging to 16 orders in which the norm for most usually is accepted to be only 1 ovary. In some species the frequency with which 2 ovaries occur is quite high; for example, the probability is 24% in Ring Doves and 50% in mature hawks (718, 853).

Kiwis assemble clutches of 2 or 3 eggs (usually 2) by ovulating 1 egg alternately from each ovary (monoallochronic; see 1,403, 1,407); this also appears to occur in Goshawks (*Accipiter gentilis*; see 1,407). Although the mode of ovulation apparently is unknown or unspecified in other species with two functional ovaries, monoallochronism is the likely practice. In the Brown Kiwi, in which 2 ovaries normally are found, the single oviduct engulfs oocytes from either ovary. In the absence of a right oviduct in many birds with two functional ovaries, oocytes ovulated from the right ovary drop into the body cavity and are absorbed, since a mesentery usually separates the right ovary from the left oviduct (989).

The asymmetrical germinal population of the gonadal territories in the embryos of most avian species may be due primarily to unequal development of the presumptive gonadal areas, or a differential rate of mitosis or degeneration of the germ cells. The view that the asymmetry is caused by differential primordial germ cell migration (see treatment in 989) no longer is favored (see 901). [In crocodilians, the right ovary (and oviduct) usually is larger and contains more follicles of pre-ovulatory diameter than the left one (759).]

PASSAGE THROUGH THE OVIDUCT

INFUNDIBULUM AND FERTILIZATION. The infundibulum of the oviduct is its thin, fimbriated, funnel-shaped anterior segment or ampulla, with lips continuous with the ventral and dorsal ligaments and an epithelium consisting of both ciliated and non-ciliated cells (about 7-9 cm long). It surrounds the follicle and is closely applied to the ovary in such a manner that when the follicle ruptures and the secondary oocyte passes through the surface epithelium of the ovary, it does not lie free in the splanchnocoele (body cavity) but is guided into the infundibulum by the "ovarian pocket" (414, 453, 511; see also p.149).

The walls of the infundibulum are composed of the peritoneum, a thin layer of longitudinal muscles, with a pseudostratified columnar ciliated epithelium covering the tops and sides of its folds, and a non-ciliated, simple, columnar epithelium. It possesses specialized tubular infoldings ("glands") that play a role in prolonging the survival of the spermatozoa (510, 511, 622, 851).

Soon after the secondary oocyte enters the oviduct, 2 outer layers are laid down over the perivitelline layer, the "continuous layer" and the "extravitelline layer." Their exact origin in the oviduct is unknown; it may be that their formation (and that of the chalazae; see pp. 154, 155) is a continuous process that normally starts in the infundibulum and is completed at lower oviductal levels (944). The extravitelline layer is 3-8 micra thick and is composed of a delicate meshwork of fine fibrils arranged in concentric sublayers. The continuous layer is about 50-100 nm thick, with little structure except for granules about 7 nm in diameter. All told, the central yolk mass is invested in 4 covering layers, the so-called "vitelline membrane of the ovum" (949), of a thickness variously estimated at between 4 and 24 micra. Only the innermost of these layers, the cytolemma, is a true cell membrane (622).

The fragile cytolemma and strong perivitelline layer of the ovulated secondary oocyte permit considerable squeezing and deformation as the oocyte is grasped--engulfed by extension of the fimbriae by vascular engorgement and contraction of their muscle fibers. The oocyte then is passed along by muscular contractions, possibly aided by the muscles of the dorsal and ventral supporting ligaments (622, 944). The epithelium of the oviduct is ciliated throughout its length; the cilia tend to beat toward the cloaca and thereby may assist the passage of the developing egg (441, 622). During this period the infundibulum, which normally is quiescent until the secondary oocyte is liberated, becomes extremely active and will engulf any suitable object (28, 510), sometimes even a follicle, in which case ovulation occurs within the oviduct (see 947).

If spermatozoa are present, fertilization begins in the upper thin-walled neck of the oviduct, where the mucous membranous lining is many-folded (378, 414, 453). Fertilization usually is by polyspermy, and it is speculated that this also occurs in chelonians (see 757). Fertilization first becomes possible in the 2nd meiotic metaphase. As spermatozoa penetrate and become embedded in the perivitelline layer (activation), the 2nd polar cell is extruded, thereby completing the maturation divisions, with the production of the mature ovum or ootid. However, the spindle for the 2nd maturation division (equational) is formed and arrested in metaphase even before ovulation occurs (511, 622).

Fertilization takes place within 15 min after ovulation, before the secondary oocyte reaches the magnum (pars albuginae; see 348). Penetration of the spermatozoa is followed by fusion of one of them with the female pronucleus (amphimixis). Since the female is the heterogametic sex in birds, the sex of the future embryo is determined before ovulation, rather than at fertilization, as in mammals. Supernumerary spermatozoal nuclei in the Rock Pigeon divide and form an outer ring of nuclei around the first cells of the embryo. With the formation of the blastoderm, these nuclei disappear and are replaced by nuclei derived from the zygote (997).

BLASTULATION. A subsequent series of mitotic cellular divisions beginning 5 h after ovulation divide the thin germinal disc into an increasingly large number of cells (meroblastic cleavage), forming the blastoderm (378). Supernumerary sperm pronuclei also divide but subsequently degenerate (see 622). The 4-8-cell stage is reached while the developing egg (technically speaking, the zygote) is still in the isthmus (511). By the time of oviposition, the blastoderm has attained a diameter of nearly 5 mm and consists of a double layer of cells overlying the central sub-germinal cavity (414, 622). At that time, two areas are distinguishable, a central area pellucida and a peripheral area opaca, which give rise to embryonic and extra-embryonic structures, respectively (see 622). According to van Tienhoven (989), all avian embryos are in about the same stage of development at the time of oviposition, because the eggs of all species are in the oviduct for about the same length of time after fertilization in the infundibulum. Within that paradigm, differences in periodicity of oviposition would be determined solely by differences in the periodicity of ovulation.

MAGNUM. After a stay of $\frac{1}{4}$-$\frac{1}{2}$ h, the infundibulum starts each ovum on its passage toward the vagina by peristaltic contractions. Before leaving the infundibulum, however, the ovum receives its first albumen layer, a thick, gel-like secretion deposited as it traverses the neck or caudal region. After leaving the thin-walled neck, it traverses the highly-glandular and highly distensible magnum (2.3 mm/min avg. rate of transit; 944). This is the cranial (upper) portion of the oviduct, and is the longest of the 5 oviductal regions, being about 33 cm long (441, 453, 510). It readily is distinguished from the infundibulum by its dull, white color, greater external diameter, and markedly thicker wall.

The magnum is characterized by mucosal ridges with secondary and tertiary folds. It is lined with tubular glands formed by invagination of epithelial cells and by unicellular glands. The latter are composed of the goblet and ciliated cells (the former filled with an acid mucopolysaccharide mucus), whereas the former are composed of non-goblet, non-ciliated cells that secrete albumen granules. The latter appear to coalesce to form large masses that are secreted during the ovipositional phase (510, 845, 847, 860, 944). It appears that there is sufficient water-soluble protein present in the magnum at the time of ovulation for the formation of the albumen of 2 eggs (see 944).

[There is a direct dose-response relationship between estradiol and the increase in weight and size of the oviduct in Budgerigars. But as in the domestic fowl and Canary, neither progesterone nor prolactin appears to have a synergistic effect with estradiol on this growth. Although prolactin appears to play no role in the development of the oviduct of Budgerigars, progesterone acts directly to influence the development of the tubular glands of the magnum (847).]

ALBUMEN DEPOSITION, STRUCTURE, COMPOSITION, FUNCTION. In a 3-4-h stay in the magnum, the yolk becomes coated with a series of concentric layers of albumen (the egg white). There is a concomitant pre-eminent enlargement of another ovarian follicle and completion of defeathering in the course of brood-patch development (414; see pp. 179, 180, **The Brood Patch**, and pp. 561, 562, **Incubatory Temperatures and Brood Patches**). The albumen is synthesized and secreted in the oviduct under the influences of estradiol and either progesterone or testosterone. It consists of 88% water, about 10% proteins and amino acids, and small amounts of minerals, and comprises 20-25% of the total energy content in the egg for nidifuges as opposed to 40-50% for nidicoles (see p. 166, **Egg Composition**; 975). There are some 40 proteins of 12 major types; of these, 54% consist of ovalbumin, 13% of ovotransferrin, 11% of ovomucoid, 8% of ovoglobins G_2 and G_3, and 2% of ovomucin (770, 945). With but few exceptions, the oviductal cells that are involved in the synthesis of individual proteins have not been identified conclusively (945).

At the time of leaving the magnum the developing egg appears to possess only a single thick layer of albumen, jellylike in consistency, with little evidence of stratification, and constituting half of the albumen's final volume (701). In reptiles, chelonians at least, the albumen persists in this form in oviposited eggs. In developing avian eggs, however, the albumen eventually stratifies and differentiates into a complex structure of 4 layers, partly through hydrolytic and gel hydrational processes (770). These processes apparently occur as the egg traverses the isthmus and shell gland (510).

[The fact that estrogen injection stimulates the tubular gland cells in the oviduct of young hens to synthesize and secrete large amounts of albumens has made the domestic fowl system a model one that is very actively being employed for gene sequence studies. Such studies have revealed that the ovalbumin and ovomucoid genes of the domestic fowl hen--the only species in which they have been sequenced--each possesses 8 exons separated by 7 introns, of greatly differing length; ovotransferrin possesses 17 exons and 16 introns (see 651).]

Concerning the structure and composition of the albumen layers of the developing egg, there are 3 outer layers. In sequence, these are the inner, fiber-free, liquid layer or thin albumen, the middle, gel-like, thick or dense layer, which appears to contain some structural organization, and the fiber-free, outer, thin or fluid layer. The main difference between these layers consists in the amount of ovomucin that they contain. At each end of the egg, the thick albumen, comprising 60% of the total egg white, extends outwards forming the "albumen ligaments," which are fixed to the shell membranes by mucin fibers (348, 510, 622, 949).

The 3 outer layers are separated from the yolk by the chaliziferous layer, which surrounds the yolk and consists of the innermost thick, viscous albumen. This includes twisted, fibrous, ovomucin strands or chalazae that originate in the chaliziferous layer and end in the thick white near the albumen ligaments, 2 strands at the pointed end of the egg and 1 at the blunt end, parallelling the egg's long axis (949). The chalazae only become apparent as the ovum approaches the caudal levels of the magnum to be completed in the isthmus and shell gland (see 944). They are believed to be supportive structures that stabilize the position and orientation of the yolk and developing embryo in the albumen, and are considered to result from a combination of enzymatic degradation of the innermost dense layer of albumen and rotation of the ovum during oviductal transit, which leads to the segregation and twisting of the ovomucin fibers into strands (718, 770).

The albumen forms a dense wet mantle that covers the embryo and its membranes during their early development when they are particularly vulnerable to dehydration. One of its chief functions is as a storage depot of the embryo's water supply (roughly 2/3rds of it; see 508). It also is an important store of protein. The amount of the latter in the albumen varies considerably among avian taxa, whereas the water content is relatively constant (838). The albumen supports the yolk, perhaps preventing collapse and flattening, and it has bactericidal and fungicidal properties. In the presence of this colorless, viscous albumen and the possession of a hard, calcareous shell, avian eggs are comparable with those of tortoises, some turtles, some gekkonid and dibamid lizards, and crocodilians (see 336, 364, and pp. 538, 539, **Eggs of Oviparous Reptiles**).

[It has been proposed that the evolution of rigid eggshells in reptiles is related to the greater protection that they afford against predators and pathogens. A large, enclosed reservoir of water in the form of albumen presumably was a necessary coadaptation. since the relative impermeability of the eggs to water would impede efficient absorption of that substance from the environment (672). The "parchment-shelled" eggs of reptiles, on the other hand, have the capacity to transport water rapidly, and customarily absorb much water (364; see also pp. 538, 539, **Eggs of Oviparous Reptiles**).]

ISTHMUS AND SHELL MEMBRANES. Continued peristalsis thrusts the developing egg posteriorly into the isthmus (avg. transfer rate, 1.0-1.4 mm/min; see 944, 947). This is shorter, being only about 8-10 cm long, much less glandular and more muscular, but thinner-walled (shallower ridges), than the magnum, from which it is distinctly demarcated by a sharp translucent line that is free of tubular glands and covered by a cuboidal epithelium. The glandular elements of this region are distinctive and contain extremely high concentrations of both calcium and citric acid, which probably function in the calcification of the mammillary knobs during shell formation (see p. 156, **Mammillary Cores and Knobs**).

In a 1-1½-hr stay in the isthmus, the developing egg becomes tightly enclosed in the inner and outer shell membranes 477, 500). These are composed of a meshwork of keratin fibers cemented together with albumen, with a polysaccharide covering. The two membranes differ in the diameter of the fibers, the mesh of the weave, and their total thickness, all these parameters being larger in the outer membrane. The latter is about 50 micra thick as opposed to 15-20 micra for the inner membrane. There is a general correlation between the spaces separating the fibers and the size of the species or its eggs (822). The inner side of the inner membrane is lined with a thin film that appears to be continuous, rather than merely an extension of its fibers (478, 492).

[The eggs of crocodilians and many chelonians also have a pair of shell membranes that lack mineral inclusions and separate the albumen from the shell. Those of crocodilians, however, are 10 times as thick as those of birds (759). These membranes are known to consist of a protein-carbohydrate complex in crocodilians (glycosaminoglycans) and marine turtles (759, 770). The eggs of oviparous squamates, on the other hand, do not have shell membranes and their shells contain mineral inclusions (673 757). Monotreme eggs are enclosed in an uncalcified, ovokeratinous shell membrane about 70 micra thick which is permeable to nutrients and capable of distension. Its latticework is sufficiently open to be penetrated by erythrocytes (1,307, 1,317).]

The shell membranes are secreted by the less-densely-distributed glandular cells that line the lumen of the isthmus. The inner one surrounds the albumen in intimate contact with the thick layer at the region of the albumen ligaments. The outermost of these membranes has a rough texture that provides a receptive surface for the calcareous shell (414). Soon after the egg is laid, the spaces between the loose meshwork of fibers of the shell membranes become filled with gas, so that these membranes apparently represent no significant barrier to gas diffusion (478, 492). In the course of incubation these membranes become dehydrated, with a concomitant increase in their permeability to water. At the same time there is a decline in the oxygen tension in the capillary bed of the chorioallantois (see pp. 168, 169) and a resulting increase in the driving force for oxygen exchange. These changes account for the increase in oxygen permeability to the peak value attained during incubation (427).

MAMMILLARY CORES AND KNOBS. The shell membranes come to cover the shell from the inside. They are loosely fused together at infrequent intervals, except at the air cell at the broad end of the egg (226). Among other things, these membranes serve to contain the egg contents during shell formation. As the egg contents and shell membranes pass into the distal end of the isthmus, approaching the shell gland, organic granules, the mammillary cores, become attached by fibers to the rough-textured surface of the outer membrane, and this also is true of developing chelonian eggs (757, 770), and probably those of crocodilians as well. These cores consist of a protein-mucopolysaccharide complex, rich in acidic groups (477, 500, 620).

The mammillary cores are the sites of formation of the first calcite crystals, the "spherulite crystals." The latter act as nuclei or "seeds" for the massive further growth of calcite crystals, inward, outward, and sideways, to form the shell (226, 822). Nucleation with these seeding crystals already has taken place by the time the egg reaches the shell gland (510). [During incubation, calcium begins to be resorbed from the shell beginning at the tips of the mammillary knobs, that is, the knob-like structures formed by crystalization of calcite on the mammillary cores. In late stages of incubation, as withdrawal of calcium from the shell ceases, the fiber connections between the mammillary knobs and the shell membrane weaken and the membranes peel from the shell (236).]

SHELL GLAND---ALBUMEN "PLUMPING"--THE SHELL. Next, roughly 4½ hours after engulfment by the infundibulum, the egg, at about the 16-cell stage, passes to the shell gland (pars calcigera, or "uterus," which is about 8-10 cm long). This consists of the short segment of oviduct immediately caudal to the isthmus and of similar diameter, through which the oocyte passes relatively rapidly, plus the succeeding muscularly-walled, dilated, highly-vascularized, expandable, pouch-like segment. The pouch is a permanent structure, not merely a product of distension by the egg. It contains both tubular and unicellular glands, presumed to secrete the watery "albumen" (510, 944).

By the time of entry into the shell gland, the shell membranes have come to fit quite loosely over the developing egg (477, 500). The latter may remain in the shell gland for about 20 h, while practically all of its thin or watery albumen is formed (a process referred to colloquially as "plumping") together with its calcareous shell, outer cuticle, and any shell pigments (453). The shell gland terminates in a narrow annular zone that lies immediately anterior to the vaginal spermatzoal glands, measuring some 0.5-1.0 cm in width, the so-called "recessus uteri," having mucosal folds that are intermediate in width and length compared with those of the shell gland, and the glands are fewer and shorter than those typical of the shell gland (944).

[Oviducts of marine chelonians are very long--4.6 to 6 m in *Lepidochelys olivacea* as compared to less than 0.8 m in the domestic fowl--and complements of developing eggs move through them in single file, occupying from 1-2 m of their length (771). Only a slight difference in the degree of calcification between the 1st and last egg in a clutch has been noted (770, 771). Calcification of the shell commences about 72 h after ovulation and is completed in about 6 or 7 days. In the Green Sea Turtle, the shell-forming segment is about 155 cm long and calcium deposition occurs simultaneously on the shells of 50-60 eggs within it, all along its length (770).]

During the first 5-8 h in the shell gland "plumping" occurs, as water and salts enter through the shell membranes and are added to the albumen at a fairly constant rate. By this action, the volume of the albumenous layers of the developing egg swells to about twice its prior value (701). As a result the shell membranes become stretched, increasing the distances between the mammillary knobs. Concomitantly, there is an enlargement of the calcite crystals that radiate in all directions from the mammillary cores, the continued growth of which forms the shell.

Plumping apparently is an essential preliminary to the main process of shell calcification, namely the laying down of calcium carbonate to form the palisade or spongy layer of the shell, about 270-370 micra thick. Calcification begins slowly and increases in rate gradually during the first 5 h in the shell gland, as the seeding sites--mammillary knobs or mammillae--are formed. The apices of these knobs are embedded in the outer surface of the outer shell membrane, from which fibers enter the knobs. The size and shape of the latter are characteristic for the species (622). After formation of the mammillae, calcification occurs at a constant rate over the following 15-16 h (until 2 h before oviposition), probably with one column of calcite forming over each mammilla (see 701). Shell calcification is thought to have basic features in common with bone calcification (477, 500, 510).

[Eggshells average about 300 micra thick and consist of about 98% calcium carbonate (about 1.6-2.4 g or 40% of the weight is calcium; 323, 500), in the form of calcite crystals, small concentrations of Mg and P, together with a matrix of 1-3% organic matter, principally a protein-mucopolysaccharide complex that is distributed throughout the cystalline layer but concentrated in the outer 1/3rd (101, 226, 348, 946). The function of this matrix is not firmly established.]

Medullary Bone

LABILE CALCIUM BUFFER SUPPLY. The calcium requirements for shell formation in laying birds are so great (a daily turnover equalling about 10% of total body Ca; 948) that a special mechanism--a dynamic equilibrium between blood, bones, and calcifying shell--has evolved to accommodate them. During the period of reproduction, the marrow cavities of those bones of the hen that are relatively highly vascularized are invaded by a whole new system of secondary bone of a labile, storage-type, called medullary bone.

This bone acts as a buffer supply for calcium (but not solely in this capacity; see p. 159, **Signs of Calcium Insufficiency**) that is largely responsible for the provision of calcium for shell formation when absorption from the gut is insufficient (477, 500).

Medullary bone formation by osteoblasts (bone-forming cells) is stimulated experimentally in pullets by the synergistic action of a high level of estrogenic and androgenic hormones in the blood, and its maintenance requires a constant estrogenic stimulus (477, 500). [Additional hormones, possibly from the thyroid gland, may be required for the normal development of medullary bone (500).] Both the formation and destruction of medullary bone proceed simultaneously and continuously at adjacent sites on the bone spicules; it is the relative rate at which the two processes occur during egg production that changes in relation to the demands of calcium for shell formation (1,148).

Medullary bone consists of outgrowths of fine interlaced trabeculae (spicules) from the endosteal surface of the marrow cavity of the shaft of long bones. These outgrowing trabeculae gradually advance between the sinuses and blood vessels as laying progresses, leaving the vascular pattern unaffected (500). By the time of the 1st ovulation in the pigeon, medullary bone has invaded the entire marrow cavity. It possesses a greater ratio of calcium to P and a higher concentration of mucopolysaccharides than does ordinary bone (348, 500), and its formation correlates with the size of the ovarian follicles (346, 348). [The bone marrow of birds, unlike that of mammals, contains large amounts of lymphatic tissue (514).]

The retention of dietary calcium and phosphate rises markedly about 10 days before a pullet starts to oviposit. During this period calcium phosphate is absorbed from the intestine and contributes to the formation of medullary bone in the hen's marrow. The resulting increase in skeletal weight, most of it medullary bone, is about 20% (510). Vitamin D promotes net retention of both calcium and P and has some specific action in connection with the deposition of calcium salts in bone (443). There are also marked changes in the intestinal absorption of calcium during oogenesis. When the shell gland is inactive, about 40% of the dietary calcium is absorbed, whereas during times of intense shell formation, absorption rises to 72% (see 510). There is a large and clearly demonstrated fall (about 20%) in the calcium content of the venous blood from the shell gland within a few hours of the egg entering it (946).

During the period of oviposition the level of ionic calcium in the blood is roughly the same as in the non-laying hen or in the male. On the other hand, the level of phosphoprotein-bound calcium (20-30 mg/ml) is twice the normal value. The high value of phosphoproteins (largely phosvitin) in the plasma at this time correlates with yolk formation, not shell formation (477, 500, 942). In addition to the storage of calcium in medullary bone and the yolk, it also is stored in the albumen and extra-embryonic membranes (see K. Simkiss, 1967, 1980, in 759).

MEDULLARY BONE DECALCIFICATION. When the eggshell is being formed, breakdown of medullary bone is initiated by more numerous and more active osteoclasts (bone destroying cells), probably under the influence of parathyroid hormone and possibly also prostaglandins (932). The material obtained in this way is used in the formation of the eggshell (97, 477). If dietary calcium levels are 3.56% or higher, most of the eggshell calcium is derived directly from the intestinal contents. At a concentration of only 1.95%, 30-40% of the eggshell calcium is derived from medullary bone. Medullary bone may, however, be a particularly important source of this calcium during the night and early morning hours, when the calcium content of the digestive tract is low (510). Under duress, up to 10-12% of total body bone substance of the hen can be released per 24 h (324, 477, 500). The hens of all species that have been studied have comparable capabilities.

Hens increase their calcium intake by about 50% before and during oviposition, as a result of a complex suite of hormone-regulated responses (17). The level of blood calcium, for example, appears to control the release of adenohypophysial gonadotropins preparatory to ovulation, while decalcification of medullary bone undoubtedly involves both ovarian steroidal (under gonadotropic influence) and parathormonal activity (324). The transport capacity of the small intestine for calcium also increases markedly during the laying period (226).

It is during the "plumping" period that marked changes begin to occur in the medullary bone of the Rock Pigeon. Domination there by osteoblasts transforms to a domination by osteoclasts and this medullary bone destruction continues throughout the period of shell calcification and for 4-5 h after the 1st of the 2 eggs is laid. Then, quite suddenly, another cycle of 20 h of medullary bone formation and extensive subsequent destruction begins (477, 500).

SIGNS OF CALCIUM INSUFFICIENCY. If insufficient calcium is supplied in the diet, too much calcium is withdrawn from the hen's bones. She then lays eggs with progressively thinner shells, followed by complete cessation of ovulation and laying. The latter probably ensues because of reduced secretion of gonadotropic hormones from the adenohypophysis (anterior pituitary). The mineral drain from the bones under such conditions may deplete them of almost 40% of their calcium and over 50% of their original mineral matter (477, 500). This may prevent a hen from perching or discourage walking and induce secondary hyperparathyroidism (also induced by an excess of P). Unexpectedly, most of the resorption occurs in cortical, not medullary, bone, as in the early stages of the deficiency the newly-formed medullary bone is calcified at the expense of the cortical bone. Although there is some demineralization, the amount of medullary bone remains constant or increases, suggesting that medullary bone does not function solely as a buffer reservoir of calcium (441, 443, 455).

However, in an advanced state of calcium deficiency, medullary bone is poorly calcified. As the deficiency proceeds, particularly if laying is maintained with hypophysial extracts, calcification of the new medullary bone becomes progressively poorer until, eventually, the matrix remains uncalcified and appears histologically as osteoid tissue. This advanced state of calcium depletion is never reached in birds with a low laying potential; the skeleton is "protected" as ovulation is held in abeyance by the inhibition of secretion of LH-releasing hormones by the hypothalamus, and by hormonal action on the hypophysis itself (see 1,148).

WITHDRAWAL OF EGGSHELL CALCIUM. About 100 mg of calcium and other minerals are withdrawn from the eggshells (and, if necessary, the yolk) and used to build the growing bones of the embryo between the 13th day of incubation and hatching, which accounts for the change from about 22 mg of calcium in the unincubated egg's internal contents to about 125 mg of calcium in the hatchling. Before day 13, calcium withdrawal is but slight. Calcium resorption from the inner surface of the shell is clearly associated with the chorioallantois, specifically with the acid-secreting "intercalating cells" distributed throughout its ectoderm, and possibly also with the "capillary-covering cells" (see pp. 168, 169, **Chorioallantoic Membrane**; 97, 923, 1,053, 1,150). Plasma calcium concentrations rise steadily from 2.42 mmol/l beginning on day 16, reaching a plateau of 2.61 mmol/l that is maintained through days 18 to 20. At hatching the level falls to 2.55 mmol/l and 1 day later it is 2.52 mmol/l (1,148).

[Withdrawal of calcium from the shell also occurs among crocodilians and chelonians (666). Squamates, on the other hand, obtain both calcium and Mg from rich stores that are present in the yolk, not from the shell. This may have been a critical factor allowing the evolution of viviparity in many species of squamates but not in reptiles with rigid eggshells (673; but see 759, 765 for other alternatives), a view supported by the fact that viviparity otherwise has evolved independently in numerous vertebrates (see 896). A lesser dependence of crocodilian than avian and chelonian embryos on eggshell calcium permits experimental embryological studies using shell-less and semi-shell-less culture of crocodilian embryos to later developmental stages (759).]

About 5% of the shell supplies the domestic fowl embryo with about 80% of its calcium requirement and some bicarbonate (226). The mechanism for this is unknown, but after the middle of the incubatory period the eggshell is significantly weakened by thinning (235). Hormones of both the ovary and parathyroid glands (whose major function is to effect calcium homeostasis) apparently cooperate in the regulation of the calcium of the body for bone construction and destruction, and for eggshell secretion (28). Furthermore, during at least the last half of the incubatory period the parathyroid glands of the embryo contain a hormone capable of resorbing bones, modifying renal excretion, and inducing hypercalcemia (923).

OUTER CUTICLE. The precise origin of the outer cuticle of the shell of most eggs is uncertain. It is a partly vesicular structure about 10 micra thick, composed principally of a rather resistant proteinaceous material (about 90% peptide), fat, and polysaccharide, that apparently protects the egg contents from penetration by microorganisms without impairing gas exchange (427, 601, 949). It also is responsible for conferring on the egg its water-repellant properties and reducing loss of water, an important feature for terrestrially breeding animals (see 622). It varies greatly among species in thickness and chemical composition and imparts to the surface of the egg its characteristic texture and appearance (622, 822). In certain species, such as the Emu and penguins, the cuticle is overlaid by a specialized layer, the "cover," of uncertain function (see 1,053).

DEVELOPMENT OF THE EMBRYO begins in the shell gland. Four h after entering this gland, the blastoderm has grown from the 16-cell stage to approximately the 256-cell stage (511). By the time of oviposition the pre-primitive-streak blastoderm can be seen lying on the surface of the yolk, adhering to the inside of the perivitelline layer (336). Tiny yolky droplets within the cells of the blastoderm probably supply much of the nourishment of the embryo until the end of gastrulation. [In the Rock Pigeon, gastrulation occurs about 5-7 h before oviposition (511).] Subsequently most of the embryo's nourishment is obtained from the extraembryonic yolk via the blood vessels of the yolk sac (336). A portion of this yolk, the "residual yolk" (see p. 196, **Yolk Reserves**) supports the early existence of the nidifugous hatchling (see pp. 193-199 for definitions).

[Chelonian embryos develop to a stage of mid-to-late gastrula. Differentiation then ceases until the eggs are oviposited, though arrest is not absolute and cannot last indefinitely (681, 757). The embryos of The Tuatara also are reported to be at the gastrula (or earlier) stage (755). Crocodilian embryos, on the other hand, often are of considerable size at the time of oviposition, making it very difficult to obtain early stages for study (658, 659). Their stage of development at oviposition is not invariant but may be as advanced as roughly equivalent to the 18-somite domestic fowl embryo (754, 759).

Squamatan embryos often have 20-30 somites, a well-established blood circulation, and distinct limb buds at oviposition, equivalent to a domestic fowl embryo at Hamilton-Hamburger Stage 16-17. Less frequently they are oviposited as gastrulas (754, 763). In certain squamates the eggs spend so much time in the oviducts that the species appear to be in evolutionary transition from oviparity to viviparity (acompanied by a reduction in the degree of cacification of the eggshell and in the thickness of the shell membrane), and the eggs may hatch within a few days of oviposition (673).]

The calcium and carbonate for crystal formation in the shell are derived from the blood plasma and secreted by the extremely richly vascularized mucosa of the shell gland, which is supplied by 3 arteries. The evidence suggests that the calcium and the carbonate are formed by two entirely different sets of shell-gland cells, calcium from the ciliated epithelium and carbonate from the tubular gland cells (946). The shell gland contains very little calcium, and so does not store this element. The mitochondrial fraction of the shell-gland mucosa, and to a lesser extent the microsomal fraction, appear to be most active in the transport of this calcium to the shell structure (324). During the main period of shell formation, about 5 times the total circulating calcium in the hen is removed from the blood every hour, amounting to about 100-150 mg. Calcium deposition is associated with the excretion of large amounts of phosphorus in the urine. The formation of the pores (from 6,000-17,000 in domestic fowl eggs; see 427, 478, 492, 500) and the regulation of their numbers by the shell gland is not well understood (226).

The main part of the shell, the palisade or spongy layer (70-80% of the shell thickness), is composed of columns of tightly, but imperfectly, packed calcite crystals, extending from the mammillary knobs to the cuticle. The "true shell" (exclusive of membranes and cuticle) consists almost exclusively of calcite, with small amounts of Mg, P, and citrate and traces of Na and K (500). The upper part of the palisade layer is very compact, with a lamellate pattern produced by the rhombic cleavage of the calcite crystals, the zone of "Streifenmuster" or "Fischgrätenmuster" (herring-bone pattern). A surface crystalline layer of about 5 micra in thickness is superimposed on the palisade layer. In many species it confers a characteristic surface texture to the shell (822).

THE PORES of the shell are funnel-shaped and oval to circular in cross-section in most species, about 6-23 micra in diameter at their inner ends and 15-65 micra at their mouths. They are the surface openings of the canaliculi that run up between the imperfectly-packed crystals where groups of knobs come together (477, 478, 492, 500, 622, 946). [The relationships are very similar in crocodilian eggshells (759).] In the majority of species the canaliculi traverse the shell radially without branching, but they branch extensively in all planes in the Ostrich. The pores often are grouped more closely at the blunt end of the egg (622). The surface openings of the pores sometimes are covered with secreted organic or inorganic particulate matter similar to that of the cuticle (also seen in crocodilian eggshells; 759), but containing radial cracks, through which gaseous exchanges can occur (478, 492, 622). On the average, there are about 154 pores/sq. cm, occupying a total surface area of about 2.3 sq. mm (see 1,053).

The diffusive capacity (permeability) of the eggshell is determined by the number and aggregate geometry of the pores. It increases with egg size, over a range of species, but does not change during the course of incubation (478, 492). The shell provides the embryo with protection against physical injury and microbial infection, while oxygen uptake and carbon dioxide and water losses occur by diffusion in the gas phase through its pores (435). [Pores also exist in the calcareous shells of chelonian eggs but not in the parchment-like shells of squamates, some turtles, and the Tuatara; 673).]

GROUND COLOR PIGMENT is due to the secretion of porphyrins (related to blood and bile pigments) by the shell gland epithelium. It is deposited during the final stages of shell formation, and appears to be distributed evenly throughout the shell and cuticle and to be absent from the shell membranes. Blotches, streaks, and other surface markings, on the other hand, are acquired after the shell has been completed, several hours before oviposition (414, 510, 944). In neither case have the cells of origin in the shell gland been identified positively. Ground color pigmentation occurs mainly in the calcified palisade layer of the shell. When pigments occur on the surface of the cuticle, they form the characteristic mottling of the species. In all species examined, the pigments are deposited as crystals throughout the calcified region, but most heavily in the outer parts (622).

The precise involvement of the various parts of the shell gland in the secretion of the shell remain obscure. Thus, it is not firmly established which cells transport calcium (nor whether the transport is active), although the ciliated cells appear to be implicated (see 944, 946). Uncertainty also attends the elaboration of carbonate and the organic matrix precursors, although the tubular gland cells would appear to be involved in the former (see 946). Nor is it known how these precursors come together in the lumen of the shell gland to form the shell. We also are ignorant of the physiological control signals that initiate and terminate the processes of nucleation of the outer shell membrane with calcite crystals, plumping, formation of the true shell, and of the cuticle. The driving force for shell formation could be either calcium transport, carbonate formation, or the secretion of organic matrix. In any event, the organic matrix is believed to play an important role in shell calcification, with which it is closely linked (510).

[As opposed to the single day required for the oviductal development of most avian eggs, maturing of oviductal chelonian eggs, as determined by transformation from soft to rigid shells, requires 7-10 days for trionychids, 14-20 days for temperate kinosternids, chelydrids, and emydines, and 17-25 days for many batagurines and tropical kinosternids (757).]

VAGINA AND OVIPOSITION. Finally, 26-28 h after ovulation, through the mediation of a muscular contraction of the shell gland, the completed egg passes through a relaxed shell gland-vaginal sphincter into the vagina. The latter is a relatively-short, S-shaped mucous-gland-lined tube that possesses a highly-developed circular muscle layer. Typical vaginal glands are short, simple tubules that occur only in the vicinity of the junction

of the shell gland and are separated from one another by relatively great distances. These glands store clumps of spermatozoa for 12-22 days or longer. Although the mechanism of spermatozoal release from the glands remains obscure, some control over it is exercised by the ovary.

In the vagina the egg is rotated through 180° on its long axis, whereupon surface markings may be given a spiral configuration (see 336 and 414). Within a few sec in some birds but as much as hours in others, the vaginal muscles relax, and the resulting distension (initiating the "bearing-down" reflex) allows the egg to enter the cloaca through an aperture a little dorsal to the rectum, whereupon it is oviposited, usually with the pointed end leading. However, oviposition results from the coordinated activity of both the shell gland and the vagina; the vagina itself appears to be incapable of expelling the egg (622, 947). In this connection, both the shell gland and its junction with the vagina have a more abundant nerve supply than other parts of the oviduct and the majority of the ganglion cells are located in this vicinity (944). In domesticated species such as fowl, the hen characteristically oviposits during the 1st half of the light period of the normal day, with the 1st egg being laid early in the day and successive eggs being laid later on successive days (921, 948). Rock Pigeons generally lay the 1st egg of a clutch at 17:00 h, ovulate 3 h later (with spermatozoal penetration occurring at the same time), and oviposit the 2nd egg 40-44 h after the 1st (997, 1,011). Sora Rails (*Porzana carolina*) oviposit in the very early hours of daylight (216).

[In a comparison among domestic fowl, Japanese Quail and domestic Mallard Ducks on a 14L:10D light regime with the light period from 05:00 to 19:00 h, the fowl oviposited between 06:00 and 14:00 h, the quail between 14:00 and 19:00 h, and the ducks between 01:00 and 06:00 h (1,014). On a 16L:10D photoperiod, domestic fowl ovulated the 1st egg in a sequence between 7 and 8 h after lights-off, with successive subsequent ova maturing and being ovulated slightly later each day until the final egg was ovulated 15-16 h after lights-off. Ovulation occurs about 15-75 min after oviposition. If the length of the dark period is reduced, oviposition comes more nearly to approximate the time of lights-off (see 510, 1,140).]

Not a great deal of information is at hand concerning the immediate factors that govern oviposition, but it is known to be delayed by removal of the entire post-ovulatory follicle or merely its granulosal cells, or by stimulation of the telencephalon (947, 989). The contraction of the shell gland seemingly is regulated by the secretion of a hormone by the pre-ovulatory follicle 1½-2 h before it is ovulated, and it occurs regardless of whether or not an egg is present in the shell gland. This hormone either acts directly on the shell-gland musculature or indirectly through stimulation of the secretion of arginine vasotocin by the neurohypophysis. The concentration of the latter increases more than 40-fold immediately prior to and during oviposition. (see 414, 495, 510, 920, 989, and K. Shimada *et al.*, 1981, in 989).

PREMATURE AND DELAYED OVIPOSITION. Oviposition can be stimulated to occur prematurely by electrical stimulation of the pre-optic area of the hypothalamus, and it occurs within a few min after intravenous injection of arginine vasotocin (see 510). Interestingly, though oviposition is delayed by removal of the recently ruptured follicle, ovipositional behavior, the rise in body temperature, and an increase in corticosterone all occur at the time of the normally expected oviposition, yet fail to occur afterward, when the egg eventually is laid (see 989).

THE ROLE OF PROSTAGLANDINS. In addition, there is convincing evidence that prostaglandins have an important function in the physiology of avian oviposition. These substances are known to be able to stimulate the release of hypophysial hormones both by direct action on the gland and by acting on the hypothalamus; acting at the latter site, ACTH, FSH, LH, and prolactin can be released (1,029). Prostaglandins also are known to cause contraction of the muscle of the shell gland both *in vivo* and *in vitro*, and relaxation of the shell gland-vaginal sphincter. In fact, intrauterine injection of prostaglandins induces premature oviposition within a few min and administration of indomethacin or anti-prostaglandin serum inhibits spontaneous oviposition. Moreover, plasma levels of the prostaglandins increase significantly around the time of oviposition in the domestic fowl and Turkey.

Contraction of the shell gland correlates with a preferential binding of prostaglandin (PGF-2-alpha) to the plasma membranes (sarcolemmas) of its smooth muscle cells. Prostaglandins may act in concert with arginine vasotocin to produce the full contractile tension required for oviposition, although release of the latter hormone does not appear to be the stimulus for the increase in plasma prostaglandin levels at that time. Certain observations suggest that prostaglandins are the hormones in the ruptured follicle that induce the transport of the developing egg through the oviduct. However, the ruptured follicle does not appear to be the exclusive source of prostaglandins, as they also appear to be produced in the shell gland itself, a production that is augmented in vitro by estradiol but abolished by the simultaneous presence of progesterone (see 622, 920, 932, 989, 1,142-1,147).

[In connection with the above, injection of hypophysial extract, presumably containing oxytocin as the active substance, induces ovulation (sometimes even nest construction) in many chelonians in 20 min to 6 h, and induces premature expulsion of the egg or embryo in several species of squamates. Injections of synthetic oxytocin or arginine vasotocin have induced oviposition in 53 species representing 7 families, yielding about 90% of all mature oviductal eggs in viable condition. Such hormonal induction also can cause the oviposition of premature eggs with incompletely calcified shells (682, 757, 989). Arginine vasotocin also simulates parturition in a viviparous lizard (see 920).]

[The oviduct of the Green Sea Turtle also is divisible into 5 segments, the infundibulum, aglandular segment, magnum, shell-forming segment, and vagina. Only the magnum and shell-forming segment actively engage in the synthesis and/or secretion of the albumen, shell membranes, shell, and cuticle. Throughout its length, the oviduct is lined by a pseudostratified columnar epithelium compounded of ciliated, non-secretory, and (except for the infundibulum) secretory cells. The latter secrete a strongly sulphated acid mucin in the magnum but a non-sulphated acidic mucin in the shell-forming segment (770).]

HEN'S ENERGY REQUIREMENTS AND EGG ENERGY CONTENT. During the period of oogenesis and oviposition, the hen's energy expenditure peaks and is 15-85% greater than that of the male in all species studied (257). For example, the hen's respiratory rate is augmented 64% during shell calcification and its body temperature also peaks during egg formation (see 510). In terms of the standard metabolic rate the excess energy requirement for egg formation in several birds with nidicolous young is estimated at 31-58% (257, 648, 729, 975). In Boat-tailed Grackles (*Quiscalus major*), for example, the figure is only 31% (365), in hawks and owls it is 39% (975), in Blue Tits (*Parus caeruleus*) the value is 40% (232), while in house sparrows it is 44-47% (1,352). For the duck and Brown Kiwi the figure is 160-216% (257, 648). It is estimated to range from 71-113% in 7 galliform species and from 156-239% in a selection of 4 anseriform species. For comparison, the excess energy requirements of typical passerines at other periods of the reproductive cycle in terms of standard metabolic rate are 2-12% during ovarian and oviductal egg growth, 25-50% during incubation (see also pp. 176, 177, **Incubation**), and 200-300% during the nestling period with 4 young (975).

In terms of daily energy intake for normal function without gain or loss of body weight, the daily maximum cost of egg production is estimated at 13-16% in passeriforms, 21-30% in galliforms, and 52-70% in anseriforms (729). The energy content of the egg itself in terms of standard metabolism is lowest for passerines (45%), intermediate for raptors (103%) and galliforms (126%), and highest for anseriforms (180%) and gulls and terns (320%; 975); in general, the eggs of nidifuges are loaded with almost twice (1.97) the caloric content as those of nidicoles (329).

OVIPOSITION BY CONFINED BUDGERIGARS. Female Budgerigars provided with NBs (nestboxes) and exposed to male vocalizations oviposit sooner after entering the NB (a median of 7½ days) under a 14L:10D photoregime than under regimes with shorter periods of light (850). But oviposition will occur even if the hens are kept in very dark surroundings or total darkness, but within hearing of males (850). In fact, Budgerigars are the only birds known in which vocalizations, particularly Soft Warble, promote ovarian development and ovulation (67). [Breeding ceases when strong light is introduced (27).] It also has been shown that the sensitivity of the Budgerigar female to male vocalizations exhibits a diurnal rhythm (846, 1,047, and pp. 121, 122). The waves of follicular development and atresia in the ovaries of species of wild birds kept under conditions designed to enhance reproductive performance suggest that ovarian competence is present throughout the year, just as in domesticated species (622).

Three to 8 eggs (averaging 14.3 x 18.3 mm and 2.0-2.8 g) customarily are laid in the hollow, one every other day, usually in the afternoon. Development of the embryo begins before oviposition but halts and only recommences on the beginning of incubation (see p. 167). Clutch size in any given species is known to vary with a number of internal and external environmental factors (314; see also pp. 594, 595, **Ovarian Functional Adaptability**). For example, some hole-nesters adjust clutch size to the size of the nest cavity (see 814). Species with larger eggs relative to the size of the females produce more eggs than expected from relations between female weight and clutch weight, and the reverse (with smaller males) also holds (794). It is said that a confined Budgerigar pair's first clutch may contain as many as 8 eggs but that subsequent clutches usually number only 3 or 4. More commonly, clutch size increases with age (e.g., in the Great Tit, *Parus major*; 810).

THE DISTINCTION BETWEEN DETERMINATE AND INDETERMINATE LAYERS is, as yet, poorly drawn, as comparisons between species have not been made with the same experimental regime. Furthermore, some birds appear to respond to tactile stimuli from the eggs, others to visual cues from the clutch (222). The designation "determinate layers" has been applied to hens of a species that lay a certain number of eggs, which does not become augmented when eggs are removed. The number may be reduced, however, in various unfavorable circumstances, in which case atresia of the remaining follicles occurs. All 3 species of the present studies are determinate layers.

Two different control mechanisms appear to determine the clutch size in determinate layers. In some species, for example the Brant (Branta bernicla) and Snow Goose (*Chen caerulescens*), the number of follicles that grow to ovulatory size usually corresponds with the clutch size. In other species, of which lovebirds are examples, the number of follicles that mature is said to be larger than the clutch size. When the last egg of the clutch is laid, atresia sets in and the unovulated follicles are resorbed (3).

The designation "indeterminate layers" has been applied to the hens of species in which the clutch size may show little variation when the eggs are left in the nest, but if the eggs are removed, the number of eggs laid exceeds the normal clutch size. Extreme cases of indeterminate layers are the Khaki Campbell Duck (*Anas platyrhynchos* var. *domesticus*), Japanese Quail, and domestic fowl and Turkeys, all domesticated species in which egg production has been increased by selective breeding. After oviposition begins, the domestic fowl hen lays eggs in long sequences (series of eggs laid on successive days), but after about 6-10 weeks, the sequences decrease in length (969).

EGG COMPOSITION. Species with nidifugous or precocial hatchlings (see pp. 195-198, **Nidifuges**) generally load their eggs with significantly more yolk (providing more energy) and significantly less albumen (providing less water) than do those with nidicolous young (329). Such eggs consist of 75-82% water and their size ranges from 9-27% of adult body weight. They generally contain about 30-40% yolk (of which 50% is water) but the value attains 60-61% in kiwis and some megapodes (see 329, 772, 974, 1,403, 1,406, 1,408); the albumen content is about 53½% (329).

It has been suggested that the amount of yolk increases with increased precocity of the young, but this relationship now is regarded as an oversimplification. Although the eggs of species with nidifugous hatchlings have the highest percentages of yolk (and lipids), there is a complex overlapping in the percentages of yolk in the eggs of all other hatchling types (838). The greater amount of energy stored in these eggs, as compared to those of nidicoles, may offset partly the somewhat higher respiratory rate and longer period of embryonic development of nidifuges, but a substantial portion of the yolk reserve is available to the chick after hatching (975 and p. 196, **Yolk Reserves**). Each 1% increase in yolk content of an egg is associated with a 0.033 kcal/g increase in its energy density (see 1,150).

In species with nidicolous or altricial young (see pp. 193-195, **Nidicoles**), such as the Budgerigar, the water content of the egg is greater, at about 82-89% (81½% in Peach-faced Lovebirds) and the egg size ranges from 4-10% of the adult body weight. The eggs of parrots are relatively small, amounting to about 8½% of adult body weight for Peach-faced Lovebirds (634). The higher water content of the eggs of nidicoles compared to those of nidifuges may provide additional water for the young nestling, as the allofeeding parents usually supply primarily food (329). The yolk content of the eggs of nidicolous hatchlings is only about 15-25% (23.3% in parrots generally, 21-25% in Budgerigars, and about 24% in Peach-faced Lovebirds; see 226, 239, 245, 329, 543, 634, 975); the albumen content is about 70½%, and the albumen contains more water than that of nidifuges (see 329). Translated into terms of energy density, that of eggs of nidifugous hatchlings is roughly 62% higher than the value for those with nidicolous hatchlings, while the corresponding energy content compared to adult standard metabolic rate averages about 100% greater (257).

The Embryos After Oviposition

TEMPERATURE AND DEVELOPMENT----ONSET OF SENSORY RESPONSES. The embryo may remain in the blastoderm stage for a week or more, but eventually dies if not incubated. The optimum incubatory temperature for domestic fowl eggs is 37-38°C in forced draft incubators and about 1° higher in still air, only about 3°C below the body temperature of the hen. Relatively minor long-term deviations from the incubatory temperatures that are optimal for survival can result in large decreases in hatchability, with greater resistance to cooling than to overheating, but the findings in this domain are divergent and complex (see 1,290). Reports for a wide range of other species quote an average incubatory temperature of 34.0 ± 2.4°C in one series (for daylight hours only), and a range of 34-36°C in another. Eggs of the domestic fowl and several other domestic species do not hatch after continuous exposure to temperatures below 35°C or above 40½°C, and overheating is a real danger and "uncomfortably" close at all times (see 427, 527, 1,290).

Some development will occur at a temperature as low as 27°C, which is the upper limit of the 25-27°C "physiological zero temperature" range (737). But this temperature does not support development of the circulatory system. If the egg is maintained for any length of time at higher temperatures, but below 35°C, development usually is anomalous, particularly that of the heart. The lower limit for successful hatching of passerine embryos is said to be approached at about 34°C (427, 527).

At 25°C, the blastoderm fails to develop beyond the primitive streak stage (see 336). Below "physiological zero temperature" (25-27°C; 214, 527) but above 0°C--since ice crystal formation causes irreversible damage--there is a wide range of relative safety in cold torpor, at least for moderate periods of exposure in blastular and perhaps early gastrular stages (718). The optimum holding temperatures for storing eggs--for as long as several weeks prior to incubation--fall in the range of 11-13°C (see 427). [Gottlieb refrigerated batches of domestic fowl eggs at 1.7-3°C for 6 days, and of Peking Duck eggs at -1.1-2.2°C for 3 days, to kill embryos in advanced stages of development and synchronize and render more accurately known the timing of development of the surviving embryos (1,274).]

RESPIRATION

YOLK-SAC MEMBRANE---AMNION---CHORION---ALLANTOIS. As in reptiles (757), the trilaminar yolk-sac membrane, the most primitive and widespread of vertebrate extra-embryonic membranes, is the first membrane to differentiate during ontogeny. Expansion of the exocoelom into the mesodermal layer of the yolk sac results in the separation of somatic and splanchnic mesodermal layers. The inner splanchnopleure (vascular splanchnic mesoderm plus endoderm) becomes the definitive yolk sac, whereas the outer splanchnopleure (avascular somatic mesoderm plus ectoderm) becomes a part of the chorion.

The yolk-sac mesoderm is the initial site of hematopoiesis and angiogenesis (blood and blood vessel formation, respectively), in accord with its role in providing an efficient movement of stored yolk nutrients to the embryo. Its area vasculosa serves as the respiratory organ during the early phases of embryonic development, until the chorioallantoic membrane forms (786). The yolk sac also is a site of synthesis of specific proteins and amino acids, a source of lymphoid precursor cells for the thymus and bursa of Fabricius, the major site for glycogen storage (under insulin control), a site for calcium storage, and a temporary excretory organ. It seems likely that much of the calcium that accounts for the progressive rise in calcium concentration in the plasma during the 3rd week of incubation is transported to the yolk. The yolk materials required by the embryo are taken up by the endoderm, transferred to the mesodermal blood vessels, and then transported to the embryo (see 1,053, 1,150).

In reptiles and birds, the amnion and chorion are developed together as upwardly projecting folds of the extra-embryonic somatopleure that eventually close over the dorsal surface of the embryo, completely enclosing it in the amniotic cavity. The surface of the fold facing the embryo lines the amniotic cavity and becomes the amnion; the surface facing away becomes continuous over the dorsal surface of the embryo and the exocoelom (outer cavity) and is the chorion. The latter completely envelops the other fetal membranes and the embryo and is in a unique position to play an important functional role in the passage of substances into and out of the egg in all amniotes (786).

As fluid is secreted into the exocoelom the embryo comes to float on top of the yolk, lying on its left side just below the shell membranes. In this position it can develop without adhesion, desiccation, or distortion, which presumably are the selective advantages that account for the evolutionary development of the exocoelom in reptiles (see 786, 1,053). The embryo is connected to the extra-embryonic parts only by the stalk of the yolk sac and the neck of the splanchnopleuric allantois.

The latter begins to grow out of the embryo's right side after about the 4th or 5th day of incubation, as a bud from the hindgut into the exocoelom, that subsequently becomes continuous with the urogenital sinus and urinary bladder. Its expansion and subsequent fusion with the chorion appear to depend on the functional differentiation of the mesonephric kidney during the 4th day (see p. 181, last paragraph). Its evolutionary origin probably was causally related to its function as a urinary bladder for the storage of mesonephric excretions, which pass caudally into the cloaca and thence into the allantoic sac. At first, ammonia and uric acid are stored, as the sac increases in volume to a maximum of 7 ml on about the 13th day; thereafter, water is re-absorbed, urates are precipitated, and the volume of the sac declines. From about day 11, the albumen begins to be absorbed, partly by flowing into the amniotic cavity and partly into the yolk sac, to which the albumen sac also is joined at the yolk-sac umbilicus (155, 336, 786, 1,053). Adult avian urine usually is creme colored and contains thick, mucoid material, a colloidal solution of uric acid and urates, in which form it is transported through the tubules (442, 522).

CHORIOALLANTOIC MEMBRANE. Up to the 10th day, the allantoic capillaries lie under the 2-layered chorionic epithelium but by day 12 they have become incorporated completely into the epithelium. They are separated from the inner shell membrane by extremely thin cytoplasmic extensions of "capillary-covering" cells that are found between the capillaries. The thickness of the tissue barrier between the inner shell membrane and the capillary lumen decreases from 4.3 micra at day 8 to less than 0.8 micra after the 12th day (702, 1,053). By the 9th day of incubation the chorioallantoic membrane--the fusion between the mesenchymatic layers of the chorion and the underlying allantois--has invested about half of the inner surface of the inner shell membrane.

When fully developed, the dense capillary network of the chorioallantoic membrane covers 70-80% of the entire inside of the eggshell (703), underlying the inner shell membrane and in contact with the continuous, thin film that lines it. In most species, this is achieved after completion of about 55% of the incubatory period, at which time the gaseous uptake resistance of the chorioallantoic membrane attains its maximum value (234, 435, 478, 492). In the Peach-faced Lovebird, this does not appear to occur until after about 80% (day 18) of the incubatory period, and the corresponding figure for another nidicole, the Brown Pelican (*Pelecanus occidentalis*) is at least 70% (see 1,275).

[The developmental interrelationship between the avian proamnion, ectamnion, and somatopleuric headfolds differs considerably from the condition in chelonians and the Tuatara, but is quite similar to the pattern in crocodilians (786). The amnio-chorion develops earlier in reptiles than in birds, appearing first with the head fold in pre-somite reptiles but after the 12-somite stage in the domestic fowl. It may act as a positioner of the reptilian embryo, holding it close to the eggshell and enhancing respiration, but also holding it slightly away from the eggshell and preventing adhesions that might arise upon dehydration. However, since there is so little variation in the amnio-chorion, despite huge differences in hydration risks, its primary function in reptiles may be to provide the space universally required for the growth of the dorsal region of the embryo.

The chorioallantois forms and functions in much the same manner in reptiles as in birds, except that expansion may cease and retraction occur prior to pipping. In most chelonian species, pipping occurs while the allantois still covers the posterior 50-75% of the carapace, but in kinosterids the allantois usually withdraws completely before pipping, which may be delayed for 2 months after this withdrawal (see 757, 774). It is the chorioallantoic membrane that becomes modified to form the fetal portion of the chorioallantoic placenta of viviparous reptiles and eutherian mammals.]

The chorioallantois plays the part of a lung in the developing embryo. Its reticulate capillary plexus is fed with unsaturated venous blood (estimated at 20% saturation) from the allantoic artery and drained of arteriolized blood (91.7% saturated in 16-day-old embryos) by the allantoic vein (435, 703). Originally there are paired allantoic arteries and veins but both left vessels degenerate and are lost by the 8th day. Since the width of the capillaries is approximately the size of the RBC, the elliptical corpuscles are deformed to various degrees within the capillary walls and flow through them in zig-zag fashion. This type of movement greatly lengthens the effective path length between the arterioles and the venules and produces a "stirring" effect. As a result, the time of contact between the RBCs and the environmental air is lengthened, with a consequent increase in the diffusive capacity of the chorioallantoic membrane (703).

In the 16-day-old embryo, the chorioallantoic membrane (or the film lining the inner cell membrane) offers twice as much exchange resistance for oxygen as does the eggshell (or an equal amount), whereas the resistance of the eggshell is 5-6 times that of the chorioallantoic membrane for carbon dioxide. The eggshell is responsible for virtually the entire resistance to water vapor. Normally the latter is believed to be lost at a constant rate throughout incubation (see 478, 1,053).

TWO BASIC PATTERNS IN THE ONTOGENY OF OXYGEN CONSUMPTION. The resistance of the chorioallantoic membrane for both oxygen and carbon dioxide declines during later development (see 478 and J. Piiper *et al.*, 1980, in 435). In general, there appear to be two basic patterns in the ontogeny of oxygen consumption. Nidicolous (altricial) embryos show a roughly exponential increase throughout development, with a substantial rise upon hatching; nidifugous (precocial) embryos also show a roughly exponential increase during development, but a plateau is reached several days before hatching (after passage of about 60-70% of the incubatory period), associated with a similar stabilization of growth rate. The plateau period may be one of developmental maturation, leading to the nidifugous condition by the time of hatching (see 320, 545).

Oxygen consumption is not constant throughout the day, but follows a rhythmic pattern with a peak at around 19:00 h (1,053). Nor is it the same in both sexes. Males consume 74% more oxygen than do females between days 10 and 19. The difference is due partly to the greater growth rate in males, which averages 55% higher than in females; the remaining difference correlates with the appearance of sex hormones in the circulatory system of the embryo. As one consequence of these sexual differences in respiratory rate, female embryos have a higher survival rate than do those of males in conditions of oxygen shortage. About 35% of the total uptake by the egg on day 6 is accounted for by the allantois and yolk sac, as compared to only 5% by day 19 (see J.A. Shilov, 1973, in 1,150).

To a first approximation parrots follow the general pattern of other species with nidicolous young, but owing to the longer incubatory periods the total embryonic energy metabolism in relation to egg weight is greater than expected in such species and approaches the values typical of species with nidifugous young (634).[Oxygen consumption by chelonian embryos follows the avian nidifugous pattern. Thus, oxygen consumption by *Kinosternon subrubrum* embryos increases very little during the last 3 weeks of development (757).]

As an example for a nidifuge, oxygen consumption by the domestic fowl embryo increases slowly during the 1st 10 days of incubation. Between the 10th and 14th days it rises steeply to a plateau value of about 600 ml per diem (900 ml per diem after hatching), at which level it remains until internal pipping occurs. This value of oxygen consumption represents the maximum amount of oxygen that can be obtained by passive diffusion through the pores of the eggshell. The vigorous muscular actions and movements of hatching, however, require 200-350 ml more of oxygen per diem than can be provided by simple passive diffusion (478, 492). In the case of parrots, though the total embryonic energy metabolism approaches that of nidifuges, both the pre-pipping and hatching levels of oxygen consumption are lower than those in nidifuges with eggs of the same size, and the same is true generally of pre-pipping oxygen consumption of nidicoles as compared to nidifuges (634).

THE RELATIVE GROWTH RATE of Peach-faced Lovebird embryos (egg weight about 4.2 g) decreases throughout the incubatory period; the rate is about 80% per day after passage of 35% of the incubatory period, and less than 20% per day during the last quarter of incubation. In the much smaller Zebra Finch, another species with nidicolous young, with eggs only 25% as weighty, values are 150% per day after passage of 40% of the incubatory period and decline to 5% per day during the last quarter. For comparison, in Eurasian Quail, with nidifugous young and eggs weighing 8-13 g, the relative growth rate is about 45% per day after passage of 40% of the incubatory period and declines from about 25% to less than 10% per day during the last quarter of incubation (see 1,275).

PRODUCTION EFFICIENCY. A typical egg of the Peach-faced Lovebird contains 20.31 kJ of chemical potential energy, 13.94 kJ contributed by the yolk and 6.36 kJ contributed by the albumen. At the time of hatching, the potential energy of the chick, including its yolk reserve and membranes, is at least 10.01 kJ, amounting to 49.3% of the energy contained in the original egg. For the yolk-free hatchling, the energy content is 44.8% of the chemical potential energy of the egg contents used during incubation. This value, equivalent to the total production efficiency, is higher than the values (26-37%) for mammals for producing tissue from milk at the time of weaning (see 1,275). This result is not unexpected, since, as functioning ectotherms, avian embryos theoretically should have higher production efficiencies than endotherms (1,294).

AIR CELL. Separation of the shell-membrane layers as water is lost during incubation (see pp. 175, 176, **Hydration**) leaves a compensating volume of gas in the air cell at the broad end of the egg, continuous with the gas between the fibers of the shell membranes. The air cell increases in size at a constant rate (inasmuch as water vapor is lost at a constant rate) until it occupies about 15% of the internal volume of the egg at the end of incubation (478, 492). It provides a slightly cooled zone in which vaporized metabolic water is partially re-condensed, with a net reduction in loss to the environment (1,150). The embryo pips the chorioallantoic and inner cell membranes into this air cell on about the 19th day. It uses the air therein to aerate its bronchial system, the air sacs, and parabronchi, initiating a rapid development of the parenchymal mantle, accompanied by a rapid increase in heart rate (185, 226, 702, 705). Respiratory movements can, however, occur many hours before internal pipping (1,053).

[Air spaces also occur in chelonians with rigid-shelled eggs, but their location is variable and can change with orientation. As in birds, they reflect the state of hydration of the egg, increasing in volume as water is lost (673, 681, 757). Air spaces also were reported in the eggs of developing Nile Crocodiles (*Crocodylus niloticus*) and are to be expected in the eggs of all crocodilians as long as the shell membranes are intact. Air spaces do not form in the parchment-shelled eggs of squamates, since these are free to deform with changes in hydration (673, 757).]

RESPIRATORY MOVEMENTS---AERATION OF THE PARABRONCHI. The lung becomes functional and increasingly takes over the gas exchange as the few blood capillaries between the arterioles and venules increase enormously in number and infundibula sprout from the tertiary bronchial atria. The latter give off numerous air capillaries, that surround the developing blood capillaries and form a 3-dimensional network of gas exchanging tissues (702). Simultaneously there is a decrease in the chorioallantoic gas exchanges, although the degeneration of the chorioallantois would not seem to be initiated until 10 h after the initiation of breathing (1,053).

The oxygen requirements of the embryo are 25 ml/h prior to breathing, 35 ml/h prior to active hatching, and about 40 ml/h at the moment of leaving the shell. The above-described manner of ventilation of the parabronchi with air provides the additional few 100 ml of oxygen per diem required for the vigorous movements of hatching (478, 492). After hatching, at least in homeothermic endotherms, a further substantial increase occurs. The glucose made available by the dramatic mobilization of glycogen stores of the liver just before breathing commences appears to be necessary for the proper functioning of the central nervous system. A marked rise in the glycogen stores of the brain has been noted at this time (see 1,053).

The manner of ventilation of the parabronchi also is viewed as an essential intermediate stage in avian ontogeny, which occurs in all species. The presumption is that the gradual aeration (or fluid filling) of the air capillaries as they sprout as open tubes is necessary, since the interfacial tensions in preformed capillaries would not permit a sudden inflation from the collapsed state (702). Aeration of the tertiary bronchi in limited areas can be recognized by the change in color of the lungs from dark to bright red (1,053). The attainment of the stage of lung aeration is signalled by a cheeping of the chicks of many species (336, 426). Inflation is completed in both lungs after about 6 h in domestic fowl embryos, 4 h in duck embryos, and 9 h in Bobwhite Quail (*Colinus virginianus*; 1,053). This occurs at about 24-30 h before hatching in the domestic fowl embryo and about 48 h earlier in Mallard embryos.

At first the respiratory movements are irregular and intermittent and accompanied by a low-level, low-frequency sound (the "silent" phase of respiration). Gradually regular patterns of medium amplitude breathing emerge and come to dominate the pattern. Finally, both frequency and amplitude increase and each breath often is accompanied by a readily detectible clicking sound at 3-4 Hz in bursts of about 1-10 clicks. These accompany breathing in all species investigated and are produced by bouts of bill clapping. At hatching, the breathing rate is about 1.5-1.7 Hz (see 737, 1,053).

There seems to be little doubt that avian embryos cannot vocalize before the trachea and the syrinx are cleared of fluids, but the relationship between the 1st calls and the 1st breaths has not yet been elucidated. Duck and domestic fowl embryos sometimes vocalize before their lungs are aerated and the latter can do so even before breathing movements begin. The air sacs and the primary bronchi may be clear of fluids when the embryos call, although the lungs are not yet aerated. In view of the structure of the avian respiratory system, air might be drawn through the syrinx without necessarily involving the lungs (1,053).

In fact, even before aerating its lungs, the chick embryo executes periodic respiratory movements that begin 2-3 days earlier. Lung inflation defines the beginning of the paranatal stage (pipping to hatching) in which oxygen is obtained by both diffusion and convection. During this stage there is a gradual transition between diffusive respiration, via the chorioallantois and eggshell, to convective breathing via the developing capillaries of the parabronchial lungs. During the same period the ductus arteriosus (between the pulmonary and aortic arches) and the intra-atrial foramina gradually become closed off, forming the avian double circulation (1,053).

The chorioallantoic blood circulation continues to supply oxygen until the chick pips the eggshell, removing most of its diffusive resistance. Then the chick begins to breath the outside air directly. Therewith, the parabronchial lungs become the predominant sites for gas exchange and convection becomes the only mechanism for gas transport to the blood-gas barrier (435). Blood pressure rises markedly during hatching to at least 43/23 mmHg (systolic/diastolic) and continues to increase in the immediate post-hatching period, and the heart rate increases from about 4.3 to 4.9

Hz or more (1,053). Since the only circumstance in which ventilation of the lungs with air can occur simultaneously with gas exchange by a chorioallantois is through ontogeny in a hard-shelled egg, viviparous avian development seems to be ruled out (702), even had there been selection for the intermediate stage of egg retention, which seems unlikely (1,402).

[LUNG INFLATION IN REPTILES. The circumstances appear to be quite different in reptiles, in which sudden inflation of the lungs occurs and internal pipping into an air space, such as is typical of avian eggs, is not the usual procedure. For example, when air spaces are not present, crocodilian hatchlings may not breathe until the shell, extra-embryonic, and shell membranes are broken and the fluids drain from around the head. The time elapsing between initiation of breathing and emergence from the shell ranges from only a few min to 24 h, so that the transition from chorioallantoic to pulmonary respiration can be very rapid, as in mammals.

However, the extent of chorioallantoic perfusion in the time between first breathing and hatching is unknown. Since crocodilian embryos can vocalize for many hours prior to pipping in response to certain stimuli (see pp. 575, 576, **Vocalizations and Care of Young**), it is suggested that the oxygen in air bubbles is used prior to pipping. These bubbles form beneath the shell membrane and move about in the albumen so as always to lie beneath the uppermost inner surface of the egg. Although high humidity may be required during the early stages of incubation, it is suggested that lower humidity may be essential during later stages of crocodilian embryogenesis to facilitate water loss and the formation of air spaces within the shell. These would enable internal breathing and maturation of the respiratory system, and would provide the extra oxygen required for pipping (759). The circumstances in megapodes may not be greatly dissimilar (772).]

PERIODS OF CONTINUOUS INCUBATION by many birds are interrupted periodically by a bird's rising, assuming a stooping posture, and looking down at its eggs. The bird may then turn around in the nest and face in a new direction, and it may shift and/or turn the eggs with its bill before resettling. Domestic fowl hens, for example, shift their eggs every 10-60 min, Black-headed Gulls (*Larus ridibundus*) about every 40 min, Herring Gulls (*Larus argentatus*) every 140 min, and Mallards at least once every 50 min. Among passerines, the incubating female Mountain White-crowned Sparrow (*Zonotrichia leucophrys oriantha*) was noted to change the egg position frequently and randomly (482). Resettling on the eggs typically consists of a sequence of behavioral patterns, which Beer termed *chest-dropping*, *waggling*, and *quivering* (movements by which close contacts between the brood patch and eggs are re-established). During the act of resettling or while looking down at the eggs, before or after shifting them, the bird may vocalize briefly. Movements of the bird in the nest in other acts also may change the position of the eggs.

During the pre-hatching and hatching periods, marked changes in attentiveness have been noted in many species; the duration of bouts of continuous incubation becomes shorter and the periods between them lengthen. Rising and resettling (and the proportion of incomplete settling sequences) increase in frequency, and the rate of shifting of the eggs also tends to increase. Increased vocalizing occurs in some species and, where both parents incubate, they also exchange with each other more frequently. Ring Doves spend more time on a nest with fertile, developing eggs than with infertile eggs. Some changes in the incubatory pattern in late stages may be induced by movements of the protruding bill and egg caruncle of the embryo during pipping.

With the 3 species of the present study, attentiveness to the eggs was most noteworthy among the Cockatiels, a species in which both parents incubate the eggs (see Part 3 and Chap. 4, Parts 1 and 2). Even the non-incubating bird visits the nest periodically and displaces the sitting bird long enough to make a thorough, close inspection of the eggs, particularly in later stages of incubation. The incubating bird also participates in all such inspections (see 1,290).

TURNING OF THE EGGS by the hen is particularly critical during the 1st half of the incubatory period, particularly between the 4th and 7th days. At first it prevents premature adhesions involving the extra-embryonic membranes, such as the premature fusion of the chorioallantois with the inner shell membrane (23, 427). These early adhesions can lead to various anomalies later in development, such as disruption in the uptake of albumen or aberrant positioning of the embryo within the egg. These reduce the probability of successful hatching (see 737). Turning in later stages prevents adhesion of the allantois and yolk sac, which would prevent the retraction of the yolk sac into the abdomen, prior to hatching. Yolk remaining at that time is utilized by hatchlings, particularly nidifuges that may have difficulty feeding during the first few days after hatching (245).

With each turn of the egg, the yolk rotates, bringing the lighter portion bearing the developing embryo always to the uppermost position. Once the extra-embryonic membranes have fused with the inner shell membrane and egg contents (about midway through incubation), this rotation no longer occurs, and the latter becomes fixed with respect to the shell. At such time an egg free to roll assumes a stable equilibrium position (with its center of gravity lowermost) determined by the asymmetrical weight distribution of its contents (427, 737).

Domestic fowl eggs commonly are incubated artificially at 37.8°C in a relative humidity of 40-80% and turned 3-4 times daily by hand or 8 times automatically, except during the last 10-15% of the incubatory period (late on day 17 or early on day 18). Turning of artificially incubated eggs in close imitation of the jostling that they receive from the incubating parent(s), i.e., of an irregular nature and around different axes, promotes the survival of embryos better than smooth, slow, regular turning. Alternated rotation of about 45° from 1-4 times/h is a common practice toward this goal. Eggs should not be rotated always in the same direction as this can result in rupture of the yolk sac, disruption of the chorion, allantois, and shell membranes, twisting of the chalazae, and rupture of the blood vessels (see 492, 1,052, 1,274). Irregular turning may provide tactile and proprioceptive stimulation to the embryo to a far greater degree than regular turning (see 427, 1,290).

[The same situation occurs in developing crocodilian embryos with respect to excretory functions by the yolk sac and allantois (759) but the opposite situation prevails with respect to the turning of the eggs. About 24 h after crocodilian oviposition a critical period ensues, as the vitelline membrane (a non-cellular membrane that separates the yolk and early embryo from the albumen) or dorsal surface of the blastoderm becomes attached to the inner aspect of the shell membrane (665, 666, 754, 759). If the eggs are turned after attachment, the embryos are unable to rise to the top of the yolk mass and may be crushed or "drowned" by the heavy yolk. Movements in the first few days also tend to shear the embryo from the embryonic disc and rupture blood vessels of the extra-embryonic membranes. But after the 4th week of incubation the embryo and extra-embryonic membranes are more resistant to damage.

Similar cautions, and for much the same reasons, are expressed for the handling of chelonian eggs at a time between 1 h and 2-3 days after oviposition. It is suggested that the apposition of the membranes may accommodate the respiratory needs of the embryo during the several days preceding formation of an extra-embryonic respiratory system and that it largely-to-completely determines the subsequent embryonic orientation. Both chelonian and crocodilian eggshells become chalk-white at the points of adhesion to the shell membrane (681, 757, 759).]

GASEOUS REGULATORY CAPACITIES---HYDRATION. Most embryos are said to develop in similar gaseous environments within the shell. Since passive processes of diffusion in the gaseous phase are responsible for gaseous exchanges across the pores of the eggshell (see 427 and 435), the diffusion resistance of the shell is constant throughout incubation. A typical domestic fowl egg takes up about 6,000 ml of oxygen and gives off about 4,500 ml of carbon dioxide and 11,000 ml of water vapor over the 21 days of incubation, decreasing in weight at a relatively constant rate from about 60 to 51 g over the same period (478, 500). Lipids form the major energy source for the developing embryo, with about 80% of the consumption taking place after the 14th day. Since complete metabolism of 1 g of fat yields about 1.07 g of water, the 2.5-3.0 g of lipid consumed during incubation can supply about 2.7-3.2 g of the 8-9 g of water that is lost. Water balance does not come under neurohypophysial control until the final week of incubation (1,053, 1,150).

Recent studies suggest that the embryos have regulatory capacities for dealing with variation in gaseous exchange, and that these capacities contribute importantly to survival (226). Nevertheless, hatchability of domestic fowl eggs is very sensitive to deviations in oxygen concentration outside of the range of 15-40%, and drops by about 15% for every percent rise in carbon dioxide concentration above 1% (427). In this connection, if gaseous exchanges across the shell are restricted, embryonic heart rate is proportionately reduced and pipping and hatching are delayed (705).

The interior of the egg is fully saturated with water vapor, and the maintenance of a constant level of hydration throughout incubation seems to be important for survival of the embryo. In the case of Budgerigar eggs incubated artificially at 41.7°C, a high relative humidity was recommended, with turning of the eggs at least 6 times per day, whereupon 80-90% development could be expected (see H.B. Fell, 1939, in 338). In general, it can be asserted that hatchability of artificially incubated eggs is greatest when the total water loss over the entire period of incubation is between 10-12% of the initial egg weight, and that this is achieved within the range of 40-47% relative humidity (427). Higher levels, even periodic sprinkling, are recommended for some eggs, for example, those of ducks and geese (1,053). The relative humidity, of course, governs the rate of aqueous loss from the fully saturated egg through the constant diffusion-resistance barrier presented by the pores of the shell.

There are many effects of deviations in water loss, but they are poorly understood. Eggs can, however, hatch after sustaining water losses 3-4 times greater than normal, but the size of the hatchlings is much reduced (see K. Simkiss, 1980, in 674). Individual variations in parameters can be great. For example, in Peach-faced Lovebirds, the water vapor conductance of eggs of different individuals varies by a factor of at least 7. Though this results in a large range of gas tensions in the air cell, these appear to be tolerated well by the embryos (1,275). [The developing eggs of petrels, which have relatively long incubatory periods (a ubiquitous feature among procellariiform birds), lose about the same amount of water as those of birds with much shorter incubatory periods. This is accounted for by the fact that the former eggs contain far fewer pores and are incubated at lower temperatures (508, 532).]

In naturally incubated eggs of a wide variety of birds, the calculated and measured loss of water from eggs during incubation averages 15-18.6% (the higher values being for procellariiforms) of initial egg weight, which is considerably higher than the optimum mentioned above for artificially incubated eggs (274, 478, 492, 524). About 75% of this loss occurs before the onset of internal pipping (see A. Ar and H. Rahn, 1980, in 524). It is suggested that the behavior of the incubating parent(s) is important in maintaining the humidity of the air in the nest within close tolerances, and that in many environments, the water loss of eggs may be crucial in determining the survival of a developing embryo (478, 492).

The water loss from the egg compensates both for the reduction in solid content, mostly yolk, by catabolism and for the production of metabolic water. As a result both the fresh egg and the pipping embryo have the same relative level of hydration. Since the eggshell is rigid, the volume of water lost is replaced by an equal volume of air in the air cell (see p. 171). The number of pores present in the shell apparently represents an optimum value arrived at in the course of evolution. It presumably is a value that balances the the opposing tendencies of having many pores, favoring oxygen exchange, and few pores, favoring conservation of water (see 427).

GUARDING NESTBOX----INCUBATION----BROOD NUMBER----PARENTAL ENERGY COST. Breeding Budgerigar hens become very pugnacious in guarding their NBs (nestboxes) against the intrusions of other birds, though occasionally 2 hens will share a NB (137). Some workers report that incubation often or usually starts with the laying of the first egg (67, 171, 1,056), others between the 1st and 2nd eggs (843), still others with the laying of the 2nd egg (104), or that it is an individual matter (185). It seems beyond doubt that variability in incubatory habits of the hens also occurs in the wild, as the nests examined by Cayley contained chicks varying between the two extremes of having young in all stages of development to having young of almost uniform size (1,056). In any case, once incubation has commenced, the female spends 45-60 min/h of daylight in the NB (67). In general, in species in which only one parent incubates the eggs, the parent usually spends 60-80% of the daytime activity and the entire night on the eggs (28). In general, during the very late stages of incubation, attending parents primarily supply insulation and protection from predators, rewarm eggs allowed to chill, and protect the egg from lethal overheating in very hot environments (729).

Numerous experiments and observations have illustrated that the incubating parent treats the eggs, in essence, as an extension of its own body core. Feedback from the clutch via the broodpatch leads to adjustment of the tightness of contact of the broodpatch with the eggs, while shifting the eggs, gular fluttering, panting, shivering, elevating the feathers, etc., take place, as required to maintain constancy of incubatory temperature as the external thermal regime varies (737). Computation of mean parental energy cost of incubation for House Wrens at an ambient temperature of 22°C and with excellent nest insulation, yielded a figure of 0.067 kcal/h, which is approximately 19% of the productive energy available to the female (see 60, 738). For the Herring Gull the figure is 25% at ambient temperatures of 12-28°C (738). For Zebra Finches incubating at 29.1°C, the energy of incubation amounts to 11% of standard metabolic rate (975), and food consumption increases 13.6% over existence energy requirements during control periods (see A.J. El-Wailly, 1966, in 975).

Much higher values are obtained in some other species. For example, the free-living Blue Tit hen incubating a clutch of normal size (10-13 eggs) at an ambient air temperature of 0°C increases her metabolic rate by 50-90% (664; see a further discussion of this topic on pp. 403, 404, **Insulation**). For fasting Wandering Albatrosses (*Diomedea exulans*) incubating in alternate shifts of several weeks, the cost was estimated at 120-200% of standard metabolic rate (826). The parental contribution diminishes progressively during the later stages of incubation as the heat production of the embryos increases (see R.H. Drent, 1967, in 729). The heat produced by developing House Wren embryos contributed about 10% of the total requirement (see 60). On the last day of incubation by the Herring Gull, the embryo contributes 75% of the total heat requirement (411 of 545 cal/h; see R.H. Drent, 1970, in 975).

FEMALES INCUBATE. In contrast to the habits of Cockatiels and Peach-faced Lovebirds (see Parts 3 and 4, Chap. 4, Part 2, and Chap. 7, Parts 1 and 2), many male Budgerigars do not enter the NB during the incubatory period. Though some males spend a great deal of time in the NB with their mates in confinement, only females incubate the eggs (ascertained by Brockway and by Hutchison by observing birds nesting in NBs with one-way viewing panels; 67, 860). In general, incubating hens in the wild typically undergo a regulated loss of weight and reduction in food requirements. These changes allow the hen to resolve conflicts in the allocation of time between foraging and nest attendance (257). On very hot days, incubating Budgerigar females in the wild perch briefly at the nest-hole entrance (171).

INDUCTION OF INCUBATORY BEHAVIOR. The period of oviposition involves a transition from courtship and nesting activity to incubatory behavior that is accomplished by a marked reduction of plasma levels of LH and steroidal hormones in both sexes (928). Although much is known of the hormonal correlates of behavior in the pre-incubatory period (see, for example, 414), the hormonal control of incubatory behavior has been controversial, despite 30 yr of intensive and very active research. As mentioned on p. 148, a compelling recent postulate is that a surge in prolactin concentration serves the dual function of inhibiting ovulation and stimulating the initiation of incubation (1,106). According to this scheme, hens generally would be expected to increase greatly their incubatory behavior during the 24-h period preceding the laying of the last egg, in consequence of which they would begin to incubate after the laying of the penultimate egg. This behavior is found in many passerines (see 1,106).

It usually is presumed that, in the wild, tactile and visual stimuli of the eggs and nest induce an increase in prolactin secretion, which, at least in part, induces incubatory behavior and subsequent care of the young (927). But with the exception of an affirmative reply in the case of the domestic fowl hen, in which prolactin clearly plays a key role (see

1,000), there still is no accord on the answer to the question, "does prolactin induce incubatory behavior?" Discord on this issue in other species may not be resolved definitively until the neural pathways for incubatory behavior have been identified and their degree of dependence on prolactin assessed (748).

Whatever the identity of the factor that induces incubation, there is much evidence suggesting that this period of the reproductive cycle is associated with a decrease of gonadal activity, very likely induced by prolactin, the greatly increased secretion of which is well established (see p. 148 and below). Three types of more or less direct correlational evidence support the view that testicular and ovarian hormonal secretory activity are diminished during incubation (260, 748). This evidence involves cessation of singing and overt sexual activities in many species, regression of secondary sex characters, and regression of the gonads.

There is a clear annual cycle in the secretion of prolactin in wild European Starlings. Levels of LH are highest during nest building and gradually decline during the subsequent stages of breeding, whereas prolactin concentration increases steadily during periods of nest building and oviposition, and peaks during incubation. Prolactin levels also are high in hens when feeding their nestlings, but decline to basal values when breeding is completed. A reciprocal relation between prolactin and LH also is quite well marked in the domestic fowl hen in which circulating prolactin levels rise during the period of oviposition and are further elevated during incubation, but not during brooding (see 1,000,1,135).

Estradiol induces the gathering of nest material and nest construction in female Canaries (928). In the confined bird, prolactin levels rapidly rise 8-10-fold at the beginning of incubation and then decline to 50% of peak value midway through the nestling period. Thus, in both species high levels of prolactin secretion occur during both incubation and feeding of the young. This may not apply to all species with nidicolous young, though, as there is a fairly rapid decline in prolactin after hatching in Pied Flycatchers.

On the other hand, though prolactin levels also are high during incubation in species with nidifugous young, the levels generally decline very rapidly after hatching (748, 928, 931). Male and female steroidal hormones appear to be present in both sexes of Rock Pigeons and Ring Doves and to be important in regulating behavioral patterns (1,000). Plasma testosterone and 5-alpha-dihydrotestosterone levels increase 4 h after pairing experienced Ring Doves males with females in breeding enclosures (935). Mating and nesting are accompanied by an increase in plasma levels of LH and estradiol but the former peaks after pairing with the female and then falls to a low level during incubation and brooding (see 928, 1,000). During courtship, the plasma estradiol concentration in the female increases; it decreases during nest building and then drops steeply to undetectable levels during incubation (989).

Strong courtship and nesting behavior are induced in castrated male Ring Doves injected with testosterone or estradiol. Only the testosterone-induced Bow-cooing and incubatory behavior were slightly more frequent in the group treated with estradiol. LH-releasing hormone also synergizes with estradiol in the female to elicit courtship behavior, with low doses of the latter inducing nest soliciting and squatting. The anti-androgen, cyproterone acetate, reduces Bow-cooing in the male and nest soliciting in both sexes (see 1,000).

Progesterone appears to be important in the induction of incubatory behavior in Ring Doves, rising from 0.5 to about 3.0 ng/ml of plasma from the 1st to the 5th day of courting. Its level is low, however, during incubation (1.1 ng/ml), while estradiol is undetectable (see 900, 989). The results of experiments in which progesterone was injected into intact birds suggest that for the induction of incubatory behavior progesterone has an important function in the male under certain social conditions and in the female under all conditions tested (see 989). Prolactin levels in the male and female are low during courtship and oviposition, nor are they high at the beginning of incubation. They increase markedly between the 7th and 15th days of incubation, secretion apparently being stimulated by visual and tactile cues from the nest and eggs. Thus, although prolactin may be involved in the maintenance of incubatory behavior in the Ring Dove, the absence of an increase in plasma concentrations at the start of incubation raises doubts concerning its importance in the induction of this behavior (748, 922, 928).

The cyclic pattern of hormone changes in the male Rock Pigeon begins with high FSH and androgen titres, which lead to the initial courtship display. This is followed by an estrogen-activated phase of nest demonstration, after which a further peak in FSH leads to nest building. This is succeeded by the onset of incubation, which is induced by progesterone. The restorative effect of testosterone on castrated males is antagonized by simultaneous administration of progesterone (see 1,000).

The increase in plasma levels of prolactin during incubation by Ring Doves and Rock Pigeons causes the crop sacs to hypertrophy (from 0.5 to 3.0 g) in preparation for milk production for the allofeeding of the young (748, 928, 1,000). Parental prolactin levels remain elevated during the first few days after hatching, when the young are allofed by regurgitation of crop "milk," but are much lower after the crop glands regress. There is much more prolactin present in the adenohypophysis of "lactating" than in "non-lactating" pigeons (see 1,000).

As the young of columbids are weaned onto grain, prolactin concentration decreases in parallel with crop-sac regression. In general, high prolactin secretion is sustained in those birds that both cease oviposition and become broody, except that once eggs have accumulated in the nest, their presence seems to be an important stimulus for maintaining high levels of prolactin secretion (748). Prolactin injections activate incubatory behavior in members of both sexes in a dose-dependent fashion (see 752).

[The ovary secretes primarily female sex hormones, such as estriol and progesterone, while the testes secrete primarily androgens. These are involved in the induction of numerous secondary sex characters. In addition, in at least some species, the gonads secrete gonadotropins characteristic of the gonadal secretions of the opposite sex (442).]

THE BROOD PATCH. Administered prolactin acts synergistically with administered gonadal steroids, or in some cases, estrogen acts in synergism with progesterone (depending upon the level of circulating prolactin) to control the development of the brood or incubative patch, a clear indication of differential local hormonal sensitivities in the integument (319, 847). This development consists of a defeathering of any down, increased vascularization and intercellular fluid, epidermal thickening through hyperplasia (cell multiplication) of cells in the epidermis and dermal connective tissue, and increase in tactile sensitivity in the ventral apterium, which becomes well endowed with superficial non-myelinated nerve fibers. The thickening and softening of the skin of the brood patch region allow it to fit the contours of the eggs more closely than otherwise would be the case (see 269, 414, 427, 561, 748, and pp. 561, 562, **Incubatory Temperatures and Brood Patches**). In 2 species of phalaropes (*Phalaropus tricolor* and *P. lobatus*), in which the males are the sole incubators, the brood patch can be induced by administration of a combination of testosterone and prolactin, but not by estrogen and prolactin (989).

Generally speaking, steroidal hormones combined with prolactin appear to exert their chief influences on defeathering and vascularization, whereas steroidal hormones combined with progesterone affect mainly epidermal thickening and sensitivity (427). In Budgerigars, however, treatment of ovariectomized females with estradiol plus progesterone results in defeathering that is advanced in relation to vascularity when compared with intact breeding females, whereas defeathering and vascularity do not differ from the condition in the latter birds when the treatment is with estradiol plus prolactin. The latter treatment not only is most effective in inducing defeathering and incubatory behavior of Budgerigars, but also in inducing the later phases of nesting behavior (847). Refeathering of the patches may be delayed until the postnuptial molt or, following egg loss, after as little as 10 days in Canaries (427).

The chronology of the morphological changes in the formation of brood patches differs widely in different species (see 414). In passerines, defeathering and histological changes usually are completed by the time the clutch is completed. In galliforms, on the other hand, defeathering may not be completed until the middle of the incubatory period and full histological development of the brood patch may not be attained until the eggs hatch (975). In Rock Pigeons and domestic fowl hens, the eggs are incubated against a patch of skin devoid of feathers, which never becomes feathered in the adult (1,000).

In female Budgerigars, brood-patch development is coincident with oviposition and incubation, not with nesting behavior. Defeathering begins at the junction of the abdomen and thorax and usually precedes an increase in vascularity. It then spreads anteriorly and posteriorly about 5 days later. Feathers also are lost from the center of the crop region and eventually the ventral surface becomes defeathered completely in 11% of females. The crop consistently becomes more vascular than the abdominal-thoracic region. The median total period of defeathering was about 10 days (range 7-13 days). The brood patch is completed by the time of oviposition of the 3rd or 4th egg when incubation usually is well established. By the time that chicks have hatched, the entire brood patch is completely refeathered (860). I have noted no brood patch development in either Cockatiels or lovebirds. In both species, the ventral plumage can be parted widely at the mid-line allowing close epidermal contact with the eggs.

Brood patches are in close contact with the eggs during incubation, and they facilitate the transfer of the necessary heat for embryonic development. In addition, the brood patch provides an increasingly sensitive surface in contact with the nest and eggs. This source of tactile stimulation, among others, influences nest-building behavior in some species. In any event, the latter correlates temporally with brood patch development (see 414, 542, 860) and nest attentiveness (influenced by feedback from cold eggs; 527) in many species; in others it is influential in determining clutch size, by way of the central nervous sytem and the adenohypophysis (348, 414).

SOME EVENTS OF EMBRYOGENESIS

HEMOGLOBIN SYNTHESIS. A few days after incubation commences, the fertile eggs begin to change from having a fragile, whitish-tan appearance to a dull, full white, as they become more opaque with the development of the embryo (185). A synthesis of hemoglobin can be detected at 35 h. Some workers have detected 7 embryonic hemoglobins, others only 6 (see 1,053). By the 16th day, the embryonic hemoglobins have been replaced almost completely with adult hemoglobins (704). [From 2 to 7 adult hemoglobins have been detected, though HbI and HbII are present in concentrations considerably in excess of the others. However, several species have but one adult Hb, including the Rock Pigeon and the Cuckoo (*Eudunamys scoloracea*; 1,053). Chelonian (*Emys orbicularis*) embryos have 3 types of hemoglobins that adults lack; adults have 3 other types (757).]

BLOOD PRESSURE---HEART RATE---THYROID---PINEAL. A very low blood pressure in the vitelline arteries can be recorded as early as 46 h after incubation begins. By the 20th day the pressure, possibly under the control of circulating catecholamines, has risen to a value of 36/22 mmHg (systolic/diastolic; 515). The absolute embryonic heart rate is quite variable and increases from 2.3 to 3.7 Hz, or from 3.6 to 5.4 Hz, from the 3rd to the 20th day, according to some workers using different techniques; according to others it declines after the 10th day to about 4.3 Hz in conjunction with an increased cardiac output (see 516, 1,053, 1,150 and pp. 172, 173).

On the 2nd day the head region begins to bend into a cranial flexure at the level of the mesencephalon, followed by further cervical flexure at the junction of the trunk and head on the 3rd day (1,150). The ductus venosus is lost on the 7th day. The primary pineal evagination is formed during the 1st 3 days of incubation, and the gland grows rapidly from day 8 and attains the usual hatching size by the 12th day (see 1,120).

AMNION--ALLANTOIS---ADENOHYPOPHYSIS---LUNGS---LIVER---ELECTRICAL ACTIVITY. The earliest indication of amnion formation is evident in the 8-9 somite stage (about 33 h) as a horseshoe-shaped ectamniotic thickening near the anterior margin of the mesoderm-free proamnion (786). The allantois appears in the 28-30-somite stage (52-55 h) and expands slowly and protrudes into the exocoelom during the 3rd day. The Rock Pigeon adenohypophysis begins to form after about 60 h (see 997). The lungs first appear early on the 3rd day and develop out of the lung-bud stage on day 4, while the air sacs begin to sprout on day 8 (702). The liver differentiates at about day 6 or 7, perhaps earlier, whereupon the synthesis and storage of glycogen can begin. Electrical activity has been detected from the spinal cord as early as the 4th day, and, from this day onward, the embryo takes up its characteristic crescent shape, seemingly determined by the precocious development of the central nervous system. However, no spontaneous electrical activity has been recorded for the brain before day 13 or 14 (see 1,053, 1,150).

THE TERTIARY BRONCHI are fully formed by the 18th day and the air capillaries are fully developed between the 19th and 20th days (517; see also p. 196, **Respiratory System**). The bursa of Fabricius first appears on the 5th day as a sac-like evagination of the dorsal wall of the cloaca (631). The mesonephros begins to form urine during the 4th or 5th day and ceases to function by the end of incubation (718). The metanephros begins to develop on about the 4th day, shortly after the mesonephric (Wolffian) duct fuses with the cloaca. Optical-system axons grow into the tectum and presumably form synaptic connections there between days 6 and 18 and have already developed to an advanced stage before hatching. The initial formation of functional retino-tectal connections occurs in the absence of patterned visual stimulation or of visual experience (1,021).

THE GONADS of all vertebrates, with the possible exception of teleosts, begin as sexually bipotential primordia located to each side of the midline of the embryo. The undifferentiated gonad consists of an outer region of cortical tissue and an inner region of medullary tissue (1,027). Chromosomal constitution has crucial consequences for the course of gonadal differentiation which, in turn, dictates the development or regression of the genital ducts. If the bird is a genetic female, the cortical tissue proliferates and becomes the ovarian tissue, and the medullary tissue fails to proliferate; if it is a genetic male, the medullary tissue proliferates at the expense of the cortical tissue (see 1,027).

[One can summarize the facts of vertebrate sexuality, particularly that of mammals and birds, by saying that the homogametic sex (producing one type of gamete; the male in birds) is the neutral sex in ontogeny and is the most easily reversed by experimental intervention, both morphologically (in early life) and behaviorally (in early life and in adulthood), and that the heterogametic sex produces the organizing hormones (1,027).]

OVARIAN DEVELOPMENT starts on the 3rd day, when primordial germ cells (future oocytes and spermatocytes) and mesenchymal cells are incorporated into the germinal epithelium. Synthesis of hormones begins shortly after the gonadal anlage of both sexes appear and there is some evidence that this begins earlier and is more active in the female. Cells containing neurosecretory material are found in the Rock Pigeon nucleus lateralis externus hypothalami on the 4th day. This is the earliest stage for which neurosecretory activity has been reported in a vertebrate, and the activity shows rhythmic changes and is maintained throughout embryogenesis. Between the 4th and 6th days, while gonadal tissue is in the indifferent state, estrogen and estradiol are synthesized. The right ovary and Müllerian duct develop indifferently at first (see 997, 1,053). Regression of the germinal epithelium of the right ovary is initiated during the beginning of the 5th day in domestic fowl and songbird embryos (347, 490), while regression of the right oviduct begins on about the 7th day (622). These sexual differentiations are caused proximately by differential steroidal secretions (741).

During the 6th and 7th days, primary sex cords form, giving rise to the medulla and medullary-interstitial cells. The germinal epithelium proliferates during the 8th to 11th day, forming the cortex and the secondary sex cords. Control is extra-hypophysial until the 13th day (940). Unless exposure to steroidal sex-hormones takes place during the embryonic period, differentiation of the neural substrate underlying sexual behavior takes place in the masculine direction (see 1,027).

The ovary develops earlier but at first grows more slowly than the testes. The latter are larger than the former until about the 7th or 8th day; after this stage, it is the ovary that grows at the greater rate (see 792, 989, 997). By the 16th to 18th day, sexual dimorphism is well established in domestic fowl embryos (490, 625), whereas the embryonic ovary of the Rock Pigeon is differentiated into cortex and medulla on the 9th day and the oocytes already have invaded the cortex (997).

SECRETION OF ESTROGENS by the left ovary (beginning between the 2nd and 6th days) apparently inhibits the medullary tissue of the right gonad and destroys its potential to develop (851, 940). In the control of sexual differentiation (demasculinization) of the brain, cells of the hypothalamus appear to be targets for estrogens. Beginning on about the 9th day the Müllerian ducts begin to regress in the male, probably as a consequence of the secretion of some non-steroidal testicular secretion, and they are vestigial by day 13. The right Müllerian duct of females also regresses during this period, probably as a consequence of some secretion of the left ovary (see 1,027).

There is evidence that the gonads have the potential to secrete hormones even before morphological differentiation occurs. Even at an early age ovaries probably secrete more estrogen than do testes, even more than those of adult laying hens (see 1,027). However, the production of steroids in the early female embryo must be accomplished without hypophysial involvement, since the hypophysial-ovarian axis becomes established only at about the middle of the incubatory period (see 951). In the case of the duck embryo, both the syrinx and the genital tubercle begin their divergent development in males and females on the 13th day. Testosterone is first present in the embryo on day 5½; from day 7½ through 17½, males produce more of the hormone than do females (see 1,027). The testis can produce androgens independently of the hypophysis until about 13½ days. After that, the hypophysis becomes essential for androgenic production, but operates independently of the hypothalamus (989).

[In both birds and mammals, the gonad of the heterogametic sex appears to outgrow the gonad of the homogametic sex during the major part of its development. The sex-determining mechanism in both birds and mammals appears to be one of dominance determination. In birds it is the precocial development of the bipotential gonadal rudiment that leads to the formation of an ovary; in mammals, precocial development yields a testis (792).]

MOVEMENTS---VISUAL RESPONSES---EYE OPENING. The avian embryo is in movement for almost the entire incubatory period, and the greater part of these movements are active rather than passive. From the time they begin and for the greater part of the incubatory period, these movements are almost entirely spontaneous, in the sense that they can occur in the absence of any sensory input. After about 15 days, though, there is a deterioration in the spontaneous motor performance. The movements are believed to originate in discharges from nerve cells in the spinal cord augmented by activity in the brain, with specific influences from different brain regions appearing at different stages (communication is established between different parts of the nervous system very early in development). Spontaneous movements can, however, develop in the absence of descending influences from the brain, and there is no doubt that these early motor rhythms reflect fundamental endogenous tendencies (1,268, 1,277).

Motor columns in the spinal cord differentiate earlier than the sensory areas, as a result of which the chick and most other vertebrate embryos are motile before they can respond to tactile stimulation (and the same sequential order prevails in the brain; 1,277). Active movements begin at about 3½-4 days and occur in 3 somewhat overlapping phases. In the 1st phase, movements begin in the head region and gradually come to involve the entire corpus. In the 2nd phase, beginning at about 13 days, these whole-body movements break up into random, jerky movements of all parts of the body. Nevertheless, they retain a periodicity, in that spells of activity alternate with spells of stillness that decrease in duration with age.

In the 3rd phase, beginning around day 17, these small, jerky movements alternate with cycles of large, slow stereotyped movements and coordinated activity of the kind that bring the embryo into the hatching position and later become hatching movements. These bring the embryo's head out from under the yolk sac and turn it, pushing the bill through the inner shell membrane into the air cell (see 1,053, 1,150, 1,268, 1,277).

[All studied vertebrate embryos perform movements when undisturbed. In the chelonian, *Chelydra*, the form of the movements is much like that of chick embryos. Motility in members of this group, as well as in the lizard, *Lacerta vivipara*, is cyclic, activity phases alternating with inactivity phases, suggestive of a non-reflexogenic basis. Definite evidence for the latter is derived from the existence of a pre-reflexogenic period in both forms. A pre-reflexogenic period does not seem to exist in mammals, in which spontaneous movements also are cyclic, aimless, and uncoordinated, as in the chick and reptiles (1,277).]

Intrajoint (ankle) coordination is present by at least the 7th day of incubation, apparently even before reflex arcs are functional, and interjoint (knee-ankle) coordination is present by the 9th day. Brief episodes of alternating flexions and extensions of the legs occasionally are seen in 9-day embryos. Normal articular cavity formation of the joints and the fine sculpturing of their cartilaginous surfaces require the mechanical action provided by these movements (1,071). Between active amniotic movements and passive recoil of the yolk, the embryo is thrown into a "swinging" movement that becomes quite violent at the time when amniotic contractions are at their height on the 10th day (600, 1,053, 1,167, 1,271).

Embryonic motility can be affected by unnaturally strong light as early as the 3rd day; at first, the light increases motility, but on the 8th or 9th day the effect becomes inhibitory (see 1,290). Motile responses similar to food soliciting behavior can be elicited in the Rock Pigeon by photic stimulation of the body on the 11th day, whereas a visual response begins on the 15th day (see 997), and on the 17th-18th day in the domestic fowl. Levels of illumination that reach the eyes of quail and duck embryos in the wild during the last few days of incubation are sufficient to elicit the pupillary reflex. Continued illumination of eggs during the whole or a certain part of the incubatory period of several species speeds up development and advances the time of hatching (see 1,290).

A strong rocking of the incubator, a loud noise, or a very strong light seldom fails to produce violent wriggling movements involving the entire body, accompanied by eye movements and strong vocalizations or clapping of the bill (1,272). Hearing of experimental low frequency tones is detected first on days 11-12, in the form of electrical activity in the cochlea (see 1,150, 1,290). Embryos of both Mallard and Wood Ducks (*Aix sponsa*) have been shown to develop a selective responsiveness to a component of the maternal call (largely repetition rate in the former and descending frequency modulation in the latter) prior to any auditory experience, but specific auditory experience is required to maintain the selectivity. While self-stimulation is sufficient to do so in Mallard ducklings, the young of a Wood Duck must be exposed to the calls of siblings to maintain it (see 1,267).

The final maturation of electrical activity in the optic lobes occurs later than in the cerebral hemispheres, even though the latter are the last parts of the brain to develop, and both maturations occur after hatching. By about half way through the incubatory period, the embryo has come to lie at right angles to the long axis of the egg, on its left side and on top of the yolk, into which it is beginning to sink slowly. Swallowing movements begin at about the same time. By about day 14, though, the body begins to turn lengthwise of the long axis of the egg. From the 11th or 12th day, the eyes open only occasionally and between the 11th and 16th day they are covered by the yolk sac. But once the head begins to be lifted out from under the yolk, the frequency of eye opening increases until the time of hatching (1,053).

INTESTINE----SENSORY RESPONSES----FLUID INGESTION AND DIMINUTION. The establishment of the Budgerigar intestine occurs in 3 stages. From the 1st to the 5th day, the primitive intestinal loop and the duodenum form, from the 6th to the 13th day, the parrot-specific pattern is laid down, and from the 13th day to hatching, the tract grows in length and volume (see C. Joos, 1941, in 441). The first indication of an esophageal dilatation (the crop) is seen on the 6th day (441). There is a marked increase in the maturation rate of the alimentary tract of the domestic fowl during about the last 6 days of incubation (1,053). The onset of sensory responses seems always to occur in the sequence: non-visual photic (see p. 184), tactile (or cutaneous, coinciding with the establishment of the cutaneous reflex arc), vestibular (at 8 days, though this is controversial), proprioceptive (10 days), auditory (11-12 days), visual (15-18 days), and olfactory, and, as noted on p. 184, seems to be preceded by motor functioning in all vertebrates (see 419, 1,053, 1,290).

[The sequences of sensory development in birds and mammals suggest that the tactile-vestibular-auditory-visual sequence of sensory development also may have characterized the embryos of the reptilian ancestors of birds and mammals, the archosaurs and therapsids, respectively (1,278 and pp. 534-537, **Reptilian Ancestry of Birds**). As a general rule, one can distinguish 3 phases in the responses of vertebrate embryos to tactile stimulation: at first, local stimulation elicits only restricited local responses; in a 2nd phase, the whole body responds with so-called total or mass movements; in a 3rd phase, the response becomes a specialized adaptive local action, e.g., leg withdrawal (1,277).]

Two or 3 days before hatching but perhaps beginning as early as day 13 (usually beginning when the incubatory period is 70% completed), the embryo ingests the amniotic fluid and the residual albumen--the so-called "breakfast of the chicken"--with concomitant aeration of the amniotic cavity. Imbibition usually is completed about a day before hatching and a limited amount of digestion of this fluid, which is particularly rich in proteins, occurs. The allantoic fluid diminishes rapidly from the 13th day, so that, by the 19th day, virtually none remains. In this way, beginning at about 17 days of incubation, the free fluid of the egg diminishes rapidly, a necessary precondition for breathing and hatching (702, 1,053). [On the contrary, there remains in hatching turtles a viscous mixture of albumen and allantoic and amniotic fluid, including urea (757).] For a chronology of albumen and yolk utilization during embryogenesis, see reference 950.

HORMONAL CONTROL OF GROWTH by the thyroid has been demonstrated. The thyroid arises as a mid-ventral diverticulum of the pharynx on the 2nd or 3rd day and colloidal droplets form intracellularly by the 8th day; secretion of thyroxine, and, presumably, triiodothyronine begins on the 10th day (see 1,053). The thyroid achieves the adult appearance on day 14. Secretion of thyroxine and triiodothyronine is regulated by the neurohypophysial hormone, thyrotropin. Although growth rates and metabolic rates can be depressed, and hatching retarded, by antagonists of thyroid secretions, injections of the hormones do not accelerate growth. But the uptake of amino acids by developing bones is stimulated by triiodothyronine. Treatment of the embryo with triiodothyronine or thyroxine also induces a small (less than 1 h) advance in the onset of pulmonary respiration and a 4-5-h advance in the time of hatching (see 1,053).

INCUBATORY PERIOD----HATCHING INTERVALS----NUMBER OF YOUNG. The incubatory period (the period elapsing between the laying and hatching of the last egg) varies between species and is roughly proportional to egg size. It lasts about 17-20 days in Budgerigars (843, 860) and 17 days in Rock Pigeons (997). In general, eggs are more tolerant to interruptions of incubation (i.e., low temperatures) both early and very late in the incubatory period than at intermediate times (28, 427). The eggs of Budgerigars tend to hatch at the same intervals at which they are laid. In one study, oviposition occurred every 2.2 ± 1.1 days and hatching every 2.6 ± 1.5 days (uncorrected for hatching failures; 843). Five or 6 young are successfully reared by many pairs but the best results are obtained by restricting the brood to 3 or 4 (137, 185). According to Blackmore (see 137), it is safe to allow laboratory Budgerigars to raise 6 broods of 4 chicks per yr; Fell recommends 2-3 months of rest between laying for pairs maintained as a source of eggs for embryological studies (see H.B Fell, 1939, in 338).

The Young and Their Care

PIPPING----YOLK-SAC WITHDRAWAL----EXTRA-EMBRYONIC BLOOD CIRCULATION. No gradual buildup of well-coordinated pre-hatching and hatching behavior has been observed in the avian embryo. Rather, the sequence of events, beginning at 17 days and ending at hatching, seems to be triggered sequentially by changes in the internal milieu (1,277). Pipping of the egg, the formation of the first hole or cracks in the shell, normally is an indication that the embryo has begun to breathe through its lungs (162). The bill clapping that can be heard as clicks at this time and in the preceding hours or days accompanies the operation of the newly functioning respiratory system, the first movements of which may, and apparently often do, precede penetration of the bill into the air cell (23, 427). These clicking sounds also function in clutch synchronization in some species (see 427, 474, 1,053, 1,290, and p. 191).

The partial pressures of oxygen (98-114 torr or roughly 15%) and carbon dioxide (33-43 torr or roughly 5%) in the air cell just prior to internal pipping are approximately the same in a wide range of species and are nearly identical with those found in the lungs of adult birds (478, 492; see 545 for a different view, according to which the partial pressure of air-cell oxygen correlates positively with egg weight). Just prior to external pipping, the lungs meet about 40% of the total oxygen requirements of the chick (1,053).

Visschedijk has suggested that it is the attainment of characteristic pressures of oxygen and carbon dioxide within the air cell that triggers external pipping. In keeping with this suggestion, the time of pipping can be accelerated by decreasing the oxygen concentration and/or increasing the carbon dioxide concentration in the air cell (the former normally decreases and the latter normally increases as incubation progresses). The opposite changes retard external pipping (see refs. to A.H.J. Visschedijk in 427, 478). [The positive identification of the pulmonary stimulus itself, however, remains an intractable problem. It seems very likely that it also is gaseous, but whether it is a high carbon dioxide concentration or a low oxygen concentration, or a critical ratio of the two remains to be elucidated (1,053).]

[Of great interest in this connection is the fact that the ambient gas composition in the center of the deep nests of marine chelonians (80-160 eggs) at late stages of development (partial pressure of oxygen at about 80-110 torr and of carbon dioxide at 30-50 torr) is remarkably like that given above for the avian air cell and like that in the mound nests of megapodes (772, 774)]

The yolk sac, containing unused yolk which the hatchling can continue to draw upon for nourishment, tends to be fully withdrawn into the body cavity about 14-20 h before hatching (apparently by the abdominal musculature under hormonal control of uncertain identity; 336, 1,053). The yolk sac must be fully drawn in and lung ventilation must be well established before hatching. Failure of these processes to be completed is one of the reasons why precociously hand-aided hatchlings often fail to survive. The situation is much less critical for most chelonian hatchlings, where a fairly large external yolk sac (except in kinosternids) is not internalized into the coelom until after hatching, concurrently with the unfolding of the carapace and plastron (681, 757). As mentioned above, in the domestic fowl chick, at least, blood circulates in the extra-embryonic (allantoic) blood vessels until a few min before, or even after, the chick has begun to cut around the shell prior to its emergence (see 162, 435).

HATCHING. The final activities of cutting around the shell and emergence of the chick appear to be independently controlled by a non-gaseous stimulus, seemingly hormonal. Thus, thyroidal hormones accelerate or specifically stimulate active hatching, though it also has been suggested that progesterone is the responsible hormone (see 1,053). Since hatchability of eggs is critically dependent upon ambient temperature, humidity, and the gaseous environment, nest humidity and temperature appear to be crucial external factors in determining hatching success (see 435).

Up to the time of hatching, the embryo is in a state of "stupor without awareness." If the head of a chick is pulled out of a hole in the shell and allowed to hang over the edge, the embryo continues to show active and inactive periods. During the active phase the chick will vocalize, open its eyes, and periodically raise its head for a brief time. However, muscle tonus is lacking and to all outward appearances the chick is comatose, except for the periodic movements. During the active motility periods, the chick remains in this non-vigilant state. If touched or pricked on the wing, it moves the wing but is not aroused (1,303).

Rapid maturation of neural circuits in the brain may be triggered by the great variety of stimuli and the enormous stimulation that arises when the neonate first opens its eyes and rises to its feet (see 1,053). Behavioral patterns associated with hatching are remarkably similar in a wide variety of species with nidicolous and nidifugous young. To a large extent interspecific differences in development and hatching are matters of timing, and the relative duration of different events is not always consistent from one species to another (247, 737, 1,053).

There are several notable exceptions. Embryos of the Brush Turkey (*Alectura lathami*) do not achieve the usual hatching position with the bill pointing upward toward the air cell and tucked under the right wing (see below). Instead, hatching is from a position with the head pointing downward toward the small end of the egg. In addition, Bobwhite Quail are able to hatch without the use of the legs (see 1,053). Megapodes eggs lack an air space (but may possess a movable bubble), have a high gas conductance, have abnormally thin shells, and lose the egg caruncles (see p. 189) before hatching. The embryo remains in the head-between-legs position, breaks the whole eggshell to pieces by a combined action of the legs and wings--without the aid of the bill--and emerges legs first, keeping the head between the legs during the climb to the surface (247, 427, 772).

Fork-tailed Storm-Petrel (*Oceanodroma furcata*) adults assist the chicks in emerging by removing pieces of the shell, while Eastern Bluebird (*Sialia sialis*) females forcibly remove the young. Sanderlings (*Calidris* alba), Stone Curlews (*Burhinus oedicnemus*), and other waders also assist their chicks in hatching (see 579, 1,150). In some species (if not all) of Procellariiformes, sometimes in the Rock Pigeon, and in some other species, external pipping precedes internal pipping, perhaps brought about by the bill striking the shell during tucking movements (1,290)., In the Wedge-tailed Shearwater (*Puffinus pacificus*) star-fractures (see p. 189) appear in the shell 5-6 days before the completion of hatching (524).]

Hatching itself often is a relatively quick operation, but successful emergence depends to a great degree on the attainment of the proper starting position, which is the end result of a sequence of events that commence many days beforehand. Even minor aberrations in these events can greatly decrease the probability of a successful outcome (427, 737, and refs. therein).

THE TYPICAL PRE-HATCHING POSITION for birds is with the embryo lying on its side with its neck arched under the air cell. The tarsal joints are in the pointed end of the egg, with the toes resting against the head. The head itself is withdrawn and tucked beneath the right wing, with the bill directed toward the air cell at the blunt end. This position is attained from the previous one by "tucking," recognizably coordinated movements of the head, trunk, and wings that are regarded as preparatory to emergence from the shell, and occur at about 16-17 days of incubation (see 600). [Through means not yet ascertained, some chicks pip and hatch at the small end of the egg, as Brush Turkeys normally do (see above; 1,274).]

Once tucked, the embryo gradually shifts position so that the bill and right shoulder penetrate into the air cell but remain covered by the chorioallantois and inner shell membrane. The next significant events after assuming this so-called "draped" position are the critical ones of wearing a hole through the chorioallantois and inner shell membrane by head and bill movements. These allow the embryo's lungs and air sacs to be ventilated with oxygen transported to the lungs by convective or bulk flow. Breathing among nidicoles generally is weaker than among nidifuges at this stage, since the atria of the tertiary bronchi are less well developed, and the nidicoles also engage in shorter bouts of bill clapping (see 427, 478, 492, 1,150, 1,159).

The first cracks in the eggshell typically are made many hours prior to the hatching climax (usually about 6 h after internal pipping; 478, 492). The interval between external pipping and hatching is 15.4 h in the House Wren, 20 h in the domestic fowl, 41 h in the Laughing Gull (*Larus atricilla*) and Bobwhite Quail (1,150, 1,290), and 5-6 days in Bonin Petrels (*Pterodroma hypoleuca*; 278). The procedure is rather prolonged in some species; the mean period required for Great and Blue Tits is roughly 3 days, while for Herring Gulls and Greater Black-backed Gulls (*L. marinus*) it requires 3¼ days (489). In Forster's Terns (*Sterna forsteri*), it ranges from 1 to 5 days, with a mean of 2.82 days (483). Once the shell is pipped the embryo enters a relatively quiescent period which persists until 3 or 4 h before the domestic fowl embryo emerges from the shell (1,053). In 6 species of parrots, intervals between pipping and hatching of a few hours to 3 days have been reported (634). [I noted a case in Peach-faced Lovebirds in which it required less than 40 min (see pp. 727, 728).]

At the time of pipping, the rate of water vapor loss increases (524), since such loss no longer is limited by the number and size of pores in the eggshell. A series of bumps or star-fractures (revealing the path of the bill tip during tucking in some species, often termed "starring" or "cracking") may begin to appear in the shell as early as 64 h before hatching and 35 h before the first penetration of the egg shell. In the majority of species, however, tucking leaves no trace on the shell.

THE PIPPING MOVEMENTS consist of vigorous lifting or oblique back-thrusting of the head and bill against the shell. These are achieved by contractions of the transiently-turgid hatching muscle (the M. complexus), which extends from the vertebral column to the dorsal surface of the head, and may be influenced in its development by thyroid hormones. Such movements are significantly more frequent at this stage of the embryo's development and are accompanied by increased respiratory rates. Vocalizations also commonly are heard first at about this stage.

The pipping movements are accompanied by coordinated alternating treading movements of the legs and extension of the forelimbs. These acts impart a rotary component to the movements of the embryo and help to hold the body of the embryo tightly in place inside the egg. The movements serve to force the egg caruncle--developed in all birds--against the shell and to crack it. In a rather sharp transition after enlargement of fractures to a distinct pip-hole, the actual hatching movements begin, all of which bring pressure against the shell (see 427, 737, 1,053, 1,150, 1,159). The formation and refinement of intra- and interlimb coordinations are apparent during early embryonic development (see 1,267). It has been suggested as a general principle that intrajoint coordination tends to precede interjoint coordination, which, in turn, precedes interlimb coordination, with homologous limbs preceding homolateral limbs. There also is evidence for cephalocaudal and proximodistal progressions in movement (see 1,268).

[Extirpation of the right forelimb does not necessarily prevent hatching but, with few exceptions, embryos without normally functioning legs fail to hatch, being unable to turn in the shell. Since the food soliciting posture of young chicks can consist of extension of the limbs, neck, and body, it might be derived from hatching movements (see 1,053, 1,159).]

THE "EGG CARUNCLE," loosely referred to as the "egg tooth," is an epidermal knob of horny cells containing hydroxyapatite (795), formed principally by a hyperplastic stratum corneum, and structurally unrelated to the dentition. It usually occurs only on the tip of the upper mandible, but some birds, such as terns, megapodes, and the American Woodcock (*Philohela minor*) have caruncles on both mandibles (403). In Budgerigars, the egg caruncle usually is lost on the 7th day (67), but in some species it persists beyond this time (318).

[A similar epidermal caruncle is found in the testudines, The Tuatara, and crocodilians but is not always employed in hatching. It is to be distinguished from the true "egg teeth," which are formed as part of the premaxillary dentition and have an analogous function in oviparous squamates (said to be double in some geckos), and persist even in viviparous species (336, 602, 673, 759). Both egg caruncles and true egg teeth are present in neonate monotremes (see Fig. 102 in 1,308). The egg tooth is attached to the symphysis of the premaxillae whereas the caruncle lies dorsally, overlying the anterior nasal region. Rudiments of egg teeth are exhibited by the embryos of marsupials; pouch young of some marsupials are said to exhibit the anlage of a caruncle but no vestige of an egg tooth (see 1,308, 1,342).]

Pipping movements are accompanied by an increase in oxygen uptake by the embryo, a gross depletion of triglycerides within the hatching muscle, and a marked mobilization of hepatic glycogen. The latter decreases by as much as 66%; the decrease probably is mediated by catecholamines, and continues until at least 24 h after hatching (324). Inasmuch as air capillaries develop rapidly in the parabronchi after internal pipping, oxygen uptake by the lungs gradually takes over from chorioallantoic gas uptake. Once pipping of the eggshell has occurred, lung function is well enough established to allow the significant increase in oxygen consumption (roughly 50%) required for the final efforts of hatching. On hatching, the lung becomes the sole site for gas exchange, and convection is the only mechanism by which gas reaches the blood-gas barrier (see 435). The smooth transition from passive gas transport to active gas transport requires 24-36 h in the domestic fowl chick (478, 492).

THE HATCHING MOVEMENTS soon acquire a strong counterclockwise rotary component (as viewed from the blunt pole) in all species thus far studied. Strong head thrusts accompanied by deep, rapid exhalations (depressing the bill toward the chest), together with the turning components, result in a circular puncture locus, as the shell is chipped steadily and progressively around its circumference. The chick is able to push off the shell cap and emerge after about 48 min, when the puncture locus extends about 2/3rds of the way around the egg. This is achieved by vigorous heaving movements of the shoulders coupled with strong extensions of the tarsal joints into the pointed end of the egg. Each sequence lasts 1-3 sec and is repeated every 11-30 sec (247, 427, 1,053, 1,159). The degree of rotation varies with the species, depending largely upon the strength of the shell and shell membranes, but 2, or even 3, rotations might occur, if needed to complete the severance of the cap, even in experimentally manipulated domestic fowl embryos (427, 1,053). If the embryo is in an abnormal position or unable to rotate, hatching will fail (336).

HATCHING VERSUS WALKING MOVEMENTS, AND NEURAL CIRCUITRY. A neural circuit that is capable of programming the extension of all 3 leg joints in alternation with flexion of all 3 is used during these hatching movements. Although the pattern of muscular activity is simple, it is quite similar to the pattern seen in the cat hindlimb during walking. However, the behavior of hatching, taken as a whole, differs markedly from that of walking, inasmuch as the head, trunk, and wing movements of the former seemingly are unsuited for the latter process. Even though the posture of the embryo and the positions of the legs during hatching are quite different from those in the walking hatchling, it is not unlikely, reasoning from considerations of economy, that the same neural pattern-generating circuit for leg movements is used in both (600).

POSSIBLE INFLUENCES OF EGG ORIENTATION ON HATCHING. In the equilibrium position assumed by the egg prior to hatching, the embryo is oriented in such a position that the first penetration by the egg caruncle is uppermost. Drent makes the reasonable suggestion that this may have functional significance, especially in view of the fact that one of the stimuli that elicits loud, distinctive distress cheeping is the turning of the egg from its resting position (427). Such cheeping induces the Bar-headed Goose (*Anser indicus*) parent to return to the nest and turn the eggs or, if already sitting on them, to rise and jostle them (see I. Würdinger, 1970, in 427). On the other hand, artificially incubated guillemot eggs hatched normally when they were fixed in a position with the pipping hole facing down.

Rising, egg shifting, and calling by the incubating adult all increase with pre-natal calling by the embryos, and with a strong temporal correlation. Peaks of calling by the parents and chicks occur during emergence from the shell. In some species the egg turning and shifting may ensure an adequate oxygen supply or facilitate the breathing movements of the embryo. According to the results of one study, domestic fowl embryos are incapable of turning around to pip on the upper half of the egg in eggs whose position has been fixed with the site of the future pipping hole facing downward, whereas those of another study were that a certain amount of passive turning could occur on days 19 and 20 (see 1,150, 1,290).

Vocalizing prior to and during hatching may serve as an obvious signal to the parent of ongoing hatching, as birds are said to settle differently and more lightly upon hatching eggs than otherwise, and there are progressively stronger correlations between chick calls and certain parental activities (see above) as hatching approaches (427, 737, 1,290). Calls during hatching appear to suppress aggressive behavior by adults; 15 of 26 Laughing Gulls sitting on unpipped fostered eggs at the normal time of hatching pecked a fostered hatchling, although none of 31 birds incubating a pipping egg did so (see 1,290 and M. Impekoven, 1976, in 1,150). It is said that nidifugous and semi-precocial embryos begin to vocalize with lung ventilation, 1-3 days before hatching, whereas nidicolous embryos are silent until hatched (see 1,150). However, I often have heard Cockatielian and lovebird embryos vocalize within the shell many hours before hatching (see also 3, 27, for lovebirds). [Some, perhaps all, hatching crocodilians vocalize when ready to emerge from the buried nest, which leads the parents of many species to open the nest and even the eggs (see pp. 575, 576, **Vocalizations and Care of Young**).]

Prehatching vocalizations exchanged between embryos are believed to play an important role in the synchronization of hatching of the eggs of the clutches of many species, particularly among the large clutches of nidifugous birds, and this also is thought to be true of parental calls. For example, it has been demonstrated that naturally occurring parental calls synchronize the hatching of Mallard embryos. In the absence of such calls, late-hatching chicks might be left behind in the nest and not survive (see 1,290). The eggs of sandgrouse (typically 3) achieve semi-synchronous hatching despite the fact that oviposition is spread over 5 days and incubation begins with the 1st egg (830). These matters have been the object of considerable study and literature, to which the reader is referred for further treatments (see 1,053, 1,290).

RESIDUAL YOLK is the yolk that remains at hatching, which may amount to up to 50% of the original yolk volume in some species (427). After about the 15th day of incubation, the yolk begins to diminish noticeably in size and gradually is withdrawn from both ends of the shell, finally coming to lie over the embryo's ventral surface, between the legs; from this position it is withdrawn into the body cavity (1,053). After being drawn in by the abdominal musculature, the yolk sac remains as an outpocketing of the intestine for up to 4 weeks, though it usually is vestigial by the 5th day in the domestic fowl chick (718, 1,053). A remnant of the yolk sac and yolk duct often persists in the adult as the vitelline (Meckel's) diverticulum of the ileum (near the apex of the umbilical loop; 441). In parrots, it usually is a rudiment that is invisible to the naked eye, containing numerous Peyer's patches and lymph follicles (322; 341).

Carbohydrates and triglycerides are absorbed from the residual yolk through the yolk-sac membrane and enter the blood plasma very rapidly via the omphalomesenteric vessels during the 1st 4-5 days after hatching. These nutrients supplement the dietary intake, particularly among nidifuges (see pp. 193-198 for definitions), which generally have twice as much residual yolk as nidicoles on hatching (329, 427, 1,013). In nidicolous hatchlings of 31 species, the yolk sac averaged 8% of wet weight (see 365).

The young of most species apparently use most of their residual yolk reserves at a fairly even rate over the 1st 4-5 days after hatching (see 975). By 7-8 days, virtually all the nutritive value of the residual yolk is exhausted (324). The approximately 5 g of residual yolk that remain in the Rock pigeon hatchling (nidicolous) ordinarily are consumed within 5 days, but are not essential for survival (519). The yolk sac of the Boat-tailed Grackle hatchling (also nidicolous) comprises 19% of its wet weight and 49% of its total energy content, or 68% of initial energy of the yolk, enough to sustain growth and maintenance of the chick for a day or more without being fed (365). Almost half the weight of kiwi hatchlings (nidifugous) may consist of food reserves (e.g., 112 g yolk and 43 g fat in a 319 g chick), which they live off of largely for the 1st 2 weeks (see 1,403).

The yolk reserve of the domestic fowl hatchling may function as much as a supply of protein as it does as an energy source. The yolk is assimilated at the rate of about 1 g of dry weight per diem, representing 5.9 kcal of metabolizable energy,, which would supply most of the White Leghorn's basal metabolic rate of 6.8 kcal/day. Thus, the yolk reserves apparently give the hatchling substantial energetic independence, allowing it to get on its feet before having to meet all of its energy needs by its own foraging (see 975).

[During the final 2-3 weeks (82-95-day incubatory period) of development, the crocodile (*Crocodylus*) egg swells and a series of cracks form in the rigid outer shell aligned with the longitudinal axis of the egg. Fragments also may flake off, but the flexible inner shell membrane usually remains intact (665). Similar observations were made on the eggs of the American Alligator (*Alligator mississippiensis*; see 673) and some chelonians (681). If not already cracked by swelling, the growing and moving embryo strains and cracks the eggshell. The extra-embryonic and shell membranes are punctured by the egg caruncle and the slit is widened, frequently by the embryo pushing its snout through and then opening its jaws. The embryo then pushes through its entire head and neck; after a few min, one quick forceful thrust, sometimes assisted by the claws, forces the entire body out of the eggshell.

The ruptured extra-embryonic membranes progressively detach from the shell membrane but remain attached at the umbilical region for about 1 day. Eventually they shrivel and fall away. At the time of hatching, the abdomen is distended by the yolk sac and residual yolk, which are withdrawn into the body cavity through the umbilicus, together with the embryonic intestines, several days before hatching. The residual yolk serves as a food supply for a few weeks, until the hatchlings begin to feed (759). The Nile Crocodile hatchling is said to have a yolk sac about the size of a domestic fowl egg, with a clump of yolk as big as a walnut remaining after 8 weeks; traces of yolk remain even after 6 months (685).]

MORNING HATCHINGS---HORMONAL CORRELATES OF CHICK CARE. Avian eggs tend to hatch in the early morning, as the freeing movements of the chicks usually are most vigorous then (Nile Crocodile eggs also tend to hatch during dawn; 679). Thus, the hatchling can be fed without a long delay. At least one of my Cockatielian hatchlings may have been lost because of an untimely hatching that left it unfed and perhaps unbrooded through the night and too weak to be allofed in the morning (see pp. 703, 704, **Hatchling Succumbs**). [Though lovebird, Cockatielian, and Budgerigar hatchings in the colony often occurred in the equivalent of early morning, they also occurred at all times through the daytime period.]

In addition hatchlings are much more vulnerable to low temperatures than are the embryos at any stage of prehatching development (28). Since hatchlings are wet when they emerge from the shell, the generally greater warmth of the morning as opposed to the night hours should be more favorable for drying out. Newly hatched Budgerigar chicks are naked or have a few strands of down; they leave most of their neossoptiles (down) inside the shell with the extra-embryonic membranes (819).

With the exception of circumstances for the Ring Dove, little is known about the hormonal correlates of behavior associated with nestling care. In the Ring Dove, hormones can increase markedly the likelihood of allofeeding and brooding the young, but their effects interact strongly with experiential and situational factors. Experienced doves allofeed the young when stimulated by prolactin alone, but inexperienced ones also require the administration of progesterone. Once established, care of the young doves apparently becomes relatively independent of hormonal inducing stimuli (260), but this view is not held by all (see 430). It is unknown to what degree the findings for Ring Doves apply to other species.

NIDICOLES VERSUS NIDIFUGES

Nidicoles

NIDICOLOUS OR ALTRICIAL YOUNG (as opposed to nidifuges; see pp. 195-198), exemplified by those of most passerines, represent one extreme of neonatal condition and are found in 80% or more of all avian species (221, 329). They hatch in an early stage of development in possession of relatively little or none of the initial yolk reserves of the egg (see p. 192). They generally are blind, psilopaedic (bare-skinned), helpless, and with bodies having high thermal conductances until they are fairly well grown (975). Their ability to regulate heat production develops at a variable, though species specific, time after hatching and may not be complete until the end of the nestling period. Use of the designation, **nidicolous** emphasizes the "nest-sitting" or "nest-dwelling" behavior of the young, whereas use of the alternative designation, **altricial**, emphasizes the dependence of the neonate upon its parents for nutrition. Nidicolous development is believed to have been an essential step in the evolution of avian brains to higher levels of intelligence (46, 342). [Brain weights in nidicolous hatchlings amount to 2.9-3.6% of bodily weight, as opposed to 4.2-7.2% in nidifugous ones (246).]

SIZE AND WEIGHT COMPARISONS. With few exceptions (for example, among hemipode-quails of the genus *Turnix*) the smallest nidifugous neonates are considerably larger than the smallest nidicolous ones. Nidicolous hatchlings generally weigh about 2/3rds the weight of the fresh egg (an average value of 64.67% has been reported for 6 species of parrots; 28, 329, 430, 634). In the case of Budgerigars, the latter amounts to nearly 2 g (137). Whereas no nidifuge has an egg weight of less than 4 g, the eggs of most nidicoles are less weighty (329). The shells account for 5-10% of fresh egg weight in nidicoles and 11-15% in nidifuges (718, 975). [The comparable figures for chelonians with rigid eggshells are 60-75% for the neonate itself (only 50% in marine chelonians, which have parchment-like shells; 775), 11-20% for the shells, and 82% for the sum of both in 9 species; the sums in 24 avian species averaged 76% (757).] Yolk-free *Agapornis* hatchlings contain about 85% water (634).

THERMAL RESPONSES. Nidicolous hatchlings usually cannot respond metabolically to ambient temperatures below 35-40°C, in which case they are unable to maintain their body temperatures above that of their surroundings. Although this can result in their being chilled to unusually low body temperatures, many young nidicoles show an extraordinary resiliency in the face of chilling. For example, a 2-day-old Vesper Sparrow (*Pooecetes gramineus*) left at a temperature of 18-20°C for 8 h recovered fully, and similar recoveries have been documented in many other species. In the absence of foraging parents, European Swifts (*A. apus*) undergo nocturnal hypothermia, in which their body temperature drops from the normal 38-41°C almost to the nest temperature of 21°C and recovers again the following morning (see 1,150; see also pp. 204-208, **Thermoregulation**).

GROWTH---ALLOFEEDING--EFFICIENCY OF FOOD UTILIZATION. The nidicolous way of development appears to be a highly adaptive arrangement that permits rapid development--generally with a growth rate about twice as great as that of most eutherian mammals (994)--at a relatively low energetic cost (37). Moreover, the production of nidicolous young also makes it possible for the main portion of the energetic cost--care of the young--to be shared by the parents, and, indeed, it is found that most chicks that grow rapidly are allofed by both parents (994). The parent almost invariably delivers the food into the nestling's mouth. Gull (semi-nidicolous) and heron nestlings can, once they are a few days old, pick up food regurgitated onto the ground in front of them. Birds of prey initially allofeed the nestlings directly, but at a later stage, the young tear the food items to pieces themselves, and the adults merely bring the prey to the nest (1,150). In most species with nidicolous young, the latter are brooded for a relatively small portion of the day, even on the day of hatching, so that brooding is said to reduce the feeding potential of the parents by less than 50% (975). [Ar and Yom-Tov (329) find neither the incubatory nor nestling period to correlate with the mode of reproduction, i.e., nidicolous versus nidifugous.]

Inasmuch as nidicoles are protected from the environment and brooded, a relatively greater proportion of their food is converted into protoplasm than would be the case if they needed to expend energy in thermoregulation. Moreover, much of their food is converted into protoplasm directly, rather than passing in large part through the intermediary of yolk (37). Thus, the facts that most nidicolous hatchlings are immature, with relatively short incubatory periods (a minimum of about 9-11 days in, for example, the Red-billed Quela (*Q. quela*; see 101), allow the egg to be relatively small, with a minimum of stored food and little or no residual yolk (17, 427).

In the case of the nidicolous young of terrestrial birds, at least, a further economy is achieved by virtue of the fact that basal metabolic rates and maintenance costs (compared to adults, on a per gram basis) before the onset of endothermy are relatively low, which favors even further the conversion of a large portion of the food into protoplasm (see 37). The basal metabolic rate increases during the developmental period (generally paralleling the development of homeothermy) and may exceed the adult level before fledging. Rock Pigeons and Ring Doves are exceptional in that the basal metabolic rate initially is 2-3 times the adult level and remains high until the young are more than half grown (975). The adequacy of a small avian egg may have been a key factor in the evolution of very small bodily size, with its many challenging bioenergetic requirements (see E. Witschi, 1956, in 37).

PARROT EMBRYOS AND CHICKS CONSTITUTE A NOTABLE EXCEPTION among nidicoles in that the incubatory periods are relatively long, development is relatively slow (1, 634, 1,275), the eggs are more yolky (see p. 166, **Egg Composition**), and the yolk contains a higher percentage of solids (about 46½%; 634) than typically is the case with the eggs of nidicolous hatchlings. In essence, birds with nidicolous hatchlings have traded energetic commitments--to the manufacture of eggs (see pp. 164, 165, **Hen's Energy Requirements and Egg Energy Content**) and early development of endothermy--for increased parental care responsibilities after hatching (226). The fledging period of nidicoles often is roughly of the same length as the incubatory period, sometimes longer but seldom shorter (see 230).

Nidifuges

NIDIFUGOUS OR PRECOCIAL YOUNG, exemplified by those of galliforms, represent the other extreme of neonatal condition, which appears to be limited to ground-feeding, terrestrial species and to inshore-feeding waterfowl. These usually consume vegetation, seeds, or insect larvae that are found on the ground or the benthos of an aquatic habitat. Except for shorebirds, more young are raised than among species with nidicolous offspring. Birds that are specialized to feed on prey that must be searched for, or pursued, by flight or even by rapid movement on the ground, usually have nidicolous young which are fed by the parents (975). Males contribute substantially to incubating eggs, feeding young, brooding young, and/or guarding young in virtually all species other than ducks, grouse, and bustards, and may be able to help guard more than one brood at a time (1,266).

Use of the designation, **nidifugous** ("nest-fleeing") emphasizes the fact that the chicks leave the nest, whereas use of the alternative designation, **precocial**, emphasizes early maturing, that is, the advanced stage of development of the neonate (some precocial young, however, are nidicolous, for example, those of the Adélie Penguin, *Pygoscelis adéliae*, and those of the Herring Gull). Nidifugous young generally respond to cooling by a marked shivering thermogenesis (heat production), the major means of adult avian chemical thermoregulation, but their capacities to maintain a constant body temperature are imperfectly developed and vary among species. Thus, they usually require warmth at night (23, 155, 221, 222, 245).

Only in species with nidifugous young, with their comparatively small brains (246), can development of the brain at hatching achieve adult functional capability. The nidifugous condition doubtless was the situation in the young of early avian ancestors, considering their evolutionary origin from reptiles, but it has been preserved in relatively few groups (72, 221, 226, 245, 329, 342). The earliest direct evidence in this regard is the finding of fossilized avian eggs (652, 653), presumably those of the chicken-sized, *Gobipteryx minuta*, from the Late Cretaceous (Campanian) Barun Goyot Formation in Mongolia. These contained well-preserved skeletons and Martin concludes that it is likely that the chicks were well formed and precocious at hatching (652). In general, species with nidifugous young nest on the ground, those with nidicolous young in trees (245).

NIDIFUGES HATCH IN AN ADVANCED STATE OF DEVELOPMENT, with a downy coat, with well-developed nervous and muscular function, including large, well-developed leg muscles (providing for thermogenesis as well as mobility; 559), and with relatively mature tissues with low water content. The standard metabolic rate typically increases to a peak soon after hatching, often to several times the adult level, and then gradually declines to the adult level with growth (975). The shortest known incubatory period for a nidifuge is 12 days (*Turnix*; see 230); Brown Kiwis require 74-84 days (1,406). Most nidifuges grow slowly, at about the same rate as do eutherian mammals (994), and none of the rapidly growing species develops flight at an early age (e.g., gulls, terns, and pond ducks; 975). Nidifugous young may begin preening on the 1st day, whereas preening does not begin until about the 5th day after hatching in some nidicoles (see 1,053).

YOLK RESERVES. Up to 50% of a nidifuge's initial yolk reserves may be available for continued nourishment after hatching (comprising up to 34% of chick weight; 1,406). This permits long journeys between nest and foraging area, or extended survival if the foraging parent is late in returning (427). In addition, nidifuges vary in their sensitivity to unfavorable conditions during the week(s) after hatching. The tissues of nidifugous young generally have a lower water content and greater reserves of stored fat (needed as insurance against poor initial foraging conditions) than those of nidicoles. Capercaillie (*Tetrao urogallus*) chicks suffered heavy mortality in bad weather late in the 1st week after their yolk sacs had been consumed, whereas Blue Grouse (*Dendrogapus obscurus*) chick survival was unaffected by the reduction in foraging time brought about by the need for additional brooding in cold or wet weather (see 1,150).

RESPIRATORY SYSTEM. Differences in the development of the atria of tertiary bronchi are evident at 2 or 3 days before hatching in nidifuges as opposed to nidicoles. The atria of the former are large, with a thick mesenchymal mantle, whereas those of nidicoles are less well developed and surrounded by only a relatively thin mesenchymal sheet. As a result, nidifuges have a relatively large gas exchanging surface at the time of hatching, as compared to nidicoles, and require a less extensive postnatal development to attain the adult condition. However, the posthatching development of the avian lung is strictly proportional in all structures. In both nidifuges and nidicoles, the number, branching pattern, and topographical positions of the secondary bronchi are fixed from the time the embryo aerates the amniotic cavity (702). [The myelin sheaths are visible as early as the 15th day of incubation in nidifuges; a nidicole (e.g., the magpie) does not attain this stage until 3 days after hatching (342).]

VOCALIZATION. Nidifugous and semi-nidifugous embryos begin to vocalize shortly after internal pipping (into the airspace), 1-3 days before hatching, whereas nidicolous embryos are thought not to vocalize (as opposed to bill clapping) before emergence from the shell. Vocalization increases in frequency, intensity, and complexity as hatching is approached (see 1,150, 1,290). As will be noted in Chap. 4, Cockatielian embryos may vocalize before hatching, and this also is true of lovebirds (3, 27).

THE ABILITIES OF NIDIFUGOUS HATCHLINGS vary somewhat independently across species. They typically, but not invariably, are open-eyed and mobile from the first and feed themselves from the time of hatching with varying degrees of parental assistance, usually by the hen among cursorials (994). Ducks and shorebirds, for example, follow the parents but depend on them only for brooding and defense. Quail lead their young to feeding areas, even to individual prey items. Other species may make food available to the young by scratching the ground, as do domestic fowl, or by cutting vegetation, as do some swans. Members of another group of nidifugous young are fed actively by their parents, as among grebes (1,150).

THERMOREGULATION (see also pp. 204-208). Nidifuges usually require a central source of heat from which they can venture to take exercise and forage on readily-procured food (444) after their down dries. The heat conductances of the bodies of the hatchlings vary in relation to their capacity to thermoregulate. Hatchlings of Leach's Petrels (*Oceanodroma leucorhoa*) and Pigeon Guillemots (*Cepphus columba*), for example, can maintain high body temperatures and have low heat conductances--comparable to those of adult birds of similar size (975), whereas the ability of Japanese Quail hatchlings to maintain a high body temperature is poor.

Amongst ducks, brooding may last for 2-21 days, until full thermoregulatory abilities are established; it appears to vary with the natural cold-adaptedness of the species, because diving ducklings require less brooding than do dabbling ducklings. Velvet Scoter (*Melanitta fusca*) ducklings are brooded at night, as are Eiders (*Somateria mollissima*) at times during the high tide roost, and both are brooded more in bad weather than in good (see 1,150).

Most nidifugous chicks have a very good thermoregulatory ability by the end of their first week (1,053). Willow Ptarmigan (*L. lagopus*) chicks respond to cold by shivering of the leg muscles from the day of hatching, but after the 3rd day the pectorals also are activated. As in growing nidicoles, the ability to regulate heat production is preceded by increases in erythrocyte number and hemoglobin content, as well as by changes in blood sugar and liver glycogen (see 1,150).

Hatchlings bred in cool environments tend to have a greater thermoregulatory capacity than those bred under warmer conditions (538); the capacity generally is greater in ducks (particularly sea ducks), intermediate in galliforms, and least in shorebirds, particularly gulls and terns (975). The greater thermal independence of young diving ducks has led to the evolution of loose family ties and the formation of communal broods of up to 50 young (see J. Koskimies and L. Lahti, 1964, in 975).

In this connection, though young domestic fowl apparently have capabilities for both shivering and non-shivering thermogenesis, they must be kept warm even after the first few weeks of brooding. The optimum environmental temperature for their growth is 35°C, only 3°C below the incubatory temperature (37, 481, 519). [Ambient temperature in Gottlieb's artificial brooders was only 30-33°C, but chicks were maintained there for at most 50 h (1,274).] Nidifugous hatchlings usually are dried and warmed by being brooded; nestlings are escorted to foraging areas and vigorously and persistently defended by parents (155, 488). In most nidifuges the fledgling period may be roughly of the same length as the incubatory period; it rarely is shorter but often is longer, and even very much longer (see 230).

EXAMPLES OF CARE OF NIDIFUGOUS YOUNG. Nestlings of Rock Ptarmigans (*Lagopus mutus*) are brooded extensively during the 1st week after hatching and are able to forage only for about 1½ h daily until homeothermic capacities are developed sufficiently for independence (see 975). Black Duck (*Anas rubripes*) hens must brood the ducklings during early- and mid-rearing when the temperature falls below 10°C; the brood-bond lasts over 40 days. Brooding females also alert the ducklings to predators, select the rearing wetlands, and escort the brood to the best foraging patches (528). Brown Kiwi chicks do not eat in the first 72-84 h after hatching. On leaving the burrow on the 5th to 8th day, they are escorted by the father (who incubates unilaterally). They feed but sparingly until 9-12 days (see 1,406). In Baird's Sandpiper (*Erolia bairdii*) and some other nidifugous shorebirds, the body temperature of the chicks is thermolabile; they commonly forage and are active without stress even when body temperatures drop from 37°C, the value attained with brooding, to 30°C. Lowering body temperature reduces energy requirements for a free existence, and therefore is adaptive. A similar situation probably occurs in many other species with nidifugous young (see D.W. Norton, 1973, in 967).

The highly precocial chicks of Egyptian Plovers (*Pluvianus aegyptius*) hatch from an egg under sand (incubatory period of about 30 days) and leave the nest permanently by the end of the day of hatching. Parents bring the chicks small arthropods in the bill and also expose food for them by turning over stones and employing other foraging devices. At any sign of danger in their open-sand-bar island habitats, the chicks crouch low and are covered with sand by the parents. Buried chicks are cooled by wetting them or the overlying sand with water-soaked ventral feathers of the parents. Even 3-week-old chicks may receive such parental care. The young are fledged after about 35 days (230). In addition to brooding their young for a few days, adult sandpipers lead them to foraging areas, warn them of approaching predators, and lead predators from the vicinity of the young by distraction displays (963).

ACHIEVEMENT OF FLIGHT. Although many nidifugous young acquire endothermy and the ability to walk at an early age, with few exceptions, they do not fly until they are almost full grown. Accordingly, the development of their pectoral muscles and flight feathers usually is comparable to that of nidicoles (245). Examination of the taxonomic distributions of these two extreme categories of neonates reveals a pattern of great evolutionary conservativeness (see also pp. 376-388).

[For a finer categorization of nidifuges versus nidicoles, based on parental attendance, the ability of hatchlings to acquire food, the amount of down, locomotor ability, development of vision, yolk content of eggs, etc., see refs. 221, 245, 543. Even taking into account these variables, a few species are not conveniently categorized because their young have unusual combinations of nidifugous and nidicolous features, for example, the Hoatzin and the Bearded Bellbird (*Procnias averano*).]

THE CHICK-BROODING POSTURE of many birds differs from the typical incubatory posture in that the carpal joints are out of their pockets in the body plumage and the wings are extended slightly downward, i.e., "drooped." While eggs are incubated ventrally, nidifugous and semi-nidifugous chicks usually are brooded between the wings and the side of the body, and sometimes under the tail or just anterior to the broodpatch. In certain birds with nidicolous young, the brooding posture may differ but little from the incubatory posture. Some studies suggest that a certain amount of parental neglect of eggs begins after the 1st chick has hatched (see 1,290).

Members of all 3 species of the present study brooded chicks at the sides, rear, and fore. Whereas this was typical of Cockatiels and Budgerigars, it was less frequent in lovebirds. In all 3 species, the tendency to brood in this manner increased as the chicks grew, as it became increasingly difficult to brood them and less necessary to supply parental bodily heat (e.g., p. 275, **The Sheltering of the Chicks**). There was no evidence that experienced parents tended to neglect eggs after the 1st hatching. Eggs usually were cared for attentively until hatching was overdue in the one that was laid last (see Chaps. 4, Part 2, and Chap. 6).

CHICKS OF WIDELY DIFFERING AGES & SIZES----HUDDLING---MOIST EXCRETA. Inasmuch as Budgerigar eggs are laid every other day, and incubation may commence almost immediately, hatching often occurs every other day. The 1st chick to hatch from an 8-egg clutch then is 2 weeks older than the last one. Thus, the latter sometimes gets hidden under and among its older broodmates. Nevertheless, the youngest chicks seldom are neglected (5, 104, 138, 843). In nests averaging 6 chicks in the wild, Cayley noted that the young of some broods were in all stages of development, from practically naked to nearly fully-fledged birds; in others they were of almost uniform size (1,056). At about 5-7 days of age, the chicks begin to sit up, stretch up their necks and orient their heads toward the allofeeding parent, while wriggling their wings and vocalizing (843). When sleeping or immobile, they huddle together in a little heap, resting (interlocking) their long necks on one another's. The youngest individuals typically are at the bottom of the heap, and the oldest on the top (67).

[According to Rutgers, after all of the young have hatched and one peers into the NB, "they will be found neatly in a row or circle ranged according to age" (104). During 174 h of observation, Stamps *et al.* (843, 844) apparently noted no such arrangement. Nor did I in 3 broods of 3, 4, and 3 chicks. Rutger's description may nevertheless have some basis, since my direct, more-or-less continuous observations of the care and behavior of Cockatiel nestlings have disclosed a not dissimilar practice, particularly during feeding (e.g., p. 688). In both species, the tendency for a roughly circular or arcuate arrangement according to age may depend on the fact that the brooding parent tends to keep the youngest chicks sheltered in the breast or chest feathers, with the older ones under the wing(s).]

Budgerigar chicks achieve a weight of 12-15 g at an age of only 7 days and about 30 g at 14 days (137) [The faster growing Ipswich Sparrow (*Passerculus sandwichensis princeps*) nestling also averages about 2 g in weight as a hatchling but achieves a weight of about 20 g at 7 days, which is 79% of the weight of breeding adults (558).] Chick weight at 10 days (17.9-19.4 g) is about 50% of that at 22 days (38-38½ g), by which time but little further increase occurs (843). The droppings of the chicks (and incubating and brooding hens) are more moist than those of nonbreeding adults.

ALLOFEEDING THE YOUNG

MALE ALLOFEEDS HEN---"BUDGIE MILK"---DRIED RESIDUES HAZARDOUS. Parrots are exceptional among granivores in that they do not allofeed their chicks on insects in the wild as do most granivorous and frigivorous birds (309, 334, 444). The male Budgerigar regurgitates food to the hen directly from his crop by retroperistalsis (620). She then allofeeds the chicks in similar fashion, as they lie on their backs. The parents wait at least 3 sec between food regurgitations, with most intervals being 5-10 sec (843). The food, at first, is said to consist of a colostrum-like, very protein-rich material, "budgie milk." This apparently consists partly of material derived from the proventriculus or "glandular stomach" (see p. 105, **The Proventriculus**, and pp. 741-743), probably formed under the influence of the hormone, prolactin. As mentioned above, the latter also causes broodiness and is involved in the development of incubative patches (23, 135, 137, 260, 442). [The proventriculus is an avian development; only the muscular stomach (gizzard) is found in reptiles (28).]

As the chicks grow older, they receive less "milk" and more hulled, softened, and partly digested, whole or broken seeds. If necessary, in the case of inexperienced or insufficiently attentive parents, it is recommended that dried food be removed carefully from the head and mandibles of the young. The upper mandible in the chicks is very pliable and easily becomes malformed when encumbered by dry residues (185).

LESS FOOD PER CHICK IN LARGER BROODS. The energy required by nidicoles after endothermy is established (see pp. 205-208) varies with brood size. Offsetting the greater energy conservation in larger broods, in which the relative rate of heat loss is less, is a decrease in the amount of food that each nestling receives compared with what is received in a small brood. In the House Sparrow, for example, the adults provide more food for broods with 3 young than for broods with 1 or 2, but above 3 young the amount of food provided remains constant, so the share of each individual declines (see D.C. Seel, 1969, in 967).

NIGHT FEEDING----FATHER GRADUALLY TAKES OVER CHICK CARE. The chicks of Budgerigars are said to be allofed during the night, based on the observation that their faint vocalizations can be heard from time to time as they solicit food (5). The first feedings occur about every 15 min, and the interval lengthens with age. While the nestlings are small, the hen keeps them covered and warm as she incubates the remaining eggs.

It is said that the hen virtually stops feeding the chicks as they approach and achieve fledging. The male parent then is thought to take over most of this activity gradually, often allofeeding the chicks directly at the nest entrance. What little food fledglings receive from the parents usually is from the male (5, 843), but such feeding is said to be rare both in the field and in confined flocks (171, 893). If either parent should die, the other often will succeed in rearing the chicks alone (185).

DIFFERENTIAL PARENTAL ALLOFEEDING AND NESTLING BEHAVIOR

As a result of the recent, detailed studies of Stamps and her coworkers (843, 844), much interesting and significant new information has been obtained concerning the parental breeding and nestling behavior of Budgerigars, as detailed below. Twenty nests of dye-marked chicks were observed through the rear walls with one-way viewers (car-window film on Plexiglas). Observations totalled 174 h during 3 breeding seasons (Mar.-Sept.) in outdoor flight enclosures, and were carried out from 07:00 to 11:00 h. There were 223 viewing periods, 80% of them for 30 min, at 2-3-day intervals, beginning with the 1st hatching and ending with the last fledging. [Stamps *et al.* gave their results counting the day of hatching as the 1st day; I have expressed the results in terms of chick ages, i.e., the day of hatching is taken as the 0th day.]

SOLICITING AND AVOIDING FOOD. It was unnecessary for hatchlings or young nestlings to solicit food by cheeping in order to be allofed by the parents, but by an age of about 10 days, prior solicitations were more or less mandatory. There were significant differences in the average ages at which male and female nestlings began to solicit; for females the age was 8.1 ± 3.4 days, while for males it was 10.8 ± 4.7 days. Additionally, up to an age of 9 days the female nestlings solicited more frequently (2.73 ± 2.38/h) than the males (0.97 ± 1.62/h). A small nestling avoided further parental allofeeding by turning away its head as a parent sought to grasp its bill to initiate or continue an allofeeding bout.

COMPETITION----ALLOFEEDING BOUTS----CHICKS ALLOFEED EACH OTHER. Greater size, agility, and motor control made it possible for older nestlings to run toward the parents, lunge for the parents' bills, and physically displace smaller broodmates. It was found that, in general, both the number of regurgitations of parental food per bout of allofeeding of the young and the number of regurgitations per unit of time declined with increasing age of the nestlings. The latter occasionally were observed to allofeed their broodmates, usually younger ones (a phenomenon also known among Purple Gallinules, *Porphyrio melanotus*, nestlings; see J.L. Craig, 1975, in 1,150); without exception, such allofeedings followed either mutual solicitations for food or a solicitation by one chick of another.

ALLOFEEDING OF YOUNG BY THE HEN, even an inexperienced one, was very markedly selective. Thus, a hen generally began an allofeeding bout by approaching and feeding the youngest or smallest nestling first, then the next-smallest one, etc. (also noted by K. Banz and A. Wenner in domestic and feral Budgerigars; see 843). It is this selectivity of the female that appears to ensure that the youngest nestlings are not neglected in the presence of older and much larger broodmates. In fact, it was found that, although youngest nestlings were underweight at 10 days of age (relative to their older broodmates at the same age), by 22 days of age they had achieved comparable weights and they fledged at the same age (33-34 days). In comparisons of rates of allofeeding of 10-day-old nestlings, it was found that the hen allofed the undersized ones almost 100 times as frequently as the largest ones. A consequence of this great selectivity was that in most broods, the larger a chick was at a given age, the slower its growth in the subsequent period.

The hens were highly tenacious in completing the allofeeding of a given younger nestling, despite competitive interruptions and distractions by older or larger nestlings seeking to be allofed. In pursuing this strategy, it was necessary for the hen to ignore or respond differentially to the rates and age-related properties of food solicitations, even disregarding vocalizations by the older chicks before the youngest chicks had begun to solicit for food. As another consequence of this selectivity of the hen among members of the brood, her rate of allofeeding the chicks was lower than that of an allofeeding male, whose choices typically were non-selective (see below). Only once did a hen ignore the vigorous solicitations of a young chick (3 days old) and allow it to starve.

The distribution of parental allofeeding of the chicks was such that through 9 days of age the hen delivered 96.1 ± 4.1% of all regurgitations to the young (9.26 regurgitations per bout), from 10 to 21 days of age she delivered 86.4 ± 14.3% of them (3.01 per bout, and shorter bout lengths), while from 22 days until fledging, her deliveries amounted only to 63.7 ± 24.6% (only 2.18 per bout, and still shorter bout lengths). The hen virtually never allofed fledged young. In cases where the male had participated in allofeeding the younger chicks, he delivered 56.6 ± 27% of all regurgitations to chicks 22 days old and older, whereas in cases where he had not, his deliveries to young of that age class numbered only 26.9 ± 41% of all regurgitations. In only 3 cases did hens rear their offspring without male assistance in feeding them (one of these hens produced no 2nd clutch, and the other two delayed an extra month before ovipositing again, presumably as a consequence of the greater cost of their brooding efforts).

Parental allofeeding of young also was influenced by the sex-ratio bias in the brood. In the case of the hens, however, the only influence was with chicks 22 days old and older. Hens tended to allofeed these young more frequently in broods in which females predominated. But there was no evidence that young of either sex of a given brood were allofed selectively at this time (i.e., neither sex was favored).

ALLOFEEDING BY THE MALE PARENT was almost diametrically opposed in several of its aspects to allofeeding by the hen. Allofeeding by males was governed entirely by the solicitations of the chicks, to which the males responded unselectively, regardless of chick age (including the bout lengths and feeding rates). Accordingly, since the older chicks solicited more frequently than the younger ones, they also were allofed more often. Furthermore, a male parent was much more likely to be diverted to the allofeeding of another nestling when interrupted by the competitive activities of the young, giving the older nestlings an additional advantage.

As a consequence of the male's participation in the allofeeding of a brood, the young of the brood were allofed 3 times as frequently (3 times as many regurgitations per unit of time) as those allofed by a female alone. But because of compensatory parental allofeeding behavior, growth and fledging success within the broods were unaffected. Thus, from 22 days of age to the time of fledging, each parent tended to compensate for excessive or deficient allofeeding rates of the other; if one allofed the young more frequently, the other allofed them less frequently, suggesting either that the parents cooperate in achieving an optimum allofeeding rate or that the behavior of the chicks ensures it.

A male's inclination to allofeed the brood could be assessed from the frequency with which it entered the NB--the more visits therein, the greater the inclination to allofeed. The sounds of nestlings soliciting for food within the NB appeared to stimulate the entry of the male, and once inside, a male tended to allofeed most frequently the most vigorously vocalizing young. Once a male had begun to feed his nestlings, the frequency of their solicitations tended to increase within a day, showing that the nestlings were influenced by the fact that they were allofed in response to vocalizations. If both the hen and chicks were soliciting, a male allofed the nestlings in preference to his mate. Although the rate of allofeeding chicks by a male usually exceeded that of his mate--because he exercised no discrimination--when the male was obliged to make a choice between allofeeding his mate or the young, his allofeeding rate decreased to the lower level typical of allofeeding by his mate.

The fact that female chicks began to solicit food earlier than males by an average of 2.7 days, and at almost 3 times the rate of male chicks (up to an age of 9 days), greatly influenced brood care. Thus, since the feeding of the young by male parents was in response to their solicitations, males tended to feed broods in which female young predominated much earlier and at higher rates than those in which males predominated. In consequence of such additional care, the solicitation rates in female-biased broods escalated to the point where chicks of such broods were being allofed 3 times as frequently as those in other broods. Moreover, this allofeeding tendency persisted until the time of fledging, even though chicks of both sexes were soliciting after an average of 11.8 days of age, and at equal rates after an average of only 9 days. Since there was no evidence that female chicks were allofed preferentially after the solicitations of the sexes had become equalized, it seems unlikely that the differential male behavior was a specific response to the presence of female chicks.

PHENOMENALLY RAPID GROWTH. A young nidicolous parrot or passerine hatchling, "is a veritable growth machine, permitting prodigious metabolism of an efficiency not found elsewhere among the higher vertebrates" (246). It has been suggested that the achievement of this condition was an important step in the evolution of small eggs and birds (565) and that the growth rate in passerines has been maximized (see 557). Although parrot chicks follow the nidicolous pattern, their growth is somewhat slower than that of typical nidicoles and their relative growth rate decreases throughout the incubatory and nestling periods (634). As a group, the overall growth of nidicoles is 3-4 times as rapid as that of nidifuges (245). In most nidifuges, however, the flight apparatus--the integument, wings, and pectoral muscles--grows more rapidly than the body as a whole and the major feathers unsheath soon after they begin to grow, whereas the head and some visceral organs grow more slowly (559). In one view, the length of the post-hatching period of development in species with nidifugous young is determined by the rate of growth of the chicks' legs (see 559).

Reflecting the preoccupation of nidicoles with eating and growing is their possession of relatively large-sized intestines (10.3-14.5% of body weight, as compared to 6.5-10.5% in nidifuges; 245, 322). Generally speaking, growth rates among terrestrial species are inversely related to the precocity of the chick, a relationship thought to be mediated by the balance between embryonic and differentiated function in the chick's tissues, particularly skeletal muscle (535). [Commercially raised nidifuges have achieved a remarkable efficiency; up to the age of 6 weeks, it is claimed that Turkeys convert food into tissue almost weight for weight (481).]

This capacity of a chick to receive and digest large amounts of food extremely rapidly and efficiently is highly adaptive and would appear to be one of the great advantages of the nidicolous condition (245; see also pp. 193-195, **Nidicoles**). It permits a phenomenally rapid rate of post-hatching development during a generally comparatively brief growth period (parrots being somewhat exceptional) and at minimal energetic cost (albeit at a sacrifice of early neural development). Since the young do not employ endogenous heat for temperature regulation at this stage (see p. 205), and assuming a fixed energy income or nestling energy allocation, a larger percentage of the energy from their food can be used in growth than is the case for nidifugous young (17). On the other hand, one study suggests that, at least in some nidicoles, rapid growth is not directly dependent on energy saved for lack of engaging in thermoregulation (548).

[Experimental studies have revealed that post-hatching growth within a given species can be influenced by quality of diet, quantity of food, temporal pattern of food availability, temperature, brood size (influencing quantity of food and temperature), egg size and composition (larger eggs generally producing larger, more rapidly-growing chicks), position in the hatching sequence, age and experience of parents, and individual variability in the quality of parental care (245).]

BROOD SIZE AND PARENTAL STRESS. The Pied Flycatcher is another species in which only the female incubates and in which both parents usually participate in the feeding. Accordingly, the endocrine correlates of their brood size are of interest in the present connection, and perhaps even more pertinent for Peach-faced Lovebirds, in which the male parent allofeeds the young nestlings extensively, even as hatchlings (see pp. 752, 766, 767). There is a significant positive correlation between brood size and plasma levels of corticosterone, indicating that large broods produce increased parental stress, and this appears to be associated with increased mortality. Moreover, single females have significantly higher levels of corticosterone than females that have an assisting male at the nest. Increased parental mortality might be an indirect consequence of the high corticosterone levels, which reduce the effectiveness of the birds' immunological defenses against diseases and parasites (749).

THERMOREGULATION

TERMINOLOGY. The terms **ectotherm** and **endotherm** refer to the predominant source of an organism's bodily heat, i.e., whether that source is external, say, solar radiation or warm substrates, or internal, i.e., metabolic. In the latter case, thermoregulation is achieved by a balance between a high (tachymetabolic) and controlled rate of production of metabolic heat and its dissipation to the environment. Ectotherms, on the other hand, generally produce bodily heat at a much lower (bradymetabolic) rate. The terms, **homeotherm** and **poikilotherm** (and **heterotherm**) refer to the degree to which an organism regulates deep-body (core) temperature.

Poikilothermy describes a pattern of thermoregulation that is characterized by large variations in deep-body temperature that are the results of changing environmental conditions; **homeothermy** is the maintenance of a "constant" deep-body temperature in a varying environmental regime (where the body temperature varies by no more than ± 2°C); while **heterothermy** refers to a pattern of thermoregulation by an endotherm in which daily or seasonal variations in deep-body temperature exceed the arbitrary range of ± 2°C that defines homeothermy (see 410). Examples of the latter are birds that practice facultative hypothermia.

Accordingly, a rigorous characterization of thermoregulatory capacity would employ both types of terms, for example, a **homeothermic endotherm** (warm-blooded in common and archaic usage), a **poikilothermic ectotherm** (cold-blooded in common and archaic usage) etc. But even these terms must be applied cautiously to specific organisms, rather than as general characterizations of all members of diverse or closely related groups. Even within a genus, some species may be endothermic and others ectothermic (412).

CHANGEOVER FROM ECTOTHERMY TO ENDOTHERMY--DIURNAL METABOLIC PATTERNS. A constant body temperature maintained through thermoregulation is one of the outstanding features of the constant milieu intérieur of adult birds. Most nidicolous hatchlings can regulate their body temperatures at high ambient temperatures. Their metabolic rate varies directly with ambient temperature, a typical poikilothermic response; there usually is a gradual transition to the homeothermic pattern. The capacity to avoid heat stress actually may decline with age as conductance and evaporative surface area of the mouth relative to bodily weight both decrease. Budgerigar chicks are able to dissipate heat by panting at least by the 9th day, and this ability has been observed well before the onset of shivering thermogenesis (or calorigenesis) in many nidicoles (by the 2nd day in White-crowned Sparrow chicks and even in some hatchlings; see 975, 1,150), indicating that a central temperature sensor is functioning and can stimulate motor activity (245, 442).

[In general, adult birds appear to lack mechanisms of non-shivering thermogenesis, i.e., in excess of standard metabolic rate (see p. 57) and calorigenic effects of food digestion and absorption (422). However, adipose tissues from a Ruffed Grouse (*Bonasa umbellus*) and two Black-capped Chickadees were found to show the typical features of brown fat, the multilocular fat involved in non-shivering thermogenesis in many mammals (507). The mechanism of non-shivering thermogenesis in young birds is not understood fully but there is evidence of thyroid involvement and free fatty acids appear to be its universal substrate in avian and mammalian neonates.

Surgical cutting of various areas of the hypothalamus, which controls the rate of production of thyrotropin, leads to impaired response to temperature changes in adult birds, affecting both thermogenesis and thermolysis, depending on where the cuts are made (see B.M. Freeman, 1971, in 518). The maximum increase in heat production by shivering in the Rock Pigeon (which begins at 20°C) achieves about 5 times the basal level, which is sufficient to stabilize the core temperature of a resting bird at ambient temperatures down to -70°C (see 1,004).]

The striking changeover from **poikilothermic ectothermy** of the young chick to **homeothermic endothermy** of the adult does not occur until about 10-11 days of age (45, 442; see also S.C. Kendeigh, 1939, in 488). This compares with 6-7 days in several sparrows and the Cattle Egret (*Bubulcus ibis*) and 9-12 days for wrens (see 37). Diurnal metabolic patterns in the domestic fowl chick appear first at 7-8 days (334).

Large nidicolous nestlings, including those of raptors and seabirds, can regulate their body temperatures fully at a relatively much earlier point in their development than can small ones, because large size and the growth of a heavy coat of down in most species enhance heat conservation (see 975). In early stages of Rock Pigeon development, the squabs are virtually devoid of insulative feathers, yet are left unattended for considerable periods by both parents in a relatively flimsy, uninsulated nest. It is felt that the lipid-rich crop milk (up to 51% of total solids) is a very important source of energy for thermoregulation under these conditions (1,000). [Semi-nidicolous chicks appear to be able to maintain adult body temperatures within a few days of hatching (278).]

The changeover to homeothermy and endothermy are clearly associated with the appearance of muscle tremors (thermogenesis in birds being a function primarily of skeletal muscles; see 559) and development of insulative plumage, but nestmates and effective nest linings allow many nidicoles to develop significant thermoregulatory capabilities in advance of well-developed plumage (245, 422, 546). As an example of the influence of nestmates, endothermic responses of nestling Piñon Jays (*Gymnorhinus cyanocephalus*) to low ambient temperatures (0°C for at least 1 h) within a nest were seen first at 8 days of age for broods of 3, but not until 10 days for broods of 2. Isolated chicks did not show a response before the age of 12 days (585).

If one reckons the time from the beginning of incubation (the inclusive age), the changeover, in general, would be at 27 to 31 days. The earliest noted shivering in Peach-faced Lovebirds and Black-masked Lovebirds (*A. personata*) occurs at an inclusive age of 27½ days (5 days post hatching). By 29-32 days, shivering was continuous in nestlings removed from the nest (634). Upon the same basis, a figure of 20-29 days is quoted for typical nidifugous young to acquire sufficient body temperature control to be independent of parental brooding or shading (28).

[At ambient temperatures of 27.5-32.8°C, nidicolous young behave as ectotherms, their temperature following that of the environment and exceeding it by only 0.5-1.6°C (155). In some nidicolous young, the changeover to endothermy begins as early as the 3rd day. Vesper Sparrows are able to increase their heat production and maintain their body temperature in response to declining temperatures at an age of only about 6 days (37). Several nidicolous non-passerines respond metabolically to low temperatures when they have achieved as little as 25% of adult weight (see 546). In some passerines, the changeover takes about one week (23, 97), in others, the young may not develop effective thermoregulation until the end, or after the end, of the nestling period (see 349).

Nidicolous birds that hatch in very hot environments usually are brooded very attentively by the parents (497); some of these nestlings, however, have evaporative cooling mechanisms that are functional on the day of hatching (37; see also 518). Because of the immaturity of their immune systems and their inability to regulate their body temperature at the time of the changeover, nestling parrots are more susceptible to disease than their parents. It is not uncommon for such young to succumb to infections (for example, papova virus) from organisms carried by, but not affecting, the parents (141).

European Swift chicks are unique in being able to revert to poikilothermy (in this case, reversible hypothermia) in times of food shortage and to live on stored fat for as long as 21 days (28). The reversion does not take place, however, until after several days, i.e., until after severe weight loss has occurred (245). This is reminiscent of the responses of Poor-wills starved at 5°C. They do not become torpid until after a 20% weight loss (see ref. 326 and J.T. Marshall, 1955, therein).]

ONTOGENETIC DEVELOPMENT OF THERMOREGULATION. King and Farner point out that the categorization into nidicoles and nidifuges tends to obscure the fundamentally important principle that young birds from relatively early embryonic stages develop under essentially homeothermal conditions (349). Thus, whatever the capacities of the embryos or young may be, they appear to be complemented universally by parental behavior (brooding, shading, etc.), so that even nidicoles spend much of the embryonic and nestling periods in such thermal conditions (37). For example, the thermal environment of passerine hatchlings is maintained within a range of 34-36°C, similar to the incubatory range. Body temperatures of young rarely are allowed to fall below 30°C, and they may be as high as 39°C in very young birds during brooding (see 975). Nestling body temperatures increase and become more narrowly regulated as the young grow.

EMBRYONIC HEAT PRODUCTION. From the beginning of incubation, there is a gradual change in the thermoregulatory contributions of the adults and the young or embryos to the latters' homeothermy. For example, heat production by the embryo increases continually throughout the incubatory period. This heat production begins to raise the egg temperature above incubatory temperature on about the 9th day and there is a rapid increase after the 10th day, concomitant with incipient thyroidal activity (519).

In the case of the Herring Gull, heat production by the embryo exceeds heat loss after the 13th day of incubation at 38°C, and may provide up to 75% of the heat required for incubation during the final days, but the embryos apparently show no response to cooling (see 975). Embryos of 3 species of nidifugous shorebirds (*Calidris* spp.) that were nearly ready to hatch contributed 35-40% of the total daily incubatory cost (see 427, 737, 967). The domestic fowl embryo can respond to a small reduction in the ambient temperature by a transient rise in metabolism beginning on the 19th day. The Mallard embryo can elevate the egg temperature 4°C above the 37.5°C environment of the incubator at the end of incubation. Western Gull embryos also appear to be able to regulate their body temperature to some extent (35; see also 422, 518).

Since incubation and brooding may be interrupted frequently, even regularly, it is essential that the embryos and chicks up to a certain age be able to tolerate temporary periods of hypothermia, during which they behave essentially as poikilotherms (see pp. 193-195, **Nidicolous or Altricial Young**). Budgerigars are one of the species with nidicolous young in which this ability has been noted (see A. Böni, 1942, in 349), but the ability is widespread. The tolerance gradually diminishes as the young attain full thermoregulatory capacities (37, 349).

HEAT FOR TEMPERATURE REGULATION IN NESTLINGS is derived largely from shivering, and the onset of homeothermy is closely paralleled by the appearance of shivering and closely tied to the maturation of skeletal muscle for locomotion (see 975). The thermogenic stimulant may well be thyroxine, and differences in thyroidal glandular activity upon hatching correlate with thermoregulatory ability (see 1,053, 1,150). The domestic fowl hatchling, however, also can respond to low temperatures by non-shivering thermogenesis, though not through the use of brown adipose tissue, of which it has none. The ability to shiver develops rapidly after hatching and probably is responsible for most of the thermoregulatory heat produced after 1 week. A similar situation exists in other chicks, both nidicoles and nidifuges.

[Adult domestic fowl exposed to cold ambient conditions, shiver before their core temperature becomes lowered, suggesting the existence of peripheral thermal sensors. Nevertheless, some workers believe that control of avian body temperature through skin receptors is relatively unimportant in most birds compared with its role in mammals (see 595, 1,109).]

BEHAVIORAL RESPONSES. Nidifuges generally are able to pant or gular flutter, but most nidicoles show lesser abilities to increase heat loss by these methods (389, 1,013). The domestic fowl responds to heat exposure by panting, which commences at a lower body temperature than in the adult (518). Nestling Red-tailed Tropic Birds (*Phaethon rubricauda*) placed in the sun pant before the deep-body temperature increases, indicating that the stimulation of peripheral receptors alone is sufficient to elicit this response (497). Nestling Cactus Wrens of all ages breathe open-mouthedly and increase their respiratory rates at high ambient temperatures, so that even very young birds can maintain their body temperatures below an ambient temperature of 44°C. In addition, Cattle Egrets gular flutter, even as hatchlings, when they barely can hold up their heads. Passeriform hatchlings, however, have little ability to regulate their body temperature at air temperatures below 35°C or above 40°C (see 37). Most avian hatchlings show behavioral responses to temperature changes. They will huddle and reduce their activity to a minimum at low temperatures (e.g., see 35); in domestic fowl chicks, this leads to a 15% reduction in energy expenditure (see 1,053). Consequently, young birds in large broods may be able to produce enough heat for homeothermic endothermy earlier than broods of fewer young, which lose relatively more heat (see 1,150).

THE PRINCIPAL ONTOGENETIC EVENTS that are believed to contribute to the ability to thermoregulate are: (1) the rapid decrease in the surface-to-volume ratio with increasing size, which decreases the thermolytic surface per unit of thermogenic tissue weight--in some passerines, this effect can reduce heat loss to 40-50% of the value in hatchlings, and in domestic fowl chicks the same principle accounts for the rise in body temperature in the first few days after hatching (as the yolk sac is converted to metabolically active tissue); (2) improvement of the insulation of integumental structures by the development of contour feathers, which primarily reduces the energetic cost of thermoregulation; (3) increase in the capacity to produce heat by shivering and non-shivering thermogenesis with the growth and maturation of the major skeletal muscle masses; (4) the development and beginning of function of the air sacs; and (5) the development of nervous and hormonal control mechanisms, including the development of a central, presumably hypothalamic, temperature sensitive regulatory center. The neurophysiological basis appears to be fully developed at an early age (see 37, 349, 975, 1,150).

FEATHERING---EYE-OPENING---AVOIDING BEING HANDLED. The down feather papillae are first recognized as dome-shaped elevations of dermal tissue, enclosed within a thin layer of epidermis. After a short period of rapid elongation, the base invaginates into the dermis; by the time of hatching, each papilla is located in a tube-like follicle lined with epidermis and opening onto the surface (337, 795). When the follicle has reached its maximum length, cell division becomes localized to a collar at its base, and this constitutes the germinal region of dividing cells that are responsible for further feather growth. In many species, some of the feather follicles in each pteryla (a tract of contour feathers) do not develop until sometime after hatching, so that the pterylae in chicks are relatively smaller than in adults and the apteria larger (795).

Papillae gradually become visible in certain regions of the Budgerigar integument and are easily seen at about 6 days. Within another 2 or 3 days, the various tracts are well defined. The white down feathers, themselves, begin to cover the nestling on about the 9th to 12th day, at which time wing-feather papillae become visible. A feather papilla within a feather follicle produces succeeding generations of feathers throughout life (441), as it goes through cycles of growth (anagen), followed by a rest period (telogen) in which the completed feather remains anchored in the follicle and the germinal cells stop dividing (795). But a single papilla may produce different types of feathers, depending on the age of the bird and the season (443).

The eyes of Budgerigars are fully open at about 11 days and, not coincidentally, the chicks then actively seek to avoid being handled (67). They tend to stand erect and face into the corners of the NB. [The proper time for banding birds of normal size is said to be when the opening eye slit just begins to show (185).]

SEVENTEEN DAYS TO ONE MONTH. At 17 days, $\frac{1}{2}$-$1\frac{1}{4}$-cm pin feathers are on the head, wings and tail (441). Wing and tail feathers have developed by about 3 weeks, and the quills of other feathers are well-formed (137). During this part of the nestling period the young receive large amounts of food (estimated at about 85% of the bodily weight per diem for starlings; 23). At about 20 days of age, the chicks have achieved a weight of 20-25 times their hatching weights (185). When the feathers appear, the hen ceases to brood the young at night and sleeps outside the NB. At about 1 month of age, the juvenal plumage is complete, though the flight feathers are not fully grown. At about this age (but certainly within one week of it) the young leave the nest. At this time, the forehead and back of the head have a slightly dark, barred appearance (67, 136, 137, 171). The testes grow only slowly during the 1st 30 days, during which time bodily growth essentially is completed. Testicular growth ceases during the period of 30-40 days of age, after which it commences exponentially (1,228).

FLEDGING. Budgerigar chicks bred in small enclosures leave the NB earlier than those bred in large aviaries. In the latter, no chick leaves the NB until it also can fly back (5). Newly fledged young do not fly well; they tend to locomote by climbing, sidling, or walking, whichever is appropriate. When flying, they seem to be unable to sustain themselves for more than a few sec and are clumsy at landing. By the end of the first week after fledging, they make rough but adequate landings, and fly without plummeting downwards (67). In the wild, even month-old young will fly from the NB if disturbed (171).

FLEDGLING FEEDING. After leaving the NB, confined young are allofed decreasingly by both parents. Within 7-14 days after fledging, they are able to fend for themselves and the parents cease allofeeding them (5, 10, 136). In this connection, the young of most temperate passerines are totally self-feeding when they are 25-30 days old and usually are completely independent after 30-45 days. Tropical species allofeed their young, at least to some extent, for much longer periods, sometimes up to 50-60 days of age. Patterns of attaining independence of parental feeding in the young of seabirds are quite diverse; the young of many species are wholly independent on fledging, others exhibit delayed maturity and are allofed to some extent or exclusively by the parents for many months thereafter. In one view, the complete acquisition of self-feeding is delayed in species in which foraging requires special skills or which occupy habitats in which the food supply is very sparsely distributed. In another, the extension of parental care is related to the replacement value of the young (525, 975).

By the time Budgerigar parents have ceased to allofeed the chicks, most hens will be incubating their next clutch. In this connection, a single pair raised 23 broods in 40 months in the laboratory (311). [The longest unbroken breeding period of a bird reported in the wild is 9 months in *Langonostica senegala* in Senegal (see M.-Y. Morel, 1964, in

312).] In the wild, young are capable of feeding themselves before they leave the nest and become independent (fledged) on leaving the nest or shortly thereafter (171).

Food for the fledglings should be placed on the enclosure floor (in shallow trays). At that time, the ceres (see pp. 73, 74) of both sexes are pinkish-lilac. The upper mandible of the young bird is darkened by a considerable amount of melanin, which usually disappears by the end of the 2nd month (67). During this period of sexual immaturity, the gonads are quiescent and many of the species-typical behavior patterns are absent.

SEXUAL MATURITY. Juvenal plumage frequently is molted after a few weeks and replaced by feathers more like those of adults; the wing and tail feathers, however, usually are not lost in this first molt (443). By 3-4 months of age, the barring usually is lost, as the young acquire the adult plumage, pair, and become physiologically capable of breeding. The development of species-specific behavior generally parallels the growth and differentiation of the gonads, and gonadal steroid injections usually induce precocious adult behavior (260, 1,228).

[In general, small avian species become sexually mature sooner than large ones. Most temperate passerines and many non-passerines first breed at an age of just under 1 yr (28, 63, 67, 137, 314) but there are many nonpasserines that can reproduce within 6 months of hatching (350). Several lines of evidence show that young birds in the wild are prevented from earlier-than-normal breeding by environmental restrictions rather than by physiological limitations (1,150). Numerous cases within at least 27 species are known of reproduction by somatically immature birds (paedomorphosis), for which the subadult appearance may lead to reduction of aggression by adult male conspecifics (see 1,321).]

In the Rock Pigeon, rapid growth of the gonads begins at an age of about 7 weeks and reaches a maximum at about 18 weeks; oviposition can begin at about 120 days. The juvenal molt in the Rock Pigeon starts at about 50 days, with the shedding of the 1st primaries. The breaking of the voice (Stimmbruch), at about 56 days, falls between the shedding of the 1st and 2nd primaries. The juvenal molt proceeds very slowly and ends after maturation, at an age of 6 months (see 997). [In the breaking of the voice, the pitch drops from 3,000 to about 250 Hz and the peeping solicitations transform into the adult "Whoo" calls. The time of the voice breaking (53 ± 5 days) can be advanced by the application of androgens, delayed by castration, and completely inhibited by hypophysectomy (997).]

Although Budgerigars will pair and breed at an age of 5 months, it is best not to breed males until 8-10 months of age, and females until 8-11 months (137, 138). Spermatozoa have been found in juveniles as early as 52 days after leaving the nest (311). Once a male reaches maturity, the testes seem to remain active, provided the individual can hear the vocalizations of other males (67, and p. 122). Spermatogenesis (sperm formation) is under the control of an endogenous (internal) rhythm, since spermatozoa are formed even if the birds are kept in almost total darkness (350, 414). [Virtually all terrestrial birds first breed in the season following their birth, with the exception of swifts (2 yr), many parrots (2-3 yr), and raptors (3 or 4 yr; 34, 314, 740).]

Comparisons of hormonal and behavioral development in juvenile Zebra Finches yields interesting parallels. Thus, behavior patterns that are known to be testosterone-dependent in adult males, such as song, courtship, and copulation, first occur at times that are characterized by maxima in testosterone production. The beginning and end of the sensitivity phase for sexual imprinting in males coincide with the first 2 maxima in testosterone production, whereas the onset of the sensitive phase for song learning (template learning) is accompanied by increased estradiol-17-beta production (746). The latter result correlates with the finding that the brain areas responsible for the control of song in adults (see pp. 269-273) are differentiated under the influence of this hormone during a "sensitive phase" in the first few postnatal days (716).

An age-related decline in reproductive capabilities has been observed in both female and male Japanese Quail coincident with a drop in fertility and hatchability. Spermatozoal production decreases in the aging male and a higher proportion of testicular abnormalities are found. Additionally, there is a lowered incidence of copulation, indicating that both behavioral and physiological components of reproduction are affected (see 746). Female egg production declines with age and by 2 yr none is observed; male reproductive capability declines sharply after 1 yr of age, accompanied by great reduction in testicular weight, but can be reversed in 80% of birds with testosterone implants. It appears that aged males that remain active are able to utilize available testosterone more efficiently (746).

FAMILY GROUPS. As with geese and most parrots, the young usually remain with the parents until the latter breed again. This accounts for the families that often are observed (1, 45, 62, 84). In many other species the parents are less accommodating (80), in others they are even more so.

[Extended periods of post-fledging parental care seem to occur in those species (e.g., eagles) that have low reproductive rates that trace to small clutches and long reproductive periods (314). Most species of seabirds do not begin to breed until an age of 3 yr or older (19, 525, 740). The cygnets (young) of Bewick's Swan may stay with their parents for years, and do not breed until they are 4-5 yr old. Royal Albatrosses (*Diomedea epomophora*) and Fulmars (*Fulmarus glacialis*) do not breed until they are at least 8 yr old; individual Royal Albatrosses breed only in alternate years and take longer than 12 months to rear their single young (see 352). Sexual maturity is delayed until as late as 9-12 yr in other large albatrosses and condors, among which only the most experienced birds reproduce successfully (see D. Amadon, 1964, in 740). There is general agreement that deferment of breeding beyond 2 yr of age occurs mostly in populations in which the breeding adults have difficulty bringing food to the colony at a high enough rate to raise young successfully. This occurs only in species with high adult survival times and small broods (316).]

LEARNING DURING BROODING. It has been evident to those who have hand-reared Budgerigars that a great deal of learning must occur during the process of their brooding by the parents (2). Many of the Budgerigar's supposed "instincts" are revealed to be behavior traits acquired from the parents during the nestling period. Others are acquired between the ages of fledging and weaning. There are, in fact, a number of species in which chicks are cared for long after the completion of physical growth, suggesting that the components of development related to experience are important to chick survival and perhaps for eventual recruitment into the population (245). Many deviations from "normal" behavior that are encountered with hand-reared birds, trace to the interruption of the orderly learning process. However, the deficiencies caused by these interruptions usually can be made up later (2).

RENESTING. Many species including Budgerigars, Cockatiels, and lovebirds have the capacity to renest after the loss or abandonment of a clutch or brood. This behavior is particularly important in species that breed at high latitudes or altitudes where the summer is brief and only one brood can be reared in a season. However, the nest must be lost before photorefractoriness or other phenomena that terminate reproduction set in. In female Mallards, circulating levels of LH increase 3-fold within 24 h of the loss of a clutch, and the diameters of ovarian follicles increase significantly within 3 days. Circulating estrogen and LH levels in White-crowned Sparrows in Alaska increase following clutch or brood loss that results in the induction of vitellogenesis and preparation for a 2nd nesting.

Renesting males also exhibit an increase in plasma levels of LH and testosterone. This could be important in the re-establishment of a territory or even the pair bond. These increases may be enhanced by reciprocal behavioral interactions that serve to synchronize mates in their attempt at renesting. The increases may be involved in the delay of the onset or the overt effects of photorefractoriness, since testosterone can delay the onset of post-nuptial molt and testicular regression (see 928 and pp. 309-313, **Courtship and Courtship Displays**).

Common Disorders and Longevity

Although many disease-causing organisms have been found in birds, many more undoubtedly await discovery. Much remains to be learned of the effects of diseases on wild populations, and of the relationships between diseases and such factors as nutrition, quality of habitat, population density, and the geographical distribution of the host. There is highly suggestive evidence that increased plasma corticosterone levels in brooding wild birds induced by stressful conditions, for example, unassisted brooding or artificially enlarged broods, may greatly increase their susceptibility to infectious diseases, with serious consequences (1,124). Such diseases pose the most serious clinical problems in the care of cage and aviary birds. These sometimes are difficult to diagnose and their origins often cannot be traced (457). Change of environment can cause much stress; death within 1 or 2 days of acquisition is very common, and said to be the most common cause of death in lovebirds (787).

The extensive system of air passageways in the avian respiratory system facilitates the rapid spread of air-borne diseases, and magnifies the toxic effects of air pollutants and irritant materials (see p. v, last paragraph). The nasal chambers and turbinates provide only limited protection against these, and the air sacs form a ready-made reservoir for the nourishment of pathogens and the retention of exudates (449). In addition, birds are vulnerable to traumatic hemorrhage of the bronchial airways, and this often leads to sudden death.

Nothwithstanding these susceptibilities, parrots, and the Budgerigar in particular, are fairly resistant to many infectious diseases (137, 449) and it generally is the case that infectious organisms seldom spread systemically from superficial pyogenic foci (sites of pus formation), except for those caused by pasteurellae, Escherichia coli, and certain staphylococci (449). Primary diseases of the ear and eye and their adnexa (adjunct parts) are rare in confined birds, although secondary involvement is not uncommon (456). Also pertinent is the fact that a genetic background exists for susceptibilities and resistances to a broad spectrum of avian diseases (430).

RESPIRATORY AILMENTS---MYCOPLASMAL AND FUNGAL INFECTIONS. The confined Budgerigar is sensitive to drafts and very susceptible to respiratory ailments. Colds, asthma, brochitis, and pneumonia may well account for most losses (2). Upper respiratory tract diseases usually are the source of cerebral infections through extension to the sinuses and thence to the base of the brain (457). Parrots rarely recover from true pneumonia; despite apparent recovery, death usually ensues from heart failure with pericarditis in the convalescent period (450).

A bird with involvement of the respiratory tract at any level is liable to show tail-dipping on the slightest exertion, or even at rest when the involvement is marked (449). Pneumonia produces severe shortness of breath; the bird sits without movement, puffed up and with its eyes closed (185). Mycoplasmal infections also have been described in Budgerigars and Cockatiels, for example, in lower respiratory tract disease, and may be of widespread occurrence among confined birds (141, 457). Whether they result from a primary pathogen or a secondary invader in viral or stress disease is still an open question (141, 449).

With the exception of aspergillosis, not a great deal is known about fungal diseases of parrots. *Candida albicans* can cause mild to severe abnormalities of the bill in all parrots, particularly lories, but is successfully treated in its early stages with Nystatin, with a follow-up of large amounts of vitamin A (448, 787). Although it is primarily a disease of the upper digestive tract in birds, it also can infect the small intestine (451), spreads quickly to the air sacs (787), and also is known to attack the lungs (1,265). There are a few records of candidiasis of the crop in parrots, including Budgerigars, in which it causes debility; listlessness and ruffled feathers occur in chronically infected passerines (461).

One of the commonest infectious respiratory conditions in birds and in the Budgerigar in England is aspergillosis. It is caused by the fungi *Aspergillus* spp., usually *A. fumigatus*, which probably are the commonest causes of diseases of the lungs and air sacs (457). It seems likely that members of all avian species are susceptible, particularly at a time of confinement (461). The fungi are ubiquitous and grow rapidly on almost any damp plant matter, so that opportunities for infection are widespread (449). Although inhalation is the usual route of infection, the fungi can gain access by way of the alimentary tract or through cutaneous wounds and can infect the embryo by penetration of the eggshell. In parrots and parakeets, especially Budgerigars, the disease usually is chronic (449).

The clinical signs range from debility and varying degrees of dyspnea (difficult or labored breathing) to sudden death. Treatment--by hygienic management--is unlikely to be successful in most cases, as the lesions frequently are too far advanced by the time the disease is suspected or diagnosed (461). There is only one known case of skin mycosis (*Microsporum gypseum*) in a parrot, and that in a Budgerigar (461).

VIRAL INFECTIONS. During their lifetimes birds may become infected with and become reservoirs for numerous species of viruses. Some cause serious avian diseases, for example, Newcastle disease, leukosis, and avian pox; others, like those responsible for encephalitis and equine encephalomyelitis, frequently produce no symptoms in the avian host (458, 491). Infectious avian encephalomyelitis is transmitted from the hen to her progeny via the egg (1,053). Overt cases of encephalitis that are not of bacterial origin are caused chiefly by viral infections, many of them not yet well understood (457). The presence of serum-neutralizing antibodies in birds provides an index of encephalitic viral activity (491).

Although viruses undoubtedly play a greater role in the diseases of confined birds than now is realized, there is no common infection of Budgerigars (141). Papova virus, when it occurs, causes great mortality in nestling Budgerigars. The adults are unaffected but carry the disease and pass it on to the nestlings. Avian pox apparently is confined to birds; it frequently is seen in domestic poultry and captive game birds but also is known in wild birds, including many species of passerines (491). Canary pox is a slowly spreading, highly-fatal, acute disease with evident skin lesions, particularly around the eyes, and respiratory symptoms. It has been reported in Budgerigars and isolated from outbreaks of natural disease in lovebirds (see 458).

Recovered Canaries appear to be solidly immune and preventative vaccination has given favorable results. A possible connection of Budgerigar pox virus with French molt is still under investigation (447). Pox virus often causes wart-like lesions about the head or on the feet; it is one of the few viral agents that regularly produces upper respiratory tract exudative lesions and also is responsible for some oral lesions (449, 491). All South American parrots may have pox, but become ill to varying degrees, depending on the species (see 451). Unfortunately, a pox vaccine that immunizes one species may infect another. Up to 20-30% of the yearling Wood Pigeons examined in South Sweden were afflicted with pigeon pox. Death rates were high whenever the lesions proliferated to the bill, damaging it and making feeding impossible (1,150).

Newcastle disease is a severe, often-fatal mixoviral infection with respiratory involvement, diarrhea, and depressed appetite. The virus is spread chiefly by exudates, excreta, and offal of infected birds, airborne or otherwise. It has a wide range of natural hosts, including a number of species of special interest to aviculturists. In some areas it is a primary problem in the maintenance of domestic poultry flocks. Imported exotic game birds and other species have been shown to be a means of introducing new strains of the virus into these flocks (491).

The leukosis complex comprises a group of diseases characterized by lesions that result from an abnormal proliferation of the precursors of various blood cells. It has long been established that the causative agents in domestic fowl are filterable. Diseases of this complex have been recognized in other species, including Canaries and various parrots (458). The cutaneous form of leukosis has been seen in 2 Budgerigars (462). Leukosis still frustrates the search for prevention and cure in poultry, causing losses of up to 15% of commercial stocks (481).

Outbreaks of the natural disease, often with high mortality, have been recorded in passerines and in 31 species of parrots distributed among virtually all families and subfamilies. Among confined birds, the parrots undoubtedly are most susceptible. Control can be achieved by stimulation of immunity in birds at risk by vaccination. Both living and inactivated viral vaccines are being used. The former are recommended for parrots but immunity often is transient and certain vaccine strains of reduced virulence may cause fatal disease in some confined birds (458).

PSITTACOSIS (ORNITHOSIS). Cockatiels and lovebirds are commonly infected with the highly contagious psittacosis (parrot fever or chlamydiosis). [In non-psittacines this is referred to as "ornithosis."] It is caused by the filterable micro-organism, *Chlamydia psittaci*, an obligate intracellular parasite (141, 459). Inasmuch as the infection tends to be relatively benign in some parrots, they are accepted as natural reservoirs of chlamydiae (459). The disease is of frequent occurrence in wild birds in Australia and South America and is thought by some investigators to play an important role in the regulation of populations (491).

Psittacosis is essentially a systemic disease, associated with a febrile septicemia and usually, when severe, accompanied by gastroenteritis and splenomegaly (enlargement of the spleen; 457). Some strains of the organism produce overt signs of disease no different from those of other febrile systemic avian illnesses, for example, ruffled feathers, lack of molt, depression, "sleepiness," poor breeding, lack of appetite, watery, sometimes green, excreta, recurrent gram-negative infections, and rapid loss of weight. On the other hand, many strains produce little effect other than the build-up of measurable antibody (449, 459). The disease is relatively rare in captive-reared Budgerigars (185).

Infected birds usually shed the organism throughout a household or aviary, through the medium of nasal discharges and excreta. It is believed that some birds rid themselves of the infection in 2-3 months; most remain carriers or develop the active disease state, though there are few obvious clinical signs. Susceptible birds may acquire the infection by way of either the respiratory or gastrointestinal tract. Certain strains cause illness and death only when an epizootic or superimposed bacterial or helminth challenge supplements the chlamydial infection (449). Among parrots, mortality is usually very high in lorikeets, rosellas, some of the South American parrots (especially *Amazona* spp.), and parakeets of disease-free ancestry. All strains of chlamydiae tested are susceptible to tetracyclines, which arrest the maturation and multiplication of individual particles (459). Administration in the feed is an effective route.

Nestling mortality of up to 75% occurs in infected flocks of Cockatiels, with or without the deaths of adults, whereas a high death rate usually occurs in both the adults and young of lovebirds (141). Owners of infected birds should be alert to their own persistent flu or respiratory ailments that resemble pneumonia; however, most exposed people do not become clinically ill, and the disease is curable (141, 185).

BACTERIAL INFECTIONS cause diseases in either or both of two ways: by the production of toxins, or by the destruction of tissues. The commonest source of bacterial infections in birds may be the animals' own commensals, which may cause the disease when the bird is chilled or upset, or has the even tener of its life otherwise disturbed (457). Bacterial infections are common in Budgerigars, Cockatiels, and lovebirds, both as primary infections and as secondary opportunistic invaders (141). They are probably the most common cause of upper respiratory disease and enteritis. Chicks usually are protected passively from infectious agents for up to 4 weeks by circulating antibodies absorbed, probably intact, from the yolk, having been produced by the hen. A primarily antigenic response develops rapidly and progressively after hatching and is mature after 3 weeks (1,053).

Infectious enteritis is the most common affliction of confined birds and is most frequently caused by the gram-negative bacterium, *Escherichia coli* (451, 457). As in other parrots, gram-positive bacteria (cocci, bacilli) predominate in the gastrointestinal and respiratory systems, and in the skin and feather follicles of Budgerigars. The best-known bacterial disease of wild birds is botulism. *Clostridium botulinum*, type C, the causative agent, thrives on decaying organic matter in low-oxygen environments. It produces a toxin during growth which, when swallowed by the bird, has paralytic effects on the nervous sytem ("limberneck"), with often fatal consequences in large numbers of birds in limited areas (491).

Except in carnivores and insectivores, the presence of gram-negative bacteria is generally considered to be abnormal, particularly in granivorous and fructivorous species, except during the breeding season, when insect food is taken (141, 457). These bacteria are potentially pathogenic and are most often the causes of diseases of confined birds. *Salmonella pullorum*, for example, is the cause of pullorum (bacillary white diarrhea), which is generally considered to be a disease of young birds. Though it may start in the intestines, salmonellosis (most commonly *S. typhimurium*) is as much and as frequently a disease of the kidneys, and characteristic changes usually also occur in the liver (457).

Of the recognized septicemic organisms, the most serious in cage and aviary birds are *Pasteurella multocida* and *P. tularensis*. The former organism causes fowl cholera, which reaches epizootic proportions in wild birds, with the loss of large numbers of birds in limited areas (491). Although tuberculosis (caused by *Mycobacterium avium*) is a well nigh ubiquitous and cosmopolitan disease of birds, parrots, particularly Budgerigars, are fairly resistant; a high incidence is found in the Wood Pigeon (*Columba p. palumbus*, and wild birds also commonly are affected; 449, 457).

The causative agents of pseudotuberculosis (*Yersinia pseudotuberculosis*) and plague (*Y. pestis*) share common antigens and confer a degree of cross immunity (457). Pseudotuberculosis is an insidious, almost invariably fatal disease spread by rodents and wild birds. It is prevalent in cold and damp weather, and can be diagnosed only after a necropsy and bacterial tests. The most common symptom is the discoloration (pallid) of the liver, spleen, and other internal organs, and the presence of lesions and yellowish-white spots and abscesses in these organs. The intestines often are full of undigested blood. Infected birds die quickly in a fit (834).

THE MOST COMMON BACTERIAL ISOLATES---THREAT OF MAN HIMSELF. The most common isolates are enterobacteria (especially *Enterobacter*, *Klebsiella*, and *Salmonella*) and non-enterobacteria, such as *Pseudomonas*. The low numbers of gram-negative organisms often found in the cloacas of otherwise healthy birds may represent normally harmless colonizers of the gut that could cause disease under stressful conditions. On the other hand, infections by gram-positive bacteria, such as *Staphylococcus aureus*, probably are more common than is presently realized, particularly in Budgerigars and Cockatiels (141).

Man himself can be a source of infection to confined birds through two principal routes. Anyone with a respiratory infection might transmit it to his birds. Hemolytic staphylococci derived from throat infections pose the greatest threat. Staphylococci readily prove septicemic and may start an epidemic in confined birds. Similarly, contamination of the hands with gram-negative organisms derived from feces poses a special danger. The common colon bacillus, *E. coli*, normally present in human feces, causes fatal enteritis in many avian species. It appears quite likely that many such outbreaks have been associated with personal hygiene failures leading to the contamination of hand-mixed foods left standing in bowls in heated aviaries (457).

[Most liver diseases in birds are caused by bacteria (142). Pathological studies over the years have revealed that almost all sick birds have liver damage (141).]

PROTOZOAL PARASITES. Budgerigars, Canaries, and other birds that have been bred in confinement and away from other species, and normally kept in indoor enclosures or indoor aviaries, are seldom troubled with parasitic diseases. Birds kept in outdoor aviaries are more commonly infected, being exposed, as they are, to infection from free-living wild birds by way of the excreta, molted feathers, or direct contact, and being more liable to be bitten by the insect vectors of blood parasites (460). Protozoal parasites may become dangerous in confined birds when they are exposed to stressful circumstances (451), inasmuch as healthy birds can carry a heavy burden of parasites, sometimes of several different species. Intestinal protozoa, for example, are relatively common in parrots, particularly *Giardia* in young Budgerigars and Cockatiels. Giardiasis, the resulting overt disease, often is accompanied by bacterial enteritis, especially infections by *E. coli*; secondary acute hepatitis is known in Cockatiels (460).

Microsporidial infections have been reported in Peach-faced Lovebirds and Blue-masked Lovebirds (*A. personata*; see 452), and trichomoniasis is known in Budgerigars in India (see 460). Coccidiosis (*Eimeria*, *Isospora*, *Caryospora*, *Aratinga*, etc.), as a rule, is not a problem in confined birds, though Budgerigars occasionally are infected and show prominent symptoms (451, 460). It generally affects birds kept in outdoor flights, since it usually is transmitted to them by wild birds. Poultry flocks also are susceptible (491). The symptoms of coccidiosis are loose and bloody excreta and weakness and loss of appetite. It is cured easily by the administration of sulfa drugs (185).

Trichomoniasis (infections with parasitic flagellated protozoans) and avian malaria (*Plasmodium*, *Haemoproteus*, *Leucocytozoon*), on the other hand, are rare in confined birds. *Trichomonas gallinae* lives in the upper digestive tracts of doves, pigeons, hawks, eagles, and other wild birds, and in domestic fowl and Turkeys. It causes the disease "frounce" (eliminable with Emtryl) characterized by emaciation and yellow caseous nodules in the upper alimentary canal (see 709). Severe losses from trichomoniasis have been reported in Mourning Doves (*Zenaidura macroura*). A number of fatal cases of avian malaria have been observed in nature and chronic infections may persist for several years; many species of birds apparently are infected with malarial parasites as nestlings (491). Trypanosomes (*Trypanosoma* spp.) have been found in a wide variety of birds, especially passerines, but infections normally are light.

HELMINTHS (nematodes, trematodes, cestodes) can be detected by the presence of their eggs in a bird's excreta. Nematodes (roundworms, most commonly *Ascaridia columbae*) of the respiratory, circulatory, and alimentary systems have been reported in many avian species, including parrots, sometimes causing massive infections. Roundworms living in the alimentary canal debilitate their hosts and cause local intestinal irritation and inflammation, finally causing blockage and rupture (436, 834). Their natural hosts probably were members of the Columbiformes but there is little doubt that almost any species of confined bird is likely to be infected if exposed to their infestations (460, 787). The embryos of nematodes within their eggshells are very hardy and, although desiccation and direct sunlight are fatal, they can otherwise remain viable for months, perhaps even for 1 or 2 years (787).

A great number of different species of cestodes (tapeworms) occur in birds. Because an intermediate host is involved in their life cycles, they are more frequently encountered in insectivores and carnivores than in graminivores, granivores, and fructivores, such as parrots and finches. However, the incidence of infestation is high in freshly captured nectarivorous parrots (787). There is little evidence of an adverse effect other than in domesticated waterfowl (436). Anseriforms are susceptible to parasitism by a great number of helminth species, with mature birds often bearing very heavy infestations of cestodes (1,150). Clinical signs are indefinite and may range from general debility to diarrhea, resulting in weakness and death. Therapeutic treatments may do more harm than good, but Mebendazole and Yomesan fed to the nectarivores are very effective (787). Special attention should be paid to proper feeding and to the elimination of intermediate hosts (460).

Trematodes (flukes) generally have complex life cycles and are unlikely to be found in confined birds, unless they have been captured recently or are kept in elaborate outdoor aviaries containing stagnant water. They are of primary concern only in waterfowl and other aquatic birds in which schistosomal blood flukes occur frequently. "Swimmer's itch" ("cercarial or schistosome dermatitis") in man is caused by a developing stage of trematodes (Cercariae) in fresh-water areas; the adult stage of most of these reach maturity in avian mesenteric blood vessels (436, 460, 491). The common oviductal fluke (*Prosthogonimus*) is pathogenic in domestic fowl and occurs in a wide variety of wild birds, in which it could be an important factor in the determination of population size (491). For controlling the pathogenic effects of helminths inhabiting the alimentary tract, the importance of proper feeding cannot be emphasized too strongly (460). Specific medication for the eradication of these parasites, where feasible, can be diagnosed by a veterinarian through microscopic examination of the excreta. The nontoxic, new, and easily employed helminth eradicator, Piperazine, is an excellent expellent for birds (185).

MITES----LICE----TICKS----FLEAS----FLIES----MOSQUITOES. Mites and biting and chewing (feather) lice (Mallophaga), widespread and of many kinds, are the plague of the breeder, but most are easily controlled with insecticide dusting powders and sprays. The feather louse, *Afrimenopon waar*, has been recorded from Peach-faced Lovebirds (see 835). Clinical signs of the former are anemia, often fatal, and night restlessness caused by irritation, whereas those of the latter are evidence of irritation, such as restlessness and continuous preening and ruffling of the feathers (460).

Nestlings of the colonial Red-winged Blackbird (*Agelaius phoeniceus*), Yellow-headed Blackbird (*X. xanthocephalus*), and several oropendolas are infested regularly by body mites, whereas those of a non-colonial blackbird, the Bobolink (*Dolichonyx oryzivorus*), rarely or never are (573). The blood-sucking mite, *Ornithonyssus bursa*, infesting European Starling hatchlings moves from site to site on the chicks as they mature, always infesting the sites that are the most difficult to preen at the time (1,150). Living primarily on feather debris, avian lice ordinarily do not suck blood and therefore usually are not involved in disease transmission. Mites, however, can be involved in the transmission of encephalitis from bird to bird (491).

Budgerigars most often are affected by Cnemidokoptic mange (*Cnemidokoptes* spp.), susceptibility to which may be hereditary (141). On the other hand, they seldom are troubled by red mites (*Dermanyssus avium*), which are common in Cockatielian flocks and infest nestboxes by the thousands. Mite infestations of the mandibles and legs (e.g., "scaly face" and "scaly legs," caused by *Cnemidokoptes pilae*), are by far the most common cause of bill and leg deformities in Budgerigars (448, 451). Cnemidokoptes mite infestation also commonly involves the eyelids and all parts of the face of Budgerigars and the eyelids of Canaries (456, 787). Mites that gain access to the auditory passageways may cause wryneck (vertigo or postural and flight imbalance). Eye infections of lovebirds, of whatever etiology, are uncommon (834), but the mite, *Pellonyssus viator* has been found in the eyes of Peach-faced Lovebirds (see 835).

For control of mites, a 30% pyrethrum powder (not containing DDT, derris root, or rotenone) should be dusted under the wings and around the vent. There also are available excellent Freon sprays packaged for mite eradication. The combination of a good spray and dusting is most effective. Effective medications are Aureomycin salve, sulphur-base skin lotion, or any of the trade-name products, such as Sca-Fade or Scalex (185). In the cases of quill and feather-follicle mites, there is no satisfactory treatment.

Birds are attacked mainly by soft ticks but they are not important parasites. Some ticks require several hosts to complete their life cycle; one species is the vector of a spirochete infection of poultry. Tick infestations have been a cause of breeding failures in Brown Pelicans, have caused up to 15% desertions by nesting pairs in the large seabird colonies off the coast of Peru, and have caused up to 75% of Peruvian Boobies (*Sula variegata*) to abandon their chicks in individual colonies (573).

Fleas infrequently are seen on birds but often are abundant in nests, and feed on the blood of nestlings (491). The maggot stage of calliphorid fleas is another nest-inhabiting parasite that feeds on the blood of nestlings and frequently causes extensive mortality. The hippoboscid flies (louse flies) live among the feathers and feed on the blood of the host. They are known to transmit one type of avian malaria (*Haemoproteus*); several species of black flies transmit another type (*Leucocytozoon*) in ducks, with a resultant high mortality in young birds. The endangered Puerto Rican Parrot (*Amazonia vittata*) is parasitized by the larvae of philornid flies (myiasis; 615), while dipteran larvae (*Protocalliphora* spp.) also infest hawks and owls (710). Mosquitoes serve as vectors for several avian diseases; culicine mosquitoes transmit avian malaria (*Plasmodium*) and birds can be a reservoir of mosquito-borne human encephalitis virus (491).

ATHEROSCLEROSIS. Different breeds of Rock Pigeons develop spontaneous atherosclerosis at significantly different rates, making them a very valuable animal model for the study of this disorder. White Carneau and Silver King have a high incidence of aortic atheromatous lesions, while Racing Homers and Show Racers are relatively resistant to the disease. Plasma cholesterol of White Carneau and randomly bred Rock Pigeons quadrupled in response to the 0.5% cholesterol contained in an atherogenic diet; lesion prevalence was increased and more aortic surface was covered with atherosclerotic plaque. Atherosclerotic lesions located near blood vessel branch points are more likely to progress to plaque formation than those at other locations.

On another diet containing 0.5% cholesterol, plasma cholesterol levels increased by a factor of over 7 during the 12-week experiment. Lesion thickness and lumen stenosis increased progressively during this period, with severe involvement of the carotid bifurcation. Diet-exacerbated lesions could be brought into regression by withdrawal of dietary cholesterol. Since the various breeds and strains of Rock Pigeons appear to be excellent media for the study of genetic, nutritional, and environmental factors in atherosclerosis, this species is coming into increasing favor for research (see 998).

BUDGERIGARS ARE "PHENOMENALLY" SUSCEPTIBLE TO NEOPLASMS (tumors), more so than any other vertebrate. The incidence in confined birds is from 15-24%, and about 67% of these are malignant and involve the skin (all as carcinomas) and subcutaneous tissue (75% as fibrosarcomas) or the kidneys (75% as adenocarcinomas; 137, 453, 455, 462). Older birds show a high incidence in both the ovary and testes, and a lesser but still considerable incidence of involvement of the oviduct.

Neoplasia of the ovary (and of the testes) is essentially a disease of the older bird, although cases are known at only 2 yr of age (453). Tumors of the hypophysis, liver, spleen, and skin, also are common (135, 454, 455, 462). Tumors of the bill occur infrequently and almost exclusively in Budgerigars; they are predominantly fibrosarcomas (448, 451). Primary neoplasia of the eye and adnexa are rare (456). Lipogranulomas are amongst the most commonly found tumors and often are quite amenable to excision (456). Approximately 90% of the benign tumors involve the skin and subcutaneous tissues (462).

These various types of tumors account for over 30% of the deaths of confined Budgerigars. They may have either a hereditary or an environmental basis, or both. In recent years, improvements in surgical techniques have greatly improved the success rate for removal of large abdominal tumors in Budgerigars (141). Tumors occur far less commonly in other confined birds.

FEATHER-PICKING. Feather-picking and other forms of self-mutilation are virtually unknown in Budgerigars (141). In some instances feather-picking by other birds has been controlled by adding 2-4% salt to the diet for a few days (443; see pp. 709-711, 714, 715, 754, 756, 757, 763, 768, 801 for treatments of feather-picking in Cockatiels and lovebirds).

FRENCH MOLT. Young Budgerigars primarily, but also Cockatiels and lovebirds are susceptible to French molt, a feather disease of uncertain origin (but see p. 214 for a possible association with Budgerigar pox) that also occurs in the wild state (2, 141, 447). In 1887 the Red-rumped Parrots in the Adelaide Hills succumbed to French Molt (the first recorded case in the world) and feathers were not renewed after molting in the otherwise healthy birds. The destruction by predators was so extensive that the species was quite rare even 20 yr later (1,264).

The disease may be characterized loosely as a condition in which the flight and tail feathers of young birds often are poorly formed, and drop out or break off at about the time when the birds are ready to be fledged. In severe cases the secondaries also may be lost, and in extreme cases practically all the feathers are shed, leaving a virtually naked bird. An interesting feature of the disease is that the flight feathers are shed symmetrically; if a particular feather in one wing is lost, the corresponding feather in the other wing also falls out (447). The clinical picture is hazy and undefined.

Many claim that the ailment is congenital or of genetic origin (185). Hart believes it to be the result of a dietary deficiency coupled with an indirect action of hereditary factors (an intolerance to a specific dietary lack; 185). There also is evidence that implicates excessive vitamin A in the development of French Molt in Budgerigars (443, 447). Thus, cod liver oil not only may supply excessive quantities of this vitamin, it may also contribute to the destruction and, hence, deficiency of vitamin E, which also may be a contributing factor. The most reasonable view is that of Schofield, who regarded a nutrient failure to the growing feathers to be the immediate cause and suggested that genetic, nutritional, and environmental factors also are implicated (see F. Schofield, 1955, in 447). A successful method of prevention is said to be spraying often and thoroughly, to kill mites, and offering a widely-varied diet (2). Hart recommends feeding a scientifically-balanced supplement with the basic diet, and limiting pairs to 2 broods of no more than 4 chicks each per yr (185).

THYROIDAL DISEASE---DIABETES---GOUT---EGG-BINDING---CATARACTS--CYSTS. Thyroidal disease (caused by iodine deficiency) and obesity are common problems with Budgerigars. The disease usually is accompanied by degenerative changes in certain vital internal organs. Diabetes mellitus appears to occur most commonly in Budgerigars and Cockatiels (141). It can cause skeletal deformities by disturbances in the production of estrogen.

Although the etiology remains obscure, it is thought that various types of gout can develop from both excessive and insufficient protein consumption. The disease is characterized by the extracellular deposition of uric acid and urates in synovial cavities, the sheaths of tendon, connective tissue spaces, fairly large fasciae, and elsewhere. Gout may run an extremely protracted course, extending over months, but almost always eventually is fatal (135, 465). The disease often starts in one or a few joints and usually is evidenced by hot joints that are swollen and painful. Parrots are the most frequently affected birds. Although the prognosis is poor, treatment is partly dietary, partly systemic drug therapy, and partly local (465).

Budgerigar flocks that have a high incidence of lipomas also have an increased frequency of egg-binding, which, in any case, is frequently seen in Budgerigars (and Canaries; 142, 453). The obstruction usually occurs in the distal portion of the oviduct (in the shell gland or the vagina). In this connection, obstruction of the oviduct is one of the most common diseases of the avian reproductive tract (453). Cataracts occasionally are found in old Budgerigars and other parrots but are more frequent in Cockatiels (445). Their etiology (cause) is unknown but may be similar to that of mammalian senile cataract (456). Removal of cataracts rarely is justified, however, except in cases where they occur bilaterally (446). Cysts (or dilation) of the oviduct, and skin swellings caused by lipomas (fatty tumors), also sometimes develop in Budgerigars (135).

DISEASES OF THE URINARY SYSTEM commonly are diagnosed only at necropsy and have been found in practically every avian species. Little is known regarding the clinical manifestation of these diseases and there appears to be little agreement concerning their incidence; one estimate for parrots is 7% (see 452). Types of affliction range from acute infectious nephritis (kidney disease) to deforming neoplasms. Reminiscent of the refractoriness of nervous system diseases to diagnosis (454), it is virtually impossible to make a diagnosis of acute renal disease on the basis of individual examination alone, nor to differentiate between the various acute renal diseases from a single necropsy. Paraphrasing D.L. Coffin, no symptom is diagnostic and no treatment is worthwhile (see 452). Treatment of urinary tract diseases at the present time must be considered to be in the experimental stage. The fact that the nephritic condition usually is secondary to another disease doubtless accounts for the variable signs and symptoms. If the primary cause can be eliminated, there may be a chance of spontaneous recovery (452).

APOPLEXY---SHOCK---HEMORRHAGE---RUPTURE. A bird that lies on its side on the enclosure floor or the floor of a flight and appears to, but does not, have a broken leg, probably is suffering from apoplexy. This condition often is caused by lack of vitamin E (185). A wheatgerm oil supplement is recommended as a preventative, and cortone acetate as a cure. Many species of birds, like many other wild animals, easily become shocked or stressed. Even merely after improper handling, a change of enclosure or ownership, or a medicinal injection, a bird may be found dead within 1 or 2 days of hemorrhages, usually of the small intestine but sometimes of the kidney or nervous system (450, 452, 457). Also the stress may trigger the activity of a latent pathogen of the intestinal tract, causing death from infection as a secondary effect (such hemorrhages also are known to occur in Man and dogs; 450).

Hemorrhages may be caused by dietary deficiencies, injury, diseases of various organs, and especially may occur agonally (in death throes or agony; 457). Death from rupture of the liver, for example, commonly occurs in all avian species, particularly in those that are highly pigmented, in which the metabolic strain on the liver is greater; fatty liver is the commonest cause of rupture (450).

AVITAMINOSES, the afflictions consequent upon vitamin deficiencies, are manyfold, too many to be treated here in detail. The most important deficiency diseases of the nervous system belong in this category, particularly those due to deficiencies of the B-complex vitamins. The following treatment is based primarily on that of Tollefson (443). Vitamin A is a dietary essential for all birds, either directly or via conversion from carotene. Vitamin A deficiency results in epithelial changes in the respiratory, alimentary, and reproductive tracts, and the eye, with resulting infections. It also leads to a low hatchability rate and high hatching mortality. It is the most common cause of oral lesions in the larger parrots and also causes xerophthalmia and keratitis (451, 456). In Eclectic Parrots (*Eclectus roratus*) and lorikeets such lesions often lead to susceptibility to candidiasis (monilliasis), particularly in newly imported birds (787)

Vitamin D is required for normal calcification of bones in young birds. It also promotes net retention of calcium and P in the body. The amount required depends on the calcium/P ratio in the diet. A deficiency can cause rickets, osteomalacia (bone softening), and cessation of oviposition. A deficiency of vitamin A causes encephalomacia and muscular dystrophy in chicks and steatitis (yellow-fat disease) and white muscle disease in adults.

A deficiency of vitamin B_1 (thiamine) results in severe anorexia, retarded growth, general weakness, leg paralysis, nervous derangements and death. A deficiency of vitamin B_2 (riboflavin) causes curly toe paralysis; it also causes degeneration of cells lining the duodenal crypts of Lieberkühn and changes similar to cellular anoxia in metabolically active cells of the pancreas and duodenum (also caused by deficiencies of thiamine, niacin, and pantothenic acid). A deficiency in vitamin B_6 has profound effects on the metabolism of proteins and amino acids and causes reduced production and hatchability of eggs. Severe deficiency results in anorexia, rapid weight loss, and death. A good source of these vitamins, used by many birds, are the excreta (787).

Vitamin K is essential for normal avian blood coagulation. Its deficiency in growing domestic fowl chicks produces severe intramuscular and subcutaneous hemorrhages and initiates a moderate hypoprothrombinemia in laying domestic fowl hens (514). Vitamin K can be supplied both in the diet and by intestinal bacterial synthesis; sulfonamides can act as vitamin K antagonists. Deficiency of pantothenic acid retards the growth and development of feathers, causes dermatitis, granulation of the eyelids, tissue necrosis, liver damage, spinal-cord changes, and decreased hatchability of eggs.

Biotin deficiencies cause poor hatchability of eggs, perosis and, perhaps, swelling and ulceration of foot pads and fatty liver and kidney syndrome. A deficiency of choline causes fatty liver and perosis. Folic acid is an antianemia factor. A deficiency of this vitamin in domestic fowl chicks results in perosis, retarded growth, poor feathering, depigmentation of feathers, and anemia. A deficiency in vitamin B_{12} results in poor hatchability of eggs and bone abnormalities. Vitamin C (ascorbic acid) is not generally considered to be essential in the diets of most birds, but certain birds, including some bulbuls and shrikes, require it.

DIETARY CAUTIONS. There are many constituents or contaminants in food products that may exert unfavorable effects upon nutrient requirements, nutritive status, or nutrient utilization (332). Raw soybeans that contain antitrypsin activity depress growth, and other protein fractions can both depress growth and and cause pancreatic hypertrophy in the domestic fowl. Cotton seed may contain a toxic yellow pigment, gossypol, the toxicity of which can be reduced by adding iron salts to the diet.

Linseed meal contains a potent pyridoxine antagonist that depresses growth. The castor bean also contains several growth depressants. The saponins in alfalfa impair growth and egg production in domestic fowl, influences which can be counteracted by dietary cholesterol. The tannins, widely distributed in plants, for example, certain varieties of sorghum, are growth depressants in domestic fowl chicks and also depress egg production. Lastly, nutmeals contaminated with aflatoxin (a mycotoxin) have caused widespread death in domestic Turkeys and Mallards.

[An inexpensive new Budgerigar seed, that incorporates medicinals and antibiotics, now is available to breeders. It is claimed that the new seed gives full protection against pneumonia, ornithosis, and other infectious diseases, and stimulates food intake and growth (185).]

AFFLICTIONS OF WILD BIRDS have been touched upon briefly in the above treatments. Additional evidence is sparse and has been reviewed by Herman (491). More is known of the incidence of ectoparasites than of other causative agents, probably because they are most amenable to field study. Notable studies include the classic of Lord Lovat on strongyosis (nematodes) in Red Grouse, a virus epizootic among Manx Shearwaters (*P. puffinus*), and ornithosis among Fulmars in Iceland (see 352). None of the 1,500 wild Budgerigars that were handled by Wyndham (171) had a gross external or internal sign of disease or injury.

According to McDiarmid (355), the most prevalent diseases among wild birds in Britain are tuberculosis and aspergillosis. Although Lack (181) sees disease as most commonly a secondary rather than a primary cause of death among wild birds, McDiarmid believes that "the ecologist....too often inclines to....attribute mortality and fluctuations in populations to such factors as availability of food, weather conditions, and predation" (355). At the very least, disease and severe ectoparasitic infections represent a significant energy drain that could well make the difference between starvation and survival in marginal situations (573).

A good example of the potential severity of ectoparasitic infections is that of Pearly-eyed Thrashers (*Margarops fuscatus*) by the larvae of a tropical fruit fly (*Philornis deceptivus*). First-year mortality may be as high as 80% in nestlings that suffer heavy infestations (615). Cavity- and burrow-nesting swallows often are plagued by vast numbers of bedbugs (Cimicidae), ticks (*Acarina*), and fleas (*Ceratophyllus*) swarming in the linings and walls of their nests. These can induce mass colony desertions or prevent the repeated use of otherwise favorable colonial nesting sites (see 1,221). Endoparasitic infections appear to affect juveniles most severely. One study of 46 Canada Geese goslings yielded 14 species of parasites, including 5 protozoans, 4 nematodes, and 2 cestodes (see 1,150).

Perhaps the most striking example of the effects of disease on avian populations is the extinction or severe declines in populations of indigenous forest birds on the Hawaiian Islands caused by the introduction of avian malaria and birdpox. Avian malaria also appears to have led to a shift in the habitat of some native Hawaiian birds to higher elevations or more xeric locations where contact with the mosquito vector is minimized (see 1,324).

LONGEVITY. Just as in the wild, the death of confined birds from old age is very rare. Though the confined Budgerigar is said to have an average life of but 3-4 yr, proper care leads to much greater longevity; 10-11 yr of age is near to the practical limit, but there are records of birds living to an age of 21 yr (137, 464). Some confined cockatoos have attained over 100 years of age, for example, the celebrated "Cocky Bennett," a White Cockatoo (*Cacatua alba*) of Tom Ugly's Point, George's River, New South Wales (28, 1,056). Humboldt asserted that he found one venerable parrot in South America that spoke in the literally dead language of the extinct Atures tribe of Indians (see 1,056).

PART 3. COCKATIELS

Introduction

POPULARITY SECOND TO BUDGERIGARS. Like Budgerigars, Cockatiels (*Nymphicus hollandicus*, or "goddess of Holland"), also called Quaarion and cockatoo-parrots, are native to Australia (which was called New Holland in the 18th century). These handsome little parrots are second only to Budgerigars in popularity as cage and aviary birds, and, perhaps, in abundance in Australia, as well (127).

FIRST DESCRIPTIONS. The first European to describe Cockatiels in the wild (in 1839) was the same John Gould mentioned in pp. 41, 42: "I have seen the ground quite covered with them while engaged in procuring food, and it was no unusual circumstance to see hundreds together on the dead branches of gum trees in the neighborhood of water, a plentiful supply of which would appear to be essential to their existence." Their occurrence, however, had been reported during 1770 by the naturalists of the Cook expedition along the east coast of Australia (New South Wales; 32).

BREEDING IN CONFINEMENT---IMPORTATION---NAME DERIVATION. Cockatiels were bred first in Europe in 1845 or 1850 (127, 138). By 1864, they were being imported from Australia in considerable numbers, while by 1884 they were very well established as breeding birds in European aviaries. The name "Cockatiel" was coined by Jamrach, the importer, from the Dutch *Kakatielje*, which, in turn, derives from the Portugese, *Cacatilho* or "little cockatoo."

The Birds in the Wild

DISTRIBUTION---HABITATS---TEMPERATURES ENCOUNTERED---FLOCKING. Cockatiels are widely distributed throughout Australia, particularly in the interior, but generally are more numerous in the north, and only occasionally are coastal, probably when driven there by inland drought conditions. They are considered to be accidental to Tasmania. Cockatiels exhibit a decided preference for most types of open, lightly-timbered country adjacent or close to freshwater, such as open woodlands and savannas threaded by water-courses and bordering water holes (1, 11, 32). In their various habitats they are exposed to night temperatures as low as 4.5-10°C (in winter, surface water frequently freezes in Australian deserts) and daytime shade temperatures that may exceed 43°C (32); they are said to endure cold "better than almost any other parrot" (1,259).

Large flocks of Cockatiels are common, especially during seasonal migrations. Flocks in the north may be made up of many hundreds of individuals. Like most birds that fly in large flocks, the male, the female, and juveniles show little difference in plumage while in flight (62; see also p. 226, **Wing Stripes**). [As a general rule, dense vegetation discourages the flocking habit, while open vegetative formations, such as those occupied by Cockatiels, encourage flocking (28).]

NOMADIC IN NORTH, MIGRATORY TOWARD SOUTH----ADVANTAGES OF FLOCKING. Cockatiels lead a highly nomadic existence in the north (where the monsoonal rains produce a wet season from about Dec.-Apr.; 63), continually on the move in search of favorable conditions for food and water. They become migratory toward the south, where the weather patterns are more regular. They appear in Victoria, much of New South Wales (west of the Great Dividing Range), and southern South Australia in the Spring (Sept.-Dec.). Sometimes they remain to breed, and then move back northward to breed again from April to July or August (32), but nests can be found at any time of the year following rains (139). Only during years with exceptionally low rainfall do Cockatiels invade the coastal regions.

It is the scarcity of food and water that forces many birds of Northern Australia to congregate in flocks (63). Thus, a flock can search the ground more quickly for the richest pickings, sound the alarm more quickly at the approach of a predator, and confuse an attacking predator, who would most likely capture an injured, sick, or differently colored bird (127, 573). Individual birds of flocks also have more time to eat and, if food occurs in localized patches, local enhancement might give flock foragers a significant advantage over solitary birds. The benefits of flocking may, however, be partly offset by aggressive social interactions. Dominant birds may force subordinates to the periphery of the flock, drive them into inferior habitats, or even force them to leave the flock (see 432, 573). When a particularly rich food supply is at hand, or drought forces Cockatiels to congregate near the few remaining sources of water, feeding flocks may consist of hundreds to thousands of individuals (127). Such large flocks easily break up into smaller groups.

NO DISTINCT GEOGRAPHICAL RACE--SHORT BREEDING CYCLES. The thorough intermingling of populations brought about by a nomadic existence has prevented Cockatiels from forming any distinct geographical race (unlike the somewhat different circumstances that are said to apply for Budgerigars; but see p. 231, **Coloration**); consequently, new species are not forming. As with Budgerigars, because of a nomadic existence and a premium on time, natural selection has favored a shortened breeding cycle (73, 127).

NOISY, POWERFUL, GRACEFUL FLIERS---WING STRIPES. Flocks of Cockatiels on the wing are noisy and conspicuous and usually can be heard before they are sighted. Their flight call is a distinctive, soft, melodious, warbling *weel, weel*, terminating with an upper inflection, and is a field mark by which they can be identified before they are sighted (1,055). The flying bird easily is recognized by its characteristic white wing stripes. They consist of 4 or 5 yellowish spots on the inner webs of both the primaries and secondaries and are present in adult females and in the immatures of both sexes but are lost in adult males (1,056). The sight of these and the oft repeated flight call may keep the members of a flock in close contact with one another (127). When alighting after a flight (or taking off), whether to forage or perch, the flock behaves almost as a unit.

Flight is graceful and typically very swift and direct, the backward-swept, pointed wings being moved with a deliberate, regular motion. Their slim, streamlined silhouette is very similar to that of members of the genus *Polytelis* (33, 1,056). Cockatiels are said to be as fast on the wing as any parakeet (104). They are powerful fliers, and throughout the day they often take long flights from the open-plain foraging grounds to water (139), of which they require an abundance. Sometimes such flights have proved to be valuable indicators of the presence of water to travelers in arid regions.

DRINKING---FOOD AND FORAGING. Cockatiels, like Spotted Sandgrouse (Pterocles namaqua), always are exceedingly cautious as they come in to drink at a water-hole in the early morning and in the evening. They may circle for quite some time before they descend to drink (127, 1,206). "After a few hasty gulps the whole flock is off and away." They drink by immersing the bill as far as the gape corners. Fluid enters the buccal cavity by rapid rostro-caudal movements of the tongue and accumulates on the floor of the pharynx between the tongue and the larynx. Accompanying rostral movements of the larynx maintain the airway between the choanae and the trachea. Lastly, the head is raised and the fluid flows laterally to the larynx and into the relatively narrow parrot esophagus (presumably with a reflex closure of the choanal slit and glottis; 322, 442, 620). [Cockatiels can, however, live for a long time without drinking, provided that they do not have to fly far or greatly exert themselves (127). Like Budgerigars, they utilize metabolic water.]

Cockatiels normally are almost exclusively ground foragers (127). They generally congregate in pairs, small families of 6-8 birds, tight flocks of 12-26 individuals that keep fairly close together, or larger flocks of up to several hundred birds. A group of foraging birds may call down other flocks of passing Cockatiels by giving their *weel, weel* flocking call (127, 1,055). They search for exposed, small sun-dried seeds that lie upon the ground. These fall from grasses, herbaceous plants, trees, and shrubs, on the forest floor or in open grassland. The tiny seeds are hulled by rotating them with the tongue while the forward edge of the lower mandible works against the inside of the hook of the upper mandible (127).

Cockatiels also have an appetite for fruits, berries, and the nectar of flowers from trees, and are particularly fond of *Acacia* seeds, which they obtain either among the branches or on the ground. Sometimes Cockatiels even raid standing crops, such as ripening sorghum, millet, wheat, panicum, and sunflowers. For that reason there is an open season on them in Queensland, whereas elsewhere they are protected by law.

[The *Acacia* (400 species in Australia) fossil record is only fragmentary but may go back to the Eocene. There is a suggestion that the common association with *Eucalyptus* began in the Miocene. However, unlike the eucalypts, some *Acacia* species are widespread in arid Australia and are dominant in most of the taller communities (68, 1,072). *A. aneura* is by far the most abundant representative, occurring across the arid zone, excepting the extreme west and northwest, and dominating in shrublands and woodlands that are 2-6 m in height. The species prefers sandy or skeletal soils where the mean annual rainfall exceeds 170 mm, with a predominantly summer incidence. In drier areas it is replaced by hummock grasslands, where it may occur as an emergent (1,072).]

SILENT FORAGERS----BLEND WITH GROUND COVER----NOT ADEPT CLIMBERS. The soft-colored, foraging birds blend so well with ground cover that they are easily overlooked, particularly in the shade of trees (1, 139). They are generally silent when foraging, though they sometimes exchange soft chattering notes (32). Cockatiels are natural acrobats, but since only a small proportion of their diet comes from trees, they are not adept climbers among trees and branches, where they use their bill as a "third foot" (127). They are not timid in trees and usually will allow a close approach, say, to within a few meters. On the ground, it is a different matter, for there they are extremely timid; they fly upward at the slightest disturbance (127).

SEEK SHELTER IN TREES---PERCH TOGETHER QUIETLY. When disturbed, foraging Cockatiels seek temporary shelter in nearby trees. They very noticeably avoid perching on leafy branches, preferring large, dead eucalypts, upon which they perch lengthwise on stout outermost branches (11, 127, 1,055). Their degree of gregariousness is such that most birds of a small flock perch together on the same branch. The perched birds do not, however, come into contact with each other; they are "distance animals," maintaining an "individual distance," as opposed to "contact animals," and this is true of the members of most species of flocking birds (315, 419). If restricted space requires close perching, they will squabble and soon fly off. Their gray color helps to camouflage them, both in these locations and in nesting places. Roosting quietly on perches is said to occupy more time than any other single activity of Cockatiels (127).

BREEDING HABITS IN THE WILD

FOLLOW THE RAINFALL---BREED DIRECTLY---TIMED TO ENSURE MAXIMUM FOOD. The breeding season varies with the weather in arid regions, as the nomadic flocks follow the rainfall. A heavy rain in the spring initiates breeding and assures a plentiful supply of food for the young. Avian breeding seasons, in general, are adapted to the environment in such a way that the young will be raised at the time of maximum food supply, even though this may entail nest-building and egg-laying in least favorable climatic conditions (56, 80, 101, 730). In some larger birds of the temperate and polar zones, adhering to such a practice may entail incubating while the snow is deep (312, 730).

Since adults remain paired throughout the year, they, like Budgerigars, can proceed directly to breeding. Inasmuch as the ovaries are in a state of full development for most of the year, the hen can oviposit within about 4 days of finding a suitable cavity. Even though individual nest-holes may be in trees scattered over a wide area, the breeding pairs continue to forage and travel to and from foraging and watering places as a flock (127). Adult cockatiels molt annually, usually just after the spring breeding season (32).

'ECSTATIC' EXCITEMENT IN RAINFALL----FRENZY OF MALE SEXUAL DISPLAY. Following the colorful account of Smith (127), when a thick, black rain cloud darkens the sky, Cockatiels call excitedly to one another as they fly from perch to perch. Upon landing, they spread their wings fully to the side, with the tail open, and teeter forward to hang almost vertically downward. As rain starts to fall, particularly after a dry spell, the birds fly about in 'ecstatic' excitement, giving their flight call of *weel*, *weel*. They perch with the wings and tail spread wide and catch the falling drops, even hanging upside down to wet their undersides (as do also Black-masked, Red-faced, and Madagascar Lovebirds; 3, 4, 27).

Smith likens their fluttering, posturing, and shrieking to the wild, excited abandon of young children who have found a muddy puddle in which to splash. Once the birds are sopping wet, they sit drying and preen themselves and their mates' heads. The excitement of these events usually elicits a frenzy of sexual display by the males and they sing and give the *wher-wetit-whew* and *were-it*, *were-it* calls to their mates. The male starts to search for nest-holes, accompanied by the hen. If the rain continues long enough, the pair sets to nesting in earnest. My confined birds bathed both by sitting in water and head ducking, and sometimes did both simultaneously. But head ducking apparently is practiced infrequently, as it appears to have escaped notice (1,054).

THE NEST SITE

NEST HOLE PREFERENCES. Cockatiels are secondary cavity nesters, nesting predominantly in large, plentiful tree hollows, 37.5-75 cm deep, customarily with only one pair to a tree. Nests are preferably in dead eucalypts, usually 1.8 m or more above ground, not far from water, and often in the hollow spout of a broken branch (32, 127, 1,056). Black cockatoos are known to prefer tree hollows cracked with age (46). These are unlikely to become swamped in heavy downpours of rain. [Ceylon Hanging Parrots are said to prefer a deep, natural cavity in a tree trunk (preferably a dead Areca palm; Arecaceae) with a narrow entrance at the top, with a vertical chamber 50-150 cm deep and 8-10 cm in diameter (1,263).]

VERY CAREFUL EXAMINATIONS of prospective nest sites by hole-nesters is common practice, and Black cockatoos probably are not the only ones with a preference for cracked hollows. The latter would help to account for the preference of Cockatiels for nest sites in dead trees. Although Cockatiels are said not to be very selective as to height, shape, and size of their nest cavities (32, 127), there is no information as to a possible preference for cracked ones. On the other hand, when nest cavities are well-protected from rain and wind, completely-enclosed (except for the entrance), uncracked cavities are preferred (484). This is the preference, for example, of Thick-billed Parrots.

EUCALYPTS SENSITIVE TO MICROHABITAT CHANGES. In palearctic and nearctic woods, there is severe competition for nesting holes, which determine the maximum number of nesting pairs (105, 313). I would suggest that a continuous abundance of dead eucalypts and dead branches in living eucalypts, for nesting sites, is assured for most Australian parrots and the Continent's many other hole-nesters by the fact that a very precise correspondence exists between each eucalypt species and a particular microhabitat. In fact, Australian vegetation, in general, is affected by changes in soil type to a much greater extent than on other continents (283). The resulting extreme sensitivity of eucalypts to changes in their microhabitat, such as changes in nutrient status and edaphic moisture relationships (68), probably makes them exceptionally vulnerable to unfavorable conditions. The greater abundance of hollows in old eucalypts (805) accords with this view. [Wombat State Forest in central Victoria, Australia has been logged intensively for over 100 yr. Trees with hollows now are rare there and their shortage is affecting the numbers and breeding success of hole-nesting birds (see 806).]

[On cracking clays, species of *Acacia* and/or *Casuarina* replace those *Eucalyptus* species that are dominant on "normal" soils. On solonized soils, the high calcium content, particularly in the subsoil, is inimical to many species of *Eucalyptus*, which are calciphobes. *Melaleuca* and *Casuarina* replace eucalypts in more humid areas; multi-stemmed mallee species of *Eucalyptus* (with large lignotubers) occupy the less humid but non-arid solonized soils. On well-drained soils of extremely low nutrient status, forest, woodland, or mallee species of eucalypts may overtop the heathland to form communities of sclerophyllous forest, sclerophyllous woodland, and mallee heath. The actual dominant species of *Eucalyptus* or *Acacia* usually differ from one edaphic complex to the next, but in some cases the same species may be represented as edaphic ecotypes.]

TERMITES---FUNGI---AN ABUNDANCE OF HOLLOW LIMBS AND TRUNKS. Perhaps this vulnerability of eucalypts to the microhabitat accounts for the fact that they and the related *Angophora* trees of Australia have the unusual habit of periodically shedding branches and parts of branches (153). In addition, storm damage and droughts lead to many dead limbs on a variety of trees of inland Australia. Termites eat out exposed trunks and the centerwood of dead and broken branches, and trunks attacked by fungi rot locally. Some fungi decompose heartwood but leave the sapwood firm (484).

These agents provide an abundance of hollow limbs and trunks for hole-nesters in living trees. The successes of parrots in Australia doubtless owe, in part, to the ready availability of such nesting hollows (153). In fact, the possession of many relict responses by Cockatiels (see Chap. 4) --and perhaps by many other Australian hole-nesters--may owe largely to greatly lessened selective pressures on hole-nesters in locales where nest holes are abundant (recall, in this connection, that the eucalypt fossil record in Australia extends back into the Eocene; see pp. 55, 56).

REPRODUCTION

OVIPOSITION---LONG-LIVED SPERMATOZOA---INCUBATION. Four to 7 eggs (about 19 x 24.5 mm and 5.6-6.9 g) usually are laid--1 every other day--on the decayed wood dust or dead leaves (or bare wood) that naturally line the nest bottom. Although confined Cockatiels may copulate right up to the time an egg is laid (6), their spermatozoa are extremely long-lived (stored in the oviduct; see p. 123, **Storage and Transport of Spermatozoa**) and may fertilize eggs laid a month or more after deposition (127, 1,054). As in many parrots, both Cockatielian parents incubate the eggs. The male is said to incubate from early morning to late afternoon in the wild. Confined males incubate the eggs for most of the day, but the female often relieves him and they sometimes are together in the NB for hours.

The hen spends the entire night on the eggs. At this time, the male often stands outside the NB or near the entrance (6). The events that transpire in the NB, when both birds are together there, form the basis for some of my most fascinating and significant observations, and correlate closely with some other extraordinary Cockatiel behavior. (see Chap. 4 and Chap. 6, Part 1).

HATCHING---FEEDING---GUARDING THE CHICKS. Incubation lasts 17-23 days, and the birds are noted for sitting on the eggs very tightly. Hatchlings may begin to solicit food by cheeping shortly after emerging from the shell. Both parents usually will be allofeeding them within 2 h (9), but a hatchling can go 9-12 h before receiving its first meal (9, 11). Most of the allofeeding is said to be performed by the male. The parents keep constant guard until the chicks are about 5 days old, after which there are times when both are away from the NB (6, 32).

HISSING---STRONG PARENTAL DRIVE. As in many different species of hole-nesting birds, both sighted young and incubating adult Cockatiels make a hissing, snake-like sound when disturbed (105). This is the type of aggressive or defensive sound that is most widespread among animals, so it is likely to have been one of the first communicatory sounds used by land animals.

In soliciting food, older Cockatielian nestlings usually make a harsh, hoarse-rasping sound, described by Courtney as a "repetitive, insistent wheezing noise" (30), but I have noted that they also sometimes solicit food with a low whine. The identical hoarse-rasping sound used in soliciting also is emitted (more commonly than hissing) when chicks are disturbed, either after their eyes have opened, or by still-blind chicks that join in the chorus begun by sighted ones.

The parental drive of Cockatiels is very strong, and they usually will not abandon the young in the face of danger. The Allens found wild Cockatiels, especially the female, to be so reluctant to leave the nest that hens sometimes had to be prodded from their hollows (32). The young leave the nest about 4-5 weeks after hatching.

Affinities, Morphology, and Characteristics

COCKATIELS AS PRIMITIVE COCKATOOS. Although Cockatiels are a key species for deciding the evolutionary relationships of Australian parrots, their phylogenetic relation to other parrots remains uncertain (30). Because they bear the more streamlined body and long tail of typical Australian parakeets, but share an erectile crest and many other features with the cockatoos, Cockatiels have long been regarded as a possible link between the two groups (11). It recently has been suggested that Cockatiels are most closely related to cockatoos, and that they are, in fact, a primitive cockatoo. Cockatoos presumably evolved from a Cockatiel-like ancestor related to parrots of the genus *Neophema*, the grass parrots or parakeets (30, 31; see, also, 819). This view receives support from the recent finding that the shape of the Cockatielian egg is closer to that of the cockatoo egg than to that of any other parrot (176).

REPORTED TO HYBRIDIZE WITH ROSELLAS AND GRASS PARAKEETS. There are reports (104, 138) of hybridization of Cockatiels with two other frequently ground-foraging graminivores, the Eastern Rosella and the Blue-winged Grass Parakeet (*Neophema chrysostoma*), which are the least specialized of the Neophemas. If valid, such hybridizations would be supportive of the recent suggestions (see 819 for further discussion of parrot hybrids).

SIZE---WING SPAN---COLORATION--METABOLIC PARAMETERS. Cockatiels are long, slender, graceful, streamlined birds with an overall length of 25-35 cm, and wing spans of up to 40 cm. Half of this overall length is a tapering (graduated), 15-cm-long pointed tail. They are the only crested parrot with such a tail. Mature Cockatiels are sexually dimorphic, with the female generally more robust than the male. The plumage pattern is somewhat reminiscent of some features of the cockatoos of the genera *Callocephalon* and *Calyptorhynchus*. The plumage of the male is generally dark grayish-brown, passing into gray on the rump and upper tail coverts, with a bright yellow facemask. On each cheek, a rich marigold-orange circular patch is bordered by white. These are the ear coverts, which are modified contour feathers. They minimize turbulence in flight and, in so doing, also protect the ear itself (318, 418, 1,056). Although geographical variation is negligible, as is to be expected in a species with such pronounced nomadic habits, birds derived from Queensland are said to be of a noticeably darker shade of gray, especially the males (1,056).

The female is much drabber. She also is generally gray but the facemask is a much duller yellow, tinged with the background gray. Her cheek patches are dull orange and have no white border. Members of both sexes have large, white shoulder patches that extend across the wing coverts (overlapping contour feathers that complete the flight surface).

The undersides of the birds are paler, particularly in the female, and are sometimes washed with brown. The bottom of the female's tail and her thighs are barred dark gray and yellow, in contrast to the solid dark-gray-to-almost-black of the male. The irises (irides) are dark brown, the bill, dark gray, and the legs, blackish-gray. A 5-cm-long, dainty, wispy crest adorning the heads of both sexes can be raised and lowered at will.

Immature birds resemble the female but their tails are shorter and the cere is pinkish rather than gray. Sexing by morphology cannot be accomplished with certainty until the first molt, which occurs at about 5-6 months of age (except by plucking tail feathers and observing their replacements). Behavioral sexing can, however, be achieved at about 3 months, when the males usually begin to sing and warble (787). [In general, the female and juvenal plumages retain more primitive features than that of the adult male, which often has been secondarily acquired during evolution (155; see also pp. 374, 375).]

THE METABOLIC PARAMETERS OF COCKATIELS, as measured by Gavrilov and Dol'nik (see 967) under the same conditions as for Budgerigars (see pp. 57, 58), are as follows. The standard metabolic rate of birds averaging 85.6 g in weight is 35.8 - 0.895T kcal/bird/day. The corresponding lower critical temperature for the birds is 24°C and the basal metabolic rate at that temperature is 14.2 kcal/bird/day. The corresponding existence metabolic rate is 48.8 - 0.967T kcal/bird/day (see p. 57 for definitions).

COMPANIONABLE----LONG-LIVED----PROLIFIC----AVOID CLOSE CONTACT. Confined Cockatiels are good-tempered and become very companionable. They are hardy and adaptable, and perhaps the easiest birds to habituate (most notably the males) and breed. There are reputed to be millions of owners of Cockatiels (32). The birds usually are very prolific. Many live to be 20 yr old; if housed in aviaries, they may even achieve 25 yr of age. They are friendly to people for the most part and, when not breeding, also coexist peacefully with conspecifics and other birds.

However, they avoid close contact with one another; even mates never clump together like, say, lovebirds. Should two birds happen to touch, they typically raise their crests in mild alarm and quickly move away 1 or 2 steps. Then, 'contented and relaxed,' they sit with lowered crests and slightly fluffed feathers--the attitude of 'composure and well-being.' They are said to be highly discriminating in their selection of a mate (see 787).

STRONG PAIR BONDS---IMPACT OF MATE LOSS. The pair bonds of Cockatiels are particularly strong, with the birds being very loyal to their mates. Accordingly, a bird may take some time to adjust to a new companion. [In fact, the majority of Australian birds seem to pair for as long as both birds survive (68).] The pair bond is strengthened by mutual head allopreening, in which they indulge frequently, close attendance upon one another, and sexual union, as often as several times a day, except when the birds are molting (127).

A Cockatiel parted from its mate may 'grieve' for as long as 6 months, during which time interest in the opposite sex may appear to be lacking. When separated from original mates, it is said that some hens may never oviposit again, though they may accept the attentions of other males (6). Extreme cases are known in other birds in which a surviving bird of a pair never remates (for example, among confined swans and geese; 14).

MATING RECOMMENDATIONS. Other observers have recommended that one carry out Cockatielian matings to one's advantage, since, in their experience, birds did not pair for life (11). They even found certain males to be promiscuous, particularly when their mates were unresponsive to their attentions (127). Prospective mates should be paired months in advance to give them adequate time to become well acquainted with each other. Complete strangers sometimes form an almost immediate union, but if a previously mated bird can still see or hear its previous mate, it may not pair with a new companion. [Incompatability of mates is very common in Cockatiels (and cockatoos) and often shows up first in the form of feather-picking (141).]

MATE FIDELITY---TOLERANCE FOR INSPECTION AND SURVEILLANCE. My experience, in the very special circumstances where parent Cockatiels were housed together with successive broods in a colony situation, supports the view of great mate fidelity. Cosimo, the family patriarch, never showed any inclination to court or copulate with any of his juvenile or adult daughters, while remaining closely attached to Carmen, his mate. The same probably cannot be said for parent male lovebirds. In fact, the males of many "monogamous" species actively pursue a strategy of seeking copulations with other females (227).

Because it is easy to habituate Cockatiels, and because they are relatively tolerant to disturbances--for example, they may permit frequent inspections of the NB and close surveillance of the enclosure--a certain amount of information has been at hand on the breeding habits of the birds (6, 9, 11). Thus, something has been known of how they adopt a NB, their oviposition and incubation, how they allofeed their young, etc.

CONTINUOUS OBSERVATIONS CAST FORMER INTERPRETATIONS IN A NEW LIGHT. My studies have shown that most of what transpires within the NB cannot be appreciated fully, sometimes not even suspected, unless continuous observations are made. This is because activities usually are inhibited when the birds are aware of a foreign presence, as when one lifts a lid to peer inside the NB; they instinctively "freeze," with eyes fixed on the intruder, no matter how well habituated they may be. Continuous observations (through Plexiglas sidewalls and in broadly exposed nests) have cast most of the former interpretations of the behavior of Cockatiels in the NB in a new light (see Chap. 4 and Chap. 6, Part 1).

INTERACTIONS WITH HUMANS AND ONE ANOTHER

EXCITABLE---EASILY FRIGHTENED--SENSITIVE TO ROUGH HANDLING. Despite being relatively friendly and peaceable by disposition, Cockatiels are very excitable and very easily frightened. Unhabituated birds will shiver and shake when nervous and being closely watched (9). They also are sensitive to rough handling and become very wary of changes in their surroundings (6; see also p. 295). When angry, upset, or encroached upon, Cockatiels hiss or make "Donald-duck-like-sounding" complaints. Some observers find females to be more easily provoked and more inclined to bite than the males (6). Like Budgerigars, the confined Cockatiel is very susceptible to colds and sensitive to drafts (6). It is said that confined Cockatiels seldom show much homing ability and quickly become hopelessly lost.

BEST REPUTATION OF CONFINED BIRDS. Of all confined birds, Cockatiels have the best reputation, and are the most popular after Budgerigars. They have endearing personalities, are among the most affectionate, companionable, and easily trained of the smaller parrots, have a gentle disposition and charm, and are longer-lived than most of the commonly confined birds. To Bates and Busenbark (2), Cockatiels are the most charming and persistently affectionate of all birds. They recommend no bird more highly. In their judgement, the bond of affection that a Cockatiel holds for its owner probably is greater than that held by any other bird, and one of the strongest shown by any kind of animal companion.

Adding greatly to the attraction of Cockatiels is their enjoyment of being scratched and caressed about the head. As noted above, they commonly groom one another on the head, particularly mated birds, and this is an important aspect of their social behavior (137). The female is said to be most docile and trustful, whereas the male tends to be independent, sometimes with a very bold curiosity. The males characteristically talk, whistle, and peer endlessly into mirrors, whereas females take note of their reflections, at first, but quickly lose interest (6).

"WATCHDOGS"---WHISTLING. Certain individual Cockatiels become "watchdogs." One or more of these birds usually signals my getting up from a chair, or moving while seated, with a double chirp or whistle. Often they whistle in unison when I walk by or away from their enclosure. Such close attention from one's birds can hardly fail to create a feeling of attachment. Additionally, the birds whistle almost every time they hear certain familiar sounds--a siren outside, a door closing, a paper bag being crumpled, a cupboard door closing, a page being turned, the clicking of a light switch, and even the tones of a pushbutton telephone.

FORAGING---STRETCHING----MANIPULATIONS---'COMPLACENCY'---CURIOSITY. Cockatiels have other endearing mannerisms and habits. One is the intent, yet alert, way they forage on the enclosure floor, sometimes with tails held high, and often in a group. Another, is the way they stretch their wings when the lights go on in the morning, just as we stretch our arms and yawn. Yet others, are their compulsion to investigate, chew, and dismantle everything within reach, both inside and just outside the enclosure, and the way they unhinge small food trays and peer after them with a 'quizzical, disarming innocence' after the trays have fallen.

They also strut about on the enclosure floor, "mouthing" objects that catch their fancy, particularly feathers, and they find it greatly rewarding to unweave the woven mats that cover the enclosures. They resemble most parrots in the delight they take in chewing on fresh branches (11). Still others endearing mannerisms are the way they sit complacently bathing in water, and the curiosity with which they poke their heads out of the enclosure bars to investigate outside happenings.

ATTENTION-GETTING PECKS---SQUABBLING---TENDER ATTENTIONS BETWEEN MATES. Cockatiels' interactions with one another also are quite appealing. They give their mates attention-getting pecks followed by lowering or appropriate cocking of the head to solicit grooming. They have short-tempered disputes over perching positions, and they engage in other impatient squabbling and peck threats when paths unintentionally cross or space is invaded. Then there are the tender attentions and the competition between parents during the incubation of the eggs and, sometimes, in the rearing of the young (see Chap. 4, Parts 1 and 2, and Chapter 6, Part 1).

In addition, the touching solicitude of a bird for a sick mate is most readily noted in Cockatiels (2). Some of these appealing mannerisms and habits will be recognized as also being characteristic of many other parrots; taken together with the vocalizations described below, they contribute to the special appeal of Cockatiels. In this connection, as with most parrots that flock, but particularly the cockatoos, if one member of a flock of Cockatiels suddenly is hurt, the others hover about it for a while before leaving (1,055).

VOCALIZATIONS

VOCALIZATIONS REPORTED IN THE LITERATURE. One author describes Cockatielian vocalizations as a prolonged, warbling *queel, queel*, terminating with a pronounced upward inflection (1), another attributes to them a shrill *keoroe, kreeou* (or *curryou! creeou!*) (2). The whistle of the male ranges in tone and sometimes sounds like whistling for a dog--*whew, whew*--ending with an upper inflection, while the females possess a high, shrill *eeek, eek, eek* (6). Others describe the male's mating call as a loud, repetitive, 2-tone, 2-syllabic whistle that may last several minutes, and the female call as more of a chirp, less frequent and less persistent (9; see also p. 228, **'Ecstatic' Excitement in Rainfall**).

[The differences in song between males and females does not trace to great structural differences in their syringes. They trace, instead, to the fact that song is primarily under the control of hormones and the nervous system (28; see also pp. 269-274, 439, 440).]

The most detailed accounting of the vocalizations of adult Cockatiels has been made by R. Zann (unpublished thesis) who distinguishes the calls, as follows (see 824):

1. *Screech*--a prolonged, high-frequency distress call;
2. *Weurp*--a low, short *weurp-weurp* given in response to moderate alarm stimuli that do not precipitate flight;
3. *Weep*--a prolonged *wee-up*, the most common call given on the wing;
4. *Hiss*--a short, low, snorting sound given as a threat in defense of the nest;
5. *Copulation call*--a low, repetitive call given by the female;
6. *Terrestrial-courtship call*--a long, complex call given by the male when close to the female, most commonly during courtship;
7. *Bill-wiping call*--a prolonged, pulsating, high-frequency call in which the bird wipes its bill toward the end of the call.

I would add to this list the repetitive squeaks made both during allofeeding of the female by the male and during allofeeding of the young by both parents. A young male, Lothair (see Table 4), of the 7th brood of Carmen and Cosimo, frequently uttered these sounds unassociated with either allofeeding or soliciting for food (accompanied by marked, visible fluttering of the thorax).

[I refer to call #5 as Coition Sounds. It is very easy to be misled into believing that the male utters this call during coitus, but all observers other than Zann agree that the call is uttered by the female at that time, and I have confirmed this origin repeatedly. However, a seemingly identical call also is uttered by the male at other times during breeding, and very infrequently at other times also by the female (see treatment on pp. 412-414, **Coition Sounds**). Coition Sounds, though not pre-coital, would appear to belong in the category of "mating songs," which, following Robinson, "...unlike territorial songs are as a rule, low monotonous songs with no rising and falling inflections and may easily be overlooked." They "...are prevalent in Australia and of vital importance to resident territory holders." In this connection, female song is very common among Australian birds but restricted essentially to resident territory holders (960).]

WEALTH OF CALLS AND SONG. None of the above characterizations adequately describes the rich vocal repertoires of my breeding male Cockatiels. They have a wealth of different passages in their calls and song. Similarly, my non-breeding adult males often engage in long-lasting vocalizations. The complexity of these utterances is very great, and, following the definitions given below, they would appear to qualify as song.

SONG AND SUBSONG VERSUS CALL NOTES. Avian songs usually are complex, species-specific, learned vocalizations consisting of "a series of notes, generally of more than one type, uttered in succession and so related as to form a recognizable sequence or pattern in time. Thus, the song as a whole displays the features of accent, increased duration, increased rhythmical complexity....which are not discernible to anything like the same extent in call notes" (76). From another point of view, the term "song" usually is reserved for loud and sustained vocalizations delivered seasonally by males in possession of a breeding or courting territory, which usually are discontinued as the testes regress (426). Songs often show individual differences, and sometimes dialect patterns.

Subsong is a loose aggregation of variable-to-stereotyped random "warbling" notes. It is uttered at low volume by young birds prior to the emergence of the fully developed song pattern and usually with a greater length and frequency range, often while the birds doze. It is believed to be of the nature of vocal practice and has been noticed in many passeriformes and in the Orange-winged Amazon (426, 1,269). I have noted it frequently in lovebirds.

Calls usually are shorter than songs, often considerably less complex, inherently simpler to produce (require little modulation), and may contain harsh or grating notes rather than pure tones (247). Moreover, calls develop normally in the absence of full neuromuscular control, whereas song requires a degree of training or practice under auditory feedback (see 1,150). Some calls are seasonal and sexually specific, whereas others are heard the year around or are produced by both sexes. Moreover, stereotypy is typical of many of the calls of all birds, so that on successive repetitions and in different contexts these vocalizations show little or no gradation in amplitude, length, or structure. The context in which the calls are delivered, the identity of the calling individual, and the response elicited from conspecifics suggest the type of information conveyed and the function of a call (426).

Calls that do not convey information about position share certain characteristics: they are of long duration, have no sudden changes in pitch, and begin and end gradually. Social calls, which must be locatable easily, have the opposite characteristics. Calls used in agonistic interactions with conspecifics or denoting alarm or arousal, often occur in a series of gradations and thus presumably are capable of reflecting a broad range of moods. In contrast to songs, calls often convey information that must be sent and received correctly with no practice (258, 419, 429). Species differences in both calls and songs often have provided the clues to the discovery of sympatric species (1,320).

The wealth of parrot vocalizations, in general, probably is not appreciated. For example, the Eastern Rosella (which is reported to hybridize with Cockatiels; 104) has 19 known calls (62). Estimates of the number of different vocal signals or call types in birds' repertoires range from 5 to 40 (103). One Great Tit had as many as the latter figure (109), Plumed Guinea Fowl (*Guttera plumifera*) have about 20 (see 1,205), while White-crowned Sparrows and Brown Noddies (Laridae; *Anous stolidus*) have only 9 (1,218, 1,353). The number of visual signals probably equals or exceeds the number of vocal ones (419). Brereton proposes that the number of calls is a measure of the complexity of a species' social organization (see 171).

AN IMPRESSION OF IMPORTANT INFORMATION CONVEYED WITH GREAT URGENCY. One of the fascinations of the calls and songs of Cockatielian males is their resemblance to human speech, in the sense that many of their vocalizations give the very strong impression that important information is being conveyed with great urgency. Others have similar impressions from other non-songbirds, such as jacamars and certain tinamous, motmots, and trogons; the simplicity and purity of tone of some of the utterances of these birds give an impression of sincerity and depth of feeling that, in certain moods, are more moving than the brilliant, and seemingly more studied, song of many songbirds (101).

PART 4. PEACH-FACED LOVEBIRDS

Affinities and Group Characteristics

Lovebirds (genus *Agapornis*) belong to the family Psittacidae (Table 1c), a group with signs of a rapid and recent speciation among some members (27). The family is so diverse, that it usually is subdivided into 4-6 subfamilies (1, 27, 819). Lovebirds are classified by Smith in the subfamily Psittaculinae (Table 1c), for which no common name exists, although von Boetticher's designation "coral- or red-billed parrots" may be most apt (27).

This family also includes the genera, *Psittacula, Tanygnathus, Eclectus, Prioniturus, Psittinus, Bolbopsittacus, Psittacella, Geoffroyus, Alisterus, Aprosmictus, Prosopeia, Polytelis*, and *Loriculus*. Accordingly, it forms a subgroup of Peters' and Forshaw's subfamily, Psittacinae (see Table 1a,b). Taken as a group and disregarding occasional exceptions, members of the subfamily Psittaculinae are distinguished from all other parrots in a number of characteristics (27, 819), of which the following are most pertinent here.

(a) Contrary to the usual circumstances in birds, in which the male is much more aggressive than the female (261), probably related to a lower androgen production of the ovary compared to the testes (260), female psittaculines are dominant. They tend to be larger and stronger than the males and, as is characteristic of dominance in parrots, to take the initiative in selecting the nest site, and to defend it against other birds. [In many passerines, the male is dominant early in the season and the female later, with correlated changes in the courtship displays (296).]

(b) Psittaculines have a strong dislike of touching each other (they are "distance animals"). Lovebirds tend to be exceptions ("contact animals;" 315).

(c) Characteristic (b) has been overcome by the development of courtship displays, whereby the male generally disarms the hen by approaching her in a "devious" manner.

(d) Psittaculines are very gregarious, usually forming large flocks and nesting in loose colonies.

(e) The tail often has a red, orange, or yellow pattern at its base. When spread, this carries a message of threat (or dominance) to other parrots.

Paleogeography and Paleoclimatology of Africa, Influences on Avifauna

ROTATION AND DRIFT----INTERMITTENT CONNECTIONS WITH EURASIA. Prior to the early Jurassic period, when Africa and South America rotated away from North America (with the opening of the Atlantic Ocean), Africa was broadly connected with southwestern Europe (184). Beginning at about 148 mya, and continuing for almost 70 million yr, Africa rotated counterclockwise relative to Europe. In the early Paleocene epoch, Africa and Europe were connected via Spain, and Africa may also have been connected broadly with Asia through Arabia. The Continent has been of approximately the same shape since at least 100 mya (259) and has maintained much of its present outlines (29 million sq. km) since the middle of the Eocene epoch, some 50 mya (1,052). Since about 15-10 mya it has drifted at a rate of about a few cm per yr, perhaps with a slight rotation (see 1,326).

From the early Paleocene into the late Eocene epochs, Africa and Europe seem to have become more widely separated. Following intermittent re-establishment of direct connections between Africa and Eurasia, direct dispersals were possible at various times during the Cretaceous and Tertiary periods (184, 186, and above), leading to a greater mixture of Laurasian and Gondwanan faunal elements than is found in South America (1,098). The apparent intermittency of such connections can be judged by the exchange of mammals between Africa and Asia at the ends of the Oligocene, Miocene, and Pliocene epochs, but even then the connections must have been filter bridges or "sweepstakes routes," since the fauna as a whole did not become deeply involved in the interchanges. The much greater mobility of birds than of, say, mammals, would have ensured a more continuous history of exchange (153, 154), and the African Continent has been exposed repeatedly to invasions by well-adapted newcomers (166, 1,293). Comparatively speaking, the Continent is at a peak of sophistication and complexity of its "faunal evolution," whereas that of Australia is primitive (based upon evaluations of their Carnivora; 784).

MARINE CONDITIONS---DEPOSITION AND EROSION---TECTONIC ACTIVITY. Though Africa now is separated from southwestern Asia by the Red Sea trench and the Gulf of Aden, the Arabian block has been essentially a unit in African structure through most of geological time. The Tethys Sea extended across the northern fringe of Africa through the Persian Gulf on many occasions, and the northwestern part of the Continent was invaded extensively by the ocean during portions of the Paleozoic and Mesozoic eras. In Triassic times, the African Continent was the site of widespread continental deposition. In the Jurassic period, marine conditions encroached upon the present Continent on its eastern side and the Tethys Sea broke across Arabia and Ethiopia for the first time since the Precambrian, forming a "trans-Erythraean trough," but leaving an unsubmerged "Arabo-Somali massif." During this period, southern Africa apparently was undergoing general erosion but a substantial basin of deposition existed in the western half of the equatorial belt, in which fresh- and brackish-water fossils occur (1,293). Triassic-Jurassic times also saw intra-continental down warping and the development of regional tensional structures (rifting; 1,382).

During the Cretaceous period, general warping of the entire Continent took place. In the south, there was broad uplift accompanied by marginal monoclinal flexion that permitted the seas to invade the ancient landmass, first on the eastern side and later in the west. In eastern Africa there was only a minor change in the Jurassic shoreline, but the sea withdrew from the Somali-Yemen area. The Atlantic margin of the present Continent began to take shape, and by mid-Cretaceous times the Atlantic and Tethys Seas became united across an area that stretched from the Gulf of Guinea to Algeria, separating the main mass of Arabo-Africa from the west African shield area. In a broad belt between latitudes 10° and 30°N, deposition took place yielding a complex of sandy sediments known as the Nubia sandstone or "continental intercalaire."

In Egypt there was a progressive southward advance of the shoreline during the Cretaceous, followed by regression of the sea in the Paleocene epoch. During the Jurassic and much of the Cretaceous periods, the Continent as a whole was subjected to extensive erosion, reducing it to a landmass of low relief. The main direction of sedimental transport was to the continental margins and adjacent ocean basins. The planed off landscape has since been warped extensively but still is traceable in strongly uplifted areas where it has escaped subsequent erosion (1,293, 1,382). Early in the Paleocene epoch, mountain building in the Tethys area and general uplift to the south led to withdrawal of the invading seas. The Tethys was drastically reduced in size and there were broad terrestrial connections to India and Europe; tenuous links also may have existed with the Iberian peninsula and Madagascar. This Paleocene uplift initiated the dissection of the newly elevated surfaces and a fresh cycle of planation began.

The seas advanced once more in the Eocene, virtually isolating Arabo-Africa again. The early Oligocene epoch was marked by a gradual withdrawal of the sea, particularly in northern Africa. Uplift became general and mountain-building activity associated with the folding of the Alpine chain reduced the size of the Tethys Sea very substantially. Toward the end of the Oligocene, there also was folding and elevation of the Atlas region, resulting in the complete emergence of Tunisia, Algeria, and Morocco. From the middle Eocene until the end of the Miocene, the western trough of the Tethys between northern Africa and Spain was divided into two parts, separated by an upfolded landmass--the "Betic massif," at times reduced to a string of islands but probably fully emergent by the end of the Oligocene.

ISOLATION OF ARABIA---UPLIFT, VOLCANICITY, AND PRESENT-DAY RELIEF. At that time there was almost certainly some kind of land connection between northern Africa and emergent Europe, even if not a continuous one. The floors of both troughs were fully submerged again in the early Miocene, which was characterized by renewed marine invasion. The Tethys/Mediterranean Sea could flow through the Gulf of Suez and flooded the Red Sea trench, while waters of the Indian Ocean extended into the Gulf of Aden; Arabia became isolated partially from Africa for the first time. The land connection was not cut finally until some time during the Pleistocene epoch.

In the interior of Africa, the 25 million yr that elapsed between the major Paleocene uplift and that of the late Oligocene saw an extensive planation that resulted in the development of the "African" peneplain which is so prominent a feature of the landscape of the Continent. Warping during the late Oligocene emergence was followed by dissection, so that by early Miocene times quite considerable relief had been produced in the eastern African region. Uplift occurred again in the late Miocene, causing the seas to withdraw from the continental margins, bringing about the virtual isolation of Arabia from Africa, although partial isolation must have resulted from the earlier Miocene rifting. Post-Miocene uplift, volcanicity, and faulting together greatly modified the interior of the Continent, producing the relief and form of today (1,293; see pp. 244-251).

WITHDRAWAL OF HUMID FORESTS---SPREAD OF SAVANNA & SCRUB VEGETATION. Humid forest evidently covered nearly all of Africa except, perhaps, for the south, until Neogene times (184). Tectonic activity was strong in Africa in the early Pleistocene, during which epoch it would seem that the only land connection between Africa and Eurasia was the narrow Isthmus of Suez, whose dimensions varied considerably with fluctuations of sea level, even being cut through completely at times. As a result of post-Miocene movements, the surface of Africa has much the highest average elevation of any of the continents (1,052). The increased elevation and hotter, drier conditions eliminated much of the Miocene rainforest and facilitated the spread of savanna and scrub vegetation.

VIOLENT TECTONIC ACTIVITY--INCREASED RAINSHADOW EFFECT. Continental uplift since the end of the Miocene epoch has been of the order of 1,200 m, with the altitude of eastern Africa increasing a full 2,400 m. This has resulted in a substantially cooler, drier climate, since the mean temperature drops by about 0.6-1°C for each rise of 100 m. Half of the uplift occurred about 12 mya, when vast areas of southern and eastern Africa were elevated. Extensive volcanic activity then created the high peaks of Ethiopia and East Africa (259, 1,335). Extending southward from Ethiopia down the rift valleys, the volcanic field further increased the rainshadow effect, and brought greater drought and temperature extremes (184).

Especially around 2 mya and into the early Pleistocene epoch, extensive mountain building took place, and the development of the Rift Valley in Northeast and Central Africa produced the huge troughs that now are occupied by Lake Malawi, Lake Tanganyika, and others. Lake Victoria was formed between its two arms. Large new volcanos rose in the Rift Valley neighborhood, and also in the Central Sahara, in Tibesti. Most of the spectacular present-day African topographical features were formed in this period of violent tectonic activity. West Africa was almost unaffected, so that nearly all of this part of tropical Africa remains below 1,000 m, while by far the greater part of tropical and South Africa is higher, mostly at 1,000-1,500 m. The geological erosion, arising from this richly varied topography, has brought about the distribution of different types of soils, with their characteristically associated vegetation, in any particular set of climatic conditions (259, 1,052).

INFLUENCES OF ANTARCTIC GLACIATIONS. Climatic effects of polar ice sheets now are known to be virtually restricted to the corresponding hemisphere, and the interactions of the hemispheric atmospheric circulations are much more complex than had been anticipated. For example, unlike other late Cenozoic climatic variations, the mid-Brunhes global change, 400,000-300,000 yr ago, shows opposite trends in the Northern and Southern Hemispheres (see also p. 30, **Circumantarctic Current**). In the Northern Hemisphere the climate shifted to more "glacial" conditions and Earth became more arid; in the Southern Hemisphere, an opposite trend brought a halt to the severe cold, and a humid ("interglacial") period ensued.

Since Peach-faced Lovebirds are endemic to Southwest Africa, I confine attention here to the influences of Antarctic glaciations, but a succession of glaciations in the Northern Hemisphere after about 3½ mya exerted comparable influences in Africa north of the equator. The timing of late Pleistocene and Holocene climatic changes in the southwest Pacific, however, leads similar fluctuations in the Northern Hemisphere by several millenia, as does that of the changes in sea surface temperatures. A probable explanation of the asynchrony in temperature trends is the rapid freezing and melting of Antarctic sea ice, in comparison with which the northern continental ice sheets respond slowly. The faster response of Antarctic sea ice apparently causes southern high and mid-latitude land and sea temperatures to fall or rise more rapidly than equivalent northern latitude temperatures (see 259, 1,153, 1,326, 1,327, 1,400).

Ice cap development in the Antarctic definitely was in progress by 30 mya, and gradual development probably was occurring as early as 40-38 mya, at a time when warm-temperate moist climates prevailed in high Arctic latitudes (972, 1,326). Combined faunal and isotopic evidence have been interpreted as indicating an increase in Antarctic ice volume and a concomitant major global cooling event in the mid-Oligocene (see 567). However, the first Antarctic sheet of major proportions may not have been in place until the early Miocene epoch, about 15 mya. Thereafter, it fluctuated tremendously in extent, reaching massive proportions at least 3 times and collapsing--perhaps even disappearing--on an unknown number of occasions.

The western ice sheet probably underwent rapid expansion about 6½-5 mya--the "Terminal Miocene Event," in coincidence with the transient drying up of the Mediterranean--the Messinian "crisis." The effects of this dramatic expansion are thought to have been considerable on the African environment, stimulating evolutionary change, and they may have been felt on a global scale. In addition to having provided a bridge between Europe and Africa, the cold interlude of the terminal Miocene impacted upon a very different topography from that of earlier times, inasmuch as it followed a period of active mountain building in the circum-Mediterranean and Himalayan areas, as well as uplift and rifting in eastern Africa (see p. 241).

In the Cape Province, the vegetation underwent a replacement of tropical and sub-tropical forest by "fynbos" shrubland cover, and the fauna of the Continent underwent drastic changes, possibly including the first appearance of hominids. Some of the faunal changes, particularly among bovids, elephantids, carnivores, and rodents, probably had their origin in the major faunal interchange that accompanied the Messinian "crisis." Southern ocean microfossils also indicate cooling periods at 10.2 and 8.9 mya--not yet reflected in the Antarctic record (186, 282, 285, 1,334).

With the initiation of early Miocene Antarctic glaciation, the cold Benguela Current began to bathe the West African Coast. Upwelling along the coast intensified significantly from the early upper Miocene onward and the Benguela current increased progressively thereafter, bringing significant aridification of the southwestern hinterland. Glaciation was so extensive by the Pliocene epoch (about 5 mya) that it would have brought a much drier climate to the tropical West African coast. There was a possible disappearance of the ice sheet between 3 and 2½ mya, and a short-lived but severe cooling about 2.4 mya, which, perhaps, occasioned an ice buildup that overrode the Transantarctic Mountains (which rise to some 4,600 m; 184, 1,331, 1,382)).

The history of the Congo basin rainforest provides an example of the influences of these Antarctic ice-sheet fluctuations on the African flora. From being very extensive in the middle Miocene epoch, about 15 mya, rainforests shrank about 9 mya, then expanded 8.8-6.4 mya, and contracted dramatically about 5.2 mya. Forest expansion resulted 5-3½ mya, followed by another contraction, 3.2-3.5 mya. A brief, warm, moist period was followed by dramatic cooling and drying 2.4 mya, marked by the opening of woodland and the increase of savanna. There are clear connections between the Antarctic ice advances and Continental cooling at 5 and 2.3 mya (186, 1,335).

PLEISTOCENE CLIMATIC FLUCTUATIONS---EXTINCTIONS---MIGRATIONS---RADIATIONS---SAVANNA-ADAPTED AVIFAUNA. Finally, fluctuations of the Pleistocene climate (drier than now during glacial ages, and wetter during interglacial ages) also had important effects on the African tropical rainforest flora and fauna. [These fluctuations also account for many extinctions and relict distributions elsewhere, for example, in the Antilles (see 206 and pp. 37-39).] The drier phases of the ice ages apparently correspond to periods when African deserts and savannas expanded. Concurrently, the forests that required near ever-wet conditions were reduced to comparatively small refugia in which a limited number of forest species could survive. In the interglacial periods, wetter climates prevailed at lower altitudes, and forests expanded, while savannas and deserts contracted (259). These climatic vicissitudes seem adequate to account for the extinctions that impoverished the African flora (for which there is both direct and indirect evidence) and increased the areas of tropical savanna and grasslands (184).

The changes in habitat and climate doubtless caused a marked disappearance of numerous animals from some parts of Africa by extinctions and immigrations (12, 152). The continent has few endemic avian taxa above the species level; most of these taxa have less than 10 species and 40% of all endemics have been recovered as fossils from the Eurasian Cenozoic era (106, 438). The habitat and climatic changes also placed limits on potential radiations of many birds, particularly insectivores and frugivores. Thus, the fact that savannas and deserts covered very much larger areas of Africa in the past than they do today, helps to explain why the avifauna of Africa is particularly rich in some families adapted to desert or savanna conditions, for example, larks and weaver birds, and relatively poor in some typically sylvan families, such as trogons or broadbills (259). None of the wet periods accompanying the marked Pleistocene climatic fluctuations was sufficiently extensive and prolonged to exterminate South Africa's rich, open-country, "savanna-adapted" avifauna (153).

A DYNAMIC AVIFAUNA FAVORED. Certain of these Pleistocene African changes would have provided isolating mechanisms, such as the rift valley systems. These seemed, at first, to have been inadequate to account for the speciation that has occurred in lovebirds (12), in which fairly uniform evolutionary trends can be discerned among the living forms, from *A. cana* through *A. personata nigrigenis* (3). More recent work has elucidated the geographical pattern of various types of African sylvan regions in the late Pleistocene. This pattern favored a dynamic avifauna with a high rate of both speciation and extinction.

Vast spreads of forest in wet periods and of *Acacia* in dry periods created islands of opposite vegetational types. In these, speciation could take place and new species could specialize to cope with increasing pressures as "islands" shrank. The specialization could have taken either of two routes. It could have been a precarious one of adapting to new habitat, within the shrinking islands (population reduction in accordance with the extent of an available habitat carried the risk of extinction if that habitat disappeared). Or, it could have been an opportunistic change in habits, that carried the species into a new niche in the expanding vegetation outside an ecological island (165, 259).

Accordingly, the patterning of geographical changes in Africa has provided opportunities for both arid and humid-country species to undergo active speciation in the Pleistocene. In a more general overview, it is thought that many different groups of flora and fauna "respond by synchronous waves of speciation and extinction to global temperature extremes and attendant environmental changes" (186).

Present-Day Africa

TOPOGRAPHY. Most of the Continent consists of deserts, scrublands, steppes, savannas, open woodlands, or uplands. Volcanic peaks in central and eastern Africa reach considerable heights (Mt. Kilimanjaro, 6,900 m;

Mt. Kenya, 5,200 m). The northern coast consists of macchia vegetation and deserts. The Atlas Mountains give northwestern Africa additional vegetational types, increasing the range of avian habitats. Deserts, semi-deserts, and arid scrubs cover about 43% of the Continent.

Southern Africa is essentially a high tableland, with a narrow coastal plain rising abruptly through a series of plateaux that are bisected deeply by the main river valleys. In the south, the ranges of the Langeberg and Swartberg Mountains run parallel to the coast and contain the Little Karoo Plateau (350-800 m) between them. The main escarpment rises a little further inland in the Roggeveld, Nieuweveld, and Stormberg Mountains, with the Great Karoo Plateau (> 1,000 m) beyond them. In the west, the escarpment rises in the Tiras Mountains and Khomas Highlands of Namibia. Fully half of southern Africa lies at elevations of over 1,000 m (835, 1,292).

THE IMMENSE SAHARA DESERT in the north includes some of the hottest and driest areas and the greatest expanses of sand (only 1 mm of rainfall per year in the eastern portion; see 1,390). It occupies nearly 8 million sq. km, as large as Australia or the U.S.A., and is almost wholly incapable of supporting any avian migrants for significant periods because of its extreme barrenness. The total area of its oases is negligible on a continental scale, and the highlands, which rise to over 3,000 m, are hardly less barren than the lower desert that surrounds them (1,052).

The aridity of the Saharan belt (15-23°N) in contrast with other areas in this latitude, is caused by a cross-circulation of the summer monsoonal system (low-level equatorial westerlies and tropical easterly jets) in the exit region above the Sahara (1,326). To the south, the Sahara grades into subdesert, grass and scrub savannas, and finally more or less dense arboreous savannas. In the south there are the Kalahari and Namib deserts and the Karoo subdesert steppes. In the east there are the Nubian, Danakil, and Somali deserts, as well as Man-made deserts in Kenya and Tanzania.

THE KALAHARI DESERT is a huge, arid to semi-arid, sand- and marl-filled basin. It is the largest onshore Cenozoic depocenter in southern Africa, a huge shallow depression into which sediments have been moved by internal drainage (main input from the Okavango River and it tributaries into the Okavango Graben and Makgadikgadi Depression) and aeolian agencies. It is dominated by extensive systems of parallel, gentle, mostly linear dunes. These are 30-150 m apart, often kilometers in length, and fixed by savanna vegetation. They occur throughout the Kalahari from the Orange River to southern Angola and southwestern Zambia, forming an arc that corresponds approximately to the pattern of outblowing trade winds around the South African anticyclone. Dune crests are active in some areas of the southwestern Kalahari, where rainfall averages only 100-150 mm annually. Past periods of aridity and dune formation were associated with, and probably changed by, a larger and more intense anticyclonic circulation and higher windspeeds than at present.

With the exception of the dunes of the Namib Desert, the sand dunes of the southern African subcontinent are formed from the surface sediments of the Kalahari Beds (primarily mostly lithified)--the Kalahari Sands (unconsolidated, quartzose)--which cover an area of 2½ million sq. km between the Orange and Congo Rivers. The Kalahari sands had a much wider distribution in the past, reaching far into the Orange Free State, Mozambique, and possibly western Namibia. Although the precise provenance of the surface Kalahari sands is uncertain, it seems fairly well established that they have been redistributed by the wind a number of times during the late Cenozoic era. Thus, their widespread distribution in southern and south central Africa points to a number of periods of very extensive aridity in the same interval.

The Kalahari has acted as a major sedimentary basin since the Cretaceous period. Many of the sediments have been calcreted and silicified. It appears that the antiquity of arid climates in southwestern Africa parallels that of the Sahara. Thus, the Kalahari has had a long history of arid and semi-arid climates, including at least 3 periods with more intense and more expansive aridity than at present. Some limited periods of sub-humid climates occurred in the Pleistocene epoch. The amplitude and extent of the climatic oscillations varied between the Kalahari and the Namib. In the Namib, they were of low magnitude and extent, while in the Kalahari, there was much greater contrast between the massive expansions of aridity, as evidenced by the distribution of fixed dunes, and the widespread Late Glacial humid period in the southern Kalahari (see 1,329, 1,331, 1,382).

THE NAMIB DESERT extends along the southwest coast for over 2,800 km. The Namib sandstone rises cliff-like up to 200 m above the crystalline basement near the coast and up to 200 m above the foreland of the Great Escarpment in the east. This sandstone pedestal gives the dune field an elevated appearance and exaggerates the height of the dunes. Conditions in the north vary from "extreme, hyperarid desert" to "desert," and from hot to mild. It apparently has experienced no climate more humid than semi-arid (350-450 mm of summer rainfall) since the end of the Miocene, was hyperarid throughout the Pliocene, and underwent a progressive desiccation during the Quaternary. The Lüderitz-Bogenfels area, which supported a varied large-mammal population in the Miocene, now is an area of extreme aridity.

Five rivers were active on the sandstone beneath the Namib dune field in Miocene-Pliocene and Pliocene-Pleistocene times. After an erosional stage, decreasing run-off led to the accumulation of large alluvial fans, which were the main source of the blown sand and the centers of dune-field development. Even the channels of the Tsondab and Tsauchab Rivers, alone, could account for all the Namib dune sand, without even considering erosion along the Great Escarpment. The Kuiseb River appears to have played a significant role as the northern boundary of the main Namib Sand Sea for at least the duration of the Quaternary, except in the immediate coastal tract, where the high energy, unidirectional south-southwesterly wind regime is dominant.

The northern terrain subdivision of the Namib desert consists principally of bedrock and extensive flat, gravel surfaces, with scattered sand accumulations along the coast. The central subdivision is a vast extent of tremendous sand dunes of both longitudinal and barchan type. Some of the former, which are 1-3 km apart, crest at up to 275 m, possibly making them the highest dunes in the world. The southern terrain subdivision is mostly a flat rock platform with low rock ridges and shallow deposits of sand and gravel. The thick, red-brown sandstones of the Tsondab Sandstone Formation represent the accumulation of a major sand sea in the central and southern subdivisions over a period of some 20-30 million yr prior to the middle-to-late Miocene.

The Namib Sand Sea Dunes are the only active desert dunes in southern Africa today. The main linear forms may be out of phase with today's resultant dune-forming winds, and possibly are being reworked. The sand cover in the interdune valleys of the central subdivision is not very deep, and the underlying Namib Sandstone, which is exposed over large areas in the southern subdivision, is everywhere to be found. The inactive dune fields of the Continental interior are dominated by longitudinal forms; all are degraded and vegetated (1,307, 1,329, 1,331-1,333, 1,382).

GRASSLANDS cover about 40% of Africa in both subtropical and tropical regions, and they vary greatly from one region to another. Africa's savannas, steppes, arid plains, and subdeserts stretch in an arc approximately across the Continent. There are savanna woodlands and arboreous savannas, but there also are woodlands that do not fit into any definition of savanna--one may say that woodlands form a transition between savannas and forests. Most of Africa's lowland or equatorial rainforests are located in the Congo drainage basin. They extend from the Albertine Rift Valley in the east to the Atlantic Ocean in the west, and a broad strip continues along the Gulf of Guinea from Ghana to Sierra Leone. The gallery forests around rivers and lakes and the coastal mangrove and lagoon forests also are a type of rainforest. African lowland, transitional, and montane forests are of mixed composition, but above these belts the mountains are clothed generally by less diverse communities or even are dominated by a single species.

THE MOUNTAINS OF TROPICAL AND SUBTROPICAL AFRICA are, in great proportion, bare, having been eroded down to bedrock. Best preserved are the higher vegetational zones of the "tropical" (in the geographical sense) regions. There are isolated, mountainous highland areas scattered throughout Africa and in various climatic regions, but they are mostly concentrated in the eastern parts of the Continent, from Ethiopia to Natal. Many of these, such as those of East Africa, the Camerouns in the west, and the Ethiopian highlands in the northeast support relics or outliers of sylvan faunas. The coastal zone of the southernmost part of Africa, from immediately north of Cape Town on the Atlantic side to Port Elizabeth on the Indian Ocean, is unique in many ways, above all in its flora. Around the Cape, distinct plant associations dominated by one or a few species have given way to an incredibly complex mosaic of plants, generally low vegetation of the macchia type. Among vertebrates, only the birds can compare in their singularity with the flora of the Cape (1,155, 1,292).

THE CLIMATES OF THE SOUTHERN AFRICAN SUBREGION are dominated by seasonal or permanent aridity. Though 74% of the area, which includes the range of Peach-faced lovebirds, is classified as arid or semi-arid, it possesses a wide, extremely varied range of biomes. Consequently, it probably is the most complex portion of the entire Afrotropical region to deal with from the zoogeographical point of view. Avian habitats range from absolute, fog-bound desert in the extreme west, and a variety of semi-deserts and savannas over the interior plateau, to a humid littoral strip, as well as localized evergreen forests in the south and east. The wide diversity of biomes underscores the existing complex distributions, parapatric species combinations, and high levels of subspeciation (1,286, 1,331).

RAINY SEASONS. Rain in southern tropical Africa falls in roughly the same period as in the southwest, mainly from November to March or April, with May to September dry, and some rain again in October. During the rainy season, the easterly winds from the Indian Ocean bring warm, nearly-saturated air inland. Forced up over the Drakensberg Range and the plateau behind it, the air is cooled and parts with much of its water vapor as rain. When it reaches the Kalahari Desert it still has enough vapor to produce some thunderstorm rain, and if it is not released there, it will fall farther west, where the higher land of Southwest Africa (Namibia) cools it. The air that descends to the coast warms up as it progresses, so that at sea level it is so far below its saturation point that even the cold Benguela current (locally > 10°C) can produce only an occasional fog (1,297). In addition, upwelling suppresses oceanic evaporation and contributes to the prevalence of the more arid climates of the equatorial zone (1,325).

[Mid-latitude western coasts of continents generally are dry because the return portions of the major oceanic gyres bring cold waters from high latitudes along that portion of the coast. The Benguela current is an example of such a current. Onshore winds, which normally would bring moisture-laden air onto the land, are cooled as they pass over the cold Benguela current and lose most of their moisture. They then are so far below their saturation point that they cannot do better than give rise to an occasional mist (1,297). This accentuates the normal dryness at these latitudes caused by the dry descending air of the low-latitude cell and results in the extreme aridity of the Kalahari (and Atacama in South America) desert (987).]

In the greater part of northern tropical Africa, the single rainy season is mainly from May to September. In the remainder there are two distinct rainy seasons, one centered around May, the other--a minor one--around late October; everywhere else the single rainy season is succeeded by months of unbroken drought and a high saturation deficit, aggravated over vast areas by the absence of dew. In these main rainfall regimes, the rains tend to be less reliable in areas of lower mean annual rainfall.

UNRELIABILITY OF RAINFALL. Even in the part of eastern Africa with a double rainy season, but a mean annual total of about 600 mm, the wettest year in a series can register 6 times as much rain as the driest, while in a locality in Namibia (Southwest Africa) rainfall can vary by a factor of 10, from 75 to over 750 mm. In Sénégal, during 3 of 4 months, June to September, in which rain is expected, in individual years during the period 1953-1964 no rain was registered and in another month there were only 12.4 mm (1,052).

While changes in reliability of precipitation occur over distances of several 100 km in Namibia, in some mountainous parts of eastern and northeastern Africa, the regime may change from a copious and reliable rainfall to a low and unreliable one within 50-100 km. Consequently, there is a corresponding change from a regularly productive environment, where birds may be sedentary and breed during regular seasons, to sporadically productive areas where rainfall is unreliable and where birds must be opportunistic and take advantage of good conditions whenever they occur (259).

The cause of the instability of rainfall and its local nature in desert and dry mountainous regions is the attendant high degree of insolation (which is much more effective on dark, bare soil than on light-colored soil with some vegetation). Thus, dry air means clear skies and clear skies mean excessive receipt of solar radiation by day and emission of radiation by night--two processes that are responsible for some degree of precipitation. [The rapid cooling at night tends to cause a temperature inversion, so that the air near the ground is colder and heavier, and remains there.]

The rapid daytime heating of the land induces large-scale rising air currents which rise high enough to cool by adiabatic expansion and even reach dewpoint, forming clouds. These usually are of the cumulus type, since the release of heat within them still further increases the rate of air ascent. These clouds often produce rain, but it is rain that rarely reaches the ground and, indeed, one can see it evaporating in wispy tails to the clouds as it descends. But when it does reach the ground, it tends to be torrential and brief, of thunderstorm type, and comparatively local in extent (1,297).

RAINFALL IN THE SOUTHERN DESERTS. The Namib desert receives an annual average of less than 50 mm but benefits from sea fog and dew, and supports a scanty vegetation in some areas. In the northern part there is no seasonality to precipitation; in the southern portion, winter precipitation is the rule. The northern part of the Kalahari receives summer precipitation and has neither the climate nor vegetation of true desert, but from 22°S latitude southward to the Orange River it is more nearly true desert and receives only little and unreliable rainfall in the summer. Average annual rainfall is 450-650 mm. South of the Orange River, the Karoo subdesert receives both summer and winter rains (1,307, 1,331).

Over much of central southern Africa, annual rainfall is less than 250 mm, and the semi-arid areas of the Karoo Plateau and Kalahai Basin would be called "desert" in Australia. It is a feature of the entire south African region that it is much subject to droughts. In the drier regions rain may fail for 5 or 6 or more yr. Conversely, the total precipitation in the whole of an average year may fall within the period of a few days or even hours. Thus, floods and droughts may alternate with devastating effects in many parts of the country and occasional hailstorms sometimes inflict a high mortality on small birds (835).

AQUEOUS HABITATS. Of pertinence to the avifauna are 3 kinds of aqueous habitats: the open water of rivers, the still surfaces of lakes and pools, and marshy places of all kinds. In the northern tropics, the zone that includes the waters important to migrants is between roughly 10° and 15° N latitude. These waters depend on the summer rains. By the time that the migrants arrive, the rains have filled the hollow places and by the time that they leave most of these places have faded away. There are the areas in Sénégal flooded seasonally by the river, the great flood plain of the upper Niger (the Inundation Zone) 1,000 km to the east, about 400 Nigerian lakes of 20 ha or more another 1,000 km eastwards, while across Tchad and in the Sudan it is the rain-fed waters that attract and maintain the migrants through the winter. These waters diminish in volume constantly and many of them dry up soon after the turn of the year. All across this belt the natural ephemeral pools now are augmented by small and primitive man-made water catchments.

TEMPERATURE REGIMES. Most Palearctic migrants (largely north of the equator and below about 1,300 m) experience a mean temperature of over 23°C during the coolest month of their stay. [It has been estimated that on the average they require from the African ecosystem only about 60% of what they require while in the Palearctic.] By day, for the great majority of the migrants, not only in the tropics but also in South Africa, the mean temperature exceeds 27°C and often 32°C. Over a large part of northern tropical Africa the temperatures approach those above which certain birds have been shown experimentally to increase their metabolic rate to counter heat stress (see pp, 80-83). South of the Sahara, and below 1,500 m, the mean nightly January minima are nowhere below 10°C, and most nights are no colder than 14°C. Lethally cold snaps at night are almost unknown. This is an area where, for the greater part, summer and winter in the usual sense also are unknown, where there is little or no variation in the length of day, and where any alternation is between a dry season and a rainy season.

The rainy seasons vary in date and locality and in some parts show two peaks of wet weather separated by a short dry interval (56, 1,052).

Throughout the southern African region temperatures are influenced as much by elevation as by latitude and also by the cold Benguela current (see p. 248), which washes the west coast. Over about 60% of the area mean temperatures do not exceed 21°C, while on the west and south coasts and in the high hinterland of the Republic of South Africa they average 18°C and less. In the Kalahari basin it becomes exceedingly hot in the summer; high temperatures are reached then in all the main river valleys. By contrast, much of the country suffers severe frosts in winter, and snowfalls are regular on mountains of any height (835).

RAINFORESTS, MOIST WOODLANDS, SAVANNAS, AND TROPICS. Rainforests cover 6-7% of Africa. A rainforest belt fills much of the Congo Basin and extends westward toward Cameroun, and thence still further west to Guinea in blocks along a coastal strip. No migrant avian species lives in these forests exclusively and less than 6 species even have been detected in them. In West Africa, going north from forested areas, one encounters the "moist woodlands" comprising first the Southern Guinea Savanna. As the rainfall diminishes northward, this is succeeded by the Northern Guinea Savanna and then the heavily disturbed Sudan Savanna. Further north in the Sahelian zone, acacias become the dominant trees. Important elements there for the birds are *Savadora persica*, *Maerua crassifolia*, and *Balanites aegyptica*, all of which fruit in the dry winter. This is the driest zone before the vegetation becomes discontinuous and fades into the Sahara.

It is the drier zones, with the lower biomass of vegetation that accommodate far more migrants for the winter than the more humid densely vegetated zones to the south. This generalization applies both to arboreal feeders and ground foragers. These parallel vegetational zones persist from the Atlantic almost to the Red Sea, with the surface hardly anywhere reaching an altitude of 1,000 m, until the pattern is broken by the mountain masses of Abyssinia and Eritrea. Thence, southward through Kenya the broken topography and consequent patchy rainfall induces a great variety of vegetational types, terminating in full desert on the Namibian coast (1,052, 1,292).

As a consequence of the influences of Antarctic ice-sheet fluctuations on the African climate and rainforests, many groups of organisms that are represented abundantly in the New World tropics and in the stretch of tropics from southern Asia to northern Australia are relatively poorly represented in tropical Africa. The tropical flora of Africa, for example, is unexpectedly scanty, and this is true particularly of the rainforest component of the flora, with its meager showing of orchids, palms, bamboos, and aroids--plant groups that abound in other tropical lands (659).

AVIFAUNAL COMPARISONS WITH AUSTRALIA. There are some broad parallels between the non-passerine birds of Africa and Australia, in the avifaunas as a whole, in individual groups, and in distributional patterns. But there are also basic differences, some attributed directly to differences in the two continents as living areas. Africa, with its larger avifauna, has 4 times the land surface area of Australia and greater contact with Eurasia. Though there is no avian fossil record, the mammalian record indicates that faunistic interchanges occurred between Africa and Southern Eurasia at the ends of the Oligocene, Miocene, and Pliocene epochs, and these have tended to diminish the distinctiveness of their respective faunas (1,255, 1,293). Presumably, these were times when the barrier of the Tethys sea became narrowed. Since birds are able to cross water gaps much better than can mammals, the avian history of Africa must have been one of periodic and frequent interchanges with the northern continents.

Africa has received continued waves of avian colonists, with the result that the avifauna has been built up as a series of superimposed "strata." As each new family became established, there must have been a period of intense competition and a resorting and redivision of adaptive zones and niches, until stability was re-established (1,255). Avian parasitic habits in Africa seem to be far in advance of those in Australia, probably because the opportunities are far greater. The trends and differences that exist in parasitic behavior on these Continents are compatible with an evolutionary spread from Gondwana (1,257).

Climatic and vegetational belts are distributed zonally from the coast inland in both Africa and Australia, and these belts underlie the major faunal divisions. Since Australia has only one desert, there has been much more limited opportunity for geographical isolation and speciation than in Africa. The latter continent has a remarkable diversity of savanna and desert birds, in comparison with but few species of ground-dwelling, arid-zone birds in Australia. The former include sand-grouse, coursers, francolins, larks, pipits, and vultures, an avifauna basically different from that of Australia. These have been derived both internally and by interchanges with the adjacent Eurasian deserts. A major difference in the avifauna of the two continents is in the parrots. In contrast to the uniquely rich and diversified avifauna of Australia and New Guinea, Africa has only about half a dozen groups of parrots, mostly inhabiting woodland and savanna. The great diversity of structural types, monotypic genera, and distributional patterns shown by Australian parrots is largely lacking. On the other hand, the African hornbills and barbets that, to a degree, occupy the niches of parrots, do show specializations in habitat similar to those shown by the Australian parrots (815).

The Australian avifauna has had a history of development in isolation similar to the South American one. Extensive areas of sea, and the Indonesian Islands have provided a "faunal filter" along which only a few Eurasian groups have been able to pass (see pp. 23-39). Colonization of Australia has been predominantly along the same lines of latitude, along climatic belts, rather than from north to south. The later arriving Australian birds, and the rodents amongst the mammals, both provide evidence of having colonized Australia in several "waves," as can be seen from their showing several "levels of difference" from their Oriental counterparts today. No fewer than a dozen families of Eurasian birds are represented in Australia by only 1 or 2 species (1,255).

Lovebird Evolutionary Forerunners

AFRICAN FORERUNNERS PROBABLY CAME FROM EURASIA. The lovebird ancestor probably was a member of the genus, *Loriculus* (the hanging parrots or parakeets), or a *Loriculus*-like species that underwent adaptive radiation (4). It was perhaps recognizable as belonging to the genus *Agapornis* by the time of the Miocene epoch. Among contemporary members of the genus *Loriculus*, the behavior of *L. galgulus* is markedly similar to that of the 3 most primitive species of *Agapornis* (*cana*, *pullaria*, and *taranta*) and shows some similarities to that of *A. roseicollis* and *A. personata*. But *L. vernalis*, shows greater affinities than *L. galgulus* to the latter two species (79).

Lovebird forerunners probably came to Africa from tropical-subtropical Eurasia millions of years ago, probably in more than one invasion (4). Thus, waves of immigration of other fauna clearly are discernable at identifiable points in the past (and are good potential indicators of global warming and cooling cycles; 186 and pp. 242-244). On the other hand, the preponderance of evidence indicates that Africa has played a minor role in contributing to the Eurasian avifauna through dispersal in the opposite direction (106).

The lovebird forerunners spread across the once-damper Arabian peninsula in the Pliocene, adapting to and colonizing across the northern African savannas and south (in the east) to the southern savannas (4, 12). Following the climatic deterioration of the late Cenozoic, the African and South Asian populations were isolated from each other by intervening areas of hot, dry climate.

The Birds in the Wild

DISCOVERY---IMPORTATION---GEOGRAPHICAL RANGE. Peach-faced, Rosy-headed, or Rosy-faced Lovebirds (Agapornis roseicollis)--called "lovebirds" because of the way they snuggle together on perches, and because they pair early and normally remain paired for as long as both members survive (3)--were discovered in 1793 and, at first, were regarded as the same species as the Red-faced Lovebird (*A. p. pullaria*). They were imported into Britain for the first time in the early 1860s (834)

They inhabit a vast area of arid coastal plain and savanna. Their range includes most of Namibia, but in the Namib Desert the birds are found only where there is permanent water. The range extends into Gordonia in the northern Cape and across the Orange River into the northern parts of Little Namaqualand, Bushmanland, and the Kenhardt district. In the north the birds were said to be found as far east as Lake Ngami but there is no recent report of Peach-faced Lovebirds in Ngamiland. The northeasterly limit of their range lies in the neighborhood of the Waterberg. To the west of this it extends through Ovamboland and the central Kunene valley into southern Angola (*A. roseicollis catumbella* occurs in the Benguela district), where it reaches as far north as Sa da Bandeira in the interior and Novo Redondo on the coast (see 3, 12, 27, 279, 834, 835).

Peach-faced Lovebirds are abundant almost everywhere they are found, and appear to be entirely isolated from other lovebird species (3, 12), as are the other species from one another (i.e., the species are allopatric). [For reasons not clear, certain vegetational types, particularly *Brachystegia-Isiberlinia* woodland, appear to be effective barriers (12).] It is noteworthy in this connection that the 10 species of the genus *Loriculus* --their phylogenetically nearest relatives--also are mostly allopatric (79). The geographically nearest relative of Peach-faced Lovebirds is the Black-cheeked or Nyasa Lovebird (*A. personata nigrigenis*) in the eastern Caprivi, at a distance of at least 500 km (835).

Practically none of the range of Peach-faced Lovebirds receives an average of more than 400 mm of rain annually, usually between October and March. The weeks at the start of the rains, as in most parts of Africa, are the hottest of the year. The variability of rainfall is extreme, both locally, for most of it falls in erratic thunderstorms, and from year to year in any one locality (598). Thus, in one and the same breeding season, the conditions for breeding may be very different even in neighboring districts and even where the monthly totals are about the same, because with the low amounts of precipitation involved very much depends on its distribution.

HABITAT---WATER AND DRINKING. Peach-faced Lovebirds frequent dry, open country of deciduous woodlands and "bush," steppe, desert, and subdesert country, at elevations from sea level up to more than 1,500 m, and tolerate extreme climates (12, 27, 259). Though they prefer mountainous country with a long, severe dry season, they are seldom found far from water--to which they require daily access--and are avid bathers. They drink by dipping the scoop-like lower mandible into the water and then ingesting by means of rapid, piston-like movements of the tongue, with or without upward tilting of the head (3). The absence of water probably limits their inland range into the Kalahari Desert (27). It is easy to find their water sources by following their evening flights to the drinking pools (1), though these may be "of small compass and strangely situated" (see C.J. Anderson, 1872, in 311).

In most of tropical Africa, vegetative growth is not limited critically by temperature, as it is in temperate Europe or North America. In consequence, temperature has relatively minor effects on food supplies and the behavior of birds. On the other hand, the temperature falls by about 0.6-1°C per 100 m increase in altitude, and Peach-faced Lovebirds prefer mountainous country.

INTERBREED ONLY IN CAPTIVITY. The amazing mutual exclusiveness of different lovebird species, which seem nowhere to hybridize in the wild, may account in part for the fact that they have not developed effective species isolating mechanisms (mechanisms that prevent interbeeeding; 3). Thus, the different lovebird species interbreed readily in captivity, giving highly fertile hybrid offspring. [Analysis of hybrids between such closely related species sometimes provides unexpected insight into the inheritance and evolution of plumage and other characters, for example, ancestral properties (440; see also pp. 528, 529, **Relict Behavior in Hybrids**).]

INCREDIBLY DEXTEROUS FLIERS---FLOCKING---FLIGHT CALLS---FORAGING. To the distinction of belonging to the group of fastest creatures on earth, namely, birds, lovebirds add that of incredibly dexterous flight. The birds are capable of rapid, sharp turns and move at remarkable speed along paths winding through the trees (they even can fly backward for several cm in still air). One is lucky to catch more than a glimpse of their red heads as they approach and their azure-blue rumps as they depart. B.P. Hall remarked that they "travel like express trains" (see 311). The birds tend to negotiate short distances by climbing, sidling, or walking, rather than by flying, particularly when the tendency to locomote is not very strong (and the progression is downward; 3).

Peach-faced Lovebirds usually travel in flocks of about 5 to 15-20, but flights of many hundreds are seen at certain seasons, such as when favored foods are ripening or abundant (7, 835). They utter rapid, repeated, shrill notes when in flight, or when disturbed or alarmed. As with other parrots, they tend to be most vociferous on the wing. They forage on seeding grasses, the seeds of *Albizzia* and *Acacia* trees, berries of many types, on the flowers of *Albizzia*, on the buds and foliage of various other plants, including *Euphorbia* spp., and they may become pests on grain and millet crops (1, 12, 27, 834, 835). [It is said of lovebirds' closest relatives (genus *Loriculus*) that "A hanging parrot is strictly arboreal, never venturing near the ground when at liberty" (1,260).] Most activities, including feeding, tend to be confined to the morning and late afternoon hours during very warm weather, but sexual activities seem to be less affected by temperature (3).

Morphology and Characteristics

MINIATURES OF THE LARGE PARROTS. Lovebirds are beautiful, colorful, bright-eyed, noisy, gregarious little parrots. All but the Madagascar (Gray-headed; *A. cana*), Abyssinian (Black-winged; *A. taranta*), and Red-faced species are highly social. These same 3 exceptional species are the only ones in which the sexes are dimorphic. In both respects, the 3 species resemble the probable ancestral hanging parrots more than do the other lovebird species (3). Lovebirds can be likened to miniatures of the large parrots, inasmuch as they are short and stocky, with a large bill and a relatively blunt tail.

PROMINENT HEAD--LARGEST LOVEBIRD--SOCIALITY--AGGRESSIVENESS--MONOMORPHIC. Lovebirds are somewhat comical in appearance, one's first impression being that their heads are all bill and forehead. The prominence of the head correlates with its exceptional importance in the interactions of the birds with one another. Their brains are relatively quite large, approaching in size those of the much larger Rock Pigeons (1,283).

Peach-faced Lovebirds are members of the largest (50-61 g), one of the most social and adaptable (least specialized), probably the noisiest, and certainly the most aggressive species in the genus. Not coincidentally, in view of their size, they conform with Bergmann's Rule, in that they experience the lowest cool-season temperatures (12). [According to Bergmann's Rule, races of warm-blooded vertebrates from cool climates tend to be larger than races of the same species living in warm climates (see 974).]

From head to tail, the overall length of Peach-faced Lovebirds is 12½ to 17½ cm. As implied above, the sexes are essentially monomorphic (identical in appearance). Breeder hens, however, have wider, flatter, longer abdomens (caused by oviductal development) than males (also true of Budgerigars and Cockatiels), and the latter are said usually to have fractionally bolder and brighter heads and a slightly sharper, acid green color than the hens (834). [In monomorphic species the males usually outlive the females, a difference that probably is associated with reproductive cost; that may account for the generally earlier entrance of females into the breeding populations (314).]

METABOLIC PARAMETERS of lovebirds as measured by Gavrilov and Dol'nik (see 967) under the same conditions as for Budgerigars (see p. 57) are as follows. The standard metabolic rate of birds averaging 48.1 g in weight is 27.4 - 0.685T kcal/bird/day. The corresponding lower critical temperature for the birds is 26°C and the basal metabolic rate at that temperature is 9.6 kcal/bird/day. The corresponding existence metabolic rate is 44.1 - 1.030T kcal/bird/day (see p. 57 for definitions).

BODY COLORATION. The soft, beautiful shade of apple green or bright grass-green of the body of Peach-faced Lovebirds--paler in the breast--gives way to a brilliant azure- or peacock-blue rump and upper tail coverts. The latter are short feathers that cover the bases of the quills and help to clothe the body (coverts form the main insulation in most adult birds). The face is a soft rose-pink, tinged with gray at the edges of the cheeks, and capped by a vivid rose-red crown. The cere is feathered and unobtrusive. More color mutations have been bred and become established in this species than in any other bird except the Budgerigar. The best known of these is the recessive known as Pastel Blue, in which the body is sea-green, the rump blue, and the facial area a palest peach (787, 834).

The irides are dark brown and the legs and feet are gray. The thick, deep bill is of horn color (whitish-green), and is one of the strongest bills among lovebirds (but there is no obvious correlation between bill size and food; 12). The orange-pink and blackish bands of all but the innermost quils of the spread tail present a very beautiful appearance. This colorful appendage probably is used in signalling, to coordinate flock movements (3; see also p. 262). It is of interest in the latter connection that many species have evolved conspicuous rump and wing markings that function in flock integration (351), and that the color and pattern of the outer tail feathers are evolutionarily very conservative (3, 12).

IMMATURES---CALLS. Immatures are recognized readily by their duller, more olive-green coloring, their light greenish-gray, orange-tinged faces, and the dark-black saddle marks on both mandibles. Those present on the lower mandible, however, usually are hidden beneath the feathers at its base. The call is a shrill, metallic screech repeated several times in quick succession. Like many other birds, they repeat the call even faster when they are alarmed, agitated, or distressed (101, 109). This correlation makes it easy to judge the birds' moods in their various interactions.

MOBBING NEST DEFENSE. Peach-faced Lovebirds protect the immediate vicinity of their nests against predators with a highly-developed "mobbing" defense (3, 27, 573). At first, they sit upright and squeak slowly but loudly. If the predator or other source of annoyance continues to advance, the birds utter faster, higher-pitched squeaks, and eventually also beat their wings rapidly, with the body erect. They might also approach and attack an intruder, if it were not too large (3, 27). [No parrot is known to defend an exclusive territory, as do most other hole-nesters and other birds.]

Lesions in the medial archistriatum (see pp. 348, 349), which, with its associated fiber tracts, may be involved in escape behavior in many or all birds, markedly reduce the frequency of mobbing displays in response to unfamiliar objects, and simultaneously decreased avoidance and withdrawal behavior of Peach-faced Lovebirds (and increased some approach behavior). Such lesions reduce the number of calls emitted in response to the presence of a novel object and increase the speed with which the birds begin to consume food in the presence of the novel object. When no novel object is present, lesioned birds are somewhat slower to eat than controls, indicating, at the least, that their appetite for food is not been increased by the lesions. On the other hand, lesions of the hyperstriatum increase mobbing displays and probably increase the inhibitory effect of novel objects on feeding (1,283). [For a discussion of the possible mechanisms that are disrupted by medial archistriatal lesions, see 1,283. In mammals, similar results have been produced by ablating or lesioning the amygdaloid complex, which is thought to be the homologue of the avian archistriatum.]

REPRODUCTION

THE ADAPTIVE SIGNIFICANCE OF AVIAN COLONIALITY, in general, is not yet understood fully; nor is avian coloniality a simple or unitary phenomenon. Not all breeding colonies are adaptive for the same reasons, and the same can be said for roosting colonies (573). Nor do all individuals necessarily participate in a given roost for the same reason (778). In the cases of "rainbreeding" birds, however, accounting for their coloniality would appear to be less problematical than in most other cases, and it is true generally that colonial breeding is particularly frequent among birds whose food supplies are patchily distributed and unpredictable in space and time (837).

Wild Peach-faced Lovebirds breed in February and March and are strongly colonial. The strong tendency toward mutual stimulation in their colonies may contribute to achieving an immediate response to favorable conditions and thus enhance the effects of other environmental stimuli, may help to synchronize the group, and may accelerate ovulation (see 63, 67, 312). This also is true of some highly colonial passerines, which appear quite suddenly and establish breeding aggregations numbering in the hundreds of thousands or even millions of birds, and in which virtually all of the females may begin incubation within a span of 1 or 2 days. Such breeding synchronization enhances the exploitation of the extremely abundant but ephemeral resources upon which the vast colonies feed (see 968).

Such "social facilitation" of breeding success through numbers is known as the "Fraser Darling" effect. This effect apparently even was manifested in my colony, where all the mated pairs sometimes bred simultaneously, whether experienced or facilitated or not. For example, in July and November-December, 1985, and again in January, 1987, all 5 mated pairs on hand were incubating clutches concurrently.

[Apparently most birds breeding in Namibia (Southwest Africa) are opportunistic, breeding at the beginning (or end) of the rainy season, egg-laying always being so timed as to secure the most abundant food supply for the young at all times. In essence, the birds "keep step with the vegetation ....breeding when the vegetation flushes, whether just before or after rain has fallen....When the vegetation is awaiting rain, the birds wait too. In a bad year many miss a breeding season altogether." A few species (the largest raptors and scavengers), however, avoid the rains and breed in the driest and coldest months (598).

As in Australia, observers of "rain-breeding" birds in some parts of Africa have gained the general impression that even very slight showers premonitory of the actual "rains" may serve as a powerful stimulus to breeding, and that in some circumstances, particularly in semi-arid country, rainfall and humidity may stimulate birds directly. Moreau's impression was that "showers at the end of a drought stimulated the birds to sing and that a continuance of rains stimulated them to build....In all these cases it is possible that the stimulus, by sight, sound or feel of rain was direct...." If the rains broke off unexpectedly, so did the birds (598). However, birds of the Kalahari desert, though highly nomadic and ultimately dependent on rainfall for breeding, apparently are unable to respond reproductively to rain as rapidly as Australian birds (see 1,086).]

In their recent discussion of breeding synchrony and the Fraser Darling effect, Wittenberger and Hunt conclude that "the physiological mechanisms associated with initiation of breeding should be designed to facilitate breeding at the best possible time" (573), a conclusion fully concordant with observations of the breeding behavior of "rain-breeding" birds in the wild (312, 730). [One of the suggested bases for breeding synchrony, in general, is that it is a female sexual strategy for ensuring male investment in offspring by minimizing chances for cuckoldry (see 573). Recall, in this connection, the sexual promiscuity of confined male Budgerigars.]

Colonial nesting improves defenses against predators, including mutual vigilance and the advantages of massed arrivals and departures from the colonies. [As a general rule, proportional loss to predators decreases as the number of nests at risk increases, once a colony becomes large enough to swamp the exploitive capabilities of all predators in its vicinity (64, 573).] Colonial nesting also gives the young greater protection through synchronous fledging, gives them access to their contemporaries almost from the moment of their birth, enhances communication about sources of food--"information centers"--and increases the efficiency with which the sources are exploited ("local enhancement;" 351, 573, 793, 968, 1,280),

In foraging by local enhancement, a small group that has found a good foraging place may swell into an enormous flock in a matter of minutes, while a veritable swarm that is unsuccessful can dwindle to nothing with equal rapidity (see 968). One consequence of such fluid foraging behavior is that flock size may be quite variable and responsive to local conditions. Thus, mixed-species flocks of seed-eating finches in the Mohave Desert of California increased in aggregate size as the winter progressed and the food supply dwindled and became more patchily distributed (970).

Coloniality makes it possible for Peach-faced Lovebirds to form pairs very early, even at an age of only 2 months, while they are still in their juvenal plumage (3, 4). It also offers the lovebird young the opportunity for considerable practice at bill-fencing with their contemporaries, an activity at which they quickly become skilled (3). On the debit side, the presence of large numbers of interacting individuals and the close proximity of large numbers of active nests provide opportunities for various subtle forms of behavioral manipulation and cheating (see 607), result in increased competition for resources, as well as risks of rearing the young of others, cannibalism, and increased transmission of ectoparasites and diseases (537, 837). [In another view, mostly discordant with that expressed above, it is suggested that colonial or communal breeding is more likely to arise as a consequence of special social factors rather than strictly ecological ones, and that it ought to be expected to appear in environments with stable rather than erratic conditions (823).]

COLONIAL BREEDING, FLOCKING, AND SEXUAL INDISTINGUISHABILITY. The indistinguishability between the sexes of monogamous species, like Peach-faced lovebirds, may be related to flocking and colonial breeding habits (605). Thus, animals that spend their time during the breeding season in groups, such as colonial breeders and group foragers, may benefit from sexual indistinguishability (and the benefits should increase with group size) because the sexual competition that results from group living is at some times, at least, disadvantageous to all individuals in the group. For example, competition within a flock creates disturbances that lower the efficiency of food gathering and reduce attentiveness to predators.

A number of selective pressures are envisioned that might act to effect convergence of one sex's phenotype onto that of the other (605). Included among these is a possible preference for indistinguishable mates in response to their greater parental ability (which plays a large role in the 3 species of this study). On the other hand, a counter selective pressure for dimorphism exists among opportunistic breeders, since it allows for rapid pair formation and breeding in unpredictable environments. If one were to be guided by these considerations alone, one would conclude that opportunistic breeding played a greater role in the evolution of Budgerigars and Cockatiels than of Peach-faced Lovebirds, since the former two species are slightly dimorphic sexually, whereas the latter is monomorphic.

["Sexual indistinguishability" implies "the absence of sex-specific, continuously displayed characteristics perceived by conspecifics during some stage of the life cycle of a species" (605). "Sexual monomorphism" is descriptive of an overall similarity in appearance but does not specify indistinguishability. Of 151 monogamous species examined with respect to appearance and social structure, 52 were classified as sexually indistinguishable, 32 as barely distinguishable, and 67 as distinguishable. Of the 52 indistinguishable species, 47 were colonial breeders and/or flock feeders during the breeding season, while of the 67 clearly dimorphic species, 64 were territorial or solitary (605).]

FIRST KNOWN BREEDINGS---PROBABLY OPPORTUNISTIC BREEDERS IN THE WILD. Peach-faced Lovebirds doubtless are the most widely bred and highly domesticated species of the genus, because of the readiness with which they come into breeding condition and nest (834). They have almost as long a history of domestication as do Budgerigars. According to Prestwich, the first recorded breeding was by Brehm at the Berlin Aquarium in 1869, the same worker who was the first to record the carrying of nesting materials thrust between the rump feathers (see 12, 27, 104). The first known British breeding was by Cronkshaw in 1895, and Peach-faced Lovebirds must have been bred almost annually since the turn of the century. The confined birds not only are very easily bred, they breed more or less continuously.

The continuous breeding of confined Peach-faced Lovebirds strongly suggests that, like Cockatiels and Budgerigars, they are opportunistic breeders in the wild. In other words, they probably nest when circumstances are favorable, and not only according to the season (27). In this connection, the breeding seasons of birds in arid African regions, though tied to the rainfall, generally are less dependent upon it than in Australia, being more or less regular and related to the seasonal changes in neighboring mesic areas (598). However, in the driest parts of Namibia, some birds are known to nest after rain, no matter the time of the year (see G.L. Maclean, 1966, 1971 in 312). Their dependence on rainfall seems to be less dramatic, though, and the irregularity of their breeding, less pronounced than in central Australia (312). I found it virtually impossible to discourage breeding in the conditions under which I kept my mated pairs of all 3 species (as discussed in subsequent chapters).

DUETTING. An interesting correlation between the behavior and ecology of lovebirds is the singing of duets by mated pairs. Much of the song of birds living in climatic conditions that are uncertain--typically caused by erratic rainfall--is related to the preservation of the pair bond, rather than the defense of territory (109). The ability to initiate breeding on the first sign that food supplies are about to become favorable, such as when rains begin, depends on pairing having existed beforehand.

This is where the function of duetting comes into play, since it seems to maintain and consolidate the pair bond. Duetting is found in all birds in all regions where rainfall is irregular or uncertain, such as Mexico, parts of Australia, and equatorial Africa. Thus, the existence of duetting illustrates the close integration between the nature of a bird's activities and its habitat (109).

NEST LOCATION. Unlike most parrots, which simply oviposit in essentially empty cavities, Peach-faced Lovebirds sometimes build elaborate cup-shaped nests in crevices of cliffs, holes in trees, and suitable sites in buildings. They thereby convert places otherwise quite unsuitable for most parrots of their size into dry, warm, enclosed, smooth-shaped quarters (27). When exploring possible nesting sites, they are able to "walk" up vertical surfaces, such as a cliff, using flapping wings for support and propulsion (see 835).

But the birds also are opportunistic, very often taking over the woven and domed nest chambers of certain weaverbirds (1, 12, 27). No effort is expended to refurbish or add material to these appropriated nests, perhaps because they are rather small inside. This is in contrast to the way they care continually for the nests they build themselves (a trait not unfamiliar to us). Each of these communal nests customarily contains many breeding chambers. Although the lovebirds drive off the prior owners of the appropriated nests, they do not interfere with the weavers' use of the remaining nests.

HIGH NEST-BUILDING DRIVE----HANDLING AND PREPARING NESTING MATERIALS. The drive to build a nest is high throughout the year in the presence of nesting material and a nest site, that is, it is more or less independent of a specific reproductive stage. However, because of conflicting demands on the female's time, the amount of such activity peaks just before and after the period of oviposition, and when the young are developing in the nest. With access to standard-sized nestboxes, the females build a rather well-made, cup-shaped nest in which the eggs are deposited. Any intruding bird is threatened or attacked (3). Lovebirds and their closest relatives, the hanging parrots (genus *Loriculus*), are the only Old World parrots that build nests (3, 4, 79).

Female Peach-faced Lovebirds elaborately handle and prepare nest material (3, 27). The methods employed are both instinctive (also stimulated by implanted estrogen; 440) and brought to perfection by continuous practice (3, 27). In fact, there seems to be a critical period, sometime before the age of 6 months, during which the birds must have material with which to practice stripping, otherwise they never achieve the ability to cut normal strips (440). Similarly, if their rump feathers are shaved before they have been through a nesting cycle, their subsequent tucking behavior never becomes normal (3).

The female Peach-faced Lovebird first cuts green bark, fresh palm or bamboo leaves, or grass (or any other available nesting material) into straight, 2-6-cm-long strips of uniform width, "with almost postage-stamp-like elegance." She does this by means of a serial hole-punching action of the upper and lower portions of her bill (3, 12). Then she softens these strips by running them back and forth through her bill several times while chewing on them (27, 138). One end of the strips then is tucked between or under her ruffled (erected) lower back and rump contour feathers for the return flight to the nest. The females of some species of hanging parrots also carry nesting strips in the same manner (see 79). The females of some other species of lovebirds also do so, but not on an exclusive basis (3, 12).

The strips are held in place by a contraction of the muscles that regulate feather mobility, which pulls the feathers together tightly (27). Several strips are tucked before the hen takes off for the nest. Any strips that are dislodged on the return flight are not recovered. Once the hen has the strips of nesting material within the nest, she usually chews and nibbles them until they become soft and pliable. Then she uses them to construct a comfortable, high-sided basin (27).

The habit of carrying nesting materials between the feathers is shared with only a few parrots, including hanging parrots (1, 4). It is believed to represent a primitive trait of all lovebirds that has given way to carrying materials in the bill in other species (3, 12). Most lovebirds that build nests usually use small pieces of material rather than strips and, except for species with white eye-rings, their nests are comparatively primitive (2). [A case of "luxuriance," the condition where hybrids or intergrades exceed the parental forms in characters that do not necessarily confer adaptive superiority, is known in lovebirds. Thus, 7 F_1 hybrids of female *A. roseicollis* x male *A. personata fischeri* consistently cut significantly longer strips of nest material, by a wide margin, than did either parental type (440).]

PRIMARILY HOLE-NESTERS---CONSTANT ADDITIONS TO THE NEST. Although representatives from all 3 parrot families build nests, some, such as the Monk Parakeet, even employing sticks (707, 819), parrots are regarded as being primarily hole-nesters, like woodpeckers. Their nest-building habits presumably arose fortuitously and are unrelated to the similar activities of other birds (4). The fortuitous occurrences that are thought to have given rise to nest building involved chewing on bits of wood, bark, and leaf (which keeps the bill sharp and properly worn down), and preening (which keeps the feathers clean and properly arranged; 3). In fact, some parrots that do not build nests, "accidentally" leave bits of material in their feathers when they start preening directly after chewing. It is suggested that the transport of nesting material may be a primitive feature, since it is known in all groups of parrots (819).

Unlike in many birds, especially among the passerines, Peach-faced Lovebirds do not neglect structural details of the nest after oviposition is completed (101). They make constant additions to the nest during the nesting period (138). Dead young, droppings, and broken eggs, are not removed; they merely are covered with nesting material, and cracks through which light enters are sealed in the same manner (3). Even in the absence of a clutch or brood, the NB is a favored sleeping quarter.

DETERMINATE LAYERS---INCUBATING---ASYNCHRONOUS HATCHING. Unlike many non-parrots, like the House Sparrow and Bobwhite Quail, lovebirds cannot be induced to lay additional eggs by removing eggs as they are oviposited (4). Lovebird clutches usually contain 3-8 eggs (averaging 17.3 x 23.8 mm and 4.24 g; 1,275) and incubation usually lasts 21-24 days. The eggs are incubated solely by the hen. The male often sits at her side in the nest and allofeeds her. He not infrequently spends the entire night with her.

Three to 5 young usually are reared but broods as large as 7 are known (834). Since oviposition usually occurs every other day, and incubation may begin immediately, eggs also tend to hatch every other day. In one view, asynchronous hatching evolved as a mechanism of brood reduction--through selective starvation of late-hatched chicks--in birds that often encounter fluctuating food supplies from season to season; it appears to be common in a number of polygynous species. Following this mode of incubation, only the largest nestlings would be expected to survive in years of food scarcity (218, 224, 314, 954, 1,357).

An extension of this scheme links brood reduction with the laying of an extra egg, to allow for the contingency of an infertile or inviable egg (see 1,106). Another possible selective advantage of asynchronous hatching is that it allows a reduction of peak energy requirements for the brood (115). It also has been suggested that hatching asynchrony minimizes the consequences of nest failures that result from predation (812). Thus, young from the 1st eggs to be laid may escape nest predation that occurs late in the nestling period. The minimizing of losses from predation is most likely to apply when food is in adequate supply (813).

In a quite different interpretation, hatching asynchrony is regarded as an epiphenomenon engendered by (1) the conservative nature of the hormonal mechanisms that govern oviposition and incubation, and (2) selection for the potential to control clutch size. Within this paradigm (which applies only to species in which the female parent incubates), most birds are expected to begin incubation after the laying of the penultimate egg, irrespective of clutch size; the behavior is regarded as being independent of the advantages or disadvantages of the resultant hatching patterns. Hatching asynchrony then is predicted, regardless of the reproductive strategy. The implication of this analysis is that birds that evolve survivalist strategies will do so by making adjustments in the feeding or provisioning of offspring, rather than through the elimination of hatching asynchrony (1,106).

ALLOFEEDING THE NESTLINGS---NIGHT FEEDING----GROOMING AND SCRATCHING. The hatchlings are said to be allofed almost immediately by the hen. Partially-digested, or merely softened, food, regurgitated from the crops of their parents, comprise the diet (see pp. 740 *et seq.* for details). Feedings occur while the young are lying on their backs, bellies, or sides. At first, the chicks only utter soft "peeps," but it is not long before fairly well-developed young are clamouring loudly for food. Based upon the same evidence as for Budgerigars, namely that Peach-faced Lovebird chicks can be heard soliciting for food during the night, it has been suggested that they are allofed at night (834; not observed in this study).

While still in the nest, the chicks groom themselves and each other (sometimes even before feathers have developed), and are also allogroomed by the parents. Interestingly, the nestlings are said to scratch their heads at first by reaching their legs forward under their wings, but to change to scratching by reaching up and over the wing upon fledging (3). The only instances that I noted of chicks scratching their heads, occurred in 16-, 19-, and 25-day-old chicks; the 1st scratched under the wing, the latter 2 over it. But the reverse sequence has been reported in the development of 2 species of water thrushes (*Seirus*; see 957). Also of interest in this connection is the fact that lovebirds also scratch the bill by bringing the legs over the wing, but clean the feet with the bill by bringing them under the wing (1,351).

FLEDGING--JUVENILE PAIRING--SEXUAL MATURITY--RENEWED PARENTAL BREEDING. After 35-43 days, when they begin to venture from the nest, the young are already fully feathered. Like the fledging young of most hole-nesters, they are capable of strong, sustained flight at this time (105). These fledged young return to the nest frequently during the day and roost there during the night.

Just as in colonies in the wild, young birds, including broodmates, may form pairs as soon as they are independent of their parents, even at about 2 months of age, while still in juvenal feathers (3, 4). Sexual maturity is reached at about 80-120 days, though some females do not begin to nest until well over a year old. The adult feathers develop at about 4 months of age. It is not unusual for the parents to begin breeding again, before the young have left the nest.

SEXING

A PROBLEM EVEN FOR EXPERTS---THE PELVIC BONE TEST. Sexing juvenile Peach-faced Lovebirds can be a problem even for experts. The skillful stripping of nesting material by females would be a sure mark of identification if all females became expert at this as juveniles. Some females, however, take many months to learn to strip. But even an inexperienced female attempting to strip gives a far more convincing performance than a male of the same age. However, females may not even begin to try stripping until they are old enough to breed. Exceptions occur when the young copy the stripping activities of their mothers or, sometimes, their fathers.

The pelvic bone test is fairly reliable when the birds--even juveniles --are tested in a standard posture, the most favorable of which is perching upright. It is based on the fact that in the majority of birds neither the ilium nor the ischium meets ventrally in a symphysis, so that the pelvic outlet is not ringed by bone (338). The resulting space between the thin, needle-like pubic bones or pubes (and the distance of each from the rear of the sternum) is larger in females than in males, increasing and becoming more flexible during the breeding season. This appears to be an adaptation for oviposition. [It is of interest in this connection that in species in which the pelvis of the female is compressed dorsoventrally (narrow and flattened), the eggs tend to be elongated (as in grebes), whereas those species in which the pelvis is deep (such as gulls and raptors) lay eggs that are more nearly spherical in shape (622).]

In this test, a lightly constrained bird perching on a finger of one hand is tested with the tip of the small finger of the other hand. One gently feels the abdomen just in front of the vent. There, immediately beneath the skin, one contacts the two relatively sharp free ends of the pubic bones. In the female, these free ends much more nearly straddle the tip of the small finger than in the male. It is cautioned, however, that the pubic bones of some hens that are out of breeding condition may be very close together, while those of some adult breeding males are as wide apart as those of young hens coming into breeding condition (834).

FEMALE DOMINANCE---SPREAD TAIL FEATHERS. The most convenient method may be one to which H.H. Jacobsen has called attention (see 27, 834). Among mated pairs, it was noticed that the hen characteristically tends to advertise her sexual dominance by keeping her tail feathers slightly spread; the males signal their submissive state relative to that of their mates by keeping their tail feathers tightly compacted. Although this is a constant feature of lovebird social behavior, it is not 100% reliable, even in mated birds, unless the birds are habituated to the presence of the observer. The test is less reliable for juveniles. [For the most complete discussion of sexing methods, see 27.]

INTERACTIONS WITH ONE ANOTHER AND HUMANS

MOST POPULAR LOVEBIRD---EXTREMELY SOCIABLE---COLOR MUTATIONS. Confined lovebirds have very engaging, expressive personalities and very colorful, lively, playful behavior, including comical antics and acrobatics (8). They are very hardy and long-lived. Peach-faced Lovebirds are the most popular species, requiring but a minimum of care and space. They are extremely sociable and will live and breed very well in a large community. The total number of combined color mutations now bred in Peach-faced Lovebirds can be second only to those of Budgerigars (27).

TALKATIVE---ACTIVE---REQUIRE LITTLE ATTENTION. Although they do not become habituated nor acquire speech as easily as Budgerigars or Cockatiels (see pp. 276, 277), a well-habituated lovebird is much more entertaining. The birds are very easily hand fed and make delightful companions from time of acquisition. "If you want a talkative, active, beautiful little bird that lives happily with virtually no attention, the lovebirds are for you" (8). [But the hand-reared bird rarely, if ever, learns to talk.] A lively relationship is carried on between 2 birds (just as between 2 kittens), regardless of sex.

Phillips gives an accurate, colorful description of some of their vocalizations. "...a peculiar jumble made up of a prolonged series of squeaks, chips, shrieks, chitters and warbling notes that the birds give for minutes at a time. The ‘song’ was usually performed by birds that were otherwise quietly perched. Often they were fluffed or almost ruffled.... and most often had their eyes half-closed or closed. Despite this slumberous look the notes were exceedingly loud, and the birds bobbed, bowed, and jerked with the effort. It gave the general impression (except for volume!) of subsong...." (1,283).

AGGRESSIVE AND PUGNACIOUS----SPITEFUL, PERHAPS EVEN VINDICTIVE. Aside from the fact that lovebirds, in general, are very destructive to woodwork, the only difficulty with keeping Peach-faced Lovebirds is that, despite being sociable, they are aggressive, with very pugnacious, and even fierce, temperaments. They are best kept to themselves, as they ordinarily cannot be trusted with other birds, sooner or later killing or maiming them (7, 8, 27). Generally speaking, they should not be housed with Budgerigars or Cockatiels; they can harass even a Blue and Gold Macaw (*Ara ararauna*), a bird many times their size (8). Single, unmated Peach-faced Lovebirds generally should not be allowed to remain in a breeding colony; an unmated female, for example, will try to enter the NB of a brooding female, and perhaps kill her or the young (787).

Several workers have gone so far as to characterize Peach-faced Lovebirds as being "spiteful" (7, 104, 787, 834), and Rutgers also refers to "spiteful" and "bad-natured" Budgerigar hens (138). Students of animal behavior would be inclined to challenge such descriptions (where the term "spiteful" is used to refer to an emotional state, as opposed to its other use to refer to effects on fitness; see 140), because the observers attribute motives to the birds that generally are regarded as being limited to humans. But I not only endorse this characterization, I would go further. I have observed Peach-faced Lovebird behavior that appears to merit the characterization, "vindictive."

BITING STRONGLY INHIBITED. Peach-faced Lovebirds have developed strong inhibitions against biting each other, and such attacks ordinarily are confined to the toes (3). However, much more serious aggression--"fierce fighters among themselves"--is known (27, 104, 141, and Chaps. 3 and 5); breeding birds, not only do not tolerate, they will kill unrelated birds with which they are housed (138). Accordingly, it is not advisable to house strangers together. This is particularly ill-advised if one bird is in its home enclosure and the other is new to it, or if one bird is an adult and the other is a young stranger. But, as we shall see, in some circumstances, even a younger sibling of another brood, who is not a stranger, can be in mortal danger (see pp. 647, 648, **Titus Severely Injured**).

ENCLOSURE SHARING. Whenever two or more Peach-faced Lovebirds are to be housed together, the birds should be brought together for the first time in an enclosure unfamiliar to all of them, or a young bird should be given the advantage of its home enclosure. In very special circumstances, Peach-faced Lovebirds will get along with both Budgerigars and Cockatiels. But these associations must be cultivated beginning with young juvenile or fledgling lovebirds in enclosures that favor the movements or numbers of the other birds, or involve "well-acquainted" colony members.

Cyrano, a male lovebird, whose courtship behavior and mating are described in Chapter 3, was housed for months with 4 Budgerigars; Flavia and Zenobia, 2 of his younger sisters, annoyed Cockatiels in only minor ways when allowed to visit frequently with them. Moreover, their oldest brother, Jagatai, was housed with 4 Cockatiels for many weeks after the colony was transferred to the laboratory. After that, he was housed for months with 2 of them, Carmen and Cosimo. He was dominant but very tolerant. He only occasionally "bothered" them, and then usually only when they were copulating (see pp. 413, 414, **Attacks during Copulation**). During a span when Carmen was ovipositing, however, she aggressively repelled and vehemently attacked Jagatai. Thus, even a Peach-faced Lovebird retreats under attack by a breeding Cockatiel.

Still later, the Peach-faced Lovebirds, Jagatai and his mate, Aspasia, lived harmoniously for weeks with the young, mated Cockatielian pair, Kirsten and Rimski. I eventually terminated this arrangement when, after a squabble, I detected Aspasia with a mouthful of Kirsten's feathers. After that, for several weeks, I housed a juvenile pair of lovebirds from the 5th brood of Cassandra and Cyrus (see Table 4) with both Kirsten and Rimski and a young pair of Budgerigars (Hepheistus and an unnamed female).

FAMILIAL BATHING. Whereas flighted lovebird pairs might be occupied with other activities and overlook or ignore a large bowl of water during flighting, quite a different situation usually prevailed when a family of 4 or more individuals were flighted (for example, Petra and Ramses and 5 offspring; see pp. 728, 729). On such occasions, when one member of the family chanced upon the bowl of water and bathed by head ducking (see p. 184, **Bathing by "Head-Ducking"**), the others often joined in, perching together around the rim of the bowl and casting water far and wide.

PART 5

THE COLONIAL SITUATION

COLONIAL BEHAVIOR. The appealing traits of Budgerigars, Cockatiels, and lovebirds are not appreciated fully until one experiences their company in a colonial situation, specifically when one has them all housed within sight and sound of one another. In this situation, the colony, like a flock, takes on an identity through its behavior as a whole. To me, the greatest pleasure of the birds' presence comes in the late morning, afternoon, and evening, times when members of the colony take to engaging in choruses of 'contented' warbling.

In this group singing, most or all of the lovebirds are sounding their most attractive warbling notes, with members of pairs usually responding to one another, and sometimes all in concert. At the same time, the Budgerigars also are sounding their most melodious and soothing subdued warbles. Sometimes the male Cockatiels also join in. The appeal of the combination of these sounds is so great that one is more than usually reluctant to take leave of the birds at such times. The circumstances provided by colonial housing of the birds may have been a contributing factor to the relative ease with which I was able to breed all 3 species in "transparent" NBs and/or on the enclosure floors or in open nestbowls.

'WELCOMING' CHORUS. But leaving such an appealing ensemble also has its reward. For, on my return, the key no sooner turns in the lock than there arises a chorus of 'welcoming' whistles from the Cockatiels and chirps from the lovebirds and Budgerigars, as would gladden any heart. The lovebirds often joined into the chorus of "watch-dog" whistles and chirps of the Cockatiels with chirps of their own. Without the contributions of the Budgerigars, the first chorus referred to above would lose much of its charm, as also would the 'welcoming' chorus without the contributions of the Cockatiels. A chorus of whistles and chirps also usually was set off every morning, when I picked up the tray of water bowls and departed to clean and refill them.

A REMOVED OR LOOSE BIRD, OR OPEN DOOR, EXCITES THE ENTIRE COLONY. The colonial situation also leads to interesting expressions of excitement and anticipation, and reveals the great and constant alertness of the birds to the presence and activities of one another. When a Cockatiel is removed from its enclosure and handled, or merely is allowed to perch at an open enclosure door, all of the other Cockatiels immediately begin to whistle excitedly. If the Cockatiel is flighted in the room, the other Cockatiels set up a great din of whistling and hooting, and clamber about on the front faces of the enclosures, seeking to get out.

The lovebirds usually enter vigorously into this excitement with their shrieks. A similar situation prevails if a lovebird is removed or allowed to perch in an open enclosure doorway, particularly if it is a fledgling or juvenile. All of the other lovebirds begin to shriek, but the Cockatiels do not always participate. Virtually the only way to restore tranquility is to rehouse the bird. Phillips noted the same effect when a Peach-faced Lovebird was loose in his aviary: "then a great outburst of wing beats and chitters arose from all the birds in the room, and the displays were intensified by the residents of any cage the stray neared or alighted on" (1,283). If all the Cockatiels are out, the lovebirds become fairly quiet, since they no longer are being "set off" by the whistles of still-housed Cockatiels. Often such excitement as described above is elicited merely by opening and fastening open an enclosure door, or even a side-pane, of a lovebird enclosure, without an occupant exiting or even approaching the exit.

EASILY PANICKED. A very great deal of caution must be exercised when a family of birds is housed in quarters of modest dimensions, and when several enclosures containing families are in close proximity. The unexpected sight of any large object --a paper bag, a book, a clipboard--can panic the birds, especially the Cockatiels, and unsettle the entire colony. Similarly, fast movements--turning a page, turning one's head, or raising a book (even at the other end of the room)--can lead to panic.

Any unfamiliar object brought into an enclosure, even a large honey seed-stick or sprig of spray millet, and especially a large seed bell, can start a panic. Members of all 3 species of birds may be panicked by a sheet of paper brought into their enclosures. So, the paper usually must be folded or rolled into an inconspicuous size and cautiously spread on the enclosure floor. These sensitivities and reactions are not specific to parrots or the colonial situation, but only become more severe in colonies; they are characteristic of birds in general (101). The best strategy is to flight birds and make major changes in an enclosure in their absence.

NIGHT FRIGHTS

HEALTHY IN EVENING, DEAD IN MORNING---MOST SEVERE PANICS AT NIGHT. Boosey has called attention to cases in which birds that were in seeming perfect health in the evening are found dead the following morning, presumably from extreme fright. Although external lesions are conspicuous by their absence (454), such birds have extensive bruising on the skull, as revealed by autopsies. [Apparent hemorrhage in the skull, however, is a common postmortem artifact arising from capillary rupture consequent to right-heart failure (141, 450).] Extreme fright also may cause death through increasing the blood pressure to so marked a degree that the aorta or a thin-walled atrium ruptures (23). The causes that are suggested are the panicking of the birds by sudden noise, mice running along the perches, a cat jumping on top of the aviary, or the sudden light from the headlights of a passing car (138, 454).

In the case of my colony, the most severe panics occurred at night. These were set off by even very mild earthquakes, by an accidental fall of a bird or other object, or by any other uncommon disturbance. When this happened, every bird in the colony panicked and flapped about frantically. Mobile young in nestboxes even recoiled off the walls and the roof. Once birds lose their bearings, the panic feeds on itself. Every new struggle of one bird panics all the others. The quickest way to restore tranquility is to turn on the lights. Speaking to the birds reassuringly also is helpful.

NO FRONT COVERS---MAINTAIN DIM NIGHT-LIGHT. The danger of panics is an important reason for not covering enclosures at night. When the enclosures were covered, the panic was likely to continue until the covers were removed and there was adequate light. But removing the covers, in and of itself (as well as restoring them), can further panic recently panicked parrots. So, for colonies, at least, enclosure covers are dispensed with. The best, and quite adequate, solution to this problem is to keep a dim light on at night. It must be sufficiently bright for the birds to recover their bearings quickly after a panic has been precipitated.

DAYTIME DISTURBANCES CAUSE EERIE SILENCE. Incidents that panic a colony in the dark may have the opposite effect in the light. A food tray falling during the day results in an eerie total silence, as do many other unexpected sounds, whether familiar or not, for example, a sneeze. My mere act of standing up, and my walking over near to a noisy colony, usually results in an eerie silence. No matter how habituated the birds have become, in the colonial situation they retain the cautions and responses of wild birds. The daytime responses depend very much on the mood and activities of the colony. One notable exception is a jarring or other movement of the enclosures, which almost always leads to panic; another is bringing large objects near to or into an enclosure.

COMMUNAL FORAGING BY COCKATIELS. A most interesting example of an activity that keeps the Cockatiels on edge is "community foraging" on the enclosure floor. Cockatiels on the floor, in numbers, become extremely sensitive to movements and sounds, no matter how well habituated they may be, consonant with the extreme timidity of wild birds foraging on the ground (see p. 227, last sentence). We also noted above that wild Cockatiels take temporary refuge in dead trees when they are disturbed during their foraging. One sees the equivalent response in a confined group. If the group is foraging, no matter how intently, I need only talk to them--even just one word--or turn my head (in any way but very slowly) and look at them, and they are likely to go scurrying up the sides of the enclosure to the top perches. Needless to say, a greater disturbance precipitates an even more marked exodus.

If only 1 or 2 Cockatiels are foraging, especially if they are well habituated, I sometimes can move and talk freely without disturbing them. With 3 birds foraging, the situation usually is touch and go, but again it depends to a large extent on the degree to which the individuals have been habituated.

MANDIBLE GNASHING. Another activity that achieves prominence in the colony but that otherwise might pass unnoticed, is the rubbing together or gnashing of the mandibles. This is very much in evidence after the lights are turned out for the night, when a chorus of dull, rasping mandible-gnashing sounds often is to be heard from most colony members. Lovebirds are known to hone the blunt end of the lower mandible by rasping it against the corrugated inside of the tip or hook of the upper mandible, probably to keep the latter in good working order. Because the hook is laminated with alternate bands of hard and soft keratin, this grinding action produces a file-like surface (see 3, 819). Additionally, continued abrasion of the constantly growing horny material enclosing the bill-tip organ is necessary if it is not to overgrow the openings of the touch papillae, and the mandible gnashing that accompanies this may be typical of all parrots (801).

Part 6. VOCAL MIMICRY AND MANIPULATION

ARTICULATING ABILITY

Though birds generally utter far more complex sounds than do mammals (127), they are poor at imitating sounds that are not determined innately (but not the sounds made by other birds) and are not distinguished by their ability to learn manipulations (39, 488). Though parrots generally have harsh, unmelodic call notes, their unusual abilities to imitate the human voice and perform manipulations, and their adaptability to training have been among their main attractions. Further, the best mimics among parrots are said to be those that are exceptionally affectionate (101, 109).

The talking ability of the African Gray Parrot, perhaps the best mimic among parrots as regards quality or fidelity, is mentioned in ancient Greek and Roman writings, for example, by Ctesias, around 400 B.C. (24, 109, 127, 174). Although the African Gray is not generally regarded as having an outstanding repertoire, at least one astonishing exception is known (184). Macaws (*Ara*) also may become gifted speakers and have pleasant, soft, speaking voices (439). Only recently has mimicry by parrots in the wild been recorded, for example, by Australian King Parrots (*Aprosmictus scapularis*) and Palm Cockatoos (1,056). One should bear in mind in connection with mimicry that a bird need not reproduce the precise waveform of a human's sound, but only an approximation of the amplitudes of the several harmonics, which can be accomplished with an infinite number of other waveforms (480, 498).

Parrots apparently owe much of their ability to mimic to a highly-developed, specialized organ, the syrinx (vocal organ), and a fleshy, muscular tongue that can protrude from its resting place within the lower mandible, be pressed against the palate, and shunt vocal energy through the nose (as does Man during nasal speech). By means of its intrinsic muscles, the tongue can coordinate lingual action during phonation, altering the volume and shape of the oral cavity and articulating crudely, especially during soft, mumbling vocalizations (155, 441, 1,284). In this connection, it has been suggested that the large size and unique specialization of the nucleus intermedius of the hypoglossal nerve in parrots is correlated with the large mass and complexity of their lingual musculature, rather than with any syringeal specialization (see 441).

The syrinx, as in songbirds, is controlled by intrinsic muscles and well-defined brain nuclei that can exploit its complex structure. The former directly alter syringeal configuration, greatly increasing the independence of syringeal components and simplifying the control of sound modulation (258). In particulars, however, different species may use different techniques of sound production and modulation. The anterior chambers in the vocal tracts of birds are not as complex as those of Man, although, in theory, it should be possible to lengthen and shorten the avian trachea by means of extrinsic muscles (207).

NEURAL CONTROL OF SOUND PRODUCTION

AVIAN VOCALIZATIONS are controlled by a highly localized, interconnected system of neurons. The following pathways are traversed in the innervation of the muscles of the trachea and syrinx (largely after Nottebohm; 241). A major auditory projection from Field L of the caudal medial neostriatum abuts on the borders of a relatively large telencephalic nucleus, the hyperstriatum ventralis pars caudalis (see also treatment beginning on p. 348, **The Avian Brain**, et seq.). In the sense that neurons of this nucleus show properties that would be expected if it were involved in the perception and production of learned vocalizations, this nucleus might be functionally analogous to Broca's area for speech control in the frontal lobe of Man. Two areas adjacent to Field L project directly into the caudal hyperstriatum ventrale and to the borders of a smaller telencephalic nucleus, the robustus archistriatalis, which also is involved in song production. Both the nucleus robustus archistriatalis and the hyperstriatum ventralis pars caudalis connect with the cranial motor neurons that innervate the syrinx.

[Field L is the tonotopically organized primary auditory projection area of the telencephalon, which consists of a map of isofrequency contours oriented approximately perpendicular to the layering. It represents chiefly the spectral contrast of calls, not the spectral peak, and it enhances contrast by suppressing sidebands. Thus, even though some species-specific calls of Helmeted Guinea Fowl (*Numida meleagris*) contain frequencies extending over a range much wider than that of the tonotopic area of Field L, they activate only restricted frequency bands within it. Frequency-modulated signals produce extremely high contrast representations in the tonotopic map of Field L (1,205).]

THE NUCLEUS MAGNOCELLULARIS OF THE ANTERIOR NEOSTRIATUM comprises another part of the song control system (see 493). For example, this nucleus seems to be involved critically in song learning by juvenile Zebra Finches but not in the maintenance of song by adult birds. The experiments that led to these findings not only demonstrated the existence of a neural region that is important for song learning, as opposed to maintaining the production of an already learned song, they also revealed perhaps the sole known instance in which the lesioning of a specific brain region is effective only during part of the period of development of a learned behavior. Since a high proportion of the cells in the nucleus magnocellularis in adult male Zebra Finches accumulate androgens, the findings also suggest that hormonal action is involved in song learning. It seems likely that the nucleus magnocellularis is involved in the formation of an auditory-motor transcription (and less likely that it acts as a conduit for auditory information relevant to song-related feedback), but only during a restricted period of development, since it clearly is not on the main vocal motor output path in adulthood (1,269; see also 747 for a probable role of estradiol).

In birds that learn their songs, such as the Canary, the size of the hyperstriatum ventralis pars caudalis changes with the season and song capability (partly controlled by gonadal hormones). This nucleus projects to the center of the smaller forebrain nucleus, the robustus archistriatalis, which has been likened, in terms of connectivity, to layer V of the mammalian motor cortex. The latter nucleus goes through similar, though lesser, seasonal changes. Nottebohm has hypothesized that these seasonal volume changes reflect cyclical growth and retraction of dendritic segments and, consequently, increases and decreases in the number of synapses, and that these changes correlate with facilitation of the learning of new motor coordinations for song in the spring, and loss (forgetting) of song elements in the fall (see 1,269). [In the Ring Dove, which does not learn its songs, the basic components of the vocal control system include at least one forebrain, one midbrain, and a medullary nucleus, each of which has a counterpart in the Canary (751).]

[In connection with changes in nuclei in the avian central nervous system, many studies of mammals have revealed effects of differential environmental exposures or treatment. Thus, deprivation of visual stimulation causes a variety of changes in occipital cortex, including reduced diameters of cells, altered electrical responses, decreased numbers of dendritic spines, lesser weight and thickness, and differences in enzymatic activity. "Compensatory" changes may occur in other cortical regions. Differential experience with cagemates and with stimulus objects also lead to a variety of modifications in the rodent brain, particularly in the cerebral cortex, including changes in weight and thickness of the cerebral cortex, number of glial cells, and size of the perikarya. However, it has not yet been possible to establish functional relationships between the cerebral and the behavioral effects of differential experience in mammals (1,249).]

THE NUMBER OF NEURONS in the nucleus robustus in male Zebra Finches is approximately twice that in females and the soma diameters and dendritic field sizes are larger. Both the nuclei magnocellularis and robustus (and a tear-shaped region within the parolfactory lobe) in Canaries are several times larger in adult males (which sing) than in adult females (which do not; 1,048). The former nucleus undergoes a sharp decrease in volume and a 50% loss of neurons between 25 and 53 days of age in Zebra Finches, even though other song control nuclei (n. robustus and hyperstriatum ventrale pars caudale) are increasing in gross nuclear volume at the same time. One possible explanation for this phenomenon is that extensive neuronal death is occurring. Another is that the neurons involved in the final song pattern redifferentiate and migrate outside the borders of the nucleus. Both suggested mechanisms normally are features only of embryonic or early postnatal development (1,269).

Furthermore, the total volumes of the hyperstriatum ventrale pars caudalis and nucleus robustus of Canaries correlate with the number of syllables in their songs and with the size of their song repertoires, and in Marsh Wrens (*Telmatodytes palustris*) they also correlate with the size of the song repertoires (see 1,048, 1,269). These are the first discoveries of direct relationships between variation in the volume of a localized neural substrate and the complexity (or amount) of the specific learned behavior that it controls. On the other hand, in the White-browed Robin Chat (*Cossypha neuglini*), a species in which females participate in vocal duets with males, there is less sexual dimorphism in the volume of vocal control regions than in Canaries and Zebra Finches (see 1,269).

SELECTIVE ATTRITION. In the case of the male Swamp Sparrow (*Zonotrichia georgiana*), a phase is exhibited (prior to the development of the adult performance of stabilized song) in which their vocalizations contain up to 5 times as many song types as in the mature state. During the intervening period, the components of the adult song are derived from this enlarged repertoire by an actively selective process of attrition. This has been analogized with the concurrently occurring neuronal cell death and related regressive phenomena during development; in both cases there is an initial overproliferation of units followed by their subsequent cell death.

COMPARING MOTOR OUTPUT WITH AN AUDITORY MEMORY. These phenomena are thought to represent a general principle underlying the epigenesis of both behavioral and nervous systems (1,291). This progressive development of song frequently has given rise to the concept that the process entails a phase of motor learning during which auditory feedback is used to match the sounds of the species' song with the motor (articulatory) patterns necessary to pronounce these sounds. Several experiments have shown that young birds must be able to hear their own incipient vocalizations in order to be able to compare their motor output with an already established auditory memory or template of song (see 1,269).

[Post-hatching treatment of female Zebra Finches with estrogen masculinizes both their undirected singing and the song regions of their brains, but not their courtship activities (including directed song) or copulation (see 741). Both alpha-androgenic and estrogenic hormones interact in the control of the sexually dimorphic development of the neural song-control system of this species and in its control in the adult. These relationships and similar findings in Canaries suggest that these two classes of hormones interact at all stages of life to modulate singing behavior in oscine songbirds (though hormonal control may be context specific; see 745).]

POSSIBLE SELECTIVE RESPONSE. The smaller nucleus, the robustus archistriatalis, in turn, projects via the occipito-mesencephalic tract to the midbrain dorsomedial nucleus of the intercollicular region and to an even smaller pool of hypoglossal motor neurons. The latter give rise to the tracheosyringeal branch of the hypoglossus nerve, which innervates the muscles in question. Units in this nerve and its motor nucleus are known to respond to pure tones and various naturally occurring song elements in anesthetized adult male Zebra Finches, reflecting auditory activity in the telencephalic vocal control nuclei. It appears possible that motor neurons in this nucleus respond selectively to auditory stimuli that are similar to the sounds produced when the units themselves fire during vocalization.

LATERALIZATION. Whereas there are massive ipsilateral projections between the nuclei described in the foregoing, only weak contralateral projections have been reported, suggesting that each side of the hyperstriatum ventralis pars caudalis exerts predominant control over the ipsilateral half of the syrinx; cross-talk also must occur, though, because the song elements on the two sides are rigidly coordinated. Lesion experiments with Canaries suggest that the left hyperstriatum ventralis pars caudalis normally prevents its right counterpart from acquiring a major role in song control, but that destruction of it frees the right side from this constraint. The left side of the syrinx seems to produce the vast majority of elements of a song, and because the contral connections of the vocal-control system seem to be overwhelmingly ipsilateral, the system would appear to be lateralized throughout (see 241, 1,250, 1,269).

Some recent studies by McCasland (1,252) employed two novel techniques for further investigations of asymmetry in vocal control; neither technique involved neural lesions in the vocal control system. One study, involved the recording of neuronal discharge patterns in the hyperstriatum ventralis pars caudalis during sound production; it indicated that the right side is not a silent partner of the left side in the control of song, as both sides are active during singing and give surprisingly similar discharge patterns. The other study involved the use of bronchial plugs to block airflow past the corresponding tympanic membrane; it was concluded from this study that all of the qualitative features of song syllables--duration, frequency, interval, modulation, complex elements, and two voices--can be produced independently by either half of the syrinx. Though McCasland's results are not conclusive, Nottebohm's model of asymmetry in syringeal sound production and its neural control may require modifications to account for the non-concordance (see also 1,250).

ONLY CONSPECIFIC TOTAL INTELLIGIBILITY? Nottebohm's findings led him to suggest that avian song may be totally intelligible only to to an animal with a neural system that is capable of producing the same vocalizations (493). One recalls, in this connection, experiments with hybrid crickets, which suggest that the male neural circuit that generates the courtship song pattern is specified by the same genes as the female circuit that recognizes the song; they may even be identical circuits (see R.J. Hoy and R.C. Paul, 1973, in 1,030). Also pertinent is the proposal that the perception and production of speech sounds in Man are inextricably interrelated (see 1,269).

VOCAL CONTROL IN PARROTS. If asymmetrical neural control of behavior has evolved as an adaptation that facilitates the accomplishment of complex, learned tasks, it is not an essential concomitant. Thus, the Orange-headed Amazon is capable of learning complex vocal sounds, yet there is no difference in the effect produced by sectioning the right as opposed to the left hypoglossal nerve. This can be understood in terms of the fact that the 2 tracheosyringeal nerves in parrots anastomose and exchange motor fibers on the trachea. As a consequence, both tracheosyringeal nerves innervate the syringeal muscles on both sides (1,284). This situation has been confirmed in Budgerigars, in which the recurrens branch of the vagus also appears to send fibers to the syrinx, though they may not be involved in vocal control. Thus, the parrot syrinx apparently lacks the ability to regulate two sound sources independently, and there appears to be no asymmetry at the syringeal level (see 1,250, 1,284).

Furthermore, in Budgerigars, and presumably in all parrots, the projection from the nucleus robustus archistriatalis to the midbrain dorsomedial nucleus of the intercollicular region, and to the hypoglossal motor neurons, is bilateral rather than ipsilateral. This explains the finding that stimulation of the left or right hyperstriatum ventralis pars caudalis of Budgerigars evokes activity bilaterally in the tracheosyringeal nerve, in contrast to the predominantly ipsilateral responses in Canaries and Zebra Finches. In brief summary, there is no evidence for neural asymmetry in vocal control by parrots, though members of some species have an indisputed ability to learn many complex vocalizations (see 1,250 and above and below).

MIMICRY BY OTHER BIRDS. Virtually the only birds other than parrots that can imitate strange sounds are the songbirds (21 families of Passeres or "Oscines;" 28, 43, 45, 396), in most of which cultural inheritance of songs is the rule. Among these, some birds will mimic a wide variety of avian and other sounds, whereas others are limited to learning a small variety of sounds similar to those that normally are uttered by conspecifics; the copying, however, may occur with a greater or lesser degree of accuracy (655). [Vocal development among the suboscines, however, requires no imitation of conspecifics (see 1,128).]

EXTREMELY FINE CONTROL OF THE OSCINE SYRINX is permitted by isolation of its flexible portions and specialization of the functions of intrinsic muscles. Some species have repertoires of hundreds of songs, a few have over 1,000 (see 258). In Marler's words, "The interspecies complexities in bird song exceed what one usually thinks of as limits to the competence of genetic mechanisms" (670). Generally speaking, Oscines have a wider frequency range and more varied kinds of modulation than non-passerines. A remarkable example of interspecific mimicry in the wild is provided by the Marsh Warbler (*Acrocephalus palustris*), individuals of which mimicked an average of 76 other species including a total of 212 different species (see 655). The facility of the Hill Mynah (*Gracula religiosa*) for vocal mimicry is even greater than that of parrots, and comes so close to duplicating human tonal qualities that a listener might be deceived into believing that a person was speaking (439, 480).

A lyrebird (*Menura superba*), living over 19 yr on an Australian farm, could imitate almost any barnyard sound, even chains rattling and a cross-cut saw. A similarly talented Australian Spotted Bowerbird (*Chlamydera maculata*) could imitate wood-chopping, sheep walking through dead branches, etc. (28). Among over 50 mimetic Australian species, the best performers inhabited wooded country and were strongly territorial (see A. J. Marshall, 1950, in 23). There is no other country in which mimicry is so prevalent among birds, perhaps linked, in no small measure, to the varying, challenging climatic conditions (960).

IMPROVISATION appears to be an important source of variety in avian songs, as judged by findings of certain laboratory studies. It has been considered to have a major influence on song development in Dark-eyed Juncos (*Junco hyemalis*). This might also be true of Song Sparrows (*Melospiza* melodia) and Swamp Sparrows, as these species invent syllables even when trained on a variety of models. Although this may account for the great individual variation in the songs of wild Song Sparrows, the extent and role of improvisation in the wild are as yet uncertain (655, 670).

BIOLOGICAL SIGNIFICANCE OF VOCAL MIMICRY

A PHYLOGENETIC TREND. Avian vocal development appears to show a phylogenetic trend from strategies that are independent of auditory input, and in which genetic and other developmental influences predominate, to more open and environmentally dependent vocal ontogenies, in which learning is manifested (426). The possession of the latter properties by parrots is one of several respects, related to the phylogenetic state of development of the central nervous systems, in which parrots are advanced as compared to other relatively primitive types, such as members of the Columbiformes and Galliformes (see also pp. 343-346, 350).

Since with few exceptions, avian vocalizations seem to have evolved for purposes of communication (to announce the presence of predators, to repel rivals, attract mates, stimulate oviposition, etc.), it seems reasonable to conclude that all intervening stages in vocal learning also must have served an adaptive function in communication. Since vocal imitation and vocal learning (as a strategy for vocal development) may have evolved concomitantly, vocal ontogenies that are strictly dependent upon the imitation of other individuals may be considered as secondarily adaptive specializations (426).

WIDESPREAD ENHANCEMENT OF VOCAL DEVELOPMENT USING AUDITORY INPUT. At any rate, regardless of the precise mode of origin of vocal mimicry, there is little cause for surprise over its occurrence. Thus, all experimental studies of song development among songbirds have revealed that juveniles must be exposed to normal adult songs in order for song development to proceed along normal pathways (see 603, 604, 655). Though the juveniles have innate tendencies to learn their species-specific songs, the tendencies are inadequate to develop these songs on their own (1,320). Over 300 avian species are known to modify or enhance their vocal development using auditory information, including feedback (228). For example, imitation plays a crucial role in song development in several wren species (see 544), and song dialects in many species may result from dispersing birds copying their established neighbors' songs (604).

THE SELECTIVITY IN LEARNING SONGS exclusively from individuals with whom they are bonded or can interact (mates, parent-offspring, juvenile-non-conspecific tutor, socially bonded conspecific rivals), by members of some species, finds its counterpart in avian vocal mimicry of Man by birds. Thus, when speech was used as a method of social interaction in controlled experiments with European Starlings, the birds mimicked only the humans who were the actual interactants, rarely mimicking the female spouses of the investigators (211). As in duetting or mimicry by other species (212), European Starling mimicry may function to define particular social relationships.

SOME EXAMPLES suggestive of the biological significance of vocal mimicry are the following. The parasitic Widow Bird (*Tetraeunura fisheri*) sings both species-specific phrases and vocalizations that are learned from the host species (see 1,268). The females of mated pairs of various cardueline finches were found to recognize the flight calls of their mates. Moreover, the flight calls of the members of each mated pair were found to be virtually identical. This indicates that learning and modification of calls by vocal mimicry had occurred, and that it took place well after the birds had reached reproductive age (248, 820). Similar convergence in songs between mates also is known in several duetting species (249, 250). Furthermore, in the majority of songbirds, neighboring males have songs that are more similar to one another's than they are to those of more distant males; males usually respond most vigorously to song that most resembles their own (see 544, 603, 604). In addition, it is believed that specific vocal mimicry plays an important role in the functioning of certain host-parasite systems, as with several viduine finches that learn to sing the songs of their host species (251; see also 426).

Interspecific song mimesis by songbirds in the wild also is known in: European Goldfinches (*C. chloris*), which imitate a wide variety of sympatric species and use the imitations in their advertising songs; Indigo and Lazuli Buntings (*Passerina cyanea* and *P. amoena*, respectively), which regularly imitate one another in a zone of sympatry in Nebraska; Song Sparrows, which mimic other species in both the field and the laboratory; and Lincoln Sparrows (*Melospiza lincolnii*), which mimic sympatric Mountain White-crowned Sparrows in California, possibly learning this mimicry during interspecific aggression (see 712). Lastly, mimicry in a territorial songbird may possibly correlate with lack of competition from conspecifics, "the surplus energy finding outlet in imitation of other sounds in the environment" (960). It has been suggested that large song repertoires may advertise individual fitness (712).

DECEPTIVE MIMICRY. In another category is presumed mimicry, apparently deceptive, of male territorial advertising and defense songs by female Black-headed Grosbeaks (*Pheucticus melanocephalus*) and Eastern Bluebirds. The very infrequent uttering of these male songs by the females in critical situations induces their mates to return to the nest, primed to defend the nest against a non-existent intruding male (509 and ref. therein to E.S. Morton *et al.*, 1978). Another suggested deception is that of a male Village Indigobird (*Vidua chalybeata*) in mimicking a local stud's songs at a vacated call-site. In that way, he may deceive other competing local males and increase his chances of taking over and maintaining the vacated site (603).

PRESUMED VOCAL LEARNING IN NON-PSITTACINES OR NON-OSCINES is known in only a few birds. One example concerns mimicking of a local species by Emerald Toucanets (*Aulacorhynchus prasinus*), another is the occurrence of learned songs in populations of Little Hermit Hummingbirds (*Phaethornis longuemareus*). A 3rd example is that of mimicry among Greater Prarie Chickens (*Tympanuchus cupido*), the Sharp-tailed Grouse (*Tympanuchus* phasianellus), and their hybrids. In the 1st and last examples, the syringes are of the simple type, the configuation of which changes as a unit, with no evidence of the existence of intrinsic syringeal muscles. Hummingbirds, on the other hand, are one of the few groups other than passerines and parrots to possess intrinsic syringeal muscles (258; see 426 for other examples).

Vocal Mimicry and Manipulation by Budgerigars, Cockatiels, and Lovebirds

BUDGERIGARS. It is precisely the ability of Budgerigars to imitate the human voice, and their great adaptability to training, that have made them the most popular confined bird in the world. Their power of mimicry was discovered first during the last part of the 19th century, most probably in Germany. But it is only over the last few decades that this talent has been developed fully (136). Male parrots generally are said to be far superior mimics, but there apparently is no proved sexual difference for Budgerigars (127). However, the males are said to make better pupils, by virtue of being better tempered, more easily habituated, and biting less readily and less hard than do the females (137, 138).

A few birds develop "astounding" vocabularies, sometimes exceeding 100 words (109, 439), and Budgerigars seem to have the best memory for prolonged phrases of sound of any parrot (127). They display marked individual differences in their ability to learn and mimic the human voice. Some start to talk soon after being taken into a household, others may not start for weeks or months; some never succeed (126). Women and young people are the best tutors, because of their clearer, higher voices.

Except for the large parrots, Budgerigars are the best imitators and talkers (5). Though some characterize their voices as hoarse-sounding whispers, at best, others find them to be high and thin (104). Budgerigars readily learn to respond to commands and to perform simple acts, for example, lying on their backs and feigning being dead, opening match boxes, climbing ropes, operating a see-saw, and riding toy cars.

COCKATIELS. Cockatiels of both sexes become quite good talkers and whistlers, although their voices have a somewhat shrill, "reedy" quality, not unlike that of a child with a slight head cold. They can be trained to repeat words and phrases and recite poetry. The males even can be taught to whistle complete bars of simple tunes. Though they may not be able to repeat as many words nor as many different sounds as can Budgerigars, most of the sounds they are able to learn are reproduced with greater fidelity (6, 32, 104, 127, 1,055).

Cockatiels find it very rewarding to manipulate small objects of every description, and will occupy themselves in endless antics with bells, mirrors, musical perches, small chains, etc. They have been taught to open objects with their bills, to turn handles, to open and close small doors, to work small mills with their feet or bills, etc. (127).

LOVEBIRDS. Members of both sexes of Peach-faced Lovebirds are equally vocal. They definitely cannot be considered to be "good talkers" (8); teaching them to talk requires considerable effort. Moreover, their voices are harsh and unpleasing at close range (439) and their shrieks "can be quite excruciating" (138). Habituated individuals have an exceptional talent for learning manipulative feats and have provided many owners with almost endless diversion. Various species of lovebirds now are preferred for trained acts; they walk tightropes, push tiny carriages, climb and descend ladders and ropes, ring bells for rewards, etc.

CHAPTER 2. HOUSING AND CARE

HOUSING

The studies were carried out in two phases insofar as housing and lighting conditions were concerned. In the 1st phase, beginning in 1981, the colony was housed in my living quarters (Fig. 2a), where early morning lighting was provided through windows by external natural dawns, and artificial daytime lighting was discontinued abruptly (referred to as "lights-off"). Only enclosures A-F were employed in the 1st phase. The 2nd phase began on September 22, 1984, when the colony was transferred to the laboratory and housed in an air-conditioned room (Fig. 2b), with only artificial lighting, and with both "dawn" (referred to as "lights-on") and "dusk" (lights-off) occurring abruptly on a fixed schedule. Enclosures A-N were employed during this phase.

ENCLOSURES. In the 1st phase of the study, enclosures A-F (Fig. 1a) were mounted on a 60-cm-high stand, all facing toward north windows. Having the enclosures only 2.1 m to the side of my work-chair (Fig. 2a), made it possible to keep all members of the colony under continual scrutiny. All enclosures were fabricated of iron-wire mesh or hardware cloth. Enclosure A (45 x 60 x 90 cm; 2½ x 5-cm mesh) generally housed Cockatiels, which could stick their heads through its mesh. It contained 7 natural, bark-covered branches of differing diameters (perches of various sizes are desirable to facilitate exercising of the birds' toes).

Enclosures B and C (45-cm cubes) were used to housed all 3 species. Enclosure B was made of 1¼ x 2½-cm mesh and enclosure C of 2½ x 2½-cm mesh. Adult lovebirds and Budgerigars could stick their heads through the latter mesh. Enclosures D (22½ x 35 x 35 cm), E (35 x 40 x 50 cm), and F (25 x 32 x 32 cm) were standard birdcages with vertical wire bars spaced 1 cm apart. All 3 were used to house Budgerigars and lovebirds; the latter housed a pair of Cockatiels in one study. The home perch stood atop enclosure D in the 1st phase of the study. Each of the enclosures, B-F, was supplied with at least one irregular or tapered natural-branch perch up to 3 cm in diameter (which also served to provide wood and bark for chewing). A 10-cm "crawl space" separated enclosures B and C from enclosure A, and a 7½-cm space separated enclosures D and E.

Enclosures G-N were added for the studies in the laboratory. Enclosures G, H, and J (25 x 30 x 38 cm), K (21 x 26 x 30 cm), and M (25 x 40 x 40 cm) also were standard birdcages with vertical bars 1-1¼ cm apart and outfitted in the same manner as enclosures B-F. Enclosure N (45 x 60 x 45 cm, 1¼ x 2½-cm mesh) housed various birds and was outfitted with 4 large perches after the manner of enclosure A. The enclosures in the laboratory were placed on tables 75 cm high, and on top of one another in the arrangements shown in Figs. 1b and 2b, with the home perch on top of enclosure J. NBs (nestboxes) are shown in Fig. 1a but not in Fig. 1b, since, except for the breeding Budgerigar pair, Lucretia and Lysander, in enclosure F, all incubating and brooding at the laboratory was carried out in open nestbowls or on the floors of the enclosures. My work-chair was at a distance of 1-2½ m from the various enclosures.

BEDDING AND ACCESS. The removable base-pans of the enclosures contained coarse wood shavings (#3 sawdust), which were renewed as necessary. Paper toweling often was placed on top of the shavings or wire-mesh bottoms of enclosures that housed Cockatiels and Budgerigars, but not on those housing lovebirds. Enclosure A had a 45-cm-square hinged door. Similar doors on encosures B, C, and N were 22½ cm square.

ILLUMINATION. Until September 22, 1984, a single 15-watt fluorescent lamp, at a distance averaging about 1.2 m (Fig. 2a) illuminated all of the enclosures from the upper front. This provided an illuminance level of from 45 to 80 lux (meter-candles) at the front faces of the various enclosures. At my domicile, this light was turned off manually at from 24:30 h to 01:30 h and turned on manually at from 08:00 h to 09:00 h. This artificial illumination was supplemented by very low level indirect sunlight from two windows (with blinds closed), located as in Fig. 2a, that never exceeded 12 lux. At the laboratory (2.1 x 4.62 m), illumination was provided by 3 banks of 70-watt fluorescent ceiling lamps at locations shown by the arrows in Fig. 2b. These provided an illuminance level of from 160 to 270 lux at the front faces of the various enclosures. The lights were operated automatically on a schedule of 09:30 h to 24:30 h or 02:30 h. I always was present at the time of "lights-on." Nighttime illumination was provided at a level of about 0.1 lux.

ENCLOSURE SHIELDING. Coarse-woven, multi-colored throw mats, of the type often used on automobile seats, or light, white toweling, covered the enclosures on the sides and tops. By leaving open only the fronts and a 15-cm depth of the sides and tops, large parts of the enclosures always were protected from drafts. This is a very important consideration for Budgerigars and Cockatiels, because of their susceptibility to colds, as well as for convalescing birds; even the hardy lovebird is susceptible to colds in a draft. Infrequently, a bird would catch a claw on these mats or toweling, with momentary panic but no other ill effect.

ENRICHMENT OF ENVIRONMENT. To provide a stimulus-rich environment, with objects accessible to the birds' dominant senses (facilitating recreation and exploration), the enclosures contained an assortment of suspended swinging perches, mirrors, spray-millet holders, miniature chains and rings, and bells. Such objects are essential, whether the birds are kept for research, commerce, or companionship. It even is desirable to change and relocate objects in enclosures from time to time to provide novelty. They serve to prevent boredom, which often turns the attentions of birds into unwholesome channels, including self-inflicted wounds (see 127 and 439). Contrary to what one might expect, considering the inquisitiveness of parrots, the ingestion of foreign bodies (parts of the above objects) does not appear to be a common problem (451).

THE DANGER OF SELF-INJURY is heightened by the fact that birds (and also reptiles)--unlike mammals--appear to be relatively insensitive to pain. Exceptions are in areas such as the bill, nares (nostrils), eyes, ears, and vent region. Physical abuse is tolerated in most other areas. For example, birds tolerate skin suturing without any form of local or general anesthesia, and seldom indicate pain by movement or sound (135).

AVOIDANCE OF OBESITY. Obesity is one of the more common problems encountered in confined birds, especially in Budgerigars (463). Dieting often is a valuable method of reducing weight to the normal range. However, birds in richly structured environments, or housed in colonies, are unlikely to become obese, even when unflighted and on unrestricted diets. The many

Enclosure Assemblies

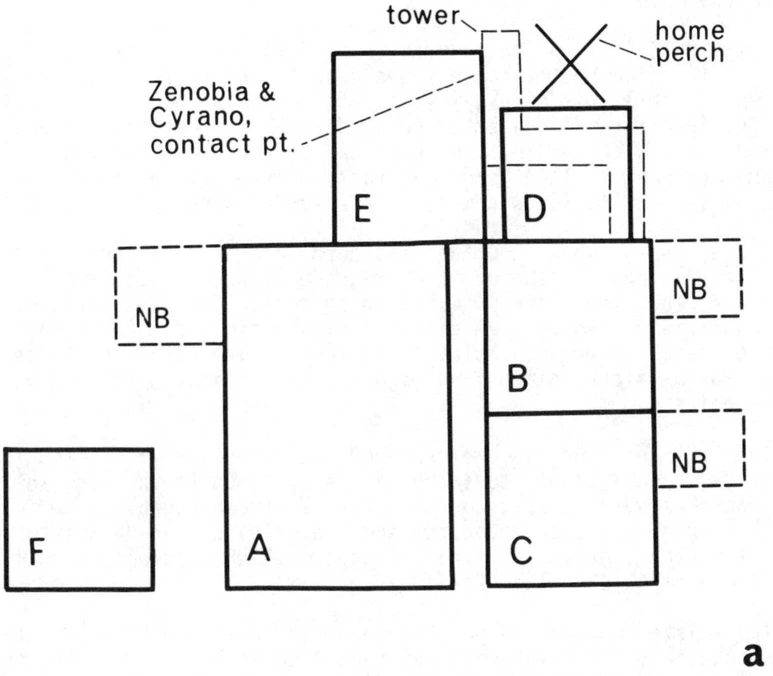

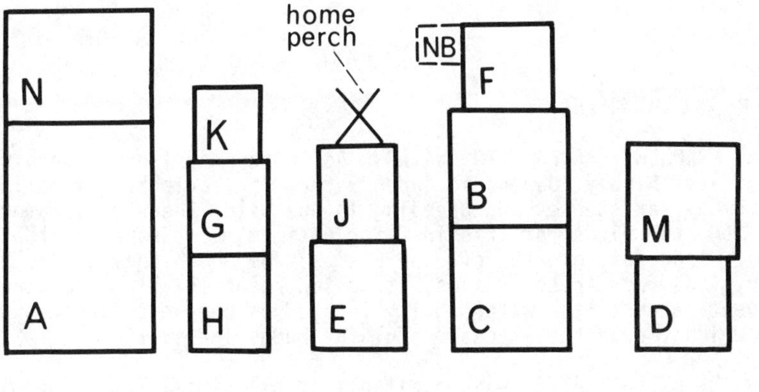

Figure 1

outlets for activity and interest tend to keep them constantly occupied and on the move.

A "HOME PERCH" atop enclosures D or J (a wooden, dowel-and-slat-frame, commercial, wine-bottle holder) was used to return flighted birds to their enclosures. All birds usually alighted on this perch (see p. 296, **Training to Specific Sites**) after being disturbed at another perch. To return a bird to its enclosure, the perch was carried to the vicinity of the enclosure entrance. The bird generally entered its enclosure voluntarily, although several failures sometimes preceded a successful transfer.

NESTBOXES (NBs) were of the standard, commercially-available variety. These were constructed of outdoor-grade plywood, with tops hinged at the front or rear. They were modified to suit specific applications. Those for the Cockatiels had 23 x 28-cm floor dimensions and a 25-cm height, with a 7½-cm-diameter entrance hole. Those for the lovebirds and Budgerigars had 15 x 20-cm floor dimensions and a 21-cm height, with 5-cm-diameter entrance holes.

The entrance holes were centered midway on the front face (one of the 2 narrow faces) at ¼th to 1/3rd of the distance to the top. The entrance-hole perches were of 1½-cm doweling and extended roughly 5 cm into and out of the NBs for the lovebirds and Budgerigars, and 9 cm into and out of them for the Cockatiels. The "transparent" NBs had one sidewall replaced with 1/8th-cm-thick, clear Plexiglas.

The distance of the perches below the entrance holes is not critical for Cockatiels or lovebirds, but should be at least 5 cm beneath the bottom of the hole for Budgerigars (67). The theory and practice of NB construction and design--of vital importance for breeding success with some birds--is discussed in detail by Smith (27). In this connection, it is preferable to have the examination door at the side or rear of a NB at a height of about 15 cm.

CARE

WATER AND BATHING

ALLOW FREQUENT ACCESS TO WATER. As noted earlier, the birds of this study are highly dependent upon water, particularly rainfall, for their day-to-day existence and breeding in the wild. There, rainwater is important to the birds for drinking, for optimum maintenance of their feathers (142), and for growth of the plants from which they derive the bulk of their food. For these reasons, it is important to allow the confined birds frequent access to water (daily intake has been estimated at about 5% of body weight, or about ½ teaspoonful for Budgerigars; 15).

FRESH DRINKING WATER was available at all times. Water for birds in enclosures A, B, C, and N was supplied in 13½-cm-diameter x 5-cm-deep glass bowls, about 250 ml per bowl. Small, white, plastic, roughly hemi-circular water cups (commercial food trays), either 6¼ cm in diameter x 4¼ cm deep or 12 cm in diameter x 4½ cm deep, were used in the other enclosures, depending upon the number of birds present. Fresh tepid water was supplied each morning from storage bottles filled the morning before and left standing. Fresh tapwater generally is too cold for avian bathing. Cockatiels, for example, showed a preference for bathing in tepid water.

VITAMIN AND IODINE SUPPLEMENTS. As a vitamin supplement, commercial liquid vitamin drops (such as Avitron) were added to the water, one drop per 250 ml for non-breeding birds, and two drops per 250 ml for reproducing birds. Supplemental iodine is highly desirable for Budgerigars since they appear to have a species-susceptibility to displasia and hyperplasia of the thyroid gland, which may be accompanied by difficulty in breathing, food regurgitation, inactivity, feather problems, and other symptoms (137, 443, 455). Two drops of a solution of KI (5 mg/ml) were added to 250 ml of drinking water for all birds. [Iodine preparations also are available at animal supply stores; less than 20 micrograms of iodine per week are required (445).]

CLEANING AND PLACEMENT OF WATER CONTAINERS-----FREQUENCY OF RENEWAL. All water containers were rinsed and brushed thoroughly on each use, to remove residues and scum. The latter consist primarily of microorganisms that grow up daily on the vitamin supplement and the minerals that are present in hard tapwater. Positioning of water containers was such as to minimize contamination with falling debris and droppings.

The hulls, shells, food scraps, and droppings that fall into the drinking water of birds housed singly, in pairs, or in small families ordinarily are not harmful, provided only that the water is renewed, and the containers cleaned, daily. Soiled water should be removed when the birds are retired for the night or in the early morning. Renewal of drinking water twice or more per day, as is sometimes recommended (9), is unnecessary for a single bird or small groups. Nor need one renew water after it has been bathed in, on the notion (9, 10) that such water thereafter is unclean for drinking. Careful drinking-water hygiene becomes necessary only when there is a very real danger of the transmission of infectious agents, in the presence of ailing birds or newcomers.

"DIRTY" WATER--INFECTION AND INFESTATION. Many birds, including those of this study, "will drink almost any water, however dirty" (3), without ill effect. In this connection, water consumed in the wild generally is teeming with microscopic life and, comparatively speaking, birds are highly resistant to infection, even from open, superficial wounds (which are easiest to treat and heal most quickly). [Cleanliness and sterility of surgical wounds, nevertheless, is highly desirable in all operative procedures (135).]

It not only usually is impossible to avoid entirely infection or infestation of confined birds, it is undesirable. This is because birds that are reared in a near-sterile environment develop virtually no immunity. As a result, they are highly susceptible when they do become exposed to pathogenic organisms.

WATER RESORPTION AND TASTE---BATHING MOVEMENTS. Most birds must allow water to flow passively into the buccal cavity. After filling and closing the mouth, the head is raised, and the water flows to the esophagus under the influence of gravity. But some birds, including some parrots (Budgerigars included; see p. 47), can drink actively without raising the head (134). Water resorption occurs in the large intestine and the cloaca (the terminal chamber into which the digestive tract and the urogenital ducts empty; see pp. 49, 110, 111). Water probably has a specific taste to most birds, as it does to the domestic fowl and many mammals (see 397)

According to Bates and Busenbark, most parrots must learn to bathe (2). These authors state that if confined birds bathe only by head ducking (see below), then "good bathing habits were not taught when the birds were most responsive to learning." It is well established, however, that birds do not have to be taught bathing movements, any more than to shake or scratch their heads (14, 23, 28, 41, 101, 230, 488). Only the amusing bathing movements misleadingly referred to as "good bathing habits" need be taught. On the other hand, the young bird does have to learn through experience or parental example in which medium to perform the bathing movements --water, dust, or sunlight (101).

The Cockatiels bathed both by sitting in the water and by head-ducking (see below). Some Cockatiels are known to jump into a bowl of water and splash about (127). Although Cockatiels are known to soak themselves in water when breeding, and thereby humidify the nest, the birds that I observed appeared to dry out before taking over the care of the eggs.

The lovebirds bathed only by head-ducking and, in fact, untrained lovebirds never are seen to stand in water (3). Rather, they stand at the water's edge. Budgerigars usually do not bathe in deep water (5, 10) but they 'relish' rolling in wet greens (5) and avidly "attack" wet grass. I sometimes observed my Budgerigars bathing by head-ducking (see also 67 and p. 46, **Bathing**). In partially-covered outdoor flight areas, birds of many kinds usually choose to be out in a gentle rain; they often hang upside down, flap their wings, and squawk excitedly (141).

BATHING BY "HEAD-DUCKING". When a bird bathes by "head-ducking," it first dips its head and shoulders into the water. By vigorous head movements, the adhering water then is shaken and rubbed off onto the body. At the same time, the feathers are ruffled and the wings are spread and shuffled. Thus moistened, lovebirds, for example, fly heavily to a perch. There, they beat their partly-folded or extended wings at high speed (wing whirring) and alternately shake and preen their bodies (3). As they dry out, they progressively shake less and preen more. Although it is stated that Cockatiels "...have not been observed actively water bathing" (819) by head-ducking, some of my Cockatiels sometimes bathed in this manner.

BATHING FACILITIES. The small water cups that were used provided ample space and depth for the lovebirds to bathe by head-ducking, while 14-cm bowls are big enough for Cockatiels to sit in and bathe. But even birds that readily drink water that is dirty on the surface, usually will not also bathe in it (3), and Peach-faced Lovebirds and Cockatiels tend not to be exceptions. So, if the water surface becomes heavily soiled during the day, and it is desired to encourage the birds to bathe in the afternoon or evening, the water should be changed when necessary. It matters little how much debris is at the bottom, if the surface is clean.

THE LEGS AND THERMOREGULATION. The unfeathered parts of the legs, and to a lesser extent, other unfeathered surfaces, represent a principal route of heat loss, particularly in members of species whose bodily insulation enables them to withstand low environmental temperatures (349). In connection with avian bathing habits, it is noteworthy that heat loss in some birds with their legs immersed in water is over 4 times as great as when the feet are in air at the same temperature. Vasoconstriction of the skin vessels diminishes the heat loss, whereas a vasodilation of the same vessels increases it. Vascular arrangements that facilitate countercurrent heat exchange serve to minimize such losses in the limbs of aquatic birds. Panting or gular fluttering (mechanisms that dissipate heat at high air temperatures; see pp. 81-83) decreases or stops when the feet are immersed in water (37, 320, 1,004). The importance of the legs, generally, in thermoregulation can be assessed from the fact that heat loss in domestic fowl is 40-50% greater while standing than while sitting, when the legs and feet are enclosed within the ventral plumage (see 37, 349). Further evidence comes from the behavior of several species of hummingbirds when hovering and perching; with changing low ambient temperatures, they cover their feet and toes by varying amounts in a special patch of downy belly feathers, gradually exposing them as the temperature rises (506).

FOOD, DIETARY SUPPLEMENTS, AND FEEDING

GRIT OR GRAVEL. Sharp-edged grit or gravel was provided in ordinary food trays and supplemented with bird mineral mix (but some parrots will ignore it unless it is scattered on the floor; 787). The grit trays were cleaned of seed hulls or shells ("topped off") or renewed every 1 or 2 weeks, as necessary. A new supply of mix almost always is the object of great attention and vigorous competition among Peach-faced Lovebirds, and not much less so among some Budgerigars. Though grit or gravel (or oyster shell) is not absolutely essential for granivorous birds (13, 14, 521), because hard seeds make a fairly good substitute for grit (see, for example, 588), it is highly desirable. Grit greatly aids the trituration (grinding) of food in the rhythmically-contracting muscular stomach and increases the latter's motility (521). It also makes digestion in this organ and in the small intestine (chemical and enzymatic breakdown) more efficient. For example, in the domestic fowl, grit increases the digestibility of whole grains and seeds by about 10% (659). It is recommended that minerals be supplied separately from grit, inasmuch as mineralized grits could result in excessive mineral intake, with possible kidney damage (443).

[Crocodilians also swallow stones and other hard objects ("gastroliths") that become resident in the muscular stomach and doubtless aid in the trituration of coarse food (659).]

Unlike most graminivorous birds, parrots of this habit typically not only remove husks, they also fragment seeds mechanically with the mandibles (322). In the case of fig seeds (*Ficus ovalis*) only a very fine crack is made in the hull by Orange-chinned Parakeets (*Brotogeris jugularis*; 588). The muscular stomachs of graminivorous parrots have a particularly well-developed epithelial koilin ("keratinoid") lining (322). The muscles of the muscular stomach in many species are fairly readily modifiable to meet the needs (hardness of food) of the diet (341, 442, 620). Accordingly, if a bird manages to survive long enough (without, or with inadequate, grit) for its ventricular musculature to adapt, it may become independent of grit. This was true of the lovebird, "Jaws" (see pp. 315, 316), which lived for years without grit. Removal of the muscular stomach, in fact, has little influence on digestion if only soft food is given (521).

DIETARY SUPPLEMENTS AND EXCESSES. Minerals and trace elements, some of which also can be obtained from certain types of grit, serve as dietary supplements. It was unnecessary to spread grit or gravel on the enclosure floors for the birds of this study, as some claim (6, 10). If grit is made available to sick birds, it should be monitored closely. The reason for this is that such birds sometimes overeat grit, leading to impaction (141). Caution also must be exercised in feeding parrots table scraps, such as pastries, as insufficiency of roughage in the diet can lead to wasting or atrophy of the gizzard and gut muscles (135).

Commercial distributors assert that a charcoal supplement aids digestion and combats hyperacidity, through "sweetening the stomach." I know of no experimental evidence for this conclusion. Boosey (138), in his remedy for crop sickness, includes powdered charcoal together with 1 part of bicarbonate of soda and 2 parts of bismuth bicarbonate, but he presents no evidence for its effectiveness. On the debit side, charcoal adsorbs vitamins A, B_2, and K from the intestinal tract, thereby creating vitamin deficiencies (443). Hart recommends against including it in grit for Budgerigars (185). The most telling contra-indication is that charcoal is not used by veterinarians in treating birds.

These supplements are given to breeding birds, primarily to supply the needed additional calcium for eggshells and the bones of the offspring. The chicks of many species of passerines are allofed fragments of teeth, bone, and eggshells to supplement the calcium in their normal insect diets (245). Parrots are particularly prone to calcium deficiency, because their diets usually are high in oil-bearing seeds, which have a low calcium content. Furthermore, constituents of the oils may combine with calcium to form insoluble soaps (443). Calcium metabolism is linked with those of phosphorus and vitamin D (see pp. 158, 222), and adequate amounts of these also are necessary for proper calcium utilization (135).]

But diets too high in calcium also cause problems--for example, kidney failure, gout, and failure to absorb trace elements. Young domestic fowl hens being reared on high calcium diets exhibited a nephrosis syndrome with renal failure and visceral urate deposition (gout complex). The parathyroids also were smaller than normal. Heavy supplementation with calcium but without increased Mn and Zn interferes with absorption of the latter trace elements and leads to perosis (slipped tendon and bone deformities; 443).

NEED FOR CHEWING MATERIAL. It probably is best to employ cuttlefish bone and/or mineral blocks routinely. [The major constituents of cuttlefish bone are 85% calcium carbonate and 4% protein (443).] But, if mineral mix is supplied, these substances are not necessary, as some assert. Sufficient chewing material must be present, however, to prevent overgrowth of the keratinized surface covering of the bill, the horny bill or rhamphotheca (see p. 97). This covering grows constantly in parrots and is worn down, in pace, by feeding, grooming, climbing, and purposeful rubbing on parts of the enclosure or a cuttlefish bone. The various seeds in the diet and natural wood perches usually provide sufficient chewing material. If Budgerigars are given a choice between whole and hulled seeds of various kinds, they prefer the whole seeds (443), the dehusking of which helps to keep the horny bill worn down.

NUTRITIONAL REQUIREMENTS FOR REPRODUCTION and the replacement of bodily tissues of adults seem to be very similar for all avian species thus far studied (726, 928). They include 13 essential amino acids and adequate amounts of nitrogen for the synthesis of non-essential amino acids. There are, in addition, 13 essential trace elements and 13 necessary vitamins. Some members of the Passeriformes require dietary ascorbic acid (vitamin C). All others are believed to synthesize it in the kidney (see 998). Also needed are linoleic or arachidonic fatty acids (employed in the synthesis of prostaglandins), alpha-linolenic acid, and an adequate supply of minerals (e.g., about 1% Ca and 0.7% P; 443) and energy. As an energy source for growing chicks, carbohydrates can be replaced completely by protein (or amino acids) and by triglycerides but not by fatty acids alone (245,

324). Species with heavy plumages, such as many seabirds, may require large amounts of sulphur-containing amino acids to support feather growth.

A PROPER DIET is the most important single factor that ensures a long, healthy life of the confined bird. Many studies have shown that malnutrition is a leading cause of disease and is accompanied by a lowered resistance to parasites. A good policy is to offer a wide variety of seeds, fruits, and vegetables to parrots. Any serious deficiency in carbohydrates, fats, proteins, vitamins, minerals, or water may lead to both characteristic and non-specific symptoms. In mild deficiencies, only non-specific symptoms may be seen, making it difficult to pinpoint the nutritional problem (142, 443, 726). [For exhaustive discussions of diets and dietary recommendations, see 443].

Malnutrition frequently causes breeding failures, with caloric status seemingly monitored sensitively, and reproductive activity modulated, by the hypothalamo-hypophysial system. Malnutrition in young birds delays sexual maturity and suppresses gonadal function. It reduces fertility and productivity in adult birds--that of females more promptly and drastically than that of males, whose reproductive potential is relatively resistant--and may stop gonadal function entirely if the deficit is severe and prolonged. In this connection, gonadal function will continue in malnourished birds supplied from endogenous energy sources, if supported by hormone therapy (729). Domestic fowl roosters on a protein-deficient diet have smaller testes and lower circulating levels of LH and testosterone, while female Mallards and Red Grouse lay fewer eggs. Domestic fowl cockerels maintained on a diet deficient in essential fatty acids also had smaller testes and lower circulating levels of LH, while hens produced smaller eggs than controls, with a hatchability of virtually zero (728, 729, 1,123).

In hot weather, birds consume less, thereby usually reducing their protein intake and increasing the need for protein-rich supplements (see p. 288, **Rations for Chicks and Breeding Birds**). Excessive amounts of food and lack of exercise result in obesity and gout (135, 443). If a bird is nutritionally sound, the chances for successful treatment of non-nutritional ailments are greatly increased (141).

FREEZING SEEDS AND NUTS. In the interests of preservation, all seeds and nuts are best stored in a deep freeze. Besides preserving vitamins and nutrients, this treatment kills insects. [Of course, if the birds were to eat the insects, the latter would provide a rich source of animal protein.] The commonest insect in seeds is the Saw-toothed Grain Beetle (*Oryzaephilus surinamensis*). Although the latter is harmless to birds, birdseed contaminated with mites may be harmful (134).

CONTAMINATED SEED. Woerpel and Rosskopf (141) have found that most seed mixes, especially sunflower seeds, are contaminated with gram-negative bacteria (*Escherischia coli*, *Enterobacter*, *Pseudomonas*), which are the most serious causes of disease in confined birds. Innoculates of bacteria isolated from these mixtures were fatal to some experimental birds. Unfortunately, freezing of the seed mixes usually does not eliminate bacteria, though it may greatly reduce their numbers. On the other hand, seed mixes obtained from health food stores consistently were found to be uncontaminated. [It should be mentioned in this connection, that Man, himself, is a potential source of infection, particularly via the medium of the normal biota of his mouth (141).]

Foods and Feeding

DAILY RATIONS. All of the birds received a daily ration of parakeet seed, shelled, raw sunflower seeds (a favorite of Budgerigars), fresh or frozen corn, fresh spinach, carrots, celery, or broccoli, and whole-grain bread. As a rough guide to quantity, adult, non-breeding Budgerigars consume about 6-7 g (1 to 2 full teaspoons) of whole seed per day (137, 443, 445). [Terrestrial birds in the weight range of 10 to 90 g generally eat 10-30% of their body weight per day (155).]

In addition, Cockatiels and lovebirds were fed unshelled safflower and sunflower seeds, and, every few days, all got fresh lawn grass, very thoroughly rinsed. All seeds were fed separately in standard pet-shop trays that hooked onto the enclosure mesh or snapped between the bars. This practice facilitated the monitoring of food consumption and preferences (see, also, 787). It is said that sunflower seeds offered to brooding Cockatiels should be soaked for 24 h and then left another 24 h until they have started to sprout, because the dry, hard seed is difficult for the young to digest (787). I have found that with soft food always available during brooding--at the least corn and bread--the proper processing of sunflower seeds can be left to the devices of experienced Cockatielian parents. The necessary treatment of the seeds certainly would be simplified by prior sprouting, though, and this might be very desirable with broods numbering more than 3.

[Parakeet seed consists of common or proso white millet (*Panicum miliaceum*), canary seed (*Phalaris canariénsis*), and hulled oats (*Avena sativa*). Imported canary seed and millet are said to be superior to domestic varieties (185).]

COD LIVER OIL AND EGG BINDING----EXCESS FATS AND OILS. Supplementing parakeet seed with vitamin D_3 (via cod liver oil) in the winter helps to prevent egg binding (127). This disorder should be avoided at all costs, as the prognosis for an afflicted bird is unfavorable. Egg binding is seen most often in Budgerigars, Cockatiels, finches and Canaries (142). The larger parrots, at least, such as macaws and cockatoos, develop atherosclerosis when fed imbalanced diets of sunflower seeds (323), presumably because of the high oil and fat content, which have been said to "upset the liver" (1,259). Cockatiels have been known to suffer bone fractures on a diet of sunflower seeds alone (142).

RATIONS FOR CHICKS AND BREEDING BIRDS. Most basic commercial seed mixtures, consisting exclusively of cereal grains (family Gramineae), are inadequate for chicks and breeding birds, although certain combinations of grains can provide a well-balanced diet (245). Cereal grains contain both less and less-nutritious protein than do the oil seeds. Their seeds usually are deficient in lysine, arginine, methionine, and tryptophane, low in vitamins A, B_2 and B_{12}, and calcium, and lacking in vitamins C and D (443, 445). In Budgerigars, cereal grains result in low egg production, poor hatchability, high chick mortality, and poor growth rate of surviving chicks (137). My breeding birds receive plentiful quantities of corn (every 3-4 h) and fresh vegetables, several times per day, a small amount of parakeet condition food, and a few drops of wheat-germ oil mixed in with their seeds. High-protein supplements are highly desirable, for example, milk, boiled or dehydrated eggs, ground meats, cheese, fish and liver meals, alfalfa leaf, soybean meals, etc.

A proper diet, sufficient space, and lack of disturbance are the three most important inducements to breeding. A sudden improvement in the quantity of food, including the provision of fresh, green vegetables, even can stimulate the formation of sperm and eggs in some birds (323, 723, 928). In the case of the Piñon Jay, in fact, the availability of green pine cones appears to be essential for testicular recrudescence (see 989). Similarly, in the Red Crossbill (*Loxia curvirostra*), the initiation of breeding appears to be dependent on sporadic crops of cones of coniferous trees, and relatively independent of the annual photocycle, while the vernal vegetative growth, which constitutes the major food item in the spring, may regulate directly gonadal growth and the onset of nesting by California Quail (*Lophortyx californicus*; 1,123).

It is not simply the lack of a natural environment, per se, or appropriate nutrients that frequently inhibits reproduction in confined birds; the stress of confinement also may inhibit the secretion of gonadotropins. There is some involvement of the central nervous system in this inhibition, involving visual information along a pathway from the retina to the archistriatum, to the tractus occipito-mesencephalicus, to the hypothalamic region (936). On the other hand, it also has been suggested, and supported by some data, that the depression of circulating levels of reproductive hormones, and subsequent delay of gonadal development and onset of breeding in birds maintained on nutritionally deficient diets, may be brought about by stress-induced elevations of plasma ACTH and corticosteroid levels in the blood; these could inhibit gonadal function directly (see 1,123).]

Temporary deficiencies in the diets of chicks do not, however, have long-term deleterious effects, so long as maintenance requirements are met. A remarkable finding is that domestic chicks maintained on protein, amino acid, or energy-deficient diets at levels that are just sufficient for maintenance, can be kept at a physical age of about 10 days for months. Return to an unrestricted, nutritional diet restores normal growth and development with little subsequent effect on adult bodily size or egg production (245). Similar results have been obtained with several other nidifugous species.

TREATS AND FLAVOR PREFERENCES. As treats, I give spray or foxtail millet (*Setaria italica*) on the stem, which is the food the birds prize most highly. Low suggests that the basis for the preference for this food is that birds find it very rewarding to extract the seeds from the sprig (787). This also could be the case with other grains in the ears and could be one basis for the preference for seed sticks. On the other hand, my birds exhibited the same preference for loose grains of spray millet as for the grain on the stem, so that it may be the ease of dehusking that plays the most important role. But the avidity with which this food is sought out and consumed makes it difficult to avoid the conclusion that taste plays a role in the preference. I also give Budgerigar fruit treat or seed treat and honey seed-sticks. The latter also are greatly prized.

Preferences for sugars exist in many birds, particularly parrots and the Budgerigar (397, 802). The data suggest that nectarivores and fructivores are more likely to respond positively to sugars than do insectivores and graminivores, most of which respond negatively or show no preference (513). Saccharin and dulcine lack the quality of "sweetness" for birds (343 413). Birds either are indifferent to or dislike salt solutions, parrots and pigeons falling into the latter category (397, 802 1,005). Although many birds have a wide range of tolerance for acidic and alkaline drinking water, Rock Pigeons markedly reject sour and bitter solutions, preferring low concentrations of salt and high concentrations of sucrose (513, 802). Other birds have notorious appetites for salt (28) but generally reject bitter substances (513; see also 417). Bobwhite Quail have the capacity to discriminate between sweet, sour, salt, and bitter solutions at 10 days of age (see 1,150).

PEANUT BUTTER. Peanut butter is praised for its nutritive value, particularly in emergencies for sick birds and for the hand-feeding of chicks (2). However, there is nothing special about the peanut, any more than there is about chicken soup. Almond or cashew butter probably would serve quite as well. The high nutritive value of the nut and seed butters derives from the fact that the nuts already have been homogenized or pulverized by mechanical action. As a result, a sick bird is spared this work. [Birds ordinarily digest foods more quickly, more completely, and more efficiently than do most animals (28).]

A large part of the work of pulverizing the peanuts, normally performed by muscular contractions of the gizzard--which takes over some of the functions of our teeth--is by-passed, and high-energy food is available directly for efficient digestion in the small intestine. On the debit side, peanuts are low in calcium and high in phosphorus. A diet consisting solely of peanuts would lead to hyperphosphatemia and hypocalcemia, with danger of lethargy, feather-picking, vomiting, diarrhea, and eventual parathyroid hyperplasia (swelling) and death (142).

FREQUENT FEEDING FACILITATES HABITUATION. Because of the various demands of delivering treats and fresh vegetables, and checking and replenishing food trays, especially at times when the birds were breeding, I usually attended to the birds' needs 8-12 times per day. The more frequently birds are fed, the better acquainted one becomes with them and the better habituated they become to one's presence. [Petra and Ramses, the founders of the lovebird colony, became accustomed to being fed fresh corn in a tray in the corn-perch corner (Fig. 3b). Petra, in particular, would raise a great ruckus in this corner when the tray was empty, and this usually did not abate until after I supplied fresh corn.]

ABUSE OF FOOD TRAYS. Lovebirds are incorrigible when it comes to unhooking and spilling food trays, in which case the trays either must be wedged in or weighted. Flat, heavy containers also can be used and placed on the enclosure floor. If large trays are used for lovebirds, the birds will be encouraged to go to nesting in them. Except for treats, only large, 12-cm-diameter hemi-circular plastic trays were used for the Cockatiels. The birds easily unhooked these at one end but could not readily unhook the other end, once a tray had been tilted.

REFECTION--EATING OF EXCRETA. Many mammals and some birds, including Budgerigars and Cockatiels, make up for vitamin deficiencies in the diet by eating small quantities of their excreta, a practice known as "refection." Bacterial action in the intestines of birds, and after the excreta are voided, produces many B-vitamins, including two that often are deficient in the diet, vitamins B_2 (riboflavin) and B_{12} (cyanocobalamine) (127).

Unless Budgerigars are allowed to eat some of their own excreta (which they void 25-50 times per day; 142, 445), they begin to suffer anemia for lack of vitamin B_{12}. Some breeding birds derive as much as 10% of their daily energy expenditure from eating the excreta of their young nestlings (28). By contrast, Cockatiels are said to be so supremely efficient in their digestive mechanisms that they often can manage on rather poor diets (both when confined and in the wild). They are said to extract "practically every molecule" of the scarce necessities from grains (127).

ULTRACONSERVATIVENESS OF BIRDS WITH REGARD TO FOOD ACCEPTANCE

CREATURES OF HABIT---CHANGING THE DIET. Birds have the reputation of being creatures of habit. They are very reluctant to change their diets and accept new foods (137). Visual properties and surface textures of foods appear to take precedence over all other qualities for many birds. Thus, birds often avoid food of changed texture and food or water of different color tint, because of the emphasis on appearance that accompanies keen eyesight. Accordingly, it is necessary to make dietary changes gradually (137, 443, 802). New food items must be given day after day, until, after cautious sampling, they are accepted. One may even have to resort to various subterfuges to get non-breeding adult birds to accept new foods (2, 7), such as "meating off" and allied techniques (439). The avoidance of new foods may be moderated if the food shares characteristics of familiar foods (see 1,150).

Many birds have their choice of food "fixed in their brains" (135). They select food both instinctively and through imprinting by the parents during their youth. The habits acquired then affect them throughout their lives (443). Budgerigars, for example, readily accept canary and millet seeds, the seeds that were regurgitated to them by their parents, but often will die of starvation rather than accept strange seeds. It also is said of black cockatoos (*Calyptorhynchus*) that "....they will sooner die of starvation than take to new foods" (1,259). Yet if strange seeds are included in the diet allofed to nestlings by hand, the birds will accept a wider range of seeds when they become adults (135). Furthermore, if adult Budgerigars are presented with a wide choice, they will consume a variety of seeds other than those in their regular diet (443). Adult Rock Pigeons also show marked and persistent individualistic food preferences that probably are determined by imprinting on the foods eaten during youth (1,013). Domestic fowl chicks are most likely to accept new stimuli as potential sources of food in their 3rd or 4th days, which is about the time that they first forage after depletion of their yolk sacs (1,150).

ADULT ANIMALS HIGHLY CONSERVATIVE. Not only birds, but most adult animals, including ourselves, are creatures of habit (see also pp. 342, 343, **Advantages of Behavioral Stereotypy**). It probably is more appropriate to say that adults are highly conservative in their behavior. Young animals, on the other hand, tend to be curious and rather indiscriminate, often taking their cues from their parents. It is virtually universal for young birds early in their feeding development to show curiosity and exploratory pecking at various objects, usually those contrasting with the background, regardless of whether these are edible or not. They gradually come to concentrate their pecks on edible items, usually those of the right size and shape. The appearance of solidity is likely to be the most general cue that elicits pecking from a visual omnivorous feeder (see 27, 247, 1,150).

ORIGIN OF CONSERVATISM. We meet the rationale for conservatism in such expressions as, "never argue with success," "if it works, don't make changes," and "keep to the beaten track." Simply stated, it is adaptive to continue in a practice after the manner that already has proved to be successful. Animals that tend to stray from the "beaten track" more often meet with disaster, and are likely to leave fewer offspring, than those that do not. That is why today's survivors tend to be conservative; they are the descendants of conservative ancestors. "Nature liquidates deviationists much more consistently and drastically than does any totalitarian dictator" (469).

Some of the mammals I have studied are almost as conservative as birds. For example, consider the behavior of White-footed Mice (genus *Peromyscus*). My enclosures for mice had duplicate facilities for food and water on opposite sides. A mouse typically adopted and used only one of the two identical food sources and water bottles. The others usually were not touched until the ones adopted first became exhausted. If I kept restocking the ones being used, they were the only ones used; the others simply were 'ignored' (1,391). Even when I progressively added salt to the water in the bottle being used, a mouse was extremely 'reluctant' to switch to the bottle with pure water. This conservativeness is one reason why it has become so difficult to bait-trap domestic rats; they tend to avoid new (unproven) food sources; less conservative rats were eliminated long ago.

The birds that impress us as being creatures of habit simply are behaving in the same conservative way as do their free-living relatives. Some of the anecdotes about birds that are cited as examples of their lack of insight and 'stupidity,' more appropriately illustrate the ultraconservativeness of their behavior. In other words, it is not so much a question of the merits of alternate courses of action not being perceived by a bird, as it is of the animal's not seeking alternate courses.

SELECTION OF OPTIMUM FOODS. Birds generally prefer certain foods, not only because of their physical properties, flavor, and availability, but probably also because of their nutritive value in relation to dietary needs (23). Many herbivorous and granivorous species selectively consume emerging green shoots, leaves, flower buds, or even algae in the spring; this vernal growth contains higher levels of proteins than old growth, and higher levels than most seeds. Most omnivorous species survive on vegtable matter and seeds during the winter and then switch dramatically to emerging green growth in the spring. During the period of oviposition, the diet of females may consist entirely of invertebrates that are rich in essential amino acids and calcium. The otherwise granivorous Song Sparrow and Red-winged Blackbird apparently consume mostly insects during yolk depositional and ovipositional phases (1,123). Iceland ducklings of different species take slightly different foods, thus showing a degree of ecological separation of the species even in the duckling stage (see 1,150).

But one cannot expect confined birds to select optimum food items from a wide variety of possibilities (513). Captured Dark-eyed Juncos given a choice of dyed seeds preferred those with the shortest handling times or had no choice when the handling times were similar (208). Comparable results were obtained with various species of finches, members of which preferred seeds yielding the most kernel weight per unit of husking time (253). European Blackbirds (*Turdus merula*), foraging preferably in the winter and spring, favored fruits with greater energy content, metabolizable energy, relative digestibility, and lower seed handling time, whereas in the fall, seed handling times alone formed the basis for preferences. Members of several avian species feeding on fruits prefer those with large amounts of pulp, regardless of nutrient content. [Fruit pulps often contain substances that function to attract and feed dispersers, but relationships between fruit size, composition, and consumption by dispersers of seeds are likely to be complex (see 1,322).]

On the other hand, Rock Pigeons offered a diet of kaffir (*Sorghum vulgare*), maple peas (*Pisum sativum*), hemp (*Canabis sativa*), maize (*Zea mays*), and vetch (*Vicia sativa*) exhibited stable but idiosyncratic individual patterns of food selection (see 998). The birds also are able to correlate the positive or negative after-effects of foods with the appearance of the food. Thus, an habituated bird that has, after much coercion and coaxing, eaten peanuts for the first time, will, after some hours, but usually not before, become extremely eager for them (1,011).

SOCIAL FACILITATION (contagious behavior in which the action of one animal may release identical behavior in another; 102) or observational learning plays an important role in food selection by some birds in the wild (28, 110, 303, 473). But there are species differences in the ability to profit by watching other feeding individuals. For example, Wood Pigeons "look to see what other individuals are finding and eating and they copy each other's feeding actions...." (see R.K. Murton, 1971, in 432). Similarly, young Rock Pigeons follow the male parent to his feeding grounds, where they note what he, or other adults that are present, are eating. This learning from parental example often is shown at an earlier age if food is placed near the nest, so that the parents can be seen eating while the young still are in the nest (1,011).

Similarly, in experimental studies, the relatively social, flock-feeding Great Tits rapidly assimilated the feeding characteristics of individuals they observed, and naive gull chicks may learn to take new foods by responding to the feeding actions of their siblings (see 1,150). Sometimes observational learning even produces local traditions in feeding, as in the consumption of fruit buds by Redpolls (*Acanthis flammea*) in New Zealand and in the U.K. On the other hand, confined Greenfinches (*Carduelis chloris*), which normally are rather solitary feeders in nature, were relatively uniformly influenced by the learning experiences of other individuals. It seems likely that the potential for observational learning to be an important determinant of dietary preferences is associated with the tendency to forage in aggregations. Since many granivorous species, including those of these studies, forage in flocks over much of the year, such learning may be widespread (see 968).

In addition to social facilitation, parental behavior can have a strong and important influence on feeding by the chicks, even in nidifuges that start to feed themselves immediately (28, 101, 247). Red Junglefowl hens (*G. gallus*), for example, normally adopt a particular stance by which they point to available food for the chicks (252). After the young are old enough to wander away on their own, the hen still indicates food sources, but by exaggerated and apparently stereotyped pecking movements. Domestic fowl cockerels communicate both the presence and preference ranking of food to hens, who are most likely to approach when highly preferred foods are being advertised (1,100).

Captive-born birds whose food selection is not learned from parents or companions might eat the same foods eaten by wild birds, if given an appropriate variety and enough time. In practice, they sometimes sample and adopt foods that would be ignored or not be available in the wild, just because of coming into daily contact with them. But these other foods might not provide an adequate diet. Many species of chelonians also become imprinted on familiar foods and choose an unbalanced diet (see 757). [For an additional treatment of effects of social facilitation and observational learning on feeding, see 303.]

Although there are characteristic species differences in feeding behavior, it is far from clear how these differences arise. The situation is complicated by the fact noted above, that it probably is not usual for specific preferences for food to be wholly inherited directly; rather, they probably depend in part on learned individual feeding behavior (351). The development of feeding preferences may be quite complex even in species with restricted diets, and must be even more so in those with highly varied diets (351, 419). Accordingly, it may be more than a coincidence that species with highly varied diets also have a reputation for considerable intelligence (419; e.g., crows, ravens, titmice, and parrots).

INSTINCTIVE FEEDERS. Mallard chicks are good examples of purely instinctive feeders. Ducklings 1-6 days old consume animal food almost exclusively. As they mature, they take increasing amounts of plant food (23). Many adult birds, and even young domestic fowl chicks, seem to be able to make fine distinctions in selecting protein-rich foods (28; see D.G.M. Wood-Gush, 1955, in 351). Wild Red Grouse and Rock Ptarmigan are more selective for foods rich in N and P when the nutrients are in short supply, and the hens are particularly selective in the spring before ovipositing (727).

Other examples are provided by hand-reared young Piñon Jays, that recognize piñon seeds (*Pinus edulis*) instinctively (254), as well as Loggerhead Shrikes (*Lanius ludovicianus*) and American Kestrels (*Falco sparverius*), both of which appear to have an inborn recognition of mice (255, 256). Comparative studies of prey attack in different species indicate that innate components are present whenever the young bird would be at risk from the prey or where the prey item might escape regularly (1,150). Parental example alone apparently plays little, if any, role in early food preferences (prey recognition) in certain species, and experience alone seems to play a greater role in prey manipulation than the actual recognition of them (247). This is evident particularly in birds that prey on fishes. In some species, the increase in the proportion of insects in the diet is simply a reflection of increasing adaptedness in capturing such prey. The nearly 3-fold increase in the relative intake of insects by young Australian Wandering Whistling Ducks (*Dendrocygna autumnalis*) has this basis (see 1,145).

[In this connection, members of many avian species may recognize their specific niches instinctively (28, 95) and seem to be intolerant of even slight deviations from the standard niche. In other species, habitat selection may involve imprinting, conditioning, habituation, and social influences (96).]

THE ROLE OF TASTE. Though seemingly playing a lesser role than color, taste probably also is important in food selection (see also pp. 289, 290). Domestic fowl fed diets deficient in calcium or Na developed specific appetites for diets or solutions that corrected their deficiencies (see 397, 513). Similarly, pheasants maintained on a calcium-deficient diet can select a calcium-rich grit over grits having a lower calcium content (97).

Taste preferences also are evident in British thrushes (see 1,322). Such tastes may be at work in the attention that confined birds give to cuttlefish bone and mineral blocks, particularly when ovipositing and brooding. [On the other hand, one of my breeding male Cockatiels began to consume or demolish the white plastic frame of a mirror, raising the possibility that color plays a role in the attention to cuttlefish bone and mineral blocks.]

ULTRACONSERVATISM WITH REGARD TO LOCATION

Birds may be even more conservative with regard to location than with regard to food (see also 134). Cockatiels, for example, are extremely conservative about investigating and adopting new or supplementary quarters. Thus, when I installed a passageway between enclosures A and C, at a time when the latter was empty, several days elapsed before the birds would enter enclosure C, even when coaxed with spray millet. Similarly, mated birds may take several months to settle down and breed after a major change in their surroundings, such as movement to a new enclosure or the installation of a NB (141).]

LOCATIONAL CONSERVATISM IN LOVEBIRDS. When the male lovebirds, Jagatai and Ogadai, were placed in enclosure E (see Fig. 1), several days elapsed before they spent time at the rear of the enclosure. They began to use the food tray near the floor of the right-front corner of the enclosure, which was nearest their former quarters in enclosure D, and scarcely touched food at the left-bottom corner. Even when I switched tray foods daily, between sunflower seeds and birdseed, they concentrated on the rations in the right tray for weeks.

When the lovebird pair, Petra and Ramses, were transferred to a new enclosure after the move to the laboratory, for many weeks they ate almost exclusively from the mid-level food trays and essentially ignored food in the bottom trays. As a result, they consumed shelled sunflower seeds and forsook unshelled ones. When I switched the trays, they ate the whole seeds in the mid-level tray and ignored the shelled ones in the lower tray. Whole-grain bread was eaten from a mid-level tray but not from a lower one. They were aware of the presence of the foods in the lower trays, though, because they occasionally partook of them, and Ramses would visit a lower tray for a preferred food, like corn.

LOCATIONAL CONSERVATISM IN COCKATIELS. The situation was similar when the Cockatiels were placed in a new enclosure. They ate from the mid-level trays but would scarcely touch food in trays 20 cm directly below them. That meant that the Cockatiels were not eating shelled sunflower seeds, but they ate them avidly when I put them in a mid-level tray.

The pairs, Isabella and Ferdinand, and Kirsten and Rimski, showed even sharper locational preferences, with their diet determined almost entirely by the location of the foods. Similar results have been obtained with Budgerigars (443). In cases where such locational preferences threaten proper nutrition, it is necessary to rotate the trays periodically or give a complex mix at the preferred locations.

Enclosure, Perch, and Foraging Locations, Flighting, and Identification

ENCLOSURE LOCATIONS. The enclosures at my domicile were placed in indirect sunlight, since long periods in direct sunlight must be avoided. They were protected from drafts by placing them near a corner of the room, against a wall (Fig. 2a; the adjacent door was kept closed). This location was far from the air vents and opposite a north-facing window. With a thermostatically controlled lower temperature (never below 20°C), there was no need to cover the enclosures at night (undesirable, in any event, for the reason mentioned on p. 266). The window blinds were kept closed at all times and the birds did not become fully active until the lights were turned on in the morning. Generally this was at 08:00 h to 09:00 h, roughly 7 h after they were turned off.

PERCHES AND BROWSING LOCATIONS. Perches and browsing locations were underlaid with paper to catch excreta. The need for this protective paper and the need to flight the birds made it difficult to prevent pair-bonded lovebirds from breeding. Habituated lovebirds with access to paper nesting material attempt to breed whether they have a NB or not. The only way that I could prevent pairs from rearing one brood after another--given that keeping mates together and flighting and maintaining the birds in good health were prerequisites--was to remove eggs as they were laid, or leave offspring housed with their parents (see pp. 728-730, **Unfacilitated Clutch in the Presence of Fledglings**, et seq.)

TRAINING TO SPECIFIC SITES. Training the birds to use only the protected perches and browsing areas was achieved very simply. Fledglings were habituated to use the home perch and shelf perch by placing them there by hand. These sites soon became favored. All other perching and browsing sites were adopted by the birds without my intervention, usually by following their parents or older siblings. The birds also were trained to avoid unprotected sites at my living quarters. Birds alighting at such locations were offered a finger to perch upon. They then either were carried to permitted sites or flew off to them voluntarily. Eventually, merely a motion of the hand toward the birds rousted them from unprotected sites.

PAPER-STRIPPING AND PERCHING SITES. The favored lovebird paper-stripping sites at my living quarters were the chairbacks to the right of my chair and a position under the tower in front of enclosure D (Fig. 2a). Next preferred sites were the shelf of the front window frame and the top of the kitchen door. Next favored were the side shelf (lying 23 cm below the ceiling) and the top of the lamp shade. Paper was draped over all of these sites. In the laboratory, the preferred sites were beneath the perches along the wall and on the tops of enclosures J, K, and N.

The favored lovebird perching sites, after the home perch, were the fluorescent light arm and the ceiling lamp fixture. The tops of all door frames also were popular, even though perching on them appeared to be uncomfortably restricting. The Cockatiels also used all these perching sites, favoring the home and shelf perches and the top of the kitchen door, followed by the door frames, light arms, and ceiling lamp fixture. They browsed mainly on the side shelf. Cockatiels do not strip paper, though they will peck and tear it into pieces. Having complete freedom of perching sites at the laboratory, the birds utilized every possible perch.

Enclosure, Perch, and Foraging Locations

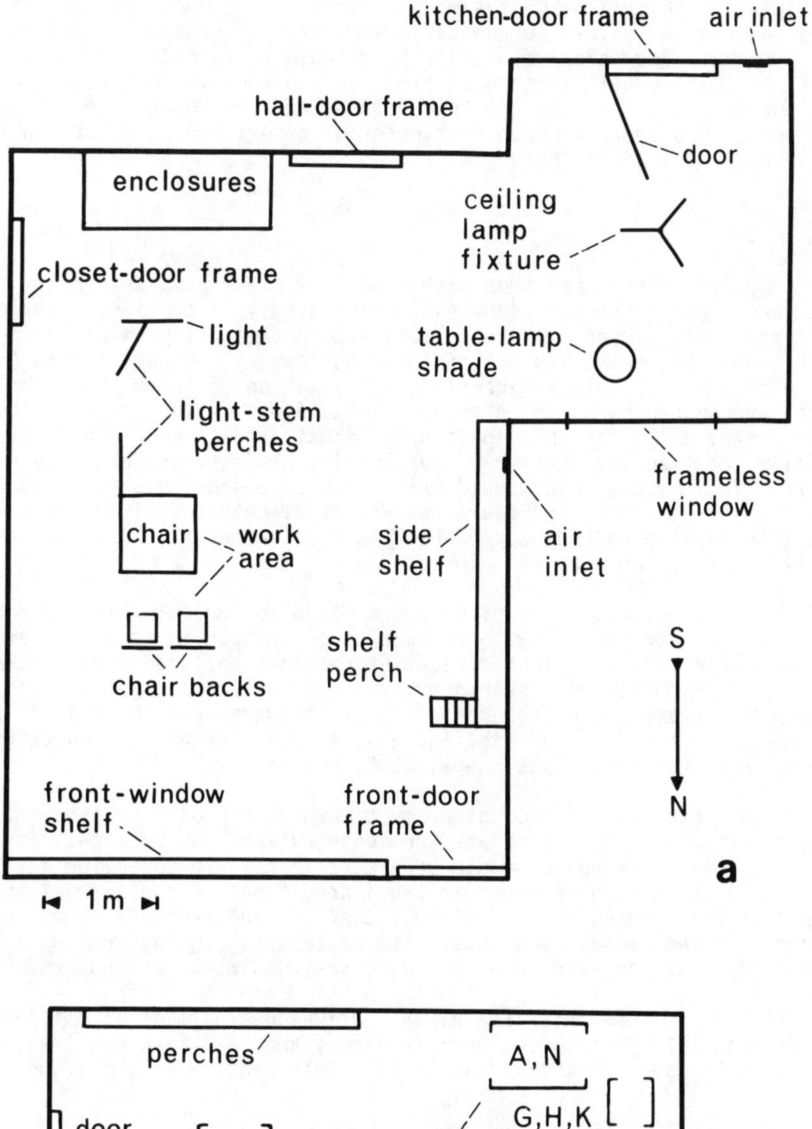

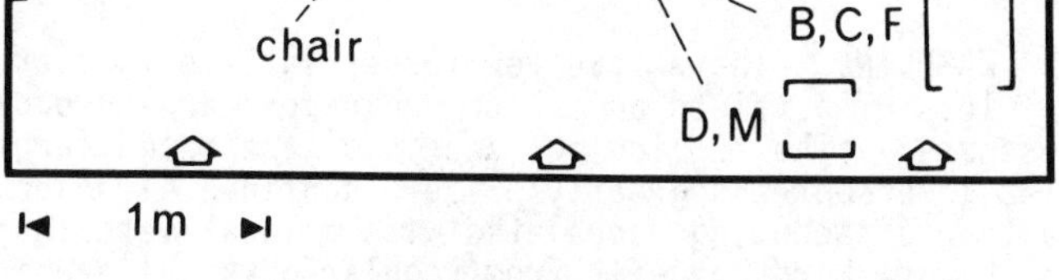

Figure 2

PREDICTABLE ACTIVITY. On the whole, birds flying about in my living quarters developed fairly predictable activity patterns and could be tracked very easily. The lovebird matriarch, Petra, for example, was most predictable of all. Usually, she just stripped paper on the chairbacks or on top of enclosure B (beneath the tower) and then returned to her enclosure. If the enclosure door was open, she entered; otherwise she waited in the vicinity until I admitted her.

FLIGHTING

Confined birds provided with food *ad libitum* have a tendency to overeat and become obese (439, 443). Accordingly, food either should be restricted or, preferably, opportunities for flighting should be provided. Accustomed to being let out of their enclosures for free flight exercise, my birds almost always accepted an invitation to leave their enclosures. Some even paced back and forth or climbed about on the front of the enclosure 'nervously' in anticipation or 'frustration.' Accordingly, flighting usually was achieved simply by opening or fastening open the enclosure doors. The birds then could exit and browse and fly as desired. If only certain birds in an enclosure were to be flighted, I discouraged the others from leaving as they approached the door. After the birds to be flighted had exited, the door was closed.

PERIODIC FLIGHTING. The birds were flighted periodically--as frequently as once or twice daily in certain studies--both for exercise and to observe social interactions. These interactions included those between parents and members of their current and prior broods, between siblings of different broods, between broodmates, between pair-bonded or breeding pairs and a broodmate or sibling, and, in the case of the Budgerigars, between unrelated birds (see Chaps. 3, 5, and 7).

Prior studies of flighted multi-brood parrot families or, indeed, those of any bird, are, to my knowledge, almost non-existent. Most of the interactions I studied would be almost impossible to follow in the wild, and impractical to produce in usual conditions of confinement and breeding. In some cases, it is unlikely that the interactions I observed would occur in the wild, yet they are no less intriguing and instructive in their implications--and sometimes more so--than **what does happen** there.

IDENTIFICATION OF FLIGHTED BIRDS. Using combinations of clipped tips of right and left primary feathers (remiges) and tail feathers (rectrices), I was able to identify individual birds fairly readily at a distance.

HEALTH AND VETERINARY CARE

NORMAL BLOOD BASELINE. There are few losses in life that are as hard to bear as the loss of a valued animal companion or ward through negligence or thoughtlessness. [The following sections are based largely on refs. 135, 141, 142.] Persons who greatly prize a confined bird should take the simple precaution of becoming acquainted with a local veterinarian with an expertise in birds. Birds benefit from regular physical examinations, including weighing, and, above all, determination of the normal blood baseline (the normal biochemical and cellular composition of the blood). This is a particularly important datum because there is a considerable variation in the blood baseline of normal birds, so much so that caution has to be exercised before changes even in a known baseline are attributed to disease (514).

"HIDE" SYMPTOMS. Birds are unique among endothermic vertebrates in their manifestations of diseases and injuries, and in their responses to them. They possess an extraordinary ability to compensate physiologically for diseased conditions and other afflictions, and they show signs of pain and discomfort to a much lesser extent than do mammals. "It is seldom possible to get even a 'cheep' when a diseased organ or limb is handled" (457). [In this connection, although the presence of pain receptors is established (1,006), there is a relative poverty of sense receptors in the skin, a condition promoted by the protective effect of plumage (28).]

The sick bird often maintains itself in the compensatory state of apparent good health for a surprisingly long time. A period of "sustained subclinical illness" may last for as long as 2 weeks after an infliction is acquired and before one can detect overt symptoms of illness.

SMALL DIFFERENCES MAY HAVE FATAL CONSEQUENCES. Birds apparently live so close to their limits of tolerance, that even small variations in their health may have fatal consequences. Often, they appear to be healthy when they are quite near death. Death frequently comes as a surprise and shock to an observer. Sudden death apparently often results from a massive dilatation of a vein or the right atrium, as the sick bird strains to maintain normal-appearing activity. These same influences often result in congestion of the lungs and even hemorrhage into the lung substance, either of which may prove fatal (450). Even excited healthy birds are susceptible to ruptures of vessels of the chambers of the heart, for example, as a result of the emotional excitement of territorial battles (28).

THE "PRESERVATION RESPONSE" refers to the behavior of birds in tending to "hide" illnesses. Its adaptive value is greatest in flocking and highly social animals. Among them, overtly abnormal individuals or misfits are at risk of being killed or driven from the group by their companions (eliminating unfit birds eliminates their specific genes from the gene pool). In addition, if they are conspicuous, they become more vulnerable to predators. Thus, "predators can spot unusual individuals, follow them through crowds, and track them down" (605).

DISEASES USUALLY WELL-ADVANCED WHEN DETECTED. Taking into account the tendency of birds to hide infirmities, the inability of most observers to detect subtle signs of illness, and the fact that gross physical examination alone often cannot assess a bird's physical status, the disease process usually is well advanced, and the bird may be seriously or critically ill, by the time physical illness is obvious. And, the smaller the bird, the more severe the disease condition can become before it is recognized. The chance of recovery of critically-ill birds is increased substantially if they are cared for in the optimum environment of the avian hospital.

DIAGNOSTIC BLOOD MICROANALYSES. A major factor that has contributed to the success of modern avian medicine (almost as important as the availability of broadspectrum antibiotics) has been the development and use of laboratory instruments and techniques that make possible the analysis of micro-quantities of blood (usually obtained from clipped toenails). These have literally revolutionized avian medicine by making it feasible to do serial blood testing and obtain sophisticated diagnostic cross-sections of blood parameters. [In a similar vein, the development of micro-radioimmunoassays for both hypophysial and steroidal hormones in serial blood samples have made possible "field systems" for endocrinological studies and field experiments on members of wild populations (1,149).]

By supplementing hematology and blood chemistry with bacteriological testing, the veterinarian achieves a level of diagnostic capability almost equal to that of the hospital physician. These revolutionary diagnostic procedures have been complemented by significant improvements in avian surgical treatment and diagnostic procedures, using microsurgery, electrosurgery (bloodless cutting), fiberoptic endoscopy, and blood transfusions. [A Budgerigar donor, for example, can give up to 0.15 ml of blood.]

[Several avian species are much better able to tolerate severe blood loss than are mammals. Circulating blood in avian species ranges from about 4.8 to 13% of total body weight (see 442, 515, 1,002). Most Rock Pigeons survive blood loss of 8% of total body weight during prolonged hemorrhage. After hemorrhage of about 50-70% of total blood volume, blood pressure and cardiac output fall, but partial recovery occurs within ½-4 h, when blood pressure achieves about 80%, and cardiac output about 55% of control values. This is accomplished by continuous hour-long shifts from the extra- to the intravascular compartment. Such hemodilution can be carried out continually during bleeding (1,002). As much as 75% of blood volume may be removed from domestic fowl without fatal consequence (see 320, 515).

INDIVIDUAL DIFFERENCES IN BLOOD PARAMETERS. The crux of the issue regarding veterinary care is that animals, particularly vertebrates, cannot be treated like production-line products. Each animal, whether a Man, a mouse, or a bird, is an individual unto himself. Thus, in addition to changes with age, and sexual differences, the normal blood parameters of avian conspecifics vary from one individual to another, sometimes very markedly.

For example, the amounts of heterophils, lymphocytes, glucose, total protein, and lactic dehydrogenase, not uncommonly vary by a factor of 2 among confined birds. Some parameters, for example, uric acid, thyroxine, and creatinine concentrations, vary by a factor of as much as 5. When a comparison can be made between the normal baseline values and the values in a sick bird, it becomes possible to make prompt, informed diagnoses and detect even subtle changes. This approach is a cornerstone of programs of preventive medicine for confined birds. In the absence of a baseline for comparison, valuable time usually is lost.

Though the veterinarian rarely can pin-point the cause of a disease from hematological analyses alone, such analyses can provide the objective data needed to assess severity and to recognize the involvement of vital organs. In the absence of such comparative data, the veterinarian often is forced to make decisions upon the basis of insufficient knowledge.

DAY-TO-DAY CHARTING OF BLOOD PARAMETERS. Sequential blood testing now allows even day-to-day charting of changes in blood parameters when following the course of a disease. This makes it possible to take full advantage of the clinical pathology laboratory. Being able to assess quickly the efficacy of treatments and the validity of diagnoses facilitates making therapeutic changes much more rapidly than otherwise would be feasible. This ability often is crucial to the survival of the bird.

SYMPTOMS OF ILLNESS. Avian clinical symptoms that are indicative of illness, even incipient, are listed below. Many of these are comparatively easy to recognize, though patient and careful observations frequently are required. If the possessors of birds were to become familiar with the normal habits and behavioral routines of their birds, they would be in a position to detect many of the subtle changes that usually are warning signals of disease onset. It is a particularly sound policy always to be alert to the condition of a bird's eyes. If they are bright and alert, it is a good indication of good health (138).

1. reduction in appetite or drinking
2. cessation of eating or drinking
3. excessive eating
4. changes in routine or habits
5. decreases in overall activity
6. decreases in amount of preening
7. general inactivity
8. fluffed feathers
9. droopy wings
10. a low posture on the perch
11. falling off the perch
12. inability to perch (bird on the enclosure floor)
13. equilibrium problems (rocking to and fro or appearing unsteady while perched)
14. changes or decrease in vocalization frequency
15. changes in vocal quality
16. feather loss without replacement
17. incomplete maturation of new feathers
18. feather-picking
19. weight loss
20. vomiting
21. closing of either or both eyes
22. discharges from either or both eyes
23. changes in clarity of eye color
24. any swellings or enlargements
25. frequent sneezing
26. discharges from nostrils
27. plugged nostrils
28. audible and/or congested breathing
29. open-mouth breathing
30. rhythmic back and forth movements of the tail with breathing (while perched)
31 crusty, white deposits on feet
32. excessively dry and flaky skin
33. changes in amount, consistency, or color of droppings
34 a soiled or "pasted" vent
35. any bleeding (an emergency situation requiring immediate attention)

EARLY DETECTION AND PROMPT ACTION ARE ESSENTIAL to ensure successful treatment and survival. As soon as a bird is found to be ill, the most important first step is to place it in a separate "hospital" enclosure (with food and water) in an ambient air temperature of 29.5-32.2°C (using a heat lamp, an ordinary light bulb, or a heating pad; see 185). In cases of concussion, however, the bird should be kept in rather cool surroundings (454). Neither vitamins nor medications should be added to the water of a critically ill bird, as some birds refuse to drink medicated water and it is important to keep the bird drinking (141, 443). Moreover, changes in intestinal flora resulting from antibiotic administration can have serious consequences (443). [Healthy birds at rest easily can sustain a water loss of 15% (see G.A. Bartholomew and coworkers, 1954, 1956, in 423).]

TRANSPORTING A SICK BIRD. Inasmuch as the diagnosis and treatment of the sick bird cannot occur without first bringing it to a veterinarian, this should be done at the earliest opportunity. Bearing in mind that sick birds are highly susceptible to stress of any kind, the following recommendations for transporting the birds should be followed (445).

1. bring the bird in its own enclosure
2. remove any water from the enclosure
3. do not remove any droppings or otherwise clean the enclosure
4. cover the enclosure; if the weather is cold, warm the car in advance
5. bring all medications and food that have been used, past and present

CHAPTER 3. CHALLENGING THE LOVEBIRD PAIR BOND

Introduction

The portions of this Chapter derived from experiment and observation deal primarily with the incredible persistence of a male lovebird in the face of seemingly insurmountable obstacles. His perseverence, despite hundreds of rebuffs and attacks, a few of which even crippled him, gives one some insight into the "character" of Peach-faced Lovebirds. The account helps to set the tone for observations of the social and reproductive behavior of parrots, with which much of the remainder of the book is concerned. The circumstances that led to many of the particular events detailed here were as unplanned as the events were unforeseen. The results have come from daily observations of the behavior of confined and flighted members of over 36 broods of offspring and their parents for in excess of 10,000 h, during the course of 5 years.

PAIR-BOND MAINTENANCE IN THE FACE OF REPEATED CHALLENGES. In a broad sense, the present Chapter concerns the formation and maintenance of a lovebird pair bond, a kind of association that, aside from that in Man, has reached its most extensive development in birds (488). Its contents are highlighted by observations of the maintenance of a heterosexual pair bond between lovebird broodmates in the face of repeated challenges by an unmated broodmate brother. Through unwavering efforts, the latter attempted to insinuate himself into their affairs, including their activities during breeding.

PARROT FAMILIES USUALLY REMAIN TOGETHER. This kind of intense broodmate sexual competition may well arise in the wild, because parrot families commonly remain together until the next breeding season. In the current view, non-helpers (in cooperative breeding) typically disperse from the parents and each other and attempt to breed independently (638). The persistence of parrot families hints at the possibility of cooperative breeding in the wild. This view receives support from these results, which include 5 cases in which bachelor males courtship-fed breeding females while the latters' mates looked on without interference,(see discussion on pp. 331-333). Other cases of persistence of close family groups are known, for example, among House Martins (Delichon urbica); the young of a 1st brood may sleep within the nest even with 2nd- and 3rd-brood nestlings present, but they also assist their parents with the rearing of the young (1,150).

The extent to which inbreeding occurs in families of parrots is not known, but it appears commonly in confined lovebird families (4) and appears to occur in wild Silver Gulls (*Larus novaehollandiae*; 68). Although sibling breeding generally is undesirable, because "inferior" offspring often result, such breeding is not intrinsically unfavorable. My entire family of over 60 lovebirds began with an initial inbreeding of two siblings, Petra (14 months old) and Ramses (17 months old). [When the word "siblings" is used in the following, it is understood to refer to brothers and/or sisters from different broods, otherwise the term "broodmates" is employed.]

Lovebird Pair Formation (Mating)

PAIR-BOND FIDELITY--BREAKING THE PAIR BOND--TELLING THE SEXES APART. Most birds probably incline naturally toward living in pairs (101). This can be understood in terms of the fact that the combination of endothermy and oviparity place extreme constraints on reproductive strategies. The rapid production of large eggs lessens the likelihood that the female alone can accomplish all the nest building and the extensive care required for brooding and feeding the young. Accordingly, the chance of reproductive success is enhanced if both parents engage in this care. In essence, then, the pre-eminence of monogamy among birds can be viewed as a consequence of the evolution of endothermy in an oviparous stem stock (431).

It is estimated that 91% of all avian species are monogamous (34), although more cases of polygamous relationships continue to be discovered as more species are studied intensively. As is characteristic of other parrots, monogamy also is the habit of lovebirds. They seemingly form pair bonds--psychological bonds between males and females--very quickly. As with many other birds, best known among which are geese and swans, they practice permanent monogamy, i.e., they ordinarily remain paired for as long as both birds survive (see 28, 101, and below). Such enduring pair bonds even may be favored by natural selection, since periods of adjustment not infrequently are needed for effective breeding, following a change of partners.

For example, the more lengthy periods required for the pair bonding of newly-formed pairs of Semipalmated Sandpipers (*Calidris pusilla*) delay hatching, which often results in greater chick mortality (see 272, 730), and pairs of experienced Great Tits breeding together for the 1st time had significantly poorer success than pairs that had remained together for a 2nd season (810). Black-legged Kittiwakes (*Rissa tridactyla*) that keep their mates from one breeding season to another are likely to breed earlier, oviposit larger clutches, and raise more young to fledging than are members of the species that do not (see 739), and Arctic Skuas (*Stercorarius parasitticus*) bred earlier and more successfully when paired birds had bred together previously. Similarly, Fulmars showed a drop in breeding success (from 70 to 50%) on taking a new mate following the disappearance of a previous one. Members of several species "divorce" their partners if their reproduction has been poor (see 1,150). Long-term pair bonds also may have advantages outside of the breeding season (see D.K. Scott, 1980, in 646). Even female-female pairs exhibit mate fidelity, for example, in Ring-billed Gulls (*Larus delawarensis*; 586).

[In the cases of some long-lived seabirds, for example, Leach's Petrel (see 552), repeated pairings are a consequence of site tenacity, rather than mate fidelity (201). The same may apply to some migratory hawks (525) and Brown-headed Cowbirds (534). In Semipalmated Sandpipers site tenacity only secondarily often results in mate fidelity (272).]

It was this life-long fidelity of lovebirds that prompted the French to characterize them as "Inseparables" and the Germans as "Unzertrennlichen." To break the lovebird pair bond, the birds must be separated from one another for at least several weeks and be unable to hear or see each other

(3). It already has been noted in Chapter 1 (p. 261) that even juvenile lovebirds may form pair bonds. Since male and female Peach-faced Lovebirds look and sound alike at all ages, they presumably distinguish each other's sex by their behavior (29). The way in which they hold their tail feathers probably is one of the cues (27; see also p. 262, **Spread Tail Feathers**).

[It seems very likely that sexual dimorphism of birds first arose as a means for quick identification of sex and avoidance of costly reproductive errors, which is still its sole role in some birds (28). Among sexually dimorphic parrots, the pair bond is established and maintained by a sexually oriented display, and it relaxes considerably or may be disrupted following breeding in confinement. For the largely sexually monomorphic species, on the other hand, the pair bond is initiated and seems to depend for its maintenance primarily on a sexual behavior including clumping, mutual grooming, and shared territorial defence (see 819 and pp. 308, 314).]

INTERACTIONS SHAPE CHANGES IN BEHAVIOR. Pair bonds begin with the first contacts between the prospective partners. They are subsequently maintained and strengthened by behavior (for example, greeting ceremonies) that modifies the subsequent interactions of the birds. Thus, the time course of changes in behavior between mated birds depends characteristically upon the nature of their interactions, rather than merely upon the passage of time. Both the initiation and maintenance interactions between paired birds evolve from the pre-existing repertoire of modifiable behavior of the species (163). The interactions that become selected are those that can be assimilated best into the species' total behavior pattern.

MATE CHOICE---FACILITATING ROLE OF DISPLAYS---THE DISPLAYING SEX. Although Darwin dealt extensively with the evolutionary significance of mating systems, until the last 20 yr, the subject has been a comparatively neglected one. The neglect traced both to disputes about the reality and nature of sexual selection, concerning which our understanding had made but limited headway since Darwin wrote, and, subsequently, to the tendency to assume that the non-monogamous mating systems were simply the by-product of unequal sex ratios, in which case attention focussed on the basis for the differential mortality (315). The more recent view generally has been that mating relationships are the result of either variations in the quality of the habitat or variations in the quality of the females and males, which allow individuals to acquire additional mates. A recent analysis, however, accounts for the evolution of monogamy, polygyny, polyandry, and polygyny-polyandry in terms of specific patterns of sex ratio, survivorship, ages at first reproduction, and annual fecundity (1,316; see also pp. 578, 579, **Double and Multiple Clutching**).

["None of Darwin's theories has been so heavily attacked as that of sexual selection" (1,226). Though some of the criticisms were justified, time has proved Darwin to be correct in principle, and the label "sexual selection" has helped to bring together and organize a vast body of scattered observations (1,230). In Darwin's definition, sexual selection "depends on the advantage which certain individuals have over others of the same sex and species solely in respect of reproduction" (107). In one recent definition, sexual selection is the consequence of the within-sex variance in mating success that results from intrasexual competition and/or opposite-sex choosiness (140).]

Of the considerable attention that has been devoted to avian mating systems in the last 20 yr, the primary interest has been in polygamous species and cooperative breeding (227). Considerable attention has focussed recently on the proposal that monogamously-mated males are selected to pursue a mixed strategy in which they actively seek opportunities to fertilize females other than their mates.

MATE CHOICE---SEXUAL SIZE DIMORPHISM. While the facilitating roles of displays of plumage and song are well known, the process of pair formation in monogamous species has received comparatively little attention. Furthermore, although previously the opinion prevailed that mate choice and sexual selection were of minor importance in evolution, mate choice now has come to be regarded as an important evolutionary agent; it could be a potent force in the evolution of pre-mating reproductive isolative mechanisms (see 154, 662, 1,230, 1,381), though there is still very little evidence of female choice in Darwin's original sense (choice of the most beautiful and striking males; 613).

Further, sexual selection must be the cause of sexual size dimorphism, which cannot arise from ecological selection (ecological factors can act only secondarily, if at all), and it seems likely that sexual selection can be a potent force in the evolution of elaborate, highly ritualized display behavior. Reverse sexual dimorphism is not strongly associated with foraging behavior; it is found in monogamous and polygamous species in which acrobatic displays are used to establish a territory or attract a mate, and in polyandrous species (see 613, 963, 1,319). [Size dimorphism in shorebirds is independent of the mating system. One finds monogamous, polygynous, and polyandrous mating systems in species with normal, reverse, or no sexual size dimorphism (1,319).]

In many birds (but not in lovebirds) pair bonding is initiated by an aggressive or dominance display by the male, with the female signalling her acceptance or subordination with some submissive gesture. Among boobies and gannets, the male performs a distinctive ritualized "advertising display" on or near the nest site (163). In robins, it is the female who courts the male, by crouching submissively before him and resisting being driven out of his territory when he attacks her (97, 101). In the White Throat (*Sylvia communis*), courtship is mutual (97).

FACTORS INFLUENCING CHOICE---FIGHTING. In southern cormorants, the female tends to pair with the male that manifests the greatest sexual, nest-building, and display activities (see 29). Fighting or threatening possible rivals commonly occurs (80). In some species, for example, Peregrine Falcons, there appear to be extreme compatibility requirements between mates (28). In others, for example, the Song Sparrow, mate selection seems to be largely a matter of chance. Events described here shed additional light on how the pair-bond is formed in some parrots.

[The entire complex of behavior in pair formation usually is stimulated by steroidal sex-hormones (80; see also p. 309). In Zebra Finches the combination of estrogenic and alpha-androgenic hormones appears to be involved in successful establishment and maintenance of pair bonds, whereas nesting success seems to be largely determined by estrogens (745). Not all aspects of reproductive behavior in all species necessarily are linked directly to hormonal control. For example, male mounting behavior in the White-crowned Sparrow is said to be activated in direct response to a social cue; males in any reproductive or endocrinological state will respond to the solicitation displays of females by mounting and copulating (see ref. 25 in 895).

On the other hand, it has been proposed that interactions between male White-crowned Sparrows as they establish territories in the spring, result in an increase in testosterone secretion to a high circulating level that is maintained during the period of intense aggression. Since the circulating level of androgen correlates positively with intensity of aggression, short term changes in plasma levels of androgens could be important in regulating agonistic behavior during establishment and maintenance of a breeding territory, and in access to, or attraction of, a female. Only mated females have elevated circulating levels of LH and estrogen (1,123). For a treatment of plasma hormonal levels in Pied Flycatchers breeding in the field, see 1,124.

The mechanisms regulating reproductive behavior and physiology can differ between the sexes in some vertebrates. For example, in Asian Musk Shrews (*Suncus murinus*), reproductive behavior in the male coincides with testicular growth and depends on testicular androgen, whereas sexual receptivity in the female precedes ovarian recrudescence and is independent of gonadal hormonal control (see 895).]

PAIRING IN FLOCKS. The procedure of pair bonding is more difficult to identify when the pairs are formed by birds within flocks. Individual associations gradually are formed, with both members contributing through displays which apparently serve to attract attention and arouse sexual excitement (488). Consider the situation where a flock of unacquainted lovebirds is formed in an aviary. Each bird apparently attempts to interact socially with a number of others in exploratory encounters, attempting to groom, sit closely with, and otherwise engage the attention of its new companions. Certain of these initial encounters prove to be more congenial than others, and the participating members come to prefer each other's company. Preferences gradually strengthen until, in just a few hours, lifelong pair bonds seem to have become established (3).

COURTSHIP PROCEDURES AMONG TITS. In the Great Tit, the stimulated male attacks indiscriminately and obtains a mate on the basis of differential response to attacks (see R.A. Hinde, 1952, in 488). The pair-bonding displays of male Blue Tits begin while the birds are still in winter flocks. The males raise their slight crests, while facing the hens, and shiver their wings. But pair formation is gradual. In a later stage, the male leads the hen from one possible nest hole to another, enters and looks out, seemingly inviting the female also to enter. Finally, when she does enter and accept a hole, nest-building begins and courtship ends (97, 101; for other examples, see 41, 101, 105, 213, 225, 488, 1,124).

DUCKS OF MIGRATORY SPECIES GENERALLY PAIR ON THE WINTERING GROUNDS and remain together until incubation begins in the following summer. During this time, males accompany their mates continually and repulse any unmated males that approach too closely; otherwise the females would be subjected to repeated harassment and even forcible attempts at copulation. Early pairing probably is a response to the intense competition for mates, which arises because males outnumber females by about 3 to 2. The lesser number of females probably results from higher reproductive costs incurred by females while incubating eggs and accompanying broods. The universal basis for pair formation in ducks is feminine 'inciting' behavior, which induces males to attack nearby rivals; in early stages of courtship, a female indicates her choice of mates by inciting a particular courting male to attack the other males in her vicinity (see 1,266).

LOVEBIRDS OF EITHER SEX CAN TAKE INITIATIVE---"DOGGEDLY" PERSISTENT. As will be seen, lovebirds of either sex may take the initiative in pairing. Birds of both sexes can be "doggedly" persistent in pressing their attentions to that purpose (see p. 316, *et seq.* and Chaps. 5, and 7).

CEMENTING THE PAIR BOND. Beyond such initial interactions as those described above, the most important early activity that cements a pair bond in many species is courtship feeding. Other contributing activities are courtship ceremonies, territorial maintenance, nest construction, group singing, and singing in duets (63, 101). After a songful male has won a mate, he usually sings much less or, in many species, hardly at all. Even if he continues to sing, he usually ceases when the female begins to incubate. The paired male also frequently becomes more aggressive toward other males, or even toward intruding females (see 101).

DUETTING, by definition, is restricted to mated birds. It is characteristic of species in which the sexes are monomorphic, in which pairing is for as long as both birds survive, and in which the members maintain territories for the greater part of the year, usually in densely vegetated tropical regions. In special circumstances, duetting is characteristic of birds engaged in pair formation. It seems to be unknown in birds that form only brief pair bonds (109, 199, 479, 960). The functions of duetting in order of decreasing importance appear to be: recognition, location, and maintenance of contact with the mate; mutual stimulation; aggressive maintenance of territorial integrity; and mutual reassurance after disturbance (479). Duetting is common among Australian birds, and in birds such as Magpie-larks (*Grallina cyanoleuca*) and Butcher-birds (*Cracticus torquatus*) is "....of the utmost importance as a bond between the birds and also in synchronizing the sexual rhythms" (960).

NATURE, GENERAL SIGNIFICANCE, AND EXAMPLES OF PAIR BONDS. The nature of the pair bond in birds has not received a great deal of attention from students of avian behavior (488). Following one definition, the pair bond is a reciprocal "mutual attachment" between two heterosexual, sexually mature organisms, such that aggressive tendencies are largely suppressed and sexual ones enhanced (see 28). According to another, it is the special relationship between members of a pair that facilitates cooperation, principally in one or more phases of the breeding cycle (163); still another sees it as a "grudging truce," in which acts of generosity are regarded with mild skepticism (646). The general significance of the pair bond, however, is clear. Pair formation "implies that a number of social responses....become more or less limited to one individual; at the same time, other responses (e.g., aggressive ones) become inhibited toward the partner" (144, 188).

In some pair-bonded birds, one sees little more than a simple recognition and tolerance of the mate at a time when intruders are poorly tolerated. Thus, the Cliff Swallow (*Petrochelidon pyrrhonata*) quickly recognizes and accepts its mate on arrival at the nest, while vigorously repelling any other bird. But it does not associate with nor defend its mate from attack when away from the nest (488). In other mated birds, close-association food-sharing, feeding of one partner by the other, mutual preening and displays, defense of the mate, and dual singing are much in evidence (101, 488). In some cases, members of duetting pairs modify their calls to resemble each other's (see 98). In still other cases, for example, Black Ducks and Adélie Penguins, something akin to human affection is strongly suggested (28). We shall see many of these elements, and others, in Peach-faced Lovebirds.

PAIR BOND DURATION-----MORE LASTING THAN IN MAMMALS. Usually paired birds stay together only for a season, for weeks or months (488). In some cases, the pair bond is of shorter duration and does not last even through the rearing of the the brood. In extreme cases pairing lasts only for minutes or hours after copulation (488). Yet some birds pair for years or for as long as both birds survive, for example, parrots, Blue Tits, House Sparrows, Fulmars, albatrosses, Herring Gulls, and many others (28, 97, 431; see also p. 304).

Among birds that remain paired from one breeding season to the next, there are some in which the mates remain together the year around. Others separate after completing breeding and come together again at the beginning of the next season. The pair bond of birds is more lasting than that of mammals, probably because male birds often assist in rearing their young, which seldom occurs among mammals (28)

COURTSHIP AND COURTSHIP DISPLAYS

BRIEF AND UNSPECTACULAR, OR LENGTHY AND FLAMBOYANT. The preliminary behavioral activities of, and exchange of stimuli between, the sexes that lead to mutual attraction and stimulate physiological readiness for sexual union, thereby increasing the probability of eggs being fertilized, are called "courtship." In birds that pair for life, as do most parrots, courtship tends to be brief and unspectacular. In species that pair anew each year, courtship displays tend to be lengthy and often are flamboyant (84).

[The action of stereotyped behavior in causing specific hormonal secretion now is established firmly (see 414). Many experiments have revealed a preeminent role of androgens in the control of courtship activities (see also p. 306), but other hormones also could be involved, for example, the gonadotropins (260). There is highly suggestive evidence that the nature of avian mating systems (e.g., monogamy versus polygamy) is regulated proximally by temporal patterns of hormonal secretion. For example, subcutaneous implants of testosterone in males of monogamous species resulted in a substantial number of the males becoming polygynous (1,358). Moreover, the influence of androgens upon sexual behavior is quite evident also in less advanced mammals and reptiles, and comparable relationships probably exist in amphibians (295). The capacity of the male gonad to produce androgens probably is as old, phylogenetically, as is the testis itself.]

DERIVATION---ROLE IN SEX RECOGNITION---INVOLVEMENT OF NESTS. In sexually monomorphic species, courtship behavior provides a means of sex recognition. The more dissimilar the sexes are in color, the more rapidly sex recognition occurs, the less the degree of male aggression toward the female, and the more different are the sexual displays of the courting birds. These displays appear to have arisen as modifications of the various types of behavior that appear in conflict situations, primarily intention movements (often locomotion), redirected activities, and displacement activities (419). [Some piscene displays are little more than ritualized locomotion (595)]

Courtship displays include such activities as manipulating bits of nesting material, passing a stick to the hen, picking up and dropping pebbles and bits of vegetation, various types of feather raising or lowering, preening and cleaning movements, and even mock nest-building (28, 419). For some species, courtship stimulation derives from building the actual nest, for still others it derives from displaying the nest hole.

[To some doves and pigeons, the sexes are visually indistinguishable. Rock Pigeons readily engage in courtship with unknown individuals, regardless of sex. Experiments suggest that individuals rely on behavior elicited over a period of time to establish sex and cannot assess the sex of all unknown conspecifics (605).]

USUALLY PROVINCE OF MALE---SPECTACULAR AND DRAMATIC. Except in a few species, such as the Painted Snipe (*Rostratula benghalensis*), in which the sexual roles are reversed, courtship activities are the province of the male (and are abolished by castration). The male also usually has a more conspicuous coloration. He exhibits his inducements before the female with a great assortment of devices, varying according to the species.

"He may posture so as to reveal his gaudiest nuptial plumage; spread his tail and erect his crest or inflate brilliantly-colored pouches; parade, dance, fly with dizzying acrobatics; sing his most fetching songs...; bring tid-bits of food--anything, it seems, to impress" his prospective mate and suppress her non-sexual responses (28). These postures, vocalizations, etc., stimulate specific responses by the female, whose receptivity is controlled by ovarian endocrine secretions (mainly estrogen, presumably in synergism with progesterone; 260). Without the female responses, the male could not continue his displays and reach the next stage (155), as these responses have pronounced stimulatory effects on his endocrinological state, including maturation of the testes (see 928). [A similar dependence of male courtship acts on immediately preceding acts of the female have been documented in the lizard, *Varanus bengalensis* (885).]

Some hormonal correlates of behavior in the male Rock Pigeon are of interest in this connection. Exogenous testosterone favors the sexual-appeasement component of the introductory courtship display, that is, Bowing, whereas exogenous FSH encourages the aggressive attacking and chasing component. Further, testosterone allows the male to distinguish his mate and behave differently toward her than to a rival male, while if affected by FSH, a male is predisposed to attack all intruders indiscriminately. These results reinforce the view that, at the beginning of Rock Pigeon pair formation, endogenous levels of FSH are elevated and cause aggressive components of the courtship display to predominate (390).

EFFECTIVENESS OF DISPLAYS---COST TO MALE. The effectiveness of courtship displays often is enhanced by their strangeness, eyecatching nature, and dramatic suddenness of presentation. Every kind of behavior that enters into the ritual plays its part as a stimulus, the sum of which controls the reproductive cycle (155). Courtship exertions often cost the male dearly in terms of energy and weight. The usually-less-conspicuous female assumes the domestic role in the nest, where her drab coloration affords a degree of protection against predators.

SYNCHRONIZATION AND DURATION OF SEXUAL DISPLAYS. In the course of mutual sexual displays, behavior becomes increasingly synchronized as the pair bond strengthens. There are clear reciprocal interactions mediated by visual and auditory cues between members of a pair that are important in promoting and synchronizing the reproductive efforts of males and females (1,123, 1,124). At first, in the absence of coordination and synchronization, vocalizations and visual displays usually are clumsy, but they improve progressively toward eventual perfection. Sexual displays reach their climax, of course, with coitus, which is characterized by submissive behavior of the female.

Sexual displays continue in various ways for greater or lesser periods during incubation and brooding. They serve to maintain the pair bond, taking their place with other kinds of behavior that begin on hatching of the eggs. Thus, they play a more far-reaching role than merely serving to prepare the birds for the sexual act (155), which, itself, serves to maintain the pair bond in some species (23).

CONFLICTING TENDENCIES---AT FIRST AN ENEMY. A courting male usually has three mutually incompatible drives or tendencies: to attack, to flee from, and to behave sexually toward, his prospective mate. These result in a 3-way "bitter-sweet" conflict of opposing influences, though the disadvantage of being overly hostile probably limits the degree to which aggressiveness evolves (27, 351, 419, 1,231). "Submissive" postures of the female, of course, help to suppress the male's tendency to attack. The actual behavior shown at any stage in courtship (and the species differences in display) depend largely on the relative strengths of these 3 conflicting tendencies (104, 296, 351, 419).

However, in many birds, notably in certain grouse and other polybrachygynous forms (forms in which there is an absence of pair bonds, persistence in seeking mates by males, and failure of males normally to participate in parental care), little if any distinction can be made between the agonistic and sexual displays of the male. The sexual displays of polygynous and, particularly, polybrachygynous species generally are characterized by unusually strong aggressive and copulatory elements in the males and marked submissiveness in the females (1,231). In this connection, some threat displays in gulls apparently are derived from a combination of attack and flight behavior (467). In a very interesting result, it was found that electrical brain stimulation through two electrodes, stimulation through one of which alone elicited attack and the other flight, might cause threat behavior when the stimuli occurred simultaneously (468).

To any animal, a member of the same species is, at first, an enemy. For that reason, the female must be led progressively to accept the male (155). In many gulls, the courted female responds to the hostile displays of the male by approaching him. Both birds then proceed with apparently hostile displays, often ending with a retreat by the female. On her subsequent returns, the intensity of the hostile encounters gradually decreases and the participants eventually mate. "Love and war, eroticism and aggression, are closely allied partners in the breeding behavior of many birds..." (28).

MATING. Mating follows successful courtship and implies pair formation, but not necessarily sexual union. The latter usually follows shortly thereafter but may be delayed a considerable time, during which specific ceremonies may be engaged in repeatedly. These ceremonies apparently serve both to maintain and consolidate the pair bond and to synchronize the production of ripe sex cells (13, 14, 296, 489). Coitus is repeated very frequently in birds that form lasting pairs, and continues throughout the period of oviposition in many species (155, 489).

SOLICITATION BY FEMALE LOVEBIRD--FUNCTIONS OF COITUS. The female lovebird solicits and accepts the male for coitus by holding her head tilted to one side, with the feathers of the cheeks, throat, and wrist (carpus) ruffled. Coitus in parrots seems to serve other functions besides fertilization, namely, pair-bond maintenance, and arousal and synchronization of physiological processes involved in breeding (4).

SOCIAL FACILITATATION. Courtship and other social activities also can have a stimulating and synchronizing effect within a flock or breeding colony of, say, lovebirds or Budgerigars (see also p. 293). Performance of courtship or nesting behavior by one pair or group of pairs can stimulate other pairs to do the same immediately, thus leading to closely synchronized activities. By this means, groups may achieve an immediate response to favorable conditions and minimize the period of their vulnerability to predators during breeding (even for adults, mortality usually is greatest during the breeding season; 312).

COARSE AND FINE ADJUSTMENTS-----FEMALE CONTROLS KEY EVENT. The male usually is more susceptible to environmental stimuli than the female, and stimulates the latter by means of courtship and other behavioral interactions, particularly during the early part of the breeding cycle (312, 730, 860, 1,123). Thus, full gametogenesis in the male is stimulated merely by increasing daylength in many north temperate birds (155, 312). In migratory species, the males tend to arrive at the breeding grounds earlier, and with the gonads in a more advanced state of development than in the females, and with elevated circulating levels of LH and testosterone (350, 431, 928). Since the female often plays an active role in patrolling and defending the territory, it is possible that the elevated plasma levels of testosterone in the subsequently arriving females induce aggressive and territorial behavior similar to that of the male (928).

The male in all lovebird species is prepared to inseminate his mate (has attained the "culmination phase" of the reproductive cycle; see 414) long before she is in readiness; to him falls the "coarse" adjustment in the timing of the breeding season. Although the female receives part of the environmental information only indirectly, she is more sensitive to the critical factors; to her belongs the fine adjustment. Female lovebirds, e.g., at first respond overtly to the males' courtship solicitations with 'indifference,' active avoidance, or aggression (3). Gradually they show an ever increasing tendency to behave sexually, until, finally, they permit copulation.

Though dependent upon receiving the appropriate stimuli, both from the male sexual displays and from environmental cues, such as proper temperature, nest sites, food, nesting material, rain, etc., the female controls the single, critical event--the laying of the first egg--which "starts" the breeding cycle (101). It also is apparent that sexually active females have pronounced stimulatory effects on the endocrine state of the male, including maturation of the testes in European Starlings, increase in plasma levels of LH and testosterone in Ring Doves and Rock Pigeons, further increases in plasma levels of testosterone in White-crowned Sparrows, etc. (see 1,124 and pp. 113-118, **Hormonal Control**).

GIVING THE REPRODUCTIVE CYCLE FLEXIBILITY. Appropriate habitat, hormonal stimulation of nest-building, and interpair displays often are essential to stimulate the final stages of oocyte development, ovulation, and fertilization. Thus, acting primarily through the medium of the female, the general rigidity of the reproductive cycle can be mitigated, giving the flexibility needed to adjust breeding activities to the most favorable conditions (155).

INFLUENCES OF RITUALIZED ACTIVITIES. The highly species-specific ritualized activities of pair formation and the immediately subsequent activities, such as displacement actions, intention movements, and threat postures, have very important influences in the maintenance of reproductive isolation, for example, between members of closely related species. These behaviors tend to confine breeding to pairs whose members share specific behavioral and morphological features (28, 406).

In large part, this is because ritualized activities increase the complexity of the mating pattern and tend to extend the length of the courtship period. Often, mating behavior is the primary or sole isolative mechanism (88, 296). Because courtship behavior involves complementary actions on the part of the interacting birds, "wild hybrids are rare in avian species with definite pair formation and engagement periods, but fairly common ....in genera and families without pair formation" (88).

AUDITORY SIGNALS AS BARRIERS TO GENE FLOW. In general, auditory signals are more effective in preventing hybridization than visual ones (109). Mistakes are forestalled while the birds are still at a distance, and even out of sight. For example, so far as is known, the main or sole factor preventing interbreeding between two populations of Nightingale-wrens (*Microcerculus philomela*) in Costa Rica is their highly distinctive types of song (109). In fact, it is possible, though by no means established, that the abilities of songbirds to learn songs and establish populations with their own isolating dialects--culturally transmitted (learned) vocal traditions--account for the great number of oscine species (see G. Thielcke, 1972, in 28). Some instances of interspecific hybridization may trace to similarity of songs, for example, the hybridization that occurred when the North American warbler *Virmivora pinus* extended its range northward into that of *V. chrysopter* (1,320).

OTHER FUNCTIONS OF COURTSHIP AND COURTSHIP DISPLAYS. In many species, the courtship songs and displays serve primarily, not for mate selection or pair formation, but to warn intruders or competing males of the occupancy of the territory (28). Some displays function primarily to guide the prospective mate, for example, the nest-site displays of many hole-nesters and the song of many passerines (351). In some species, there are group courtship contests that determine which males succeed in breeding. Though perhaps implicit in the above treatment, it should be pointed out that courtship also brings the bird doing the courting into sexual readiness through self-stimulation (see also pp. 121, 122). In adult Mallards, for example, blood levels of male hormones correlate directly with intensity of the male's displays and sexual behavior (28).

COURTSHIP FEEDING

OCCURRENCE, DISTRIBUTION. Courtship activities are not confined to periods before or during pairing. In some species, like Budgerigars (67), constant interactions between the paired birds seem to be important. In lovebirds, courtship feeding--usually feeding of the courted female by the male--may occur at any time of the year. The female sometimes solicits food from the male by gently bobbing the head and calling, as do Abyssinian Lovebirds (see 27). In most cases of courtship feeding (also commonly referred to as "nuptial feeding"), the female adopts an attitude and uses calls that are almost identical with those of a young bird soliciting food from its parents (181). There are many examples that could be cited to show that psychological relationships are far more important than the nutrient value of the food that is transferred (29, 181, 667).

In nearly all birds, including various species of hanging parrots (genus *Loriculus*; see 79) the male feeds the female. In Cockatiels, however, among pairs that engage in much courtship and allofeedings, the female allofeeds the male (e.g., see pp. 410-412, 690, 691). In some species, including Budgerigars, courtship feeding is closely associated with copulation. Courtship feeding seems to be restricted to monogamous species, among which the females usually dominate their mates early in or throughout the breeding season (540). Within monogamous species, this behavior is found mainly among the species in which members of both sexes allofeed the young (51).

MAINTAINING THE PAIR BOND---INCREASING FITNESS. Courtship feeding occurs among birds that feed their young by regurgitation, or with their bills, or with food carried in the talons. Among such species it is most common in those in which the parents remain together for the breeding season (28). Like sleeping side by side and mutual grooming, courtship feeding stimulates and helps mated pairs maintain the psychological relationship and faithfulness of the pair bond. This maintenance generally is highly adaptive, because the losses of eggs and young that occur in many birds would be greatly increased if only one parent participated in their care. [However, in the hole-nesting Eastern Bluebird, at least, experimental studies indicate that parental care by the males does not significantly influence female reproductive success (777).]

Courtship feeding also can serve to increase a male's fitness, inasmuch as it is a direct manner of contributing to the quality of "his own" eggs; it can increase a female's fitness by augmenting her energy intake at a critical period of her annual cycle. Smith recently has pointed out that courtship feeding is strongly correlated with female dominance over the male, and that the associated soliciting displays are more appropriately viewed as "demand behavior" than begging (540). The present studies with Cockatiels strongly support this view; among Cockatiels, the male usually is dominant, and when courtship feeding occurs (observed in 2 of 5 mated pairs) in such circumstances, the female allofeeds the male. [Allofeeding of the Cockatielian male by the female also occurs during brooding (see pp. 410-412, 690, 691).]

ACCOMPANIED BY EXCITEMENT---SYNCHRONIZES BODY RHYTHMS. Courtship feeding occurs much more frequently with the onset of breeding (usually in the spring or summer in temperate climates). It always is accompanied by excitement. Courtship feeding could aid in suppressing inhibitions over close bodily contacts, and in synchronizing the bodily rhythms of the pair (3, 63). Thus, it may be one of the activities that brings the female lovebird into breeding condition--the "right combination" that "unlocks the door for reproduction" (13)--and serves to prepare the birds for allofeeding the young (101).

ASSOCIATIONS WITH COITUS---WHO FEEDS WHOM. Courtship feeding usually is a necessary prelude for sexual union in some birds. In others it occurs during coitus, or even afterward (28, 101). For Common Terns (*Sterna hirundo*), it is an important factor in determining the number and size of the eggs. With very rare exceptions, including Buttonquail (genus *Turnix*) and, as mentioned above, Cockatiels, the male allofeeds the female, even in cases where the parents share incubatory duties (28, 29, 706). Favored morsels often are offered.

ALLOFEEDING THE INCUBATING AND BROODING LOVEBIRD HEN. Courtship feeding occurs all through the period of sexual activity of lovebird pairs. Afterward, it gradually changes over into the much more extensive allofeeding of the hen as she incubates and broods the young (3). Food regurgitated by the male may be the sole source of nourishment for a female Peach-faced Lovebird during some extended periods of incubation. It has been suggested that courtship feeding appeared in adults in a new context, as an extension forward of this allofeeding during incubation (29, 51).

REDIRECTED COURTSHIP FEEDING. A seemingly healthy male Budgerigar sometimes will regurgitate moist seed and attempt to allofeed its mirror image, a favorite enclosure trinket, or even shiny objects. This behavior probably is a neurosis. The bird may spend most of the day filling its crop with seeds, only to regurgitate them later. Such birds often lose weight and deteriorate through starvation (451, 454). Other imprinted birds sometimes develop an unnatural pair-bonded relationship with their owners, to whom they regurgitate food. They may even copulate with an owners' hand (141, 451, 454). Both redirected courtship feeding and redirected copulation have been reported in the Blue-crowned Hanging Parrot (*Loriculus galgulus*; 79).

Cyrano's Early Social Interactions

HATCHING OF THE FIRST AND SECOND BROODS. With this introduction to breeding preliminaries, we are ready to trace the threads of the activity and interactions of the juvenile lovebirds, Cassandra, Cyrano, and Cyrus. These broodmates were the 2nd brood of Petra and Ramses, and hatched during the days of January 23 and 24, 1983. Their older brothers, Jagatai and Ogadai, hatched on the previous November 12 and 16. [The eggs of the 2nd brood hatched on consecutive days because they had been replaced by substitute eggs as they were laid, so that Petra could not begin to incubate them almost immediately, as she otherwise would have done. With this manipulation, the eggs were expected to hatch at roughly the same time, instead of every other day, at the same spacings as the ovipositions.]

ENCLOSURE EXPLORATION---FLIGHTINGS---CYRANO'S ALTERED BEHAVIOR. When the chicks were 37 days old, Petra and Ramses allowed them to leave the NB and explore enclosure B for the 1st time. Three days later, they took their 1st flights in the room, and were facile fliers within 48 h. For roughly the next 5 weeks, they were flighted daily with their parents, frequently accompanied by, but not closely socializing with, their older brothers, Jagatai and Ogadai.

By the 11th week, it was clear that Cyrano was behaving differently from his broodmates. When the family was being flighted, he sometimes did not stay close to them. I did not realize it at the time, but this probably was because Cassandra and Cyrus had begun to form a pair bond and did not welcome his presence. [Recall, that I could identify individuals from combination of clipped tips of primary wing feathers and tails.] In any event, I planned to give Cyrano to a friend, Bill Murphy, who had a very pugnacious 4-yr-old female Peach-face Lovebird, appropriately named "Jaws". Bill's plan was to house Jaws with Cyrano in the hopes that they would mate, and that Cyrano's presence also might mellow Jaws' personality. Since Cyrano was well habituated and might have been expected to be handled a great deal, I clipped his wings before giving him to Bill.

AN ILL-FATED VISIT. On April 19, 1983, Cyrano was moved to a small enclosure next to Jaws' large one. After a few days of adjustment for both birds, Bill introduced Cyrano into Jaws' enclosure for a short period each day. This was when Cyrano's misadventures began, as Jaws attacked him incessantly. Cyrano's only means of escape were to hop, jump and sidle away, since he could not fly. Not only was Cyrano continually pursued by Jaws during these visits, he also was ill prepared to defend himself because it was his first exposure to fierce, sustained aggression.

In a very short time, the tip of a toe had been bitten off Cyrano's left foot. In consequence, Bill decided to promote the pairing more cautiously. A more spacious enclosure and floorstand were provided for Cyrano. Since this was placed on the other side of the room from Jaws' enclosure, Cyrano no longer was adjacent to Jaws at all times. The aftermath was that, one morning a few weeks later, Bill found Jaws dead on the floor of her enclosure.

SOCIABLE LOVEBIRDS MORTALLY SUSCEPTIBLE TO ISOLATION STRESS. The most surprising aspect of this outcome is not so much that Jaws died, but rather the speed with which it happened. A remarkable but little-known fact about the more sociable lovebirds, such as Peach-faced Lovebirds, is that if an individual is deprived of the normal social contacts but kept within sight and sound of other lovebirds, it gradually becomes ill and eventually dies of stress. Death usually occurs in about 6 months (3). So, it was not an entirely unexpected result that one of the birds died, but rather that it occurred so soon after they were separated.

I am inclined to believe that the death of Jaws was no coincidence. Not having been near another bird of any kind for 4 years, she may have been greatly affected by Cyrano's close presence for over 1 month, even though she was very hostile toward him when they were housed together. However, the matter cannot be resolved; I learned of her death long after the fact, and had no chance to examine her for signs of stress.

CYRANO RETURNED---HOUSED WITH BROODMATES----SEEKS TO SOCIALIZE. When I was informed of what had transpired, I thought of the excellent opportunity to ascertain how Cyrano's family would react if he were to be returned to their enclosure. Would they recognize him? Would he be accepted, or would they repel and attack him, as they would have responded toward a stranger? So, I was quite agreeable to reclaim Cyrano when Bill suggested it. On July 7, 1983, approximately 11 weeks after leaving the colony, Cyrano was returned. Meanwhile, Petra and Ramses were breeding again, and the 1st egg was due at any time, as could be judged from the bulge in the area of Petra's vent.

It would have been pointless to return Cyrano to the family in enclosure B, because Petra and Ramses already were becoming less tolerant of the presence of Cyrano's sister and brother, Cassandra and Cyrus. Instead, I put the 3 broodmates together in enclosure C, which was new to them all, beginning on Cyrano's 1st night back. Needless to say, I kept a watchful eye on Cyrano's condition and all interactions between the 3 broodmates.

As might have been expected, Cyrano was treated as an intruder, even though he very likely was recognized. In the next 24 h there were bouts of squabbling between Cyrano, on the one hand, and Cassandra and Cyrus, on the other, with Cyrus being responsible for most of the aggression. To give Cyrano some respite, and to find out how Cassandra would treat him if she were to be alone with him, I put Cyrus back with his parents for the 2nd night. The following morning I found Cyrano perching next to Cassandra, but not touching her. Though she tolerated his being nearby, she would not allow him to perch in contact with her, in the usual fashion of lovebird mates and broodmates.

The few days following Cyrus' return from his overnight absence with his parents in enclosure B were marked by his continued aggression toward Cyrano. However, despite being repelled at every advance, Cyrano continually sought to socialize with his broodmates. Cassandra, herself, was not antagonistic; Cyrano's intrusions and attempts at courting merely appeared to be unwelcome. The closest liaison Cyrano could achieve occurred at night, when he slept on a perch just below the mated pair.

INTERACTIONS WITH FAMILY MEMBERS. Cyrano's disadvantages numbered more than being treated as an intruder and having an injured foot; he still was incapable of flight, from having had his primaries clipped. This meant that I could not observe his interactions with his parents and siblings under conditions of being flighted. These interactions were of great interest because one would expect less aggression to take place outside, than within, a confined space, such as a small enclosure.

Placing Cyrano on the home perch (see Fig. 1a) by hand was one step toward a solution, as he then could interact with his relatives there, or on top of the enclosures. Unfortunately, the others spent little time there; when they flew off, Cyrano sometimes tried to accompany them, but he always came crashing down. His falls were not serious, though, because he could maneuver sufficiently to alight at the nearest available high point.

UNABLE TO FLY, CYRANO REMAINS AN OUTSIDER. The family members had taken to spending most of their time on the shelf perch and the side and front window shelves (Fig. 2a). So, I also placed Cyrano at these locations by hand, and kept guard nearby to prevent an accidental fall. This practice allowed Cyrano to participate more in family activities, but he remained an outsider. This was perhaps not so much because the others avoided him, as because he could not accompany them in flight. When Cyrano encountered another bird, as he followed on foot or when one alighted near him, the other bird usually pecked at him. As a result, Cyrano tended increasingly to skirt the fringes of the group and to be very wary. This was the situation that prevailed more or less in the following 5 months, until Cyrano again was able to fly.

GAINING ATTENTION BY TOE-CARESSING. Within the next 10 days, Cyrano made considerable progress in his attempts to socialize, and it became evident that his main objective was to court Cassandra. He adopted an effective new tactic. Since Cassandra and Cyrus would not tolerate his perching next to them, he perched at the next-nearest location, on a branch that lay just beneath their favorite perch position. There, he was close to them, yet comparatively immune to attack.

Then he began to make cautious overtures to Cassandra. He would reach up to her feet and very gently caress one of her toes in his bill (just as a bird cleans its own toes), sometimes also vocalizing softly. In the following, I refer to this simply as "caressing" her toes, and I reckon the number of elapsed days during the next months from this 1st day on which it occurred. I little anticipated at the time that in the coming weeks and months Cyrano would employ this tactic hundreds, even thousands, of times.

At first Cassandra was alarmed when Cyrano made contact with her toes, and she pecked at him vigorously. These pecks gradually became less frequent as she came to tolerate his attentions. Sometimes she only discouraged him by touching beaks lightly. Cassandra's initial responses of repelling Cyrano vigorously are easily accounted for, because toes are the focal points of attack via biting and pinching in most aggression and intimidation between lovebirds. For that reason, Cassandra was very sensitive initially to contacts made with her toes.

TOE-CARESSING AS NORMAL ATTENTION-GETTING BEHAVIOR. At the time Cyrano employed this tactic, I viewed it as an innovation to cope with the existing circumstances, since this behavior had not been reported previously in the literature. It was not until a year later that I discovered that precisely this form of toe caressing is used, though infrequently, by both lovebirds and Cockatiels to gain the attention of a conspecific (see pp. 814, 815, **Attention Getting by Toe Caressing**).

ENDLESS COURTING, BUT A SOCIAL OUTCAST. Having at hand a comparatively safe, effective way to get Cassandra's attention, it became Cyrano's major activity in the following weeks, and he often vocalized softly to her at the same time. All through the day, every day, at every opportunity, Cyrano now sought her attention hundreds of times and got chased or threatened away by Cyrus almost as often. By the 4th day of Cyrano's ceaseless courting, Cyrus' reactions in repelling him had flagged noticeably. Mere discouraging bill pecks became much more frequent and chases much less so.

Cyrano not only was excluded from other interactions with Cassandra, he was in the position of a social outcast. A good example occurred one day when Cassandra and Cyrus were bathing. As they took turns head-ducking at the edge of the water bowl, Cyrano stood by, 'eagerly' awaiting a chance to move in and take his turn, as he had done with them in his youth. But it was not to be. Each time Cassandra or Cyrus backed off and Cyrano attempted to advance, he was chased away. This was unusual behavior because, ordinarily, with 3 young broodmates, all 3 birds would have bathed. By the time the pair had finished their long baths, Cyrano seemingly had either been thoroughly intimidated or had lost interest, as he did not bathe.

COURTSHIP FEEDING BEGINS--REGURGITATING FOOD. Then, a new element of behavior entered the picture, as Cyrus began to courtship-feed Cassandra frequently. Cyrano's situation then became most pitiable. Previously, I was witness to Cyrano's actions but could only imagine or presume to guess at their object. But with the onset of courtship feeding, I not only could identify with him, I was privy to each 'disappointment' or failure.

Let me explain that in order for one lovebird to allofeed another, food must be regurgitated from the crop by retroperistalsis (103). This act is seen as a convulsive bobbing of the head, something like the convulsions one goes through when one retches. Every time Cyrano saw Cyrus courtship-feed Cassandra, and often at other times as well, he also sought to allofeed her. But in order to be prepared to offer food after getting her attention by caressing her toes, he first had to regurgitate the food. Since this behavior is so readily recognized, his regurgitations always gave me advance notice of his intentions, so that I could not fail to recognize his countless failures. It was this heightened awareness that made his situation appear to be so pitiable to me.

It is possible, but unlikely, that not all of Cyrano's head-bobbing served to regurgitate food, since head-bobbing also can have a purely display function (3, 4). But at later times when Cassandra accepted his attentions, Cyrano never failed to allofeed her after head-bobbing.

CYRANO EMBOLDENED---HIS FIRST NOTED ALLOFEEDING OF CASSANDRA. Apparently encouraged by his successes at toe caressing, Cyrano became emboldened. By the evening of the 8th day (i.e., the 8th day after adopting the toe-caressing tactic), undaunted by hundreds of failures to allofeed Cassandra, he began to try to edge his way onto the night perch next to her. But Cyrus would not tolerate his near presence. Cyrano had to continue to be contented with sleeping solitarily at his customary position on the lower branch.

Nonetheless, these proved to be the days of Cyrano's first notable progress. In checking the locations of the birds on the morning of the 11th day, before I turned on the daytime lights (but in a room by no means dark), I watched him edge over to Cassandra along the side of the enclosure and allofeed her for several min, while Cyrus looked on at her side. In view of the ready and lengthy acceptance of food by Cassandra, it seems likely that Cyrano had been allofeeding her on other early mornings as well. The allofeeding probably would not have lasted so long and progressed routinely, had it been occurring for the first time. It will be seen in Chapters 5-7 and below that there are sound reasons to believe that there had been previous early morning allofeedings of Cassandra by Cyrano.

CASSANDRA AND CYRUS SQUABBLE---CASSANDRA BUILDS A NEST. On the 12th day, additional new interactions commenced. Cassandra and Cyrus then began to have more frequent squabbles, pecking each other's bills and 'scolding' vigorously by high-pitched shrieking. This might have been partly because of influences of Cyrano's presence. More likely, it simply represented increased agonistic interactions associated with premature attempts of Cyrus to achieve sexual union with Cassandra. Such behavior of lovebirds during early breeding is not uncommon. At any rate, the pair continued to treat Cyrano as an outsider. He still was not allowed to perch adjacent to them. In fact, he never achieved that degree of acceptance by them.

On the 17th day I observed Cyrano allofeeding Cassandra for the 2nd time. His routine of caressing her toes and seeking to allofeed her during the day had continued unabatedly. As often as Cyrus chased him away and attacked him, he returned, with no sign of having been in the least intimidated. By the morning of the 19th day, however, yet another new development surfaced. There was a great flurry of excitement, as Cassandra attempted to strip paper at every opportunity. She also occasionally accepted food from both Cyrus and Cyrano.

CYRANO AND CYRUS GRAPPLE. Cyrano even became so bold as to hold his ground and return Cyrus' pecks. And their contacts then were no longer of the momentary type, with Cyrano fleeing more or less in panic. Rather, they had fights that could last several sec or more, with both birds grappling and feathers flying. Though this did not at all present the usual picture of restrained Peach-faced Lovebird combat, bitter fighting is not unknown in the species (see pp. 264, 265). But after about 2 h of these agonistic encounters, all birds settled into their usual routines. At times like this, I kept a watchful eye on the trio, because in unrestrained fights within some lovebird species, the birds are known literally to "tear each other apart" (3). As will be seen in Chapter 5, the birds did not confine their biting to the toes, although this has been the maximum extent of aggression noted by most workers.

CYRANO EXCLUDED FROM NESTING AREA. In the most notable change of the next 3 days, the left-rear corner of the enclosure floor below the sleeping perches (Fig. 3b; enclosures B and C had similar floorplans) became the focus of attention of Cassandra and Cyrus. This area was being prepared as a nest, and Cyrano was excluded from it. Cassandra then spent a great deal of time attempting to strip paper, at which she was not as yet very proficient, and to chew off pieces of the outside enclosure cover.

Since Cassandra kept mostly to the nesting area, from which Cyrano was excluded, only Cyrus courtship-fed her there. Although Cyrano's opportunities to secure Cassandra's attention diminished somewhat, because Cassandra spent more time on the enclosure floor, he still had many opportunities to make the effort while she was grasping the side and chewing on the outside enclosure cover. But when he tried to get her attention then, she was too intent to be diverted from her efforts, and his overtures were ignored.

CYRANO CRIPPLED. A marked change in circumstances also was signalled by an increased ferocity of Cyrus' attacks. On the 22nd day, he crippled Cyrano --still at a disadvantage from not being able to fly--with bites on his left foot. This put Cyrano at a still greater disadvantage for the next week or so. Although much concerned for Cyrano's safety, I did not isolate him, because, as yet, Cyrus only attacked when Cyrano intruded. Despite a great improvement in Cyrano's condition after 4 days, much of his daytime activities had to be confined to skirting the fringes of the nesting area. There, Cassandra and Cyrus were intensely occupied, as she continued to try to strip paper and chew the outside cloth, and he "tagged" after her, copying her activities, including almost continual chewing of paper.

CYRANO INTIMIDATED BY CASSANDRA. Cyrano's intrusions into the nesting area then were cautious and tentative. His closest approaches occurred when Cyrus was allofeeding Cassandra. At these times he edged as close as safety allowed, ever ready himself to offer a portion of food. He regurgitated (and then reswallowed) food time after time, at virtually every promising opportunity to allofeed her, but without success. The usual outcome was that he was chased off by Cyrus. At this relative nadir of Cyrano's courtship endeavors, on the 28th day, I ascertained the status of his relationship with Cassandra in the absence of Cyrus. When I removed Cyrus to another room, Cyrano succeeded in taking up a position near Cassandra on the perch, but she pecked at him when he tried to come closer. Thus, intimidated, he became even less aggressive in seeking to socialize with her than he had been when Cyrus was present.

CYRUS TEMPORARILY "FALLS FROM GRACE"---FEMALES DOMINANT. But a great surprise came 80 min later, when I returned Cyrus, because Cassandra also rejected him. As often as he approached her, she repelled him. After about 1 h, she allowed him to perch near her, but not in contact with her. It required another 2 h of courtship by Cyrus to recover his former prerogatives as her mate. This episode lends emphasis to the previously noted (p. 239) fact that the female Peach-faced Lovebird is the dominant member of the mated pair (3). The manner in which Cyrano was intimidated by Cassandra's rejection in Cyrus' absence also is very suggestive of this dominant role (and that of female Budgerigars also, for that matter; see pp. 777, 778, **Cesare Excluded**, *et seq.*) in the acceptance of a male's attentions during pairing, a phenomenon well known in gulls (472).

NEST-BUILDING ATTEMPTS CONTINUE. In the next 10 days, Cassandra spent a great deal of time trying to strip paper, trying to tuck strips of anything available between her rump feathers (though there was no need for transport by flight), trying to chew material from the outside cover, and trying to build a nest on the floor in the left-rear corner. At all these tasks she did very poorly. After repeated failures, I gave her strips of paper for nest building. Meanwhile, Cyrano had continued to toe-caress and try to allofeed Cassandra at every opportunity, but with little more success than she herself was having at nest-building. Cyrus usually accompanied and imitated Cassandra, but he frequently was diverted to chase Cyrano from the nesting area. The latter still was favoring his left foot.

BREEDING BEGINS. Beginning on September 1, 1983, with their first noted successful sexual union, intensive breeding activities of Cassandra and Cyrus began. Further copulations occurred several times in the next week, and oviposition occurred every other day, beginning on Sept. 7th. Although I did not facilitate this breeding by providing a NB or nutritional supplements (other than cuttlefish bone), neither did I discourage it, because I wanted to determine to what extent Cyrano's presence and intrusions would be tolerated. I gave Cassandra a shallow nestbowl with paper strips, placing it at the rear-corner location that she had selected as the IA (incubative area). Although she did not incubate continuously, she spent a great deal of time in this bowl sitting on her eggs. Typically she sat 'contentedly,' softening fragments of paper by chewing interminably on them.

HOUSED WITH BUDGERIGARS. Meanwhile, Cyrano had become even more of an outcast; both members of the pair began to attack him. On September 11, the day on which Cassandra laid her 3rd egg, I removed Cyrano to enclosure D. At that time this housed the Budgerigar pair, Cornelia and Cesare. Since Cyrano still favored his left foot, and could not fly, he was much less dexterous than the Budgerigars. Accordingly, their safety was not at risk, though he did bully them, at first, and prevailed in every dispute.

RETURNED TO THE COMPANY OF THE MATED PAIR. Cyrano remained with the Budgerigars for 5 days, until the 16th of September. By that time, Cassandra had abandoned her eggs, and it was safe to return him to enclosure C. In fact, with the termination of breeding activities, Cyrus' tendency to engage in sexual fighting waned, and the milieu was far different from the one that Cyrano had left only 5 days earlier. The markedly different climate was heralded already on Cyrano's 1st night back, when the pair bathed and he was allowed to participate after they had finished. The next week saw essentially a repetition of the activities of the week preceding Cyrano's first noted allofeeding of Cassandra, in the sense that his numerous unsuccessful efforts to allofeed her were fairly well tolerated.

To assess the situation again in the absence of Cyrus, I removed him for 20 min. Cassandra immediately allowed Cyrano to allofeed her, but she still would not accede to letting him do so while perched beside her. Rather, he had to perch on the branch below, or on the left side of the enclosure. The return of Cyrus immediately restored the status quo. The next 2 weeks, however, found Cyrano succeeding in allofeeding Cassandra many times, sometimes even with Cyrus perching right next to her. In fact, she occasionally even chased Cyrus away as Cyrano allofed her. But she never let Cyrano perch beside her, nor did Cyrus cease to chase and attack him. At least once during these 2 weeks, the trio bathed again, first Cassandra, then Cyrus, and lastly Cyrano.

BREEDING AGAIN. On October 15, one month after Cassandra had abandoned her previous clutch of eggs, and I had reunited the trio, Cassandra and Cyrus were breeding again, and the 1st egg was imminent. Out of concern for Cyrano's safety, I returned him to enclosure D with the Budgerigars, Cornelia and Cesare. I did not facilitate breeding with their 2nd clutch, either, giving them a nestbowl, but no NB. It was during this period that events took place that eventually culminated in Cyrano's mating. These events are treated below, but first I consider Cyrano's interactions during family flightings.

FAMILY FLIGHTINGS. The 3rd brood of Petra and Ramses consisted of 2 females, Flavia and Zenobia. At that time they were over 2 months old, having hatched on August 6. They already were in their juvenal feathers and independent of their parents. I sometimes flighted the entire family of 9 lovebirds together, to observe their interactions as a group. But I concentrated on concurrent flightings of the 2nd and 3rd broods (Cassandra, Cyrus, and Cyrano, and Flavia and Zenobia, respectively). Sometimes I flighted Cyrano only with Flavia and Zenobia, who were prospective mates for him.

CYRANO AND ZENOBIA---REMAINING QUESTIONS. On Cyrano's very first encounter with Flavia and Zenobia they showed a very friendly interest and seeming curiosity over one another. However, because of Cyrano's inability to fly, and the fact that the rest of the family always pecked at him on close approach, he had become very skittish. He had developed the habit of breaking into headlong retreat whenever intimidated by any bird. Even though he followed Cassandra and Cyrus boldly on foot during these flightings, he fled from them whenever he was threatened or confronted.

After a short visit with Flavia and Zenobia, Cyrano's skittishness prevailed, and he fled. The consequence of this overt act of subordination was that Flavia and Zenobia appeared to become emboldened to chase and threaten Cyrano whenever they afterwards encountered him. In fact, they often sought him out and pursued him. On October 24, however, only about 2 weeks after his most successful allofeedings of Cassandra, Cyrano was bold enough to stand his ground when he encountered Zenobia on top of the enclosures, even though he still could not fly. She proved to be receptive, and he courtship-fed her forthwith. This was the opening wedge that eventually led to their pairing and numerous breedings.

I had several remaining questions to ask of Cyrano. One was whether he would make any further progress in courting Cassandra. Or, would his initial success with Zenobia influence his former determined behavior in that regard? Since Cyrano already was thoroughly accommodated to being housed with the Budgerigars, would he now prefer to be in the company of the latter birds?

SECOND RETURN---A COOL RECEPTION. On November 2, I removed Cassandra's eggs and nestbowl, in which her interest, in any event, had been waning rapidly, and returned Cyrano to her enclosure. This time, he was much less well received than previously, as can be judged from the following incident. During the 1st day of reunion, Cassandra and Cyrus took long baths, taking turns repeatedly at head ducking. Having been accustomed to joining in at such times during the period of his last sojourn with them, Cyrano also attempted to bathe. But they chased him off repeatedly. Cyrano persisted doggedly, as if desperate to maintain his former gains, but to no avail. They just as determinedly drove him off. When they finally did finish bathing, though, Cyrano also took a bath, contrary to the previous outcome (when he apparently had lost interest by the time they finished bathing).

PREFERS TO BE HOUSED IN ENCLOSURE D. In the next few days, Cyrano appeared to answer one of my questions many times. He seemed to prefer the company of the Budgerigars. Whenever he was flighted with his broodmates (although he, himself, still could not fly), he sought to enter enclosure D with the Budgerigars--pulling at and struggling with the sliding lift door. If both enclosures C and D were open, he joined the Budgerigars in D. If placed in enclosure C, with or without Cassandra and Cyrus, but with the door open, he promptly left and joined the Budgerigars in enclosure D. However, we may not consider this behavior to provide an unambiguous expression of a preference for being housed with the Budgerigars, because the dominant factor determining his choice may have been a conservativeness for location (see p. 295), namely being housed in enclosure D.

COURTSHIP-FEEDS CASSANDRA REPEATEDLY. Ten days after his return, Cassandra accepted food from Cyrano for several min, as he perched beneath her. Three days later, and again 10 days later, she accepted food from him for over 5 min and for about 2 min, respectively. Cyrano allofed her through the enclosure mesh as he perched outside, while Cyrus looked on. However, the pair otherwise were becoming ever more aggressive toward Cyrano, and they re-injured his left foot, though not seriously. The next day Cyrano courtship-fed Cassandra twice. Once, he was inside the enclosure with her, with Cyrus looking on; the 2nd time he allofed her from the outside.

AIRBORNE AGAIN. Two days later, Cassandra laid the 1st egg of her 3rd clutch, still accepting food from Cyrano through the bars 2 days after that, as the 2nd egg was about to be laid. That same day (Nov. 30) marked a milestone for Cyrano. For the first time in almost 8 months, he could stay airborne for short periods. A week later, he could gain altitude, and after another week he had regained completely his flight capabilities. But by then, Cassandra and Cyrus were becoming very aggressive; after they injured him yet again on December 2, this time on his right foot, I removed him permanently and returned him to enclosure D with the Budgerigars.

It had been established that Cassandra would accept food from Cyrano during the period of early incubation. Would she also do so while brooding chicks? That question would not be answered until over 4 months later, as described on pages 329-331 (**An Unexpected Aftermath**). There it is found that Cyrano not only succeeded in allofeeding her during brooding, but, in a limited sense, he became dominant over her. At that time Cassandra solicited food from Cyrano and was not merely refused, but ignored.

Success Along Another Avenue, Cyrano Mates with Zenobia

UNUSUAL PAIR-BONDING CIRCUMSTANCES. I now trace the formation of a sibling pair bond under the unusual circumstances of the pairing birds being able to interact with one another freely only during limited periods. Most of the time they were separated from one another to a greater or lesser degree, but they always could see and hear each other. These studies probe the question, "What are the requirements, as regards amounts and types of contacts between two siblings, such as courtship feeding, grooming, sleeping side by side, companionship in flight and in foraging, vocal exchanges, visual exchanges, etc., for the formation of a pair bond?" Some fascinating, but not entirely unexpected, answers were obtained.

FLAVIA PAIR BONDED WITH ZENOBIA. Between October 24, when Cyrano first allofed Zenobia, and December 2, when I returned him to the company of the Budgerigars in enclosure D, he and Zenobia were not flighted together. However, Cyrano had been housed only 10-15 cm from the enclosure-B tower (to which Zenobia had access) from October 24 to November 2 and, again, beginning on December 2. Since I temporarily discontinued studies of Cyrano's interactions with Cassandra and Cyrus on December 2, I turned to an investigation of Cyrano's interactions with his younger sisters, Flavia and Zenobia.

These sisters already had established a homosexual pair bond. They groomed one another and slept next to one another, as do all broodmates, but, in addition, Flavia was courtship-feeding Zenobia. Any progress that Cyrano might be able to make in advancing his relationships with them, once again, would have to be made in the face of the various ties of a pair bond. But, of course, a homosexual pair bond does not present the formidable obstacles to an intruding bird of the opposite sex that are presented by a heterosexual one. In fact, as a rule, homosexual bonds eventually break up spontaneously (4).

CYRANO ALLOFEEDS ZENOBIA AGAIN. After returning the injured Cyrano to enclosure D on December 2, I did not flight him for a week. During this time, he was able to vocalize with Flavia and Zenobia, both when they were in the adjacent tower (Fig. 1a) and when they were foraging near his enclosure when being flighted. At the latter times, they showed great interest in Cyrano, and he in them. The last time that Flavia allofed Zenobia was on the morning of Dec. 9, on the same day that I later flighted them and opened the door to Cyrano's enclosure to flight him also. Shortly after Zenobia left her enclosure, she sidled around on the front of Cyrano's enclosure near the entrance. Cyrano screeched excitedly and defended the entrance by pecking at her. But his pecking quickly gave way to courtship feeding, although this was only the 2nd time he had allofed her.

CYRANO PAIR-BONDS WITH ZENOBIA. On December 13, both Flavia and Zenobia entered Cyrano's enclosure, but Cyrano allofed only Zenobia. He now had become very aggressive toward the Budgerigars, seemingly trying to expel them from the enclosure, which doubtless was regarded as a prospective nesting site. On the very next day, Zenobia showed the first sign of defending her pair-bonded relationship with Cyrano, by chasing Flavia away from him (so-called "sexual aggression"). We can date the formation of the pair bond between Zenobia and Cyrano from this day. In this connection, Brockway considered pair formation in Budgerigars to be completed when an individual either preened or fed another and both showed a prolonged tendency to remain near each other (67).

PAIR BOND FIRMLY ESTABLISHED. Cyrano allofed Zenobia several times in the next 5 days, either in his enclosure or through the mesh of her enclosure. He also had friendly exchanges (non-aggressive bodily contacts and vocalizations) with her through his enclosure bars, when only she and Flavia were flighted. On the other hand, he repelled any attemps by Flavia to intrude. Cyrano also made a first attempt to copulate with Zenobia on the enclosure floor. Although she seemed to be receptive, he was unsuccessful, perhaps because sexual union is most readily achieved when the female perches on a branch or other support. Even in the most favorable of circumstances, newly-formed pairs attempting to copulate tend to be awkward and make many "mistakes" (3).

Cyrano's pair-bonded relationship with Zenobia became strengthened in the next 2 weeks. Whenever they were flighted together, or permitted to interact, Zenobia kept close to him and frequently repelled Flavia, who continued to vie for his attention. Their favorite retreat was the floor of Cyrano's enclosure (the prospective nesting site) where he frequently attempted to copulate with her. Meanwhile, he continued to courtship feed her. It was also during this period that Cyrano developed the habit of plucking the bars of his enclosure with his bill, like the strings of a harp (later engaged in even more frequently by Flavia)

Zenobia and Cyrano's pair bond became firmly established during the month of January, 1984. At that time, he sometimes tried to keep her within his enclosure by guarding and repelling her from the entrance as she sought to leave. Their most intensive effort at coitus occurred at mid-month. As usual, this took place on the floor of enclosure D.

MAINTAIN PROXIMITY---AGGRESSIVE TOWARD CAGEMATES. When housed in enclosure C, Zenobia spent ever more of her time in the horizontal section of the tower (Fig. 1a), which was the position at which she was closest to Cyrano. Likewise, he perched and slept close to or on the front face of his enclosure, where he also was closest to her in the tower. Late at night, they often made brief, low 'contented,' warbling chirps in near unison with one another (duetting). Zenobia did so even with her head turned back over her shoulder in the sleeping posture. These vocal exchanges probably serve to cement the pair bond (63). An indication that their pair bond had continued to strengthen was that both birds became more aggressive toward the birds with which they were housed. Zenobia repelled Flavia from the horizontal section of the tower during most of the day, usually allowing her to enter only late in the evening and at night, when they slept there side by side.

TRANSFERRED TO A LARGER ENCLOSURE. Cyrano's hostility to the Budgerigars now became intolerable. Not only did he expel one or both of them from the enclosure several times when Zenobia was present and the door was open, he became excessively aggressive toward them at other times. Being able to fly then, and with his legs and feet healed (except for the lost claw), he was a formidable antagonist for the relatively dainty Budgerigars in the confined space of enclosure D. A change was necessary. These problems were the catalyst that also led to a more flexible arrangement for Zenobia and Cyrano.

On February 8, I exchanged Cyrano and the Budgerigars for Jagatai and Ogadai who had been housed in the larger enclosure E. This change also would prove to have interesting consequences for Flavia. In the larger enclosure, the Budgerigars easily evaded Cyrano. And Cyrano less frequently crossed paths with them, because now he could come into direct contact with Zenobia, albeit only through a $1\frac{1}{4}$ x $2\frac{1}{2}$-cm space. The opportunity for such contacts tended to divert and monopolize his attention.

FACILITATING DIRECT CONTACT. The ability to make direct contact was achieved by placing enclosure E flush against the tower (Fig. 1a). I also placed a small ladder along the right side of enclosure E, by the top of the tower, inclined downward at about 30° from the horizontal. This provided a platform on which Cyrano could perch, without having to cling to the bars. Another ladder was placed underneath the first, flush against the right side of enclosure E, adjacent to the tower. This latter ladder allowed Cyrano to climb and perch along the right side at any level. It now was very easy for Cyrano to perch directly across from Zenobia, at any desired height. [Zenobia could cling to the mesh of the vertical section of the tower at any height and perch horizontally at its base.]

TOWER DEFENDED BY ZENOBIA---CYRANO USUALLY NEARBY. With the new arrangement, Zenobia's temporal commitment to the tower, especially the highest vertical section, became even greater, and her occupancy of it more nearly exclusive. Then she usually would not permit Flavia beyond the turn to the horizontal section, except at night, when they slept together. She protected her perch with such tenacity that she often went hungry, foregoing food rather than leaving the tower unguarded in Flavia's presence. As will be seen below, Zenobia's protectiveness of her pair bond with Cyrano was not ill founded.

HOUSED IN CLOSE PROXIMITY. Zenobia and Cyrano then were housed practically side by side. They interacted almost all through the day and evening. They perched next to each other, followed one another when flighted, and touched bills through the 1¼-cm space. Sometimes they created a great racket with rapidly repeated shrieks, seemingly venting their frustratiuon at being so close to one another, yet unable to achieve more intimate contact. At other times they duetted melodiously.

CLOSER CONTACTS---ALMOST ALL PAIR-BOND INTERACTIONS ACHIEVED. After a few days of the new arrangement, I made yet another change to allow more intimate contacts. I provided a 2½-cm-square cutout between enclosure E and the top of the tower. Cyrano then could allofeed Zenobia through this opening, which also allowed a certain amount of allogrooming of each other's heads. The change also led to a lesser amount of shrieking, but by no means eliminated it. Taken together with the contacts that occurred during flighting, Zenobia and Cyrano could achieve almost all of the interactions of a pair bond except sleeping side by side at night.

CYRANO SEEKS TO ENTER HIS OLD ENCLOSURE. One might have expected that with the much more advantageous arrangement of enclosure E, Cyrano would not seek to return to enclosure D, which then housed his older brothers, Jagatai and Ogadai. But this reasoning does not take into account the ultraconservative nature of avian behavior.

Cyrano's ultraconservativeness or, if one prefers, his being a creature of habit, was expressed in the form of repeated efforts to return to enclosure D, even though it was occupied by his brothers, with whom he was not on particularly friendly terms (as they never had been housed together). For the next 2 weeks, he sought to enter enclosure D every time he was flighted. Even when I sought to return him to enclosure E from the home perch, he always flew, instead, to the enclosure-D entrance. I always found it necessary to catch him manually to return him to enclosure E (as opposed to transferring him on the home perch; see p. 282).

FLAVIA FORCEFULLY ENTERS ENCLOSURE E. During this period, Cyrano entered enclosure E voluntarily only when he followed Zenobia, as she went into it to feed. In fact, when I flighted Cyrano with his older brothers on February 17, he lost no time in entering enclosure D and bathing there. The likelihood that Cyrano had become possessive over enclosure E was suggested the next day, after he followed Zenobia into it. When Flavia also sought to enter, Zenobia and Cyrano both repelled her from the entrance. It required a tenacious struggle on Flavia's part to force her way into the enclosure. Though Zenobia doubtless was trying to keep Flavia away from her mate, Cyrano, Cyrano's actions could have been an expression of his possessiveness over either enclosure E, or Zenobia, or both.

FLAVIA, A "FORCE" TO BE RECKONED WITH. One appears to be seeing in Flavia's behavior expressions of the same strong determination noted above in Cyrano, in his interactions with his broodmates, Cassandra and Cyrus. Again, the loyalties of a pair bond were the barriers to acceptance. But in Cyrano's youth, Cassandra was the only unmated female lovebird in the colony. In Flavia's case, the field of prospective mates was much broader. In addition to Cyrano, her older brothers, Jagatai and Ogadai, also were present. Though these brothers were homosexually pair bonded, Flavia by no means ignored their presence.

I had flighted Flavia with Jagatai and Ogadai on several occasions. At such times, they never tolerated her company, though she sought repeatedly to socialize with them. But these occasional flightings did not provide opportunities for the sustained pressure on the pair-bond loyalty that Cyrano was able to exert in the case of Cassandra and Cyrus. Moreover, if I had housed Flavia with her older brothers, it would have provided no great challenge for her. Nor was it a promising area for study. It was a foregone conclusion that, in time, she would have formed a pair bond with one or the other of them. Furthermore, I wished to keep Flavia unmated, to provide a means of challenging the pair-bonded association of Zenobia and Cyrano.

However, Flavia did not remain a passive pawn to my plans. When I flighted her with Zenobia and Cyrano, she usually spent a considerable amount of time visiting the front of enclosure D, where Jagatai and Ogadai had been housed since February 8, 1984. Though she busied herself stripping paper there, she often also sought to socialize with her brothers. They usually descended to the enclosure floor, in close proximity to her (separated only by the 1-cm-spaced bars), shrieking and milling about excitedly the entire time. At other times, they merely watched with apparent interest, often pacing back and forth. Although they reacted to Zenobia in a similar way when she stripped paper there, Zenobia took little or no note of them. Occasionally only one of the brothers descended to the enclosure floor when Flavia or Zenobia was present.

FLAVIA PENETRATES ENCLOSURE D. The following noteworthy events occurred on March 22. Flavia was visiting near enclosure D in her usual fashion, when a great din of lovebird vocalizations began. On investigating, I was greatly surprised to find Flavia inside enclosure D with Jagatai and Ogadai. The left plastic sidepane (the cover designed to prevent debris from being scattered outside the enclosure) had been dislodged and she had entered through the empty space that normally contains a food cup, inserted from outside. There she stood on the enclosure floor at one end, 'challenging' Jagatai and Ogadai, who were backing up against the opposite end. All 3 of them were 'scolding' excitedly with rapidly repeated shrieks, the one at the other two, and vice versa. It was not hard to get the gist of the communications being exchanged.

I happened to be reading at the time. Not realizing, at first, the interesting opportunities that were presented by this situation, I simply flushed Flavia from the enclosure (I needed only to speak, for her to leave voluntarily) and replaced the sidepane. I assumed that it had been dislodged inadvertently, and went back to my reading. To my great surprise, the very same events were repeated in their entirety a few min later. Clearly, Flavia had learned how to remove the sidepane and enter enclosure D. Instead of letting her repeat the feat a 3rd time, and watching her accomplish it, I closed off the crawl space between enclosures D and F by packing some newspaper between them. Having acted in haste, I repented at leisure; I had to wait an entire month to see her repeat the act.

EVEN NON-MATED FEMALES DOMINATE MALES. Flavia's actions on that day appeared to demonstrate an ability to learn an unusual manipulation after only a single successful performance. More significantly, they gave striking evidence of the active role a female lovebird may take in initiating pair bonding, even in the face of an existing (homosexual) pair bond. Recall that Zenobia also had taken the initiative with Cyrano by invading his space in enclosure D when he was housed there with the Budgerigars. The mere fact that a female lovebird would venture to invade the space of pair-bonded males in the fashion demonstrated by Flavia implies that females dominate males even outside of heterosexual pair bonds.

ZENOBIA "TAKES OVER." Roughly one month after transferring Cyrano and the Budgerigars to the larger enclosure E, I twice placed Zenobia in the enclosure with him by hand, to test his reaction to her sudden presence. In both cases, and on a number of subsequent occasions when she entered his enclosure voluntarily, Zenobia simply "took over" immediately, just as if it were her home enclosure. Regardless of how agitated or aggressive Cyrano became, she remained unintimidated, pausing in her ongoing activities (see below) only to trade bill pecks with him, if and when self defense became necessary.

EATING AND DRINKING OCCUPY ZENOBIA'S ATTENTION. On these occasions, eating and drinking had the highest priority with Zenobia. Her hunger and thirst usually were so great after her long protective vigils in the tower, that she ate and drank for up to 10 min. And the more she ignored Cyrano, the more agitated and aggressive he became, and the more frequently he shrieked. In his calmer moments, he merely sought her attention by nibbling on a wingtip. But Cyrano eventually lost interest and, when the enclosure door was open, flew off to other pursuits, as treated below.

MORE ABOUT FLAVIA. A full 2 months after installing Cyrano and the Budgerigars in enclosure E, I flighted him together with Flavia and Zenobia. On that occasion, Zenobia joined Cyrano in enclosure E after he returned to it from being flighted, rather than before he left it. After Cyrano courtship-fed her, she left and Flavia approached. The latter repeatedly entered and exited from the enclosure. But she never ventured into it more than several cm from the entrance. She was exhibiting the more cautious approach to venturing into Cyrano's enclosure that Cyrano sometimes had adopted in approaching Cassandra and Cyrus.

STRICT TOWER-OCCUPANCY RULES. Throughout this period, Zenobia enforced very strict tower-occupacy rules on Flavia. She excluded her from the upper vertical section at all times, and often kept her out of the horizontal section in the early morning. As the day wore on she usually let Flavia move over into the latter section. Despite the disputes that often were precipitated, as Zenobia enforced these restrictions, she and Flavia continued to sleep side by side, and were close companions when flighted together. They also were close companions when flighted with Cyrano, at least during those periods when he flew off elsewhere by himself.

THE FAVORITE ACTIVITY OF MY FLIGHTED LOVEBIRDS when I was in the vicinity of the enclosures, was to alight on my head and shoulders. Usually they scrambled all over me, as well, chattering, nibbling on my ears and at blemishes on my skin, picking on hairs, and sometimes even giving me painful nips. On one occasion, I watched Cyrano closely in a mirror, while he and Zenobia were in my hair. He was going through motions very similar to those of copulation, suggesting that the similar footing in my hair to that on a female's back sometimes stimulated copulatory behavior. In Chapter 6 (see pp. 722, 723, **Unusual Sites for Coitus**, and pp. 746, 755), I describe how these attentions toward me originated and one of their unusual consequences.

An Unexpected Aftermath

I now have traced the course of Cyrano's social interactions, beginning with their early phases, including his injuries and his outcast existence. He persevered in courting in the face of seemingly insurmountable obstacles, finally managing repeatedly to allofeed his brother's mate. This had seemed a highly unlikely eventuality in view of the known social behavior of lovebirds. He then acquired a mate, Zenobia, though his contact interactions with her were restricted greatly, since she was housed separately. Cyrano subsequently made further progress in courting Cassandra, the object of his initial attentions, and developed a more friendly relation with Zenobia's broodmate, Flavia. At the same time, he preserved his pair bond with Zenobia, with whom he eventually bred repeatedly.

CYRANO REJECTS FLAVIA'S ATTENTIONS. On the day (April 21) that I detected how Flavia removed the sidepane of enclosure D, she spent some time perched on the top of Cyrano's enclosure. Even though Cyrano was perched next to Zenobia, who was in the tower, he had friendly vocal exchanges and bill contacts with Flavia through his enclosure bars. Although Zenobia was agitated and climbed and paced about in the tower, these exchanges continued for several min. When I flighted Cyrano to see if he would socialize with Flavia, he interacted with her in a not unfriendly way, though Flavia occasionally pecked at him.

In the next 7 weeks I flighted Cyrano concurrently with his two sisters a number of times. The only noteworthy events, as regards Cyrano and Flavia, were that Flavia: bathed alone in Cyrano's enclosure several times; sometimes stripped paper with Zenobia and Cyrano atop the kitchen door; and, now and again, either precipitated or merely partook in excited vocalizations with the pair. When, on May 30, I again flighted Cyrano and Flavia together alone, to assess the status of their relationship, Flavia repeatedly sought Cyrano's company. But he flew away each time she approached, evidencing no interest in socializing with her.

CYRANO AND CASSANDRA. Cyrano's subsequent relationship with Cassandra provided an unexpected aftermath. On April 21, Cassandra was brooding 3 chicks whose eyes had just opened. This also was the day that Cyrano socialized in a very friendly fashion with Flavia (see above). When I later flighted Cyrano alone with his mate, Zenobia, he left her and flew down to the left side of enclosure C. To my surprise, Cassandra and Cyrus came over to the enclosure side near him, and Cyrano allofed Cassandra time after time. Not only did Cyrus look on without interfering as Cyrano allofed her, the two males took turns at allofeeding her. After witnessing this episode, Zenobia descended and engaged in aggressive bill-pecking through the enclosure mesh with both Cassandra and Cyrus.

In the preceding days there had been no opportunity to observe interactions between Cassandra and Cyrano because Cassandra spent almost all her time in the nest with the chicks. She received most of her food from Cyrus. By this time I had become accustomed to the act of an incubating lovebird female accepting food from a male other than her mate. But with each passing day of incubation Cassandra and Cyrus had become more hostile to Cyrano and more protective of their eggs. It was possible that this hostility would increase further after the young hatched. But that proved not to be the case, and I was quite unprepared to see the mated pair that had repelled Cyrano so frequently, approach him in a friendly manner, and to see Cassandra accept food from him.

IGNORES CASSANDRA'S SOLICITATIONS. In the next 5½ weeks, I flighted Cyrano alone, with Flavia and Zenobia, and even with Cassandra and Cyrus. During the flights without Cassandra and Cyrus, he visited outside their enclosure 11 times and allofed Cassandra 7 times. But on 2 of these visits, he just watched Cassandra as she perched near him on the enclosure side, as she obviously was expecting to be allofed.

I was astonished at the events that transpired on a 3rd visit. Instead of merely waiting passively, Cassandra solicited food from Cyrano by extending her open bill toward him through the enclosure mesh, but he totally ignored her. The events of the last month had, indeed, wrought a remarkable change in Cyrano's relationship with Cassandra. Whereas, previously, his every action seemed to have as its focus the allofeeding of Cassandra, his new relationship with Zenobia altered the situation to the point that he might quite ignore Cassandra's solicitations for food.

INTERACTIONS DURING FLIGHTING. On 3 occasions when I flighted Cyrano with Cassandra and others, neither Cassandra nor Cyrano solicited the attention, nor encroached upon the space, of the other. On one of these occasions, Zenobia behaved aggressively toward Cassandra. On another, Cyrano pecked at Cyrus' tail, whereupon Cyrus boldly chased him off, showing that Cyrus still was dominant, at least in Cassandra's presence.

To ascertain how Cassandra and Cyrano would interact when alone, I flighted only the two of them on May 30. Cyrano became greatly excited as he milled around her on the home perch for several min, chattering incessantly and often shrieking. But she neither encouraged nor discouraged him, no matter how close to her he came. She just perched quietly. This behavior of Cyrano toward Cassandra was in marked contrast to his lack of interest in Flavia only an hour earlier. Even after Cyrano was returned to his enclosure, some 10 min elapsed before his excitedness waned. Cassandra obviously had either stimulated or frustrated him.

ZENOBIA AND CYRANO. During the same 5½-week period, Cyrano's relationship with Zenobia changed very little. They frequently perched next to one another (he in enclosure E, she in the tower) during the day, and he courtship-fed her from time to time, sometimes in long bouts. When they were flighted together, she continued to enter his enclosure and spend most of the time eating, customarily ignoring him. He, in turn, usually became agitated, sometimes pecked at her, and almost always created a din with his shrieks before he left the enclosure.

After Zenobia had eaten, or if she had eaten before being flighted, she and Cyrano frequently flew about together. Zenobia sometimes flew with her sister Flavia and left Cyrano to his own devices. In short, Zenobia and Cyrano still behaved as if pair bonded, but the "bloom was off the rose" for them.

FLAVIA AND ZENOBIA. Technically speaking, one perhaps should consider the homosexual pair bond between Flavia and Zenobia to have been broken from the time that the latter paired with Cyrano. In the actuality, it weakened only gradually. The first change I noted was that Flavia stopped allofeeding Zenobia. They remained on very friendly terms, however, except when Flavia encroached too close to Cyrano in the tower. They continued to sleep side by side, often flew together when flighted, and sometimes allogroomed one another.

They also shared the common plight of frequently being excluded from enclosure B and being confined to the tower. This was because their parents, Petra and Ramses, with whom they were housed, were brooding and caring for the chick, Titus, during this period. He was the sole chick in their 4th brood, and the parents seemed to be more than normally protective of him, often chasing Flavia and Zenobia into the tower. As will be seen in Chapter 5, the two sisters, apparently as a consequence of their being rigorously excluded from the company of the new family (the parents and Titus) behaved toward Titus in a manner that I feel justified to describe as "vindictive;" they attacked him viciously at every opportunity, once almost fatally.

DISCUSSION -- LOVEBIRD FINDINGS

Before embarking on a discussion of the significance of the events described in the earlier sections, I emphasize again the following caveat. Since the studies described above were carried out with only a few confined birds, all descendants of an original sibling pair, the results do not necessarily apply to the behavior of wild Peach-faced Lovebirds, nor even to all confined ones. The chances are very good, though, that they are representative. But aside from questions of breadth of applicability, they illustrate **what can happen.** This would seem to be the topic of greatest interest as concerns the potentials of Peach-faced Lovebirds to adapt to, and survive in, changed conditions.

COURTSHIP FEEDING AND OTHER ALLOFEEDING

COURTSHIP FEEDINGS AND ALLOFEEDINGS NOT PAIR-INVIOLATE. The finding that stands out from the interactions of Cassandra, Cyrus, and Cyrano is that courtship feedings and allofeedings are not pair-inviolate during the care of eggs and brooding of young. Essentially all the other activities engaged in by courting and breeding Peach-faced Lovebird pairs are carried out only with the mate. Recall that, while Cassandra would accept food from Cyrano, she would not engage in any other pair-bond interaction with him, such as mutual grooming or perching side by side while sleeping.

This result is not entirely unexpected, even though the acceptance of food in other birds often is the equivalent of saying "yes" to the suitor (101), and even though courtship feeding probably is one of the most important activities that maintains the pair bond (4). So long as the pair bond were not threatened, it even could be considered adaptive for an incubating or brooding hen, at least, to accept food from a non-mate.

COOPERATIVE BREEDING AMONG NON-PARROTS. Lovebird parents probably consume more food than normal during the fledging of young, much more during the phase of oviposition, and very much more when brooding chicks. Two males could do a much better job of supplying food to the hen than one at these times of great demand. In fact, many cases are known among monogamous birds where bachelor males and unmated females, not necessarily related to the young that they aid, sometimes attach themselves to mated pairs, though this rarely is found during courtship (13, 21, 101, 209, 607, 638). The only previous suggestion of cooperative breeding among parrots is based only on sightings of more than a pair of birds at the nests of Red-sided Parrots (*Eclectus pectoralis*) in Australia (see 638).

The overwhelming majority of the known cases of helping behavior occur in group-territorial species, though this behavior also is known in many species that occupy the arid and semi-arid habitats in Australia and Africa, including numerous nomadic species (219, 638, 647). The exceptional known instances of helping in colonial species include a few kingfishers, a few swifts, and many members of the Old World family, Meropidae, the bee-eaters (607). In some cases of communal breeders, the helpers participate in all flock activities except breeding (608). In addition to assuming part of the breeding burdens, they also contribute to flock and familial welfare by assisting in the detection of predators. Far from being a rare social system in birds, cooperative breeding is known in some 3% of all living avian species, belonging to a wide variety of taxonomic groups (647, 1,369). Many of these represent societies that sometimes are faced with severe ecological conditions that limit their behavioral options, as well as those in which competitive conflicts of interest reach extreme limits (638). In essence, grown offspring remain "at home" only when the cost of doing otherwise is prohibitive (1,370).

TELESCOPING THE BROODS, BENEFITS TO THE YOUNG ADULTS. In both group-territorial and colonial species, it frequently is the young of one brood that help to feed those of the next one (50, 53, 68, 101, 219, 607). This makes it possible for breeding pairs to telescope more broods into each breeding season (609). The young birds of the previous brood receive the benefits of parental care and experience for a much longer period than otherwise would be the case, hastening their behavioral development, and they also receive valuable experience in foraging and in the rearing of young. Such experience could be extremely beneficial to the young birds of long-lived species that frequently are subjected to harsh breeding conditions, and can be viewed, in some cases, as an essential alternative strategy to gain eventual breeding status. A male helper may even inherit the territory and mate with the brooding female the next year. In addition, the helpers receive the benefits of remaining in a familiar area, with the added safety afforded in a family group (see 607, 780).

One would not be justified to assume that the contribution of helpers is primarily the feeding of the nestlings. In the case of Florida Scrub Jays (*Aphelocoma c. coerulescens*), the food delivered to the nestlings was not the basis for the positive correlation between the presence of helpers and the production of young jays. The greatest contribution of the jay helpers to nestlings and fledglings stemmed from their anti-predator behavior. It has been pointed out that the main advantages of group living, including helping behavior, may accrue between breeding episodes, rather than during the rearing of the nestlings. In the case of the jays, the personal benefit to the helpers may be a gain in their safety as a result of recruitment into the flock of younger, naive birds (see 780).

COURTSHIP FEEDING LEAST INTIMATE. Important as courtship feeding might be in bringing the hen into breeding condition, it clearly is a less intimate interaction than either grooming or sleeping side by side. As Skutch recognized, mutual preening may establish more intimate relations than courtship feeding, which is more quickly accomplished (101). If we equate courtship and other allofeedings to a dinner engagement, our own social practices are not inconsistent with those of lovebirds.

JAGATAI A SPECTATOR TO THE 3RD BROOD OF CASSANDRA AND CYRUS. The conclusion that Cyrano's allofeeding of Cassandra may be likened to the allofeeding of reproducing females by bachelor males is supported by subsequent observations. For example, in January, 1985, after the colony was housed at the laboratory, Jagatai, an older brother of Cassandra and Cyrus, was housed with the Cockatielian pair, Carmen and Cosimo, in the upper half of enclosure A. At the same time, Cassandra and Cyrus were rearing their 3rd brood (3 chicks) in enclosure M, on top of enclosure A (before the acquisition of enclosure N, as in Fig. 1b). Jagatai could squeeze almost half of his body out through the top mesh (2½ x 5 cm) of enclosure A and observe all that took place in the enclosure M, above.

HEIGHTENED INTEREST AS CHICKS APPROACH FLEDGING. When the chicks were quite young, Jagatai paid only normal heed to the occurrences in the enclosure above. But his interest rapidly heightened as the chicks became well-feathered and more vocal. He spent long periods, with his body half extended from the top of enclosure A, intent upon the family activities occurring above. Since he was the only unmated lovebird in the colony, I naturally interpreted this behavior as a sign of a very keen interest in the maturing young, perhaps as a possible source of a future mate (and, indeed, one of them--Aspasia--eventually became his mate; see pp. 834-838).

JAGATAI'S URGE TO ALLOFEED CASSANDRA. But his subsequent behavior ultimately supported a quite different interpretation. I periodically flighted Jagatai alone during the period of heightened interest, both to observe his behavior with colonial members and to reduce any isolation stress he might be experiencing. He usually spent almost all his time at the right rear side of enclosure M, next to the nestbowl containing the young and Cassandra. The nestbowl was out of my view and I assumed, at first, that he simply was further exercising his interest in the young. But when I checked the activity at that location, I found Jagatai allofeeding Cassandra through the bars, with an unconcerned Cyrus looking on. As subsequent observations amply confirmed, his real interest was not at all in the chicks, but in the opportunity to allofeed a brooding hen.

CASSANDRA ALLOFED, BUT CHICKS' TOES NIPPED. I flighted Jagatai with Cassandra and Cyrus daily after that observation. Until the chicks could fly, I placed them on the home perch at the same time, to investigate further any interest Jagatai might have in them. Jagatai fed Cassandra many times during these flightings, even after she started to oviposit her 10th clutch. He was continually attentive to her but repeatedly and unprovokedly nipped the toes of the chicks whenever they came near. Not only that, Jagatai repeatedly chased away Cassandra's mate, Cyrus, whenever the latter intruded, or even came near, just as if he, and not Cyrus, were her mate. Cyrus, of course, usually was otherwise occupied, since that was the time in the breeding cycle when the male parent is fully occupied escorting and otherwise overseeing the perching or fledging chicks.

SIBLING DOMINANCE HIERARCHIES? The interaction of Cyrus with Jagatai was quite the opposite of his interactions with Cyrano. Thus, Cyrus was dominant to his broodmate-brother Cyrano in such interactions, but subordinate to his older brother, Jagatai, in precisely the same cirumstances. Accordingly, just as interactions between a mated pair of offspring could be disrupted by a parent (as Petra or Ramses could disrupt interactions between the mated Zenobia and Cyrano), so also could those between a flighted, mated pair be disrupted by an older sibling (at least insofar as 2 males are concerned). This suggests the existence of a hierarchy of dominance between successive broods, when allowed to interact as a family from the times of fledging onward. It also suggests that a bachelor lovebird's urge to allofeed a brooding sister (perhaps any brooding conspecific) is very strong, and that brooding (and ovipositing) lovebird hens are highly receptive to being allofed by bachelor male siblings.

LOVEBIRD PERSISTENCE

CONTRASTING CYRANO'S BEHAVIOR AT TWO AGES. Considering the significance of other topics in more or less the order in which they were treated, one might ask, first, why Cyrano desisted so readily in his efforts to socialize with Cassandra and Cyrus during flightings as a fledgling and juvenile, but was so persistent in courting Cassandra 3 months later. At 11 weeks of age, he was becoming a loner during flights, whereas at 22 weeks, he sought endlessly to re-enter the circle of activities of Cassandra and Cyrus.

I suggest that Cyrano's sexual drive was weak at the age of 11 weeks primarily because of his youth. In addition, Cassandra probably discouraged his attentions, and he was able to sleep and mutually allogroom with the family since he still was an accepted member thereof. At 22 weeks, on the other hand, he was approaching maturity, he had been living in isolation for 11 weeks, he was not being strongly discouraged by Cassandra, and he no longer was accepted as a family member.

CYRANO'S PERSISTENCE IN COURTING ANOTHER'S MATE. How is one to interpret Cyrano's indomitable pursuit of Cassandra's attention and company? May we draw a parallel with the dogged persistence of an infatuated human suitor? In the most general sense, I believe so, and one would be even more justified to pursue human analogies after learning of another case of dogged persistence of lovebirds, as related in Chapter 5.

When I wrote on page 303 that Cyrano's behavior gives one some insight into the character of lovebirds, I was referring mostly to his dogged persistence. This trait of lovebird males in certain situations has not escaped notice by others. Thus, Dilger has remarked that their intense courtship bouts are "characterized by extreme persistence despite repeated thwartings...." (3).

DOGGED PERSISTENCE NON-ADAPTIVE IN THE ABSENCE OF PROGRESS. Cyrano's dogged persistence would, of course, have been non-adaptive in the face of an utter lack of progress. But Cyrano had made progress, though apparently only very slowly, at first. I have also observed a clear-cut relevant example of this sort of behavior in White-footed Mice. Mice trying to gnaw their way through a stainless-steel barrier made no progress, whatsoever, and they did not persist very long in such a futile endeavor. But if they were making any progress, however slight, say, against a much softer aluminum barrier, they persisted doggedly.

Cassandra's actions in trying to chew nesting material from the outside enclosure cover also is relevant. She persisted in this effort month after month, even though her bill cut very poorly through the plastic material and she obtained very little of it. However, she was making substantial apparent progress, because she was cutting through the binding fiber that held the weave together, so the woven bundles were falling loose. An example familiar to naturalists is that of a persistent male songbird eventually succeeding in taking over the territory of a less determined one.

BIRDS FLY RELUCTANTLY FROM DANGER----ADVANCE MORE LIKELY THAN FLEE. Cyrano's persistence in the face of the danger of being injured by Cyrus (and sometimes by Cassandra, as well) recalls to mind Hudson's remark, "birds ever fly reluctantly from danger." Moreover, Skutch comments, birds "frequently approach danger and try to keep it in view. To advance toward their enemies is more characteristic of birds than to flee from their enemies" (see 10). [Yet both the structural and behavioral adaptations of birds are regarded as being developed better for flight or concealment than for fighting (488).] Though the "enemies" and "danger" referred to in these observations, were meant to relate primarily to predators, Cyrano's behavior suggests that the comments may not be entirely inappropriate for lovebirds in relation also to conspecifics.

EARLY MORNING BEHAVIOR

COURTSHIP FEEDING. One is tempted to see a plan behind Cyrano's first observed successful allofeeding of Cassandra, considering that she probably would be most hungry in the early morning and that Cyrus, just rousing from sleep. probably would be least inclined to attack him then. Subsequent findings were to discourage any such interpretation. It is necessary to invoke nothing more than Cyrano's great tenacity in seeking to gain Cassandra's attention and allofeed her (and not necessarily even the latter), coupled with what was later to be discovered to be normal very early morning behavior among breeding lovebird pairs.

Recall that, other than tending to maintenance activities, Cyrano did little else during the period in question than seek to allofeed Cassandra. [This calls to mind Welty's comment that "Two urges dominate nearly all the waking activities of a bird: hunger and love--self preservation and race preservation." (28). The hypothalamus controls both urges.] And, since he had to sleep alone, it is very likely (being less comfortably ensconced) that he sometimes, if not usually, became active before the other birds very early in the morning. In keeping with his behavior during the remainder of the day, he very likely would have tried to allofeed Cassandra at that time. His success in being able to do so probably owes its attainment to the following two aspects of lovebird behavior.

A TIME OF "TRUCE" AND COURTSHIP FEEDING. First, the early morning period is a time of "truce" among Peach-faced Lovebirds, when overt aggression is strongly inhibited and may never occur. This was first noted in subsequent studies (see p. 649, **Early Morning Aggression Taboo and Relocations**), in which Petra and Ramses reared the single chick, Titus, in the presence of Flavia and Zenobia. Accordingly, in allofeeding Cassandra early in the morning, Cyrano apparently had nothing to fear from Cyrus. Second, the first activity in which breeding lovebird pairs engage very early in the morning, is the allofeeding of the female by her mate.

This came to my attention much later, after the colony was transferred to the laboratory and all mated lovebirds were housed as individual pairs. And much the same was found to be true of mated Budgerigar pairs in breeding condition. Accordingly, not only would Cassandra have been predisposed to be allofed, and hence to accept food from Cyrano early in the morning, but Cyrano would have been very strongly motivated to allofeed her at that time. While it is true that Cyrano was not Cassandra's mate, he was attempting to court her in every feasible manner. Viewed in the light of these later findings, it can be regarded as fairly certain that Cyrano had allofed Cassandra on mornings previous and subsequent to my first observation of an occurrence. Moreover, it also is very likely that his persistent efforts to allofeed her during the day, as well, were prompted and sustained by his successes in doing so in the early morning. In that sense, the way for his ultimate daytime allofeedings probably was paved by the early morning ones.

INTERACTIONS DURING BREEDING AND PAIR BONDING

CYRANO'S CHALLENGES DID NOT PREVENT BREEDING. These studies show that the company of a bachelor broodmate vying for a hen's attention does not necessarily inhibit a mated lovebird pair from coming into breeding condition. Cassandra began ovipositing clutch after clutch through the periods of Cyrano's presence, and her failures with some of these were not the result of infertility. Rather, the main problems would appear to have been lack of appropriate diet (leading to thin-shelled eggs) and of a suitable nesting location. I did not supply either, at first, since I was not seeking to facilitate breeding.

MALE BROODMATE POORLY TOLERATED BY A BREEDING PAIR. Along the same lines, it seems very likely that the presence of a male broodmate in the same enclosure would be very poorly tolerated by a breeding pair. This was evidenced by the increased ferocity of Cyrus' attacks on Cyrano, as incubation progressed, and the fact that Cassandra also began to attack him. At that time, Cyrano's allofeeding of Cassandra from outside the enclosure during such periods did not present a threat to the breeding pair. On the other hand, it will be seen in Chapters 5 and 6 that lovebird pairs do tolerate the presence of a preceding brood during the rearing of the next one, though they are very protective of the latter.

REJECTION MORE INTIMIDATING THAN A COMPETITOR'S ATTACKS. Events on the 28th day after Cyrano first solicited Cassandra's attention by caressing her toes were both revealing and somewhat unexpected. When Cyrano courted Cassandra in the presence of Cyrus, he persevered despite repeated rebuffs by the latter. But when Cyrano courted her when they were alone together, and she repelled him with pecks, as he sought to perch next to her, he was easily 'discouraged.' The ease with which he became intimidated by this rejection suggests the very great influence of a female's behavior in encouraging or discouraging further courting by a male in the formation of pair bonds.

Cassandra's temporary rejection of her mate, Cyrus, when I returned him after an 80-min absence, was reminiscent of the way a female lovebird often rejects her mate when he begins to solicit sexual union. In fact, subsequent studies showed that, when a parent male lovebird (or a member of the immediately prior brood) is removed, even very briefly, from an enclosure in which eggs are being incubated or chicks brooded, his mate usually attacks him briefly on his return. [In some woodpecker species, the members of a pair seem to be always "on a wartime footing," forever bickering and avoiding each other, as if "resenting the fact that a second bird is necessary for reproduction" (28).]

FEMALE INITIATIVE. Flavia's behavior was noteworthy in several respects. The manner in which she removed the sidepane to enclosure D, and the significance of her learning so quickly, are treated on pages 823-825, **Flavia's Forced Entry Into an Enclosure**. Her interactions with her male siblings strongly support the conclusion, based on her sister Zenobia's behavior, that female lovebirds often or even characteristically take the initiative during pair bonding. The results for Flavia are, perhaps, more impressive, because she challenged both homosexual and heterosexual pair-bond loyalties, whereas Zenobia did not have to cope with either type.

A FEMALE OUTCAST. Flavia, more than any other bird except Cyrano, often found herself in the role of an outcast. Many were the occasions when she was caught in the tower between Zenobia, who vigorously drove her back down the lower vertical section (away from Zenobia's mate, Cyrano), and Petra and Ramses, at its entrance, who vigorously drove her back up (away from their chick Titus).

COURTSHIP BEHAVIOR OBSCURED. I suggested earlier that Flavia and Zenobia appeared to become encouraged to chase and threaten Cyrano after he fled from them in an open act of subordination. And, I mentioned that they often sought him out thereafter and pursued him. It appears to be most likely that Cyrano's skittishness was obscuring the fact that Flavia and Zenobia were not being aggressive so much as they were trying to court him. This suggestion is supported by Zenobia's acceptance of being courtship fed on the one occasion when Cyrano stood his ground, and by the fact that she subsequently took the initiative in their mating interactions. It was Zenobia's seeking out of Cyrano's company in enclosure D that led to their mating. Significantly, the last time Flavia allofed Zenobia occurred on the day that Cyrano subsequently also courtship-fed Zenobia.

FACTORS IN LOVEBIRD PAIR-BOND FORMATION

NEITHER MUTUAL GROOMING NOR SLEEPING SIDE BY SIDE ESSENTIAL. Since Zenobia and Cyrano formed their pair bond under most unusual conditions, and under my close scrutiny over a considerable period, knowledge of these conditions, and of the progress of the mating, gives new insights into lovebird pair bonding. It seems quite likely that neither the opportunity for extensive mutual allogrooming nor to sleep side by side is essential to the formation or maintenance of the pair bond. [Mutual allogrooming is known to occur among unmated adults of Peach-faced Lovebirds and *A. personata* (835).] The bond between Zenobia and Cyrano became established only on the basis of courtship feeding, short periods of contact in Cyrano's enclosure and during flighting, very limited mutual allogrooming, and the continuous existence of channels for visual and vocal exchanges.

EVIDENCE OF STRENGTHENING OF THE PAIR BOND. Many events in the course of the next few weeks strongly suggested that the pair bond between Zenobia and Cyrano became strengthened continually. [This is known to occur in cormorants, for example, in which the pair bond is furthered as the birds cooperate in nest-building, fighting, and display activities.] But one still must recognize the possibility that many or all of these events merely were manifestations of mate retention or evidence of preparations for breeding.

The events in question were: increasing aggressiveness of both Zenobia and Cyrano toward Flavia when all 3 were together; attempts at, and possible achievement of, sexual union between Zenobia and Cyrano; Cyrano attempting to prevent Zenobia from leaving his enclosure; increased time spent by Zenobia and Cyrano in closest proximity to one another (in their respective enclosures); development of 'contented' warbling exchanges; and increasing aggression toward enclosure mates--and even expulsion of enclosure mates (the Budgerigars).

To all intents and purposes, the pair bond appeared to have become fully estabished long before it became possible for Zenobia and Cyrano to expand the sphere of their interactions. As a result of subsequent housing modifications they were able to groom each other's heads and courtship feed at will through the hole between their adjacent enclosures, and to maintain close proximity to (but not extensive contact with) one another.

MAINTENANCE ACTIVITIES VERSUS THE PAIR BOND. Although thirst and hunger had priority for Zenobia over attention to Cyrano, when Zenobia joined, or was placed with him in his enclosure, this priority in overt behavior does not imply that thirst and hunger take priority over maintenance of the pair bond. The reason why Zenobia was thirsty and hungry, in the first place, was because she had neglected drinking and eating to protect her pair-bonded relationship with Cyrano while she was in enclosure B. She did this by guarding the tower to prevent Flavia from coming near to Cyrano during the day. When she was alone with him in his enclosure, there was no threat to the pair bond, so attending first to maintenance needs did not directly endanger this relationsip.

LIMITATIONS OF SIMPLE, SHORT-TERM CHOICE EXPERIMENTS

Simple short-term choice experiments are inadequate to assess a matter such as enclosure preference, if a bird has lived in one of the enclosures in the recent past. In the first test of whether Cyrano preferred enclosure C, with his broodmates, or enclosure D, with the Budgerigars, the apparent early preference for enclosure D (where had lived for 18 days) may have been either real or only an expression of conservativeness.

In a 2nd test, between enclosures D and E, there can be little doubt that Cyrano's preference for enclosure D (his home for the prior 2 months) was purely an expression of conservativeness, since the conditions in enclosure E were much more favorable to his relationship with Zenobia (in both tests he was housed with Budgerigars). To obtain conclusive answers from enclosure-preference tests with almost any mammal or bird, the tests should be carried out under conditions where no aspect of conservativeness of behavior comes into play. [Other of my studies have demonstrated the existence of a great and long-lasting attachment to and possessiveness over (and defense of) both prior housing quarters and IAs, even in preference to being flighted.]

AN ANALOGY WITH CHEMICAL REAGENTS. In closing this section, I would like to draw an analogy between my colony of lovebirds in their various groups in different enclosures, and chemical reagents on a shelf in the laboratory. Just as one can predict the chemical product to be expected from mixing any two given reagents, so also was I able to predict the type of interaction to be expected from flighting any two separately or jointly housed lovebirds. For example, I could predict the outcome of flighting Cyrano with his mate Zenobia, as opposed to the object of his first courtship attentions, Cassandra, or Zenobia's sister, Flavia, or his mother, Petra, or one of his older brothers, Jagatai or Ogadai, etc.

DISCUSSION -- GENERAL

BERRILL'S PORTRAIT OF AVIAN LIFE. The Canadian zoologist, N.J. Berrill has written, "To be a bird is to be alive more intensely than any other living creature, Man included. Birds have hotter blood, brighter colors, stronger emotions. They are not very intelligent--they live in a world that is always in the present, mostly full of joy....with little memory of the past and no real anticipation of what is yet to come--intensely conscious of sight and sound, strongly swayed by joy and anger and sometimes petrified by ecstacy or fear" (20).

How well do the lovebird portraits of this Chapter fit Berrill's colorful assessments of avian life? I believe that the answer must be "poorly." By changing key words, the events that transpired between Cyrano and his siblings would not be greatly dissimilar from those of human love triangles. And chapters that follow depict many additional, perhaps even more convincing, similarities between the behavior of Peach-faced Lovebirds and Man.

Avian Behavior and the Avian Brain

AVIAN BEHAVIOR

AVIAN BEHAVIOR AND HUMAN BEHAVIOR. Since lovebird behavior bears similarities to human behavior, it is pertinent to inquire whether birds are motivated like humans. Does consciousness, as we understand it, exist in birds? Does it influence their actions? Or are resemblances to human behavior misleading? Although I grant the likelihood of "physiological continuity between men and [other] animals in brain function," and even of "comparable continuity in mental experiences" (98), in my opinion we still fall short of being able to give definitive general answers to these questions. Readers interested in a extensive treatment of these topics are referred to the recent thoughtful analysis of Griffin (98) and to the related Dahlem Conference Report (99).

VARYING DEGREES OF EVOLUTION OF AVIAN BRAINS. One of the problems associated with answering such questions is that avian brains have undergone widely varying degrees of evolution. The disparities between them have to be related to very different levels of mental processes (155). These disparities can be seen in the relative development of different parts of avian brains, as measured, for example, by the cerebral indices of Portmann and Stingelin (the divergences in which parallel differences in avian intelligence; see 28 and 342).

In fact, the range and variety in appearance and behavior among the gamut of extant birds--so "exceedingly specialized in diverse directions ..."--are so great that the concept of "the brain of a bird" becomes threatened seriously (43), and perhaps even that of "a bird" itself (384). It is no more valid to lump all species of birds together, in discussions of intelligence, than to lump all mammals together (I take this liberty for convenience).

COMPLEX MECHANISMS AT WORK---AVIAN-MAMMALIAN DIFFERENCES. Although direct conscious control of bodily motions may be greatly reduced in birds, their activities are not merely the results of sequences of simple reflexes. Complex mechanisms of the nervous sytem often are at work, and birds can show great intelligence in many tests (39). In their performances of visual and other discriminative tasks, they are truly competitive with the most intelligent of mammals (83).

In Heinroth's words, the "chain of instinctive activities....is not quite complete; gaps have to be filled in by the individual's use of his own experience. The more gaps there are, the better the opportunity for intelligence to work" (41). And though every kind of bird does admittedly have a large repertoire of more or less stereotyped, relatively inflexible responses (perfected fixed action patterns), so too has every kind of mammal (351, 419). Those of birds often are enormously complicated and they usually are more conspicuous. But the differences between the fixed action patterns of birds and mammals are largely ones of degree (see also R.E. Lockley's remarks in 808).

REVISING VIEWS ON VERTEBRATE BRAINS. Although there are wide varieties in perceptual capacities and motor skills across the various groups of vertebrates, and these are reflected in the functional organization of their brains (1,091), there also are many striking similarities in functional organization. Following the treatment of Webster (400), until two decades ago it was thought that mammalian forebrains had evolved *de novo* in the synapsid-mammal, independently of those of other vertebrates. In this view, only mammals had the concurrently evolving visual, auditory, and somesthetic projections to the dorsal thalamus and thence to the neocortex. In non-mammalian vertebrates, it was believed that projections from these sensory systems terminated at midbrain levels.

Further, it was thought that the non-mammalian cerebrum was dominated by the olfactory system. Cells of striatal structures, presumably the equivalent of the neurons of the basal ganglia of mammals (on the basis of cytoarchitecture), coordinated the olfactory input and projected it to the lower brain centers. The non-mammalian cerebrum was considered to have but vague indirect control of bulbar and spinal cord levels. Only mammals were thought to have direct pathways carrying motor information from the cerebrum to the spinal cord and bulbar nuclei.

Recent investigations of the sensory and motor systems of the avian brain have provided a far clearer picture of the overall organization of the avian nervous system and have elucidated numerous similarities to the more widely studied mammalian nervous systems. The reevaluation of the older ideas has followed the striking results of modern experimental neuroanatomy, particularly those obtained with the use of powerful new silver techniques of selective staining of degenerating nerve fibers (even those that are unmyelinated) and boutons (terminations). When a particular structure is lesioned, the pathways of the degenerating fibers of severed axons then may be traced. Complications resulting from inadvertent damage to axons passing the lesion site can be circumvented by utilizing autoradiographic tracing techniques (retrograde transport of the enzyme horseradish peroxidase and anterograde transport of amino acids). Several previously unsuspected neural projections have been revealed.

DIRECT RETINAL PROJECTIONS TO THE DORSAL THALAMUS exist in all vertebrates and auditory projections thereto in all amniotes (reptiles, birds, and mammals). Second, confining attention to amniotes, there are large sensory projections from the dorsal thalamus to the ipsilateral (same-side) cerebral hemispheres in all amniotes and direct spinal-cord projections to discrete nuclei in the dorsal thalamus. Rather than the non-mammalian cerebrum being dominated by olfactory information, there are olfactory projections to only a limited portion of the cerebrum. On the other hand, there are large projections from the cerebrum to lower brainstem structures.

[Among the more striking features of the avian telencephalic (end brain) efferent systems are their striking similarities to certain descending projections and their distributions in mammals. Some forebrain constituents have axonal distributions identical to those of the mammalian neocortex: projections on the thalamus, optic tectum, red nucleus, tegmentum, pontine nuclei, medial and lateral reticular formations, nuclei cuneatus and gracilis, and spinal cord. The small amount of information available concerning the sub-telencephalic efferent systems also suggests rather remarkable similarities to the major mammalian pathways projecting upon the spinal cord, as, for example, the rubrospinal tract. But not all of the intrinsic neurons of the avian neostriatum and hyperstriatum ventrale (see pp. 348, 349) can be related to intrinsic mammalian neocortical cells; some components, e.g., the visual Wulst, may be without mammalian equivalents (386).

In terms of cellular structure, the avian brainstem is readily comparable to the brainstems of reptiles and primitive mammals, such as opossums (*Didelphis* spp.). Reptiles, however, apparently lack inferior olive and pontine nuclei; in mammals and birds these nuclei are present and include projections to the cerebellum (see 889).]

THE BRAIN OF PTEROSAURS. Pterosaurs were Mesozoic archosaurs that paralleled birds in becoming active flyers. Their wings were skin webs supported by a greatly elongated 4th finger. The presence of a hair-like body covering on some well-preserved specimens suggests that they were endothermic (877). The brain of Pterosaurs is remarkably similar in appearance to avian brains, presumably as a consequence of similar sensory and neural adaptations to the demands of active flight. Thus, the olfactory apparatus is reduced greatly compared to the primitive archosaurian condition; the cerebrum and cerebellum appear to be enlarged and in contact medial to the optic lobes; the optic lobes are well developed and situated laterally; and there are very large flocculi (posterolaterally-directed lobes on the lower sides of the cerebellar hemisphere), larger than in extant birds of comparable size, suggesting a high degree of muscular coordination in maneuverability in flight, takeoff, and landing. In the advanced pterosaurs, culminating in *Pteranodon*, the tail was almost completely suppressed, as in modern birds; thus, an advanced nervous system had allowed inherent stability to be sacrificed for improved maneuverability (1,050). However, despite the avian-like specializations of parts of the pterosaurian central nervous system, the brains of pterosaurs are not believed to have been developed to the advanced level of avian brains (877).

IDEAS REGARDING AVIAN BRAIN REQUIRE REVISION. In view of the foregoing considerations, multiple sensory projections to the dorsal thalamus and thence to the cerebrum must be regarded as a much more general characteristic of vertebrates than previously believed. This means that the dominance of forebrain structures in the control of behavior, long established for mammals, also may occur in other vertebrates.

Moreover, because many specific dorsal thalamic nuclei of non-mammalian vertebrates project to structures previously regarded as striatal, it has become necessary to entertain the idea--now well established for birds (see pp. 348 *et seq.*, beginning with **The Avian Brain**)--that these striatal structures are homologous to mammalian neocortical areas. [Only the paleostriatal complex now is regarded as a clear striatal homologue; the bulk of the cells are neither homologous nor functionally analogous to the mammalian corpus striatum.] If one is guided by the nature of the projections whose existence already has been established, it seems possible that the same representational fields of telencephalic cells have evolved into the teleost epistriatum, the reptilian dorsal ventricular ridge (see pp. 350, 351), the avian neostriatum, hyperstriatum, and ectostriatum (see pp. 348, 349, and the mammalian neocortex (399; see pp. 353, 354).

In the light of the above findings, earlier ideas regarding the avian brain, both neuroanatomical and functional, require complete revision. No longer can it be regarded simply as a nervous structure concerned with elaborating stereotyped responses (fixed action patterns) as a result of cognitive decisions on the part of the optic tectum (see pp. 355-361, beginning with **The Optic Tecta**) and other brainstem structures. Nor can one any longer entertain the notion that birds are "eye-brained" in the same sense that many fishes were thought to have been "nose-brained" (28). Now that the underlying similarities of the neuronal projections between parts of the brains of members of different vertebrate classes have been established, the next major challenge is to try to understand the differences, rather than the similarities, in the anatomy and function of avian and mammalian visual forebrain structures.

ADVANTAGES OF BEHAVIORAL STEREOTYPY. There is a consensus among behaviorists that the behavioral repertoires of birds are far more stereotyped than those of mammals. In Thorpe's words, "a bird without instincts would be almost a contradiction in terms, an imaginary animal bearing little relation to the real thing" (39). This stereotypy of avian behavior, compared to that of mammals, is attributed to a lesser ability of the avian brain to modify the drives that result from the interactions of hormones and neurophysiological processes (23).

On the other hand, one should not be too hasty in denigrating stereotyped behavior. Highly stereotyped behavior has its advantageous aspects. Thus, stereotyped acts tend to optimize the signal-to-noise ratio in given conditions and thereby to facilitate signal detection (36; see also 384). Szarski takes the position, "there is no evidence that a plastic behavior is always superior to a rigid one. I am convinced that the rigid, inherited reactions are usually more efficient in the struggle for life." He suggests that "plasticity is favored only in organisms which live in a variable environment, whereas in the majority of species one generation after another lives in identical conditions where the inherited reactions can be highly efficient. The process of individual learning of necessary skills is time consuming, requires a large expenditure of energy, and is often dangerous" (1,314).

Another most important aspect of stereotyped behavior for birds is discussed below. Indeed, Armstrong's analysis of the learning of mimicries suggests that stereotyped behavior in birds is so advantageous, that the trend of development with age is to eliminate flexibility (109). In other words, decreases in learning ability with age very likely do not merely reflect decay in versatility and originality. Rather, they can be viewed as being due to positive processes, which have evolved because of the advantages of stereotyped behavior. The older we get, the more we become creatures of habit, but for good reason.

RESPONSES TO NOVEL SITUATIONS--LEARNING---BIRDS VERSUS MAMMALS. Though birds and mammals are outstanding among all vertebrates in their flexible responses to novel situations (369, 476), most birds are less flexible than mammals in their selection of responses and less able to make adjustments to such situations (488). Hasholt and Petrak take the view that some changes in avian behavior in response to unusual stimuli are the results of "short circuits" between neural pathways. Inasmuch as birds have only limited numbers of reflexes, and these are assumed to have been tailored to deal with ordinary situations, these authors feel that "unusual stimuli....may produce peculiar manifestations" (454).

Birds are second only to mammals in their ability to learn and to mold species characteristic behavior through individual experience. Indeed, this ability to modify behavior is essential (351). Parrots, in particular, are advanced in this regard. They easily establish connections between sounds and events, remember them, and even establish anticipatory associations (109). Birds are "rat-like" in serial reversal performances, show no qualitative difference from mammals in probability learning, and respond in similar ways to rats in reward shifts. Phenomena that are taken by some theorists to demonstrate selective attention are found in Rock Pigeons as well as rats. Differences between Rhesus Monkeys (Macaca mulatta) and Blue Jays (*Cyanocitta cristata*) in object discrimination learning are primarily quantitative, but transfer of sameness and difference by Rock Pigeons from one problem to another does not attain the level achieved by Rhesus Monkeys. Thus, there is but little evidence to suggest the existence of qualitative differences in the learning capacities of birds and mammals (see 1,091).

INDIVIDUAL INFLEXIBILITY--ADAPTABILITY AS POPULATIONS. Although a strong case can be made for insightfulness and insight learning in birds (treated in detail in 28, 39, and 143), most birds indubitably fall short of mammals in their abilities to form concepts and use tools. On the other hand, the individual inflexibility of birds is offset by a well-developed behavioral adaptability as populations. This is seen in the many adjustments birds have made to the environmental changes produced by Man (488). This is one of the areas in which **what can happen** has happened.

STORED PATTERNS. Athough we may not yet be able to give definitive answers to the questions raised at the beginning of this section, we can indulge in informed speculation. In Jerison's view of flying vertebrates (59), "The bird or bat (or Pterodactyl) in flight may be thought of as a more or less conscious machine, following instructions to move through space defined by a map in its head, rather than as a machine pre-programmed....extensive conscious perceptual worlds appeared only with the evolution of mammals and, to a lesser extent, birds."

"INTELLIGENCE," defined by Jerison is "the integrative functions of the brain," that is, "the capacity to learn new response patterns in which sensory information from various modalities is integrated as information about objects in space." Jerison elaborates, however, that "....dimensions other than learning may also be considered as the basis for intelligence in animals, in particular, dimensions of perception, imagery, and consciousness." ["The core process of learning is the detection and storage (memorization) of spatial and temporal correlations between events" (1,013).]

In this connection, after reviewing learning processes in reptiles, Burghardt (358) concluded that "....there is no type of problem learned by all birds and mammals that is beyond the ability of all reptiles." Following Jerison, again, only in the sense of how numerous and complex are the things that can be learned and retained can data from studies of learning provide a basis for defining animal intelligence. In a more conventional definition, "intelligence" is a measure of the degree to which an individual can adaptively modify its behavior, or a measure of the degree to which an individual can learn, as the result of experience (28).

BATS, MICE, AND INTERNAL MAPS. Experiments with bats clearly demonstrate that some sort of internal map or stored pattern representing the familiar environment must exist in the brain (98). Thus, when flying in thoroughly familiar surroundings, bats rely so heavily on spatial memory ('ignoring' their echolocational input) that they often collide with newly-placed obstacles and avoid the locations of obstacles recently removed. Moreover, neurophysiological experiments based on neurally processed auditory input have shown that simple but systematic maplike arrangements of responsive cells exist in the auditory cortex of owls, pigeons and bats (see 98, 386).

I have observed the same type of behavior in White-footed Mice during nightly activity in a dimly-lit outdoor sand-and-rock vivarium. The mice customarily spent a portion of the night repeatedly running a complicated closed course of their own choosing through the rocks and sand. When a new obstacle was inserted in their path, they invariably collided with it, and they continued to avoid or jump over locations where obstacles or voids had been during earlier circuits.

As mentioned on page 103, Jerison also suggests that maps of the sensory and motor surfaces of the body of all vertebrates are repeated again and again in different parts of their brains, enlarged in larger species, following the enlargement of the bodily surfaces that are represented. Brodman's area 19 in the Owl Monkey (*Aotus trivirgatus*), for example, is known to contain 6 separate visual field representations, each of which appears to be a functional unit involved with distinct visuomotor and perceptual behaviors (1,366). In Jerison's view a difference in map enlargement or amplification in two species implies a difference in their capacities to process information derived from a bodily surface, such as retina, basilar membrane, muscle, or skin. The brain encephalization quotient is then identified essentially with the amplification factor (1,102). Jerison's views would seem to be supported by the finding that the order of both increasing neuronal convergence of ganglionic innervation and increasing dendritic complexity follow the order of increasing bodily size (1,355).

IMAGERY IN NEST BUILDING---SPATIAL DISCRIMINATIONS--ABSTRACT CONCEPTS. Findings such as those described above give compelling reasons to speculate on the possibility that some animals "consciously think about their orientation" and surroundings (98). But entirely different approaches lend weight to the belief that birds are capable of imagery, a "higher" intellectual function. For example, if one contemplates the vast variety and complexity of avian nests, built by means of a few simple fundamentally innate operations, it is suggested (101), though there is room for doubt (1,273), that we must agree with Thorpe's view, "....the bird must have some 'conception' of what the completed nest should look like, and some sort of 'conception' that the addition of a piece of moss or lichen here and here will be a step towards the 'ideal' pattern, and that other pieces there and there would detract from it" (102). In the case of nest-building by the Long-tailed Tit (*Aegithalos caudatus*), Thorpe has shown that responsiveness to at least 18 distinct stimulus situations is necessary.

Similarly, the Colliases concluded that nest-building ability depends on practice "appropriately directed by the growing structure of the nest itself." and that "a mental image of a properly built nest based on experience" may be necessary (668). Beer puts the same interpretation on the behavior of the Laughing Gull in its restoration of the artificially removed rim of its nest: "Thus even the simple form of a gull's nest can be viewed as the result of deliberate actions guided by something like comparison between conception and perception" (739).

Even more direct and convincing evidence comes from Pastore's studies with Canaries (143; see, also, 28). In order to learn the manipulations required to obtain food, the birds had to make spatial discriminations, remember, form concepts, and behave with insight. In the same category are the results of Braun's studies (366) with an African Gray Parrot which was able to form the abstract concepts of "3" and "4" (it was trained to pick up 3 or 4 pieces of food after hearing 3 or 4 auditory signals, respectively).

In more recent studies with an individual of the same species, after 26 months of speech training the bird acquired a vocabulary consisting of 3 adjectives for color, 2 phrases for describing shades, 9 nouns, and functional uses of the word "no." The bird became capable of combining these vocalizations correctly so as to identify proficiently, request, and/or refuse more than 40 objects by means of verbal labels. The same bird also acquired a limited understanding of abstract class concepts. It routinely could decode and reply successfully to queries concerning either color or shape for objects that possessed both properties (colored and shaded keys, wood, and rawhide). For example, scores on queries that required such answers as "rose wood" or "3-corner hide" were at better than the 80% level (1,378).

Other experiments have shown the ability of Rock Pigeons to learn to categorize a bewildering array of quite detailed figures and photographs in a way that suggests that the birds form abstract concepts concerning the visible displays. For example, they can master the concept of symmetry of form and learn to discriminate a picture of a particular person seen for the first time (369, 373, 1,009). Whether or not these performances are to be regarded more properly as relating to perception rather than to intelligence, they point to similarities between avian and mammalian (at least, human) performance (1,091). Birds also have been taught to open boxes serially until up to 6 or 7 baits had been found and then to stop, with the bait distribution among the boxes being varied between trials (see O. Koehler, 1943, in 419). They can adopt win-stay lose-shift strategies, form expectations, and possess mechanisms of selective attention; it is uncertain whether Rock Pigeons exhibit a dichotomy between short-term and long-term memory stores (see 1,091).

It is increasingly coming to be appreciated that the mental capabilities of many species of wild birds probably have been underestimated, for example, their memory of past events and individual recognition. On available evidence, it would appear that some birds, at least, engage in highly complex forms of reciprocity (see 780).

COMPARISONS OF LEARNING ABILITIES. In a series of 29 spatial discrimination reversal tests, Yellow-crowned Amazons (*Amazona ochrocephala*) and Red-billed Blue Magpies (*Urocissa occipitalis*) made fewer errors than Bob-white Quail or domestic fowl chicks but there was no significant difference between the performances within the 1st two or last two species. The performances of Hill Mynahs in a separate study seemed to be superior to those of the parrots and magpies. In brightness discrimination reversal tests the magpies were superior to the mynahs, which were considerably superior to the parrots, which were superior to the chicks. On the other hand, domestic fowl performed very efficiently in serial reversals involving a pattern discrimination. It seems clear from these non-uniform results that serial reversal tests alone are unreliable as general measures of learning abilities. In learning-set formation studies mynahs and Blue Jays achieved the best results, Carrion Crows (*Corvus corone*) performed at a lower level, and Rock Pigeons at the lowest level (see 1,091).

LOVEBIRD AND HUMAN MENTAL PROCESSES. Let me be guided, for the moment, only by my studies of Peach-faced Lovebirds. Of the existence of "conscious awareness" in these birds, following the criterion of "versatile adaptability of behavior to changing circumstances and challenges" (98), I see little room for doubt. But I would go further; I am hard put to find a substantial basis for concluding that their mental processes, as assessed from their social interactions, differ from those of mammals in any way but degree. In fact, quoting Heinroth again, "As we pursue our studies of the behaviour of birds, we come more and more to recognize that our own behaviour toward our family and strangers, the emotions of love and hate, are in some ways a much simpler business than we imagine" (41).

Many studies of behavior have drawn parallels between the behavior of Man and birds in general, that is, not confining the comparison to any species. For example, quoting Welty (28), "in fundamentals, avian and human courtship patterns are not widely divergent....the hotsprings of love run deep and pervasive in the clay of all vertebrates. It is not surprising that their external bubblings appear to be much the same, whether in a university graduate, an Australian bushman, or a lowly sparrow."

EVOLVING AVIAN BRAINS AS ARTISTS, COMPOSERS, AND ARCHITECTS. On the same theme, Skutch notes, "If we deny that birds possess the capacity for aesthetic enjoyment, then the exquisite details of the plumage of many, the beautiful songs that others pour forth, not only in the breeding season but at other times, and the tastefully decorated gardens of the bower birds all remain incomprehensible to us" (101). The foregoing remark of Skutch's takes on all the more poignancy and significance when one considers that the plumage, gardens, and songs, of which he speaks, evolved largely through sexual selection, which appears to be one of the keenest forms of competition among birds.

In essence, the evolving brains of birds have been the artists, composers, and architects of these marvelous works. Since we find the works, themselves, to be wondrous--and they are but samples of the potential output--must we not hold the corresponding capacity of the avian brain, itself, in even higher esteem? [In a lesser and more limited sense, one could say that insect brains were the major artists and chemists that directed the evolution of flower types and fragrances (see 1,254, 1,376).]

FREEDOM OF EXPRESSION---AESTHETIC SENSITIVITY. And the seeming element of the gratuitous in the painting of the bower, and of the purely decorative in the songs of birds suggest a degree of freedom of expression--free choice, if you will--which is one of the prerequisites of artistic expression. As our knowledge mounts, it becomes increasingly difficult to deny that birds possess some aesthetic sensitivity (109). [Craig and Saunders agreed, on the basis of analysis of the songs of a single remarkable bird, that the Wood Pewee exercises aesthetic choice (see 109).]

SOME BIRDS POOR AT COMMUNICATING INFORMATION. I have limited my impressions to those gained specifically from Peach-faced Lovebirds. Some impressions of Skutch (101), gained from the breeding behavior of birds other than parrots, are less favorable. He finds some paired birds to be well able to communicate moods and emotions, but to be severely handicapped in their ability to communicate information and "exchange ideas." He concluded that the admirable cooperation of paired birds depends on the fact that the instinctive activities of the two partners fit together like lock and key. For all the satisfaction that constantly mated birds find in each other's company and their distress when separated, they "have not reached the higher stage of psychic development at which joy is enhanced by the sharing of good news." These remarks of Skutch were prompted specifically by the fact that the brooding females he observed let their mates remain ignorant for hours, and even days, of the critical fact that the eggs had hatched. However, other birds do find ways to communicate this information, for example, the Cedar Waxwing (*Bombycilla cedrorum*). And such information routinely becomes known among many or most parrots, including those dealt with here.

ROLES OF MANIPULATION, MIMICRY, AND COLONIALITY. It is believed that the ability and performance of coordinating hand and eye by Man's ancestors was a crucial contributing factor in the perception of relationships and the development of the brain, speech, and abstract thought. Among birds, we also find suggestive associations. Thus, many parrots use their feet to hold food, and all use their bills as a third foot. Crows and ravens also use a foot to secure food while they peck, and Carrion Crows, Rooks (*Corvus frugilegus*), jays, Jackdaws, and Great Tits are among the few birds known to be able to pull up food suspended on a string (109). [But the latter is child's play compared to some of the remarkable feats of Canaries (143; see p. 345).]

All of these birds are mimics, suggesting the possession of some capacity for detachment and some freedom from stereotypy. And the bower birds, with their remarkable manipulative skills in painting their bowers, are among the most exceptionally gifted among all mimics (109). These examples include many birds with a reputation for great intelligence, suggesting that it is not inappropriate to draw parallels with Man's evolution.

In fact, in Armstrong's view, "a step has been taken along the road which Man took toward speech and abstract thought" (109). It is noteworthy, in this connection, that parrots, the most intelligent of birds, also possess the most varied manipulative skills. Not only do many of them manipulate food with the feet and use the bill as a third foot, almost all of them also manipulate their food with a prehensile tongue. Moreover, Peach-faced Lovebirds and Budgerigars--among the most intelligent of parrots--are strongly social or colonial. Vertebrates that live in complex social groupings, "where each one is crucially dependent upon cooperative interactions with the others....need to have internal models of the behavior of their companions....to think consciously about what the other one must be thinking or feeling" (98).

THE AVIAN BRAIN

PROGRESSIVE ENLARGEMENT OF THE CEREBRAL HEMISPHERES is one of the conspicuous phenomena of vertebrate evolution from fishes to endotherms (342). The functions that first appeared in the evolution of mammals and birds probably were governed by these forebrain structures more than by other parts of the brain. Evolution of the avian brain to higher degrees of complexity has been accompanied by a tendency to concentrate the mass of the higher centers in the front parts of the cerebral hemispheres, either in the dorsal or basal parts. The functions governed by these parts of the cerebral hemispheres generally were sensory-motor functions and coordinating or integrative functions related to information processed by distance-sense modalities (401).

In other words, avian brains evolved in ways appropriate to control the changed behavior required for life in arboreal, and subsequent, aerial habitats. This is not to imply that the altered structure of avian brains was necessarily a key innovation for venturing into these habitats. Generalizing from findings in mammals, avian brain structure may have been acquired secondarily, as a consequence of selective pressures that came into play after the initial occupancy of the habitats (297, 402).

FRONTAL DEVELOPMENT A CRUCIAL PREREQUISITE. The dorsal zone, the neostriatum, hyperstriatum ventrale, and sagittal elevation, is involved in the enlargement of the centers for most forms of complex behavior. The basal centers, the paleostriatum and archistriatum (basal dorsal ventricular ridge; see pp. 350, 351), have played a more passive role and have been more or less compressed by the process of frontal development. It appears that the structural transformation of the hemispheres that led to frontal development was a crucial prerequisite for progressive evolution of higher degrees of complexity of avian brains (342).

[The 5 major constituents of the avian telencephalon are the paleostriatum, archistriatum, neostriatum, ectostriatum, and hyperstriatum. It appears that only the paleostriatum derives from the subpallial or striatal part of the embryonic telencephalon and that all the other avian "striatal" structures derive from the dorsal part, and so are of pallial or cortical origin (derived from dorsal portions of the enlarged anterior neural tube) and, as mentioned above, are homologous to the mammalian neocortex. An additional subpallial telencephalic nucleus, the nucleus basalis, occurs rostral to the paleostriatum. This nucleus receives a direct bilateral input from the principal sensory trigeminal nucleus and projects, in turn, to a region of the hemisphere dorsal to the archistriatum. Thus, the immediate ascending target of the principal trigeminal nucleus is a telencephalic nucleus in birds, rather than the nucleus ventralis posterior medialis of the thalamus, as in mammals (1,236).

The neostriatum is the largest single cell mass and probably is a sensorimotor coordinating center, the paleostriatum probably is a motor coordinating center; the paleostriatum primitivum appears to be homologous with the mammalian globus pallidus; and the evidence is suggestive for a homology between the paleostriatum augmentatum and at least part of the mammalian caudate-putamental complex, both of which regions are rich in cholinesterase and dopamine, and receive their major afferents from overlying pallial regions (386, 1,236).

The archistriatum may be divided into 4 major regions: anterior, intermedium, posterior, and mediale. The latter two are clearly limbic and may be homologous with the mammalian amygdala, principally in showing a wide distribution to the hypothalamus. The former two divisions may be somatic-sensorimotor rather than limbic in function, possibly comparable to the sensorimotor neocortex of primates (see 386). It is suggested that the archistriatum probably facilitates any bodily reorientation tendency established in the neostriatum by novel or significant stimulation, and may be involved in escape behavior in many or all birds (395, 1,283). The ectostriatum lies laterally and ventrally in the anterior neostriatum and receives a direct projection from the thalamic nucleus rotundus (see p. 357).]

SIZE. On the anatomical side, the small size of the avian brain once led to the belief that the mental powers of birds also were miniscule. Hence the disparaging expression, "birdbrain." This now is known to have been a total misapprehension. Avian brains are not small in relation to the sizes of the birds themselves. When proper allowance is made for bodily size, even birds with the lowest degree of brain organization have brains 6-11 times larger than those of extant reptiles (28, 59; 342). The precise significance of the increased number of neurons in relatively larger brains is not established fully. The large number of neurons may allow greater computational complexity, increased intelligence, or increased learning ability; or the size of a neural structure may be related to the number of neural maps of sensory surfaces that it embodies and the relative magnification of the sensory surfaces within these maps (see 59, 1,048, 1,102).

RELATIVE BRAIN WEIGHTS. The avian brain, like the mammalian brain, is a relatively large, highly evolved, complex organ. Many avian brains even are relatively larger than those of some mammals, particularly those of rodents. For example, the brain of the House Sparrow comprises 4.4% of its total bodily weight, as compared to only 2.8% in a meadow mouse (28). In general, avian brain weights corrected for bodily weights (brain weights divided by the 2/3rds power of bodily weights) fall in roughly the same range as those for mammals (59).

POORLY DEVELOPED-CEREBRAL CORTEX---DOMINANCE OF HYPERSTRIATUM. Nor is the relatively poor development of the thin, non-fissured, cerebral cortex of the bird a valid criterion by which to judge the potentials of birds for intelligent behavior. Although the same basic subdivisions of the forebrain (telencephalon plus diencephalon) appear to be present in all vertebrates (99), the cerebral cortex plays a much lesser role in the mental processes of birds than of mammals.

A structure unique to the avian telencephalon, the **hyperstriatum**, dominates in these processes. The latter is a portion of the enormously expanded, very massive, bottom layer of the cerebral hemispheres. This is the evolutionarily oldest portion of the vertebrate forebrain. The hyperstriatum has descending connections to all important visual centers of the midbrain and thalamus (512). Its dominance and major role in information processing have been demonstrated in tests involving the "insight" detour problem (36), maintenance and shifting of attention (47, 392), acquisition and retention of visual patterns and various visual discriminations (45, 475, 512), reversal learning (383, 395, 476) and imprinting (see 1,091). In fact, in a number of avian species there are direct relationships between the relative size of the hyperstriatum and both performance on the "insight" detour problem and the ease of learning a multiple spatial reversal problem followed by a brightness discrimination (383).

Related probable functions of the hyperstriatum are the organization of the fine degrees of orientation to visual and auditory stimuli and the production of arousal to fine stimulus differences (395). In addition, the hyperstriatum may be inhibitory in suppressing gross orientation tendencies facilitated by the archistriatum (see p. 349) in respect to extraneous stimulation.

The hyperstriatum seems to be particularly sensitive to hormonal control (28). It is most highly developed in birds that are noted for intelligent behavior, being well developed and differentiated in the raven, crows, owls, woodpeckers, and parrots, especially lovebirds (particularly in the mediocaudal portion of the hemispheres; 383), as compared to, say, the less intelligent game birds, fowls, pigeons, and some waders (28, 45, 155, 342 383, 476). [Mayr and Amadon (501) considered that "....Corvus ranks above other birds in brain development."] Hartshorne's suggestion that vocal imitation is the most unequivocal manifestation of intelligence in birds is pertinent in this connection (see 102).

THE DORSAL VENTRICULAR RIDGE OF THE TELENCEPHALON. Certain more or less specific and doubtless homologous regions of the telencephalons of both reptiles and birds are implicated as sensory linkages between the principal sources of sensory information and particular brainstem structures that modulate important behaviors. These have been designated collectively as the "dorsal ventricular ridge" (DVR, defined on p. 351). This structure, which is divisible into anterior and basal regions in all members of both groups, includes a series of areas, each of which receives information from one of the major sensory modalities (1,048).

Although not established with certainty, all available data indicate that the DVR in birds and reptiles is pallial in origin and homologous to mammalian neocortex (see pp. 353, 354), excluding the primarily occipital visual cortex, which may be homologous to part of the dorsal cortex in birds and reptiles. The DVR of birds has expanded to the point where it is difficult to recognize boundaries between it and other portions of the pallium. It is not yet clear whether the DVR of reptiles is organized in a similar manner to that of birds. Ridge evolution may have proceeded independently in different orders of birds, reptiles, and mammals, in which case similarities in its internal organization and many of its neuronal cell types would be the result of parallel evolution (homoplasy; 1,236).

Efferents that connect the striatum (basal telencephalon) with the brainstem reticular formation place the anterior DVR in a position to modulate the activity of motoneurons, while those that connect the basal DVR with the hypothalamus and nuclei in the autonomic nervous system place the anterior DVR in a position to modulate effector systems concerned more with the internal milieu. Visual, auditory, and somatosensory information are carried through thalamo-telencephalic projections to its anterior region. Visual projections (see also pp. 355-356, **Avian Visual Pathways**) seem to terminate laterally within this anterior region, somatosensory projections in a central region of it, and auditory projections in it medially. Each modality is represented at least once, but birds may have 3 distinct auditory areas (see p. 91, **Field L**) and 2 visual areas (see pp. 355-361) within the anterior dorsal ventricular ridge. Olfactory information is carried through either the accessory or lateral olfactory tract, depending upon the species, to the basal DVR (archistriatum), but the terminations in the archistriatum of birds have been little studied.

The overall implication of the rather formidable set of connections that issue from the anterior DVR is that sensory information that reaches it can be distributed to 2 major regions of the brain, the underlying striatum (basal telencephalon) and the basal DVR or archistriatum. These structures, in turn, issue along 3 major pathways. First, predominantly striatal projections reach the brainstem reticular formation through the optic tectum, and thereby place the anterior DVR in contact with major descending motor pathways. Second, there are striatal projections that engage the ridge in a series of feedback loops through a variety of thalamic and brainstem structures. Lastly, there are projections from the archistriatum to the hypothalamus (1,048).

[Although there are some complications, including the fact that the DVR is not part of the striatum, the avian anterior DVR is defined, after Ulinski, as including the hyperstriatum dorsale, hyperstriatum ventrale, neostriatum, ectostriatum, nucleus basalis, and the temporo-parieto-occipital area. These structures are located topographically between the dorsal and middle ventricular sulci. The basic developmental pattern seen in the telencephalons of the different groups of reptiles and birds is sufficiently similar to define the dorsal ventricular ridge universally (including both its anterior and basal components) as "that part of the telencephalon that develops between the dorsal and middle ventricular sulci" (1,048).]

AVIAN-CROCODILIAN SIMILARITIES. The intrinsic organization of the anterior DVR in crocodilians and birds differs from that in squamates, The Tuatara, and chelonians. The anterior DVR shows a different pattern of origin in the two groups. In the pattern of neuronal populations characteristic of the latter groups, a cell cluster zone is separated from the ependyma by a distinct cell-poor periventricular zone in the anterior DVR. In crocodiles and birds, on the other hand, there is no distinct cell cluster zone near the ventricle. Instead, isolated neurons and clusters of touching neurons are scattered throughout the ridge. Radially-oriented connections are, however, present and interconnect Field L (see p. 270) of the caudal medial neostriatum and the hyperstriatum ventrale, and connect the ectostriatum with overlying structures. Such connections could serve to spread information that is carried to the anterior DVR within radially-oriented sectors.

Three major types of neurons are present in *Alligator*--juxtaependymal, aspiny, and spiny, the latter with stellate-shaped dendritic fields that bear a variable number of dendritic spines. In birds, however, the majority of the clusters are of the 3rd type, having stellate-shaped dendritic trees and bearing dendritic spines. The basal DVR in crocodilians has been little studied, so that its organization cannot yet be related to that of either the basal DVR of other reptiles or to the archistriatum of birds (1,048).

AVIAN CEREBELLUM---SPINAL CORD INTUMESCENTIA--DESCENDING TRACTS. Stable flapping flight requires integration of the continuous proprioceptive muscle input with the output from the motor centers, in order to maintain accurate control over the repeated contractions and relaxations of opposite muscle groups. This integration is carried out in the cerebellum. Reduction in the size of the tail, while enhancing maneuverability led to a decrease in flight stability. Flight maintenance and maneuvering of an aerodynamically unstable bird requires a control system capable of continuous supervision and almost instantaneous minor corrections of the movements of the wings and tail. The need for these flight perfection mechanisms of the brain again would have been met by the cerebellum, integrated with the vestibular, visual, and somatic motor systems (see 618, 1,050).

The large, remarkably well-developed avian cerebellum (together with the medulla composing the metencephalon) is built on the reptilian plan. It is, however, larger and much more differentiated, through a multiplication of cortical folds and an augmentation of gray matter and fibers in the more central parts (342). Though it lacks the lateral lobes of the mammalian brain, all the major cell types seen in the mammalian cerebellar cortex are present (386).

Numerous tracts project to the cerebellum, including fibers from the spinal cord, vestibular nuclei, pontine nuclei, trigeminal nuclei, optic tecta, and forebrain. As indicated above, the cerebellum plays crucial roles in the maintenance of equilibrium and in the precise control and coordination of movements (much more demanding in 3 dimensions than in 2), and it is involved in the regulation of muscle tone (512). It receives its most important input from the vestibular organs of the inner ear (418). The cerebellum has been retained in its complex form in the flightless ratites (291). In contrast to the primarily motor centers, the cerebellum cannot release movements directly; its influence is strictly regulatory (342). In the Budgerigar, it is longer than it is wide and has 10 well-developed transverse primary folia (gyri; 441). [Recent evidence overwhelmingly favors an essential role for the mammalian cerebellum in the learning and memory of discrete, adaptive behavioral responses to aversive events (1,389).]

Certain parts of the avian spinal cord, namely the cervicothoracic and lumbosacral enlargements (intumescentia) have achieved a higher degree of development than in the mammal. Some aspects of flight and walking movements, respectively, are coordinated in these two intumescentia rather than in the brain (386, 454). Although the cervicothoracic enlargements generally exceed the lumbosacral one in size, the reverse is true for cursorial birds (386). Detailed comparisons of the laminar organization of vertebrate spinal cords reveal that there are remarkable similarities in the descending pathways from the brainstem to the spinal cord in the toad and bullfrog, Tegulizard (*Tupinam nigropunctatus*), Rock Pigeon, and American Opossum. All have rubrospinal, reticulospinal, and vestibulospinal tracts, terminating in comparable areas of the spinal gray matter (888).

MONOAMINERGIC SYSTEMS IN AVIAN BRAINS. The monoamines (norepinephrine, dopamine, and serotonin), whether as putative neurotransmitters or neuromodulators, have been implicated specifically in the control of many fundamental brain functions in vertebrates, such as the regulation of temperature and endocrine function, control of sleep and wakefulness cycles, and control of motor activity. They also are involved in various affective disorders. A crucial role for catecholamines (epinephrine, norepinephrine and dopamine) and serotonin in the hypothalamic control of body temperature and reproductive cycles has been suggested by many studies. For example, microgram quantities of serotonin injected intraventricularly in diverse mammals produce profound elevation of body temperature (891).

As regards monoaminergic systems in avian brains, but few data are available. It would appear, however, that the overall organization of such neuronal systems in birds is similar in many ways to that found in chelonians and various mammals (see pp. 131, 132, **Synaptic Transmitters and Releasing Factors**). In the brain of the domestic fowl, for example, the serotonin cell bodies are located in the raphé region, whereas the catecholamine cell bodies are scattered more laterally in the tegmentum of the brainstem, as they are in chelonians and mammals. In addition, lesion experiments in Budgerigars and Rock Pigeons have shown that some of the catecholaminergic neurons of the brainstem appear to project to the various areas of the telencephalon; the detailed organization of these presumed telencephalic afferents remains to be ascertained (891).

There also are topographically organized projections of dopaminergic groups from the midbrain tegmentum to the striatum (basal telencephalon), which has a characteristically high concentration of dopamine. The striatum also has relatively high concentrations of several other substances related to transmitter metabolism, such as acetylcholinesterase, suggesting that it contains a relatively large number of cholinergic neurons or terminals. The axons of the monoaminergic systems characteristically are thin and bear many varicosities or presynaptic elements (terminaux en passant), and have widespread projections within the telencephalon (1,048).

MAMMALIAN NEOCORTEX. The telencephalon of all mammals is characterized by a large, laminated cortex or neocortex (also referred to as "isocortex," to avoid implications of evolutionary history). This consists of a greatly expanded, folded and fissured, outer layer of the cerebral hemispheres, that has enlarged laterally and finally curved ventrally so as to envelop the entire forebrain. It consists of a well-differentiated, structurally unique, characteristic 6-layered cellular array about 1-3 mm thick, organized into columns or modules of neurons; other cortical regions possess fewer layers. Its convolutions provide space for the increased dendritic arborizations that exist in larger brains (1,102). It is suggested that this "stacking" of neurons in layers, combined with a parallel palisade-like orientation of apical dendrites, makes possible great economy in the expediture of axonal material, and thereby permits a greater number of neurons per unit volume to be connected with one another in cortical tissue than in subcortical gray matter. However, the essential functional characteristics of neocortical tissue as opposed to subcortical neuronal groupings have escaped definition thus far (1,233).

The neocortex contains characteristic pyramidal neurons (in layers 2, 3, 5, and 6), and it receives large and specific projections (inputs) of dorsal thalamic fibers (399, 400, 1,048, and below). Spiny stellate neurons are major post-synaptic targets for these thalamic afferents, and this likely also is the case in the anterior DVR of reptiles and birds. The pyramidal neurons also receive direct thalamic inputs; since their dendrites often extend radially across several cortical layers, their output can be modulated by a sample of all major cortical inputs, whereas the output from a stellate cell is more likely to be dominated by inputs to the particular layer in which it is situated (1,048). Based on studies in Rhesus Monkeys, in which synaptogenesis occurs concurrently in different layers of the visual, somatosensory, motor, and prefrontal areas of the cerebral cortex, it would appear that the entire mammalian cerebral cortex develops as a whole, rather than in an hierarchical sequence (1,207).

Considered from the point of view of design features of sensory linkages in mammals versus reptiles and birds, the overall functional organization of the pallium or cortex is such that a component of it participates in sensory linkages with the brainstem reticular formation and the hypothalamus in all 3 groups. In reptiles and birds, the component in question is the anterior DVR; in mammals it is the neocortex. In all 3 cases, projections bearing relatively complex kinds of sensory information are received from the thalamic sensory nuclei and issue to the underlying striatum. The projections of the striatum include pathways that run through the midbrain tegmentum and terminate in the optic tectum (birds) or superior colliculus (mammals). [In mammals, the superior colliculus receives visual information both directly from the retina and from the visual cortex; the latter's unique contribution is binocular information and directional sensitivity (1,362).]

Since these pathways complete a linkage through the tecto-reticular pathways with the brainstem reticular formation, they place the pallium in a position to modulate the activity of many groups of motoneurons, generating and modulating coordinated movements involved in relatively complex species-specific forms of behavior. The existence of some similarities in the design features of the anterior DVR and the neocortex, such as the presence of modality-specific areas, modes of vertical or radial organization, and both topologically and non-topologically organized maps, suggests that these features have evolved independently in response to common functional demands (1,048).

In a relatively primitive mammal, such as the opossum, which has acquired relatively little neocortex, almost all of the cortex is accounted for by the motor area and the cortical targets of the thalamic sensory nuclei; in the Tree Shrew (*Tupaia glis*), in which the visual system has undergone remarkable development, as well as in the Bush Baby (*Galago senegalensis*) and domestic cat, about half of the neocortex seems to be primary visual cortex (1,362). In contrast, in Man, the greater part of the neocortex is devoted to association area (1,344); it has become the seat of "higher" intellectual functions--reasoning, imagery, complex learning, flexibility of reactions, etc. The current overall conception of the evolution of the neocortex is that many of the populations of neurons of the mammalian neocortex were present in ancestral vertebrates. The numbers of neurons in each population apparently have increased in the evolutionary lines leading to birds and mammals, and the gross configurations of each population have changed. In Ulinski's view (1,048), however, efforts to homologize specific components of the forebrains of mammals with those of the DVR (see pp. 350, 351) have had but little success.

AVIAN-MAMMALIAN HOMOLOGIES. Though apparently different in the major detail of the hyperstriatum versus the cerebral cortex, we are nonetheless justified to say that the brains of birds and mammals follow a fundamentally similar pattern of organization (45, 367, 376, 386). Even the difference in this major detail has been deeply eroded. Some populations of cells in the avian hyperstriatum have been found to be homologous with populations of cells in the mammalian cerebral cortex (52, 372, 374, 376).

These homologies extend to the afferent (incoming) and efferent (outgoing) relations with other cell populations, cell types within the populations, synaptology, electrophysiology, histochemistry, and other fundamental characteristics that make each cell population a unique entity (376). One now is justified to assert that the major neural connections of the avian external striatum (hyperstriatum and neostriatum) are quite similar to many of those of the mammalian neocortex (386). Such relationships had been suggested by W. Stingelin in 1972 (see 23), who regarded the whole Wulst (see p. 358) to be homologous to the mammalian neocortex.

CONSERVATIVE CEREBRAL EVOLUTION. The deeper one probes, the more evanescent become the purported differences in functional roles of homologous avian and mammalian brain structures. Although the pattern of cell assemblies differs in birds and mammals (e.g., clonal versus lamellar), the identities, sequences of development, and functions of homologous neurons do not appear to differ in any major way. Thus, in fundamental aspects, the combination of the avian thalamus (a visceral brain center) and telencephalon seem to participate in information processing and transformation in a manner still indistinguishable from that performed by the combination of the mammalian thalamus (also a visceral brain center) and cerebral cortex (367). In brief, cerebral evolution has been much more conservative than was realized by earlier students of the comparative anatomy of the nervous system (99).

REBUILDING OF LOCAL CIRCUIT INTERNEURONES. Not to be lost sight of, though, is the fact that there is constant rebuilding--as opposed to synapse turnover--of the adult avian forebrain, or at least rebuilding of parts of some of its neural circuits, probably only local circuit interneurons. In this process, new neurons form, migrate, and incorporate themselves into existing networks. Comparably rapid post-natal neurogenesis does not occur in mammals, although there might be rebuilding or "fine wiring" at a lower rate, but there is no evidence for it in Man (241).

AVIAN VISUAL PATHWAYS

No discussion of the avian brain and avian behavior would be complete without a consideration of the role of communication between the hemispheres of the brain. Because of the bilaterally symmetrical structure of vertebrates, the mirror-image hemispheres have to interact and cooperate with each other to achieve organized behavior. These actions are accomplished via the nerve pathways between the hemispheres, the "commissural" and "decussational" connections.

Since vision is the pre-eminent sense in birds, the neural pathways serving it achieve particular prominence, with the diencephalon or "between brain" (consisting of epithalamus or subthalamus, thalamus, and hypothalamus) being much more highly differentiated than that of reptiles. The anatomy of these pathways probably tells a significant story with regard to the workings of the avian brain. The avian visual system is remarkably complex, involving a variety of subcortical visual centers that relate directly with the retinal fibers. The optic lobes are relatively enormous in size, though only a limited portion of them actually is related to the visual system (386). Their supraventricular portions (or superficial laminated rinds) make up the optic tecta, which contain the primarily afferent and associated interneuronal and efferent zones. [By contrast, most bats (excepting the pteropodids) have voluminous colliculi posteriores and other well-developed auditory relays (785).]

THE OPTIC TECTA of the mesencephalon or midbrain generally are conceded to be homologous with the retino-recipient layers of the mammalian superior colliculus, which is implicated in form vision (among other functions; 1,363). The tecta are elaborately laminated structures, more so than is any other in the avian nervous system (386). These structures far exceed the superior colliculi of mammals in relative size and/or complexity, indicating a functional emphasis upon the midbrain (376, 386). The optic tecta appear to play a major role in controlling responses to both visual and non-visual information related to pattern discriminations, the guidance of neck and whole-body movements, as in tracking moving objects, and in the orienting of visual attention (the tecta also appear to be the main sensory-correlative centers in reptiles; see 371, 892).

Visual information is carried from a retina to the contralateral tectum via massive projections of the axons of retinal ganglion cells. The manner of information processing in the tectum is determined initially by the organization of the retinotectal projection and the manner in which the terminations occur in the tectum. Subsequent processing is effected by neuronal interactions within the deeper layers of the tectum itself and with afferents from other regions of the brain (892). [In mammals the tectum is a "relay" in at least two visual pathways to the thalamus and neocortex: one to the lateral geniculate body and one to the pulvinar nucleus (1,362).]

Unlike the situation in primates and megachiropteran bats, in which the visual representation on one optic tectum (superior colliculus) is restricted to the contralateral half of the visual field (hemifield of space), in birds and all other vertebrate groups so far examined an optic tectum receives a complete representation of the visual field of the contralateral retina. The latter representation of the retina and visual field is topographical, with proportionately larger areas subserving the fovea: the anterior retinal quadrants are represented anteriorly and dorsally, whereas the superior quadrants are represented posteriorly and dorsally (1,210).

The tecta connect to many parts of the brain. There are important projections to the nucleus isthmoopticus upon which there is an ordered representation of the retina via the lateral optic tract and tectum. Regions of the isthmooptic nucleus project via the medial optic tract to the contralateral retina supplying centrifugal fibers to the parts thereof from which they receive impulses via the tectum. The tectum also projects to the nucleus rotundus (topographically in chelonians; 892), which does not appear to receive any other important afferents, and to the central ectostriatum and paleostriatum augmentatum via the lateral forebrain bundle. Among other projections, important fibers also pass to the opposite tectum (512, 513, 1,008, 1,210). Rhesus Monkeys probably have at least 12 separable and differently specialized maps of their retinas at the level of the visual cortex alone (see 1,102).

THE TECTOFUGAL VISUAL PATHWAY AND DECUSSATION. The course of the highly developed tectofugal optical pathways in vertebrates was a subject of great controversy throughout most of the latter half of the 19th century. Did the nerve fiber bundles from the retina of one eye decussate (cross over) completely in the optic chiasm en route to the optic tectum of the contralateral (opposite) brain hemisphere? Or was decussation only partial, with some of the fiber bundles terminating in the ipsilateral hemisphere? These questions are answered on pp. 359, 360, following descriptions of the tectofugal and thalamic pathways.

THE COMPLETE TECTOFUGAL VISUAL PATHWAY is remarkably similar to the mammalian tecto-thalamic-circumstriate system (386). It projects massively and topographically from the retinal ganglion cells to the superficial layers of the contralateral optic tectum. There seems to be a conversion of visual units with small receptive fields into movement-sensitive units with very large fields within the tectum. Fibers from a deep, central, gray layer of the tectum project primarily ipsilaterally via a discrete fiber bundle to the nucleus rotundus of the thalamus, a specific visual relay and major lemniscal terminus. It is the largest and most prominent nucleus in the avian thalamus and appears to be homologous with the nucleus lateralis posterior thalami of mammals. At least in Rock Pigeons (and chelonians), a given region of the rotundus receives information from all points in visual space (receptive fields of 120-180°), but the projection may be organized according to the laminar position of neurons within the central gray (see 376, 1,008, 1,048). [There also is evidence of direct projections (that do not synapse in the thalamus) from the optic tectum to the hyperstriatum ventrale in domestic fowl chicks (see 1,091).]

From the various subdivisions of the nucleus rotundus, the pathway projects massively with little change in unit properties and in a topographically, but not retinotopically (retinotopy is lost in the tecto-rotundal projection), organized fashion to the core region of the ectostriatal nuclear mass in the ipsilateral telencephalon. Fibers from the ectostriatum, in turn, project selectively in the periectostriatal belt, which may be the major avian center controlling perception of form and motion. There is general agreement that the rotundal-ectostriatal pathway has units with large receptive fields that respond to the movement of small stimuli anywhere in the receptive fields (367, 370, 1,048). From the periectostriatal belt, efferents project to the neostriatum intermediale laterale, the hyperstriatum, and a restricted portion of the archistriatum intermedium dorsalis, which sends efferents back to the tectum (see 1,008).

There also is suggestive evidence of another major source of visual input to the ectostriatum and of projections of the hyperstriatum back upon many structures receiving retinal input, such as the ventral geniculate (internal lamella), visual areas of the dorsal thalamus, and the optic tectum (see 386). Lesions of the ectostriatum, the nucleus rotundus, and other levels of the tectofugal visual pathway disrupt visual localization and orientation and produce severe deficits in learned responses and color discrimination in Rock Pigeons. The thalamofugal system apparently plays a minor role in these functions (see 892, 1,091).

THE SMALLER THALAMOFUGAL VISUAL PATHWAY is topographically organized and appears to be homologous with the mammalian geniculostriatal pathway (386). Both this pathway and the tectofugal one are discrete at all neural levels in birds (892). They are present in all vertebrates and may trace back at least to the presumed time of separation of the reptilian ancestors of mammals (the middle Carboniferous), reflecting a main trend of evolution of vertebrate brains (385, 892).

[Northcutt cautions, however, that it is not clear whether retino-thalamo-telencephalic input to the dorsal cortex exists in all reptilian orders, or exactly what cell group(s) give rise to the projection, and that there are insufficient data on the similar pathway in birds to ascertain whether it is homologous with the retino-geniculostriatal pathway of mammals (1,236). Not only do extrageniculate pathways to visual cortex exist in parallel with geniculocortical pathways, but even the latter pathways are a complicated array of at least 3 parallel, distinct, and independent neural chains, the W-, X-, and Y-cell pathways (1,365).]

Embryological studies suggest that the medial pallium in birds consists of thin hippocampal and parahippocampal cortices. The dorsal pallium is divided into a rostral segment, termed the Wulst, and a caudal dorsolateral, corticoid plate. The Wulst consists of lateral and medial divisions; the latter seems to be more closely associated with the medial cortical areas than the former, but its connections are understood poorly (1,236).

[The lateral Wulst or "visual Wulst" is a prominent, multilayered, dorsomedial elevation of the telencephalon that lies medial to a longitudinal groove, the vallecula, and is quite reminiscent of the granular 4th layer of the mammalian visual cortex. It contains exclusively stellate neurons and is composed of the hyperstriatum dorsale, the h. intercalatus superior, and the h. accessorium, i.e., excluding only the ventral portion of the hyperstriatum, the h. ventrale. It appears to be a broad cortical zone with several afferent sources and different efferent projections (386). One of the most notable of the latter is a substantial descending, topographically-organized projection on the optic tectum. This, and its columnar arrangement, render the similarity of the avian Wulst to the mammalian visual cortex even more likely (see 386, 1,008, 1,048, 1,233). It now is recognized that in many mammalian species the visual cortex is not required for form vision; its unique contribution appears to be that of providing high-acuity vision (1,363).]

The nerve fibers of the thalamofugal pathway in the bird originate in the retina, whence they project to a complex of nuclei in the contralateral, anterior, dorsal thalamus (including the nuclei dorsolateralis anterior and pars lateralis). Thence, they bypass the ectostriatum, to enter the overlying visual Wulst (see below), projecting to massive terminal fields, primarily to a broad, bilaminate band of granular cells (nucleus intercalatus hyperstriati accessorii) intercalated between the hyperstriatum dorsale and the hyperstriatum accessorium (376).

From the Wulst, efferents are sent to the nuclei in the dorsal and ventral thalamus, to the pretectum, to the optic tectum, and to the periectostriatal belt. These Wulst efferents offer a pathway by which the thalamofugal system may exert a modulating influence on the more extensive tectofugal system via the periectostriatal belt and optic tectum, and upon other cell groups that receive retinal input (1,008). Thus, the nucleus dorsolateralis anterior also receives feedback from the Wulst (371). A smaller number of axons and terminals project from the thalamus to the contralateral Wulst via the dorsal supraoptic commissure, ending in homotopic regions (see p. 360, **Recrossing Thalamic Axons**).

SOME TYPES OF VISUAL INFORMATION DIFFERENT from that carried by the fibers of the tectofugal system, are carried by those of the thalamofugal system. The receptive fields increase in size with progression through the tectofugal system, often extending over virtually the entire monocular visual field, and color-coded responses are most obvious in the rotundus. Based on such findings it has been suggested that tectofugal units typically respond to general stimulus dimensions, such as color and luminance, and the wide-field characteristics of many units also may be indicative of attention-directing functions toward new stimuli.

On the other hand, units with small receptive fields are found at all levels of the thalamofugal pathway, and binocularly-driven units are known only in the Wulst. The narrow receptive fields (usually less than 10°) of these thalamofugal units could transmit more specific information, encoding details of stimulus size and spatial localization, and be involved in contrast and pattern analysis (368, 1,008). Such information apparently directs the fine head or eye movements that serve to hold images on the central retina for examination (371). Lesions of the Wulst or of the anterior dorsolateral thalamic nuclei (thalamofugal pathway) cause little or no impairment of intensity or pattern discrimination in Rock Pigeons but produce deficits in response to difficult visual tasks, such as reversal of learned discriminations and discrimination of threshold-approaching stimuli (see 892, 1,008 and pp. 349, 350 **Dominance of Hyperstriatum**).

HIGHER ORDER PERCEPTION WHERE PATHWAYS REJOIN. In some birds the thalamofugal system rivals and exceeds the corresponding system of some mammals (367, 368). In the pigeon, at least, the visual information is greatly modified at the thalamic relay, that is, the nucleus dorsolateralis anterior (368, 371). Higher order perception probably occurs where the tectofugal and thalamofugal pathways rejoin (371), such as in the periectostriatal belt. Thus, there is a topographically arrayed projection within the telencephalon between the Wulst and the periectostriatal belt, which provides an anatomical substrate for interactions at the telencephalic level between the tectofugal and thalamofugal visual systems (386). It is suggested that the parallel transport of visual information along these anatomically separate pathways precludes the occurrence of interfering cross-talk between different stimulus dimensions (371).

A CONCLUSIVE CASE FOR PARTIAL DECUSSATION IN MAN had been made toward the end of the 19th century. In time, it became recognized that in Man and other primates, decussation in the optic chiasm is only partial; a large ipsilateral retinotectal projection is present. On the other hand, decussation seemed to be complete in birds and the lower vertebrates, possibly including some primitive mammals (57). In the latter groups, each eye sees either largely or entirely separate fields, giving very good vision over a very wide angle (97; 340° in the Rock Pigeon, with a 25°-30° width of binocular overlap; see 432, 1,009). The vision then is either preponderantly or completely panoramic, as opposed to binocular.

[In the visual pathways of other mammals than primates and megachiropteran bats, the visual cortex generally receives visual input from the nasal portion of the contralateral retina and the temporal portion of the ipsilateral retina. In the production of this pattern, neurons that originate in ganglia in the nasal part of the retina decussate in the optic chiasm to the contralateral geniculate nuclei, whereas neurons originating in ganglia in the temporal part of the retinas do not cross over at the optic chiasm and proceed to the ipsilateral lateral geniculate nucleus (993).]

DECUSSATION IN BIRDS. There was a strong tendency to accept the thesis that decussation was complete in most birds and less advanced vertebrates, because binocular vision played a lesser or insignificant role for them. In fact, Ramon y Cajal long ago lent strong support to the view that the visual neural pathways in birds decussate completely in the optic chiasm (57). This could have meant that there was relatively limited cross-talk between avian brain hemispheres concerning visual information.

On the other hand, most birds with monocular vision also may have good binocular-stereoscopic vision (57, 97). For example, the binocular field in the Rock Pigeon is about 24° wide, while it is 60-70° wide in owls and hawks (513). That being the case, cross-talk between the hemispheres would have to occur for binocular convergence to take place. Numerous neural pathways that could come into play in such cross-talk were recognized (see p. 360).

Be that as it may, studies in the 12-day-old domestic fowl chick, in 1964, showed that a small, inconspicuous bundle of optic fibers does not cross over (48), and this also could be seen in retrospect from a similar study in 1951 (see 48). [Most of the ascending auditory fibers also cross over--in the medulla--before being passed on to higher centers (418).] Since then, incomplete decussation also has been found in Rock Pigeons (1,093), snakes, turtles, and some lizards, whereas it is thought to be essentially complete in other lizards, *Sphenodon*, and crocodilians. The ipsilateral projections most commonly are to thalamic sites, are relatively variable in different groups, and are most extensive in squamates. Although the factors that determine the extent of crossing over remain to be elucidated, an involvement of the degree of overlap in the frontal visual fields has been questioned (see 1,048).

[The extensive cross-talk that occurs in the more primitive mammals takes place via the abundant interconnections in the corpus callosum, and this structure also plays a primary role in interhemispheric processing of visual information in the cat (in which it is the sole route for such high-level transfer) and primates, as shown by split-brain studies (1,364). This structure is absent in the oviparous monotremes, for example, the Duck-billed Platypus, in which decussation is "practically complete, a few fibers only passing to the ipsilateral side of the brain," and a similar condition exists in the Echidna, *Tachyglossus aculeatus*, where only 1% of the fibers have an ipsilateral destination (the apical lateral geniculate nucleus; 1,308).

RECROSSING THALAMIC AXONS. In this connection, there is no indication that any fiber of one optic nerve of the Barn Owl joins the tract on the ipsilateral side from the bundle decussating in the chiasma (57, 374). But thalamic axons recross to the Wulst posterior of the contralateral telencephalon via the dorsal supraoptic commissure. Moreover, it has been shown convincingly that this commissure provides a primary vehicle of interocular transfer of visual information (concerning color and patterns) in Rock Pigeons, serving in a sense as a forebrain commissure at the thalamic level (see 383, 393). The Wulst posterior bears a striking resemblance to the striate cortex (area 17) of mammals and its efferent connections also are amazingly reminiscent of those of the mammalian striate cortex (367, 374).

Thus, it would appear that the Wulst of the Barn Owl, like the visual cortex of mammals, is the first site of integration of information from both eyes. Since the optic pathways of hawks, kites, and ducks have been shown to bear great similarities to those of the Barn Owl (see 367), it is likely that many other birds also achieve binocular-stereoscopic vision by recrossing of thalamic axons, rather than by partial decussation of primary retinal fibers, as in most mammals (367, 374).

RETINOTOPIC PROJECTIONS AND STEREOSCOPIC VISION. The relative sizes of the discrete retinotopic projections ("retinal maps") on the Wulsts of Barn Owls, hawks, kites, and ducks appear to be directly proportional to the degrees of binocular overlap, and, therefore, presumably proportional to the degrees of stereoscopic vision (see 367). In the Barn Owl's Wulst, neurons exist with selectivity for stimulus orientation, for direction and speed of movement, for binocular stimulation, and for binocular disparity. On the basis of similarities with the cell properties of the mammalian visual cortex, Pettigrew and Konishi (374) suggested that they have homologous functions. A very similar situation exists in the Rock Pigeon Wulst except that neurons responding to tactile stimulation also are present (see 372).]

FUNCTIONAL ADVANTAGES OF BINOCULAR VISION AND STEREOPSIS. Despite extensive neurophysiological and psychophysical studies of binocular vision, its functional advantages and those of stereopsis are in dispute, and there is no clear understanding of the selective factors that determine the extent of eye frontality and binocularity of vertebrates, in general, or in birds, in particular. Walls' suggestion (405) that there is a universal tendency toward binocularity and attendant benefits of steropsis also is questioned (800).

It has been proposed that the relative widths of the panoramic and binocular fields are determined by the interaction of separate selective pressures that are not of universal occurrence but predominate only in certain modes of existence. In this view an animal's "praxic space," in which visually-controlled activities involved in directed locomotion, prey capture, nest building, and other manipulations of the environment take place, is the principal determinant of binocular field size (833). This supposes that visual fields are determined more by such factors as the possession of prehensile limbs and the diet, than by fundamental problems of vision *per se*, from which any general predictive relationship may be discerned (800, 833).

NON-TRANSFERABILITY OF LEARNING AND MEMORY BETWEEN THE EYES

VISUAL CLIFFS AND MOVING OBJECTS. A behavioral consequence of the almost complete crossing-over of the visual input (despite integration in the Wulst for binocular convergence) was shown by Zeier in young domestic fowl chicks (47). A chick raised on a glass floor-pane above the deep side of a visual cliff lost its fear of deep sides. But if it was raised with one eye covered, the changes in the brain that were associated with loss of fear using the exposed eye could not prevail during the use of only the other eye. In other words, the loss of fear was not "transferable to the other eye." When the blindfold of the chick raised with one eye covered, was switched to the other eye, the chick feared the deep side.

This non-transferability of learning between eyes does not apply to all types of behavior but generally is observed when the task to be learned is rather difficult to perform (393). A somewhat different type of result is obtained if Rock Pigeons are trained with one eye to respond positively to a line tilted at 135° and negatively to one tilted at 45°; they respond in an opposite manner when tested with the other eye (178). Rock Pigeons trained on color and pattern discriminations showed interocular transfer when the discriminations were performed simultaneously but non-transferability when they were performed successively (1,018). If chicks in the same type of experiment are "imprinted" to follow a moving object, interocular transfer of the following response occurs readily. Zeier suggests that responses compatible with normal behavior are more readily transferred from eye to eye than responses that run counter to innate tendencies (47, 393).

SEED CACHES. In a related experiment, Sherry, Krebs, and Cowie (see 99) allowed Marsh Tits (*Parus palustris*) to store hundreds of seeds with one eye covered, and then permitted them to recover the seeds with either the same eye or the other one. Using the other eye, the birds were much less likely to find the stored seeds (i.e., to visit the storage areas), suggesting that memory is important in the recovery process, and that there is little "transfer of memory between the eyes." Eurasian Nutcrackers (*Nucifraga caryocatactes*) dig through as much as 130 cm of snow for stored hazel nuts; the hippocampal cortex, thought to be involved in the consolidation of long-term memory, may play an essential role in the memory of cache locations (see 28, 351, 419, 536). Studies of Clark's Nutcracker (*N. columbiana*), which carries pine seeds up to 23 k to caching sites, buries about 7,700 separate seed caches per year, and must recover over 1,000 of them, support the view that the caches are found by means of memory (536).

HOW BIRDS DEAL WITH THEIR VISUAL WORLD. Based on his extensive further studies with Rock Pigeons, Zeier proposed that, in certain circumstances, at least, birds probably experience their visual world primarily with one eye and its corresponding brain hemisphere (via a hemispheric representation of the retinal image; 57, 59). They then 'analyze' the situation with the other eye and the opposite hemisphere. If something stored in one of the hemispheres predisposes them to give a certain response, this hemisphere ignores conflicting information from the opposite one, unless it is very urgent or compelling.

In other words, Zeier suggests that one hemisphere tends to become dominant in ordinary conflict situations; it suppresses the other hemisphere, in the sense of neither taking into account the information the latter is receiving, nor informing the latter of what it, itself, is doing (393). But there is sufficient crosstalk (probably via projections from the contralateral thalamus) to allow Rock Pigeons to perform some simple tasks requiring integration between the hemispheres. Not to be lost sight of in this connection is the fact that stereoscopic vision, in species that otherwise are inclined to use the eyes separately--sparrows, finches, flycatchers, titmice, chickadees--is especially in evidence during normal flight (195).

[It is of interest to compare Zeier's proposals with current views of visual neural processing in cats and primates (though not specifically addressing the matter of **interhemispheric** integration); experiments "suggest that more or less independent processing can occur within each visual area itself, as well as both visual areas. Thus, a particular area might process a number of different features locally in parallel, not necessarily processing each individual percept or partial percept in a unique segregated anatomical locus....One processor might abstract features from another processor and could produce classes of neural interactions....that might provide the substrate for a particular aspect of visual perception" (1,363). Of course, Zeier's proposals do not specifically address the matter of **intrahemispheric** neural processing of vision nor exclude the possibility of a complexity in birds equal to or exceeding that in mammals.]

Cerebral Asymmetry

BRAIN HEMISPHERE SPECIALIZATION AND CONSCIOUSNESS. Nottebohm (241, 426; see also 1,250) has demonstrated a marked cerebral asymmetry of control of vocalization in songbirds, control being concentrated almost entirely in the left half of the brain. This was demonstrated, for example, by the loss of most of the components of songs, subsong, and calls by Canaries and Chaffinches after sectioning the left hypoglossal nerve. If the left tracheosyringeal nerve of the Canary is cut, 80-100% of the song syllables are replaced by faint clicking sounds, by silence, or by an unmodulated note, whereas if the right nerve is cut, 80-100% of the song syllables remain virtually unchanged. This result suggests that most song elements are produced by the left tympanic membrane, and that denervating the left syringeal muscles prevents the modulation of this sound source. In both Chaffinches and Canaries, the elements elimated by right nerve section are briefer, less complex, and of higher frequency than those influenced by left nerve section. Moreover, the songs are to a large extent learned in songbirds, including the species mentioned in the foregoing.

This parallels the situation in Man, in which the production and comprehension of language is far more likely to become aphasic (disrupted) after lesions to the left cerebral hemisphere than to the right one (at least after about 14 yr of age, when language functions finally are fixed in the left hemisphere; 1,021). And Thorpe long ago, and Marler recently, compared the development of song by a bird to the learning of speech by Man (102, 121). Nowhere else in the animal Kingdom, except for the remote parallel of the development of speech in children, is learning known to play such a dominant and complex role in the development of behavior as in avian vocalizations (121).

[The type of mental processing by Man that one observes when the left hemisphere is in command has been characterized as being verbal, sequential, analytical, logical, and computer-like, whereas that of the right hemisphere contrasts in being non-verbal, spatial, synthetic, insightful, and Gestalt-like. Correlations indicating mutual interference between the right and left forms of mental processing provide the basis for the suggestion that a distinct operational advantage can now be seen to having these two rather different and somewhat antagonistic mechanisms for the cerebral processing of information set apart in separate hemispheres" (1,276).]

Both avian song and speech involve the processing of rapidly-modulated sound sequences and selective developmental attrition (1,291). Furthermore, many investigators view speech as a prerequisite for consciousness and believe that one cannot empirically divorce human intelligence from language or compare human intelligence directly with that of non-linguistic animals (1,091). Accordingly, these findings seemed, at first, to raise interesting possibilities. If such specialization of the hemispheres could have been shown to be a reliable correlate of consciousness, a new tool for probing, or at least identifying candidates for studies of, consciousness in non-human animals would have been at hand (99).

But the apparent absence of neural asymmetry in vocal control by parrots (see p. 273, **Vocal Control in Parrots**), and its presence in domestic fowl (which do not learn their vocal repertoire), the rat, and some other vertebrates (see 122, 1,251, 1,284), speak against the existence of such a correlation. [In domestic fowl, e.g., the left tracheosyringealis nerve innervates the entire syrinx, whereas the right nerve innervates only the right syringeal half (see 1,284).] However, in a much broader context, cerebral asymmetry is seen to have major significance for many branches of biological science and medicine. It provides a coherent substrate for the study of important comparative and phylogenetic issues and impinges upon the entire spectrum of brain-behavioral research from the synapse to the sentence, with the potential to lead to innovative approaches to various aspects of the biology of normal function and disease (100, 1,251).

AVIAN BRAINS SPECIALIZED FOR HIGH-SPEED DECISION MAKING

To me, a most relevant message regarding the function of the avian central nervous system that is conveyed by the fact of a paucity of direct connections from retinas to both hemispheres, and the findings concerning transfer of loss of fear and memory between the eyes, is the following. The avian brain has become specialized for high-speed responses at the expense of drawing upon its complete sensory input and/or complete store of pertinent information.

[The less advanced vertebrates seemingly employ this same strategy, and the lack of inter-ocular transfer also has been shown in goldfish trained on a successive visual discrimination problem (1,018). Their forerunners, however, were exposed to less selective pressure for responses at such high speeds and, in any event, the less advanced vertebrates would have had to deal with much less stored information. Support for the primitiveness of the complete decussational mode is the fact that the frog optic nerve fibers form their connections in the contralateral tectum during early embryonic development, whereas connections with the ipsilateral tectum only are formed during metamorphosis (1,021). A further finding of interest in connection with the high-speed decision making of birds is the possibility that some information from the tactile, auditory, and visual sense modalities may reach the telencephalon from sites in the midbrain and hindbrain without an intervening thalamic relay (see 1,091).]

MAMMALIAN BRAINS GENERALLY NOT SUFFICIENTLY FAST-ACTING. The mammalian brain organization (having achieved extensive inter-hemispheric cross-talk) is superior for reasoning: "....when the spectrum of possible challenges is broad, with a large number of environmental or social factors to be considered, conscious mental imagery, explicit anticipation of likely outcomes, and simple thoughts about them are likely to achieve better results than thoughtless reaction" (98). But these processes generally cannot be carried out fast enough for the needs encountered in rapid flight, which frequently involve times measured on a scale of only msec.

NO TIME FOR THE LUXURY OF CROSS-TALK. Natural selection has led to something of a compromise. Many of the pathways for extensive inter-hemispheric cross-talk of the mammal have been passed over in the bird in the interests of high-speed decision making, and vice versa. In many of the situations that call for "split-second" decisions encountered by birds, there probably is no time for the luxury of extensive inter-hemispheric interrogation and integration. The tremendous capacities of mammals for storing, retrieving, and integrating the information that makes possible intelligent decisions confer no advantage in critical, life-threatening situations that require decision-making at speeds too great to allow the use of these capacities.

ADVANCED CAPACITIES SUITED TO NEEDS. It would be difficult to account for the following specializations, if the avian brain, itself, operated at an unexceptional pace:

(a) "enormous" eyes that provide large, "eagle-eyed" sharp images (28; 344);

(b) eyes capable of high resolution over a visual angle of 70-80° (344);

(c) thick, elaborately-organized retinas--the ultimate in retinal organization (405)--that assimilate detail at high speed (45; 344), perform many of the complex functions of the visual system that are relegated to the higher centers of the nervous system in mammals (415), that confer a temporal sensitivity to fluctuations in light level far exceeding that of Man (1,009), and that allow ready recognition of small details over a large part of the visual field (177; 344)--the owl retina (along with the retina of mammals) would appear to have attained the ultimate limit of visual sensitivity dictated by the quantal nature of light (800);

(d) a striated ciliary eye muscle that apparently can produce changes in the curvature of both the lens and the cornea (800; M. ciliaris; also possessed by reptiles) that leads to extremely rapid focussing of images on the retina (23, 488);

(e) striated iridial sphincter and dilator muscles (also possessed by reptiles, at least testudines; 887) that make it possible for pupils to be constricted with tremendous rapidity, the response being completed before the pupil of a human eye even would begin to respond (41, 624, 800);

(f) strong powers of near and far focussing or accommodation, and involving actions of both the lens and cornea (800); the accommodation range typically is 20 diopters, but is as great as 50 diopters in a number of aquatic species and as little as 0.6-10 diopters in owls (see 800) [The refracting power of a lens (diopter) is expressed as the reciprocal of the focal length in meters.];

(g) extensive saccadic deflections (small, rapid, jerky movements) of the eyes of some species, e.g., Rock Pigeons, possibly in maintenance of a sharp and constant vigilance; these occur in short bursts at frequencies of about 30 Hz with an amplitude of 3°-15° and durations of about 250 msec and probably are essential for pattern vision (195, 394, 800);

(h) more rapid nerve impulses for fibers of a given diameter, by virtue of higher body temperatures than mammals (28; but not necessarily greater standard metabolic rates; 423); and

(i) inner ears with 10 times (50-100 times, according to Greenewalt's studies; 480, 498) the resolution of Man's in detecting sound fluctuations or perceiving time intervals (28, 36, 45, 345, 418, 513), vocal response times to audition with standard deviations of only 2.9 msec, roughly 8 times the accuracy of Man (479), and the ability to produce song notes of duration only just under 2 msec (480). ["Astonishly short" latent periods to auditory stimuli of only 5-11 msec have been observed in processing by the rostral region of the neostriatum (418).]

[Even aside from the matter of rapidity of action, avian visual systems seem far superior to those of mammals, at least of Man, though this is not generally conceded. Thus, in direct comparison tests in the field, Delius (375) found that Skylarks (*Alauda arvensis*) could recognize each other clearly by vision at 30 m or more whereas an observer could only do so unreliably even with a 30x telescope; they could detect Merlins (Pigeon

Hawks; *Falco columbarius*) flying overhead at heights where an observer positively could not resolve them without the aid of 8x binoculars; and, most remarkably, they could detect minute, usually camouflaged, insect prey in dune sand and vegetation, over 10 times better than an observer aided by a 5x magnifying lens. Free-ranging Rock Pigeons appear to have even better vision (369), leading to the belief by Delius and Emmerton that because of the limitations of psychophysical techniques the laboratory measures of pigeon visual capabilities are but "a pale reflection of the real performance of the pigeon's visual system."]

ACCESSORY OPTIC SYSTEM----RAPID RESPONSES TO PERIPHERAL STIMULI. Before leaving the topic of speed of decision making, it is appropriate to take note of the existence in most vertebrates of high-speed neural channels for sensing and commanding orientation to objects in the peripheral field of vision. The accessory optic system and the accessory optic nuclei are major central targets of retinal axons and their subsequent projections. The largest component of the accessory optic system is the medial terminal nucleus, which occurs in most sighted vertebrates. One of the most striking features of this nucleus is the large size of the retinal axons that enter it, and the distinctiveness of a separate tract from the retina to the accessory optic nuclei, called the "basal optic root" (BOR) in Rock Pigeons (see 367). The nucleus upon which the BOR terminates centrally is called the "nucleus of the basal optic root" (nBOR). The nBOR, in turn, sends a direct ipsilateral projection to the vestibulo-cerebellum (see 367, 1,008).

In 1948, Herrick (359) proposed that the BOR of amphibia provided an early, very-high-speed input channel to the nBOR, sensitive to peripheral movements, and of great survival value. Since the BOR projects, in turn, on the oculomotor complex, Herrick postulated that it resulted in rapid orienting movements of the eyes and neck to the source of the peripheral stimulus.

Karten and his coworkers (367) have adduced substantial evidence that seems to confirm fully the validity of Herrick's proposals, both in Rock Pigeons and in members of a variety of other classes of vertebrates. Thus, they not only demonstrated that the nBOR projects directly on the vestibulo-cerebellum and confirmed the pathway on the oculomotor complex proposed by Herrick, they also discovered a direct projection on the oculomotor complex. Pursuing the thesis that whatever applies in birds and mammals was likely to be true as well in other vertebrate classes, they also demonstrated the existence, and cerebellar projection, of an accessory optic nucleus in catfish, goldfish, and chelonians.

Prompted by the prominence, and large size of the axons, of the retinal fiber tract of the accessory optic system, Karten and coworkers also examined the BOR tract itself. It was found to contain 4,500 heavily-myelinated axons that constituted 0.15% of the entire optic nerve. Moreover, these fibers could be shown to arise from a specific population of retinal ganglion cells found predominantly toward the retinal periphery rather than in regions of high visual acuity. These are the "displaced ganglion cells of Dogiel" (DCGs), whence the more specific designation DCG-nBOR. They apparently are the specific mediators of movements of the eyes in response to peripherally-moving stimuli; all of their features are consistent with Herrick's original proposals.

Recordings from the cells of the nBOR of rabbits and Rock Pigeons indicate that they are triggered by large stimuli, at least 30° in diameter and often covering the entire monocular visual field, that they respond preferentially to very slowly moving stimuli and patterns with a random texture, that they show some degree of directional sensitivity, with little response from the region of the area centralis, and that they do not adapt (see 367, 1,008).

Presumably the DCGs react to stimuli in relative motion and signal to the nBOR as to the relative size, speed, and direction of movements of objects as they first appear in the periphery of the visual field, eventuating a foveopetal movement. In this view, the nBOR is involved in image stabilization following both self-induced motion and absolute motion of the target, achieved through compensatory eye and hand movements (see 1,008). Inasmuch as the nBOR is among the first of the central visual structures to develop ontogenetically and, thus, probably is of phylogenetic antiquity, Karten proposes that the DCG-nBOR probably is a primitive mechanism of visual function.

A BROADER PERSPECTIVE ON INSTINCTIVE RESPONSES BY BIRDS

ALLOWING FOR SPEED OF DECISION-MAKING. It is recognized that largely stereotyped and instinctive behavior may be as adaptive as intelligent behavior (28 and above). It follows from the above considerations that a valid comparison of the powers of the brains of birds and mammals has to take into account more than just our interpretation of the appropriateness or adaptedness of birds' responses. It also has to allow for the crucial aspect that has played a much greater role for the bird than for the mammal --speed of decision-making when msec decisions are critical--in hunting, in escape, in avoidance, etc. This is a respect in which avian brains are far superior to those of mammals, with the possible exception of bats. [The latter maneuver primarily by audition rather than sight and there is an emphasis on tectal (midbrain) systems (83).]

[Although the auditory time-resolving abilities of birds are comparable to those of bats (418), the superiority of the avian neurosensory system, as adapted for maneuvering in flight, is suggested by the fact that the principal nocturnal predators on bats are owls (195).].

MANY INSTINCTIVE ACTIONS CAN BE ACCOUNTED FOR when viewed from this broader perspective. They are seen to be the consequences of an otherwise highly beneficial compromise in the mode of operation of the brain. The daily survival of the individual bird was much more important than, say, the occasional loss of a few eggs or chicks, or broods thereof. It was much more adaptive for the birds to act fast in critical situations than to act best in non-critical ones.

[Our pride and self-esteem have led us to overvalue enormously the worth of infants. Objectively viewed, rather than babies being our most precious commodity, they are one of our more expendable commodities. They are only "potential reproducers," that can be replaced easily in less than a year. Contrariwise, adults are "bona fide reproducers," whose vast stores of knowledge and experience take many years to replace.]

NEXT YEAR IS ANOTHER YEAR. In this connection, Drent accounts for the abandonment of artificially enlarged broods by parent European Starlings as follows: the threat to the parents' survival would not be offset by the benefit from survival of the brood, when account is taken of the likelihood of raising a brood during the next season (60). Similarly, Sooty Shearwaters (*Puffinus griseus*), swallows, boobies, martins, Laysan Albatrosses (*Diomedia immutabilis*), and Wood Pigeons, and many birds of prey simply abandon their young if the time for migration arrives before the young have become independent. Or, they abandon the eggs in times of food shortage, including when the foraging parent fails to return on schedule and when the weight loss of the incubating bird is excessive (526; see, also, discussions and refs. in 28, 101, 427 737). Many cases are known of mass abandonment of young by breeding colonies in times of food shortage, and mid-winter abandonment of small roosts among winter-roosting colonies of passerines is common, probably when local food patches become exhausted (573). The basis for such behavior is obvious: why gamble, when next year is another year.

In essence, natural selection has set limits to parental devotion in those species in which the young are dependent upon adult care. Parental devotion extends to the limit consistent with parental survival, but not beyond that point (101). "When survival of the parent is pitted against the survival of the progeny, the former prevails" (737). In another view, that includes the alternatives of parental investment in future progeny, parents should continue to invest in a particular offspring only as long as incremental gain in that offspring's prospect for survival outweighs the cost of continued investment to the parent (530).

I would agree with Welty that "flight has proved to be an enormously successful evolutionary venture, but one that has cost birds dearly in mental development" (28), but I view it from a somewhat different perspective. He sees flight as a "substitute for cleverness," in the view that birds solve many of their potential problems merely by flying away from them. I see the mental cost as the price that has had to be paid for the ability, itself, to exploit flight, that is, for the ability to make decisions at high speed. At the same time, I suggest that the cost has not been as great as usually is assesed, by emphasizing the advantages of highly stereotyped behavior.

COMPARING BIRDS AND MAMMALS

BIRDS HAVE "CONQUORED" EVERY PORTION OF THE WORLD. Perhaps we have identified another important factor that allowed birds to achieve the distinction of conquering "every portion of the world, including the most remote oceans, the wastes of the Antarctic, the depths of the deep caves, the top slopes of the Himalayas, the mud bottom 60 m below the surface of the sea, and the darkest recesses of the jungle" (174, 309), and become numerically the most successful terrestrial vertebrates.

Their vision, hearing, digestion, remarkably efficient respiration, endurance, flight efficiency, mobility, etc., not only are generally superior to those of mammals, birds also make the quickest decisions. Many birds see near-ultraviolet light--only physiologically destructive wavelengths are not transmitted--and some species detect the plane of polarization of light. Birds also can sense changes in magnetic fields, in some cases as small as 0.02% of that of the earth, detect changes in atmospheric pressure of 1 mbar, and hear infrasound down to 0.05 Hz (118, 191, 200, 377, 657, 671, 800, 1,007-1,010).

A CONSERVATIVE ESTIMATE OF 100 BILLION BIRDS. Let us use numerical success as a crude measure of the "brain power" of endothermic vertebrates, if only as an exercise. In this way we seek to allow both for appropriateness and speed of brain-guided responses. Consider the fact that birds comprise 9,021 extant species, belonging to 166 families and 27 orders. By contrast, only 4,060 species of mammals are recognized (89, 804).

The world population of birds was conservatively estimated in 1951 to exceed 100 billion (10^{11}) individuals (28, 87, 111, 313). That this was indeed highly conservative may be judged from the recent estimate that there may be 70-75 billion birds today in Africa alone (259). Just two species of mallard duck may well exceed 100 million individuals, Chaffinches over 200 million, and blackbirds and starlings in the continental U.S., in winter, 500 million (88, 313). The total population of terrestrial birds in the U.S. is estimated at between 5 and 6 billion (155).

Roughly 5 billion Palearctic migrants, not including incalculable numbers of waterfowl, winter in Africa. Four-fifths of these occupy a receptive area of some 20 million sq. km south of the Sahara (between 16° N and 15°S latitude), where about 1/3rd of the breeding birds of Europe spend their winters. Single flocks of Bramblings (*Fringilla montifringilla*) and blackbirds have been estimated to number 11 and 25 million birds, respectively (28, 1,052). Birds even rival or exceed reptiles and mammals in the numbers and varieties of their aquatic forms (309). There are over 390 species from 21 families and 9 orders that swim habitually (28).

Paleontological Comparisons

AN EVEN RICHER AVIFAUNA IN THE PAST. Thus, if one were to accept numerical success as a yardstick of "brain power" of endothermic vertebrates, one probably would have to give birds the edge over most mammals. This conclusion would seem to be bolstered when one takes into account the fact that, from the point of view of diversity and structure (but not of brain size; 59), avian evolution achieved virtually its present status in the major radiations of early Tertiary times. The avifaunas were even richer in different types then than they are today (49, 55, 308). The surviving avian species are estimated to represent from less than 1% to about 5-6% of those that existed in the past 140 million yr (31, 308).

MAJOR RADIATION IN CRETACEOUS PERIOD. There apparently were several major radiations in the course of very early avian evolution, each of which gave rise to a variety of forms with diverse morphological and ecological adaptations. Aside from members of the Hesperornithiformes (unknown after the Cretaceous period), which were small predators of the epicontinental seas that resembled modern grebes, these earliest radiations are entirely unknown (574). The living paleognathous birds, the ratites and tinamous, may be survivors of such an archaic radiation (616). The Mesozoic avian and mammalian faunas consisted primarily of bizarre reptile-like forms with no clear relationship to extant taxa. A major radiation of terrestrial avian species took place in the Cretaceous period; at that time the basic structure of birds was established and about 40 species in 20 families are known (106, 308, 309, 334). Even in early Cretaceous, the indications are that birds were widespread, with a substantial number of the major avian lineages already in existence. Only 2 or 3 modern orders have been discerned in the late Cretaceous period, the Charadriiformes and possibly some members of the Procellariiformes and Pelecaniformes, but no Mesozoic fossil can be referred to a contemporary family

(574, 590, 1,094). Indeed, the Mesozoic birds assigned to the Charadriiformes might all be assigned to extinct orders if they were fully known. They and their close relatives may contain the progenitors of the entire Tertiary radiation (652).

THE EARLIEST PALEOCENE BIRDS appear to represent a continuance of the basic patterns in these late Mesozoic "shorebirds." Thus, the earliest representatives of many orders, like the Anseriformes, Phoenicopteri, and Galliformes, show similarities with shorebirds and waders (see 652). A major radiation of neognathous non-passeriforms probably was underway before the end of the Cretaceous period, reaching its height in the early Cenozoic era. Starting within that radiation, one basic line, that of the passeriforms, underwent its own radiation from mid-Cenozoic to the Holocene epoch and became the dominant group in later Cenozoic and Recent avifaunas (616). Various aquatic birds were well established by the end of the Cretaceous period, but ducks, gulls, and petrels had not yet entered the record (308). All toothed birds apparently became extinct, and teeth did not reappear when birds reradiated (652).

Far less is known concerning avian radiations in the Paleocene epoch than about the Cretaceous radiations. Since great diversity and differentiation is seen in the avifauna of the Paleocene and Eocene epochs, including both terrestrial birds and waterfowl, and all existing major forms appeared during the Tertiary period, one is compelled to conclude that most of these 20 families of the Cretaceous period (see p. 369) probably also had their origin in that period (106, 652).

In the most reasonable view, the birds of the Paleogene subdivision of the Tertiary period generally comprise extinct taxa that have to be regarded as mosaics of modern families, or that, if fully known, would show trends culminating in very different taxonomic groups later in the Tertiary period. [Later Eocene to Oligocene records are still the oldest for many families, such as the Anatidae, Ciconiidae, Gaviidae, and Cuculidae. Most modern genera should be even younger (652).] The Paleogene groups that were numerically important and most diverse in their membership were not the same as those of today (290, 652).

Clearly, however, some birds of truly modern aspect date back at least to the Oligocene epoch (members of the genera *Limosa*, *Totamus*, *Pterocles*, *Bubo*, *Asio*, *Sula*, *Phalocrocorax*, *Puffinus*, *Buteo*, and *Anas*), and many birds that presently are confined to the Old and New World tropics were widely distributed in middle latitudes then; these may have evolved under tropical conditions in high latitudes but shifted into medial latitudes as the tropics contracted (see 652, 1,094). In another view, by the Paleocene epoch, and certainly by the early Eocene, many different modern families were represented (574, 590); 32, or 57%, of the families that arose in the Cretaceous period and Paleocene and Eocene epochs having survived into the Holocene epoch (616).

MEMBERS OF ORDER PASSERIFORMES NOT YET PRESENT. The order Passeriformes might have diverged before its record indicates, but the bulk of its radiation must have been in the Miocene epoch or later (652; see p. 371). Relatively far fewer passeriform families (only 22.8%) than non-passeriform families (67%) are known before the Pleistocene. Of course. this may be a preservation sampling bias in favor of the latter groups (616). The most important Paleocene avifauna at present come from the late Paleocene epoch of France, including a sizable and diverse group of owls and the gigantic flightless *Gastornis*, which closely resembles *Diatryma* (652).

MOST MODERN AVIAN ORDERS (26 of the 32 known orders are found as fossils), both contemporary and extinct, date back to the Paleocene and Eocene epochs. Perhaps all had appeared by the end of the Eocene, an epoch of greatest importance in the evolution of birds. Modern families began to appear and more of them arose then than at any other time. There are 20 families from deposits of undoubted Eocene age and 8 more in the phosphorites of Quercy (the latter are deposits that filled sink-holes in the Karst topography of the departments of Tarn-et-Garonne, Lot, and Aveyron, to the southwest of the central French massif). Only 6 new living families appeared during the Oligocene, when a trend toward drier conditions developed that continued during the Miocene and on into the Pliocene epochs. Only in the Oligocene do the first extant genera appear with certainty (308).

PASSERIFORMES APPEARED IN THE EARLY MIOCENE, when tropical or semi-tropical conditions prevailed as far north as the 50th parallel. All of the non-passeriform families, most, if not all, passeriform families, most Recent families, perhaps even all the families that have ever existed, and most modern avian genera probably were established by the end of this epoch (308, 309, 334, 616). The fossil record of 20 extant avian families begins in the Miocene epoch but the birds within these families were often rather primitive within the taxa (290).

Essentially all extant genera probably were established by the end of the Pliocene epoch. Nine new families appeared then, including the tinamous, Ostriches, emus, rheas, and Ospreys (*Pandion haliaetus*; 308). Extant species are not known to occur prior to the late Pliocene and most of them are of Pleistocene or more recent occurrence (290).

21,000 NEW SPECIES IN THE PLEISTOCENE EPOCH. Virtually all living species of birds appear to have arisen at various times during the Pleistocene epoch (308) and the quality of the Pleistocene fossil record is far superior to that of any other geological period (290). Avian evolution in this epoch, which was a period of constant change, is estimated to have given rise to roughly 21,000 new species. This can be attributed to the fact that the geographical isolation resulting from Pleistocene glaciation was one of the most effective barriers to gene flow in the recent history of birds. The speciation process apparently was more or less completed by the end of the 4th glaciation in the Northern Hemisphere.

The late Pleistocene birds included not only today's depleted avifauna but thousands of species that failed to adapt to the marked environmental changes (308). At least 6 orders and suborders and 40 families have become extinct (309). Only minor specific and subspecific variations, mainly the latter, have occurred in the post-glacial Recent epoch (the last 11,000 yr).

BIRDS "BROKE OUT" EARLY, MAMMALS DEVELOPED PROGRESSIVELY. By contrast with birds, many more mammalian families, both relatively and absolutely, first appear in the fossil record of the Cretaceous, Paleocene and Eocene, but fewer of them survived into the Holocene epoch (616). During the late Cretaceous period, there were only 6 orders present, including about 5 families of placentals, 3 families of marsupials, and 6 families of multituberculates. At the end of the Cretaceous period, most of the marsupials became extinct. Before the end of the Paleocene epoch, at least 40 families (seemingly mostly diurnal forms) were in existence (see 1,281, 1,301). Many of these mammals belonged to primitive orders that became extinct by Oligocene times (652). Rodents and bats, the two orders of mammals with the greatest number of living genera and species are about equally old, appearing in the late Paleocene and early Eocene epochs (the chiropteran species, *Icaronycteris index*), respectively, long after the oldest known primates and multituberculates had become numerous and diversified.

By the time that rodents were becoming abundant and ecologically varied, the bats already were totally volant and, compared with the rodents, highly precocious (782). Although the Eocene epoch was an era of major evolution for mammals, these were only distant ancestors of modern types. The ancestors of birds broke out early from a primitive base (in which the rigorous conditions for flight were fulfilled) into perfected, exceedingly-specialized types (501). Their adaptive radiation among the vertebrates has been rivalled in recent geological time only by the teleosts (351, 419). [We see evidence of the different evolutionary history of birds from that of mammals in the fact that no living bird is especially primitive. All contemporary members of the class are highly specialized for their respective habitats. On the other hand, mammals include a range of representatives from fairly primitive to highly advanced. Thus, the monotremes, though in some respects specialized, have retained many reptilian features of the therapsids (see 106).]

Mammals, on the other hand, developed progressively, with many failures and evolutionary dead-ends. Ordinal and familial diversity increased rapidly through the Paleocene and Eocene epochs to reach respective all-time highs of 26 orders in the late Eocene and 116 families in the early Oligocene epochs (excluding bats and odontocete plus mysticete whales). The total ordinal and familial diversity underwent a decline in the latter half of the Oligocene, with secondary rejuvenation in the early Miocene. A general decline from the Pliocene epoch to the present has left only 18 extant orders (1,301).

Most modern mammalian families were not differentiated until the early Oligocene or end of the Miocene epochs. Many of these appeared almost at the same time in Europe and North America (652). These were separated by long lines of descent from the primitive forms that were contemporary with the "modern" birds of the Eocene epoch (28, 55, 155, 308, 616). Relatively few of these Eocene mammalian families are still living. Concerning the total number of mammalian orders and families per continent, there has been a remarkable uniformity from the early Oligocene to Recent epochs, despite major faunal "turnovers" in the late Cretaceous period and the Eocene through early Oligocene, and early Miocene epochs, suggesting the existence of some manner of faunal equilibrium (1,301).

A high number of first appearances of mammals occurred in the late Eocene to early Oligocene and in the first half of the Miocene epochs. [A dramatically rapid and severe deterioration in temperature and equability in the early Oligocene is followed by a spectacular decline in the number of first appearances of mammalian families during the middle 1/3rd of the Oligocene.] But unlike the case for birds, the greatest number of living families of mammals do not appear in the fossil record until the Miocene. Some mammalian families probably did become differentiated in the Pliocene epoch, whereas it is not clear that any avian family did. In neither case is it likely that any family emerged after the Pliocene (616). In short, it is clear that there has been a much more marked mammalian than avian faunal turnover since the Eocene. The two histories resemble one another, though, in showing the repeated evolution of distinctive adaptive types separated by either geography or time, as seen in the close similarities of the foot-propelled divers or of the wing-propelled divers (652).

CHAPTER 4. REPRODUCTIVE CYCLES, RELICT EGG-CARE, AND AVIAN EVOLUTION

PART 1. EGG CARE BY ANCESTRAL BIRDS

Introduction

I now consider some facets of Cockatielian behavior and reflect on their implications. In turning our attention from Peach-faced Lovebirds to Cockatiels, we change between birds about as unlike as cats are from dogs, both in their personalities and in many aspects of their behavior. But an even greater change is made from another point of view. Although one may have peered closer than ever before into the social interactions of lovebirds in Chapter 3, nothing about the actions of the birds, taken by themselves, would greatly surprise a student of avian behavior.

By contrast, this Chapter deals with behavior that is unprecedented in any bird. Again, the findings depend upon both experimental manipulations and close, lengthy, more or less continuous observations of the birds' behavior. In this case, the primary concerns are with the ways in which Cockatiels care for their eggs and react to some simple experimental manipulations of them. Most of the observed responses probably are rarely, if ever, called forth during Cockatielian hole-nesting in the wild, in which case they might fall entirely into the category of **what can happen**. Their compelling interest is that they apparently harken back to primitive patterns of egg care of ancient birds and their post-reptilian ancestors.

Just as it was desirable to introduce Chapter 3 with considerations of courtship, courtship feeding, and the pair bond, the reader will benefit by beginning the present Chapter with considerations of parental egg care. The most pertinent questions have to do with the manners in which birds care for and incubate their eggs, how ancestral birds probably accomplished it, and how avian parents that share in the incubation of their eggs exchange with one another, that is, how they "change the guard."

Parental Care of Eggs

INCUBATORY PATTERNS FOR SINGLE CLUTCHES RARELY ADAPTIVELY RELEVANT. When one tries to account for the manner in which parent birds of various species take part in the incubation of single clutches of eggs, one enters hopelessly tangled webs of competing factors. Incubatory patterns of birds under these circumstances rarely appear to be adaptively relevant. It is not difficult to arrive at a probable reason for this. A stage must have eventuated when there was no further need for both members of mated pairs in evolving primitive avian stocks to participate in the incubation of a single clutch of eggs (29), which is believed to have been the practice of ancestral birds (see pp. 375, 376). [In cases of rapid multiple-clutching, however, incubatory patterns are adaptively relevant (see 963).]

I would suggest that the major factor in this emancipation was the transition to the use of nests in which the eggs had greatly increased protection from both predators and the elements. Almost in one fell swoop, the welfare of many birds no longer depended importantly on continuous incubation and attendance of their eggs. Incubatory patterns then were set free to change more or less vicariously (i.e., along adaptively irrelevant lines).

SIDE EFFECTS OF FREEDOM FROM THE NEED TO INCUBATE

MARVELOUS COURTSHIP HABITS---ADAPTIVELY IRRELEVANT ORNAMENTS. Some side effects of this freedom have been spectacular. Release of the male from participation in incubation, and eventually from being involved in any way with the nest, opened the way for the evolution of marvelous courtship habits and splendid adornments (29). These accumulated largely through sexual selection of completely arbitrary, even deleterious, male traits, save for the traits having maximum visual stimulatory value to the female.

FIRST STEP TOWARD POLYGYNY. It also doubtless was the first step from monogamy toward promiscuity and polygyny (34), since emancipation of males favors the development of a highly polygynous mating system (227; see also 431). The latter practice is found in at least 5% of North American passerines (431), among which its evolution is promoted by patchy resource distribution in "2-dimensional" habitats (see 954, 973). Constraints among birds are sufficiently great, however, that relatively few species have become polygamous or promiscuous (primarily among species with nidifugous young; 646), though many normally monogamous species occasionally are polygynous and some are polyandrous under certain environmental conditions (431). In extreme cases, males developed abundant, brightly-colored, progressively exaggerated, nuptial plumes (a process known as hypertely). Although the bearers of these would have had the best chance of mating and reproducing themselves, the size and unwieldiness of the plumes would have seriously impeded performance of parental care at the nest.

[Polygyny is a far more frequent dominant mating strategy than polyandry (431). Since polyandry requires very uncommon male behavior and since resources required for females to reproduce are greater than for males, mated females of the vast majority of species are unlikely to achieve it (227). True polyandry occurs only in birds with markedly nidifugous young (34) and is found in fewer than 1% of the species studied to date. Though restricted primarily to the orders Gruiformes and Charadriiformes, it also is known in Harris' and Galapagos Hawks (Parabuteo unicinctus and *Buteo* galapagoensis, respectively), the Hedge Sparrow or Dunnock (*Prunella modularis*), and the Acorn Woodpecker (*Melanerpes formicivorus*; 159, 431, 964, 1,323). In the latter 4 species the polyandry is of the cooperative (as opposed to the classical) type in which all members of the breeding unit contribute to the care of a single nest (1,323). Among polyandrous species, sexual role reversal in the conventional sense appears to be essentially complete in the American Jacana (*Jacana spinosa*); their polyandrous system also appears to be the most advanced (highly evolved; 964).

Sexual role reversal also has occurred in cassowaries (*C. casuarius*), phalaropes (Phalaropidae), buttonquail (Turnicidae), the plains wanderer (Pedionomidae), the Variegated Tinamou (*Crypturellus variegatus*), painted snipes (Rostratulidae), and Bensch's Rail (*Monias benschi*). Generally speaking, it has evolved when the reproductive output of females is limited by their ability to obtain mates (see 1,266). The mating system of the Hedge Sparrow is extraordinary, with monogamy, polyandry, polygyny, and polygynandry all occurring (see 1,323).]

ALOOFNESS FROM NEST--EXAGGERATED ORNAMENTATATION RELATIVELY INNOCUOUS. As implied above, some of these male birds never could have become so ornate if the survival of the species depended on their attendance at the nest (101). In such birds, one virtually always finds that the males remain aloof from the nests (but they ceased to tend the eggs before, rather than after, acquiring the adornments). In general, the more brightly colored the male of a species, the less likely it is that he will participate in nest-building, incubation, and the rearing of the young (28).

Although one could imagine that the extreme conspicuousness of its males might have maneuvered a species into a precarious condition, and such males often do show poorer survival (374), in most cases exaggerated sexual differences seem to have been relatively innocuous (88). The adaptively irrelevant ornaments have not been eliminated by natural selection because they did not decrease the species' reproductive efficiency below the critical point (101).

[These brilliantly-colored birds court in the near vicinity of one another, often in leks, using primarily visual signals (releasers). They have adapted themselves so well to their environment, by such expedients as nesting in cavities or emancipating the male from the need for his presence at the nest, that the visual conspicuousness of the male to predators is offset. Moreover, the flesh of many brilliantly-colored birds is unpalatable (109). Additionally, many of these birds eat very nutritious fruits, as a consequence of which they have need to spend only a relatively short time foraging (126).]

HORMONAL BASIS FOR SOME SEXUAL ADORNMENTS. The various secondary sexual plumage changes and acquisition of other nuptial adornments often have a steroidal hormonal basis, and their periodic appearance coincides with the appropriate period of the breeding cycle. But if a permanent plumage difference between the sexes imposes no disadvantage, it may have a genetic basis, so that hormones are unable to alter the inherited sexual type (347, 414).

In Witschi's view, the hormonal control of secondary sexual characters that develop seasonally, represents a relatively ancient evolutionary mechanism. Direct genetic determination is believed to be the stable type of control, which is being evolved in many species (347). Another type of control, operating at the neurophysiological level, is the mediation of hypophysial activity by the hypothalamus, in turn by tracts in the central nervous system, in turn by behavior and environment (see pp. 124-134).

INCUBATORY PATTERNS. Equal sharing of all kinds of parental care is practiced in all groups of extant birds, from the most primitive to the most advanced (22), but is most prevalent among non-passerines (227). Out of some 160 families, representing the majority of extant birds, members of both sexes usually incubate the eggs in 54% of the cases, including most marine birds, many non-passerines in various orders, and members of 40% of the 293 species of passerines found in North America (including mostly species with monomorphic sexes; 527, 582).

The female, alone, incubates the eggs in 25% of cases, and the male, alone, in 6% of them. In these instances of incubation by a single parent the nests tend to be bulky and well-insulated (115; including the ratites --except Ostriches--some charadriiforms, some gruiforms, a few galliforms, and nonparasitic cuculiforms). The male, the female, or both, incubate in the remaining 15% of the families. There is no reliable information on the sex of the incubating parent(s) in some 20 families (23). Uniparental care is most likely to develop in groups with slight to moderate parental care needs (i.e., with nidifugous young) and a phyletic history of shared incubation (431). [Male European Starlings delay the onset of incubation until after the period in which the risk of cuckoldry exists (582).]

BOTH PARENTS PROBABLY INCUBATED. Since characteristics that are held in common by a group of organisms are likely to have been present in their common ancestry, this modern-day distribution of incubatory practices reinforces other lines of reasoning that lead one to believe that both parents participated in incubation by ancestral birds (see, 527, 962-964). [Indicative of the primitiveness of shared incubation is the fact that the alternate care of the eggs and hatchlings by ciclid fishes is strongly reminiscent of the pattern of equal sharing by birds (101).]

In some cases, the ancient avian stock evolved in the direction of greater participation in incubation by the male, in others toward greater participation by the female; in most lines, though, the ancestral condition was conserved. The evolution toward greater participation by the female in many species may reflect the greater extra-bond mating opportunities of males, coupled with the relatively small energetic cost of spermatozoal production (431). But even in cases where the male now only occasionally incubates the eggs, both parents most commonly build the nest and care for the young (21, 23, 46). Allofeeding of rapidly growing young by both parents is the usual situation, irrespective of the degree of precocity (1,150). In some species the male is the chief architect of the nest (81).

Conservativeness of Behavior and Its Basis

The retention of the presumed primitive incubatory practice in the majority of birds emphasizes the conservative evolutionary character of this type of behavior. Indeed, though parental care reaches its highest and most elaborate development in birds, it is more conservative than many avian structural features, some of which have a very superficial basis (22). One can go further: habits and behavior generally seem to be deeply rooted; usually they are the products of very ancient evolution (38; see also 486) and involve complex aggregations of spatially and sequentially organized movements (488).

SPECIES-SPECIFIC BEHAVIOR REMOVED FROM DIRECT GENE ACTION. "There is no doubt that species-specific behavior patterns are extraordinarily stable genetically" (569). Although all aspects of behavior now are recognized to be under genetic influence (403, 569), species-specific behavior is likely to be far removed from the direct action of the genes. The structure of the underlying genetic system is such that single mutations can alter behavior drastically only rarely or not at all. This is a consequence of the enormously varied patterns of causal sequence by which gene mutations usually effect changes of behavior (299). Yet, notwithstanding the relatively minor influence of single mutations, behavior, like other phenotypes, is accessible to genetic analysis and manipulation (see below). One behavior pattern for which the genetic basis (but not the neuronal basis nor the mechanism of its establishment) is known is the so-called hygienic behavior of the honey bee, which depends on the presence, in the worker bees, of two genes (1,282).

[On the other hand, a single gene mutation can lead to rather extensive interrelated changes in the structure and function of the central nervous system. Thus, Siamese cats possess a mutant gene that specifies the structure of tyrosinase, in consequence of which their fur is pale and the pigmentation behind their retinas is reduced. This pigment deficiency apparently induces inappropriate projections of the optic nerve fibers, leading to a cascade of neurological defects in centers involved with vision--in the thalamus, in primary and secondary visual cortex, and perhaps even in higher areas. As the result of the abnormal ducussational mode of neurons from retinal ganglia (at the optic chiasm), Siamese cats either can see only the nasal part of their visual field (see pp. 355-361, **Avian Visual Pathways**), or their visual field representation has two domains of monocular input rather than binocular input (see 1,021, 1,036, and M. Foster, 1965, therein).]

As an example of deeply-rooted behavior, there is a much greater uniformity in the courtship displays, nesting and incubatory habits, and care of the young by Darwin's finches than there is in, say, the shapes of their bills (25). The fact that behavior is likely to be far removed from the direct action of genes does not, however, imply the absence of behavioral variability. In fact, genetic selection experiments have demonstrated the existence of considerable genetic variation within a species with respect to behavior, providing raw material for the process of natural selection (569). But only very few data on the mutability of behavioral traits are as yet available.

HORMONES. Another aspect of the conservativeness of behavior relates to its ultimate hormonal control. A well-known maxim of comparative endocrinology asserts that the evolution of hormonal control mechanisms rarely involves the appearance of new molecules, rather pre-existing molecules find new uses after pre-existing cells acquire new sensitivities, say, through the evolution of new receptors (760, 905, 1,178). The fundamental basis for this circumstance, as with behavior, is that steroidal sex-hormones are the products of complex sequences of biochemical reactions, and are far removed from the direct actions of the genes that determine these reactions (1,162). Thus, it has been proposed that the role of steroids as regulators of genomic activity is of prechordate origin, and that steroids secreted by the gonads came to play an essential role in reproductive processes very early in vertebrate evolution (see 905). Moreover, the cellular mechanisms of the action of gonadal hormones on the brain seem to be uniform across species (see ref. 45 in 895).

SUPERFICIAL CHARACTERS EASILY ACTED UPON. Structure and behavior tend to be linked through the course of evolution; one scarcely can be considered successfully without due attention to the other (488). Long ago, however, Lorenz and Tinbergen recognized that the ways in which birds display their striking adornments usually are more ancient than the adornments themselves (see 29). Since, within groups of closely related species, the same display posture may be used to exhibit different structural characters, the movements would appear to be more primitive; the structural features were evolved later and made the movements more conspicuous (296, 419). [Similarly, bobbing, which in members of the primitive genus, *Anolis*, serves to display the gular fan, persists in many lizards in which the fan has become vestigial or even is entirely lacking (as in iguanids; 868).]

Indeed, most superficial characters, such as the shapes of the bill and wing, webbing of the feet, curled rectrices, tail rackets, frontal crests, and feather gloss are easily acted on by natural selection and are of no great use in classification (46, 97, 502). On the other hand, color pattern may be extraordinarily conservative and the genetic persistence of signal markings suggests the likely retention of associated behavior patterns despite divergent speciation (see 819). It now is widely recognized that "....a system of classification based wholly on structural characters is not always natural" (486).

BIRDS ADHERE "TENACIOUSLY" TO ANCESTRAL INCUBATORY PATTERNS. In the family Columbidae, for example, the incubatory pattern is characterized by the male incubating the eggs for a continuous period in the middle of the day and the female incubating at other times, with the eggs constantly covered (within this practice, each pair establishes its own characteristic pattern; 978). Lorenz regarded this behavior as being typical of all members of the order, and considered it to be a more general phenotypic trait than any morphological one by which to classify pigeons and doves in a common taxon (991). The validity of this generalization has been upheld by several studies of wild and feral species and by anecdotal reports of the Passenger Pigeon (*Ectopistes migratorius*; see 978).

The surprising unresponsiveness of incubatory patterns and habits to ecological conditions constitutes an impressive confirmation of their conservativeness (21, 60). Incubatory habits do not change even in extreme climates, where a change clearly would be highly advantageous (at least, in the short term). [In contrast, the clutch size of introduced species adjusts readily to the new conditions (314, 353; see also pp. 594-597, beginning with **Ovarian Functional Adaptability**).] A well-known case involved the Crested Mynahs (*Sturnus cristatellus*) that escaped from captivity in Vancouver, Canada, in about 1895. Because they persisted in the regime of incubation that was appropriate to their tropical home, but ill-suited to the rigors of Vancouver (where their attentiveness to the eggs at midday was only at the 20% level), their incubatory success was poor.

Although the Crested Mynahs established themselves as a feral population in the city (and on Vancouver Island, and are casual in parts of Washington and Northwestern Oregon), they did not enjoy the spectacular spreading success that was achieved by the European Starling after its introduction to New York in 1890 (23, 60). [See also the similar results of experimental studies with the same 2 species by S.R. Johnson, 1971, in 60.] "On the whole .... birds adhere stubbornly to their ancestral patterns of incubation, which change less readily than certain other habits in adapting to new conditions" (101).

In connection with the above, it is of interest to note that the metabolic level of birds generally appears to be correlated more closely with bodily weight and taxonomic position than with the climatic characteristics of the regions in which they reside, if the influence of differences in thermal acclimation are excluded. Thus, in general, comparable species from markedly different climates tend to have similar body temperatures when tested under similar conditions. Accordingly, it would appear that shifts in metabolic level are not involved significantly in the process of avian adaptation to cold, although the same cannot be said of species that must contend with severe heat (see 37).

SOME REPTILIAN ANALOGIES. A similar conservativeness is seen in the evolution of thermal preferences in most ectotherms. For example, in many reptiles (including most lizards) closely related species from different climates have nearly the same activity temperature ranges (body temperatures at which they are active), whereas the activity temperature range may differ considerably in different species from the same locality (363).

Another impressive example derives from similarities in nest building and ovipositional habits of crocodilians and freshwater chelonians. Although the probable common ancestor of these forms dates back to some 280 mya, aspects of the ancient reproductive behavioral pattern have been conserved to a striking degree. For example, members of both groups dig the nest with the hind feet and check the fall of the eggs into the nest with the hind feet in the same manner (659). [On the other hand, lizards dig the shallow depressions or burrows in which they deposit their eggs with either the forelimbs in alternation or both fore and hind limbs (938).]

Another measure of this great conservativeness is the fact that all chelonians dig the nest cavity exclusively with the hind feet. Although the Gopher Tortoise (*Gopherus polyphemus*) is capable of digging a 9-m burrow with its forefeet, it excavates its nest cavity with its elephantine hind legs, "removing scarcely a few grains of dirt with each stroke ...." At no time during the digging is the hole under visual inspection, yet dirt rarely is brushed back into the nest, owing to the "exceptional stereotyping and replication of the movements of the hind legs and the body" (683).

CONSERVATIVE EVOLUTION OF THE CENTRAL NERVOUS SYSTEM

ONE OF THE LEAST VARIABLE BODILY SYSTEMS. Breeding habits and other patterns and elements of avian behavior (like courtship and copulation in lizards; 94) can be as valuable, if not more valuable, indicators of ancient conditions as some physical characters (but they have to be applied just as cautiously). The reason for this is not far to seek: the fundamental structural basis of behavioral patterns is the organization of the central nervous system (albeit few structural correlates have been found). This most complex of all tissues probably makes up the least variable of all bodily systems. Because of this link between the structure and functions of nervous systems and behavior, and because behavior, in its turn, makes adaptation possible and, therefore, influences phylogenetic selective processes, the evolution of brains and of behavior ideally should be studied together (1,232). [Probably not coincidentally, the avian central nervous system is relatively infrequently subject to hereditary abnormalities (135). It is not, however, less susceptible to lesions, with figures for the incidence of these varying from 0.7-10% (454).]

BRAIN EVOLUTION & INTEGRATIVE MECHANISMS ARE BASICALLY CONSERVATIVE. In fact, the five subdivisions of the brain (telen-, dien-, mesen-, meten-, and myelincephalon) are partially developed even in the most primitive known vertebrates, and all vertebrates pass through primitive 3- and 5-vesicle stages (182). Several cytologically distinct cell groups characterize the pallium and subpallium in every vertebrate radiation and a pallium divided into lateral, dorsal, and medial formations and a subpallium divided into striatum and septum appear to be primitive characters and to be homologous among all vertebrates (1,236). The evolution of the vertebrate brain, particularly the forebrain, is characterized primarily by more or less progressive modification of neuronal subsystems, rather than by a progressive increase in size of the central nervous system or in the number of its constituent neurons. Increases in telencephalic size and differentiation of telencephalic cell masses appear to be restricted generally to the dorsal or lateral pallium and may be correlated with the origin or hypertrophy of thalamo-telencephalic pathways (1,233, 1,236).

One can assert that brain evolution is basically conservative, that adaptations are mostly minor, and that once achieved, adaptations tend to persist (59). Even diversity in brain size is conserved. Thus, the amount of diversity is determined by the average brain size of a species, regardless of whether the size is influenced by allometry with bodily weight alone, or by allometry plus encephalization (1,102).

The evolutionary inertia of the central nervous system can be traced to the difficulty of evolving and altering central nervous patterns, mainly the higher level integrative mechanisms, upon which selection can act only in an indirect manner. These involve complex widespread connections between neurons (299, 1,384), perhaps even--following the "doctrine of mass action"--an extensive and diffuse network of neural structures (see 401). It would appear to be much easier to initiate and establish a change that involves only one or a few closely related "terminal twigs" in the embryonic development of the widespread connections between neurons, than a change that depends upon harmonious modifications in many "widely separated branches" (299).

Testifying to this complexity is the fact that the vertebrate brain requires a much larger amount of genetic information to specify its development than does any other organ. At least 170,000 different types of messenger RNA molecules in the mouse brain, for example, presumably code for a like number of different brain proteins (see 862). In fact, a complete genetic specification of the neuronal organization of the brain of Man, which contains approximately 100 billion neurons, with an average of about 1,000 direct synaptic connections per neuron, would require an amount of genetic material far in excess of the total amount present (see 993, 1,379).

Perhaps the marked evolutionary conservativeness of the nervous system should be viewed largely as an extreme manifestation of a fundamental evolutionary conservativeness of all organ systems, imposed by the constraints of intrinsic genomic regulatory mechanisms and supragenomic developmental mechanisms, including ontogenetic buffer mechanisms (concerning these mechanisms, see 980, 981, and below). The earlier an embryological event occurs, the greater the number of subsequent embryological processes that will be dependent upon it, and the greater the likelihood that it will be conserved in the evolution of new forms of embryos (1,238).

Evolutionarily speaking, ontogenetic buffer mechanisms integrate mutations of highly interactive genes into phenotypes in which the gene products still interact smoothly (981). Morphological, neurological, or behavioral patterns may be so narrowly and steeply buffered that they manifest themselves under all but lethal developmental conditions. "One assumes that the strongest kind of developmental buffering results from multiple genes which can act in alternative combinations to increase the likelihood of the same end result" (1,278). Although supragenomic mechanisms (an example of which is selective neuronal death) act in the development of all organ systems, they play critical roles in the development of the nervous system (993).

[Among plants, comparable circumstances at the organismic level have been interpreted convincingly from the Darlintonian point of view: a progressive and cumulative modification of genetic systems may be traced, generally, from the open "ideal ancestral" genetic system to increasingly inflexible configurations, driven by the unceasing selection of conservative devices that ensure that minimal departures occur among progeny from the already-tested, adapted parental genotypes (1,075).]

BEHAVIOR ENCODED INDIRECTLY. Take, for example, the evolution of a complex, instinctive behavioral pattern like nest-building. Since this doubtless involves a multiple array of changes in many areas of the brain, such changes could not have sprung full-blown from a single gene mutation. A great many studies in comparative behavior are consistent with the view that single mutations generally bring about only slight, inconspicuous changes in behavior and therefore usually are not recognizable, though exceptions are known (569). Genes would appear to encode behavior and the underlying neural circuitry in only a very indirect manner (132, 1,384), and behavioral differences may be polygenic in nature even in very early evolutionary stages (569). Gottlieb does "not think it is possible to overestimate the self-realizing potency of the genetic and cytoplasmic material with regard to neural and behavioral development" (1,278).

Findings in behavioral genetics indicate that changes in behavioral patterns arise, in general, step by step through complex alterations in a highly effectively stabilized system of genic interactions (569). One expects, then, that the whole central neural pattern also must have been assembled step by step, with each genetic change having been made in terms of, and with reference to, all others (299). In fact, genetic analyses of evolutionary divergences in behavior, in general, tend to support the existence of polygenic inheritance, regardless of whether the behavioral differences concerned are between subspecies ("ecological races") or between closely related species. Consistent with these views is the finding that the geotactic reaction in *Drosophila melanogaster* depends on several genes that "are distributed over most of the *Drosophila* genome" (569).

CONSTRAINTS ON NATURAL SELECTION----CONSERVATION OF ORGANIZATION. As Simpson has stated, "as each configuration is derived from the last, and from all previous ones, each can only be a modification or addition to what was already there" (298). Accordingly, many otherwise entirely feasible evolutionary possibilities cannot become realized because they are unachievable within the established framework of embryonic development (299). In wider perspective, there are numerous factors in the genetics, developmental physiology, demography, and ecology of an organism that make the achievement of optimal adaptations unrealizable (779).

The relationships most pertinent to the present discussion are subsumed in Stebbins' principle of "conservation of organization," as follows. "Whenever a complex, organized structure or a complex integrated biosynthetic pathway has become an essential adaptive unit of a successful group of organisms, the essential features of this unit are conserved in all the evolutionary descendants of the group concerned" (108). Applying this principle specifically to the nervous system: a particular neural input-output relationship once established in particular neural networks is realized by homologous networks in the descendant species of an evolutionary series (401).

[In connection with the above discussion, it should be borne in mind that most of the identified functions of the brain that are at all well understood are functions of minute amounts of tissue; current knowledge of the brain in the large is both very limited and paradoxical (401). Thus, whereas extensive brain damage can have apparently trivial effects on measured behavior, suggesting a dispersed basis, the activation of very small regions of the brain can be highly effective in eliciting elaborate behavior patterns, more consonant with a localized basis (see 401, 488).]

MORPHOLOGICAL CHANGES MORE READILY ACHIEVED. On the other hand, morphological changes (changes in size, shape, color, etc.) are much more readily achieved than behavioral changes, even when they also involve a coordinated pattern of alterations. There is a growing body of inferential evidence that the major morphological changes of adaptive radiations are more likely to involve other modifications than changes in structural genes (599, 610).

It is of interest in this connection that birds are remarkably conservative in their pattern of genetic divergence, as determined by electrophoretic analyses of proteins within congeneric species, as compared to the divergences found in most other vertebrates; for example, amphibian congeners are roughly 10-20 times more divergent in their protein composition. It is suggested that the relatively high, stable body temperatures of most birds provide an extreme internal physiological environment to which only a small number of alternative forms of an enzyme or other proteins are well adapted functionally (650).

Genes tend to control embryonic development by processes that already are intrinsically adaptive. To take a simple example, the sizes of the eye and orbit (eye socket) in many vertebrate species are not achieved by separate genetic control of the absolute size of each. Instead, the orbit adjusts through a considerable range to fit the size of the eye (as shown in transplantation experiments; 299). Similarly, the forms of some bones are controlled to some extent by the functions of the attached and associated muscles (305).

In a like manner, the sizes of sensory and motor nuclei in the brains of vertebrates tend to adjust to changes in the size of the "end-organ load" that they come to innervate (133). Similar correlations are to be seen in the spinal cord. These are well evidenced in reptiles, among which are to be found profound differences in the shape and development of the trunk, tail, and extremities. For example, loss of limbs in snakes and limbless lizards is accompanied both by a reduction in the indices of encephalization and an absence of cervical and lumbar enlargements of the spinal cord (878, 888). Such supragenomic determinations of size and form based on function enormously reduce the requirements for explicit genetic instructions, while also automatically ensuring adaptedness (1,238).

Accommodations to end-organ load occur all through embryonic development, but the most impressive examples of the lability of morphology, as opposed to behavior, come from domestic fowl and cagebirds. Some examples of hereditary abnormalities, based on one or a few mutations, are extra toes, extra legs, no legs, absence of one kidney, absence of the uropygial gland, hermaphroditism, and wing reduction (28, 440, 1,050). In some vertebrates, notably amphibians and mice, the number of vertebrae in the spinal cord can be increased or decreased in response to environmental temperature. Retaining the potential to add vertebrae by retention of prolonged inductive ability gives tremendous plasticity to the evolution of changes in bodily length (1,239).

Another instructive example concerns the reappearance of ancestral morphological characters in Guinea Pigs (*Cavia*). Like all caviid rodents, Guinea Pigs have only digits II-IV on the forefeet and digits I-IV on the hindfeet. Several atavistic mutations restore all 5 ancestral digits, and it would appear that the genetic basis for these digits probably is latent in all cavies. The mechanism of reappearance of the digits has been described as the effect of a "polygenic system of thresholds," wherein the transition from the normal to the ancestral condition is controlled by one gene associated with several modifiers. Apparently a small change in a developmental parameter (e.g., diffusion of a morphogen) can cause the reversion to the ancestral digit number. Reversion also can be induced by a variety of environmental agents, such as age and nutritional state of the mother, and temperature, probably merely by altering developmental parameters in a fashion equivalent to the alterations produced by the atavistic mutations (see 982).

Similarly, an acceleration in the rate of side splint development in the legs of horses can lead to formation of the original toes, of which the splints are vestiges, and an increase in the rate of fibular growth in domestic fowl embryos leads to re-creation of an ancestral pattern of ankle bones below, since the fibula apparently retains a capacity to induce ancestral ankle-bone differentiation when it comes into sufficiently close proximity with the ankle bones.

Through such channeling of variation and the imposition of constraints, development is thought to become "an evolutionary force in its own right and not just a contributor to the random pool of small-scale variation that makes natural selection the only force of evolutionary change." In connection with the above it is felt that even morphological changes that arise initially as effects of single mutations probably would be poorly "canalized" and therefore subject to later stabilization through establishment of modifiers, in that manner establishing a subsequent polygenic basis (983). [For treatments of epigenetic control in development, see refs. 1,239, 1,246.]

Even so great a change as the evolution of flightlessness probably could have been achieved merely by retaining the skeletomuscular structure of infancy into adulthood (neoteny)--probably by the alteration of just a few regulatory genes--and neoteny may be fairly widespread in birds (1,321). Thus, flightlessness has arisen independently many times in the Hawaiian Islands and "an untold number of times on oceanic islands the world over....a testimony to the tremendous potential of organisms to independently evolve convergent or parallel adaptations in response to similar selective processes" (190). However, based upon numerous lines of evidence, including DNA-DNA hybridization studies and tarsal morphology, the ratites (including tinamous) probably should be regarded as being a monophyletic taxon derived from an ancestral stock more primitive than carinates (see 1,161, 1,247), though not a flightless stock.

RETINAL NEURAL CIRCUITRY LAGS PHOTORECEPTOR ADAPTATIONS. An impressive example--one of several instances among reptiles--of the much greater adaptive lability of visual cell morphology than of retinal neural circuitry is furnished by the gekkonid lizards. The latter include representatives with vision spanning a range of adaptedness from diurnal to nocturnal and some members appear to be in evolutionary transition to strictly nocturnal forms from a most recent diurnal ancestral stem stock. But the nocturnal species that already have achieved fully nocturnal retinal visual cells (rods) and nocturnal vision, still retain vestiges of diurnal retinal neural function. The retinal bipolar and ganglion cells continue to display a type of connectivity that also is adapted to serve diurnal visual cells (functionally duplex phases of dark adaptation; 1,373). If this interpretation is valid, it would open the possibility of establishing a timetable of evolution of retinal types through assessment of the state of retinal neural connectivity as compared with the coexisting visual cell types.

RIGIDLY PATTERNED CIRCUITRY---ONTOGENETICALLY PLASTIC ROUTING. But the fact that many morphological changes are much more readily achieved than behavioral ones should not be taken to imply that there is a high degree of rigidity in the functional capability of the underlying neural circuitry and the resulting adult behavior. The differentiation of the organization of the nervous system appears to proceed to advanced stages without the benefit of functional activity, sensory feedback, or environmental stimulation. But the very fact that the links between the genotype and the phenotype in the ontogeny of behavior are complex and indirect--more so than in the development of any other biological process--confers a notable susceptibility of synaptic patterns to various kinds of modulating influences of environmental and experiential factors in late stages and in their final perfection (570, 1,277, 1,278).

This susceptibility of behavioral ontogeny is enhanced by a rather extended period of plasticity of nerve cells insofar as their interplay is concerned, particularly in the formation and consolidation of selective routes within the genetically-determined neural circuitry. It is primarily the high degree of specialization of the neural units themselves that sets relatively rigid limits on their developmental potentialities (570). In brief, the overall pattern of the neural circuitry is laid down more or less rigidly but there is a great plasticity of the synaptic and dendritic details of the wiring (1,036), the ontogeny of impulse routing within the pattern, and the resulting adult behavior (570).

That there may exist plasticity of impulse routing, even in the adult, is suggested by the findings that (a) mammalian neurons react to partial denervation, injury, or sensory disuse by the sprouting of new axonal collaterals and synaptic terminals from intact axons, by the enlargement of synaptic endings, by the reorientation of dendritic branches, and by an increase in the numbers and sizes of dendritic spines (see 1,361); and (b) there is an androgen-regulated plasticity of the dendritic length of motoneurons in a sexually dimorphic nucleus in the spinal cord of adult male rats (1,160).

In their organizational effects, the perinatally-acting steroids appear to function by changing "thresholds for behavioral responses rather than by grossly changing the course of neural pathways....the essential 'wiring' for these behaviors persists...even the earliest paper of the proponents of the 'organizational theory' anticipated that the effects of the perinatal hormones on the nervous system would be subtle rather than gross" (1,026). Similarly, activational effects of steroids leading to altered neuronal and synaptic efficiency within developmentally fixed neural pathways (1,030) may lead to changes in utilized neural circuitry. A plasticity also appears to exist in the triggering mechanisms for certain functions; for example, depending upon circumstances, the central nervous system may exploit any convenient and appropriate signal to trigger reproductive behavior (895). It has yet to be demonstrated that the changes in neural circuitry effected by experience consist of more than merely facilitation or enhancement, maintenance, or inhibition of neural circuits that are more or less rigidly patterned by genetic factors (1,034, 1,276).

[Recent progress in the fields of biochemistry, physiology, and morphology has revealed that there is no reliable criterion for defining a nerve cell, since long neurofibrils and Nissl bodies are not specific to neurons. Neurons and "neuro-epithelial cells" may contain, besides synaptic vesicles, endocrine-like granules, and endocrine cells may contain synaptic-like vesicles. Even action-potential-like depolarization of an excited cell membrane has been detected in pancreatic islet cells and some other endocrine cells, as well as in the skin of toad larvae. In fact, a multifaceted analysis of the cytological features shared by neurons, endocrine cells, and neuroepithelial or sensory cells has led to the view that both the cell types, on the one hand, and the hormones and neurotransmitters secreted by them, on the other, should be regarded as forming continuous spectra, and to the proposal to designate the latter two categories of cells as "paraneurons" (see 1,164, 1,278).]

IMPRESSIVE SIMILARITIES BETWEEN AVIAN AND MAMMALIAN BRAINS. To bring our treatment into sharper focus, let us now consider some concrete general examples of the evolutionary conservativeness of (or inherent constraints upon the evolution of) the central nervous system. First, it is found that sensory mechanisms in the central nervous systems of birds and mammals still can be recognized as being merely elaborations of the same constructions found in reptiles (386). The more caudal subdivisions of the central nervous system have evolved in a fairly stable manner that allows relatively facile inter-class comparisons to be made. But the modifications of the ancestral reptilian forebrain structure pose problems.

Whereas in birds the resulting organization still appears to be relatively comparable to that of contemporary reptiles, the recomposition of the reptilian forebrain in mammals has been very extensive. The latter recomposition culminates in the abrupt emergence of a neocortex in the pallial mantle and seemingly profound changes in the composition of the thalamus and corpus striatum (1,233). Yet despite the long lines of divergent evolution of birds and mammals, many details of their brains are impressively similar. In fact, the well-known differences in the forebrain reflect dissimilarities in the final patterns of alignment of the constituent nerve cells. The cells that can be identified reliably are found to fall into populations with striking parallels in the two groups (52, 367).

SIMILARITIES IN NEURAL VOCALIZATION CONTROLS. Additional evidence comes from some "amazingly close similarities" between both peripheral and central neural control mechanisms for vocalizations in toadfishes, several species of frogs, several species and orders of birds, and 3 orders of mammals (396). Of course, the key feature of this finding is not that homologous networks are involved in the central mechanisms for vocalizations in the evolutionary series. "It would be an unnecesarry burden for the evolutionary process to have evolved new systems to solve a problem already solved by an existing system" (59). The key feature is that the "amazingly close similarities" have been retained in these particular evolutionary lines, despite the fact that the lines diverged as long as 350 mya. A comparable situation is found to exist with regard to the neuroanatomical organization of the auditory system; for example, there are gross similarities up to the thalamic level in amphibians, reptiles, birds, and mammals, though the auditory capacities of the latter two groups are far more advanced (1,091).

It seems clear from the foregoing that the evolutionary inertia of behavioral patterns is just an expression of the generally highly conservative nature of the evolution of the nervous system itself. Changes in behavior and changes in the nervous system, being in the main a result of nervous system function, now often are regarded as different manifestations of a single phenomenon (108).

BEHAVIOR AND RELATEDNESS

Since patterns and elements of behavior can be valuable indicators of ancient conditions, it follows that they also can give clues to relatedness and homologies. In fact, the study of the kinds and diversity of organisms (systematics) is one of the fields of biology in which comparative behavior is most deeply involved. As Simpson stated, similarity of behavior "may be used....as evidence on existing degrees of phylogenetic relationship. It thus adds importantly to the total evidence, anatomical, physiological, and otherwise, and it may well be decisive when other evidence is equivocal or conflicting " (298).

Marler stresses the necessity of knowing the functions of behavioral characters in order to employ them most judiciously for taxonomic purposes. He points out that releasers (i.e., color, patterns, and forms of structures, as well as behavior), involved in reproductive isolation and selected for specific distinctiveness (e.g., song and courtship displays), are of limited use above the species level. Characters that are selected for moderate specific distinctiveness, and which include mobbing, preflight, and aggressive displays and sounds not involved in reproductive isolation, are useful for delineating genera and families (958).

BROAD APPROACH DESIRABLE---SOME INDICATORS UNRELIABLE. Currently, when there is a disagreement between the evidence provided by morphology and behavior, below the level of orders, taxonomists are increasingly inclined to give greater weight to the behavioral evidence (111, 297). However, neither a strictly behavioral nor a strictly morphological approach is desirable for attacking evolutionary problems, and one must exercise great caution with both (111, 403). All available characters should be used simultaneously and critically (155, 406, 486).

Unfortunately, it is extremely difficult to find behavioral characters that are free of suspicion of having been acquired independently in different groups. Just as with many morphological characters that are readily affected by function and adaptation, some behavioral characters are particularly subject to multiple, convergent origins (111). Thus, while behavior often is of systematic value, it must be used just as cautiously as any other kind of character (486). Methods of food-getting, locomotion, and nest-building, being subject as they are to heavy selective pressures, are notoriously unreliable (28).

LOCOMOTORY MORE CONSERVATIVE THAN PERCEPTUAL COMPONENTS. For this reason, a very broad approach is desirable, particularly making use of studies of function and causation. The locomotory components of behavior patterns (as opposed to "methods of locomotion," themselves) tend to be more conservative in evolution than the perceptual components or releasers

(297). For example, in Burmese Red Junglefowl (*G. gallus spadiceus*) a lack of social experience has little influence on motor aspects of behavior, but much influence on the way in which the motor patterns are released, oriented, and integrated; thus, fighting and mating movements of birds reared in social isolation may appear to be well correlated by the animal expressing them, yet fail to be appropriately coordinated with respect to the birds' social companions.

The regions of the brain that are thought to have particularly important effects on these "higher-order" aspects of motor performance are those regions that also are considered to be "higher-level" (and later to develop). There is a growing consensus that genetic predispositions buffer the organism from modifications of the lower levels of motor control by experience. It is consistent with these findings that many early events of motor development occur with a high degree of specificity in the absence of environmental (sensory) influences that contribute to later performance. For example, neuromuscular connections form before the motoneurons connect to interneurons, with sensory neurons connecting with interneurons still later (see 1,268).

As will be seen below, essentially all of the "relict" egg-care responses of Cockatiels that make up the signposts to ancient avian, proavian, and pre-avian nesting and egg-care habits are locomotory. It can be suggested that because the muscles employed in these responses are used in many other movements and actions, the responses--even as relics--continue to be expressed fully, rather than having become vestigial. In contrast, most of the relict human reflexes and spinal automatisms and their effector muscles are vestigial (see pp. 523-526, **Relict Responses in Man**).

HEAD SCRATCHING, DRINKING, AND "TAIL FLICKS." A classical example cited by Heinroth for the greater reliability of a behavior pattern than of appearance in assessing relatedness concerns Old World hornbills and New World toucans. Though both look superficially alike, their method of scratching suggests that they belong to different groups: toucans reach under the wing to scratch their heads, hornbills reach over it (41). Recent studies of head scratching of 16 diverse species in 4 genera of Darwin's finches strongly support the thesis that this behavior is evolutionarily conservative. All adults scratched over the wing, despite ecological and behavioral divergences and morphological differentiation of heads and bills (231).

While the head-scratching behavior pattern can serve as a useful guide for assessing relatedness between birds, as suggested by Heinroth, it cannot be accepted as definitive, because of many exceptions and the possibility of adaptive convergence (23, 31, 74, 111, 957). Thus, it is suggested that the mode of head scratching is more likely to be determined by the nature of the food source now, or in the immediate evolutionary past, than by phylogenetic relationships (819).

A perhaps more impressive example of the use of behavior in classification is that which discounted the relatedness of sandgrouse (Pteroclidae) to grouse (Tetraonidae). Like pigeons (Columbidae), sandgrouse drink by sucking up water in long draughts (see p. 47). Most other birds, however, take up water by mouthsful, then lift the head and let it run down the throat (see p. 227). Sandgrouse, at first, were thought to be aberrant grouse. Only when their unusual drinking behavior was noticed, were they studied carefully. As a result, they next came to be regarded as aberrant pigeons that had taken to living on the ground, and on sand in treeless deserts (174, 297). Subsequently, it was argued that the sandgrouse had their closest affinities with the plovers (Charadriidae; see 835). Recent DNA hybridization studies place sandgrouse as a sister group of a large part (including plovers) of the order Charadriiformes (899).

[In this connection, one recalls Shaklee's speculation in 1921 that the evolution of the avian forebrain centers for feeding was advantageous, in that this allowed adaptations to changing foods. In contrast, such adaptability has not been a factor in the evolution of drinking mechanisms, the central control of which has remained sub-telencephalic (see 395).]

Another very good example concerns the precise patterns of tail flicks that are made by passerines moving through foliage. These patterns are rather conservative and have proved to be very useful in assessing relatedness at the subfamily and family levels. Most wood-warblers, for example, have a down-up flick (296, 406, 957).

BEHAVIOR PERMITS FINER DISCRIMINATIONS. Numerous examples could be given in which traditional systematic groupings have been altered in recent times on the basis of behavioral criteria (see 297). In fact, in a number of cases the use of behavior has permitted a much finer discrimination in classification than was possible with morphological criteria, particularly in the cases of so-called "sibling species" (very similar species). In several cases, behavior gave the first clues to the discovery of these species, and it also has given clues to the affinities of groups of otherwise uncertain relatedness (297, 406). There are many behavior traits that are characteristic for entire higher taxa (genera, families, orders, or classes); in their genetic basis and phylogenetic history these appear to be completely equivalent to the morphological characters that have a similar taxonomic distribution (297).

Parrots and Ancient Behavior

Parrots are distinctive ancient or primitive birds that have no close relatives. They are classified by themselves in an exclusive group (see Table 2). There is, perhaps, no other order of birds that embraces so large a number of interesting and engaging members, nor are there many groups more sharply set apart from all others (1, 24, 61). The similarity of appearance of parrots, with a fossil record going back at least to the Eocene (293 and p. 1), is one of the characteristics that is taken to indicate a very ancient origin and an early loss of links that connected them with other groups (61).

EVOLUTIONARY RELATIONSHIPS OBSCURE EVEN AMONG THEMSELVES. But despite the similarity of appearance of parrots, the individual structural elements are combined in so many different ways that that it is difficult to assign priorities to characteristics in attempting to assess the affinities of parrots with other groups of birds. Indeed, despite the unusually abundant material, the subject of parrot affinities always has been and remains one of the most difficult and enigmatic problems in ornithology (275). In fact, even the determination of evolutionary relationships among the parrots themselves is one that presents many difficulties. Although studies of albumins, erythrocyte antigens, and eye and muscle proteins have all demonstrated unusual diversities of patterns within the group, these studies have provided but limited systematic guidance (see 819).

PARENTAL CARE AND ANCIENT HABITS. When we consider that parrots are an ancient group, that incubation by many species of parrots follows the primitive pattern (although the brooding habits of relatively few species are known, and the female alone incubates in many species), that the evolution of breeding behavior is conservative, and that the aspects of parrot breeding about which the most is known are remarkably uniform, parental care by parrots looms large as a field in which to seek clues to the reproductive habits of ancient birds.

[The courtship displays of parrots generally are simple, ovulation (but not oviposition) is spontaneous, most species are monogamous and remain mated for long periods, parrots nest primarily in cavities--which are much the safest kinds of nests (and in which the occupants are often noisy)--their eggs are white, relatively thin-shelled (indicating that they must be treated very gently), and oval (in some cases tending toward rounded), their oviposition is determinate (see pp. 165, 166), the newly-hatched young are blind and naked (nidicolous; see pp. 193-195), juveniles generally are duller in color than members of either adult sex, and the sexes generally are monomorphic (1).]

COCKATIELS NOT HIGHLY SPECIALIZED. Of the two species of parrots--Cockatiels and Peach-faced Lovebirds--the latter are relatively highly evolved. Contrariwise, nothing about the body structure, appearance, or known habits or biology of Cockatiels suggests a high degree of specialization. The differences in coloration between the sexes are minor and almost entirely a matter of degree, and obvious courtship displays are lacking. Nor does anything that is known of the origin, evolution or relatedness of Cockatiels (Chap. 1, Part 3) contradict the view that many ancestral characters may be retained. In this connection, the habit of hole nesting in dead eucalypts by the ancestors of Cockatiels and many other Australian parrots might well date to 65 mya, and have provided a very stabilizing influence on their behavior and morphology.

EGG CARE BY COCKATIELS SUGGESTS RETENTION OF ANCIENT ADAPTATIONS. Considering the otherwise unexceptional behavior of Cockatiels, it came as a surprise to discover a rich repertoire of unprecedented, sometimes quite extraordinary, responses. These relate to the ways in which they care for their eggs in nestboxes large enough to accommodate both parents, and in shallow, open depressions or nestbowls on an enclosure floor.

Most of the observed Cockatielian responses suggest retention of very ancient adaptations for egg care in very primitive nesting conditions, namely, open nests on flat, level ground. All of them reveal an extraordinarily high degree of attention to the eggs. Since Cockatiels are relatively unspecialized, and their incubatory pattern itself is of the ancient type, one is alerted to the possibility that the same applies to many elements of their patterns of normal and relict egg care.

COMPARING COCKATIELS AND LOVEBIRDS. Comparisons of the behavior and properties of embryo, hatchling, and adult Cockatiels and Peach-faced Lovebirds support the thesis that Cockatiels retain many primitive characters. First to be noted is the fact that Cockatielian embryos seem to be very tolerant of having their development interrupted for long periods (which also is true of reptilian embryos in certain stages under certain conditions; see p. 543). Several disturbances and colony panics occurred during the care of the eggs of the 1st brood of Helena and Homer in an open nest. As a result, the clutch apparently was left unattended for a full 5 or 6 nights (ambient temperature, 27°C) at various times during the incubatory period. Despite this, one chick hatched and a 2nd pipped but could not rotate to complete hatching. [Similarly, a 5-egg clutch of the Budgerigar hen, Lucretia, hatched, even though nighttime incubation only commenced after the 5th egg was laid (see p. 787, **Incubatory Behavior**).]

Second, Cockatielian hatchlings, though they may be somewhat uncoordinated at first, are able to sit and hold up their heads to solicit and crawl "on all fours" within a few hours after hatching. On the other hand, lovebird hatchlings, like most parrot hatchlings (634, 707), are unable to hold up their heads. They jerk and flop about vigorously in an uncoordinated manner; coordination is not achieved until several days after hatching. Budgerigar nestlings occupy an intermediate position. Although they are unable to stretch up their necks and orient their heads toward their parents until an age of 6-8 days (843), they are coordinated in their movements much earlier. They voluntarily withdraw from being allofed on their backs and turn over onto their bellies at only 1-2 days of age.

Third, Cockatielian chicks can tolerate a much longer delay before being allofed and usually are not fed until several hours after hatching. Fourth, Cockatielian chicks rhythmically jerk the head and neck as they are allofed, beginning with the 1st feeding. This behavior would appear to harken back to a time of avian insectivory when primitive nidicolous hatchlings snatched pieces of flesh held in the parents' mouths. On the other hand, lovebird and Budgerigar chicks are passive in this regard until they are able to sit up while being allofed.

Fifth, Cockatielian hatchlings are covered with a moderate coat of down and are much more tolerant to exposure than those of lovebirds. A hatchling of Carmen and Cosimo was displaced accidentally from the nest and exposed for several hours (ambient temperature, 27°C) yet survived (see p. 697, **Hatchling in Distress**). A hatchling of Helena and Homer was exposed for part or all of its 1st night at 27°C, and part or all of its 2nd night at 30°C, yet survived (see p. 706, **Chick in Distress**). Lovebird hatchlings and chicks, on the other hand, are almost naked (as are those of Budgerigars) and seem unable to tolerate even a brief chilling to 27°C, though they may survive for some time before succumbing to its deleterious effects. Sixth, the females of some of my Cockatielian pairs characteristically allofed the male during both courtship and breeding, whereas, among lovebirds, this is known to occur only among mates of the 3 primitive species, *A. cana*, *taranta*, and *pullaria* (3, 4, 27).

Nest-Exchange Ceremonies

ENSURE RECOGNITION---AS AN EXPRESSION OF EMOTION. When one surveys the manner in which birds exchange with one another in the incubation of the eggs, so-called patterns of "nest-relief," one finds that it often involves elaborate ceremonials or rituals. In some birds, these nest exchange ceremonies ensure the recognition of the returning partner, appease the incubating bird, and lead it to surrender the eggs. In others, they may be only a spontaneous expression of emotion that takes place when mates who have been separated for hours or days come together again--a renewal of the courtship rites that help to hold the pair together (101).

RELUCTANCE TO SURRENDER EGGS. In over 20 examples cited by Armstrong (29), mostly involving large sea birds, there is no instance in which a bird that was incubating eggs behaved as if it were anxious to surrender them to an incoming mate. Rather, the dominant theme is one of great possessiveness. The sitting bird is reluctant to give up the eggs. On the other hand, small terrestrial birds that breed in areas teeming with predators, such as antbirds, often make the changeover silently and discretely (101). Their survival would otherwise be threatened. On balance, the evidence of current behavior suggests that ancestral birds that were covering eggs also were reluctant to surrender them to incoming mates.

EXAMPLES OF NEST-EXCHANGE CEREMONIES. Very few nest-exchange ceremonies or rituals are sufficiently unspecialized to be regarded as models for the primitive method. In the Gray Heron (*Ardea cinerea*), there are vigorous wing-flapping, clamourous cries, upward neck stretching, hoarse shouts, and mandible snapping. Adélie Penguins bow, make soft gurgling sounds, and describe circles in the air with their heads. The arriving bird indicates its readiness to make the exchange by the rate of repetition of its displays, while the incubating bird may indicate its readiness to leave the nest by its displays, ceremonies that usually limit the exposure time of the highly vulnerable eggs or chicks to only about 3 sec (577). Screamers jerk nesting material over their shoulders. Brown Pelican males point their bills to the sky and wave them from side to side, while females poke their bills vertically into the nests.

Louisiana Herons (*Hydranassa tricolor*) elevate their plumes, and the departing bird presents its mate with one or more sticks. Avocets bow, utter twittering sounds, and throw straws and shells about. Failing in this gentle persuasion, there follow pushing, vehement calling, and a flicking of large pebbles at the non-yielding mate. American Coots (*Fulica americana*) and dabchicks bring weeds to the sitting birds. Turnstones (*Arenaria interpres*) throw small pebbles over their shoulders, Stone Curlews exchange pebbles, and gannets bow, fence with their bills, and often exchange festoons of seaweed (29).

Even in Ring Doves, which have rigidly prescribed continuous periods of incubatory time, nest exchange normally is "cooperative" only 66% of the time and "conflicting" on the other occasions (see 752). In 87% of the exchanges, the non-sitting bird was the initiator (90% of the time when in large outdoor enclosures; see 978). In the remaining 13% of cases the incubating bird left the eggs unilaterally and generally was replaced by the mate within 5 min. In cooperative exchanges, the incoming bird most frequently (44%) approached and touched the sitting bird with its bill, next-most frequently (27%) the sitting bird yielded without contact, and next most frequently (8%) the incoming bird attempted to push the sitting bird off the nest without jumping on the latter's back, which occurred next-most frequently (5%). Non-sitting males entered the nest area far more frequently than did non-sitting females (978).

Since members of both sexes determine when to exchange with the other on the basis of the time of day, and when to surrender to the other on the basis of the duration of the time spent incubating, if the mates' time schedules are thrown out of phase, they will "vie for the nest" for a period of time determined by the amount of disruption of the phasing (752). In the case of a female White Stork (*C. ciconia*) and male Black Stork (*C. nigra*) at a zoo in Germany, the differences in the nest-exchange ceremonies were sufficient to be regularly disruptive at exchange times (101).

NO MORE ADAPTIVE THAN INCUBATORY PATTERNS. It is difficult to escape the conclusion that nest-exchange ceremonies are no more adaptive than incubatory patterns, and for essentially the same reason. Just as there came a time in the evolution of birds when there was no further need for both sexes to incubate the eggs (since there no longer was a need for strictly continuous incubation), it also came to matter very little precisely how nest exchanges were achieved, or, for that matter, whether they were achieved at all. As a result, neither incubatory patterns nor the nest-exchange ceremonies of many evolving stocks appears to have come under the close control of natural selection (i.e., selection for survival value).

DERIVED FROM DISPLACEMENT ACTIVITIES. It is no mystery to fathom how the various bizarre nest-exchange ceremonies mentioned above became established. In 'emotional' situations or times of nervous tension, such as when the normal outlet for instinctive behavior is blocked, birds tend to engage in activities that appear to be functionally irrelevant--the so-called **displacement activities** (351, 406). Among the commonest of these are feather raising or lowering, preening and cleaning movements, and toying with pebbles, leaves, or grass (29, 351). These, then, are some of the displacement activities to be expected of the 'frustrated' and agitated incoming bird, unable to acquire the eggs from its mate. [Two other fundamental evolutionary sources of displays are intention movements and autonomic responses (406).]

One can understand, in much the same terms, the fact that the nest-exchange ceremonies in some birds briefly recapitulate the formation of the pair bond (29, 101). Indeed, an intention movement or displacement activity of one species may be part of the courtship performance of a related species (296). It seems quite likely, then, that nest-exchange patterns, like incubatory patterns, became established more or less vicariously from the time when they ceased to be critical to the welfare of the species.

Cockatielian Egg Care Yields Clues to Ancient Practices

COCKATIELIAN PATTERNS OF EGG-CARE AND PRIMITIVE BEHAVIOR. It will be found, in the following, that the nest-exchange practices of confined Cockatiels, though they sometimes involve prolonged maneuvering, do not involve bizarre displacement activity or excessive noise. Cockatielian actions include only subdued vocalizing, hissing, preening, pecking, and gentle pushing. But great attentiveness to the eggs usually is the dominant theme. Cockatiels have been observed employing 8 principal types of actions that have led me to regard their patterns of egg care and nest exchange in large nestboxes and shallow open areas as our best available models for ancient practices.

PATTERNS OF COCKATIELIAN EGG CARE

DISCOURAGING OR REPELLING THE INCOMING BIRD. The 1st type of action indicates a high degree of possessiveness over the eggs, and a great reluctance to surrender them to the incoming bird. This is the kind of behavior that one would expect if the previous practice had been to possess the eggs at all times (see pp. 547-553, **Individual Unaided Incubation of Separate Clutches**). The incubating or guarding bird sometimes merely adopts a threat posture toward the incoming bird, sometimes hisses at it, sometimes pecks at it, and occasionally vigorously repels it (e.g., see pp.

420, 421, 430, 455-464, 469-472, 474, 476). Sometimes this temporarily 'discourages' the incoming bird, typically it does not.

"STEALING" THE EGGS. The 2nd type of action aims directly at egg take-over. One must regard this action as a more primitive approach than the indirect methods that employ distractions and irrelevant displacement activities. One approach, nudging the mate off the eggs, is not unique to Cockatiels. For example, Black-headed Gulls, Ruddy Ground Doves (Columbigallina talpicti), Wood Pigeons, nightjars, and male goatsuckers sometimes gently push a 'recalcitrant' mate off the eggs, and Laughing Gulls may thrust a sitting mate from the nest (see 28, 29, 41, 101, 978). The other approach appears to be unique. Cockatiels are the only known birds whose nest-exchange practices involve direct contact with the eggs. The 'impatient' incoming bird of either sex sometimes literally "steals" the eggs out from under its sitting mate (e.g., see pp. 457, 460, 461, 474, 495).

DIRECTED SEARCHES FOR EGGS---THE "DISTANT VISUAL SEARCH." The 3rd type of action is highly adaptive for nesting on a yielding substrate. Cockatiels, Peach-faced Lovebirds (see pp. 737, 738) and Budgerigars (see pp. 779-781) are the only known birds that display the following behavior. On returning to a nest and finding their entire clutch of eggs missing, they often show signs of distress, and search the incubative area and its near environs for the missing eggs. The searches consist of both visual scanning of the "ground" and probing and/or ploughing in the shavings with the bill. Since these birds are hole-nesters, and Cockatiels and Budgerigars customarily oviposit in very shallow or no bedding, it is evident that these searches for buried eggs must be relics of ancient egg-care patterns that were adaptive for nesting on a yielding substrate. [Members of 3 species of the genus *Charadrius* are known to use the bill to probe for and recover adventitiously or artificially buried eggs (328, 1,396, 1,397).]

The 4th type of action, known only for Cockatiels, has been observed both in NBs and in open nests on enclosure floors. It is a component of the egg search pattern that I refer to as the "distant visual search," wherein the bird raises its head on high or climbs to a vantage point and peers at the far ground surrounding the incubative area (e.g., see pp. 430, 481). This is another component that appears to have been conserved from an ancient pattern of egg care. It implies that at some time in the past the ancestors of birds nested in shallow scrapes on a flat substratum that was sufficiently compact to allow the eggs occasionally to roll or be displaced an appreciable distance from the nest. The Cockatielian behavior leaves little doubt that missing eggs are the object of the search pattern. [The possibility that the behavior represents a search for a possible nearby predator responsible for the absence of the eggs seems to be ruled out by the fact that no alarm or search occurs as long as a single egg of a clutch remains.]

ROUTINE SEARCHES FOR EGGS. The 5th type of action is highly adaptive for primitive nesting conditions. Cockatiels and Peach-faced Lovebirds are the only known birds to behave in the following manner--another behavior that would appear to be a holdover from ancient times. They routinely search for and recover errant or buried eggs in a bedding of wood shavings. The searches are carried out by gently probing or "ploughing" with the bill (e.g., see pp. 428-433, 452-454, 464-466, 469, 721, 722, 738, 739). This type of relict behavior also might have had a multiply adaptive basis. Thus, Egyptian Plovers also probe about in the sand around their buried eggs (230). In that case, though, they appear to be testing the substratum temperature, and this might also have been a practice of early ancestors of birds (see Part 3). Thus, routine probing of the nesting substrate with the bill might have functioned in the early ancestors of birds both to locate buried eggs and to monitor the substrate temperature (such as in decaying vegetational debris; e.g., see pp. 550, 551, 568, 629-631). In this connection, it has been suggested that avian facial cutaneous receptors may be important for measuring the temperature of the nest, eggs, or nestlings (60).

BURSTS OF SCRATCHING ON SMOOTH SURFACES. The 6th type of action is observed when a smooth metallic surface makes up the floor of the nest or enclosure. When the wood shavings have been brushed aside, an egg rolls about freely. In this circumstance, the bird attempting to cover or incubate it unleashes a quick burst of foot-scratching movements. Never otherwise seen, these movements are unmistakably intended to scrape out a depression to accommodate the egg(s) (see pp. 819, 820, **Scratching on Smooth Surfaces, A Relict Response to Freely-Rolling Eggs**). Clearly, this is not an adaptation for hole-nesting in decayed leaves or wood dust. Eggs would scarcely roll freely in them. Rather, it appears to be another relict adaptation for nesting on fairly compacted, flat, level or very gently sloping ground. Only relatively hard, compacted soil would fail to yield to a burst of such scratches. Usually a shallow scrape would be formed. [In this connection, it is of great interest that long claws are adaptive both for a scansorial habit and for walking over soft ground; those for the former habit are more strongly curved (334).]

Even the merest of nest scrapes could play vital roles in keeping a clutch together in a configuration for best contact with the incubating bird, providing a favorable surface for the eggs to attain stable equilibrium (see p. 174, **Turning of the Eggs**, and p. 475, **Adjusting Egg Orientation and Placement**). Thus, murres of the genus *Uria*, which lay their eggs on bare rocky ledges, suffer the greatest losses from eggs rolling off the ledges or into crevices from which they cannot be retrieved (see 427). Members of many species with the primitive habit of incubation by both parents oviposit in little more than a slight concavity in the substrate (527).

The behavior of lovebirds also is of great interest in this regard. Thus, when incubating a clutch of 4 eggs on the flat, smooth floor of an enclosure, Petra proved to be quite incapable of keeping the eggs bunched at all times; instead, eggs continually were rolling out from under her (see p. 727). Even a slight depression would have tended to keep the eggs grouped. She, also, scratched the substrate in an apparent effort to produce a concavity. She was able to accomplish this without rising from the eggs, a practice that also has been described in Egyptian Plovers (230).

STRONG DISINCLINATION TO EXPOSE EGGS IN BRIGHT LIGHT. The 7th type of action is known only in Cockatiels, Peach-faced Lovebirds, and Budgerigars (e.g., see pp. 434, 435, 477, 487, 495, 496, 721, 735, 782, 783, 789). It is most strikingly exhibited by Cockatiels. The latter are strongly disinclined to leave their eggs exposed in bright light, in the same circumstances in which they will leave them exposed in the dark. This is believed to be the most ancient of the relict egg-care responses. It would appear to harken back to an early post-reptilian stage (that of the "pre-aves;" see Table 3), before avian ancestors were endothermic and incubated their eggs. I would suggest that at that time the development of the embryos was hastened by both surface heat and exposure to direct low-angle solar radiation (i.e., in early morning and late afternoon). Standing and crouching over the eggs during the day then would have been for the purposes of concealment, for shading from midday solar radiation, and for allowing exposure to low-angle solar radiation.

Related, but not as striking, behavior is seen in Peach-faced Lovebirds and Budgerigars. The lovebird hen is more attentive to the daytime shielding and sitting over the eggs in a "transparent" NB (nestbox) or open nestbowl than in an opaque NB. Absenting the eggs in the latter case does not leave them exposed to light and view, whereas in the former two cases it does. In the case of Budgerigars, a female not fully in incubatory condition incubated her exposed eggs of 2 clutches only during the day. She returned to them promptly each morning within 15-45 sec of "lights-on" and abandoned them every night after "lights-off."

DEFECTIVE EGGS ROLLED AWAY AND/OR HIDDEN. The 8th type of action also is known in extant ground-nesting birds. Cockatiels nesting on an enclosure floor roll exposed, defective eggs (or eggs "presumed" to be defective) out of the nest to a distance, or to a nearby location at which the eggs are partly or completely hidden (e.g., see pp. 483, 484, **Responses to a Plethora of Scattered, Exposed Eggs**, and p. 492). Since Cockatiels are hole-nesters, this also appears to be a relict adaptation for nesting on flat, level ground. [Many ground-nesting birds are known to retrieve displaced eggs by rolling them back to their nests with their bills.]

PRIMITIVE FORERUNNERS NESTED ON FLAT, LEVEL GROUND. It should be emphasized that the observed relict responses do not appear to reflect behavior that characterized some particular period of the evolutionary past. Rather these relics appear to be records of practices at various past times, extending back to early post-reptilian stages. Taken in combination, the last 6 types of actions are adaptive for a primitive condition of nesting at the surface of flat, level or very gently sloping ground. But some responses suggest the use of a substratum that was sufficiently compact to allow the eggs to roll with only weak resistance, whereas others suggest that there was a time when the substratum was sufficiently loose to have allowed eggs to become intentionally or accidentally buried or hidden in it (see pp. 621-639, **A Synthesis of Avian Evolution**).

The existence of these responses in Cockatiels suggests that they were adaptive for the manners of nesting of ancient forerunners of Cockatiels. The behavior patterns have survived, though perhaps rarely or never elicited during hole-nesting in the wild today, because of their adaptive neutrality and the highly conservative nature of the evolution of parental egg care. Their survival in the lineage to Cockatiels implies, the absence of any significant selective pressure for altered egg-care responses.

COCKATIELIAN RELICT EGG-CARE BEHAVIOR---MODELS FOR ANCIENT PRACTICES. Consider also the combined implications of the following: (a) Cockatiels belong to an ancient group; (b) they are relatively unspecialized; (c) the evolution of avian breeding habits is conservative; (d) Cockatielian nest-relief practices include direct physical takeover of the eggs themselves; and (e) other components of Cockatielian egg care, both those occurring spontaneously and elicited experimentally, appear to have been conserved from times when the eggs were laid on the surface of flat, level ground in primitive nests. A very strong case seems to be built for regarding large elements of the egg-care response repertoire of Cockatiels to be relics of ancient practices of all birds, even for regarding elements of the Cockatielian response repertoire as models for ancient practices.

ADDITIONAL PERSPECTIVES FROM RELICT EGG-CARE PATTERNS. Nor is there any reason to doubt that close scrutiny of the ways other parrots care for their eggs and respond to experimental manipulations also will reveal that they have conserved many elements of ancient behavioral repertoires (see, e.g., pp. 737-739, 779-782). Should this prove to be the case, relict patterns of egg care might well provide some useful perspectives for avian classification. Other patterns of avian relict behavior and recapitulation of ancestral stages very likely also remain to be detected, some of which might prove to be more revealing than those of egg care.

CLASSIFICATION CHAOTIC ABOVE LEVEL OF ORDERS. The classification of birds as to orders seems to have reached a fairly stable position (501). Aves is the best known and most completely described class of animals, and the techniques of DNA sequencing and hybridizing and multi-locus electrophoretic approaches are beginning to yield spectacular advances. But despite these facts, avian classification presently is in a state of chaos for categories above the level of orders and very little information exists on the genetic relationships of different taxa (43, 49, 97, 111, 486). Until the recent effort by Cracraft (587), there had been no attempt to present a comprehensive scheme of phylogenetic relationships (specifying concepts of genealogy) of the higher avian taxa since that of Fürbringer in 1888.

"It is characteristic of the present status of avian taxonomy that the relationship of species and subspecies within a family can be worked out down to the most elaborate details, while it is as yet impossible to give a clear cut diagnosis for the family as a whole, or to state its nearest relatives...." (502). Any proposed arrangement of avian families is open to question at many points (486). Even above the genus level, classification is far less well advanced than that of many other animal groups (106, 428). In the words of one worker "....the present classification of birds amounts to little more than superstition...." (206), " The currently accepted arrangement of birds in no way reflects the probable evolutionary history of the class....we are still a long way from being able to promulgate a truly satisfactory classification" (574); in those of another, "....our understanding of the phylogeny and relationships of avian orders and families is still in its infancy " (421; see also p. viii). It even has been suggested that "ornithology has not fully appreciated the scientific importance of classifications" (587). On a more optimistic note, "....there is now every reason to believe that we are finally getting near the objective of every bird taxonomist: to have a relatively sound view of the phylogeny of birds" (590).

Insofar as relict elements of primitive egg-care patterns are concerned, the most promising other birds to study, from a purely practical point of view, may be certain sandgrouse (Pteroclidae; which are terrestrial granivores with nidifugous young; see pp. 193-198) and hole-nesting and ground-nesting pigeons (Columbidae; which, also are granivores but have nidicolous young). Parrots may be most closely related to the latter group (see, for example, 106, 1,285), with which they share syringeal features (1,284).

Ancestral Birds

To give focus to the following observations of Cockatielian egg care, I preface them with a hypothetical scheme of the properties of ancestral birds and their nesting habits (see Table 3). I have deduced these from known facts about *Archaeopteryx* and primitive behavior of extant birds, supplemented by the implications of my present findings, and by *a priori* considerations. We now turn back to the time of archaic birds, not greatly different from *Archaeopteryx*, in the middle to late Jurassic (Portlandian), well over 150 mya.

REGARDING *ARCHAEOPTERYX*. According to Lowe (see 1,212), Savile, Brodkorb, Martin, and Tarsitano, but disputed by Walker, *Archaeopteryx* is not likely to be ancestral to any group of living birds (193, 308, 652, 1,050, 1,188, 1,203). New information from the skull of the Eichstätt specimen (for example, the seeming absence or extreme reduction of the squamosal bone) is thought to serve more to isolate *Archaeopteryx* than to provide clues to the origin of birds. In addition to the skull specializations, those in its tarsometatarsus (a compound bone in the foot that bears the toes)--fusion of the metatarsals without the characteristic tarsal cap of contemporary birds--suggest that *Archaeopteryx* is on a side-branch of avian evolution. It may have been a late-surviving relic of an even earlier stage of avian evolution that very likely was contemporaneous with birds of more typical avian construction (574, 652, 653, 1,191). On the other hand, there is nothing in the construction of the quadrate, which is more reptilian than previously thought, or its articulation ("normal" archosaurian type) that would debar *Archaeopteryx* from direct ancestry of contemporary birds, and the otic capsule is highly avian in nature (1,188).

According to Martin's analysis of the articulation of the femur with the pelvic acetabulum, *Archaeopteryx* may have been able to sprint for short distances on the ground (likely maximum speed of about 2½ m/sec; see 1,200), and have been a good jumper, but it (or its predecessors) was unlikely to have been a primarily cursorial ground dweller, as it did not have a "fully-improved" bipedal posture (193). He suggests that the latter did not appear until relatively late in avian evolution, perhaps not before the Cretaceous. In this connection, bipedal sprinting and jumping capabilities and the fully-improved bipedal posture may have been fostered by a frequent need of ancestral birds (of Table 3, capable of bursts of true flight and in possession of the supracoracoideus pulley system) to initiate flight by running take-offs when on the ground, in the fashion of many contemporary birds.

Other studies (308, 597, 652) support the supposition of more arboreal than terrestrial habits. Thus, the skeletal proportions of *Archaeopteryx* are similar to those of modern arboreal birds, such as the Chachalaca (*Ortalis vetula*, Cracidae), the Hoatzin, and touracos (Musophagidae), and the distal end of the posteriorly-directed hallux is arched. On the other hand, one should bear in mind in this connection that some animals that are highly specialized in form and behavior for arboreality are nonetheless exceptionally skillful at bipedal running. An example is the abbess lizard (genus *Corytophanes*; 659).] It also has been suggested that *Archaeopteryx* was an inherently unstable biped; even slight movements of the tail presumably would generate instability, so that *Archaeopteryx* could lunge forward and downward instantly in pursuit of prey (1,184). The manus is sufficiently developed for use in climbing and quadrupedal landing (1,203).

ARCHAEOPTERYX figures prominently in the identification of the digits of the avian manus. All modern embryologists favor the indentification of these as being homologous with digits 2-3-4 of the primitive tetrapod limb, with a developmental pattern of digital reduction that is typical for amniotes, whereas paleontologists generally have identified the avian digits as being homologous with digits 1-2-3, because the phalangeal number of the 3 digits of *Archaeopteryx* corresponds to the phalangeal formula of digits 1-2-3 in the primitive reptilian morphotype. It is asserted that if *Archaeopteryx* falls in the avian ancestral lineage, its digits must be homologous to the digits of all extant birds, namely 2-3-4, whereas if the digital formula is 1-2-3, it cannot be considered to lie in the avian lineage but, rather, to be either a theropod or derived from a pentadactyl theropod relative (1,315; see also p. 535, **Archosaurians as Probable Ancestors of *Archaeopteryx***).

"AGE OF CYCADS"---JURASSIC FLORA AND CLIMATE. From the standpoint of its vegetation, the Mesozoic is known as "The Age of Cycads." The Jurassic vegetation was less diversified and less affected by its geographical position than that of any other stage in geological history. The Jurassic was a period when stragglers from the Paleozoic world disappeared. More modern and familiar types became increasingly abundant, hardly distinguishable from plants that now are subtropical or tropical (85). The vegetation differed essentially from today's in the absence of both angiosperms and broad-leafed trees.

Jurassic trees were dominated by members of the order Cycadeoidales. Some species of these were dwarf trees resembling dwarf palms (cycadophytes). They reached a height of about 180 cm, and had columnar unbranched trunks, each terminated by a crown of leaves arranged in a spiral. Other species were branched profusely and perhaps were shrubs. Still others developed gigantic basal tubers that protruded somewhat above ground level. The pinnate leaves resembled those of ferns in most characters. In some species the leaves were as much as 275-305 cm long, but 30-60 cm was the common length. The strobili, sometimes occurring by the hundreds in the axils of branches, each bore both ovules and microsporangia. There also were abundant, large--sometimes gigantic--conifer-like trees of familiar habit (araucarians), large luxuriant ferns, and small-to-large pine-like or yew-like podocarps with hard, stiff (sclerophyllous), needle-like or blade-like leaves (85, 719). The wide distribution of these trees across low and middle latitudes implies broadly-zoned, well-watered, equable climates. These seemingly afforded ancestral birds a world comparable to an "ultra-mild greenhouse" (82).

THE HABITATS OF *ARCHAEOPTERYX* lay on the island formed by the Central German Swell and the London-Brabant-Massif, on the Bohemian Island, and perhaps on some smaller offshore islands. The just-emerged coastal territories must have been occupied by wide, flat plains cut by dry drainage channels. Inselbergs might have developed on high areas that were exposed to weathering and erosion, and cliffs might have been present along shorelines and on offshore islands.

The terrestrial flora preserved in the Solnhofen lithographic limestones display xeromorphic characteristics. Leaves were covered by thick cuticles, and in the stem-succulent conifers, *Brachyphyllum* and *Palaeocyparis*--by far the most abundant land plants--they were reduced to scales that restricted evaporation. These stem succulents must have been shrubs, not exceeding 3 m in height. They had only a woody central cylinder, whereas for the most part the stems and branches were occupied by water-storing tissue. Even the fern-shaped leaves of *Cycadopteris* (Pteridospermae) show a topside leathery cuticular coating, whereas stomata lie in sunken fields on the underside.

The ginkophyte, *Furcifolium longifolium*, exhibits thorns at the base of the clustered, bifurcate leaves, which also can be regarded as a xeromorphic feature. Evidence of trees is absent from the Solnhofen limestones. No large piece of driftwood that might have originated from a log has been found, only remains of branches with a maximum thickness of 3-4 cm. A warm semi-arid tropical climate with long dry and short rainy seasons is suggested for the entire late Jurassic period (nearly 20 million years) on the Central and Western European islands (1,180).

VISUAL SYSTEM OF ANCESTRAL BIRDS. As noted above, it is believed widely that the first birds were arboreal (308, 334, 597, 1,185). Early adaptations of the eyes for an arboreal existence would have been an increase in size and at least some degree of overlapping vision, associated with the reduction of the snout in size and width (333). In Jurassic woodland habitats, visual information from the mottled background of leaves, bark, and changing lights and shadows, would have changed whenever there was motion. It is suggested that in order to maintain some constancy of the visual input from such habitats, ancestors of birds would have required additional representation of the retinal images in the brain (59), such as is found today in the Wulsts of pigeons, hawks, kites, ducks, and owls (see 367).

[There would have been many advantages to the use of color in this representation, and a constructed "real" space with objects in it (59). The fact that an arboreal existence leads to characteristic specializations in the central nervous system is shown by adaptations of Tree Shrews and the Gray Squirrel (*Sciurus carolinensis*). Since they have developed similar arboreal habits but had no common arboreal ancestor, the common ecological influences must have played a large part in the characteristic differentiation of their thalamic and cortical centers (1,344).]

As a result of increased retinal representation, greater visual acuity, increased limb dexterity for grasping, climbing and clinging among branches, and the need to improve coordination between rapid movements of the forelimbs and visual information about the spatial position of small, rapidly-moving prey, the brain in the ancestors of birds had to become enlarged, together with concomitant adaptive modifications of the sense organs and external morphology. There would have been increased demands on the brain, both as a visual information-processing center that supplemented the processing that took place at the retinal level, and as a coordinating center (the cerebellum; 59, 333, 407, 990).

ACTIVITY. Ancestral birds did not have the endurance and very high rate of metabolism required for sustained powered flight. They were primarily gliders but were capable of brief bursts of graceful, high-amplitude, gently-flapping flight with good control and maneuverability (59, 77, 169). Although they nested on the ground, they were adapted well for an arboreal existence, and their activity was mostly in and between trees in woodlands. There, they presumably fed chiefly on large insects, other invertebrates, and small arboreal and terrestrial lizards and amphibians (308, 309, 334). [Since the mammals of the time probably were nocturnal, any small mammal prey would have had to be taken during twilights or plucked from under heavy cover.] The possibility that *Archaeopteryx* also fed along the shorelines of shallow lagoons, preying on small fishes (1,184) also merits consideration. Poisoning by planktonic blooms is believed to account for the abundant fossilized remains of fishes and many other forms, even pterodactyls, in the Solnhofen limestones (1,181; see pp. 564-566), and *Archaeopteryx* also would seem to be a possible candidate.

Supplementation of the gliding of ancestral birds with brief, gently-flapping flight would have enabled them to remain in the trees and have provided a wider choice of landing sites (193). I would suggest that almost all "flights" may have continued to be initiated from the trees, in updrafts, or after a long terrestrial run followed by shallow climbing, as the wing-flapping abilities of "ancestral birds" (at the stage indicated by Table 3) may have been insufficient for facile takeoff from level ground. The need for running takeoff from the ground may well have been a factor in the retention of advanced bipedal sprinting adaptations.

Ancestral birds climbed these trees in reptile-like fashion, with the aid of the hook-like, very sharp wing claws of the manus (possibly also used for grooming; 1,198), except that climbing probably was largely or exclusively upward. Wing claws are still a very common feature of birds (e.g., birds of prey, game birds, geese, the Ostrich, the Hoatzin, and even several passerines; 23, 28, 44, 308, 795, 796). The birds were relatively lightly built, had a bipedal posture and a long, counterbalancing tail, were fleet-footed, bipedal sprinters and good jumpers, were tree perchers, had teeth, and were homeothermic endotherms. The latter condition is essential for conventional incubation and brooding.

BREEDING AND NESTING. It was a time before the evolution of the bewildering array of ecological and behavioral adaptations for breeding that we find in extant birds. Birds did not yet build elaborate nests, nor did paired birds allofeed one another. The newly hatched 1- or 2-day-old young could fan out from the central nesting area and feed (nidifugous young). The pair bond consisted largely of sharing incubation and the care of the hatchlings and young nestlings. A very great reproductive advantage was conferred on birds that continued to remain in consort after prolonged periods of repeated sexual union and oviposition, and cooperated in the demanding and crucial task of caring for the eggs, and protecting, grooming and escorting the young.

EGGS AND NESTS. At that time the eggs were oval, camouflaged (cryptically colored), hard-shelled (as opposed to leathery, for many living reptiles; see pp. 538, 539, **Eggs of Oviparous Reptiles**), and large and yolky (the eggs of contemporary species with nidifugous young are larger and average 35-40% yolk, as compared to only about 15-25% in those with nidicolous young; see p. 193, **Nidicoles versus Nidifuges**). They were oviposited in slight scrapes on essentially flat, level, well-drained ground.

[Nightjars, sandgrouse, and many other contemporary ground-dwellers nest in this way; European Nightjars (*Caprimulgus europaeus*) are so well camouflaged that they sit very tightly and do not leave the nest until a predator is very close. Some statistics on Red Grouse are of interest in this regard. The hen customarily builds a shallow scrape with a shallow lining of moorland vegetation. Of 163 nests examined, more than 75% were on hard well-drained ground, and about 67% were on flat, as opposed to sloping ground (382).]

The use of a very shallow scraping and soft bedding facilitated keeping the clutch together in a small area that could be covered by one bird. Needless to say, the birds also were camouflaged (cryptic or disruptive coloration) to blend into the background--the greater their exposure, the more highly developed the protective coloration (46).

HYPOTHETICAL EGG CARE BY ANCESTRAL BIRDS

EGGS REQUIRE CLOSE ATTENTION. The eggs in these circumstances were highly vulnerable to loss, and required very close attention. They easily could roll away or become embedded in the substratum when the parents altered their sitting positions and yielded them to one another on the "changing of the guard." For this reason, birds that tended their eggs very carefully had an adaptive advantage over birds that did not.

ERRANT EGGS RECOVERED. Eggs that rolled off to the side, even at some distance, were carefully nudged back into the incubative area, a behavior well-known in many of today's ground-nesting birds (e.g., doves, hawks, grebes, gulls, terns, etc.). Eggs that settled into the substratum were resurfaced. And the incubative area and its neighborhood were checked periodically by carefully pecking prodding, and scraping for eggs that might accidentally become hidden from view in the yielding substratum. These were wedged out gingerly and retrieved or merely resurfaced.

[The degree of cryptic coloration of the eggs would have been established by natural selection, depending upon whether or not the number of eggs of a given coloration that were lost to predators exceeded the number of errant eggs that were lost through being overlooked by the incubating pair.]

RELUCTANCE TO SURRENDER EGGS TO MATE. During daylight, the eggs were virtually continually covered by one member or the other of the mated pair. An incubating bird was very possessive of the eggs and surrendered the clutch to its mate only 'reluctantly,' largely because of its need to forage. An incubating bird "unprepared" to surrender the clutch frequently threatened and even repelled its mate.

HEN PROBABLY NOCTURNAL INCUBATOR. Guided by the habits of contemporary birds, many of which oviposit shortly after sunrise (for example, see 216 and A.F. Skutch, 1952, in 489), it is suggested that the eggs were laid shortly before or after dawn. In addition to lesser vulnerability to predation, ovipositing at this time would have allowed the last 10 h of shell calcification, which then is occurring at its maximum rate (see p. 157), to be completed with a minimum of movements by the hen. Since the eggs would have been oviposited in the nest, the female would have spent the night on the nest and would have been the nighttime incubator. The male then would have tended to become the principal diurnal caretaker, because he customarily would have taken over the care of the clutch in late morning or very early afternoon (after he, himself, had foraged), when the female went off to forage. Such an arrangement is particularly advantageous when the parents have to forage for extended periods.

EGGS CHECKED CLOSELY. When not repelled, a bird (assume the male for convenience) returning to the incubative area after foraging usually made a close check of the eggs being incubated (see the method employed by Cockatiels on pp. 457, 462, 474-476, 488), just as the hen periodically checked them herself. While waiting for the female to surrender the eggs, he became the retriever of errant eggs. He prodded gingerly about the incubative area for any eggs that might have become buried, and recovered any that rolled away. When the male recovered an errant egg, he incubated it himself, taking up a position of vantage to the side of the hen.

CARE OF EXPOSED EGGS LIKELY TO BE TAKEN OVER BY THE MATE. When the hen adjusted her position, if an egg rolled out from under her, or merely became exposed, on the side of the male, he alertly took over its care, and vice versa. The hen, alone, recovered errant eggs on her other side. But when she did so, she became vulnerable to the "pilfering" of eggs that became exposed on the side of the male, as she turned slightly or stretched to reach an errant egg. The eggs covered by the male were similarly vulnerable to takeover by the hen. [It is of interest in this context that the female mates of a polygynous Common Rhea (*Rhea americana*) male only oviposit in the vicinity of the male's nest, whereupon the male chases off the females and rolls the eggs into his nest (1,266).]

TAKING OVER THE CLUTCH. When the hen's hunger overcame her urge to incubate the eggs, she departed. If one recalls from Chapter 3 how readily Zenobia endured hunger and thirst to remain near Cyrano and prevent Flavia from socializing with him, one can imagine that this might, on occasions, have taken considerable time. [In this connection, many examples of parental solicitousness to the young, to the point of self-deprivation of food, could be given.] At such time as the hen left, the male followed one of two likely courses of action. If he already was incubating one or more eggs, he maintained his position and merely rolled the nearby exposed eggs under himself, next to the egg(s) already there. If he was not incubating any egg, he took over and incubated the vacated clutch.

Alternatively, an 'impatient' male might gently push or otherwise displace a recalcitrant hen from the eggs, or "steal" all of the eggs out from under her. With the eggs being so great a focal point of attention, natural selection would have tended to confer a reproductive advantage on birds that treated the eggs very gently.

DEEPER SCRAPES AND HOLLOWS. This would have been a very effective, adaptive method of egg care during times when predation was not severe, particularly in the equable Jurassic climate. But in less favorable times, pairs that established their incubative areas in deeper scrapes and hollows, but still with adequate drainage, would have possessed an adaptive advantage. Their clutches would have been more "cohesive," less vulnerable to predators, less exposed to the elements, and more effectively covered by the birds' bodies. The deeper the hollow, the greater the advantage, and the lesser the need for camouflaged eggs and continuous coverage and vigilance. Similarly, pairs that came to use other measures that gave the eggs greater protection--those that took the early steps toward nest-building (see W. Makatsch, 1950, in 28)--also would have left more descendants.

CLOSED NESTS---A PREMIUM PLACED ON HOLE NESTS. In many birds, the two lines of development eventually led to fully-developed habits of primary and secondary hole nesting and the building of closed, concealed, or inaccessible nests. In this connection, from the point of view of the reproductive success of their users, hole nests are far superior to other types and generally demand a close pair bond (126, 313, 314). Among passerines, nests in marsh habitats are least secure, with nesting success increasing progressively in ground-nesting, tree-nesting, and hole-nesting species (740). Of the hatched young of the hole-nesting Red-breasted Merganser (*Mergus serrator*), 91% survived, as compared to 58% for 6 species of open-nesting ducks (181, 1,051). Only half of the eggs in open nests of birds in temperate North America hatched, as opposed to 2/3rds in hole nests (354). Nesting losses in the tropics may be even heavier. The comparative safety of hole nests also is suggested by the patently non-secretive behavior of many hole-nesters. Thick-billed Parrots, for example, often call from their nest entrance and while en route to it (484).

[It has been suggested that one of the bases for the relative breeding success of hole-nesting birds is the free use of nest boxes, in which rates of predation and partial nestling losses are lower than in natural cavities, and that the proportion of eggs laid that give rise to fledglings is roughly the same in natural cavities and open nests. Although losses of the total nest contents seem to be higher in open nests, interference competition (see below) and nestling losses due to hyperthermia and nest parasites may reduce breeding success in natural cavities more than they do in open nests (1,354).]

Hole nests undoubtedly were the first type of tree nest to be exploited by evolving ancestral bird stocks. The premium placed on such nests is illustrated by the fact that contemporary hole-nesters fight savagely over them, sometimes with fatal consequences among Tree Swallows (*Tachycineta bicolor*; 1,220). Interspecific fighting is common, for example, between Pied Flycatchers and Great Tits in Sweden (155, 313, 1,124), and cavities even may be defended when not in use during post-breeding periods (240). In the case of frugivorous toucans (Rhamphastidae), it requires the continuous defense efforts of members of both sexes to maintain possession of the scarce nest holes, and defense of the hole begins well in advance of the breeding season. A deserted female would soon be evicted from her hole by a competing breeding pair (see 1,266). Large hole-nesting species dominate smaller ones in competition for nest sites, and the smallest species tend, in consequence, to be relegated to inferior nest holes (1,354).

Increased levels of plasma corticosterone in Pied Flycatchers are attributed to stress resulting from intense competition for nest holes (1,124). Juvenile harassment--chasing juveniles from the colonies--by Purple Martins (*Progne subis*) would appear to be a strategy of unrelated breeding birds that reduces competition for hole nests in subsequent years by preventing the imprinting of juveniles on the nesting sites (708). Hole-nesters tend to nest early, though the reasons for this are not clear (740). It has been proposed that hole-nesting species generally tend to be brood reductionists, laying smaller eggs last, to facilitate the elimination of the last chick to hatch (see 1,106 and pp. 260, 261). Hole nesting by small birds is rare in the tropics, probably because wasps and bees quickly appropriate small cavities (174).

INSULATION. Of course, the insulation provided by closed nests also conserves heat, facilitating the maintenance of more uniform incubatory temperatures at higher average values, reducing maintenance costs of the young, and allowing lesser parental attentiveness (527). Higher incubatory temperatures made possible a reduction in the period of achieving maturity of the brood, and, in consequence, a reduction of vulnerability to exposure and predation (313). Members of some species of birds appear to possess a range of nest insulating capabilities, providing a substratum of adaptability upon which natural selection can act (see 527). The nests of hummingbirds, for example, are very thick in cold climates (see 974).

In addition, closed nests may conserve energy for the parents; in some birds, winter energy expenditures may be reduced by as much as 40% (28, 967). In fact, heat conservation within a closed nest can be so great as to overwhelm the effect of heat loss from an incubating bird to the eggs. Incubation entails an increase in resting or existence energy expenditure (of from 6-30% for various passerines)--over that of non-breeding adults--

only for birds that normally roost within the nest cavity (see 257, 547). Inasmuch as the pressures of predation and bodily heat loss affect small birds most severely, it is they who build or occupy the solidest and warmest nests (28, 155).

In general, one can conclude that the energy expenditure of incubating hens usually is low compared to that during other portions of the annual cycle (648) and in some cases, at least, the metabolic rate of a bird at rest may be able to supply a large fraction, if not all, of the heat required for incubation (729). On the other hand, restricted foraging time during incubation could significantly limit reproductive performance (648).

[Many avian species orient their nests so as to obtain the warmth of the morning sun; others situate them so that they are shaded during the hottest periods of the day, or at all times (some even build a pebble wall around the nest); still others minimize the impact of wind by situating the nest on the leeward side of vegetation or other objects or exploit the cooling effects of winds (see 737, 967). Large compartmented nests provide significant thermal insulation and energy savings in both breeding and non-breeding seasons (591).

With the limited fasting endurance inherent in small bodily size, hummingbirds can be expected to take the greatest advantage of vegetation, topography, orientation, and airflow patterns in order to conserve heat and energy reserves (974). Thus, they generally reduce overhead radiative exchange by building their nests beneath vegetation (overhead shelter can cut radiative losses in half), and 70% of Andean Hillstar (*Oreotrochilus estella*) nests in rocks were facing east, receiving solar radiation in the early morning but not receiving an excessive solar load in the afternoon. In at least one hummingbird species, the relocating of the nest during the breeding season ameliorates the microclimate around it, with an energy-sparing effect on the incubating bird (see 576, 974).

Cactus Wrens even reorient the entrance to their covered nests according to the season, to gain heat in the winter and admit cool air in the summer (562). The extent to which their nests were orientated with the entrance facing into the cooling southwest winds during the hot part of the breeding season correlated with higher percentages of the young successfully leaving the nest (see G.T. Austin, 1974, in 967). Desert Larks (*Ammomanes deserti*) locate their nests so as to receive solar radiation during the cool mornings, be shaded during the hot midday hours, and receive cool northwestern breezes in the late afternoon (see Y. Ora, 1970, in 967).]

SAFER NESTS OPEN MANY EVOLUTIONARY PATHWAYS. With this advance in nest security came emancipation from the needs for oviposition at any particular time of day, for camouflaged eggs, cryptic coloration of the incubating parent(s), and for continuously covering the eggs, making possible the incubation of the eggs exclusively by one parent. In addition, possibilities were opened for the evolution of polygyny, which is seldom encountered in species in which both parents play vital roles during incubation (227), and for larger clutch size (averaging 6.9 eggs in hole-nesters, as compared to 5.1 in open-nesters; 28; see also specific examples in 707, 1,051).

The greater safety of the nest also allowed the alternative of slower development of the eggs and young (with less food needed per individual; 34, 707; see also D. Lack, 1948, in 313, and discussion by Drent, 427). In the case of the hole-nesting parrots, natural selection has favored neither rapid growth nor early maturation of function (634). A longer period of achieving maturity makes possible the enhancement of family bonds and increased education of the young (28 and p. 211).

It is thought that a long period of evolution usually is needed to take advantage of the safety and seclusion of the nesting site (105). But considering the reluctance with which the eggs often are given up by one parent to the other, even today, it is easy to imagine how a member of one sex or the other might expeditiously have taken over exclusive egg incubation, when the species had become emancipated from the need for covering the eggs continuously.

COCKATIELIAN BEHAVIOR LAID THE FOUNDATIONS. This outline of egg care by ancestral birds, though conjectural, is not implausible. However, since one can formulate an almost endless variety of seemingly plausible hypotheses in this realm, it probably would have been regarded as highly speculative at any time before the results of the present study were known. It is the behavior of the birds treated here, primarily the Cockatiels, that has laid the foundations for the above outline and lends credibility to it. Thus, aside from the fact that I have not given many enlightening, convincing, and sometimes amusing, details, this outline is largely a description of the care of many clutches of eggs by 3 mated Cockatielian pairs, as described below.

PART 2. COCKATIELIAN EGG CARE

Birds and Experimental Conditions

APPROACHES EMPLOYED WITH MAMMALS. In my laboratory studies of the behavior and learning of mammals (e.g., see 1,391), all detection of activities and responses either was accomplished automatically, without the presence of an observer or disturbance, or by using closed-circuit infra-red, deep red, or daylight television. In most such cases, I used wild animals and had as few interactions with them as feasible. I sometimes studied them continuously for weeks without intruding on them, without the need even to replenish food or water.

HABITUATED BIRDS ESSENTIAL. In the current studies of parrots, I was always in the presence of the birds, frequently feeding them, and not infrequently making experimental changes. Wild animals generally do not behave normally under these conditions, perhaps least of all in their breeding activities. Undistracted, confined wild birds are no less aware of, and influenced by, an overt observer than birds in the field. In fact, even the birds most accustomed to my presence usually were influenced by my movements. The reason why it was possible to observe "normal" interactions of these birds was that they were habituated to my presence. It was almost as if I were in a blind. This being the case, their preoccupation with each other and higher priority activities in which they were engaged often resulted in their taking little or no notice of me as long as I did not move. This also sometimes tends to be true in the wild. Thus, Cayley notes of wild Budgerigars in certain circumstances, "the birds were exceptionally tame, being far too busy carrying out their domestic duties to worry about intrusion" (1,056).

Of course, the critical importance of using birds habituated to the presence of an observer when carrying out close observations is well known. In 1952, Julian Huxley remarked that, "Only when birds have come to lose their fear, can a human observer really begin to be let into the secrets of their lives, and discover the degree of their intelligence" (see 26). The results of Len Howard's lengthy observational studies of many wild birds flying freely in and out of her cottage in Sussex, England (26), prompted and amply justified Huxley's remarks.

THE ADVANTAGE OF THE "TRANSPARENT" NESTBOX AND OPEN NESTBOWLS was not that the birds occupying them were unaware of my presence and the fact that they were being observed. They were no less wary and aware of such matters when they were in the Plexiglas-sided nestboxes or open nestbowls than when they were out in the enclosures. The advantage was that I could watch all their activities at times when they were fully occupied with each other and the eggs or young, without my having to move or otherwise intrude upon them.

On the contrary, when I had to lift the cover of an ordinary NB to observe them, or even when I moved in the vicinity of a Plexiglas-sided NB or open nestbowl, they often turned to look at me and "froze." I easily could have observed wild birds in the NB unobtrusively using closed-circuit television, but with very much less flexibility. And the crucial experimental avenues opened up by being able to manipulate the eggs and chicks of habituated birds almost at will without disrupting breeding would have been closed off.

PREVIOUS STUDIES IN "TRANSPARENT" NESTBOXES. Nestboxes with a transparent wall were used previously both by Eisner (129) and by Brockway (67), but apparently with only limited success and unaccompanied by experimental manipulation. Thus, several species of otherwise-easily-bred finches either would not nest in nestboxes backed by a glass panel or were too skittish to be observed under the conditions employed. Only the Bengalese Finch (*Lonchura striata* var. *domestics*), a long-domesticated (at least 200 years) form of the Sharp-tailed Finch (*Lonchura striata*), bred sufficiently reliably and was tolerant enough of disturbances to permit observations of its parental behavior (129).

In a study in 1964, Brockway (67) used nestboxes with a glass side to confirm that Budgerigar males do not partake in the incubating of the eggs, even when they spend time in the NB with the female (but see a contrary indication by Hart in ref. 185), but the result is mentioned only in passing. In 1969, Brockway used nestboxes with panes of one-way glass built into the walls. By this means she was able to ascertain that male Budgerigars commonly continue previously initiated courtship of the female within the NB (67). Again, the technique apparently did not warrant extensive application, and the result is referred to only as an aside.

Subsequently, Hutchison made successful observations of the behavior of nesting Budgerigars within NB's (in unspecified conditions of illuminance) through a one-way plastic back from a darkened hide. She studied relationships between nesting behavior and the development of the ovary and oviduct (860). Continuous observations were made each day over one 2-h and one ½-h periods. In very recent studies, "transparent" NB's were used by Stamps *et al*. (843, 844) in studies of parental care of nestlings and parent-nestling interactions of Budgerigars. NB's were backed with Plexiglas and one-way viewing film and their contents viewed in the dim light obtained through the entrance holes. Twenty nests were viewed over 3 breeding seasons for a total of 174 h in predominantly ½-h viewing sessions every 2 or 3 days, with results cited in on pp. 200-203. No previous investigator studied breeding lovebirds, Cockatiels, or Budgerigars in open nestbowls or NB's with walls that were transparent as viewed from both sides.

It is evident from the results of the above-cited studies (843, 844, 860) and the present ones that a wealth of significant information probably remains to be obtained concerning the activities of incubating and brooding birds within cavities, and concerning their responses to experimental manipulations. Present-day techniques of closed-circuit television are more than adequate for remote viewing of birds that are found to be intractable to direct visual observations.

SUPERFICIAL AIDS TO MONITORING NESTBOX ACTIVITY. When a tightly-fitting hardwood perch is mounted just below the entrance of a plywood NB, it acts like the string of a musical instrument, with the NB acting as the sounding board or body. As a consequence, the sound of any scraping or other contact with the perch is magnified manyfold and easily heard from a distance. These sounds alerted me to any contacts of birds with perches, as well as movements to and from nestboxes.

Minor movements within the opaque Cockatiel NB were detected by mounting a flat, 5 x 7½-cm stainless-steel mirror against the back wall of the enclosure at NB height. Looking in this mirror, I could see the reflections of objects in the room. Since the NB was in direct contact with the wire-mesh sidewall of enclosure A (see Fig. 1a), suspended by two hooklets, any movements within the NB were transmitted to the enclosure side, and thence to the suspended mirror, roughly 45 cm away.

Even though the movements of the mirror might be only thousandths of a cm in amplitude, the fact that my eyes and the imaged objects were over 2.7 m away led to easily perceptible magnified displacements of the images. Any appreciable movements within the NB were evident to me instantaneously. [At the time of use of this system, enclosure E was not yet atop enclosure A, so there was no bird atop the enclosure that might have produced interfering movements; see Fig. 1.]

Cockatielian Courtship, Sexual Union, and Egg Care

BREEDING BEHAVIOR DOUBTLESSLY VARIABLE. Before beginning a chronological description of my findings with 3 pairs of breeding Cockatiels and many clutches of eggs, I summarize briefly the current knowledge most pertinent to the material to be treated. It should be emphasized that the breeding behavior of most, if not all, birds, whether confined or free-living, undoubtedly is variable. Some aspects of behavior doubtless adapt to the particular circumstances that the birds encounter and are influenced appreciably by individual differences, including age and experience. Accordingly, with but few exceptions, I do not question some differing results of others. Primarily, I add findings that enlarge the spectrum of known behavior, probably both **what does happen** and **what can happen**.

CONTINUOUS OBSERVATIONS YIELD GREATER INSIGHT. The chief contributions of the following material are observations of the events that transpire during incubation in nestboxes and open nests. These contributions fall into two main categories. First, there are the observations of parental actions and interactions during egg care, uninfluenced by experimental intervention. These permit one to draw more enlightened, and often quite different, conclusions from the ones drawn in the past, that were based largely on peeking into a NB from time to time.

CLUES TO PRIMITIVE ADAPTATIONS. Second, there are the observations of egg care after experimental manipulations. These are mostly of an unprecedented nature. Together with some of the observations in the first category, they give clues to the primitive adaptations of nesting and egg care by the ancestors of Cockatiels. These include facets of behavior whose implications may apply to the immediate reptilian ancestors of birds.

Supplemented Literature Accounts

COURTSHIP ACTIVITIES

OBVIOUS, ELABORATE COURTSHIP DISPLAYS LACKING. Male Cockatiels will court throughout the year, and some females are able to breed the year around (127). These birds lack the obvious elaborate courtship displays that are common in many other species. [This primitive characteristic is one of the features that allies Cockatiels with cockatoos (30).] One display is described as being given only when a female is first introduced to a male that had led a bachelor existence for some time (1,056). It consists of a series of hops while following the female along the ground, accompanied by a low warbling variation of "the usual shrill call note." [Cockatielian males also are said to make an "unmistakably characteristic" hop when viewing themselves in a mirror (60).]

Another display is described as a rather subtle series of maneuvers by the male. He is said to approach the female with lowered head and depressed crest, lifting his shoulders, and holding his wings lifted and out from the body with their tips folded across his back, forming a flat, heart-shaped surface. In the culmination of this display, he holds his head very high and utters a mixture of whistling song and the "characteristic melodic Cockatiel call," *coo-ee, coo-ee*, several times in succession. Except for the position of the wings, this is very similar to the cringing attitude taken when soliciting preening (32, 127, 1,054).

MUTUAL PREENING---EXPLORING NEST SITE---COURTSHIP FEEDING. Other courtship activities include: mutual preening, especially about the head, which soon follows courtship and contributes to establishing and maintaining the pair bond; the male flying to and fro in the near vicinity of the nest-hole and displaying and twittering at it; exploratory activity in the vicinity of the nest site; and a thorough inspection of the nest site, itself, including singing, bill tapping, and chewing wood from the walls and around the entrance hole. Within a few days of pairing, the female usually solicits for copulation (6, 32, 127, 1,054).

On the subject of courtship feeding and supplemental allofeeding, there is no consensus in the literature, most of which is anecdotal, except if it be that such activity occurs infrequently. Sturman and Schults noted mutual allofeeding in courting pairs and assert that the male may allofeed the hen during periods when she spends much time in the NB with the chicks (9). Smith cites the unique case of a hen that solicited food from and was allofed by all the males with whom she was paired (32). Some workers are of the conviction that Cockatiels, like all cockatoos except those in the genus *Calyptorhynchus* (in which the male allofeeds the sitting hen), do not courtship feed or allofeed (30, 32, 127 1,054).

ALLOFEEDING OF STRONGLY DOMINANT MALES. I have observed courtship and allofeeding as routine activities between adult Cockatiels in 2 of my 5 mated pairs; both pairs engaged in it very extensively during courting and one during brooding (the other pair did not breed). It was always the hen who allofed the male, usually only in response to his solicitations, though little encouragement was required. Since such feeding sessions sometimes occurred as frequently as 50 times per day during courtship, the male sometimes might have obtained a large fraction of his nourishment by this means. On the other hand, it was evident that some sessions of the courtship feeding, but not of the allofeeding during incubation and brooding, were only mock feeding, that is, little or no food was transferred.

The failure of most other workers to observe either courtship or supplemental allofeeding, aside from the fact that it is not invariable behavior of all pairs, might be partly explained as follows. Much of courtship feeding occurs in the NB, and many pairs, particularly unhabituated ones, will not begin preliminary breeding activity unless a NB is present. Others have pointed out that courtship feeding that is confined to the nest site easily may be overlooked (e.g., see 706). Insofar as allofeeding during the incubatory and brooding phases is concerned, all such feeding usually occurs in the NB. However, my breeding birds that did not courtship feed did not allofeed at other times either.

My results are in accord with S.M. Smith's thesis (540) that it is the dominant member of a pair that receives food from the mate, but only during the period of dominance. The failure of 3 of my pairs to engage in allofeeding might have been a consequence of a lesser strength of the dominance relationship among them. The likelihood of applicability of this explanation is strengthened both by direct observations of dominance relationships (see below) and the fact that qualitative behavioral differences of this nature (i.e., some mates allofeeding and others not) are rare within a species, and in many cases even between closely related species.

In general, intraspecific behavioral differences are only quantitative, as, for example, differences in frequency of occurrence or intensity of a particular kind of behavior (569; see also 16). Extensive investigations of genetically determined behavioral differences in various races and breeds of dogs failed to detect even a single behavioral difference by which any two forms could be distinguished clearly without overlap. Through artificial selective breeding, certain behavioral traits were enhanced or weakened, but nothing new arose (592).

The direct observations referred to above concern the strength of the dominance relationships between members of the pairs that did not courtship feed, as opposed to those that did, as assessed primarily by interactions at the food trays. In the cases of the courtship-feeding pairs, the male always was able to drive the female away from a food tray or a choice item and partake first himself. With one of the non-courtship-feeding pairs, Helena and Homer, Helena was unusually aggressive at the food trays and exceedingly reluctant to be displaced by Homer. Contrary to the usual circumstances among Cockatielian mates, usually it was he who yielded, rather than she. Moreover, Helena was the only hen who groomed her mate's head aggressively over an extended period (intermittently for over 40 min) in an effort to acquire a clutch from him. The hen, Carmen, usually only did so defensively when her dominant mate, Cosimo, allogroomed her head in efforts to displace her from the eggs (e.g., see pp. 455, 456, 459, 460, 471, 474).

In the case of another non-courtship-feeding pair, Isabella and Ferdinand, competitive interactions over possession of the clutch were the most sustained and vigorous of all those I have witnessed, suggesting the absence of a strong dominance relationship. I once found it desirable to rescue a chick from them and foster it with Carmen and Cosimo when it was at risk during their tenacious "wrestling" for possession of the clutch (see p. 489). It may be that the male of pairs formed in the wild characteristically is dominant, whereas confined birds sometimes pair by default and have less stable dominance relationships. In this connection, the female of my other courtship-feeding pair, Kirsten, had her choice of a mate among her 3 brothers. With 2 non-courtship-feeding pairs, Helena chose from among 2 brothers and Isabella mated with Ferdinand by default.

Dominance of the male also is reported in Crimson Rosellas (1,264), a member of a genus (*Platycercus*) in which hybridization with Cockatiels has been claimed, and in which genus the two species in question (*P. elegans* and *P. eximus*) also hybridize with one another (see 104, 138, 1,264). From Forshaw's description of how "the male bird examines the nesting site and spends the next few days forcing his mate to enter the selected....hole in a tree," it seems that Red-rumped Parrot males also are dominant (1,264).

[In view of the fact that, except perhaps among buttonquails (51), it is the male who usually allofeeds the female, some of the observers who noted occasional courtship feeding among Cockatiels may have assumed that food was being transferred to the female from the male, rather than vice versa. On the other hand, one also must consider the possibility that the female of such pairs was temporarily or typically dominant over the male and that members of either sex may be dominant among Cockatielian pairs.]

It is evident that neither parent could undertake most of the allofeeding of a large brood unless it also either ate periodically itself or was allofed by the other. Since male Cockatiels sometimes do almost all of the daytime incubating and feeding of the chicks, and may tend them almost continually, the occurrence of unobserved allofeeding by the female is not unlikely. Allofeeding even might be widespread among those hole-nesters in which one of the mates spends the entire day in the nest. In this connection, it is likely that the Brown Kiwi hen sometimes allofeeds the unilaterally incubating male, who incubates for 74-84 days and leaves the nest burrow daily for only about 90 min in the early morning and again after dark. Thus, hens have been seen to enter the nest with live food in their bills (1,406, 1,408). [There is an indication that the relaying of food from one Cockatielian parent to the other to the chicks may serve a role in food processing (e.g., see pp. 690, 691 **Parental Division of Labor**).]

SEXUAL UNION

EVEN THROUGH THE TIME BROODING. Many observers have noted that Cockatiels sometimes engage in sexual union several times per day, even through the time of oviposition, incubation, and rearing the brood. Post-ovipositional copulation probably serves to maintain or strengthen the pair bond. [But an egg could not be fertilized by sperm from an immediately pre-ovipositional union, since the albumen is secreted and the membranes and shell are formed after fertilization (see pp. 152-157).] Individual periods of coitus usually last 1 or 2 min or more.

MALE OPENING AND CLOSING OF THE BILL---FEMALE SOLICITING. One worker observed coitus several times in a captive pair and noted that the male opened and closed his bill throughout the act of copulation, in the same way that Sulphur-crested Cockatoos (*Cacatua galerita*) do when at the nesting hollow in the company of the female before oviposition (30). This is said to make a soft tapping noise when the mandibles touch, which Courtney refers to as the "bill-clicking display." Smith describes the hen's soliciting as, "crouching low on the perch with wings slightly away from the body....and the back perfectly horizontal....she holds her crest down and keeps her head twisted on one side." The male mounts her back with both feet, lowers his tail to one side, and copulation takes place. According to Smith, other males, even if sitting on the same perch, appear to be disinterested (127, 1,054; but see p. 412, **Attacks During Copulation**).

COITION SOUNDS

EMITTED BY THE HEN DURING COITUS. During coitus, Cockatielian hens utter repetitive, slow, soft squeaks (also described as a continuous chirp).

Other parrot hens also are known to engage in such vocalizations during copulation, for example, Abyssinian Lovebirds (27). Over the course of 5 yr I confirmed that the female produces these sounds, either by listening from within a few cm of the heads of copulating, habituated pairs, or by mildly disturbing the female (beneath her bill) with a finger or pencil. The sounds were much the loudest at the level of the females' heads, and ceased momentarily when she pecked at the finger or pencil. As mentioned above, males usually open and close their mandibles rapidly during copulation (which I refer to as "Mandible-fluttering"), and these movements are not synchronized with the quiet chirps or squeaks of the female.

EMITTED BY THE MALE AFTER COPULATION--ATTACKS DURING COPULATION. The same sounds made by the female during coitus sometimes are made by the male after coitus, particularly if the birds have been disturbed in the act. I observed this on a number of occasions when Carmen and Cosimo were housed with the male lovebird, Jagatai. On 2 occasions, Jagatai attacked them as they copulated, by pecking Cosimo on his back, whereupon Cosimo jumped off Carmen's back in great alarm. On 5 other occasions, I listened within 3 cm of their bills as they copulated, with their heads practically up against the enclosure side. On these latter occasions, Cosimo was not disturbed enough to interrupt the sexual act.

[Attacks on copulating pairs by another male also are known in other species, for example, Rock Pigeons, but only by males in breeding condition. Goodwin observes, "....natural selection seems to have favored males that show an instantaneous aggressive response to the sight of others of their kind copulating. That this is the correct explanation is suggested by the behavior of the interfering male towards the female of the copulating pair; his apparent 'indignation,' his ferocious pecking of her head, and his desisting and displaying to her as soon as she rises..." (1,011).]

On the 7 occasions noted above (and on an 8th apparently involving no disturbance), when Cosimo jumped off Carmen's back, he was greatly agitated. He then also emitted Coition Sounds, but in a louder, more alarmed tone. So great was his agitation, that he sometimes continued emitting sounds for at least an additional 90 sec. He also often emitted Coition Sounds after copulating, during the fledging period of their 6th brood.

On another occasion Heloise and Julian, a young, inexperienced 5-month-old male (of the 3rd brood of Helena and Homer), were copulating for the first time in the lower portion of enclosure A where they were housed with a male sibling, Marcus, and a younger uncle, Lothair. Upon this occasion Marcus approached and began to attack Julian vigorously by pecking at his head from above. The latter turned his head and defended himself just as vigorously. Throughout their encounter, Heloise continued to emit the Coition Sounds without break or change in rhythm, apparently being unaware of the conflict occurring above. Marcus also came over from another part of the enclosure to attack this pair on at least one other occasion as they copulated, and Homer also disturbed Isabella and Ferdinand, grooming Isabella about the eyes several times during copulations (see p. 674).

[Jagatai's and Marcus' interferences were, of course, unprovoked. Both deliberately came over to attack the copulating pairs from far sides of the enclosures. On a 3rd occasion, Jagatai followed the same pattern but was unable to approach closely from an upper perch, as on the 1st 2 occasions. After hesitating and duly 'deliberating' in their vicinity, he approached them on the same perch and bit Carmen on a toe, instead. As she became startled, Cosimo jumped off her back without uttering Coition Sounds.]

On the other hand, a markedly subordinate bird, such as a juvenile offspring, will not attack a copulating pair and will be tolerated by them in close proximity. In May-September, 1986, I housed Lothair, a juvenile male of the 7th brood of Carmen and Cosimo, with his parents. As the parents came into breeding condition, Lothair was attacked and pursued with increasing frequency and vehemence, mostly by Cosimo. During this period I usually flighted Lothair every morning. As Carmen and Cosimo began to breed, they usually copulated during Lothair's absence. One day, when I failed to flight him, however, they began to copulate in his presence. Lothair immediately approached and perched 2 cm distant from Carmen's left side, taking evident note of the proceedings. After about 15 sec there, he hastily circled the perimeter of the enclosure and perched in equal proximity at her right side. [Throughout the act, the older siblings of Lothair, in enclosures C and N (Fig. 2b) whistled; see below and pp. 838-840.] Seeking to be allofed himself, Lothair also pressed in his head as closely as he dared every time Carmen allofed Cosimo during the following brooding. Lothair eventually became dominant over and attacked Cosimo. Although Cockatiels often may squabble with their offspring, this is the only such instance of offspring-parent dominance of which I am aware.

EMITTED AT OTHER TIMES. Virtually the identical, repetitive slow, soft squeaks uttered by the female during coitus also are one of the utterances or calls of the courting and breeding male (and even juveniles). These sounds were made by all of my breeding males during the periods of oviposition and incubation and by virtually all juvenile males, at one time or another. For example, for many weeks, Rimski, and much later, Casimir, 4th-brood sons of Carmen and Cosimo, made them almost daily. [Subsequently, Rimski paired and copulated many times with his fostered-broodmate niece, Kirsten.] In one case, when Julian uttered Coition Sounds, it stimulated Cosimo, who was brooding day-old chicks at the time, also to utter them. The sounds usually are made with only very small-amplitude movements of the mandibles. There is no contact with the female at these times. Females rarely make the Coition Sounds at other times (see p. 427).

Independent verification of the resemblance of the Coition Sounds uttered by the female during copulation, and the similar sounds uttered by the male after copulation and during courtship, appears to come from the birds themselves. It was the habit of all the adult offspring (of both sexes) of Carmen and Cosimo (from 4 to 6 of which were present at any given time) to whistle excitedly at times when Carmen and Cosimo were copulating and Carmen was emitting loud Coition Sounds. These same vocalizations of the other adults of the colony also were elicited when Cosimo emitted loud Coition Sounds after copulation and, particularly, when he emitted them from the nest during the courting period, before the onset of oviposition. At first, I thought it was the Coition Sounds alone that stimulated the whistling, but subsequently I noted that offspring who could see Carmen and Cosimo copulating began to vocalize even before loud Coition Sounds were emitted. Sometimes this was my first indication that copulation had commenced (see also pp. 838-840).

OVIPOSITING ELSEWHERE THAN IN A NESTBOX

Many observers have noted instances in which Cockatiels (and other parrots; 27) have oviposited at various places on enclosure or aviary floors "because their nestbox was unsuitable" or none was provided. In the usual breeding accommodations the presence of a NB acts as a stimulant, and most pairs will not nest without one (9, 127). In the circumstances in which my birds were maintained (see pp. 280-291, 296-298)--perhaps partly facilitated by the colonial situation--the opposite condition held: I was unable to prevent the birds from ovipositing, incubating, and rearing young, even in the absence of the stimulation of a NB or any other facilitation of breeding (see Table 4, broods labelled "unfacilitated").

EGGS OVIPOSITED ON THE ENCLOSURE FLOOR. All the birds that I isolated as mated pairs without NB's--including 3 pairs of Cockatiels and 9 pairs of lovebirds--proceeded to oviposit and incubate clutches in the open on the enclosure floor (although I sometimes ultimately provided shallow nest-bowls lined with shavings). Five of the 9 lovebird pairs hatched eggs and brooded their chicks at least twice. One Cockatielian pair hatched eggs but failed to brood the chicks. The experienced pairs, Carmen and Cosimo and Helena and Homer, fledged 9 broods in open nests. A case also is known to me of a Cockatielian pair that reared a brood of 5 in an open nest on the floor of a small enclosure (personal communication from Jim Northern).

NESTING ON ENCLOSURE FLOORS, AND ANCESTRAL PRACTICES. I consider this behavior, and numerous other patterns of egg care discovered in the 3 species of parrots of this study to be relics of the distant past. They are of a very primitive nature and appear to reveal ancestral practices, suggesting that distant ancestors of Cockatiels made a transition directly from ground nesting to hole nesting. Most of the responses probably rarely occur in normal breeding conditions, either in confinement or in the wild.

CARE OF THE EGGS

IMPRESSION OF A CONGENIAL EXCHANGE CEREMONY. As is well known, male and female Cockatiels share in the incubation of the eggs and brooding of the young. As was noted on page 376, sharing of incubation is believed to be the primitive pattern of avian egg care. The general impression among observers is that there is no "exchange ceremony" as the incoming Cockatiel takes over from the incubating bird. It is said that the former may just sit next to the latter and that they may congenially split the clutch and share in the incubation. More typically, it is said that as one bird settles into the nest the other arises and departs. As we shall see, my studies suggest that such behavior is the exception rather than the rule.

MALE, THE PREDOMINANT DAYTIME INCUBATOR. Essentially all references to free-living birds state that the male incubates from early morning to late afternoon, and the female for the remainder of the 24 h. One observer notes that an occasional confined female is the sole incubator (1,054). I would judge that the female dominates the male in such cases. No one has observed a nest site of free-living birds throughout the day or timed the parents' attentiveness, so these observations only can be regarded as being indicative of the predominant habits of confined birds.

The only quantitative data that exist for outdoor nesting are for the care of week-old chicks (rather than eggs) in a nest-hole in a log in an Australian aviary (32). During the day, the male spent a total of almost 4 h either inside the nest hole or perched near the entrance. The female spent only about half as much time there. Together, they made about 114 trips to the nest-log.

[In connection with apportionment of egg and chick care, it is interesting to note some results obtained with Band-tailed Pigeons (*Columba fascia-*

ta) using radiotelemetry (217). During the nesting period (late May to early July), males were found on nests from approximately 8:00 h to 17:00 h, during which time females were at the foraging sites. Females were found on the nests at other times.]

On the other hand, observers of confined birds assert only that the male incubates for most of the day. The female often relieves him and they sometimes spend hours together in the NB (6, 9, 104). The birds are very curious, alert, and easily frightened. At the least disturbance, their heads appear at the NB entrance to investigate. According to Rutgers (138), the hen will leave the nest quickly if disturbed by sudden or unusual sounds; but if she can look out and see what is happening from her position on the eggs, she probably will remain sitting quietly.

In the case of the birds confined in the outdoor aviary in Australia, the female incubated throughout the night and the male exchanged with her periodically during the day (32). One observer found that both birds stayed in the NB together on the days when eggs were laid, with the male incubating the eggs that were present (6). A number of observers have noted that the parents often share in incubating a divided clutch (6, 9, 127).

LOOSE SITTING FOR FIRST FEW DAYS. It is said that the eggs may be sat upon either very loosely or very little for the first few days, but usually will be incubated tightly starting when there are 3 or 4 eggs (6, 9, 127). Accordingly, the first few eggs may hatch almost simultaneously. It also has been remarked that, when the hen is reluctant to incubate the eggs, the male often chases her into the nest (9).

DEFECTIVE EMBRYOS DISCARDED---NESTBOX KEPT UNSOILED. After the first hatchings, it is said that the male often cares for the chicks in the NB at night, while the hen incubates the remaining eggs, and that the parents become reluctant to leave the NB and often can be found together in it. If a chick is unable to complete hatching (usually for lack of sufficient moisture), the parents discard the egg from the NB. The parents keep the NB unsoiled during the incubatory period by voiding well away from it. At night, the male usually perches outside the NB or very near its entrance (6, 9, 127).

NOT ADVISED TO SYNCHRONIZE CLUTCH OR DISTURB NESTBOX. Although the incubation of Cockatielian eggs has been delayed for up to 9 days (9), one is advised not to synchronize the clutch by removing the eggs as they are laid, and restoring them later (6). If this is done, the eggs should be stored at 11-13°C. Although some workers recommend turning the cooled eggs at least twice per 24-h period (9, 127), I am aware of no documented study that supports the need for this practice for eggs that are stored at low temperatures (for the rationale for turning eggs during the period of incubation, see p. 174). If the pair is experienced or of sufficient age, synchronization of the clutch is scarcely necessary; if it is not, synchronizing the clutch probably will be to no avail.

[I have found that eggs stored at room temperature for more than 2 days will not develop normally, even if turned several times per day. In one case an egg stored at room temperature for 4 days with turning several times per day developed to term but the embryo did not complete hatching. Presumably such eggs must be agitated many times per day, as is done by the parents before steady incubation begins.]

If one's objective is successful breeding, it is wise not to disturb the nest (6, 439): even inexperienced birds usually will perform better than their owners. Thus, inquisitive owners are advised either not to disturb the NB of breeding birds at all, or, if it is inspected, to do so daily. Habituated birds become accustomed to daily attention, but if inspections are sporadic, the birds are likely to become disturbed and desert the nest (2, 439).

VARIABILITY OF EGG CARE. Judging from the findings reported here on the care of the eggs by Cockatiels, there generally is a great deal of qualitative variability (just as there is variability in courtship activities). This probably is very much dependent on the relative and absolute ages and experience of the paired birds, on the degree of dominance or lack thereof of one member of the pair, on the properties of the enclosure and NB, on the diet, and on environmental circumstances, particularly the ambient air temperature and relative humidity.

NO PRIOR HINT OF RELICT RESPONSES. On the other hand, concerning events that transpire within the NB, prior findings have been rather unenlightening, because birds interrupted in their activities usually "freeze" in a position of eyeing the observer or camera (as can be seen from most existing photographs of Cockatiels in the NB). Concerning the newly-discovered relict egg-care responses, not a hint of them is to be found in the literature, nor, with one exception, could any of them have been inferred from the known egg-care habits, as they have been reported in the past. Informed observation of Cockatiels nesting and incubating eggs in the open on enclosure floors, of which there is none in the literature, probably would have given at least another hint.

The First Clutch of Carmen and Cosimo

ATTENTION TO THE NESTBOX. The opaque NB (Fig. 3a) became an object of great attention by both birds in the few days after its installation on October 11, 1982. Cosimo enlarged the entrance hole to such an extent that the perch was carried away in the process, necessitating making a new perch hole just beneath the former location. Both birds sometimes were inside the NB together, but Cosimo typically spent much of the morning alone in it, and Carmen spent long stretches of time in it after noon. Neither bird spent the night in it.

COSIMO SINGS AND IS COURTSHIP FED. During those times, Carmen customarily courtship-fed Cosimo several times per day, most notably in the evenings. He sang softly and melodiously from the NB several times per day, including a song that I had not heard before. Sometimes he sang still another new song from his position on an enclosure perch in front of the NB, at times when Carmen was inside.

[The song of birds generally attains its greatest complexity, volume, and vigor during the breeding season (28, 155). The prominence of Cosimo's song at this time can be understood in terms of its important role in stimulating Carmen's sexual behavior and the process of synchronizing his and her reproductive cycles (see pp. 309-312). Male song is primarily under the control of the male sex hormones, appearing and reaching its greatest amplitude when the testes develop (155).]

[On every weekday throughout the first phase of this study (until Sept. 23, 1984), excepting only during summers, I was absent at the University for 2-4 hours in the afternoons, during which time no observation was made. On weekends and during summers, the period of absence usually was only 1-2 h.]

OVIPOSITION BEGINS

DESULTORY COVERING OF THE FIRST EGG. On the 9th day after installing the NB, the 1st egg was detected by lifting the hinged top and inspecting the interior. The IA (incubative area) was at the position marked "X" in Fig. 3a. Reckoning time henceforth in days of incubation (days after the laying of the 1st egg), Cosimo joined Carmen in the NB on the first day (i.e., the day after ovipositing) at 23:30 h. After a few min, during which much movement was detected with the mirror, he left. At 23:47 h, he exchanged with her for 5 min, while she went out and ate.

When Cosimo exchanged with Carmen at 10:00 h on the 2nd day, he followed her out of the NB but stayed out only briefly. He exited again for 30 sec shortly after noon. Then both entered the NB briefly, and Cosimo sang a few soft notes. They both exited for about 30 sec, re-entered for 2 min, and then exited again and fed for 15-20 min. Thereafter, both entered the NB but Cosimo exited immediately and stayed out for about 15 min. Seven min after he returned, both exited.

Both were still out of the NB when I left at 13:18 h, but only Carmen was out when I returned at 15:00 h. Cosimo poked his head from the NB to investigate. At that time, I flighted Carmen for 1 h. Since Cosimo exited the NB after 50 min, I returned Carmen to the enclosure and she took over the care of the egg. Cosimo remained outside. At 16:30 h, Cosimo entered the NB and subdued vocalizations were heard. Carmen exited after about 20-30 sec but she returned at 16:52 h and remained inside for 30 min.

I have accounted somewhat in detail for many of the movements on the 2nd day only to give the reader an impression of the sporadic incubatory habits of Cockatiels in the early days of oviposition (although this was their 1st clutch, these habits also obtained with subsequent clutches). It will be found below that on these 1st few days the eggs usually only are guarded or shielded, rather than incubated. In other words, the birds usually merely crouch over the egg(s) in very loose contact, as compared to the way they incubate in low profile, tightly contacting the eggs on later days. During most of the periods when the birds were in the NB together, there was much movement (judged from viewing the mirror). The significance of this movement also is revealed below.

FLIGHTINGS. I usually flighted Carmen for 1 h each day, and the other birds also were being flighted during the same period. It is noteworthy that, no matter how much noise and other disturbance were created outside by the flighted birds, Cosimo never was prompted to budge from the NB or even peer out. But whenever I serviced the enclosure, and caused even slight noise or movements, he peered out of the NB entrance hole.

OVIPOSITION COMPLETED

COSIMO BEGINS EGG ATTENDANCE IN MORNING. In the ensuing days, a total of 4 eggs were laid, one roughly every other day. I was checking the NB

Nestboxes & Enclosures A, B, & C (top views)

enclosure A

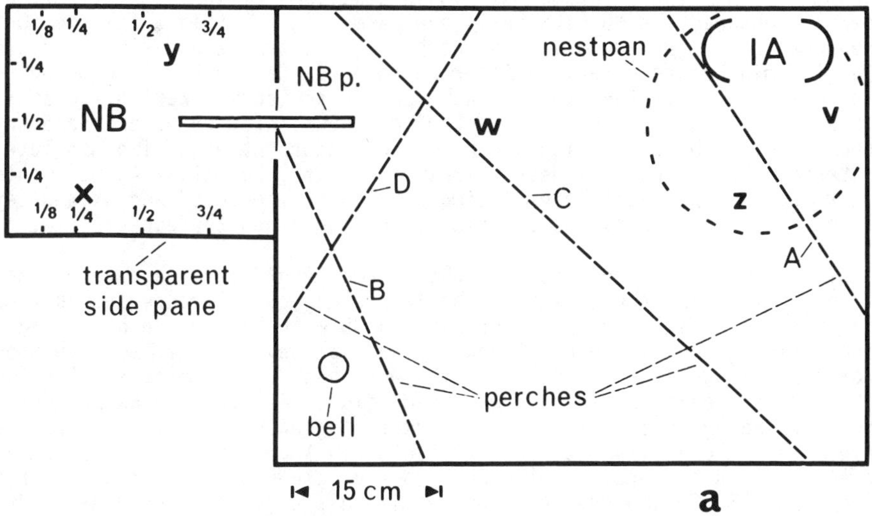

a

enclosures B & C

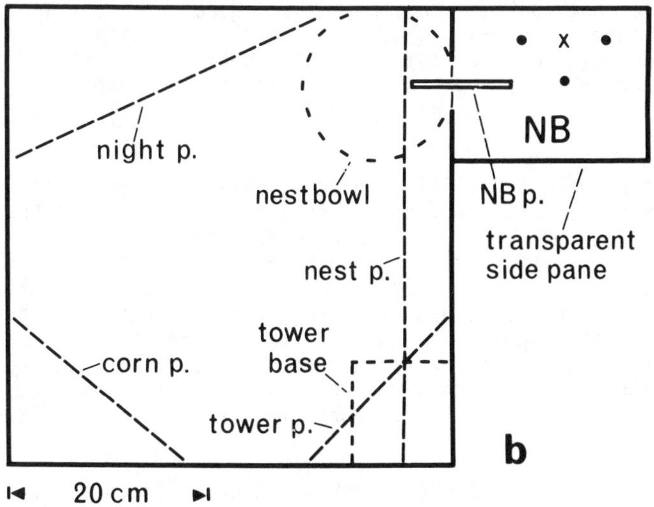

b

Figure 3

for eggs only on the infrequent occasions when both birds were out and busily occupied, deeming it more important not to disturb them (especially as this was their 1st clutch) than to have close knowledge of the precise timetable of oviposition. The presence of the 4th egg was confirmed on the 9th day. During the days of oviposition, Cosimo generally began, or sought to begin, attendance of the eggs in mid-to-late morning.

CARMEN INCREASINGLY RELUCTANT TO RELINQUISH CLUTCH. At first, Cosimo merely entered the NB cautiously and Carmen left within a few sec. On subsequent days, he began to scratch at the entrance and sing unusual song for 1-2 min before entering. After he entered, Carmen usualy came out within a few sec. By the 8th day, however, these tactics were of no avail. As late as 11:24 h, when he poked his head into the NB and some throaty sounds were heard, Carmen would not surrender the eggs. Two min later, he entered the NB and some deep chirps were heard, but still Carmen would not surrendered the eggs. After Cosimo subsequently entered and exited several times in close succession, she finally relinquished the eggs to him.

NESTING TOGETHER. The situation when Carmen took over the care of the eggs from Cosimo in the evening was less-clear cut, because she customarily spent several late evening hours in the NB with him before he exited. During this time much movement usually took place, as detected with the mirror, and squabbling sounds sometimes were heard. Only months later, when a NB with a Plexiglas sidepane was used, did I realize that Carmen must have been spending much of these hours trying unsuccessfully to acquire the eggs from Cosimo, who tenaciously retained them. On one unusual occasion, after Carmen had acquired the eggs in the late evening, she began chirping from the NB. Cosimo responded by leaving his perch and temporarily joining her.

During these 10 days, Carmen and Cosimo often were in the NB together for long periods (many min, even 1 h or more) during the morning and afternoon, again with much movement taking place. They not infrequently were also both outside together. There were some occasions when Cosimo directly followed Carmen out of the NB and others when Carmen already was out (and had been out for some time) and Cosimo came out and voided, or engaged in other activity. On these occasions, the farther along it was in the incubatory period, the more promptly Carmen was likely to take over the care of the eggs.

UNILATERAL DECISIONS. On the basis of subsequent observations, the following generalization about the behavior of the Cockatiels in the colony can be made. The Cockatiel male (the dominant sex) may leave the eggs at any time that he is in the NB alone, whereas the female infrequently does so. When the male exits, the female characteristically takes over the care of the eggs. She does so very promptly after the arrival of the 3rd egg, but not necessarily with dispatch when there are only 1 or 2 eggs. If it were not for this attentiveness of the female, the eggs often might chill. [Either Rock Pigeon parent will go to the nest and incubate out of turn, if it sees its mate away from the nest or if it sees the eggs exposed (1,011).]

'COVETING THE BROOD.' However, one cannot conclude that the male is "derelict" in his "duties" on the occasions when he leaves the eggs unilaterally. On many future occasions when Cosimo left the NB and Carmen sought to take over the eggs, he turned around and raced back, hardly ever failing to "head her off" and regain the eggs himself (or, sometimes, the eggs and chicks both). Sometimes, when he exited, Carmen was eating, or otherwise occupied, and did not take immediate notice. When I arose at such time to approach the NB for a closer look, Cosimo raced back, mounted the outer perch, and guarded the brood from there.

Thus, the male may leave the eggs and/or chicks unilaterally for one reason or another, but he usually continues to 'covet' them. On some occasions, he forsakes his apparent reason for leaving the NB, rather than let the hen acquire the eggs or chicks by default (or he protects them, on my approach). On many occasions during her brooding, after leaving the NB, Carmen also raced back to it when she saw me approach, and entered and 'protected' the brood.

CARMEN EXPELS COSIMO. In the next 10 days, up to the time of hatching, nothing noteworthy occurred that cannot be dealt with more effectively in discussing the care of clutches in a "transparent" NB. I would mention only that; (a) Carmen and Cosimo usually exchanged egg care several times during the day (with Cosimo contributing in most of the care), (b) that it became increasingly difficult for Cosimo to acquire the eggs from Carmen in the morning, and (c) that Carmen sometimes would expel Cosimo from the NB with aggressive hisses when he was reluctant to surrender the eggs. [One must keep in mind in this connection that this was Cosimo's 1st breeding experience, whereas Carmen had been bred before I acquired her.]

NESTBOX SANITATION. As mentioned above, I usually flighted Carmen for 1 h after Cosimo exchanged with her in the late morning. Her first act was to fly to the top of the kitchen door and void. It is well known that parent Cockatiels avoid fouling the nest. On more than one occasion when Cosimo exited the NB briefly, he went to the farthest perch and voided.

"FORAGING." Carmen's favorite activity when she was flighted in the morning was to roam about a great deal on the floor (carpet), even to the exclusion of eating, though she did drink. Her roaming on the floor is the counterpart of ground foraging in the wild. This always was accompanied by regular pecks at the carpet, as if it were replete with seeds. But it is unlikely that more than an occasional seed was acquired in that way.

HATCHING BEGINS---COMPETITION INCREASES--WANING OF CONTINUOUS CARE. On November 8, on the 19th day, the 1st chick had hatched, and by the 22nd day, there were at least 2 chicks, judging by their cheeps. The 4th chick hatched sometime during or before the 25th day, about 17 days after the last egg was laid. During the days of caring for the chicks, with eggs still present, Carmen continued to have great difficulty in periodically taking over the care of the brood from Cosimo during the day. She had to hiss aggressively to expel him. On each return, he, himself, experienced like difficulty in recovering the brood from her. Though he did not appear to vocalize while attempting to do so, there usually was a great deal of movement in the NB, and the birds often were inside together for long periods.

By the 4th or 5th day after the 1st chick had hatched, both birds were out of the NB together on several occasions, which is known to be customary at that time. This is accounted for by the fact that continuous incubation of near-term eggs is unnecessary, and the chicks need to be allofed only periodically.

THE LESS-EXPERIENCED COSIMO EXHIBITS MORE 'CONCERN.' Being out of the NB together usually occurred when Cosimo left the NB after Carmen already was out. At these times, when she did not automatically take over the care of the eggs and brood, as she customarily had done before any egg had hatched, Cosimo appeared to become nervous and 'confused,' and usually returned to the NB within less than a min. After entering and exiting several times, or even after the 1st time, he sometimes pecked at Carmen, trying to get her to take over the care of the eggs and/or brood. She usually did not yield on such occasions, though, with the result that both parents sometimes would be outside together for many min. Cosimo's needless 'concern' probably was a consequence of his inexperience. As mentioned above, this was his first breeding experience.

CHICK LOSS ATTRIBUTED TO INEXPERIENCE. At the time of confirming the presence of 4 chicks on the 25th day, 2 of them were so tiny compared to their broodmates, that I feared for their safety. Two days later, both of these chicks were found at the bottom of the IA, squashed and desiccated. In the light of subsequent findings, it seems resonable to attribute this outcome, also, to Cosimo's inexperience (as he was the major daytime caretaker). I did not realize that at the time, though, and resolved to try to synchronize the next clutch by removing the 1st 3 eggs and replacing them when the 4th egg was due. But for this misguided resolve, the foundations for many of the subsequent findings might never have been laid. [The care of the chicks is treated in Chap. 6, Part 1.]

The Second Clutch of Caremen and Cosimo

IMMINENCE OF ANOTHER CLUTCH SIGNALED BY VOCALIZATIONS. The first indication that a 2nd clutch might be imminent was noted when the oldest chick was 20 days old. On that day, Cosimo launched into a continuous bout of singing from the NB while Carmen was being flighted. Two days later, they copulated, and 3 days after that Cosimo sang again from the NB--a quiet, melodious song. The 1st egg of the 2nd clutch was laid on December 8, 1982, when the oldest chick of the first brood was 30 days old, 7 weeks after the laying of the 1st egg of the 1st clutch.

FIRST EGG BURIED. My plan was to remove the 1st 3 eggs of the clutch until the 4th was due, and to bury them in the NB, in 3 of the corners. Accordingly, I buried the 1st egg in the corner near the IA (the latter marked **X** in Fig. 3a), heaping about a $1\frac{1}{4}$ cm depth of shavings over it. Roughly the same depth of shavings also covered the floor of the NB, except in the IA, where the birds had shaped a shallow depression.

[Whenever a change of any kind was made within a NB during these studies, including handling of the chicks, the entrance-hole was closed with a cardboard partition. This prevented the birds from entering or witnessing anything that transpired within the NB during the change.]

BURIED EGG RECOVERED. To my astonishment, when I checked the NB about 3 h later, I found that the egg I had buried had been restored to its original position in the IA and was being incubated. Before this observation, instances of the recovery (by digging with the bill) of artificially or adventitiously buried eggs apparently were known only in 3 species of the genus *Charadrius*, which includes several species that intentionally bury their eggs (328, 1,396, 1,397). [Members of some species routinely dig up eggs that they, themselves, have buried (see 328); some birds may return displaced eggs to the nest or IA.]

A PROPITIOUS CHOICE OF BURIAL SITE. It will be found, however, that the Cockatielian behavior pattern that led to the recovery of the egg is more remarkable than I had guessed at the time and have suggested above. In fact, if I had buried the egg in any other corner, it probably would not have been found, except accidentally. The behavioral pattern for recovery of missing eggs includes even other relict responses previously unknown in any bird. Some of these responses subsequently also were found in the female Peach-faced Lovebird, a very distant relative within the parrot order (see Table 2), and also in the female Budgerigar, suggesting that such latent relict responses are widespread among parrots.

PLANS FOR A "TRANSPARENT" NESTBOX. Upon this finding, I resolved to investigate the matter intensively using a NB with a transparent sidepane. Accordingly, I did not bury any other egg of this clutch, but allowed the birds to proceed without further experimental manipulation. A total of 4 eggs were laid, 1 every other day. As with the 1st clutch, these were incubated in the area marked with an **X** in Fig. 3a. Rather than describe the egg-care behavior for this 2nd clutch, I shall leave such considerations for detailed treatments when the results obtained using a NB with a transparent sidepane are described. It need only be mentioned that Ferdinand and Helena, the chicks of the 1st brood, continued to be cared for and allofed all through the period when the 2nd clutch was being incubated.

EXCITEMENT OCCASIONED BY IMPENDING HATCHING. On the 20th day of incubation of the 2nd clutch, Cosimo joined Carmen in the NB at 10:30 h and unaccountably did a great deal of singing. Both birds then spent practically the entire day in the NB. Judging from subsequent findings, it can be suspected that the parents had detected either the faint bill clapping sounds of a chick nearing hatching, or its vocalizations or sounds of hatching, and were tenaciously competing for the eggs. That the events of hatching excite many incubating birds, and sometimes lead them to refuse to surrender the clutch to a would-be exchanging parent, is well known (14). Probably, Carmen and Cosimo also spent some time participating together in the incubation of a split clutch, as described below.

ANOTHER CHICK LOST. On checking the NB at 05:18 h on the 21st day, the 1st chick was found to have hatched and was already dried out with fluffy down. A 2nd chick was present on my checking 2 days later, and the last hatching occurred on the 6th day after the 1st. The hatching of the last chick was delayed so lengthily, however, that the chick did not survive. Again, I would suggest that, if Cosimo had been more experienced, this chick would have survived without difficulty. I take this view because, as will be seen, the brooding of Cockatielian chicks by experienced parents (see p. 675, *et seq.*) is a most orderly and systematic procedure that leaves very little to chance. In this connection, it is well known that Cockatiels are very successful in rearing their broods.

COSIMO DOES NOT LEAVE THE BROOD UNILATERALLY. It should be mentioned in Cosimo's favor, however, that he was a most attentive parent in most respects. During the period of late incubation and first hatchings of the eggs, when the 2nd brood was of mixed composition--eggs and chicks--whenever Cosimo left the NB and found that Carmen was out being flighted (she usually was perching on the home perch or shelf perch, or "foraging" on the carpet), he immediately returned to it.

SECOND BURIED EGG RECOVERED. It would have been unwise to breed the birds again to begin the experiment with the "transparent" NB immediately, so when Carmen oviposited again on February 13, 1983, I removed both the egg and the NB. After the NB and egg had been absent for 1 day, I repeated the test described above: I restored the NB with the egg buried in the same corner, near the IA, to see if, after a 24 hour hiatus, the egg still would be recovered and incubated. Indeed, it was. When I checked 4 h after the return, Cosimo was crouching over the egg in the IA. Many months were to pass before circumstances were favorable to begin the following planned experiments.

The Third Clutch of Carmen and Cosimo

THREE PAIRS HOUSED TOGETHER. In the period between the time the 2nd brood of Carmen and Cosimo were reared in early 1983, and March, 1984, the 3 pairs of Cockatiels were housed together in enclosure A. One of the 2 males in the 2nd brood of 3 had been given away, leaving 6 birds: Carmen and Cosimo, and the pairs of the 1st (Ferdinand and Helena) and 2nd (Homer and Isabella) broods. Ferdinand paired with his younger sister, Isabella, and Homer paired with his older sister, Helena. The members of each pair copulated from time to time and socialized almost exclusively with their mates, the socializing including perching near one another, sleeping near one another, mutual allogrooming, etc. But members of the young pairs did not courtship-feed one another.

CARMEN COURTSHIP-FEEDS COSIMO---USE OF "TRANSPARENT" NESTBOX. During the month of March, 1984, I noted a great deal of courtship feeding of Cosimo by Carmen. This occurred 15-30 or more times per day. Cosimo typically would bow low and present his bill pointing upward to solicit food from Carmen. He appeared to be receiving most of his nourishment from her during this period. Since Carmen and Cosimo were observed to copulate on February 19, 1984, and again on the following March 11, 18, and 28, and courtship feeding was intense, I began the experiment on egg care in a "transparent" NB.

ADOPTING THE "TRANSPARENT" NESTBOX

On March 28, at 19:11 h, I installed the Plexiglas-sided NB (Fig. 3a), bedded with a 2½-cm layer of wood shavings (#3 sawdust). [Some breeders recommend a 7½-cm layer of cedar shavings, noting that eggs can become buried and tiny chicks smothered in a 7½-cm layer of sawdust (11).] The side facing toward me was constructed of 5/32-cm, clear Plexiglas. The NB immediately became the focus of attention and competition on the part of all 6 birds. After observing their interactions for 35 min, I flighted the 4 siblings for 1 h to simplify the situation.

PARTITIONING THE ENCLOSURE. The next evening, I partitioned enclosure A into upper and lower halves with ½-cm thick plywood and left Carmen and Cosimo in exclusive possession of the upper half, with the NB. The following is a brief description of their behavior in relation to the NB prior to the partitioning, with mention of the 4 siblings only when they interacted with Carmen and Cosimo. This is of interest both in relation to the competition with the young, and the interactions between Carmen and Cosimo.

RESPONSES BY FAMILY. Carmen was the first to approach the new NB but she retreated. Cosimo then approached it and drove away Homer. Carmen mounted the outside perch, with Cosimo close by, pecking at it. Then Cosimo took over the perch and Carmen stood by. Cosimo left and Homer returned, driving Carmen away when she approached. Cosimo then returned and drove Homer off, and he and Carmen mounted the perch together. They defended the area against the others, and Cosimo began to peck and claw around the periphery of the entrance hole. When Cosimo left, Ferdinand mounted the perch and drove Carmen away as she approached. At this point, I flighted the 4 siblings.

Carmen and Cosimo then made external inspections, sometimes poking their heads partway into the entrance. At 19:52 h, 41 min after installation, Carmen entered the NB and inspected its inside, and even settled in momentarily in an incubative posture. At this time, Cosimo was on the outside perch. Then Carmen was frightened out by seeing me raise my arm. At 20:00 h, Cosimo stretched his head and neck into the NB but retreated. Carmen entered and left again. After much hesitation, Cosimo finally entered the NB at 20:05 h. He pecked about, dunked his head, bill first, into the shavings, and then left. At 20:15 h, he entered again and inspected the interior for 3 min. He did this again 10 min later, but only briefly.

At 20:40 h, I let the 4 siblings back into the enclosure and covered the entrance to the NB with a sheet of cardboard. The birds pecked away at this until I removed it at 20:52 h. While the others explored the NB entrance, Carmen and Cosimo chewed on a mineral block, which I had newly installed, driving the others away when they approached. At 23:00 h, Carmen entered the NB and explored in it for 2 min. After she left, Cosimo entered for 2 min, and, again, 15 min later, for a brief visit. At 23:30 h, however, Homer entered and let Ferdinand join him without conflict. At 23:40 h, for the first time, both Carmen and Cosimo visited the NB together. After a few min, Cosimo left, followed shortly thereafter by Carmen.

CARMEN AND COSIMO ISOLATED---COURTING AND COITUS. The next morning the NB got a great deal of attention, mostly from the males, and mostly a matter of chewing and pecking at the entrance borders (see also 9, 127) and perch. This continued throughout the day. At 17:10 h, Cosimo was inside and Carmen was guarding the entrance from the outside perch, repelling any of her approaching offspring. At 19:30 h, I partitioned the enclosure, leaving Carmen and Cosimo in the upper half with the NB. I also trimmed 4 cm from their tails to facilitate their movements in the NB. At 22:30 h, they were both inside it, giving it a thorough going over--inspecting, pecking about, etc., but they did not spend the night in it.

The next morning, Carmen and Cosimo copulated for about 1 min, shortly after lights-on. This ultimately proved to be their favorite time for sexual union. They more or less ignored the NB that day but copulated again at 17:20 h. At 23:30 h, both birds approached the vicinity of the NB and "fussed around" at the entrance. Shortly thereafter, Cosimo jumped in, and Carmen followed a few min later. Cosimo poked around in the shavings quite a bit, scattering them with twists of his head. Then he exited, and Carmen also poked around into, and scattered, the shavings. Then she also left. They had spent a total of about 5 min in the NB during these latter visits. Again, they did not sleep inside the NB.

COITION SOUNDS STIMULATE VOCALIZATIONS. The above described events took place on March 30, 1984. The enclosure had been partitioned the day before. The 1st egg of Carmen's 3rd clutch was not to be laid for almost another 2 weeks, on April 10. Accordingly, I touch only on the highlights of the intervening period. First, Carmen and Cosimo copulated 1 or more times almost every day throughout this interval. On some of these occasions, Carmen's Coition Sounds stimulated the 4 offspring in the part of the enclosure beneath to raise a great din of whistling. As noted above, the same responses to Carmen's Coition Sounds during copulations and to Cosimo's similar utterances during courting were noted in her offspring on many subsequent occasions during their other breeding cycles (even when the offspring themselves were incubating or brooding; see pp. 838-840, **Persisting Recognition of Parents by Offspring by Either Sight or Sound**). [In this connection, Cockatiels, like Budgerigars and lovebirds, often are stimulated to breed by observing the actions of nearby pairs (127).]

IMMINENT BREEDING---ATTENTION TO NESTBOX. Second, Carmen continued to courtship-feed Cosimo. He also ate himself, including much scraping and chewing on the cuttlebone. Third, Cosimo's courting also was signalled by his breaking out into loud, protracted song--for the first time, early on the morning of March 31. Fourth, heavy consumption of birdseed, mostly by Carmen began on April 1. By April 8, the consumption of shelled sunflower seeds also had increased greatly.

There was a great deal of entering, "fussing about" in, and leaving the NB through this period. This included frequent occasions when both birds, or only one or the other, on entering and seeming to have settled down for a long visit, got up and left abruptly (as if merely "checking out" the facility and testing the prospective incubative area). Although both birds engaged in both activities, Carmen favored settling down into the incubative posture, whereas Cosimo favored inspections and pecking about in the shavings. Sometimes Carmen sat with her tail and rear underside leaning high against a wall or corner, a posture that has been described by others as an "egg-laying" posture (6). It proved also to be an occasional incubative posture. In the following, I confine attention to visits to the NB that were either lengthy or of exceptional interest.

INVITATION TO ADOPT NESTBOX. At 19:35 h on March 31, Cosimo spent 10 min in the NB poking around in the shavings, in a preview of one of his methods of locating buried eggs. On April 3, he had been "fussing around" in the NB until just before midnight, when he settled into the future IA, which had been more or less cleared of shavings (Fig. 3a, area marked Y, this being the area least accessible to my view). He then began singing softly, melodiously, and almost continuously, for 25 min.

Carmen was far from the NB entrance, but approached the outside perch when his singing began. She hesitated there for 15-20 sec, and then, acting as if uncertain of what to do, entered and exited from the NB 14 times in just the next few min. These brief visits continued at a much lower frequency until her last visit at 24:25 h, when Cosimo followed her out and ceased singing. It seemed as if Cosimo's singing was an invitation to Carmen to adopt the NB. Cosimo's songs on this occasion were highly varied, and included virtually his entire repertoire, but no Coition Sound.

A CONTINUED FOCUS OF ACTIVITY. On April 4, at 22:45 h, both birds repeated the same routine, except that this time Cosimo sang for only 2 min, rather than 25 min, and that they left the NB after Cosimo had been inside for only 7 min. At 23:30 h, Cosimo again sang from the NB, this time for 5 min, but Carmen was indecisive. She approached the NB twice, as if to enter, but withdrew each time.

The next day, at the early hour of 18:10 h, Cosimo again sang softly from the NB, and Carmen joined him for a full 10 min. Later that evening (23:05 h), they were in the NB together again and Cosimo launched into a session of the Coition Sounds followed by other soft vocalizations. Carmen entered and exited several times during the latter singing. The usual routine, of Cosimo singing from the NB and Carmen entering and leaving repeatedly, took place yet another time about 30 min later (23:40 h).

EARLY COMPETITIVENESS. Some overt evidence of competitiveness over the IA --just the faintest hint of the vigorous jousting and jockeying that lay ahead--surfaced on the afternoon of April 7. Singing softly, Cosimo joined Carmen in the NB and pecked her away, as she "brooded the future IA," the care of which he took over himself.

COITION SOUNDS BY A NON-COPULATING FEMALE. An unusual event occurred very late the next night (24:35 h). Cosimo had again been singing softly from the NB (for about 8 min), and Carmen was mostly ignoring him. When she finally came over near the NB, she began emitting Coition Sounds. These continued as she entered the NB. After about 2 min both birds exited. This occasion, and later ones on the evenings of the same day and the next day, were the only occasions when I heard a non-copulating female utter these sounds. Males, on the other hand, often may do so during the periods of sexual maturation, oviposition, and incubation.

COSIMO'S SELF-FEEDING INCREASES---MORE INCUBATIVE-AREA COMPETITIVENESS. While I was replenishing the food and water the next morning (activities requiring 60-75 min), Carmen and Cosimo entered the NB repeatedly, and spent about half the time inside. At about this time Cosimo's self-feeding greatly increased and Carmen allofed him much less frequently. On the afternoon of that day, Cosimo again rousted Carmen from her favorite spot in the IA, with a pecking attack.

NESTBOX DARKENED---FIRST NIGHT OF USE. By April 8, the NB was becoming an irresistible attraction to them. That evening, I covered the sidepane with black cloth to darken the interior, to ascertain whether they then would spend the night in it, which they had not as yet done. This seemed to heighten further their interest, which was already at a very high level. Between 19:25 and 20:56 h, when I stopped recording their actions, both had entered and exited many times, often being inside together. On one of these occasions (19:55 h), while Cosimo was inside, Carmen stood on the inner perch, with her head out of the entrance and uttered the Coition Sounds. Four times (20:50, 20:56, 21:50, and 23:10 h), Cosimo sang softly from inside. On the last of these occasions, Carmen courtship-fed him. At 23:43 h, they engaged in sexual union for 2½ min. They did not, however, spend the night in the NB.

I removed the black-cloth cover from the sidepane during the next morning. But the great attention to, and the brief visiting of, the NB continued. During the late evening, beginning at 23:15 h, there were hints that they might stay in the NB for the night (the 1st egg was laid the next morning). Thus, both birds spent longer periods than usual inside, but still entered and exited repeatedly.

At 23:50 h, for the 3rd and last time, Carmen again uttered the Coition Sounds. At the time, Cosimo was nearby, but not in contact with her. She continued to utter the sounds while mounting the inside perch. For the first time she, but not Cosimo, spent the night in the NB. This was ascertained by checking at 05:30 h; by the time of the next check, at 07:15 h, she had exited.

Responses to Experimental Manipulations

OVIPOSITION BEGINS. Except for exiting to eat, Carmen spent most of the morning of April 10 in the NB. At 11:20 h, I detected her 1st egg. As the center of the IA (incubative area) had almost been cleared of shavings, the egg was practically in direct contact with the NB floor. Cosimo merely was crouching low over it, leaving it almost fully visible beneath him. When the pair left the NB, I replaced the fresh Cockatielian egg with a full-weight lovebird egg, of which I then had a plentiful supply (the avg. wt. of the fresh lovebird eggs was about 4.3 g, as opposed to 5.6 g for the fresh Cockatielian eggs). By 11:30 h, Cosimo was back over the egg but Carmen entered and readily acquired it from him, gently tucking it under her breast with the underside of her bill.

FIRST OBSERVATIONS OF RESPONSES OVER A MISSING CLUTCH

EGG SEARCHES. At 17:45 h, I found Cosimo crouching loosely over the egg. When he left the NB, I buried the egg beneath 1¼ cm of shavings, 5 cm from the far rear corner of the NB and 2½ cm out from the far sidewall (between the corresponding 1/8- and ¼-way labels in Fig. 3a). After a few min, Carmen entered the NB. She scanned the entire NB bottom, apparently in search of the egg, walking around while doing so. Then she sat in the IA. After a few min, she rose slightly and pivoted 360° while looking beneath herself, as if again searching for the egg. She also pecked about briefly in the IA before settling into it once more. [Although I say "as if" and "apparently" in search of the egg, the markedly different behavior of the birds at such times (and subsequent findings) leave no doubt as to the object of their actions.]

At 18:16 h, Cosimo entered the NB and Carmen exited. When he found no egg, he looked repeatedly all about the bottom of the NB. Then he began to plow up the shavings in the IA by running his bill gently through them, with its tip scraping the floor. He exited at 18:20 h, without having found the egg. Five min later, Carmen re-entered the NB and momentarily settled into the corner near the IA. She spent another min pecking gently in the IA before exiting. Two min later, Cosimo returned and, again, visually examined the entire NB floor. Finding nothing, he next raised his head on high, cocking it sideways from time to time, and seemed to be carefully scanning all 4 walls of the NB. Again, he tested the IA by gently running his bill through the shavings like a plow. After 9 min, he exited.

RESTORED EGG ACCEPTED ROUTINELY. Not wishing to interfere excessively with the birds' activities at the time, I restored the lovebird egg to the IA at 18:52 h. [It is of incidental interest, in this connection, that if all the eggs and/or chicks are taken from a breeding Cockatiel hen, she usually will begin to oviposit another clutch within a week (127).] Cosimo came in a few min later and promptly settled down on the egg without prior search behavior, just as if it never had been missing. Carmen relieved him in routine fashion 10 min later. By 19:15 h, Cosimo was back again, and they resumed their normal routine of egg care typical of that for the 1st 2 or 3 eggs of a clutch.

PREVIEW OF SEARCH ROUTINES. This experiment had given tentative answers to several questions and revealed several interesting new facets of the egg-recovery responses of Cockatiels. Since, as a result of subsequent experiments, these answers now are firm, I do not qualify them in the following discussion. First, where do the birds search visually? They look everywhere in the NB, even ostensibly at the walls at all heights. Second, where in the shavings do they search in attempts to find a concealed egg? They usually search only within the IA and around its periphery. Third, how do they search in the shavings? The female usually merely pecks about gently, whereas the male typically both pecks about and gently plows through the shavings with his bill.

ONLY CERTAIN EGGS RECOVERED. Why did they not find the egg this time, whereas they had found 2 other buried eggs with dispatch? I previously had thought that they had searched the entire NB floor until they found the buried egg(s), but it had become evident that the 1st 2 eggs were found because they were at the periphery of the old IA (in the corner near X in Fig. 3a). Had they been placed in any of the other corners, they would not have been found by a direct search. This was confirmed by many further experiments.

Relict Egg-Care Behavior Revealed

NO NEED TO RECOVER EGGS IN NEST HOLES. How do these findings correlate with the ecology of Cockatiels? Cockatiels, today, are strictly hole-nesters. They do not line or pad their nests in any way, but oviposit on bare wood, decaying wood dust, leaves, or other organic matter that is naturally present in the hollows. When there is an excessive depth of loose material, confined birds remove it (as also do Budgerigars, e.g., see p. 778; **Fostered Egg Ignored**). Consequently, it is highly unlikely that a Cockatielian egg in the wild ever gets buried or hidden from view.

Similarly, it is unlikely that Cockatiels ever have a need to recover eggs at a distance from the IA. Thus, the tree holes used by Cockatiels rarely are spacious, because large holes are at a premium and become appropriated by the many larger hole-nesting Australian birds. Moreover, an accidentally missing or displaced egg in a nest hole would not be found along the walls of the cavity, at any height. Accordingly, the conclusion is inescapable that the observed responses are relics of a time past, before Cockatiels nested in tree holes (a type of behavior termed "obsolete" or "archaic" by Provine; 132).

RESPONSES ADAPTIVE FOR SURFACE NESTING. Being relict responses, however, does not automatically imply that the responses are ancient or primitive. It only implies that they are of a time past. One is led to conclude that the Cockatielian egg-recovery responses are primitive and very ancient, because they are, without exception, adaptations of a type that would be expected in birds that nested in shallow scrapes on flat ground. That mode of nesting very likely was the primitive mode employed by birds. Since the eggs of birds that nest in constructed, cupped nests or burrows do not roll away or get buried (except intentionally), their possessors rarely have a need to search or dig for them.

"DISTANT VISUAL SEARCH". Cosimo's response of seeming to search the NB walls, and elevating his head, is simply the search pattern for eggs that might have become displaced to distant locations. Of course, this cannot happen in the NB, but the behavior pattern is stereotyped. It harkens back to the time when, on flat ground, eggs could have rolled, been blown, or otherwise been accidentally displaced a considerable distance and become to some degree obscured. If the "distant visual search" represented a search for a possible predator responsible for the loss of the eggs, one also would expect it to occur when all but 1 egg of a clutch was missing, but it does not (perhaps because a predator already would have struck). These first observations of Cockatiels searching for a missing egg do not firmly establish the relations that I have outlined, but many subsequent observations substantiate them and very greatly broaden the picture.

SERENADING---EGG NOT CARED FOR ATTENTIVELY. On that same night (Apr. 10), at 22:43 h, Carmen joined Cosimo in the NB, as he crouched low over the egg, but she stayed for only a moment. At 23:00 h, it was she who was crouching over the egg, when Cosimo entered and serenaded her very softly. She let him take over the care of the egg, but only for a few sec, after which he exited. When he returned and perched in the entrance, Carmen exited. At 23:13 h, Carmen again was within the NB with Cosimo, as he crouched over the egg and serenaded her. She exited after about one min, but was back again and crouching over the egg 26 min later. Just earlier, Cosimo had entered the NB several times and sung softly.

COMPETITION--EGG SHIELDING---EGG NOT CARED FOR AT NIGHT. At 12:12 h, Cosimo entered the NB and tried unsuccessfully to peck Carmen off of the egg. Eight min later, he succeeded in doing so, and sat over the egg himself for a few sec. From being able to observe the birds at all times within the NB, it was evident that that they were sitting on the egg very lightly. They were, in essence, shielding and guarding it, rather than incubating it. Both birds were out of the NB at 1:10 h, when the lights were turned off. They were still out when I checked 10 min later (using a dim pencil beam from a flashlight) and at 7:22 h (when the eggs were cold), so the eggs were not incubated that night (unless they left their perch positions within a few min of the lights being turned off, Carmen and Cosimo infrequently moved from these positions during the night).

SECOND OBSERVATIONS OF RESPONSES OVER A MISSING CLUTCH

CONTROL EXPERIMENT WITH COCKATIELIAN EGG. Since the buried egg of the day before was a lovebird egg, but on the previous 2 occasions it had been a Cockatielian egg, I repeated the buried-egg experiment with a Cockatielian egg, to rule out the remote possibility that olfaction and the fact of the egg being a foreign egg played a role. Accordingly, when Cosimo exited the NB at 15:00 h on April 11, I buried their 1st egg in the identical position of the lovebird egg the day before, 5 cm from the far, rear corner. When Cosimo returned at 15:08 h, he missed the egg, even as he 'peered' in from the outside perch, as could be seen from the 'alarmed' manner in which he turned his head and scanned the bottom of the NB.

URGENT SEARCHES. When Cosimo entered the NB, he looked all around in it, high and low, and even poked his head out the entrance and looked at the enclosure floor below the NB entrance. Then he began "nuzzling" around the IA with his bill. When he exited, around 15:11 h, Carmen took his place, and she, also, examined the NB bottom for the missing egg. After Cosimo joined her for a few sec, they both exited. At 15:19 h, Cosimo returned and searched again visually and by nuzzling, and 3 min later Carmen made another visual search. At 15:22 h, Carmen returned and made still another visual search, and also pecked around sporadically in the IA.

EXPOSED EGG RECOVERED. At 15:36 h, I attempted a different type of experiment. I left the buried egg in place (the egg laid by Carmen), but buried a lovebird egg against the transparent sidepane at the ½-way point (see Fig. 3a), with its top surface slightly exposed--just enough to show a conspicuous white area. Cosimo came into the NB on two occasions, beginning at 15:47 h, and made very extensive searches of the NB (recall that the egg still was missing from the IA), looking up, down, and around. Sometimes, he seemed to be looking right at the exposed tip of the buried lovebird egg, and he almost touched it twice. He also nuzzled around again in the shavings in the IA.

Cosimo entered and searched the NB still a 3rd time, but without doing any nuzzling in the IA. On the occasion of this last search, Carmen joined him briefly but did not, at that time, notice the exposed tip of the egg. When she came in alone, though, a few min later, she spied it immediately and matter-of-factly wedged it out of the shavings with the side of her bill. She then nudged it gently to the IA, with the underside of her bill, and crouched over it.

TREATMENT OF RECOVERED EGG. When Cosimo joined her, a moment later, and discovered the egg, they both gave it great attention, as if they were cleaning it. Then Carmen crouched over it and Cosimo settled down at her side. Both now seemed very relaxed, as opposed to the way they were pacing and searching the NB earlier. Cosimo left after 2 min but returned almost immediately and pecked Carmen off of the egg, and then stood over it. But then she pecked him away, in turn, and crouched over it. By 16:12 h, Cosimo had taken over the care of the egg again.

NON-ADAPTIVE TO PROBE BEYOND INCUBATIVE AREA. This experiment settled the question of whether the results were influenced by the egg being that of a lovebird (17.3 x 23.8 mm) rather than of a Cockatiel (19 x 24.5 mm). It was immaterial. It also greatly reinforced the previous findings, including the fact that the birds usually do not probe for missing eggs much beyond the periphery of the IA, even when they make prolonged and repeated searches. Searching into the substratum much beyond the periphery of the IA would not, of course, be adaptive for birds nesting in shallow scrapes on a loose or lightly-compacted substratum. In such circumstances, there would be little likelihood of an egg getting buried outside the IA, and time and energy spent searching outside of it would be wasted.

EGG RESURFACING PREVIEW. In addition, the experiment raised the possibility--later dispelled--that the male does not recognize an egg without seeing a considerable portion of its profile, whereas a female seemed to recognize one from its color or from seeing just a small portion of it. The experiment also previewed the way in which Cockatiels bring buried eggs to the surface, namely, by wedging them out with the side of the bill (as opposed to, say, digging around them or extracting them with a foot).

RESPONSE TO OUT-OF-PLACE, SUPERNUMERARY EGG. At 17:30 h, that same day, I tried a different type of experiment. I put a 2nd lovebird egg in the NB on the surface of the shavings at precisely the same spot where the first lovebird egg had been almost totally buried (at the ½-way position, adjacent to the sidepane). Cosimo was the first to enter the NB, but when he noticed the 2nd egg, he became startled and left the NB in haste.

He returned shortly, however, but acted very confused and "mouthed" the 2nd egg. At this time, Carmen also entered, and she also acted very confused. She pecked hesitatingly at the egg. Both birds continued to act confused, and, in a seeming displacement activity, they pecked at each other. Then Cosimo nudged the 2nd egg over to the IA (against Carmen's seeming opposition), and they both stood bending over the 2 eggs, making a great fuss over them and inspecting them closely. At 19:40 h, I found Carmen crouching over both eggs.

INFLUENCES OF LOCATION AND MENTAL STATE. It would seem from these results that both Carmen and Cosimo were 'confused' over the presence of a 2nd egg far from the IA. They doubtless would have accepted the egg routinely if it had been in the IA. At any rate, the egg certainly got a greatly different reception from that accorded to an egg when they were in the mental state of missing a solitary egg or an entire clutch. Both treated the egg, at first, as if it were a foreign object. Cosimo appeared to be more readily reconciled to the addition of the egg than was Carmen, though she accepted it readily enough once it had been moved into the IA.

THIRD OBSERVATIONS OF RESPONSES OVER A MISSING CLUTCH

WOULD THE BIRDS SEEK A MISSING EGG AT A KNOWN PREVIOUS LOCATION? It had become clear at that time that the birds would not engage in active searches for missing eggs much beyond the borders of the IA. However, they already had recovered both a buried egg that was partly exposed and an unburied egg, from the ½-way point against the sidepane. Would they dig at this location, even though it was far from the IA, if the eggs were missing again? To seek an answer to this question, I removed both eggs from the IA later that same day, at 20:40 h, and buried only one of them 1¼ cm deep at the ½-way point against the sidepane. In addition, I "stored" Carmen's 1st egg by burying it against the sidepane, 5 cm from the rear corner.

EGG PRESENCE NO LONGER TAKEN FOR GRANTED. When Carmen started to enter the NB, a few min later, she immediately missed the eggs and stopped short in the entrance, eyeing the entire floor of the NB. It would seem that Carmen and Cosimo no longer were taking the presence of the eggs for granted, but checked for them even before they entered the NB, just as if they were nesting in a colony and confirming that they had returned to the right nest. Then Carmen entered and sat in the corner by the empty IA, with her tail and rear underside high up against the corner. Following that, she dug and scratched around vigorously in the IA, while pivoting 360°.

CARMEN EYES CORRECT LOCATION BUT WILL NOT PROBE. When Carmen exited the NB, Cosimo tried to stop her. Then he looked into the NB and also seemed to miss the eggs. Entering, he looked all around in the IA and then exited. At 20:48 h, Carmen re-entered and settled down in the IA. Then she arose and came over to the precise spot where the egg was buried (and had been found twice before). She eyed the ground over the egg very carefully with her head cocked sideways. But she would not peck or probe there. On her following visit to the NB, she scratched vigorously all around in the IA, while also pivoting.

FRANTIC SEARCHING WITH VOCALIZATIONS. When Cosimo entered the NB shortly afterward, he vigorously plowed up the entire IA with his bill. As he swept his bill from side to side ("bill-sweeping"), shavings were scattered into the air, right and left. Although he searched the IA again and again, he did not extend his search beyond its immediate vicinity. [Clearly, an egg that was buried anywhere within or near the IA would have been found and resurfaced with dispatch.] At 21:40 h, Cosimo came in again and made a thorough "distant visual search" with his head held high, this time also pecking at and scraping his bill across the NB walls. Widening his search area around the periphery of the IA, he again cast shavings far and wide. Then he resumed a frantic distant visual search and pecked at the walls, before returning again to the IA. Following that, he broke out into loud vocalizations.

Meanwhile, Carmen had entered and exited 3 times, while he was so engaged, and she, too, searched the IA. On the 2nd of these visits, she also cast the shavings far and wide. Several times they were both engaged simultaneously in frantic searching, he on high and she in the IA. At 21:15 h, both, again, were searching visually in the NB. Carmen exited with little delay, but Cosimo, who continued to sing--now in a medium voice with many modulations--settled into the IA. A few min later, at 21:18 h, he yet again pecked and ploughed in the IA,.

ACTIVE PHYSICAL SEARCHING CONFINED TO INCUBATIVE AREA. The results of this experiment convinced me that the birds generally would not search for missing eggs by digging and plowing in places much beyond the periphery of the IA (say, beyond 2-3 cm), even though they might be searching frantically for them, and even though they might have found buried eggs previously at locations outside the IA.

There would seem to be little doubt that Carmen was examining the surface of the shavings above the buried egg for signs that the egg might have been there, and that she looked there because she had dug up an egg at precisely that location earlier in the day, and also had found another egg there on the surface. Any sign of an egg surely would have released her wedging-out activity. But the searching procedure appears to be highly stereotyped: active physical searching is reserved for the IA and its periphery.

[A notable exception is when a NB is explored before an IA has been established. At that time, exploratory pecking by the pair could occur anywhere on the floor of the NB. Budgerigars behave similarly in their NB exploration (see pp. 777, 778, **Behavior in Relation to the Nestboxes**).]

ANOTHER PARTIALLY-EXPOSED EGG RECOVERED. That same evening, at 21:22 h, I repositioned the buried egg with its tip showing to the extent of 5 mm. Carmen came in immediately afterwards, noticed the egg immediately, wedged it out with the side of her bill, and nudged it gently back to the IA. Being in possession of an egg, the pair settled into their normal routine, with no sign of 'concern' over the absence of the 2nd supernumerary egg. Carmen happened to be the one to find the egg again this time, because I exposed it after Cosimo left the NB, and she rarely failed to enter when he left. But Cosimo was, by far, the more vigorous searcher.

An Influence of Light: Clues to the Earliest Pre-avian Egg Care

RESPONSES TO "LIGHTS-ON" AND "LIGHTS-OFF". Later that same night, at 24:52 h, Carmen was still in the NB, having been there for about an hour. It looked very much like she had settled in for the night. However, no sooner had I turned the lights out than I heard the tell-tale rustling on the NB perch that signalled movements on it. When I turned the lights back on a moment later, Carmen already was off the NB perch and moving toward perch A (Fig. 3a). That perch was on the far side of the enclosure, and it was where she and Cosimo usually spent the night, and from which they often voided.

But as soon as the lights came back on, Carmen turned around, hastily retreated to the NB, and again crouched over the egg. I waited for a few min, until after she was well settled, and then turned the lights off again. Once more, the rustling on the perch began almost immediately and, sure enough, when I turned the lights back on after a few sec, she was sidling across the rear enclosure wall toward Cosimo on perch A. But as soon as the lights came on, she promptly reversed her path, returned to the NB, and again crouched over the egg. Again, I waited a few min until after she was settled, and repeated the experiment, with precisely the same result. The next time I turned the lights out (the 4th time), she did not exit immediately, and I retired for the night. But at 08:30 h that morning, I found her on perch A with Cosimo.

THE CRUCIAL DIFFERENCE---EXPOSURE OF NESTBOX INTERIOR. How is one to interpret these responses? First, recall that when I turned out the lights on the previous night, Carmen and Cosimo were not in the NB, and the egg was temporarily unattended. Since that was the 1st night after oviposition, the night of the experiment was the 1st night that Carmen was crouching over the egg in the "transparent" NB at the time of lights off. Accordingly, it was the 1st opportunity for the response to occur with an egg of the 3rd clutch. But I had never noted any such response during the care of the 2 previous clutches. The crucial difference, of course, was that this was the 1st time that the interior of the NB and an egg were exposed to bright light and external view.

[It has been suspected and suggested that some parrots prefer dark NB's, and that this is the basis for the preference for a NB with north-facing entrance holes (in the northern hemisphere), and for nestboxes with extremely deep interiors (27). However, a number of other factors also influence the location and orientation of nests in different species and habitats (60, 158).]

CLUE TO ANCIENT PRACTICES OF EGG CARE? It now seemed evident that one of the reasons why the birds were crouching or sitting lightly over the 1st egg, to the degree that they were, was because the egg was exposed to light and view. I felt sure that these responses to lights-on and lights-off were giving an important clue to practices of egg care in the remote past. Perhaps the main purposes for covering the eggs in daylight at some primeval time were to guard them and shield them from the direct sun and the eyes of predators, not to incubate them. In the dim light of night, the eggs did not require close attendance; they could be guarded without the parents actually being in their immediate vicinity.

LIGHT RESPONSES OCCUR DURING INCUBATORY PERIOD. Many times subsequently I observed the responses of leaving the eggs at the time of lights-off, or sometimes merely mounting the inside NB-perch or other nearby perch, and returning to them at the time of lights-on. Even during the period of incubation and very tight sitting, Carmen sometimes promptly left the eggs of this clutch at the time of lights-off. For example, this occurred on the nights of April 18 and 19, when she was incubating 3 eggs. On these occasions, she also returned immediately when I turned the lights back on, etc. The difference is that, on these latter occasions, she was only delaying a short recess (usually for the purpose of voiding) until after the lights were off; she would return to the clutch, anyway, within 30-60 sec. On the other hand, with only 1 or 2 eggs present, she usually left the NB for the entire night after lights-off.

[In an opaque NB, the eggs are neither exposed to view nor in bright light, so that the crouching or tightly-sitting birds "have no reason" to delay a brief exit for voiding until after dark. Recall that Cockatiels keep the NB "spotlessly clean" while incubating; they void outside of it. It is of interest to note in this connection that in the burrow-nesting Bonin Petrel the single egg of the clutch is not left uncovered by a parent during the day but the incubating bird usually leaves the nest briefly twice during the night. Since the adults of this species do not appear to soil the burrow during the incubatory period, it is suggested that these absences also are for the purpose of voiding or other maintenance activities (532). Rock Pigeons also retain excretory products during incubation; a female voids a very large mass of excreta shortly after her long incubative session, upon exchanging with her mate (1,011).]

LIGHT RESPONSES BY OTHER HENS. These responses to light occurred with 2 other breeding Cockatielian pairs, and in an even more convincing fashion. On one occasion, the responses were repeated so consistently that I found it superfluous to continue to elicit them. For a time the above-mentioned interpretation of this behavior eluded me. Obviously, the urgency of sitting over the eggs was gone, once there was no light (i.e., at night) but was restored in bright light (i.e., during the day).

Successive Stages of Cockatielian Egg Care Recapitulate Equivalents of Ancestral Evolutionary Stages

MANY PRIMITIVE FEATURES RETAINED. The impediment to deciphering the probable significance of the responses to light, at first, was that I kept thinking in terms of the act of crouching over or sitting lightly on the 1st 1 or 2 eggs during the day as being for the purpose of incubation. In that case, it would have been maladaptive not to continue to incubate them at night. Why not incubate the eggs around the clock and shorten the incubatory period?

But Carmen and Cosimo were giving me the answer, because they were not incubating the 1st egg; they were merely crouching low over it in very light contact, that is, they were only shielding and/or guarding it. Before advancing the proposed interpretation in detail, I introduce the following working hypotheses: I postulate that Cockatiels retain, among other primitive characters, a great many behavioral features that trace back to very ancient times in the reptilian-avian evolutionary lineage.

Further, I would suggest that Cockatiels adopted their current hole-nesting habit tens of millions of years ago, directly succeeding the most primitive nesting habit, namely, nesting on the surface of flat ground. As a result of the very safe and otherwise highly advantageous mode of nesting in holes, there has been no selective pressure to eliminate or alter the elements of egg-care behavior that are adaptive for nesting on flat ground, i.e., these elements have remained adaptively neutral in the hole-nesting Cockatiels. [Some workers have described such a response as "a phyletic holdover, with no real selective cost or benefit."] Accordingly, the earlier elements of egg-care behavior, though no longer required, underwent little or no secondary modification (i.e., they are ancestral, rather than derived, characters in this regard).

It was noted earlier that because of the highly conservative nature of the evolution of the central nervous system, behavioral evolution also tends to be highly conservative, particularly aspects of behavior that relate to vital breeding functions, such as egg care. In essence, the evolution of behavior tends to occur in hierarchical steps, each new facet being an elaboration or extension, rather than an outright replacement, of those that came before.

EGG CARE EVOLVED IN A SEQUENCE OF STAGES involving ever increasing attentiveness. Early reptiles merely buried their eggs deeply at shaded sites and left them entirely uncared for. The stem-reptiles in the avian lineage buried the eggs in shaded sites at very shallow depths, guarded the nest site closely, and shielded it from excessive solar radiation. Pre-aves oviposited at partially shaded surface sites and shielded and closely guarded the eggs, concealing them with vegetational debris during their absences. Finally, pro-aves and ancient and modern birds added incubation to the care of the eggs (see pp. 621-637, **A Synthesis of Avian Evolution**, and Table 3).

I further postulate that during the progress of each breeding cycle the sequence of appearance of egg-care behavior in many extant birds recapitulates the equivalents of the evolutionary stages of egg care (and even early chick care) of their ancestors. Since Cockatiels have retained, to an exceptionally great extent, primitive ground-nesting adaptations, they are ideal experimental animals for reconstructing these ancient adaptations and the probable sequence in which they were elaborated.

The interest in this phenomenon does not attach so much to the elucidation of the adaptations themselves. Some of these already are familiar from the habits of contemporary ground-nesters. Rather, the interest attaches to the fact that the neural circuitry for primitive ground-nesting behavior has been retained within the central nervous system of modern-day hole-nesters. The circuitry apparently has been retained for tens of millions of years, notwithstanding the fact that egg-care adaptations for ground nesting are very unlikely to be needed during the course of hole nesting.

ACCESSIBILITY OF NEURAL CIRCUITS. In a sense, I am proposing something akin to the Haeckelian "ontogeny recapitulates phylogeny," except that the phylogenetic sequence of appearance is not being recapitulated by an ontogenetic sequence but, rather, by the order of appearance of certain elements of an adult cyclic breeding pattern. I would suggest that what is involved here cosists merely of changes in utilized circuitry in the central nervous system, all of which circuits still are laid down (just as is that of, e.g., the human grasp reflex, which can be elicited in infants; see pp. 524, 525, **The Palmar Grasp Reflex**).

Inhibitory neurons are present from the earliest embryonic stages at which neural networks begin to generate bursts of activity, and inhibitory mechanisms underlie the precise adjustments resulting from sensory input that occur in post-hatching behavior (see 1,053 and S.M. Crain in Discussion and refs. in 1,277). During embryonic development in many organisms, some coordinated behaviors may be expressed only under permissive conditions. "That is, the neural circuitry may be present at a particular stage of development but the behavior may be produced only if neural inhibition or specific physical barriers are removed....thus, it must be kept in mind that the absence of behavior at one stage does not necessarily indicate the absence of the underlying neural circuitry" (1,337).

Elaboration of circuits and mobilization of successively-utilized pathways would appear to be consequences of physiological changes--principally changes in hormone levels--and the "opening" of antecedent pathways, in part, by the lifting of inhibitory influences, probably following more or less strictly hierarchical sequences. "....membrane or other micro or molecular changes could affect excitatory threshold conductance, and resistance to impulse transmission, or endogenous discharge properties, all within the already established morphological networks" (1,295). There is no question here of extensive reorganization of embryonic structures, the necessities for which, among other things, make it impossible for ontogeny truly to recapitulate phylogeny or ontogenetic stages thereof. In this connection, it has been suggested that, in the maturation of sensory neural pathways, early stages involve competition within a system; as new pathways become functional the new competition results in the disruption of stabilized circuitry and provides the basis for a more advanced organization (see 1,268).

There are obvious parallels here with the integration of nest-building behavior patterns of Canaries into functional sequences, in which the performance of one specific activity (and the accompanying altered endocrine state) leads to the stimulus for the next one (406). In the case of nest-building movements by Great Cormorants (Phalacrocorax carbo), the development of behavior during breeding proceeds as a rule in ascending "stages;" at the conclusion of a breeding season these "stages" are traversed in a descending order, only to develop again and again in subsequent years (505; see also A. Kortlandt, 1955, in 1,268).

Parallels also may be seen with the progress of female Ring Doves through the reproductive behavior cycle. The latter, for example, appears to be effected from one phase of breeding to the next by changes in endocrinological state consequent, at least in part, on past and current changes in stimuli to which the hen is exposed, some of which are imposed by the environment or her mate and some of which result from her own activity (714). The reproductive development of the male during the cycle similarly depends on a sequence of transitions in behavior that are related both to hormonal changes (including a massive surge in circulating testosterone, which field studies also have detected in other species; see 744) and the behavior of his mate (744, 750).

The above proposals regarding the early-occurring organization of central neural pattern-generating circuits are not inconsistent with the occurrence of extensive regressive changes in neuronal and glial cells during the later developmental organization of pathways of peripheral connectivity in vertebrate nervous systems (see 1,103). That these central circuits are laid down and can function before, and independently of, fully functional peripheral organization (pathways) is indicated (a) by the well-known occurrence of "impulsive" or spontaneous movements in the domestic fowl embryo before it is possible to elicit reflexogenic movements, (b) other findings in both vertebrates (birds, monkeys, mice) and invertebrates (crickets, locusts, moths, lobsters) that show that sensory input is not necessary for the development of motor circuits and normally-patterned locomotory movements, and (c) several studies that suggest that altered sensory input does not modify previously established motor connections; nor is any case known in which reflexes play a role in patterning embryonic motor behavior (see 1,337 and pp. 183-185).

It is becoming increasingly evident that, in general, regressive processes, often involving competition and functional mechanisms at the level of end organs, are an important feature in the ontogeny of vertebrate nervous systems. Various aspects of neurogenesis appear to depend as much on the elimination or loss, or suppression, of previously formed characteristics as on the attainment or formation of new characteristics. "Regressive processes such as cell death and the loss of synaptic connections may have arisen phylogenetically as necessary epigenetic mechanisms to compensate for individual nonheritable variations....during ontogeny." In the absence of such epigenetic canalizing mechanisms many mutations might lead to maladaptive quantitative mismatches between neurons and their targets (1,336).

HORMONES AND THE NERVOUS SYSTEM

ORGANIZATIONAL EFFECTS. In connection with the above postulate of the "opening" of neural circuits in hierarchical sequences by the actions of hormones, steroids are known to exert profound influences during pre- and perinatal life on the development of neural tissues destined to mediate sexual behavior, with resulting permanent modifications of such behavior and of sexual differentiation. Thus, testosterone and estradiol can organize neural circuits neonatally into a "male" or "female" brain (see 611, 1,027, 1,030). These are the so-called "organizational effects," which are characterized by a critical period and a high degree of irreversibility. These effects reflect direct actions of hormones on the growth of neural connections. In the Canary and Zebra Finch, close correlations can be drawn between aspects of the behavioral and neuronal differentiation (743). Of greater interest in the present connection are the so-called "activational effects" that have been observed in adult animals (260, 391).

ACTIVATIONAL EFFECTS are influences of hormones on behavior that are mediated in adulthood by a central action at the level of the brain. It is believed currently that steroids activate behavior by acting on the brain cells in a fashion similar to the action described in peripheral structures, such as the domestic fowl oviduct, the rat uterus, etc. Steroids would enter the brain cells passively, be transformed enzymatically to metabolites having higher and lower hormonal activities, bind to low-capacity, high-affinity cytoplasmic receptors, be translocated to the cell nucleus, etc. (743, 916, 1,022, 1,030). Activational effects have become the best-documented of the two types of effects. A small number of areas seem to be of paramount importance in the endocrine control of behavior. Thus, the preoptic-hypothalamic continuum (preoptic area and anterior and posterior hypothalamus) is one of the major sites of androgen and estrogen binding within the brain.

[No study has yet linked any normal developmental change in internal neuronal properties, such as threshold, refractory period, responsiveness, ionic conductance, size or form of the action potential or its ionic basis, size of synaptic area, or surface area of postsynaptic neurons, with a specific change in the functioning of a neural circuit involved in generating patterned motor output (1,337).]

Testosterone implants in the preoptic and anterior hypothalamic regions lead to the induction of copulatory behavior and/or sexual display in the domestic fowl. Implants of progesterone in these regions or in the lateral forebrain area of Ring Doves induce incubatory behavior in both sexes and inhibit courtship behavior in the male (see 989). In members of the latter sex, both courtship behavior and aggression are induced by testosterone (which becomes converted to estrogen; see p. 116) implants in the same areas, but the two effects could not be dissociated (260, 262, 989); only implants in these specific areas are effective in restoring sexual behavior in castrated males (744). Restoration of nest-material collection, chasing, Bow-cooing, Nest-cooing, and copulation, after castration of male Ring Doves, could be achieved only by implanting androgen in certain regions of the hypothalamus (see 989, 1,000). Specific binding sites for progesterone are present in both the cytosols and nuclear fractions of the hypothalamus of the domestic fowl hen (as well as in the hypophysis and in the magnum of the oviduct; 1,133).

Estradiol implants in the nucleus medialis hypothalami posterioris of ovariectomized Ring Doves stimulated sexual crouching and nest soliciting, and this nucleus is the crucial area in the mediation of courtship by estradiol (265). Strong copulatory responses are elicited in young domestic fowl chicks by testosterone implants in the preoptic region (263, 264). The aromatase system that converts testosterone to 17-beta-estradiol is present in the preoptic area of male Ring Doves. The estradiol so formed probably is involved in inducing nest-oriented courtship behavior. The 5-beta reductase system also is present and apparently is involved in regulating the sensitivity of the brain to androgens (see 1,000). [Aromatization of androgens to estrogens in the central nervous system of turtles may supply the active hormone for central neural integrative activity related to reproduction, and specific areas of the brain are known to concentrate steroidal sex-hormones in lizards (genus *Anolis*; see 1,318).]

THE VARIETY OF POSSIBLE NEUROCHEMICAL EFFECTS OF ESTRADIOL serve to generate a model of steroidal hormonal action on neurons. First, there are alterations in oxidative metabolism of neural tissue, and of the hypophysis as well, that may provide increased amounts of energy for neuronal function. Second, there may be hormonally-induced alterations in synthetic and degradative enzymes for neurotransmitters and releasing hormones. Third, there also may be hormonally-induced alterations in the number of postsynaptic receptors for neurotransmitters. Thus, genomic effects of steroidal hormones may well result in altered neuronal and synaptic efficiency within developmentally fixed neural pathways (1,030), leading to changes in the utilized circuitry.

CONTROL OF VOCAL BEHAVIOR. Similarly, the nucleus intercollicularis of the midbrain is involved in the control of vocal behavior in a number of avian species in at least two orders, and the central mechanisms that control avian vocalization are now one of the best understood systems of the neuroendocrine control of behavior. Gonadal hormones act directly on neurons in some nuclei of the vocal system. Testosterone apparently acts at several levels to control passerine singing behavior, in addition to its control of syringeal musculature (260). Song learning is affected by the hormonal state of the young bird but is not rigidly constrained to an age-dependent sensitivity period; rather the sensitivity period follows the crystallization of song, whenever it occurs, and it may re-open seasonally. Early singing by young male Zebra Finches can be induced by injections of testosterone but there seems to be a point prior to which juvenile song cannot be induced, perhaps because components of the central nervous system have not yet matured (see 1,150).

Estradiol implants in the nucleus intercollicularis restore the Nest-coo in ovariectomized Ring Doves, testicular implants have the same effect in castrated males, and lesions in the nucleus reduce Nest-cooing in otherwise intact males, all of which suggests that one function of the nucleus intercollicularis is to mediate Nest-cooing (265, 751, 989). Castrated Rock Pigeons bearing testosterone implants in the anterior hypothalamus undergo the vocal break at the same age as do controls (997).

In addition, there are good reasons to believe that steroidal binding in the hyperstriatum ventrale is related to the control of vocalization in songbirds and indirect evidence suggests that hormonal effects there take part in the imprinting of young nidifuges (260). There also is a distinct nucleus, the nucleus magnocellularis neostriatalis anterioris, of songbirds that strongly accumulates (binds) testosterone. Since this nucleus projects to an area involved in song control, this uptake may relate to androgenic modulation of song. Lastly, nest material collection by Ring Doves is activated by testosterone acting in the preoptic-anterior hypothalamic area and, secondarily, on the ventral neostriatum intermediale (266).

Technical advances in recent years have allowed the accurate placement of electrodes in different regions of the avian brain, with the observation of the effects of selective electrical stimulation and electrolytic lesions. The results of these studies highlight the complex nature of the control mechanisms that regulate reproductive behavior. There are clearly areas in the brain that exert a direct and immediate effect on sexual display. Steroidal sex-hormones may affect behavior and reproduction through these centers or by other means. Changes in FSH and LH are both causes and consequences of the steroidal secretions. Stimulation of specific areas within the hypothalamus of Japanese Quail, e.g., causes the release of LH, while electrolytic lesions lead to gonadal atrophy (see 1,000, 1,132).

EGG CARE BY PRE-COURTING, COURTING, AND COPULATING COCKATIELS. In the light of this introduction, consider that the most primitive pattern of egg care after oviposition and burial or concealment is simply none at all--the predominating method among extant reptiles. This is the equivalent of the 1st phylogenetic stage of egg care. It is recapitulated in the egg care of non-courting, adult Cockatiels (and even juveniles). When experienced Cockatiels are in non-breeding condition between broods, and they accidentally expose a buried egg, or are given an egg, the egg usually is an object of great interest. They may touch it and move it about, repeatedly tuck it beneath themselves momentarily, and even compete mildly or vigorously for it, but they usually do not relocate it to a former IA, and they do not shield or guard it. The physiological state of the bird has not opened (i.e., lowered the threshold for activation of, or disinhibited) the neural circuitry that leads to stimulation of guarding, shielding, or incubating response.

But once experienced Cockatiels have begun to court, and coitus has occurred, hormonal concentrations change, and neural circuitry corresponding to the next stage in the phylogenetic pathway begins to be mobilized. Then, the birds shield and guard fostered eggs during the day, but leave them at night (but in a NB the eggs may be guarded from the inside perch or nearby). They care for the eggs the more attentively during the day, the farther along the hen has progressed toward the phase of oviposition. In this case, one is dealing with the state of egg care reached at the time of laying the 1st and 2nd egg. This is the equivalent of the 2nd phylogenetic stage of egg care.

Contemporary Timing and Sharing of Egg Attentiveness

Inexperienced Cockatiels may shield or guard the 1st egg or 2 very little or not at all, particularly at night (see pp. 473-476, 480, 481, 486, 487, 491, 495, 496). Similarly, when a Bengalese Finch occasionally lays but one egg (5 or 6 eggs is most common), the egg is not incubated (130); endocrine control has not yet opened the neural circuitry that leads to the "release" of incubatory behavior. After the laying of the 2nd egg, though, the circuitry has "opened" and the 2 eggs are incubated. The first Brown Kiwi egg may be left unattended for 2-6 days (1,406).

Ostriches, rheas, rails, and woodpeckers usually do not begin incubating the eggs until shortly before completion of the clutch, although males of the Common Rhea begin incubating on about the 3rd day. Incubation begins with the penultimate egg in the Red-billed Quela and Bobolink. Ducks, geese, gamebirds, and most passerines do not begin to incubate until the last egg is laid, or 10 days afterward in the Rock Partridge (*Alectoris graeca*) and the Bobwhite Quail (28, 155, 216, 954, 968, 1,266). The Great Tit hen, for example, does not begin to incubate until 0.33 ± 1.55 days before completing the clutch, while for the Blue Tit the figures are 0.62 ± 1.25 days, and the incubation may begin gradually (489).

Snowy Plover (*Charadrius alexandrinus*) males incubate 16.6 ± 3.0% and females incubate 10.3 ± 2.7% of the time during the day during the period of oviposition. Sustained incubation typically begins after the last egg is laid. The males then incubate 9.5 ± 3.3% and the females incubate 79.7 ± 3.4% of the daytime period. The males are believed to incubate at night (73 dusk checks of the nests showed 90.4% male occupancy; 1,130). Attentiveness of Wilson's Plover (*C. wilsonia*) was low during the ovipositional period and consisted mainly of egg shading by the male during the heat of day, with little warming of the eggs at night. During this period, the male's share of the attentiveness was 63%, whereas during incubation it was only 30%, with the male incubating at night (1,222).

Black-headed Gulls that are nesting in isolation from other pairs abandon the clutch regularly at night up to 16 days after clutch completion, and nighttime incubation sets in only gradually. Though this behavior has been interpreted solely in terms of nighttime vulnerability of the parents to predators (see 737), the readiness with which it occurs also may reflect gradual or delayed attainment of the 3rd phylogenetic stage of egg care. This also may be the basis for the incubatory behavior of Mountain

White-crowned Sparrows. They begin some degree of daytime incubation beginning with the 1st egg but delay nocturnal incubation until after they have laid the penultimate egg (1,106; see also p. 444).

On the other hand, some birds begin to sit on or crouch over the eggs from the time the 1st egg is laid. This is true of storks, grebes, divers, pelicans, gannets, herons, raptors, and sandgrouse. It sometimes is true also of the Sociable Weaver (*Philetairus socius*), though usually incubation begins with the 2nd egg. However, these instances of sitting on or crouching over eggs, beginning with the 1st, may be primarily a matter of shielding and protecting the incomplete clutch (158, 968, 1,266). This is recognized in Rock Pigeons, which sit in the nest, in turn, from the time the 1st egg is laid, but usually do not begin to incubate until the arrival of the 2nd egg (1,011). Continuous nest attendance in many of these birds is essential to prevent depredations by corvids and other predators as well as for preventing interference by conspecifics among colonial nesters (1,266).

In the case of indeterminate egg-layers, it is believed that the tactile stimulus of the full-sized clutch of eggs somehow stimulates the anterior pituitary to secrete prolactin. This induces regression of the ovarian activity (i.e., inhibits the ripening of follicles; see p. 148) and initiates (opens the neural circuitry for) broodiness or incubation of the completed clutch (28; see also pp. 569-571, **Within an Endocrinological Framework**).

If inexperienced Ring Doves are injected with progesterone, they will incubate eggs; if, in addition, they are given prolactin, they also will allofeed the young; but they do neither if given prolactin alone (28). Thus, the influences of oviposition and antecedent breeding behavior can be achieved, or substituted for, by progesterone but not by prolactin. Both given together open the neural circuits for incubating and early brooding, and the presence of the eggs and young stimulates the appropriate behavior. Incubating and brooding, in turn, lead to the opening of the terminal neural circuits for later care of the young.]

NEED TO REOPEN NEURAL PATHWAYS EACH BREEDING CYCLE. With each successive breeding cycle, all the neural pathways for successive behaviors in courtship, nest-building (perhaps), coitus, oviposition, incubation, and brooding, have to be opened anew in proper sequence. Once opened, or made accessible, the length of time for which they remain open, after completion of the clutch, varies in members of different species whose oviposition is indeterminate.

In many small birds, the neural pathways for stimulating oviposition remain accessible for a time after completion of the clutch. In these the loss of an entire clutch can be made up with only a brief delay, with the 1st egg of the replacement clutch being laid within 4-5 days (see E. Stresemann, 1927-1934, in 28). In the Song Sparrow, the first replacement egg is laid in only 5 days, an average of 6.2 days are required in the Great Tit, 6-7 days in Pied Flycatchers, 8 days in European Starlings, and 7.7 days in lapwings (22 cases; 313, 489). In other indeterminate ovipositors, the neural circuitry for oviposition is closed upon the completion of the clutch, and all the breeding preliminaries usually have to be repeated in sequence to reopen them.

[Similar phenomena are known in reptiles. For example, some lizards roll their eggs about to various ends, such as in burying one in a nest, to more favorable substrates, and to relocate a disturbed nest. But only females that had recently oviposited exhibited these behaviors. Green Anole females that had not oviposited recently ignored nearby eggs, either being rolled by a maternal female or placed near them, in circumstances in which females that had oviposited recently would have cared for the eggs (938).]

SHORTENING INCUBATORY TIME WITH BOTH CLIMATIC AND SURFACE HEAT. Returning now to the main thread, namely, the matter of the pre-avian method of egg care at which I hinted above. The method of egg care suggested by the Cockatielian responses to lights-off and lights-on is that of oviposition at the surface, utilizing both climatic heat and surface heat (indirect and direct solar radiation), rather than bodily heat, to accelerate embryonic development, as opposed to utilizing essentially only climatic heat in nests located at a shallow or considerable depth. This is the postulated 2nd phylogenetic stage of egg care.

It is significant that Cockatielian hens do not leave the eggs until after lights-off and resume shielding them after lights-on (either when the latter occurs shortly after turning them off or the next morning). This suggests very strongly that, in the corresponding ancestral stage, eggs were shielded by the parental body in the period before sunset and beginning again after sunrise. Such a practice suggests that the early morning and evening shielding were for the purpose of concealment from overhead (and high-angle) view, while at the same time allowing exposure to direct, low-angle solar radiation.

One reaches this conclusion because, if concealment alone were the function of this behavior, it would have been adaptive for the ancestors to have achieved it merely with a covering of vegetational debris, which would have freed the pre-aves to forage or engage in other essential activities, even if only in alternation. The practice of warming the eggs by means of direct and indirect solar radiation (including exposure to low-angle insolation) but leaving them unattended at night, presupposes that the ancestors at that stage were ectothermic. Accordingly, it is proposed that the Cockatielian light responses harken back to very ancient, post-reptilian times--the ectothermic pre-avian stage of Table 3--before eggs were incubated by bodily heat.

SHIELDING, SHADING, CONCEALING, GUARDING, AND INCUBATING EGGS

The practice of standing or crouching low over the eggs by the pre-avian ancestors of birds would have been to guard them, shield them, prevent excessive exposure to high-angle solar radiation, and allow direct exposure at low angles. Judging from the fact that diurnal birds today generally are active during the brighter half of civil twilight (the interval between sunset or sunrise and the time when the true position of the sun is 6° below the horizon), there would have been a total period of not less than 22 min, at the equator, to 27 min, at 30° latitude, and up to 65 min at latitudes up to 60° (1,052), before sunrise and after sunset, when both pre-avian parents could have foraged, before and after standing over the eggs to allow exposure to direct, low-angle insolation. These also are times when many insects are most active. [The probable critical need for shading from high angle radiation is emphasized by the fact that crocodile (Crocodylus) embryos, for example, are susceptible to midday overheating and direct solar radiation even during the short periods when the nests are unpacked by investigators to inspect the eggs (665).]

Presumably, the eggs merely would have been concealed with a thin cover of vegetational or other ground litter in mid-morning and late afternoon when the ambient temperature was favorable for embryonic development. At such times both parents could have foraged. At night, the eggs probably were buried under a well-insulating and warming layer of decaying vegetational debris (see pp. 630, 631, **Warmth Provided by Decomposing Vegetational Debris,** *et seq.*) and continued to be guarded, but there would have been no need to stand directly over them. In fact, such close guarding might have been maladaptive, in needlessly exposing the parents and revealing the position of the nest to nocturnal predators. The importance of a surface covering over eggs at night, even only from the point of view of insulative protection, can be appreciated from the findings on heat loss from domestic duck eggs. During the initial stages of development, heat is lost principally by evaporative water loss across the shell, but in the 2nd half of the incubatory period, this proportion declines, to less than 10% toward hatching. With exposed eggs, both convective losses and radiative losses increase in importance, from about 25% each on day 12 to about 45% each on day 26 (see V.V. Khaskin, 1961, in 1,150).

Contemporary Practices

Various practices of contemporary birds are of interest as regards these postulated practices of avian ancestors. For example, when the hole-nesting Blue Tit enters the nest cavity in the evening, she immediately removes the nesting material that usually is left covering the eggs during the daytime. She then begins to incubate the eggs. But during the early part of the period of oviposition, she incubates only a short time before standing in the nest cavity and remaining standing in sleeping posture for the rest of the night. Just before leaving the nest in the morning, she oviposits and then again covers the eggs with nesting material. As the clutch grows, she incubates increasingly longer, until, during the last nights of the ovipositional period, she incubates continuously all night (664). Similar behavior has been described in the Coal Tit (*Parus ater*; see S. Haftorn, 1966, in 1,053). Of this interesting mosaic of elements of past habits of egg care, the most interesting in the present connection is that of guarding the eggs from within the nest cavity during nights in the stage prior to all-night incubation, as does the Cockatielian hen at times.

Mountain White-crowned Sparrows attend the eggs irregularly during the period of oviposition. Females begin to tend the eggs on the day the 1st egg is laid, with most visits occurring at midday, when the hens sometimes shield the eggs from the sun by standing in an upright position over them, often with the wings spread beyond the nest rim and panting heavily. Periods of absence from the nest tend to be long in the cold hours of the morning and brief at midday when exposure of the egg to solar heat can be critical and attentiveness by the female is essential. As oviposition continues, the number of visits to, and total time in, the nest increases markedly. The eggs generally are neglected at night until after the penultimate egg is laid, when steady incubation commences. But even during the incubatory period, the embryos are exposed to low temperatures (17- 30°C) for short periods when the hens leave the nest to forage in the near vicinity. Hatchability regularly is above 90% and mean daytime attentiveness during the incubatory period is 74½ ± 1.4% (1,108).

Many contemporary open-country birds in temperate and tropical regions shade their eggs by standing over them to keep them cool in hot summer weather, for example, Common Nighthawks (*Chordeiles minor*), Lesser Nighthawks (*C. acutipennis*), Three-banded Sand-Plovers (*Charadrius tricollaris*), and Wilson's Plover (28, 214 1,222). Double-banded Coursers (*Rhinoptilus* africanus) and Yellow-wattled Lapwings (*Vanellus malabaricus*) may leave the eggs unattended at air temperatures of 20- 30°C. When air temperature and body temperature are about the same, they merely shade the eggs, whereas if air temperature exceeds body temperature, they maintain contact with them (60, 158). In the latter case, the action of keeping the eggs cool is shifted to one of keeping the parent cool, so that it can prevent the ambient heat from reaching the eggs. Egg attentiveness of Dusky Flycatchers (*Empidonax oberholseri*) in the summer in the high Sierras (about 3,000 m altitude) of California is greatest at midday, and this may be a general pattern of behavior of open-nesting birds at high altitudes that has evolved because of the susceptibility of the eggs to damage by direct, high-angle insolation (277).

Desert-nesting Mourning Doves practice facultative hypothermy (271). In air temperatures of 44-46°C, they maintain the eggs at 40°C or below by close contact with their relatively cool bodies, maintained near 38°C. White-winged Doves (*Zenaida asiatica*) behave very similarly in the deserts of Arizona (see 427). The Three-banded Sand-Plovers in Southwest Africa scarcely ever leave the exposed eggs uncovered in direct sunlight when shade temperatures are 49°C or more, and they are not easily frightened off the nest (see J.D. Macdonald, 1957, in 311).

Seven species of Charadriiformes nesting in the Salton Sea area of southeastern California transported water to their eggs and chicks via the ventral plumage after belly-soaking (214). Their nesting environment is one of the harshest in the world. The summer nesting season is characterized by intense solar radiation, an almost total lack of cloud cover, open ground temperatures exceeding 50°C almost daily, and the maximum daily air temperature in the shade reaching or exceeding 37.8°C on an average of 110 days per year.

The birds do not avoid the hottest season. They oviposit on the ground, sometimes without nest lining, and generally avoid vegetation and other sources of shade (presumably as an anti-predator strategy). Egg temperatures are maintained below lethal levels by 100% attentiveness, minimum exposure time during nest exchanges (even a 1-min exposure of eggs during nest exchanges can lead to marked temperature changes), and belly-soaking (also probably important in cooling the attending bird, cooling the chicks, and maintaining nest humidity). Even a 2-min exposure to high temperatures and solar radiation can destroy a clutch. For example, a brief, rapid climb of temperature to 47.7°C was lethal for a hatching Black-necked Stilt chick (*Himantopus mexicanus*; 214).

Brown Thrashers (*Toxostoma rufum*) spent only a small portion of their time shading their young when temperatures were below 30°C but the amount of time increased sharply at higher temperatures. At times when the sun shone on the nest, they did not begin to shade until ambient temperatures reached 20°C; thereafter the time spent shading increased exponentially with the amount of sunlight striking the nest (223). Whenever possible, the nestlings occupied a shaded portion of the nest. In the case of Herring Gulls, which are 98% attentive to the eggs (738), lethal internal egg temperatures were reached in an abandoned nest within 2 h on a sunny morning when air temperature in the shade was only 18°C (737). [The Herring Gull nest is on the ground and the eggs lie in a bed of dry grass (738).]

A nesting Gray Partridge (*P. perdix*) hen observed closely in a large aviary during the ovipositional period (in conjunction with detailed temperature measurements) treated the eggs in such a manner as to compensate for the temperature regime that prevailed at the times of her inspection visits. In cool conditions, the eggs merely were concealed with a layer of straw. As the temperature increased, she added a layer of earth. Finally, at high temperatures, she covered the eggs with earth by day, and opened the nest, allowing it to cool, through the night (see P. Krüger, 1965, in 158). In the same vein, during the ovipositional phase, the Black-tailed Godwit (*L. limosa*) hen places an insulating cover on the eggs at night, particularly at low ambient temperatures when there is danger that the embryos might freeze; the parents do not otherwise visit the nest at this time (see H. Lind, 1961, in 737). Many extant birds also protect nestlings from direct sun for hours, by standing over them with wings spread (28).

[Covering unattended eggs, for whatever purpose, is well known in Temperate Zone species of grebes and waterfowl (Anatidae) as well as in S. American screamers (Anhimidae) and tinamous (Tinamidae), at least 13 species of waders (Charadrii) in the tropics, and kiwis (Apterygidae; see 1,150, 1,406; see also p. 527).]

SHADING EGGS AND THERMAL PROBLEMS. It could be argued, based on contemporary analogies, that eggs that were shaded by an ectothermic, non-feathered early post-reptilian ancestor of birds might not have been protected effectively for very long periods from the heat of direct insolation, merely by the interposition of the body and a thin layer of vegetational debris (though they would, of course, have been shielded from the lethal effects of direct exposure). Since the shading body and vegetation eventually also would have heated up, they would have become less effective as heat shields. For example, even shaded eggs buried partially or totally at shallow depths in dry sand could overheat fatally on an average day at the Salton Sea (214, and p. 445).

In fact, in the absence of ameliorating convective effects (calculated increase in rate of heat loss of 10%/m/sec increase in wind speed; see 967), even contemporary birds, with the full advantages of advanced homeothermic mechanisms can encounter severe heat loads when shading eggs and young with their bodies (157). Thus, desert and non-desert inhabiting avian species alike are capable of tolerating body temperatures approximating 46°C (controlled hyperthermia) only for brief periods (829).

Available mechanisms of regulation of body temperature by incubating and brooding birds that are shading eggs or young include: insulative feathers; cutaneous evaporative cooling and evaporative cooling by panting and/or gular flutter; postural orientation with regard to the sun (to minimize heat gain) and wind (to maximize convective cooling); appropriate modification of plumage, such as compression of the contour plumage, exposure of the thinly feathered sides of the thorax by holding the wings out from the body, and elevating the scapular feathers so that convection is increased while a barrier to solar radiation is maintained (see 37, 497, 829); frequent relief at the nest; standing in water; and adjustment of contact with the eggs between the extremes of merely shading them to sitting on them tightly (214). For example, nesting Spotted Sandgrouse in the Namib Desert stand over the eggs, face into cool oceanic winds, and droop their wings from their sides, exposing the thinly feathered axillary areas and increasing convective cooling (830), and probably facilitating cutaneous water evaporation (see 1,219).

[The Namib is one of the most "total" deserts in the world. Its barren gravel plains and naked sand dunes are said to be matched only in the harshest parts of the Sahara and the Middle East (835 and p. 246). In connection with the above, reflectance of sunlight (visible solar radiation) is high (9-88%) from very light-colored to albino birds but low (3-15%) from dark-colored or black birds, but increases in the near infrared (422).]

REDUCED METABOLIC RATES---HYPERTHERMIA. As in a number of desert homeothermic endotherms, 3 species of desert-nesting sandgrouse (*Pterocles* spp.) appear to have lower metabolic rates than expected on the basis of allometric relations, leading to lesser food requirements and lesser metabolic heat production and heat loads. The birds also time their periods of physical exertion to the cooler periods of the day when metabolic heat can be dispersed most readily by passive means; they are reluctant to fly during the heat of day. Certain species maintain a body temperature of 41°C despite ambient air temperatures in excess of 51°C. Other species tolerate some measure of hyperthermia. Thus, female *P. alchata*, *P. coronatus*, and *P. senegallus*, incubating eggs in full sunlight in Morroco (males generally incubate at night), increase their insulation at an ambient temperature of 40-41°C but do not gular flutter until ambient temperature exceeds 50°C, as opposed to commencement of gular fluttering at an ambient temperature of 43-45°C in *P. namaqua* and *P. bicinctus* in the Namib desert. Moreover, the hyperthermic Morrocan species were virtually immobile during daytime incubation (830).

MILDER CLIMATES: LESS DEMANDING REQUIREMENTS FOR BODILY SHADING. At the times in question, however (perhaps the early Jurassic period or even earlier), climates were much milder than today. [Although the climates of the late Permian were cool and seasonal, a gradual upward shift in the paleotemperatures began and continued into the early Cretaceous period (182, 413; see also pp. 573, 621).] Requirements for bodily shading may have been less demanding in times of greater equability, particularly in view of the effectiveness of free and forced convective (and conductive) cooling for small animals (and eggs). Furthermore, both parents doubtless cooperated in the shading and other care of the eggs.

MILDER CLIMATES: SELECTIVE FORCE FOR EVOLUTION OF SURFACE NESTING. In fact, I would suggest that it was precisely the advent of the equable climates of those times, with their higher average surface temperatures, that was the crucial change. It would seem to have been the factor that facilitated the evolutionary transition from burying the eggs at depths (at which losses through predation were reduced and exposure to lethally high temperatures and other environmental fluctuations was avoided) to employing exposed surface nests and giving the eggs and young close parental care.

FEATHER PRECURSORS AS SHADING AIDS. Further, there is no reason to preclude the presence of precursors of feathers in the form of feather-like modifications of scales in the stem-reptilian ancestors of birds and/or the following pre-avian stage. The existence of elongated and enlarged body scales as feather precursors and shields (particularly when raised) against the heat of direct solar radiation has been suggested by Regal recently (170; a primordial function of feathers proposed earlier by Cowles; 633). Such elongated, raised scales could shade the body and absorb heat on their exposed surfaces, dissipating it to the air. They would have had the effect of slowing the rate of heating of the body in the sun and of producing a lower body temperature for an animal in equilibrium with heat loads and sinks, thereby permitting the extension of exposure times and activity, and pre-adapting the animal for the evolution of endothermy (170, 1,182). There also are cogent reasons to believe that the first feathers--evolved from scales for their insulative properties--as suggested by Fürbringer in 1888, were of the down-feather type (795). In this connection, reptiles would appear to be preadapted to tolerate excessive cutaneous temperatures, since behavioral thermoregulation can be initiated solely by the stimulation of central receptors (1,109).

[In one view, the insulation afforded by plumage would have become advantageous only after an intensification of metabolism that had decreased the dependence of a nascent homeotherm on solar heating, since feathers would have retarded the absorption of solar radiation (966). However, this would appear to be valid only: (a) as applied to modified scales in the highly specialized feather form (as in *Archaeopteryx* and contemporary birds), rather than to a very primitive insulative change in scales; (b) on the unlikely assumption of an absence of mechanisms of controlling the erection, and/or separation, or orientation of modified scales (or the entire body) to suit the thermal regime (gradual, progressive control of feathers is well known in in birds, as is control of mammalian hair); and (c) on the assumption of climatic conditions far less favorable to ectotherms or nascent endotherms than those of the Mesozoic. The conditions probably did not apply to stem-reptiles and/or pre-aves. In this connection, once heated, lizards with enlarged, raised scales, basking near heat lamps in the laboratory, turn so as to obtain maximum scale shading. There is no orientation at which the scales intensify the uptake of heat (1,182).

It is of interest, in connection with feather precursors, that thecodont-like tetrapods (*Longisquama insignis* sp. nov.) of the lower Triassic period possessed long dorsal plumes made up of individual, prominently-bordered, feather-like appearing structures (180; for a discussion and review of other fossil evidence of feather-like structures and avian-like reptiles or possible reptile-bird transitional forms, see 170, 289).

Of interest also is the fact that the origin and early evolution of insect wings very likely traces to an initial thermoregulatory function in increasing body temperatures by the absorption of solar radiation, allowing longer and more vigorous periods of activity in the climates of the Devonian or early Carboniferous period (see Table 1). They could have functioned very effectively in this capacity at the small bodily sizes of the earliest insects, particularly if the early "wings" could have been moved in the adjustment of orientation (1,234). Though heat conductivity in the highly specialized wings of contemporary insects is quite small, although the basal regions are important in thermoregulation, the fossil record suggests that the wings of early insects were thicker and more heavily venated and contained more hemolymph than do the wings of contemporary forms (see 1,234).]

SURFACE NESTING

ADVANTAGES. The advantages of surface nesting and employing the heat of solar radiation directly are that they shorten an otherwise very long embryonic period and that they more closely circumscribe the time of occurrence of the embryonic period (see also pp. 593, 594, 629-631). The shorter the length, and the more certain the time of occurrence of embryonic development, the shorter would be the period of vulnerability of the eggs and the more control the reproducing animals would have over the extent of exposure of the eggs to unfavorable conditions.

BRINGS POWERFUL SELECTIVE FORCES INTO PLAY. The practice of ovipositing at the surface of the ground in shallow scrapes, rather than in protected, non-surface sites, would have brought powerful new selective forces into play. The ultimate reason for this is that unattended eggs in surface locations, even if concealed with a covering layer of vegetational debris, or other material, would have been very much more vulnerable to predation and the elements than unattended eggs that were buried in deep nests or otherwise concealed at non-surface locations.

The very significant threat that predation can pose is illustrated by the fact that the continuous incubatory habit of many monogamous avian species is primarily a response to predation pressure (see also pp. 555-557, **The Great Vulnerability of the Eggs and Young**). For example, in the absence of an incubating parent, predation is heavy on the nests of the solitary species, the Green Sandpiper (*Tringa ochropus*) and the Common Loon (*Gavia immer*), especially by corvids (431). Biparental care, of course, allows eggs to be attended almost continuously without imparing adult health. An extreme example of biparental care in response to the pressure of predation is seen in 43 of 45 species of hornbills. Among these, the female is sealed within the nest chamber and receives food from the male through a small hole (see A.C. Kemp, 1978, in 431).

IMPLIES CLOSE PARENTAL ATTENDANCE TO EGGS. But there would have been no advantage to shortening and more closely circumscribing the period of vulnerability of the eggs if their vulnerability were excessively increased during the shorter period. In other words, a shorter period of embryonic development utilizing direct solar radiation would have been unproductive unless accompanied by very close, virtually 100%, attendance of the parents to the safety of the developing embryos. This is evident merely from the fact that even a single period of overheating of eggs would doom a clutch. Accordingly, it was mandatory that eggs laid in exposed surface scrapes receive extremely close parental attention. The powerful new selective forces, to which I refer above, are those for this close parental care.

CLOSE ATTENDANCE TO EGGS IMPLIES A CLOSE ATTENTION TO HATCHLINGS, which would have represented a greater investment of reproductive effort than the eggs. If parents were in close attendance to eggs they would have been present at hatching time, in which case it would have been adaptive to groom and protect the hatchlings. This degree of attention to the hatchlings would very likely have led to escorting them to foraging grounds and back to the nest (with its many advantages as a site for spending the night together).

In other words, it is suggested that the evolutionary transition to direct-solar-radiation-assisted development of embryos at surface sites would have been accompanied by development of the practices of grooming and protecting hatchlings, and escorting nestling (nidifugous) young. If one were to be guided solely by the present-day care of birds with nidifugous young, one would conclude that the young at that time probably were escorted to and from hunting grounds, where they could have shared in parental kills, rather than having had food brought to them at the nest.

MONOGAMY A LIKELY PREREQUISITE. One can carry one step further the implications of surface nesting and utilization of the heat of direct insolation by the early post-reptilian ancestors of birds (pre-aves of Table 3). Thus, the requirement for very close parental attention to eggs and young by ectothermic ancestors implies that both parents shared in the care. Only in this way could the safety of the eggs have been assured at all times, through the medium of the parents alternating in attendance during periods of greatest heat stress or other critical demands. Even in less demanding circumstances than those envisioned, it has been argued that avian reproduction typically is maximized when both parents invest their time and energy in its pursuit (34).

Even if shared parental care were not necessary to allow foraging (if one parent fasted the entire period), it would have been a means of obviating the problem of thermally overstressing the shielding parent when the sun was high in the sky (see pp. 444-447). Accordingly, the transition from nesting in non-surface sites to nesting in surface sites implies both parental care of the eggs and of the early post-hatching young and the monogamous sharing of this care. Accordingly, monogamy was a likely prerequisite for the evolution of surface nesting and endothermy in an oviparous stem-reptilian stock. [If an insectivorous parent brought food to the brooding mate, the likelihood that the young also were fed at the nest would be greatly increased.]

A NEST OF HERBIVOROUS DINOSAUR YOUNG. This scheme receives strong support from a recent discovery concerning herbivorous, duck-billed, ornithician dinosaurs (Hadrosauridae, the latest and most specialized family of ornithipods to appear; 877). These creatures, 9½-16½ m in length, had extremely large forebrains for dinosaurs, and their cranial crests suggest that they engaged in complex patterns of social behavior (407, 877). An apparently bowl-shaped nest of fossilized skeletons of 15 young was found in Late Cretaceous sediments (of 70-80 mya) in Montana (168). The evidence suggests that these reptiles nested in large, densely-packed colonies and guarded their eggs. In fact, even the practice of reproduction based upon the production of a small number of relatively large (energetically expensive) eggs would appear to be strong presumptive evidence of an extensive investment of parental care in its various forms (1,175).

From the wear on the teeth of the young, it could be concluded that they had been chewing and grinding food for some time. Moreover, the nestlings (about 100 cm long) already had grown to about thrice the size of hatchlings (about 30-35 cm long). It seems reasonable to conclude from these findings, that the young of these reptiles received parental care and protection over a period of, at least, months. It is not unlikely that they were fed at the nest, at first, and escorted between the nest and feeding grounds when they were old enough to forage (they appear to have been relatively fast runners; 168). In this connection, it is of interest that iguanas often sleep and forage together for at least several months after hatching, and confined newborn colubrid snakes tend to aggregate selectively with conspecifics (see 602). [The stem-reptilian ancestors of birds, however, doubtless were predators and there is no reason to believe that the nidifugous hatchlings or nestlings of a predaceous grade of preavis were fed by their parents.]

EVOLUTION OF PARENTAL CARE AND INCREASED TERRESTRIALITY IN ANURANS. In concluding this discussion of surface nesting, it gives additional perspective to recount briefly portions of McDiarmid's evolutionary scheme for the evolution of parental care and increased terrestriality in anurans (frogs), which occurs in roughly 10% of all species (see also pp. 577, 578, **Anuran Parental Care**). His scheme gains considerable support from the spectrum of parental care habits of contemporary anurans, principally among tropical species that oviposit on land (601; see, also, 606).

"As the selective advantages of increasing parental care manifested themselves, initially eggs, and then eggs and larvae were tended by one of the parents. In some situations selection favored male attendance; in others it favored that of the female parent. As selection for maintaining or providing the larvae with a suitable 'aquatic habitat' out of the water became stronger, parental care became more and more important. As a result, the nature of parental care expanded from an initial one of egg attendance only, to include attendance of later stages, larval transport, and brooding."

In the case of the stem-reptilian to pre-avian ancestors of birds the transition was from oviposition in shallow excavations, and burying eggs for the entire period of incubation, to ovipositing at the surface and concealing, excavating, shielding, and guarding the eggs, as required; in the case of anurans, it was from oviposition in water to oviposition on land. Both transitions brought very similar selective forces into play and both probably were largely responses to predator pressures. It is important to recognize, however, that there are fundamental differences between parental care in anurans and birds, chiefly the facts that anuran parental care is less costly and not crucial (606).

SECOND EGG LAID. Resuming the topic of egg care by Carmen and Cosimo, at 20:30 h on the day after the 1st experiment in which the lights were turned on and off in alternation late at night, Carmen had not yet entered the NB, but 1 h later she was inside. At 21:50 h I was surpised to find both parents busily inspecting objects in the IA, whereupon I realized that the 2nd egg probably had been laid, and that they likely were inspecting the 2-egg clutch. Shortly thereafter, Cosimo was trying to exchange with Carmen in the care of the eggs, but she would not surrender them (see treatments on p. 455 *et seq.*). While they were competing, he bent down under her and nudged one of the eggs to under himself, but when Carmen detected this, she leaned over, nudged the egg back, and sat over both eggs.

I found Cosimo crouching over the eggs at 22:15 h. When I approached the NB, he mounted the inside perch, and when I reached toward the lid, he exited. In the same circumstance, Carmen just would have hissed at me. The basis for the different behavior was that Carmen was habituated and not intimidated by my presence, whereas Cosimo was very skittish. However, at a later time in the incubatory period, or when chicks were present, Cosimo was much more likely to hold his ground. As I mentioned above, if I approached just after he exited the NB, he sometimes raced back to the NB and 'protected the brood.'

I MOVE THE EGGS. At any rate, I substituted another infertile lovebird egg for the newly laid Cockatielian egg and buried the latter in the corner, against the Plexiglas sidepane, near their other buried egg. But instead of putting the 2 substitute eggs in the IA, I placed them both at the rear between the ¼- and ½-way points (where I would have a better view), to ascertain if the birds would tolerate a change in the location of the IA.

DISPLACEMENT OF INCUBATIVE AREA NOT TOLERATED. When Carmen entered the NB a few moments later, she moved only one of the eggs back to the IA and crouched over it, leaving the other one just to her rear. In time, she also would have gathered the other egg in, but the lack of urgency lends emphasis to the fact that a single egg tends to be sufficient to stimulate and satisfy the the egg-incubatory instincts of Cockatiels. One egg most certainly is sufficient if no other egg is visible. When Cosimo entered the NB at 22:28 h, however, he took over the care of the eggs and restored the remaining displaced egg to the original IA.

'CONTENTED' WITH SINGLE EGG. In the last experiment on the preceding day, I had found that, even though the birds were in possession of 2 eggs for a period of 2 h before both eggs were hidden from them, they were quite 'contented' after recovering only one of the eggs. They did not continue to search, as they did before either egg had been found. Did this mean that 1 egg was sufficient to satisfy their egg-care instincts in any circumstances? Or did it mean that 1 egg was sufficient only because, to that point, Carmen had laid only 1 egg? Recall that the 2nd egg was an extra one, that I had added. Although a proof is necessary, we can guess that 1 egg is sufficient in any circumstances, since Cosimo presumably had no way of knowing that Carmen had not oviposited a 2nd egg.

But now that a 2nd egg had been laid, an experiment was possible to answer this question (at least, as far as Carmen was concerned). When Cosimo left the NB at 16:50 h, I took one of the eggs from the IA and buried it in the same location used in the other experiments (at the ½-way point, against the sidepane). But I left just the tip of one end showing. When Carmen entered the NB at 16:55 h, she did, indeed, visually inspect the IA. But then she settled in over the remaining egg. Perhaps she missed the 2nd egg, but, if so, she seemed 'contented' just to have the single egg that remained.

When Cosimo relieved Carmen a few min later, he also took over the care of the remaining egg, with no evidence of 'concern' for the missing one. In the ensuing 45 min, Carmen and Cosimo exchanged with each other several times, but on no occasion did either show evidence of 'concern' over the missing egg. At 17:45 h, when Cosimo left the NB, I exposed 5 mm of the end of the newly-buried egg. On entering, Carmen noticed the egg immediately and recovered it in the usual way.

A PATTERN OF NEST EXCHANGES DEVELOPS. During the nest exchanges in the previous 24 h, I had noticed a pattern developing. When one bird entered and its sitting mate was agreeable to the exchange of egg care, the exchange was accomplished without incident. If not, however, the incoming bird "pecked away" its mate. But if the incubating mate was reluctant to surrender the eggs, it "outpecked" the incoming bird.

COCKATIELS ROUTINELY SEARCH THE INCUBATIVE AREA.

ROUTINE SEARCHING---BOTH INCUBATING AND EXCHANGING BIRDS SEARCH. Until that time, searches for eggs had been observed only after all eggs were missing from the IA. It appeared that no further searching took place after a single egg had been recovered. The possibility remained, however, that incubating birds routinely search for buried eggs from time to time, and even that intended exchanging birds routinely search for buried eggs while waiting to be allowed to make an exchange.

The incubating bird often is noted to peck about at the periphery of the IA, turn around in it temporarily, and "fuss about" among the eggs. And an incoming bird does not always sit immobile at the side of the incubating bird, but may busy itself pecking about while waiting. If the incubating bird were to search routinely for buried eggs, that would help to explain why birds that are searching for missing eggs do not extend their search beyond the periphery of the IA. Perhaps they tend to search only as far as they can reach without leaving the eggs. In other words, the search area may be stereotypically determined.

DISTANT BURIED EGGS NOT FOUND---NEARBY EGGS PROMPTLY RECOVERED. The following series of experiments sought answers to these questions. First, beginning at 19:45 h, on the same day, I buried both of the eggs against the sidepane, one on each side of the ½-way point. The by-then-familiar spate of searches of the IA and distant visual searches ensued, mostly by Cosimo (Carmen rarely was seen to perform the "distant visual search"), but no probing for eggs extended to locations much beyond the periphery of the IA, so no egg was found.

Accordingly, I reburied the eggs against the far sidewall, also on both sides of the ½-way point, one egg being essentially within, and the other on the border of, the IA. When Cosimo entered the NB, he started to search in the IA but stopped abruptly and settled over it. He already had found the closest egg and had stopped his directed (as opposed to routine) search. When Carmen relieved him at 20:25 h, she also was 'content' to crouch over the single egg.

IMPLICATIONS OF RECOVERY OF SECOND EGG. What would it mean if they were to find the buried egg at the periphery of the IA? It would mean either (a) that they did, indeed, miss the 2nd egg and still were searching for it, though with much less urgency, or (b) that they routinely search the IA from time to time. This experiment would not permit a decision between the two alternatives. But a positive result would, in itself, be exciting, because both alternatives have interesting implications.

The positive result came at 21:00 h, when the other egg that I had buried also was found to have been restored to the IA. The result was not quite conclusively positive, though, because the remote possibility remained that the egg merely was found accidentally. Perhaps the movements of the incubating bird exposed the buried egg accidentally.

MORE DISTANT BURIED EGGS RECOVERED. To eliminate this possibility, I buried one of the eggs at the 1/3rd-point against the far sidewall, sufficiently distant from the IA to eliminate the possibility of its being recovered accidentally, as a result of movements of the incubating bird. When Carmen entered the NB at 21:08 h, she crouched over the remaining egg, with no sign of missing the 2nd one, and likewise for Cosimo, when he exchanged with her not long afterwards. At 23:20 h, I had another answer to my question; they had found the egg buried at the more distant location.

This result ostensibly ruled out the accidental uncovering of eggs as an explanation, and left the two alternatives mentioned above. To decide between them, I buried still a 3rd egg at the same position (the 1/3rd-point). If they had recovered the other egg at that position because they were keeping track of the number of eggs, and missed it, they would not continue to search. But if they searched routinely, they would not cease doing so. When I turned out the lights at 01:02 h, both Carmen and Cosimo exited from the NB (as I had come to expect during the care of the 1st few eggs). They were still out at 06:00 h the next morning (Apr. 13). At 08:45 h, I had an answer to the last question. They had found the 3rd egg.

ANCESTORS PROBABLY BURIED OR CONCEALED EGGS. The presumption then was strong that Cockatiels routinely search the substrate in and around the IA, and all subsequent studies supported this conclusion (also found to be true of Peach-faced Lovebirds, but not of Budgerigars; see pp. 738, 739, **Tests for Systematic Routine Searching**; pp. 781, 782, **No Routine Search**). This is persuasive evidence that, at some time in the past, the ancestors of Cockatiels buried or concealed their eggs. One also could take the view that it implies only that the ancestors of Cockatiels once nested on a yielding or lightly compacted substratum, into which eggs might sometimes have sunk from sight. But I feel it would have been maladaptive to nest on such a substratum, in which the eggs were vulnerable to such loss, unless the vulnerability were outweighed by an advantage, namely, the facility with which the eggs could have been both concealed and recovered on such a substratum.

INFLUENCE OF PLEXIGLAS SIDEPANE? As a last experiment in the series, I explored the possibility that the presence of the transparent, and partly reflective, Plexiglas sidepane accounted for the failure to dig up fully buried eggs next to it, rather than the eggs being too distant from the IA. One manner of accomplishing this would be to bury both eggs against the far sidewall at more distant locations than the 1/3rd-point. Accordingly, at 14:30 h, I buried the eggs directly across from Carmen's first 2 eggs. These had been buried against the sidepane (one in the corner and the other 5 cm out from the corner) ever since shortly after they were oviposited. One of these newly-buried eggs was only 4¼ cm further away than the egg that they had discovered that morning in a routine search.

Both birds, but particularly Cosimo, then made the most frantic of all searches witnessed until that time. The entire IA was thoroughly pecked, plowed, and excavated. There were distant visual searches, the walls were pecked and scraped, and there was much pacing back and forth inside and outside the NB. But Cosimo's excavations and plowing fell just short of reaching the nearest buried egg.

It was apparent that their searching would not ordinarily extend much beyond the confines of the IA. A location just 4¼ cm farther from the IA was too far away. Since it then had become clear that this finding also applied to eggs that were not buried against the sidepane, it appeared unlikely that the presence of the sidepane was the determining factor. This conclusion was supported by a later finding, in which an egg buried next to the sidepane was recovered (see p. 466, **More Likely to Search Distant Locations When Ranging After Chicks**).

CARMEN DETECTS BURIED EGGS BUT DOES NOT EXCAVATE THEM. Another aspect of their searches was revealed in the last experiment. Carmen appeared to detect visually the presence of her 2 eggs that I had buried against the sidepane. These could be seen from outside the NB, viewing them from the right side of the enclosure (e.g., from near the bell; see Fig. 3a), since they rested directly against the sidepane.

On 3 separate occasions, Carmen seemed to detect the eggs visually from outside the NB, judging from her alert stares in their direction. Each time that this occurred, she entered the NB with dispatch, went directly to the location of the eggs, and peered closely at the surface of the shavings above them. But, apparently because she saw no sign of an egg, she would not peck or dig in the area (just as in the earlier experiment, when an egg had been buried at a previously used location; see p. 432). It would appear from these results that searching for buried eggs is, indeed, a highly stereotyped activity.

At about 16:00 h, roughly 1½ hours after I had buried the eggs against the sidewall, I uncovered about 8 mm of the tip of each. Carmen was next to enter the NB, and she detected and recovered the eggs immediately. [Again, since I had made the last change after Cosimo exited the NB, she was taking his place. I rarely could make an experimental change after Carmen left, because she customarily remained with the eggs until after Cosimo entered to exchange with her.]

DEFECTIVE EGGS ARE DISCARDED. It is well known that many birds discard damaged eggs. In some cases, the lovebird eggs I was using as substitutes for the Cockatiel eggs were too light in weight, because they had dried out. [In one case, Carmen and Cosimo pecked a hole in one of these light eggs, and I replaced it.] On April 14, at 18:55 h, I noticed that Carmen was crouched or sitting in the NB but that one of the eggs seemed to have been discarded behind her. I suspected that her 3rd egg had been laid and that, perhaps by comparison, the light egg was 'judged' to be defective and discarded.

Three h later, I got a glimpse of her 3rd egg, and when Cosimo entered the NB shortly thereafter and crouched at Carmen's side, he also ignored the egg to the rear. At one point, Carmen arose and examined the eggs carefully, and Cosimo joined in beside her. Such joint careful examinations of the eggs were seen many times subsequently. Later, after I substituted another light-weight lovebird egg for her 3rd egg, and restored the 1st light-weight egg to the IA, I saw Carmen discard an egg again with a backward kick (I also saw lovebirds violently expel defective eggs). Later, the other light-weight egg also was discarded, but one of them eventually was accepted again (the unaccepted light-weight egg was found to be cracked).

[It will be seen, below (e.g., see pp. 483, 484), that Cockatiels nesting in the open on an enclosure floor usually do not discard defective eggs in so incautious a fashion. When feasible, they roll them out of the nest to a distance and/or try to conceal them under an overhanging object. Otherwise, they peck a hole in them at a point of damage and lift them out of the nest on the inserted bill, and discard them (see p. 699).]

COMPETITION INTENSIFIES--ALLOGROOMING AS A FORM OF PERSUASION. On the midnight before Carmen laid her 3rd egg, I saw what appeared to be tender interactions between Carmen and Cosimo. They were 'tenderly' grooming one another, often sitting side by side, interacting closely, and using gentle persuasion (competitive interactions in their mildest form) to acquire the eggs from one another. This was suggestive of the gentle interactions of a human couple, or the playful cavorting of young mammals. If these scenes were what they appeared to be, they were merely the "calm before the storm." But, as tempestuous as Cockatielian nest-exchange interactions can become, with rare exceptions, the eggs are treated very gently, though they typically get moved about scores to hundreds of times every day.

It will be found in the following, that in competing for eggs, Cockatiels of both sexes, but chiefly the male (the dominant sex), employ allogrooming of the head and neck as a form of gentle persuasion. Usually, it is the male who grooms the sitting female until she surrenders the eggs, but the female sometimes allogrooms the male, in return, as a countermeasure (depending upon her degree of subordination). This unilateral or mutual allogrooming sometimes escalates into vigorous defensive allogrooming, gentle pecking, and, eventually, vigorous pecking with raised heads.

It has long been recognized that mutual allogrooming is a widespread, ritualized form of agonistic behavior that "bridges the narrow gap between sexual behavior and aggressive attack" (29), but it apparently has not been reported previously as occurring in competition over the care of eggs. Peach-faced Lovebird males may tenderly groom the incubating female for extended periods over all exposed portions of her body, but in that case the behavior is unilateral and has no aggressive overtone (see p. 721).

ADJUSTING TO COSIMO'S SCHEDULE. With the laying of the 3rd egg, i.e., beginning on the 4th day of incubation of the substitute lovebird eggs, subtle to not-so-subtle changes in the behavior of the birds became evident. They then were entering the equivalent of the 3rd phylogenetic stage of egg care, in which the eggs were being incubated by day and by night, not just crouched over, sat on lightly, and/or guarded by day. For one thing, Cosimo became more steadfast in his care of the eggs. Instead of his becoming 'nervous' when I approached the NB while he was incubating the eggs, he simply eyed me calmly. If he was up on the inside perch, he settled down protectively on the eggs, instead of continuing on out of the NB. From this time on, I no longer could depend on being able to make ready substitutions and manipulations of the eggs, but had to adjust the timing of my experimental manipulations more to Cosimo's schedule.

On more than one occasion while incubating the 3 eggs, Cosimo vocalized and Carmen came into the NB and exchanged with him. On these occasions, he customarily returned within a few min and reclaimed the clutch. On another occasion, I saw him leave unilaterally, void, and return, within an interval of only 15 sec, without Carmen replacing him.

COSIMO REPELS CARMEN WITH A FURY---CARMEN NOT INTIMIDATED. As a prelude of things to come, on the same morning that the 3rd egg was laid (Apr. 14), Carmen mounted the NB perch with the intention of entering the NB. When Cosimo saw her at the entrance, he hissed and jumped up on the inside perch. He then pecked her away with a fury more appropriate to repelling a predator. It was just as if Carmen had been a complete stranger, or as if I had stuck my finger into the NB entrance.

Such an unfelicitous welcome might temporarily postpone Carmen's entrance, but it had no lasting effect of intimidation. In this particular case, Cosimo exited unilaterally 8 min later (I took advantage of his absence to substitute a lovebird egg for the 3rd Cockatielian egg) and Carmen took over the care of the eggs. When Cosimo returned, she did not oppose his entrance. He unceremoniously pecked her off the clutch, but she contested for the eggs for some time before surrendering them and leaving.

WHITE MARBLES FOR EGGS. At this time, I performed my last egg-manipulation experiments on the clutch, using colored marbles. At 15:20 h on April 14, I replaced the 2 light-weight lovebird eggs with 2-cm-diameter white marbles, leaving the lovebird egg of normal weight (this was the only lovebird egg of normal weight that was available at the time). Cosimo was the first to chance upon the new "eggs," and, as often occurs, he examined the clutch carefully before settling down on it. At that time, the clutch was being incubated very tightly, not just being shielded or guarded by loose contact. At 16:50 h, I heard Cosimo singing softly from the NB and noticed that Carmen also was inside. Since his singing continued unabatedly, he might have begun to sing after she arrived, rather than having enticed her in with his song.

INSPECTING EGGS AS IF INVENTORYING A TREASURE. Carmen also accepted the marbles and incubated the clutch again that night, as she had the night before. Beginning at about that time, and continuing on through the remainder of the incubatory period, the inspections of the eggs (or marbles), when the birds joined one another in the NB, reminded one of the attentive inspection and inventorying of a treasure hoard. The significance of this behavior is discussed on pages 475, 476 (**Adjusting Egg Orientation and Placement**, *et seq.*). There can be little doubt, however, that late during the incubatory period the birds are listening for the respiratory or bill-clapping sounds that alert them to impending hatching.

A GREEN MARBLE. It was not until 21:43 h on April 15 that I had the opportunity to make a further change in the clutch. At that time, I removed the lovebird egg and replaced it with a dark green marble. I also buried a purple marble at the ½-way point against the far sidewall in the IA, and a black marble in the front corner in the IA. When Cosimo returned 1 or 2 min later, he eyed the green marble warily from the outside perch and would not enter the NB. Carmen came over and eyed it too. Nor would she enter. Then both peered in together, hesitatingly. When Carmen stepped halfway in, Cosimo pecked her rump in an apparent attempt to get her to enter completely. Finally, she entered and incubated the marbles, including the green one, and Cosimo joined her. [For a recent treatment of egg recognition by birds, see 496.]

"STEALING" THE CLUTCH----RELUCTANCE TO SURRENDER EGGS. Both birds were in the NB together at 22:52 h, and Cosimo was singing softly. They had found the purple marble and incorporated it into the clutch. As I watched, Cosimo "stole" the clutch out from under Carmen by getting her to rise temporarily. He acquired all 4 marbles in what eventually proved to be a typical fashion of acquiring eggs from a non-cooperative mate. He rolled them out from under her, one by one, to under himself, and then settled down upon them. Carmen and Cosimo then jockeyed around for several min contesting for the marbles. Even though Cosimo had possesion of the "clutch", Carmen was not discouraged, not even when he kept pecking her away gently. But the time in the evening was late; it was not an hour at which Carmen was easily discouraged from acquiring a clutch. At 23:02 h, Cosimo finally surrendered the marbles and left the NB.

In the next hour, Carmen and Cosimo spent a great deal of time in the NB together, disputing the care of the eggs (marbles) and examining and tending to them. At 24:15 h, when one would have expected Cosimo to be very receptive to surrendering the eggs for the night, he once again rose from the clutch and repelled Carmen from the NB entrance with a rapid volley of sharp pecks. She drew back momentarily but then pressed on, and he allowed her to enter. Again, they examined the eggs carefully together. Sometime before 24:30 h, Cosimo exited, and Carmen settled down on the "clutch" for the night.

"DIVING IN," "MANDIBLE-FLUTTERING," AND CONTINUED HEIGHTENED COMPETITION

THE EGGS RESTORED---INCUBATION COMMENCES. Carmen had laid her 3rd egg sometime during the early morning of April 14. So, on the morning of April 16, at 08:05 h, when the laying of the 4th egg presumably was imminent, I restored the 3 eggs that had been buried at the rear of the NB (but not turned periodically). I also removed the black marble, which had remained undiscovered in the corner. In the eventuality, no 4th egg was laid.

ABNORMAL DEVELOPMENT OF EGGS STORED BY BURIAL. The 3 eggs proved to be fertile, but the development of #1 and #2 was abnormal, in proportion to the time that they had been buried at room temperature. The 1st egg developed only partially, the 2nd egg appeared to have developed almost normally, but was not internally pipped (the inner shell membrane, enclosing the embryo, was not broken). The 3rd egg, which had been unturned for only 2 days, hatched and yielded a normal chick.

[If an egg is stored at room temperature, rather than being cooled, it appears to be necessary to impart to it a similar amount of agitation to that received from the frequent attentions of the parent in the few days before steadfast incubation begins. Storage of eggs at room temperature for longer than 4-5 days may lead to abnormal development, regardless of whether they are agitated.]

"DIVING IN." Cosimo was able to take over the care of the eggs early that morning because I had coaxed Carmen out of the NB, so as to have the opportunity to restore her eggs. When Carmen returned to the NB at 08:35 h, Cosimo again became aggressive, but this time his pecks only were directed in her general direction, and Carmen even pecked back at him once. Then she made her typical entrance, which I describe here for the first time.

Whereas, when Cosimo entered, he always just hopped down off the inside perch to the open area at the side and rear of the IA, Carmen always "dove in" under Cosimo--nudging under him in a continuous movement directly from the perch to the eggs. This was a maneuver that invariably stimulated Cosimo to rise to accommodate her. It mattered not how adamant in retention of the eggs he might have been just a few sec before, or he might become a few sec afterward. Both birds entered the NB in these characteristic ways, whether the other was present or not.

The maneuver of "diving in" that caused Cosimo to rise from the eggs, formed the basis for a device that Carmen used time and again to gain possession of the clutch. This gave her, at least, a temporary advantage. Her actions were as follows. After a vigorous but unsuccessful session of competition with Cosimo for the clutch, Carmen simply would turn away and leave the NB. But no sooner was she outside of it, and Cosimo had settled back onto the eggs, then she turned around, re-entered, and "dove in" onto the eggs. Cosimo invariably rose and surrendered the clutch to her--but often not for long.

When Carmen "dove in" at 08:35 h, she and Cosimo first went through their usual routine of examining the eggs closely. As far as I could tell, this differed not at all from the way they had examined the marbles. Then there followed some shuffling about as each bird attempted to roll the eggs under itself. Carmen finally gained possession of the clutch and settled in on it. Fifteen min later, Cosimo was back and Carmen allofed him once. He then gently pecked her to make her rise from the eggs, then rolled them out from under her to under himself, and settled over them. As Carmen sat beside him, they interacted tenderly with mutual allogrooming and gentle pecking. But this soon gave way to sharper pecking with raised heads. Eventually, Carmen departed.

Cosimo then incubated the eggs very attentively most of the evening. When Carmen appeared at the entrance at 24:10 h, she encountered no opposition and dove in onto the clutch. Then they "cavorted" mildly and Cosimo left. It was mainly the "cavorting" of the birds that was responsible for the many extended movements that I had detected earlier with my mirror system, during the incubation of the 1st 2 clutches.

[I use the verb "cavort" in this connection to signify that the birds competed for the eggs in a more or less mild manner. This included any combination of shoving, gentle pecking, grooming of one another's heads (described on p. 460), stealing the eggs out from under one another, Cosimo grooming Carmen's crissum (an action that invariably led to Carmen's rising from the eggs), etc.]

THE "MANDIBLE-FLUTTERING" DISPLAY. Lastly, I describe "Mandible-fluttering"--a rapid opening and closing of the bill--and the circumstances in which it occurs. Mandible-fluttering almost always occurs in parental interactions that concern the eggs and/or chicks within the NB (or within an IA on an enclosure floor). The incubating or brooding bird usually Mandible-flutters whenever the mate enters the NB. Once inside, or on the way in, the arriving bird also Mandible-flutters. They also may Mandible-flutter when examining the eggs, and often when competing for the eggs.

On one occasion, Cosimo Mandible-fluttered between audible song phrases, while in the NB with Carmen and the clutch (see p. 463, **Cosimo Steadfast**). The male often Mandible-flutters while copulating, and the female usually does so immediately afterward. Either bird also would Mandible-flutter when I approached the NB or the IA. This display apparently has several functions, among them appeasement, expressing agitation or 'concern,' and as a recognition signal.

Courtney (30) refers to Mandible-fluttering as the "bill-clicking display" and asserts that it makes a soft tapping noise as the upper and lower bills touch (also referred to as "bill-clapping"). The situation may be more complex, though, since close observations reveal that the bird performing the Mandible-fluttering also usually is fluttering the throat synchronously. It took a long time in the noisy background of the colony before I succeeded in hearing the sounds made by Mandible-fluttering.

SOFT "POPPING" SOUNDS, POSSIBLY MODULATED. Even though I sometimes could listen within 2-3 cm from the bills of my male birds, while they were copulating near the side of an enclosure (i.e., perched next to the side), the ongoing Coition Sounds of the female drowned out the male's vocalizations accompanying his Mandible-fluttering. It was only during moments of quiet, when I stimulated Mandible-Fluttering in a bird sitting on eggs on an enclosure floor, that I succeeded in hearing the sounds. Each flutter of the mandibles produces a soft "pop," such as we make when we open and close our lips rapidly. Perhaps the birds modulate these sounds to alter the messages conveyed, by expelling or drawing in air at the same time.

COMPETITION REACHES ITS HIGHEST PITCH. During the next few days, after the restoration of the 3 bona fide eggs, competition for them ever intensified. April 17, for example, was only the 2nd full day of incubation of the *bona fide* clutch. But as far as the birds were concerned, it was the 8th full day, since one must reckon the time spent incubating the substitute eggs, as well. As an example of the frequency of competition, on the night of the 17th, from 19:30 to 22:30 h, Carmen and Cosimo were in the NB together competing for possession of the eggs on 6 different occasions.

I have selected a period of 88 min on the night of April 21 and the morning of April 22nd, as an example of what transpires in the NB on occasions of peak competition. As far as the birds were concerned, this was the 12th night of incubation, over halfway through the incubatory period (but only the 6th day for the *bona fide* clutch).

ALLOGROOMING THE CRISSUM. Before recounting this, though, I describe the two devices that Cosimo frequently employed to acquire the eggs from Carmen when she would not surrender them voluntarily. In the first of these, Cosimo allogroomed Carmen's crissum (the plumage surrounding the vent). He merely pushed under the base of her tail, and she invariably raised the rear of her body. Cosimo then proceeded to allogroom her crissum, all the while pushing upward. The result was that the eggs became exposed and Cosimo could roll them out from under her and take over their care himself.

It is likely that this device derives from allogrooming of the vent region for utilitarian purposes, particularly during the period when sexual unions are occurring frequently. In fact, mutual crissum-allogrooming is a known courtship activity of some parrots (484). This would serve the purpose of clearing feathers from over the vent so that the passage of sperm would not be impeded. Even though the tissue in the neighborhood of the vent is everted (to expose the cloaca) during coitus, excessive feather growth of the crissum could interfere with the passage of spermatozoa.

ALLOGROOMING THE HEAD. In the second device, Cosimo allogroomed Carmen's head. In this action (seemingly performed mostly by the male), the male allogrooms, without solicitation, every area of the female's head--incessantly and interminably. As the allogrooming proceeds, the female's early receptivity turns to annoyance, thence to discomfort, then pain, and ultimately to 'desperation' for relief. At that point, she counterattacks by pecking at the male, twists, turns away, shifts her position to avoid the male's attentions, rises for the same purpose, or flees the NB. If she counters vigorously by pecking, the male usually pecks in return just as vigorously, but ceases allogrooming her for the moment.

ALLOGROOMING BIRD "STEALS" THE EGGS. After harmony has been restored, the male simply initiates the process again. But in cases where the female shifts her position, in an effort to draw away from the onslaught of grooming, or raises her body, the male siezes on her moment of distraction to steal one or more eggs out from under her. He does this by the usual method of nudging them along with the underside of his bill, until they are located under his body. Sometimes the female will be in the process of recovering a stolen egg at the same time that the male is stealing the next one. This same tactic of incessant head grooming also was used by Cosimo to hasten Carmen's departure from the NB when a chick was being brooded.

DIVIDED CLUTCH MERELY IN THE NATURE OF A TRUCE. In my experience, the sharing of a divided clutch by the birds in a single IA, each of them incubating a portion and sitting side by side, is not usually an acceptable solution to either bird. It is of the nature of a truce, tolerated only until the remainder of the eggs can be acquired. Judging from my observations, my birds reached the impasse of incubating a divided clutch at least twice daily, from the time of laying of the 3rd egg onward. [As experiments with Helena and Homer were to reveal subsequently, there is little or no competition when mates incubate portions of a split clutch in separate, non-proximal IA's. Each bird then incubates his portion of the clutch throughout the day. The male abandons his portion at night but the female continues to incubate hers.]

COMPETITION AT ITS PEAK. I now turn to an example of competitiveness for the clutch at its peak. The time is 23:00 h on April 21, 1984, a time of the day at which Carmen would not readily surrender the eggs. At that time I noticed that the birds were cavorting in the NB. As I watched, Cosimo began to allogroom Carmen's head. After continuing this activity for 2 min, he departed. Eight min later he hopped back into the NB and they began jockeying for position over the eggs. Although Cosimo at first "muscled" Carmen off the eggs, she was able to recover them.

GAINING AND LOSING THE CLUTCH. While distracting Carmen by allogrooming her head, Cosimo rolled an egg out under himself. However, Carmen noticed it and rolled it right back under herself. Cosimo then began to allogroom her head endlessly. She kept ducking, twisting and turning, withdrawing, pecking his head away, and showing her distress vocally, but he was relentless. Finally, she surrendered the eggs. Cosimo covered them and stopped allogrooming her. When Cosimo was distracted momentarily, as I shifted my position to get a better view of the proceedings, Carmen took advantage of the situation and recovered the eggs, whereupon Cosimo left the NB.

LONG CONTINUED EGG EXCHANGES--INCUBATING A DIVIDED CLUTCH. Cosimo returned in about 6 min and again "allogroomed" Carmen off of the eggs. But again, she managed to recover them, and he commenced again to allogroom her head. As she became increasingly distressed and distracted, he rolled 2 eggs out from under her to himself. But when she noticed this, she rolled them back. Having lost the eggs, Cosimo resumed allogrooming Carmen's head. Several min later (23:42 h), he still was allogrooming her and she still had the eggs. Six min later, he stopped allogrooming her momentarily and tried to roll the eggs out from under her. Failing in that, he resumed allogrooming her until, finally, she surrendered the eggs.

[The reader may be puzzled over how it is possible for such exchanges of eggs to occur in the sight of both birds. The answer is that the birds never contest directly for the same egg. That would be highly maladaptive, because of the great danger of damaging the eggs. Accordingly, when one bird is removing an egg, the other merely watches until the act is completed. Only then does the other bird make its move to regain the egg, at which time the first bird also merely watches, or appropriates another egg.]

Cosimo then took over the care of the eggs and leaned snugly into the adjacent corner. The eggs were under his chest, and his tail and rear underside were pressed high against the walls in the corner. Somehow Carmen managed to come back onto the eggs, but Cosimo succeeded in rolling one of them out from under her. Then he also managed to take over the other 2 eggs, and Carmen allogroomed him briefly. Shortly thereafter I became aware that Carmen had obtained 1 of the eggs, and she and Cosimo were sitting side by side incubating the divided clutch. This truce lasted but a few min, as Carmen somehow managed to obtain the other 2 eggs, and incubated all 3 of them (23:53 h). But Cosimo got her to rise, by allogrooming her crissum, whereupon he rolled the eggs out from under her to himself and incubated them. Carmen, with no egg, just sat quietly next to him.

By 23:59 h--49 min into the competition--Carmen had gradually displaced Cosimo from the eggs and he was back to allogrooming her incessantly, working over her head ever so thoroughly. After about a min of this vigorous attention, Carmen would tolerate no more of it. She surrendered the clutch and departed. But she was barely out of the NB before she turned around quickly, dove back in, and took over possession of the eggs. Undeterred, Cosimo resumed the tactic of allogrooming her off of them again, whereupon he regained the clutch. Then Carmen went back to sitting at his side without an egg. At 12:02 h, Carmen was allogrooming Cosimo and managed to work her way into the corner and acquire the eggs, but not for long. Cosimo succeeded in rolling 2 eggs out under himself, and, again, they sat side by side, head-to-tail, with the clutch split.

Eight min later, they were still sharing the split clutch, but Cosimo had turned about enough to reach and allogroom Carmen's head, and she also was grooming his. This continued for almost 4 min, as he allogroomed every spot on her head--forehead, cheeks, bill, chin, etc. Then, at 12:14 h, Cosimo departed and Carmen gathered in his 2 eggs.

Seven min later, however, Cosimo jumped back in and unceremoniously "muscled" Carmen off the eggs. Unphased by this action, she, in turn, displaced him and re-acquired the eggs. But then, he repeated the act and displaced her. Shortly after, they were vying directly for the eggs (but never simultaneously for the same egg). Cosimo managed to roll one out under himself, and they sat side by side, head-to-tail, again sharing the split clutch.

COSIMO SURRENDERS THE CLUTCH. Six min later, I noticed that Cosimo had turned toward Carmen again and was allogrooming her head interminably, as she tried to avoid his attentions. But Cosimo was still incubating one of the eggs. After 3 min of this activity, Carmen seemed to have yielded, and perched on the inner perch facing halfway out the entrance. Twenty sec later, she backed in and their competition began anew. Finally, after another 7 min, Cosimo left (24:30 h), and I turned out the lights. At 09:45 h that morning, Cosimo jumped into the NB, engaged with Carmen in momentary pecking of each other's bills, and "muscled" her off the eggs.

NON-SITTING BIRD FREQUENTLY CHECKS THE EGGS. Both birds always maintained a great interest in the eggs. They never were taken for granted. On many occasions, the non-sitting bird would enter the NB merely to make a quick check of the eggs, as if the mate were not entirely trustworthy. On these occasions, Carmen just dove in; Cosimo just jumped in and used the crissum-allogrooming routine. In each case, the incubating bird yielded readily, and both inspected the clutch with great attentiveness (see pp. 475, 476, **Adjusting Egg Orientation and Placement**, et seq.). Without further ado, the bird that had initiated the inspection session often exited.

FURTHER EVENTS OF THE INCUBATORY PERIOD

COMPETITION CONTINUES, COSIMO INVESTIGATES ANY CONTACT WITH PERCH. I touch only on the most notable features of the remainder of the incubatory period. April 22 was another day of intense competition for the eggs, but I will not repeat detailed desriptions of interactions like those already described above. Every time that Carmen touched the outside NB perch or mounted it, Cosimo stretched up and looked out to investigate. When he verified that it was Carmen, he settled back.

IF COSIMO EXITED AFTER CARMEN'S DEPARTURE, SHE RETURNED. When Carmen dove into the NB at 16:15 h, Cosimo yielded, sang softly, and exited. At 16:30 h, he was singing on the outside NB perch. Then he jumped into the NB and continued to sing, followed by his Mandible-fluttering. When Carmen exited, but found that Cosimo had followed her out of the NB, she returned to and cared for the clutch. When I turned off the lights at 24:30 h, Carmen popped up onto the inside perch momentarily, but did not exit. [Movements and positions after the lights were turned off usually were followed with a pencil-beam flashlight.]

COSIMO REPELS CARMEN VIGOROUSLY. On April 24, I witnessed an extraordinary occurrence. Carmen tried to re-enter the NB at 10:30 h, which was a time of the day when Cosimo often possessed the eggs uncontestedly. Cosimo stretched up from his position on the eggs and pecked her away from the entrance. When Carmen persisted, Cosimo mounted the inside perch and aggressively pecked her completely off the the outside perch by stretching almost all the way out of the entrance. But Carmen, characteristically, was not daunted in the slightest, and the entire episode was repeated with the same vigor 4 more times.

As Carmen approached for the 6th time, Cosimo jumped up and guarded the entrance before she could get to it. After backing off for 2 min, Carmen Mandible-fluttered while approaching, and Cosimo allowed her to enter. He still pecked at her, though, but after a session of cavorting, he surrendered the eggs and exited.

GENTLE HANDLING OF EGGS---A SPLIT CLUTCH. Later that day, I was impressed again with how gently the eggs were handled. At 21:44 h, both parents were standing in the NB with the eggs between them, as Cosimo was allogrooming Carmen. With the most gentle manipulations, he surreptitiously moved 2 eggs over under himself, while only briefly interrupting his allogrooming. At 22:00 h, both birds seemed very 'contentedly' to be incubating the split clutch. At 24:15 h, i.e., 135 min later, Cosimo mounted the outside perch and sang softly while looking into the NB. Then he jumped in, while continuing to sing, and remained for 5 min. He did not attempt to reacquire the eggs.

COSIMO STEADFAST. During the next day, at 19:42 h, Cosimo sang softly from the NB as Carmen entered it, but I did not know whether she was answering his call. Shortly after 23:11 h, he used the crissum-allogrooming device to acquire the clutch. He jumped into the NB 45 min later and sang softly. It was on this occasion that he Mandible-fluttered between audible phrases. When I flighted Carmen and the 5 offspring of her 1st 2 broods at 17:15 h on April 26, Cosimo did not budge from his tight sitting on the eggs, despite the great disturbance going on within view outside. This tenacity proved to be characteristic of incubatory behavior by both Carmen and Cosimo when within the NB during the other's flighting; no matter how much excitement took place outside the enclosure, the incubating bird did not leave the eggs. On the other hand, Cosimo was quick to leave the eggs and attack an intruding Cockatiel approaching from outside the enclosure.

COMPETITIVE INTERACTIONS WHEN A CHICK COULD BE HEARD. On April 27 at 11:28 h, Cosimo Mandible-fluttered while on the outside perch and then sang softly after jumping into the NB. On the night of May 1, Carmen and Cosimo engaged in another long, highly-competitive contest for the eggs, beginning at about 23:00 h and ending when they retired at 24:47 h. It is very likely that they could hear a chick breathing or bill-clapping at that time (see also 127), since one of the eggs hatched 35-40 h later.

A CHICK HATCHES---COMPETITION CONTINUES UNABATEDLY. During the 18th day of incubation (May 3), I noticed that both parents were spending much of the morning in the NB together. At 17:15 h that afternoon, I found a hatchling being very attentively cared for by them. It was difficult to fathom exactly what was happening, as there was a great deal of activity and both parents were very excited. But it soon was evident that they were competing for both the eggs and the shells, as each kept gathering in both (Bengalese Finches also have been observed to compete for shells, but as a food item; 129). Although the parents handled the hatchling very gently when they were attentive to it, it did seem to me that the chick suffered some rough moments while they were distracted by competing for the eggs and shells. [There are many avian species among which the impulse to incubate is so strong that the young may be neglected as the brooding of empty shells continues (1,175).]

COMPETE FOR THE HATCHLING TOO---EGGS JOSTLED. It soon became evident that the parents were competing for the hatchling too. At such times, the eggs also came in for some careless treatment, as the birds jockeyed about. At first sight this behavior might appear to be selectively disadvantageous. But even if an egg were to become cracked or slightly damaged at that late stage of incubation, the damage might have little influence upon the hatching of a contained chick, so the parental behavior at that time cannot necessarily be regarded as maladaptive.

There was some mutual grooming taking place at 17:25 h, but no evident concern to allofeed the hatchling, which was doing much cheeping. By 17:35 h, however, both parents were of a mind to allofeed it, and in the competitive jousting to do so, and amid a great deal of cheeping, the process seemed to be generally disrupted. Despite all, however, the hatchling was obtaining food from both parents. It was fully capable of holding its head high and jerking it up and down ("pumping") when no more than 3-4 h old.

Aside from the continuing competition for both the eggs and the chick, the only other notable development on that day was that, with a chick present, Carmen jumped into the NB instead of diving in. In subsequent days, it was not unusual for one parent to be incubating the eggs while the other allofed the chick. But both participated in both activities. As mentioned above, the other 2 eggs were fertile but did not hatch, apparently because they had not been turned after I buried them in the NB.

FOURTH OBSERVATIONS OF RESPONSES OVER A MISSING CLUTCH

RESPONSES AT LATER STAGES. All the previous experiments on responses to missing clutches had been carried out during the early days of an incubatory period. At that time, the urge to incubate and otherwise tend to the eggs was at a high level. No other non-maintenance activity distracted the parents or competed with the care of the eggs for their attention. These experiments had shown that the parents routinely search the IA for possibly buried eggs during the early days of incubation. What would happen if similar experiments were performed long after the eggs were due to hatch and the birds were occupied with the care of one or more chicks?

RESPONSES IN PRESENCE OF A CHICK. On May 10, 1984, precisely one month had elapsed since the 1st egg of the 3rd clutch had been laid, and 27 days had elapsed since the 3rd egg had been laid. Since hatching normally takes place after 17-22 days, the remaining 2 eggs were at least 5 days overdue.

In addition, the birds were occupied with the care of a week-old nestling. The time seemed propitious for ascertaining how parents would react over a missing clutch when the incubatory urge was waning and a chick was present.

FOUR EGGS BURIED. Would the presence of a chick substitute for missing eggs, as the presence of a single egg did? At 22:25 h, I removed the 2 eggs that were long overdue to hatch and buried 4 full-weight lovebird eggs under $1\frac{1}{4}$ cm of shavings. Two were buried against the far sidewall and 2 against the sidepane. One pair was in the rear corners and the other pair at the $\frac{1}{2}$-way points. This placed one of the eggs at the $\frac{1}{2}$-way point well within the IA

NO DIRECTED SEARCH, BUT SIGNS THAT THE EGGS WERE MISSED. Carmen was the first to enter the NB. She showed no sign of agitation over the absence of the eggs. But she did pivot once in the IA before settling in there in her usual position. When Cosimo came to the entrance, Carmen held her wings out slightly from her body and began to sway, in a typical threat posture. Since this was decidedly atypical for her in this situation, it suggests that she was affected by the absence of the eggs. Cosimo entered despite the hostile reception, and seemed not to be disturbed when his customary check of the IA beneath Carmen revealed no egg. Although he made no directed search, he did stand in the IA, apparently 'confused,' for several sec before leaving the NB.

A CHICK SUBSTITUTES FOR ABSENT EGGS. Carmen was already outside the NB and seemed undecided about whether to return when Cosimo followed her out. She stayed out with him and both ate for 2 min. After Cosimo visited the NB briefly, Carmen entered and settled into the IA. So far it was evident that either the urge to search for missing eggs had waned, or the presence of a chick substituted for the absent eggs. The latter is the likely explanation. This is to be expected, since, to say the least, the parents' investment in a chick is greater than their investment in an egg (the loss of a chick is a greater detriment to successful reproduction than the loss of an egg).

A NEAR EGG RECOVERED. Except for the fact that the birds pivoted several times in the IA, their behavior during the evening gave no indication that they missed the eggs. By 15:20 h of the following day, they had recovered the egg from the $\frac{1}{2}$-way point in the IA. This could have been either accidental or the result of continued routine searching. In either case, it seemed evident that routine searching for eggs at this time had lower priority than when eggs, alone, had been present.

A DISTANT EGG RECOVERED---ROUTINE SEARCHING HAD CONTINUED. As a critical test of whether routine searching still was taking place, I now buried the egg on the same side, but further back, at the $\frac{1}{4}$-way point. This was 2 cm farther away than the most distant egg ever recovered by Carmen and Cosimo (which had been at the 1/3rd-way point). Again the parents showed no evident concern over the missing egg. Notwithstanding this, by 9 h later they had recovered the egg at the $\frac{1}{4}$-way point. Evidently routine searching still was occurring. I let them retain the egg overnight.

THE RECOVERED EGG COVETED---I BURY IT FARTHER AWAY. As usual, both birds spent the night in the NB with the chick. Carmen did not leave the NB until 11:00 h the next morning; she spent the entire time incubating the egg. Cosimo had been the only one to allofeed the chick until then on that morning. When Carmen exited, Cosimo, at first, started to follow, but then remained and incubated the egg. Between the two parents, the egg was incubated until noon. Whenever Cosimo mounted the perch, and I arose with the thought of removing the egg, he backed down and covered the egg and protected the chick (they did not sit over their chicks, as lovebirds usually do, but kept them at their side, front, or rear, or under their wings). Finally, when I flighted Carmen at noon, I managed to get Cosimo to leave the NB. This time, I reburied the egg even farther away, against the sidewall, 4¼ cm from the corner (Fig. 3a).

MORE LIKELY TO SEARCH DISTANT LOCATIONS WHEN RANGING AFTER CHICKS. All 4 eggs now were buried so far away from the IA that previous experience suggested that they would not be found by either routine or directed searches. Nevertheless, by the afternoon of the next day (May 13, 15:45 h), they had found the egg at the ½-way point against the sidepane. This indicated that they were not inhibited from digging near the sidepane. It also suggested that they were more likely to dig at locations more distant from the IA when they were ranging after a chick, as opposed to when they merely were incubating eggs, and this would have been adaptive.

DISTANT VISUAL SEARCHES BY COSIMO. I removed the newly-recovered egg, leaving 3 eggs still buried at remote locations. To my surprise, when Cosimo returned to the NB, he looked in all directions for the missing egg. But he looked only on high (distant visual search). Afterward, he left the NB, but returned twice in the next few min, each time repeating the distant visual search. After that, there was no further directed search.

EGG ACCIDENTALLY UNCOVERED. Two days later (May 15 at 14:15 h), the 4 sibling Cockatiels in the lower part of enclosure A (beneath the partition) panicked while I was servicing their enclosure. This created a great deal of excitement in the colony, and frightened Carmen and Cosimo. As they clambered into the rear-sidepane corner, they accidentally exposed the egg that was buried there.

After they "settled down" and noticed the egg, they resurfaced it and "fussed" about with it briefly. But over 30 min later, during which time they were mostly busy caring for the chick, they had not moved or otherwise tended to the egg. Then Cosimo moved it a fraction of a cm toward the IA, and he and Carmen moved it another fraction further, but they did not return it to the IA nor incubate it. It was evident that they no longer were in an incubatory phase (i.e., the 3rd phylogenetic stage of egg-care). Later, I removed all the eggs and temporarily discontinued the studies on searching for and recovering eggs.

OBSERVATIONS OF RESPONSES OVER A MISSING, SOLITARY CHICK

CHICK REMOVED SURREPTITIOUSLY. I mentioned above that a chick is a "much more valuable property" than an egg to a pair of breeding birds, since it represents a greater investment of time and energy, and has a much better chance of becoming a breeding adult. This being the case, it was of great interest to ascertain how Cockatielian parents would respond to the absence of an only chick. Accordingly, on May 13, at 21:48 h, when both parents were out of the NB occupied with eating, I removed the chick without either of them being aware of the action.

Cosimo happened to be on an enclosure perch at the time and Carmen was on the enclosure floor. After I left the vicinity of the NB, and put the chick in another room, Cosimo came down off the perch and pecked at Carmen. He appeared to be trying to get her to return to the NB. However, Carmen demurred, and they both commenced to forage for 10 min.

CHICK MISSED---THOROUGH VISUAL SEARCH---COSIMO PUZZLED OR INDECISIVE. Thereafter, Cosimo entered the NB and looked about for the missing chick. Not finding it, he went back to the entrance. From there, he first looked down at the enclosure floor beneath the NB entrance, and then all about in the enclosure. Not seeing the chick, he came out onto an enclosure perch with a good view (perch a, Fig. 3a) and scanned the entire enclosure floor. Following this, he foraged on the floor for about 1 min and returned to perch A.

He stood on perch A for about 20 min, moving about very little, and mostly staring intently at an area of the enclosure floor, as if in a daze. Meanwhile, Carmen was foraging and pacing, unaware of the chick's absence. At 22:25 h, both birds were grooming themselves, after which Cosimo again stared intently without moving (i.e., he was not searching). Carmen continued to forage and tray-feed, and Cosimo joined her on the floor.

COSIMO SEARCHES AGAIN---CHICK RETURNED. At 22:34 h, Cosimo returned to the NB and looked in from the outside perch. Then he again looked down at the enclosure floor in the area beneath the NB perch. After just perching there for another min, he joined Carmen on the floor and followed her around as she foraged. Finally, almost 1 h after I removed the chick, Carmen entered the NB, took a brief look about, and exited. Cosimo entered afterward. Again, he looked all about, before sitting in the IA for a few sec and exiting. Both birds were foraging on the enclosure floor at 22:45 h, when I unobtrusively restored the chick to the NB.

COSIMO SPIES THE CHICK---TRIES TO CHEW THROUGH SIDEPANE. About a min later, as Cosimo stood on perch B, he heard the chick calling from the NB. This precipitated another bout of scanning the enclosure floor. Descending, he continued to search on the floor and then returned to perch B. Following that, he looked about outside the enclosure. Suddenly, he spied the chick through the NB sidepane and frantically tried to reach it by sticking his head out through the enclosure mesh, within 2-3 cm of the chick. However, he was unaware that the chick was in the NB (possibly influenced by the fact that he had already searched there repeatedly), because he began to chew frantically on the edge of the NB, near the chick. For the next 10 min he kept chewing on the NB, biting on the wire mesh, and trying to force his way through it.

COSIMO SEES CARMEN WITH CHICK, REUNION FOLLOWS. Meanwhile, Carmen had mounted to the entrance to the NB and, after about a min, entered it. However, once inside, she paid very little attention to the chick and did not allofeed it. She seemingly never had taken note of the chick's absence, in the first place, even though she had visited the NB once while it was gone. In a displacement activity, Cosimo then attacked the nearby bell vigorously (see Fig. 3a). He could not see into the NB at that time, because the bell was in his line of sight. After frantically trying again to get closer, by forcing his way through the enclosure mesh, he spied Carmen and the chick. Then he apparently realized that both of them were in the NB, because he proceeded directly to enter it, and began to allofeed and allogroom the chick. The scene gave the impression of a very happy reunion.

FRANTIC REACTIONS WHEN A CHICK IS PERCEIVED TO BE IN DANGER. The events of this single episode, in which, in essence, only Cosimo participated, suggest the following tentative conclusions. Whereas Cockatielian parents may evidence great concern over the whereabouts of a missing chick, they do not become frantic in their reactions. But they do become frantic if the chick is perceived to be, or believed to be, in danger. Further experiments along these lines with older nestlings support this view (e.g., see p. 695, **'Concerned' Parents**).

The Fourth Clutch of Carmen and Cosimo

THE OBJECTIVE---TO OBSERVE CARE OF NORMAL-SIZED BROOD. The 3rd brood of Carmen and Cosimo had consisted of but a single offspring, the male, Marco. It was evident that some aspects of the ways they cared for him (see pp. 681-686, **Chronological Accounts of the Third Brood**) were much influenced by the fact that they had only the one chick to brood. Accordingly, I bred Carmen and Cosimo again in the "transparent" NB, with the objective of observing the care of a brood of normal size.

To this purpose, I left the NB in place, to facilitate further breeding. I also continued a close scrutiny of their courtship behavior. [I viewed the presence of Marco as a welcome variation from the more usual circumstances during courtship.] The forthcoming eggs of the 4th clutch were not removed or otherwise manipulated, but an additional experiment with the courting birds was performed using substitute eggs, just before Carmen began to oviposit.

Preliminaries to the Fourth Clutch

VIGOROUS DISPUTES OVER INCUBATIVE AREA. For reference, Marco hatched on May 3, 1984. The first signs of preliminaries to breeding again were noted on the evening of May 15, when Cosimo began chewing on the borders of the NB entrance-hole. Later that same evening, both he and Carmen pecked about in the IA. Two days later, they seemed to be vigorously disputing for occupancy of the (empty) former IA. Marco generally was off to the side at those times. After another 2 days, I noticed that food was being consumed in 2-3 times the normal amounts (Marco then was 16 days old). The next day (May 20) both birds were busily chewing on a mineral block (oviposition, which began on June 15, was still almost a month away).

VOCALIZATIONS BEGIN. The earliest and most notable behavior preceding the 4th clutch occurred on May 21, when Carmen and Cosimo were in the NB together at 24:18 h. At that time, Cosimo began making urgent-sounding repetitive squeaks, identical with the female Coition Sounds. These soon graded over into the singing of almost his entire song repertoire, a very rich collection, indeed.

DAYTIME SINGING OUTSIDE, EVENING SINGING INSIDE, THE NESTBOX. In the following weeks, Cosimo was full of song--"singing up a storm" on many occasions, morning, afternoon, and evening, usually from outside the NB. On many other occasions, between May 24 and June 13, he sang softly from the NB, never at an earlier time than 17:30 h, and often very late in the evening. If the objective of this singing was to invite or encourage the female to adopt the NB, it was somewhat superfluous, inasmuch as the NB already was adopted and being used for the care of Marco. Indeed, Carmen seemed to ignore his soft singing from the NB, in the sense that it did not stimulate her to join him there.

MUTUAL SERENADING BY BREEDING MALES. A most interesting development was that Isabella and Ferdinand were courting and incubating eggs in the lower part of the same enclosure during this period. The singing of one breeding male not infrequently stimulated that of the other. On these occasions, they sometimes sang across the partition to one another, simultaneously and for long periods. One bird often had his head out through the enclosure bars looking at the other; at most their heads were only a few cm apart. Seemingly, the male (as well as the female) receives stimulation from his own song during breeding (as is known to be the case for Budgerigars; see pp. 121, 122).

POSSESSIVENESS OVER EMPTY INCUBATIVE AREA. I noted the first sexual union on May 29 and the last on June 13, spanning the period of intensive singing. Cosimo first began tending to the IA and "brooding" it for extended periods on May 25, when he sang softly from it at 23:00 h. Thereafter, he did so frequently, even when Marco was within the NB. He showed possessiveness over the IA on June 1, as he pecked at Carmen when she tried to enter the NB. He also rose and made ready to peck at Marco when he entered, before recognizing him. After allowing Marco to enter, he pecked away Carmen from the entrance twice more. On June 3, a similar scene ensued, when he interrupted his "fussing" in the IA to peck weakly at Marco when he entered, and again at Carmen when she merely looked in.

CARMEN AND COSIMO PREFER PRIVACY. Carmen gave the IA much less attention but sometimes "plastered" herself into the IA corner, as she sometimes formerly did while ovipositing and incubating. There was only a small amount of mutual allogrooming, but, beginning on June 5, Carmen courtship-fed Cosimo roughly every other day. An indication of a desire of the courting birds for privacy (noted on many subsequent occasions with all 3 species of these studies) was seen on June 13, when they were together in the NB. When Marco joined them, they promptly left; when Marco left, they promptly returned.

DISCOVERY AND CARE OF BURIED EGGS BEFORE LAYING COMMENCES

It appeared likely that Carmen was about to begin to oviposit, so I took the opportunity to ascertain whether, at that time, they would recover eggs that were buried in the IA, and, if so, whether they would care for them. The old IA had not been kept clear of shavings, perhaps because Marco's movements in the NB tended to keep the shavings more or less evenly distributed. Accordingly, on June 14, at 16:16 h, I buried 4 lovebird eggs $1\frac{1}{4}$-cm deep at the $\frac{1}{2}$- and 3/4-way positions, 2 against the far sidewall, and 2 about 5 cm out from it. All 4 of them were squarely in the old IA. Within 75 min, one egg had been found, within 82 min, a 2nd one, and within 4.75 h, a 3rd one. The last egg, at the $\frac{1}{2}$-way point against the sidewall, was not found until after 24 h.

EGGS CARED FOR AS IF THEIR OWN. Carmen and Cosimo proceeded to behave toward these eggs just as if they were their own clutch, including all the different kinds of competition for them: stealing them out from under one another, splitting the clutch, protecting and shielding the eggs, diving in, Mandible-fluttering, Cosimo heading Carmen off from the NB to get back to the eggs first, etc. That night, Carmen did not incubate the eggs, but guarded them from the inside perch. Marco slept in the NB, as usual. From the pair's behavior, one would never have surmised that the clutch was a fostered one.

MARCO, A TOLERATED BUT INHIBITORY PRESENCE. It is interesting to note that Marco was tolerated completely, though Carmen and Cosimo easily could have excluded him from the NB. He often was in the NB when his parents crouched over or guarded the eggs, or competed for them. His presence, however, tended to be inhibitory, particularly for Carmen. When Marco entered the NB during a session of competition for the clutch, a "truce" sometimes would ensue, and prevail until after he left. On some of these occasions, Carmen left the NB and characteristically would not return until after Marco had departed. The eggs thereby were left in Cosimo's care by default.

At other times, Carmen's attention to the eggs had higher priority. On the 2nd night after adding the eggs, e.g., Carmen sat lightly on them and Marco slept off to the side (she had laid the 1st egg of the new clutch earlier that evening). As was his usual habit during the incubatory period, Cosimo slept outside the NB, either nearby or on perch A (Fig. 3a).

OVIPOSITION COMMENCES

The 1st egg of the new clutch was oviposited during the evening of June 15, only about 30-32 h after the substitute eggs were buried in the IA. As mentioned above, Carmen covered this egg together with the other 4 eggs that night. On the morning of June 16, I removed the 4 substitute eggs, noting that the IA still contained a 2-cm depth of shavings.

CARMEN EXITS NESTBOX BRIEFLY AT LIGHTS-OFF. In general, the care of the eggs of this clutch proceeded no differently from that of the preceding one. Some noteworthy repetitions and differences are mentioned below. As before, on the first few nights, Carmen left the egg(s), and usually the NB, as soon as the lights were turned off for the night, but returned to them within 1-2 min. If the lights were not left off for the night but were turned back on again after she had taken her temporary leave of the NB but before she had returned voluntarily, she hastened back and sat over the egg(s).

TOLERANCE FOR MARCO DIMINISHES. I found Marco's presence becoming disruptive at that time and placed him off to the side in enclosure F. However, I returned him for a visit of several hours every afternoon or evening. In that way, I could assess changes, if any, in the parents' tolerance for him during their care of the new clutch. He continued to be tolerated very well until June 31, 4 days before the first chick hatched. On that day Cosimo tolerated his mere presence well enough, but pecked him away when he approached too closely. He also began to intercept Marco and peck him away if the latter approached the NB, and he also barred Marco's entrance from within the NB. Cosimo's only previous intolerant behavior toward Marco was in pecking him away when he solicited to be allofed.

FOUR EGGS FOSTERED INTO THE CLUTCH. A notable modification of the usual circumstances was that I fostered 4 eggs of the 2nd clutch of Isabella and Ferdinand into the clutch of Carmen and Cosimo. One of these was added every other day, namely, on the days following Carmen's ovipositions, just as they were oviposited by Isabella. The reason for this was that Isabella did not begin to care for her eggs during the night (i.e., she did not incubate the substituted lovebird eggs) until after her 4th egg was laid. The presence of these additional eggs seemed to intensify the normal competition for the clutch between Carmen and Cosimo, as described below.

A LIGHTS-OFF TEST. During the early period of incubation I carried out an experiment with Cosimo that involved turning the lights off as he sat over the eggs. It was noted earlier that during the early days of incubation in the transparent NB, Carmen customarily vacated the eggs and voided as soon as the lights were turned off. The experienced hen returns shortly thereafter and begins to sit on, or crouch over, the eggs for the night, but, as will be seen, the inexperienced hen may not. The question to be answered was, "Would a male sitting or crouching over the eggs late in the evening also vacate them, if the lights were turned off prematurely?"

Accordingly, on several successive nights, I performed this test with Cosimo, as opportunities presented themselves, namely, at 23:00 h, 23:03 h, 21:56 h, 22:28 h, 22:00 h, 22:45 h, and 24:01 h. The answers were clear; Cosimo did not vacate the eggs promptly (as Carmen almost always did). In fact, a few min after turning off the lights, whether or not I turned them on again, Carmen made her way to the NB, entered, and took over the eggs from Cosimo. He yielded them to her readily on these occasions, and, it would seem that both birds were behaving as if lights-off signalled that it was time to exchange the care of the eggs for the night.

[On the other hand, in later experiments involving the males, Ferdinand and Homer, the male bird incubating or brooding late in the evening sometimes showed the light responses--leaving the eggs or chick(s) when the lights were turned off and returning to them shortly thereafter when the lights were turned back on (e.g., see p. 496, **Neither Parent Broods Hatchling at Night**).]

INTRUDING COCKATIELS PROVOKE COSIMO--COMPETITION INTENSIFIES. Sometimes Cosimo directly poked his head under Carmen to inspect the eggs, without a first recourse to grooming her crissum. It also is of considerable interest that, if a Cockatiel was climbing about outside the NB, in sight of Cosimo as he incubated within, Cosimo rushed out of the NB on the attack, whereas if it was a lovebird climbing about, he merely became alarmed. On June 21, with 6 eggs in the clutch, competition for them definitely was becoming intense. Even Marco's presence in the NB (during his daily visits) and his occasional bumping into his parents, did not deter Carmen and Cosimo from competing for the eggs.

COMPETITION PEAKS. By the time that I added Isabella's 4th egg to their clutch, competition between Carmen and Cosimo was more intense than ever before. Even though there were enough eggs present for each bird to care for a clutch of 4, Cosimo was so tenacious in retaining all 8 eggs, that he would not tolerate even a temporary splitting of the clutch. Carmen now faced a very formidable operation, indeed, to acquire the clutch for the night, particularly as she sometimes began to contest for it as early as 21:00 or 22:00 h, when Cosimo was extremely reluctant to surrender it.

On such occasions, Cosimo would groom Carmen's head relentlessly in his efforts to drive her from the NB. Even after he succeeded in getting her up onto the NB perch, paused half-way out, or in the process of leaving, he would peck her rump to hasten her departure. On those occasions when she turned and dove back into the NB and onto the eggs, he surrendered them to her, but following that he would "punish" her with incessant head allogrooming and drive her away again. Even when she only sat on the outside perch, and was not in the act of entering, he got up from the eggs and gently pecked her away.

REMOVED EGGS NOT MISSED---COMPETITION REMAINS INTENSE. On June 25, I returned Isabella's eggs to her, leaving only the 4 belonging to Carmen. Carmen was the first to return to the NB afterwards. She took over the care of the clutch without the slightest sign of having missed the other 4 eggs. Nor did Cosimo show any sign of missing them on his next visit. They probably would have behaved no differently had only 1 egg remained instead of 4. Their vigorous competition for the eggs in the late evenings continued as before, with the exception that, on June 26, Cosimo tolerated a brief splitting of the clutch.

FIRST CHICK HATCHES

A CHICK HATCHES--EXTREMELY DIFFICULT TO ACQUIRE THE BROOD. The 1st chick hatched early on the morning of July 4. When Cosimo came to the NB at 09:30 h and spied the egg-shell halves lying to the side and rear, he hesitated to enter. When he did enter, Carmen pecked at him aggressively. After inspecting the eggs, he left, but returned 3 min later. Cosimo then was able to acquire the chick and eggs from Carmen only with the greatest of difficulty. This usually entailed about 1 h of intermittent but vigorous effort, with extensive allogrooming of Carmen's head and back, and some allogrooming of her crissum.

CHICK TENDED BUT ALLOFEEDING DELAYED. But even after Cosimo came into possession of the chick and eggs, Carmen did not leave the NB. She waited over 1 h at his side. He surrendered the chick and eggs to her again at 11:45 h but returned and reacquired it 25 min later. When Carmen dove in for an inspection at 12:35 h, he left again, but returned within 10 min. At this time, the hatchling was extending its head vigorously, and both parents attended to it with bill contacts, but there was no sign of its being allofed. Cosimo eventually acquired the chick and eggs for the afternoon at 12:50 h, but Carmen remained in the NB until 13:25 h.

Carmen was the first to allofeed the hatchling, at 22:34 h. Her head bobbed very gently in passive response to the hatchlings pumping. Most of the meal was trickled slowly into the chick's bill (see pp. 675-678, **Feeding of Hatchlings**). She had the usual difficulty reacquiring the chick and eggs from Cosimo late that evening, but the competition was relatively mild, with much back-and-forth stealing of the eggs. [The care of Cockatielian chicks is treated in Chap 6, Part 1]

The First Clutch of Isabella and Ferdinand

TWO PAIRS OF MATED SIBLINGS HOUSED TOGETHER. As the reader will recall, on March 29, 1984, I partitioned enclosure A into upper and lower halves and placed the 2 mated, sibling Cockatielian pairs, Isabella and Ferdinand, and Helena and Homer, in the lower section. It was not my intention to facilitate breeding of these pairs. I already was well occupied with the breeding of Carmen and Cosimo and lovebird pairs. I was soon to learn, however, that, if other circumstances are not unfavorable, compatible Cockatielian pairs are likely to breed in the absence of a NB, just as will lovebird pairs. Considering the many primitive characters posessesd by Cockatiels, the ease with which they will oviposit and nest on the floor of an enclosure is another piece of evidence that points to the practice of nesting on the surface of flat, level ground as being the primitive method for birds.

A STIMULATORY INFLUENCE OF PARENTAL VOCALIZING? It is not unlikely that the frequent singing by Cosimo and the Coition Sounds of Carmen had a stimulatory influence on the 2 pairs in the lower part of the enclosure (see pp. 121, 122 for a description of such influences in Budgerigars). As was already mentioned, these pairs usually set up a din of whistling when they heard the Coition Sounds of their parents (see pp. 414, 838-840).

SEXUAL UNION. The first sexual union of Ferdinand and Isabella was noted in the evening of April 12, a 2nd in the evening 6 days later, and a 3rd in the evening 4 days later. All occurred between 06:00 and 09:30 h. From then on, until the completion of their clutch, they copulated virtually every day between 16:00 h and 23:55 h, with the exception of 5 days, when copulations occurred in the morning. Their routine was unorthodox but very effective. Isabella sat in a large food tray, facing the enclosure side, and gripping a side wire tightly in her bill. Her vent protruded over the rear of the tray. Ferdinand then mounted her in the usual manner.

PREPARING A NEST----FERDINAND ATTACKS HOMER----COITION SOUNDS. During this period, there had been a great deal of "fussing around" (mostly pecking at and tearing up paper, sitting, and exploring) in the right-rear corner of the enclosure by Isabella and Ferdinand (the enclosure floor there was covered with layered paper). On 3 occasions, Ferdinand had chased Homer tenaciously all about in the enclosure, and attacked him, amid loud vocalizations. Homer was so greatly intimidated and agitated by the attacks, that he cried out repeatedly in fright and alarm for over a min afterward. On at least one occasion, Ferdinand uttered the Coition Sounds while foraging in the company of Isabella. In the next few months, he uttered this call more times than all the other 5 Cockatiels combined.

OVIPOSITION BEGINS. Isabella laid her 1st egg shortly before 15:30 h on May 16. At that time, I removed Helena and Homer to enclosure F. I placed a 22½-cm-diameter pie pan, 3-cm deep, on the bottom of enclosure A at the right-rear corner (dashed circle labelled **NP** in Fig 3a), where the pair had been preparing a nest and where Isabella oviposited. I also closed off the enclosure wall in the vicinity of the corner with cardboard. I placed the egg on a 2-cm bed of wood shavings at the rear corner of this pan, which was adopted immediately as a nest.

NEST PREPARATION----FERDINAND "FULL OF SONG"----EGG CARE. Later that day, Ferdinand began the preparation of the new nest, picking around and clearing in the prospective IA (**IA** in Fig. 3a), and singing, leaving little doubt that the Cockatielian male adopts and prepares the nest. As with Cosimo, on such occasions, he was "full of song." He frequently scraped the bottom of the nestpan with his bill, just as Cosimo had "plowed" in the IA of the NB. He was very gentle with the egg, crouching very lightly over it and occasionally moving it about. Isabella joined him several times for a few sec. He gave the IA a thorough further treatment as late as 23:20 h. The egg was left unattended that night, but Ferdinand was back in the nest singing softly, early the next morning. He "fussed" and pecked about in the IA, and swayed his head while doing so--scattering shavings all about. On one occasion, when he was crouching over the egg alone in the nest, at 11:30 h, Isabella joined him for short periods.

SINGING INTENSIFIES---COMPETITION BEGINS. As the day wore on, Ferdinand's singing increased in frequency and duration. He displayed many songs, variations, and modulations, just as his father, Cosimo, had done. Interest in the nest and egg also increased progressively, with both Isabella and Ferdinand making many short visits, and Ferdinand doing most of his singing from the nest. From 23:00 h to midnight, interest in the nest reached its highest pitch, with many visits, much singing, and loose sitting on the egg by both birds. The first signs of competing for the egg were noted at 23:28 h, when the parents "stole" it back and forth, out from under one another. Between visits to the nest, both Isabella and Ferdinand spent much time consuming cuttlefish bone and mineral block. The last visit to the nest was at 24:01 h. The egg also was left unattended on that 2nd night.

SECOND EGG LAID---ALL FACETS OF EGG-CARE BEHAVIOR EXPRESSED. The 2nd egg was laid on May 18, and the birds gradually settled into sitting loosely on the clutch. One by one, all the facets of egg-care behavior evidenced by Carmen and Cosimo appeared. On this particular day I saw:

(a) alternation in the care of the eggs;
(b) careful positioning of the eggs before sitting over them, and occasionally tucking them in;
(c) Ferdinand vocally warning off Isabella, and then pecking her away from the IA;
(d) Isabella climbing down the enclosure side, head first, diving under Ferdinand and displacing him from the eggs, followed by his "muscling" or "bulldozing" her off of them;
(e) Mandible-fluttering during virtually all interactions;
(f) frequent inspections of the eggs by the non-sitting bird;
(g) one bird waiting in the nest at the side of the other to acquire the clutch from the other;
(h) Ferdinand jumping into the nest, just as Cosimo jumped into the NB; and
(i) Isabella pressing her tail and crissum high against the enclosure sides in the corner while sitting on the eggs.

At no time did either bird allofeed the other. The birds were off of the eggs when I turned the lights off, though Ferdinand had been crouching over them and singing as late as 23:27 h.

COMPETITION INTENSIFIES---FERDINAND HIGHLY VOCAL. By May 19, competition for the eggs had increased in intensity, and Ferdinand used the head-grooming tactic several times to displace Isabella. They then frequently "stole" the loosely-sat eggs back and forth out from under one another and, for the first time, they also sat on a divided clutch, one egg for each. They had become much more vociferous in the nest, with Ferdinand sometimes uttering "duck-squawk" 'complaints' after he had lost the eggs to Isabella and was trying actively to reacquire them from her.

Sometimes, I received the impression, after Ferdinand lost the eggs and left the NB and vocalized, that his singing was a displacement activity--an expression of frustration over having lost the clutch. Such vigorous singing from a perch, while Isabella was sitting loosely on the eggs, did not appear to be an effort to influence her. Sometimes, after the laying of the 2nd egg, such vocalizing evolved into an interchange with Cosimo, in the upper part of the enclosure. On 1 or 2 occasions when Ferdinand sang softly from the nest, Isabella paid no noticeable attention, at first. But as his calls became more urgent-sounding, she joined him, if only for a few sec, and he then tended to cease vocalizing.

ADJUSTING EGG ORIENTATION AND PLACEMENT. With a better view of the eggs in the completely open nest, and with habituated birds, I was able to witness and appreciate more fully the tremendous attentiveness of the birds to the orientation and placement of the eggs, which had so impressed me when observing Carmen and Cosimo incubating in the NB with the Plexiglas sidepane.

[In the early stages of incubation, before the extra-embryonic membranes have fused with the inner shell membrane, the parents' frequent turning or jostling of the eggs functions to prevent adhesions and premature fusions. After each rotation during this period the contents of an egg rotate freely within the shell, bringing the lighter portion of the yolk bearing the blastoderm to an uppermost position (see p. 174).

After the extra-embryonic membranes and shell membranes have fused (first chorion with allantois, then chorioallantois with inner surface of inner shell membrane), about halfway through the incubatory period, the egg contents become fixed with respect to the shell and no longer rotate freely within it. From this time onward the contents of the egg also are distributed in a more markedly asymmetrical fashion, to the extent that when allowed to rotate freely, an egg will settle into a stable equilibrium position. The predominant assumption of this position apparently plays an important role in the embryo's attainment of the proper prehatching position and in its making its way from the shell in the hatching process (427). It is well known that in some avian species the parents are responsive to the prehatching vocalizations of the chicks, sometimes looking down, rising, turning the eggs, resettling, calling, or returning to uncovered eggs (see 427, 1,053).]

The attentions of the parents to the eggs after the middle of the incubatory period--the many close inspections that impressed me so--apparently serve to jostle and space the eggs so that they are free to oscillate sufficiently to settle into a stable equilibrium position. Close attention to the eggs in the last hours and days before hatching also may play an important role in the terminal incubatory behavior of the parents, insofar as the physical treatment of the eggs is concerned (see discussion and refs. in 427), and in the preparation of the parents for allofeeding and otherwise caring for the young. A close TV surveillance of the precise manipulations performed by the parents in the course of incubation might well reveal changes in the nature and extent of their attentions that are consonant with the different requirements of the eggs in the early and late stages of embryonic development.

NESTS WITH FLAT, BARE BOTTOMS AVOIDED. Many workers warn of the danger of eggs getting cracked or broken through collisions, and the consequent need to avoid a perfectly flat or totally unlittered nest bottom (see discussion in 27). Parrots with bare-floored nestboxes "provide this litter themselves," when a source for it is available. Thus, if strips are fastened inside the NB, most, if not all, parrots will chew bits from them and shape a simple nest pad (27). It is well known that the walls of the entrance-hole are a frequent object of the chewing attentions of nesting parrots.

I would suggest that this desirability of avoiding perfectly flat nest bottoms may be quite unrelated to the danger of the eggs becoming cracked by rolling up against one another. In fact, the eggs of a given Cockatiel-ian, lovebird, or Budgerigar clutch become jostled against one another scores of times every day as the parents gather them in, shift the position of the entire clutch by shoving them about, and, in the case of Cockatiels, compete for them.

It seems much more likely that the requirement for a non-smooth nest bottom is, rather, because the presence of a thin layer of wood dust allows the eggs to rotate with slight parental prodding, yet at the same time provides enough frictional barrier to free rolling that the eggs will hold close to their equilibrium positions once such positions have been attained. It is not unlikely that the very close attention that I often observed being conferred consisted of the parents gently and slightly nudging the eggs about until they reached a stable equilibrium position (an unstable equilibrium position would be one in which the eggs were out of balance but were prevented from attaining balance by friction or contacts).

NO NOCTURNAL INCUBATION---COMPETITION PEAKS. On the night of May 19, it appeared likely that Isabella would care for the eggs for the night, particularly in view of the fact that her 3rd egg was due to be laid the next day. Nonetheless, she came off the eggs as soon as the lights were turned off. As a matter of fact, she never incubated or crouched over the eggs of this clutch at night, that is, she never progressed beyond the equivalent of the 2nd phylogenetic stage of egg care. She oviposited for the 3rd (and last) time on May 20, but the birds did not begin daytime incubation of the eggs for another week.

In the following weeks, competition for the eggs, while perhaps not reaching a higher pitch than that achieved by Carmen and Cosimo, occurred much more often, lasted for longer periods, and was more vocal. There was much more back-and-forth stealing of the eggs and alternate displacments of one bird from the clutch by the other. It was particularly easy for Isabella to roll the eggs out from under Ferdinand, when he pecked at the shavings and the bottom of the nestpan. Isabella, herself, rarely engaged in such activities. All the tactics and actions employed by Carmen and Cosimo in competition for the eggs also were employed by Isabella and Ferdinand, although Ferdinand was more sparing in his employment of crissum grooming, and was not so 'relentless' in his head grooming. The differences in behavior from that of Carmen and Cosimo, including the failure of Isabella to allofeed Ferdinand, are consistent with the view that Ferdinand was much less dominant over Isabella than was Cosimo over Carmen.

ISABELLA, THE MAJOR DAYTIME INCUBATOR. Beginning at the time when Isabella began to incubate the eggs in the morning, after the lights came on, she became the major daytime incubator. This status was achieved only after many prolonged competitive bouts for the eggs. Isabella eventually became so highly possessive of the clutch, that she usually began to Mandible-flutter if Ferdinand even approached the vicinity of the nest. When he was in the nest pecking about while she sat, she pecked him away if he even brushed accidentally against her.

UNSATISFIED AT NIGHT, INCUBATORY URGE STRONGER DURING THE DAY. The reason for this change in the distribution of daytime incubation probably was the total absence of nighttime incubation. Isabella almost always came off the eggs shortly after the lights were turned off, and, with few exceptions, she began to incubate them again in the morning very shortly after the lights were turned on (though it had been Ferdinand who first entered the nest in the morning until after the 3rd egg was laid).

It seems likely that Isabella's urge to incubate persisted at a very high level during the day because, in the absence of nocturnal incubation, her "needs" for the stimuli of incubation were not being met, i.e., she had accumulated an "incubatory debt." Her consequent much greater tenacity in seeking and retaining the eggs during the day led to an increase in the length and intensity of the bouts of competing with Ferdinand for their possession. The fact that Isabella usually eventually prevailed was not so much because Ferdinand surrendered the clutch to her more readily, as it was because she, herself, was so persistent. Not only was her accumulated "incubatory debt" greater than his, but he was less dominant over her than was Cosimo over Carmen.

The same phenomenon was observed in tests of the nest-site and brood-site fidelity of Helena and Homer, in which the parents were inhibited temporarily either from incubating the eggs or brooding the chicks when the eggs or chicks were displaced from the nest. Once the eggs or chicks had been returned to the nest, subsequent incubation and/or brooding was intensified (see pp. 498-510, **Oviposition-Site Fidelity** and **Brood-Site Fidelity**). This phenomenon was observed in brooding parents of all 3 species of this study with regard to allofeeding. Whenever all nestlings were removed from the parents for more than about 15-20 min, the parents accumulated an "allofeeding debt." In consequence, they allofed returned nestlings more promptly, more vigorously, and more lengthily, the longer had been the period of absence.

PROMPT, PERSISTENT RESPONSES TO LIGHTS-OFF AND LIGHTS-ON. No bird illustrated the responses to turning the lights on and off as sharply, or over such a lengthy period, as did Isabella--both in terms of responses to sequential test cycles, and from day to day. I have mentioned already, that she came off the eggs shortly after the lights were turned off every night, and that she returned to them in the morning shortly after the lights were turned on (at least, from the time of laying of the 3rd egg).

EVIDENCE OF LEARNING OR ACCOMMODATION. On several nights, when I tested her by turning the lights off and on sequentially, she seemed to learn that I would be turning them on again not very long after they went off. She began to wait longer, or even until I left the room, before leaving the eggs. But even if she had been learning, her waiting did not persist; the urge to leave the eggs in the dark apparently was too strong to resist. Specifically, she waited much longer before leaving the eggs, on May 23-26, than on May 22, when she had responded promptly to each of the 4½ test cycles. By May 27, she was responding promptly again. [On that night, she left and returned during 5½ cycles but did not return to the eggs to end the 6th cycle.]

SHIELDING FROM LIGHT MUCH MORE URGENT THAN DEPARTING IN DARK. On May 28, she responded to 4½ cycles, whereupon I ceased testing. During these tests, she left the eggs within an average of 86 sec after the lights were turned off, and returned to the eggs within an average of 10 sec after they were turned on. Shielding the eggs from light thus appeared to be very much more urgent than departing from them in the dark. [I waited an average of 40 sec after she left the eggs before turning the lights back on, and an average of 24 sec after she re-covered the eggs, before turning them back off.]

Breeding Failures By Young or Inexperienced Birds

FIRST BREEDING SELDOM SUCCESSFUL. "Successful nesting and rearing of families are not all instinctive traits" (2). It is a well known phenomenon that breeding attempts by birds that are young or inexperienced--sometimes even after a 1st or 2nd attempt--often end in failures. Ring Doves with previous breeding experience laid eggs sooner, incubated more efficiently, raised their young more efficiently, and reared more young to maturity. In all respects in which one could measure the efficiency of behavior, the experienced birds were superior (1,279).

Bates and Busenbark seldom expected success during a confined pair's first breeding season. They point out that, with many species of birds in confinement, "dismal" failures may occur 2 or 3 times per season for 2 years before "the learning process can be successfully instilled" (2). Some pairs of 4-month-old Cockatiels are known to have produced fertile clutches, but "the parents often prove incompetent and their precocity comes to nothing" (127). "Inexperienced birds not infrequently let the chicks die, one by one...." (787). Some aspects of the breeding performance improve with age alone, independently of the experience that normally is gained with increasing age, whereas other aspects improve with the greater experience of breeding acquired with age (1,150).

Inferior reproductive abilities of young parents are well known in wild birds, "Either young birds have a lower chance of finding a mate or lay fewer eggs, and/or they care less efficiently for eggs and young" (see 101, 827). One proposed explanation for this involves "reproductive restraint," in which young breeders are thought to refrain from expending maximal parental effort to forestall associated risks, in the interests of future reproduction (827). Although some field data may support this view, I favor the more conventional explanation, though I express it more explicitly, in terms of the need for an hierarchical opening of the neural pathways involved in reproduction, as discussed below.

[When the Parrot Society in the United Kingdom took a census among breeders of Cockatiels in 1969, it was found that 58% of the eggs in 86 clutches, averaging 5 eggs each, produced chicks. All the young were reared in only 3 cases but no datum is given for parental age or experience (see 778).]

"NEEDING EXPERIENCE," A MATTER OF A NEED FOR PRACTICE. In the cases of birds that are "too young," by definition, not all the organ systems that take part in breeding have not yet reached a sufficient state of maturity, (imperfect maturation of reproductive skills; see 827). When incubatory or brooding failures are attributed to birds being "inexperienced," one does not mean that birds that fail to hatch eggs profit from the experience of losing a clutch or that the birds that feed hatchlings inadequately profit from the experience of losing chicks.

In other words, by "needing the experience," one does not imply that the birds need to learn from their mistakes, in the same sense that Man does. A Cockatielian hen does not begin to incubate at night because eggs of the previous clutch that were incubated only during the day did not hatch, nor do Cockatiels begin to allofeed a 2nd hatchling because the unfed first one did not survive. Birds generally are unable to form judge-ments as to what is a "mistake" and assess cause and effect, at least not where the incubation of eggs and the raising of chicks are concerned.

What is involved primarily in the "need for experience," is the need for practice, that is, for preliminary uses of the processes and pathways in the motor, reproductive, and nervous systems that are involved in the reproductive processes in question, referred to more generally as "reproductive experience in the broadest sense" (827). This was referred to by Lehrman as "the animal's learning how to do it better as it breeds over and over again" (1,279). Thus, Cockatiels that fail hopelessly as parents one year can become model parents the next year (127). [In the same vein, the experience of having built one nest often facilitates the construction of a 2nd one (28).]

[It is thought to be of particular interest in future studies of motor patterns during development (as distinct from during reproductive cycles) to ascertain the extent to which the selective practicing of motor patterns (1) inhibits or retards the development of formally or functionally similar motor patterns, or (2) facilitates the development of related patterns that involve diverse motor dimensions (or, conversely, inhibits functionally antagonistic motor patterns; 1,268).]

NEURAL PATHWAYS BECOME AVAILABLE IN HIERARCHICAL SEQUENCES. The fact that a bird may be well past maturity does not imply that the processes and pathways in question already are fully established and prepared for use in successful reproduction. Some pathways and processes serving functions that come later in the sequence of reproductive acts apparently are not available, as a rule, until those that come earlier have been used, that is, the mobilization of such processes may follow an hierarchical course. And, it may take more than one use (practice), or an optimum use, of the prior processes and pathways, to "open up" subsequent ones. With Cockatiels, one use, or an optimum use, may be sufficient, because it is said that old birds that have never been bred almost always prove to be ideal parents (127). [I would suggest that one may think of the neural circuitry that is laid down as providing the innate or instinctive component of the governed behavior, and the acts facilitating the "opening" and functioning of the circuitry as the learned or experiential component (see 1,276 and 1,279 for related material).]

Some findings that are highly suggestive of the influence of experience in the alteration or facilitation of the neural circuitry for reproductive acts by experience (primarily nest-building experience) were obtained with Ring Doves by injecting progesterone into experienced and inexperienced birds that were in breeding condition. The median time that it took for experienced birds to stand on the nest after being put in the enclosure was 1 min, compared to about 1 h for inexperienced birds. Similarly, the median elapsed time before the experienced bird actually was sitting on the nest was about 25 min, compared to 25-26 h for inexperienced birds. In addition, the number of birds that eventually found the eggs--in the same circumstances--was substantially higher among the experienced birds. If the birds are not in breeding condition to begin with, only 20% of inexperienced birds will sit on eggs that are provided, whereas 75% of the experienced birds do so (1,279).

INEXPERIENCED, AND TOO YOUNG, 3RD PHYLOGENETIC STAGE NOT ATTAINED. Let us think in terms of the elaboration of neural circuits and the mobilization of unused pathways in the nervous system being consequences of changes in hormone levels and the opening of antecedent pathways. The pathways that lead to the equivalent of the postulated 2nd phylogenetic stage of egg care by birds (namely shielding or crouching over the eggs by day and guarding by night) had been established in Isabella and Ferdinand, but the pair never achieved full expression of the 3rd stage. In this stage the eggs are incubated by sitting tightly on them both by day and by night. At most, they only began to incubate the eggs by day after about 12 days.

Although Cockatiels begin to form pairs at a very young age, they very rarely breed before they are 1 yr old (6), and Bates and Busenbark point out that one should not come to expect success in breeding them until the birds are a full 2 yr old (2). Ferdinand was about 19 months old, and Isabella about 17 months old. Accordingly, they not only were an inexperienced pair, they might still have been too young for successful breeding.

COSIMO YOUNG, BUT CARMEN MATURE. In this connection, it is noteworthy that Cosimo was less than 1 yr old at the time he first was bred successfully, but he had the benefit of a very much older and experienced partner. In fact, it is said to be good policy in Cockatielian breeding to arrange to have an experienced bird paired up with an inexperienced one (127). I got the impression on many occasions that Carmen's not infrequent hesitations and 'uncertainties' in her responses (none of which was observed during subsequent breeding) to Cosimo's actions had their basis in the fact that he behaved and responded in an immature or inexperienced manner. [The age of the male is more important in determining the number of fledged and surviving young of the biparental-caring, hole-nesting Great Tit than is the age of the female (810).]

DIURNAL SHIELDING URGE PERSISTS AFTER NOCTURNAL INCUBATION CEASES. The egg care of the 3rd phylogenetic stage not only is the last to be exhibited by breeding birds, it also is the first to be abandoned by hens whose incubatory urges are waning in the care of overdue or infertile clutches, or clutches that are losing parental attention for other reasons. For example, the 3 juveniles of the 5th brood of Carmen and Cosimo disrupted the care of Carmen's next clutch and destroyed 2 of the eggs before I removed the young on the 14th day of incubation. As a consequence of this interference by the young, the attentiveness of the parents to the remaining eggs waned. On the the 18th day, I found the eggs unattended and at room temperature (27°C). But within min after turning on the lights, Carmen resumed incubating them (after the usual brief period of stretching and grooming). Incubation by both parents during that day was desultory.

Again on the morning of the 19th day I found the eggs unattended and at room temperature. Once again, Carmen returned and incubated them within min of the lights being turned on. This behavior not only shows that the urge to incubate during the night (a component of the 3rd phylogenetic stage of egg care) is the first to wane, the prompt morning incubating of the eggs shows that the urge to shield the eggs from exposure during the day (a component of the 2nd phylogenetic stage of egg care) still remains strong. I observed precisely the same type of behavior repeatedly in lovebirds and, strikingly, during the Budgerigar hen Lucretia's care of her 2nd and 4th clutches (see pp. 782, 783, 789, **Daytime Incubation Only**).

INEXPERIENCED BIRDS COMMONLY DO NOT INCUBATE AT NIGHT. The lack of breeding success of immature or inexperienced birds commonly is caused by their failure to incubate the clutch at night. In the present case, it is clear that the failure to achieve the 3rd phylogenetic stage of egg care was a limitation imposed by Isabella's youth and/or inexperience, since the nighttime incubation by Cockatiels is carried out by the female. It will be seen below (p. 407, **Nocturnal Incubation Begins**) that, in the care of their next clutch, about 6 weeks later, Isabella achieved the 3rd phylogenetic stage of egg care. At that time, Isabella and Ferdinand incubated an egg to hatching, but they did not appear to have progressed to the point at which they could properly brood a hatchling (I fostered out their hatchling, the female, Kirsten, to Carmen and Cosimo).

TESTING EGG-CARE RESPONSES. In any event, since this 1st clutch was not destined to hatch (though it was fertile), because it had not been incubated tightly during the day and not at all at night, I used the opportunity that was presented, to test the responses of Isabella and Ferdinand to missing clutches, and to the presence of supernumerary eggs. Some of the results were quite unexpected, but they generally confirmed and extended those obtained in similar experiments with Carmen and Cosimo.

Lastly, it should be mentioned that there are anecdotal accounts of two cases in which fostered eggs were accepted, incubated to hatching, and the chicks fledged by Cockatielian pairs consisting of males over 2 yr old and young or immature females (1,101). But details of the reproductive histories, particularly the degree to which the foster parents might have achieved breeding condition before receiving the eggs, are not available.

FIFTH AND SIXTH OBSERVATIONS OF RESPONSES OVER A MISSING CLUTCH

EGGS REMOVED---FERDINAND "PLOWS UP" INCUBATIVE AREA. At 22:10 h on May 30, I took the 3 eggs of Isabella and Ferdinand from the IA and buried them diametrically at the most distant point in the nestpan--fully 20 cm away--under 1 cm of shavings (location z in Fig. 3a). Based on similar experiments with Carmen and Cosimo, one would not have expected these eggs to be found by pecking or probing, and, indeed, they were not. Ferdinand was the first to return to the nestpan. When he detected the absence of the eggs, he promptly nuzzled (pushed his bill into) and plowed all through the IA and its vicinity, but he did not come close to approaching the far side, where the eggs were buried.

REPEATED FAR-AND-WIDE VISUAL SEARCHES--PARTLY EXPOSED EGGS RECOVERED. Ferdinand also carried out a "distant visual search," that is, he raised his head and looked out of the nest around the enclosure floor. After that, he climbed to a perch and also examined the enclosure floor from that vantage point. Meanwhile, Isabella entered the nestpan and also searched everywhere visually for the eggs. Finding nothing, she left, but she returned another 5 times and repeated her visual search each time. Both birds also searched on foot everywhere outside the nestpan, and Ferdinand peered down and outside the enclosure from various points along the sides from on the floor. They were still 'agitated' and searching visually for the eggs 15 min later.

At 22:25 h, I exposed the surface of 1 egg (by reaching in with a thin dowel and brushing some shavings off of it). Ferdinand spotted it immediately, climbed down hastily from perch C (Fig. 3a), and wedged it out of the shavings. In the process, he exposed a 2nd egg, and recovered it also. After nudging the eggs over to the IA, he sat on them. Since he seemed to be 'contented,' with just the 2 eggs, and did not search for the 3rd one, I exposed it too (in both cases, the exposure was to the extent of about 25% of the egg's volume). Again, he spied it right away, came over, and recovered it. Since it was Ferdinand who recovered all these eggs, it confirmed my belief that there was no significance to the fact that it was Carmen who usually recovered exposed eggs in the NB in earlier experiments.

EGGS BURIED AGAIN---MORE VISUAL SEARCHES. On the next day, at 17:50 h, I buried the eggs again, at the same locations (z in Fig. 3a), to see if the experiences of the day before would lead the birds to dig there for them. Again, Ferdinand was the first to enter the nest, by backing down into it along the sidewall. Again, he searched the IA for the eggs, turning around several times, but he did not peck or plow (though, in time, he doubtless would have). Then he raised his head and looked about. After that, he climbed the rear wall to perch **A** (see Fig. 3a). Isabella came over near the nest on perch **C** and looked into the IA for the eggs. Though she did not descend, she returned to a near position 3 or 4 more times and looked for them. Then, both birds perched on a food tray at the front of the enclosure. All this transpired in less than 5 min.

RECOVERY AND CARE OF ADDITIONAL PARTLY EXPOSED EGGS. Three min later, I exposed a small patch of one egg. Ferdinand noticed it the first time he looked down into the nest. He descended, recovered it, nudged it to the IA, and sat on it. Again, he seemed to be 'contented' with only the one egg, though he did peck about a little in the IA. After he settled in, I exposed small patches of the other 2 eggs with the dowel, frightening Ferdinand off the egg as I did so. He returned to the egg shortly thereafter, but he did not notice the inconspicuous, small, exposed patches of the other 2 eggs. Although he seemed somewhat restless, he sat on the single egg without making any effort at a further search. Again, this suggests that 1 egg is sufficient to satisfy the urge to incubate. Whenever Isabella came near, Ferdinand raised his head and hissed at her.

At 18:13 h, Ferdinand sang softly from the nest, but kept hissing at Isabella every time she came near. This behavior strongly suggests that, at that time, at least, such soft singing was more in the nature of 'contentment' song or self stimulation than a form of invitation to the hen. A full 20 min later, Ferdinand noticed a 2nd egg and recovered it, also. Even though it lay adjacent to the 3rd egg, as he wedged it out, he overlooked the latter--of which only a small patch of white surface was exposed. At 19:48 h, he still responded by hissing when Isabella came near. At 19:52 h, 18 min later, he noticed the 3rd egg and also recovered it.

CAREFUL CONTACTS WITH EGGS. Among other things, this experiment showed that Cosimo's failure to recognize an egg from a small white patch, in an experiment on April 11 (see p. 431), cannot be generalized to conclude that male Cockatiels must see a greater part of an egg profile than must females, in order to recognize or investigate it. Later that night, at 20:55 h, Isabella and Ferdinand competed very actively for the eggs. But they were so careful in their contacts with them that, because of their very slow movements, they gave the impression that they were wrestling.

SEVENTH OBSERVATIONS OF RESPONSES OVER A MISSING CLUTCH

BURIED EGGS RECOVERED AFTER VISUAL SEARCHES. It remained to confirm that this pair would recover eggs that were buried in the IA (rather than at a previously unused location). At 19:45 h, on June 3, I buried the 3 eggs 1¼ cm deep in the IA, just where they lay. When Ferdinand looked down into the nest from perch **C**, he missed the eggs immediately and searched all about for them, visually, from the perch. Descending to the enclosure floor, he searched further on foot. After that, he perched on a front food tray. Isabella also missed the eggs when she looked into the nest from perch C. She was beginning to descend to the nest, when Ferdinand pushed her aside and descended himself (had they been lovebirds, the female would have pushed the male aside). He pecked and nuzzled in the IA and promptly found all 3 eggs, which he resurfaced and incubated.

RESPONSES TO A PLETHORA OF SCATTERED, EXPOSED EGGS

ANOTHER RELICT RESPONSE ELICITED. I was considering terminating studies with the 1st clutch of Isabella and Ferdinand, when I decided to attempt an experiment of a different kind. To that end, I flighted the birds on June 5, at 20:20 h. While they were out of the enclosure, I added 6 lovebird eggs to the 3 Cockatielian eggs, and spread the 9 eggs out evenly on the surface of the shavings in the nestpan. Then, I returned the birds to the enclosure, and settled down to watch. The most reasonable expectation was that the birds would gather the 9 eggs into the IA and incubate them. That did happen eventually. but the events that transpired in the interim were of a quite unexpected nature. They disclosed the existence of still another relict response that suggests that the ancestors of Cockatiels nested at the surface of flat, level ground.

GATHERING IN EXPOSED EGGS. When Ferdinand spied the eggs from perch C, he eyed them repeatedly, but did not descend to the nest. My guess was that he was more concerned over the number of eggs, than he was with their locations. Isabella also eyed the eggs, but only once. At 20:36 h, Ferdinand descended to the nest, gathered in the 4 eggs that were closest to the IA, and incubated them. About 20 sec later, he nudged over the next-closest egg, but had some difficulty adjusting (getting "comfortable") on the clutch of 5 eggs. Then he nudged over still a 6th egg, leaving only the most distant 3 eggs, at the other side of the nestpan. At 20:40 h, he ventured over to their vicinity and nudged over still a 7th egg. He then did a great deal of additional adjusting--weaving from side to side--trying to position himself "comfortably," or in good contact with the eggs.

DISPOSING OF EXPOSED, "DEFECTIVE" EGGS. Meanwhile, at 20:55 h, Isabella noticed the 2 eggs lying off to the side (near location z in Fig. 3a), and descended forthwith to them. I thought she would either incubate them herself or, possibly, restore them to the IA. To my surprise, she did neither. Instead, she rolled the eggs, one at a time, out over the inclined 3-cm-high rim of the nestpan and to a distance of about 15 cm away, and left them there (right next to each other). At 21:12 h, I put the 2 eggs back at their initial positions at the far side of the nestpan (Ferdinand left the clutch briefly when I intruded). Four min later, Isabella again noticed the 2 exposed eggs in the nestpan. Reacting as if alarmed, she descended hastily and removed the eggs again. But this time, she merely tucked them under the protruding rim (by about 2 cm) of the nestpan.

COMPETING FOR A NINE-EGG CLUTCH. To ascertain what Isabella would do a 3rd time, I again restored the 2 eggs to their original exposed positions. But before Isabella noticed them, Ferdinand came over and gathered them into the clutch. He now was covering a solid mass of 9 eggs, upon which he spread his wings slightly and crouched down very low. At 21:30 h, Isabella joined him and they began to compete for the eggs, incuding "stealing" them from one another, one by one. Isabella finally gained possession of the entire clutch, but had trouble accommodating them all. Eight min later, Ferdinand returned, and their competition for the eggs resumed. There were 3 more spirited bouts of competition for the clutch that evening, the last at 22:30 h.

IMPLICATIONS OF EGG-DISPOSAL BEHAVIOR. A reasonable explanation for Isabella's behavior, on discovering the exposed eggs, is that she regarded them as defective eggs that had been discarded by Ferdinand, as is the Cockatielian habit (in fact, this pair subsequently discarded a defective egg from their 3rd clutch by rolling it from the nestpan and tucking it under the far side of their water bowl; see p. 492, **Cracked Egg Removed to Inconspicuous Position**). Many other birds remove or eject defective eggs, for example, lovebirds (see p. 720, **Discarding Defective Eggs**), Herring Gulls, and Mourning Doves; removal of shells from nests is common (1,375).

It appears likely that Isabella was hastening to dispose of the eggs, to avoid attention being drawn to the nest. This is an unlikely response for a hole-nesting bird, but a highly adaptive one for nesters on the surface of flat, level ground. As such, its existence reinforces the interpretations of all the other relict egg-care responses of Cockatiels, described in the foregoing, namely, that the ancestral nesting habit was to employ scrapes on the surface of flat, level ground. The present result also is noteworthy in that the non-attending parent removed the eggs, whereas, except in the colonies of some species, removal of shells is known to be carried out only by the parent actually engaged at the nest (see 1,374). Thus, the behavior also suggests that primitive egg care may have involved closer biparental attention than exists in most extant birds.

EIGHTH OBSERVATIONS OF RESPONSES OVER A MISSING CLUTCH

FRANTIC, VIGOROUS, DAYLONG SEARCHING. I again flighted Isabella and Ferdinand at 09:20 h the next day. While they were out of the enclosure, I removed the nestpan and eggs, and placed a fresh multi-layer of paper on the enclosure floor. My intention was to terminate the experiment. When I returned the birds to the enclosure, 20 min later, they perched for a few min and then descended to the corner, where the nestpan had been.

Both birds, but particularly Ferdinand, then began a frantic, vigorous search for the eggs, pecking and tearing up the paper flooring in the former nest corner in the process. This continued for 20 min. During that time Ferdinand also searched the enclosure floor on foot, and mounted the perches and looked inside and outside of the enclosure in every direction. Their searching continued, on and off, throughout the day. By 22:30 h, the multi-layered paper in the nest corner was in shreds.

THE NESTPAN RESTORED, FERDINAND RECOVERS THREE BURIED EGGS. In view of the vigor of the responses of Isabella and Ferdinand, continuing over a period exceeding 13 h, it was desirable to carry out additional experiments with them. At 23:55 h, I returned the nestpan and their 3 eggs, but buried the eggs in the IA. To my surprise, when Ferdinand descended into the nest, 6 min later, he first pecked and plowed at the far area, where I had buried and exposed eggs on the two previous occasions. After leaving the nest for 30 sec, he was back pecking around in it, and soon located and resurfaced all 3 eggs. After he began incubating, he sang very softly and melodiously (he also had sung very softly and melodiously from the corner earlier in the day, at a time when the eggs still were missing).

FERDINAND "HEADS OFF" ISABELLA BUT SHE TAKES OVER THE CLUTCH. When Ferdinand became alarmed, over some slight disturbance, and left the eggs, at 24:15 h, Isabella started for the nest. But Ferdinand raced back and sat on the eggs before she could get there, and similar events recurred a few min later. But Isabella persisted the 2nd time, and took over the care of the clutch, while Ferdinand continued to peck around in the nestpan. As usual, Isabella left the clutch at the time of lights-off.

NINTH AND TENTH OBSERVATIONS OF RESPONSES OVER A MISSING CLUTCH

EGGS BURIED AT FAR SIDE. As a last experiment with the eggs of the 1st clutch, I buried the 3 eggs at the far side of the nestpan at 09:45 h the next morning (June 7). This was the location where they had been buried and exposed before. It also was the spot where Ferdinand had scraped and probed the night before, when I had returned the nestpan and eggs after a 13-hr absence. Both Isabella and Ferdinand were pecking around in the nest 5 min later but did not locate the eggs. Sixteen min later, Ferdinand excavated an area no more than 1¼ cm to the right of one of the eggs, before leaving the nestpan.

THOROUGH, VIGOROUS SEARCHING---EGGS EVENTUALLY FOUND. Eight min later, Ferdinand again excavated the entire IA. His pecks into the shavings were by no means carried out as cautiously as Cosimo's, as he sent the shavings flying far and wide with vigorous sideward casts of his head. Isabella also was pecking around, but daintily. When Ferdinand came back for another search, but found Isabella already in the nest, he left (they sometimes backed down into the nest from the enclosure sides, and were unaware of the other's presence until they alighted).

Forty min later, at 10:54 h, Ferdinand found all 3 eggs and wedged them out (I had buried them in a close cluster). After nudging them over to the IA, he sat on them and sang softly. Isabella took over the care of the clutch 25 min later. Five min after that, Ferdinand evicted her from the eggs with low pecks near her legs, but she regained the clutch within 8 min.

One can suggest two explanations for Ferdinand's initial search at a point distant from the old IA, after the nestpan had been removed for 13 h: either he remembered where the eggs had been buried on two previous occasions, or he no longer recognized the existence of an established IA. [The distance (about 12 cm) from the old IA to the location where he searched, was the same as that from the IA to the ½-way point at the sidepane in the NB of Carmen and Cosimo.] After the pair had incubated eggs again in the old IA, and I again buried the eggs at the far side, it took Ferdinand over 1 h to find them (though he had come close to finding them much earlier). This suggests that the latter alternative may be the correct one, since if it were a matter only of his remembering the previous burial location, he probably would have found them sooner.

FIRST EGG OF SECOND CLUTCH LAID---FERDINAND VOCALIZES. Two days later, while Ferdinand was sitting on the eggs, he "sang up a storm" of Coition Sounds. It was then that I made the final decision to remove the eggs and let the pair proceed with the preliminary activities for a 2nd breeding. Although Ferdinand still appeared to search for the eggs after that, his activity was so desultory that it could just as well have been for the purpose of preparing the nest for a 2nd clutch. The likelihood of the latter is suggested by his resumption of soft singing and continuous loud singing, and the fact that the 1st egg of their 2nd clutch was laid a week later, on June 17.

The Second Clutch of Isabella and Ferdinand

DISCOVERY AND CARE OF BURIED EGGS BEFORE LAYING COMMENCES

DAILY SEXUAL UNIONS. Although the first clutch was not finally removed from the nest until June 9, Ferdinand had been making the Coition Sounds as early as June 7 and June 8, and had copulated with Isabella on June 8. From then on, into the period of oviposition of the 2nd clutch, he made the Coition Sounds and copulated with her frequently--at least once or twice per day. June 14 was the day I had buried 4 fostered eggs in the IA of the NB of Carmen and Cosimo, as Carmen was about to lay the 1st egg of her 4th clutch. Inasmuch as Isabella and Ferdinand were courting, and also about to begin their 2nd clutch, I performed a similar experiment with them. Would they search routinely for buried eggs at that time, and what would they do with them when they were found?

ALL ELEMENTS OF COMPETITION REAPPEAR. On June 14, I buried the 3 unhatched eggs of their 1st clutch $1\frac{1}{4}$ cm deep in the IA. These were found 8 min later by Ferdinand. There ensued a very vigorous and vocal competition for them with Isabella. The subsequent loose, fairly attentive (but not strict) daytime sitting on the eggs was similar to that characterizing the early days of their 1st clutch. Although all the elements of competition for the eggs reappeared, Isabella did not sit on them promptly when the lights were turned on in the morning. Once again, she did not sit on the eggs at night, but this could not, as yet, be regarded as significant. As was noted earlier, even experienced breeding Cockatielian pairs sit on eggs loosely, at first, and usually only guard them at night.

CARE OF THE SECOND CLUTCH

VIGOROUS COMPETITION FOR FIRST EGG. Isabella laid the 1st egg of her 2nd clutch on the afternoon of June 17. When I discovered it, I removed the 3 eggs of their 1st clutch (used in the test described above). There ensued so great a competition for the newly-laid egg, and "fussing" and pecking around in the nest, that it appeared possible that the birds were searching for the missing 3 eggs, which would have been unprecedented. However, that this was not the case is indicated by the fact that their vigorous competition continued unabatedly after I restored 2 of the eggs (for a test period of 4 hr).

DIM PROSPECTS FOR NOCTURNAL INCUBATION---I FOSTER ISABELLA'S EGGS. It was of great interest to see whether Isabella would shield or guard her 1st egg that night. The answer was a definite "no." She abandoned the egg 3 min after I turned the lights off, at 24:05 h, returned to it 2 min after I turned them back on, and left it again for the night after I turned them off again. The next morning she did not crouch over the egg until 10:46 h. It seemed quite likely that it would be some time before she would begin nighttime incubation of her eggs. For that reason, I fostered her eggs into the 4th clutch of Carmen and Cosimo, but I replaced each with a substitute, as it was laid.

MORE PRIVACY PROVIDED. Because of the great activity and noise from the colony, and the presence of the enclosure F and Helena and Homer off to the side but in view from their nest, I gave Isabella and Ferdinand more seclusion during their breeding. I installed a wood cover over the top of the nest at a height of 15 cm, and a wood partition at the open side. Thus, though the nest was still on the enclosure floor, it was effectively closed in everywhere but at the front, where the opening measured 12½ x 22½ cm. I still had a clear view of the interior.

COMPETITION CONTINUES-----NO NOCTURNAL INCUBATION. Competition between Isabella and Ferdinand for the eggs of this clutch continued in the pattern seen with their 1st clutch. All the already-described tactics were seen, although different ones were emphasized at different times. Descriptions are confined to the most noteworthy events of the competitions for the eggs, of vocalizing, and of egg care. The greatest interest, of course, attaches to Isabella's care of the eggs. When would she start to shield or incubate them at night? As will be seen, when Isabella eventually did begin to incubate consistently at night (entering the 3rd phylogenetic stage of egg care), she did so with an attentiveness and tenacity not seen even in an experienced hen like Carmen (see below).

LATE-EVENING VOCALIZING---NOCTURNAL INCUBATION BEGINS. Every day during the period of oviposition, and continuing irregularly for a week afterward, Ferdinand became tremendously vocal late in the evening, usually between 23:15 h and midnight. His utterances on these occasions customarily consisted solely of Coition Sounds. The last copulation that I witnessed, however, was on June 17 at 20:00 h. Isabella oviposited the 1st egg on that same day. The first indication of a change in Isabella's egg-care habits came on June 19 (actually the early morning of June 20), the day that she laid her 2nd egg. That night, she sat loosely over the eggs for a full 31 min after I turned off the lights.

Isabella did not sit over the eggs the next night, but she returned to them as soon as the lights were turned on the next morning, which was the same day (June 21) that she laid her 3rd egg. That night, for the 1st time, Isabella incubated the eggs all night. But she left them immediately when I turned on the lights at 08:00 h, and they remained unattended until Ferdinand took over their care 2½ h later. It appeared that Isabella would incubate the eggs again that night, but a slight panic in the colony frightened her off of them early, and she did not return to them.

HIGHLY TENACIOUS INCUBATION AND COMPETITION FOR THE CLUTCH. Isabella laid her 4th egg on June 23, a date that marked the turning point in her egg-care behavior. Not only did she incubate the eggs all night, then and thereafter, she also retained them tenaciously every morning, sometimes even past noon. On June 24, for example, she would not surrender the eggs until 13:17 h. The following morning saw a repetition of this behavior; Ferdinand failed repeatedly to acquire the eggs from her, even after as many as 7 attempts. On June 25 and 26 he could not acquire the eggs until noon and 13:30 h, respectively. Isabella was incubating the clutch very tightly as well as very tenaciously. She usually crouched down very low on the eggs, with her eyes closed and her bill pointed straight down and touching the bottom of the nestpan.

In view of Isabella's then attentive egg-care habits, I restored her eggs (that had been fostered to Carmen and Cosimo) and removed the substitute ones. So tenacious was Isabella's egg care, that she sometimes even resisted letting Ferdinand merely check the eggs. On the morning of July 5, for example, he began to check the eggs at 10:22 h. While he was doing so, Isabella pecked at him sharply. Upon that, Ferdinand repelled her with vigorous pecks, in an a most determined fashion. To my surprise, instead of retreating, Isabella unleashed a "torrent" of sharp pecks, whereupon he retreated. But he returned a few sec later and unceremoniously "bulldozed" her off the eggs, despite her continued attempted resistance.

In the case of Isabella's great tenacity in the daytime incubation of her 1st clutch, I suggested that it had a basis in the accumulation of an "incubatory debt," for lack of nighttime incubation. But she was equally tenacious with her 2nd clutch, even though she then had begun to incubate at night. The difference was that her tenacity with the 2nd clutch was exhibited mostly in the morning and early afternoon, rather than throughout the day, as with the 1st clutch.

The possessiveness of the birds for the clutch then was such that, if either one even approached the nest, the other began to Mandible-flutter excitedly. Such a strong possessiveness of each member of a breeding Cockatielian pair for the clutch strongly suggests that the pro-avian ancestors of Cockatiels practiced rapid double-clutching, with each member of a pair incubating its own clutch exclusively (see pp. 560, 561, **Considerations Relating to Endothermy, Incubating Eggs and Rapid Double-Clutching**).

HATCHING IMMINENT, GREAT EXCITEMENT AND COMPETITION. On July 6, at 15:30 h, I noted that Isabella was incubating the eggs. At 17:55 h, Ferdinand entered the nest and began to contest for them. Though he "muscled" her off of them, she quickly reacquired the eggs. Ninety min later, they were engaged in very spirited competition. Ferdinand managed to acquire the eggs, but Isabella struck back determinedly. In an unusual act, usually practiced only by the male, she began head-allogrooming him relentlessly. But, instead of being driven off, he responded in like fashion.

Seventeen min later, the issue still had not been resolved, and both birds were behaving very aggressively. My guess was that they were stimulated to great excitement by hearing one or more of the embryos bill-clapping, breathing, or vocalizing. A few min later, they had split the clutch in a temporary truce that lasted about 20 min. Then, they resumed vigorous competition. Eight min later (20:18 h), they split the clutch once more. By 20:25 h, spirited competition again ensued and lasted until Isabella finally surrendered the clutch and departed, 21 min later. When I managed to check the eggs, I heard an embryo cheeping faintly in the first-laid egg. [Bengalese Finch pairs become very difficult to flush from the nest as the time of expected hatching approaches (even when the eggs are infertile). Sometimes, Eisner had to push them off the eggs (129).]

A COLONY PANIC---THE CLUTCH TEMPORARILY ABANDONED. At about 02:31 h the next morning an unknown disturbance panicked the colony, and Isabella abandoned the clutch for the night. After waiting 1 h, I fostered the egg with the "peeping" chick into Carmen's clutch and made hasty arrangements to incubate the other 3 eggs. Unfortunately, they became overheated accidentally and did not hatch. I returned the eggs (then with a loudly cheeping chick in one of them) later in the morning, but Isabella did not return to them until 10:40 h. In the light of later findings, there need have been no concern over the eggs becoming chilled. During the summer months, the nighttime ambient air temperature in my living quarters generally was 27-30°C. Subsequent studies revealed that Cockatielian eggs may develop normally and hatch after being left unattended for several nights at these temperatures (e.g., see p. 502, **Egg Hatches Despite Four Full Nights of Chilling**).

BOTH PARENTS DETERMINED TO ACQUIRE THE CLUTCH. At 20:05 h that same day (July 7), Isabella and Ferdinand launched into a vigorous bout of competition for the clutch. It is best described as a "free for all," as Isabella tried to get Ferdinand to give up the eggs (one of which was near hatching) and he tenaciously resisted. At one point, she was draped over the top of his head trying to maneuver him off the eggs in a virtual "tug of war." By sheer persistence, she acquired the clutch 15 min later, but Ferdinand then pushed beneath her and lifted her bodily off of it. Again, she shoved him away, after which they split the clutch. Isabella finally left the nest at 20:28 h, after an 18-min struggle.

HATCHED CHICK CLUMSILY ATTENDED. At 20:34 h, a chick had hatched and was squirming and wriggling about with great vigor. Ferdinand was attempting to care for it (at 20:56 h) but was not up to the task, as the hatchling kept squirming out from under him. [Experienced birds usually do not sit on a chick, but nestle it between a wing and the body or keep it just in front of them.] There was no evidence of an attempt to allofeed the chick, but allofeeding usually is delayed for several hours after hatching. When Isabella attempted to approach the nest, Ferdinand "hissed her away." With the chick still cheeping at 21:45 h, Ferdinand tended to it and Isabella seemed totally unconcerned.

A "MONUMENTAL" STRUGGLE for the hatchling and eggs ensued between 22:00 h and 22:25 h, such as I had never seen before nor since. Isabella and Ferdinand were crawling over each other like wrestlers, respecting neither the eggs nor the chick. Isabella sometimes was hanging over Ferdinand's back, attempting to groom the chick, while he covered the eggs, and both were shoving against one another, slowly but with relatively great force. Insofar as I was able to ascertain, the hatchling was not being allofed. After Ferdinand left for a time, Isabella retained the chick under her wing (not under her body, as lovebirds do). She was so engrossed with it that she paid no heed to me as I watched closely.

THE HATCHLING FOSTERED. At 22:40 h, Ferdinand returned and started in anew competing for the brood. After witnessing another 5 min of "wrestling," I decided to foster the hatchling to Carmen and Cosimo to bring the number in their brood up to 4 or 5. It might, perhaps, have survived with Isabella and Ferdinand, but there was a reasonable doubt, and I wanted to observe Carmen and Cosimo caring for a brood of normal size. At the time, I still was hopeful that the other 3 fertile, though overheated, eggs of Isabella and Ferdinand would hatch.

NO INDICATION THAT THE CHICK WAS MISSED. I also was considering the possibility of returning the chick to Isabella and Ferdinand after it had been properly cared for and allofed by an experienced pair. It is most interesting to take note of the fact that Isabella and Ferdinand showed no sign of 'concern' or 'distress' over the loss of the hatchling, though they had just finished competing spiritedly for the brood for 30 min. As I found many times subsequently, either a hatchling or an egg will satisfy the parental instincts of incubating and brooding Cockatiels. Somewhat to my surprise, the vigor of the competition for the remaining 3 eggs during the next day seemed not much less than that for both the chick and the eggs the day before. Though Isabella and Ferdinand split the clutch on several occasions, such truces usually were short-lived, although one lasted for 65 min and another for 90 min.

RESPONSES TO A FOUR-DAY-OLD CHICK---ALLOGROOMING BUT NO ALLOFEEDING. On the evening of July 11, 4 days after removing the chick as a hatchling, I returned it to Isabella and Ferdinand. The latter still were incubating their remaining 3 eggs, close to being overdue. If they had been experienced birds, they would have lacked only the stimulation of caring for the chick I had removed for 4 days. In that event, they doubtless would have been capable of caring for it at the time it was returned to them. If they could not care for it, it would suggest, but not prove, that they could not have cared for it at the time I removed it, either. In fact, as will be seen below, they could not even care for a hatchling at the time the eggs of their 3rd (following) clutch were due to hatch.

When Isabella and Ferdinand saw the chick in the nest, both eyed it 'inquisitively' from a perch above. Ferdinand then pecked Isabella, prodding her to descend. But she only pecked him in return. Then Ferdinand descended and tended to the chick, himself--allogrooming it, sheltering it in front of his chest, and then nestling it under his left wing. Each time Isabella approached closely--her curiosity seemingly overcoming her caution--Ferdinand left the chick. It was evident that he was yielding a free path for her to take over its care. When she did not, he returned to it immediately each time and continued to shelter it, himself.

After 30 min, of advances and retreats, Isabella, at last, remained in the nest when Ferdinand made way for her. But it soon became evident that her interest lay entirely in the eggs, not the chick. At first, she pecked lightly at the latter, seemingly out of curiosity, but she gave no indication that she would care for it. Rather, she then gathered in the eggs and incubated them, but ignored the chick. It seemed that, just as Isabella earlier had lagged behind Ferdinand in attaining the 2nd phylogenetic stage of egg care, so too was she then lagging behind him in the maturation of the appropriate phylogenetic stage of chick care (earlier she had attempted to allogroom the hatchling and cover it under her wing, but these tendencies already had been lost).

[It should be pointed out at this juncture that the seeming ignoring of a hatchling by parents, whether experienced or not, usually is no criterion upon which to base conclusions. Many times subsequently I saw lovebird and Cockatielian parents give fresh hatchlings little or no attention or food for hours with no ill effect on the survival of the chick. In the present instance, the conclusion drawn is based primarily upon the difference in attentiveness of the parents.]

CHICK RETURNED TO ITS FOSTER PARENTS. It is quite possible, but perhaps unlikely, that Ferdinand would have allofed and cared for the chick at that time, as well as 4 days earlier (if he had not been preoccupied in competing with Isabella for the chick and eggs), but I gave higher priority to studying the care of a brood of 4 by Carmen and Cosimo (whose 4th egg did not hatch). I also wanted to ensure the survival of a 2nd generation bird. For these reasons, I returned the chick, the female Kirsten, to its foster parents, Carmen and Cosimo.

The Third Clutch of Isabella and Ferdinand

Recall that the 1st egg of the 2nd clutch of Isabella and Ferdinand was laid on June 17. By July 14, their attention to the unhatched eggs had waned so greatly that I considered the clutch to have been abandoned and removed it, the nestpan, and the remainder of the nest (its top and side-wall). I was not planning to breed the pair again until after moving the colony to laboratory quarters in late September. However, the birds had other plans. Despite my not facilitating their breeding (neither with nesting facilities nor nutritional supplements), they proceeded almost immediately with the production of their 3rd clutch.

COITION SOUNDS, COITUS, AND NEST PREPARATION. I cover their activities only briefly, since the early breeding behavior of this pair already has been treated twice, above. Even on the night when the 2nd clutch and nest were removed, Ferdinand sang softly from the enclosure floor at the position of the old IA. During subsequent days, he spent much time pecking and "fussing around" there among the remaining shavings and layers of paper, usually uttering the Coition Sounds. He continued to utter these sounds even after the last egg was laid (3 times in the 8 subsequent days). On July 27, when he was singing softly there, Isabella joined him. They spent considerable time together in the old IA on many occasions. Both the amount of time they spent there and Ferdinand's vocalizing, increased as the days passed. The birds were observed to copulate on July 17, 19, 25, 29 (twice), 30, August 2, and 4.

EGGS LAID---INCUBATION BEGINS ON FOURTH NIGHT. On the morning of August 2, Isabella laid the 1st egg of her 3rd clutch, and a 2nd, 3rd, and 4th followed every other day thereafter. I substituted for the 1st 2 eggs (turning the stored eggs 2-3 times per day) with lovebird eggs, but returned them on the morning of August 5. I also restored the entire nest arrangement after the 1st egg was laid (at a time when the birds were being flighted). As described above, the birds only crouched or stood over the 1st 2 eggs desultorily. But beginning on the night after the 2nd egg was laid, Isabella incubated the eggs every night.

LESS INTENSE COMPETITION--UNSUCCESSFUL ATTEMPTS AT NEST EXCHANGE. Although all the aspects of competition for the eggs that were seen with the 1st 2 clutches also were seen with the 3rd clutch, the intensity of the competition did not reach the heights seen during the care of the 2nd clutch. For example, Isabella was far less possessive of the eggs during mornings. Grooming in the nest much more often was accommodating and solicited, rather than relentless and unsolicited, and no longer frequently had the object of driving the other bird off of the eggs. Ferdinand's behavior, at times, was reminiscent of Cosimo's, in that he sometimes left the eggs unilaterally, leaving it to Isabella to take over their care.

An interesting event occurred on the night of August 17, when Isabella came off the eggs at 22:30 h and Ferdinand did not take over their care in her absence. She went to his side where he perched, and began to peck at him, seemingly trying to get him to descend to the nest and care for the eggs. Instead of complying he pecked back at her. After incubating the eggs again 3 times for short periods, and returning each time to Ferdinand and pecking him, she ceased her apparent efforts to effect a nest exchange and returned to the eggs for the night at 22:55 h.

CRACKED EGG REMOVED TO INCONSPICUOUS POSITION. There was no highly vigorous, prolonged competition for the eggs as normal hatching times neared, as there had been with the 2nd clutch. The basis for the different behavior was that no egg of the 3rd clutch hatched or reached the stage where breathing of the embryo or other sounds could be heard within the shell. On August 23, the birds discarded their 3rd egg (which was cracked and had coagulated material protruding). They rolled it over the 3-cm-high rim and out of the nestpan and tucked it into an inconspicuous position under the far side of the water bowl, a full 40 cm away from the IA.

The next day I attempted an experiment with Ferdinand. On some past occasions when I wished to inspect or spray the eggs with water (see below), I would reach into the enclosure toward Ferdinand, and he would oblige by coming off the eggs. On the 24th of August, though, he reacted quite differently. As I reached toward him, he came off the eggs and attacked me vigorously and vociferously (but harmlessly). In addition, Isabella came to his support, hastily descending from her perch toward the nest. When I approached again, a short time later, Ferdinand began singing, including a stanza of Coition Sounds. Again, when I reached in toward him, he attacked me, and Isabella once more hastened down toward the nest.

[Ferdinand was my best habituated male Cockatiel at the time, who easily could be picked up bodily from within his enclosure. His pecking attacks were not damaging. Isabella also was habituated, but she always fled if I tried to pick her up or invited her to perch on my finger. Thus, it was unusual for her to approach me rather than flee. The fact that she hastened toward my hand and the nest illustrates the great influence of the urge to protect the eggs at this time. The habituated birds, Helena and Homer, also typically attacked me if I reached toward the nest as they incubated or brooded.]

EGGS FERTILE---MAY NOT BE STORED AT ROOM TEMPERATURE. An examination of the eggs showed that the first-laid contained a well-developed embryo, still within the shell membranes. The 2nd contained a poorly developed embryo, the 3rd was infertile, and the 4th contained a fairly well-developed embryo. The causes for the failures of these eggs to hatch, as determined by subsequent tests, is that Cockatielian eggs (and doubtless most other avian eggs), will not remain viable when stored at room temperatures (say, 20-30°C) for longer than 1 or 2 days, unless they are subject to frequent agitation of the type delivered by the birds themselves, even in the 1st few days. In order for the eggs to remain viable, they must be stored at about 11-13°C, in which case turning is unnecessary (see p. 167).

HUMIDITY CONTROL. The importance of maintaining eggs in constant conditions of humidity is treated on pp. 175, 176. I share the view of other workers that in most circumstances eggs fare best if left to the devices of the birds (see also the discussion of egg desiccation by Smith; 127). Increased humidity in dry, indoor environments probably is attained best and easiest by periodic moistening of the shavings or other bedding at the periphery of the NB or nestbowl, but this is a matter for future study. The latter method is one I have employed with moderate to excellent success with the eggs of lovebirds and Cockatiels that were incubated in either open nestbowls or nestboxes. The humidity is more easily controlled in the latter. On the other hand, with 5 lovebird clutches incubated in the open on enclosure floors at a relative humidity of 35-50%, without spraying or other moistening, roughly 50% hatching of fertile eggs was achieved (broods labelled "unfacilitated" in Table 4).

REACTIONS TO A FOSTERED HATCHLING

FOSTERING A HATCHLING. During the late evening of August 26, the opportunity arose to study the reactions of Isabella and Ferdinand to a fostered hatchling (from a clutch of Helena and Homer; see p. 496) in a circumstance in which their own eggs were due to hatch, as assessed timewise from the oviposition dates. Since the eggs were laid on August 2, 4, 6, and 8, not all of them were overdue on August 26 (incubatory times range from 17-23 days). Accordingly, if Isabella were experienced or mature enough, she might have been expected to care for a fostered hatchling.

ISABELLA ALARMED, PICKS AT THE HATCHLING AND THEN IGNORES IT. In fact, the hatchling alarmed Isabella, and she threat-postured at it. When she did approach closely, she was intent on taking over the eggs, not the hatchling. She repeatedly picked at the hatchling in a manner that was not suggestive of parental care. Except for the threat posturing and repeated picking at the hatchling, Isabella's responses were not greatly different from those of experienced Cockatiels toward hatchlings. Before a hatchling's down has dried, sometimes even for several hours, an experienced bird also tends to ignore it, give priority to the unhatched eggs, and to merely touch the hatchling from time to time with its bill (see the behavior of Helena and Homer on p. 496 *et seq.* and p. 703 *et seq.*).

A RACE TO THE EGGS. Before finally settling down on the eggs (but ignoring the hatchling), Isabella twice left the nest. Each time this happened, Ferdinand, who maintained interest in the proceedings, started down toward the nest from his perch. But, each time, Isabella turned back when she noted his movements toward the nest. She then sat on the eggs before he could get to them, whereupon he returned to his perch.

SOUNDS MADE BY THE EMBRYO MAY PLAY A ROLE. Judging from Isabella's behavior, she was less prepared to care for this fostered hatchling than to care for the hatchling of her 2nd clutch. She actually had attempted to groom the latter and brooded it for a time under her wing. Yet she was older and more "experienced." It seems likely that one of the facilitating factors, possible necessary, that brings inexperienced breeding Cockatiels into condition to feed and care properly for hatchlings, is the stimulation of the sounds of the embryo's bill-clapping, breathing, cheeping, and hatching over a period of about 2 days. Perhaps a total absence of these sounds leaves inexperienced parents unprepared for hatchling care.

In the case of the 2nd clutch, the birds were stimulated by (or, at least, exposed to) embryonic sounds, but perhaps were insufficiently mature or experienced for this stimulation (or exposure) to prepare them to care for a brood. In the present case, the birds were somewhat more experienced but lacked entirely an exposure to sounds of maturing embryos. Further studies are needed to expand our knowledge of these matters.

The First Clutch and Brood of Helena and Homer

PAIRS HOUSED SEPARATELY. Of the 1st 5 offspring of Carmen and Cosimo, Helena and Homer were the first to mate and copulate. They were observed in sexual union in the lower part of enclosure A as early as the evening of April 12, 1984, and again on the mornings of April 13-16. They probably would have bred, and nested on the enclosure floor, had they not shared the space with Isabella and Ferdinand. When Isabella laid her 1st egg, on May 16, I transferred Helena and Homer to enclosure F, with multi-layered paper on its floor. This enclosure was positioned at the same height as enclosure A (Fig. 1a), just to its left, leaving the sibling pairs within sight of one another.

HOMER VERY VOCAL. As in the cases of the other breeding Cockatielian pairs described above, the first signs of imminent breeding were long sessions of song by the male. The first of these was noted on the evening of June 1, when Homer sang so vigorously in his enclosure that, when I flighted him (Helena declined to accompany him), he continued to vocalize from the home perch (Fig. 1a). He sang at length again on June 7, 13, 16, 17, and July 4. On June 16, I flighted him again (again Helena declined), at which time he uttered Coition Sounds. These were heard again, for only the 2nd time, on the evening of July 5.

ADDITIONAL COPULATIONS---NEST PREPARATION. Another series of copulations occurred on the mornings of June 24-26, 28-30, and July 6, the afternoon of June 24, and the evening of June 28. Additionally, Homer began to prepare a nest at the left-rear floor of the enclosure on June 26 (as usual, this was at the most sheltered position). Although I provided shavings, he preferred a more or less bare nest, with most of the shavings at the periphery. From that time on, Homer spent a great deal of time in the nest, often accompanied by Helena, and often exchanging with her. But the time that Helena spent in the nest, alone, was small by comparison to his.

RESPONSES TO EGGS FOSTERED PREMATURELY

BURIED EGG DISCOVERED AND CARED FOR. Since it seemed likely that an egg might be laid at any time (although this did not occur until July 30), I assessed their stage of preparation for egg care by providing an egg prematurely. Accordingly, at 20:50 h, on July 6, I buried a lovebird egg in their nest area under a handful of new shavings (and I added a 2nd egg 2 days later). The egg was discovered at once by Homer as he pecked about in the nest, and he promptly crouched over it, with Helena at his side.

MILD COMPETITION---ANOTHER RELICT EGG-CARE RESPONSE. Both birds were greatly affected by the presence of the egg, and within 1 h were competing mildly for it. By the time Helena was able to acquire it (21:50 h), the IA was denuded of shavings and the egg rolled and slid freely on the metal-tray floor. It was at that time that another relict egg-care response was released. She unleashed a flurry of rapid, bilateral scratchings (with both feet but not simultaneously), in an apparent effort to create a depression for the egg to nestle into. [Less than 2 months later, I elicited the same responses from Carmen 7 times (see pp. 819, 820, **Scratching on Smooth Surfaces, A Relict Response to Freely-Rolling Eggs**).]

The newly-prepared IA and nest came to occupy nearly ¼th of the entire enclosure floor, greatly restricting the birds' freedom to compete for the eggs, and otherwise interact with one another. Nevertheless, it was evident that many of the same competitive activities in relation to the eggs were occurring between Helena and Homer as had been observed with the other 2 pairs.

NO NOCTURNAL EGG CARE. Both birds often were present together on the enclosure floor, and there was considerable vocalizing at times of interacting. Helena clearly had not progressed beyond the equivalent of the 2nd phylogenetic stage of egg care, as she did not sit on or over the fostered eggs at night. Homer performed most of the daytime care. The eggs typically were taken over by the birds in mid-morning and abandoned in the late evening, being crouched over or sat on loosely for most of the day.

VIGOROUS COMPETITION---LATE EVENING EGG CARE. Additional series of copulations occurred on July 14 (twice), 15, and 18 (twice). There was some unusually vigorous competition for the fostered eggs on the evening of July 22, when Homer engaged in a vociferous pecking match with Helena, as he tried to unseat her from them, succeeding after 6 min. Homer also was becoming very protective of the eggs against me. He pecked and hissed at me for the first time on July 23, as I renewed their supplies. This also was a period when they began to sit over the eggs until very late in the evening, for example, until 23:50 h (Homer) and midnight (Helena) on July 22 and 27, respectively. Sometimes Homer was the late evening caretaker, at other times it was Helena.

THE EGGS ARE LAID

"STEALING" THE FIRST EGG FROM EACH OTHER. On the morning of July 28, Helena took over the care of the fostered eggs early (09:10 h) and pecked at me as I renewed the food and water. The next day, I noticed that Helena spent almost the entire day on the enclosure floor, either on the eggs or in Homer's company when he sat on them. On July 30, Helena left the fostered eggs and attacked me again, as I serviced their enclosure, revealing, in the act, that her 1st egg had been laid.

I substituted an infertile Cockatielian egg for the 1st egg, and removed the 2 lovebird eggs. From that day on, I was attacked virtually every morning, both when I removed their trays and when I returned them; almost always, it was by Helena. The day of laying the 1st egg also was one of much more intense competition than usual, as Helena and Homer kept "stealing" the egg from one another in the late morning.

SOME PENDING QUESTIONS. Helena had been incubating prematurely fostered eggs for almost a month, without caring for them at night. Since her 1st egg finally had been laid, a great deal of interest attached to the questions of when she would begin to incubate at night (achieving the 3rd phylogenetic stage of egg care), and what the new morning pattern of egg care would be. Recall that Isabella was very possessive of the eggs in the morning hours, either covering them as soon as the lights came on, or not surrendering them until late, after sitting on them for the entire night.

EGG ABANDONED AT LIGHTS-OFF. That 1st night, Helena left the egg the instant the lights were turned off, and she did not return to it when they were turned back on. The next morning she returned to the egg within about 20 sec of the lights being turned on. Not only did she continue to attack me when I renewed their supplies, she came rushing over on the offensive if I merely approached the enclosure. Again, the next night, she was off the egg "like a shot" when the lights went off, and, again, she did not return when they were turned back on. Again, she returned to the egg promptly the next morning. The pair competed vigorously for it at 11:45 h, with Mandible-fluttering, vocalizing, "stealing" the egg back and forth, pecking, and shoving.

Late on the evening of August 1, Helena oviposited again. As before, she left the 2 eggs as soon as the lights were turned off, and returned to them the next morning as soon as they were turned on. Exactly the same responses occurred on the next 2 evenings and mornings (Aug. 2-3 and 3-4), with the 3rd egg having been laid at about 10:30 h on Aug. 4. With 3 eggs present, the day of August 4 was marked by a great deal of competition, including much "stealing" of the eggs back and forth.

NOCTURNAL INCUBATION BEGINS---"LIGHTS-ON" RESPONSE APPEARS. It was not until one night later (Aug. 5-6, 5 days after laying the 1st egg) that Helena incubated her eggs at night for the first time. Accordingly, that morning I removed the substituted eggs and restored her own. Thereafter, Helena incubated the eggs attentively on all but 5 nights (on 2 of which she was frightened off by panics). During this period, when she (like Carmen and Isabella) left the eggs temporarily just after the lights were turned off, I had several opportunities to test whether she would return promptly if I turned the lights back on. In almost every case, she did.

Candling of Helena's eggs revealed that only the 2nd and 3rd were fertile. Since the 1st egg was laid on July 30, the 1st hatching was expected on August 15 or 16, at the earliest, and August 21, at the latest. However, Helena had been off the eggs for 7 hours on the night of August 14, and for the entire nights of August 17, 18, 23, and 25 (judging from her positions when the lights were turned off, and again when I first checked in the mornings, which usually are fairly reliable indicators). Accordingly, I had given up hope for the clutch as early as August 21, and had stopped moistening the eggs and shavings to maintain the humidity. [Although the birds bathed from time to time, they usually had dried out before returning to the eggs.]

A HATCHLING NOT PROPERLY CARED FOR

SECOND EGG PIPPED, THIRD EGG HATCHES. In view of the above history, I was astonished when the 3rd egg hatched on August 26 at about 22:51 h. I subsequently found that a term chick also had developed in the 2nd egg. This chick had pipped the shell at one point (a large, bloodstained hole; see discussion on pp. 698, 699, beginning with **Mutilation of an Unhatched Chick**) but apparently had not been able to rotate within it to complete hatching (probably because of insufficient moisture). Since I had given up hope for the clutch days before, I had not been checking the eggs for signs of imminent hatching.

NEITHER PARENT BROODS HATCHLING AT NIGHT. When I turned out the lights that night, Homer promptly left the eggs and chick and mounted to a perch. Helena, however, did not exchange with him. When I turned the lights back on, Homer promptly returned to the eggs and chick (one of the few times when a male exhibited the response to light changes). Accordingly, I left the lights on until Helena exchanged with Homer for the night. The exchange occurred at 23:55 h. After waiting 5 min, I turned the lights off again, and she remained with the chick and eggs. But, since she left again within 15 min, and it appeared that the hatchling would be exposed all night, I tried to foster it with Isabella and Ferdinand, as described above, but without success (subsequent studies were to show that a Cockatielian hatchling that had been fed could tolerate being exposed all night at 27°C; see pp. 706, 707, **Chick in Distress**).

CARMEN AND COSIMO RETREAT IN ALARM FROM A FOSTERED HATCHLING. When I returned the hatchling to Helena and Homer, Homer came down to tend it, but, again, left as soon as the lights were even dimmed (without being turned off). As a last resort, I placed the hatchling with Carmen and Cosimo, who were courting again (Carmen subsequently oviposited on Sept. 9). But after eyeing the hatchling alarmedly from a perch, both Carmen and Cosimo retreated to the farthestmost point on a sidewall of the enclosure. Clearly, they were unprepared to care for a chick. In this connection, it is known that if domestic fowl hens are placed with chicks, they do not become broody unless they already have oviposited or have received hormone injections (see N. Collias, 1946, in 348). In this case, Carmen was 2 weeks shy of ovipositing, and Cosimo seemingly was equally unprepared to accept the chick.

UNCARED FOR, THE HATCHLING SUCCUMBS. Accordingly, I kept the hatchling warm for the night and returned it to Helena and Homer in the morning. But they did not brood it. Even though the chick was dry and fluffed out, Homer treated it as if it were a fresh, wet hatchling (see pp. 703-705), either ignoring it off to the side or occasionally touching or pecking at it with his bill. Helena was off on a perch and took no part in the proceedings. As subsequently elucidated, the explanation for Homer's failure to allofeed the hatchling probably was that, after an entire night without nourishment, the chick was too weak to sit up and solicit food. A Cockatielian hatchling will not be allofed, even by experienced parents, until it is able to do this, and "pumping" also may be a prerequisite (see pp. 704, 705, **Abrupt Transition to Allofeeding Hatchling**). The hatchling succumbed later that day.

[Although the pair's timing may have been thrown off, since they had been shielding and incubating fostered eggs for over 3 weeks before Helena laid her 1st egg, had she been experienced, she probably would not have abandoned the hatchling for the night, in which case it might have survived. Homer's abandoning it for the night apparently was normal Cockatielian behavior. Subsequent studies suggested that under no circumstance would Homer care for eggs at night (see, e.g., pp. 498-500).]

The Fifth Clutch and Brood of Helena and Homer

During the 2 weeks preceding the fledging of the 4th brood of Helena and Homer (see pp. 715, 716), consisting of 2 chicks, I had been removing Homer from enclosure A (lower section) much of the day and most nights to spare the 2 chicks from his incessant feather-picking. I also thought that his absences might discourage continued breeding, as I was desirous of resting the parental pair, inasmuch as they had raised 3 broods in essentially continuous succession. Accordingly, I removed their shallow nestpan (22½-cm diameter x 3-cm deep) and turned down the open face of an aluminum chassis (15 x 19 x 30 cm) that had served as a partial shelter for the nest. The chassis then became essentially a "mound" covering all but a 3½-cm edge of the former location of the nestpan. However, despite this change and Homer's frequent and sometimes lengthy absences, the pair was not deterred from breeding again. Their "nest preparation" under those circumstances consisted in pecking about and spending time on the enclosure floor in the position at the side of the chassis within nearest reach of the former location of the nest, which then merely had a paper covering.

The pair frequently had copulated in the morning within 45 min of my returning Homer to the enclosure after his nightly absences, so I was not surprised when Helena laid the 1st egg of the next clutch on October 9, 1985, and 3 additional eggs on following alternate days. Each egg was laid at the side of the chassis closest to the former nest. The 1st 2 eggs were unattended in this "new IA" when I detected them, the last 2 were being crouched over or incubated by Helena. I removed each egg when the opportunity arose and placed it in another room at 20-23°C and 35-40% relative humidity. I also turned these eggs 3-4 times daily.

OVIPOSITION-SITE FIDELITY

HOMER INCUBATES IN THE OLD INCUBATIVE AREA. Three hours after removing the 4th egg on October 15, I returned the clutch, the eggs of which had been stored for 2-6 days, with turning (see above). Before doing so, I flighted Helena and Homer and restored the nestpan and chassis to their customary positions and condition and placed all 4 eggs in the restored nest (Fig. 3a, at position **v**). When I returned the parents, Homer took over the eggs and incubated them tightly almost from the moment that he detected their presence. Helena also showed an interest in them and competed mildly with Homer for them by rolling eggs out from under him. At first, it appeared that she also was intent upon caring for the eggs in the nest but that proved not to be the case. Her interest was directed elsewhere.

HELENA SEQUESTERS AN EGG IN THE NEW INCUBATIVE AREA. Helena's intentions became clear when she succeeded in acquiring an egg. She nudged the egg up the almost vertical side and over the 3½-cm-high rim of the nestpan and then rolled it over as near as feasible (**w** in Fig. 3a) to the location at which she had oviposited the clutch. This was at a total distance of 40 cm from the old IA (**v** in Fig. 3a) where I had placed the eggs (she could bring the egg no closer because of the presence of a metal block anchoring the nestpan). Thereupon she proceded to incubate the egg attentively (sitting on it tightly and immobilely, with her head lowered to the substrate and her eyes frequently closed) and made no effort to acquire an additional egg from the remaining clutch of 3.

EGGS INCUBATED BY DAY, UNATTENDED AT NIGHT. After Helena had incubated the sequestered egg for 20 min I restored it to the clutch. At first Helena merely continued to sit in the new IA but within 15 min she secured another egg in the same manner, rolled it to the new IA and proceded again to incubate it. Homer, meanwhile, held fast to incubating the remaining eggs. After I restored the egg to the clutch again 30 min later, Helena continued to sit in the new IA and did not attempt to reacquire an egg. On a few occasions when Homer came off the eggs as he heard the calls of the 2 young of the 4th brood from an enclosure above, Helena made no effort to take over the care of the eggs or acquire another egg. However, late that evening, after Homer came off the eggs for the night, she rolled another egg out to the new IA and incubated it there for the night, leaving the 3 eggs in the nest unattended that night (room temperature, 27°C). At the time of lights-on, the following morning (09:30 h), Homer resumed incubating the 3 eggs in the nest. When Helena came off her egg and ate and groomed 25 min later, I restored the egg to the clutch. In the following 40 min Homer left the eggs briefly 3 times and Helena made no effort to take over their care, though she would have done so promptly in normal circumstances. She did enter the nest once and inspect the eggs, but instead of incubating them, she spent her time sitting in the new IA. At 11:45 h, however, during a temporary absence of Homer from the nest, she began to adjust the positions of the eggs. Homer returned promptly though and reacquired the eggs. She, again, returned to and settled into the new IA.

Twice more, the last time at 12:05 h, Helena entered the nest when Homer was absent briefly and nudged the eggs about in a manner suggesting that she was intent on transferring another one to the new IA. But she retreated on each occasion when Homer returned. At 14:00 h, for the 1st time, she gathered the eggs and stood over them briefly. It was quite evident from her behavior that she would not accept the old nest as the IA for the new clutch, but remained attached to the new IA. Homer, on the other hand, had never incubated eggs in the new IA, as each had been removed before he had the opportunity to do so, or before it came to his attention. Homer left the eggs as usual late that evening and they remained unattended (for the 2nd night); Helena, again, spent the night sleeping in the new IA.

A few min after lights-on the next morning, Helena entered the nest and nudged the eggs about briefly before departing. Homer took over incubation of the eggs within 5 min and sat on them tightly for almost the entire day. In uncharacteristic behavior that morning, Homer left the eggs in agitation during the flighting of the young of his prior broods. During the few min of his absence Helena twice entered the nest and sat on the eggs lightly for 5-10 sec. But she spent much of the afternoon and evening sitting in the new IA. Moreover, whenever she was sitting there, she defended the area vigorously, just as if it were a nest containing eggs, hissing and striking out at me whenever my hand came near her as I serviced. Three times that afternoon she entered the nest and interacted with Homer over the care and possession of the eggs. The 1st time she distracted him by grooming and tried several times to roll away an egg but each time he recovered it. The 2nd time she merely examined the eggs. The 3rd time she displaced him from the eggs and gathered them in under herself momentarily but then left.

HELENA OVIPOSITS IN THE NEW INCUBATIVE AREA. When I entered the room at 10:00 h, after an absence of 90 min, Helena was standing alongside Homer in the nest and there was an egg in the new IA. This proved to be a freshly oviposited one, leaving little doubt that Helena still did not accept the old nesting area. Although she visited the nest and perched near it several times, her major interest late that evening was in incubating the freshly laid egg in the new IA and she spent most of the time there. In order to ascertain the pairs' behavior when in possession of two nests, each containing eggs, I did not transfer the fresh egg to the nest.

INCUBATING A DIVIDED CLUTCH. That night Helena incubated the fresh egg (#5) in the new IA and the clutch of 4 eggs was left unattended (for the 3rd night). The following day was the most serene day of Cockatielian incubatory behavior that I ever had witnessed. Both birds incubated their eggs almost uninterruptedly for 14 hr, neither ever approaching the other's nest. Homer took over the clutch within 5 min of lights-on, came off of them and groomed for a few minutes at 09:55 h, and again for a few min at 10:50 h. I only witnessed Helena leave the eggs twice during the entire day, both times for 90-120 sec while she ate and drank. Hardly any food was consumed from the food trays that day.

Shortly after 23:45 h both birds left their eggs, mounted to a perch and copulated. Again that night, Helena incubated her 5th egg whereas Homer left the clutch unattended (for the 4th night) and perched above.

Notwithstanding the fact that the eggs were abandoned each night, there was a good chance that they would hatch, as the nest temperature during the night was 25½-27°C.

ALL EGGS COMBINED IN THE OLD INCUBATIVE AREA. The next morning Homer took over the clutch in the nest within 3 min of lights-on. When Helena left her egg and groomed and ate, including some time spent at the mineral block, Homer visited the new IA. He nudged the 5th egg as if to translocate it to the nest but did not do so. While Helena was busy at the mineral block, I transferred her 5th egg to the nest with the others. When she returned to the new IA, Homer was temporarily off of the eggs. Finding no egg in the IA, Helena went immediately to the nest and nudged the 5 eggs about. After two quick visits to, and returns from, the new IA, she finally settled in again in the new IA, despite having no egg. But she spent most of that afternoon on a perch, a strong indication that she had abandoned the new IA. Homer steadfastly incubated the clutch, and the afternoon passed almost as serenely as the day before, except that Helena visited him twice and examined the eggs.

COMPETITION FOR EGGS IN OLD INCUBATIVE AREA. At 17:35 h that evening, Helena entered the nest next to Homer and showed a much greater interest in the eggs than before, nudging them about and even briefly sitting on them. She returned at 22:35 h, after Homer had exited and was eating, and began to incubate eggs, though they were scattered at first. But just as she finished gathering them and began to incubate the entire clutch, Homer returned and evicted her. Fifteen min later she returned and initiated a remarkably tenacious succession of bouts of unsolicited head-grooming of Homer--designed to displace him from the eggs--that continued on and off for the next 47 min. Homer repeatedly responded aggressively to her unsolicited attentions with such rough grooming and pecking that she cried out several times and pecked vigorously in defense. Only once did she succeeded in displacing him briefly.

Several times she desisted from head grooming Homer and left the nest, once returning to the new IA briefly. It was quite evident from her behavior, which I had never before seen adopted by a female (usually only the dominant male aggressively and incessantly employs the head-grooming displacement tactic), that she was intent on taking over the incubation of the clutch for the night. This behavior provided another piece of evidence illustrating the existence of a much lesser dominance relationship of Homer over Helena than, say, of Cosimo over Carmen, consistent with the fact that Helena never allofed Homer (see discussion on pp. 410-412).

COPULATION FOLLOWED BY NIGHTTIME INCUBATION. Finally, at 23:47 h, Homer yielded the clutch and mounted to an upper perch. Helena promptly took over the care of the eggs. Then, quite unexpectedly, she behaved ambivalently, leaving the eggs briefly, and then returning several times before finally mounting to the perch near Homer. This behavior suggested that, despite her tenacity in acquiring the eggs, she was not going to incubate them that night. But the correct explanation was evident shortly thereafter when she began to solicit copulation from Homer who seemed to be only reluctantly cooperative. These pre-copulatory maneuvers culminated in coitus after about 2 min. Helena then returned to the 5 eggs in the nest and incubated them for the night for the 1st time. Since she never before had laid more than 4 eggs it seemed unlikely that an additional egg would be forthcoming and that this was the basis for her solicitation of copulation. Nevertheless, a 6th egg was laid in the nest with the others, but only after another 5 days. The subsequent care of these eggs proved to be unexceptional; from that time on Helena accepted the old nest as the IA.

IMPLICATIONS FOR ANCESTRAL EGG CARE. I have recounted this remarkable behavior in considerable detail because it very strongly suggests or illustrates a number of features of Cockatielian egg care that have significant implications for their ancestral behavior and the evolution of their egg-care behavior. First, it shows that female fidelity to the site of oviposition is greater than that to the eggs and/or a former nest site. Since it is extremely unlikely in nature that a clutch oviposited at one site will come to lie at another, this oviposition-site fidelity ensures that time and energy will not be invested in the incubation of another hen's clutch, without any risk of the hen's own clutch being abandoned. [Similar results, with the same implications, were obtained with a lovebird hen; see pp. 730-732, **Oviposition-Site Fidelity**.]

Second, it strongly supports the previous finding that one egg is sufficient to satisfy the incubative instincts of Cockatiels (as also for Peach-faced Lovebirds and Budgerigars), as Helena was 'content' to translocate and incubate but a single egg from the nest, and to incubate but the single egg that she had laid in the new IA, even though additional eggs were present in the nest. Third, it shows that a mated pair of Cockatiels will accept a condition in which the clutch is divided for long periods and care independently for the 2 sets of eggs--in fact they did so far more harmoniously than I ever had seen Cockatielian mates participate in the shared incubation of a single clutch. Clutch splitting by two Cockatielian mates in a NB, on the other hand, is merely a temporary expedient, with both birds seeking to acquire the other's eggs at every opportunity.

Fourth, it shows a strong degree of stereotypy and independence of the egg-care behavior of the male, and, to a lesser extent, of that of the female. Thus, Homer's behavior did not deviate from that seen when he and Helena cooperated in clutch care. His apparent lack of oviposition-site fidelity is inconclusive, however, since it is not evident that he was aware of the existence of the new site of oviposition before he began incubating the eggs in the nest. Similarly, despite being in the presence of her mate, who was incubating the eggs throughout most of the day, Helena gave the eggs no care at night.

Members of some avian species, particularly those that breed in crowded colonies without substantial nests, will abandon the nest site and incubate the eggs at another location, should the eggs be moved. Members of other species tend strongly to exhibit nest-site fidelity, even though the eggs have been relocated in full view nearby outside the nest (see 1,150). Some of the studies referred to appear to have been designed and interpreted solely within the framework of whether the birds recognize their own eggs, without making allowances for the influences of nest-site fidelity.

Perhaps the most extensive study is that of Howell and Bartholomew (1,151) with eggs and chicks of Laysan Albatrosses and Black-footed Albatrosses (*Diomedea nigripes*) nesting on Midway Island. The former nest in raised bowls of sand, about 8-15 cm high, and usually including bits of vegetation; the nests of the latter generally are lower and shallower and often consist only of a depression in the sand. Although members of both species often nest near one another, the colonies are not crowded. Care of the single egg and chick is biparental but the periods of individual care last for days.

The findings of Howell and Bartholomew bear a number of similarities to those of the present study but, inasmuch as short-term periodic alternations of egg and chick care were not characteristic of the species, only individual responses of parents in sole attendance could be observed (except for an occasional nest exchange between mates). Briefly stated, these albatrosses do not retrieve displaced eggs or chicks, even when they are located immediately adjacent to the nest site. The Laysan Albatrosses usually displayed nest-site fidelity (12 of 15 cases), whereas only 3 members of the Black-footed species did so, with the other 10 individuals incubating the displaced egg at the new site. Members of both species showed nest-site fidelity (for an empty nest) when chicks less than 2 days old were displaced from the nest.

New nests at a distance of 1½-5 m provided by the investigators and stocked with the egg from the nest site were accepted at first by all but 4 of 11 Laysan Albatrosses placed upon the nests by hand. However, all but 3 birds returned to the old empty nest within 30 sec to 3 h. The 3 exceptional birds remained on the new nests for at least 5 days before observations were terminated. Similar results were obtained with Black-footed Albatrosses; 4 of the relocations appeared to be long-lasting (3 of them over 6 days) but the other 7 birds returned to the old empty nests within a relatively short time (a few min to over 4 h in one case). [Experiments on brooding-site fidelity of Cockatiels are described below.]

CARE OF THE FIRST CHICK

EGG HATCHES DESPITE FOUR FULL NIGHTS OF CHILLING. Despite the fact that egg #4 had been allowed to chill overnight for the first 4 nights, as it was incubated only during the day, it hatched early on the morning of the 20th day after the clutch was restored (the 16th day after Helena began to incubate the entire clutch at night). [Egg #6 also hatched, eggs #1, 3, and 5 were infertile, and egg #2 contained a dead advanced embryo.] Although I had not listened for the cheeping of the chick within the shell of the egg the day before, I was alerted to the imminence of a hatching by the fact that Helena repeatedly visited the nest the day before and spent long periods within it at Homer's side. Experience showed this to be typical behavior of the female when a chick can be heard bill-clapping, breathing, and/or vocalizing within an egg.

HATCHLING UNFED UNTIL IT SAT UP AND SOLICITED. Inasmuch as I was able to observe the care of this hatchling in considerable detail and the results reinforce and amplify previous findings, I describe it at length. When first detected at 09:35 h, the hatchling still was partly wet and sprawled out on its belly, with its limbs contracting coordinatedly. As noted on previous occasions, the large piece of empty shell, containing the excreta, was discarded from the nest but the cap was left within it. The chick cheeped faintly and continually at the rate of about 3 times every 4 sec, and it continued to do so for the next 2 h. Homer had exchanged with Helena and the chick was in front and to his side. However, as noted on previous occasions, aside from infrequently touching the hatchling with his bill, Homer ignored it, making no effort to brood or allofeed it.

Helena paid no evident attention to the hatchling, usually perching above. After 50 min it was evident that the chick, still not dry, was becoming more and more steady and coordinated. Once it almost sat up at Homer's side and, as it did, Homer reached for and touched its bill. After 75 min elapsed, Homer still was ignoring the chick but he accidentally gathered it in under his chest while recovering an exposed egg (the chick got shoved under by the moving egg). Twenty min later, the chick was exposed again, and when it stood up momentarily, Homer seized it by the bill as if to feed it, whereupon the chick began to cheep loudly at about 5 times the previous steady rate. Upon hearing this, Helena hastened over to the nest but, as Homer threatened her, he released the chick, which fell over without having received any food. After 99 min, the chick was in front of Homer partly covered by his chest.

The chick's down then was beginning to fluff, almost fully dry, and it almost was able to sit up steadily, whereupon it also almost got allofed. By then Helena was showing a definite interest in the chick and the eggs; when she tried to allofeed the hatchling, Homer pecked her away. After 111 min, both parents were competing to allofeed the hatchling. When Homer huddled down tightly over the eggs and surrendered the chick to Helena's care, she gave it its first food in a trickle-feeding session (see p. 676) lasting over 40 sec, her head bobbing gently and passively as the chick pumped. After Homer tucked the chick under his chest, Helena tried to displace him from the chick and eggs. Failing in that, she perched on the rim of the nestpan. On several occasions when the chick was exposed, it "dug in" under Homer's side. After 138 min, Homer departed and ate, and Helena took over the care of the chick and eggs. A few min later, however, he returned and unceremoniously "bulldozed" her from the nest. Although she pecked at him, she yielded but remained perched at the side of the nest.

HATCHLING DRY & STEADY ON ITS FEET---COMPETITION---A 2ND HATCHLING. By this time (after 147 min) the chick was very steady on its feet, thoroughly dried out and fluffed, and huddled against Homer's side. Helena also took a position at Homer's side and competed with him mildly for the chick and eggs by allogrooming his head, which he did to her in return. After just over 3 h, Helena fed the chick in several long sessions by both trickle-feeding and tongue-flick allofeeding (see pp. 675-677). By mid afternoon the chick could sit up easily and it was evident that it was in excellent condition. Egg #6 hatched in the late evening 3 days later. When detected early on the following morning it was dry, had food residues in its crop, and was strong and coordinated enough to huddle with its head over the lowered neck of the older chick.

BROOD-SITE FIDELITY

Since Helena was known to possess oviposition-site fidelity and Homer was known to possess nest-site fidelity, it was of interest to investigate and compare their brood-site fidelity. Accordingly, as a first test, when the youngest of the 2 chicks was 2 days old and the remaining 4 eggs still were being incubated attentively, I removed those eggs from the nest and placed them at the site where Helena had laid all but the last egg (see pp. 498-500).

[At times when the parents were incubating and/or brooding, my manipulations of the eggs and chicks were carried out by: (a) reaching in and performing the operation as the parent(s) pecked at me harmlessly; (b) causing the parent(s) to leave the nest by brushing my hand along the table top in front of the enclosure; or (c) causing them to leave the nest by bringing a large brush near the enclosure or, if necessary, using it to brush along the table top. Almost any strange, large object brought near the enclosure, or a brushing, scraping, or crumpling sound, usually would alarm Cockatiels and cause them to climb to the perches.]

DISPLACED EGGS NOT CARED FOR. Following this, both Helena and Homer peered down at the eggs from their perches and Helena showed her state of agitation by Mandible-fluttering several times. Within 30 sec, Homer descended to the nest and allofed the chicks. After 5 min (measuring from the time of removal of the eggs), Helena descended to the eggs, tucked them under her breast, Mandible-fluttered, and sat on them for about 15 sec before returning to the perch. After 10 min, she descended again, ate at a food tray for 40 sec, and took over the care of the chicks from Homer. On leaving the nest, Homer visited the eggs, nudged them about, and gathered, but did not incubate, them. Instead, he returned to the nest and the company of Helena and the chicks. In the next 1 h, Homer once visited the eggs and nudged one under himself but left immediately. Helena visited them twice, sitting on them once for about 1 min and once momentarily.

EVIDENCE FOR AN "INCUBATORY" DEBT. After 90 min, when it was evident that the eggs would not be incubated outside of the nest, I began the 2nd test by merely exchanging the eggs and the chicks. Immediately thereafter, Homer hurried back to the nest and incubated the eggs tightly for the next 92 min. He huddled very low with his head low and his eyes closed, not having been seen to raise his head or open his eyes once, despite the outside sounds of chicks being allofed and the movements of Helena and the chicks, mentioned below. The impression given was that Homer had accumulated an "incubatory debt" in the preceding 90 min and was wasting no time in paying it. He was not to be diverted by outside events of lesser urgency.

HELENA BROODS, HOMER INCUBATES, BUT AT SEPARATE LOCATIONS. Meanwhile, Helena, on a perch directly above the chicks, ignored them for 5 min before descending and brooding and allofeeding them, just 35-45 cm distant from Homer. Helena's care of the chicks continued without interruption for the next 87 min. When it became evident from the steadfast behavior of the parents that there was little prospect of learning more in the circumstances, unless I were to leave the chicks out overnight, I began the 3rd test; I removed the eggs from the nest and enclosure but left the chicks as they were, outside of the nest. Homer returned immediately to the nest, looked about for the eggs, and pecked about in the shavings, alternately sitting and moving about. After about 2 min, he left the nest, taking notice of the chicks outside as he departed. After another min, Helena also descended to the nest, was joined momentarily by Homer, and then followed Homer out to the food trays. Neither showed any interest in the chicks.

DISPLACED CHICKS ENTIRELY UNATTENDED----MILL ABOUT IN CIRCLE. In this 3rd test, I left the chicks out for a period of 1 hr, during which time they were ignored almost totally and were entirely unattended. Helena visited the nest at least 10 times, sometimes repeatedly entering and leaving restlessly, sometimes followed by Homer, and both of them pecked about in it. They both ate at the food trays from time to time and foraged actively about the enclosure floor, repeatedly passing next to, and pecking in, the vicinity of the chicks, but ignoring them almost totally.

Meanwhile, the chicks milled about very restlessly in a circle, while leaning on one another. When a parent came very near, the older chick (6 days old) solicited for food, evidently sensing their near presence by heat or shadow (eyelids still closed). Though Homer may have brushed against them several times and repeatedly was in their near vicinity, he totally ignored their presence, except for not colliding with, or stepping over, them. The picture was almost identical for Helena, with the exception that she twice responded to the older chicks solicitations by reaching over toward its bill with hers, but doing no more.

RESTORED CHICKS ALLOFED IMMEDIATELY BY BOTH PARENTS. When I returned the chicks to the nest, Homer spied them almost immediately and dashed in and allofed the large one. Helena followed him and perched briefly on the nestpan rim before also allofeeding the chicks. Within 30 sec both parents had fed both chicks and were sitting together in the nest brooding the chicks. As the only remaining fertile egg (#2) was 10 days overdue, I did not return the eggs.

DISPLACED CHICKS AGAIN UNATTENDED--VISITS TO EMPTY NEST, INSTEAD. For the 4th test on the following day, at a time when Helena was in the nest with the chicks, I removed the chicks for 64 min and placed them outside the nest in the same position as before, at a distance of 35-45 cm from the center of the nest. Both chicks had ample food in their crops. The following events were almost a repeat of those of the 3rd test. The chicks again milled about restlessly in a circle. Both parents repeatedly foraged and passed in their near vicinity and, as before, the older chick solicited several times. At no time, however, did either parent respond nor appear to take any notice of the chicks.

As before, both parents visited the nest and sat briefly and/or pecked about in it. Homer appeared agitated and whistled every few sec almost the entire time that he was on the perches or clinging to the enclosure sides. Several times, as on the preceding day, he pecked at Helena, in the manner usually employed to urge her to tend to some task that needed attention. In addition, both bathed lengthily. It seemed evident that at that time, at least, the chicks would not be cared for when outside of the nest, despite the fact that Helena had brooded them for 87 min the day before at the same location, at a time when Homer was incubating eggs in the nest.

RESTORED CHICKS ALLOFED IMMEDIATELY BY HELENA. When the chicks were returned to the nest, neither parent noticed their presence for 4 min, as they foraged about on the enclosure floor or perched. As soon as Helena noticed them, however, she descended immediately and allofed them. Homer continued to whistle periodically and appear agitated and, though he visited the nest twice for brief periods, it was not until 1 h after I returned the chicks that he settled down in the nest with them and fed them.

DISPLACED CHICKS UNATTENDED A THIRD TIME. The 5th test on the following day was a repetition of the 4th one, in which I removed the chicks for 1 h. Again, both had ample food in their crops. Both parents were temporarily out of the nest at the time but the chicks otherwise still were receiving almost continuous attention from them. The events that transpired were very similar to those of the day before, except that the parents did not bathe, and Helena again responded twice to the solicitations of the older chick for food; once she extended her bill toward that of the chick, the other time she actually grabbed its bill momentarily. Again, Homer was agitated and whistled periodically but did not peck at Helena. Again, the nest was visited many times and the parents repeatedly foraged and passed in the near vicinity of the chicks but almost totally ignored them.

RESTORED CHICKS ALLOFED BY BOTH PARENTS. When I returned the young to the nest. both parents were perching above. Within 90 sec, Helena returned to the nest and began immediately to allofeed the chicks. Within another 90 sec, Homer had joined her and both were busily feeding intermittently for the next 12 min. As usual, Homer spent almost the entire remainder of the day with them. In essence, his only lengthy absence from the nest was during the 1-h experiment. Again, there was no reason to believe that the chicks would have been cared for had they been left outside the nest.

EGGS RETURNED---CHICKS DISPLACED AND IGNORED---EGG "INCUBATORY DEPT." For the 6th test, it was desirable to attempt to ascertain whether the presence of Homer sitting attentively in the nest incubating eggs during the 2nd test had influenced Helena to brood the chicks. That was the only time she had allofed and brooded the chicks outside of the nest, and the only time that Homer had incubated eggs since the tests began. Accordingly, on the following day, at a time when the chicks had ample food in their crops and Homer was brooding them in the nest, I transferred the chicks to the customary outside position where the first 5 eggs had been oviposited and restored the 4 eggs to the nest. Both Helena and and Homer noticed the eggs immediately, but it was Homer who descended hastily, glanced at the chicks as he passed them, gathered in the eggs, and began to incubate them.

During the next 70 min of the experimental period, he never left the nest or yielded the eggs to Helena, as she sought repeatedly to exchange with him. Most of the time he sat tightly on them, with head lowered and eyes closed. Twelve min after displacing the chicks and restoring the eggs, Helena descended to the the nest, eyeing the chicks in passing, and made her 1st effort to exchange with Homer, amid much Mandible-fluttering and pecking about in the nest. Helena spent most of the time foraging on the enclosure floor and eating at the food trays. Every time Homer exposed the eggs, as he rose and adjusted their positions, Helena hastened to the nest and attempted to exchange with him or acquire an egg, but without success. The absence of the eggs for 2 days apparently had increased the incubatory urges of both Helena and Homer.

As before, Helena often foraged in the near vicinity of the chicks, many times immediately adjacent to them, but almost totally ignored them. They presented a very forlorn sight as they milled about, pushing against each other blindly, stumbling, falling over, occasionally soliciting for food, yet being almost totally ignored by their parents. Yet these same parents would have been caring for them attentively had they been displaced by only 20 cm to just inside the nestpan. Aside from the fact that when the older chick solicited, Helena once touched its bill with hers, and a 2nd time almost began to allofeed it, she gave the impression of not even being aware of their presence. The eggs seemed ever to be of sole interest to her.

RESTORED CHICKS TENDED TO IMMEDIATELY. When I removed the eggs and restored the chicks after a 70-min absence, Homer immediately returned to the nest and tended the chicks. When he left, 3 min later, Helena literally rushed into the nest, perhaps under the impression that the eggs still were there. She allofed the chicks repeatedly in many sessions for the next 3 min before leaving and returning briefly several times in succession. When she did not return the last time, Homer took over the care of the chicks, and the brooding situation was back to normal.

ONE CHICK RECOGNIZABLE---ALLOFED FOR THE FIRST TIME WHEN DISPLACED. By the next morning, at an age of 10 days, the eyes of the older chick were opening, it was feathering and flapping its forelimbs, and Homer was beginning to feather-pick it. The 7th test was merely a repeat of the 4th and 5th tests, in which the chicks were transferred to outside of the nest for about 1 h, at a time when both parents had been attending to them. Although both parents first returned to the nest, and Homer again passed immediately adjacent to the chicks on his way to it, it was soon evident that the situation was altered markedly, probably because the older chick had become recognizable. Within 2 min, Helena visited the chicks and spent over 40 sec reaching for and grasping the older chick's bill in hers, although she did not feed it, probably because it did not respond by pumping.

After Helena visited the nest briefly, whereupon Homer left, she joined Homer on a perch, but within 2 min she was back with the chicks, allofeeding the older one repeatedly (the smaller chick was hunched over and not soliciting). At first, Homer gave every indication that he would ignore the chicks again. After sitting in the nest for 11 min, he spent a full 9 min eating corn only 2-3 cm from the chicks (which did not solicit) but without paying any attention to them. After eating seeds, perching and spending 4 min in the nest, without any preliminary, he left the nest and went directly to the older chick and allofed it repeatedly before returning and eating corn. Helena joined him directly and allofed the younger chick too. It was quite evident that their attachment to the nest was no less strong, but that they then probably readily recognized the older chick and accepted the younger one by association.

TEST REPEATED WITH UNRECOGNIZABLE CHICK---MOSTLY IGNORED. The 8th and final experiment sought to resolve the question of whether recognition of the young was the key factor in determining whether they would be allofed in an out-of-the-nest location. While the results were not entirely clear-cut, they indicate an answer in the affirmative. Since the smaller chick was 4 days younger than the larger one, it still was entirely unfeathered and its eyes were not yet open. Accordingly, since it was in the same condition that its older sibling was in on the day of the 4th test when both of the young were ignored, it could be used alone for the test. At a time when Homer was in the nest with the chicks, I reached in and removed them, as he pecked at me harmlessly and left the nest. I then placed the young chick in the same location as during the previous tests and held the older chick out in a warm, isolated location.

As the chick was bent over resting, Helena was on a perch and Homer was chewing on the mineral block, and, for the next 5 min, eating corn from the enclosure floor, only 3-5 cm from the chick, which was sitting up and grooming part of the time. Meanwhile, Helena descended to the nest and looked about and pecked about in it, raised her head and looked about, and mounted the rim and looked about, but apparently not at the chick. Then she left the nest and looked right at the hunched over chick but turned away and joined Homer at the food trays. Three min later, Helena passed near the chick, which had its head up at the time, and she reached over and grabbed its bill momentarily but then continued on her way. Both parents then mounted to the perches. In the next 20 min, both parents groomed themselves, foraged, and Homer visited the nest once. Generally, Helena followed his lead in these activities. Through much of the time the chick was bent over resting.

Without any preliminary indication, after 32 min, Helena descended from the perch, went over to the chick, and very briefly allofed it 4 regurgitations. Although Homer also approached the chick, he did not allofeed it. After an additional 23 min of perching and foraging, in which the often-sleeping chick was ignored when the parents were in its near vicinity, Helena visited the nest and pecked about for 4 min before being joined by Homer. When they both left the nest at that time, mounted to the perch, and began grooming themselves, I restored the younger chick to the nest.

Up to this time, the behavior of the parents was somewhat equivocal. Homer had ignored the chick and Helena had given it some brief token feeding in the 1 h in which it was outside the nest. But the chick was hunched over most of the time and not soliciting, so the absence of parental feeding might have been for lack of soliciting or lack of pumping in response when Helena allofed it briefly. Accordingly, the interpretation of the 1st part of the experiment would depend very much on what transpired after the chick was returned to the nest.

RESTORED UNRECOGNIZABLE CHICK ALLOFED IMMEDIATELY. The results after returning the chick to the nest were clear-cut. Within 30 sec of its return, Helena noticed it in the nest from above, descended immediately, and began to allofeed it vigorously. As soon as the feeding began, Homer became aware of it and hurried down and also allofed it. Both took turns feeding it over much of the next 5 min as Homer also settled into the IA in his usual location. After Helena left the nest and the chick was hunched over at Homer's side, Homer reached over and allofed it again the moment it raised its head. It is clear from these results that both parents were inhibited from feeding the chick (or were disinclined to do so) while it was outside of the nest, Homer, as usual, much more so than Helena. The thesis that this was for lack or recognition was in no way contradicted. But once the chick was restored to the nest, the urges to allofeed it that were inhibited or absent during the 1 h of its displacement returned or no longer were checked, and feeding proceeded with great vigor.

DISPLACED RECOGNIZABLE CHICK ALLOFED---STUMBLES IN ROTARY MOTION. For the last phase of the experiment, I returned the older chick to the enclosure, placing it at the usual position outside the nest. At this position the chick generally was out of sight of Homer within the nest (since an anchoring block was between them). Through most of the remainder of the experiment the older chick (referred to hereafter only as "the chick") sat up quietly with its head raised most of the time and often groomed itself. At first, the chick also was out of Helena's sight, as she was facing the other way as she groomed herself on a perch.

As the chick stumbled about in a rotary motion (moving in a circle about its original position), it came into Homer's view but he paid no apparent attention to it. Although the chick might have been able to see Homer and its sibling in the nest, it made no progress toward the nest, but continued to move in a circle about its original location. Its crop was only about 1/10th the size it would have been after a feeding (about the size of 2 kernels of corn) and the chick was long overdue to be allofed.

After about 9 min, during which time Helena had faced around but continued her grooming, she spied the chick. On seeing it she, at first, contemplated jumping down off the perch, and twice almost did so, but instead climbed down the side of the enclosure. She went over to the chick and grasped its bill in hers but did not allofeed it. Instead, she foraged about for 4 min and remounted to a perch. Two min later, however, she descended again and allofed the chick in several long sessions, at the sound of which Homer was stimulated to allofeed the younger chick.

HOMER IGNORES RECOGNIZABLE CHICK AT PERIMETER OF NEST. Four min later, after Helena had remounted a perch, I placed the chick at the rim of the nestpan, directly in front of Homer. The latter behaved as if "rooted" to the IA and continued to allogroom and allofeed the younger chick, paying absolutely no heed to the chick outside. Again, the latter engaged only in rotary movements about the location at which I placed it, and did not even face preferentially toward the nest.

HOMER TENDS TO RECOGNIZABLE CHICK AT INSIDE RIM OF NESTPAN. After 20 min, when it was clear that Homer would not budge from his position, I placed the older chick just inside the nestpan rim, without disturbing Homer, who just hissed and pecked at me. Within 1 min, Homer was reaching over and tending to the older chick by allogrooming the underside of its neck and picking 6 or 7 feathers from it, after the loss of each of which the chick recoiled abruptly. Then Homer allofed it in 4 lengthy bouts, at the sounds of which Helena descended from her perch and also allofed it. After she finished, Homer resumed picking feathers from its neck. Thereafter, he remained in the nest with the chicks for several hours.

Again, the results of the last phase of the experiment are consistent with the interpretation that recognition of the outside chick determined whether it would be allofed or not by a parent. They also indicate that, just as one egg is enough to satisfy the incubating instincts of a Cockatiel, one chick is enough to satisfy its brooding instincts. Homer not only displayed all the signs of being ‘contented’ to sit in the empty IA when he once again had a chick at his side, he gave no sign even of noticing the 2nd chick, even though it was at the perimeter of the nest, only 6-8 cm from the chick inside the nest.

PARENTAL CARE OF NESTLINGS OUTSIDE THE NEST INHIBITED. The overall picture that emerges from these tests is that, despite very strong urges of brooding Cockatiels to feed and brood chicks when they are within the confines of the nest (brooding area), they are inhibited from performing the same acts for chicks that are outside of the nest, unless the latter are recognizably their own, or are associated with chicks that are recognizably their own. [A related phenomenon is known in Rock Pigeons. Brooding parents usually will adopt fostered young before they are well-feathered, even if they are very different in appearance. But once their young are well-feathered, the parents recognize them individually and usually attack strange young of similar age (1,011).]

Additionally, the vigor and duration with which chicks are cared for and time is spent with them in the nest, immediately following periods when both chicks and nest are all but ignored, indicates that the strength of these urges becomes augmented continually through the periods during which they are not satisfied (accumulation of an "allofeeding debt"). This phenomenon was observed repeatedly whenever chicks and parents of all 3 species of these studies were separated by me by any means, such as when I removed chicks or the parents to give the chicks respite from parental feather-picking. On reuniting the family, vigorous allofeeding of the chicks almost always ensued immediately.

Both aspects of this behavior clearly are adaptive and ensure that Cockatiels will not invest time and energy in caring for chicks other than their own, and that chicks that are neglected, for any reason, will be compensated for the food and care, of which they might have been deprived during the period of neglect. The strong urge of brooding Cockatiels to allofeed chicks, particularly after periods when the opportunity to feed has been inhibited, is emphasized by the fact that hearing a chick being allofed by one parent attracts and stimulates the other parent also to do so.

BEHAVIOR ADAPTIVE FOR NESTING IN SHALLOW SURFACE SCRAPES. It is of considerable interest to note that the chicks, whether alone or together outside the nest, never strayed from their initial locations, always merely rotating or milling about in a circle. Even a mobile chick with its eyes opening, and unattended at the perimeter of the nest, made no effort to enter the nest, engaging only in rotary movements. This behavior obviously would be highly adaptive for nesting in small, shallow scrapes on flat, level ground but would be of lesser value in deep scrapes and hole nests. It adds to the corpus of findings that indicate that the primitive nesting mode of Cockatielian ancestors was in shallow scrapes on flat, level ground. Homer's behavior in ignoring the chick just outside a nest only 3½ cm deep is consonant with this view of the primitive mode of nesting, rather than of nesting, say, directly on the surface. In the latter case, it would have been maladaptive to ignore the chick just outside the nest area (unless, perhaps, if the primitive mode of nesting had been in closely-packed colonies).

[I remind the reader that the primary significance of these behaviors and relict responses is not that they reveal the primitive mode of avian nesting, a subject upon which there can be little debate. Rather, it is in the revelation and implications of the highly conservative nature of the behavior patterns, inasmuch as they have been retained after many, probably tens of, millions of years of hole nesting, for which they are essentially adaptively neutral.]

The 2 chicks of this brood were reared and fledged routinely, except that, inasmuch as Helena also began to feather-pick them, apparently having learned the habit from Homer, they both were very severly denuded of almost all but their primary and secondary feathers. However, Helena's feather-picking became more pernicious than that of Homer; when her allofeeding of the older chicks greatly declined, her entire attentions toward them was to feather-pick tenaciously, whereas, with Homer, allofeeding them usually carried highest priority. An effective solution to this problem proved to be to remove Helena to another enclosure for long periods, whereupon Homer was kept so occupied allofeeding the chicks that he had much less time to feather-pick them.

[In the rearing of the sole chick of the 8th brood of Carmen and Cosimo, I ascertained that after picking a feather from the chick, Cosimo consumed it in its entirety, or merely consumed the pulp at its base, in the same manner as Helena and Homer consumed the feathers that they picked from their chicks (see note on p. 709). In Cosimo's case, however, the habit was not manifested in so extreme a form and the chick was not heavily denuded.

In the case of the adult pair, Kirsten and Rimski, in which Rimski was strongly dominant, I many times observed Rimski nuzzle his bill into the back of Kirsten's neck, pluck feathers from her by their bases, and chew them. When he engaged in such behavior, he usually had to pursue her to obtain feathers, and he plucked them despite her loud vocal complaints. Though the pair were observed to copulate a number of times over the course of 2¼ years, no egg was laid.]

OVERVIEW AND SUMMARY -- PARTS 1 AND 2

The care of 17 clutches of eggs by 3 pairs of Cockatiels has been observed, as well as the responses of the birds to fostered eggs, to the loss of all eggs, to changes in the number and positions of eggs, etc. Upon the basis of these studies, it is postulated that the changes in egg care by breeding Cockatiels recapitulate the equivalents of the evolutionary stages in egg care by the ancestors of birds, as follows:

Postulated Phylogenetic Stages of Egg Care by the Ancestors of Birds

Stage 1. INCUBATION BY CLIMATIC HEAT: eggs uncared for after oviposition. This is the mode of egg care of most reptiles and was that of the distant reptilian ancestors of birds (see Part 3). The equivalent of this stage in Cockatiels is lack of care of fostered eggs in the earliest stages of breeding.

Stage 2. INCUBATION BY CLIMATIC HEAT AND SOLAR RADIATION: by day the eggs were closely guarded, shielded from view, shaded from solar radiation impinging on them at high angles of incidence (i.e., during midday) but not from that at low angles, and concealed during absences; by night the eggs were buried and the nest site guarded from a distance. This is the mode of egg care postulated for the **pre-avian** ancestors of birds (see Table 3). The equivalent of this stage in Cockatiels is loose sitting or crouching over the first-laid eggs by day and merely guarding them by night.

Stage 3. DAY AND NIGHT INCUBATION BY BODILY HEAT: eggs incubated by day and by night. The equivalent of this stage in Cockatiels is fully-developed incubatory behavior.

RESPONSES OF NON-BREEDING COCKATIELS TO EGGS. The equivalent of the 1st phylogenetic stage of egg care is seen in non-breeding Cockatiels and those that are beginning to court. Such birds almost always show an interest in eggs that they encounter prematurely. They may examine and touch such eggs, and even move them about, but they do not take over their care. Parents that "refuse to sit the eggs" (32) have not progressed beyond stage 1. Juveniles show a great interest in eggs, instinctively rolling the eggs under themselves using the underside of the bill, and even gathering them, as well as competing for them with "raised-head" pecking. They also may destroy eggs by pecking them.

DAYTIME CROUCHING OVER EGGS IN EARLY STAGES. The equivalent of the 2nd phylogenetic stage of egg care is seen in many birds that are in advanced stages of preparation for breeding and the early stages of egg care. Before the time of oviposition, such birds, for example Cockatiels, accept fostered eggs and crouch low or sit lightly over them during the day. They may guard such eggs at night but do not sit or crouch over them. Birds caring for the first 2 or 3 eggs of a clutch often behave in the same manner. In extreme cases, hens may more or less ignore the eggs for the first few days. [It is well known that members of many avian species that sit on eggs loosely, at first, gradually sit on them more tightly or closely as the incubatory period progresses (129).] Mountain White-crowned Sparrows exhibit egg care intermediate between the equivalents of the 2nd and 3rd phylogenetic stages. They begin daytime attendance and some degree of incubation with the laying of the 1st egg (incipient 3rd phylogenetic stage) but do not incubate at night until after the laying of the penultimate egg (1,106).

INCUBATION COMMONLY BEGINS WITH THIRD EGG. The equivalent of the 3rd phylogenetic stage of egg care usually is attained by female Cockatiels only after they have oviposited 3 or more eggs of a given clutch. [In the Bengalese finch, it usually is attained only after the laying of the antepenultimate egg (130), but it is common among passerines to begin incubation with the 3rd egg (14).] Attainment of the equivalent of the 3rd stage normally appears to depend on physiological and neural processes accompanying oviposition. It usually is not reached by female Cockatiels after lengthy care of fostered eggs. Inexperienced and immature females, having attained the 3rd phylogenetic stage of egg care, may also shelter and groom hatchlings, but often do not allofeed them (this is the most common cause of chick loss; 127, 787). Experienced birds that have attained the 3rd stage brood the young.

[In exceptional cases, the 3rd phylogenetic stage can be attained by Cockatielian hens that have not oviposited. If fertile eggs are fostered on a hen that has spent day after day continually sitting in the nest, but without ovipositing (almost always young birds), she and her mate may accept and incubate them, and successfully rear fostered chicks (127).]

[A PROTRACTED CASE OF BREEDING MATURATION. One of the most protracted cases of sexual maturation and progression through stages of egg and chick care is that of White Storks. As yearlings, these birds commonly fail even to migrate back to Europe, spending the summer breeding season of the adults in their African winter quarters. In their 2nd year, they migrate and may visit nests, but do not oviposit. Third-year storks may pair, copulate, and oviposit a few eggs, but few of these birds successfully hatch and rear young. Though successes increase in number in the 4th year, some pairs do not produce fledglings until the 5th year (28).]

INDIRECT ASSESSMENT OF 3RD PHYLOGENETIC STAGE IN MALE. Since nighttime incubation of eggs by Cockatiels has become the exclusive province of the female, attainment of the equivalent of the 3rd phylogenetic stage by the male has to be assessed using as a criterion whether or not he sits on the eggs tightly, that is, whether he actually incubates them. The indications are that males probably lead females in attaining the 2nd and 3rd phylogenetic stages. Yet the male is dependent upon the presence of the hen, and interactions with her, to progress beyond the 1st stage.

Relict Egg-Care Responses and Primitive Nesting Habits

NON-ADAPTIVE EGG-CARE RESPONSES AS RELICS OF ANCESTRAL BEHAVIOR. A number of previously unknown egg-care responses of Cockatiels seem to have little or no adaptive value for hole-nesters. They appear to be relict responses that trace back to the times of remote ancestors of Cockatiels. Taken together, these responses indicate that the pre-hole-nesting forerunners of Cockatiels nested in shallow scrapes on flat, level ground.

1. LIGHTS-OFF AND LIGHTS-ON RESPONSES. Cockatiels in the equivalent of the 2nd phylogenetic stage of egg care, typically the female, leave the eggs when the daytime lights are turned off. Birds in the early phases of the 3rd stage, usually the female but sometimes the male, not infrequently leave the eggs temporarily when the lights are extinguished. If the lights are turned back on while the birds are temporarily off a nest of exposed eggs, they promptly return to them.

   This appears to be the most ancient of all the observed relict egg-care responses. It suggests that there was a time in the evolution of Cockatiels (the **pre-avian** stage of Table 3) when the eggs were cared for closely during the day but not at night. Such a habit can be accounted for on the assumption that the eggs at that time were not incubated by bodily heat. That is the basis for believing that the response is one of great antiquity, not long after divergence from the line of birds' reptilian ancestors. Eggs that required shielding, shading, and close guarding by day, but not by night, must have been located in surface nests, such that they would have been exposed to view and to solar radiation if not shaded or concealed.

2. DEFECTIVE EGGS ROLLED AWAY AND/OR HIDDEN. Cockatiels incubating in open nests on the enclosure floor will roll defective eggs out of a shallow nest to a distance. They sometimes attempt to conceal such eggs under overhanging objects. Since these acts would serve to reduce or eliminate the possibility of attention being drawn to the nest or sitting bird, they indicate that at some time in the past the ancestors of Cockatiels nested on flat, level ground.

3. VISUAL SEARCHES. Cockatiels caring for eggs search visually for missing clutches by 3 methods: they raise their heads and scan the vicinity; they mount to vantage points and examine the ground near and far; and they make direct nearby ground searches on foot. These behaviors suggest that, at some time past, eggs could get lost or scattered by rolling away, being blown away, or being accidentally displaced. This implies that the ancestors of Cockatiels nested on flat, level ground or in shallow scrapes thereon.

4. SURFACE SCRAPING WHEN EGGS ROLL FREELY. Cockatiels attempting to sit over eggs that roll freely on flat surfaces respond with a surface-scraping action, not otherwise seen. This suggests that their ancestors, at one time, nested on flat substrata that yielded to vigorous scraping in the preparation of a shallow nest-depression.

5. ROUTINELY SEARCH BENEATH THE INCUBATIVE AREA. Cockatiels incubating or sitting loosely on eggs on a substratum of wood shavings routinely search the shavings for buried eggs by pecking, scraping, and "plowing" with the bill. They also generally quickly detect and recover eggs buried with only small patches of surface exposed. Other species that find it necessary to detect eggs buried intentionally (usually with the foot) or otherwise also

employ the bill for this purpose, rather than the feet, for example, *Charadrius vociferous*, *C. pecuarius*, *C. alexandrinus* and *C. dubius* (328, 1,396, 1,397, and p. 527, **Egg-Burying Behavior in the Charadrii**).

6. NON-ATTENDING BIRD APPROPRIATES EXPOSED EGGS. Among incubating Cockatiels, the non-attending bird is alert to eggs that may become exposed beneath or to the side of the attending bird. The non-attending bird appropriates such eggs and incubates them itself. This behavior suggests that, at some time in the past, the ancestors of Cockatiels nested in shallow scrapes on flat, level ground, in which eggs easily could come out from under, or become exposed at the side of, an attending bird (as they easily do on flat, or even shallowly-concave, surfaces).

Ancestral Double-Clutching

Other egg-care behavior of incubating Cockatiels indicates that, at some time in the past, members of both sexes incubated separate clutches, rather than alternating with each other in the incubation of a single clutch.

1. A SPECTRUM OF RELUCTANCE TO SURRENDER THE EGSS. There generally is a reluctance of the attending bird to surrender the eggs to its mate. Depending upon the sex of the attending bird, the time of day, the stage of the incubatory period, and the experience and maturity of the birds, this reluctance varies from being mild to being very strong, with the eggs retained by force.

2. PHYSICALLY DISPLACE THE EGGS AND THE MATE. The birds not only physically displace one another from the eggs, they also physically displace ("steal") the eggs by direct contact.

3. TEMPORARILY SPLIT MULTI-EGG CLUTCHES. As a temporary expedient, the birds frequently split multi-egg clutches and individually incubate the separate portions.

BEHAVIOR PROBABLY OCCURS INFREQUENTLY IN THE WILD. Although these behaviors are seen in confined birds without the need for experimental facilitation, it is probable that they occur infrequently or rarely in the wild. While confined birds usually are provided with a NB large enough to accommodate both of the parents and the brood, such spaciousness is not typical of the nest-hollows used in the wild, where competition with larger birds limits the size of attainable nest holes.

"COZY" CHAMBERS PREFERED. Wild parrots frequently are reported as nesting in extremely small cavities, and certain hole-boring parrots bore rather restricted chambers in which to rear their young (27). The nest-building lovebirds bring more filling material for large cavities than for small ones, preferring small-sized cozy chambers. It is said that Cockatiels are not very selective in picking a nesting chamber. A hole at any height will do if need be, and the size of the entrance and diameter of the in-side cavity are practically immaterial (127), while the shape is quite variable (32).

It seems likely that Cockatiels breeding in the wild are not able to sit side by side in the IA. Where space is limited, they would not meet with the circumstances that precipitate competition for the eggs (except, possibly during nest exchange). Furthermore, the non-incubating parent Cockatiel is said to perch some distance away from the nest-hole (127).

ALLOGROOMING AND NEST EXCHANGE. It was noted that Cockatiels, particularly males, utlize incessant head allogrooming--beginning in mild form but eventually escalating to a vigorous pursuit--as a tactic to displace their mates from the eggs. A mate reluctant to surrender the eggs sometimes responds by reciprocally grooming the incoming bird. Mutual allopreening is known to be a widespread, ritualized form of agonistic behavior that "bridges the narrow gap between sexual behavior and aggressive attack" (29), but allogrooming on the head apparently has not been reported previously as a tactic employed in competing for the clutch.

Mutual allogrooming upon nest exchange may well be a fairly common practice. For example, it has been reported in Fork-tailed Storm-Petrels. Thus, prior to exchanging roles, birds spend many min together (32.8 ± 38.4 min) engaging in behavior similar to that during courtship, which "is characterized by quiet periods in which the birds rest side by side and by occasional outbursts of calling and mutual grooming" (579). Inasmuch as these nest exchanges take place at 1-5-day intervals (averaging 2.3-2.6 days), there is little likelihood that the attending bird is reluctant to be relieved or that the grooming is employed as a form of persuasion. However, the grooming clearly could have evolved to an essentially ritualistic behavior from more primitive, aggressive, competitive nest-exchange behavior by birds exchanging with one another more frequently.

This interpretation tends to be supported by the observation that on one occasion a female petrel yielded a freshly-laid egg (oviposited about 30 min earlier) to her mate directly after being groomed by him on her forehead. In only 7 of over 500 cases did petrels decline to be relieved, and in these cases they were in their 1st or 2nd day of a session of incubation (579). [Peach-faced Lovebird males may tenderly allogroom the sitting female for extended periods over all exposed, feathered portions of her body, but this behavior has no aggressive overtone (see p. 721, **Gentle, Thorough, Attentive Allogrooming by the Male**).]

Vocalizations Associated with Breeding

COITION SOUNDS. It was mentioned earlier that repetitive, slow, soft squeaks of the female during coition were known. I have found these sounds to be associated with irregular movements of the mandibles, or, in certain circumstances, with no movement. One female made these sounds in or near the NB, usually in the presence of the male, but not immediately preceding coitus. On the other hand, males make sounds virtually identical to the females' Coition Sounds during the periods of courtship, oviposition, and incubation, often from the nest, and occasionally in the company of the mate. [Spectrographic analyses may reveal differences between the male and female sounds, but both are referred to here as Coition Sounds.]

There is little or no indication that the female reacts overtly when the male makes the Coition Sounds. There doubtless is internal stimulation of both the bird making the sounds and of the bird hearing them, and the sounds probably serve to maintain the birds physiologically and psychologically in breeding condition during the periods of oviposition and incubation. Ferdinand uttered Coition Sounds frequently and at great length, but Cosimo and Homer employed them only sparingly.

SONG. As mentioned in Chapter 1, the songs of male Cockatiels are many and varied, and sometimes are uttered in an urgent-sounding manner. The breeding bird, in particular, has a very rich repertoire, with probably more than 10 different songs. All breeding and courting males were highly vocal, and their singing generally occurred all through the periods of courting and incubation. Again, females infrequently responded overtly to singing males, and the function of the song probably is to maintain the birds in breeding condition until the chicks hatch.

SOFT, MELODIOUS SINGING FROM THE NEST. Soft, melodious song often is uttered from the NB, usually by the lone male. At different times, this may serve as an invitation to the female to adopt the nest and breed (see also 127), as an invitation for nest exchange or as "contentment song." On one unusual occasion, a female (Carmen), incubating in the late evening, uttered soft chirps and was joined briefly by her mate.

[Among Warbling Vireos (*Vireo gilvus*), song delivered in the nest by the male has a long and regular cadence; males sing in short bouts only when they are alone, away from the nest, and are patrolling their territories. Changes in their singing were related to: establishing contact with a potential mate; integrating courtship behavior to occur only in the vicinity of the nest; as a means for monitoring a bird's activity and location; and in coordinating movements of birds to and from the nest (1,127).]

Male Dominance

SEEN IN ALMOST ALL INTERACTIONS. The male Cockatiel apparently typically dominates his mate but the degree of dominance may vary greatly and may influence significantly a mated pair's interactions and breeding behavior; for example, a weakly dominant male is not allofed by his mate. The dominant role of the male is seen in almost all interactions between members of a confined mated pair. The male plays the chief role in adopting and preparing the nest (just as does the dominant female lovebird), sometimes when the female seems to have no interest (see 9, 127). [In one report of Cockatiels in an outdoor aviary, the female was seen to enter the newly-installed nest-hollow first. This forward behavior of the hen probably can be attributed to her already having been in an advanced stage of arousal. Thus, she laid her 1st egg only 2 days later (32).]

MALE UNILATERALLY LEAVES THE EGGS OR BROOD. The male usually dominates at the food tray and the perch, and tends to prevail in all disputes over choice items and locations. Though it does not occur frequently, the male may unilaterally leave the eggs or brood. He then leaves it to the female to take over, as she almost invariably does. And, if she does not, the male may "encourage" her to do so by pecking or prodding her. But, occasionally, it is the female who leaves the eggs and pecks the male in an effort to get him to take over their care.

PRODS THE FEMALE TO PERFORM CERTAIN TASKS. In circumstances in which an unusual action may be called for, the male usually attempts to bring about the action, by pecking or prodding the female. Examples of this were seen when I fostered a hatchling to Isabella and Ferdinand (see p. 493), and when Cosimo sought to get Carmen to enter the NB in the presence of a green marble that I had substituted for an egg (see p. 457).

BRUSHES THE FEMALE ASIDE TO PERFORM OTHER ACTIONS. In the case of an action or goal that the birds find to be rewarding, the male may just brush the female aside as he hastens to perform or achieve it. The female infrequently unilaterally leaves the brood before the chicks are several days old. Exceptions to male dominance occur in the NB when eggs and/or chicks are present. The female always prevails late at night and early in the morning, though the male does not necessarily surrender readily; very long sessions of competitive interactions may precede his inevitable surrendering of the brood.

Allofeeding

ALLOFEEDING OF THE MALE BY THE FEMALE was seen first in the experienced breeding pair, Carmen and Cosimo, and subsequently in their inexperienced offspring, Kirsten and Rimski. This consisted exclusively of extensive allofeeding or mock-allofeeding of Cosimo and Rimski by their mates. This extensive allofeeding of the male by the female correlates closely with male dominance. It was not seen to occur in the other two breeding pairs (Isabella and Ferdinand and Helena and Homer), in which male dominance was much less pronounced, with consequent frequent lengthy disputes at food trays. Allofeeding of the male by the female occurred routinely throughout the day, as many as 50 times during the periods in which it took place. Such allofeeding may correlate with the fact that the male spends much of the daylight hours in the NB with the eggs and chicks (see the further treatment on pp. 690, 691, **Carmen's Allofeeding of Cosimo**).

Adding to the interest of the phenomenon of courtship feeding and allofeeding of the male by his mate, Carmen continued to allofeed Cosimo after the weaning of her 4th brood (as she was ovipositing another clutch on the enclosure floor). During these allofeedings of Cosimo, the young would crowd over near Carmen and also solicit. But Cosimo would take time out from being allofed to drive the young away with pecks. The same phenomenon was observed when 2 males of the 7th brood of Carmen and Cosimo (already 5 months old) continued to be housed with their parents (see also p. 414).

A phenomenon consistent with the practice of Cockatelian females allofeeding the male, was observed when Ferdinand and Isabella were housed with their parents, Carmen and Cosimo, in October, 1984, after the summer breeding of both pairs. When Carmen courtship-fed Cosimo, Ferdinand approached her (his mother) on 3 different occasions seeking also to be allofed, whereas Isabella paid no heed. On one of these occasions, she only approached after Cosimo had been fed 9 times, whereas Ferdinand paced about excitedly in the near vicinity almost the entire time. In similar circumstances and on many occasions, the juvenile son, Lothair, extended his bill as close as he dared to Cosimo, as Carmen allofed the latter.

Interpreting Behavior

CLOSE, LENGTHY OBSERVATIONS FACILITATE INTERPRETATIONS. Although the interpretations placed upon behavior by the observer sometimes must be drawn and accepted with caution, the closer and more continuous the observations, the more evident and reliable the interpretations. I can say with confidence, e.g., that after exiting the NB Cosimo pecked at the heedless Carmen, to try to get her to take over care of the eggs, on occasions when she did not cooperate on her own (nor after being pecked), because of witnessing other occasions when she yielded to his prodding. Having come to recognize the types of pecks delivered when one bird seeks to have its mate perform some act, certain interpretations can be made with confidence, as when Ferdinand pecked Isabella to try to get her to go down to the nest containing a 4-day-old chick that I had newly-returned to them.

SOME INTERPRETATIONS OBVIOUS. On the other hand, some behavioral interactions are so obvious that they scarcely require an interpretation as to what is transpiring. Changes of intention fall into this category. I have described instances where Cosimo changed his intention to leave the NB, and hastened to "head off" Carmen as she sought to replace him, instances where he "headed off" me by hurredly returning to a guard position on the outside perch, and instances when he retreated from the inside perch to sit over an egg or guard a chick.

Similarly, Carmen changed her intent to leave a brood several times and raced back to the nest to protect it. All 4 brooding lovebird hens often raced back to the NB or nestbowl to guard the the brood when I approached just after they left (as I sought to make an inspection). There were occasions when almost all of my breeding Cockatiels, but particularly the females, could be made to change their intent about leaving their eggs (temporarily or for the night) when the lights were turned off, simply by turning the lights back on.

Can Cockatiels Count?

PRESENT EXPERIMENTS NOT DESIGNED TO TEST COUNTING ABILITY. On page 112, I mentioned the fact that Budgerigars appear to be able to count to 7 or 8. The present studies were not designed to test the counting ability of Cockatiels, but they might have been expected to give some suggestive results. In some cases, the results suggested that the birds could count (for example, the alarm of Carmen and Cosimo at the presence of a 2nd egg, and the temporary alarm or confusion of Isabella and Ferdinand on finding nine scattered eggs, instead of three grouped ones), but the experiments--not being designed to answer this question--were inconclusive. In other cases, such as those in which eggs were added to clutches and accepted routinely, the results suggested that the birds could not count.

EGG MANIPULATIONS ILL SUITED FOR TESTING COUNTING ABILITY. The only conclusive result obtained here, through manipulating Cockatielian eggs, is that such an approach is inherently unsuitable for studying the ability of Cockatiels to count (and, probably, of other parrots, also). The reason is very simple. The presence of just one egg ‘satisfies’ the instincts of Cockatiels to incubate. They stop directed searching for missing eggs after the first one is found, and they do not initiate directed searches as long as at least one egg remains.

INATTENTIVENESS TO NUMBER OF EGGS NOT MALADAPTIVE. This would not appear to be maladaptive behavior in determinate-laying birds (see pp. 165, 166) that nest under conditions in which the eggs are unlikely to be lost.

If one were to speculate on the adaptedness of this behavior in the ancestors of Cockatiels, one would, again, have to conclude that the behavior was not maladaptive. One concludes this because Cockatiels now routinely search for buried eggs under conditions in which burial is possible, and this appears to be a very ancient behavior pattern. Thus, being "programmed" to find missing eggs routinely, it is immaterial whether the birds are attentive to the number of eggs that are present. On the other hand, it is suggested below that, for pro-aves, practicing rapid double-clutching, it would have been adaptive to be 'content' with only a single egg, or the smaller of 2 clutches.

Sensing of Position and Spatial Relations

EGGS 'RECOGNIZED' THROUGH SIDEPANE. The amazing exploits of some birds in finding large numbers of hidden caches of seeds or nuts is well known, and the findings described here do not rival them. We noted two occasions in which birds (Carmen and Ferdinand) either eyed or dug in precise locations where eggs previously had been buried. A feat of Carmen's was much more impressive in terms of 'awareness' of spatial relations. Three times Carmen spied missing eggs buried against the transparent Plexiglas sidepane within the NB. Each time, she entered the NB from the outside position from which she had detected them, went to the precise spot where the eggs were buried (within 4 cm of each other), and eyed closely the surface of the shavings above them. Clearly, she had discerned from outside the NB the precise location of the eggs within the NB.

COSIMO FAILED TO PERFORM A SIMILAR FEAT on a more urgent occasion. From outside the NB, Cosimo spied a missing chick inside it, also by seeing it through the sidepane. Apparently, not realizing that the chick was inside the NB, he tried frantically to reach it by a direct route, as he attempted to peck and chew his way through the NB corner and sidepane.

Some Notable Adaptive Behavior

PARENTS INTENSELY COMPETITIVE BUT HIGHLY SUCCESSFUL. It has been noted at great length that vigorous competition for the eggs (and hatchlings) frequently occurs between Cockatielian mates. Although one's first inclination may be to regard such a situation as maladaptive, this obviously is not the case. The contrary appears to be true. It would appear that, as a consequence of the intense competition, the clutch (and brood) are very little neglected. All observers extol the success of confined Cockatiels as breeders--"usually superb parents" (9), and "one of the parrots easiest to breed in captivity" (32). The care of broods of 4 and 5 chicks by Carmen and Cosimo was a marvel to behold, in the precise and methodical way in which they managed the young (see pp. 686-695, 702).

"DIVING IN" AND CRISSUM-GROOMING, EQUIVALENT ACTIONS. Three adaptive behavioral features that act to ensure the safety and unfailing care of the eggs, in the face of intense competition for them, are worth mentioning again. For the female, there is the action of "diving in," which never fails to release an immediate surrendering of the eggs by her mate, no matter how possessive he might otherwise have been. For the male, there is the action of grooming the crissum, which never fails to induce the female to rise up off the eggs. In essence, these acts are equivalent; the female dives under at the front, the male at the rear.

NEVER CONTEST SIMULTANEOUSLY FOR SAME EGG. But the most important safety feature probably is the fact that the birds never contest physically for the same egg at the same time--only in turn. If they were to do so, it would bring the thin-shelled eggs into jeopardy. One bird may "steal" an egg in plain sight of its mate with impunity. Only after the act is completed, does the mate "steal" the egg back, again with impunity.

JUVENILES CONTEST SIMULTANEOUSLY, PECK OPEN AND EAT EGGS. It is interesting to note that this safety feature does not characterize the actions of juvenile birds. They express great interest in eggs that are presented to them, and will contest directly and simultaneously for the same egg. In the case of the 3 juveniles of the 5th brood of Carmen and Cosimo, who were left housed with the parents as they incubated their next clutch of 4 eggs, the young showed the usual great interest in the eggs but eventually pecked open and ate two of them, before being removed (see p. 700). But this is **what can happen**. In normal circumstances, juveniles of such age probably do not come into contact with eggs. Even when the parents begin another clutch while still caring for the previous brood, they may protect the eggs from the young.

Recapitulation of Evolutionary Stages of Egg Care

THE IMPORTANCE OF TIMING OR "ORDERLY" SEQUENCE. It is well known that timing, or "orderly" sequence of exposure (underlying changes in hormonal concentrations and, in my view, making neural pathways accessible in sequential fashion), is important in the determination of responses of some breeding birds to eggs and chicks. "If either internal or external forces should throw the train of instinctive behavior off its schedule, aberrant behavior may result" (28).

RESPONSES TO A HATCHLING ENCOUNTERED OUT OF BREEDING PHASE. No observation more forcefully illustrates the importance of timing and the inflexible stereotypy of Cockatielian breeding behavior than the responses of Carmen and Cosimo to a hatchling that appeared when the birds were out of breeding phase. I gave them this hatchling during their courting phase, at a time when the so-often-irresistible urge to brood is absent. Though they were highly attentive parents in the preceding month, as they reared their 4th brood, they not only were alarmed at the intrusion of a hatchling, they fled to the farthest corner of the enclosure see p. 497).

[In a comparable situation, Tricolored Blackbirds (Agelaius tricolor), building a nest, simply ignore fostered young, and may even incorporate them into the structure of their nest, as if they were inanimate objects (28). On the other hand, they will accept fostered nestlings during, or shortly after, egg-laying. In the case of Mallee Fowl (*Leipoa ocellata*) there would appear to be no period in the breeding cycle when a chick is "recognized" or attended to. If a chick appears on the surface of the nest mound while the male is tending to the mound, the chick simply is scratched out of the way with the building material (see 1,053).]

RECAPITULATION OF EVOLUTIONARY STAGES---MAY BE WIDESPREAD. The present results carry us farther than merely conveying an appreciation of the importance of timing. They suggest that the sequence of progressively increasing parental egg care by Cockatiels recapitulates corresponding stages of egg care during Cockatielian evolution. The remarkable responses to light changes were a principal guiding factor in this development. They may be the oldest of the present-day relict egg-care responses.

The contemporary recapitulation of evolutionary stages in the development of certain behavioral patterns may be a widespread phenomenon in birds, if not in many vertebrates. Thus, there is some indication that this also occurs in relation to nest utilization (see, for example, the behavior of female American Robins and European Mistle Thrushes in 28), and it is suggested strongly by Cockatielian breeding behavior, as treated in Part 1 of Chapter 6. Even seemingly trivial changes can be highly suggestive. For example, early in the incubatory period in open nestbowls, both Cockatiels and lovebirds tend to leave the eggs at my slight disturbance; at a later stage they are steadfast in remaining on them.

PREFERENCES FOR NEST SITES MAY RECAPITULATE NESTING HABITS. One also may be seeing a manifestation of the recapitulation phenomenon in preferences exhibited for nest sites, such as when Cockatiels and lovebirds revert to the primitive method by nesting on the enclosure floor when a NB is unavailable. The behavior of the Peregrine Falcon also may reveal evolutionary stages. If a cliff is unavailable, it will nest in a tree, following a probable ancestral mode. But if neither a cliff nor a tree is available, it nests on the ground, in the most primitive mode (28). Similarly, Marbled Murrelets (*Brachyramphus marmoratus*) are known to nest in various types of cavities, on tree branches, and on open ground, depending upon nest-site availability, with cavities probably being preferred (see 1,126). This last approach has obvious limitations, because of the adaptability of birds to unusual circumstances. Thus, in some situations birds will use highly unsuitable nest sites.

UNCOVERING "FOSSILIZED BEHAVIOR." These results also emphasize the fact that it is insufficient for students of avian behavior merely to make close detailed observations of **what does happen**. One often must "dig" to uncover "fossilized behavior," that is, one must perform experiments to answer specific questions and uncover relict responses. "The challenge is to activate their neural circuitry and tap the motor output" (132). As interesting as are the answers to **what does happen** (in both the field and in field-simulating conditions in the laboratory and zoological garden), they represent only fragments of the total picture. Being able to assemble these fragments into a cohesive whole more likely than not depends upon information about **what can happen**, which often may be more interesting and enlightening than **what does happen**. Much more of the past may have been preserved in the central nervous systems of vertebrates than is realized.

Normally Accessible, Normally Inaccessible, Vestigial, and Adventitious Relict Behavior

PERSISTENCE OF NEURAL CIRCUITS FOR RELICT BEHAVIOR. The neural circuits for the egg-care responses of Cockatiels normally are accessible, though they probably are used very infrequently in present-day circumstances in the "cozy" hole-nests often occupied by the birds in the wild; the behavioral responses that they effect, simply are not elicited. These circuits persist and remain accessible because the corresponding fully-manifested behaviors, though very infrequently elicited, were neither selected against nor lost through random mutations (because of the intrinsic evolutionary inertia of the central nervous sytem).

Since the muscles employed in the responses are used in numerous other activities, as doubtless are the neural circuits, as well, there was no selection against retention of the related motoneurons in the spinal cord, such as occurs, for example, in some flightless birds (see 132). In this connection it is known that the same neural pattern-generating circuits for movements of invertebrates may be employed in more than one behavioral response. In fact, complex sequences of coordinated invertebrate behavior (e.g., cricket ecdysis) result from the coordinated and controlled incorporation of many simpler units of behavior (see 600).

[In connection with the above remark on the likelihood of multiple uses of specific neural circuits or parts thereof, Bekoff suggested "that a neural circuit which is developed to produce one type of behavior at one stage of development may be used to produce another at another stage." It was suggested specifically that the pattern-generating circuit that produces the leg movements of hatching in the domestic fowl embryo also may generate the walking movements of the hatched chick, despite the fact that the two behaviors are quite distinct (1,337; see also pp. 190, 191, **Hatching Versus Walking Movements, and Neural Circuitry**).]

THE IMPORTANT ROLE OF INHIBITORY CONTROL IN BEHAVIOR has become ever more evident in recent years. Increasingly sophisticated techniques have indicated an earlier onset of inhibitory contributions to patterned movement in various vertebrate species than often was suspected from prior studies (see 1,268). "The behavioral studies of descending inhibition of cutaneous reflexes in decerebrate animals teach us the important lesson that behavior can be just as much as expression of inhibitory as of excitatory control" (1,360). Some relatively clear-cut examples of central neural inhibition serve to introduce the following treatments of human and avian relict responses.

The neural circuit that is responsible for generating the temporal pattern of the calling song of crickets (genus *Teleogryllus*) normally is suppressed until the final molt to adulthood. Lesioning of the mushroom bodies of the brain of the last larval stage results in the activation (disinhibition) of the neural circuit for the song pattern, whereupon the tiny larval wing primordia begin to undergo the stridulatory movements that produce sounds with adult wings. The contraction patterns of the muscles matched those of the adult during the production of calling song (596).

Adult-type abdominal grooming can be elicited from late-instar cockroach nymphs, but only after decapitation, and the adult motor patterns of flight and walking can be elicited from normally quiescent Phrate Moths (*Manduca sexta*) by an antagonist of gamma-aminobutyric acid. The reflex that elicits micturition and defecation in nursing kittens when the mother licks the perineal region becomes suppressed by supraspinal inhibitory controls after 4 weeks of age. It can be reactivated by transecting the spinal cord, after which the animals respond once more to perineal stimulation (see 1,337).

Another example provided by cats is less clear-cut. In 6 of 9 cats that were deprived monocularly from birth, single neurons in the superior colliculus contralateral to the deprived eye could be activated only by visual stimuli from the ipsilateral (experienced) eye, despite the fact that the ipsilateral colliculus receives a major input from the contralateral (deprived) retina. But if the visual cortex was removed (including areas 17-19), most of the collicular units then could be activated within 15 min by input only from the deprived eye.

This very strongly indicates both that the visual cortex must suppress retino-collicular input and that the suppression is by an inhibitory synaptic mechanism. Moreover, since stimulation of the deprived eye does not evoke activity in cells of the visual cortex, the cortical suppression of the retinal input must be accomplished by impulses that descend spontaneously over the cortico-collicular pathway. There are precedents for similar effects in invertebrate systems and in the frog (1,371). [In the other 3 cats, in certain "patches" of the contralateral colliculus, retinal input from the deprived eye was not suppressed but, instead, dominated the input to collicular neurons.] There also appear to be classes of synapses that are "dormant" or otherwise ineffective but apparently not maintained in that state by inhibitory control. If normally functioning afferent nerve fibers to certain cells are blocked or cut, some of the previously ineffective (alternate) fibers immediately establish effective drive of the cells (1,372).

RELICT RESPONSES IN MAN

NEURAL CIRCUITS PERSIST BUT THE EFFECTOR MUSCULATURE IS VESTIGIAL. The best known relict responses and perhaps most of the known vestigial relict responses occur in Man and are frequently encountered and dealt with by neurologists and neurosurgeons. These are treated briefly in the following. In many well known cases the neural circuitry for these responses persists and remains accessible. But the responses no longer are manifested fully, that is, they have become vestigial. Again, the persistence of the neural circuitry traces to the intrinsic evolutionary inertia of the central nervous system and/or the employment of the circuitry in multiple functions (see above). On the other hand, the more labile effector systems --primarily the corresponding musculatures--usually no longer are adequate to achieve fully-manifested relict responses. [An impressive example of the conservation of neural circuitry in the total absence of corresponding peripheral targets is seen in the flightless Mexican Grasshopper (*Barytettix psolus*). Though some flight muscles are missing, the motoneurons previously responsible for innervating them still send axons (with "blind" synaptic terminals) to their former locations, and the stretch receptor persists (1,385).

THE PROTECTIVE SUPERFICIAL REFLEXES. In this category are the relics of several protective reflexes that can almost always be elicited by stimulation of the skin of young individuals (the *protective superficial reflexes*). [Their absence in a young adult raises suspicion of early multiple sclerosis.] All of them have complex central neural pathways (146, 147).

Perhaps the best known of these vestigial relict responses are:

(a) the reflex contraction of the abdominal muscles when the overlying skin (epigastric, mid-abdominal, and lower abdominal) is lightly stroked or scratched--the *superficial abdominal reflex*;

(b) the retraction (elevation) of the ipsilateral testicle by the reflex contraction of the cremaster muscle, upon scratching the skin of the inner side of the thigh--the *cremaster reflex*;
(c) contraction of the external anal sphincter, when the peri-anal skin is pricked or stroked--the *superficial anal reflex*; and
(d) the flexion (bending) of the toes toward the sole of the foot, when the sole is stimulated--the *normal cutaneous plantar* (sole of the foot) *reflex* (147).

These superficial reflexes almost always are abolished in people with pyramidal tract disease. [The pyramidal tract consists of fibers arising in the anterior cerebral cortex and passing down through the brainstem to the medulla, where most of them decussate (cross to the opposite side) and pass down the spinal cord.]

THE NORMAL CUTANEOUS PLANTAR REFLEX is the most interesting of the group. I describe it more fully because it normally is lost temporarily (the neural circuitry temporarily becomes inaccessible or inhibited) during development. In this response, a stimulation of the outer border of the sole with a blunt point or thumbnail (or by pin-drag) leads to the above-described flexion of the toes, and sometimes of the foot.

PRESENT IN NEWBORN, GIVES WAY TO BABINSKI REFLEX, REAPPEARS LATER. Though this response may be obtained in 93% of normal newborn infants by careful technique (145), it soon gives way to the quite different Babinski reflex (see pp. 525, 526). The normal cutaneous plantar reflex does not reappear until the 2nd or 3rd year of life (upon completion of myelination of the pyramidal tract; 146, 149). This reflex is thought to be a vestige of a formerly fully-manifested reflex to remove the foot, when stepping on an offending object, and to loosen the skin of the sole, so that a sharp offending object would penetrate less readily (148).

To recapitulate, I now have considered fully-manifested Cockatielian relict responses with normally-accessible neural circuitry, human vestigial relict responses with normally-accessible neural circuitry, and a human vestigial relict response with neural circuitry that becomes temporarily inaccessible during development. I now consider well-manifested relict responses in Man, for which the neural circuitry normally is accessible only during a short period of infancy, after which it becomes contrally inhibited. These are the rooting and the palmar grasp reflexes of newborn infants. The persistence of these reflexes beyond the normal period is a sign of neural disorder. They not uncommonly reappear in old age following organic brain damage.

THE PALMAR GRASP REFLEX. The palmar grasp reflex is assessed by placing one's finger or other suitable object in the infant's hand on the ulnar side (the side opposite the thumb). This results in an involuntary flexion of the fingers and a grasping of the object. In premature infants, the grasp reflex is barely present at the fingers at 28 weeks, but by 9 months it becomes stronger, as the shoulder and elbow assist in the traction response (145). The involuntary response of term infants disappears at 3-4 months (sometimes as many as 6) and is replaced by voluntary purposeful grasping. Persistence of the involuntary grasp reflex is one of the early signs of complete infantile hemiplegia (paralysis on one side of the body).

In adults, the palmar grasp reflex may be "released" (the neural circuitry disinhibited) on the contralateral side in the presence of a frontal lobe lesion. The release (which also can be effected in stuporous and encephalitic patients) occurs when a finger is pressed into the subject's palm, between the thumb and the index finger or when the palm is lightly touched and stroked gently in a movement from the center of the palm outward between the thumb and the forefinger. Depending upon the amount of damage to the frontal lobes, and also on how much paralysis has been caused by concurrent damage to the motor areas of the brain, various components of the grasping reflex can be elicited.

Deep pressure in the palm elicits a strong, maintained flexion (grasping) of the fingers. The subject is unable to release such a grasp, even though he makes a strong attempt to do so. If the subject's eyes are covered, and the finger is withdrawn, he sometimes gropes for it (150, 1,309). If the finger is moved sufficiently slowly, the subject's hand and arm follow while just clinging to it (the *magnet* reaction). The same kind of grasping-approaching automatism can be seen in the foot of patients with frontal lobe damage in response to pressure or a light touch on the sole.

These actions are very powerful and often not under voluntary control. They pervade the frontally-brain-damaged subject's behavior, often to his great embarrassment. Thus, when opening a door, the subject may find himself unable to release the doorknob. The grasp reflex is so powerful that he has to reach over with his other hand to pry loose his fingers. The contact-approach-reflex of the foot often is exaggerated to the degree that, when walking, the frontally damaged subject often is hampered by the "slipping clutch syndrome:" when he starts to walk, his foot seems to be glued to the ground. Several sliding movements on the ground typically have to be made before the foot can be freed sufficiently to walk forward (1,309).

THE ROOTING REFLEX. If the cheek of a newborn infant is stroked lightly, he will move his head toward the stimulus and will form his mouth so as to take in the stimulating object. This movement toward the source of stimulation is known as the *rooting reflex*, and it functions to assist the neonate in locating a nipple at the time of feeding. Within a few months after birth, this response no longer can be elicited (1,303).

DISSOLUTION describes rooting and sucking reflexes that have become involuntary automatisms in Man in the presence of frontal-lobe damage. For example, one such subject, upon being touched lightly on the side of the cheek near the mouth with a finger, opened his mouth and gaped toward the finger. As the stimulation continued, he turned his head, his mouth made contact with the finger and sucking movements occurred. If such a subject is asked why he is performing this act, he may show surprise and embarrassment, reply that he was unaware of his action, or even deny it, yet be unable to cease doing it (1,309).

THE BABINSKI SIGN, RESPONSE, OR REFLEX. The last example concerns a response in humans, for which no strong case can be made for its being a vestigial relic. The neural circuitry for this response normally is accessible only during infancy, or in the presence of a lesion or disease in a certain portion (area 4) of the motor cortex or the descending corticospinal tract fibers--the pyramidal tract. (146). This reflex was first described by Babinski in 1896, and probably is the most important single clinical sign in neurology.

The Babinski reflex, like the normal cutaneous plantar reflex, is elicited by stimulating the outer border of the sole of the foot with a blunt point (the foot must be kept warm). It consists of an initial deliberate upward dorsiflexion (extension) of the hallux (great toe), sometimes followed by the spreading or fanning out of the other toes. It often is combined with a slight contraction of the flexor muscles of the leg and thigh (including the so-called hamstring muscles), producing flexing of the foot at the ankle and flexion of the knee and hip (146, 147).

THE BABINSKI REFLEX IN THE INJURED. Besides the normal appearance of the Babinski reflex in infants, it can be elicited in adults following injury to the pyramidal tract and contralateral hemiplegia (complete paralysis of the opposite side of the body). [A common cause of such hemiplegia is cerebral apoplexy resulting from thromboses (blood clots) or hemorrhage (146).] Appearance of the Babinski reflex in the newborn infant is abnormal and suggests brainstem and spinal cord injuries (145). Pyramidal tract lesions also bring other weak or latent reflexes to the surface; the lesions disinhibit the neural circuitry by releasing the inhibitory influence of the pyramidal tract on the reflex arcs. This is seen clearly in the exaggeration or hyperactivity of certain normal stretch reflexes, especially the deep ones ("tendon" or muscle-stretch reflexes; 150).

BABINSKI REFLEX UNLIKELY VESTIGIAL RELIC. Some workers have speculated that the Babinski reflex in humans is a vestigial relic of reflexes of the foot, from times when the hallux was an opposable member. This seems quite unlikely, however, in view of the fact that the infant or lesioned chimpanzee (among others), with its opposable hallux, has a Babinski response similar in all details to the human one (148, 149).

The significance of the Babinski reflex is the following. It illustrates a case in which the neural circuitry for a response: (a) is present, and accessible during a certain period, in the infant; (b) is present, but normally inaccessible (inhibited), in the adult; and (c) can be rendered accessible (disinhibited) in the adult by specific neural embarrassment. It is a reflex whose neural circuitry becomes "closed" or inhibited by activity of the higher centers of the nervous system, specifically by impulses from the corticospinal (pyramidal) pathway (146, 148).

SPINAL AUTOMATISMS represent vestigial spinal-mechanism relics that normally are held in abeyance or inhibited by the higher centers. They can be manifested when these inhibitions are abolished by severe spinal cord disease or by decerebrate states at the midbrain level (losses of parts of the midbrain). Examples are the *spinal flexion reaction*, also called *spinal withdrawal* and the *shortening reflex*, the *mass reflex*, and the *crossed extensor reflex*. They cannot be elicited after spinal injury until the stage of "spinal shock" has subsided; the exact mechanisms by which they become accessible are unknown (150).

OTHER PRESUMPTIVE RELICT AND VESTIGIAL RELICT BEHAVIOR IN BIRDS

VESTIGIAL RELICT BEHAVIOR OF THE BLUE-CROWNED MOTMOT. The appearance of a possible vestigial relict response during breeding is illustrated in the courtship of the Blue-crowned Motmot (*Momotus momota*). The approach of a courting bird to its mate holding a leaf or twig in its bill may be a vestige of ancestral nest-display behavior, inasmuch as the underground burrow of these birds now is not lined (28).

VESTIGIAL RELICT BEHAVIOR OF THE PAINTED SNIPE. Another possible vestigial relict response was noted during the brooding of a pair of Painted Snipes, birds that appear to be sequentially polyandrous. In this species only the male incubates the clutch; the female neither helps her mate nor incubates alone, and the pair bond appears to break down after the laying of the last egg. In 1 out of 15 observed breeding pairs, the male abandoned the nest. The female thereupon began to incubate the eggs in his place but she ceased after about half a day (273). The female's response would appear to be a vestigial relic harkening back to an ancestral period when females also incubated.

EGG-BURYING BEHAVIOR IN THE CHARADRII. Deliberate covering of eggs in the Charadrii (waders) occurs in at least 13 tropical and subtropical species in 4 families (see treatment on p. 580, **Covering the Eggs with Various Materials**). The taxonomic distribution of this habit among these waders suggested to Maclean that the habit arose independently in the taxa in which it occurs, a view that he feels is supported by the fact that different motions are employed in the covering; the Glareolidae use the bill, whereas the plovers and seedsnipes use the feet. The evidence suggests that the primary function of the behavior is concealment but that in many cases the function of insulation from solar heat may secondarily have assumed the major role. Some observers suggest that the covering response is released in part by the sight of exposed eggs.

Maclean did not find it surprising that egg covering is most highly developed in species of Charadrii that inhabit tropical and subtropical regions, where predator pressure may be higher and the danger of overheating on direct solar exposure is greater than elsewhere. Nevertheless, he found it difficult to understand "why it should have evolved at all," because most of the Charadrii and many other ground-nesters that occupy habitats very similar to those of the egg-covering waders "can survive perfectly well without covering their eggs" (328). I would suggest that the egg-burying habit in some species of Charadrii, like many of the egg-care responses of Cockatiels, survives from the times of ancestral birds and earlier, when concealment of the eggs was essential upon temporarily absenting nest scrapes on the ground.

This conclusion is supported by the otherwise paradoxical fact that the egg-covering species have tended more strongly to retain another primitive character, namely cryptic coloration of the eggs. Thus, the eggs of many species that do not cover them during absences are less cryptically colored than the eggs of the species that practice covering. This interpretation also is supported by the fact that the northern hemispheric forms that no longer practice egg burial have retained the ability to find and uncover adventitiously or artificially buried eggs (see 328, 1,396, 1,397).

Within the framework of the interpretation of egg covering as relict behavior, the problem shifts to one of accounting for retention of the habit only in many of the Southern Hemispheric Charadrii. Loss of the behavior pattern in Cockatiels is readily accounted for by its maladaptedness in birds that nest in holes in trees. Thus, contrary to the circumstances that usually prevail in nest scrapes on the ground, (a) a considerable effort usually would be required to transport or make available material for covering eggs in tree holes, and (b) the general snugness of hole nests (often imposed mandatorily by competition) is such that little space would be available in which to store the covering material while incubating.

RELICT RESPONSES EXPRESSED ADVENTITIOUSLY. Some known phenomena reveal that when even vestiges of ancestral behaviors are lost through selection or random mutations, the corresponding neural circuitry for these behaviors is not lost, but merely becomes by-passed or otherwise normally inaccessible (though doubtless participating in other pathways). In some cases, the neural circuitry for relict behavior is not accessible normally at any time nor under abnormal circumstances, but becomes accessible adventitiously, or in certain defined conditions (atavism).

Several cases of adventitious relict behavior are known in birds. For example, on a very few occasions, Peach-faced Lovebirds have been seen to perform the highly-ritualized displacement grooming that apparently is extinct in all but the relatively primitive Madagascar Lovebird (3). Moreau found an observation of A. Hampe's to be of extraordinary interest. The latter reported that a male, hand-reared Fischer's Lovebird (*A. fischeri*), a member of a species that otherwise is known to carry nest material only in the bill, tried to insert some material between the feathers of the rump. Carrying nesting material thrust amidst the feathers (anywhere a bird can reach, except for the flight feathers) is the presumed ancestral method (see 3, 12). Dilger sees a clear evolutionary trend from cutting small bits of material, which the birds tuck over the entire body, to cutting long strips, which they tuck only amidst the rump feathers, to carrying material only in the bill (3). [Note that tucking nesting material anywhere between the feathers would provide for very effective transport in ground-nesters gathering material in the vicinity of the nest, with no need to fly back to the nest site.]

[Cases of adventitiously expressed anatomical relics are known in many animals, for example, the rarely appearing vestigial claws on the wings of ducks, hawks, cranes, rails, and crows (28), extra toes in llamas, hind legs in whales, wings in secondarily flightless insects, plaice colored on both sides, and conservation of the tail, fur, 4 or more nipples, a divided uterus, a cloaca, and even gill slits as cervical fistulae in Man (see 1,242). Numerous examples of the appearance of apparently primitive or ancestral plumage variants expressed both adventitiously and in hybrids could be given (see refs. to C.J.O. and J.M. Harrison in 430). Similarly, in some chelonians, developmental anomalies, e.g., the appearance of inframarginal scutes, reflect the early or pre-Triassic fossil record (681).]

RELICT BEHAVIOR IN HYBRIDS. In still other cases, the neural circuitry for relict behavior appears to be present in different species and subspecies (or members of one sex) but, being more or less inaccessible, the corresponding behavior rarely is expressed. The circuitry becomes accessible, and the corresponding behavior becomes expressed, in hybrids or intergrades (440). Thus, a few highly ritualized aspects of courtship behavior of the parent species appeared in incomplete or simplified forms in a hybrid Shelduck (*T. tadorna*) x Goosander (*Mergus merganser*). These were regarded as reversions to more primitive, less ritualized conditions (572). Also, dabbling was regarded as the ancestral method of feeding, since the hybrid dabbled like Shelducks, whereas Goosanders dive for food.

In another example, most hybrid lovebird males (*A. roseicollis* male x *A. personata fischeri* female) regularly cut and carried strips of nesting material to the NB (nestbox), sometimes in greater volume and with greater proficiency than some females (see 1,156). Normally males only learn these acts mimetically from the females, although very rarely they appear adventitiously (see also pp. 259, 260, 827). Hybrid females consistently engaged in the unexpected displacement acts of grooming or head-scratching in non-sexual situations, especially when tucking nesting material. This is regarded as relict behavior, since displacement head-scratching in non-sexual contexts is seen only in *A. cana*, *taranta*, and *pullaria*, the most primitive members of the genus; displacement grooming at any time is seen only in *A. cana*, and strictly during courtship thwarting (3, 12, 79).

In addition, on the very few occasions when a single hybrid female oviposited (only a total of about 4 eggs were laid, and at widely spaced intervals), she immediately covered the egg with fresh nesting material (a behavior never otherwise seen in lovebirds) but never incubated it (1,156). I regard this as the most significant of these relict responses, one that presumably recapitulates a primitive component of pre-incubatory egg care in which the eggs were concealed during absences from surface nests (see pp. 443, 444, 629-631). Of course, the concealing of eggs before the onset of incubation is normal behavior in some birds (e.g., see pp. 444, 446).

RELICT BEHAVIOR IN TERMS OF THRESHOLDS AND DIMINISHED REACTIVITY. These hypotheses concerning the basis for, and the release of, relict responses find substantial support in Manning's genetic studies of *Drosophila*, though her conclusions are couched in somewhat different terms (593). Thus, she developed the thesis that mutations of single genes produce only small threshold alterations in behavior, which accumulate in the course of evolution. If the frequency of a behavior decreases, it is because of a diminished reactivity, and thus an increased threshold; only in extreme cases might this result in the complete disappearance of the behavior in normal environmental conditions.

Manning asserts that a great many evolutionary changes in behavior can be ascribed to threshold changes (for the activation of the neural circuitry). For example, the change of emphasis within a behavior pattern could result merely from threshold changes on the motor side of a mechanism, such that particular muscle groups were activated earlier, or later, for a longer or shorter period of time, etc. In other words, the neural circuits for ancient behavior patterns persist but their accessibility may change and therewith the behavior patterns may become altered or may become relics that are infrequently manifested. In some cases the circuits persist and remain accessible but no longer become accessed for the relict behavior in the normal course of events.

MAY HAVE BEGUN TO TAP REPOSITORY OF RELICT BEHAVIOR. I would suggest that we only have begun to tap a rich repository of circuitry for relict responses in the central nervous systems of vertebrates. The wealth of human reflexes, and Cockatielian, lovebird, and Budgerigar relict egg-care behavior probably give only a hint of these relics. The clues that they may provide could fill in many blank areas in the evolutionary picture that heretofore have been presumed to be beyond knowing.

Provine (132) has suggested that the most promising places in which to begin "this excavation for the artifacts of our behavioral past" is in animals that have undergone fairly recent major structural and behavioral evolutionary changes. The implication is that very ancient behavior is much less likely to be recoverable. The unprecedented wealth of normally-accessible and apparently very ancient relict egg-care responses retained by

Cockatiels suggests that one can aspire optimistically to recover behaviors of a much more distant past. In the most favorable circumstances, it may be possible to reach back many tens of millions of years.

PART 3. THE FORERUNNERS OF ANCESTRAL BIRDS

EVOLUTIONARY CONSERVATIVENESS. Some readers will be unfamiliar with the evolutionary conservativeness of many facets of behavior, and the evolutionary stasis, even of entire organisms. They may find it difficult to envision the possibility of "looking back" to the times and habits of ancestral birds--over 150 mya--merely by observing the manner in which Cockatiels normally care for their eggs and chicks and respond to simple experimental manipulations.

Yet, I find the relict responses of Cockatiels to be much less astonishing than the "amazingly close similarities" that exist in the neural control mechanisms for vocalizations of certain toadfishes, frogs, birds, and mammals, referred to on page 385. These latter similarities harken back to neural features of common vertebrate ancestors of an even much more distant period, the Devonian, over 350 mya.

Much the same point can be made concerning the vertebrate eye and ear, considering the latter as an organ of balance and motion perception (the vestibular organ). The eye is "a finished product, a perfect apparatus," even in cyclostomes and fishes. Well-developed orbits and channels for the optic nerves are found in fossils of the most ancient known fishes, the ostracoderms, of 400 mya. The vestibular organ reached such a high state of perfection, even in fishes, that its basic structure has remained unchanged "all the way up" the evolutionary scale to mammals (28, 195, 799).

Some invertebrates hardly differ from their ancestors of 500-200 mya (a condition of evolutionary stasis within a lineage or clade known as "bradytely"). Some Tertiary ant species appear not to have changed since 50 mya (78), and the anaspidid syncaridan, Anaspides tasmaniae, is barely distinguishable from fossils of *Anaspidites antiquus* from Triassic deposits in New South Wales (1,097). Even the species-specific characteristics of the crustacean Triops (*Apus cancriformis*) appear to have existed in the Triassic period (1,242). In the case of vertebrates, the skeleton of the opossum has scarcely changed since the Oligocene, possibly not since the late Cretaceous, the lizard-like Tuatara is almost identical in structure with ancestral Jurassic forms of over 135 mya (86), and several extant species of hexanchoid sharks border upon being anatomically identical with their late Jurassic predecessors from the Solnhofen and Eichstätt limestones (1,096).

At the "molecular" level, homologies between genes that began to diverge several 100 mya still can be recognized. Vertebrate immunoglobulin genes apparently are descendants of an ancestral gene of 330 base pairs that existed in some pre-vertebrate lineage more than 500 mya (194). All the immunoglobulins of vertebrates apparently evolved from the "IgM" type of fishes. Moreover, at the cytogenic level, extensive regions of the present-day human and mouse genomes may have remained intact after 60 million years of species divergence (1,350).

COCKATIELS AND BREEDING AND PROPERTIES OF PRE- AND PRO-AVES. I believe that the Cockatielian findings guide us much farther back along the path into the past than to the times of ancestral birds. They appear to be giving us clues to the breeding habits and properties of **pro-aves** and the early post-reptilian forerunners of birds--**pre-aves**. I use the term

Table 3. PROPERTIES OF ANCESTRAL BIRDS, PRO-AVES, AND

Property	Stem-Reptilian Ancestors	Pre-aves	Primitive Pro-aves
Thermoregulatory type, body temperature	ectothermic	same	endothermic (primitive mammalian grade, ranging about 30-32°C)
Surface insulation	keratinous scales	feather-like scales	primitive feathers
Ovarian, ovulatory, and ovipositional conditions*	2 ovaries, polyautochronic, single clutching	2 ovaries, polyautochronic, sequential multiple-clutching	2 ovaries, polyallochronic rapid double-clutching
Incubating parent	non-incubatory	non-incubatory, shielded in alternation	both, each a separate clutch
Source of heat	indirect solar (climatic)	direct and indirect solar	primarily parental body
Care of eggs	nest site attended and protected	shielded and attended (2nd phylogenetic stage of of egg care)	incubated (3rd phylogenetic stage of egg care)
Egg exposure	buried at shallow depths in shaded sites	shielded, shaded, concealed at surface sites	same, except bodily shading not required
Care of hatchlings and young nestlings, or hatching condition	groomed, protected, escorted (2nd phylogenetic stage of care of young)	same	groomed, warmed, protected, and escorted (3rd phylogenetic stage)
Mode of feeding	terrestrial-arboreal predator, primarily on small vertebrates and arthropods	same, but with increased arboreality	primarily arboreal predator on small vertebrates and arthropods
Mode of aerial activity	terrestrial, locomotor jumping	terrestrial jumping and "tree"-to-ground jumping	terrestrial jumping, arboreal jumping and parachuting

THEIR EARLY POST-REPTILIAN AND REPTILIAN FORERUNNERS

Advanced Pro-aves	Ancestral Birds	Cockatiels
endothermic (mammalian grade, ranging about 36°C)	endothermic (primitive avian grade, ranging about 38°C)	endothermic (41-42°C)
feathered	same	same
same, except monoallochronic ovulation	mostly one ovary, single eggs periodically, single clutching or seql. mult.-clutching	same, except exclusively monochronic ovulation
same	both, alternately on single clutch	same
same	same	same
same	same	same
same	eggs in various types of nest sites and nests	eggs within hole nest
transitional, some groups evolving nidicolous young	nidicolous and nidifugous young among different groups	groomed, warmed, protected, and fed (4th phylogenetic stage)
primarily arboreal predator, mostly on flying and flightless insects	wide range of foraging methods on plant and animal matter	primarily plant parts
arboreal jumping, parachuting, gliding; low-amplitude, slow, wing-flapping flight	same, with capability for bursts of high-amplitude, wing-flapping flight	sustained true flight

***Polyautochronic ovulation** = both ovaries concurrently ovulate 2 or more oocytes in roughly the same numbers.
polyallochronic ovulation = 2 or more oocytes are ovulated alternately, first from one ovary and then from the other one in successive reproductive episodes.
monoallochronic ovulation = 1 egg ovulated alternately from each ovary
monochronic ovulation = a single functional ovary exists (see 914).

---

pro-aves to refer to the ancestors of birds that had reached the stage of incubating their eggs, and **pre-aves** to refer to those in the pre-incubatory but post-reptilian stage. The immediate reptilian ancestors of birds, from which **pre-aves** arose, are termed the **stem-reptiles**.

For the reader's convenience, the entries in Table 3 compare the postulated properties of pro-aves at two stages--**primitive** and **advanced**--to those of (a) their immediate reptilian ancestors, the stem-reptiles, (b) their early post-reptilian, non-incubating ancestors, the pre-aves, (c) ancestral birds, and (d) Cockatiels. It will be helpful to refer to this Table in the following treatments. It is recommended that for preliminary orientation the reader first read the **Synthesis of Avian Evolution** and the **Summary** on pages 621-639.

REPTILIAN ANCESTRY OF BIRDS

DIPHYLETIC ORIGIN OF TETRAPODS? By way of introduction to the reptilian ancestry of birds, we note the speculation that the origin of tetrapods was diphyletic, with separate parallel lines having led, one to birds and the other to mammals. One of the bases for this proposal is that germ cell formation, which occurs very early in development, is fundamentally different in the two orders of the class Amphibia, the Anura and the Urodela: "germinal plasm" containing specific cytoplasmic organelles, the germinal granules, are present as early as oogenesis in anurans, whereas in urodeles the primordial germ cells develop epigenetically, arising from arbitrary, common cells of the animal (ectodermal) moiety of the blastula. Another basis is the pronouncedly different manner in which the mesoderm forms in members of the two orders: it forms predominantly or completely internally in the Anura but essentially externally in the Urodela. These circumstances indicate that a very ancient bifurcation occurred in the phylogenetic history of these two groups, possibly even a diphyletic origin from different groups of ancestral fishes (1,237).

In one view, based on anatomical and paleontological evidence, anurans and urodeles have evolved respectively from osteolepiform and porolepiform osteichthyan fishes in the Devonian or Silurian period, 450-400 mya. It is suggested, further, that all of the amniotes are derived from the osteolepiform line (see E. Jarvik, 1968, in 1,237). Embryological evidence, however, may not support the latter conclusion. Rather, it is possible that the amniotes are derived from two separate, parallel lines of evolution, with the osteolepiform line giving rise to the remote ancestors of birds and the porolepiform line to the remote ancestors of mammals. This suggestion is based on a presumed differential origin of primordial germ cells--from the totipotent, ectodermal moiety of the embryonic anlage in mammals, and from the primary hypoblast in birds. However, since recent studies with avian chimeras have suggested an epiblastic rather than a hypoblastic origin of the primordial germ cells, there may be no essential difference in the methods of germ cell origin in the two classes (see 1,237).

ARCHOSAURIANS AS PROBABLE ANCESTORS OF *ARCHAEOPTERYX* To follow the clues to the properties of pro-aves, we begin by recognizing the likelihood that *Archaeopteryx*, the earliest known bird, evolved from the Archosauria (a superorder or subclass of reptiles). It might have evolved from a small bipedal coelurosaurian dinosaur (suborder Theropoda) of the late Triassic or Jurassic period (28, 70, 75, 1,192), when coelurosaurs of slender build already were common (640), or from a procompsognathid theropod of the late Triassic/early Jurassic, such as *Syntarsus* (1,195). Perhaps the most likely candidate is a member of a new group of archosaurs (the "Avimorpha" of Tarsitano; see 1,203), the late Triassic *Megalancosaurus*. The latter apparently was arboreal, with a large manus, with claws morphologically similar to those of pterosaurs, and "much smaller and more lightly built than any coelurosaur" (see 1,203).

Some workers feel that the hypothesis of an archosaurian line of descent is not supported by the developmental pattern of digital reduction in the domestic fowl embryo (see 1,189), although there is admittedly great similarity of the carpus and digital proportions in coelurosaurs and *Archaeopteryx* (44, 69, 75). But many characters that previously were regarded as avian, recently have been found in various theropods of the Mongolian late Cretaceous, such as a furcula, an ossified sternum, an opisthopubic pelvis, and an ascending process of the astragalus (see 1,194).

Another possibility, for which there has been less support, is that birds derived from a much earlier pseudosuchian thecodontian ancestor, shared with crocodiles, and dating back to before the advent of either the ornithician or saurischian stocks, necessarily earlier than the loss of clavicles in crocodylomorphs (169, 179, 653, 669, 1,203). Percentage differences between avian and crocodilian globin sequences place the time of divergence in the middle Triassic; the same studies suggest that the crocodilian avian lineage diverged from a line leading to mammals and squamates during the late Paleozoic-early Mesozoic eras (see 1,312). Of all the Triassic reptilian groups, only the thecodonts display the slim, counter-balancing tail and the enlarged hindlimbs expected of reptiles that lept about in vegetation (659). There also is an extensive radiation of small Triassic archosaurs that share crocodilian features, such as *Cosesaurus aviceps* (but perhaps a prolacertid lepidosaur; see 1,194), whose possible avian affinities deserve consideration (652).

The presence of "resorption windows" (and differently-formed septa of the inner walls of the tooth-bearing bones) in the teeth of crocodilians and Cretaceous birds, but not in dinosaurs, has been advanced as evidence that the common ancestor of birds and dinosaurs was unlikely to have had a fully thecodont implantation of its teeth (teeth set in deep sockets in the jaw bones), and must have existed before the late Triassic period (193). However, neither this nor other similarities between crocodilian and avian teeth (triangular crowns, separation of an expanded root from the crown by a distinct waist, etc.) is present in *Archaeopteryx*. Accordingly, Howgate suggests that it is just as parsimonious, if not more so, to derive the teeth of *Archaeopteryx* from either a pseudosuchian thecodontian or a theropodan ancestor (1,208; see further treatment on p. 584).

[Whereas arguments for the coelurosaurian origin of birds were based primarily on features of the post-cranial skeleton (because of early lack of information on the skull of *Archaeopteryx*), the skeletal characters supporting the avian-crocodilian relationship are almost all cranial (193); both cranial and post-cranial characters support the procompsognathid theropodan affinity (1,195). There are other lines of evidence that point to close affinities between avian and crocodilian ancestors, in addition to the many mentioned herein. Thus, the crocodilian thymus more closely resembles that of birds than that of any other reptile (761), and there are the following molecular avian and crocodilian correlations: (a) immunological similarities between pancreatic polypeptides, between sequences of myoglobin, and between sequences of the alpha- and beta-chains of hemoglobins; (b) hybridizations of DNAs for alpha-crystallins; and (c) similarities in organizational patterns of genomic DNA (see 1,312).]

THE FOREBRAINS OF COELUROSAURS, for example, the late Cretaceous Stenonychosaurus and *Dromiceiomimus*, show evidence of having been atypically large, filling the cranial cavity, and of having been by far the largest brains in relation to bodily size of any known reptile (comparable to the brains of extant ratites). In fact, the "encephalization quotients" of these extremely fast-running, agile, bipedal predators, as well as of *Archaeopteryx*, fall within the lower part of the mammalian-avian range (see 407, 618, 877). In the case of *Stenonychosaurus*, the orbits were directed anterolaterally, indicating a partly binocular visual field, and the optic lobes appear to have been shifted ventrolaterally, as in birds, due to the enlargement of the cerebral hemispheres (see 877).

As factors that resulted in selection for very large brain sizes in the coelurosaurs, Hopson suggests their predatory feeding habits (preying on relatively small, fast-moving prey), extremely fast running speeds and great agility of movement, and the evolution of grasping forelimbs associated, in some species, with binocular vision (407, 618). In this view, larger and more complex brains evolved at this stage as adaptations for coping with the information-processing requirements of specific ways of life, for example, to improve the coordination between the rapid movements of the manus and visual information about the spatial positions of small, rapidly-moving prey (see also 59, 766, refs. to R. Bauchot and coworkers in 407, and p. 399, **Visual System of Ancestral Birds**).

[A small size of the reptilian ancestors of birds may have facilitated the evolution of endothermy, since metabolic rate increases as size decreases, and since the greater surface-to-volume ratio accompanying small size facilitates heat loss in warm climates (413).]

More generally, it is suggested that the possession of larger brains by endotherms than by ectotherms traces to the facts that: (1) because of the much greater maintenance energy needs of evolving endotherms, selection favored individuals that were more intensely active over longer periods of time; and (2) in consequence of selection for increased levels of activity, there also was selection for more complex perceptual abilities and precise sensorimotor control mechanisms in endotherms, both of which faculties required larger brains. "...if the brain required by a vertebrate is primarily a function of its total level of activity and, therefore, reflects its total energy budget, then coelurosaurs appear to have been metabolically as active as living birds and mammals...." (407).

PINEAL BODY OF COELUROSAURS. Additionally, the only dinosaur known to possess a pineal-like structure (i.e., a locus or foramen for the pineal body in the cranial space) is the coelurosaur, *Dromiceiomimus*, which even may have been endothermic (see 407, 413, 877). Since most extant birds have well-developed, secretory pineal bodies, both the encephalization quotients and the evidence for a pineal-like structure support the thesis of an avian derivation from coelurosaurs.

[The pineal body has been remodeled extensively, distinctly, and independently along separate evolutionary lines, especially within the classes Chondrichthyes, Osteichthyes, Reptilia, Aves, and Mammalia, with the mammalian pineal organ incorporating the most recent progressions in a long phylogenetic development. Few neuroendocrine organs have undergone such profound phylogenetic changes in structure and function. The reptilian parietal eye-pineal complex is most closely related to the primitive central nervous system in developmental origins and histogenetic relationships. Within the extant Reptilia, separate lines of evolutionary remodeling of the pineal body are seen in the Testudines, Sauria, Serpentes, and Rhynchocephalia, such that the pineal body may be only partially homologous between groups. Crocodilians are the only extant reptiles with neither the glandular nor the photoreceptive part of the pineal complex (879, 1,171).

In cyclostomes, fishes, amphibians, and lizards the pineal body is a functioning photoreceptor supplied with indole-containing sensory cells that resemble retinal cones and may transduce photic information into a neuroendocrinological response. The pineal body of marine chelonians may be among the largest known. That of the Green Sea Turtle contains a considerable amount of melatonin, the serum levels of which are sensitive to light changes (771, 1,171). However, the evolutionary transformation from a primarily sensory structure to a glandular one appears not to have progressed as far in chelonians as in ophidians, many birds (see pp. 68-70), and mammals (879). Available data suggest that the reptilian parietal eye-pineal complex may have physiological effects extending to the gonads, with seasonal timing and ambient conditions being critical for such effects to be demonstrable. For example, the pineal body can modify ovarian activity in *Anolis*, the ovary has a seasonal dependency of responsiveness to effects of pinealectomy, and melatonin can reverse the ovarian effect of pinealectomy.

It has been suggested that the physiological evolution of the pineal body in reptiles, and possibly in tetrapods generally, has involved the replacement of neural pineal projections affecting monaminergic control mechanisms with essentially secretory and endocrinological pineal activities, still affecting primarily monaminergic control mechanisms (involving pathways that contribute to the regulation of arousal and sleep phases; 779). Although the mammalian pineal body generally had been thought to control target tissue exclusively through the release of melatonin into the circulation, the discovery that mammalian pinealocytic processes project to several brain areas raises the possibility that these processes deliver chemical messages directly to specific target sites in the central nervous system (971). In this connection, although arginine vasotocin, the presumed ancestral neurohypophysial peptidic hormone (see pp. 127, 128), is not found in the neurohypophysis of mammals, it has been extracted from the pineal bodies of cats, rats, and cows (1,023, 1,167).]

EGG CARE PRECEDING BIPARENTAL INCUBATION

Introduction

Inasmuch as birds evolved from reptiles, an attempt to trace the evolution of avian egg care should have as its starting point the egg-care habits of birds' primitive reptilian ancestors. This is not, however, to imply that the immediate reptilian ancestors of birds--the stem-reptiles --possessed the same egg-care habits as the more ancient reptiles from which they themselves evolved. In fact, the present analysis suggests the contrary; the evolutionary transition of reptiles to birds apparently involved changes in egg care, leading to the stem-reptiles, that long preceded the achievement of endothermy in the pro-avian stage.

The most primitive type of post-ovipositional egg care, which doubtless was characteristic of the primitive reptilian stock of the Pennsylvanian epoch (Carboniferous period), some 300 mya--is simply none at all. Accordingly, one has no problem in fixing the nature of the limiting condition. Any effort to fill in the gaps between no egg care and the recognized primitive avian pattern of biparental incubation of a single clutch would benefit from a consideration of the spectrum of egg types and egg care of contemporary reptiles, and these are referred to repeatedly in the subsequent treatments. Existing patterns not only span a wide range, they would appear even to encompass the stages leading to pre-aves (see Table 3). Moreover, crocodilian egg-care habits differ very little from those deduced independently for the stem-reptiles, by reasoning from the implications of Cockatielian relict responses and *a priori* considerations (see pp. 623-628, **A Synthesis of Avian Evolution**).

Reptilian Eggs, Nest Sites, and Egg Evolution

EGGS OF OVIPAROUS REPTILES fall into 3 broad categories on the basis of their shell structure, including considerations of the shell membranes, and their sensitivities to the moisture content of their surroundings. The eggs of most squamates consist of a large yolk mass enclosed by an extraordinarily small volume of albumen in a thin enclosing layer, and a vitelline membrane. External to this is a thick, parchment-like and highly extensible shell membrane, with few or no external calcareous deposits (763). In some species, much of the surface of the shell membrane appears to be naked and exposed directly to the environment. The development of embryos within such eggs is closely coupled with the moisture content of the surroundings. These eggs probably most resemble those of the primitive reptilian stock from the Lower Pennsylvanian--which are believed to have reproduced by way of relatively naked, massively-yolky, amniotic eggs, with embryos capable of undergoing direct development in terrestrial settings. [Except as otherwise noted, this treatment of reptilian reproduction is based on refs. 672-674 and 757 and work cited therein.]

By contrast, the eggs of many chelonians have somewhat pliable shells with a more highly structured, well-developed calcareous layer. The latter is penetrated by numerous channels (spaces between closely apposed shell units, i.e., structural units of the shell) through which gaseous exchanges occur and water presumably passes. A large mass of yolk is surrounded by a relatively thick albumenous layer, over which lies the single, multilayered shell membrane. The development of these eggs is relatively independent of the moisture content of their surroundings.

At the other end of the spectrum of reptilian eggs is "the most marvelous 'invention' in vertebrate history" (790)--the hard-shelled eggs of all crocodilians, some chelonians, and a few lizards. These are comparable in many respects to avian eggs. Those of crocodilians, in particular, have many close parallels with them. Such eggs are rigid and non-compliant. A large yolk mass is surrounded by a thick envelope of albumen, external to which is a pair of shell membranes. The calcareous shells are highly organized and structured, and are as thick as those of avian eggs of comparable size.

Insofar as is known, the shells consist of calcite crystals (hexagonal structure) in the crocodilian and lacertilian eggs but, except possibly in *Malacochersus tornieri*, almost entirely of aragonite (orthorhombic structure) in chelonian eggs, with only small amounts of calcite. Very little is known of the oviductal environment in which reptilian eggs become calcified, but the existence of concentric rings passing through groups of aragonite crystals suggests that shell deposition occurs in pulses (770). The present-day development of such eggs is essentially independent of the moisture content of their surroundings.

REPTILIAN NEST SITES. Nests of the earliest reptiles doubtless were in or near surface locations. Eggs of extant oviparous reptiles usually are deposited in a warm environment in sheltered subterranean regions. In the vast majority of cases a hole is made in the ground and filled after oviposition. Eggs also are placed in dry humus at the bases of small trees, beneath rocks, in trash piles, under the bark of trees, or under other suitable objects, are buried in sand, friable soil, or mounds of (or level) decaying or rotting vegetation, or are buried above ground in rotting wood, where a relatively constant temperature obtains (602, 763). Many burrowing snakes and amphisbaenians oviposit in anthills or termitaria; some eublepharid and diplodactyline lizards place their eggs in rock crevices above ground, some anoles gather their eggs in clusters of 2-4 in bromeliads (large epiphytic air plants), while some chelonians (*Sternotherus odoratus*, *Rhinoclemys annulata* and *R. punctularia*) leave their eggs at the surface in shaded grass, uncovered or only lightly covered with leaves (681, 763, 868).

Shallow burial or surface deposition generally is consonant only with relatively short incubatory periods (see 871). However, the incubatory period of the chelid, *Platemys platycephala*, is 150 days and its single egg is deposited in a shallow groove or directly on the ground. The relatively enormous egg is partially covered with sand or earth, or neither, but, in any case, is buried under decaying leaves (883). Sometimes, particularly with large numbers of eggs in harsh surface environments, the nests are in laboriously constructed tunnels or holes at a considerable depth below the surface of the ground, say 60-90 cm. Hatchlings in such deep nests require 3-7 days to dig and climb to the surface (758); even in only 10-cm-deep nests in damp, compacted soil, the quick, agile hatchlings of the Tuatara require 8-10 h to wriggle to the surface (755).

Not all reptiles oviposit large clutches. Those of lizards range from one to about 70 eggs; some iguanids may produce clutches of 20 eggs several times per season (868, 874, 1,348). In general, there is a significant correlation between female lacertilian snout-vent length at maturity and mean clutch number, both inter- and intraspecifically, as well as between clutch size and age at first reproduction (see 897, 1,348). Lizards that mature early have shorter adult life expectancies, are almost always multiple-brooded (practice sequential multiple-clutching), and produce relatively small clutches (1,348).

Clutch size in all members of the Gekkonidae is only 1 or 2 (monoautochronic), clutches of 2 occur in the Eublepharinae, but of only 1 in the sphaerodactyline geckos. Clutch size is 1 in anoline iguanids and 2 in the

Gymnophthalmidae and Pygopodidae. Clutch size is a maximum of 2 in some chelonians, and is only 1 in the African Tortoise (*Malacochersus tornieri*) and the chelid mentioned above. Egg size and relative clutch weight are positively correlated with female bodily size among species of the Gekkonidae (681, 686, 764, 874, 897). In the latter cases, oviposition occurs only at intervals of 1 or more weeks (90, 93, 94, 897, 912). [Geckos are pantropical in distribution and evolved in tropical environments; species occurring in non-seasonal tropics produce eggs the year around. Most species are nocturnal or crepuscular, coming out only at dusk or night to feed on insects and retreating to crevices under bark or rock in the daytime. (874).]

The single-egg clutch of *Anolis aeneus* (see below) usually is deposited in a shallow hole dug in moist soil (858). Members of several species of *Anolis* also will deposit their eggs in communal sites (see 938), but the multiple-egg clutches of other reptiles seldom are deposited in sites where soil or sand comes into contact with their entire surfaces. Even in those species that oviposit in a subterranean chamber, the volume of the nest cavity usually greatly exceeds that of the contained eggs, an important consideration in the equalization of gas exchanges for all of the eggs (774).

In fact, gas exchange requirements in a fixed environment may limit clutch weight and place a lower limit on incubatory times for all large contemporary reptiles and also may have done so for dinosaurs (see 774). Reptilian nest sites generally are located where the relative humidity is high (usually greater than 75%) and the temperature is moderate. During the course of incubation in such sites, the eggs are vulnerable to attack by a variety of organisms, such as ants, larval dipterans and other invertebrate and vertebrate predators. Bacteria, molds, and fungi also may have deleterious effects.

OVULATION---OVIPOSITION. It is common for a clutch of eggs to be derived more or less equally and concurrently from the two ovaries and oviposited *en masse*, usually followed by weeks or months of ovarian quiescence. One to 3 clutches usually are produced per annum and well-defined seasonal reproductive patterns are the rule in temperate species (874). Some species, especially northern and high-altitude ones, produce a clutch (or brood) only in alternate years. The Green Sea Turtle in some regions only produces a clutch every 3 yr, whereas in others it oviposits 7-12 times/yr (875, 1,318). In tropical regions, some species produce more than one clutch (or brood) per annum (914) and year-around reproduction is common in tropical lizards. Many anoline species are reproductively opportunistic (858, 874).

The reproductive habits of many species of the primitive lacertilian genus, *Anolis*, practically all of which are arboreal and all of which are diurnal, are of particular interest. In these species, only one of an hierarchical series of developing follicles matures and ovulates at a time in each ovary, and there typically is an alternation of ovulation between the two ovaries, which also hypertrophy, in turn (monoallochronic ovulation). Reproduction occurs at frequent intervals throughout the breeding season of up to about 9 months, one egg being laid at a time at about 1-2-week intervals. After copulating, a female Green Anole is unreceptive (receptivity being ovarian dependent) until the largest follicle is ovulated and another follicle in the contralateral ovary develops. In the Green Anole and *A. aeneus*, oviposition occurs at intervals of 10-14 days (764, 858, 867, 898). Since ovulation from a given ovary occurs 3-4 days before oviposition from the contralateral oviduct, and the total time for egg production by one ovary and its oviduct is 20-28 days, oviductal maturation of an egg requires some 16-25 days (compared to 1 day in birds; see also p. 153, **Blastulation**, and p. 162, note near bottom). Mean intervals as low as 6.9 days (*A. onca*) and 7.7 days (*A. limifrons*) between ovipositions are known in confined animals (897). In some species, a 2nd ovulation never occurs from an ovary before the previously ovulated egg has been laid. A postovulatory corpus luteum persists in one ovary of Green Anoles until oviposition of the egg in the ipsilateral oviduct (900, 914).

[Removal of the largest follicle (8 mm) in this species results in the compensatory growth of only the next-largest follicle (3 mm), which is in the contralateral ovary (suggesting that ovarian autoregulation is not operative). Removal of the 2nd-largest follicle (i.e., the largest follicle in the smaller ovary) or the entire smaller ovary induces no compensatory follicular growth in the large ovary. On the other hand, removal of both the largest and next-largest follicles results in compensatory growth of follicles in both ovaries--the 2nd, 3rd and 4th largest in the larger ovary and the 2nd and 3rd largest in the smaller ovary, suggesting that the larger preovulatory follicles control gonadotropic delivery to the smaller vitellogenic follicles. Smaller, previtellogenic follicles exhibit synchronous growth in the two ovaries (897, 911).]

This pattern of ovulation is found in only 3 other genera of lizards (*Chamaeleolis*, *Chamaelinorops*, and *Phenacosaurus*) comprising the remainder of the anoline genera of the tribe Anolini (*Tropidodactylus* has been synonomized with *Anolis*), all of which are highly successful inhabitants of arboreal niches (874, 914). On the contrary, no member of the other 10 genera of the subfamily Anolinae (family Iguanidae) exhibits the reproductive pattern of *Anolis*, nor does any member of the other 7 iguanid subfamilies (914, 953). In a few reptiles (e.g., the Painted Turtle), one ovary ovulates more eggs one year than does the other; the latter then ovulates more the next year (see 900; among extant forms, this may be the closest approach to the condition of polyallochronic ovulation).

[The anolines are unique among iguanids in their possession of subdigital adhesive pads. The latter are functional only for relatively light-weight lizards, unburdened by a heavy clutch (897); certainly they are of great importance in obtaining purchase after a leap, even if of lesser importance in maintaining purchase. They would appear to have been a key innovation in the successful radiation of the group, permitting its members to adopt highly acrobatic locomotory behavior and to exploit fully the spatial heterogeneity of arboreal habitats (881). In fact, although an upside-down stationary position usually is avoided by amphibians and reptiles, anoles and certain other lizards prefer the head-downward resting posture (875).

Specialization for their acrobatic arboreal habits is believed to be one of the factors that led to evolutionary reduction in clutch number to very few eggs or only 1 in anolines, presumably conferring the maximum possible agility on gravid animals. This probably was facilitated by the fact that the center of distribution of the tribe was subtropical, which permitted multiple clutching over a period of 9-10 months (953). Non-acrobatic, less versatile, relatively slow-moving, arboreal lizards without toe pads, e.g., *Polychrus*, *Basiliscus*, *Iguana*, and *Chamaeleo*, have large numbers of eggs in their clutches and tend to have large relative clutch weights (ratio of clutch weight to total body weight), for example, as high as 0.40 in *Polychrus acutirostris* (897, 953, 955).]

Single-egg clutching through most of the year also occurs in the comparatively large tropical, terrestrial Whiptail Lizard (*Cnemidophorus arubensis*), in seeming conflict with the correlations proposed above for the practice of single-egg clutching among anolines. However, in the case of the Whiptail Lizard, the single egg is exceptionally large and the species also is exceptional in being largely herbivorous and perhaps sustaining strong adult-juvenile competition. The life style of the Whiptail Lizard is much less dependent upon great agility than is that of anolines. Accordingly, the competitive advantages conferred on larger hatchlings may have resulted in selective pressure on females to produce large eggs, irrespective of the burden they constituted, culminating in the production of but a single egg of the maximum size that could be accommodated (952).

REPTILIAN NEST ENVIRONMENT AND EMBRYONIC DEVELOPMENT. Most reptilian embryos probably are not exposed to wide fluctuations in temperature, either in the course of a single day or during the entire course of development, owing to the moderating effects of the nest environment in which the eggs usually are laid. The widest reported diel temperature fluctuations for chelonian nests apparently are 8°C (22-30°C) for Panamanian Painted Turtles at a depth of 11-18 cm, and 6-8°C (28-36°C) for the Texan *Trionyx muticus* in 10-17-cm-deep nests in broad sandbars; the narrowest is only 1°C in many nests at a depth of 60-90 cm (681).

Unlike birds, oviparous reptiles represent various extremes between types in which most of the development occurs before oviposition, so that hatching occurs within only a few days (as in *Opheodrys vernalis*), and those in which several months (2-4 months in most temperate species) to over a year elapse between oviposition and hatching (as in *Emys orbicularis*; 914). [Squamates occupy an intermediate position, 40-50% of the developmental period occurring *in utero* (1,402). Monotremes exhibit the former extreme type of reptilian development; the eggs are oviposited at about the 19-20-somite stage and hatch within 10-11 days (1,307, 1,317).] Normal development usually can proceed over a range of temperatures, say 28-34°C, but very few reptiles develop normally above 34°C. Some lizards living in environments in which the ambient temperature rises above 40°C deposit their eggs in microhabitats at temperatures of 35°C or less (754). Each species appears to have an optimum temperature for embryogenesis. For example, incubation of American Alligator eggs gives the best hatching success at 30-32°C (759). A temperature of 28-30°C probably is safe for all chelonian eggs (681).

[Both male and female heterogamy, as well as temperature-dependent sex determinism, are found in various reptiles, with the American Alligator and *Crocodylus porosus* known to be included in the latter category. For example, at temperatures greater than 34°C, all *C. porosus* embryos develop as males, at less than 30°C, all develop as females, while between 30 and 34°, members of both sexes develop (see 66). Heteromorphic sex chromosomes have not been found in crocodiles (see 792). Reptilian sex chromosomes seem to have evolved recently, since they appear independently in several lineages. This implies that environmental sex determination was the ancestral condition (363, 995).]

Embryos of tropical species are less tolerant of departures from their thermal optima than are those of temperate forms. Thus, the embryos of temperate-zone squamates can be incubated in the laboratory over a temperature range of 20-30°C, whereas embryos of the tropical *I. iguana* die when the incubation temperature varies more than 1 or 2°C from 30°C (see 763). In some species, relatively small departures from the optima cause developmental asynchronies that only lead to inconsequential developmental anomalies (postnatally benign terata, e.g., changes in the number of scale rows or tail abnormalities). Large departures from the optima, on the other hand, generally result in appreciable increases in embryonic mortality, often caused by lethal terata or fatal behavioral abnormalities (such as hatchling crocodiles that swim with their heads under water; 681, 759).

The temperatures of the nests of some species of chelonians, and other reptiles that oviposit large numbers of eggs, gradually rise as a consequence of metabolic heating (see p. 544, note in last paragraph), and it is suggested that the temperature optima for successive stages of development follow a rising pattern. In such nests, a temperature gradient from the center to the periphery would be expected in the late stages of development (757). The embryos of Tuataras, like those of amphibians, appear to be tolerant of wide diel temperature fluctuations and extremes (754).

It is well-known that long periods of chilling of eggs to temperatures that are sufficient to arrest embryogenesis completely have no adverse effect in many reptiles. In the case of squamates, the subsequent development of such cold-arrested embryos is obtained only in the presence of a functional blood circulation (763). On the other hand, exposure to low temperatures that are insufficient to halt embryogenesis completely leads to anomalies or is fatal. For example, embryos of *Chelydra serpentina* became arrested at 10°C, malformed at 15°C, and gradually weakened and died during very long periods at 20°C; if the latter embryos were transferred to 26°C after 80-88 days, they hatched normally (757).

Exposures of crocodilian embryos to temperatures below 26°C for long periods are lethal (759). Little is known of the tolerance of embryos to departures from their optimum temperatures, insofar as the durations of these departures are concerned. The embryos of temperate squamates can tolerate brief exposures to temperature extremes similar to those withstood by the adults. On the other hand, temperatures even slightly higher than the range for normal development induce serious malformations in near-term squamatan embryos (764). Some chelonian eggs are known to have survived relatively brief exposures in soil at 4.9°C (*Chelodina expansa*) and in artificial nest beds to 46°C (*Malaclemys terrapin*; 681).

It seems clear that the most critical consideration for the incubation of reptilian eggs is that continually developing embryos in late stages (as opposed to embryos whose development is arrested fully) not be exposed to wide diel fluctuations, because of their susceptibility to asynchronous development of different organ systems or components thereof. But embryos also are susceptible to abnormalities in the aqueous and gaseous environments (759). This often translates into burial of unattended eggs at 10-20-cm depth in well-insulating substrates (soil, humus, compacted vegetation) or 60-90 cm in less-well-insulating substrates (sand, gravel).

[The critical demands on the nest environment are illustrated by physical environmental effects on survival of eggs of the Desert Iguana or Northern Crested Lizard (*Dipsosaurus dorsalis*) as defined by their temperature and moisture requirements. Open washes near Palm Springs, Calif. are suitable for successful incubation (requiring from 45 days at 36°C to 82 days at 28°C) at depths below 20 cm in midsummer, but other soil microenvironments in the same region are unsuitable. For example, the soil beneath moisture-consuming shrubs is intolerably dry for eggs. Further north, in Rock Valley, Nevada, the soil is moist enough but not warm enough in the spring and late fall, and warm enough but not moist enough in midsummer.

Still farther north, in Smyrna, Washington, conditions for eggs are even less tolerable. Eggs in nests at a 30-cm depth would not develop because the soil temperatures are always too low. At a 10-cm depth the eggs could start developing in about the 3rd week in May but a substantial part of each day is too cold for development at this depth. Eggs deposited at a 5-cm depth would complete only a maximum of 43% of their development before overheating lethally. Eggs laid at a depth of exactly 7½ cm might be able to hatch if deposited as soon as favorable conditions set in. However, the precision of depth measurement by the female would have to be on the order of the dimensions of the egg and no unusual hot or cold spell during the summer could be tolerated. Otherwise, the eggs would either overheat or fail to complete development. In brief, it is suggested that there is no room for error in either inconstant climate or the siting of the Desert Iguana nest (871).]

Some additional specific figures are given for orientation, as follows. Mean hourly nest temperatures of American Alligators during the course of a single day averaged over 3 seasons ranged from 29.3-30.5°C, whereas the mean hourly temperatures over 4 periods during each of the nesting seasons varied from 26.9-29.9°C, 27.3-30.7°C, and 31.7-33.1°C (676). Diel air temperature variation above the nest could be as great as 9.3°C. Laboratory studies indicate that allowing alligator eggs to cool only retards development. Thus, with eggs removed from the nest and exposed for many days to the prevailing air temperatures, hatching merely was greatly retarded (659).

The 25-cm-deep nests of the temperature-sensitive tropical lizard *I. iguana* have a diel temperature range of 30-32°C (675). Temperatures in the adjacent sand in another study of the same reptile ranged from 27.8 to 31.4°C (see 678). [Nest emergence of the hatchlings of this species is facilitated by visual cues between them as they peer from their escape tunnels; they show group-coordination activities in leaving the hatching site, migrating from islets, and, later, in foraging and selecting sleeping sites (721).]

In the temperate Race-runner Lizard (*Cnemidophorus sexlineatus*) in North Carolina, temperatures in nests in sawdust piles fluctuated over a range of 4°C and averaged 32°C (see 678). In the case of the Galapagos Marine Iguana (*Amblyrhynchus cristatus*), the temperatures in nests at a 40-cm depth ranged from 28-30°C (677). Hognose Snakes (*Heterodon nasicus*) develop normally at 27.8°C and 32.8°C, but in 11 fewer days (59 instead of 70) at the higher value. For eggs of marine chelonians in the incubatory range of 26-32°C, a 1°C decrease lengthens the incubatory period by 5-8½ days (773).

NEST HUMIDITY--AMBIENT GASES. In regard to the moisture content of nests, and water exchanges therein, there is evidence that reptilian eggs in natural nests exchange water with the environment. Apparently the eggs of most reptiles lose water by evaporation while simultaneously absorbing liquid water from the substrate. [Water can be lost even under saturation conditions if the heat produced by the embryos is sufficient to raise their temperature above that of their surroundings. In nests of Green Sea Turtles, there is a temperature increase of 2-6°C during the course of incubation (681).] In the flexible, parchment-shelled eggs of squamates and some chelonians, eggs exposed to favorable moisture conditions customarily absorb water and swell appreciably. Such eggs have a high percentage of hatching success and produce larger hatchlings than those exposed to less favorable conditions.

The somewhat flexible-shelled eggs of many chelonians, on the other hand, are much less dependent upon external water, and the percentage of hatching success is not unduly reduced by exposure of the eggs to dry conditions. Nonetheless, favorable moisture conditions lead to larger hatchlings. In the case of the rigid-shelled eggs of crocodilians, some chelonians, and a few lizards, excess aqueous uptake is more or less precluded and aqueous loss is greatly restricted. Such eggs are essentially independent of moisture conditions and neither hatching success nor the size of hatchlings is influenced notably by variations in nest humidity. It has been suggested that the only major difference between the eggs of birds and those of crocodilians (and the hard-shelled eggs of chelonians) is imposed by the nest site; avian nests favor aqueous loss whereas crocodilian nests favor aqueous gain (see 759).

In general, it appears that, with the possible exception of eggs incubated in humus-rich soils, where microbial respiration may reduce the oxygen content of air in the spaces between the eggs, the composition of air in shallowly-sited nests usually does not depart appreciably from that of the overlying atmosphere. It is known, however, that when large numbers of eggs are deposited in a single nest chamber, particularly when it is at a considerable depth below the surface, as in the nests of some chelonians, there may be a notable depletion of oxygen and accumulation of carbon dioxide. In the nests of marine chelonians, as noted on p. 187, the composition of the ambient gas is remarkably like that of the gas in the avian air cell. Species that oviposit massive clutches may be restricted to nest sites in sandy soils to ensure adequate porosity for air circulation (by simple diffusion through the sand; 681, 750). Influences of ambient gas composition on reptilian embryonic development remain to be determined.

NESTS OF HERBIVOROUS DINOSAUR EGGS. The only dinosaur eggshells whose pore structure (radial, unbranching) has been examined are those of 3 herbivores from Upper Cretaceous deposits in southern France (*Hypselosaurus priscus*) and the Gobi Desert (*Protoceratops andrewsi* and an unspecified sauropod). The shell conductances of these eggs were 4-100 times greater than predicted for avian eggs of the same size (360-2,064 g; 335-1,900 ml). This indicates that the eggs developed in high humidity environments, either underground or in well-insulated, surface mounds. In any event, the nests must have been vastly different from the nests of most birds.

In the case of the *Protoceratops* eggs, the clutches were deposited in 3 layers, with sand between the layers. This strongly suggests that hole nests were employed, and contemporary hole-nesting Nile Crocodiles in Zululand also deposit their eggs in 3 layers (see p. 575), and include no organic matter in their nest holes. The nests of *Hypselosaurus*, on the other hand, were associated with fossilized rushes, similar to those incorporated into some crocodilian nest mounds, and there is evidence that a nest hole was not excavated. The clutch of a single female was divided into as many as 5 groups totalling about 50 eggs (2,064 g per egg) laid out along evenly spaced parallel lines, a practice that probably facilitated respiratory gas exchanges. A single clutch of 13 eggs also is known for this species (probably near the maximum size for an assembled clutch) and numerous apparently complete clutches of up to 6 eggs each were found belonging to the unspecified sauropod (see 772, 775).

REPTILIAN EGG EVOLUTION. Accounting for the evolution of the cleidoic egg (shell penetrable by gases only) among the reptilian antecedents of birds appears not to present formidable problems. The deposition of eggs on land rather than in water probably evolved as a protective adaptation for avoiding aquatic predation (see A.S. Romer, 1957, in 786). The eggs of the earliest reptiles probably contained a large mass of yolk encased in several layers of jelly, the outermost of these having been dense and tough. These probably were oviposited in moist locations where aqueous exchange could occur freely and from which aqueous absorption was essential for development. The parchment-shelled, extensible eggs of oviparous snakes and many lizards probably come closest to approaching the ancestral condition.

The evolution of a progressively thicker, more protective, and isolating calcareous layer is believed to have occurred in response to selective pressures having their origin in egg depredations, particularly by microorganisms and invertebrates. Indirect evidence of the threat posed by bacteria, molds, and fungi is seen in the anti-microbial properties of egg albumen (see also p. 619, 1st complete paragraph), and these deleterious agents may be a major source of mortality of the more naked reptilian eggs, even today. As eggshells progressively thickened and became more complex in their structure, their resistance to the transport of liquid water increased, their dependence on external water and their transpirational loss of water during incubation decreased, and their internal reserves of water in the yolk and, particularly, the albumen increased, pre-adapting the eggs for development above the ground.

Ultimately, there evolved rigid-shelled, cleidoic eggs such as are seen in many contemporary reptiles. The latter approach closest to the avian level of organization and it is assumed here and by workers in the field that the rigid-shelled eggs of the stem-reptilian ancestors of birds also approached the avian condition.

CLUE OF RELUCTANCE TO RELINQUISH EGGS. Having considered contemporary reptilian egg care and nesting habits, as well as reptilian egg evolution, I now address the question of "what was the antecedent pattern of egg care of the endothermic ancestors of primitive birds--the pro-aves?" The answer to this question will provide an intermediate reference stage for analysis. Breeding behavior in many avian species that practice biparental incubation gives us a clue to the answer. I have referred several times to the fact that incubating members of such species often are reluctant to surrender the eggs to incoming mates (except where, understandably, there has been strong selective pressure against such behavior). And among these species, Cockatiels would appear to be the most reluctant (compare the findings in Part 2 for Cockatiels with other examples of nest-relief behavior on pp. 390-392). It is this behavior that provides a crucial clue to a pattern of egg care of egg-incubating ancestors of birds, tracing back to earlier times even than those of ancestral birds.

The often great reluctance of Cockatielian mates to surrender eggs to one another implies an ancestral pattern of egg care in which members of both sexes incubated the eggs but did not surrender them to one another. The current reluctance of the birds to surrender the eggs is seen as a relic of instinctive elements of egg care of those earlier times. It would appear to be an expression of the persistence of pathways of organization in the central nervous system for the more ancient pattern. Ancestors possessing such egg-incubatory behavior would, of course, also have possessed some degree of endothermy.

Individual Unaided Incubation of Separate Clutches

EACH PARENT INCUBATES A SEPARATE CLUTCH. This more ancient pattern, that is implied by current behavior, must have been one in which each member of a mated pair incubated a separate clutch, probably within sight of one another in a territory. In other words, there apparently was a time when members of both sexes cooperated in the incubation and care of their eggs, each caring for a separate clutch as its exclusive responsibility. Not only does this conclusion seem to be mandated by the noted reluctance to give up the eggs, it is not difficult to perceive the selective advantages of the practice (see pp. 562, 563). It is of interest in this connection that both members of mated pairs of Egyptian Plovers make preliminary scrapes (15 cm in diameter by 5 cm deep) in the sand-gravel nesting substrate before one finally is chosen to receive the eggs (230). This is consistent with the possibility that at some ancestral stage the male prepared and/or managed a separate nest.

[Very close proximity of the two nest sites probably would have been counterproductive and selected against. This is inferred from the facts that predation is the single greatest cause of reproductive failures in most species of extant birds (see also pp. 555-557). Furthermore, predators that find nests are in the habit of searching around them, and may even return and check the nest sites day after day (see Tinbergen *et al.*, 1967, in 313). For example, Weasels (*Mustela nivalis*), which are the main predators of nesting Great Tits living in Whytham Woods near Oxford, apparently hunt selectively in the vicinity of their last meal (432). A practice of separating the nests widely to reduce the rate of food consumption in the breeding area (963) would have been unlikely by the largely arboreal, insectivorous, pro-avian ancestors.]

PROBLEMS POSED BY INDIVIDUAL UNAIDED INCUBATION. Let us ask, first, how a pro-avis of one sex could have incubated a portion of the eggs without aid from the other. And, let us make the reasonable assumptions that pro-aves were Crow-sized or Rock Pigeon-sized (the size of *Archaeopteryx*), incubated their eggs for a matter of weeks, and had a body temperature of about 32°C (primitive pro-aves) to 36°C (advanced pro-aves). [Judging from the size of *Archaeopteryx* (weight estimated at 220-330 g and wingspan at 58.8 cm; 1,209), the first birds were smaller, as adults, than most dinosaurs were as hatchlings. The smallest known dinosaurs generally had adult live weights of about 2-3 kg, although that of *Campsognathus* is estimated at only 532-638 g (408-410).]

CONTINUOUS INCUBATION BY SINGLE PRO-AVIAN PARENT UNLIKELY. The stem-reptilian and pre-avian ancestors of pro-aves probably could have remained inactive and gone without food for relatively long periods, when necessary, just as contemporary viviparous reptiles commonly cease feeding during their gravid periods, when they are more vulnerable to predation (765). [The possibility exists that the stem-reptiles and pre-aves sustained a metabolism approaching that of living birds and mammals (407), but I make the more reasonable assumption that they were ectotherms.] However, a small, crow-sized animal, with the high energy cost of primitive endothermy and a continuous need for large quantities of food, would not have been able to fast while incubating continuously, even allowing for the likelihood that energy reserves were accumulated before the start of breeding. [The duration of fasting that a bird can tolerate is related inversely to bodily size (974).]

Energetics

Among contemporary birds, sitting on the eggs and fasting for several days in succession usually is feasible only when the parents alternate in egg care (28). Of course, when the young are nidifugous and forage for themselves shortly after hatching, an incubating parent is able to fast longer, since it needs no reserve to allofeed the young. All small birds, whatever their diet, take food repeatedly throughout the day (155, 433), and according to one estimate, a 25-g bird typically can store, at a maximum, only sufficient energy for 2 days of normal activity (257).

A striking illustration of the great expense at which birds sustain high body temperatures, is the fact that the Western Fence Lizard (*Sceloporus occidentalis*) can live for a month on the amount of insect food an insectivorous bird consumes in a day (689). Correspondingly, the minimum power input required by a Budgerigar for level flight is 3½ W, whereas the maximum aerobic power of a Desert Iguana of the same size is only 0.4 W (see 776). It has been estimated that the annual existence energy budget of a population of birds is 10-30 times greater than the corresponding budget of an ectothermic population of animals of the same size and adult bodily weight, or, on the basis of individual daily metabolic energy expenditure, 20-40 times that of an iguanid lizard during its activity season (see 776, 870, and R.T. Bakker, 1975a, in 408). The average cost of the daily activities of a 380-g bird is estimated at 74% greater than that of a mammal of the same size (973). [The existence energy is a measure of the energy expenditure associated with normal activities, including reproduction (519).]

In general, the standard metabolic rate of a bird is 6-10 times as great as that of a reptile of the same size at the same body temperature (361, 404). Moreover, even during rest phases, the standard metabolic rates of small birds (0.46-1.5. J/h in some finches) are 80% of the rates in the active phases of the daily cycles (442). [The standard metabolic rate is the minimum rate of heat production in a resting animal at a given temperature, while not digesting or absorbing food (422; see p. 57).]

The daily food consumption by an insectivorous bird amounts roughly to 40% of its bodily weight, but a large fraction of the weight of the food is accounted for by water (23). The limited data available for total energy expenditure and maintenance metabolism requirements of birds indicate that the latter functions require as much energy as all other activities combined (257, 648). Such a costly way of life is feasible for birds, of course, only because of the higher rate at which they can harvest resources.

Other illustrations of the expense incurred in sustaining endothermy are the facts that: (a) during winter in a pine plantation England, a Coal Tit must visit 1,000 trees daily in order to capture 2 average-sized insects every 5 sec for 96% of the day in order to meet its energy requirements (315); (b) in midwinter a Coal Tit may lose 10% of its bodily weight overnight, despite the insulation of its roost cavity (232); (c) hummingbirds high in the Andes need to visit 1,500-2,700 flowers each day to meet their food needs; and (d) confined Common Bushtits (*Psaltriparus minimus*), one of the smallest passerine species in the world (weighing 5½ g), consume 80% of their body weight in mealworms per day at 20°C (302).

PARENTAL ENERGY EXPENDITURES. The highest levels of energy expenditure occur when parents are feeding young; the hen's foraging rate also is very high during incubation (114, 257), and female warblers, at least, forage at higher speeds than do males (see 713). An extreme example, for a small bird, is that of the European Swift, which is estimated to fly 16-18 h/day and travel as many as 960 km while gathering insects for its young (155). In this connection, foraging in flight is the most energetically-costly method of avian food procurement (257). This conclusion is supported by studies with Savannah Sparrows, which suggest that aerially foraging species expend relatively more energy while rearing their young than do ground-foraging species of comparable size (437).

The Willow Flycatcher (*Empidonax traillii*), a sit-and-wait predator, may engage in more than 1,000 foraging sorties or longer flights per day throughout its breeding season (557). In the cases of typical broods of various species, it is estimated that parents must increase the amount of energy acquired while foraging either 2-3-fold or 3-5-fold, depending on whether the care of the young is biparental or unilateral (257, 648). The increased energy expenditure of the foraging female may, however, be relatively modest: in confined Savannah Sparrows, it is only 11% above existence levels (437); in Purple Martins, in which only the females allofed the young frequently, the daily energy expenditures by the females exceeded those of the males by 28% and averaged about 340% of standard metabolic rate (67% of the time was spent in flight). For House Wrens, in which both parents allofeed the young, the daily energy expenditure ranges from 220-540% of standard metabolic rate (1,158). Female Great Tits increase the length of their working day as the nestling period progresses and the young require more food (see 975).

As total brood mass of the 1st broods of House Martins increases, both parents increase their delivery of food to the nestlings, but the male responds at a more rapid rate. Whereas the female's energy expenditure is independent of brood weight, despite her increased delivery of food to larger broods, the male's energy expenditure increases with brood weight. With 2nd broods, the female's metabolic costs remain independent of brood weight, but at a higher level, whereas the costs to the male are proportional to brood weight, as well as being at a higher level. At constant brood size, the combined parental costs of the 2nd brood are 35% greater than for a 1st brood. Although the 2nd broods are smaller (avg. of 2.9 eggs, as opposed to 3.5 for 1st broods), rearing of the chicks still requires more work of the adults (1,158).

Birds as large as penguins, albatrosses, and Argus and Golden Pheasants (*Argusianus argus* and *Chrysolophus pictus*, respectively), can fast for many days while incubating (101). A fasting period of 60 days was recorded for a male emu in a zoo, and the incubating, winter-breeding, male Emperor Penguin (*Aptenodytes forsteri*) fasts for up to 115 days at temperatures as low as -40°C, as it incubates one egg (which has the distinction of being the smallest avian egg relative to adult bodily weight) supported between the foot webbing and the brood patch (28, 323, 431, 539). The bodily weight of the incubating penguin decreases from about 35 kg to 20-23 kg during the incubatory period. [For a treatment of weight changes in adults, and female survivorship during reproduction, see 975.]

A PROBABLE SOLUTION TO ACHIEVING INDIVIDUAL UNAIDED INCUBATION. The most likely manner in which individual unaided uncubation was achieved by pro-aves would have been for each parent to have left its clutch temporarily, as necessary, in order to forage. Selection would have favored the offspring of parents that left the eggs at different times, leaving the remaining incubating parent to keep watch over and defend the temporarily uncared-for eggs.

A contemporary example of vigilance over vacant nests is seen in the Yellow-wattled Lapwing; the eggs are left apparently unattended for long periods after sunrise, but as environmental temperatures rise, they are attended for longer and longer periods, until they are attended almost continually in the heat of day. During periods of inattendance, one or both parents invariably appeared if the nest was approached by intruders (see 1,053). As will become apparent in the following (see pp. 621-637, **A Synthesis of Avian Evolution**), there are compelling reasons to believe that avian ancestors from the stem-reptiles to the advanced pro-aves of Table 3 nested on the ground among trees and foraged in the vicinity of the nest(s)--increasingly in the trees above. Accordingly, both parents might well have been absent from their nest(s) concurrently and still maintained close nest vigilance, just as do the Yellow-wattled Lapwings. [In this connection, there are many modern-day species of birds in which the male guards the nest and eggs or young from an inconspicuous nearby perch, even when the female is within the nest (28).]

In the case of the ectothermic pre-aves, which sited their surface nests in locations that were more or less exposed to solar radiation during the midday hours, both parents doubtless attended the eggs closely in alternation during this period and foraged intensely preceding and following it. This is precisely the strategy employed by some open-nesting contemporary birds, for example, the Dusky Flycatcher nesting in the high Sierras of California (277). On the other hand, being homeothermic endotherms and not dependent on direct solar heating for shortening incubatory periods, primitive pro-aves probably sited their nests in locations that were well shaded during the midday hours. Their most intense foraging probably occurred in the hot midday periods when the eggs were least in need of parental bodily heat. This is the practice, for example, in Great Tits and Field Sparrows (*Spizella pusilla*) with broods of small young, which are not in need of parental bodily heat at this time (see 1,150).

BURYING OR CONCEALING EGGS DURING ABSENCES. But for pro-aves of such habits to have survived in the Jurassic milieu, they would have had to conceal their portions of the clutch with soil or vegetational debris during their absences, even though the mate customarily was keeping watch. This presupposes a very simple, unstructured scrape or hollowed-out nesting site that would not have been conspicuous after the eggs were concealed and the parent had left. In a contemporary example, the 15-cm-diameter by 3-cm-deep nest-scrape of the Egyptian Plover in a sand-gravel substrate is covered with sand when a parent absents itself, leaving the covered nest essentially level with the surrounding sand (230).

Many ground-nesting birds, such as game birds, grebes, and some waterfowl leave the eggs covered with down or plant material during their absence. In a study of the care of nests by Eared Grebe, *Podiceps nigricollis*, in South Africa, parents that covered their nests completely during their absences had only 10 of 46 nests preyed upon, whereas those that did not lost 48 of 58 clutches to predators (see 427). [Arid-zone birds in this category include seedsnipes and the Australian Dotterel (*Peltohyas australis*; 158).] Many others, that breed in scrapes or loosely-constructed nests on the ground, do not cover their eggs. Birds in the latter category include Ostriches, rheas, emus, loons, geese, grouse, pheasants, cranes, and numerous shorebirds (101).

A POSSIBLE RELIC OF ANCIENT, EGG-BURYING HABIT when leaving the nest may be seen in the following behavior. As birds in the last-mentioned category walk away from the nest site, usually after a session of incubation, they often pick up whatever small, loose objects that they find in their paths and toss them backwards in the general direction of the nest (101).

ABSENTING THE EGGS. In connection with this postulated scheme of pro-avian egg care, consider the habits of some extant birds. Quail, including the Bobwhite, and tinamous may leave their eggs daily for one or 2 h in the heat of day (or for even longer in very warm weather) while they eat, drink, groom, etc. Birds that take more frequent recesses rarely are absent for more than 1 h at a stretch (101). Contemporary ground-nesting birds, often with little nest structure, conserve energy by having only 1 or 2 relatively short foraging periods (967). Several species of tyrant flycatchers and swallows incubate their eggs for only half the daylight hours; they spend the rest of the time away from the nest. Members of other species, like Rock Pigeons, incubate almost continuously (28).

TOLERANCE OF EMBRYOS TO CHILLING AND OVERHEATING. In a large number of species incubation takes place for only part of the time. Periodic absences often are long enough for the eggs to cool to ambient temperature, particularly in those cases where only one parent incubates the eggs. It has been suggested that the cooling characteristics of eggs may greatly restrict the permissible lengths of inattentive spells, making it necessary for some birds to divide inattentive time into many brief intervals rather than a few long ones (737). In both Herring Gulls and House Wrens the eggs warm more slowly after resumption of incubation than they cool upon its interruption (723, 737). Although Herring Gulls do, indeed, usually restrict their absences to less than 1 min, many other species leave their clutches unattended for 10-60 min or more (975).

In fact, recent studies indicate that many avian embryos experience wide fluctuations in temperature during their development; they are resistant to chilling but rather susceptible to overheating. In an extreme example of such fluctuations, the attentive incubating Mountain White-crowned Sparrow female maintains the eggs at 34-38°C in severe high altitude weather conditions, but egg temperatures often undergo rapid fluctuations between 17.8° and 43°C during her frequent foraging trips which average 7.8 ± 0.5 min, as opposed to incubatory bouts averaging 19.6 ± 2.7 min. This tolerance of the embryo to chilling allows the females to forage during the coldest hours of the day and to shield the eggs at midday, when exposure of the nests to heat loads often is critical (482, 1,108; 2-day-old chicks left unattended in a nest in full sunlight were dead within 20 min; see 975). Similarly, repeated excursions of egg temperatures to low values, sometimes during outright periods of neglect by the hens of Dusky Flycatchers during inclement weather in the high Sierras of California did not seem to affect embryonic survival (277).

In more typical cases, when the weather is mild or warm, developing avian embryos suffer no harm from periodic absences. Physiological adaptations that permit egg neglect and slow growth of chicks are commonplace in marine and freshwater colonial birds (563). In some species, the physiological adaptations of the embryos to chilling are found to a surprising degree, particularly among procellariiforms (28, 202). In an extreme example of this, the Fork-tailed Storm-Petrel embryo, which can tolerate more frequent and extended periods of parental neglect than any other known avian embryo, can survive up to 7 continuous days of chilling at 10°C or a total of 28 days of such neglect on the breeding grounds (the Barren Islands in the Gulf of Alaska). The eggs normally are incubated at 29.7°C in deep burrows for an average of about 50 days (552, 1,152). The steep decrease in metabolism as the egg cools is such that even after 28 days of neglect at burrow temperatures, the metabolic cost to the embryos is only about 4% more than without neglect. A low conductance of the eggshell to water vapor appears as an adaptation in some such species (466). In the case of calidrine sandpipers (genus *Calidris*), though egg chilling upon the prolonged absence of a foraging adult seldom is fatal, it leads to asynchronous hatching and reduced chick viability (see D.W. Norton, 1972, in 963).

This tolerance to occasional interruptions of incubation doubtless is an adaptation to long-distance foraging on unpredictable food supplies by the incubating parent. But even the one-day-old domestic fowl embryo can survive an exposure of 76 h to ambient air at 0°C (518). However, as a general rule, long interruptions of incubation at low ambient temperatures usually retard embryonic development and often are fatal, sensitivity increasing in later developmental stages. Lethal overheating temperatures are 42.4-48.3°C for domestic fowl embryos, depending on age, 1 h at 41.1-43.9°C for House Wren embryos, and 1 h at 43°C for embryos of Heermann's Gull (*Larus heermanni*; see 214, 518, 1,150).

FORAGING by primitive endothermic avian ancestors would have had to be much more sustained and systematic than that of their ectothermic ancestors (though their needs would have been somewhat ameliorated in the mild Jurassic climate) and would have required a total of at least several hours each day. For comparison, small and medium-sized birds, in normal weather, require at least 20% of the daylight hours for foraging during the time of incubation (but thick-walled and closed nests often retard cooling of the eggs; 101).

RELIANCE ON SOLAR HEAT? Because of the need for sustained systematic feeding, solar radiation and climatic heat could not have been relied on to keep the eggs at, or somewhat below, the body temperature of a pro-avis (see Table 3) during parental absences, even during the most favorable times of the day (because of the inevitability of poor weather, even in the mild, equable conditions of the Jurassic and early and middle Cretaceous periods). Contemporary tropical birds whose eggs are not exposed directly to the sun can rely on heat from indirect solar radiation to accomplish incubation of the eggs only during midday (159).

[Amongst extant birds, daylight incubation by climatic heat alone is possible only in the hottest of regions, such as the Dead Sea Basin, lower Iraq, and Seistan. Although probably also practiced by the Dead Sea Sparrow (*Passer moabiticus*), exclusive solar incubation by day has been demonstrated only in the Red-billed Quelea or Dioch in a semiarid region near Lake Chad (see P. Ward, 1965, in 311).]

CLUE OF COCKATIELIAN TEMPORARY TRUCES. This outline of the postulated egg-care habits of pro-aves receives other support from the behavior of Cockatiels. One facet of the support is the habit of Cockatielian mates to tolerate temporary "truces" in their competition for the eggs during periods when they divide them between themselves. This can be seen as a "compromise" between a relic of the pro-avian practice, of **possession of some of the eggs all of the time**, and the later practice of ancestral birds, of **possession of all of the eggs some of the time.** Once one recognizes the probable existence of an ancient practice of sole possession of separate clutches by each member of a pair, it becomes very likely that the practitioners had a lower body temperature than that of modern birds.

CLUE OF ROUTINELY SEARCHING FOR BURIED EGGS. The other facet of the support is the fact that Cockatiels of both sexes routinely search for, resurface, and recover eggs buried in wood shavings in and around the IA (incubative area). This is fully concordant with, and suggests, a prior practice of egg care in which eggs, kept in shallow scrapes in a yielding substrate, were concealed under vegetational debris while parents were absent foraging for extended periods, and were uncovered upon the parents' return. Accordingly, the egg-care pattern immediately antecedent to incubation-sharing by ancestral birds probably was one in which each pro-avian parent individually incubated a separate clutch.

Recall that, guided by the fact that most extant reptiles leave their eggs unincubated and unattended, it was assumed as a working hypothesis that this also must have been the habit of the ancient reptilian ancestors of birds (i.e., those preceding the stem-reptiles of Table 3). A question that ultimately must be addressed, then, is how the unassisted incubation of a separate clutch by each pro-avian parent could have developed from a reptilian pattern in which the parents neither incubated nor attended to the clutch (which, for extant reptiles, generally leads to extremely variable, and sometimes very lengthy, periods of embryogenesis).

[As noted above, despite generally leaving their eggs unincubated and unattended, extant reptiles usually are more discriminating than most amphibians in selecting and/or constructing suitable sites for their eggs (91), foreshadowing the elaborate parental-care behavior of birds. Moreover, as noted on p. 450, at a much later time (in the late Cretaceous period), some reptiles, such as duck-billed dinosaurs, appear to have been giving their young extensive parental care (168).]

PRE-AVES---EARLY NON-INCUBATING POST-REPTILIAN ANCESTORS. In Part 2, I outlined the basis for believing that pre-aves, the early post-reptilian ancestors of birds, nested in shallow surface scrapes, making it possible to utilize the heat of both direct and indirect solar radiation and greatly shortening the period of embryonic development. It was the behavior of breeding Cockatiels that provided the first of several clues to the existence of such a stage. This first clue was the strong inclination of Cockatiels to stand over and shield eggs (otherwise exposed to light and view) in the identical circumstances in which they have no hesitation to leave them unattended when the lights are extinguished.

STANDING AND SHIELDING, A RELIC OF VERY ANCIENT TIMES. This behavior appears to be a relic of very ancient times, before the practice of parental incubation. At that time the nest and eggs would appear to have been shielded from view and direct midday solar radiation by the bodies of the standing parents, which is the habit of many extant birds in extremely hot environments. In early to mid-morning and late afternoon, it would have been adaptive for the shielding pre-aves to allow rays from the low-lying sun to impinge directly on the eggs. In the hour or more of transition between excessively hot, overhead to warm, low-angle radiation in mid-morning and mid-afternoon, it seems likely that the eggs merely would have been concealed with a light covering of vegetational debris while both parents foraged.

Considerations Relating to Endothermy

FEATHERS AND ENDOTHERMY. The bases for the coming into play of strong selective pressures on pre-aves that favored the evolution of rapid double-clutching of relatively small-sized clutches by pro-aves (see Table 3) can be traced to (a) the progressively increased parental care accorded to the eggs and (b) the practice of incubation made possible by the achievement of a primitive grade of endothermy. These factors greatly increased the probability of successfully hatching eggs and "fledging" young, and, at the same time, required that clutch sizes be relatively small in order that the factors operate effectively. It is unlikely that the achievement of a primitive grade of endothermy would have been possible, however, without the concomitant development of a feather-like surface insulation (see 170, 633, 1,046). Some aspects of these relationships are treated here.

[Selective pressures for integumentary structures with favorable aerodynamical properties associated with existence in aerial habitats or flight are considered below. I have adopted the working hypothesis, that the earliest modifications of the properties of scales toward those of feathers in stem-reptiles and pre-aves were developed initially for insulative properties, primarily as protection from heat and intense solar radiation and secondarily for heat conservation, rather than for flight. However the origin-for-flight alternative also has its supporters (see 44, 169, 193, 571, 1,183; for a discussion of hypothetical stages in feather evolution, down vs. contour feathers, etc., see 170).]

ENDOTHERMY AND SUPERIOR MENTAL POWERS----SHORTER INCUBATORY PERIODS. For the extreme specializations in foraging envisioned for pro-aves, there would have been selective advantages to the development of enlarged memory capacities and advanced information processing systems (407, 766). But for the acquisition of such superior mental abilities, adaptations that regulate brain temperature within narrow limits are a prerequisite--the brain is 1°C cooler than the body core over a variety of cloacal and external temperatures in most avian species (see 829). Generally, this translates to a requirement for endothermy (155), and the ability to vary heat production is believed to have been one of the earliest adaptations in the evolution of homeothermy, just as it is in the development of homeothermy during ontogeny (1,099). [But some ectotherms also have made progress along the lines of regulating brain temperature (408; see below).]

[The vascular plexuses of the eyes primarily serve in the regulation of avian brain temperature, and the degree of vasomotion seems to be adjusted in response to the brain temperature (see 1,004). In the case of the Zebra Finch, the rete mirabile ophthalmicum is not well developed and the birds are unable to maintain brain temperature at more than 0.2°C below body temperature during heat stress (see 829).]

FEATHER-LIKE STRUCTURES are believed to have been one of the adaptations that made endothermy possible for primitive pro-aves. In other words, feather-like insulation made it possible for these ancestors to maintain a constant high body temperature independent of the exterior temperature, guaranteeing the stability of the internal environment. But having achieved insulative feather-like scales primarily through selection for their heat-shielding properties, and also having achieved a primitive grade of endothermy, primitive pro-aves no longer would have been dependent upon the siting of nests in exposed locations with access to direct solar radiation.

Accordingly, selection would have favored the siting of the nests by primitive pro-aves in less exposed, more protected locations, in which bodily shading from midday heat would have been unnecessary. Rather, the midday period probably would have been the most favorable one for foraging, as temperatures during midday at shaded and protected sites probably would have been most favorable for the climatic incubation of concealed eggs. Following this scheme, one also can envision a transitional stage between pre-aves and primitive pro-aves in which a single parent bodily shielded nests unassistedly in less exposed sites during midday heat.

THE ADVANTAGES CONFERRED BY ENDOTHERMY and its accompanying high rates of energy flow, for survival or reproductive success scarcely need recounting, but I mention those of greatest interest in the present connection. The primary advantage derives from the consequent firmly predictable and shorter incubatory times. Thus, the evolution of endothermy was a key factor in the lifting of physiological constraints on growth rates, maximum values of which for endothermic vertebrates (except for some marsupials and anthropoid primates) are at least an order of magnitude greater than the maximum for any ectothermic vertebrate (994).

However, to the extent that eggs and young are cared for in the same location, they should be subjected to parallel selective forces (see T.J. Case, 1978, in 1,150), so that if it is adaptive to accelerate embryonic development, it also should be adaptive to accelerate post-hatching development. Accordingly, as nidicolous development evolved primarily in response to selective forces for small egg size, there would have been strong concurrent selection for rapid development of nestlings.

LESSENING AND CIRCUMSCRIBING THE PERIODS OF VULNERABILITY. The primary advantage referred to above shortens and completely circumscribes the periods of vulnerability of the eggs and young and increased risk to the parents. These are likely to have been crucial considerations, because the most powerful factor in selection for brevity of incubatory periods and quick fledging of birds, even today in fully-developed endotherms, is the hazards to which the eggs and young are exposed, especially those from predators. And smaller species are vulnerable to a greater variety of predators than are larger ones (34, 101, 219, 354, 430, 499, 1,017). Indeed, predation appears to be the single greatest cause of reproductive failure in most avian species (314; see also note on p. 547).

Selective pressure for lessening the exposure of the young to unpredictable environmental conditions may have been a key element in the evolution of the nidicolous strategy of "individual care" as opposed to the "mass production" strategy of birds with nidifugous young, although there are certain environmental conditions in which large clutch size is seen to be an advantage (329, 1,051). [Among reptiles, also, the hazards of long periods of vulnerability of slowly developing eggs are emphasized by the fact that cold climates seem to have been the most important single selective factor favoring viviparity. Other reptiles have adapted to such selective pressures by prolonged oviductal retention of the eggs, which, in fact, is the rule in oviparous squamates (765, 786).]

THE GREAT VULNERABILITY OF EGGS AND YOUNG can be judged from the fact that over 75% of the eggs of the great majority of small terrestrial birds fail to develop into independent young (28). About 88% of all nesting failures in a deciduous scrub habitat were caused by predation (see 740), and about 75% of the nest mortality in Britain (181). Of possible significance in the present connection, since the periods of concern lie within the Mesozoic era, is the fact that contemporary egg and nestling predation is much higher ("high-predation regime of the tropics;" 1,150) in more equable tropics than in temperate regions, possibly as a consequence of increased specialization or diversity of predators (see 314, 740, 1,051).

High predation rate in the tropics is another factor that may favor nidicolous development, which is relatively more common there, inasmuch as smaller energetic losses are sustained by the loss of a clutch (329). Greater predatory pressure in the tropics than in temperate regions also was cited by Maclean as a possible "important selective force for egg-covering as a concealing mechanism" in the open-nesting Charadrii (328; see pp. 527, 580, 581). E.S. Morton calculated that 39% of the nests that otherwise survive would be predated in the tropics if the dependency periods of nestlings were to be lengthened 9 days to allow frugivory (see 1,150).

[At the present time, the few arboreal predators of temperate regions--mostly crows and squirrels--are supplemented in the tropics by specialist nest robbers, such as toucans, and by a wide variety of monkeys, snakes, and other tree dwellers. The bulk of this additional mortality must fall on eggs and nestlings. The nests of Arctic species (mostly ground-nesters), enjoy greater success than do those of species in temperate regions, averaging only 2/3rds of the mortality of mid-latitudinal species. The differences are more pronounced for egg survival than for nestling survival (1,150).]

In the ground-nesting Blackish Nightjar (*Caprimulgus nigrescens*), the percentage loss of eggs (64 ± 7%) is 3 times as great as that for the loss of young (198). In certain years in Britain, Weasels have destroyed more than half the nests of tits (*Parus* sps.); foxes accounted for 89% of the losses of eggs of Ruffed Grouse in North America, while 2 species of birds of prey (Accipitres) accounted for most of the losses of their young, which amounted to 63% of the total (see 352). At least 70% of fledging failures from 228 nests of Black and White Manakins (*M. manacus*) could be attributed to predation (see D. Snow, 1962, in 1,051).

For 6 common North American passerines it has been calculated that 55% of all eggs and 66% of all nestlings are lost through predation (see 1,150). Despite the fact that Long-tailed Tits build closed nests (incorporating 1,500-2,000 feathers) with an outer layer of lichens, which tends to blend the nest with the tree trunk or branch, close the nest entrance with a feather, and disguise their visits by imitating insect hunting tactics, more than half the nests are destroyed by jays (see H. Riehm, 1970, in 737). An important factor contributing to the large egg and chick losses is the fact that nest predators typically consume entire clutches and broods during one visit (222, 564). Moreover, nests probably are most commonly deserted after being disturbed or partially robbed by a predator, because of the probability that the predator will return (1,150). Perhaps the chief adaptive advantage of brood division in species with biparental care of the young is the reduction of the incidence of predation on entire broods (see p. 563).

Among species with nidifugous young, continuous nest attendance and, hence, male parental care, is crucial to prevent predation losses in murres (Alcidae), flamingos (Phoenicopteridae), avocets (Recurvirostridae), cranes (Gruidae), and many gulls (Laridae). Predation pressure also may be an important factor in the continuous attendance at the nests of pratincoles (Glareolidae), skimmers (Rhynchopidae), doves (Columbidae) and terns (Sterninae), in addition to the obvious need to prevent overheating (see 1,266).

[Predation is similarly extensive on the eggs of many reptiles. Among chelonians, losses to predators (and microorganisms) is the fate of eggs in most nests in all but a few of the regions that have been studied (681). Excessively cold weather, storm tides, droughts, and other environmental disturbances also take their tolls (683). Chelonians subject to these heavy losses survive through their prolificness. At their extreme, they are the most prolific amniotes. Some species regularly oviposit clutches in excess of 100 eggs and sometimes more than 10 clutches per year (682). Probably fewer than 1% of hatchlings survive to maturity (683), the same survival percentage that has been estimated for crocodilian hatchlings (685).]

INCUBATORY TEMPERATURES CLOSE TO TOLERABLE MAXIMUM. Any risk of predation also tends to favor brood reduction, that is, reduction of the number of successfully reared chicks of a brood (115). The great importance of shortening the incubatory period also can be judged from the fact that the body temperatures of birds so closely approach the lethal limit. This means that the incubatory temperatures usually are close to the maximum that the embryos can tolerate (also believed to be true of American Alligator embryos; 659). [In another view, the above considerations are not taken into account. Rather, it is suggested that by regulating body temperature at the high values characteristic of birds, "natural selection has opted for water economy instead of energy economy" (422).]

INSTANT ACTIVITY AT FULL MUSCULAR POWER---EXTENDING ACTIVITY PERIOD. Two other advantages for survival, and the ones most commonly cited, are the abilities to become instantly active at full muscular power (i.e., at a high metabolic level) and to maintain fully functional sensory faculties at any time of the day or night, even in severe winters and at high latitudes. Body temperature exerts an important influence on activity and stamina, and low or even moderate temperatures may restrict greatly behavioral capacity. The "assurance by metabolic means of a stable temperature for the activity of the skeletal musculature and the digestive and central nervous systems" (869) is another way of describing the above-mentioned advantages. In other words, the homeothermic endotherm achieves a state of responsiveness, around-the-clock, that is attained by small-to-medium sized ectotherms only during their periods of activity.

Numerous physiological and biochemical studies have shown that optimum performances of the tissues of ectotherms, for example, optimum temperatures for enzyme activity, are achieved at the body temperatures that the animals prefer (maintain) during their activity (see 408). In regard to the central nervous system, many ectothermic tetrapods also have special adaptations that regulate brain temperature within narrower limits than those achieved for other tissues (408). The new degrees of freedom of movement accompanying successful adaptation to arboreal habitats also would have required a metabolic rate in excess of what is usual in reptiles, particularly as regards respiration (333).

Locomotion and activity, even at very low speeds, almost always involve substantial increments in metabolic rate. Although power input and running performance levels during burst activity may be very similar in small reptiles and mammals, and the former may even outperform and outrun the latter for short distances, even modest levels of sustained activity (beyond 1 or 2 min) quickly outstrip a reptile's aerobic metabolic capabilities. The transitional speed between sustainable and non-sustainable locomotion is surprisingly low in most lizards. Yet the impressive capabilities for burst activity conferred on most lizards by their high anaerobic energy production capacity (with a very limited dependence on body temperature but great inefficiency) are far beyond those that can be supported by aerobic systems (776). [Anaerobic burst speeds reach 2.6 m/sec in *Basiliscus* and 8.1 m/sec in *Callisaurus*, whereas sustainable speeds usually are much slower, often less than ½ m/sec. Maximum running speed in small mammals is essentially independent of their size, at about 1.1 m/sec.]

THE AEROBIC METABOLIC LIMITATIONS IN REPTILES probably are correlated with their relatively simple lungs and incompletely-double blood circulation. High levels of activity for them appear to be attainable only by anaerobic mechanisms (principally glycogen breakdown), for which their capacity is high. These, however, cannot be sustained for long at a high rate and the physical disruptions entailed may persist for hours, accounting for their lack of stamina. Accordingly, another important contributing factor in the evolution of avian endothermy, particularly in small animals, with their low thermal inertia, probably was selection for enhanced aerobic metabolism to support high levels of sustained activity (766, 776; see pp. 587-592; **The Evolutionary Sequence of Mechanisms of Predation**).

[The reptile generally depends on external heat to reach its highest level of activity and it is recognized that the practice of homeothermy enhances the ability of reptiles to detect and/or evade potential predators (363). Any factor that would allow reptiles to increase their periods of activity, particularly in a harsh climate, would confer a selective advantage (170). The adaptive advantage of being able to extend the active time can be gauged from the fact that the maximum period of activity among reptiles probably is that of lowland tropical lizards of the genus *Anolis*, which may be active during most of the daylight hours and thus are active nearly 50% of the total time during the year (see Heatwole, *et al*., 1969, in 363). The teiid lizard, *Ameiva chrysolaema*, a member of one of the most active lizard families, is active only for about 4-5 h per diem during the hot hours, being on the move foraging for more than 70% of that time (766). Times of activity are short in most other reptiles, particularly herbivorous ones, mostly ranging from 3-19% of the daylight hours for lizards and chelonians, with 32-41% estimated for *A. agama* (363).]

ENDOTHERMY NOT INTRINSICALLY SUPERIOR. It is not meant to imply that endothermy is intrinsically superior to ectothermy. It obviously is not. From some points of view, there is not even a clear distinction between animals in the two categories (411 and p. 559). Ectothermy is an indubitably highly successful strategy among living amphibians and reptiles (177, 410). A low body temperature and resting metabolic rate is highly advantageous in many habitats, not only because of the energetic saving accrued, and the retention of high capacities for short-term performance, but because a low energy budget allows a great specialization of food choice in time and space (357, 408, 869). Endothermy is likely to arise only if its costly energy budgets make possible equivalent or greater benefits (362, 412). [The efficiency of energy conversion of reptiles (over 40% in some species) is an order of magnitude higher than that of endotherms (see 262).]

In some ecological circumstances--say, abundant food but unfavorable climate--it is advantageous to be endothermic, in others--say, scarce food but abundant solar energy--it is advantageous to be ectothermic (361,

413). At the stage in evolutionary history when the immediate forerunners of primitive pro-aves became functionally committed to primary endothermy, they were outcompeted for an abundance of ecological niches by their ectothermic relatives (361), including virtually all energetically marginal environments.

Even though the evolution of homeothermic endothermy has involved the development of an elaborate system of feedback controls of the rates of thermogenesis (heat production) and thermolysis (heat dissipation; 349), most of the differences between reptiles and birds, as regards their abilities to control their body temperatures by physiological means, are quantitative rather than qualitative. But two of these differences are of crucial importance--the rate of aerobic energy metabolism, and heat conductance at the bodily surface (thermal conductance). Living reptiles have high thermal conductances and low rates of oxygen consumption; birds have low thermal conductances and high rates of oxygen consumption (361). [The overall thermal conductance of lizards is 10 times as great as that of birds and mammals and 4 times that of defeathered birds. The thermal conductance of fish is yet another order of magnitude greater than that of reptiles (1,099).]

As Bartholomew has pointed out, although members of both groups can vary these parameters, the results that can be achieved by this ability contrast sharply. The disparity hinges on differences in their rates of energy flow. With few exceptions, the best that the reptiles are able to achieve is to influence the rates of change of their body temperatures and to control local differences thereof (361; see also the treatment in 408).

It is pertinent here to consider related views concerning physiological aspects of the evolutionary transition from poikilothermy to homeothermy and homeothermic endothermy. Reasoning from the physiology of reptiles and young birds, and on the assumption that such components of physiological regulation as active evaporative cooling and vasomotor activity were inherited by avian ancestors from their reptilian antecedants, the crucial steps are thought to have been metabolic: (1) an overall intensification of heat production, with far reaching demands on various organ systems; and, then, (2) the development of chemical regulation with its underlying control mechanisms. Other components probably developed only after the higher metabolic levels were attained. The full development of feathers is thought to have been as a result of selection for both their insulative and aerodynamical properties (37).

Taking the agamid lizard *Amphibolurus barbatus* as a model for the first transitional step from the low metabolism and high heat conductance characteristic of ectothermy to the high metabolism and low heat conductance characteristic of endothermy, and reasoning from studies of the modulation of its rates of heating and cooling, Bartholomew and Tucker (966) made the following suggestions. The variable heat conductance that allows the control of the lizard's rates of temperature change, would be appropriate for a vertebrate evolving toward homeothermy but still dependent on solar radiation for attaining its activity temperature. Even a slight increase in endogenous heat production would allow greater precision of control of the rate of change of body temperature. Natural selection for increased metabolic rate ultimately could lead to the persistently high level of metabolism of homeotherms.

As heat production increased, dependence on solar heating could have decreased; ultimately any deleterious effect of integumentary insulative structures on the absorption of solar energy could have been balanced by enhanced conservation of endogenously produced heat. In this scheme, the selective factors that favored the evolution of homeothermy may have operated on the control of rates of changing body temperature as much as on the maintenance of constant body temperature (966).

INCUBATING EGGS AND RAPID DOUBLE-CLUTCHING. I call the ancestors of the pro-avian grade, in which feathers and a primitive level of endothermy had been achieved, **primitive pro-aves**. How and why did their pattern of oviposition and egg care change from that of their ectothermic pre-avian ancestors? The answer to the "how?" half of the question hinges on the fact that a primitive grade of homeothermic endothermy had been achieved. This matter is treated in detail on pp. 592-605, **The Evolutionary Transition from Primitive Reptilian to Avian Ovipositional Modes."**

Treated very cursorily, however, the achievement of endothermy and higher metabolic rates made it feasible for the first time to produce eggs at different times from the halves of the clutch oocyte complement contributed by each ovary (allochronic ovulation; see legend to Table 3), without a loss in reproductive potential. It is proposed that this was achieved by alternate ovarian and oviductal function, whereby the complement of ripe or ripening oocytes from one ovary were ovulated and oviposited *en masse*, first at one location, followed in a few days, at most, by that from the other ovary at another location, that is, by rapid double-clutching.

Not only would the time required to produce and oviposit the contributions of both ovaries separately by primitive pro-aves probably not have exceeded that required to do so simultaneously by pre-aves, because of the former's increased body temperature and metabolic rate, but the fact that clutches were incubated by primitive pro-aves also would have contributed to reduction of the length of a reproductive episode, allowing more breeding cycles per annum. This would have made it possible to reduce the relative clutch burden of gravid animals by 50% in a single step of altered ovarian function (this is not to imply, however, that the transition necessarily was abrupt).

A major egg-care departure that was necessary in order to achieve the benefits of partitioning egg production by rapid double-clutching, was that each parent would have had to incubate and otherwise care exclusively and almost independently for a separate clutch. The potential for an adjustment of this nature is seen in many contemporary birds. Many studies have led to reports of females successfully rearing young despite loss of male help, either after their mates disappeared or in rare cases when females accepted polygynous conditions. Thus, a male's full parental allocation is not essential ordinarily for some offspring to survive (1,248).

For example, unassisted female House Wrens and Pied Flycatchers are able to compensate in part for work not done by the male (in the case of the Pied Flycatchers, 3.35 ± 1.84 young/brood compared to 5.40 ± 0.89 for primary females and 5.39 ± 1.48 for monogamous females). Similarly, unassisted secondary Bobolink hens mated to polygynous males are able to compensate (for lack of assistance) in their allocation of times budgeted to foraging and delivering food to the young, and exhibit remarkable success in fledging young; they almost attain the effectiveness of the combined efforts of the male plus the primary female (see 954, 1,124, 1,223).

[Unassisted brooding Pied Flycatcher females have much higher corticosterone levels than paired females with the same brood size, but it is not known whether it is the increased foraging demands or the more intense food solicitation by the nestlings that is the primary stressing factor (1,124). Male assistance in feeding young may be essential when only one chick is reared at a time, since the evolution of a larger brood size would be expected if one parent were capable of rearing a chick unaidedly (34). Male parental care is essential whenever continuous nest attendance is required for the survival of offspring (see 1,258). Males would be expected to desert their mates whenever opportunities for new matings would lead to greater reproductive success than could be achieved by helping the current mate care for offspring (1,266).]

Although alternate ovarian and oviductal function and sequential clutching (but not rapid double-clutching) would have been possible for pre-aves, the reproductive cost to them, as ectotherms, would have been that of almost doubling the time required to produce the same number of eggs. Nor did they possess the homeothermic mechanisms (insulative integumentary structures) that would have made it possible to care independently for a clutch--most notably, in the shading of the eggs during midday periods. [Of course, once homeothermic endothermy and the incubatory practice were achieved, there no longer would have been any need to site nests in locations that were exposed to direct solar radiation.]

The answer to the "why?" part of the question, of course, has to deal both with the competitive advantages of reduced relative clutch burdens to gravid animals and the general advantages of rapid double-clutching and smaller sizes of clutches that are incubated by parental bodily heat.

INCUBATORY TEMPERATURES AND BROOD PATCHES. The incubatory temperatures of birds usually increase during the course of incubation as the brood patch becomes fully developed and/or the attentiveness of the parent(s) increases. The special morphological properties of the brood patch do not effect an increase in the skin temperature (which is about 1°C lower than the bodily core temperature) because heat is withdrawn by the eggs. Rather, they bring heat to the skin at a rapid rate. Heat is transferred between the adult and the eggs at a rate proportional to the area of contact and to the temperature gradient between the skin and the eggs. Although the central temperatures of the eggs usually range from 2-6°C below body temperature, depending upon the species and stage of incubation (averaging 4.01 ± 1.35° in 16 species; 427), the temperature at the upper surface of the eggs nearest the embryo is 1-5°C higher, essentially at that of the brood patch. The smallest gradients between brood patch and clutch temperatures occur in species with relatively small clutch weights (975).

These measurements suggest that embryos probably are maintained at a temperature differential no greater than 1-4°C below body temperature during the last half of incubation. In this connection, Witschi (see 23) quoted a temperature differential of 2-4°C as optimum for avian embryonic development, and Skutch (101) suggested that the maximum difference is only 1°C. In the case of the domestic fowl, with a body temperature of 41°C, temperatures taken beside the embryos during the early phase of incubation were remarkably uniform, rising from 37.6° to 39°C during the course of steady incubation (427). Normal egg temperatures during incubation are said to vary between about 34 and 38°C (737). One can speculate that, unless brood patches evolved concomitantly with feathers and endothermy, the temperatures of incubated embryos at the primitive pro-avian grade of endothermy probably were not maintained as close to body temperature as they are in extant birds.

On the other hand, though broodpatches occur in most orders of birds, they are not absolutely essential. They are absent in members of the Pelecaniformes, Anseriformes, many Columbiformes, and some of the Alcidae. Most species of the latter pluck the down from their ventral surfaces for nest lining, which essentially brings the eggs into contact with the body during incubation. Furthermore, the apteria of doves are bare of down, while the lack of brood patches in members of many Columbiformes and Pelecaniformes may be related to their tropical distribution and small egg weight (975).

In some extant species, in which the parents share incubation, such as House Sparrows, nutcrackers, Common Bushtits, Wren-tits (*Chamaea fasciata*), some grosbeaks, Bank Swallows, and Barn Swallows (*Hirundo rustica*), the males have no broodpatch (101, 437). It has been shown experimentally that tightly-sitting males of the latter two species can incubate as effectively as females during the day under mild temperature regimes (267, 268). On the other hand, the non-incubating males of other species, such as in the American genus of flycatchers (*Empidonax*) possess a brood patch (see 414). It is noteworthy in this connection that the distribution of broodpatches among brooding and nonbrooding passerine males strongly suggests that the brood patch is a primitive passerine attribute; behavioral deviations in incubation apparently have evolved subsequently (348).

RAPID DOUBLE-CLUTCHING: MORE EGGS ACCOMMODATED, BETTER, SAFER. But once parental incubation was practiced: (1) the eggs would have had to be very readily accessible, and, hence, would have required parental protection from numerous hazards; and (2) the number of eggs that could have been incubated by one parent--as determined by physical constraints--would have had a relatively low upper limit. By the rapid double-clutching of half-sized clutches, with one clutch being incubated by each parent, twice as many eggs could have been accommodated. This is the essence of one of the advantages conferred by this strategy. But regardless of the total number of eggs accommodated, by having each parent care for only half of them:

(1) the efficiency of incubation would have been increased (the fewer the number of eggs in an avian clutch, in general, the shorter the incubatory period, and the less their vulnerability) [Although coots, e.g., can incubate and hatch experimental clutches of up to 21 eggs as successfully as normal ones of about 9 eggs (28), the incubatory time is lengthened]; and

(2) other factors remaining unchanged, each portion of the eggs would have been safer from predators than the two portions combined, by virtue of: (a) the separate portions occupying less space, and, hence, of their being more readily concealed, less conspicuous, and less readily discovered; and (b) the care of the nest by only one adult often tends to render the nest less conspicuous to predators than when both parents share in its care (963). Skutch has postulated that the necessity to reduce the number of trips to the nest with food for the young, and thereby decrease the chances of being detected by a watching predator, is a possible basis for relatively small clutch sizes in the tropics, and for infrequent trips to the nest with relatively large morsels among forest birds (see refs. in 1,051). In this connection, lack of predation sometimes permits a relatively larger clutch size on tropi-

cal islands, when there is no compensatory influence of increased climatic stability (1,051).

[On the other hand, in certain cases, biparental incubation entails much less traffic to and from the nest than uniparental care. For example, among shorebirds, biparental caring Greater Golden Plovers (*Pluvialis apricaria*) make only 120 passages to and from the nest during the incubatory period, whereas uniparental-caring Eurasian Dotterels (*Charadrius morinellus*) breeding in the same area make about 1,400 passages. In the latter case, conflicts between needs for self-maintenance and incubation select for many short foraging recesses, whereas in the former case, shared incubation (12-h daytime periods by the males and 12-h nighttime periods by the females) allows long foraging periods at good feeding sites far from the nest (1,129).

Moreover, the percentage of Black and White Manakin nests lost to predators is the same during the incubatory and nestling periods, despite a 4-fold increase in parental visitation rates, suggesting that the predators find the nests by searching in likely locations rather than by watching the parents (see 1,266). In addition, in a 10-year study of Spotted Sandpipers, no significant difference in predation--as measured by hatching successes--was detected between nests cared for by 1 parent versus those cared for by two parents (1,323).]

LESS CHANCE OF TOTAL LOSS THROUGH SINGLE ACT OF PREDATION. It is most pertinent, in this connection, that the reduction of the chances of an entire brood being lost through a single act of predation--most likely among species with nidicolous young--is believed to be the chief basis for the practice of many avian parents of splitting their broods of fledglings between themselves (101). In fact, it has been suggested that the upper limit of clutch size among contemporary birds with nidifugous young may be set by the ability of the parents to protect the brood (167). Clearly, mere division and separation of the two portions of a clutch also decrease the chances of losing the entire clutch in a single act of predation (1,104). [Of course, in some habitats and under some types of predator pressures, close biparental cooperation and attentiveness to guarding a single brood of chicks (particularly until they become experienced), rather than caring unassistedly for divided broods (or separate clutches), could be selectively advantageous (see 1,129).] Small clutches also can be readied sooner and oviposited at more frequent intervals than large ones, which require longer periods between ovipositions (897).

"FEATHER"-ASSISTED JUMPING. We are considering a stage in the evolution of reptiles to birds--primitive pro-aves--in which primitive feathers already had evolved but primarily as an adjunct to the development of homeothermic endothermy. This is in keeping with the view that the initial development of feather-like scales was independent of adaptations for flight. Primitive pro-aves probably were largely arboreal, bipedal, fleet-footed, sprinting and jumping predators, preying on small amphibians, reptiles, insects, and mammals (the latter almost exclusively during twilights or in heavy cover). Their aerial activity probably included "feather"-assisted jumping, both terrestrial and arboreal, and parachuting from low-lying branches to the ground. In this connection, Owl Parrots are incapable of true flight, but they still occasionally climb trees and use their wings to assist in long jumps from limb to limb (174). ["Parachuting" is used to refer to descent with an absence of lift capability. As defined arbitrarily by Oliver (see 1,050) it refers to a reduced rate of fall at an angle to the vertical of less than 45°, by which definition the animal has the capability to generate lift (see 1,199). Parachuting involves balancing but generally little or no steering.]

Archaeopteryx and the Capability for Flight

OVIPOSITIONAL HABITS. In connection with the above treatment, it is pertinent to consider Ostrom's thesis that "*Archaeopteryx* was not particularly arboreal in its habits, but was a very active, fleet-footed, bipedal, cursorial predator" (70, 1,019). If this were to be correct, it would seem to imply that *Archaeopteryx* still oviposited eggs in the reptilian, pre-avian, and primitive pro-avian fashion--*en masse*--rather than 1 egg daily or on alternate days, in the predominant avian fashion. I visualize the periodic oviposition of single eggs as the ultimate adaptation of ovarian function for the achievement of advanced faculties in aerial habitats by an oviparous vertebrate, not primarily as an adaptation for terrestrial predation, nor even for ground-based leaps after insect prey. [Recall (p. 397) that according to Martin's analysis, *Archaeopteryx* was more likely to have been a sprinter and good jumper than a primarily cursorial ground dweller.]

The only information available concerning oviposition by *Archaeopteryx* is indirect and inconclusive. Although the pelvis is not avian in construction (but see 1,191), there is a discernible trend of ornithization, compared to the coelurosaurian condition, by the enlargement of the pre-acetabular portion of the ilium and by the elongation of the pubes. The same trend occurred in other theropods, without any closer relationship to the ancestral stock of *Archaeopteryx*, for example in the late Cretaceous *Adasaurus* and *Segnosaurus* (see 1,187). Wellnhofer observes that "the aperture of the pelvis of *Archaeopteryx* was relatively narrow, leaving just a small passage way for the eggs" (1,187; specimen sexes unknown). Of course, if several theropodan groups were practicing increasingly shallow burial of clutches of fewer and smaller eggs, all might be expected to show the same trend of changes in pelvic construction, reduction of body size, etc., even though not all eventually practiced surface nesting.

ALL REMAINS RECOVERED FROM MARINE SEDIMENTS. An indirect, though persuasive, argument that *Archaeopteryx* was capable of, at least, gliding flight is the fact that 4 of its 5 skeletal fossils (and a feather) have been recovered from the Solnhofen and Pappenheim lithographic limestone quarries (about 30 x 90 km in extent and up to 90 m thick) of the Lower Tithonian, little more than 48 km from one another. These quarries are in the neighborhood of the Altmünl River in or near the Langenaltheim region of Bavaria, and are restricted to the area of the Southern Franconian Alb known as the Altmuhtal. The limestones in question are strongly compacted and were formed about 150 mya from very fine-grained, chalky silt deposited in the quiet bottoms of what may be referred to broadly as "tropical" lagoons. These formed part of a subdivided marine backreef basin near the flat shores of the upper Jurassic (middle Kimmeridgian), northwestern rim of the pre-Mediterranean Tethys Sea, which cut Arabo-Africa off from Eurasia during much of the Mesozoic era and Tertiary period (75, 1,180, 1,181, 1,293; see also pp. 240, 241).

Since the Maxberg specimen was found 6 m above the level of the London one in the quarries, the species must have persisted for at least the length of time of the Solnhofen depositional series, estimated at about 500,000 yr, at most (97, 333, 1,180). In the same strata are found many pterosaurs, shells of crayfish and crabs, innumerable remains of sea lilies, jellyfish, shells of ammonites, and piscene skeletons of the genera, *Leptolepides*, *Caturus*, and *Thrissops*, with many of the fishes and other organisms apparently having been poisoned quickly by coccolithophorid blooms. *Archaeopteryx* is believed to have lived in cycad and araucaria groves in the neighborhoods of these lagoons, although they might also have spent some time on the lagoon shores (92). The Australian fossil feather impressions, and the ones from Lerida, Spain and the Kara-Tau Ridge in Kazakhstan, Russia also were recovered from aqueous sediments (see 169, 290, 308, 574, 1,383). The earliest known post-Jurassic avian fossils, those of true carinates (having a keeled sternum), also occurred in aqueous sediments (Lower Cretaceous--Neocomian; see 574).

CODEPOSITION WITH PTEROSAURS SUGGESTS *ARCHAEOPTERYX* WAS AIRBORNE. In consideration of these facts, it is hard to avoid the conclusion that airborne *Archaeopteryx* and pterosaurs were downed and perished in the lagoons for one reason or another, most likely blown in or caught in flight by monsoonal storms (1,180). [Pterosaurs also may have been poisoned directly or indirectly by coccolithophorid blooms (1,181).]

Swinton suggests that the preservation of fossils of *Archaeopteryx* was a consequence of its feeble flight capabilities (333); having left the shelter of their trees and encountered monsoonal winds, they may have been carried over the Solnhofen lagoons and perished through their inability to return to a safe perch. Saville (1,050) makes essentially the same point in remarking that birds capable of true flight may have existed contemporaneously with *Archaeopteryx*, but that they would have been much less likely to fall victim to the conditions that led to the preservation of the *Archaeopteryx* specimens.

The validity of this argument, of course, depends on the pterosaurs in question having been similarly limited in their flight capabilities. Inasmuch as some of the pterodactyloids appear to have developed unstable, powered flight (1,050, 1,109), this scenario either is unlikely or, if applicable, the flight capabilities of *Archaeopteryx* were equal to those of the codeposited pterodactyloids. The other possibility is that the pterosaurs were poisoned as a consequence of planktonic blooms (1,181), in which case *Archaeopteryx* might have been downed as described above and/or poisoned in the same manner.

[The early rhamphorhynchoids, such as *Rhamphorhynchus*, combined an unkeeled sternum with a long tail, whereas the pterodactyloids, of more recent origin, such as *Pterodactylus*, *Nyctosaurus*, and *Pteranodon* (a toothless piscivore with a 7½ m wingspan, a body of the bulk of a Turkey, and probably primarily a glider), had short tails and carinated sterna. Representatives of both groups are found in the Solnhofen limestones (1,181, 1,198, 1,204, 1,248, 1,302).]

It is true that the poor condition of the London and Maxberg specimens might be explained by a period of exposure before having been washed into a lagoon (although a surface drift of the deteriorating carcasses before sinking seems a more likely explanation; see 1,181, 1,198). But what of the fine Berlin and Eichstätt specimens? It is unreasonable to adopt the position that codeposited, almost fully-articulated, skeletons of pterosaurs and *Archaeopteryx* had widely different origins, that is, that the pterosaurs were downed in flight or blown into the lagoons, but the *Archaeopteryx* specimens merely got washed in from a postulated terrestrial habitat in the neighborhoods of their flat shores.

The complete preservation of these latter specimens suggests a rapid burial and precludes long transport (1,180). Only if the animals drowned, with their lungs filled with water and their plumage soaked, could the carcasses have sunk quickly and become well preserved. Otherwise, they probably would have floated for a prolonged time (30-40 days) and been largely decomposed (see 1,180). Bottom-site preservation before loss to scavenging apparently was made possible by frequent periods of lethality of the water to scavengers as a consequence of the direct and indirect effects of poisonous planktonic blooms (1,181). By the time of recovery of scavengers, bacterial action presumably had left only bones and other resistant structures, which slowly became silted over in the quiet bottom waters (at the rate of about 0.2 mm/yr).

ASYMMETRICAL FEATHER VANES ESTABLISH AERIAL HABITS. Even more persuasive evidence that *Archaeopteryx* was capable of, at least, gliding flight has been provided by Feduccia and Tordoff (131). The clearly evident asymmetry of the feather vanes in the Berlin specimen leave no doubt of this, inasmuch as they conform to the pattern in contemporary flying birds. In these, the flight feathers are streamlined in cross-section. The stiff quill (rachis) of each feather lies toward the leading edge, and the leading vane is thicker and narrower than the more flexible trailing one. The vanes of the feathers of flightless birds, on the other hand, are symmetrical. Thus, in addition to skeletal evidence (see, for example, 1,185), there is a substantial basis for believing that *Archaeopteryx* represents an early-to-intermediate stage in the evolution of powered flight, as opposed to being a mere glider (169).

Based on high-speed photography of birds in flight, together with wind-tunnel tests on wings and feathers, and data on the flexural stiffness of feathers, R. Norberg (1,202) has developed a new mechanical and aerodynamic theory on the function of vane asymmetry and feather curvature. This theory accounts for the automatic adjustments of the angles of attack of feathers throughout the cycle of wing beating, despite the continually varying direction and speed of the relative wind. Since the advanced structural characteristics of feathers that are necessary for this passive maintenance of optimum angles of attack were present in *Archaeopteryx*, the presumption is very strong that it could fly with true, powered, flapping flight, though probably not sustainedly.

ADVANCED PRO-AVES

Origin of Periodic Oviposition

LINK WITH GLIDING AND SLOW WING-FLAPPING AT SMALL AMPLITUDES. Advanced pro-aves represent the stage in avian evolution when eggs first were oviposited periodically, one at a time, after the fashion of contemporary birds. We now consider the question of how and why this practice of assembling clutches by periodic ovipositions at, say, 2-3-day intervals, first arose from the primitive pro-avian practice of *en-masse* rapid double-clutching, with one clutch derived from each ovary. Again, the question of "how?" is treated in greater detail on pp. 592-605, **The Evolutionary Transition from Primitive Reptilian to Avian Ovipositional Modes.**

Periodic oviposition of single eggs at 2-3-day intervals only became feasible with the further advances in endothermy and body temperature, and increases in metabolic rates, represented by the evolutionary transition from the primitive to the advanced pro-avian condition. It then became possible to assemble clutches, one egg at a time, through alternating contributions from both ovaries (monoallochronic ovulation) within sufficiently brief periods to maintain viability of the first-laid eggs and inter-clutch hatching synchrony. A need to maintain intra-clutch hatching synchrony probably was not the major factor, on the assumption that incubation began after the penultimate egg was laid (see pp. 148, 569-571).

Periodic ovulation, oviductal maturation, and oviposition of one egg every few days is regarded as the ultimate functional adaptation of the ovaries and oviducts of oviparous vertebrates for invasion of the aerial or acrobatic arboreal habitats; it depends for its attainment upon a relatively advanced degree of endothermy and its attendant high metabolic rates. But even non-acrobatic arboreality, in pre-aves and stem-reptiles, would have led to strong selection for lesser relative clutch burdens in gravid animals--both smaller and fewer eggs. It seems very likely that the culmination of this trend was not attained until pro-aves had become very well adapted to arboreal habitats and had attained relatively advanced faculties in the air, namely the ability to glide and wing-flap slowly at small amplitudes.

With the attainment of this degree of wing flapping, the strongest selection against high wing loading--leading to periodic oviposition--probably would have come into play, rather than in the relatively passive, less demanding, gliding precursor stage. In this connection, we already have noted the importance of endothermy and enhanced aerobic metabolic rate, (a) for successful adaptation to the new degrees of freedom in the arboreal and aerial habitats, (b) for supporting high levels of sustained activity in the exercise of aerial activites, and (c) during the exercise of extreme foraging specializations (333, 766, 776).

The advance in activity from the *en-masse* ovipositing, arboreal iguanids that lack toe pads, to the single-egg clutching, highly acrobatic, arboreal, anoline iguanids that possess them (see p. 541), is perhaps qualitatively comparable to the advance in arboreal and aerial activity represented by the transition from primitive to advanced pro-aves. [In this connection, it has been suggested that the physical burden of a clutch puts arboreal lizards at a great disadvantage and, as mentioned earlier, it is common for gravid reptiles to cease feeding. Laboratory experiments with skinks, which are examples of reptiles that do not decrease their food intake during reproduction, show them to be 25% slower moving when burdened by a full-term clutch, in which condition they are particularly vulnerable to predation by elapid snakes (765).]

[In the case of placental mammals, the fetuses are cradled in a firm support sling very near the mother's center of gravity and balance. She still usually is capable of high rates of activity involving hunting, running, turning, and migrations, even when at near-term stages of pregnancy. There are few data that suggest that predation is significantly more successful on pregnant eutherians than on non-pregnant individuals; most predation is upon the very young, the old, the crippled, and the diseased (1,342).]

OVIPOSITIONAL INTERVALS, SPERM VIABILITY, AND FERTILIZATION. Intervals of oviposition longer than 1 day seem to be the rule among members of the Sphenisciformes (3-4 days), Pelecaniformes (1-5 days), Psittaciformes (usually 1½-4 days), Falconiformes (usually 1½-5 days), Strigiformes (usually

2-4 days), Apterygiformes (24-33 days; range, 11-75 days), and many tropical suboscine passerine families (generally 2 days), but are rare in members of the Galliformes, Anseriformes, and non-Australian oscine Passeriformes. In most species the interval is of fixed length and it is suggested that this is regulated in some species by hierarchical sequencing of the initiation of yolk deposition (661, 1,107, 1,406, 1,408).

Only avian species with relatively small eggs oviposit large clutches with 1-day intervals between the eggs; otherwise, eggs are laid at greater intervals (115). In view of the viability of reptilian sperm in the female reproductive tract of a variety of chelonians and squamates for long periods, even years (90, 91, 93) and in poultry and many other birds, including parrots, for several weeks (see pp. 123, 124), it seems very likely that a single transfer of sperm sufficed to fertilize an entire clutch of eggs of advanced pro-aves.

EVOLUTION OF PRO-AVIAN EGG CARE. Cockatiels and members of many other avian species guard to varying degrees, crouch over, or sit loosely on, but usually do not incubate, the 1st few eggs of a clutch; in many species incubation does not begin until after the penultimate egg is laid. In the case of the Mountain White-crowned Sparrow, it is only the nighttime incubation that is withheld completely until after the laying of the penultimate egg; eggs are attended by the females but reach developmental temperatures only for brief periods during the day, beginning with the laying of the 1st egg (1,106). It has been assumed in the present treatment that this type of pre-incubatory egg-care behavior recapitulates the equivalent of egg care in the pre-avian stage of evolution, when surface nests were employed and the eggs were not incubated by bodily heat. But since the attainment of the fully-manifested functioning of the mechanisms underlying present-day incubatory egg care still appears to depend upon many birds passing through a diurnal and/or nocturnal pre-incubatory phase, this must have been an even more rigid prerequisite in primitive pro-aves, the next stage in the line of evolutionary succession after pre-aves (see Table 3).

Accordingly, the conclusion seems inescapable that pro-aves also must have gone through a pre-incubatory phase. In this phase, eggs, oviposited in surface nests *en masse* by primitive pro-aves, or one by one, by advanced pro-aves, were not incubated immediately. Instead, they probably were shielded, guarded, and concealed with vegetational debris for several days--in much the manner of the preceding pre-avian egg care. Incubation by primitive pro-aves may not have begun until after *en-masse* oviposition of the 2nd clutch, and incubation by advanced pro-avian parents very likely did not begin until, at the earliest, after completion of the egg-by-egg assembly of the 1st clutch. In the interim the eggs probably were maintained at the lower temperatures characteristic of pre-avian egg care.

In connection with the above, recall that on the very infrequent occasions when a hybrid lovebird female laid an egg, she covered it with fresh nesting material but did not incubate it (see p. 529). This would appear to reflect the most primitive type of egg care in the post-reptilian avian ancestral line (i.e., early pre-avian), not only because it is the simplest and least attentive, but because it occurred in a female that only very infrequently oviposited and usually lacked nesting cycles (all the other hybrid females totally lacked nesting cycles). In other words, it occurred in a female in which only the most primitive neural circuitry for breeding had achieved a functional state, and then only very infrequently.

WITHIN AN ENDOCRINOLOGICAL FRAMEWORK. To bring the probable route of the evolutionary transition into sharper focus, it is helpful to treat it within an endocrinological framework, namely the Mead-Morton paradigm of dual prolactinic control of the ovulatory-to-incubatory transition, although the present development does not depend upon specific endocrinological details. According to the Mead-Morton scheme, a sudden increase in prolactin levels generally both terminates ovulation and is responsible for the onset of incubation. It follows that females would be expected to increase greatly their incubatory behavior during the 24-h period preceding the laying of the last egg, which would still be in the oviduct at the time of the prolactinic surge that terminates ovulation (1,106).

If one extends this scheme back to the times of pre-aves, the pre-incubatory phase of avian evolution "immediately" preceding the transition to incubatory habits, prolactin would have played the same role of terminating ovulation, but not of initiating incubation. Instead, the 2nd function of its dual role probably was to initiate and maintain the post-ovipositional care of the eggs, namely, the shielding, shading, concealing, and guarding by day, and the concealing and guarding by night.

With the evolutionary transition to homeothermic endothermy and incubatory behavior, it is reasonable to assume, bearing in mind the well-known maxim of comparative endocrinology (see p. 377), that prolactin maintained its dual functional control. The post-ovipositional egg care initiated in the female by a surge of prolactin during a reproductive cycle merely would have graded over gradually from being solely egg-care with non-bodily incubation to egg care with bodily incubation. Prolactin is a very reasonable candidate for these functions in ancient times by virtue of the fact that it appears to have assumed more different functions during the course of vertebrate evolution than has any other hypophysial hormone (see pp. 130, 131). Thus, the possession of multiple functions suggests that prolactin must have been of very early origin and that its functions were expanded repeatedly into additional channels.

Accordingly, during the course of the evolution of homeothermic endothermy, the prolactin-induced, post-ovulatory care of the eggs during each reproductive cycle probably consisted of an early phase of daytime shielding, shading, concealing, and guarding, and nighttime guarding and concealing (under vegetational debris), and a terminal phase of day and night incubation; the early phase would have been an extension of pre-avian egg care and the terminal phase would have been that of the evolving primitive pro-avian egg care. As evolution continued, the early phase would have shortened progressively and the later phase would have lengthened. The equivalent of the early phase, characteristic of pre-avian egg care, is recapitulated today in many birds, but it does not always exclude bodily incubation. The early phase of egg care now may include daytime shielding, guarding, and incubation to varying degrees but not nighttime incubation (as exemplified by Mountain White-crowned Sparrows, Cockatiels, and, on occasion, by Budgerigars--see pp. 418, 434, 435, 470, 473, 474, 476, 477, 486, 487, 491, 495, 496, 498, 568, 701, 703, 711, 782, 783, 789, 795).

However, the transition to primitive pro-aves is postulated to have been somewhat more complex than that described above, inasmuch as primitive pro-aves are thought to have ovulated polyallochronically and practiced rapid double-clutching. But the postulated rapid double-clutching probably would have been facilitated by a dual prolactinic control of ovulation and egg care. Thus, if the female were to have oviposited 2 polyallochronically-ovulated clutches, the prolactinic surge terminating ovulation would have had to be delayed until after ovulation by the 2nd ovary. It is reasonable to assume that an increase in prolactin concentration also stimulates egg care in contemporary males of species in which solitary care by the male or dual parental care is practiced.

This assumption is supported by the comparative levels of prolactin during the incubatory period in male and female Wilson's Phalaropes, in which only the male incubates and broods (see p. 148). But whatever the endocrinological mechanism in a male, it probably is regulated both by the sight of (and contacts with) the eggs and the behavior of (and interactions with) his mate. Further support for such relationships derives from well-known studies of Rock Pigeons, in which the sight of the incubating female induces prolactin secretion in the male, bringing him into condition to incubate (provided that he had associated freely with the female during the periods of courtship, nest-building and oviposition, i.e., provided that his reproductive cycle was synchronized with that of the female; 1,225). Accordingly, in the course of the evolution of polyallochronic ovulation and rapid double-clutching from pre-avian antecedents, the male of a pair probably would have been primed for egg care at the time his mate completed laying the first clutch and probably would have taken over immediately the major role in its care.

[In many cases of single clutching, incubation begins with the 1st egg, sometimes, as in lovebirds, by the female. In such cases, the threshold level for stimulation of incubation by prolactin either has been lowered or the sight and contact with eggs provides sufficient supplemental stimuli to induce incubation. In other cases, more primitive relationships appear to persist, with greater attentiveness by the male during the period of oviposition, probably induced by higher levels of prolactin than in the female. For example, the Spotted Sandgrouse male begins to incubate with oviposition of the 1st egg. The female usually does not begin to incubate until the 3-egg clutch is complete, whereupon the male incubates by night and the female by day (often in temperatures exceeding 40°C). Neither parent normally leaves the nest during its period of attendance; both sit on the nest very closely and do not flush easily (1,206, 1,219).

Other examples of greater attentiveness of the male than of the female to single clutches during the period of oviposition but not during incubation are found in Wilson's Plover, in which the male's share of attentiveness is 63% during oviposition but only 30% during incubation; the Snowy Plover in Japan, in which it is 86% during oviposition but only 15-16% during incubation; and the Killdeer (*Charadrius vociferous*) in which it was about 80% during oviposition, when total attentiveness was low, but only roughly 50% during incubation (see 1,222).]

In the early stages of the evolutionary transition to rapid double-clutching, the female also would have participated in post-ovipositional egg care, just as her pre-avian antecedents did. But with achievement of rapid double-clutching, there would have been no surge in prolactin concentration after the laying of the 1st clutch from the one ovary, otherwise ovulation from the contralateral ovary would have been inhibited. This absence of a prolactinic surge probably facilitated the eventual yielding of the care of 1st clutches entirely to the males. The females themselves probably would not have been primed fully for post-ovipositional egg care until the occurrence of the prolactinic surge that terminated ovulation of the 2nd clutch.

At that time both primitive pro-avian parents would have given their clutches non-bodily-incubatory, pre-avian-type care, at first, as described above, before eventually beginning to incubate them. This progression would have left the two clutches desynchronized by an interim period of at least 2 or 3 days. Accordingly, selection would have favored males that prolonged the non-incubatory phase and/or females that shortened it, so as to bring the two clutches into synchrony. Greater flexibility on the part of the male in this regard would be consonant with the fact that his endocrinological control mechanisms would have been modulated to a great extent by his mate's behavior.

FEMALE NEED MERELY CONTINUE OVIPOSITION AT NEARBY LOCATION. The evolutionary transition to advanced pro-aves, females of which laid eggs periodically every 2-3 days by monoallochronic ovulation, follows by direct extension of the above scheme. With each additional egg of the 1st clutch that was laid, the male's tendencies for egg care would have waxed until, with completion of the 1st clutch, he would have begun to give it the full non-incubatory egg care characteristic of pre-aves, eventually followed by incubatory care. By the time the male's egg-care behavior and possessiveness of the clutch had peaked, the female need merely have continued to oviposit at a nearby (within sight) location. Again, selection would have favored pairs that synchronized their clutches by a lengthening of the pre-incubatory phase by the male and/or a shortening of it by the female.

A crucial difference in the egg-care behavior of advanced pro-avian parents from that in the primitive pro-avian stage (in which oviposition was *en masse*) is that pre-incubatory care of the eggs would have had to be practiced beginning with the 1st egg of each clutch. Thus, the very process of egg-by-egg assembly of clutches by advanced pro-aves required that the partial clutches be given the same degree of pre-avian type of egg-care that was accorded to complete clutches by primitive pro-aves during the period before their incubation of them commenced, otherwise the 1st eggs would have been susceptible to overheating or loss to predators. This practice would have involved no departure from primitive pro-avian egg care, in the sense that eggs were cared for from the time that they were laid, but it would have been a departure in the sense that the female would have had to begin caring for eggs before the occurrence of the prolactinic surge that terminated ovulation.

In the case of the male, the departure is minor on the likelihood that the sight of, and contact with, the eggs played a major role in releasing the pre-avian type of egg-care behavior. The resolution of the seemingly altered circumstances is achieved on the reasonable assumption that the sight of, and contact with, the eggs also had become one of the factors that released pre-avian egg-care behavior in females. This assumption also is fully concordant with practices in contemporary birds, where one or both parents will care for the eggs of a clutch to varying degrees before the clutch is completed, i.e., before the prolactinic surge induces the beginning of incubation.

With improved bodily insulation in the form of feather-like scales, greater powers of thermoregulation, the use of shaded nest sites, and a relatively low incubatory temperature, each single pro-avian parent would have been able to care unassistedly for one of the nests of eggs. Selection would have favored pro-avian pairs that nested within sight of one another and foraged at different times. By that means, one member could have acted as "watchdog" for the other's clutch, while the latter was absent. In the absence of a selective advantage for a pair to nest within sight of one another, that is, if a single parent were capable of caring unassistedly for a clutch of eggs and the young, one would expect selection to have favored females that simply abandoned the clutch to the attentions of the male, as do some contemporary birds in such circumstances (979; see p. 578, last paragraph).

The common departures of primitive and advanced pro-avian egg and chick care from those of pre-aves were:

1. Two clutches were oviposited in rapid succession, either *en masse* (primitive pro-aves) or 1 egg at a time (advanced pro-aves), the 1st clutch being cared for by the male and the 2nd by the female.
2. The clutches were incubated by bodily heat.
3. Employment of nest sites shaded at midday shifted the most favorable time for foraging to the period of midday heat, since at that time eggs could have been maintained close to incubatory temperatures without parental bodily heat.
4. Close parental attendance to eggs and young extended through the night period.
5. Young chicks were warmed in addition to being groomed, protected, and escorted.

If the pattern of pre-incubatory egg care were as described above, it would have been non-adaptive for an advanced pro-avian hen assembling a 2nd clutch, and with only one or a few eggs, to leave the egg(s) and take over the clutch of her mate during one of the periods of the latter's absence while foraging. Such behavior would have greatly increased the time of absenteeism from the egg(s) of the 2nd clutch, and would have been selected against. In other words, selection would have favored advanced pro-avian hens that were steadfast in the care of their 2nd clutches, no matter how few eggs they might have contained, at times when their mates were absent from the 1st clutches.

IMPLICATIONS OF BEING 'CONTENT' WITH ONE EGG. One may be seeing a relic of this behavior in Cockatiels. As noted in Part 2, brooding Cockatiels returning to the NB (nestbox) become agitated, and initiate a frantic search, if an entire clutch is missing. But as long as at least one egg remains, they behave perfectly normally, showing no difference in their response to that when the entire clutch is present. The same phenomenon was shown by the hen, Helena, when she would not crouch over eggs in a location other than at the site of oviposition, and was 'content' to relocate and crouch over only one of the 4 eggs of the clutch (see pp. 498-502). As will be seen in Chapter 6, Parts 2 and 3, the presence or recovery of only one egg of a missing clutch also is sufficient to 'satisfy' the incubating urges of lovebirds and Budgerigars.

ADAPTIVE FOR ADVANCED PRO-AVES, ADAPTIVELY NEUTRAL FOR DESCENDANTS. Being 'content' with one egg is not maladaptive for birds that use hole nests, because eggs are unlikely to become lost or buried in such locations. Nor would being 'content' with one egg have been maladaptive for ancestral birds nesting in simple scrapes, because Cockatielian (and lovebird) behavior suggests that their ancestors routinely searched for errant, buried eggs. Accordingly, the trait of being 'content' with only one egg would have been adaptive for advanced pro-aves but would have been adaptively neutral for ancestral birds and their hole-nesting descendants. That, and the conservativeness of the evolution of egg-care practices (and of their underlying neural circuitry; see pp. 379-385, 522-529), would explain the retention of this trait as one of the suite of primitive egg-care habits of the birds of this study, and probably of many other birds.

RAPID DOUBLE-CLUTCHING NOT ADAPTIVE FOR ANCESTRAL BIRDS

COOLER OR LESS EQUABLE REGIMES FAVORED SINGLE CLUTCHING. It will be evident that this scheme for rapid double-clutching also provides a mechanism for evolution to a stage in which both members of a pair share in the incubation and other care of a single clutch, as is believed to have been the mode of clutch care by ancestral birds (see Table 3 and pp. 371-376). A facilitating factor for this transition might have been the change from semi-tropical and tropical, equable climates of the Jurassic period to the global cooling of the last 15 million yr of the Cretaceous period (with a decline of about 5°C from Santonian to Maastrichtian, and a lowering of sea level and increased seasonality in the late Maastrichtian; 82, 182, 413, 739, 1,154). However, a change to incubating single clutches cooperatively also would have been favored in any population that colonized more temperate regions.

[Growth rings in fossil wood indicate that seasonal climates were restricted to very high paleolatitudes during the Jurassic period, but were more marked as far south as 55° N paleolatitude in the late Cretaceous period (409). A larger thermal gradient existed between the poles and the equator during the Cretaceous than in the Triassic or Jurassic periods. Although the end of the late Cretaceous (early Maastrichtian) apparently was marked by considerable warmth, cooler climates (though warmer than today) of the late Cretaceous (middle Maastrichtian) initiated a broad decline in equability that continued until the Pleistocene glaciations, notwithstanding late Maastrichtian warming (and relatively moist conditions) that continued into the Cenozoic era culminating in the early Eocene epoch (50-54 mya) with the warmest interval of the entire Cenozoic. The late Jurassic also was marked by a return to greater aridity, as indicated by several sedimentological factors, including an increase in the distribution of evaporite deposits--the late Jurassic through the early Cretaceous being an evaporite maximum period (see 413, 789, 972, 1,343).]

BODY TEMPERATURE ALSO WAS INCREASING PROGRESSIVELY with the evolutionary progression to a more advanced stage of endothermy. This factor, alone, might account for the evolution of shared parental care of single clutches. At any rate, the time eventually came when single advanced pro-avian parents no longer could assure the maintenance of a constant high temperature of clutches in surface locations, whereupon rapid double-clutching no longer would have been adaptive. From that time on, pairs that cooperated in the incubation and care of single clutches would have had greater reproductive success than those that did not.

SUGGESTIVE BEHAVIOR IN CONTEMPORARY VERTEBRATES

At one extreme of reptilian behavior, with but few exceptions, parental care of any kind is unknown in chelonians, which are considered to belong to the oldest surviving reptilian group (602). The sole known possible exceptions (unconfirmed and viewed with much skepticism by herpetologists) concern the females of 2 species of Bahamian turtles (*Pseudemys felis* and *P. malonei*) which are reported to dig the hard-packed earth from over their nests when it is time for the young to emerge. Young not aided under such conditions may have to estivate for long periods, possibly even an entire year, until conditions permit unaided emergence (688). There are only a few exceptional cases in which living oviparous reptiles incubate their eggs, but parental care of hatchlings and nestlings is found in some groups. Like almost all chelonians, "The majority of species....abandon their eggs to a predatory world and leave them to be hatched by the heat of the environment" (336; see also 720). In such cases the juveniles begin to interact independently with other animals soon after hatching (408).

Crocodilian Parental Care

ADULT-YOUNG NURSERIES. Virtually all the steps that may have been involved in the transition from stem-reptiles to pre-aves to primitive pro-aves, and on, are known to occur in extant birds or reptiles. In fact, the best-developed and most spectacular reptilian care of eggs and young is found in birds' closest living reptilian relatives, the crocodilians, in all of which such care probably occurs (602). Thus, it is deserving of close attention. Crocodilians (26 living species) are the descendants of a relatively conservative lineage that arose from thecodontian ancestors approximately 230 mya (see 759).

Predation between and within crocodilian species is common, even characteristic, and causes the habitat boundaries between species to be sharp, the degree of sympatry to be low, and selection by combat and its avoidance to be strong (see 1,095). Males contest for dominance and establish systematically patrolled mating territories. After a lengthy courtship (6-8 weeks; 680, 721) and nest-site selection, the females engage in nocturnal preparation of elaborate nests (mounds, alone, in 20 of the 26 species; 759) over periods spanning as long as 3 days in some species. The dominant larger females of the social hierarchy are the first to mate, copulate, and oviposit.

The interval between insemination and oviposition is 3-4 weeks in the American Alligator. In some species the females return to the same nest sites year after year, resting at them and defending them against the approach of other females until the time of oviposition (665, 680). Nests and nursery sites generally are well spaced by American Alligators. Female Nile Crocodiles "fought to the death" at one nesting area but communal nesting was documented at two other sites (1,095). Nests almost always are near water, shaded by foliage, frequently in deep shade where the sun cannot reach them. Those of some species, for example, the American Alligator, often are at the base of a tree (659).

NEST CONSTRUCTION AND OVIPOSITION. Depending upon the species and substrate availability, the nest may be sited in decaying vegetation, earth, or sand, or mixtures thereof. The female scrapes dirt and ground debris, or whatever material is available, together by lateral movements of her body and tail. Then she shapes and packs the nesting mound by crawling over and around it, pushing against it with her flanks, and scraping and pushing nest material with her hind feet. The hind feet also are used to scoop out a roughly 61-cm-deep nest cavity in the top of the mound with remarkable dexterity, after the nest has had time to settle properly. The hind feet also are used to manipulate and arrange the eggs while ovipositing--well above ground level in many cases--to a depth of about 30 cm, and to lower them and round off the completed nest (658, 659). Oviposition occurs at night or in the early morning. Three to 15% of the eggs become cracked in the process but develop normally if the shell membranes are not torn (759).

Nile Crocodiles average about 55-60 eggs per nest, American Alligators about 30-39 eggs (658, 659, 759). In the nests of Nile Crocodiles examined by Pooley in Zululand, the eggs almost invariably were arranged in 3 layers separated by loose soil; some other species oviposit in only 2 tiers, separated by sand or soil (see 685). In many cases the fermentation of vegetation included in these nests raises the nest temperature (averaging 28-32°C, depending upon the species) 1-5°C above mean air temperature and plays an important role in shortening the period of embryogenesis (750).

The decomposition of nest material may be enhanced by the presence of urine, voided by the female during and after nest construction (759). The hole nests of *C. acutus*, for example, become progressively warmer as incubation proceeds. In other nests, only climatic heat and metabolic heat from the developing embryos are responsible for incubation. The incubatory period in Nile Crocodiles is about 12-14 weeks (90, 659, 680, 759). Communal breeding sites are not uncommon (659, 685). [The broad-nosed group of crocodilians--having the "combat-ready design"--comprising mainly alligators, crocodylines, and caimans, is the only evolutionarily relatively stable group and has been the central core in crocodilian evolution, able to innovate on many levels (1,095).]

NEST GUARDING. It has been confirmed in virtually all species that the female remains in the close vicinity of, or immediately adjacent to, the nest, night and day throughout the incubatory period. She nearly constantly guards a fairly large territory around it by charging predators and intruders, even Man. The Nile Crocodile, for example, is frequently called upon to defend the nest against Marabou Storks (*Leptoptilos crumeniferus*) and Nile Monitors (*Varanus niloticus*; 1,016). The latter is the most successful predator on the nests of Nile Crocodiles (685), but female conspecifics also raid nests (1,095). A damaged or raided nest never is repaired or restored (685).

Sometimes the female rests her throat directly above the nest. At intervals she visits the water and then drips water on the nest from her wet body, or splashes water over it with her tail. The embryos can tolerate extremely low partial pressures of oxygen and are very resistant to increased levels of carbon dioxide (759). In some species, for example the Nile Crocodile, the female is known to fast during the incubatory period (94, 680, 685, 717). The male Nile Crocodile also remains in the general vicinity of the nest but does not approach it closely and goes off at intervals to hunt (680). Crocodilians, particularly alligators, cannot tolerate direct sunlight for long; their sites of vigil usually are shaded (659; as are the nest sites).

VOCALIZATIONS AND CARE OF YOUNG. The eggs generally hatch during a period of seasonally high water. Both near-term and hatching young of all species begin to call by squeaking or chirping loudly from the buried nest. In response to vibrations or sounds on or near the nest surface, the hatchlings call collectively, the sounds of each apparently reinforcing the others. Vocalization apparently occurs even within the fluid environment of the egg (presumably in the presence of air spaces). Nile Crocodilian chirping of young can be heard through the overlying soil at a distance as great as 20 m (see 721). Adults also communicate vocally with the young (659, 680).

Females of many species (*Crocodylus acutus*, *C. moreleti*, *C. niloticus*, *C. novaequineae*, *Caiman crocodilus*, *Alligator mississippiensis*) are known to respond to the calls of the embryos or hatchlings by opening the nests to facilitate the emergence of the hatching young (90, 91, 639, 658, 665, 680, 684, 717). They achieve this by excavating with their forelimbs and scraping and biting with their jaws (680, 717). In the case of Caimans, confined males have been reported to open the nest (see 717).

In many cases the opening of the nest is essential because of the hardened or close-packed surface material, in others it appears that the young are able to emerge without assistance (659, 665). Both males and females are known to assist the hatching of the young by breaking open the eggs between their teeth (665) or between the tongue and the palate (680). After the nest is opened and the young have emerged, the female picks up the hatchlings one by one--recovering any vocalizing strays--and carries them to the water, where they are released. This has been photographed in *C. acutus* and observed in 4 other species (see 684, 717), and the behavior also is available to the male (680, 717).

Both Nile Crocodilian parents--themselves much addicted to cannibalism (adults on subadults, and subadults on juveniles; 1,095)--remain near the crèche and defend the young against predators and other crocodiles for as long as 8 weeks, at which time the young usually disperse (680). Parental behavior is complex in all investigated species and may even include provisioning the young by the female (see 1,095). The female American Alligator is said to scoop out a wallowing pool for the young and protect them from predators. The young may remain with her for as long as 2 yr (see 91, 1,095, and G.R.M. Meyer, 1977, in 602). In all species studied, all adult crocodilians, not merely the parents, exhibit a high degree of protective behavior toward young in distress. In response to the loud, repetitive distress calls they come charging to the rescue and attack, even leaving the water to do so (659, 680, 721). Hide hunters take advantage of this behavior to lure adults by using juvenile distress calls (1,095).

SOME SNAKES GUARD AND/OR WARM THEIR EGGS. Females of several ophidian species--cobras, pythons, American Mud Snakes (*Farancia abacura*)--coil about their developing eggs. An incubating female Indian Pythons (*Python molurus*) is able to raise her body temperature over 7.3°C above ambient air temperature for many days. Thermogenesis results from intermittent spasmodic contractions of the bodily musculature (90, 91, 93). The egg temperature is kept at approximately 30°C. "This pattern of endothermy....is the most striking and incontrovertible instance of physiological temperature control available for any member of the class Reptilia....and can reasonably be characterized as physiological thermoregulation" (361). The metabolic rate of incubating Indian Python females at an ambient temperature of 23°C is about 20 times that after incubation has ceased.

A confined Indian Cobra (*N. naja*) oviposited in a nest chamber constructed with the aid of her mate. She remained in the chamber and guarded the eggs throughout the incubatory period. But she left daily for 1 or 2 h and ate, drank, and rested. In her absence, her mate kept guard over the eggs (90). Males of other species also are known to guard the eggs (see M.A. Smith, 1943, in 602). [Some lizards, such as members of the genera *Amphibolurus*, *Tiliqua*, and *Varanus*, also are, to some slight extent, endothermic. Within limits, they can regulate the amount of heat that they produce within their bodies (91, 361).] Newborn vipers (*Vipera berus*) remain with their mother for a few days after hatching (see 602).

SKINK EGG CARE. All female skinks of the genus, *Eumeces*, are either oviparous and attend their eggs or are viviparous and live at high elevations (see 1,347). The oviparous species oviposit in nest chambers in various secluded locations, such as underground, under logs or rocks, and in rotted areas of hardwood trees or logs (usually *Quercus virginianus*) under bark or under relatively thin surface strips of wood (1,347). The females of some species are said to enter their nests periodically and brood the eggs by coiling around or curving their bodies among them (90, 91). Presumably, the eggs gain heat from the sun-warmed body of the parent. In recent field studies of *E. laticeps*, *E. faciatus*, and *E. inexpectatus*, the females were found to attend their clutches virtually continuously until hatching, usually coiled around the eggs, and rarely were seen at the surface (1,347).

The females protect their eggs from mice and other small predators that approach the nest, and similar behavior is known in members of 3 other genera. A female also regathers the clutch if it becomes scattered or displaced (also true of some species of *Lacerta* and *Calotes versicolor*; see 938), sometimes preparing a new nest and moving the eggs or reconstructing an old nest (1,347). *E. laticeps* and *E. fasciatus* females even appropriate eggs from the nearby nests of other individuals (90). In the laboratory, females leave the nest on a regular basis to feed, and all eggs within given clutches (9-18 eggs) of *E. laticeps* hatched on the same day (1,347). *E. obsoletus* females turn and roll the eggs daily, help partly-hatched young escape from the egg shell by rubbing their bodies against those of the young as they emerge, insure undisturbed feeding conditions for the young, and groom them (including licking the cloacal region) for at least 10 days (90, 875); young remained with the mother for 16 days after hatching in the laboratory (see 602).

Females of *E. fasciatus* appear to regulate nest moisture by digging up moist substrate beneath the eggs, by moving the eggs to a more suitably moist site, or by voiding onto the nest (see 938). Females of the viviparous Desert Night Lizard grasp and rupture the extra-embryonic membranes surrounding the newborn young with their teeth, swallow these membranes, and sometimes seize the young, which emerge with the tail and hind limbs in advance, and draw them out (875). Though almost all of these examples involve maternal care, it is well established that most vertebrate motor patterns of breeding behavior of one sex also can be performed by the other sex (3, 67).

[ANURAN PARENTAL CARE occurs in roughly 10% of all species, and is of passing interest, inasmuch as all of it probably also traces ultimately to predator pressures. Egg attendance is the most common form of parental behavior, occurring in at least 12 families (601, 606). Male *Hyla rosenbergi* (Hylidae) guard mud nests against conspecifics (but only when population density is high), while female *Leptodactylus ocellatus* (Leptodactylidae) guard eggs against predators in a foam nest at the water surface (see 606). Some dendrobatids of both sexes remain with eggs until they hatch and then carry the tadpoles to water, but they may or may not care for the eggs. Transport of tadpoles on the back has been reported in 3 families. In other cases the tadpoles are transported in the male vocal sac or in inguinal brood pouches and subsequently released as completely, or nearly completely, formed froglets.

The male of at least some species of *Centrolenna* (Centrolennidae) is territorial and the eggs are deposited at his calling site; they must receive at least some benefit, if only as a by-product of his territoriality.

Males of *Phyllobates* desert the eggs for a week after fertilizing them. During the 2nd week the male visits them once daily for about 5 min. During the 3rd week he visits them 3 times daily. After hatching, the tadpoles climb onto his back and are transported to water (see 606, 875, 979). Attendance to tadpoles is rare but the female *L. ocellatus* follows the school of her tadpoles for some time after hatching, and the African ranid, *Pyxucephalus adspersus*, has been reported to guard tadpoles from predators (606).]

DOUBLE AND MULTIPLE CLUTCHING. In some shorebirds and galliforms the female may oviposit in rapid succession a first clutch that is incubated solely by the male and a 2nd clutch fertilized by the same or another male (sequential polyandry) that she herself promptly incubates; some overlapping in the oviposition of the clutches is not ruled out in some species. Temminck's Stint (*Calidris temminckii*) produces the 2nd clutch only 2-4 days (the shortest known interval) after the 1st and may produce 8 eggs for the 2 clutches in as few as 10 days (the ancestral Charadrii clutch number is thought to be 4; 962). Each parent usually takes sole responsibility for its clutch and brood. It would appear that if the 2nd clutch is lost, it is the female who incubates the 1st one, just as is the case if no 2nd clutch is oviposited (825). Among others, this breeding system occurs in European Red-legged Partridges (*Alectoris rufa*), Temminck's Stint, Sanderlings, Mountain Plovers (*Charadrius montanus*), and Scaled Quail (*Callipepla squamata*; 101, 431, 825, 962, 979, 1,266).

[Polygamy is somewhat more prevalent in birds with nidifugous as opposed to nidicolous young (34), but many of the former species are promiscuous rather than polygynous. Polyandry is sufficiently unusual that virtually any mating system in which a female pairs with more than one male during a single breeding season has been so termed, regardless of whether the males also pair with more than 1 female (1,266; otherwise referred to as polygyny-polyandry; 1,316). Strictly speaking, however, cases in which the females do not monopolize multiple mates, as they do in Red-legged Partridges (see below), should be excluded from the classification "polyandrous" (1,323).]

In the first 3 cases mentioned above, the males apparently can delay incubation and leave the 1st clutch unincubated (the equivalent of a pre-avian, pre-incubatory phase) for 6-12 days while continuing to court additional females and fertilize a 2nd clutch (sequential polygyny), a practice that promotes and often leads to hatching synchrony within the 2 nests. The female, on the other hand, may even exploit 2 incubating males, while going on to oviposit a 3rd clutch which she then incubates (431, 962). Eurasian Dotterel hens (*Eudromias morinellus*) may share the incubation of the 2nd clutch with the 2nd mate (see 962). In the case of Red-legged Partridges, at least, pairs remain in consort (interpreted as mate guarding) during the oviposition of both clutches. In consequence, it appears that on the average incubation begins at the same time in both nests, but there is considerable individual variation and discrepancies of up to 10 days (825).

If the female forms a persistent pair bond with one male, both clutches are located within the male's territory, but if not, they are located in different territories, usually more than 100 m apart for Temminck's Stint (962). In no species, except perhaps in the simultaneously polyandrous American Jacana, has the employed mating system reached perfection; various exceptions to the normal schedule are common and individual differences in breeding behavior exist (see 962).

Also of interest in this connection are cases of sequential polyandry in which the hen oviposits in rapid succession the 1st set of eggs on one nest for a 1st mate (beginning 10-13 days after mating) and then oviposits a 2nd clutch on another nest for a 2nd mate (see 273, 431). The Spotted Sandpiper (*Tringa macularia*) hen may provide clutches for up to 4 males in succession, and shares in the care of at least the last clutch and brood. Essentially all clutches lost to predators up to a certain point in the season are replaced. The normal role for females helping with the chicks is one of warning, of distracting, and of attacking potential predators (see 837, 964, 979, 1,323). Multiple clutching probably is more common than is realized, especially among shorebirds. It also may prove to be common among phasianids; males of a number of species sometimes incubate and/or brood young without female participation (431).

RAPID DOUBLE-CLUTCH OR MULTIPLE-CLUTCH MONOGAMY has been regarded as a derived, relatively new, and extreme form of breeding strategy, not sufficiently advantageous to all species to become prevalent (841, 962, 963). While the present treatment does not dispute an origin of this form of reproduction from the single-clutch monogamy and shared parental responsibilities of "ancestral birds," it suggests that rapid double-clutch monogamy was the most primitive form of reproduction practiced by the endothermic avian ancestors that preceded the ancestral-bird stage of Table 3 (the postulated practice of both primitive and advanced pro-aves).

[Monogamy itself is thought to be selected for only when conditions that favor alternative mating systems are not met. It is suggested that 3 preconditions must obtain before monogamy can evolve: (1) females must obtain benefits from monogamous pair bonds that otherwise are not obtainable; (2) females must be able to ascertain the true mated status of potential mates; and (3) mates do not desert (1,258).]

On the other hand, the ectothermic, stem-reptilian ancestors of birds are regarded as having practiced single-clutch monogamy, and the following ectothermic pre-avian ancestors as having practiced sequential multiple-clutch monogamy. It is suggested that single-clutch monogamy by endothermic avian ancestors became the practice only in the much later "ancestral-bird" stage. At that time body temperatures had achieved levels comparable to those of less advanced contemporary birds (see Table 3), and the consequent need for higher incubatory temperatures probably required the participation of both parents in egg care.

THE SELECTIVE ADVANTAGE OF RAPID MULTIPLE-CLUTCHING is seen as an increase in reproductive potential, but this tends to be counteracted by the loosening of pair bonds (which last only over the period of oviposition), increased losses of eggs and young because of the lesser care that can be rendered by a single parent, and increased demands on the hen in the production of more than one clutch. The distribution, amount, and dependability of food during the critical period of oviposition are thought to be decisive factors: thus, rapid multiple-clutching is found only in those species or populations that occupy very productive habitats with abundant food supplies (such as is believed to have been the case in the times of pro-aves). High predation rates also have intensified selection for multiple clutching (962-964).

It is suggested that the absence of multiple clutching in potentially qualified species derives from an opposite selective pressure towards the persistent pair bond, once the latter has developed beyond a certain strength, because the necessary "intermediate stages," that is, with looser pair bonds and weaker incubatory drive, are not favored by natural selection (963).

DIVIDING THE BROOD OF FLEDGLINGS. Many birds merely divide the care of the brood of fledglings between the two parents (101). In species with nidicolous young, in which only 3 cases of the foregoing are known, this may allow more carefully regulated parental allofeeding of the young and a finer control over the timing of offspring independence. The practice is quite widespread and may be common in species with nidifugous hatchlings and biparental care, perhaps most noteworthy in large species that nest close to, or on, the ground; it helps to reduce predation of entire broods and to improve the foraging efficiencies of the parents (see 807, 1,104).

COVERING THE EGGS WITH VARIOUS MATERIALS. Ground-nesting birds use their bills or feet to cover the eggs with down, dry earth, grass, sand, wet vegetation, and other materials. Among the Charadrii, it is a tropical to subtropical phenomenon that occurs in at least 13 species in 4 families (Jacanidae, Glareolidae, Charadriidae, and Thinocoridae). It is most widely developed in members of the genus *Charadrius* (see review by Maclean; 328). In some species, complete burial occurs only before the clutch is complete, that is, during the period when absences are lengthy. It is well known among waterfowl and is a worldwide phenomenon in the grebes (Podicipedidae) and many members of the Anatidae. Some tinamous cover their eggs with leaves or feathers when they leave the nest (see 328). Egyptian Plover chicks commonly hatch in eggs that are covered, or almost completely covered, with soaking-wet sand (230).

Many forest-dwelling birds sometimes rake over the ground litter to a considerable depth, determined by the lengths of their legs and bills. Examples of arid-zone birds that cover the eggs with nesting material while the parent is absent, are the Australian Dotterel and several seedsnipes (158, 328). The Australian Dotterel apparently covers its eggs and leaves them for long periods in warm weather, but incubates them in cool weather. Females of the Least and D'Orbigny Seedsnipes (*Thinocorus rumicivorus* and *T. orbignyianus*, respectively) cover their eggs and nestlings by kicking loose material over them whenever they vacate the nest. They use exactly the same foot movements as do Kittlitz's Sandplovers (*Charadrius pecuarius*; 328). Even birds that breed in holes and burrows, such as titmice, the Pygmy Nuthatch (*Sitta pygmaea*), and the Masked Tityra (*Tityra semifasciata*), sometimes bury their eggs under nest materials (101).

COVERING AND UNCOVERING EGGS BY KICKING SAND. Kittlitz's Sandplover often nests in a mere lined scrape in the sand. Its management procedure on human intrusion is most interesting. While rotating in the scrape, usually clockwise, it buries the eggs (and any young chicks that are present) by rapidly kicking sand in from the periphery to the center. The operation usually requires only a few sec. On returning, it locates the eggs by probing and tossing aside material with its bill and then kicks the sand backward off of them as it pivots on its breast (28, 101, 328). Sometimes nestlings are buried in the same manner, but usually with their heads exposed. Some observations suggest that the egg-covering response is released, at least in part, by the sight of exposed eggs and is manifested only when the drive to incubate is strong. Thus, egg burying may not begin until after the 2nd egg is oviposited (see 328). [Digging a nest and manipulating eggs with the hindfeet may be an exceedingly ancient behavior pattern, antedating even the rise of the thecodonts (659).]

[In this connection, whereas Cockatiels and Peach-faced Lovebirds typically use primarily the bill (and head) for resurfacing eggs and exploring and excavating in shavings, Budgerigars use both the bill and the feet (see p. 777, **Scattering Shavings**). They use only the bill in searching for eggs, but when exploring and preparing a nest, they often use the feet to dig rapidly and vigorously "down to bedrock" through a layer of shavings, scattering them far and wide in the NB. It was not until I gave lovebirds roughly hemispherical 14-cm-diameter glass bowls for nesting that I observed some of the hens using their feet and legs to excavate. Before ovipositing, they often emptied their bowls of shavings (every time I replenished them) by grasping the rims of the bowls with their bills and kicking backward rapidly and vigorously in alternation. I also occasionally observed such actions by lovebird hens on enclosure floors. In all cases, they held themselves fixed and steady by grasping objects with their bills while kicking.]

UTILIZING SOLAR RADIATION BY DAY AND BODILY HEAT BY NIGHT. White-fronted Sandplovers (*Charadrius maginatus*) and Egyptian Plovers (Cursoriinae) also cover their eggs with sand (to a depth of 2-3 mm in the latter case) by day and utilize solar heat; they partly uncover them (by about 2/3rds for Egyptian Plovers) and incubate them continually only at night (230, 328). The Egyptian Plover also covers the chicks, even when they are 3 weeks old (230).

During the day the Egyptian Plovers alternate on the nest and may sometimes achieve contact between the eggs and the broodpatch by scraping away sand with the feet while sitting. When the nest is vacated without relief, the eggs are re-covered by quickly throwing sand over the site with the bill. There usually is a period of 1-2 h in the early morning and 1-3 h straddling sunset when ambient temperatures are sufficiently moderate (within the normal limits for incubation) that the covered eggs are largely or completely unattended (230). In the event of heat in excess of that alleviated by shading the eggs (and chicks), the parents transport large quantities of water (at a temperature no higher than 27-28°C) to the eggs in the soaked ventral plumage (28, 230, 328). The eggs of Egyptian Plovers have to be wetted every few min and maintained in soaking-wet sand for as long as 6 h over the midday periods, when ambient shade temperatures may attain as high as 46°C. On cool, cloudy days no wetting of the eggs occurs, but the adults attend them continually, sometimes adjusting the sand cover with the bill, sometimes sitting on them quietly, and sometimes settling low and removing sand with the feet (230).

Crowned Lapwing (*Vanellus coronatus*) eggs exposed to full insolation regularly are buried half-way in sand during the ovipositional phase. The protection from overheating so provided has been confirmed by temperature measurements (60). [At a time when the exposed surface temperature in a desert was 56½°C, the temperature in full shade was only 32°C (155).]

ADVANCED PRO-AVES---IN THE AIR BETWEEN "TREES"

Accordingly, almost all the pieces in the puzzle of the transition from the presumed stem-reptilian egg care to pro-avian incubatory patterns are known in living vertebrates. Only the details of the historical transitions need to be filled in. To account for the next step in the evolution of birds, one must explain the evolutionary transition from the feather-facilitated, ground-to-ground and tree-to-ground jumping and parachuting primitive pro-avis to the gliding and low-speed, low-amplitude wing-flapping advanced pro-avis. In other words, one has to ascertain the reproductive advantages that could have accrued to those primitive pro-aves that made use of, and further developed, their feather-like scaled condition and higher rate of metabolism in the invasion of aerial habitats.

[In U. Norberg's (977 1,201) aerodynamic model of the evolution of avian flight, flapping frequency is rather constant, irrespective of flapping speed. An advanced pro-avis would have had to attain a particular flapping frequency (perhaps less than 2 Hz) in order to obtain the thrust and lift necessary to balance bodily weight, but even very small flapping speeds and amplitudes might have sufficed. In a contemporary bird, such as the Rock Pigeon the flapping frequency is 9.4 Hz at takeoff and 5.4 Hz at a flight speed of 12 m/sec, and the swept angles are 142° and 85°, respectively (see 1,003).]

THE ADVANTAGES OF BEING A BIRD. Suppose we consider first the advantages of being a bird. These are portrayed as follows (28). "The power of flight has opened up to birds an enormous gaseous ocean, as a means of quick, direct access to almost any spot on earth....they occupy and exploit a greater range of habitats....birds can eat in almost any 'restaurant'....they can choose to build their homes anywhere...frequently beyond the reach of predators." These capabilities unquestionably confer reproductive advantages on birds, but they do not apply to advanced pro-aves, inasmuch as the latter were incapable of sustained powered flight. Returning to our immediate interest, what were the reproductive advantages of being an advanced pro-avis? Why evolve into an advanced pro-avis, rather than remain in the primitive condition?

ADVANCED PRO-AVES ADAPTED FOR AERIAL ACTIVITY BETWEEN "TREES." As a preliminary to answering this question, let us consider first the properties of advanced pro-aves. These creatures were specialized for activities in aerial habitats within and between trees and shrubs. They could jump and glide between branches, they could jump and parachute to the ground, and they could move from tree to tree by gliding and by low-amplitude, low-speed, wing-flapping flight. Inasmuch as the body temperature of advanced pro-aves is postulated to have exceeded the primitive mammalian grade by only a few degrees (Table 3), it would have been sufficient to sustain the level of muscle physiology needed for maneuvered gliding and low-amplitude, low-speed, wing-flapping flight, but insufficient to achieve even short periods of vigorous, high-amplitude, wing-flapping flight. In other words, advanced pro-aves were superbly adapted for the exploitation of aerial habitats in the vicinity of and between trees.

LARGE FLYING INSECTS WERE THE ATTRACTION IN AERIAL HABITATS. One advantage of being able to become airborne in these spaces obviously is greater facility for escape from predators, but that is not the one that concerns us here. Numerous species of small reptiles that have taken to the trees managed to solve that problem without the development of flight. Anyone familiar with the tremendous escape agility of partly-to-largely arboreal, even fairly large (35-50-cm long) lizards (for example, species in the genera *Enyalioides*, *Physignathus*, and *Basiliscus*) in the foliage of trees and shrubs (659) would find it difficult to conceive of their being vulnerable to predators other than one another in such surroundings.

Only the partly aquatic medium-sized-to-large members of these genera often jump from trees into water (from a height of up to 4½ m). None escapes by jumping to the ground (659). The much smaller anoles also prefer to remain in the vegetation and will jump 60 cm or more from branch to branch. They usually jump to lower-lying brush but sometimes they jump to the ground (659, 868).

The question of concern here is, "what was there to be exploited in the air itself?" The answer, of course, has to be, "that greatly abundant, rich, almost-untapped source of animal proteins, the large flying insects" (see note below), of which members of the orders Coleoptera, Diptera, Hemiptera, Hymenoptera, Mecoptera, Neuroptera, Orthoptera, and Trichoptera, at least, were present during the middle Mesozoic era (768). While on the wing (except near the ground) and preceding the appearance of early avian ancestors, these insects were scarcely touched by predators other than each other, save probably for small, non-piscivorous pterosaurs, some of which were sparrow-sized (e.g., *Anurognathus*; see 413, 640, 1,248, and p. 586). An increasing reliance on arthropodan prey by early avian ancestors is consistent with their undoubted progressive size reduction (see pp. 624-627), as prey size correlates positively with predator size among vertebrate carnivores (see 1,046).

[The development of nocturnalism in many insects, which preceded reptiles and birds in the air in the Devonian or early Carboniferous (Mississippian) period by at least 150 million yr (78, 86, 1,334), may, in fact, have been primarily an adaptive response to a greatly increased selective pressure consequent upon predation by birds (782). The presence of crepuscular and nocturnal flying insects, in turn, may account for the development of flight in the ancestors of bats, some of which (the ancestors of pteropodids) apparently employed optical sensing but the majority of which probably developed or inherited acoustic sensing. Competition between paleocene primates and primitive bats also has been suggested as one of the initial selective pressures for chiropteran flight (1,339). The time of origin of chiropteran flight is unknown, although the evidence that it originated from arboreal gliding appears to be overwhelming (see 1,200).

Recent evidence of an advanced retinotectal pathway in megachiropteran fruit bats (but not members of the Microchiroptera), together with other complex details of organization of the visual system as well as more advanced encephalization and neocorticalization, link the former group with ancestral primates (see p. 356) and suggest that flight evolved independently in the Megachiroptera and Microchiroptera (1,210, 1,216). Even on other grounds, the former group had been thought to have diverged from other bats very early in the history of the order (1,216). The earliest chiropteran fossils (Microchiroptera) date from the early Eocene epoch (782). The microchiropterans are suggested to be a monophyletic group with a common ancestor in the Paleocene epoch or perhaps the late Cretaceous period; the earliest megachiropteran fossils are present in Oligocene deposits of Northern Italy (1,217).]

LARGE FLYING INSECTS---A FERTILE, LITTLE-EXPLOITED RESOURCE. The primitive pro-aves that went on to evolve the ability to glide and wing-flap at low amplitude (but with only moderate lift capability), thereby achieving the level of advanced pro-aves, had the very significant reproductive advantage of being able to exploit more fully the enormously fertile, but otherwise very little tapped resource of large flying insects.

In this connection, it is "almost" certain that *Archaeopteryx* was insectivorous (69, 308, 309, 1,019), based partly on its possession of moderately-to-very-sharp (enamel-tipped), stout, peg-like, conical teeth. Such teeth generally are regarded as being adapted for piercing and crushing prey that are swallowed whole. These teeth are especially well preserved in the recent Eichstätt specimen (see 70, 75, 1,179, 1,208). Lizards as a rule also swallow their prey whole, after making a few chewing or crushing movements of the jaws (875). [It is of interest in this regard, and supportive of the above thesis, that the teeth induced in domestic chick mandibular-arch epithelium by mouse dentary mesenchyme in tissue culture are of this simple conical type (304).]

EVOLUTIONARY DERIVATION OF THE DENTITION. Howgate (1,208) suggests that the Eichstätt and Berlin specimens of *Archaeopteryx* represent two stages along the route from an obligate carnivore to an obligate insectivore. The original tooth style would have been that common to theropods and pseudosuchian thecodonts, in which the teeth were moderately recurved and serrated, suited to cutting prey into manageable pieces. Next would have been a stage with *Campsognathus*-like dentition in which all the teeth are strongly recurved and there is a fang-like development of the most anterior teeth, designed to force whole prey down the throat.

This would have been followed by a stage corresponding to that seen in the Eichstätt specimen, which Howgate regards as a different species of *Archaeopteryx* from the other specimens (a poorer flier and more cursorial). The teeth were stouter and subcylindrical, but with short points and distinctly recurved, suggesting a facultative "whole-body" carnivore becoming adapted to a more insectivorous diet. The final stage corresponds to the condition of the teeth in the Berlin and London specimens. The teeth are peg-like, with bluntly conical tips. They occlude one another, producing steep wear facets, and appear to be adapted to crushing and slicing up insects, but no longer adapted to ingest whole, large prey.

PRO-AVES AND *ARCHAEOPTERYX*, OBLIGATE PREDATORS. It is tacit in this sketch of pro-avian evolution that the animals were obligate predators, although fruits and berries may have been included in the diet. It seems highly unlikely that any arboreal reptile that was able to subsist on plant material alone would have evolved to a pro-avis and, thence, to a bird. Whence would have come the selective pressure for flight adaptations? Herbivores tend to be predator limited, rather than food limited (95, 1,037). They are expected to live in an environment that always is favorable with respect to resources (1,032), and plant food must have been exceptionally abundant during the Jurassic period (1,301).

Moreover, the Hoatzin, which is a folivore, has almost lost the ability for powered flight (1,296), suggesting the inferiority of an herbivorous diet lacking in seeds or fruits for generating and maintaining a metabolism capable of supporting flight. Most significant in this regard is the inferiority of all gymnospermous organs as sources of nutrition for animals, taking into account the fact that gymnosperms were the dominant flora prior to the late Cretaceous period (1,254, 1,296 and below). [Plant food generally is two orders of magnitude more abundant than animal food (408).] The only selective pressure that might have led to adaptations of herbivores for an aerial niche would have been for escape by jumping, parachuting, and gliding.

DEVELOPMENT OF POWERED FLIGHT LIKELY ONLY IN OBLIGATE PREDATORS. Only for pro-aves that were obligate or near-obligate predators would selective pressures engendered by intra- and interspecific competition likely have been strong enough to lead to the development of powered flight. Indeed, a strong case has been made for *Archaeopteryx* having been an obligate predator (69, 70), and, of course, the theropods (which include coelurosaurs) were predators (169).

Moreover, fruits--few of which were present in Jurassic times--are an inferior source of food for birds, particularly during the period of egg production (34, 314), and protein-rich food is a necessity for rapidly-growing nestlings, at least before the development of their endothermic capabilities. Thus, most frugivorous birds feed insects to their young nestlings (28, 242, 309, 334). As a nestling becomes endothermic, energy costs of general body maintenance and activity as well as temperature maintenance increase, and energy derived from carbohydrates and lipids can be used for these needs (242). Thus, among those avian species that feed both insects and fruit to their young, the fruit is not brought to the young until they are a few days old and presumably past their peak requirements for proteins (1,150). [Frugivory now is well developed in many avian genera, most of which are chiefly tropical and by far the bulk of which are passerines (1,322).]

It is of interest in this connection that the phylogenetic sequence of mammals passed only through carnivorous lines (1,046), though the pertinent common feature with birds is endothermy rather than flight capability. In the same context, it has been suggested that the extensive radiations of mammals in post-Cretaceous times correlates with the ascendancy of the angiosperms and their abundant nutritious organs, particularly since fruits usually comprise an important part of the diet of small mammalian carnivores (see 1,296).

[Further support for the view of *Archaeopteryx* as having been an obligate predator is the fact that only a few living reptiles (some turtles and tortoises, and large lizards) habitually eat plant material, and among these the herbivorous lizards are carnivorous (primarily insectivorous) until they reach body weights of 50-300 g, for example *I. iguana* and *Basiliscus plumifrons*; omnivores are rare. In the families Agamidae, Gerrhosauridae, Iguanidae, and Scincidae, the few species that weigh more than 300 g are almost all herbivores (because of the greater relative energetic cost of preying on arthropods), whereas the vast majority, weighing less than 50-100 g, are carnivores (1,338). Knowledge of herbivorous reptiles is so scanty and inexact that it does not justify extrapolation to the bases for the great success of herbivory among many reptiles of the past (876). It is suggested, however, that the evolution of a large, unspecialized lizard usually requires a changeover from carnivory to herbivory (1,338). Most reptiles (about 90-95%) are primarily or entirely predators throughout their lives (356, 357, 408).]

PRIMITIVE PRO-AVIS PROBABLY MOST AGILE, SWIFT, ARBOREAL PREDATOR. It appears unlikely to me that primitive pro-aves acquired the ability to parachute to the ground or a lower limb as a result of selective pressure exerted by predators, which is the favored mechanism that has been proposed in the past. A feathered primitive pro-avis may, itself, have been the most agile and swift arboreal predator of the time and the tree its safest haven (see pp. 582, 583, concerning escaping arboreal and partly-arboreal lizards). Predators sufficiently agile to pose a threat in trees probably also could have followed an escaping pro-avis that was parachuting to the ground or a lower limb.

[It cannot be ruled out that some larger arboreal reptile, for example, a pseudosuchid, like *Scleromochlus* (92), preyed on primitive pro-aves in the "trees". Small pterosaurs (of their first evolutionary radiation, the Rhamphorhynchoidea) also might have been possible predators. They usually are visualized as having lived on cliffs near sea coasts but they might well have been partly arboreal. However, the form of the teeth of many species indicates that they fed (probably in skimming flight) on fish or other slippery animals, and this is confirmed by the fossilized marine material (or impressions) found within their fossilized rib cages and throat sacs (91, 92, 308, 1,248). The tiny pterosaur, *Anurognathus*, has a short face and peg-like teeth and probably fed on insects, whereas the lower jaw of *Pterodaustro* has hundreds of teeth resembling the baleen of a whale, and the animal may have fed on plankton. Nearly all of pterosaur remains have been found in marine beds that were laid down in epicontinental seas (39, 169, 308).

One also must bear in mind one of the possible implications of the facts of higher soil nutrient losses through erosion in the Mesozoic era and the lower rate of primary productivity inherent in gymnospermous physiology. The pertinent implication is that the total herbivore and carnivore biomass probably was notably less than that of the present day (996, 1,296). Thus, arthropods and to a much lesser degree, carrion and nests of eggs, might have been the most accessible, major food items of small predators.]

PARACHUTING AS A PERFECTION OF HUNTING BY "TREE"-TO-GROUND JUMPING. It appears much more likely that parachuting--the first significant step of avian ancestors into an aerial habitat--became developed, not as an escape tactic, but as the perfection of a means of pre-avian hunting, by "tree"-to-ground jumping, at first along ballistic paths. In this hunting tactic, pre-aves lept at the prey from vantage points on low-lying branches of trees or the stems of stout shrubs. In the event that small ground-dwellers were being taken, a pre-avis spread its limbs and extended the tail at once to slow descent, analogously to the way frogmouths (Podargidae) flutter down to the ground from a perch to catch small terrestrial prey (169). Jumps from branch to branch for purposes of transportation probably also played some role, since animals that did so would have become partly preadapted for parachuting, through an improved sense of balance and reduced reaction times (1,050).

[According to one estimate, there would be considerable risk of injury on impact with a non-yielding substrate at a speed greater than 6 m/sec, roughly the speed attained in free fall from a 2-m height with negligible air resistance (see R.J. Templin, 1977, in 1,203). Perry (1,296) points out that for an animal of weight "above approximately 10 pounds, arboreal existence is a deadly game of chance;" in practice the slowing of falls by air resistance presented by the profile of lighter animals provides a considerable degree of protection.]

In the much more likely event that volant insects were being taken, a pre-avis lept swiftly toward the nearby passing or fleeing prey, analogously to the manner in which some extant birds repeatedly sally forth from a perch to catch flying insects, and sit-and-wait basking, predaceous diurnal reptiles (*Amphibolurus ineamis, Uta, Crotaphytus, Leiocephalus schreibersi*) rush out in brief forays of only a few sec to catch passing insects (see 766). In this tactic the pre-avis would have been limited to taking only nearby volant prey, both because of very limited aerial maneuverability and because of the need to bring drag mechanisms into play as promptly as possible.

After the prey were seized in the jaws or seized with the forelimbs and transferred to the jaws, the pre-avis immediately would have spread its limbs and extended the tail to provide increased air resistance (drag) to slow its descent. Not only would limitations of structure and aerial capabilities have dictated the requirement that the earliest forays into the air be near the ground, but an abundance of coniferous shrubs and the distribution of insect prey also may have favored that strategy. Thus, some contemporary studies of flying insect distribution have shown a decrease in their abundance with increasing height above the ground (see 821).

[The arthropodan food of terrestrial birds, e.g., in Africa, can be divided loosely into 4 categories (1,052): (1) those that live in or close to the surface of the ground, if small, are sought particularly by wagtails, pipits, and chats, if larger and harder by shrikes (Laniidae), rollers (Coraciidae), and if very plentiful, by big raptors (Accipitridae); (2) those that are found in the foliage of trees and bushes, or attracted to flowers, e.g., those of *Albizzia* spp, *Acacia* spp, and *Capparis* (= *Aphylla*), which are put out even at the height of the dry season and even when a tree is leafless; (3) insects flying at low levels, the staple of such birds as, e.g., the Spotted Flycatcher (*Muscicapa striata*), and of bee-eaters (Meropidae); and (4) insects flying on high and ranging in size from the "aerial plankton" on which swifts (Apodidae) depend, to migratory locusts. Many aerial feeders sometimes forage close to the ground but sometimes much higher, for example bee-eaters and the Barn Swallow. In 1963 the live weight of ground arthropods in the acacia savanna just south of the lower Sénégal River rose during the brief rainy season from 223 g/ha in June to 656 g in Sept. and 1946 g in Nov.; the corresponding weights for insects in arboreal foliage were 2, 13, and 35 g (1,052).]

THE EVOLUTIONARY SEQUENCE OF MECHANISMS OF PREDATION

The evolutionary sequence of mechanisms of predation by the ancestors of pro-aves is visualized as having been as follows. At first, a relatively small, terrestrial-arboreal, stem-reptilian, cruising forager--the predatory mode suggested for primitive lizards (766)--searching for food or foraging areas, probed for and grasped with the manus or pounced upon arthropods and other invertebrates and small amphibians that were located on the ground and on the bases of trees and shrubs. Previously alighted, fleeing, winged insects merely were snatched at, or lunged for with the jaws or forelimbs, at the end of a short leap.[Lizards preying on insects usually make a quick dash and either secure the prey or lose it beyond the further possibility of capture (1,338).]

Such foraging habits inevitably place the locomotor emphasis on the hindlimbs, with their consequent enlargement and predisposition toward a bipedal carriage, and the prey grasping and manipulating emphasis on the forelimbs. The lack of reduction of the forelimbs, as commonly occurs in bipedal terrestrial forms, can be accounted for by these limbs also being used in quadrupedal climbing and landing on vegetation, and in steadying the body after a terrestrial leap (1,212). In this connection, in the absence of heterocoelous centra at this very early ancestral stage, the neck would not have possessed the great flexibility characteristic of birds, which is an additional factor favoring an enhanced role of the forelimb and manus in prey capture (1,198). The forelimb and manus doubtless continued to play a major role in prey capture and manipulation on into the times of both pre-aves and pro-aves.

[Concerning the paleontology of some invertebrate groups that were potential prey, all the widespread families of spiders probably attained cosmopolitan distribution during Pangean times (late Paleozoic; Pangea consisted of Gondwana and Laurasia; 1,077, 1,090). Fossils that are thought to be terrestrial snails occur in the Carboniferous period and it seems likely that the majority of extant families were differentiated by the end of the Mesozoic era (1,078). Recent findings of *Sabatinca*-like whole specimens from Lower Cretaceous amber in Lebanon and wing scales from the mid-Cretaceous of France not only confirm the presence of Lepidoptera in the Mesozoic era but indicate that this Order of insects also enjoyed worldwide distribution in pre-drift Pangean times (1,079).

Most authorities seem to agree that the majority of modern coleopterous families arose in the Jurassic to early Cretaceous periods and fossil remains from Australia are known from the Permian and Triassic periods (1,080). The Australian Odonata (dragon flies and damsel flies) include a substantial archaic component, and at least 15% of the species can be regarded as Gondwanan relics (1,082). Plecoptera (stoneflies) are known from the early Permian period (1,083). The earliest fossil remains of a water bug (Hemiptera) are known from the late Triassic period and they become quite recognizable from the early Jurassic onward (1,084). About 180 species of excellently preserved terrestrial insects are known from the late Jurassic Solnhofen limestones. Many of these insects are of large size, exceeding the size in contemporary tropical insects, suggesting that they lived in warm tropical conditions (1,181). In this connection, cockroaches of the Permian and Pennsylvanian, of which over 600 species existed, attained a length of 15 cm, and the huge dragon flies of those times were the largest known insects, with wing spans of 61 cm (1,296).]

Since intensive foragers would be detected easily by predators that were within sight of them, great agility and the ability to move rapidly to escape pursuing predators would have been doubly advantageous (955) and selected for strongly in the stem-reptiles (of course avian predators did not exist at the time in question). A greater significance of visual output to motor coordination in these rapid movements would be expected to have increased tectocerebral interactions (1,109).

In such a life style, the weight of a clutch relative to the bodily weight of gravid animals and the ability to maneuver while carrying a clutch would be expected to have influenced both the energetic costs of foraging and the probability and energetic costs of avoiding predation, especially since intensive foragers tend to travel relatively long distances in escaping from predators. Accordingly, bodily shape and the relative clutch weight (ratio of clutch weight to total bodily weight) of animals burdened with large oviductal eggs would be expected to have coevolved to maximize reproductive success while, at the same time, minimizing adult mortality (886, 955). Consequently, intensively foraging stem-reptilian avian ancestors would not be expected to have had relatively massive clutches. [The importance of the relative clutch weight is readily seen in a sampling of contemporary lizards, in which it has a mean value of only 0.176 in intensive foragers as opposed to 0.259 in sit-and-wait foragers that use crypsis in predator avoidance (955). Although bats do not appear to be hampered by the extra weight of their young, which they even carry for a time after birth, it is very rare for them to have more than one offspring per litter (see 336).]

This modus operandi continued as arboreal habitats were invaded, except that the pre-avian ancestors then began to forage more intensively; they began to jump after fleeing, winged insects during ground foraging as well as from initial, low-lying positions on the bases of trees and shrubs, from which, in any event, it doubtless would have been energetically more efficient to jump rather than climb down (see also 840). Jumping at insects from the ground or from plants (in dense tropical forests) also has been suggested as the first method of predation employed by the ancestors of bats, though at night and using acoustic sensing (1,216).

[Good jumpers among the Amphibia and Reptilia are universally of small-to-medium size. Many lizards become aware of, and snap at, their prey only when it moves. In doing this, they are in the habit of making fairly long jumps, just as many frogs pounce when snatching their food (875).]

Comparative observations of falls of parachuting and non-parachuting frogs and lizards indicate that the first requirement in parachuting is behavioral, through the development of attitude control, rather than structural changes (see 1,050). This pattern of more active foraging and invasion of arboreal habitats would have been favored by smaller size, lighter build, high surface-to-volume ratio, the possession of lesser relative clutch burdens in gravid animals, and greater speed and agility. The metabolic demands of intensive foraging would have led to selection for improved oxygen and nutrient delivery and waste removal systems and reserve oxygen capacity, including more efficient lungs and cardiovascular systems and increased aerobic metabolic energy capacities. Each of these would have improved the benefit-to-cost ratio and ecological effectiveness of intensive foraging (766, 776, 1,109).

[In this connection, scansorial (climbing) extant birds that use their tails for support (woodpeckers, wood hewers, tree-creepers, etc.), as *Archaeopteryx* perhaps did, usually start foraging near the base of a tree and move upward only (309, 334, 796). These extant birds, of course, are primarily gleaning bark and probing wood (seeking insects on the surface or in fissures in the bark). All such climbing birds have large, strongly-curved, sharp claws (309, 334), as did also *Archaeopteryx* (see particularly 1,185).

In birds that start at the base of a tree and move upward only, while foraging, the claws of the anterior and posterior digits are of about the same size; in those that move downward as well as upward, the claw on the posterior digit is considerably larger than those on the anterior digits (334). If the claws of the pes of *Archaeopteryx* are examined from this point of view, the ungual of the hallux is found to be much smaller than that of the median toe (London and Eichstätt specimens; see Fig. 7, p. 170, in 1,179), suggesting that *Archaeopteryx* climbed upward only.

It is noteworthy that tree trunks and the stems of large shrubs in open habitats could have represented thermoregulatorily low-cost, preferred microhabitats for stem-reptiles and pre-aves, just as they do for contemporary lizards. Thus, diurnal changes in the extent of shading on tree trunks favor precise temperature regulation and ensure the existence of sun and shade areas that are in very close proximity (see 363).]

In the next stage, with still lesser clutch burdens and greater agility in general, even more vigorous pursuit of flying insects was practiced. When taking such prey by leaping from arboreal surfaces, grasping with the claws of the manus and transfer of the prey to the jaws would have preceded unfurling or spreading of the protowings. More intensive terrestrial foraging included constant probing, digging, tasting, exploring, short dashes and pouncing at alighted and fleeing winged insects, and running and bipedal jumping at the latter as they flew nearby or were overtaken in flight. Both the jaws and forefeet would have been brought into play in seizing prey.

As terrestrial hunting by running, followed by jumping, led to increased aerial control of bodily orientation in these practices (see 781), "tree"-to-ground jumping occurred from increasingly greater heights. This would have led to further selection for small bodily size and on scales, which already were modified greatly to enhance solar heat shielding in one attitude and retention of bodily heat in another. The new selective forces would have been for increased protruding surface area and modified surface texture at the edges of the bodily profile and extremities, so as to increase air resistance (both frictional and parasitic drag; see 1,203). Jumping and scampering between the limbs of vegetation probably would have been employed primarily for transportation.

All jumps would have been initiated with forward bipedal propulsion (symmetrical 2-footed, using the hindlimbs, which also is the practice among lizards; 875) from more or less level arboreal surfaces, and terminated with predominantly bipedal alighting on the ground or other broad surface, but with predominantly quadrupedal (forelimbs grasping first) alighting in vegetation of all kinds. [In the case of lizards, arboreal species tend to be thin with long and fragile appendages (880). The parachuting Geckos (Ptychozoon and *Uroplatus*) are much depressed dorsoventrally with fringes of skin on the flanks, broad tails, and webbing between the digits of the front and hind feet (875).] Small lift components produced by enlarged, elongated, flattened forelimbs and elongated, protruding scales would have increased greatly maneuverability and enhanced the foraging efficiency of a primitive pro-avian jumper (781, 977, 1,199, 1,201).

Extensions and movements of the forelimbs would have increased stability and bodily control; rapid movements and twisting of them for this purpose would have led to increased lift and thrust, leading eventually to the practice of gliding. Any small animal "that can control its attitude is the potential ancestor of a glider" (1,050). The transition from parachuting to gliding would have been accomplished in part by reduction of the angle of attack to de-emphasize drag and direct the air flow over the bodily surfaces. Selection then could have led to modifications of the upper and lower surfaces and leading edges of the forelimbs, increasing lift and reducing drag and unfavorable turbulence components (see 1,203, 1,215). [Gliding has evolved at least twice in amphibians, 5 times in reptiles, and 8 times in mammals, quite apart from birds or pterosaurs. Most gliders are arboreal (1,015, 1,200).]

If the increasing lift of an evolving glider were unaccompanied by proportionately increased drag, which is likely, the glide-path length also would have been increased (in proportion to the increase in the lift/drag ratio; 977). But metastable bipedal landing (center of mass directly over one or two support points) on small branches, as opposed to quadrupedal landing on vertical vegetational surfaces, would have been highly unlikely in the absence of significant lift capabilities (781, 1,199), and might not have been practiced until flight had evolved and wing flapping could have participated in braking and attitude control (977, 1,201).

Caple, Balda, and Willis have proposed a scheme for the evolution of powered flight, beginning with an active, bipedal, terrestrial, insectivorous reptile lacking lift capabilities, that lept after flying insects. In their proposal, each stage in the evolution of wings from forelimbs is envisioned to have conferred selective advantages, derived primarily from increased control of bodily orientation (781, 1,199). However, there is no evident impediment to applying the same scheme to an avian ancestor with similar terrestrial foraging habits that also lept after insects from upright bipedal stances on branches, beginning on low-lying ones and adapting to greater heights with the acquisition of greater aerial bodily control. With the perfection of arboreal leaping after flying insects, followed by descent to the ground or gliding to a landing in a tree or shrub, downward climbing, if it had been practiced to any significant degree previously, would have ceased to play a role, with a consequent reduction of the hallux (or merely its ungual or bony claw), as seen in *Archaeopteryx*.

Caple, Balda, and Willis argued against the likelihood that true gliding (after the fashion of contemporary gliders) was an intermediate stage in the evolution of powered flight (781, 1,199). However, U. Norberg's aerodynamic model supports the mechanism and aerodynamic feasibility of a transition from gliding (with stationary aerodynamics) to powered flight (with unsteady aerodynamics). Her model confers presumptive adaptive advantages for every step along the hypothetical route to powered flight from gliding and incipient flapping, in terms of length and control of flight paths (977, 1,201). Similar results have been obtained by Rayner using a somewhat different approach (1,200). In any event, true gliding in the contemporary sense is not implied nor intrinsic to theories of the arboreal evolution of powered flight. It would have sufficed for the avian ancestors to have had a faculty for gliding, with the necessary control and stability to maintain or alter the glide direction and angle to reach a destination, that was consistent with any constraints that might have been imposed by an evolution from parachuting to powered flight (see also 990).

Aside from its employment in the taking of terrestrial prey (see next paragraph), gliding locomotion, with its greatly limited maneuverability in prey pursuit, probably was used by advanced pro-aves as a means of transportation rather than as a means for approaching volant prey. It would have conferred flexibility in the selection of landing sites after the capture of nearby passing or fleeing, winged prey. "....gliding does not provide the means for entering the flying insect-eater niche" (783). It is regarded primarily as an adaptation for energetically cheap, rapid transit between trees and tall shrubs (791, 990). The primarily vertical surfaces of these plants, rather than primarily horizontal ones, very likely were the favored landing points of pro-avian gliders, as they are today in many gliders. Most gliding mammals can land on a selected tree far from the take-off point, indicating an ability to steer, control the length of the flight path, and to pull up into a stall just before encounter with the trunk (1,050, 1,193).

Serious consideration must be given to the possibility that gliding also was employed as transportation from clifftops and other high points by advanced pro-aves in searching extended beaches for prey or carcasses, as suggested for *Archaeopteryx* in the Solnhofen habitat (1,190; see also 1,197). Even the faculty for brief periods of true flight is more likely to have evolved in ancestral birds (of Table 3) primarily as an adaptation for transportation rather than for the taking of aerial prey (as opposed to predation on marine forms by surface skimming). Thus, members of only 3 avian sub-families feed upon insects in flight, as opposed to those of roughly 40 groups that do so in other ways (34). The aerial insectivores include the slowest flying birds, such as swifts and swallows, to whom fast flight would be disadvantageous, as their insect prey fly slowly (1,200).

Thus, the ability of an arboreal, advanced pro-avian predator to glide and/or employ low-amplitude wing-flapping, for moderate increases in lift capacity, to reach a landing site at a height (rather than having to descend to the ground each time) after leaps at, or after, large flying insects would have conferred immense selective advantages. An example of a contemporary glider that employs precisely this tactic is the flying opossum (*Petaurus*), which catches flying moths by leaping after them and then glides to a landing site at angles of 20-30° (782). [Of interest in this connection is the fact that all mammalian gliders are nocturnal and all large species among them are folivores (foliage-feeders). Smaller species are frugivore-insectivores (791).]

THE EVOLUTIONARY TRANSITION FROM PRIMITIVE REPTILIAN TO AVIAN OVIPOSITIONAL MODES

The most challenging, and perhaps most fascinating, evolutionary transition to reconstruct is that from the primitive reptilian mode of oviposition of a clutch *en masse* to the predominating avian mode of periodic laying of single eggs daily or on alternate days. Even if otherwise reasonable, no reconstruction would be persuasive unless each step in the proposed transition were itself selectively advantageous. This criterion is the ultimate guide in the following treatment.

Greatly facilitating the analysis is the fact that ovarian function is known to be very highly responsive to both internal and external environmental influences, as mediated by endocrinological and local neural control (although local neural control may be merely modulating; see pp. 144, 145, p. 602, **Ovulatory Allochronism under Neural Control**, and p. 610). This suggests that if simple adaptive types of altered ovarian function are known to exist or be evokable in contemporary reptiles, birds, or mammals, it is not unlikely that they also were accessible to ancestral forms exposed to appropriate selective pressures. In some cases this realization may provide the most reliable guide to the likely evolutionary pathways of altered ovarian function within the avian ancestral lineage.

Lending focus to the analysis is the fact that the end point is known, namely oviposition of single eggs of relatively small clutches daily or on alternate days. In approaching the problem, it is assumed that the selective pressures for reduction of relative clutch weight were, at first, those for adaptedness for increasingly intensive ground foraging and increasing invasion of arboreal habitats, and later those for increasing invasion of aerial habitats.

PERIODIC OVIPOSITION BY REPTILES. It lends perspective to the analysis to recall the fact that the transition for which an accounting is sought is not in all aspects a unique one. Thus, as mentioned above, there exist today some lizards that periodically oviposit only single eggs, often of unexceptional size (the Sphaerodactylidae, some Iguanidae, and a few smaller Gekkoninae), and others that give birth to only 1 or 2 live young (e.g., the Desert Night Lizard). Moreover, in many anoles, practically all of which are arboreal, single eggs are ovulated alternately by the two ovaries and may be laid as frequently as every 7 days. Clearly, selection for reduced relative clutch weight and reduced intervals between clutches also must have been operating in the evolutionary history of these lines.

In the case of the Desert Night Lizard, which tends to avoid predation via crypsis and known escape routes (955), the selective forces in question must have been those for small size (snout-vent length of about 4.7 cm), great agility in prey capture, and predator pressures that favored parental retention of developing embryos. In most of the single-egg clutching oviparous examples, adaptedness for arboreality doubtless also played a role.

[Ballinger (874) suggests that small clutch size in the Gekkonidae may have evolved as one of the many adaptations to the tropical environment: (1) decreasing reproductive risk through greater mobility of gravid animals in their frequently-arboreal habitat; (2) permitting the production of larger eggs and young better suited to the relatively competitive conditions in the tropics; and (3) reducing nest predation, since smaller clutches would be less conspicuous than large ones. He further suggests that alternate ovulation of single eggs from the ovaries of anoles and members of several related genera (see pp. 540-542) was adaptive to the arboreal life-style of their ancestors. Moreover, the distribution of the species that practice single-egg clutching throughout certain higher taxa suggests that the practice evolved very early in the evolutionary history of each taxon (955).]

From the Stem-Reptilian Ancestors to Pre-aves

SHALLOWER BURIAL REQUIRED REDUCED CLUTCH SIZE. I begin with a consideration of the change in ovipositional habits in the transition from the stem-reptilian ancestors of birds to their pre-avian ones. The former are postulated to have buried their eggs at shallow depths in vegetatively shaded sites and merely to have guarded the nest site, whereas the latter are postulated to have oviposited at surface sites and to have guarded, bodily shielded and shaded, and concealed the eggs (with vegetational debris). It is most pertinent to this transition that progressively shallower burial of eggs, in the sequence from deep burial, to shallow burial, to surface placement, necessitates that clutch size also be reduced, despite the fact that, compared to tree nests, ground nests are conducive to holding many eggs (1,051). Thus, multi-layered clutches are feasible (and are a common contemporary practice among reptiles) in nests at a great depth, whereas only a single layer of eggs is feasible in a surface nest, and a greatly restricted areal extent is mandatory if the eggs are to be incubated by bodily heat.

ALTERNATIVES FOR MAINTAINED OR INCREASED REPRODUCTIVE POTENTIAL. Accordingly, if reproductive potential were not to have been eroded by the reduction in clutch size with decreased nest depth, the transition necessarily would have been accompanied by an increased number (or, at least, an increased percentage) of hatching successes per clutch and/or an increased number of clutches per annum, and/or an increased survivorship and lifetime reproductive success (overall fitness of the life history). All 3 of these alternatives and other requirements are consonant with the presumed selective pressures at work at the time.

Thus, decreased clutch size and relative clutch weight are consonant with selection for intensive ground foraging and invasian of arboreal and aerial habitats by relatively less-burdened, gravid pre-aves; an increased percentage of hatchings is consonant with a decrease in the length of the period of embryogenesis and increased parental care; an increased number of clutches is consonant with shorter reproductive episodes, smaller clutches (which can be readied sooner and deposited at more frequent intervals than can large clutches; 897), and with the more equable climatic regime of the Mesozoic era; and an increase in survivorship and lifetime reproductive success would have been a consequence of the greater competitive advantage in hunting and escape that would have been conferred on relatively less-burdened, gravid pre-aves. It is significant, in this connection, that among contemporary birds a variation in the number of broods a hen produces successfully during a breeding period has a far greater influence on reproductive potential than variations in clutch size, and is thought to provide the most flexibility and environmental responsiveness in fecundity (968).

[A contemporary example, in which a particular ecological adaptation offsets reduced relative clutch weight (0.195) and lower reproductive potential per reproductive episode, by conferring increased survivorship and lifetime reproductive success, is that of the saxicolous South American iguanid lizard, *Platynotus semitaeniatus*. This lizard, even when gravid, has a flat morphology and escapes from predators by entering narrow rock crevices (955).]

These considerations form the basis for considering the change in ovipositional habits in the evolutionary transition from the stem-reptiles to pre-aves to have been one of decreased clutch size and relative clutch weight, and an increased number of clutches per annum. The suggested transition (Table 3) is from annual single-clutching to sequential multiple-clutching (but it also might have been from 2 sequential annual clutches to a larger number thereof). In this connection, single-brooded squamates have larger clutches and tend to be temperate in distribution, as opposed to being tropical or temperate for multi-brooded species (see 897, 912). [In a comparison of *Anolis* and *Sceloporus*, this amounts to many clutches of a single egg each, versus 1 clutch or a few clutches of many eggs each (897).]

The occurrence of sequential double- and multiple-clutching among reptiles and birds is so common and well known that it requires no further documentation but it is of interest that it occurs even in birds' closest living relatives, the crocodilians. For example, 15% of sexually active Nile Crocodiles have 2 sets of ovarian follicles developing concurrently. Maturation of one batch of ova may then be accompanied by the development of a younger batch that will near maturity soon after the 1st batch is oviposited; the 2nd set then can be fertilized and 2 clutches of eggs may be produced in one season. This sequential double-clutching also has been reported for some individuals of *Crocodylus palustris* and is suspected in some *C. porosus* (759).

OVARIAN FUNCTIONAL ADAPTABILITY. Many studies of ovarian function in vertebrates have revealed a tremendous adaptability and potential for altered activity of virtually all quantitative aspects of ovarian function. This adaptability is evident both at the level of the morphology of the egg-producing organs and of their neural and endocrinological control. Adaptability at the morphological level apparently finds its basis in the evolution of a control mechanism whereby minor genetic alterations are capable of producing major morphological influences. As was noted on p. 151, 2 ovaries occur in 24% of Ring Doves and 50% of mature hawks, and a case is known of a domestic fowl, with 2 functional ovaries and oviducts, that laid 2 eggs daily.

Even the arterial blood supply to the ovaries can be widely variable within a species. Thus, in the domestic fowl, the blood supply to the ovaries usually is from the left gonadal-renal artery via an ovario-oviductal branch, but in some cases this branch is absent and the ovarian artery branches directly from the aorta. Occurrences such as these bespeak a system for egg production, the quantitative output of which is very labile, evolutionarily speaking. Many examples also could be given to illustrate the great degree to which avian clutch size can become independent of rigid genetic control (see 1,051, below, and pp. 596, 597).

The potential for alterations in the timing and numbers of follicles that mature and are ovulated finds its basis, among other things, in readily altered degrees of vascularity and innervation of follicles, which appear to be the factors that control follicular access of blood-borne substances. These factors allow so ready a control of hierarchical ordering of follicular maturation that clutch size in lizards, for example, Whiptail Lizards, correlates positively with female bodily size, even intraspecifically (952), and hereditary changes in litter size of mammals have been brought about merely by selective breeding.

Thus, selection for multiple pregnancies has led to strains of sheep having litter sizes ranging from 1 to 4, resulting from variations in the number of ovulations per estrus cycle, and similar alterations have been brought about in various strains of laboratory mice (911). In strains of mice selected for larger litters, the ovaries are depleted of oocytes before death (see 913). The same potential for ready alteration of ovarian function is seen in the breeding of strains of domestic fowl that produce double- and triple-yolked eggs, and the fact that oviposition in the 1- or 2-week period between the first ovulation and the beginning of regular ovipositional sequences often is erratic, with the laying of 2 eggs per day (one or both of which may be abnormal; 948).

MULTIPLE OVULATIONS. Similar alterations in the direction of ancestral ovarian function are readily induced, and counteracted, with hormonal intervention and hypophysectomy. For example, injections of FSH in laying domestic fowl destroy the follicular hierarchy and make many of the large follicles ovulable. As a result, LH injections in FSH-primed hens induce multiple ovulations. Multiple ovulations also occur when LH is administered shortly after hypophysectomy of laying hens. On the other hand, injection of FSH prior to LH injection of a hen that had been hypohysectomized 8 h earlier prevented multiple ovulations, provided that the FSH was administered within 4 h after hypophysectomy (see 989).

Induction of superovulation in mammals is well known; pregnant mare serum gonadotropin usually is injected first to set a group of follicles on the path to maturity, followed by injection of human chorionic gonadotropin some hours later to induce ovulation (1,033). There also is a large literature on the control of ovulation in cattle and dogs with progestins and prostaglandins. Ovulations can be induced even during pregnancy and they occur spontaneously in early pregnancy in equids. Such studies have tended to emphasize the importance of interactions between the thecal and granulosal cells in contributing to the regulation of follicular steroidogenesis and ovulatory control (1,044).

In many species of lizards, birds, and mammals clutch size increases with age and size of the female, and many birds oviposit larger clutches when food at the time of laying is plentiful (810, 862, 955). It has been suggested that such adjustments in birds are mediated through alterations of the output of gonadotropins, which is sensitive to caloric variations (see 912, 928, 973, and below). In some birds the number of eggs per clutch generally decreases with the onset of warmer weather and in dry years, and species generally lay more eggs per clutch in northern, cooler latitudes than toward the tropics (see 967, 1,086).

EASE OF CONVERSIONS BETWEEN SINGLE AND MULTIPLE CLUTCHING is illustrated dramatically by the reproductive behavior of the Green Sea Turtle, which only produces a clutch every 3 yr in some regions but 7-12 clutches per annum in others (see p. 540). In a recent study, clutch size reduction of roughly 20% in a California Gull (*Larus californicus*) population at Mono Lake, California, as compared to the clutch size for a population at Great Salt Lake, Utah, was explained best in terms of poorer food supplies in the spring. Egg-removal experiments showed, however, that resource limitation exerts a relative, rather than an absolute, effect (1,235). In the case of meadowmice (*Microtus*), certain factors in green plants may increase the number of oocytes per ovulation and shorten the interval between consecutive pregnancies; fertility apparently cannot be maintained on a diet of dry vegetation alone (1,299).

It frequently has been suggested that, in addition to qualitative changes in available food, a certain threshold abundance must be exceeded before the onset of breeding and egg production will begin, that the threshold level is modulated by environmental temperature and rainfall, and that the nutritional plane of the female at the time when food resources reach the threshold also is important. For example, the largest of vitellogenic follicles were observed in those female Snow Geese with the highest endogenous reserves of proteins (see 1,123). Based upon such considerations and independent studies, P.J. Jones and Ward have postulated a possible physiological mechanism of control of avian clutch size.

According to their hypothesis, all female Red-billed Quela begin egg production upon reaching a similar initial level of bodily reserves of proteins and cease when they reach some lower threshold level or begin to approach it too rapidly. Differences in clutch size, following this scheme, would arise from differences in daily rates of protein loss from the bodily reserves, assuming that the supply of energy was not limiting. With high daily protein intake during oviposition, all developing follicles may produce eggs, leading to the exceptional clutches of 5-7 eggs. With quite low daily protein intake, egg production may be sustained only by the rapid exhaustion of reserve proteins, resulting in clutches of only 1 or 2 eggs. Thus, clutch size limitations would be imposed by the demands placed upon bodily reserves of proteins and the rate at which they could be supplemented by feeding (965). One possible mechanism of action of these factors might be via influences on prolactin levels, following the scheme of dual prolactinic control discussed on page 148 (see 1,106).

Such findings concerning ovarian functional adaptability led R.E. Jones to suggest that altered follicular selection, as the result of interaction between ovarian vasodynamics and circulating gonadotropic levels, could account for the evolution of altered clutch or litter sizes (fecundity), and that relative clutch weight reduction, as an adaptation facilitating flight (or a reduction in clutch size with viviparity), led to selection against the occurrence of oogenesis in the adult ovaries of some vertebrates (911, 913). Accordingly, there appear to be substantial and highly responsive physiological mechanisms by which clutch size could have become reduced in response to selective forces in the evolutionary transition from stem-reptiles to pre-aves.

[It is of interest in connection with the above discussion to take note of the existence in many contemporary vertebrates of compensatory mechanisms that ensure the achievement of full reproductive potential in response to destabilizing factors over the short term. This is illustrated by the "law of follicular constancy" in mammals. Removal of one ovary in several mammalian species leads to a doubling of the number of ovulations from the contralateral ovary. Similarly, in mice in which one ovary ovulates fewer than the normal number of ova, the contralateral ovary compensates with increased ovulations. This can occur either through an increase in the number of recruited follicles or a decrease in the number undergoing atresia.

The phenomenon also has been demonstrated in 3 species of teleosts, one amphibian, and one lizard, all of which, unlike birds and mammals, exhibit oogenesis and folliculogenesis as adults. Similarly, removal of large, vitellogenic follicles from one ovary of several non-mammalian vertebrates including the Japanese Quail, leads to the recruitment of smaller follicles to take their place. It would appear that the phenomenon depends upon a lessening of follicular estrogenic negative feedback on gonadotropin secretion (see 911).]

From Pre-aves to Primitive Pro-aves

SEQUENTIAL MULTIPLE-CLUTCHING TO RAPID DOUBLE-CLUTCHING. The evolutionary transition from the ovulatory and ovipositional habits of pre-aves to those of primitive pro-aves is proposed to have been one of passing from polyautochronic, sequential multiple-clutching to polyallochronic, rapid double-clutching. In other words, instead of sequentially ovipositing several clutches, one in each reproductive episode, with the eggs of each clutch being derived from both ovaries, it is proposed that 2 clutches were laid per reproductive episode, in rapid succession, each of half size and each derived from a different ovary. Whereas pre-avian parents nested in more or less exposed sites and guarded, shielded, shaded, and concealed their eggs, with both parents sharing in the hatching and "fledging" of the young of each clutch before the oviposition of another, it is proposed that primitive pro-avian parents nested in well-shaded sites, and that each cared unassistedly for a separate clutch, concurrently with the other.

The advantages of rapid double-clutching through polyallochronic ovulation, from the point of view of clutch care and hatching success, particularly in the case of a clutch that is incubated, already have been dealt with in the preceding text. Here it is emphasized that the above-mentioned change of ovipositional mode is fairly readily accessible, evolutionarily speaking, and by means of it the clutch burden of gravid primitive pro-aves could have been halved in one fell swoop without any reduction in the ultimate clutch size or reproductive potential from that of pre-aves, provided only that a primitive degree of endothermy had been achieved. Such a change, of course, would have conferred a very great adaptive advantage on gravid primitive pro-aves for intensive foraging, arboreality and the early steps of invasion of aerial habitats.

IN POLYALLOCHRONIC OVULATION, there is a desynchronization of ovarian function whereby an advanced complement of oocytes in one ovary mature and are ovulated and oviposited while the maturation and/or ovulation of those in the contralateral ovary are inhibited or delayed, in the limiting case until the oviposition of the former complement has occurred. It is suggested that, while polyallochronic ovulation also would have been accessible to pre-aves, and would have correspondingly reduced the relative clutch burdens of gravid pre-aves, it would not have conferred selective advantages on them for at least two reasons.

The 1st of these reasons is that the degree of arboreality of pre-aves, and the heights on tree trunks and stems from which they jumped after prey, were as yet insufficient for a critical selective advantage to have accured to them in this regard by virtue of a halving of relative clutch weight. Second, and most important, as ectotherms it would have been maladaptive for pre-aves to hold in abeyance the development and/or ovulation of the oocytes of half of a clutch until the the eggs derived from the oocytes of the other half had been, or were well on the way toward being, oviposited. This practice would have doubled the time required to produce a given number of eggs, a loss that presumably could not have been offset by the competitive advantages of halved relative clutch weights to gravid pre-aves, in terms of lifetime reproductive success.

On the other hand, once primitive endothermy and increased body temperature had been achieved in primitive pro-aves, egg production could have proceeded so much more rapidly that the time lost by holding the development of half a clutch in abeyance would have been of very much less importance than it would have been in pre-aves. Further, the increasingly arboreally-based predation of primitive pro-aves probably would have greatly increased the selective advantages of halved relative clutch weights. Although the ovipositional condition of primitive pro-aves is described as rapid double-clutching in Table 3, it is likely that breeding would have occurred more than once annually--certainly no less frequently than it occurred among pre-aves. In fact, the number of reproductive episodes probably was increased over that of pre-aves by virtue of the shortening of breeding cycles as a consequence of incubation of the eggs by bodily heat.

OVARIAN ASYMMETRY AND CLUTCH-SIZE HALVING. Both the existence of ovarian asymmetry in birds and many other vertebrates, and the fact of the occurrence of alternate ovarian function in anoline lizards, cows (911), and some primates (but not in Man, in which ovarian function is more or less at random; 1,240), as well as the simplicity of the mechanism itself, lend credibility to this avenue of clutch-size halving. In fact, the widespread ovarian asymmetry in some vertebrate classes (see pp. 149-151) probably originated as a consequence of the disuse of one ovary, in the process of relative clutch-weight halving. Regression and vestigiality of the disused ovary probably followed as a consequence of selection for physiological economy and/or general weight reduction.

THE INDIVIDUAL PARENTAL CARE OF SEPARATE CLUTCHES by primitive pro-aves merits discussion, since it represent a departure from the pre-avian condition, in which parents shared in the guarding, shielding, shading, and concealing of the eggs. It is proposed that both primitive pro-avian parents participated in the care of the 1st of the two sister clutches, just as their pre-avian ancestors had shared in the care of the successive, temporally spaced clutches. After oviposition of the 2nd of the sister clutches, however, it is suggested that each parent cared exclusively for one clutch, and incubation may not have been begun until then. However, the parents cooperated in "watchdog" fashion, as described earlier, with one parent tending to be on its nest when the other was foraging. By the time of advanced pro-aves, however, care of the 1st of the simultaneous double clutches may have fallen exclusively to one parent, just as it does among many contemporary rapidly double-clutching species.

EGG ATTENTIVENESS AND FORAGING EFFICIENCY. It should be noted in connection with the individual care of separate clutches by primitive pro-aves, that this practice would have been facilitated by the fact that only a primitive grade of endothermy (see Table 3) had been achieved, and the incubatory temperature was correspondingly low, allowing more lengthy or frequent parental absences from the nest. As the grade of endothermy advanced, and body and incubatory temperatures rose, requiring greater parental egg attendance, so too did the intensiveness and efficiency of foraging, with more of the greatly abundant large insect prey being taken per unit of time in the shorter or less frequent absences from the nest. With the achievement of an advanced grade of endothermy and higher incubatory temperatures in ancestral birds, biparental attendance of surface nests became mandatory, particularly in less equable or cooler climates, as the embryos were much less tolerant to chilling.

In other words, as the grade of endothermy advanced and incubatory temperatures rose, the increasingly stringent requirements for egg attentiveness probably tended to be balanced by a greater intensiveness and efficiency of foraging. This made it possible to meet pro-avian nutritional needs (which also were on the increase) in less foraging time. But at the level of the ancestral bird stage, egg-care requirements overwhelmed the capacities of a single parent, and biparental care became mandatory. A transition from insectivory to herbivory (see pp. 613-618, **The Transition to Herbivory**), possibly partly as a consequence of decreasingly abundant large insect resources and a resulting lesser foraging efficiency, also may have figured prominently in the transition to biparental care.

From Primitive to Advanced Pro-aves

DAILY OR ALTERNATE-DAILY OVIPOSITION. To facilitate discussion it is assumed that the number of eggs ovulated from each ovary at the stage designated "primitive pro-aves," had been reduced to about 5, making a total of 10 in the 2 clutches oviposited *en masse* in relatively rapid succession. Further advances were the attainment of a primitive state of endothermy, of higher body temperatures, the initiation of incubation with bodily heat, and further reduction in the length of the period of embryogenesis. The stage then would have been set for evolution of the practice of periodic ovulation and oviposition of single eggs--the ultimate reproductive adaptation of ovarian and ovipositional function in response to invasion of aerial habitats (or a high degree of acrobatic faculty in arboreal habitats).

Only in the evolutionary transition to advanced pro-aves, with their still higher body temperatures, would metabolic rates have achieved levels that could have sustained the rapid syntheses needed to produce single eggs in sufficiently rapid succession to assemble clutches of 5 eggs within relatively short periods. Even if some degree of selective incubation were to have been practiced, relatively rapid clutch assembly would have been necessary to maintain a sufficient synchrony of inter-clutch hatching and/or viability of the first-laid eggs (which would have been at risk if incubation were delayed lengthily).

Large clutches presumably would have been quite infeasible in advanced pro-aves, assuming a laying interval of greater than 2 days, both because of the need for hatching synchrony and because the lengthening, alone, of the combined periods of oviposition and incubation would have greatly increased the risk of losses through predation in surface nests. Similarly, prolonging the period of brooding and exposure to mortality, at a constant risk, quickly offsets gains in clutch size (1,150). [If incubation begins with the 1st egg, asynchronous hatching will tend to lengthen the period of brooding; if it begins with the last or penultimate egg, the period of egg exposure will tend to be lengthened, though there are strategies to counter both potentially lengthened exposures to risks.]

ANOLINE MONOALLOCHRONIC OVULATION. We can receive valuable guidance in attacking this problem by considering contemporary reproductive practices among lizards. Within this group it has been noted that low clutch size and the capability of ovipositing clutches in relatively rapid succession appear to be selectively advantageous in tropical habitats, particularly in areas with relatively equable climatic regimes (such as obtained in the times of pro-aves), yet regimes with highly variable and unpredictable conditions of rainfall (897). If we pass at once to the limiting example in this category, a clutch of 1 egg, the shortest period known between successive ovipositions appears to be that of *Anolis onca*, namely about every 7 days (cited on p. 541). As this is achieved through monoallochronic ovulation, the production of each egg from an oocyte requires 14 days. Since the eggs are deposited singly and are not incubated, no question of clutch synchrony arises.

[For additional perspective concerning rapid egg production among ectotherms, the maturing, alone, of oviductal eggs of trionychid chelonians requires 7-10 days (757). The skate *Raja eglanteria* lays a total of as many as 60 eggs in pairs at decreasing intervals, beginning 18 days apart and decreasing ultimately to 4 days apart, but neither the ovulatory nor the maturational schedule is known (912).]

NO ADVANTAGE TO OVIPOSITION MORE FREQUENTLY THAN DAILY. As compared to the fastest known period of 14 days for single successive egg production by one ovary of a reptile, that for a bird is only 1 day. There would be no advantage to ovarian egg production by birds over a period of less than 1 day, since the adaptive advantage of periodic daily or alternate-daily oviposition is (a) that the burden of but a single advanced maturing oocyte or unshelled oviductal egg is present during the active part of the daily cycle, rather than a full-weight egg in the shell in the oviduct (see discussion in 1,402), and (b) the peaking of the demanding processes of shell deposition occurs during the nightly period of inactivity in the hours before early morning oviposition.

Shell calcification is a period of egg maturation that is ill suited to other activities; for example, as mentioned on page 164, the respiratory rate of domestic fowl hens is augmented 64% during this period (see 510). In fact, growth in general is asserted to take place primarily during times of inactivity (1,032). Had there been an advantage to the oviposition of single eggs more frequently than daily, many birds probably would have retained 2 ovaries and ovulated monoallochronically at least twice daily. [Members of most passerines species lay at daily intervals, in the morning, many of them soon after sunrise (see 975, 1,359).]

[Nor is it necessarily advantageous to generate clutches by daily oviposition. Some tropical passerines skip days between laying successive eggs, thereby reducing the daily energy requirement of laying (even though birds with nidicolous young expend relatively little energy on egg formation; see pp. 164, 165, **Hen's Energy Requirements and Egg Energy Content**). Most of the 32 species of suboscines examined by Ricklefs oviposited at intervals of 2 days, but all 19 oscine species oviposited daily. Since the egg sizes relative to bodily weights are substantially larger for the suboscines, the smaller ones in particular, this may account for their longer laying intervals (975). At any rate, the existence of both daily and 2-day laying intervals in tropical passerines and many other small birds is a clear indication that neither interval possesses any inherent advantage over the other, with the choice between the two being dependent primarily on ecological factors rather than physiological limitations.]

If advanced pro-aves were to have produced eggs at the maximum rate known in extant small reptiles (if not in all reptiles), it would have required 28 days to assemble a 5-egg clutch, assuming monoallochronic ovulation. If eggs deposited at surface sites were to have been shielded, guarded, and incubated, and the chicks groomed, escorted, and protected, the eggs would have to have been present in a common nest (or, at most, 2 nests, one under the care of each parent). Had such been the case, however, even allowing for the possibility of some degree of delayed incubation and self-synchronization of hatching among the embryos, the clutch(es) undoubtedly would have been excessively desynchronized (desynchronized hatchings would have been highly maladaptive, particularly among nidifugous nestlings escorted to and from foraging sites, etc.). Thus, the practice of assembling clutches by monoallochronism with eggs laid every 7 days, even if it could have been achieved prior to the time of advanced pro-aves doubtless would not have been reproductively advantageous.

But, of course, advanced pro-aves were endotherms, of higher body temperatures and metabolic rates than those of anoles, but of lower body temperatures than those of extant birds (see Table 3). If one were to assume that advanced pro-aves could have produced eggs at only twice the anoline rate, the time required for the assembly of a 5-egg clutch would have been only 14 days, under the assumption of monoallochronic ovulation (2 ovaries). This is not an unreasonable period of assembly for a clutch, as it falls within the range of some birds that oviposit on alternate days or at longer intervals, and of those with large clutches that oviposit daily [For example, as many as 13 eggs on a daily schedule by the Sora Rail (216) and 7-10 eggs on an alternate-day schedule by Common Rheas (1,266)].

ADVANCED PRO-AVES POSSESSED TWO OVARIES. One purpose of pursuing this line of approach is to emphasize that, in view of the known great adaptability and high responsiveness of ovarian function to internal and external environmental factors, and the crucial need to assemble clutches in a sufficiently short time to ensure hatching synchrony, one is led to the following conclusion: if advanced pro-aves laid single eggs periodically, they most likely possessed two ovaries and ovulated monoallochronically, which is the practice of kiwis and presumably also of other contemporary birds with two functional ovaries (see p. 151). One arrives at the same conclusion by approaching the problem from another direction: how could the polyallochronically-ovulating, primitive pro-aves, ovipositing clutches of 5 eggs *en masse*, have made the evolutionary transition to assembling clutches of similar size by ovulating single eggs periodically at intervals of, say, only 2 or 3 days?

OVULATORY ALLOCHRONISM UNDER NEURAL CONTROL. Recall that polyallochronic ovulation refers to a condition in which a complement of 2 or more ripe oocytes of one clutch is ovulated from one ovary before the oocytes of the presumptive next clutch are ovulated from the contralateral ovary. Such a differential responsiveness of the two ovaries of a single reproductive system could not reside solely in blood-borne mediating factors. Its basis must have resided in a differential responsiveness of the two ovaries that was under neural control (see also p. 610). In other words, a condition of polyallochronic ovulation in primitive pro-aves doubtlessly required that there also have existed a neural modulating system that was capable of inhibiting follicular maturation and/or ovulation in one ovary during the same phase of the breeding cycle in which the processes were occurring in the contralateral ovary.

By what simple mechanism can one envision an evolutionary transition of such a system of ovarian function to one in which oocytes were ovulated and eggs oviposited singly every 2 or 3 days? The answer would appear to be fairly straightforward. Instead of calling for neural inhibition of follicular maturation in one ovary over the entire period of time in which the process was uninhibited in the contralateral ovary, it called for short periods of alternating inhibition of the two ovaries such that single follicles matured and were ovulated during the periods of disinhibition. In other words, it called for more rapid alternation of neural inhibitory control plus the establishment or enhancement of an hierarchical regime of maturation in each ovary. The latter might itself have been a consequence of the evolution of relatively rapidly alternating neural control.

One might suggest that the same result could have been achieved with pulsed inhibition of only one of the ovaries. However, not only would that have led to elapsed times between successive ovulations and ovipositions that would have been twice as great as in the monoallochronic mode of ovulation, it also would have required the addition of a mechanism of inhibiting one ovary completely, simultaneously with inhibiting the other only pulsewise. The proposed scheme, on the other hand, merely calls for a change in the rate of alternate inhibition of the ovaries. It is more or less tacit to this scheme that the inhibitory influence on the ovaries would have been primarily one of establishing an hierarchical ordering of oocytes in advanced maturational stages, not one of lengthening the overall time required for maturation of a given selected oocyte.

[An impressive illustration of the relative ease with which the period of ovulation can be lengthened, and of the responsiveness of ovarian function to environmental factors, is the fact that merely a calcium-deficient diet will result in a slowing of follicular growth and ovulation in domestic fowl (possibly through reducing FSH secretion; see 948) to the degree that oviposition occurs only every 10-15 days, rather than daily (931). Because the process of egg formation is energetically conservative, dietary energy deprivation usually does not alter the size and quality of eggs appreciably, only the frequency of oviposition. Thus, restriction of diet to 75% of *ad libitum* levels in White Leghorn hens reduces egg production to 46-47%; in pheasants, restriction to 72% reduces egg production to only 9% (722; see also 975). Irregular oviposition with long time intervals between eggs also occurs normally in the 1- or 2-week intervals between a domestic fowl hen's first ovulation and the beginning of regular ovipositional sequences. Similarly, it is possible by selective breeding to achieve shorter periods between ovipositions (periods normally are about 24.5 h but they may become slightly less than 24 h in the middle of long laying sequences; 948).]

From Advanced Pro-aves to Ancestral Birds

The evolutionary transition from advanced pro-aves to ancestral birds involved achievement of a grade of endothermy and body temperatures equivalent to those of modern primitive birds, and total invasion of aerial habitats, except that vigorous wing-flapping flight (at large amplitudes and speeds) probably could not have been sustained for long periods. The requirement for higher incubatory temperatures (consequent upon higher body temperatures), a possibly lessened foraging efficiency, and lessened climatic equability and/or dispersal into more temperate regions, led to the need for biparental incubation of single clutches, as discussed earlier (see p. 573, **Rapid Double-Clutching Not Adaptive for Ancestral Birds**).

The change in ovipositional habits and ovarian condition hinged on the fact that the metabolic rates of ancestral birds had attained a sufficiently high level to sustain periodic production of single eggs by a single ovary at rates that previously had required 2 ovaries and monoallochronic ovulation. The conventional view of the evolutionary process of loss of a functional right ovary and oviduct would be to assume that, inasmuch as the right ovary and oviduct had become superfluous, selection favored evolving advanced pro-aves in which they regressed, so that they generally had become vestigial by the time of ancestral birds. However, unlike reproductive behavior, the presence in birds of 2 ovaries and oviducts, as opposed to only one, is a genetically relatively readily alterable property (see pp. 149-151, **Oviducts and Female Gonads**, and pp. 594, 595, **Ovarian Functional Adaptability**), so that the loss of the right ovary and oviduct by some advanced pro-avian species might have occurred over a relatively brief period, evolutionarily speaking.

[I would suggest that the uniformity of preferential reduction or vestigiality of only the right ovary and/or oviduct in birds has been determined ultimately by asymmetries in the circulatory system, and should not be regarded as a consequence of, nor evidence for, monophyly.]

The transition to biparental care of single clutches, if not entirely an obligatory response as a consequence of higher body temperatures, climatic changes, and/or reduced foraging efficiency (possibly with reduced annual reproductive potential) implies the possession of competitive advantages that increased lifetime reproductive success. These advantages could have accrued from the colonization of more favorable habitats and/or the adoption of more secure and/or better insulated nests. On the other hand, it is quite likely that some ancestral birds practiced sequential multiple-clutching.

WHY DID NOT ARBOREAL LIZARDS ACHIEVE ENDOTHERMY AND FLIGHT? For focus and perspective in relation to the scheme of avian evolution proposed in the foregoing, it is helpful to ask why arboreal lizards did not follow the same evolutionary pathway that led to birds. Of all lizards, anoles probably provide the best examples. They are of small-to-medium size, agile, practically all arboreal, insectivorous, some deposit their eggs in nests only a few cm below the surface in moist soil or loose debris, many oviposit only 1 or 2 eggs periodically, and some are said to have become gliders (1,296), in which case they would have gone through parachuting and "tree"-to-ground jumping stages.

Though these are attributes that have been mentioned repeatedly in the foregoing discussion of factors involved in avian evolution, the ancestors of lizards followed a quite different line of specialization. The answer to the question of this section may provide the strongest argument for the origin of feathers tracing, at first, to feather-like modifications of scales as adaptations for their insulative rather than their aerodynamical properties. Thus, lizards have evolved aerodynamically favorable modifications of the body, even structures such as the rib membranes of *Draco volans* and the Triassic keuhneosaurs (1,296 and p. 605). But no gliding or parachuting lizard appears to have evolved individual scales with more favorable aerodynamic properties than those found in closely related non-gliders or parachuters (notwithstanding periodic shedding of the integument).

This provides a strong indication that the earliest feather-like modifications of scales were not in response to selective forces that favored increased drag or lift. Yet scales specialized in other ways have been evolved; basking lizards that live in hotter climates have larger scales, which reduce heat uptake and allow the animals to tolerate more lengthy exposure to the sun (170, 1,182); and gliding Asian geckos have enlarged but otherwise little modified fringing scales that provide increased surface area (see 1,296).

I would suggest that the ancestors of lizards deviated from a path leading toward flight and endothermy because they never passed through a surface-nesting stage. This omission probably traced to the fact that they derive from a later reptilian lineage. The latter, perhaps, achieved the practice of shallow egg burial under somewhat less equable climatic conditions or slightly different reproductive habits. These different conditions or habits perhaps conferred lesser advantages to surface nesting and greater advantages to alternate ovarian function and multiple clutching in shallow nests, with incubatory periods of about twice those common in birds (6-7 weeks in Green Anoles; 686). [There did, however, exist early, relatively small, insectivorous Eolacertilians and even gliders (see p. 605), but these have left no trace of scales modified to confer more favorable aerodynamic properties.]

Accordingly, with no obligatory need to shade, shield, and guard eggs in exposed surface nests, the ancestors of anoles also would have experienced no selective pressure for increased insulation from solar rays nor for advanced metabolic mechanisms for achieving homeothermy. In consequence, they would not have evolved insulative, feather-like modifications of scales nor achieved primitive metabolic stages in the development of endothermy. Downward climbing, thin bodies with long, fragile appendages, and foot-pad development were favored, rather than insulative scales with aerodynamically-favorable properties for "tree"-to-ground jumping, such as for quick access to threatened surface nests.

Furthermore, having arrived much later on the scene than the corresponding avian ancestors (perhaps the late Cretaceous period, although one Triassic genus, *Paliguana*, with debatable lacertilian affinities, is known from Africa; 868; see p. 605), they probably would have found diurnal flying insects no longer as abundant, unexploited, or as readily accessible as in the Jurassic period, so that selection for "tree"-to-ground jumping as a hunting tactic for catching large flying insects in flight would have been weaker or non-existent.

[EARLY SAURIANS (LIZARDS). The Eolacertilia first emerge in the late Permian and early Triassic periods of South Africa. These include relatively small insectivorous diapsids that have been referred to the family Paliguanidae, including the genera, *Paliguana*, *Palaeagama*, and *Saurosternon*. Late Triassic early saurians, the Kuehneosauridae, have greatly elongated ribs that presumably supported a rigid membranous wing of skin, and probably were gliders.

TRUE LIZARDS. All the major groups of true lizards are represented in the late Jurassic period of a relatively small area in western Europe, but a fossil record of their primitive forerunners is lacking. The most primitive true lizards appear to be the Iguanidae, a group whose fossil record does not extend prior to the late Cretaceous period, presumably owing to the paucity of Gondwanan localities. All the major extant iguanid groups probably were diversified by the beginning of the Cenozoic era, at least. Some of the earliest fossils of true lizards appear to be gekkotans. Ardeosaurs occur in the Upper Jurassic lithographic limestones of Germany and in Upper Jurassic deposits of eastern Asia.

SEVERAL PHASES OF SAURIAN EVOLUTION have been proposed. First there was a Triassic phase in which a number of different (perhaps unrelated) prelacertilian groups exploited the insectivorous habitus, with one group assuming herbivorous habits. Only a few aspects of this phase are known--the primitive paliguanids in Africa, with normal body type, followed by gliding kuehneosaurs. After the Triassic period, the eolacertilians dwindled as the more progressive lacertilians evolved.

A Jurassic phase of lacertilian evolution resulted in the presence of all living suborders of modern lizards by the end of the Jurassic, indicating a long previous history (882). Although there certainly were lizards in the undergrowth of early and middle Jurassic forests, probably widely spread throughout the world, no record of them is known. By reason of the structure of the skull and skeleton and the accompanying arrangements of muscles and soft parts, these active reptiles were able to prey better on arthropods, other small animals, and plants of the underbrush and rock than the reptiles that they presumably displaced, such as procolophonids and protorosaurs (1,302).

In the 3rd, or Cretaceous phase of lacertilian evolution, the present family groups evolved. Some of the more primitive living families must have already been in existence in the late Jurassic period, although no record of them has yet been found. The Cenozoic era may be thought of as a 4th phase of lacertilian evolution, in which expansion of ranges occurred during periods of peak tropicality in the Paleogene subdivision of the Tertiary period. Progressive restrictions in the cooler, drier Neogene subdivision gradually led to the formation of the boundaries of the present distributions (882).]

Overview

Accordingly, in response to ever more stringent selective pressures for small size, agility, and aerodynamically favorable properties, primarily for enhanced predatory capabilities and invasion of the arboreal and aerial habitats, the evolution of ovarian reproductive physiology and ovipositional modes of avian ancestors is seen to have been guided by two main environmental factors, one external, the other internal.

The external environmental factor was increasing equability of the Mesozoic climate and eventual climatic deterioration (and/or colonization of more temperate regions). The equable climate facilitated the evolution of surface nesting and sequential multiple-clutching in some forms, namely the stem-reptiles of the avian lineage. A very much later climatic deterioration--either lesser equability or lower average temperatures--and/or colonization of more temperate regions, led to the need for biparental incubation of single clutches by ancestral birds (where independent incubation of separate clutches had prevailed previously). Many species have since become emancipated from biparental egg care, primarily as a consequence of more secure and/or better insulated nesting quarters.

The internal environmental factor was, at first, poikilothermy; later it was homeothermy, achieved with the aid of both behavioral and morphological adaptations, and eventually it became progressively refined homeothermic endothermy, accompanied by progressively elevated body temperatures and egg incubatory temperatures. The concomitantly increasing rates at which eggs could be produced made possible the evolution of alternating ovarian function (allochronic ovulation) without reduction of the capacity for egg-production. This led to the practice of rapid double-clutching with independent incubation of the two clutches by the parents.

Next, the advance of body temperatures to higher levels made possible the periodic production of single eggs by alternating ovarian function (monoallochronic ovulation) at a sufficiently high rate to maintain hatching synchrony between two clutches assembled one egg at a time, the ultimate in ovarian functional adaptation for existence in aerial habitats. Lastly, achievement of the primitive avian grade of body temperature made possible the periodic production of single eggs by a single ovary and oviduct at the same sufficiently high rate, but the heightened incubatory temperatures led to a requirement for biparental clutch care. At this stage, the 2nd ovary and oviduct became superfluous, followed by their eventual general regression and vestigiality. The combination of increased rates of egg production and concomitantly reduced incubatory times, facilitated quantitative increases in the number of clutches and broods reared per annum, either increasing, maintaining, or minimizing any reduction in, the number of young "fledged" per annum (in the latter event, counterbalanced by greater longevity with a resultant increased lifetime reproductive success).

FOLLICULAR MATURATION AND ATRESIA

Follicular Maturation and Recapitulation

BIRDS. Possible support for the above evolutionary scheme in its most general aspects appears to be at hand in the reproductive physiology of some birds, reptiles, and other vertebrates. Just as the maturation of egg-care habits in some birds (particularly in Cockatiels) during reproductive cycles appears to recapitulate the equivalents of successive stages during avian evolution, so too do follicular maturational stages in some birds (most notably Budgerigars)--in which differing numbers of follicles exist in each stage--appear to do so.

As mentioned on page 142, developing ovarian follicles in breeding Budgerigars pass first through a stage in which 10-20 follicles are larger than the others, then through a stage in which 2-5 follicles are larger than the others, and finally through a stage in which one follicle is largest, with 5-8 others forming a graded hierarchical size series. I would suggest that the stage of 10-20 follicles recapitulates the equivalents of stem-reptilian and pre-avian stages, the former when about 20 eggs were ovulated polyautochronically and oviposited in a nest buried at a shallow depth, and the latter when about 10 eggs were ovulated polyautochronically and oviposited in surface nests. The stage of 2-5 follicles would appear to recapitulate the equivalents of primitive and advanced pro-avian stages, the former when about 5 eggs were incubated in each of 2 clutches ovulated polyallochronically in rapid succession in each reproductive episode, and the latter when about 5 eggs were incubated in each of 2 clutches ovulated monoallochronically in rapid succession in each reproductive episode (at times before the right ovary and oviduct had become vestigial). The last stage seemingly is the equivalent of that in both ancestral and extant birds.

In the Canary and many other species, the earlier stage of 10-20 mature follicles may have been lost or become inconspicuous. Judging from the egg-care behavior and abundant retention of relict responses in Cockatiels, the latter would be a most promising bird for further studies of ovarian follicular maturational stages.

LIZARDS. Maturing ovarian follicles in the viviparous Desert Night Lizard appear to recapitulate early stages in its evolutionary history in even greater detail than is seen in Budgerigars (see p. 142). Thus, there would appear to have been stages when the number of ripe eggs per clutch numbered 40-80, 20-40, 10-20, 5-10, 2-3, and 1. It may, in fact, be true generally that the ovarian follicular maturational stages of reptiles recapitulate past ovipositional habits more faithfully than do those of birds, considering the less extreme (though more varied) specializations of the reptilian reproductive system and the apparent participation of large atretic follicles in steroidogenesis in some species (see 908; on the assumption that more faithful recapitulation of ovarian function depends not on adaptive neutrality of ancestral physiological mechanisms but, rather, on the mechanisms having assumed other functional roles).

MARINE FORMS. In parasitic species of lampreys (Petromyzoniformes), belonging to the Agnatha, the most ancient group of vertebrates, there is a complete commitment of the entire complement of 5,000-170,000 female gametogenic cells, all of which develop in synchrony; no stem ovogonial cell is withheld for another cycle, as all lampreys die after spawning (864). Follicles form neither corpora atretica nor corpora lutea (989). Nor is an ovogonial stem cell withheld in teleosts that spawn but once and then die, such as *Oncorhynchus* spp., or catadromous eels (866; the latter migrate downstream to the sea to spawn). In the case of myxinoid cyclostomes (Myxiniformes), members of the same ancient group, recapitulation by follicular maturation stages also appears to occur and follicular atresia is common; thus, stages are found in which the number of follicles progressively decreases, generally, to a final clutch size of about 20-30 eggs (864, 911).

In the Dogfish (*Squalus acanthias*), about 50 follicles begin to develop, a lesser number (but possibly all 50) begin to undergo vitellogenesis, and only 2 or 3 persist; the remainder undergo atresia. Several other examples among elasmobranchs could be given, for example, *Carcharhinus dussumieri*, among a number of which follicular atresia is known (see 865). In the mouse, some follicles begin to grow each day; those which ovulate in a given cycle began to grow about 19 days earlier as part of a larger pool of growing follicles. Most of these follicles continue to grow until they reach the pre-antral stage, and then undergo atresia. The few follicles that actually enter the final stages of growth appear to be selected from the pool of large pre-antral follicles, perhaps by the surge of gonadotropins in the cycle preceeding ovulation (1,043). In Man, up to 12 or more Graafian follicles may mature each month, only 1 (or occasionally 2) of which ruptures, with the others regressing to corpora albicantes without ovulation (1,033).

Follicular Atresia

Current interest in the topic of ovarian follicular atresia centers primarily on its mode of occurrence, proximate causation, and consequences, particularly the question of the origin of the responsible phagocytic cells and the role of atresia in the origin of ovarian interstitial glandular cells. The question of the evolutionary significance or ultimate causation of atresia apparently has not been addressed previously, nor has there been much concern with documenting the numbers of follicles that exist in different maturational stages. The present brief resume is based primarily on the reviews of Saidapur (894) and Byskov (908).

Follicular atresia occurs in the ovaries of cyclostomes (lampreys and hagfishes), is well known in the ovaries of elasmobranchs, is a common feature of the piscine ovary, a very common feature of amphibian, avian, and mammalian ovaries, and has been reported in many reptilian species. "One of the most intriguing mysteries of ovarian physiology is what factors determine whether one follicle remains quiescent, another begins to develop but later becomes atretic, while still a 3rd matures and ovulates" (see G.S. Greenwald, 1972a, in 911). Concerning the mode of atresia, the responsible phagocytotic activity in non-mammalian vertebrates is exhibited mainly by hypertrophied follicular granulosal cells, with contributions from thecal elements in some species. The exact mechanisms of atresia, however, are largely unknown.

IN MAMMALS: (a) follicles can become atretic at any stage in their development; (b) atresia is much less common in growing pre-antral follicles than in antral follicles; (c) once a follicle has become atretic it ceases to grow, collapses, or gradually decreases in size; and (d) a peak of atresia commonly is seen around the time of ovulation (1,042). The only common manner in which follicles of different sizes are eliminated is by extrusion of the granulosal cells of the oocyte into the intraovarian rete tubules. In the small follicles, the oocytes usually show signs of degeneration and are disposed of by various means, while the granulosal cells look healthy. In the small-to-medium-sized follicles, the follicle cells as well as the oocytes may be removed by phagocytosis.

A general pattern of atresia cannot be described in medium-sized-to-large or large antral follicles, as atresia may begin in any compartment. One of the major differences between species is related to whether or not the theca interna of atretic follicles becomes part of the ovarian interstitium (1,042). It has been suggested that atresia is brought about by a regulatory failure (change in receptor content) of follicular cells, by increased circulating levels of gonadotropins (particularly LH) or androgens, or by lack of hormonal support (FSH or estrogen; see 1,033, 1,042).

It is well documented that estrogens and gonadotropins given to hypophysectomized animals prevent atresia.

The fate of the large atretic follicles is "partly to disappear, partly to persist to form part of the endocrine mass of the ovary." Thus, large, atretic follicles of rabbits synthesize progesterone in similar or larger amounts than do healthy follicles. Whereas, in mammals, the ovarian interstitial glandular cells have a dual origin in both ordinary connective tissue of the ovarian stroma and the theca interna of developing follicles, in non-mammalian vertebrates they arise from the hypertrophied thecal cells of the large previtellogenic and early vitellogenic follicles. A steroidogenic potential of the latter thecal cells has been demonstrated in only a few species.

The decline in the total number of mammalian follicles before puberty exceeds the losses that occur in later life and is mostly from the pool of small follicles. The total loss during mammalian reproductive life ranges from about 77% in the mouse and rat to 99.9% in Man and the dog. Monotremes start their reproductive life, like other mammals, with a finite number of germ cells, but their ovaries are like those of birds and reptiles in that they are dominated by large oocytes rather than by follicles and interstitial tissues as in eutherian and marsupial ovaries.

FOLLICULAR ATRESIA IN NON-MAMMALIAN VERTEBRATES generally may occur at any time of the year and at any stage of oocyte development. An increased number of oocytes undergoing atresia are encountered in the pre-spawning period or prior to breeding, and the oocytes that remain after the cessation of breeding invariably are lost by atresia. In view of the above, and (a) the fact that withdrawal of gonadotropins (including as a consequence of hypophysectomy) is followed by follicular degeneration, (b) the fact that high levels of exogenous gonadotropins can induce ovarian hyperstimulation and superovulation, and (c) the occurrence of the phenomenon of compensatory ovarian hypertrophy, it generally is believed that follicular atresia in all vertebrates in which it occurs is related to there being insufficient levels of gonadotropins to maintain all of the follicles that have begun vitellogenic growth (see also 900, 911).

The prevailing view relating to the function of follicular atresia regards the atretic non-ovulating follicles (a) as providing additional sources of steroidal hormones (or their precursors) for reproductive processes, (b) as a source of the ovarian interstitial glandular cells, (c) as an adaptation for the temporary suspension of breeding activity, or (d) merely as degenerating oocytes lacking function. It has been proposed that substances released from atretic follicles in mice inhibit the initiation of follicular growth. In the case of atresia of ovulated follicles, it is suggested that they might have achieved an important role in the endocrinological regulation of postovulatory events.

AN EVOLUTIONARY CONSERVATIVENESS OF THE CNS PROVIDES THE BASIS. The question of how or why it has transpired that the ovaries of many vertebrates appear to recapitulate ancestral ovipositional habits is one of great interest. In Part 1 of this Chapter, it was pointed out that behavior often is very conservative evolutionarily speaking, particularly incubatory patterns. In Parts 1 and 2, I dealt with many aspects of Cockatielian egg care, of the retention of relict responses that now are adaptively neutral, and of the recapitulation of ancestral stages of egg care during the reproductive cycle. In view of these conservative features of reproductive behavior, it should perhaps come as no surprise that reproductive cycles of the ovary also may display conservative features.

The conservativeness of reproductive behavior could be traced ultimately to conservative aspects of the evolution of the central nervous system. Could such a basis also underlie the conservative features of follicular maturation stages in the ovary? The answer to this query is "yes." Thus, it was pointed out in Chapter 1 (pp. 144, 145) that each avian ovarian follicle is intensely innervated (10 or more large bundles of axons, each containing 50-100 single fibers), particularly when mature, and that the function of the nerves may include preferential selection of developing follicles, induction of ovulation, and regulation of the distribution of blood-borne gonadotropins. Aside from the persuasive circumstantial evidence of innervation of each follicle by 500-1,000 or more single fibers, additional strong evidence for neural control is the existence of alternate (allochronic ovulation) and asymmetrical ovarian function in some vertebrates, for example, anoles. As mentioned on page 602, such selectivity could not reside in blood-borne factors but must have its basis in a differential follicular responsiveness that is under neural control.

FOLLICULAR ATRESIA IN MATURE OVARIES. In view of the known complex follicular innervation in birds and mammals, it is most reasonable to conclude that the historical basis for the recapitulation of evolutionary stages of follicular maturation in mature vertebrate ovaries is the same as for the recapitulation of many aspects of avian reproductive behavior and the retention of relict responses, namely the conservative nature of the evolution of the central nervous system. Whereas the retention of some types of relict behavior can be understood in terms of adaptive neutrality, alone, such an accounting of recapitulation of events in ovarian physiology seems much less likely. I would suggest that, in species in which the presumed recapitulation of ancestral follicular maturational stages is most marked, the processes involved either have assumed new physiological roles or have retained ancient ones. Studies of the corresponding processes in many other vertebrate species may elucidate this matter.

FOLLICULAR ATRESIA DURING OVARIAN MATURATION. Taking an even broader view, consider the fact that in most vertebrates there has been a progressive phylogenetic change in reproductive strategy in response to environmental pressures. The tendency has been toward ever increasing economy or even efficiency of reproductive effort. Thus, the strategy switched away from overwhelming a hostile environment with tens of thousands to millions (among most osteichthyans; 912) of male and lightly-provisioned female gametes, and a dependence upon chance for fertilization and the survival of the embryo, toward smaller clutches, greater assurance of fertilization, greater provisioning of the eggs, and greater parental investment in the care of the embryos or siting of the clutch.

The processes of internal fertilization, ovoviviparity, viviparity, and parental care developed by a few aquatic anamniotic vertebrates and aquatic and terrestrial amniotes are well known. The minimum number of times that viviparity could have evolved in reptiles is 75, compared to 10 in members of the Chondrichthyes, 4 in amphibians, and once in mammals. In lizards, viviparity has evolved at least 30 separate times, in snakes, at least 17 times, and in amphisbaenids, probably only once. All crocodilians, chelonians, and the Tuatara are oviparous (see D.G. Blackburn, 1981, in 989). [Viviparity in reptiles is known as early as the Mesozoic era; thus, fossils of *Ichthyosaurus*, an extinct marine form, contain the skeletons of young within the body cavity (640). Reptilian viviparity often is of the aplacental type, although reptiles of at least 9 families of squamates are reported to form yolk-sac or chorio-allantoic placentas (see 989; see also p. 620, **Ovarian Function and Reproductive Mode**).]

At the aquatic level, it is thought that reduced fecundity accompanied by larger eggs in osteichthyans are adaptations to relatively sparse planktonic food in polar and deep water. Some osteichthyans oviposit on plants and guard the eggs, others guard nests of only 100-150 young. In sea catfishes (Ariidae), in which the male broods the young in his mouth, the embryos may number as few as 20 (912).

The almost universal occurrence of follicular atresia testifies to the likelihood that this was the mechanism that provided the first effective means of reduction in the number of female gametes, probably in a gradual process accompanied by a gradually greater provisioning of the eggs. Alternate ovarian function would have yielded only a 50% reduction in egg number, though possible in a shorter time span and more efficiently than atretic mechanisms. The failure of one ovary to develop in some reptiles, bats, hagfishes, elasmobranchs, and most birds suggests that alternate, and eventually single, ovarian function also has been a much used method of clutch-size reduction among vertebrates.

The atresia of large numbers of follicles in maturing ovaries of many vertebrates would appear to be a recapitulation of the equivalents of the earliest phylogenetic stages in clutch reduction by atretic mechanisms. Its almost universal occurrence (not, for example, in parasitic lampreys) suggests either that the atretic process or its consequences assumed or retained an important physiological role, or that there is great rigidity (conservatism) in the processes of oogonial proliferation and/or early folliculogenesis as modulated by the central nervous system. Although there are complicating factors, following this interpretation one would expect to find a tendency among the vertebrate reproductive systems that are of the lowest fecundity (produce the smallest egg clutches or litters) to be characterized by the greatest atresia of oogonia and/or follicles.

IRREGULARITIES DURING ONSET OF AVIAN REPRODUCTIVE ACTIVITY appear to be a consequence of incompletely established pathways for neural control and hormonal control--pathways that are not yet fully supportive of current reproductive practices. It requires 1 or 2 weeks of oviposition after the first ovulation for the domestic fowl hen's ovarian control mechanisms to mature fully. Reasoning along the lines pursued in the preceding, one would expect any deviation of ovarian function from its present pattern during this period to be in the direction of ancient patterns. And so it is. Thus, during the period under consideration, the often erratic oviposition (948) yields: 2 eggs daily or double-yolked eggs (possible throwbacks to the times of *en-masse* oviposition and autochronic ovulation); soft-shelled eggs grossly deficient in calcium (a possible throwback to times before the eggs were calcified and hard-shelled); and irregular laying with longer than daily time intervals between eggs (a possible throwback to the times before daily oviposition had been achieved but after the establishment of periodic oviposition).

[Lack of coordination of ovarian and oviductal function, as a consequence of the commercial tendency to bring hens into productivity precociously, has been suggested to account for the latter irregularity (see 948). But, reasoning along the lines pursued here, abnormalities of precocial function also would be expected to deviate in the direction of the mature functions of times past.]

ANCESTRAL BIRDS

TRUE FLIGHT----HIGHER METABOLIC RATES AND BODY TEMPERATURES. The last major step in the evolutionary sequence--that from advanced pro-aves to ancestral birds--now is considered. This entailed the achievement of the higher metabolic rates and higher body temperatures that permitted more rapid, powerful muscle contractions with lesser fatigue. These adaptations probably would have been required even for relatively brief periods of vigorous powered flight. [Providing additional perspective in this connection are observations of the characteristic differences between cold-bodied and warm-bodied fishes, namely, that the latter swim faster and more sustainedly (660).]

Selection was for those advanced pro-aves of a population with body temperatures at the upper end of the spectrum, increased wing aspect-ratios, most efficient wing profiles, greatest coordination, wing flexion of the upstroke (977), and superior wing-feather attachments (firmly based in bone), because of the many advantages conferred by the powered flight capabilities of such individuals, particularly facilitation of transport. At this stage in avian evolution, body temperatures probably were in the range of primitive extant birds (see Table 3). This latter conclusion is supported by the fact that pneumatic bones (which constitute effective heat exchangers) have not been found in the appendicular skeletons of Mesozoic birds, suggesting that they probably had lower body temperatures than most living birds (193).

HIGHER BODY TEMPERATURES AND SHARED PARENTAL CARE. Since the achievement of a higher body temperature would have entailed a correspondingly higher incubatory temperature, the strategem wherein both parents incubated separate clutches would have begun to lose its effectiveness. Thus, maintenance of a higher body temperature would have required evolving advanced pro-aves to forage more intensively and efficiently and/or for longer periods, and developing embryos would have become increasingly intolerant of being chilled (use of solar heat would have been insufficiently reliable even during midday). The waning of equable climatic regimes and/or the colonization of more temperate regions would have accentuated the problem of egg chilling and could have played a major role in accelerating the evolutionary transition to ancestral birds. Those advanced pro-aves that lived under the most temperate climatic regimes would have led the way in this transition. Additionally, a concomitant decrease in the abundance of large flying insects and the initiation of a transition to herbivory by many forms may have played roles.

It probably required only relatively small adjustments of the incubatory pattern of advanced pro-aves (treated on pp. 599-603) to achieve biparental care of a single clutch. The advanced pro-aves that followed this evolutionary path to ancestral birds never ‘risked’ having their eggs become overly chilled while they foraged (ground-nesting Rock Pigeons rarely leave their eggs uncovered for more than a few min at a time; 101). Accordingly, they would have had greater reproductive success than those that continued to leave the eggs of seperate clutches unattended, though concealed, while foraging.

NESTING ADAPTATIONS RELIEVE RIGOROUS INCUBATORY NEEDS. Two of the consequences of the need for sustained higher incubatory temperatures were selection for ancestral birds that nested in insulative structures that concealed the eggs and protected them from the elements, and for allofeeding of the incubating parent by its mate. These practices eventually emancipated many avian species from the need to be in contact with their eggs more or less continuously and/or from the obligatory participation of both parents in the care and incubation of the eggs. Incubatory and nest-exchange patterns then were set free to evolve along many channels. The former patterns proved to be most conservative; there were relatively few channels along which incubatory patterns could evolve, whereas the paths open for the alterations of nest-exchange practices were almost limitless (see pp. 373-376, **Parental Care of Eggs**).

THE TRANSITION TO HERBIVORY

PHYLOGENY OF ANGIOSPERMS. Because of the crucial role that doubtless was played by angiosperms in the evolutionary development of avian herbivory (referring to the consumption of any portion of a plant), and of the equally vital roles that birds probably played in the Cretaceous proliferation of angiosperms, this section is introduced with a brief review of some considerations of angiospermous phylogeny. This is a matter that is complicated by increasing evidence that most, if not all, of the well-known trends in angiospermous evolution are reversible, at least to some extent (but lost organs are not regained), and it remains one of deep disagreement.

However, it seems likely that there were (a) an origin in continually moist, tropical or subtropical uplands, perhaps of West Gondwana or southeastern Asia, (b) an early split into two classes, the Magnolopsida (dicotyledons) and Lilopsida (monocotyledons) in post-Barremian times, (c) a major radiation during the middle Cretaceous, and (d) a rise to dominance in tropical lowlands during a period of worldwide warming in the late Cretaceous (an increase of 5-6°C in marine temperatures in the equatorial Pacific)--perhaps in the Cenomanian to Coniacian (see 1,065, 1,245, 1,313, 1,346, and pp. 14, 15). It apparently was only as the early angiosperms evolved xylem with greater conductive efficiency (without crosswalls) that they were able to emigrate from the highlands into the tropical lowlands and there radiate quickly into varied and even extreme habitats, with their high insolation and wide fluctuations in soil moisture (1,313).

[Angiosperms have unique reproductive adaptations: the ovules are protected by a closed carpel crowned by a stigma and style which receive the pollen grains; fertilization follows soon after pollination; floral parts have evolved that attract pollinating arthropods and other animals, while the ovules are protected from these same potential seed-predators; and double fertilization (involving the fusion of 2 sets of nuclei, to form the zygote and endosperm, respectively) and a triploid endosperm may allow the rapid growth of propagules. The latter adaptations are advantageous in situations where a rapid life cycle is favored and perhaps also in that they reduce the nutritive value of the ovules at the time when the flower is attracting the pollinating arthropods. Angiosperms are involved extensively not only with arthropods, birds, and bats as pollen vectors, but also with birds and mammals as major seed vectors (see 1,300, 1,376.]

According to the classical strobilar hypothesis of angiospermous descent: (a) members of the dicotyledonous subclass Magnoliidae (magnolias, laurels, etc.) have retained the greatest number of primitive features; (b) the flower is an abbreviated, highly modified spore-bearing shoot, possibly derived from a gymnosperm-like reproductive structure, a strobilus; and (c) the earliest angiosperms may be sought somewhere in or among near relatives of the Magnoliidae, some of which are contemporary but most of which are extinct (719, 1,376). Angiosperm phylogenists generally agree that primitive angiosperms were somewhat similar to relict members of the Winteraceae (*Amborella, Eupomatia*, etc.), and that members of the extinct Mesozoic Pteridospermae or seed ferns were their likely progenitors. It is thought that primitive angiosperms were pollinated by insects (primarily beetles; 1,313, 1,376, 1,377). In a divergent point of view (see, for example, 1,306), the data that many workers regard as supportive of the strobilar descent hypothesis are thought to reflect a secondary stage in angiospermous evolution, that of a successful dicotyledonous diversification about 100 mya, but one that is not closely related to the origin of angiosperms from pre-angiosperms. In this scenario, the monocotyledons are thought to have diverged very early and to be direct descendants of the earliest angiosperms--possibly originating from a member of the extinct seed ferns.

Although some plants of the Jurassic bore seeds in closed cases or ovaries (85)--one of the essential attributes of angiosperms--the earliest certain angiosperms enter the fossil record in the Hauterivian, Barremian, and Aptian ages of the early Cretaceous period. They had monosulcate (singly grooved or furrowed) pollen and rather small, simple leaves with a poorly organized, irregular sort of pinnate net-venation. Their other characteristics are inferred rather than established (1,313, 1,377). In this connection, the Debey-Fontainer leaf type of Cretaceous angiosperms may have been derived from the *Scoresbya* leaf type of early Mesozoic gymnosperms. This type of palmate leaf with sympodial branching of segments (from several nodes behind the apex) could have given rise to both simple and compound leaves (1,345).

The earliest fossil remains of plants that could be monocotyledons give few clues to the states that were present in the earliest representatives, possibly because of deficiencies in our evolutionary concepts, including preconceived ideas of what is likely to have been a monocotyledon. Other views on the origins and relationships of the monocotyledons are: that they evolved from an aquatic, herbaceous derivative of magnoliiflorous affinity; that early forms were forest hygrophytes (growing in waterlogged soil) resembling extant members of the subclass Arecidae (including duckweeds, marsh herbs, and Panama-hat plants); that early forms resembled extant members of the Liliales (including yams); that they evolved from some extinct group of early, shrubby dicotyledons; and that they are an early and strongly specialized offshoot of the Magnoliidae (1,310, 1,311).

THE EVOLUTIONARY TRANSITION TO HERBIVORY BY VARIOUS AVIAN SPECIES at various times probably came about: (a) as large insects became decreasingly abundant and many insect species tended increasingly to crepuscularity and nocturnality; (b) as a result of increasing contacts of ancestral birds with leaves, flowers, fruits, and other plant parts that were good sources of arthropods and other invertebrates; and (c) as an accompaniment of the diversification of grasses (984) in the arid-trending world climates of the Oligocene and Miocene epochs. The latter plants are adapted to survive seasonal aridity and extremes of cold (and effects of wildfire) by the siting of perennating organs and growing points at or below ground level (988; see also p. 11).

[A not dissimilar scenario is envisioned for foraging specialization by the ancestors of bats and other mammals, although the former presumably were absent for the first 75 million yr of the evolution of angiosperms. It has been suggested that the evolution of nectarivory in bats followed upon the habit of hovering very near flowers in preying upon insects in their corollas. Pollinating systems involving bats and other mammals usually are nocturnal and include flowers that are dull-colored, odorous, and generally open, with copious nectar (782, 1,216, 1,296, 1,339).]

THE EXTENSIVE CRETACEOUS PROLIFERATION OF ANGIOSPERMOUS PLANTS very likely involved a tripartite disperser-pollinator-angiospermous co-evolutionary strategy that, by making available unprecedented amounts of nectar and fruits, created new niches for nectarivores and frugivores, as well as new evolutionary possibilities for the plants themselves. This proliferation is thought by Regal to have depended largely on the emergence on the Cretaceous scene of species of widely foraging birds acting in the role of seed dispersing vectors (1,300). This was, indeed, a time when a major radiation of birds was occurring (see pp. 369-372, **Paleontological Comparisons**). Avian pollination also may have played a significant role and seems to have been one of the major evolutionary factors in the development of the Australian and South African genera of Proteaceae after the breakup of Gondwana (1,074).

Birds that had achieved true flight capabilities and fed on fleshy or nutlike fruits adapted for dispersal by dinosaurs, or on seeds that previously may have been dispersed by wind or water, could have carried great numbers of moderately large seeds to colonization areas well outside of the traditional ranges. Plants derived from these seeds would have flourished in areas with suitable climatic and edaphic moisture conditions and distant from populations of coadapted seed predators and "pests." The key role of insect pollination would have been to allow the progeny resulting from such dispersals to produce outcrossed offspring, since wind pollination, prevalent among gymnosperms, would have been unreliable for the new populations, with members that either were widely dispersed or existed in small clusters (1,300, 1,346).

[In regard to avian seed dispersal, the seeds of fleshy fruits rarely are kept in the intestines for more than 30 min. The absolute ceiling even for very rare occasional dispersal of such seeds is thought to be about 500 km, with 100-200 km probably being the practical ceiling for most species. There have been few quantitative studies of the roles of birds and bats in the dispersal of tropical rainforest species with succulent fruits (see 1,071). Seed dispersal by ants predominates over avian dispersal and other dispersal modes on nutrient-poor soils in fire-prone habitats in Australia and South Africa. Effects of avian dispersal on plant population dynamics remain poorly known (see also p. v). However, it is known that seeds dispersed by vertebrates often are clumped, leading to possibilities for sibling and intraspecific competition (1,322). There is no concrete evidence of widespread avian nectarivory until the Miocene epoch (1,339).]

According to this scheme, the changing climatic conditions in the Cretaceous period led to many new ecological opportunities and an increased variety of competitive interactions. These led to selective pressures on plants for rapid growth strategies, new systems of chemical defense, and diversification of morphology. These favored and accelerated the diversification of angiosperms to such a degree that they outcompeted the pre-existing and previously dominant gymnospermous populations (see specific treatment below for members of the Cycadeoidales). The latter became so sparse that their wind and primitive insect pollination systems were relatively ineffective, and many became extinct (1,300).

Accordingly, a major portion of the avian transition to herbivory may have been led by a segment of widely-foraging, early Cretaceous birds through their role as angiospermous seed vectors. This probably occurred while true flight capabilities were being achieved and may have encompassed a relatively lengthy portion of the early-to-mid Cretaceous period. Mammals would appear to have been major beneficiaries of the angiospermous proliferation and the emergent properties of angiospermous coadaptations with insects and birds. Mammals doubtless also played important dispersing roles, since several subsequent striking correlations exist between the times of first appearances (i.e., diversification) of many mammalian and angiospermous groups, beginning in the last few million yr of the Cretaceous period (1,301, 1,345). Thus, some of the earliest known small, angiospermous fruits possessed glochids (hooklets or barbed hairs) that seemingly would have tangled with mammalian fur as the animals foraged among the plants for prey or edible vegetal parts (1,345). Similar "middle" Cretaceous evolutionary radiations among dinosaurs probably also were related to the diversification of angiosperms (1,343). Intense low cropping of vegetation by the herbivorous dinosaurs of those times placed a premium on adaptations of plants for rapid growth, reproduction, and colonization, which were fortes of the early angiosperms (1,404).

In connection with the above scenario, insect-damaged fossil leaves are known from as far back as the early Permian period, members of the order Cycadeoidales, with bisexual strobili with all of the characteristics of showy flowers, are known from the Triassic period, fruits are known from the early Cretaceous period (768, 1,254), and there is conclusive evidence of well established insect pollination long before the existence of angiosperms (1,254). As mentioned above, unequivocal angiospermous pollen grains and leaves first appear in the fossil record in the Hauterivian, Barremian, and Aptian ages of the Cretaceous period (see Table 1), and there is no compelling reason to believe that any considerable time gap separates these first appearances from actual appearances (1,345).

Despite the apparent major systematic and ecological radiations of flowering plants in the mid-Cretaceous, they were still early in their evolutionary development (1,394). Records of the flowers of these plants are rare. This is not unexpected, since the ephemeral nature of many of the parts of angiospermous flowers render them much more delicate than those of the Cycadeoidales (768, 1,345). However, demonstrably bisexual fossil flowers recently were recovered from Cenomanian clays of the Dakota Formation in Nebraska; these provide the best evidence available for early pollination of angiosperms by insects (1,393). Likewise, unisexual angiospermous flowers and inflorescences of higher dicotyledons recently were recovered from an eastern North American, Lower Cretaceous formation of Late Albian sediments. Combined with architectural and cuticular features of associated leaves, these floral remains suggest that sycamore-like plants with unisexual, probably insect-pollinated flowers were an important element in the mid-Cretaceous diversification of dicotyledons (1,245). Based on the fossil record, it still is not possible to determine whether unisexual or bisexual flowers are more primitive, but both seem to be representative of ancient conditions (1,393).

The Cycadeoidales reached their greatest abundance in the Jurassic period and then declined rapidly to extinction in the late Cretaceous. The ability of angiosperms to outcompete members of the Cycadeoidales derived from their phylogenetic youthfulness and modern floral structure, enabling them to produce more concentrated nectar, a higher content of proteins with greater palatability, and more intensive colors and odors, which attracted contemporary pollinators and biotic dispersing vectors. A decreasing-temperature-induced decline of cycadophytes (dwarf trees resembling dwarf palms) in the early Cretaceous also may have promoted the primary angiospermous radiation. Biochemical evolution of the Cycadeoidales, already adapted to pollination by insects, seemingly could not progress rapidly enough for effective competition, and since their primitive metabolism could not satisfy the increasing needs of herbivorous insects and birds, they became extinct (1,254, 1,345). In this connection, good evidence for the occurrence and biological implications of competition for dispersers between extant plants is meager (1,322).

On the other hand, wind-pollinated cycads have survived despite their possession of a primitive mode of reproductive biology. Members of the class Gnetopsida differ from other extant gymnosperms in chemistry, chromosome structure, reproductive morphology, embryology, and the possession of unusual growth forms (1,306). The relict genus, *Gnetum*, apparently survived by evolving energy-rich fruits, perhaps dispersed largely by birds, e.g., currently including the Chestnut-mandibled Toucan (*Rhamphastus ambiguus*), and possibly by producing seeds non-sexually by apomixis (although pollination has not been ruled out; 1,296). Angiosperms, on the contrary, under selection by pollinators and avian and other biotic dispersing vectors, as suggested above, showed an unusual genetic plasticity and progress in their further evolution of floral types, nutritious floral fructification organs, and vegetative structures (1,254, 1,296, 1,300, 1,388). The double fertilization and triple fusion of living angiosperms, which act to initiate the build-up of food reserves within the seed only after fertilization has taken place, are of particular benefit to small plants that do not have large reserves of energy. These reproductive methods are advantageous to greater or lesser degree compared to those of many gymnosperms, particularly cycads, in which food reserves often are built into the seeds regardless of the occurrence of fertilization (1,306).

[The costs of nectars, scents, and flowers, and the great diversity of complex pollination systems suggest that there are great advantages to sexuality maintained by pollination by animal vectors (1,300), and angiosperms in which large quantities of nectar are produced can be cross-pollinated effectively only by animal visitors with high energetic requirements. However, the kinds of large flowers with copious nectar that are visited by vertebrates, in general, did not occur in the course of angiospermous evolution until the end of the Cretaceous at the earliest (1,339). Although it is uncertain whether the Czekanowskiales were immediate predecessors of some groups of angiosperms, they clearly demonstrate the possibility of evolution from the pteridospermous to the angiospermous level of floral organization (1,345).]

The highly complex organization of the flowers of angiosperms represents a more sophisticated system for insect pollination than the systems developed in the Gnetales, Cycadeoidales, or other cycads. Fossil evidence indicates that until the middle of the Tertiary period all showy flowers were exclusively of regular shape and radial symmetry, with no trace of bilateralism. It is suggested that the Cycadeoidales were visited and pollinated by beetles and other insects with restricted sensory capabilities (flies, wasps, etc.), able to recognize only elementary, paleomorphic, radial floral patterns (1,254, 1,339, 1,345).

The absence of any trace of bilateral symmetry in primitive flower-like structures of gymnosperms in the Cretaceous period and earlier clearly indicates a close parallelism of the sensory evolution of pollinating insects with the morphogenetic development of floral types (1,254; see also 1,376). It is suggested that the pistil (the female reproductive organ) of the angiospermous flower developed coadaptively with insect pollinators (1,345). Floral bilateralism confers a great adaptive advantage because it secures cross fertilization by specialized pollinators (bees, bumblebees, butterflies, some anthophilous flies, etc.) with limited amounts of pollen. Thus, the visiting arthropod can approach the flower only from a certain direction and must move in a particular way to reach the food source. There is substantial evidence that this trend to bilaterality in the evolution of floral types was correlated with the genetic, chemical, and metabolic changes in the evolving plants (1,254).]

CIRCUMSTANCES FAVORING THE EVOLUTION OF LARGE-SCALE GRANIVORY are especially prevalent in pioneer or early seral (communal) stages of successions, grasslands, and arid or semi-arid savannas. The vegetation in such angiospermous communities is subjected to widely varied environmental conditions, either through the temporal transiency of early successional stages or the unpredictable stresses imposed by climatic fluctuations. Though seed production in such communities may be far less predictable than insect levels, this disadvantage is more than offset by the fact that vast quantities of seeds are produced when and where environmental conditions are favorable. In fact, the most highly developed cases of granivory, and the most closely attuned exploitive systems, occur among birds exposed to resources that provide large concentrations of small seeds at discrete intervals, and exhibit tremendous yearly variation in abundance at a given locality. These birds include the most important and spectacular granivorous avian populations (968). Moreover, although grasses and grain crops now are pollinated by wind, some of the simplest bombusoid grasses were plesiomorphically insect-pollinated, so that ground-foraging insectivorous ancestral birds would have come into close contact with them.

DIVERGENCES IN THE ANCESTRAL AVIAN AND MAMMALIAN LINEAGES

A similarly intensive treatment of the origin of mammals, from the same perspectives as those taken for birds, would require great length. However, it may be instructive merely to suggest what the main similarities and decisive divergences from the avian pathway may have been, and the possible correlations between them, with a minimum of documentation and discussion and without setting out a progression of stages.

NESTING AND INCUBATION. It would appear that the early post-reptilian forerunners of mammals adapted to the predation pressure of diurnal reptiles by becoming both smaller and nocturnal (perhaps also the evolutionary tendency of flying insects in response to avian predation pressures). The bodily weight of all known Triassic mammals has been estimated at 20-40 g, in the extant shrew-to-rat range. This is an order of magnitude smaller than that of any known middle Triassic cynodont (1,281, 1,340, 1,341). Nocturnal terrestrial-arboreal habitats invaded by early mammals or their forerunners probably had not been exploited fully by small insectivores, or even may have been vacant (1,281). This change of habitat was facilitated by tropical and subtropical climatic regimes of the late Triassic or early Jurassic period (though not necessarily uniform or equable, and rigorous in many places; 86). Like pre-aves, proto-mammals passed through a surface nesting stage. Their nests probably were hidden in inconspicuous surface burrows and underbrush, perhaps also among rocks in locations that were difficult of access, guarded by day by a continuous, contiguous presence of the resting parent(s). Embryogenesis, at first, was speeded up primarily by climatic surface heat and the heat of decaying vegetation, without the benefit of solar radiation impinging directly upon the eggs or nest surface. As homeothermic endothermy developed, perhaps beginning at a very early stage of surface nesting, parental bodily heat also hastened development.

These suggested early habits are consistent with the scenario suggested for the evolution of milk production, as expanded (1,241) from Darwin's suggestion: (1) increased proximity of the female parent to newly laid eggs, perhaps with the development of a vascularized abdominal incubatory patch; (2) enhancement of egg productivity through prophylactic protolacteal secretions from cutaneous glands, protecting the eggs and young from desiccation and bacterial, protozoal, and fungal attack; (3) ingestion or absorption of the maternal secretions by offspring, and the eventual assumption of a nutritional role for the prophylactic secretions (the gene for a nutritional factor, alpha-lactoglobulin, has evolved by duplication of the genetic material for a prophylactic factor, lysozyme; see 1,241); (4) concurrent development of suckling behavior, localized areolar regions, and an increased nutritional value of the maternal secretions.

The suggested early habits also are consistent with what little is known of extant oviparous mammals. Thus, in the springtime the female Duck-billed Platypus builds a nest of grass, leaves, roots, etc., in a chamber at the end of a long, serpentine burrow in the side of a stream bank and retires to it for some days. It appears that she lies on her back or side and curls up her tail over the abdomen; the 1-3 eggs, when extruded, come to lie in the "incubatorium" (at about 31.8°C) formed between the tail and the abdomen, and require at least 10 days of incubation to hatch. When laid, the eggs are covered with a sticky secretion of unknown origin, so that they adhere to one another and presumably to the hairs of the abdomen. The female Echidna, on the other hand, develops a pouch on the ventral surface, in which she incubates her single egg at about 32½°C. The egg apparently enters the pouch directly from the cloaca, which penetrates the pouch when the animal is in a curled-up position (1,308).

[The presence of thin, inert shells on marsupial eggs, in which the embryos remain until late in pregnancy, and an egg-tooth on the embryos are relics of their previous oviparous condition (1,308, 1,342). Pelvic structure is unknown for most Mesozoic mammals, but a few species from the late Cretaceous of Asia can be studied. The ischial arc of *Barunlestes* is very narrow and much the same is true of the well-preserved pelves of some multituberculates, possibly precluding the laying of large eggs and suggesting the birth of nidicolous young (1,342).]

HABITAT AND FORAGING. The occupancy of terrestrial-arboreal habitats, and progressively more intensive foraging, promoted homeothermic endothermy, just as it did in avian ancestors, though not of a specialization capable, at first, of coping with the high heat loads encountered frequently in a diurnal existence. But there was the added selective advantage to the early mammal that would have accrued to an active nocturnal, incipient homeothermic endotherm preying on ectotherms. A notable departure was that the arthropodan and small vertebrate prey were flightless. Prey were taken primarily during dawn, dusk, and night using quadrupedal locomotion and head and jaw-grasping movements, with corresponding adaptations of the jaws and dentition.

Accordingly, although adaptations of the visual system for nocturnal vision are not to be minimized, the sensory combination employed probably was primarily olfactory (including pheromonal cues), auditory, and tactile, rather than auditory and visual, so that jumping and pouncing played relatively minor roles in prey capture. In consequence, the hindlimbs did not undergo enhanced development (even many lizards that jump and pounce are not bipedal, and early mammals possessed an essentially modern posture, with a capability for high mobility over complex surfaces; see 1,340). [An outstanding feature of the sensory neocortex of the Duck-billed Platypus is the relatively enormous area connected with somatotopic inputs from the muzzle, consistent with its exclusive reliance on tactile information when foraging (see 1,308).]

The 3-4-fold increase in relative brain weight of members of one of the largest known mammalian groups, the triconodontids, over the most advanced mammal-like reptiles probably traces to increased musculoskeletal coordination in an arboreal-terrestrial habitat, together with greater auditory and olfactory acuity (see 1,341). With the nests hidden in burrows and underbrush--not necessarily in close proximity to foraging sites --and with neither the nests nor the ground readily visible at night, there would have been no selection for quick descent from trees by jumping and parachuting. Rather, nocturnal arboreal descents would have been quadrupedal, with the head leading the way, and would have been part of foraging activity.

OVARIAN FUNCTION AND REPRODUCTIVE MODE. In the absence of either acrobatic arboreality or invasion of aerial habitats, neither of which would have been favored in conditions of poor vision, selection for reduced relative clutch weight would have been weak. Consequently, polyautochronic ovarian function was retained. The evolution of viviparity can be seen as probably having been responsive to the same types of selective factors that may have been operative in the evolution of viviparity in lizards (see also p. 610, last paragraph), among which are: safeguarding and providing an essentially constant and optimal environment for developing embryos; expanding the period of provision of sustenance by the female; and providing greater predictability in the placement of the neonates at favorable sites (673, 1,342, 1,349, 1402). [The increased bodily size at maturity and the larger broods apparently compensate for a lower fecundity per season (1,318), and viviparity occurs mostly in those environments in which breeding seasons are so short that they allow only one reproductive episode per year (1,349).] The major departure would have been that, having occurred in an incipient homeothermic endotherm, viviparity would have been even more advantageous to the mammalian ancestor, inasmuch as it would have shortened greatly the period of embryonic development.

INTEGUMENTAL STRUCTURES. In the absence of selection for either insulative shielding from solar radiation or aerodynamically favorable properties, evolutionary modifications of scales would have been solely in response to selection for the retention of bodily heat, for which purpose hair is eminently adaptive.

In brief summary, the proposed divergences between the mammalian and avian early ancestral lineages is that mammals evolved from crepuscular-nocturnal rather than crepuscular-diurnal ancestors, hunting non-volant rather than volant arthropods, in conditions of predominantly poor rather than predominantly good vision, with a corresponding emphasis on olfaction and touch rather than sight, by locomotory means emphasizing quadrupedality rather than bipedality, nesting at the surface in hidden, protected locations rather than in exposed locations in the neighborhood of trees and other shading foliage, descending trees and shrubs head first by quadrupedal progression, rather than by jumping and parachuting, foraging during descent rather than seeking quick access to the ground or nest site, remaining terrestrial-arboreal rather than invading aerial habitats, and evolving scale adaptations that solely favored retention of bodily heat rather than those that also provided shielding from external heat sources and favorable aerodynamical properties.

A SYNTHESIS OF AVIAN EVOLUTION

USEFUL WORKING HYPOTHESIS AND DIDACTIC AND HEURISTIC TOOLS. Because of our very limited factual information about avian evolution, the above analyses and the following synthesis necessarily contain many speculative elements. However, the treatments are based on evolutionary doctrine and synthetic theory and are backed by reasonable inferences from the reproductive behavior of 3 species of small parrots and by the evidence of much other avian and reptilian reproductive behavior and physiology.

These treatments are the only existing attempts to trace the evolution of nesting and the care of eggs and young from that of the stem-reptilian forerunners of birds to that of their primitive ancestors ("ancestral birds"), topics that otherwise scarcely have been touched upon. As such, the treatments can serve as useful working hypotheses and didactic and heuristic tools, subject to elaboration and modification as additional findings become available. Their value for these purposes lies not so much in the details of the proposed evolutionary scheme, for example, those listed in Table 3, as in expanding our perspectives by bringing new considerations to bear on problems of avian evolution, heretofore largely the exclusive domain of paleornithology, with little or no consideration of the canalizing influences of reproductive biology.

ANCESTORS WELL ADAPTED FOR BOTH TERRESTRIALITY AND ARBOREALITY. It is very likely that early avian ancestors from the stem-reptiles to advanced pro-aves nested on the ground but increasingly invaded arboreal, and eventually aerial, habitats. If one bears this in mind, the apparently conflicting and sometimes highly polarized locomotory interpretations of the anatomy of *Archaeopteryx* (see for example 1,185, 1,186) favoring terrestrial cursoriality, on the one hand, and arboreality, on the other, become obviated. These early ancestors, as also many contemporary birds, were adapted well for both habitats (see also 1,193, 1,196). Though avian ancestors became increasingly well adapted for arboreality, coexisting adaptations for terrestriality long remained crucial. Though the latter were decreasingly in support of foraging, the need for them in other terrestrial activities declined only with the advent of avian arboreal nesting in the absence of terrestrial foraging, and of the extreme specializations of some groups for non-terrestrial habitats.

HARD-SHELLED EGGS----DEEP NESTS----LONG INCUBATORY PERIODS. In light of the above considerations, an appropriate starting point for a synthesis of evolutionary stages and selective pressures in the reptile-to-bird transition would seem to be at the level of the fundamental change in reproductive behavior that diverted the forerunners of the stem-reptiles of the avian lineage onto the evolutionary pathway toward birds.

Consider that the reptilian ancestors of birds very likely possessed rigid-shelled eggs and buried them in deep nests in multilayers. Such eggs of contemporary reptiles approach closely to the avian level of organization and development, including the possession of 2 shell membranes and the apparent withdrawal of calcium from the shell for the bones of the developing embryo. The shells and albumen of such eggs give physical strength, protection against microorganisms and small invertebrates, and independence from external water sources, permitting deep burial. In this connection, most hard-shelled eggs of chelonians develop slowly and, where hardness of the shell varies among closely-related species, the embryos of species with the least pliable shells develop most slowly (757).

Deep burial gives added security from predators, a relatively constant environmental milieu, as regards temperature and moisture, and accommodates more eggs (piled or in multilayers). Since temperatures are relatively low in deep nests, development is slowed and oxygen requirements can be met under the existing conditions of slower gas exchanges.

[The incubatory periods of chelonians, vary from 28 to 212 days in tropical species (28 days in *Trionyx sinensis*), and are greater than 100 days and may exceed a year in southern temperate species (420 days in *Geochelone pardalis*). Among large reptiles with eggs incubated at 25-30°C, few incubatory periods are shorter than 55-60 days (774). For the eggs of Tuataras, which develop in a 10-13-cm deep nest in friable, well-drained soil covered with loose soil and leaf litter and exposed to the sun, the incubatory period is 13-15 months (including a 5-month winter period of suspended development; 755). Most squamates require at least 3 months to develop but some take as long as 10 months (including a 3-month period of suspended development; 763, 764). Incubatory periods are highly variable in the species in which embryonic development progresses slowly (681, 757).]

Thus, the ancestors of the stem-reptiles doubtless practiced deep burial of eggs, piled or in multilayers, and had relatively lengthy incubatory periods. Since the primitive mode of avian nesting doubtless was one in which the eggs were deposited at the surface and in a single layer, it is necessary to account first for the transition of the ancestors of stem-reptiles to the use of more shallow nesting sites that accommodate fewer eggs. The selective pressure for the change would have been the pervasive one of increased reproductive success, achieved through the medium of reduced vulnerability of developing embryos in consequence of greatly shortened incubatory periods and parental attendance at nest sites.

One can envision a number of modes of accomplishing reduced vulnerability of developing embryos, merely by reflecting on the various means by which it has been accomplished among extant reptiles, for example, by the development of viviparity and more extended periods of oviductal retention of eggs before oviposition. However, the evolution of birds from reptiles probably was the product of the very specific environmental conditions and organismic substrates that prevailed during its occurrence. The selective pressures concerned would appear to have greatly influenced the evolution of some of the organisms practicing deep burial of hard-shelled eggs, yet had a lesser or no influence on others.

AVOIDING LARGE DIEL TEMPERATURE FLUCTUATIONS AND HIGH TEMPERATURES. The two critical features with regard to reptilian embryology that stand out above all others are the great susceptibility of reptilian embryos to asynchronous morphogenesis caused by excessive diel temperature fluctuations during late stages of development, and the susceptibility of embryos to exposure to high temperatures. Extreme high and low temperatures can be tolerated briefly, and low temperatures can be tolerated lengthily, at least in pre-somite embryos, in which case embryonic development simply is arrested, usually to be resumed with the return of favorable temperatures. Some emydid turtle eggs even require a period of chilling below normal developmental temperatures (757).

Similarly, relatively constant temperature regimes deviating on either side of the optimum by a few degrees Celsius merely accelerate or retard the rate of development, without other consequence. Diel temperature fluctuations, on the other hand, lead to the formation of terata that become more abnormal as the magnitude of the fluctuations increases, and become lethally affected when the magnitude of fluctuations reaches more than a few degrees. The greatest known fluctuation range for the normal development of chelonians, for example, is only 8°C (see p. 542).

STEM-REPTILES

ONSET OF EQUABLE MESOZOIC CLIMATES AS KEY EVENT----MIDDAY SHADING. Viewed from these standpoints, and with a knowledge of Mesozoic climatology, it is not a large step to the conclusion that the key factor that facilitated the transition from the deep-burial nesting habits of the ancestors of the stem-reptiles to the shallow-burial habits of the stem-reptiles themselves probably was the gradual onset of the warm, equable climatic regimes of the Mesozoic. These very likely were a product of the greenhouse effect, consequent upon a gradual increase in atmospheric carbon dioxide content to several times the present level (see 1,405). The cosmopolitanism of the biota (including vegetational uniformity at the generic level among the continents) of the early and middle Jurassic indicates conditions of world-wide uniformity (see 1,123, 1,343). Such climates had not been seen since Carboniferous times, nor have they been seen subsequently (1,302).

An illustrative example of an equable regime of paleotemperatures for a period in the late Jurassic is that in the vicinity of the Solnhofen backreef basin. This is thought to have been at the relatively high mean annual value of 28-30°C, with both annual and daily variations of less than 5°C (1,181). This identification of the key factor as being the onset of warm, equable Mesozoic climates is consonant with an increasing recognition that the timing of major biotic adaptive innovations, e.g., the origin of eukaryotes and the migration of the Charophyceae to land, with the subsequent development of a terrestrial flora, has been governed by unique events in the history of Earth's environment (see 984-986, 1,253).

As average Mesozoic temperatures gradually increased and diel surface temperature ranges decreased, possibilities were opened for speeding up embryonic development by burying eggs at shallower depths. [The more temperate the regime, the greater the day-night temperature oscillations, the deeper the eggs need to be buried to avoid overheating, and the lower the average temperature in the nest.] A prerequisite for the success of this strategy probably would have been for the shallow burial site to have been shaded from direct solar radiation during the midday hours. It is unlikely that a very-shallowly-buried reptilian egg could have survived prolonged exposures of the surface of a shallow nest to direct high-angle insolation on clear days at medial latitudes, even assuming ameliorating greenhouse effects. [Virtually every avenue of analysis of the factors that would have come into play in the evolution of avian ancestors leads to major roles for shrubs and trees, arboreality, and vegetational debris.]

On the other hand, it would not, at first, have been adaptive to site nests in permanent shade as that would have reduced the average temperature and tended to negate the advantageous features of shallow burial. The ideal burial site might have been near the base of a suitably shading "tree" (i.e., tree or shrub) in line with the midday position of the sun at medial latitudes. At equatorial latitudes, foliage would have been the primary source of shade, while at medial latitudes foliage and trunks or stems would have provided shade (recall, in this connection, that trunks and stems also provide energetically-low-cost microhabitats; see p. 589).

The habits of the female American Alligator provide a suggestive present-day correlate of this type of nest siting. Thus, her nest usually is shielded by dense vegetation and often is built at the base of a tree, a practice that also is known among Nile Crocodiles. Moreover, in regions where shores are very sparsely vegetated, a female American Alligator will build her nest as far as 75 m from the shore in order to locate it in the shade of trees (659). [Even a desert bird that characteristically nests in the open in full sunlight, such as the Spotted Sandgrouse, still shows a tendency to nest close to shrubs (1/3rd of nests), though the nest is not placed in shade (the chicks usually remain in the shade of the shrubs during the day). In one case, where a nest at the base of a shrub proved to be on ground too hard to make a suitable scrape, the eggs eventually were moved to an appropriate scrape only 30 cm distant (1,206).]

EGG BURIAL AT SHALLOW DEPTHS. Thus, in consequence of the onset of more equable climates, a powerful selective pressure would have come into play favoring certain reptiles that buried their eggs at shallow depths, in the shade of trees and shrubs. Not all reptiles could have benefited from this strategy; selection would have favored those smallest in size for at least two reasons. The first is that larger eggs of larger reptiles, if buried at shallow depths, probably would have been exposed to excessively steep temperature gradients from top to bottom. Large eggs that have long incubatory periods appear to require deep deposition and high average annual temperatures (871). Thus, reptiles with small eggs would have been favored. [In this connection, crocodilian eggs with no more than 6-8 cm of vegetational cover (as opposed to the usual 30-45 cm) are susceptible to excessive temperature gradients or overheating (665). The smallest eggs of extant oviparous reptiles generally have a maximum length of 2-3 mm, the largest, 90-120 mm (875; a 1-mm-diameter egg is known in the eutherian-like reproducing Brazilian scincid lizard, *Mabuya heathi*; 896).]

The 2nd factor has to do with the increased vulnerability of eggs buried at shallow depths; no gain would have been achieved by speeding up embryogenesis and shortening the overall length of the period of vulnerability if the risk per unit time during the shorter period were increased excessively, particularly as fewer eggs can be accommodated in shallow nests than in deep nests. Thus, the only reptiles that could have benefited from the strategy of shallow egg burial would have been those whose habits were such as to make possible the reduction of such risks.

SURVEILLANCE AND GUARDING OF NEST. Reptiles that foraged in the vicinity of the nest site could have maintained surveillance over it, guarded the eggs from predators, and ensured the integrity of overlying protective cover, probably at very low energetic costs. Fairly close guarding would have been crucial for shallow nests so predictably sited as near trees and shrubs and in the shade of foliage. Selection, then, would have favored those reptiles that restricted their foraging activities to the vicinity of, and guarded, their shaded, shallowly-buried egg clutches.

Since the female is the ovipositor, she inevitably would have been the first, evolutionarily speaking, to maintain surveillance over the less-deeply-buried nest. As the depth of burial of the nest decreased, the number of eggs accommodated also would have decreased (as the surface was approached), the vulnerability of the eggs would have increased, and selection would have tended to favor the females that devoted the most time to egg care. In time, the male parent would have begun to share in this care (see p. 626), and this would have been obligatory by the time the nests were sited at the surface. [If passive care provided by the presence of the male in a territory were adequate for the eggs, and the young required no care, selection would have favored females that deserted and mated again (see, for example, 979), and similar considerations would apply to desertion by males.]

But at a not-excessive energetic cost, this strategy would have been open only to reptiles for which adequate prey resources existed in the vicinity of the nest site, within a small enough region to allow the maintenance of adequate surveillance. Assuming that the stem-reptiles were predators, for reasons discussed in the text, the smallest reptiles would have been favored, since they could have subsisted in the smallest foraging regions. It also should be noted that the onset of warm, equable climates also probably would have tended to promote more intensive insectivory among the already predatory stem-reptiles, if only through providing highly favorable environmental conditions for insects, particularly those of large size (recall the exceptionally large size of many of the insect fossils of the Solnhofen limestones and the giant dragonflies and cockroaches of the Permian and Pennsylvanian; 1,181, 1,296). Flying insects, for example, are particularly susceptible to low temperature, rain, and strong winds (see 973).

[Present-day crocodilian females, being in a quite different size category, are able to fast throughout the incubatory period, enabling them to guard closely their predictably-sited and often conspicuous nests by remaining in their very near vicinity at all times. Many species of viviparous squamates also fast through the period of reproduction, but the activity entailed in guarding a nest is not required of them.]

SHALLOW BURIAL, ARBOREALITY, AND TERRITORIALITY. At this juncture of the evolutionary scheme, two alternatives need to be considered. The first sees the same selective pressures that favored small reptiles that buried their eggs at shallow depths in the shade of trees or shrubs and maintained surveillance over the nest site, as favoring the invasion of arboreal habitats. The reason for this is that combined terrestriality-arboreality would have made possible more effective surveillance of the nest site, both by expanding the prey-resource region in the vertical direction and contracting it in the horizontal direction, and by providing much better and nearer vantage points for surveillance, predator detection, and nest access. In brief, selection for small reptiles that guarded their nest sites would have favored those that invaded arboreal habitats.

The second, and favored, alternative is that the strategy of burying eggs at shallow depths and maintaining surveillance over the burial site may have been open only to those reptiles that already had invaded arboral habitats. Invasion of, and existence in, arboreal habitats, in and of itself, may result in strong selection for reduced size, and for females with clutches of smaller and/or fewer eggs. The latter would be a requirement in buried nests sited at shallow depths, without layering or piling and with a need to limit areal expanse and vertical thermal gradients. A small bodily size allows support by smaller branches, yields increased muscle/bodily weight ratios, tends to reduce the terminal speed of free fall in air with limbs spread, etc. (see 1,193, 1,296). Even independently of selection for agility and lightness in arboreal habitats, selection for smaller eggs tends to lead to adult size reduction, particularly in species with fixed numbers of eggs per clutch. Accordingly, following either alternative leads to the conclusion that the stem-reptiles (Table 3) were relatively small and of terrestrial-arboreal habits.

It will be recognized that selection for reptiles that home-based their foraging activities in the vicinity of their shallow nest sites and repelled potential predators from these sites would provide a basis for the origin of territoriality. But a male's remaining in the vicinity of the nest site presupposes some degree of post-ovipositional consort of mated pairs. Arboreality coupled with male territoriality provides the most likely mechanism by which this could have been accomplished; all that would have been required to achieve it would have been for the female to deposit the eggs in her mate's territory and remain there and participate in the guarding of the nest (amounting to territoriality of females as well).

It is pertinent, in this context, that by contracting the prey resource region on land and expanding it vertically into arboreal habitats, the modified resource region becomes much more economically defensible than the original terrestrial region alone. The pertinence stems from the fact that selection is known to favor male territorial defense by birds when the food resource region (or the food resources therein) is economically defensible (see 1,266). The economically greater defensibility may be visualized simply by considering a limiting case where a terrestrial-arboreal predator need only defend access of terrestrial-arboreal competitors to a single tree and, say, a 100 m sq. plot of ground, as opposed to access to, say, a 1,000 m sq. plot of ground, alone.

[In a more general treatment of related matters among metazoans, Ridley concludes that we can be certain only that territoriality stabilizes the "evolutionarily stable strategy" (in the sense of Maynard Smith and Price --"a strategy such that if most of the members of a population adopt it, there is no 'mutant' strategy that would give higher reproductive fitness;" 992) of paternal care, once it has evolved. Paternal care usually correlates with external fertilization, and an important influence of territoriality on the evolution of paternal care applies especially in piscine and amphibian lineages (979).

A territorial sense among reptiles exists in crocodilians and a few groups of lizards, including certain gekkonids, agamids, iguanids, and certain skinks. Chameleons and Tuataras probably also have territories. Side-blotched Lizards (*Uta stansburiana*) defend small, partially overlapping territories, while females defend mutually exclusive territories that generally are near or within a male's territory, in an essentially monogamous relationship (see 1,258). The territorial sense is very widespread in the iguanid genus, *Anolis* (875). Territories defended by lizards may be related to defense of mates (polygyny is common) or nest sites, in addition to food sources, refugia, or basking sites (see refs. in 873). A social hierarchy has been recognized particularly in iguanids, such as members of the genera, *Anolis*, *Sceloporus*, and large species of *Ctenosaura*. In a group of individuals occupying a territory, each animal has its own fixed position in the pecking order (875).]

Accordingly, it is likely that the habits of increasing arboreality, decreasing egg weight and number, and territoriality of the stem-reptilian forerunners were prerequisites for, rather than consequences of, evolution along the lines of shallow nest burial and effective surveillance and care of the nest. These requirements, in turn, imply that the stem-reptiles were of small size, since that would have been favored by the selective pressures for an arboreal existence, particularly in the very abundant shrub-like growth of the time. It has been suggested that the prolongation of courtship beyond the ovipositional stage was the mechanism that kept mates together and made possible biparental care of eggs by ancestral birds (752). This proposed scheme of the evolution of the reptilian forerunners of birds provides the adaptive rationale for prolonged consort, but the latter need not have entailed continued courtship.

SURVEILLANCE OF NEST SITE AND CARE OF THE YOUNG. Achievement of the stem-reptilian stage of avian evolution, as outlined above, also has significant implications for the evolution of the care of the young. Thus, a mated pair of stem-reptiles foraging on the ground and in trees and shrubs in the neighborhood of their foliage-shaded, shallow nest would have had to maintain awareness of the location of the nest, in order to guard and protect it effectively (and not prey on their own offspring, if any degree of coloniality were practiced). Under such circumstances it would have been adaptive for the pair, or only the female, at first, to check the nest site periodically to ensure its intactness and concealment.

A factor that may be of considerable significance in this connection is the fact that selective pressures that favored protecting and periodically checking the nest site by partly arboreal stem-reptiles also would have favored the evolution of "tree"-to-ground jumping and parachuting as energetically low-cost strategies for quick access to the nest site. This method of nest access might well have been the chief basis for the evolution of "tree"-to-ground jumping, which would have preadapted pre-aves for predation by jumping from trees and shrubs in pursuit of volant passing and fleeing insect prey.

But under these conditions of nest-site surveillance, it also would have been adaptive to protect, escort, and otherwise tend to the basic needs of the hatchlings and young nestlings, perhaps even to the extent of assisting them from the buried nest or digging out hatching eggs. That being the case, it also would have been adaptive to monitor the nest closely as the time of hatching approached, particularly as any sound associated with the maturation of the respiratory system or the hatching process would have been a potential marker of nest location for predators.

[The production of sounds associated with the maturation of the respiratory system may be a widespread accompaniment of pre-hatching development of embryos in hard-shelled eggs. In the eggs of stem-reptiles, movable air spaces--the forerunners of the avian egg air cell--probably would have accumulated in the upper portions in late stages of development (just as they do today as water is lost from hard-shelled reptilian eggs) and provided possibilities for pre-pipping breathing and vocalization. In this connection, it has been suggested that hearing the vocalizations of embryos or hatchlings may be one of the cues, or the only cue, by which female Inaguan Turtles (*Pseudemys malonei*) locate their nests of buried eggs (688). As noted above, even in the absence of hatching sounds some male anurans (e.g., *Phyllobates vittatus*) anticipate hatching. They visit the eggs increasingly frequently as the time of hatching approaches, after which they transport the tadpoles to water (979).]

In short, making only the reasonable assumptions that the maturation of the embryonic stem-reptilian respiratory system and/or the hatching process was accompanied by sounds, and that the eggs were buried at very shallow depths, it would have been adaptive for stem-reptilian parents to stand guard over the burial site, or to remain in its very close vicinity, from the time they first detected sounds from the maturing embryos. This could well have amounted to a period of several days and would have constituted a behavioral pre-adaptation for the shielding of eggs when clutches ultimately were sited at the surface. [Time between pipping and hatching in chelonians varies from less than 1 to as many as 4 days. Testudinids and nearly all emydids (e.g., *Terrapene carolina*) have large external yolk sacs at pipping and are not yet ready to leave the egg shell (681).]

The behavior of birds' closest living relatives, the crocodilians, provides a present-day example of some aspects of such behavior. As mentioned above, female crocodilians generally guard the nest from its very near vicinity, sometimes lying directly over it. As far as is known, all crocodilian term embryos and hatchlings chirp loudly, in response to which the females of a number of species dig out the eggs and hatchlings and even assist the hatching process. Although unstudied, there can be little doubt that sounds are associated with the respiration, pipping, and other hatching activities of other reptilian embryos. Pipping of many reptilian eggs, for example, is preceded by scratching of the inner surface of the hard shell (681) and is bound to be a noisy process in nests containing scores of hatching eggs, many of them contacting one another. [Crocodilian reproduction is perhaps even more representative of the egg-care behavior of very large Mesozoic reptiles, i.e., with nests not at great depth, in environmentally protected locations, and attended by a fasting parent.]

PRE-AVES

PHYLOGENETIC PRE-INCUBATORY PRACTICE AND COCKATIELIAN BEHAVIOR. The stage now is set for a consideration of the evolutionary transition to the pre-avian stage of Table 3. The most ancient of the relict egg-care responses probably is that to lights-off and lights-on by pre-incubating and incubating birds, mostly the females. This is evidenced most dramatically by the repeated prompt departures and returns of Cockatielian hens from and to the shielding of the egg(s) when the lights are turned off and on in several consecutive sessions at or near the end of the daytime period.

During the pre-incubatory period, the Cockatielian hen returns to the eggs promptly when the lights are turned on in the morning. Similarly, both Peach-faced Lovebird and Budgerigar hens, that are not yet or no longer fully manifesting incubatory urges, incubate or sit loosely on exposed eggs in open nests or "transparent" nestboxes throughout much or all of the daytime period, beginning promptly with "lights-on," but leave the eggs at night. These responses seemingly provide a window into the habits of the ancestors of birds at a time before the practice of incubation had come into existence, that is, in the pre-avian stage.

The extreme reluctance of the birds to leave the eggs exposed to view, coupled with the fact that the pre-incubatory females of all 3 species studied do not leave the eggs for the night until the lights are extinguished, and return to them promptly when they are turned on, has clear implications. It implies the existence of a stage in avian evolution when the eggs were laid at ground level and the parents shielded them only until the time of nightfall; the nest was not attended closely during the night, but shielding was resumed in the early morning. Sometimes Cockatielian hens only mount the inside nest perch for the night or perch nearby outside the nest in the company of the male, suggesting that their ancestors of the pertinent evolutionary stage merely guarded the eggs from a nearby perch at night.

Among a number of contemporary avian egg-care practices, it is those of Cockatiels, of merely shielding the 1st and 2nd eggs during the day, sometimes by standing, but usually by crouching or sitting loosely over them, and only guarding them from nearby at night, that most strongly suggest that the ancestral practice being recapitulated dates from prior to the time when eggs were incubated. It must date from an early post-reptilian stage, when the ancestors still were ectotherms. Had they been endotherms, it would have been adaptive for them to incubate the eggs around the clock, as do members of many avian species that no longer recapitulate any aspect of this stage of egg care (presumably because what is adaptively neutral for one species became maladaptive for another), rather than merely shield them during the day and leave them at night,

RECONSTRUCTING PRE-AVIAN EGG CARE. On the assumption that the evolutionary transition from shallowly-buried nests to "surface" nests was driven mainly by selective pressures for shorter periods of incubation, as mediated by higher average incubatory temperatures, one can reconstruct the ways in which the transition probably took place by appealing to known avian egg-care practices and the observed relict responses. These responses would appear to give us the firmest information as to how the transition was achieved.

Early morning and late afternoon bodily shielding of exposed eggs from overhead view by an ectothermic avian ancestor, rather than the mere concealment of the eggs, would appear to have been for the purpose of allowing the eggs to be warmed by the reception of direct low-angle insolation. This would have applied in the periods before ambient air temperatures had risen in the morning and after they had fallen in the late afternoon. To receive low-angle insolation, the nest site would have to have been sited on flat, level ground, with a relatively unobstructed path to the morning and afternoon sun. If the sole function of the behavior were to shield the eggs from high-angle view in the early morning and late afternoon, it would have been adaptive to conceal them by burial rather than standing or crouching over them.

Raising the average egg temperature during midday might have been achieved either solely by selecting a surface site moderately shaded at midday, with no parental attendance and with the eggs concealed and protected by vegetational debris, or by selecting a more exposed site and shading them with the parental bodies. Of these two alternatives the latter is by far the more likely, both by analogy with known widespread avian practices and from the fact that it would have provided the greatest potential for temperature control.

PARENTAL BODILY SHADING of a nest located in such a more exposed site would have required the alternate attention of both pre-avian parents, since prolonged direct exposure to solar radiation during midday would have been intolerable for one alone on clear days at low and medial latitudes. In addition, the alternate attentions and vigilance of both parents would have conferred greater flexibility of care and more effective protection from predators. This attendance to, and shielding of, the eggs by pre-aves would have had its antecedents in the guarding and periodic checking of the nest site by their stem-reptilian ancestors, particularly over the extended period of hatching.

On the other hand, between midday and the cooler early morning and late afternoon periods, there would have been periods of intermediate air temperatures that would have been optimal for embryonic development and during which parental attendance and temperature adjustment would have been unnecessary. During these times it would have sufficed merely to conceal the eggs with vegetational debris.

WARMTH PROVIDED BY DECOMPOSING VEGETATIONAL DEBRIS. Lastly, during the twilights and nights it would have been adaptive for the parents to cover the eggs with decomposing vegetational debris and to have foraged and sought a safe, nearby, overhead vigilance post. The vegetational cover would have provided a source of heat, would have retained heat already absorbed and produced metabolically by the developing embryos, and would have insulated the latter from cooler nocturnal ambient air. The periods before and after direct low-angle insolation was available may well have been optimal foraging times; at the present time, these are the periods when many flying insects are present in by far the greatest abundance (821). These various postulated parental behaviors in respect to the thermal needs of the developing embryos during different periods of the 24-h cycle are very modest when measured against the comparable behavior of extant birds in harsh climatic regimes (see pp. 444-447, **Contemporary Practices**).

Assuming fairly high average temperatures in an equable climatic regime, and a critical need to avoid large diel temperature fluctuations, it is clear that the lower nocturnal temperatures would have been the limiting factor insofar as further shortening of the incubatory period was concerned. This well may have been one of the limitations of an ectotherm's further progress along these lines that led to selection for endothermy.

Although one might be inclined to assume that the maintenance of nest warmth at night by burial in decomposing vegetation would not have been feasible, because it takes considerable time today for elevated temperatures to be generated in vegetational surface debris (after wetting), the circumstances in the Mesozoic undoubtedly were quite different. Thus, though the forest litter before the middle Carboniferous probably consisted only of accumulations of stems and branches admixed with long microphylls (leaves with single, unbranched veins) of Lepidodendrales and Calamitales, the situation probably changed drastically with the appearance of the relatively nutritious laminate (bladed) leaf. After the appearance of plants with such leaves in the middle Carboniferous period, it is suggested that forest litter consisted of an abundance of rotting vegetation with its own flora of thriving fungi and bacteria (768). [In terms of height, these Carboniferous forests equaled those of the present-day Amazon basin, Central America, and Africa; scale trees in the genera, *Lepidodendron* and *Sigillaria*, for example, attained heights of 40-52 m (1,296).]

With the surface nest already among trees and shrubs, pre-aves need only have covered the eggs with a thick layer of rotting vegetational debris for the night, as a source of nocturnal heat and insulation to keep diel temperature fluctuations low. Perhaps the deeper burial of eggs in such microorganism-rich debris in forested regions by the reptilian ancestors of pre-aves was one of the sources of selective pressures for hard-shelled, less penetrable eggs.

DECOMPOSING VEGETATIONAL DEBRIS INCREASINGLY LESS EFFECTIVE. Once this probable avenue for the provision of nest warmth at night is recognized, a possible early selective factor favoring the evolution of the practice of incubation is suggested. Thus, as Mesozoic plants invested ever increasing amounts of their productivity into chemical defenses (tannins, alkaloids, resins, phenolics, etc.) and tough, fibrous leaves that were lower in nutrients, litter decomposition would have slowed progressively (see 1,300). As a consequence, temperatures of decomposing ground litter would have tended to decrease gradually over geological time, a situation that would have favored pre-avian parents--already evolving homeothermic endothermy--that remained at the nest at night in contact with the eggs, warming them with bodily heat. Such a selection would have been exerted, albeit perhaps weakly, at first--depending largely on the safety of the nest site at night--as soon as pre-avian body temperatures exceeded the nighttime nest temperature that could have been maintained in decomposing litter.

As a present-day example of attentive diurnal egg care by an ectotherm, including possible temperature regulation, one can cite the behavior of American Alligators and Nile Crocodiles. The female normally remains at the nest with her throat lying over it; at intervals she may lie 2 or 3 m away and she makes frequent trips between the nest and water, after which the nest area becomes dampened with water dripping from her body. It is suggested that she senses when the nest site is too hot or too dry with her throat and makes appropriate adjustments (659). The Nile Crocodile also provides an example of a male ectotherm's attention to the nest site during the development of embryos; he also remains in the general vicinity but does not approach the nest itself, and goes off at intervals to hunt; the female generally fasts (680).

During the midday alternations in the shielding of the nest, the non-attending pre-avian parent could have foraged nearby. During the period when the eggs were concealed with cover, both parents could have foraged, while during dawn-to-early-morning and post-late-afternoon-to-dusk, when the eggs were shielded from medium-to-high-angle view by a parent but exposed to the low-lying sun, the parents again could have alternated in foraging. During the night the parents doubtless would have slept on a safe, nearby, overhead arboreal perch.

CHRONOLOGY OF RELICT RESPONSES

BURSTS OF SCRATCHING. The surface nests of pre-aves were the evolutionary end-product of the practice of excavating increasingly shallow burial sites for egg clutches, and burying fewer and smaller eggs. Accordingly the clutches would, at first, have been buried in earth, humus, or other substrates that were readily excavated, particularly as they probably were sited in the vicinity of trees or shrubs. Since it is improbable that eggs would have rolled freely on such substrates, it seems unlikely that the relict burst-of-scratching response dates from the time of the very beginning of the practice of surface nesting. This conclusion is reached because the response doubtless was for the purpose of excavating a shallow scrape in a surface that was compact and smooth to the degree that eggs could have rolled freely on it.

After the practice of surface-nesting had become established, pre-aves would have been emanicipated from the need to nest only on surfaces that yielded readily to deep excavation. Thereupon, they could have nested on any surface in which a shallow scrape could have been made by a burst of scratching movements with the feet, provided only that appropriate vegetational debris blending with the surroundings was available with which to conceal the eggs during absences. The purpose of the burst-of-scratching relic would appear to be to produce a depression in an otherwise fairly firm substrate, to confine and group the eggs (eggs would not roll readily on an essentially level, but yielding, substrate). Accordingly, the response probably dates from a time after the practice of surface nesting had begun.

[Note that it is not the act itself of scratching the substrate that is significant; scratching movements would be of far greater antiquity than any of the relict responses (see pp. 819, 820, **Scratching on Smooth Surfaces, A Relict Response to Freely-Rolling Eggs**). Rather, it is the specific employment of these movements in response to eggs rolling freely on a flat surface that is under consideration.]

THE DISTANT-VISUAL SEARCH, viewed as the relic of a pro-avian adaptation for locating eggs that were accidentally displaced from a surface nest, probably does not date from the beginning of surface nesting, since small eggs would not roll freely on a yielding surface. Rather, this would appear to be a relic dating from a later period, when pro-aves also were surface nesting upon less yielding substrates (which need not have been excavated to a great depth). The behavior is unlikely to recapitulate a search for a possible nearby predator responsible for the absence of the eggs, since no alarm or search occurs as long as a single egg of a clutch remains. [The lack of alarm or search behavior in the latter instance suggests that egg predators of the time either were small and posed no threat or would have struck the returning parent before the eggs were missed.]

DIRECTED AND ROUTINE SEARCHES. Pre-aves are visualized as having been engaged routinely in covering and uncovering their eggs in shallow surface nests on yielding substrates. Accordingly, the practices of both directed and routine egg searches by probing and/or "plowing" with the bill could have originated as early as the time of the pre-avian stage. The fact that Cockatiels and lovebirds confine their searches to the incubative area and its near vicinity need not imply that the practices post-date that of incubation, since it also would have been adaptive for parents that merely shielded and shaded the eggs to confine their searches for missing eggs to the yielding substrate in the very near vicinity of a surface nest.

DISPOSING OF DAMAGED EGGS. Once the practice of surface nesting had begun, selection would have favored the pre-aves that disposed of damaged eggs. When using a shallow surface nest, the most effective means of disposal would have been by removal (rather than by covering with nesting material, as cavity-nesting lovebirds do with dead chicks). Thus, selection would have favored those pre-aves that rolled defective eggs away from the nest and concealed them. Accordingly, this relict response of Cockatiels might be one of the oldest of the relict egg-care responses.

SELECTION FOR FEATHER-LIKE SCALES AND FEATHERS

In the interests of simplicity in earlier sections, I adopted the working hypothesis that the evolution of feathers was, at first, an adaptive response for the provision of greater bodily-surface insulation, primarily from external heat and secondarily for heat conservation, rather than for aerodynamical properties favorable to invasion of aerial habitats. Selection for feathers now is considered at greater length within the framework of the above treatments of stem-reptiles and pre-aves.

The stem-reptilian ancestors of birds (see Table 3) are postulated to have been terrestrial-arboreal predators, but I would suggest that they were not yet preying on flying insects by jumping from trees or shrubs to snare them and that they had little need to escape from predators by tree-to-ground jumping. First, they would have been small and agile, rendering the need to escape by that means unlikely (except perhaps for escaping from each other). It is more likely that they were the most agile arboreal vertebrate predators of their time and that trees and shrubs were places of refuge and foraging.

Second, foraging by "tree"-to-ground jumping probably was a later practice that provided an early selective pressure for reduction of relative clutch weight (because jumping, gravid animals, otherwise relatively small, agile, and slender, would have been at great risk as they landed while carrying the "dead weight" of full clutches). The principal selective pressure for "tree"-to-ground jumping at the stem-reptilian stage might have been as a fast and energetically cheap route of access to the nest site in guarding and protecting the eggs and young.

On the other hand, selective pressures for heat-conserving feather-like modifications of scales are likely to have been exerted from the time of the first invasion of an arboreal habitat, because of the advantages therein of adaptations favorable to the development of endothermy, as discussed above. The same is true of selection for small size. Similarly, any excess exposure entailed in surveillance, guarding, and midday shading of the ground over the nest site would have resulted in selection for heat-shielding, feather-like modifications of scales, particularly if concomitant selection for smaller size were occurring (since small animals have lesser thermal inertia). Accordingly, it seems likely that at the stem-reptilian grade of avian evolution, selection for feather-like scales was driven primarily by needs for greater bodily insulation, and only secondarily for aerodynamical properties to facilitate "tree"-to-ground jumping for quick and economical access to the nest site.

Selection for more effective insulation from solar radiation by means of feather-like scales would have been even greater in the subsequent pre-avian stage (see Table 3), which doubtless involved more lengthy exposures consequent upon the midday shading of eggs at surface sites. Since the primitive pro-avian stage is one in which a primitive grade of homeothermic endothermy had been achieved, late pre-aves very likely were invading aerial habitats. Jumping from tree or shrub to ground from ever increasing heights would have exerted strong selection for bodies with increased air resistance and lift. This would have favored the evolution of scales--already pre-adapted by extensive modifications that provided greater insulation--that possessed more favorable aerodynamical properties. As mentioned above, the fact that no gliding or parachuting reptile has evolved scales with appreciably more favorable aerodynamical properties than are found in related non-aerial forms strongly suggests that the earliest feather-like modification of reptilian scales were not in response to selective forces that favored increased lift or air resistance.

In summary, the first effective selective pressure for the development of feather-like scales most probably was primarily for insulation from external sources of heat and secondarily for heat conservation. The initial modifications would have made it possible to tolerate the increased solar exposure entailed in guarding and shielding shallowly-buried egg clutches, and would have facilitated the maintenance of higher metabolic rates during arboreal activity. Selective pressures for the air-resistant and lift properties of feather-like scales may have been relatively weak in the stem-reptiles and pre-aves, arising primarily from "tree"-to-ground jumping from low heights in gaining quick, low-energetic-cost access to the nest site. Stronger selection for these properties probably was a later development that accompanied intensive foraging by jumping from trees and shrubs in pursuit of prey.

ENDOTHERMY, INCUBATION, AND RAPID DOUBLE-CLUTCHING. In the pre-avian stage, the alternate attentions of both parents doubtless were essential for the shielding of the eggs, because of the susceptibility of the exposed parents to heat stress during midday. Although it might have been adaptive, even at that time, for each parent to manage a separate half-clutch, for reasons already discussed in the main text, this could not have been achieved for at least two reasons. The first of these is that just mentioned, namely, insufficient mechanisms existed for homeothermy during the prolonged heat stress that additional exposure would have entailed. The second is that, as an ectotherm, double clutching by alternate ovarian function (polyallochronic ovulation; see legend to Table 3) would have greatly increased the time required to produce 2 clutches of half size as compared to producing 1 of full size. Thus, desynchronization of the maturation of the 2 half-clutches on the right and left sides could have as much as doubled the time required to produce both clutches, as compared to that required when egg production was synchronous.

But with the achievement of endothermy in the primitive pro-avian stage--including effective bodily surface insulation--the management of separate clutches would have become practicable. Rapid double-clutching of half-sized clutches through alternate ovarian function would have been possible without reduction in reproductive potential by virtue of the considerably greater rate at which eggs could have been produced. Although the likelihood that rapid double-clutching by this means was a very early practice in avian evolution was not previously considered, the remarkable behavior of breeding Cockatiels, in steadfastly incubating a divided clutch while sitting in relatively widely spaced incubative areas (as did Helena and Homer; see pp. 498-502, **Oviposition-Site Fidelity**) or side by side in a NB, permit one to witness this type of behavior directly and appreciate the feasibility of its occurrence as an ancestral breeding practice.

OTHER COCKATIELIAN EGG-CARE BEHAVIORS perhaps even more strongly support the view that each parent incubated a separate clutch in the past, namely, the often-exhibited, extreme reluctance of an incubating bird to surrender the eggs (and chicks) to the incoming mate, and the equally great determination of the incoming bird to acquire them. These behaviors include the "stealing" of the eggs from one another, the repelling of the incoming bird from the nest entrance (just as if it were an intruder) or the expelling of it from the nest, and the practice of incessantly "grooming" an incubating mate to induce it to surrender the clutch.

FOUR MARKED DEPARTURES FROM THE PROPERTIES OF PRE-AVES characterize the postulated primitive pro-avian stage: the achievement of homeothermic endothermy; oviposition by rapid double-clutching through alternate ovarian function; independent parental care of each clutch; and incubation of the eggs. Incubation was made possible by the achievement of homeothermic endothermy, the selective pressures for which already have been discussed.

Homeothermic endothermy also made feasible rapid double-clutching and more frequent reproductive episodes.

SHIFTING NEST SITES TO SHADED LOCATIONS. The achievement of homeothermic endothermy probably would have made it possible for each parent individually to shade with its body a nest that otherwise was not fully shaded during midday. But of greater pertinence, it also probably made such a practice unnecessary, since homeothermic endotherms no longer would have needed to site their nests in locations where they received direct solar radiation. It is very likely that the development of incipient homeothermic endothermy by late pre-aves, and an increasing capability of an individual parent to shade an exposed nest without the assistance of the other, facilitated the transition to rapid double-clutching.

But, inasmuch as the body temperatures of these late pre-aves were increasing at the same time, and incubation was becoming feasible, the siting of the nests in exposed locations probably was becoming increasingly maladaptive. Thus, selection probably favored evolving late pre-aves that progressively shifted their nest sites to more shaded, protected locations and made bodily contact with the eggs for progressively more lengthy periods, perhaps only during the night, at first (promoted by more protected nest sites), subsequently also in early morning and late afternoon, and eventually also during most of the day.

ADVANCED PRO-AVES

THE TRANSITION FROM PRIMITIVE TO ADVANCED PROAVES involved further advances in the development of homeothermic endothermy and more extensive invasion of aerial habitats. The latter included the achievement of simple and maneuvered gliding, wing-flapping at low speeds and amplitudes, and advances in aerodynamically favorable properties of feather-like scales to become feathers. Flights probably were initiated primarily from trees and by terrestrial running take-offs. Increased body temperature and higher metabolic rates then had attained values capable of supporting relatively rapid egg production. This made possible the evolutionary transition to the assembly of clutches by periodic oviposition, one egg at a time--a practice that probably was selected for strongly to achieve and maintain low wing loading, most critically in flapping flight. With that development, gravid animals never were burdened with more than one maturing oviductal egg, peak shell deposition occurred during rest periods at night, and eggs were laid singly in the early morning.

THE ULTIMATE ADAPTATION OF OVARIAN REPRODUCTIVE FUNCTION for the existence of an oviparous vertebrate in aerial or acrobatic arboreal habitats is represented by the latter development. It is highly adaptive to produce eggs singly as rapidly as possible up to a rate of, but not exceeding, once per day. Accordingly, it is very likely that periodic oviposition evolved at a time when avian ancestors still possessed two ovaries, and that egg production proceeded via monoallochronic ovulation, i.e., by the ovulation and oviposition of single eggs, with a given egg originating from one ovary and the next egg from the contralateral one. In that way, the frequency of periodic oviposition could have attained twice that for egg production from a single ovary and oviduct, probably every 2nd or 3rd day.

SELECTION FOR NIDICOLOUS YOUNG AND BIPARENTAL CARE. The nidifugous condition of the young would have been the primitive condition among pre-aves, by virtue of their reptilian ancestry. But as increasing arboreality and endothermy were achieved during evolution to pro-aves, the increasingly strong selective pressures favoring smaller eggs and clutches also would have favored the evolution of nidicolous young, since their eggs can be smaller by virtue of requiring less stored nutrient. These pressures are particularly significant in the present context because they are known to be greatest in species with tropical distributions (35% of species outside the tropics develop as nidifugous or semi-nudifugous young, as opposed to only 15% within the tropics; 1,150). Achievement of the nidicolous condition of the young in many advanced pro-aves would have been one of the factors leading to selection for increasingly rapid development of the nestlings. This would have been accompanied by strong selection for biparental care, leading eventually to the predominant conditions among ancestral birds (see Table 3).

'CONTENTED' WITH A SINGLE EGG. It is to the advanced pro-avian stage that one may trace the trait of the birds of this study (and probably most birds) of being 'content' with the re-possession of only a single egg of a previously missing clutch. Selection probably would have favored pro-avian pairs that sited their surface nests within view of one another, since it would have been adaptive for one pro-avis of a mated pair to remain at its nest and maintain visual vigilance over the nest of the other member while the latter foraged.

One may assume that each member of an advanced pro-avian pair would have had a strong attachment to, and possessiveness for, its clutch. Accordingly, there would have arisen the possibility of the advanced pro-avian mates that nested within sight of one another competing amongst themselves for eggs during early establishment of a 2nd clutch that was assembled by periodic oviposition. This might have taken the form of appropriation of a departing male's clutch by the female, as she continued to assemble the 2nd clutch, with temporary abandonment of her own clutch (particularly at a time when the latter consisted of only a single egg). Accordingly, selection would have favored advanced pro-aves that had their very strong urges to care for and incubate eggs fulfilled by the possession of only a single egg, as in the case with members of the 3 species of this study.

ANCESTRAL BIRDS

The ancestral-bird stage (see Table 3) was chacterized by a return to the practice of biparental management of a single clutch, as was the practice of pre-aves and the stem-reptiles, but with the important difference that the eggs of ancestral birds were being incubated by bodily heat. As discussed below, this change is suggested to have been largely a consequence of the greatly increased body temperatures that accompanied the evolution of true flight (albeit flight not yet sustainable for long periods). In addition, with the achievement of metabolic rates supporting more rapid egg production by each ovary and oviduct, say every 2 or 3 days, the right ovary and oviduct and alternate ovarian function became superfluous, with consequent regression and vestigiality of both organs on the right side.

With the approach to a condition of endothermy and the achievement of a body temperature equivalent to the contemporary primitive avian grade (largely as a consequence of continued strong selection for shortened incubatory times and more effective invasion of aerial habitats), individual incubation of separate clutches would have become increasingly less adaptive. This probably depended largely on an infeasibility of preventing the chilling of the eggs during longer absences for foraging, occasioned by such factors as increased nutritional needs, a decreasing abundance of large flying insects, and a transition of many forms to the practice of herbivory. Biparental incubation might have been hastened as the average temperature declined or the equability of climates waned in the late Cretaceous period, and populations that had colonized more temperate regions would have led the way in this transition.

At any rate, it would appear that selection again (as postulated with the non-incubating stem-reptiles and pre-aves), but for somewhat different reasons, favored cooperative biparental care of a single clutch, with one parent always in attendance. As noted above, development of the nidicolous condition also would have favored biparental care, since, within limits, more rapid development of nidicolous nestlings can be achieved at the expense of increased parental care. Of course, this stage would have dated to long before the development of the contemporary adaptive specializations that permit extended periods of chilling of the eggs of many birds (see pp. 551, 552, **Tolerance of Embryos to Chilling and Overheating**), namely to a time when the eggs still retained something of the greater sensitivity of reptilian eggs to wide diel temperature fluctuations (see pp. 542-544, 622, 623).

COCKATIELS

Lastly, the transition to Cockatiels entailed a still further increase in body temperature and the concomitant achievement of the capability for sustained true flight, the adoption of the habit of hole-nesting in trees --probably dating back tens of millions of years, at least to the time of eucalypt origin--the achievement of an almost fully nidicolous condition, and completion of the transition from insectivory to herbivory.

Summary

STEM-REPTILIAN ANCESTORS OF BIRDS. Based primarily upon probable correlated associations of characters, 5 stages have been delineated in the line of evolution from late or post-Triassic stem-reptilian ancestors of birds to a extant bird, the Cockatiel. The stem-reptilian ancestors were small terrestrial-arboreal, bipedal, predatory reptiles, preying upon other small animals, including arthropods and other invertebrates and vertebrates. They jumped after fleeing or passing volant insects during ground foraging and from positions on the bases of trees and shrubs.

They ovulated oocytes from both ovaries concurrently, oviposited single clutches *en masse* in reptilian fashion, and buried the eggs at shallow depths in areas that were not excessively exposed. The eggs were incubated by climatic heat. The nest site was kept under surveillance by the parents as they foraged nearby, and it was guarded closely during the pre-hatching and hatching periods. The hatchlings and early young were groomed, protected, and escorted.

PRE-AVES, THE EARLY POST-REPTILIAN ANCESTORS. In an early post-reptilian stage, the pursuit of flying insects became more intensive and vigorous. It included terrestrial running and bipedal jumping, and tree-to-ground jumping from increasingly greater heights on limbs and stems. In addition to serving in predation, the latter practice provided a quick and energetically efficient means of gaining access to the nest site or ground.

Oocytes were ovulated concurrently from both ovaries and eggs were laid at the surface in relatively exposed locations. This practice led to greatly shortened periods of embryonic development, as both direct and indirect (climatic) solar heating were utilized. Eggs in relatively exposed surface locations required the close alternate attentions of both parents. Care of eggs included midday shading from the sun, early morning and late afternoon shielding from overhead view but not from low-angle solar radiation, concealment under vegetational debris during daytime absences, and concealment, insulation, and provision of heat by burial in decomposing vegetational debris during the night. Shortened periods of embryonic (and postnatal) development permitted sequential multiple-clutching. Hatchlings and early young also received close attention, including grooming, protecting, and escorting.

Exposure to solar radiation during midday shading of nest sites was the basis for the selective pressure for adaptations of scales that provided greater insulation from external sources of heat. More extensive arboreality and intensive tree-to-ground jumping led to further adaptations of scales--already modified for increased insulative properties--for increased drag and lift, and for increased retention of bodily heat to facilitate a higher level of metabolic energy capacity.

PRIMITIVE PRO-AVES. The primitive pro-avian stage saw achievement of insulative primitive feathers with improved aerodynamical properties, a primitive condition of homeothermic endothermy, and rapid double-clutching of clutches that were ovulated alternately, the 1st clutch from one ovary and the 2nd from the contralateral ovary. The animals foraged extensively in the trees, and this included jumping after fleeing and passing volant insects and then spreading the limbs and tail and parachuting in descent. Developing embryos were incubated, with each parent taking exclusive responsibility for a separate clutch.

Rapid double-clutching decreased the chances of losing the entire output of a reproductive episode through predation, while shorter incubatory periods allowed an increase in the number of reproductive episodes per season, with both factors tending to increase reproductive success. Nests were sited in protected locations, fully shaded from midday direct solar radiation. Eggs were covered with vegetational debris for concealment and insulation during periods of daytime foraging, which probably was most intensive during midday. In addition to grooming, escorting, and protecting the young, the latter were brooded at night.

ADVANCED PRO-AVES. The practice of preying on volant insects by jumping after them from positions on trees led eventually to the development of true feathers, gliding, and capabilities for wing-flapping at low speeds and amplitudes, though with only moderate lift capability--allowing landing in trees or shrubs rather than on the ground--and a more advanced state of homeothermic endothermy. Selection for maintenance of low wing loading through reduced relative clutch weight was then at a maximum. The more advanced metabolic state and increased body temperature, together with alternating ovulation and alternating oviductal maturation, made it feasible to assemble clutches by periodic oviposition, one egg at a time.

This is the ultimate adaptation of ovarian and oviductal reproductive function for existence of an oviparous vertebrate in aerial or acrobatic arboreal habitats. Members of both sexes incubated separate clutches and otherwise cared for clutches and broods unassistedly.

ANCESTRAL BIRDS. Progressive improvements in wing-flapping ability and increases in body temperature to the level in primitive extant birds, led to the attainment of true flight capabilities, though only for relatively brief periods. Flight was initiated primarily from the trees and by running take-offs from the ground, such as still is characteristic of some birds, e.g., the Common Loon, with its "appallingly high wing loading" (1,050). At the increased metabolic rate, the rate of egg production by a single ovary and oviduct achieved that previously requiring the alternate, overlapping operation of paired organs, making the right ovary and oviduct superfluous; eventually they became vestigial.

Developing embryos then required incubation at higher temperatures. The embryos were not tolerant of chilling during the increasingly long periods of parental inattendance while foraging in the increasingly less equable or cooler climates of the late Cretaceous, and to meet increased nutritional needs. As a result, cooperative incubation developed, wherein parents alternated in the care of a single clutch, rather than each caring exclusively for a separate clutch. Biparental care of the brood favored more rapid development of nidicolous young. Sequential multiple-clutching with shorter reproductive episodes maintained the reproductive potential despite the changeover from rapid double-clutching to single clutching.

MODERN BIRDS. Further increases in body temperature and perfection of flight capabilities, together with access to an enormously expanded range of habitats, led to extensive radiations yielding the diversity of modern birds. Eventually, the adaptive value of continuous attendance on the eggs came to reside largely in protection from predators, as selection increasingly favored birds whose developing embryos had greater tolerance to chilling on interruptions of incubation. With the attainment of true flight, multifaceted interactions between the widely foraging avian species (acting as seed dispersing vectors), primitive angiosperms, and insect pollinators led to the dominance of an angiospermous flora and the development of widespread and intensive avian herbivory.

CHAPTER 5. ATYPICAL PAIR-BOND FORMATION IN LOVEBIRDS

Introduction

The pugnacity and aggressiveness of Peach-faced Lovebirds are well known. In certain situations, they will kill one another and other birds. The present Chapter traces the events in the immature period of a crippled male lovebird, Titus, in the company of his parents and two older sisters, Zenobia and Flavia, from not long after hatching through the time of his mating with his sister, Flavia. I found the nature of the early behavior of these sisters toward Titus to warrant being characterized as 'vindictive,' and regard the behavior as having been a consequence of the highly favored treatment that was accorded to Titus by his parents, Petra and Ramses, to virtually the total exclusion of his sisters.

At an age of 11 weeks, Titus barely escaped fatal injury in a severe attack by his sisters. For many days thereafter, his survival depended upon continuous protective care by his parents and me, which included temporary isolation from his sisters whenever I was absent. In order for the reader to have the full background of the origin of these relationships, it is desirable to outline the entire period of Titus' youth.

Since lovebird pair formation already has been treated in the **Introduction** to Chapter 3, no introductory discussion is needed here. Some aspects of the care of young lovebirds, treated very briefly in the course of the present development, are covered in greater detail in Chapter 6, Part 2, together with a treatment of the care of eggs by lovebirds (and accounts of breeding by Flavia and Titus). Similarly, other aspects of behavior and interactions based on studies of members of the same colony are elaborated in Chapters 3 and 7. Although an example of tolerance by incubating and brooding parents to the near presence of 2 male offspring of a prior brood, and of harmonious allofeeding of chicks by all 3 males is known in Abyssinian Lovebirds (1,054; see also pp. 728-730), the circumstances and relations described below for a family of Peach-faced Lovebirds are quite different.

TITUS' YOUTH

TITUS HATCHES---SOLE MEMBER OF BROOD. Titus, the focus of attention in the interactions described below, hatched on March 2, 1984. He was the sole member of the 4th brood of Petra and Ramses. Like their 3rd brood, consisting of his sisters, Zenobia and Flavia, he was incubated, hatched, and brooded in a shallow, open nestbowl (14 x 3½ cm) on a bed of wood shavings. This was located in the open, on the floor of enclosure B, at the right rear corner (Fig. 3b). Consequently, I could observe directly all of the elements of maternal and paternal care.

TITUS CRIPPLED. I left 3 substitute eggs in the nest during Titus' nestling days to ease the weight of Petra's body on him during brooding, under the impression that the hen's weight can lead to the crippling of nestlings, which is a common belief among aviculturists. Despite this precaution, Titus' right leg was splayed out to the right side. Notwithstanding his infirmity, Titus led an almost-normal existence as an adult, with the chief exception that he was not able, unaidedly, to achieve sexual union.

[Subsequent studies were to indicate that the crippling of domestic parrot chicks usually is the product of congenital malformities, no doubt as a consequence of inbreeding, apparently quite unrelated to parental care. A total of 7 congenitally crippled birds resulted from breedings in my colony--5 lovebirds, 1 Cockatiel, and 1 Budgerigar; in all cases the malformities were in the right leg and/or foot. In 2 of the other cases, including another lovebird and a Budgerigar, the malformation was the same as that of Titus. It is noteworthy in this connection that neither Cockatiels nor Budgerigars brood their nestlings by sitting over them, as is commonly the case with lovebirds; rather they usually brood them under the breast feathers, wings, and/or tail (see treatments in Chap. 6).]

NEST CORNER GIVEN WIDE BERTH. Since enclosure B contained the tower complex (see Fig. 1a and Chaps. 3 and 7), which was much frequented by both Zenobia and Flavia, and since Petra and Ramses kept constant guard on the eggs, the period of incubation proceeded without interference from the sisters. At no time did I see either sister make an attempt to enter the nestbowl. Zenobia and Flavia had learned very quickly to give the nesting area a wide berth, inasmuch as Petra and Ramses also had courted there and had repelled their daughters whenever they approached its neighborhood.

ALLOFEEDING OF THE SOLE CHICK. The first 4 weeks after Titus hatched were fairly uneventful. Being the only chick of the brood, Petra and Ramses gave him very attentive care. Typically, he was allofed as he lay on his back. In the first few days, both parents groomed and allofed him like two surgeons working over a patient in concert at 10 times normal speed. It often appeared as if they were competing to allofeed him. It was during the course of this hectic activity that I first detected one of the two major activities of the male parent in the care of the nestlings.

PETRA ALLOFEEDS, RAMSES CLEANS. Ramses' principal activity was not direct competition with Petra to allofeed Titus. Rather, he was cleaning up after Petra as she allofed the chick. He prevented excess food from dripping down along Titus' tiny bill, removed excess food from the sides of Petra's bill, and even removed large pieces of food from within Titus' mouth, all to a vital purpose (see pp. 747-749, **Tongue-Flick Feeding, Wayward Food, and Clogged Nostrils**). This was an exciting discovery, since it was an activity previously unknown in birds. As will be seen in Chapter 6 (see, e.g., pp. 766, 767), the male lovebird parent also allofeeds very young chicks, even newly hatched ones, whenever the opportunity affords, though with lower priority than cleaning during allofeeding by the female.

TITUS' NESTLING DAYS. Attentive as Petra was as a parent, she never declined an invitation to be flighted during the periods of incubation and brooding. Another lovebird, Cassandra, on the other hand, often declined to accept such opportunities during the period of incubation. On the 11th day after hatching, one of Titus' eyes was open a tiny slit, on the 19th day, green coloration first appeared at his feather tips, and he left the nestbowl for the first time. On the 24th day, I noted him grooming himself. During this entire period, neither of his sisters was allowed to come near him.

PARENTAL PROTECTION. When I handled and examined Titus, beginning at an age of 1 week, I concurrently flighted Petra and Ramses. At such times, at first, they appeared to show no 'concern' for Titus, occupying themselves with stripping paper and other activities. On the other hand, they did show 'concern' when I serviced their enclosure during the brooding period. Ramses snapped at my fingers, protectively (but only tokenwise), after the fingers already were out of reach. Petra, however, though no less habituated than Ramses, often nipped me with her bill. At night, during this period, Titus usually snuggled his head under Petra's side, but sometimes it was fully beneath her body.

[A sexual difference in defensive behavior during breeding is well known generally among birds; the female usually is much more tenacious in her bite. When rearing subsequent broods in smaller enclosures, where my hand usually came within a few cm of the nest, both Petra and Ramses not only attacked me vigorously, they fearlessly followed halfway out of the enclosure door, snapping at my fingers and often stood perched in the entrance attacking me as I sought to reach in. Gloves then were an essential to avoid injury.]

SINGLE-CHICK BROODS AND EXCESS PARENTAL CARE. Beginning when Titus was about 4 weeks of age, an activity of Petra's began, that I have found to be typical for the allogrooming parent(s) in all 6 cases that I observed in lovebird and Cockatiel broods of but a single chick (and, often also in broods of 2 chicks). With a normal-sized clutch, the parent that does most of the grooming of the chick usually is fully occupied with allogrooming and otherwise tending the several young. When only 1 chick is present the same parent usually channels all of its excess time into caring for the single chick.

CRIES OF DISTRESS. At first, this excess attention is harmless enough and simply leads to very thorough care. But with the appearance of abundant feathering, the excess attention usually takes the form of feather-picking, which follows no set pattern (see pp. 756, 757, **Feather-Picking Begins**). This activity comes to one's attention from the continually emitted distress calls of the chicks. These calls seem not to influence the further course of action of the feather-picking parent nor to evoke any sign of 'concern' in the other parent. Nor is it unusual for both lovebird parents, which are "obsessive" groomers of chicks, to be engaged simultaneously in this activity, amid a cacophony of incessant cries of distress. These vocal responses of the nestlings to apparent pain contrast sharply with the behavior said to be characteristic of adults (see p. 299, **"Hide" Symptoms**)

FEATHER-PICKING AT A PEAK----COOPERATIVE, SIMULTANEOUS PARENTAL CARE. By the 28th day, Titus was vocalizing loudly and continually as Petra groomed his back. Day after day, thereafter, for more than a week, Petra continually feather-picked his lower back and rump, despite his continual loud cries of distress and his efforts to escape. His only relief came when I rescued him from time to time. I could do this merely by becoming a close observer, whereupon Petra usually desisted temporarily. After another 7-10 days, Titus was well-feathered everywhere but on his lower back and rump, which has been essentially "picked clean." Sometimes both Petra and Ramses groomed him simultaneously, in which case it was impossible for him to escape their attentions. While he was a rapidly-growing nestling, with a big appetite, they also commonly took turns allofeeding him in quick succession. As one parent withdrew to regurgitate more food, the other moved in and allofed.

FLAVIA SHOWS AN EARLY INTEREST. I customarily flighted all the adults in the family before removing Titus for handling. On one such occasion, after Petra and Ramses had left the enclosure, Flavia "took advantage" of their absence to snuggle up against Titus in the nestbowl. At first, I thought she was Petra, as the action was quite unprecedented for Flavia.

[For temporal orientation, this occurred long after the other sister, Zenobia, had mated with Cyrano.]

TITUS NEARS FLEDGING---MUTUAL ACTIVITIES WITH PARENTS. Three days later, Petra and Ramses showed their first 'concern' over my handling of Titus by perching on me in close proximity to him as I handled him. Also, for the first time, instead of Petra entering the enclosure directly, in her usual fashion, she flew into the nestbowl and snuggled against Titus, as I returned the bowl and Titus to the enclosure. Ramses also began to enter the enclosure promptly with Titus and Petra, whereas his prior practice had been to remain outside long after they had been returned. In all, these concerns were signs that Titus would soon be flying and would receive close parental supervision.

Petra's next activities, particularly her paper stripping and cloth chewing, signalled her preparations for another clutch. To discourage further breeding at that time, I removed the nestbowl during the day and restored it only at night as a place for Titus to sleep. He then was sleeping alone, as Petra had resumed the customary practice of perching outside next to Ramses during the night. By April 4, when Titus was 34 days old, mutual interactions began between Petra, Ramses, and Titus. These undoubtedly formed one of the bases for the 'vindictive' behavior of Flavia and Zenobia, inasmuch as both of them were excluded totally from such activities.

INDUCED ALLOGROOMING. At that time, Petra, Ramses, and Titus frequently clustered together. Petra would allogroom Titus while Ramses allogroomed either or both of them, forming a circle of intense activity. By then Ramses also began to get allogroomed by Titus. As Titus vocalized his endless complaints over Petra's feather-picking, his bill opened and closed with each utterance. By pushing his forehead against the periodically opening and closing bill of the vocalizing Titus, Ramses achieved an allogrooming of his forehead.

Since Ramses had used exactly this tactic earlier when Titus was soliciting to be fed, this was Titus' 2nd experience with the induced grooming of another bird. As Ramses continued to use this tactic on following occasions when Titus vocalized while being feather-picked or soliciting food (when his bill also opened and closed), it was not long before Titus began voluntarily to allogroom both parents, both on their foreheads and elsewhere. Several times subsequently, I observed other lovebird parents employ the same tactic to induce allogrooming by chicks.

WING-FLAPPING BY TITUS DRAWS IMMEDIATE ATTENTION. On April 5, I saw Titus turn his head back into the sleeping posture for the first time. On the next day he first flapped his wings, as I handled him. When this occurred, Ramses immediately flew to us and alighted on me near Titus. He then stayed with me and showed his concern by vocalizing in rapidly-repeated, high-pitched shrieks most of the time. Though Titus solicited food from Ramses, the latter would not allofeed him while he was in my hand. Meanwhile, Petra was busy stripping paper and carrying it back to the enclosure and took no notice. That same evening, for the first time in several weeks, Petra and Ramses copulated.

In following days, I observed the typical picture of increasing parental 'concern' with the approach of the young to flight capability. When I handled Titus then, Ramses was in constant attendance. Sometimes he "scolded" or just generally vocalized. Although Petra otherwise continued busily at paper stripping, she ceased doing so when Titus flapped his wings and immediately joined Ramses on my hand.

ALLOFED IN MY HAND----SPONTANEOUS VOCALIZATION. Usually, both parents perched adjacent to Titus on my hands, as I held him directly or in the nestbowl. Although Titus usually solicited to be allofed on these occasions, and Petra once went through the motions of regurgitating food, it was not until 3 days later (Apr. 9) that Ramses acceded and allofed Titus from his perch on my hand. Titus then had tail feathers 3 cm long, readily took short flighted jumps, and could almost maintain altitude in flight. I also noted him trying to eat seeds for the first time, and he had begun to vocalize spontaneously and take close notice of his surroundings.

PARENTAL ‘CONCERNS’ PEAK. Over the period when Titus was learning to fly, both parents usually remained in close attendance while he was in my hands. They accompanied him everywhere on his spontaneous, short, abortive flights, although Petra was inclined to leave and strip paper during uneventful moments. Parental concerns reached a peak on April 12, when Titus gained altitude in flight for the first time and repeatedly and unhesitatingly launched into flight from my hands.

FEATHER-PICKING CEASES--PARENTS MORE PROTECTIVE. On that same day, Titus began using his bill to climb, and I had to rescue him for the last time from being feather-picked by Petra. Once, when he was being handled and flighted, he flew over the top of enclosure B, out of sight of Petra and Ramses, who were inside. Both parents then rushed up into the tower, where they could keep him in view. By April 14, Titus was drinking and climbing up to the perches. By the 19th, he was eating by himself, though Ramses still allofed him regularly. Though Petra’s attentions no longer included feather-picking, she continued to groom Titus lengthily. Both parents also became more protective of Titus during this period, attacking or threatening me while I serviced their enclosure.

LIMITED FREEDOM FOR THE SISTERS----FLAVIA AND TITUS INTERACT. While these activities were transpiring, Titus’ older sisters, Flavia and Zenobia, generally were kept confined to the tower by their parents, always away from Titus. Whenever possible, though, they descended and ate and drank. To ease the problem of access to food for the sisters, I made a small food tray available to them in the tower. When Petra and Ramses were otherwise occupied, they took no step to exclude Flavia and Zenobia from the enclosure. At other times the sisters avoided attracting attention and kept at a distance from the rest of the family.

Since Titus was isolated from his sisters by this arrangement, I took an exploratory step toward finding out how the sisters would interact with him when the opportunity afforded. To that end, I manually placed Titus at the base of the tower, whereupon he started to climb into it. But Petra immediately rushed into the tower and protected him. When Flavia lunged at Titus, as he approached her, Petra chased her away.

OVIPOSITION BEGINS---TOLERANCE FOR TITUS EBBS. Petra and Ramses courted and copulated throughout this period. They also often gathered together in the nest corner with Titus during grooming and resting periods. Petra laid her 1st egg the next day, followed by an additional 6 eggs, laid at irregular intervals during the next 3 weeks. In view of this breeding activity, it is understandable that parental tolerance of Titus in the nest area began to ebb, even though they continued to perform all parental acts toward him that comprised the normal care of a fledgling.

RAMSES ESCORTS TITUS---OFTEN A TRIO. For the next 3 weeks, Ramses continued to escort Titus on all flights, usually leading him from place to place but never failing to accompany him if he took off unilaterally. In the following months, he proved to be a most attentive and protective parent. Petra, although busy stripping and gathering paper on most of these occasions, proved to be no less protective of Titus when the occasion demanded. Many times, Titus, and Ramses in turn, followed Petra on her paper-stripping forays. Titus sometimes appropriated strips that she had tucked between her rump feathers, leading to my early erroneous guess that he was a female. [The reader will recall (see pp. 259, 260) that only females normally strip paper and tuck the strips between the rump feathers. Mates usually only clumsily copy the actions of females (but see pp. 827, 828, **Learning to Strip and Tuck Paper by Lovebirds**).]

Since Petra was ovipositing during that period, she spent a great deal of time in the former nest area. Titus and Ramses typically joined her there in the early morning but the sisters always were excluded. The trio usually spent the night together on the night perch (Fig. 3b). Ramses continued to allofeed Titus and he also occasionally allofed Petra, but Petra no longer allofed Titus. All 3 birds commonly allogroomed mutually.

TITUS NOT ALWAYS WELCOME---SISTERS FURTHER RESTRICTED. Even though I removed Petra's eggs as they were laid, and none was present to be protected, she continued to attack me as I serviced the enclosure. It was easy to tell when she was incubating a freshly laid egg, because she typically would abduct her wings slightly. Between the time of the 6th and 7th ovipositions, Titus was repelled thrice--the first such occurences--as he sought to join his parents on the night perch. Each time, the repulsion was forceful and emphatic. Titus then temporarily occupied the other end of the perch. Later he was able to return to Ramses' side without interference, after which he spent over 1 min thoroughly grooming Ramses' head and neck. The next morning both Petra and Ramses occasionally repelled Titus, particularly when he sought to perch near them on the night perch.

Meanwhile the social life of Flavia and Zenobia continued to be austere. Not only were they banished to the tower by Ramses' vigilance when he was not occupied with other matters, but Ramses also paid such close attention to events in the tower that whenever I gave the sisters edible treats he rushed up into the tower and appropriated everything for himself. It can be assumed that the sisters were being excluded from the enclosure and breeding area just as any intruder would have been, since I had noticed no aggression of the sisters toward Titus. Being barely a juvenile (i.e., being barely fledged), Titus still warranted a certain amount of parental care (Ramses occasionally allofed him, weeks after a normal chick would have been weaned). But all was soon to change, as the protective instincts of Petra and Ramses were to be exercised severely.

TITUS ATTACKED BY FLAVIA. On May 14, I witnessed the 1st unprovoked attacks on Titus by a sister. At 09:30 h, while Petra and Ramses were in the tower, Flavia repeatedly attacked Titus, who usually was adept enough to avoid her (Zenobia was at her customary position at the top of the tower, close to her mate, Cyrano, in the adjoining enclosure). To halt the harassment, I flighted Flavia for 60 min, but when I returned her she resumed attacking Titus, so I flighted her again. At that time, Titus had never been very far into the tower, and had not yet adopted his subsequent habit of retreating there to the protection of his parents whenever a sister attacked him in the enclosure below.

PARENTS FREQUENT THE TOWER---TITUS ATTACKED BY BOTH SISTERS. Since I removed all of Petra's eggs as they were laid, breeding and courtship activities of the parents ceased temporarily. Accordingly, the former nest area in the enclosure ceased to be a focal point of interest and occupancy, as it had been throughout the preceding months. The attentions of Petra and Ramses then turned toward the attractions of the the tower. There, they could visit within sight of 3 of their sons (Jagatai, Ogadai, and Cyrano) and the Budgerigars.

Unfortunately, the parents' newly adopted habit of long occupancy of the tower often left Titus unprotected in the enclosure below. It then was revealed that both of his sisters were prone to attack him viciously, seemingly even more intensely than if he merely had been a stranger. Sometimes I gave Titus temporary relief by flighting Flavia when I found him isolated in the enclosure with her. That did not always solve the problem, though, because the parents sometimes also chased Zenobia out of the tower (away from her customary position at the top next to Cyrano). Then both sisters had to be flighted.

[One might wonder why I did not simply house the sisters by themselves to solve the aggression problems. The explanation is that I was not trying to solve the birds' problems for them. Rather, I was trying to probe the origin and significance of their interactions. My goal was to study interactions between groups of family members under various conditions and in different combinations, not to avoid entirely such interactions. But by flighting the sisters at critical times, I did give them and Titus the opportunity to accommodate gradually to the new circumstances.]

TITUS FOLLOWS HIS PARENTS FOR PROTECTION. In the next week I kept a watchful eye out for Titus' welfare. Titus began to accompany his parents into the tower for protection, and to flee to their company there to escape the attacks of his sisters in the enclosure. But even accompanying his parents into the tower was risky for Titus because his sisters passed close by as they fled from the tower and even were prone to attack him as they passed. Titus continued to sleep on the night perch with Petra and Ramses. Typically, he occupied the end of the perch by the left wall. That enabled him to hold on to the wall with the toes of his horizontally-extending right foot [At that time, I substituted a water tray (hung from an enclosure side) for the water bowl on the floor, because Titus often fell into the latter while escaping in panic from his sisters.] .

SISTERS BEGIN MORNING VISITS. Flavia and Zenobia customarily spent the nights sleeping together in the tower (though Zenobia was mated to Cyrano, who was in the adjoining enclosure) and remained there in the early morning. But on the morning of May 21, the sisters came down to the night perch and perched at its right end, 5-10 cm from Petra. On the following morning, for the first time, I found that Petra, Ramses, and Titus had moved from the night perch to the back of the nest perch (Fig. 3b), suggesting that they had been disturbed earlier by the sisters.

TITUS INJURED SEVERELY---HEAD AND NECK AREAS ATTACKED. Upon returning on the afternoon of May 23, I found Titus with a severe wound at the base of his skull, with the overlying feathers matted and soaked with blood. His sisters clearly were not confining their attacks to the non-lethal bites on the legs and toes that usually are seen in Peach-faced Lovebirds. Instead, their attacks obviously had lethal 'intent,' and were far more injurious even than those usually visited upon an intruding stranger. Subsequent weeks were to confirm this assessment: Flavia and Zenobia seldom bit merely at Titus' legs or toes. They almost always attacked his head and neck. Fortunately, Titus become adept at escaping, and they usually either failed to make contact or only obtained a tuft of feathers.

[Recall that Cyrus and Cyrano also had engaged in bouts of potentially lethal combat, during which feathers flew (see p. 319). Flammer (141) also has noted that attacking lovebirds may "bite the back of the skull and will often remove a portion of the occipital lobe of the brain." The identity of the species is not mentioned, but he very likely is referring to Peach-faced Lovebirds. Members of the genus, *Loriculus*, probably the lovebirds' closest living relatives (see p. 251), also attack one another by biting at the legs, feet, and head. As with lovebirds, these birds also seem to develop an inhibition against biting as they mature (79).]

TITUS GIVEN BETTER PROTECTION. The unfortunate Titus was a victim of circumstances. He never had engaged in aggressive behavior toward his sisters, and I found it difficult to conclude that their vicious attacks were motivated by anything but 'vindictiveness.' Not only did they appear to 'resent' his presence, they apparently also were 'jealous' of his favored status. If the reader is not yet prepared to entertain this interpretation of the situation, he may be won over to it by knowledge of the further course of events.

The aggressive intents of the sisters called for vigorous protective countermeasures. Beginning that same day, I never left Titus in the enclosure with his sisters when I was absent. During absences, I either housed Titus separately or flighted him. Similarly, I also flighted Titus during the morning when I was servicing the enclosures and parental protection was at a minimum.

Petra and Ramses were very attentive to Titus' safety and his wound. They tended to keep very close to him, and carefully and frequently groomed the region of his bloodied head and neck feathers for many days thereafter, until the wound was healed and the overlying feathers were normal in appearance. They also kept close track of the sisters' whereabouts and repeatedly repelled them when they ventured near Titus.

VULNERABLE WHEN PARENTS DISTRACTED. But for one small deficiency, my precautions would have been unnecessary, in view of the vigilance of Petra and Ramses. The deficiency was the fact that in the excitement of events in enclosure B and the colony, Petra and Ramses occasionally were distracted, whereupon Flavia seized the opportunity to stalk Titus. These distractions probably would have had lethal consequences for Titus, had it not been for my own precautions. From the time of the serious attack, for several weeks, the single-minded goal of both sisters seemed to be to destroy Titus (just as Cyrano acted as if the sole object of his existence was to gain Cassandra's attention and allofed her). The sisters sought out Titus and attacked him at every opportunity, sometimes by cleverly devious routes. There were more than a few times when I had to shout loudly and rush to the enclosure to dissipate a potentially lethal attack.

AFTERMATH OF INJURY. With this preamble to events of the following weeks, I now outline these events. After rescuing Titus, tending to his wound, and giving him respite by housing him for 2 h with the Cockatielian pair, Helena and Homer, I restored him to enclosure B. Petra immediately tended to him and groomed his matted feathers. The sisters, meanwhile, were confined to the tower by their parents.

DOMINANCE STRUCTURE BREAKDOWN----TITUS AND RAMSES INSEPARABLE. Since Petra and Ramses often retired from the enclosure to the tower, the structured dominance situation in the tower between Flavia and Zenobia (see pp. 325, 326) broke down. Almost any circumstances might have prevailed. Neither, either, or both of the sisters might have been at the very top of the tower near Cyrano, or in the enclosure below. Or, all of the birds might have been distributed in almost any fashion. The one constant situation that prevailed was that Ramses seldom let Titus out of his sight, and the latter customarily accompanied his father closely.

PARENT-OFFSPRING DOMINANCE IS PRE-EMPTIVE. A frequent distribution of the occupants of enclosure B found Petra in the horizontal section of the tower, with the daughters huddled together closely in the top vertical section, and Titus and Ramses together in the nest corner of the enclosure. Sometimes father and son were perched above on the nest perch or night perch. This breakdown of dominance relationships (except for that of parents over offspring) shows that parental dominance takes precedence over the dominance conferred by virtue of an offspring being a member of a mated pair. As a consequence, Zenobia was obliged to abandon her mate Cyrano, whenever either of her parents chased her from the tower, whereas Zenobia completely dominated Flavia when both were in the tower alone, by virtue of her being mated to Cyrano.

TOWER ENTERED EVERY MORNING. On the morning of May 24, the day after the severe attack on Titus, and customarily thereafter, Petra and Ramses entered the tower not long after lights-on. Unless Titus followed with alacrity, he was liable to be left alone below, when his sisters were expelled, a potentially hazardous situation for him. It was for that reason that my first act each morning was to flight Titus until the enclosure servicing was completed.

EARLY MORNING AGGRESSION TABOO AND RELOCATIONS. Although it seemed that Ramses was neglectful of Titus by leaving him and ascending to the tower, this may not have been the case. I was unaware, at first, of the fact that the very early morning, before the lights are turned on, and for some time thereafter (and probably during the night, as well), are periods of "truce" for lovebirds during which overt aggression appears to be taboo (see p. 335, **A Time of "Truce" and Courtship Feeding**). Since no aggression was observed at such times, Titus apparently was not in immediate danger when temporarily abandoned by his parents in the enclosure.

The early hours each morning, following the attack on Titus, proved to be ones of transition. Whereas, previously, Flavia and Zenobia usually remained in the tower, they now began to enter the enclosure with the light of dawn (i.e., natural dawn, hours before lights-on) and try to perch near the rest of the family. It probably was because the sisters' presence was tolerated on several early morning visits, that they began to make these visits habitually. And perhaps it was because there was no danger of the sisters' attacking Titus during early morning visits, that Petra and Ramses made no effort to exclude them. At any rate, one can attribute the new morning "lineup" (the distribution of birds between the tower and the enclosure, and on the perches) to the disinclination, if not inhibition, of lovebirds to behave aggressively toward one another in the early morning.

This disinclination also applied to aggression toward me. Thus, when I serviced the enclosures after turning the lights on, the brooding hens were disinclined to attack me and only nibbled on my fingers if I held them near. But by the time I had replenished the water and was tending to the food, the same brooding hens might attack me vigorously. When attending to the birds later in the day and evening, they usually rushed over and inflicted painful bites.

EARLY MORNING PERCH RELOCATIONS. Time and again in the following weeks Titus and his parents transferred to the nest perch in the early morning, while the sisters were found at the trio's former positions on the night perch. My interpretation of these adjustments is that the sisters attempted repeatedly to join the trio by sidling over next to Petra on the night perch (she was always at the other end from Titus, with Ramses in between). Being tolerant of their presence at this time, Petra and Ramses, with Titus following, probably usually elected to relocate on the nest perch. It is not unlikely that the switching of positions occurred more than once, as many very early morning hours were marked by a great deal of lovebird vocalizations.

ATTENTIVE FATHER-SON RELATIONSHIP. A characteristic pattern in the weeks following the attack on Titus was to find father and son, and sometimes Petra, as well, in the former nest corner, "chain-grooming" one another, or to find Titus and Ramses perched side by side. Titus usually followed his father and kept very close by. Part of Ramses' "reward" for his close association with his fledgling son was that the latter often thoroughly allogroomed his father's head and neck, but then Ramses also very attentively allogroomed Titus.

DAUGHTERS' PRESENCE DECREASINGLY TOLERATED. These close associations between Ramses and Titus usually lasted for 15-90 min, and it is difficult to avoid concluding that the associations were motivated by Titus' need for Ramses' protection. This interpretation tends to be substantiated by the fact that whenever Titus and Ramses were side by side, Ramses sometimes tolerated the presence of his daughters in the enclosure but he always watched them closely. On the other hand, when Ramses and Titus were not side by side but simply together in the same area, Ramses never tolerated his daughters' presence, but promptly chased them into the tower. Later he tended to chase them into the tower at all times, as he apparently had become more alert to their devious maneuvers to attack Titus.

TOWER GUARDED. Petra and Ramses also adopted the tactic of guarding the base of the tower from beneath, on the tower perch (see Fig. 3b). Flavia and Zenobia then had almost no opportunity to enter the enclosure unnoticed, as they were wont to do when they pressed their attacks. When Titus and Ramses were flighted together during these post-attack days, Ramses was inseparable from him. In fact, he had become so protective of Titus, that he then sometimes pecked at me and bit me when I touched Titus.

RELATIONS MUCH DIFFERENT IN TITUS' ABSENCE. It is most pertinent to these observations that when Titus was not in the enclosure, the social relationships reverted to normal. Then, Flavia and Zenobia usually were at liberty to come and go without interference (depending, of course, on the intensity of the courtship and breeding activities of their parents; in some circumstances, the courting parents even chased Titus away). In other words, when Titus was flighted, the restrictions imposed by his parents on his sisters' movements and actions no longer were in effect, since the sisters no longer posed a threat to him.

ATTACKS ON TITUS. Most attempted attacks on Titus were thwarted by Ramses, Petra, or me, before harm could be done. The most notable of these attacks in the days immediately following his serious injury, were as follows (many were not recorded). On the evening of May 27, I had to remove Titus 3 times because of Flavia's attacks when Ramses was unaccountably lax in his protection. Three days later, Zenobia descended from the top of the tower and attacked Titus from behind, as he sat next to Ramses in the horizontal section of the tower. Later that morning, Flavia also attacked him in the enclosure. On June 7, when I flighted the 3 young, both sisters pecked at Titus. On June 12, Flavia stealthily entered the enclosure from the tower, worked her way over to Titus, and attacked him before being chased back into the tower by Ramses. On June 16, I noted that Titus still needed the full-time protection of his parents.

[During the period covered in the preceding paragraph and thereafter, I had no suspicion of the significance that subsequently would attach to Flavia's behavior toward Titus during these days, so I did not keep detailed records of all attacks and attempted attacks on him. At the time I was under the impression, from the siblings' behavior and the pubic-bone test, that Titus was a female.]

On June 21, I made note of the fact that, after the trio had ostensibly settled down for the night, Petra and Ramses even began coming down off the night perch to chase Flavia or Zenobia back into the tower. On June 23, I noted the continuing pattern of Titus following Ramses around for protection. On June 30, Petra vigorously attacked Flavia but I witnessed the interaction too late to know whether it was retaliatory or protective.

FLAVIA TRYING TO COURT, NOT INJURE? On July 10, at 09:22 h, after some attacks by Flavia on Titus, I first received the impression that her attacks had decreased in ferocity. It is known from the future course of events, that at some time during July or early August, the object of Flavia's attentions toward Titus changed. Perceiving, at some point, that he was a male, she began trying to court, rather than to attack him. [Most lovebirds do not begin to exhibit sexual behavior until after the postjuvenal molt is completed, at about 4 months of age (787), which for Titus was on July 2, but pairing can occur after only 2 months (3, 4).]

Not only did I fail to perceive the change, neither did Petra, Ramses, or Titus. The parents continued with vigor to chase Flavia and Zenobia from Titus' vicinity. It seems unlikely that they would have done this had they perceived that Flavia sought to court Titus. Meanwhile, Titus continued to flee in seeming terror. In view of these circumstances, the subsequent interactions between Flavia and Titus become of great interest.

FLAVIA'S PARADOX---EARLY MORNING "LINEUPS." At some time during July or August Flavia was faced with the paradoxical situation of trying to court a male who always fled in panic on her approach. I think it is reasonable to assume, buttressed by my prior observations of the behavior of Cassandra, Cyrus, and Cyrano, that any social conciliation by Flavia would have had to be achieved in the early morning hours, when overt aggression was taboo. Consequently, the early morning perching lineups become of great interest. I kept close track of these easily, because the early morning lovebird squabbling awakened me and attracted my attention.

FLAVIA AND TITUS PERCHED NEAR EACH OTHER. It may be notable, in this connection, that the morning of July 9 was the first morning when Flavia and Titus were alone together on the night perch, though about 8 cm apart. It seemed at the time that Flavia was approaching Titus in the early morning, but not attacking him. [Some time earlier, on June 30 (over 2 weeks after Titus was injured severely), Flavia also was on the night perch about 10 cm from Titus in the early morning, but on that occasion she was perched next to Ramses. This was the only noted occasion on which the latter tolerated Flavia's near presence since her fledgling days.]

"ATTACKS" ON TITUS CONTINUE---ANY NEED FOR DEFENSE? The next interaction between Flavia and Titus came only a little over 2 h later. Flavia "attacked" Titus again (or so it appeared) and Ramses came to the rescue with a vengence. [I place the word "attack" in quotation marks because it is uncertain whether it was truly an attack, or merely an attempt to court him. After all, Titus always fled from Flavia during the day, up to the very day--and occasionally even after--he first courtship-fed her.] On July 12, for only the 2nd time, I found Flavia alone with Titus on the night perch at 07:15 h, only 7-8 cm away from him. On July 17, during the day, Ramses not only chased Flavia away from Titus and out of the enclosure, he pursued her into the tower, all the way up to the end of the top section and then nipped her rump after cornering her there.

I am convinced, in retrospect, that Flavia was trying to court Titus at this time, perhaps even much earlier. Accordingly, Ramses' vengeful pursuit and attack on her, may highlight the inability of the parents to detect her altered social intentions. But this inability, if such it was, prevailed up to the time when Flavia's changed intentions became known unequivocally by virtue of a change in Titus' behavior.

CAUGHT IN A "CROSSFIRE"---FIRST FLIGHTING OF FLAVIA WITH TITUS. By July 19, Petra and Ramses again were beginning to breed, and they chased Titus away from the former nest corner. Titus then sometimes became trapped between his parents and his sisters, usually Flavia. On such occasions, I usually rescued him merely by approaching the enclosure. Whatever Flavia's true intentions, Titus seemed to be terrified by her near approach. On July 20, I again recorded in my notes that Flavia's attacks no longer seemed to be lethal in intent (i.e., no longer targeted toward his head). Either that, or he had become so adept in escape that she could not get close to him. Titus' crippled leg generally did not hinder his movements. He was at a disadvantage only in moving on perches, along which he had to hop with one foot, or fly.

In view of the above observations, I flighted Flavia and Titus alone together to see how they would interact in non-confining circumstances. Would she fly after and attack him? The outcome was that Flavia repeatedly sought to approach Titus closely ("to no good purpose," I wrote, probably mistakenly, in my notes), but Titus fled on every occasion.

MORE ON MORNING LINEUPS---FLAVIA TRYING TO COURT TITUS. At 08:10 h the next morning, Flavia again was perched not far from Titus. But she was on the night perch and he was a 6-8 cm away on the lower night perch (about 10 cm below and parallel with the night perch). The parents were at the rear end of the nest perch. The situation was the same the next morning (07:45 h) except that Titus was on the corn perch. The situation on the 3rd morning was almost the same but then Ramses was at the left end of the night perch, just above Titus, and Petra was on the other end. In all cases, Zenobia was in the tower.

I think it clear from these early morning perching positions that Flavia already was trying to court Titus. She apparently was taking advantage of the "immunity" of the early morning hours to try to communicate her intentions. The nearby perch positions of Titus apparently were those to which he had fled by leaping when Flavia sidled close to him. As yet, there was no indication that Titus had sensed an altered intent on the part of Flavia.

ALLOWED IN ENCLOSURE TO FEED AT NIGHT. In the following week (July 25 to 31), I witnessed no notable interaction nor early morning positions on the perches, with the exceptions that Flavia was on the night perch 3 times when Titus was on the corn perch or at the rear of the nest perch. On 5 of these mornings, Zenobia also was in the enclosure. The sisters sometimes were allowed in the enclosure to eat and drink late at night, while the parents and Titus were mutually allogrooming on the night perch. At other times, Petra or Ramses came off the perch and chased them into the tower. Again, on August 1, I recorded the fact that Flavia's attacks no longer appeared to be vicious, still unaware either that Titus was a male or that she might be trying to court him.

CONTINUED PURSUIT. There was no noteworthy close approach of Flavia to Titus in the early mornings of the next week; Titus usually was to be found on the corn perch. On the evening of August 4, however, Flavia descended from the tower 3 times in close succession and approached Titus. Petra and Ramses were courting in the left-rear corner. On the first approach, Ramses was tardy in diverting Flavia, and she got quite close to Titus. The 2nd time, Ramses chased her back into the tower before she could get near to Titus. On the 3rd approach, Titus, himself, fled as she neared him, and Ramses then chased her back again. Interactions during the remainder of the week were unexceptional.

TITUS EXCLUDED FROM NEST---FLAVIA CHASED TO TOWER TOP. On August 8, I recorded that Flavia was continuing to "attack" Titus, and that his parents also had begun to attack him. They attacked and repelled him when he approached their nest corner. They again were in breeding condition. I also noted that Flavia persistently sought to approach Titus. That same evening, as late as 23:20 h, Petra repeatedly came off her "settled" perch position with Titus and Ramses, and chased Flavia back into the tower, once pursuing her all the way to the top of the upper section.

TOE "CARESSING," A NORMAL ATTENTION-GETTING ACT. It was during that 2nd week in August, late on the night of the 14th, that I made a significant observation concerning toe caressing by Peach-faced Lovebirds. [Until then, this had been done only by Cyrano as a tactic to get Cassandra's attention.] Petra had taken a very thorough bath and then took a position next to Titus on the night perch. While she was drying, she twice solicited head-grooming from Titus, each time presenting the top of her head below his bill. When he ignored her on both occasions, she twice nibbled toes on his left foot to get his attention before presenting her head again for allogrooming. Thereupon, Titus allogroomed her. I was to observe "toe caressing" many times subsequently, both among lovebirds and Cockatiels (see pp 814, 815, **Attention Getting by Toe Caressing**). It is, however, an infrequently used device, not previously reported, and, when employed, used mostly by juveniles (suggestive of an ancient origin). [Cockatiels usually get attention for allogrooming of the head by lightly pecking the bird being solicited before presenting the head.]

TITUS STALKED WITH GREAT TENACITY. The next few days were filled with significant activity. The entire social situation in enclosure B became transformed. On August 15, I recorded that Titus seemed "terrified" of Flavia. He carefully avoided being left alone in the enclosure with her, always accompanying his parents to the tower. These also were days of intense breeding activity by the parents, who courtship-fed and copulated several times. On the evening of August 18, I wrote in my notes that Flavia was continuing to "hunt down" Titus wherever he went, even though she had to dodge Ramses' protective attacks to do so. On the morning of the 19th, after eating, Flavia's tenacity was such that she descended from the tower to stalk Titus 4 times. If Ramses was positioned between them, she bided her time until she had a clear path. Titus fled each time she approached him.

TRUE RELATIONSHIPS REVEALED---TITUS SEEKS FLAVIA'S COMPANY. I then was very suspicious of Flavia's behavior. It seemed that such persistence was unlikely to have been sustained by purely aggressive urges. Furthermore, Zenobia had long since desisted from devious "planned" attacks on Titus; she only attacked him when their paths crossed (I still believed Titus to be a female). Accordingly, I flighted Flavia and Titus alone again. The proceedings this time finally exposed the true relationships. At first Flavia chased Titus and pecked at his toes as he fled from location to location. Then she lost interest and went exploring. To my great surprise, Titus thereupon began to seek her company. When she was atop the kitchen door, he sidled over (hopped and flew along it) next to her 3 times before getting pecked away (she was busy stripping paper). The true circumstances then became quite evident--Titus was a male, and Flavia had recently been trying to court, not attack, him.

TITUS COURTSHIP-FEEDS FLAVIA---CONTINUES TO FLEE WITHIN ENCLOSURE. On several subsequent approaches, Flavia tolerated Titus' presence at a distance of 2-5 cm. Then, suddenly, without other preliminary, he courtship-fed her in a bout of 5 regurgitations. Instantly, they became close companions and he continued to allofeed her repeatedly. After about another 30 min, they were interacting as pairs normally do. Sixty min later, they were perched side by side on the kitchen door and he allofed her again, on that occasion with 9 regugitations. After another 30 min of their "chumming" about, I returned them to enclosure B, whereupon Titus immediately set to eating, and Flavia got chased into the tower. Apparently Petra and Ramses were unaware that Flavia and Titus had become mates.

The influences of the enclosure milieu and his past experiences there dominated Titus' behavioral responses to Flavia during the initial period after the pair was rehoused. That afternoon, Flavia showed less interest in stalking Titus, but when she worked her way over near to him he fled. Thereupon, Petra interrupted her nest-building activity in the corner, and chased Flavia into the tower. Titus' retreat from Flavia on this occasion was not noticeably different from the way he fled on the other occasions when she approached him. Accordingly,it seemed likely that she had been courting for some time, both in the early morning and during the day.

A NEW REGIME BEGINS. At 17:30 h that evening, I flighted Flavia and Titus again. First, they perched in contact with each other on the kitchen door, later on the lamp stem (Fig. 2b). They flew about together like any mated pair. For the next month, I flighted them together 2-3 times every day, with similar results. Outside the enclosure, at least, they behaved like mates. The social interactions within enclosure B were of great interest. By 20:18 h that evening (Aug. 19), the entire tenor of the interactions within the enclosure had altered. Titus no longer fled from Flavia, nor did Ramses chase her into the tower. Fifteen min later, Flavia and Titus were alone together harmoniously in the enclosure, while the rest of the family was in the tower. When both parents descended from the tower, they just perched at its base, seemingly confused at the unfamiliar scene before them. Then they approached their nest corner, without making any effort to chase Flavia away from Titus. When Zenobia descended, she too seemed to be confused to see Flavia and Titus together in harmony. It appeared evident that all 3 birds had been unaware previously of the altered social relationship.

TOWER GUARDED BY FLAVIA---ALTERED DOMINANCE RELATIONSHIPS. Then a significant and unprecedented act took place that was to be repeated may times in the coming weeks. Flavia chased the previously dominant Zenobia back into the tower. The parents just looked on. When Zenobia descended again, Flavia chased her back again. Clearly, Flavia was protecting Titus from possible attack by Zenobia, and/or protecting her relationship with Titus by chasing off a potential competitor (sexual aggression). From that time on, Flavia dominated Zenobia in the enclosure when Titus was present, always chasing her sister into the tower, but Zenobia dominated Flavia in the tower, excluding her from the top section, and frequently also from the horizontal section.

MORE ABOUT THE NEW REGIME---MORNING FLIGHTINGS. Later that evening, all 5 birds were in the enclosure together harmoniously. Flavia still gave her parents a wide berth, but no longer fled to the tower when they approached. The parents had become much less 'concerned' over Titus' whereabouts, and Titus alternated between visiting them and keeping company with Flavia. However, after having been conditioned over a period of several months, his previously invariable daytime response of fleeing from her apparently could not be suppressed completely after just a few hours of reciprocal courting. He continued for another day to be skittish when she approached him. When I flighted Flavia and Titus again that night (22:30 h) for the 3rd time that day, they again interacted as a mated pair.

The next morning (August 20), I flighted Flavia and Titus while I serviced the enclosures. For the first time in months, Titus declined to drink from his outside water tray, which I offered to him as he perched with Flavia. Similarly, he did not alight on my head and shoulders his usual 4-5 times. He was occupied with other matters. He and Flavia were busy in the kitchen, where he allofed her atop a curtain rod. They adopted this location as a favorite perch, presumably because of its privacy and seclusion, and visited it often during subsequent morning flights. Titus did alight on me once before I finished servicing that morning, but Flavia did not accompany him. But on every subsequent morning, both alighted on me several times; Flavia often pecked gently at my ears and neck.

MORE COURTSHIP FEEDING---AN UNUSUAL SITUATION. Titus still was skittish over Flavia's attentions in the enclosure that afternoon, usually moving off when she approached. Significantly, neither Petra nor Ramses came to his rescue. They had adapted to the new circumstances quicker than did Titus. When I flighted the new pair again, Titus courtship-fed Flavia a record 13 regurgitations in one continuous bout atop the kitchen door. I watched closely from only 30 cm away. Afterward, Flavia stripped paper and was able to tuck some strips into her rear feathers. Titus still sometimes flew off when Flavia approached, but she followed after him.

Later that afternoon, I isolated the new mates alone in the enclosure while the others were being flighted. Titus still tended to flee with dispatch when Flavia approached. This was an unusual situation, indeed. Here were two birds that behaved like a courting pair outside of the enclosure, whereas the male often fled from the female when within it.

TITUS ADJUSTED TO BEING MATED. I touch only on the highlights and significant changes on subsequent days. Beginning the next day, Flavia and Titus alighted on me several times, walking about on my head, back, and shoulders, as I serviced the enclosures. I became a regular stop on their subsequent apartment tours. Though Petra and Ramses had become much more tolerant of Flavia and Zenobia, they also were more busy courting. Another clutch of eggs was imminent. By mid-afternoon, Titus was more accustomed to having Flavia perching nearby; by early evening he was sitting near her on the corn perch. Flavia continued to spend much time guarding the base of the tower, confining Zenobia therein. As on the night before, she slept in the tower with Zenobia and still was there the next morning.

Though Flavia often guarded the tower exit when Zenobia was within it, by August 22 she had become more tolerant of Zenobia's presence in the enclosure. Sometimes the sisters worked side by side trying to chew cloth from the outside cover. At other times, all 3 siblings were together almost side by side, quite harmoniously. Titus was noticeably more relaxed when Flavia was near or approaching him. All in all, this was the most peaceful day in the enclosure since the attacks on Titus had begun. What tendency Titus then had to withdraw on Flavia's approach, probably was little more than the normal submission and yielding of position by the lovebird male to the dominant female.

TITUS ATTACKED BY ZENOBIA. By August 23, Flavia was spending almost all her time during the day in the enclosure, rather than in the tower with Zenobia. By then, Titus had no hesitation to mount next to Flavia and perch at her side. Although Flavia chased Zenobia into the tower several times and guarded the entrance, Zenobia twice slipped by and attacked Titus. On one of those occasions, she nipped him on the leg. Time and again, she went out of her way to attack him. It would appear that she now was 'jealous' of Titus on Flavia's account. Her resulting behavior fits well with the "spiteful" description given these birds in the literature.

GUARD RELAXED IN TITUS' ABSENCE. The fact that Flavia was guarding the tower on Titus' behalf could easily be confirmed experimentally by removing him from the enclosure. In Titus' absence, Flavia immediately ceased her role as a guard and ascended the tower to her former customary resting place in the horizontal section. On his return, she resumed her position of vigilance at the tower base. That evening, in some temporary moments of reversion to past behavior, Petra and Ramses again chased Flavia into the tower several times, though she was not being more aggressive toward Titus than a lovebird hen normally is toward her mate.

PEACEFUL SCENES---NIGHT PERCHING. August 24 was a day of several peaceful scenes in the enclosure. Flavia and Titus usually were in each other's company, Zenobia was busy chewing cloth from the outside cover, and the parents were busy in the nest corner. Flavia and Titus often perched near each other. When Flavia was in the first vertical section of the tower, Titus perched near her at its base. Beginning early on the morning of August 27, Flavia again began to seek Titus' company on the night perch, but by the early morning of August 30, she had been able to come no closer than perching above him.

Meanwhile, the parents were very much in breeding condition. With oviposition only 2 days away, they sometimes chased their daughters into the tower, occasionally repelling even Titus when he ventured too close to their nest corner. Beginning on August 27, the parents began to copulate almost every time I flighted Flavia and Titus. This was reminiscent of the situation when the Cockatiels, Carmen and Cosimo, remained behind in the enclosure and copulated when their young left to be flighted (see p.663, **A Preference for Privacy**).

FLAVIA JOINS TITUS EVERY MORNING. All through the preceding period, Titus slept with his parents on the night perch. On the early morning of September 3 (06:50 h), lovebird squabbling awakened me in time to see Titus fly up onto the lower night perch next to Flavia (who had spent the night in the tower with Zenobia) and sit with her for almost 5 min. After jumping down, he then jumped back on at the other end, worked his way over next to her, and perched there for a short time. Beginning on September 5, Flavia began to join Titus early every morning, and I always found them perched side by side on one of the perches.

SISTERS EASILY HAND-CAUGHT FOR VISITS WITH MATES. Flavia's behavior also changed radically in another respect. Previously, when I sought to catch her by hand in enclosure B for any reason (usually flighting) she fled to the tower, where I could not reach her and had to postpone the flighting. But when I began to flight her 3 times a day with Titus, she let herself be caught easily. Zenobia responded similarly; she also let herself be caught readily for regular visits with Cyrano [When these birds subsequently were housed together as pairs, they reverted to resisting being caught by hand.]

ALLOPREENING BY FLAVIA AND TITUS---TITUS SLEEPS WITH PARENTS. Beginning on September 8, I began to put Zenobia in enclosure E with her mate, Cyrano, for most of the day, to investigate the behavior of Flavia and Titus in her absence. The pair then began to spend much time together in the seclusion of the tower. For the first time, I saw them mutually allogroom. At that time, Petra and Ramses were occupied courting and nest-building in the enclosure corner and spent much less time in the tower. Ironically, Flavia often groomed Titus at the same spot on his head where the near-fatal bite had been inflicted. Later that day, Titus courtship-fed Flavia. From then on, it was common to see Flavia and Titus allogrooming mutually while on a perch or in the tower.

On 3 nights (Sept. 19-21), I housed Zenobia in enclosure E with Cyrano and the Budgerigars. Despite the tower being free, Titus adhered to his long-established habit of sleeping with his parents, rather than with Flavia in the tower. If he was in the tower with her when I turned the lights off, he hastened down to join his parents. But Flavia always joined him on one of the enclosure perches in the early morning. On the evening of September 22, I translocated the colony to the University, ending this phase of the studies.

FLAVIA AND TITUS HOUSED AS A PAIR

FLAVIA VERY DOMINEERING. In their new laboratory setting I housed Flavia and Titus as a pair. They proceeded to engage in all the usual activities of mated lovebirds--courtship feeding, sleeping side by side, mutual grooming, and close companionship, but not coition. Flavia proved to be very domineering. She spent a good fraction of every day chasing Titus about and pecking at him. He customarily tolerated her attacks, usually retreating before her. When he stood his ground, he was punished.

CRIPPLED LEG DRAWS ATTENTION. Since Titus' right leg usually was extended to the side, it drew the attention that normally is directed only at the less-accessible toes. I often saw Flavia grab Titus' crippled leg in her bill, just as his father, Ramses, had done. This was not an aggressive act, and never did him any harm. Its significance seemed to be that it lent emphasis to the ongoing intentions of the bird that performed the act. Flavia often got Titus to move over on a perch by the maneuver of pinching one of his toes in her bill. When Flavia pursued him to the floor of the enclosure, Titus often assumed a submissive posture, lying flat on his back.

UNREQUITED SOLICITATIONS FOR COITIUS. Flavia's "hen-pecking" of Titus appeared to depend partly on his vulnerability and partly on frustration on her part, over his inadequate sexual responsiveness. Her frustration was evident from her unrequited solicitations of copulation, evinced both by crouching horizontally with wings, head, and tail raised, and by mounting the back of Titus ["reverse mounting" or "pseudomale" behavior, a frequent preliminary step to copulation in some species (23) that also was observed subsequently between the lovebirds, Andrea and Theocritus (see Table 4), in a pairing in Nov., 1986]. In normal circumstances, such spontaneous soliciting by the lovebird female is relatively rare. In the present instance, it persisted week after week.

TITUS FINALLY RESPONDS. The first of Titus' many efforts to mount Flavia were observed 10 weeks after they were housed together, when he was just over 9 months of age, as they milled about on the enclosure floor for more than 20 min. Flavia laid the first egg of her 1st clutch 6 days later. Titus subsequently became very aggressive in his efforts to copulate with Flavia, pursuing her on perches, on the enclosure floor, and even while she was incubating eggs (also subsequently attempted by Theocritus as Andrea incubated eggs)--quite the reverse roles of those described above. Successful copulation was not precluded by Titus' infirmity, since a case even is known of successful breeding of a pair of Ringed Plovers (*Charadrius hiatiula*) both members of which had only one leg (see 28). Successful copulations occurred, in the present case, after I facilitated them with an appropriate arrangement of dowel supports (see p. 773, **Sexual Union Achieved**).

INTERACTIONS WITH JAGATAI. On October 13, on one of their flightings, Flavia spent a great deal of time climbing about outside Jagatai's enclosure and trading pecks with him through the bars (Jagatai was housed alone at the time). When Titus came close on the enclosure front to join Flavia, she threatened him and chased him away. This raised the possibility that Flavia was seeking to initiate a relationship with Jagatai, since Titus was impotent at that time (I had not yet facilitated copulation). To explore this possibility, I opened the door to Jagatai's enclosure. Flavia was the first to enter, and she immediately made herself "at home." She squabbled briefly with Jagatai but little other interaction occurred. Similarly, Titus entered the enclosure and moved about in it quite uninhibitedly, without agonistic interaction with Jagatai.

Jagatai had only been housed in enclosure M for 3 days, and that might have been why he did not defend it. Nevertheless, it was clear that both Flavia and Titus were well acquainted with Jagatai from their many previous visits to his vicinity on other flightings. There was no hint of Flavia seeking to court Jagatai.

JAGATAI TREATED AS AN OUTSIDER. When the pair left the enclosure, Jagatai followed and sought several times to perch with them. But neither Flavia nor Titus would tolerate his near presence, though they were more likely to let him approach closely when they were together than when they were apart. Similar relations were observed when I flighted the trio 12 days later. On that occasion, though, Flavia once permitted Jagatai to perch adjacent to her for about 1 min, but facing in the opposite direction.

DISCUSSION

Although the central events of Titus' life are quite different from those described earlier (Chap. 3) for Cyrano, nevertheless the overall pictures possess many striking parallels:

1. both cases involved physical injury;
2. initiatives for pairing were pressed with great tenacity by the female;
3. notable turning points were marked by courtship feedings;
4. the social problems of both Cyrano and Titus ultimately were resolved by mating--in both cases without sleeping side by side with the mate;
5. taboos against early morning aggression made it possible to overcome impasses.

In large part, these parallels doubtless have to be attributed to the fact that both accounts deal with Peach-faced Lovebirds. It is difficult to envision the same events occurring with the more placid (but impatient and 'uncompromising') Cockatiels.

EASY TO BE LED ASTRAY IN BEHAVIOR STUDIES. Although I am confident of the interpretations of the events that are described here and in Chapter 3, it is important, at all times, in interpreting the behavior of nonhuman animals, not to lose sight of the ease with which one can be led astray. The matter of Titus' sex is a case in point. His interest in paper strips, combined with the pubic bone test (unreliable, at best, but particularly so in this case because of Titus' leg deformity) and the manner in which his sisters treated him initially, all suggested that he was a female. But for my being misled in that regard, I might have suspected Flavia's eventual motive of mating much earlier.

ABNORMAL BIRDS CONSPICUOUS AND PERSECUTED OR KILLED. It is well known that birds that depart even slightly from behavioral norms are persecuted by conspecifics, and often driven away or killed. Such individuals become conspicuous because of the complicated patterns of behavior of birds (territorial, peck order, courtship acts, and displays; 135).

There are many reasons for ruling out the leg deformity of Titus as a basis for his sisters' aggression, not the least of which are his parents' protection and care, the early age (of Titus) at which the aggression was manifested, and Flavia's turnabout from aggression to courting. On the other hand, as mentioned above, Flavia's subsequent overly aggressive "henpecking" of Titus probably was prompted by a 'frustration' over his abnormal behavior (in the sense of his, at first, not attempting, nor being able, to mount her).

LOVEBIRD PASSIONS AND MOTIVES COMPARABLE TO MAN'S, ATTAINED EARLIER. The most important lesson that I think is to be learned from the course of events described here and in Chapter 3, is that there should be no reluctance to conceive of other vertebrates experiencing similar passions and motives to our own. Peach-faced Lovebirds undoubtedly are exceptionally advanced in their social interactions, but the fact of a high degree of behavioral stereotypy should not be regarded as a barrier to the existence of close human parallels. And lovebirds probably reached their own advanced state of behavioral complexity many millions of years before our ancestors did.

THE SMALL ENCLOSURE, THE TOWER, AND FLIGHTING

LIMITED POTENTIALITIES WITH UNSTRUCTURED QUARTERS. It appears quite evident from the material of both Chapter 3 and this Chapter, that studies of captive birds that are limited to individuals confined in unstructured close quarters (standard birdcages) also are severely limited in their potentialities. Compared to what occurs in the wild, some aspects of behavior in confinement may be unaffected, other aspects may appear that are not normally expressed, others may be exaggerated, still others suppressed to varying degrees, and yet others totally inhibited. Even a very simple structuring of the confining quarters, like a passageway to a second enclosure, can reveal unexpected relations.

SERIALLY-SECTIONED TOWER PARTICULARLY EFFECTIVE. Each section of the 3-section, tower-like structure provided a somewhat different degree of privacy from enclosure-mates, and of access to the company of other birds in other enclosures, and serial passage was required to and from the 2nd and 3rd sections. [The tower was constructed in 3 stages, in which I added one section at a time, as the behavior in the preceeding section(s) raised new questions (see pp. 809-813, **The Tower Complex, Influences of Partitioned Living Quarters**).]

SEPARATE NEST, ENCLOSURE, AND FLIGHT AREAS PROVIDE POTENTIALITIES. Flighting provides the degree of freedom that is essential for the realization of certain interactions that may be suppressed completely in confined quarters and/or in the presence of other birds. For example, difficulties may be encountered in the breeding of parrots confined in enclosures, even though the enclosures are large (32). The combination of a NB or nest area of an enclosure, an enclosure itself, and occasional flighted access to a much larger region, provides the potentialities for most of **what can happen** and much of **what does happen**.

FEATHER-PICKING OF SELF AND YOUNG

DUE TO MALNUTRITION, OR AN "ACQUIRED VICE?" Feather-picking of young is regarded as an abnormal activity for which there is no adequate explanation or effective therapy. Many workers have suggested that it can be traced to malnutrition or is an "acquired vice" (2, 104, 138, 141). Buttner proposes that it is specifically a compensatory response to arginine deficiency at a time when large amounts of this amino acid are needed for the growth of feathers (hemp, flax, and sesame seeds are relatively good sources of arginine; see 134).

'FRUSTRATION,' INCOMPATIBILITY, OR INSUFFICIENT OUTLETS FOR ACTIVITY? Several workers have suggested that self feather-picking results from lack of activity, boredom, or frustration of breeding instincts, and that it may result from any dermatologic condition that is accompanied by pruritus (itching; 138, 448; 787). The most rigorous treatment of this problem is that of Harrison (141), which emphasizes the factors of 'frustration,' boredom, incompatibility, malnutrition, insufficient natural outlets for activity, etc.

AN EXPRESSION OF INCOMPATIBILITY OF COCKATIELIAN MATES. Though some regard the plucking of the mate's feathers around the neck and crest areas to be "expected Cockatiel behavior" (9), incompatibility of the mates is a more likely explanation. Such incompatibility is very common, especially in Cockatiels and cockatoos, and often shows up first as feather-picking (141). [Also to be borne in mind in this connection is the fact that some Cockatielian individuals have no feathers covering the head posterior to and beneath the crest (819).] Some authors recommend removing chicks that are at risk of feather-picking immediately, and raising them by hand or fostering them (9).

A SOMEWHAT DIFFERENT PERSPECTIVE. The present results cast feather-picking of the young in a somewhat different perspective, even suggesting that it may be a normal outlet for the activity of the grooming parent caring for a brood of greatly subnormal size. Thus, I have observed the most severe feather-picking by the grooming parent(s) of 4 breeding pairs with 6 broods consisting of but a single chick. Except for very young Cockatiels, the young birds vocalized loudly and incessantly during treatment, and sought every available means of avoidance, usually to no avail.

FEATHER-PICKING OF SINGLE-CHICK BROODS. Cosimo feather-picked the top of the head and the entire underside of the neck of Marco, the sole member of his 3rd brood (there were a total of 5 young in his two previous broods). It was not until a month after the rest of Marco's body was fully feathered, that his head and neck feathered out. The case of Titus was described above. He was the sole chick in Petra's 4th brood (there were a total of 7 young in the first 3 broods). Other instances are described in Chap. 6.

[Cosimo excessively groomed but could not be said to have feather-picked the 4 chicks in the 4th brood following the fledging of Marco. Some workers have noted that a hen "may pluck her brood badly one year and only slightly the next" (138). Unfortunately, figures for brood sizes have not been given.]

Another case involved Claudius, the sole chick of Cassandra's 2nd brood (there were 3 young in the 1st brood). Cassandra feather-picked the top rear of Claudius' head (the occiput and nape regions). She did the damage before feathering in the occiput region and after feathering in the nape region. On the other hand, there was no feather-picking of her 3rd brood of 3 chicks, but she extensively feather-picked the 2 chicks of her 4th brood, the 3 chicks of her 5th brood, the single chick (fostered) of her 6th brood, and the 3 chicks of her 7th brood (2 of them from fostered eggs). However, since the 2 chicks of the 4th brood hatched over a week apart, one was so far behind the other in development that they could almost be regarded as having been 2 closely-spaced single-chick broods, each of which was feather-picked, in turn.

Another example involved the female Cockatiel, Heloise, of the 2nd brood of Helena and Homer (see pp. 709-711, **Feather-Picking Begins**). Only Homer feather-picked this chick and the 2 chicks of each of the next 2 broods. Helena did not acquire the habit until caring for her 5th brood of 2 chicks (see p. 510). As I gave the chicks of these broods close attention and the circumstances were clear-cut, there is little doubt about their interpretation. The initial feather-picking appeared to be nothing more than over-grooming of Heloise by Homer. However, Homer quickly acquired a "taste" for the pulp at the base of rapidly-growing feathers and for entire tiny feathers. He ate the latter in their entirety and thoroughly chewed the bases of the former until all of the pulp was extracted before discarding the remainder and picking another. Once Helena acquired the habit, her actions were virtually identical.

Only feeding the young and nest preparation by Homer usually took priority over feather-picking, but the former two activities were interrupted repeatedly to engage in the latter. Although Homer also occasionally feather picked Helena and Heloise (as an adult), their feathers proved to be unattractive to him since he rarely succeeded in extracting the base. [In the case of the chicks he could grasp the feathers by their shafts from open tracts.] When the young were vulnerable, Homer feather-picked them so determinedly that I usually isolated him most of the time to spare them.

EXCESSIVELY GROOMED REGIONS RECEIVE STILL FURTHER ATTENTION. It seems very likely that the parents in these examples simply were, at first, bestowing all of the normal amount of grooming attention for a brood of multiple young on a single chick (when the clutches are not tampered with, single-chick broods are relatively rare). This suggests that the grooming of the young is a fairly stereotyped activity. Presumably the grooming parent perceives those body region(s) that are the first to suffer excessive grooming attention and bruising, to differ from the regions that receive more normal care. The regions that appear different then become the object of still further misguided attention. Once a taste is acquired for the pulp of the feathers, subsequent broods, even of normal size, may be at risk.

GUARDING THE EXIT TO THE TOWER

TOWER GUARDED ONLY WHEN NECESSARY. Among the several other impressive indications that Peach-faced Lovebirds readily grasp certain cause-and-effect relationships and engage in acts that have indirect consequences, was the guarding of the exit to the tower. This was done by the parents only when Titus was in the enclosure at the same time that one or more potential attackers were in the tower. Thus, over a critical period, either Petra or Ramses often guarded the tower exit (and entrance) when Flavia and Zenobia were in it and Titus was in the enclosure, whereas they were not likely to do so when he was being flighted. Similarly, over another critical period, Flavia often guarded the tower exit when Zenobia was in it and Titus was in the enclosure. But if I removed Titus during such a vigil, she ceased guarding the exit until after he was returned.

[I say "not likely" above, with reference to the guarding of the tower by Petra and Ramses, because when the parents were in breeding condition, they sometimes excluded the sisters from the enclosure. When they chased the sisters into the tower, they sometimes also "loitered" beneath the tower base (perhaps for good measure) before returning to the nest area.]

A PREFERENCE FOR PRIVACY

SMALL PARROTS PREFER PRIVACY DURING COPULATION. The Cockatielian pair, Carmen and Cosimo, usually were in the company of juveniles or mature offspring in enclosure A. Every other day or so, I opened the door to enclosure A to flight the family. On many occasions, when the parents were in breeding condition, they did not leave the enclosure and fly about with their offspring. Instead, they remained behind and copulated. When one considers the eagerness with which Carmen and Cosimo usually accepted an invitation to be flighted, this behavior bespeaks a strong preference of Cockatiels for privacy while engaging in sexual union (adaptive behavior in view of their vulnerability at the time). There also were some occasions when Carmen solicited from Cosimo when the family was being flighted, but he was not of the same mind. On those occasions, they went flying instead.

Peach-faced Lovebirds also have a preference for privacy while engaged in sexual union. This was noted first in the behavior of Petra and Ramses. While they were in breeding condition, beginning for several days on August 27, 1984 (Petra oviposited on Sept. 1 and 3), they copulated virtually every day during at least one of the flightings of Flavia and Titus. [Zenobia usually remained in the tower near Cyrano on these occasions.] Similar behavior was noted in Cassandra and Cyrus. Thus, when they were alone in their enclosure, copulation always took place on an upper perch. But when fledged or older young of a preceding brood were still being housed with them and they began a new breeding cycle, they only copulated on the enclosure floor, as far away as they could get from the young perched above. Another lovebird pair, Juliana and Nero, behaved in the same fashion.

Even more convincing behavior was noted with the Budgerigar pair, Lucretia and Lysander (see pp. 795, 796, **Privacy Preferred for Sexual Union**). In the midst of copulating, while the 4 juveniles of the 2nd brood were being flighted, Lysander dismounted and repelled one of the returning young from near the open door of the enclosure and then immediately resumed his mount and continued copulating.

MOTIVATIONS FOR THE ATTACKS ON TITUS

A CASE FOR JEALOUSY AND/OR VINDICTIVENESS. The attacks of Titus' sisters on him appeared to be vehement and vicious, and were carried out with great tenacity. They were quite different from the usual aggression of Peach-faced Lovebirds (biting of legs and toes). For that reason, they cannot reasonably be placed in the same category as aggression in defense of space against an intruder, or ordinary sexual aggression (aggression of a mated bird against a potential competitor).

It would be reasonable to draw this conclusion even if these other possible motives could not be ruled out, as they can be here. As in the case of Cyrano and Cyrus, very strong emotions must have come into play. One does not have to seek far for the motivation. The case seems particularly strong for 'bitter resentment,' if not 'vindictiveness,' by the sisters, with close parallels to human behavior.

[The circumstances accompanying the rearing of the 9th brood of Petra and Ramses (see pp. 727-730, **Unfacilitated Care of Clutches**) are supportive of the above interpretation of vindictive actions on the part of the sisters, and of the view that it traced to the highly favored treatment of Titus and the rigorous exclusion of the sisters from the nesting area and often from the enclosure. The 9th brood consisted of 3 chicks raised in a much smaller enclosure (enclosure M. Fig. 1b) in which the 2 male, 10-week-old juveniles of the previous brood (Cleomenes and Theocritus) were not rigorously excluded from the nesting area. In fact, Cleomenes, slept in the nestbowl with Petra and the eggs all through the period of incubation, allofed Petra (trickle-feeding) over a period of 5 days while she was brooding, and frequently was near the young in the nestbowl. Under these circumstances, the fledged young were not viciously attacked and pursued by their older siblings and Petra and Ramses often allowed these juveniles (then about 5 months old) to socialize with the fledglings virtually unrestrictedly within 7 days after they were fledged. But on certain occasions when the parents and fledglings were together, such as when eating a sprig of spray millet, the 2 juveniles always were excluded.]

ALTERNATE INTERPRETATION MORE REMARKABLE. K. Flammer (141) has observed lovebird adults (species not specified, but probably Peach-faced Lovebirds) to attack other birds in their enclosure, when the latter act sick or behave in an abnormal manner, as, e.g., young birds that fledge early or fly erratically. While it is quite possible that Titus' infirmity played some role in drawing the initial aggressive attention of his sisters, this could not account for all of the subsequent events (e.g., the ferocity, tenacity, and long persistence of their attacks). Nor is such an explanation consistent with the fact that Flavia eventually mated with Titus. On the other hand, if one were to assume that all the aggression by his sisters had its origin in Titus' very conspicuous disability, that would perhaps be an even more remarkable circumstance than the proposed interpretation.

INITIAL IGNORANCE OF TITUS' SEX NOT ESSENTIAL. I have suggested that Titus' gender was unknown to Flavia and Zenobia at the time when their attacks began, and that the turnabout in Flavia's intentions occurred because she perceived Titus to be a potential mate. This interpretation is by far the most likely to apply, but is by no means essential. If Titus had been perceived to be a male from the start, the waning of Flavia's aggression (through habituation) could have prepared the way for the waxing of her courting.

[It is well established in some birds with visually indistinguishable sexes, such as some doves and pigeons, that the adults must rely on behavioral cues elicited over a period of time to establish sex; they cannot assess immediately the sex of an unknown conspecific. For example, pigeons as readily engage in courtship with unknown conspecifics of the same sex as with individuals of the opposite sex (605). In the case of a fledgling Peach-faced Lovebird, it is very unlikely that sexual identity would be apparent to a conspecific until after days or weeks of interaction and maturation.]

ZENOBIA'S RENEWED ATTACKS AS MOTIVATED BY JEALOUSY. It is most interesting that, after Zenobia's attacks on Titus all but ceased, she renewed them with great vigor and tenacity after Flavia and Titus paired. As an on-the-scene observer, I could not avoid seeing these new attacks as being motivated by 'jealousy.' Titus had become favored by Flavia, displacing Zenobia as her long-time sleeping companion and cohort.

CONSCIOUS THOUGHT IN LOVEBIRDS?

I have recounted one incident in the foregoing that I believe, more unambiguously than any other, suggests the existence of conscious thought in lovebirds. This occurred on July 17, when Ramses chased Flavia away from Titus, into the tower, and all the way to the top of the last vertical section, where he nipped her on the rump. On all other noted occasions, Ramses was contented merely to chase her away from Titus and out of the enclosure (i.e., into the tower). I am inclined to regard his altered behavior on this occasion as having entailed conscious thought.

A chase to the end, after prey, is instinctive, but a chase to the end for the purpose of "punishment," warning, "or emphasis of intentions," entails a degree of determination or purposefulness that, to me, suggests the involvement of conscious thought. Must not Ramses have been thinking something like the equivalent of, "I'll teach her a good lesson this time?" In what may have been a comparable situation, F.G. Buckley describes how one Blue-crowned Hanging Parrot fighting over a perch position with another followed closely after the fleeing bird, not allowing the latter to settle until it flew off to the top of the enclosure (79). I observed similar behavior among the Cockatielian pair Kirsten and Rimski. The latter strongly dominated his mate and frequently was courtship-fed by her. His dominance was quite evident at the food trays, where he always prevailed in disputes. On a few occasions he not only pecked her away from the food tray, he chased her about the enclosure as well when she persisted in contesting with him.

NEITHER MUTUAL GROOMING NOR SLEEPING SIDE BY SIDE ESSENTIAL TO ESTABLISH THE LOVEBIRD PAIR BOND

We now have considered examples of the mating of Peach-faced Lovebirds in which one or the other of two normally-invariable accompaniments of pair-bond formation has been absent. Thus, in Chapter 3, I described how Zenobia mated with Cyrano, without the benefit of the pair ever having slept side by side with one another. In the present Chapter, I have described the mating of Flavia with Titus under conditions in which they were not observed to allogroom mutually until some days after the pair bond would seem to have become well established. [Another example of this is described in Chapter 7 (see pp. 834-838, **Lovebird Mating Between A Mature Male and a Juvenile Female**).]

SOLE ESSENTIAL ACT ALSO IS LEAST INVIOLATE. On the other hand, no case of pair-bond formation was observed in which courtship feeding was not an antecedent. Yet, as was amply illustrated in Chapter 3, courtship feeding is the only intimate act of pair-bonded birds that is not inviolate. Thus, we appear to have the unusual circumstance that the only essential act in lovebird mating also appears to be the least inviolate one. Courtship feeding is necessary but not sufficient. I would suggest that this relationship correlates with the fact that the feeding of the female by the male also is the only intimate act of the mated pair (aside from copulation) that is essential for reproduction.

PERCHING FOR THE NIGHT

In a number of instances here and in Chapter 3, I have drawn conclusions that were based on observations of perching positions in the early morning, as compared to those during or shortly after the lights were turned off the night before. The justification for drawing these conclusions is the fact that, in the absence of disturbing influences, the perching positions of these birds, particularly mated birds, usually are retained for the entire dark period, even until the lights are turned on in the morning (i.e., even until long after dawn). Accordingly, if Titus and his parents began the night together on the night perch, but were on the nest perch early on the following morning, the presumption was very strong that they had been disturbed earlier by Flavia and/or Zenobia. [On the other hand, birds that spent the night clinging to the wire of enclosure sides were much more likely to have moved about between the times of my observations.] The notable exceptions of birds that voluntarily left their resting positions before lights-on concerned Cyrano, as he sought to courtship-feed Cassandra, and Flavia and Zenobia, as the former sought to court Titus and the latter sometimes followed her.

CHAPTER 6. CARE OF EGGS AND YOUNG, AND BEHAVIOR OF YOUNG

Introduction

Parental behavior involves several functional groups of behavior patterns. These include those of egg incubation, brooding and allofeeding the young, removing egg shells and egesta, and protecting the young from predators with distraction displays and warning calls (351, 419). Where both parents have significant roles, as in the species dealt with here, their activities often bring them into close proximity, evoking tendencies to attack, flee from, and behave sexually toward one another.

Parental relations tend to be smoothed over by often elaborate ceremonies. Once the young begin to resemble adults, they may evoke aggressive behavior by their parents; this is alleviated by the adoption by the young of submissive postures (327). Another mitigating factor is that juveniles usually lack those features that are particularly significant in evoking adult aggression (351). Cockatiels, being joint caretakers of the eggs and young through most of the post-ovipositional period, evidence parental interactions to a greater degree than do lovebirds or Budgerigars.

This Chapter begins by completing the account of the rich repertoire of Cockatielian parental actions and interactions, and the behavior of the young, and continues and concludes by presenting comparable accounts for Peach-faced Lovebirds and Budgerigars.

Care of eggs and young, and behavior of young, are topics concerning which different observers of confined birds are very likely to obtain different results. These are activities that can be influenced greatly by environmental factors that are quite likely to vary from one observer's avian accommodations to another's. Such factors as enclosure size and structure, NB (nestbox) size and degree of darkness within, NB design, external disturbances, humidity, diet, and, above all, age and experience of parents, temperature, and individual differences can have large effects on the behavior of breeding birds, the care of their eggs and young, and certain aspects of the behavior of the young. There is no reason to doubt that many of these factors can have just as great an influence in the wild.

In the following, I introduce each section with a brief summary of the parental behavior and behavior of the young as they have been reported in the literature. These summaries are followed by accounts of my own observations. These generally are chronological, since such correlated accounts also cast light on the maturation and development of parental behavior.

There can be no question but that large differences in behavior are encountered among birds of the same species. Even among my own birds, behavior might vary from pair to pair and from brood to brood of a given pair. Accordingly, I usually do not call the results of other workers into question, though I sometimes discuss the basis for observed differences and matters of interpretation. For discussions of the care of eggs by Cockatiels, the reader is referred to pp. 230 and 231, and Chapter 4, Part 2.

PART 1. CARE AND BEHAVIOR OF COCKATIELIAN YOUNG

Literature Accounts

Some workers have found hatchlings to be very active and this was true of all those that I observed. Sometimes they appear to be walking on 4 legs, since they use their forelimbs (wings) for support (6). [Even some adult parrots have been known to climb about like 4-legged animals (13).] Others observers assert that hatchlings are helpless, literally lying on the floor of the NB (9, 127). In any case, they must be brooded continually when ambient temperatures are normal, as they cannot maintain their body temperature (127). They possess a moderate covering of yellow down.

The hungry hatchlings are said to "cry out for food," and generally to be allofed by the parents within 2 h (6), apparently at an initial rate of several times/h (127). But hatchlings have been known to survive without food for about 9 to 12 h (9, 11). The bill of the newly hatched chick is quite soft to the touch and tipped with a hard, white egg caruncle that is used to cut through the egg shell.

[It is thought that it is adaptively advantageous for hatching to occur early in the day, so that the hatchling can be allofed promptly (28). The fact that Cockatielian parents often delayed lengthily in allofeeding their hatchlings (as did an African Gray; see p. 676) may reflect a need on their part to process sufficient liquid food (see pp. 690, 691, **Carmen's Allofeeding of Cosimo**). Common Nighthawk chicks may not be allofed until they are 2 days old, living until then on stored yolk (28).]

SOLICITING AND FEEDING. Though, at first, they have merely a "cheeping" call, the chicks eventually solicit for food with a hoarse, throaty or raspy purr, that can be heard very clearly within a few days and becomes louder as they develop (32). The food-soliciting cheeps are followed by a succession of soft peeps in synchrony with the up and down movements of the chicks' heads as they are being allofed. These peeps also grow louder and more shrill as the chicks develop. [This makes it possible to judge the age of a chick while it is being allofed, from the sounds that it makes.] Young of fledging age use short grunts to gain parental attention before soliciting for food by hoarse rasping.

To allofeed a young chick, the parent grasps the chick's bill quite delicately with its own. A slight pinch causes the chick to bob its head up and down, whereupon the parent delivers the food in pulses into the sides of the chick's bill with its tongue (127). [The use of the tongue in feeding the young also is well known in spoonbills and albatrosses (28).]

THE FOOD---THE CROP. The regurgitated food, at first, is said to consist of crop-softened (by mucus and the uptake of water), partly-digested seeds, supplemented by a quantity of sticky, creamy fluid (6, 9, 32, 127). The contributions of a gland in the medio-caudal section of the esophagus aid in the softening of food in the Rock Pigeon but external water also is needed (998). It is suggested that proteinaceous substances (proteins, peptides, and amino acids) must be included in regurgitated material, because the rapid growth of the nestlings probably could not be sustained on the concentrations of proteins found in seeds, alone (127, 135). In this con-

COCKATIELIAN BROODS

Carmen and Cosimo

1st-4	2nd-4	3rd-1	4th-4	5th-3	6th-3	7th-5
Helena Ferdinand	Isabella Lorenzo Homer	Marco	*Kirsten Rimski Casimir Ivan	Teresa Francesca Matteo	1 male, 2 females	Lothair + 4 other males

Helena and Homer

1st-1	2nd-2	3rd-2	4th-2	5th-2
no survivor	Heloise	Marcus Julian	2 females	2 males

LOVEBIRD BROODS

Petra and Ramses

1st-4	2nd-4	3rd-2	4th-1	5th-4	6th-2
Jagatai Ogadai	Cassandra Cyrus Cyrano	Flavia Zenobia	Titus	2 fledged 2 eggs fostered to Aspasia & Jagatai	1 hatchling fostered to 4th brood of Zenobia & Cyrano

7th-1	8th-2	9th-3
unfacilitated, no survivor	unfacilitated, Cleomenes Theocritus	unfacilitated, 3 fledged

Cassandra and Cyrus

1st-4	2nd-1	3rd-4	4th-5	5th-6	6th-1	7th-3
Juliet Romeo Zoltan	Claudius	Aspasia + female-male pair	Beatrix Bion, 1 egg & 1 chick fostered fm. Titus & Flavia	3 fledged	Nero, egg fostered from Titus and Flavia	unfacilitated, Margot, Sylvia, Juliana, 2 eggs f'd fm. Z&C

Zenobia and Cyrano

1st-3	2nd-1	3rd-3	4th-2	5th-1, 1 male 6th-2, 7th-2
male-female pair fledged	hatchling fostered from Flavia & Titus, no survivor	2 fledged	1 fledged, f'd fm. Petra & Ram., 1 runt, f'd fm. F & T, succumbed	unfacilitated, 6th, Andrea 7th, 2 fledged

Flavia and Titus

1st-1	2nd-3, 3rd-2, 4th-1	5th-1	6th-2
egg fostered from Zenobia & Cyrano, after 10 days, succumbed	includes 3 chicks fostered to Zenobia & Cyrano, & C & C, & 1 egg from C & C, no survivor with F & T	no survivor	Titian, 1 runt fostered to Zenobia & Cyrano, succumbed

[Pairs, Isabella & Ferdinand, Aspasia & Jagatai, Juliana & Nero, & Lucretia & Lysander not represented. No. after brood No. = No. of hatchlings.]
*Kirsten fostered from Isabella and Ferdinand.

nection, parrots are exceptional; most granivorous (seed-eating) and primarily frugivorous (fruit-eating) birds provide the hatchlings with a proportion of protein-rich insects or other animals that are not in their normal diet (309, 312, 444).

The male is said to be responsible for the largest part of the allofeeding (6, 32), but both parents participate. As far as is known, the chicks are not allofed at night. As a chick's crop fills, it swells into a bulbous protrusion at the base of the throat (32). In older chicks, it becomes a massively distended, hanging, sac-like structure, sometimes rivaling the size of the body.

SHARING OF CARE---HUDDLING FOR WARMTH. During the latter part of the incubatory period, when both eggs and nestlings are present, the male is said to spend more time in the NB and often to care for the chicks at night, while the female incubates the remaining eggs (6). [In this connection, it has been reported that one adult Sora Rail continues to incubate the eggs during the hatching period, while the other tends the incomplete brood nearby (216)] Still later, when both eggs and chicks of greatly differing size are present, the hen attends primarily to the eggs and youngest chicks. Untended Cockatielian chicks may huddle together in the NB for warmth; there generally will be sufficient bodily heat generated within the enclosed NB for all of the birds to be comfortably warm (9).

CHICK POSTURES---DEPOSITING EGESTA. When unhatched eggs still are present and the nestlings are small, the latter usually prop their heads upon the eggs. When several chicks are present in the absence of a parent, they commonly gather together in a bunch; each typically lays its head upon the neck of a neighbor. I have found that a lone nestling will drape its neck and head over any accessible object at the right height, for example over the rim of a nestbowl. [Beyond 2 weeks of age, the nestlings often sprawl out solitarily; see p. 692, **Care of the Brood (3rd week)**.] When the nestlings are gathered in a warm cluster, they tend to shuffle themselves backward out of the cluster and deposit their egesta in a ring a few cm to the rear. As they get older, they seem to become less particular about where they make these deposits (127).

GROWTH---WAYWARD FOOD. The chick growth rate is so great that morning and evening inspections readily detect differences in feather length, etc. Within a few days, the chicks double and triple in size, and may attain half their final weight at 1 week. These fast-growing chicks require a relatively great quantity of food, keeping the parents occupied all day husking seeds, eating, and then regurgitating the partially-processed food to them (9). With so much work at hand, the fully occupied parents often regurgitate some food onto the chicks' backs and under their tongues (6). But they usually take note of this food and re-swallow it. Food also tends to coat the palate and accumulate around the chicks' bills, where it is potentially capable of leading to bill deformities (see L. Arnall, 1965, in 448). Most brooding birds remove such adhering food at regular intervals (135). If ignored, wayward food becomes sticky and hardens. It then becomes desirable to clean the chicks, lest they become injured or killed by misguided actions of the parent birds as they seek to accomplish the cleaning (6). [Regurgitated food that finds its way onto the heads and backs of lovebirds poses an even more serious problem.]

HAZARDS FACED BY THE YOUNGEST CHICKS. When incubation has been uneven, or the parents begin incubation early (say with the 1st egg), the youngest chicks can become completely hidden under and between the relatively hugh bodies of their broodmates. If one of the parents is inexperienced, such young chicks can be overlooked and become trampled and crushed to death by the older ones (as was the case with chicks in the 1st and 2nd broods of Carmen and Cosimo).

As will be seen, experienced parents cope very effectively with allofeeding and caring for chicks of widely different sizes. Such parents are said to be "most attentive" in seeking out the bills of tiny chicks, as they cry out from the enveloping pile of bodies (27, 127). It is suggested that the soft, weak cheeps of the very young are particularly alluring to the parents, ensuring that the tiny nestlings are not overlooked (127).

EYES OPENING---FIRST SIGNS OF FEATHERS---ENDOTHERMY. The parents keep a constant guard on the NB until most of the young are at least 5 days old, after which both of parents sometimes will be away from it concurrently (6). Such attentiveness to young nestlings is common (see, for example, 129). The chicks' eyes open to mere slits at about 7-10 days (6, 9, 1,054), and are fully open within a few days thereafter. At about the same time, small feather quills appear, especially in the crest, wing, and tail areas (9), and the chicks first acquire metabolic control over their body temperature (i.e., they develop homeothermic endothermy; 127). At about 8 days of age, the feet begin to take on the adult color and the voice acquires the harsh, raspy tone mentioned above.

CHICKS THREATEN INTRUDERS---TAKE ON ADULT APPEARANCE. When chicks with their eyes open are disturbed, they no longer remain silent or solicit food by cheeping. Instead, they raise the tiny quills of their crests and threaten the intruder by rocking from side to side. At the same time they hiss by forcing air suddenly from the mouth (127, 138) and often emit their raspy, persistent purr, as well (30; the same sound serves both as a threat and to solicit food). These actions are highly contagious within the brood; even the younger, still-unseeing nestlings join in (127).

By 2 weeks of age, the young begin to resemble adults, though still helpless, insofar as independent survival is concerned (9). When the young are about 4 weeks old, their bills are hard enough to crack seeds. At that time, the parents allofeed them larger portions and more frequently (32; see also 128). The young are completely feathered after about 5 weeks.

EXPLORING, AND EXITING THE NESTBOX. According to some observers, the chicks begin to explore the NB entrance or emerge from the NB after about 3-3½ weeks. But they may sit at the entrance for some time viewing the surroundings and soliciting for food, before venturing to leave (9, 127). Other observers quote 5 weeks for the approximate time of exit (6, 11, 1,054). In an outdoor aviary, the period was 4-5 weeks (32). The youngest chicks to leave moved slowly and tentatively, at first, but with ease and confidence after a few days of practice (9). Once out of the NB, chicks returned to it randomly, and sometimes slept inside for up to another week. Chicks generally flew before 6 weeks of age (127).

CARE AND BEHAVIOR OF FLEDGLINGS. Parents continue to allofeed the young until they are able to crack seeds and eat by themselves (9, 32). A fledged chick solicits food by lowering its crest and head, and bobbing its head. At the same time, it utters the raspy, insistent purr sound. As food that is regurgitated directly into its mouth is being swallowed, it utters a loud shrill piping sound and jerks its head vertically with great vigor. At 5-6 weeks of age, the young in the outdoor aviary began to show an interest in seeds and grasses (32). Chicks usually could eat and drink independently at this time (9) and were fully fledged by 7-8 weeks (6, 9, 32).

Once the older chicks are out of the NB, the male usually allofeeds them, while continuing to assist with the allofeeding of the younger ones still being brooded. Some observers claim that the male also may allofeed a hen that spends a great deal of time with the younger chicks (9). At about the time the chicks begin to fledge, the hen often starts to oviposit the next clutch (127). If a second NB is provided, she may move to it and start another clutch before the young have fledged, leaving it to the male to "feed out" the young (11).

For the birds that nested in the outdoor aviary, the parents spent progressively more time away from the nest after the chicks had developed their feathers. In fact, during the latter part of this period they did not even enter the nest hole at night, but remained near its entrance (32). Once having left the nest hole, chicks generally did not return to it, preferring to perch under it or elsewhere in the aviary. Though their first flights usually were very awkward, they became accomplished fliers after a few hours. Males acquire the bright yellow facial markings (see p. 231) when 6 months old, but the barred tail is retained until the first complete molt. The birds are sexually mature when only 6 or 7 months old but breeding is not advised until they are 10-11 months old (787).

The First and Second Broods of Carmen and Cosimo

The first brood of Carmen and Cosimo (consisting of Helena and Ferdinand) hatched in early November, 1982, and the 2nd (Isabella, Homer, and Lorenzo) in late December, 1982 and early January, 1983. Both broods were incubated and brooded in an ordinary wood NB (same as Figs. 1 and 3a, but without a transparent sidepane). I touch only upon the highlights of their care and behavior, rather than upon the figures for incubatory times, times of eye opening, feathering, and the like, which fell within the ranges of values given above. Very little is mentioned of chick or parental behavior in the first few days after the 1st hatchings, in the presence of eggs, since this topic is treated largely in Chapter 4, Part 2 (but see pp. 503-510, **Brood-Site Fidelity**).

COSIMO VERY ATTENTIVE. During the early days of incubating partly and completely-hatched clutches, Cosimo was very attentive to the eggs and/or young at times when Carmen was being flighted. He very infrequently left the NB at such times. It will be recalled that, during the pre-hatching days of the 1st brood, he was very reluctant to stay out of the NB if Carmen did not take over the care of the eggs after he left. He behaved in this manner even when continuous coverage of the chicks no longer was necessary (5 or 6 days after the last hatching), presumably because of his inexperience. He required 1 or 2 days to adjust to a situation in which chicks were left unattended by any parent, but even after making this adjustment he made frequent checks of the NB.

THREE NESTLINGS LOST---FOOD SOLICITING BY CHICKS. Three of the 8 nestlings were lost in the first few days of brooding these 2 clutches. Again, this presumably was because of Cosimo's inexperience, since he performed much of the daytime care. It seemed, and was confirmed subsequently, that unless a very young chick solicited for food by cheeping, and was able to hold its head up and compete with the older, very much larger, chicks, it would not be allofed by the inexperienced Cosimo. But soliciting and holding up the head do not appear to be essential when chicks (but not hatchlings) are cared for by experienced parents. [Sightless chicks of Bengalese Finches either must be touched by the parents or hear another chick soliciting before they, themselves, will solicit for food.]

Whenever a parent entered the NB, the cheeping of the chicks began and did not cease for some time, very likely not until after all of the chicks had been allofed (or until the parent exited). Cheeping also began whenever I disturbed the chicks in the NB, at which time they also extended their heads and necks upward.

COSIMO "RIDES HERD." The older of the 2 chicks of the 1st brood was out of the NB in only 25 days, but this was without parental approval (the chick exited while the parents were not in attendance). After I replaced this chick, Cosimo "rode herd" outside the NB entrance, and would not let either of the 2 young out until 4 days later (I handled and examined the chicks daily throughout this period). By the time Cosimo allowed them to leave the NB (the day before Carmen laid the 1st egg of her 2nd clutch), the older chick was almost flying well but the younger could not yet fly. Within 4 days the younger chick also was flying. Even as late as 11 days after the young left the NB, at a time when both were excellent fliers, Cosimo still sometimes barred their exit. Again, this "undue caution" probably can be attributed to his inexperience.

ESCORTING THE YOUNG. Before the young flapped their wings and took their first flights, I could handle them without any indication of great parental concern. But once the young began to flap their wings (and even a few days before), the parents became very agitated when I handled them. Both Carmen and Cosimo paced back and forth nervously in the enclosure and/or climbed about on the enclosure front and sides seeking to gain exit. [This was at a period of the breeding cycle when the parents in species with nidicolous young (see pp. 193-195) defend their young with the greatest vigor (see M. M. Nice, 1949, in 28).]

When the young were on their 1st flights, the parents followed after them closely. They landed with them, when they fell (after colliding with an object), guided them back to a roosting point, if they were able to fly and follow (just as the parent birds of several species escort fledglings or lead them back to the nest; see 129, 484), or stayed with them on the ground (carpet), if they could not become airborne.

CARMEN FEEDS A RETARDED CHICK. Cosimo continued to allofeed the young of the 1st brood for almost 5 weeks, and continued to groom them long after that. In the case of the young of the 2nd brood, the male, Homer, was injured at an age of 3 weeks (presumably trampled under foot by a parent in a moment of panic) and was bleeding from both of his wings and the sides of his body. My stemming of the bleeding with hydrogen peroxide, bleached and frizzled many of his feathers and may have retarded his subsequent growth; at age 6 weeks, he still solicited for food. However, Cosimo had stopped allofeeding the remainder of the brood over a week earlier and also began to ignore Homer's solicitations. Carmen then took over this function and continued to allofeed Homer until he was over 8 weeks old, but in the 8th week, Cosimo still tenderly groomed the young.

BEHAVIOR OF THE YOUNG. Some interesting features of the behavior of the young of these broods are worth noting. At age 39 days, I saw Helena mock-allofeed Ferdinand but heard no accompanying sound. The next day, Ferdinand solicited for food from his image in a mirror. This was 4 days before both young were observed to eat all kinds of seeds for the first time (previously, the only seed that I was sure they could eat was spray millet).

At 17 weeks of age, on 2 successive days, Ferdinand attempted to copulate with his 7-weeks-younger sister, Isabella, with whom he eventually mated (if he was not already mated with her at the time). On both occasions, when Isabella's brother and broodmate, Homer, heard the Coition Sounds, he came over to them from a distance and disrupted the copulation by grooming Isabella about her eyes.

Homer, himself, apparently was becoming reproductively mature 17 days later, when, at age 12 weeks, he spent much time singing to his image in a mirror. His copious singing created a tremendous din and continued unabated for an entire month, most of it to his mirror image. He also looked behind the mirror from time to time. Ferdinand, his older brother by 7 weeks, did not begin to sing copiously until a month after Homer's initial efforts.

PARENT-OFFSPRING DOMINANCE. A notable feature of the parent-offspring relationship within this family, that held as well for the lovebird families, was the dominance structure. The young tended strongly to follow and copy all activities (except copulating and singing) engaged in by the parents, whether eating at trays, foraging on the enclosure floor, bathing, chirping or whistling, etc. Contrariwise, the parents rarely followed their offspring in engaging in any activity (except chirping and whistling). In fact, they were almost guaranteed not to do so.

WHO FOLLOWED WHOM. As a consequence of these relationships, if the young were foraging on the enclosure floor but the parents were not, that meant that the young had descended first, without the parents following. If all the birds were there, however, that meant that the parents had descended first and the young had followed. This also applied for passage of the birds from enclosure A to enclosure C, in the days when a passageway connected them (see Fig. 1a).

The young were highly gregarious, regardless of whether they were broodmates or not. When one bird descended to the floor or ascended therefrom, it usually was only a matter of time before the others followed. An occasional exception was when the birds fled from the floor when I approached (which was essentially invariable). On these occasions, the most habituated birds (Ferdinand, Helena, and Carmen) sometimes either did not flee or were the last to leave.

THE THIRD AND FOURTH BROODS OF CARMEN AND COSIMO

The 3rd and 4th broods of Carmen and Cosimo were raised in a NB with a transparent Plexiglas sidepane. Observations under these conditions often gave a completely different perspective on the events that transpired in the NB, as compared to those presumed upon the basis of external and periodic brief inside observations. Since it is convenient to consider some of these findings topic by topic, rather than chronologically, I begin this section with overviews of general observations and follow these overviews with a much abbreviated chronological narrative acount.

ALLOFEEDING OF HATCHLINGS

From being able to observe directly and closely the allofeeding of hatchlings and very young nestlings (of the 5th, 6th, and 7th broods of Carmen and Cosimo and all 4 broods of Helena and Homer), the methods employed have been elucidated. The 3 methods that predominate in the early allofeedings, before the exclusive use of the familiar, vigorous pumping of the allofeeding parent and head-jerking of the chick, are designated **tongue-flick allofeeding**, **massive tongue-flick allofeeding**, and **trickle-feeding**. None of these methods has been described previously, but a variation of the latter method is known (see 128 and p. 676), and I employ the same term, **trickle-feeding**, used for it.

By the time the down on a hatchling has dried (and sometimes even earlier), which usually is in only a few hours, the chick is able to stand and balance, and even to hold up its head for brief periods. In the first few allofeedings, a parent grasps the hatchling's head in its bill by gently closing the tips of the upper and lower mandibles on the gape corners of the chick's bill. Thereupon, the chick gapes slightly (opens its mouth a few mm) and straightens up reflexly. The parent bird simultaneously raises its own head (or the parent may lift the chick's head). The chick then usually begins to cheep, and jerk its head up and down, as it actively or passively receives the food. In tongue-flick feeding, the transfer of the liquid nutrient, itself, probably is almost entirely passive on the part of the chick, whereas in trickle-feeding and massive tongue-flick feeding the transfer is mostly active.

TONGUE-FLICK ALLOFEEDINGS typically occur in brief, successive individual bouts of at most 8-12 sec each, and are carried out by the simple action of the parent, which flicks the tip of its tongue rapidly into and out of the chick's mouth. On each retraction, liquid nutrient flowing along the parent's tongue either is wiped off along the inner edge of one side, or along both inner edges at the front, of the chick's upper mandible. Thence it runs down under the influence of gravity into the chick's esophagus and crop. The tongue of the chick may pulsate during this process, but swallowing may not be necessary. The slight pulsating or jerking of the head of the parent during this type of allofeeding, during massive tongue-flick feeding, and during trickle-feeding is mostly passive, induced by active and apparently obligatory "pumping" movements on the part of the chick.

This is the precise method of delivery of the liquid food that previously has been described loosely as "the parent delivers the food in pulses into the sides of the chick's bill with its tongue" (see above). Lovebirds feed their chicks in precisely the same manner (see pp. 747-749, **Tongue-Flick Feeding, Wayward Food, and Clogged Nostrils**), and this procedure may be employed widely among parrots.

MASSIVE TONGUE-FLICK ALLOFEEDING is a variant of tongue-flick feeding in which relatively large gobs of glutinous, semi-liquid, creamy-white food are delivered into the mouth of the chick by repeated flicking of the tongue of the parent. Active swallowing on the part of the chick is essential when it is allofed in this manner. This type of allofeeding may be employed at any time with vigorously active chicks, even for the 1st allofeedings of Budgerigar and lovebird hatchlings. I have observed 2 lovebird hatchlings receive their first meal (from the father, see pp. 766, 767) in this fashion, and it appears to be the only manner in which Budgerigar chicks are allofed until they are old enough to receive semi-solid food by a simple pumping action.

TRICKLE-FEEDING typically occurs in long bouts of many sec, that often last 2-4 min. It usually involves an active flicking of the chick's tongue (which could be seen most clearly when I fed chicks from an eye dropper), in synchrony with a gentle jerking of its head. In the course of these movements, it licks off the nutrient that flows along the parents tongue, which is held motionless. This method may be employed even during the 1st feeding of a hatchling, but since it usually involves active transfer of the liquid nutrient on the part of the hatchling itself, it may not prevail in the 1st feedings.

The degree of active participation and vigor of the hatchling probably plays a role in determining which of the 3 methods is employed. If the hatchling is weak or uncoordinated, and cannot employ its tongue effectively, the parent tongue-flick allofeeds it. Otherwise, it usually is trickle-fed or massive tongue-flick allofed. The 3 methods sometimes grade into each other or alternate during a bout of allofeedings, perhaps also depending partly upon the grip of the parent on the chick's bill.

In trickle-feeding, the precise grip of the parent varies very much and is not crucial, as it is only necessary that the parent's tongue be brought within reach of the chicks tongue. In tongue-flick allofeeding, the grip must be such as to allow freedom of movement of the tip of the parent's tongue along the inner edge(s) of the chick's upper mandible. In massive tongue-flick feeding, the chick's bill is grasped only as necessary to secure its being opened, and the large gobs of food often virtually fill the buccal cavity of the chick. These 3 methods of allofeeding probably are the ones practiced generally with parrot hatchlings before the use of simple pumping of semi-solid food. Trickle-feeding is employed even with young several weeks old and it would appear that at such times the parent may be delivering primarily water.

[A particular form of trickle-feeding is known in the literature from the description by Vane (128), in 1957, when he observed the first allofeedings of a Red-lored Amazon (*A. amazona autumnalis*) fostered with an African Gray female. Inasmuch as the latter bird was thoroughly habituated, very close observations were possible.

The African Gray made no attempt to allofeed the hatchling for the 1st 24 h, though she groomed it repeatedly. In the 1st allofeeding, on the 2nd day, the chick first was lifted bodily by the head. The point of the African Gray's upper mandible was inserted gently into the small gape corner at the rear of the chick's upper and lower mandibles--the "Schnabelwulst" --thereby enlarging it ("reflection pearls," one each on the upper and lower bills just forward of the gape corners of the chick, probably guide the parent Oriental Parrot-finch, *Erythrura* sp.; 28). Liquid food then was trickled down the African Gray's tongue into the chick's mouth through the enlarged gape on the opposite side, a delicate procedure that took at least several min. Once trickle-feeding had been accomplished a number of times in this manner, a change was made to the head-bobbing, pumping method. It can be suggested that the initial 24 h delay in allofeeding of the Red-lored Amazon allowed time for the predigestion of food to sufficiently liquid form (and the mobilization of any supplemental material by secretion, sloughing, or breakdown, from the hen's body).

A similar form of allofeeding of a hen by its mate is said to be typical within the genus *Loriculus*. A male was described as "opening his beak rather wide and allowing regurgitated nectar to run from the tip of his tongue onto" that of the hen (1,260). I have observed this form of allofeeding frequently among lovebirds and their young (see pp. 747, 748). Trickle-feeding also may have been observed in Barred Parakeets (*Bolborhynchus lineola*) in which a courting pair were observed to remain in a position with their bills interlocked for "a few moments" (1,262).]

ALLOFEEDING THE COCKATIELIAN HATCHLINGS. With Cockatiels, no prompt allofeeding of a newly hatched chick ever was observed. Hatchlings usually either were merely shielded and groomed for the 1st few hours or not cared for at all. Nor could the time of the 1st allofeeding of a hatchling of the 3rd or 4th brood always be established, because the allofeeding parent often shielded the hatchling from view (but see p. 696, *et seq.* for accounts of the care of hatchlings of the 5th, 6th, and 7th broods of Carmen and Cosimo and of 4 broods of Helena and Homer). Since neither trickle-feeding nor either variant of tongue-flick feeding invariably is accompanied by readily detectable head-bobbing movements on the part of the allofeeding bird, nor necessarily by loud sounds from the chick, either type of allofeeding easily could have been overlooked. From observations of the care of 7 broods in open nestbowls, it appears that within a few days, at most, trickle-feeding, massive tongue-flick allofeeding, and vigorous pumping completely supplanted tongue-flick allofeeding.

There usually was no sharp transition to vigorous pumping, from the more delicate, gentle bobbing that often accompanied the allofeeding of liquid or semi-liquid food. Rather, the vigor of the pumping and bobbing gradually increased as the chick grew, at first being extremely gentle. With chicks of different size being present, the same parent often was slowly allofeeding liquid to a tiny hatchling in near silence, in one bout of the same session of allofeeding in which it subsequently was vigorously and rapidly "pumping" a loudly cheeping, several-day-old nestling.

ALLOFEEDING BUDGERIGAR NESTLINGS. The consistency of the food apparently has to follow the needs and digestive capabilities of the chicks. This has been noted with Budgerigars. Thus, the Budgerigar hen may be allofeeding the youngest chick a purely liquid part of the crop contents at a time when the oldest chick is receiving mostly seeds (185). "It is amazing to see, in a nest of 5, that the crop of each chick contains a different proportion of solids and liquids" (see Feyerabend and Vriends; 5).

In the light of my observations, it would appear that the allofeeding parent adjusts the liquid-to-particulate proportion, according to the age and needs of the chicks, by filtering the regurgitate between its tongue and palate. [In the cases of both Cockatiels and lovebirds being delivered gobs of food in only semi-liquid condition, I have noted the presence of some seeds that were only partly-digested or crop-softened, even in a hatchling's 1st meal.]

PASSING OF WHOLE SEEDS BY A CHICK. The role of the parent was brought to my attention forcefully on one occasion, when a young Cockatielian chick was found to have a crop prematurely filled with a loose aggregate of virtually unprocessed seeds, save for their having been husked. Subsequently, these were passed from the vent by the chick, still in undigested form (it occurred during my handling and examination of the chicks).

This inappropriate food undoubtedly was given in error by the less experienced Cosimo, rather than by Carmen. It would seem, from this observation, that a chick can pass a quantity of seeds which it is not yet prepared to digest, or which are digested too slowly. In this connection, the small young of some avian species have a low digestive efficiency and the parents probably recover substantial quantities of food by consuming their egesta. Bullfinch (*P. pyrrhula*) nestlings, for example, digest only a small fraction of the seeds mixed in with their insect diet until after some days of growth (see 1,150). [The passing of whole seeds by adults commonly is caused by pancreatitis, enteritis, intestinal irritation, or obstruction of the muscular stomach by grit (141).]

APPORTIONMENT OF ALLO-FEEDING FUNCTIONS

MALE PRINCIPAL ALLOFEEDER, AT FIRST. It has been said that allofeeding of the chicks is primarily the function of the male parent. This would be inevitable, if the male were the principal daytime incubator and brooder--as is generally agreed--since chicks have not been observed to be allofed at night (although I have found that a Cockatielian nestling in the process of being allofed will continue to be allofed in the dark, if the lights are turned off). In the cases of all the studied broods, it would be inaccurate to state that the male was the principal allofeeder. During the early nestling days, for example, Cosimo's role in allofeeding the chicks was equal to or greater than that of Carmen. But as the chicks grew older and fledged, Cosimo allofed them less and less; after fledging, he allofed them only infrequently, and Carmen did so almost exclusively.

COOPERATIVE ALLOFEEDING. Allofeeding of the chicks often was a cooperative affair, and all of the following scenarios were common. Sometimes both parents allofed the chicks in the same feeding session. When the chicks were very young, both parents were in the NB on these occasions, but, as they grew older, one parent frequently allofed them within the NB, while the other reached in to feed from the outside perch. [Generally speaking, in fact, the parents found it more convenient to allofeed from atop the inside or outside perch, as the chicks grew large.] At other times, one parent allofed the chicks and then left the NB, whereupon the other parent entered and also allofed them.

On some occasions, Carmen sat (sometimes on unhatched eggs) to the right, at the rear, of Cosimo while he allofed the chicks, and then she allofed them again after he had left. On many occasions, Carmen first allofed Cosimo in the NB (sometimes from the outside or inside perch) and then they both allofed the chicks--or she left and he then allofed them. On other occasions, Cosimo left the NB immediately after Carmen allofed him, without allofeeding the chicks. The time of most intense allofeeding, when both parents were likely to be participating together or alternately, was late in the evening (from 22:00 h to 23:15 h) when the chicks were being "loaded up" for the long night's fast. The morning allofeedings were much less urgent and, on occasions, were delayed for hours.

HEN DOES MOST SEED HUSKING. When the brood numbered 3-5 chicks, the allofeeding of them was so demanding a function that there was no competition to do so. For Carmen, the allofeeding was particularly demanding, inasmuch as she provided most of the food and Cosimo relayed the husked seeds to the young. But this apparently represented a division of labor, in which Carmen did most of the husking.

CHICK ALLOFED SIMULTANEOUSLY BY BOTH PARENTS. When the total brood consisted of only one chick, or before the 2nd egg of a multiple-chick brood hatched, competition to allofeed the sole chick was most likely to occur, and sometimes was very intense. On some of these occasions, the safekeeping of the unhatched eggs, and even of the chick, itself, seemed to be neglected in the heat of vying to allofeed it (and this also sometimes was true even with 2 chicks present; see below). On two occasions, both parents allofed a single 7-day-old chick simultaneously. One parent was positioned on each side, and their heads bobbed in unison as they delivered food at the gape corners on opposite sides of the bill. Subsequent observations of many other such allofeedings suggest that the unison is passive on the part of the parents, as their head-bobbing often merely follows the active, jerky, reflex movements of the chicks. [The opposite situation of one parent simultaneously feeding 2 chicks is known in Rock Pigeons, each chick obtaining crop milk from one side of the parent's bill. But as the chicks grow they usually thrust and push too vigorously to be fed simultaneously (1,011).]

BUNCHING, SPACING, AND COVERING THE CHICKS

PARENTAL MANAGEMENT. To me, the most impressive findings concerning Cockatielian brood management have to do with the spacing of the chicks. It seems likely that their management methods are one of the factors that accounts for their being highly successful breeders in confinement. While it may be that a high ambient temperature (in the range, 24-32°C) had some influence on the manner in which the chicks in the 4th brood of Carmen and Cosimo were spaced apart from one another, high temperatures cannot account for all of the findings. Instead, one also sees evidence of a parental management technique that facilitates the simultaneous care of tiny hatchlings side by side with comparatively huge nestlings (without the former being trampled or neglected within a pile). This view was supported by observations of the care of the 7th brood of 5 chicks by Carmen and Cosimo at an ambient temperature of only 25-27°C (see p. 702).

COMFORTABLE, AWAKE OLDER NESTLINGS AVOID CONTACT WITH ONE ANOTHER. There was scarcely any occasion, after they reached an age of 10-15 days, when the 4 nestlings of the 4th brood were bunched together with their heads resting on one another's necks or shoulders, and they hardly ever competed with one another to be allofed. Only after the oldest chick was 17 days old did the chicks tend to crowd toward the entrance hole--with extended necks and heads--when a parent arrived. Even on these occasions, though, they infrequently pushed one another aside or otherwise interacted competitively.

In other words, it appears that, in the absence of need for additional (exogenous) warmth, Cockatielian chicks may tend to avoid contact with one another. This is one adaptive mechanism that tends to assure the safety of tiny chicks in the presence of much larger ones. In the light of this knowledge, it appears likely that the 3 chicks that were lost in the first 2 broods succumbed primarily for lack of proper care by the inexperienced Cosimo, and only secondarily because they were trampled by their broodmates, i.e., the trampling may have occurred because the tiny chicks were too weak from inadequate care for the normal safety mechanisms to operate.

SYSTEMATIC, DELIBERATE, ORDERLY TREATMENT. The emerging general picture of Cockatielian parental management is that, at all times during the feeding of the brood, experienced parents keep the chicks well apart from one another, and allofeed the chicks in a highly systematic manner. They deal with one chick at a time, in turn, with no pushing, no crowding, and no disorder or confusion. In the 4th brood, there seemed to be no possibility of overlooking a chick because of its small size or a lesser ability to compete. In short, Cockatielian feeding usually was not a competitive affair, but deliberate and orderly. It presented a most impressive sight. It has been said that, because of large age differences, the youngest chick does not always receive its share of the food, gradually lags behind in growth, and often dies (787). Judging by the care of Cockatielian chicks that I have observed in 9 broods in open nests and "transparent" NBs, 7 of them at only 25-27°C (in the laboratory), one would have to conclude that the death of a relatively small broodmate, when it occurs, is not for inherent inability of parents to cope with chicks of widely disparate size, but is for lack of parental experience or crowding in the NB.

SHIELDING THE CHICKS. Except perhaps during the 1st 1 or 2 days, parent Cockatiels, unlike lovebird hens, do not shield the young chicks in the same way that they cover the eggs. Rather, the young chicks are nestled between the wings and the sides or loosely in front under the breast. Using this method, there is no danger of chicks being crushed, either accidentally or because, in a brood of only 1 or 2 chicks, they bear much of the weight of the sitting bird. As the chicks become too large to cover conveniently under the wings or breast, they are kept directly to the side, front, or rear of the sitting bird, usually in a corner or near a wall (just as when they are allofed). In the warm ambient temperatures experienced by the 3rd and 4th broods, the chicks frequently also were at the transparent side of the NB.

YOUNGER CHICKS FALL FAR BEHIND

A DAY'S HATCHING DIFFERENCE LATER BECOMES A FIVE-DAY ADVANTAGE. Despite the deliberate, systematic, non-competitive allofeeding of the chicks--the only competition between chicks was in the loudness of the chicks' vocalizations--the younger chicks fell far behind the older ones in development (and the same is true of lovebird chicks). The first chick, in particular, enjoys a tremendous size advantage. Thus, there was a time when the oldest chick of the 4th brood was practically as big as the other 3 chicks combined, though it had less than a day's head start over the 2nd-oldest one in hatching. It eventually came to have at least a 5-day advantage in development over the latter chick.

LAG TRACES PARTLY TO DIFFERENCES IN THE QUALITY OF NOURISHMENT. I would suggest that the basis for the inordinately large size discrepancy lies partly in differences in the quality of the nourishment the chicks receive. The 1st hatchling of a brood has a monopoly on the highly nutritious liquid food at a time when it is the type being allofed in greatest abundance and the parents have a plentiful supply of it. The preparation of this food requires time for predigestion and supplementation.

The younger chicks, on the other hand, are in passive competition for limited quantities of this food at a time when less-well-digested, less nutritious food is being fed in greater relative amounts. They probably receive a much greater proportion of the latter food than does the first chick to hatch.

THE ROLES OF PASSIVE AND ACTIVE COMPETITIONS. Another probable factor is that the largest chick has the longest reach, is most prominent at feeding time, and often is the 1st chick to be allofed. To the extent that there is a degree of disorder in allofeeding (some of which is inevitable), this chick enjoys the advantage. A 3rd probable factor is that the competition between the parents to allofeed the young is greatest during the period when there is only 1 chick, and greatly declines thereafter. As a consequence, the 1st chick probably gets a greater quantity of food during its 1st hours or day(s) than does any younger chick.

MARKED DISPARITY IS HIGHLY ADAPTIVE. Whatever the factors that produce the marked disparity, the result is highly adaptive: in the normal favorable course of events, the younger chicks are at no survival disadvantage. However, when conditions are unfavorable, the chicks with the best chance to survive are the ones that have received the greatest investment of parental time and resources.

NESTBOX SANITATION

DROPPINGS "PLASTERED" ON CORNERS AND SIDES. Although other workers have reported that their Cockatiels practiced no NB sanitation, Carmen and Cosimo were fastidious in this regard. They typically "plastered" the droppings of the young into the corners and along all 4 sides of the NB. This sanitation appears to have been tended to after the late evening feedings, when both parents often remained in the NB and could be seen pecking and "fussing" around in the shavings. Some droppings, of course, were overlooked. As the young approached fledging, sanitation was practiced less diligently. [I remarked earlier that both parents avoided soiling the NB, themselves.]

CLOGGING OF THE NASAL PASSAGES. When the droppings that are deposited in the NB become dry, they easily are broken up into very fine white powder, consisting primarily of urates (see p. 168). As the birds move about in the NB, the powder becomes airborne and is inhaled by them. The chicks also inhale it when they sleep with their heads resting in the shavings. This powder becomes deposited within the external nares (nostrils), which are quite small apertures that can be blocked readily by various types of foreign materials (135).

The larger the brood, the greater the deposits in the nasal passages (the cere and nostrils also sometimes harbor parasites; 135). The passages rarely become closed by this mechanism, though, because they enlarge rapidly as the chicks grow. If the caked material (visible through the nostrils) is disturbed with a tiny, blunt probe, some of it becomes expelled as a "puff" of white powder when the chick exhales. [The much more serious clogging of the nasal passages in lovebird chicks is treated on pp. 747-749.]

Chronological Accounts of the Third Brood

COMPETITION FOR AN ONLY CHICK---EARLY FEEDINGS. The 3rd brood of Carmen and Cosimo consisted of the single male chick, Marco, hatched in the late evening of May 3, 1984. Both parents were extremely attentive to the chick but also were highly competitive, in ways described fully above. It was hard to see how the chick survived the long bouts of competitive jousting and shuffling around, but it emerged apparently none the worse for it.

Because Marco was cared for at first on the left side of the sitting parent, away from the sidepane, the early allofeedings could not be witnessed. They presumably were primarily by trickling and tongue-flicking, though, because a vigorous pumping action by the parents would have been evident, even on the hidden side. The first witnessed allofeeding was not until about 26 h after hatching, and was by Cosimo, who "pumped" food into Marco's bill. Thirty min later, Carmen relieved Cosimo, amid much Mandible-fluttering, and she allofed Marco again in essentially the same manner. The chick was strong and vigorous, and easily held his head on high.

MARCO SHELTERED UNDER A WING. Since, at the time, I had not yet ascertained that Cockatiels brood their nestlings primarily under their wings or nestled beneath their breasts, I added a 2½-cm-diameter plastic ball to the clutch to cushion the weight of the sitting bird. This was accepted matter-of-factly by the brooding pair. Cosimo customarily made an early morning check of the brood, sometimes gaining access to it by displacing Carmen through grooming her crissum, but he did not necessarily (or could not) exchange with her until much later in the morning. After a 2nd day, or so, of brooding, it became quite evident that Marco was being sheltered under a wing, not under the body. Often only his head protruded in front, as if from a tightly fitting pocket.

MARCO, A LONELY FIGURE. By the 6th day, Marco usually was to be seen sitting off to the side of the incubating parent, with his head held high, giving the appearance of an independent but very lonely figure. As he dozed, his head gradually sank to the floor. He then awakened with a start and sat up again--a scene repeated many times in subsequent days. On this same day, Marco groomed himself both on his lower back and underside, presumably for the first time. The next day he began to lean his head up against the side of the sitting parent. [According to Vane (128), a fostered Red-lored Amazon was "deliberately taught to preen itself" by the brooding African Gray.]

SIMULTANEOUS ALLOFEEDING OF MARCO. The late evening of Marco's 7th day (May 10), at the time of "loading him up" for the night, was eventful. Marco was asleep and leaning against Carmen's side when he awakened with a start, as he heard me talking (at 21:39 h). Sixty min later, while Carmen still was settled in the IA (incubative area), Cosimo allofed Marco 5 times from the outside perch, before entering the NB and allofeeding him twice more. Then he left and Carmen allofed Marco still again.

Twenty min later, Cosimo returned and allofed Marco at least 7 times, followed by Carmen's allofeeding him twice. From the manner in which Carmen and Cosimo were allopreening each other's heads and shuffling about during the course of these feedings, it was evident that they were competing to allofeed. It was on this occasion, just after the 2nd feeding by Carmen, when she began to allofeed Marco for the 3rd time, that Cosimo joined in and simultaneously allofed Marco from the other side of his bill. Both parents' heads bobbed up and down in unison with each other's and Marco's. Not long afterward, a 2nd simultaneous feeding took place, and I subsequently witnessed several others, usually as parents competed to allofeed a chick, as one began to participate before the other had ceased.

HEAD-ALLOGROOMING AS GENTLE PERSUASION TO SURRENDER A CHICK. Cosimo then exited and ate, while Carmen stayed on. At 23:00 h, Cosimo returned to the NB and groomed Carmen's face continuously for 2 min; she, in turn, tried to push him away about 20 times. Then **she** groomed **his** face for 10 sec and **he** left. Since no egg was present at this time (I had buried them earlier, at the ½-way points and rear corners; see p. 424 *et seq*., **The Third Clutch of Carmen and Cosimo**), it would seem that allogrooming of the head also is used in gently persuading a mate to leave the NB and surrender a chick, not only to take over the care of the eggs.

FURTHER CARE OF MARCO. Thirty min later (23:40 h), when Cosimo was in the NB with Marco, Carmen came to the entrance, surveyed the inside scene, and left. Cosimo then called after her 4 times with a simple deep (low frequency) utterance. When she failed to return, he mounted to the inside perch and looked out into the enclosure for about 25 sec, before settling back into the empty IA. Two min later, Carmen returned for about 15 sec and then left again.

At 23:56 h, Cosimo "popped" out of the NB unilaterally, but Carmen obligingly took over the care of the brood. Marco spent the night sleeping under her raised tail. At 24:31 h, Cosimo uttered a simple 5-note call as he approached the NB, then again as he entered it, and still a 3rd time after he was inside. Then he sat with Carmen for 10 min before leaving for the night. At 09:30 h, he returned while singing softly and allofed Marco repeatedly. He also engaged in several mild "pecking" disputes with Carmen, but not in connection with the allofeedings. He did not exchange with her until 11:45 h.

MARCO'S EYES OPEN---A BURIED EGG FOUND. That same afternoon, Marco's eyes began to open. During those days, Carmen and Cosimo were "plastering" his droppings in a rear corner of the NB. The family spent the night together in the NB, with Marco between his parents, peeking out over Cosimo's back. One of the parents had found one of the buried eggs, and Carmen did not cease incubating it until almost 11:00 h the next morning. Meanwhile, both parents had fed Marco repeatedly shortly after 10:00 h.

When Carmen departed, Cosimo took over the care of the egg and also sat over it continually. The presence of just this one egg changed their behavior markedly from that of the day before; one parent always was in the NB incubating the egg. As a consequence, Marco may have been somewhat neglected; his crop was only about 1/6th full when I reburied the egg at 11:29 h.

CLOSE TURNS AND CLOSE FOLLOWING IN ALLOFEEDING. In their allofeeding of Marco that evening (May 12, 18:30 h) and on some later occasions (including the rearing of the 4th brood), they took close turns--first one, then the other, then the one, again, etc. But the non-feeding bird kept his bill very close in by the bill of the feeding bird, and seemed also to be very busy while the latter allofed (but the non-allofeeding bird's head did not bob up and down in unison with that of the allofeeder). When the feeder withdrew, the non-feeder often followed along with it, and the birds sometimes seemed to be passing food between themselves.

There were several possible explanations for this behavior:

(a) sometimes the non-allofeeder might have been keeping very close in order to be able to take its turn as soon as the allofeeder finished, possibly involving an element of competition to feed;

(b) the non-allofeeder might have been trying to maneuver to allofeed the chick at the same time, as was done twice 2 days earlier;

(c) the non-allofeeder might have been cleaning, the way the male lovebird does with very young nestlings (see Part 3), despite Marco's already being 9 days old; or

(d) the parents might somehow have been allofeeding cooperatively in a way involving transfers of food between them.

The cleaning alternative seems unlikely at an age of 9 days, though it might well occur earlier. It was not until I was able to observe closely the allofeeding of the 5th brood of Carmen and Cosimo and the 2nd brood of Helena and Homer (see p. 696 *et seq.*) that I was able to resolve this matter. The explanation was primarily alternative (a) with a contribution from alternative (b); alternative (d) also may take place, and it definitely occurs in lovebirds (see Part 3).

INCREASED PROTECTIVENESS. At about this time--after Marco was 7 days old--both parents became very protective of him. Frequently, after Carmen left the NB and I arose to get a closer look at Marco or make some change, she scurried back and dove precipitously into the IA before I could get close. But she made no effort to shield Marco in any way. He usually was on the sidepane side of the NB in plain view. Similarly, sometimes Cosimo scurried over to the NB and mounted the outside perch, when he saw me approaching.

EXCESSIVE ALLOGROOMING OF MARCO BY COSIMO. Cosimo's excessive allogrooming of Marco dated from about May 13, when the chick was but 10 days old (on the same day that I removed Marco surreptitiously and Cosimo searched frantically for him; see pp. 466-468). On that day, Cosimo groomed Marco on many different occasions--always very tenderly and attentively, but, nevertheless, excessively. Marco kept crying out and pulling away, but there was no escape for him. The same activity occurred repeatedly in the following 2 weeks, before Marco became mobile enough to escape Cosimo's attentions (Marco ventured from the NB for the 1st time on May 27).

Late one evening during this period (May 17), Carmen also devoted considerable allogrooming attention to Marco. Mute testimony to the damage that Cosimo was causing was to be seen in the deep-purple bruises on Marco's head and neck. [In this connection, the forehead and throat are favored sites for mutual allogrooming by some birds, for example, the Abyssinian Lovebird, which may strip these areas bare.]

By 17 days of age, Marco was able to move off and elude Cosimo when the latter tried to groom him in the enclosure, though he still was vulnerable within the NB. He still had occasion to cry out loudly after he solicited to Cosimo for food but got allogroomed instead. Two days later (June 1), in something of a reversal of roles, Marco groomed Cosimo on the chin and cheeks. Perhaps the last time that Cosimo groomed Marco was in the NB on June 7 (at almost 5 weeks of age).

MORNING ALLOFEEDINGS OF MARCO--COMPETITION NOT ENTIRELY IN ABEYANCE. By Marco's 10th day of age, his early morning allofeedings became of high priority. No longer was it put off even until 11:00 h. In the next week (May 13-19), Marco's 1st morning allofeedings each day were at 9:14, 9:15, 8:45, 8:36, 9:27, 9:18, and 10:07 h, respectively. Carmen was the first to feed him on 4 of these occasions, and Cosimo on the other 3, though it was Carmen who always spent the night with him.

Although competition was not intense during this period, neither was it entirely in abeyance. While Carmen was allofeeding Marco at 9:15 h on the 16th, Cosimo came to the NB entrance and she repelled him with pecks. Cosimo, being dominant, asserted himself boldly by brushing her aside. Then he also pecked her away from Marco and took over the allofeeding and allogrooming himself. Carmen merely stood close by and occasionally joined in the allogrooming.

The next day I witnessed one of the very few occasions when Carmen outraced Cosimo to the NB when he tried to divert her as she made for it when he exited. After she allofed Marco and exited, Cosimo entered and merely allogroomed him, though he fed him on many other occasions during that same day. Then, on the evening of May 19th, Cosimo, with a few rapidly-repeated sharp peck threats, discouraged Carmen from entering the NB and joining him (and Marco).

SPARE TIME FOR THE PARENTS. A change in circumstances was signalled on May 19, by the fact that Cosimo now found time to loaf and manipulate a bell, ringing it repeatedly by lifting it in has bill and then dropping it. Carmen did not give evidence of possessing such leisure time until 9 days later, when she also began to manipulate the diversified items suspended in the enclosure (see p. 280). By June 2, the 31-day-old Marco was being allofed solely by Carmen, who continued to feed him, in decreasing amounts and frequency, until June 12.

CONCERNS FOR MARCO'S WELFARE

THREATENED BY MARCO, CHARGED AT BY CARMEN. The first notable concerns for Marco's welfare were those of Marco himself (at 30 days of age), as he vocalized with a throaty purr whenever I came near the NB. Marco ventured from the NB for the 1st time at an age of 24 days. When I removed him from an outside branch-perch to return him to the NB, Carmen came charging over to protect him, but Cosimo did not (recall that Cosimo was not well habituated). This scene was repeated the very next day. On the following day, I found Marco on the floor of the enclosure. When I removed him and held him close to the front face of the enclosure, both parents came forward and climbed the front face, greatly agitated.

Later that day, Marco left the NB again and Carmen allofed him at the enclosure floor. Still later, he stood in the water bowl in 2 cm of water. When I picked him up that evening and he chirped, Carmen came scurrying over. Much later (23:55 h), when I picked him up to place him in the NB for the night, Carmen whistled and paced the enclosure, and Cosimo joined in with her. On 3 of 4 nights, beginning on the day that Marco first left the NB, both parents slept in the NB with him.

FLIGHTING THE PARENTS WHILE I HANDLED MARCO. On May 30, when Marco was 27 days old, I began to flight the parents while I handled and examined him. On the first occasion, both flew about and whistled alarmedly. Then Carmen landed on my arm, right next to Marco, and perched there "guarding" him. Meanwhile, Cosimo landed on the home perch and watched intently for 10 min. Not being habituated, he was reluctant to follow Carmen's lead. When I carried Marco and Carmen to the home perch, and placed

Marco on it near Cosimo, Carmen joined them. Later, when I returned Marco to the enclosure, both parents followed voluntarily.

By the next day, Cosimo's 'concern' had waxed to the point where he boldly joined Carmen on my hands, right next to Marco. They both flew off with Marco each time he did so, landing on the carpet with him and staying there with him. Almost the same scenes were repeated the next day (June 1). The differences were that Marco could fly somewhat better and led them on more of a chase, and that Cosimo again would not perch near Marco on my hand or arm (instead, he perched on the lamp stem by my chair).

Chronological Accounts of the Fourth Brood

ALLOFEEDING AND COMPETING FOR THE BROOD (1st week)

THE FIRST CHICK HATCHED early on the morning of July 4, and was first seen to be allofed at 14:34 h by Carmen. The feeding consisted mostly of tongue-flick and trickle-feeding and involved some very gentle head-bobbing. Both parents were seen to take close turns at such allofeeding again at 19:05 h. Each kept its bill in close to the other's, while the other fed, and they appeared to be transferring food between themselves between feedings. Both allofed the hatchling still again less than 2 h later.

COMPETITION FOR THE CHICK AND EGGS. Shortly past 22:00 h, Carmen exchanged with Cosimo after only a brief scuffle. But he came back after only a few min and competed gently with her for the chick and eggs, the competition including head-grooming and stealing the eggs back and forth. Although he managed to evict her by 22:40 h, she "dove in" 20 min later and recovered the chick and eggs. Despite a subsequent effort by Cosimo to exchange with her, she retained the chick and eggs for the night.

SECOND CHICK HATCHES. A chick could be heard cheeping within the 2nd egg early on the evening of July 4; it hatched shortly before 07:45 h on July 5 (still wet at that time). Cosimo checked the chick and eggs shortly after 10:00 h, ate for about 20 min, and then returned and cared for them for about 30 min; Carmen sat at his side. They may have split the clutch, but I believe Carmen had only empty shells. Cosimo left the NB again, but was back at 11:00 h, gently allogrooming Carmen's head for about 15 min.

FIRST ALLOFEEDING OF HATCHLING. Cosimo only occasionally checked the chick and eggs, and there was no sign of feeding the hatchling. When Cosimo allofed the day-old nestling at 11:30 h, it was by tongue-flick allofeeding and trickle-feeding, accompanied by gentle head-bobbing. Within an hour both parents were feeding one of the chicks again. Since little or no head-bobbing was to be seen, they probably were feeding the hatchling. One h later, the parents jointly allofed the day-old nestling. Both chicks were able to sit up and extend their heads within a few h after hatching.

COMPETITIVE "ROUTINE" FEEDING. In the early evening of that same day, Carmen entered the NB to exchange with Cosimo, but his resistance to surrendering the brood was so great that the parents were shuffling all about the IA, with the eggs and chicks seemingly at risk. Later, Carmen allofed the older chick while Cosimo groomed the younger one. The parents exchanged several times in the next few h but allofeeding of the chicks, if it occurred, was inconspicuous.

Carmen often sat off to Cosimo's side and rear after surrendering the chicks and eggs. At 23:12 h, Cosimo was trying to evict her by grooming her head. Next, I noticed, it was she who was grooming him, and she had the chicks and he the eggs. After Cosimo departed at 23:45 h, Carmen trickle-fed and tongue-flick allofed one or both chicks. When Cosimo returned at midnight and checked the chicks (after displacing Carmen by grooming her crissum) both chicks were vigorous and well fed.

COSIMO MORE POSSESSIVE, PROTECTIVE---NEW FEEDING ROUTINE. Cosimo allofed the chicks briefly early on the morning of July 6. Carmen allofed them 60 min later, but the feeding was disrupted by Cosimo's return. Not only had Cosimo begun to "head off" Carmen when she tried to take over the care of the brood as he left the NB unilaterally, but he also would "head me off" when I tried to get a closer look while he was out in the enclosure. Early, and again later, that evening, I saw the oft-to-be-repeated scene of Carmen allofeeding Cosimo and Cosimo, in turn, allofeeding the nestlings. Shortly afterward, both were allofeeding them concurrently. At 21:00 h, Carmen allofed Cosimo still a 3rd time, but he did not relay any food to the chicks. The latter were "flopping about" vigorously and appeared to be in excellent condition. On the whole, I would characterize the parental care of the chicks to that juncture as almost "routine," insofar as taxing their capabilities was concerned.

THIRD CHICK HATCHES. Cosimo allofed both chicks at 09:20 h on the morning of July 7. Early that afternoon, the 3rd egg hatched. About 1 h afterward, and again early that evening, Cosimo was seen to be incubating the 4th egg, with the 2 older chicks out in front of him and the hatchling under a wing. An h later, Cosimo still was sitting on the 4th egg while he and Carmen allofed and tended to the young. Again, they were mostly trickle-fed and tongue-flick allofed, and the parents seemed to be transferring food between themselves when they touched bills. When I noticed the 4th egg and the new hatchling off to Carmen's side, and I approached to try to get a closer look, she gathered in the chick before I could get there; the egg had lower priority.

FOURTH CHICK FOSTERED. Both parents allofed the chicks for about 15 min, beginning at about 20:30 h, and Carmen also allofed Cosimo, but I was unable to see the new hatchling being allofed. Later, I was able to confirm that it had been fed, and at 22:25 h I fostered the hatchling of Ferdinand and Isabella (a female, Kirsten) into the brood. At 23:00 h, Carmen was "loading up" the chicks for the night, but I could not tell whether she also was allofeeding the fostered hatchling. At my last check that night, at 23:37 h, Cosimo had the 2 older chicks off to his right side and the 2 hatchlings together under his right wing.

FEEDING CHICKS. Carmen came off the brood during a colony panic at 07:00 h the next morning (July 8) but she returned very shortly thereafter and began to allofeed the young. She could be seen to be bobbing and pumping gently when feeding the 2 older chicks but there was much less head movement as she fed the younger ones. When I moved closer, Cosimo scurried over to the NB entrance. A few min later he was inside, allofeeding the chicks himself, and he continued to do so after Carmen exited and ate, after another few min. Both parents were tending the young at 10:15 h and, though they still competed for them, it was with the greatest of gentleness. At 10:50 h, Cosimo had acquired the young and Carmen sat off to his side and rear, incubating the last egg.

TOO BUSY TO COMPETE FOR THE BROOD. Shortly thereafter, Carmen was in the enclosure eating, and the fostered chick was cheeping to be fed. In the next 60 min, for the very first time, I twice saw Cosimo voluntarily leave the NB immediately upon Carmen's approaching to enter. Clearly, the urge to eat and process food for 4 chicks had begun to take precedence over the urge to retain the brood. When Carmen entered on the 2nd of these occasions, she trickle-fed or tongue-flick allofed 1 of the 2 hatchlings, but I could not identify it. Fifteen min later, Cosimo was in the NB and Carmen was eating in the enclosure. After another 20 min, they again had exchanged places.

CARMEN RELUCTANT TO SURRENDER BROOD. On the afternoon of the 8th, they took many turns at eating and then allofeeding the chicks. Although Cosimo usually was accommodating to Carmen, when she approached or entered to exchange with him, Carmen, was not so acquiescent. Twice, Cosimo had to persuade her to surrender the brood, once by grooming her crissum, the other time by grooming her head. Though she did not offer much resistance to surrendering the chicks, she sometimes remained at the rear of the NB, often incubating the last egg, in what appeared to be a very harmonious arrangement.

ALLOFEEDING TAILORED TO SIZE. The allofeeding of the chicks took place in a very orderly fashion; the parent passed from one chick to the next as the chicks stood apart from one another, reaching upward. The 2 biggest chicks were kept apart to the side, the 2 smallest ones in front. Each was allofed by trickling and tongue-flicking and/or a gentle-to-more-vigorous pumping action, according to its size.

CHICKS LEFT UNATTENDED---GREATER COOPERATION. Though 2 of the chicks were only 1 day old, Cosimo twice (between 21:00 and 21:30 h) left the brood unilaterally, and I noted both parents were out of the NB together on still a 3rd occasion at 21:40 h. Carmen took over the care of the brood at 21:46 h. Presumably the absence of both parents posed no risk to the chicks, because the ambient air temperature was high (30°C). For probably the 4th time, Cosimo left the chicks unilaterally at 23:10 h and Carmen took over without opposition from him (such as his trying to head her off) and allofed the chicks. When the lights were turned off that night, Cosimo was in the NB with Carmen (on the inner perch) but he was in the enclosure at the time of the 7:30 h check the next day (July 9). It was becoming quite clear that Carmen and Cosimo were cooperating much more fully, with far less competitiveness, with a full brood to care for, than with only eggs to incubate. Undoubtedly, as mentioned above, this finds its basis in the greater need for eating and processing food for the young.

YOUNGEST CHICK NOT CONSPICUOUS. On that morning, Carmen allofed the chicks even before she left the NB. The young sometimes were seen to be huddled together, but when a parent came in and tended to them, they usually became spaced out around the parent. If I touched one of the chicks, it reflexly straightened up and extended its head and bill. By 10:00 h that morning, both parents had been in and out of the NB and allofed the chicks several times; once both were doing so concurrently.

Even on occasions when Carmen fed the chicks in a huddle in front of her, the allofeeding proceeded in a very orderly fashion, without any shoving. But the head of the youngest chick (within the huddle) was not to be seen at that time. Carmen exited the NB immediately when Cosimo entered to exchange with her at 11:18 h. As usual, the vigor of the feeding depended upon the size of the chick being fed. When I had an opportunity to examine the youngest chick at noon, I found it to be no less well fed than the 2nd youngest one.

PERCHING OUTSIDE AT NIGHT. Every time Carmen mounted the outside perch, Cosimo rose from his settled position and peered out of the NB and investigated. When I gave them a fresh vegetable ration at 23:30 h. both "jumped on it eagerly," after which Cosimo fed the chicks. When I turned the lights out at 01:10 h, I got the first hint of an unusual situation that transpired on some subsequent evenings. Cosimo was on the inside NB perch and Carmen was on the outside one, and they apparently held these positions throughout the night.

MORE ON ALLOFEEDING. Checking the family the next morning at 06:50 h, I found Cosimo outside and Carmen inside with the chicks. At that moment, all the chicks were cheeping for food with their necks and heads extended. At the time of lights-on (08:15 h), Carmen began to allofeed them. It took only a gentle prod near her crissum to get her to leave when Cosimo took over their care at 09:37 h. Again, on this day, the chicks were bunched in a very orderly group 30 min later, when Carmen was back allofeeding them, as well as a few min later when Cosimo joined her in the act.

Though the youngest chick kept falling behind in development, her crop was full and soft. Allofeeding continued frequently all through the day (July 10), with the parents generally taking turns. In the evening, Cosimo began to split up the brood while allofeeding. He kept the oldest--and much the largest--chick on his one side, and its 3 broodmates on the other. At the time of lights-off (24:50 h), Carmen was in the NB with the chicks and Cosimo was on the outside NB perch.

STILL "DIVING IN," MANDIBLE-FLUTTERING--HARSH VOCALIZING AT INTRUDERS. Cosimo was the first to allofeed the chicks on July 11 (at 08:45 h), and he was back making a complete "round" of allofeeding 40 min later, with Carmen waiting at his side. When he left, she also allofed a complete round, with each of the 2 rounds lasting about 5 min. Carmen still customarily "dove in" with the brood, when entering the NB, and both parents usually Mandible-fluttered on joining or exchanging with one another.

This was the day that the oldest chick's eyes opened and, for that reason, the first day that I was greeted by harsh, unfriendly vocalizations when I made an appearance (the vocalizations of the oldest chick triggering those of the others). [The chicks sometimes responded to the appearance of a parent in the same fashion. On the latter occasions, though, the vocalizations might have been food solicitations, as the same sounds are employed for both purposes by older chicks (see p. 671).] In this connection, lovebird chicks show no overt sign of fear until the eyes are open (3).

"RELAY" ALLOFEEDING. Again, this was a day of hectic eating and allofeeding, with one parent usually allofeeding and tending to the chicks while the other was in the enclosure eating. And the more and more frequently the chicks were fed, the more and more frequently Carmen allofed Cosimo. It was becoming one of the standard procedures for Carmen only to mount the outside perch and allofeed Cosimo (who was inside) from there, and for him to "relay" the food to the chicks. This type of allofeeding was even more pronounced during the rearing of their 7th brood--of 5 chicks--in an open nestbowl. On one occasion, Carmen perched on the rim of the bowl and regurgitated food to Cosimo 13 times, after each of which allofeedings he relayed food to one or another of 4 of the chicks, the youngest of which was 5 days old. The 5th, and youngest, chick--3 days old--received no directly-relayed food.

CARMEN'S ALLOFEEDING OF COSIMO

In the interest of simplicity I have alluded only briefly above to Carmen's allofeeding of Cosimo during the early care of the 4th brood. In interpreting this behavior, there seems to be no need to search beyond a reversal of the more common role of the male in allofeeding the female during courtship and the brooding of the young, just as the usual dominance role apparently typically is reversed (see pp. 410-412, **Allofeeding of Strongly Dominant Males**). Some degree of allofeeding of the male by the female, though far from common, also is known in other parrots, for example, in Budgerigars and Madagascar, Abyssinian, and Red-faced Lovebirds (3, 4, 27, 67).

POSSIBLE ROLE OF FOOD PROCESSING. On the other hand, if one examines the distribution of Carmen's allofeeding of Cosimo during the breeding cycle, there is a suggestion that food processing, rather than merely supplying food, also plays a role. Thus, almost all of these allofeedings took place during the 1st 10 days after the first hatching, when the youngest chicks were barely a week old, and the food that they were receiving presumably differed the most from mere husked seeds. In this connection, the last notation that I made of trickle-feeding or tongue-flick allofeeding was on July 10 (youngest chick 3 days old), and Carmen's relaying food by way of Cosimo virtually ended on July 15.

NO IMMEDIATE RELAYING OF FOOD. Going back to the time of the laying of the 1st egg of the 4th brood on June 15, 1984, there was no allofeeding of Cosimo by Carmen for a full 3 weeks--not until the day after the 1st chick hatched. On that day (July 5), Cosimo received 5 separate regurgitations of food in one early evening bout (a "bout" being a more or less continuous sequence of regurgitations). On the following 10 days, the numbers of observed regurgitations and numbers of bouts (the latter in parentheses) were, in chronological order, 17(3), 8(2), 29(7), 8(2), 6(2), 49(8), 13(5), 9(2), 9(1), and 5(2).

After 11 of these 34 bouts, Cosimo allofed the chicks immediately, but not at all after any of the 7 bouts on July 8, when the 2 youngest chicks were 1 day old (nor at the times when either of the oldest 2 chicks were 1 day old). With 2 exceptions in the late morning, all of these allofeedings were during afternoons and evenings. Declining to only 5 allofeedings on July 15, when the 2 youngest chicks were 8 days old, there were relatively few such allofeedings during the next 5 days, and none on 15 of the following 18 days. In essence, Carmen had ceased to allofeed Cosimo. After that, courtship feeding, coitus, and oviposition began again, but I did not facilitate the parents' resumption of breeding at that time.

PARTIAL DIVISION OF LABOR. This distribution of allofeedings of Cosimo by Carmen suggests a partial division of labor. It would appear that it fell to Carmen to do most of the seed husking, food processing, and nutrient generating in the 1st week of age of the youngest chicks, and to Cosimo to do most of the allofeeding of the chicks. Even so, Carmen did not allofeed the chicks much less than did Cosimo. There also is a suggestion that Cosimo further processed food received from Carmen before allofeeding it to a chick less than 1 or 2 days old, because he never was seen to relay food immediately to chicks of that age.

These findings raise the possibility that allofeeding of the male by the female also occurs in other parrot species (and other grain-feeders) in which the male broods the young for lengthy periods during the day. [Since all the relaying of food from Carmen to Cosimo to the chicks occurred within the NB, even as Carmen stood on the outside perch, comparable occurrences could have been overlooked in prior studies.]

CARE OF THE BROOD (2nd week)

HUDDLING, WANDERING, AND TOPPLING CHICKS. The 2nd week began on the morning of July 12, with a very orderly allofeeding of the brood at 08:55 h. Carmen allofed from inside the NB, and Cosimo did so from the outside perch. After this allofeeding was completed, the parents departed and the chicks huddled, with their heads resting on each other's necks and shoulders. On 3 different occasions on this day, and twice on the next, Cosimo allofed the chicks directly after receiving food from Carmen (the youngest chick was 5 days old).

The parents continued to keep the oldest chick off to the side by itself when they tended to the younger ones during the day and evening. The 13th of July was the 1st day that Cosimo was seen to allogroom the oldest chick excessively. It was so much larger than the other chicks that it presented a "natural" target for his allogrooming attentions.

The 4 young were still in a huddle at 06:45 h on the morning of July 14. The eyes of the 3 oldest chicks were open, and those of the youngest were just opening. During the day, the chicks "wandered" around the NB "on their own," so to speak. As they struggled to keep their balance, they often toppled over and broke their falls with their forelimbs, sometimes crawling briefly "on all fours." Cosimo continued to groom the oldest chick excessively, but not severely. When the lights were turned off at 24:22 h, Carmen had the chicks off to her side, split into 2 groups of 2 each. A short time earlier, she had barred Cosimo from entering the NB.

LATE NIGHT GUARDING OF NESTBOX: ONE PARENT EXCLUDES OTHER. I found an unusual situation on the morning of the 15th at 08:15 h. Cosimo was on the inside NB perch, and Carmen was on the outside one, and it looked like they had spent the night in these positions. This was another harbinger of things to come. The young were not closely huddled and one of them was far to the side. They continued to wander around the NB during the day and generally were spread out. As they sat resting solitarily, their heads drooped slowly to the NB floor, before they awakened and sat up with a start, or just lay prostrate. At 01:12 h, as the lights were turned off, both parents were out of the NB and the young lay prostrate, the two older ones solitarily and the other two leaning somewhat upon one another.

Late on the night of July 16, the new situation that had developed became clear. One of the parents would guard the entrance to the NB late at night and not let the other one in, and they might hold their positions for many min. The night before, it had been Carmen excluding Cosimo. On this evening, Cosimo was excluding Carmen. Even though they disputed with vigorous pecking, Cosimo held his ground and Carmen had to spend the night on the outside perch. Judging from the positions at 08:15 h on the morning of July 17, Cosimo had kept up his guard all night.

July 17 was a day of very intense eating and allofeeding by the parents, but for a period of almost 3 hours in the morning, the chicks did not receive a 2nd feeding. At 24:06 h that night, Cosimo was guarding the NB entrance from the inside and vigorously pecked Carmen away when she sought to enter. By 01:00 h, he had exited and both were outside in the enclosure together. All 4 chicks were sleeping solitarily, prostrate on their bellies, with their heads on the floor and their wingtips also touching it. Precisely the same situation prevailed the next night, as Cosimo excluded Carmen from the NB, at first, but subsequently joined her outside.

CARE OF THE BROOD (3rd week)

CHICKS CROWD TOWARD ALLOFEEDING PARENT. Both parents spent the night of July 19 outside the NB, but on the next 2 nights, they were both inside it with the young. The chicks continued to be incredibly "well behaved" during the day; they stood around solitarily in the NB, creating no "disorder"--just waiting, waiting. But they presented as lonely a sight as did Marco on similar occasions, as a sole member of the 3rd brood. Early on the morning of July 22nd (08:10 h), I found Cosimo on the inside NB perch and Carmen on the outside one, suggesting that she might have exited after I turned the lights off. The parents then customarily were allofeeding the young from the inside and outside perches. For the 1st time, I saw the young crowd together toward a parent as they reached high for food.

ALLOGROOMING BY COSIMO. As usual, Cosimo often occupied himself with allogrooming the chicks, who typically cried out. One would have expected, that with 4 chicks among whom to divide his attentions, the intensity of his grooming an individual chick would have been little more than normal in amount. Yet, judging from tiny clots that formed, he was drawing blood at numerous places on their cheeks and around their ears. These clots could be picked off or dissolved away with water; no lasting damage was caused by the grooming that caused them. On the other hand, the youngest chick ultimately was found to have been feather-picked slightly on the front of the neck.

ALLOFEEDING AND LATE NIGHT HOUSEKEEPING. On the night of July 23, Cosimo again excluded Carmen from the NB. The young, as usual, were sprawled out solitarily. During these days, both parents frequently were together with the young in the NB. Sometimes both were allofeeding the young at the same time, but, more often, one sat and waited while the other allofed. Both were participating about equally in the allofeedings.

Both parents apparently spent the night of July 24 in the NB with the young. During practically all of that week, all 4 young hissed, threat-postured, and coarse-rasped at me when they viewed me through the sidepane as I serviced the enclosures. I also noted a 3rd call, a plaintive long squeak given in distress, no different from one of the adult distress calls. As mentioned above, one of the functions that the parents tended to very late at night, after the chicks had been allofed and were standing around, was housekeeping. At such time, they would be busy pecking about in the sawdust, presumably transferring the droppings to the perimeter.

NIGHTTIME EXCLUSION. That night, Cosimo again excluded Carmen from the NB, but they spent the next night in it together. It was my impression that the only times that Carmen was able to spend the night in the NB with the chicks during this period were on those occasions when she already was inside with them when Cosimo took up his vigil. If she was out "too late," she had to stay out all night.

CARE OF THE BROOD (4th week)

CONTINUED ORDERLY ALLOFEEDING----A VERY HARMONIOUS FAMILY. The allofeeding of the young continued to be a highly orderly procedure, and gave the impression--confirmed with the 7th brood--that more than 4 chicks could have been accommodated with little difficulty. The chicks did not push or crowd, but waited their turns, though they often extended their heads and necks in the direction of the allofeeding parent. Late (23:50 h) on the night of July 26th, after the young were fed, the parents were both in the NB housekeeping and allogrooming. When I checked at 01:00 h, after the lights had been turned off, Carmen "popped" out of the NB. The late night of July 28th (between 24:30 and 01:00 h) was one of particularly harmonious interactions between family members, as the parents were busily housekeeping.

CARMEN FINDS TIME TO LOAF. Precisely 1 week after I 1st saw the chicks crowd together, reaching high for food (July 22), I also saw them crowd over to the front of the NB to be fed, and push and peck each other mildly (July 29). At that time, Carmen was doing by far most of the allofeeding, and she no longer passed food to Cosimo to be relayed to the young. July 30 was the 1st day that Carmen's parental activities eased sufficiently for her to have "spare time" to manipulate the chain and mirror (used earlier to detect movements in the NB). On the nights of both July 31 and August 1, when I turned the lights off at about 24:30 h, Carmen was in the NB and Cosimo was outside. On both occasions, they were both out in the enclosure early the next morning.

OLDEST CHICK VENTURES FROM NESTBOX. I had been handling and examining the chicks daily in my work area, and July 31 was the 1st day that the parents showed great 'concern.' Carmen, in particular, paced back and forth nervously at the enclosure front. It also was the 1st day that the oldest chick ventured from the NB. When Carmen started pacing the enclosure, I flighted both parents. Carmen thereupon spent the entire time perched near the chicks, either on my hand or arm or the tray edge. Meanwhile, Cosimo flew about the room whistling agitatedly. He would not venture any closer than the stem of the main lamp.

CARE OF THE BROOD (5th week)

COSIMO SINGING AGAIN, CARMEN COURTSHIP-FEEDS HIM. For several days preceding August 2, the parents seemingly had not spent the night in the NB with the chicks, and this pattern continued into the 5th week. On the morning of August 4, one of the 2 younger chicks left the NB for the enclosure floor, so I placed them all there. While Carmen allofed the youngest, Cosimo siezed the opportunity--for the first time in many weeks--to enter the NB and "sing up a storm." Early that evening, he sang again from the outside NB perch.

It was obvious that Cosimo was in breeding condition again, and the very next day Carmen courtship-fed him for the first time in many weeks (4 regurgitations in 1 bout; the last time she had allofed him for any purpose was during brooding, 2 weeks earlier). At that time, the young were coming forward to the NB entrance seeking food when they saw Carmen approach, but not when Cosimo approached (he infrequently allofed them). The latter was still allogrooming them a great deal, despite their continual vocal ‘objections.’

PARENTAL RESPONSES TO HANDLING CHICKS. When I handled and examined the chicks on August 4 (the oldest was the only one that could fly), Carmen perched next to them on my hand and on the holding tray, whereas Cosimo perched on the stem of my fluorescent reading lamp (Fig. 2a). When I put the oldest chick on the home perch, both parents flew over to it and stayed with it, showing absolutely no interest in the other 3 young. Was this because only the oldest chick could fly, and so was the only one that might be at risk?

To test this possibility, I brought the chick back to the tray, whereupon both parents followed, Carmen close by and Cosimo on the lamp stem. When I repeated the test, but with the 2nd-oldest chick, I obtained the same result--both flew over and stayed with it. It would appear that they tended strongly to give their attention and protection to the chick perceived to be exposed to the greatest risk, whether the risk involved flight, or not.

I obtained a similar result 3 days later. At that time I left the parents in the enclosure. Again, Carmen became agitated when I handled the chicks, and she paced back and forth at the front face of the enclosure. When I returned the oldest chick, she seemed to be perfectly contented, though she did take note of chirps coming from the other chicks. On the other hand, when I removed only one chick from the enclosure, both parents became very agitated if they witnessed the removal, and especially if they heard the chick chirp.

COSIMO GUARDS AND VOCALIZES FROM THE NESTBOX. On the night of August 5, the guarding of the NB from the inside perch by Cosimo took an extreme form. Beginning at 23:50 h, he would let neither Carmen nor the oldest chick join the 3 young in the NB, but repeatedly pecked them away. After watching him exclude them for 15 min, I caused him to leave so that they could enter. The risk of a colony panic during the night was too great, were I to leave a young bird out in the enclosure. Though Carmen did enter the NB when I facilitated it, she did not remain for the night.

COSIMO SINGS, ALLOGROOMS, & ALLOFEEDS A CHICK, GETS ALLOFED HIMSELF. Cosimo’s interest in the NB continued, as he sat in the IA and sang softly on August 7. The youngest chick also was inside and repeatedly solicited food from him. All Cosimo was willing to offer, though, was his unwelcome allogrooming. In a surprising change of attentions, he entered the NB the next morning (Aug. 8) when the same chick was alone, and allofed it 3 regurgitations. When I flighted the young that afternoon, so much excitement was created in the colony that both Ferdinand and Homer came off the eggs they were incubating. Later that day, Cosimo sang softly several times from the NB and also uttered Coition Sounds. Carmen courtship-fed him 11 regurgitations in 3 bouts.

CARE OF THE BROOD
(6th week and beyond)

ABOUT THE FLEDGLINGS. By August 9, all of the young were able to eat all kinds of seeds unassistedly. Nevertheless, Carmen continued to allofed them when they solicited, even as late as August 14. After that, she allofed them only occasionally, the last time witnessed being on September 9. Just once, on August 8, Cosimo was seen to allofeed the 2nd-oldest chick, but then did it no favor by allogrooming it also. The 3 eldest of the brood (the 3 males, Casimir, Ivan, and Rimski) could return to the NB themselves, but the youngest (the fostered female granddaughter, Kirsten) had to be returned by hand. When I reached in to touch the young birds at this time, Carmen scurried over to protect them, and Cosimo had become bold enough to threaten me with pecks.

'CONCERNED' PARENTS. If I removed one of the young from the enclosure and handled it directly outside, the parents became restless, but not to the degree that they paced back and forth or climbed about excitedly on the enclosure sides or front. If I removed it to a distance and handled it within their sight, Carmen became very restless and paced back and forth. If the chick then chirped, both parents became highly excited and vocalized. Three days later, when I removed the 4 young and held them in a tray, Carmen was much less excited if I kept them in the vicinity of the enclosure than if I carried them to my work area (Fig 2a).

During that period, Carmen was very little inclined to be flighted without the young, and was willing to be returned to the enclosure on my finger. All in all, one could conclude that the 'concern' of these parents for their young was directed toward those that were at greatest risk at the time, and increased in proportion to the perceived potential danger to them.

COSIMO EXCLUDES OTHERS FROM NESTBOX. Cosimo's guarding of the NB late at night had become a regular pursuit. Usually, when he took up his vigil on the inside perch, all the other birds were in the enclosure. He would let none of them enter, but any that already were inside could stay. On virtually all of these occasions, I eventually had to roust Cosimo from the NB to allow the young to enter, since they surely would have panicked the colony during the night if I allowed them to roost in the enclosure (they were too inexperienced and not yet entirely sure-footed). On one occasion (Aug. 14), Cosimo left the entrance and let the young enter, after having defended it for over 15 min.

BREEDING. Courtship activities between Carmen and Cosimo were at a high level all through the 6th week. Cosimo was highly vocal. Every day he sang softly and melodiously from the NB. Carmen courtship-fed him frequently. On August 12, when he sang his soft, melodious song from the NB, Carmen stood on the outside perch and Mandible-fluttered a full 10 sec. Less than 30 min later (21:52 h), they copulated for over 2 min. Although I did nothing to facilitate their breeding again, and even removed the NB on August 16, all courtship activities continued over the next few weeks. Carmen oviposited on the enclosure floor on September 7, 9, and 11. I removed the eggs as they were laid. This was the 3rd time she had oviposited on the enclosure floor when not provided with a nest.

The Fifth Brood of Carmen and Cosimo

After transferring the colony to the laboratory on Sept 22, 1984, I facilitated breeding for the 2 Cockatielian pairs, Helena and Homer, and Isabella and Ferdinand, giving the former pair a "transparent" NB and the latter pair a protected nestbowl. Carmen and Cosimo were housed in the top half of enclosure A. Though the pairs that I sought to breed--partly to study courtship feeding and allofeeding, if any, during brooding--vocalized, copulated, and brooded the empty NB and nestbowl, oviposition by Helena did not begin until 7 months later, on April 25, 1985.

UNSUCCESSFUL FOSTERING OF A CLUTCH. On the other hand, the unfacilitated pair, Carmen and Cosimo, courted and came into breeding condition in short order, laying a clutch of 3 fertile eggs. I fostered these with Homer and Helena, who were brooding an empty nestbowl at the time. They brooded the eggs attentively all through the daytime period for almost a month, and competed for them mildly, at times, in ways already described. But they never progressed beyond the equivalent of the 2nd phylogenetic stage of egg care, that is, they never incubated the eggs at night. Almost identical behavior was observed with a pair of Budgerigars, Lucretia and Lysander, for example, when Lucretia incubated a clutch during the day for 26 days, beginning promptly each morning with lights-on and abandoning the eggs each night (see p. 783, **Daytime Incubation Only**).

FIRST EGG. When Carmen laid the 1st egg of her next clutch on March 8, 1985, I provided an open nestbowl with shavings and a square of overhead screening. She continued to oviposit roughly every other day, to a total of 5 eggs. The 1st of these had been damaged and one of the parents apparently had pecked a hole in the shell at the point of damage. I did not follow in detail the care of the eggs of this clutch nor the brood. The following observations on the care of this 5th brood also are typical of the care of the 6th brood of 3 chicks during September and October, 1985.

COOLED WITHIN SHELL BY MY TOUCH, CHICK CRIES OUT. All the elements of competition for the eggs and chicks that have been described above and in Chapter 4 were observed. Having a much better and closer view, however, a number of additional findings emerged. On March 31, the 2nd egg was due to hatch and Carmen was incubating the clutch very tenaciously, not even coming off of it during the excitement when Kirsten and Rimski were being flighted. I heard a loud clicking when I checked the egg at 16:08 h, followed by a loud squawk of distress as I held it to my ear. Having had this experience before, and, again, with other eggs of the clutch, I deduced that the distress squawk of the chick was being precipitated by the contact with my fingers, as they cooled the chick through the shell, at the points where I was grasping it. Alternatively, the chick's distress call might have been elicited because of my changing the orientation of the egg (see p. 191, **Possible Influences of Egg Orientation on Hatching**).

[The frequency of one type of peep of a chick within the egg, the "distress" call, increases when an egg cools, as may happen when the sitting bird interrupts incubation. This has been shown experimentally in several species. For example, Black-tailed Godwit embryos emit distress calls in response to cooling of the egg (see 1,053). In another example, the Guillemot (*Uria aalge*), it also has been shown that the distress call of the embryo stimulates the parent to re-cover the cooling egg or to rise and roll it (60, 1,053).]

MUCH PARENTAL INTEREST AS FIRST CHICK HATCHES. At 11:00 h the next day, I noted that both Carmen and Cosimo were standing side by side in the nestbowl, apparently intent on an examination of the eggs. The likelihood that they had been watching the 1st chick hatch was suggested 30 min later when the hatched chick was in evidence. When Cosimo took over the care of the chick and eggs at 12:15 h, Carmen sat nearby, just outside the nestbowl. It was her habit to sit nearby, for a time, whenever she was displaced involuntarily (as usually was the case) from the clutch or the brood in the nestbowl, just as she formerly had remained in the NB and sat to the right rear of Cosimo when he displaced her involuntarily from the clutch or brood during the brooding of the 3rd and 4th broods.

CLOSE OBSERVATIONS OF FIRST FEEDING. I was able to get my first good look at the the hatchling at 12:50 h, by which time it was completely dried and had its head and neck draped over 2 of the eggs. The first allofeeding of the chick occurred at 14:30 h, 3-3½ h after hatching. Almost the entire meal was delivered by Carmen, but Cosimo stayed very close and also allofed for a brief time. Being able to watch closely, I was able to see that both tongue-flick allofeeding and trickle-feeding of liquid occurred, and that some semi-liquid food was delivered in small gobs by massive tongue-flick allofeeding.

The hatchling cheeped and bobbed its head throughout these allofeedings, regardless of which type was employed. When tongue-flick allofeeding occurs, the parents' bills are spread sufficiently that the flicking of the tongue can be seen clearly, whereas during trickle-feeding, the bills are much closer together and the tongue usually cannot be seen. This is virtually the only way to distinguish between these two types of feeding at a distance.

FIRST HATCHLING MAY BE AT RISK IN SHALLOW NESTBOWL----HATCHLING IN DISTRESS. As I have remarked above and in Chapter 4, Part 2, competition for the brood may reach such a high pitch during the care of a solitary 1st hatchling, that the chick and eggs sometimes appear to be at risk. [This was one of the considerations that led me to "rescue" Kirsten from the vigorously competing Isabella and Ferdinand, and foster her into the 4th brood of Carmen and Cosimo.] Although there may be but little risk to the chick within a NB, the events of the evening were to show that the situation is different in a shallow nestbowl.

When I checked the brood at 18:30 h that evening, all was in order, whereas when I checked at 23:30 h, the chick was, at first, nowhere to be seen. Then I heard it cheeping in distress, and found it fully 30 cm distant from the nestbowl hanging head down into the lower part of the enclosure (housing Homer and Helena) between the floor partition and the rear face. Evidently Carmen and Cosimo had engaged in vigorous competition for the chick and eggs earlier in the evening and had accidentally displaced the chick from the bowl (3-cm-high rim).

RETURNED TO NESTBOWL, HATCHLING IS BROODED---ADDITIONAL HATCHINGS. In the light of later studies of brood-site fidelity with Helena and Homer (see pp. 503-510), it is evident that once out of the nestbowl, the chick would have been ignored. At any rate, the hatchling's crop was practically empty and the chick itself was not warm to my touch. In all likelihood it had been out of the nestbowl and, perhaps, hanging there for some time, perhaps even for several hours. After I restored it to the nestbowl, the parents immediately resumed brooding it. The next morning, it appeared none the worse for the mishap.

The 2nd chick hatched from the 3rd egg at about 17:00 h on April 4. By 22:00 h, it already had been allofed. The next day the chick in the 4th egg could be heard cheeping, and it squawked in distress when I put the egg to my ear. It hatched early the next morning and was allofed at 09:45 h, while still wet, as usual almost entirely by tongue-flick allofeeding and trickle-feeding. On the morning of April 8th, I found an elliptical area (of about the cross-sectional area of a pencil) of the 5th egg pecked open at about the position where pipping is to be expected. The chick was clicking and it also let out a distress squawk as I handled the egg.

MUTILATION OF THE UNHATCHED CHICK. As I could not discern the chick's head or egg caruncle, I concluded that the parents had pecked open the egg, just as they had pecked open the damaged 1st egg. Accordingly, I patched the egg with a shell fragment from another egg, using non-toxic white glue. Thirty min later my error was revealed, as the chick had pipped the patch and begun to cut across it along a strip. On discovering this, I removed the patch to facilitate the chick's hatching. Unfortunately, this proved to have fatal consequences. Another 30 min later, I discovered that one of the parents (probably Cosimo) had killed the chick by pecking and mutilating its upper bill and neighboring areas of its head (causing much bleeding), and then discarded the egg from the nestbowl.

CORRELATION WITH AN EARLIER FINDING. The behavior of one or both parents on this occasion was a significant finding, which seemed to explain an earlier finding with the 2nd egg of the first brood of Helena and Homer (see p. 496, **Second Egg Pipped**). It will be recalled that a large hole merely had been pipped in this egg and that the chick failed to hatch. I also noted blood inside and on the shell of that egg, but I attributed no great significance to it at the time, as it did not occur to me that the parents might have killed the chick.

THE ADAPTIVE SIGNIFICANCE of the parents' behavior toward incompletely hatched chicks may be the following. If a chick that had begun to hatch were, for one reason or another, unable to complete hatching (in the cases cited, probably because of the inability of the chick to rotate in the eggshell and cut off the entire broad end of the shell), it would die in the shell and foul the nest-hole. Accordingly, it would be adaptive for the parents to discard the egg. But if the egg were to be discarded with a live chick inside, the cries of the chick might attract attention to the location of the hole nest. For that reason, it is adaptive also to kill the chick, which would not survive in any event.

Since the egg caruncle appears to be the focal point of the pecking attack, it would appear that parental behavior directed toward killing the chick and discarding the egg may be released when a complete egg-tooth and a fairly large part of a chick's head are visible through a large hole in the shell. During normal Cockatielian hatching, such large, circular or elliptical holes are not cut in the shell. Instead, the cut is made along a strip, and not much more than the tip of the white egg tooth usually is visible from outside, in which case it is inconspicuous, as it blends with the white shell. When the normal cut is completed, the entire broad end of the egg shell falls off and a large portion of the chick becomes visible, rather than merely a portion of the head and a conspicuous egg caruncle. [In the case of Peach-faced Lovebirds, the hatching chicks normally do cut fairly large, circular or elliptical or elliptical holes in the shell, but the parental practice is to cover incompletely hatched eggs and dead chicks with nesting material.]

Further observations relating to the hatching procedure were made with the 4th brood of Helena and Homer and the 7th brood of Carmen and Cosimo. The undamaged shell "halves" were recovered after 6 hatchings and glued together at the joints of final breakage, except in 2 cases where the chicks completed the strip by chipping with the egg caruncle. In all cases little more than a narrow strip was cut. In one case a "false start" was made just below the equator of the egg. A hole was begun there before the chick's movements allowed it to cut a strip along a longitude toward the blunt end. When the normal latitude was reached the cut was extended around in the normal fashion, though clumsily at one point (where the strip was widened), until the cap broke off about 0.4 cm from completion.

ANY SIGNIFICANTLY DAMAGED EGG USUALLY PECKED OPEN & DISCARDED. The most pertinent case indicates that if the above interpretation of killing the chick has validity, it does not describe an invariable occurrence. On the day that the chick in egg #1 of the 7th brood of Carmen and Cosimo began to hatch and the next day also, the parents spent almost the entire day in the nest together competing for and caring attentively for the eggs; sometimes they split the clutch, as was their custom at such times (as also of Helena and Homer). The embryo in egg #1 cut a roughly rectangular hole (0.4 x 0.9 cm) in the shell but was unable to cut a strip and succumbed. The parents neither mutilated this chick nor discarded the egg, which remained in the nest until after the 4th chick hatched, when I removed it. Subsequent studies of additional clutches and broods of Carmen and Cosimo revealed a more general applicability of the parental behavior toward abnormal eggs and abnormally hatching chicks. Eggs that are damaged significantly by "dimpling," crushing, flattening, or perforation, other than by a linear slit, usually are pecked open at the point of damage, lifted with the tip of the penetrating bill, and discarded from the nest.

ALLOFEEDING OF THE CHICKS AND THEIR CONCURRENT BEHAVIOR was very similar to that described for the chicks of the 4th brood (see p. 686, *et seq.*). This also was true of the behavior of the chicks in the nestbowl, as opposed to in the "transparent" NB, even though the ambient temperature never exceeded 27°C. Again, the allofeedings were very orderly, the chicks were very orderly amongst themselves, and they eventually spaced themselves apart in the nestbowl while resting, rather than huddling together.

The chief deviations were that, after the first few days, I saw very little competition between the parents to allofeed, and no instance of both parents feeding the chicks during the same period. Nor did I see any "close following" by one parent while the other allofed a hatchling or young nestling. Observations of the care of this brood thus cast no new light on the significance of the latter behavior (but see pp. 705, 706).

ALLOFEEDING OF COSIMO BY CARMEN. There also was much less allofeeding of the male by the hen. I attribute this to their having been much less possessive of the open nestbowl, as opposed to the closed NB. As a consequence, Cosimo was out eating more often and there was much less need for Carmen to allofeed him. With the earlier broods, he often had maintained possession of the NB tenaciously in the afternoons and evenings.

The only allofeedings that I observed during my infrequent monitorings occurred once or twice per day in the afternoons. At those times, Carmen allofed Cosimo as she perched on the rim of the nestbowl. Again, as in the case of allofeeding him from the outside perch, this suggests that in the wild the female may allofeed the sitting or brooding male near the entrance to the nest-hole, and that he then relays the food to the chicks.

CARE AND BEHAVIOR OF JUVENILES. Both Carmen and Cosimo continued to allofeed the young in the 7th week, long after they were ready to be fledged, and even after breeding began again and Carmen laid another clutch of 3 eggs. Since I was desirous of observing incubation and brooding in an open nestbowl in the atmosphere of a family group, I left the 3 young in the enclosure and provided a 2nd nestbowl (22½-cm diameter x 5-cm deep) at the side of the first one. Until the middle of the 7th week, the young were in the habit of perching during the day and sleeping together in their nestbowl at night. They more or less ignored the new nestbowl and eggs until that time.

After the 3rd egg was laid on May 16, Carmen and Cosimo began to incubate more attentively. This drew attention to the eggs and the new nestbowl. The juvenile, Teresa, began to enter it when the opportunity afforded and to nudge the eggs about and under herself, but she did not actually sit on them. On May 17 this same juvenile was sleeping in the nestbowl at Carmen's side in the morning. When Cosimo left the eggs during the day, as commonly occurred at that time when I disturbed him, this juvenile and sometimes her sister, Francesca, jumped into the bowl with the eggs.

On such occasions, which continued to occur during the incubatory period, Cosimo had to expel them by pecking, in order to regain the clutch (see pp. 701, 702, **Cosimo Rousts Young Forcefully from the Nest**). Neither of these young females sat on the eggs, though they showed great interest in them, nudged them about, and pecked about in the shavings (all of which are incipient manifestations of later stages of egg-care behavior). If Cosimo did not return promptly, Carmen returned and took over the care of the eggs.

On the 8 successive mornings following May 17, egg attendance was as follows: (1) the eggs were unattended, presumably the consequence of a nocturnal panic; (2) Teresa and Francesca were sleeping alone in the nest; (3) the 2 sisters were present with Carmen, who was incubating the eggs; (4) Francesca was in the nest with Carmen; (5) all 3 juveniles were in the nest without Carmen; (6) Teresa was in the nest with Carmen; (7) Teresa was in the nest again with Carmen; and (8) Carmen was in the nest alone.

On the 9th following morning, which was the 13th day of incubation of the 1st egg, I found that egg #4 had been pecked open and eaten, leaving only a half shell. After that, I monitored the condition of the eggs closely. The next morning Teresa was in the nest with Carmen again and the eggs were intact. Later in the day, though, I found egg #3 also pecked open and leaking at a time when Teresa was in the nest alone with the eggs. Inasmuch as it was evident that the remaining 2 eggs were at risk, I removed Teresa, Francesca, and Matteo from the enclosure. The planned family studies were first carried out 2 months later with the 2nd and 3rd broods of Helena and Homer (see pp. 703-715). [The eggs of yet another clutch of Carmen and Cosimo were destroyed by the 3 juveniles of the 7th brood of 5 offspring that were present when breeding began again. However, in August, 1986, I was able to accomplish the experiment with Carmen and Cosimo in the presence of Lothair, a 9-month-old male of their 7th brood. At that age, the juvenile was rigorously excluded from the nestbowl at all times by both parents, and the eggs were not damaged.]

Although 2 eggs were lost and I had to discontinue the planned family study with Carmen and Cosimo, the experiment proved to be fruitful along another avenue. The disruptive influences of the 3 young on both daytime and nighttime incubation led Carmen and Cosimo gradually to abandon the clutch. Thus, although the eggs were incubated during the next 3 nights, the urge to incubate was waning. On the morning of the 19th day of incubation, and every morning thereafter, I found the eggs unattended at the time of lights-on. Concomitantly, incubation during the day became increasingly desultory on the part of both parents. By the 21st day of incubation, the eggs were being incubated no more than 5-10 min out of every 60, and by the 23rd day, they were virtually abandoned.

The interesting results of the study relate to the sequence in which egg-care aspects waned, and to the behavior of the parents in the morning shortly after lights-on. With regard to the first result, it is noteworthy that the last facet of egg care to appear, namely, nocturnal incubation, also was the first to be lost. With regard to the 2nd result, there was a strong urge to cover the eggs promptly in the morning at the time of lights-on, just as there was to return to the nest and cover them if the lights were turned on during the night shortly after the hen had exited temporarily to void (see pp. 434, 435).

On the 1st and 2nd mornings after nocturnal incubation had been abandoned, Carmen returned to the nest and incubated the eggs within a few min of lights-on, delaying only to groom and stretch. On the 3rd morning, when Carmen did not incubate the eggs after 9 min had elapsed, Cosimo descended and incubated them. On the 4th and 5th mornings they were not incubated until Cosimo did so after about 60 min, while on the 6th morning they were not incubated at all and incubation was, to all intents and purposes, discontinued During these last days Carmen and Cosimo were engaged in breeding preliminaries, including courtship feeding, copulations, and male singing. After another week, I removed the eggs and allowed the pair to proceed, unhindered, with their next clutch.

MALE NEST VOCALIZATIONS POSSIBLY PRIMITIVE BEHAVIOR. It was most interesting to observe that each morning Cosimo spent 20-40 min during several sessions vocalizing from a crouched stance within the empty nestbowl. His song included Coition Sounds and was delivered in an "emphatic" manner that suggested great urgency. All 4 breeding males behaved in the same way, yet their mates seemed to ignore the display and did little more than occasionally join the male in the nest. Since this seems a pointless behavior for the male of a mated pair to engage in within an already-adopted nest hole in the wild, and the female seemingly ignores it, one is led to consider the possibility that this might be very primitive behavior, dating from a time when it played a role in the adoption of hole nests.

COSIMO ROUSTS YOUNG FORCEFULLY FROM NEST. Another interesting situation developed many times during the day when Cosimo sought to recover the clutch after a stint of incubation by Carmen, while the juveniles of the previous brood were still present in the enclosure. Frequently Teresa or Francesca, or both, would be sitting in the bowl alongside Carmen, or they would jump in as soon as Carmen vacated. Although Carmen might compete with Cosimo for the eggs and only give them up reluctantly, Cosimo needed only to persevere with the routines already described to displace her.

On the other hand, neither Teresa not Francesca was in breeding condition and neither responded in the same way as Carmen, nor did the "safety valve" of grooming or attempting to groom the crissum induce them to rise or leave the nest. Accordingly, Cosimo had no recourse but to roust them from the nest or vicinity of the eggs by relatively violent means, sometimes having to peck or bite them to the point where they fled squealing in pain. On the other hand, once in possession of the eggs he tolerated their joining him at his side. [Juvenile lovebirds had to be rousted from the nestbowl in precisely the same fashion by Petra as she incubated the eggs of her 9th brood (see pp. 728-730).]

The Seventh Brood of Carmen and Cosimo

In late November, 1985, 5 chicks of the 7th brood of Carmen and Cosimo hatched from a clutch of 6 eggs. The chick in the 1st-laid egg failed to rotate or hatch and merely pecked a rectangular hole in the shell, the failure doubtless being because I had stored the egg at room temperature (22°C) for 4 days (with turning 3-4 times/day; see p. 699). At last the opportunity had arisen to observe the care of a brood of 5 in an open nest. In general, it can be stated that the care of this brood was very similar to that of their 3rd brood of 4 (including one fostered chick).

The brood was reared with relative ease and with very little non-vocal competition between the chicks at times of allofeeding. As before, the young unfeathered chicks generally were sequestered according to size in the presence of one or both parents and huddled in the usual fashion in their absence. On occasion, the unfeathered young were prostrate in linear arrangement, but not necessarily according to age or size. For example, on the day when the youngest chick was 2 days old and the 2 eldest were 8 days old, the chicks often were in front of and under the breast or chest of the brooding parent. But the youngest usually were closest and sometimes the largest ones were to the side and the smallest were out of sight under the parent or its wings.

The most notable information obtained from this brood had to do with the allofeeding performances of the parents. Although my observations were neither continuous nor systematic, I was able to keep a relatively close check on the early morning feedings in the 90 min after lights-on. At first the prognosis for the youngest chick looked poor. At 23:10 h on the day of its hatching, when about 8 h old (and having had at least one tongue-flick-fed meal from Carmen 6 h earlier), it was being brooded under Cosimo and solicited for food, loudly and continuously. Cosimo, however, ignored it; instead he "loaded up" the other chicks for the night.

There proved to be no need for concern, though; Carmen (and Cosimo at least once) typically allofed the youngest chick to the point where I thought its crop would burst, before feeding any of the others. This strongly suggests that Cockatielian parents sometimes (probably depending upon the size distribution of the young) exhibit the same selectivity in allofeeding chicks that is exhibited by Budgerigar hens (see pp. 200-203, **Feeding the Young**, and p. 808, **The Selective Allofeeding of Younger, Smaller Chicks**). The brood was fledged without incident and, insofar as the time during which the parents were occupied with the chicks was concerned, I would judge that they could have accommodated at least a 6th chick and probably a 7th. In the wild, of course, a large fraction of the time would have to be spent foraging at a distance from the nest.

The Second Clutch and Brood of Helena and Homer

OVIPOSITION IN AN OPEN NEST. As mentioned above, Helena and Homer shielded and incubated a fostered clutch of 3 eggs during the day but not at night, persisting in doing so for virtually the entire month of February, 1985. Accordingly, the urge to cover eggs was strong but the birds had not yet attained the equivalent of the 3rd phylogenetic stage of egg care (see p. 511). On April 25, after the usual preliminary courtship activities and copulations, Helena laid the 1st egg of her 2nd clutch, almost exactly 9 months after laying the 1st egg of her 1st clutch (see p. 495, **The Eggs Are Laid**). A total of 3 eggs were laid in the same 23½-cm-diameter x 3-cm-deep pan used earlier by Isabella and Ferdinand (at position **v** in Fig. 3a). This was shielded on 3 sides and above by setting it within an aluminum chassis.

Breeding by this pair was particularly auspicious because the 2 members were the best habituated birds. The prospects were that I would be able to make much closer observations of their behavior than was feasible with Carmen and Cosimo. These prospects were fulfilled far beyond my expectations, as much previously enigmatic chick-care behavior was clarified and highly fruitful experiments on oviposition-site and brood-site fidelity were facilitated (see pp. 498-510). By the time the 3rd egg was laid, Helena and Homer began to incubate attentively, both by day and by night. I found the eggs cold and uncovered on the morning of May 13, the seeming result of a panic that night. [The colony was at risk of panics at that time because of the presence of the 3 juvenile Cockatiels of the 5th brood of Carmen and Cosimo in the upper half of enclosure A.] I was optimistic that the embryos would survive, though, in view of the survival of embryos of the 1st clutch after the eggs were left unattended for 5 or 6 nights.

FIRST CHICK HATCHES, RECEIVES NO PARENTAL CARE. At the time of lights-on at 09:00 h on the morning of May 16, I detected the shells of the 1st egg in the nest, but the chick was shielded from view by Helena. When Homer entered the nest at 10:15 h, the hatchling could be seen lying on its side, kicking and wriggling about. But Helena and Homer gave it no care. They hovered over it and pecked gently at its limbs, but neither made any effort to shield or allofeed it. On only one occasion did Homer nudge it closer. He was much more concerned with the care of the eggs (one of which would be hatching that night) than the chick, and restlessly kept shifting his position over them, as if continually uncomfortable.

HATCHLING SUCCUMBS. It appeared as if the interest of the parents in the chick was essentially one of 'curiosity' and that they were unprepared to care for it. Though they continued to evidence great interest in it, peck at it gently, and keep it close by, they made no effort to brood or allofeed it. They were much more occupied with competing for the eggs and shells. Judging from the relative weakness of the chick, it seemed quite likely that Helena had left it unshielded after it hatched, perhaps much of the night, just as she had done with the sole hatchling of her 1st brood.

Gradually weakening as its body temperature fell, the chick was all but lifeless at 13:15 h when I examined it. It showed no sign of being abnormal in any way. Although its demise seemed at the time to have been a result of parental inexperience, subsequent events have suggested a quite different interpretation. Thus, for example, Helena and Homer treated the 1st chicks of their next and of their 4th broods in exactly the same manner, at first, as they dried out, but the chicks eventually were cared for and fledged successfully. The difference was that the subsequent 1st chicks hatched in the late afternoon or early evening and early morning and did not lie about uncared for through much of the night, as seemed to have occurred with this hatchling.

It would appear that by the time it engaged its parents' attention the present hatchling was too weak to sit up and solicit food and, accordingly, never was allofed. In this connection, a chick of the 6th brood of Carmen and Cosimo hatched only 3-3½ h before lights-out. I witnessed one very brief feeding of it by Cosimo while it was still wet but able to sit up and solicit for food, not more than 45-90 min after hatching. It was in excellent condition the next morning and was fledged routinely.

SECOND HATCHLING IS KEPT WARM. With this most inauspicious beginning, I fully expected to see the entire clutch lost in the same way. I could not have been more mistaken. I was pleasantly surprised the next morning to find additional eggshells and a dry hatchling sitting up at Helena's left and shortly thereafter sheltered under her right wing. But, again, aside from sheltering the chick, Helena did not care for it; she just pecked gently at it from time to time. As on the preceding day, both parents were highly protective of the chick and eggs, hissing violently and striking out at me as I serviced their enclosure. When Homer joined the pair in the nest, he nudged and pecked gently at the chick but made no effort to shelter it. On the other hand, he showed great interest in the remaining egg and re-covered it promptly whenever it became exposed.

CLUMSY EFFORTS TO GRASP HATCHLING BY BILL. After leaving momentarily when Homer joined her, Helena returned and stayed close by for another 30 min. The hatchling was very energetic and stood and crawled about clumsily. In the next few min Homer sheltered the chick at first, then lost it, then sheltered it again, then lost it again, etc., as he shifted and shuffled about uncomfortably in response to the hatchling's wriggling and squirming. However, he maintained a close interest in it every time it became exposed and, for the 1st time, he almost grasped the hatchling by its bill. Ten min later he repeated this act.

HELENA'S APPETITE GONE. Meanwhile, Helena left the nest and showed her desire to be flighted by climbing about on the enclosure door. After being flighted for 15 min, she showed no sign of any special interest in eating, as she picked about 'half-heartedly' at seeds. In retrospect, the disinclination to eat probably was because it was desirable that food already consumed be further digested before being allofed to the hatchling, without being mixed with fresh food. At the time, though, the prospects for the survival of the chick did not seem promising.

ABRUPT TRANSITION TO ALLOFEEDING HATCHLING. Meanwhile, Homer grasped clumsily for the chick's bill several times and the hatchling opened and closed its mouth at the same time. Then Helena returned to the nest and competed with Homer for the remaining egg, taking over its care for the time. But she appeared to show nothing more than curiosity over the chick. Then, quite suddenly, both parents were galvanized into action by the simple act of the chick's cheeping loudly for the first time. Both crowded in toward its outstretched head and made clumsy, simultaneous efforts to feed it, but unsuccessfully (neither parent had ever fed another bird, not even each other). This observation suggests another function of the cheeping of a chick within the egg before hatching, namely, it may stimulate parents to accumulate well-digested food for the imminent need (see also p. 191, **Possible Influences of Egg Orientation on Hatching**). By 11:15 h, Homer had regained the egg and the hatchling began to cheep again.

UNSTEADY HATCHLING NEED REGAIN ITS FOOTING TO BE ALLOFED. Upon this 2nd session of cheeping, both parents crowded in again simultaneously and sought to allofeed the hatchling. All three of their bills were very close together. For the 1st time the hatchling also began to "pump" and the parents' heads began to bob alternately, as first one appeared to allofeed it and then the other. But was the chick actually receiving any food?

Two circumstances seemed likely in regard to inexperienced parents: a hatchling would not be allofed unless it cheeped; and a hatchling had to sit up and extend its head upward in order to be allofed, even when cheeping. The latter conclusion depends on the observation that every time the unsteady chick lost its balance and fell over, as it did repeatedly, it had to regain its feet (much to the my wonder) and extend its head upward before either parent would resume allofeeding. Otherwise, the parents would do nothing more than extend their bills toward the prostrate chick's bill. In this connection, Cockatielian chicks may experience considerable difficulty in sitting up again after having fallen over on their backs or sides. Studies in which I removed nestlings and allofed them a full meal by hand and then returned them to the nest showed that nestlings (perhaps even hatchlings) will not be allofed when their bill is grasped by a parent unless they respond by pumping, which is not done by sated nestlings.

COMPETING TO ALLOFEED---CHICK ALLOFED REPEATEDLY. From that time on, barring brief exits, Helena remained in the nest with Homer and the chick. The rest of the day saw the same scenes repeated again and again, every time positions were shifted and the chick became exposed. The first certain allofeeding occurred at 11:33 h. As with most of the allofeedings for the rest of the day, both parents competed mildly, sometimes vigorously, by crowding in on one another and taking close turns, often by physically displacing the other's bill. Such competitive feeding of Cockatielian chicks was observed closely in open nests on many subsequent occasions.

Sometimes the prolonged contacts of all three bills left little doubt that both parents were allofeeding the chick simultaneously. Some of the food even might have been transferred to the chick from one parent via the other's tongue. I have already confirmed that the latter method of feeding occurs commonly in Peach-faced Lovebirds (see pp. 752, 753, **Male Transfers Food to Allofeeding Hen**). Only relatively infrequently could one parent allofeed the chick without competition from the other. The chick pumped variously--from very gently to vigorously--during these allofeedings and often cheeped as well. Pumping was especially marked during tongue-flick allofeeding (as opposed to trickle-feeding). By 21:00 h the hatchling's crop was well filled. Homer was not seen to leave the nest on a single occasion for the rest of the day (at least not before 23:15 h). Though Helena left briefly several times, she ate very little, as judged from the food remaining in the trays in the morning.

I had not observed competition between Carmen and Cosimo in the allofeeding of the 1st chick of their 5th brood, but I had not remained present during the entire 1st day of its care. There seems little doubt that they did compete, as they did on many occasions with previous broods, because the hatchling of that brood got displaced accidentally from the nestbowl and had to be rescued by me (see p. 697). In any event, the present observations amply clarified precisely what had been occurring on the many previous occasions when I watched from a distance as Carmen and Cosimo allofed solitary chicks in the "transparent" NB.

Thus, the close attendance of both parents in allofeeding solitary chicks was because they were competing mildly-to-vigorously to do so, taking their turns as soon as possible, sometimes displacing one another's bills, and sometimes even allofeeding solitary chicks simultaneously. In addition, to the observations suggesting that a hatchling of inexperienced parents will not get its first meal until it solicits by cheeping, and that a hatchling may not be allofed unless it also solicits by extending its head and bill upward, I noted that the hatchling would itself seek out the warmth of a parent's body by "burrowing" under it head first from any position of peripheral contact.

RESWALLOWING FILTRATION RESIDUE. In the course of allofeeding semi-solid food to nestlings by trickle feeding and tongue-flick and massive tongue-flick feeding, or pumping, Cockatiels, lovebirds, and Budgerigars pause after each session of allofeeding and mandibulate, accompanied by manipulations with the tongue. The function of these movements is to regather the loose, large food residues left behind in the buccal cavity and swallow them before regurgitating and/or filtering again in the next session of allofeeding. The movements of the mandibles are very similar to those in the Mandible-fluttering display of Cockatiels, except that their frequency and amplitude are quite variable and may be either lesser or greater than in Mandible-fluttering. I call these movements hereafter "mandibulation" to distinguish this action from the similar display movements (designations for display movements conventionally are capitalized). If mandibulation does not follow the interaction, no food was transferred.

As a generalization, it may be stated that with Cockatielian and lovebird parents, the greater the degree of the filtration employed, the greater appears to be the amount of subsequent mandibulation. In the case of Budgerigars, which feed very young chicks exclusively by massive tongue-flick allofeeding, and remove only seeds and other large pieces of material in forming the filtrate, the degree of subsequent mandibulation seems not to vary.

The reason why it may be asserted that the chick received food from the allofeedings that occurred after 11:33 h is because after each ostensible allofeeding, the participating parent mandibulated. I already had deduced the significance of this action from close observations of Carmen and Cosimo as they allofed the 4 chicks of their 5th brood. The parents were manipulating and reswallowing the residue remaining from the regurgitate after filtering it between their tongue and palate to produce the liquid food for the chick. This was a necessary manipulation before proceeding with the next bout of allofeeding.

ANOTHER PANIC---CHICK IN DISTRESS. The next morning brought discouragement. Another nocturnal colony panic apparently had frightened Helena from the nest and she had not returned. Similarly, Carmen was frightened off of her eggs and had not returned. When I arrived the chick was in distress, cheeping loudly but being ignored by both Helena and Homer. I found both the chick and the eggs to be cool to the touch (close to or at room temperature of 27°C). I removed the chick and warmed it, noting that the crop was about half full and contained mostly semi-liquid food, including some hulled, whole seeds. Either the parents were as yet unskilled in feeding hatchlings or the latter normally receive some semi-solid food.

CHICK FED AND BROODED SNUGLY. When I returned the chick to the nest I also removed the egg and fostered it into a lovebird clutch so that the neglected chick would receive its parents' exclusive attention. [The egg proved to be the 1st one laid. Though fertile, it did not hatch.] Both parents joined the chick shortly thereafter but were not very attentive to it, at first. Then, with little preliminary attention, Homer first allofed it repeatedly and then brooded it snugly. The allofeeding session revealed that Homer's feeding skills had advanced, and the same proved to be true of Helena. He no longer waited for the chick to sit up and extend its head upward, nor did the chick have to solicit by cheeping. Rather, Homer reached down and grasped the chick's bill from whatever position, whereupon the chick straightened up reflexly, bobbed its head, and was allofed.

CHICK'S TONGUE FLICKS IN SYNCHRONY WITH PUMPING. Food was delivered both by trickle-feeding and by tongue-flick allofeeding. Ofttimes the heads of the parents scarcely bobbed at all during trickle-feeding, even though the chick pumped gently and cheeped. Sometimes during trickle-feeding the chick pumped only very gently and did not cheep. I could not ascertain, at first, whether the chick's tongue moved in synchrony with its pumping movements, but if the behavior of lovebird chicks in similar circumstances were to be taken as indicative, that would have been expected.

Such movements were confirmed the next day when Homer allofed the chick with his mandibles in an unusual orientation. They were lined up with and inserted directly between the chick's mandibles, so that the latter were spaced very wide apart. As Homer trickled liquid through the narrow gap between his mandibles, the chick's tongue could be seen to flick in synchrony with its pumping movements. It is very likely that swallowing also occurs in synchrony with these movements.

PARENTS EAT RAVENOUSLY. After I flighted Helena, she drank and picked at one corn kernel before returning to the nest, where she and Homer allofed the chick again in a brief session, partly simultaneously. Later that morning Homer left the chick in Helena's care and ate ravenously. First he picked daintily at seeds, then he hastily devoured a pile of about 15 kernels of corn. I gave him another 15 kernels and those also were consumed with dispatch. Obviously he was unusually hungry after his long fast of the preceding day.

Still later that morning Helena also consumed a pile of corn kernels with dispatch. Most of the allofeeding that day was carried out by Homer but Helena spent most of the time in the nest too, and participated to a lesser extent in many allofeeding sessions. I did not see Homer out of the nest again after the time of his morning meal, though Helena exited many times. It appeared that the chick was none the worse from the prolonged exposure during the previous night, anymore than was the hatchling in Carmen's 5th brood after a comparable misfortune 2 months earlier.

UNBROODED A SECOND NIGHT---VERY ATTENTIVE DAYTIME CARE. Before leaving that night, I took the precautions of placing a 100 watt heater outside the enclosure adjacent to the aluminum chassis shielding the nestpan, producing a 3-5°C increase in the temperature within the nest. I also increased the intensity of the dim night-light. Despite this, the chick was alone in the nest again the next morning, but there was no other suggestion that there might have been a nocturnal panic. However, at a nest temperture of close to 32°C, the chick seemingly was not in distress and its crop was over half full.

On the following morning and on all mornings thereafter until the 11th day, Helena was in the nest with the chick. It is most significant that neither on the previous night, nor at any other time when the chick was unbrooded, did it avail itself of the opportunity to seek out the warmest region of the temperature gradient in the nest (over 1°C warmer near the chassis wall by the heater). This behavior may correlate with the observations of a lack of movements of unbrooded chicks from their initial positions in the study of brood-site fidelity, though the latter chicks were outside of the nest (see pp. 503-510).

Until the 5th day, the chick received the closest of parental attention. At least 75% of this was by Homer, who took very infrequent leave of the nest, perhaps averaging only 3 absences per day. Helena continued to spend most of the day in the nest too. She customarily competed mildly to allofeed the chick and this continued to occur on subsequent days when she was present while Homer allofed it. She did, however, succeed in allofeeding it many times without interference, most thoroughly during Homer's absences. Eating by the parents continued to be infrequent, but in intensive sessions.

FLIGHTING SOLICITATIONS AND VOIDING. Both parents adopted the habit of soliciting to be flighted by clinging to the enclosure door. Their 1st activity on morning flights was to void from the home perch. The egesta of the female always were soft and voluminous, whereas those of the male often were almost entirely fluid and could not be distinguished from a stream of urine during emission. [The first egesta of non-breeding birds in the morning is known to be usually all urine (451).] With this habit established, they customarily delayed voiding until they were flighted.

This behavior also occurred, and the same differences in excreta were noted, during the incubation of their 3rd clutch and the care of their 3rd brood. The quite different behavior of the parents during flighting was consistent with their differing daytime roles in the care of the nestling. Thus, Helena was reluctant to return to the enclosure, and would stay out for hours if permitted. Homer, on the other hand, returned to the outside of the enclosure within minutes of voiding and was easily returned to it.

CHICK CARE BECOMES ROUTINE. By the 5th day, the care of the chick had become routine and parental 'concern' had waned greatly. The parents began to leave the chick alone in the nest for extended periods in the morning and early afternoon, and Helena often merely perched facing away from it on the nestpan rim. On the 6th day, 60-min absences were common and, in essence, except for allofeedings, the chick was left alone much of the morning and early afternoon. In the late afternoon, though, the vigil was taken up again, with one parent usually either close to the chick or brooding it.

During the next few days the chick, the female Heloise, was cared for by one or both parents, with intermittent absences that rarely exceeded 30 min. It is noteworthy that the attention of the parents after the first few days was one of vigilance rather than brooding, as also was noted with Cosimo and Carmen and their broods. When not allogrooming or allofeeding Heloise, the parents "brooded the nest," with the chick usually off to the side or front. Heloise presented a very lonely figure as she balanced on her feet and abdomen, sometimes rocking slowly, tilting forward, straightening up abruptly, etc.

Whereas most or all of the head pumping during allofeeding was on the part of the chick, during the 1st 2 days, active pumping by the parents gradually became more frequent thereafter. By about the 5th day, allofeeding by mutual head-pumping by both parent and chick was the exclusive method employed. One evening, after about 20 regurgitations of allofeeding by head-pumping by Homer, Helena took over for about another 20 regurgitations. I thought Heloise's crop was about to burst. The next morning Homer allofeed Heloise continuously for about 10 min in a total of about 30 regurgitations. [Another mechanism by which allofeeding of a Cockatielian chick may be terminated, in addition to the chick's ceasing pumping, could be the inability of the sated chick to maintain itself erect and engage in the prerequisite pumping action under the weight of its bulging crop.]

EYES OPEN, HOARSE-RASPING AND HISSING BEGIN. Beginning on the 8th day, when Heloise's right eye opened to a narrow slit, I was always greeted by her with hoarse-rasps and hissing whenever I came near, even when I merely entered the room in the morning before turning on the lights (a very dim light always was on at night, see p. 280). Beginning on the night of the 10th day, neither parent brooded Heloise at night, and daytime brooding often was desultory. Heloise proved to have the most handsomely feathered head of the Cockatiels that I had bred. Though the parents obviously were loafing, with the care of a single chick requiring only a fraction of their time, I had, as yet, seen no sign of feather-picking.

FEATHER-PICKING BEGINS. Almost all of the parental brooding urges were being fulfilled by allofeeding the chick and brooding the nest intensively. On the morning of the 15th day, after examining the beautifully feathered chick, I reflected on its good fortune in being a solitary offspring yet not being feather-picked, little suspecting the bizarre behavior that was to follow. On that very day, as Homer brooded the nest and Heloise squatted nearby, he began to feather-pick her in earnest. By late afternoon, Homer had denuded the entire top and rear of Heloise's head, beginning just behind the crest feathers. These were areas where feathering had been very sparse. After this treatment Heloise's head was covered with regular rows of tiny red blood clots, showing that even barely emerging feathers also were picked.

The next morning and early afternoon Homer had worked his way down Heloise's neck to the back, and by late afternoon the feathers of her back were being picked and her back near the neck was bloody. Every time I returned Heloise after giving her relief, Homer resumed his feather-picking, chewing the base of each feather thoroughly before plucking another. Finally, I removed Homer to another enclosure. In the next 4 days, I often removed either Homer or Heloise (doing so every night with Homer) to give Heloise relief and to observe Homer's behavior on reuniting them.

[Recall (p. 662) that the principal basis for Homer's (and Cosimo's, and subsequently Helena's) feather-picking was to consume the pulp at the base of the shaft, which he thoroughly chewed after plucking each feather. In this regard, each growing feather contains at its base a section of highly vascular pulp that constitutes up to 20% of the total length and, in the domestic fowl, up to 53% of the total weight. The pulps represent an extension of the blood vascular system through the surface of the body that is unique among terrestrial animals (973).]

The subsequent observations showed that feather-picking, once begun, continued for reasons unrelated to boredom. On most occasions, Homer sought out Heloise after reunion and either proceeded directly to feather-pick her or first allofed her and then feather-picked her. Homer soon began to cease feather-picking every time I scolded or approached closely, but he resumed doing so as soon as I ceased interfering. I was alerted to feather-picking, not by Heloise's distress cries, because at that early age Cockatiels do not vocalize while being feather-picked, but by the stomping of her feet on the bottom of the metal nestpan as she recoiled after the loss of each feather (this sound resonated within the surrounding metal chassis).

Helena, on the other hand, groomed Heloise in a normal fashion. After 4 days of feather-picking by Homer, and 3 successive nights during which I kept him isolated, his feather-picking decreased somewhat and remained at a lower level on following days. During these following days I not infrequently saw him quickly snatch a single feather after allofeeding Heloise and chew on its base while leaving the nest. Heloise, like her uncle Marco, often got feather-picked by her father rather than being allofed, when she solicited food.

BALANCING THE HEAD. A habit exhibited by solitary Cockatielian chicks is the attempt to bend the neck and orient and hold the head at just the proper height and angle to keep it poised in static equilibrium. I had the opportunity to observe this many times when I removed chicks for examination or isolated solitary chicks to give them relief from feather-picking. When 2 or more chicks are present, they lean over each other's backs or necks while sleeping, and have no need to balance the head to keep it from gradually sinking to the nest bottom.

PARENTAL 'CONCERNS' FOR, AND ESCORTING, THE FLEDGLING. The fledging of Heloise was without notable incident, by which time the 1st egg of her parents' next clutch was laid. It is noteworthy, though, that I was able to confirm all the aspects of parental behavior with chicks nearing fledging age and during fledging that I observed with Carmen and Cosimo and their broods (see, e.g., pp. 673, 685, 686, 694, 695). All the 'concerns,' escorting, etc., by Helena and Homer were figuratively "carbon copies" of those seen when they, themselves, were at the same age and in the care of Carmen and Cosimo. Homer's 'concern' for the fledgling at that time had greater priority than did incubation of a clutch of 3 eggs, as he came off the eggs then whenever I removed Heloise from the enclosure for flighting or isolation. Not so with Helena; she was much more likely to stay with the clutch on such occasions, though she sometimes left the eggs briefly to investigate outside occurrences. On the other hand, Homer held fast on the eggs when birds other than Heloise were being flighted, including his mate, even when great excitement prevailed.

During this period of parental 'concern,' I tried the experiment of removing the fledgling from its parents early in the morning, just after lights-on. In these circumstances, the parents showed no sign of 'concern' or alarm until after the customary early morning stretching and allogrooming. Then they launched into their typical responses to my interferences with the chick. This behavior parallels the behavior of Peach-faced Lovebirds as concerns the latters' morning "truces," that is, the fact that lovebird aggression was suppressed in part or in total in the early morning period (see pp. 335, 336).

FLEDGLING FED AND FEATHER-PICKED EXCLUSIVELY BY HOMER. It is noteworthy that as Helena approached the time of oviposition, she ceased to allofeed the fledgling, Heloise, and merely ignored her solicitations. At this time, allofeeding was taken over entirely by Homer. Although Heloise was able to eat by herself during her 5th week, the fact that only Homer allofed her greatly influenced her behavior. She often stayed very close to him, even as he brooded the nest and the eggs of the 3rd clutch. Only during the dark hours, when no allofeeding occurred, did she stay at Helena's side in the nest. At the time the 3rd egg was laid (June 24, 1985), when Heloise was 5 weeks old, the latter evidenced little interest in the eggs. Helena's nocturnal incubation of the eggs of this clutch began with the 2nd egg.

Even as the eggs of the 3rd clutch were being laid, Homer still feather-picked Heloise, whose neck and upper back were nearly bare. This became a most tenacious pursuit of Homer, who relished snatching and chewing feathers from anywhere on Heloise's body, even her upper legs, just as if they were seeds and she were a honey stick. This behavior continued for many weeks, even when Homer and Heloise were flighted together, and even after the previously denuded areas were partially or completely refeathered. Accordingly, I eventually ceased to give Homer anything but carefully monitored access to Heloise. Helena, on the other hand, exhibited no such behavior until her 5th brood (2 chicks), when she adopted precisely the same predilections for picking and chewing feathers, doubtless through Homer's continuing example.

FEATHER-PICKING CEASES----FLEDGLING TOLERATED WITH NESTLINGS. Finally, when Heloise was 2 months old, Homer not only ceased to feather-pick her, he tolerated her visits in the nest with the chicks of the next brood, beginning when they were 7 days old and continuing throughout brooding. Furthermore, he never exhibited possessiveness or antagonism by Mandible-fluttering or threatening her as she approached, which was his customary initial response when his mate Helena came near. On these occasions, Heloise took no interest in, nor even gave a sign of noticing, the nestlings, whereas, in the same circumstances, eggs often are objects of interest.

The Third Clutch and Brood of Helena and Homer

The 2nd egg of the 3rd clutch of Helena and Homer hatched in the late afternoon or early evening of July 8, 1985, I was aware that hatching was imminent, since during the morning the chick had begun to emit loud distress calls from within its shell when Homer left the clutch briefly on hearing the excitement caused by the flighting of Helena and Heloise. The latter had been housed separately 7 days earlier to spare her from Homer's feather-picking. When I discovered the presence of the hatchling at 19:45 h, it lay off to the front and side of Homer as he incubated the remaining 2 eggs. It was not yet dry and was receiving no care from Homer. Rather, Homer seemed annoyed by it and kept picking at it and pushing it away when it approached in the course of kicking and flopping about.

This was precisely the manner in which Homer had treated the weakened 1st hatchling of the 2nd brood, which eventually succumbed from lack of attention. I began to wonder whether a similar fate lay in store for this hatchling. I realized, of course, that, insofar as allofeeding was concerned, it would not be fed, because it could not yet sit up, which seemed to be a prerequisite for hatchlings. However, since Homer then was an experienced parent, and certainly was in a physiological state of readiness to care for hatchlings, I also entertained the possibility that the chick was not being cared for because it was not yet dry. That also might have been one reason why the weakened first hatchling of the 2nd brood was left unattended through the 1st hours of light after hatching.

My suspicions tended to be confirmed by the fact that when Helena descended several times for her customary periodic inspections of the eggs and nest, she not only ignored the hatchling, but Homer hissed and pecked at her. It was even less likely that Helena also was unprepared to care for a hatchling, and I knew from previous experiences that when a male Cockatiel is inadequate to a task, he welcomes, and even urges, the mediation of his mate. At any rate, Homer continually fidgeted restlessly on the eggs, endlessly shuffling about himself and repositioning the eggs under himself.

Homer's behavior during the next 60 min suggested that the sight and feel of the dry yellow down can elicit the sheltering response of the parents. Thus, there was no abrupt transition from ignoring to sheltering the chick. Instead, the transition occurred gradually, as the down dried. At 19:58 h, Homer sheltered the hatchling momentarily under a wing. At 20:17 h, Helena visited the nest and pecked at the hatchling and the shavings, as Homer pecked her away. By 20:25 h, the chick was under a wing and an egg, instead, was exposed. Homer still would not allow Helena to visit the nest unmolestedly; he kept pecking her away though she persisted tenaciously.

By 20:45 h, the chick was being sheltered frequently but not continuously. By 21:20 h, the hatchling was receiving more or less continuous care and Helena was being tolerated alongside Homer, with the hatchling between them. At 21:28 h (about 3 h after hatching), the hatchling received its 1st, but very light, meal, mostly from Helena. Apparently the chick could sit up to be allofed at that time, but it was out of my sight. At 22:00 h, Helena was eating voraciously, presumably stocking up for the night. By 22:30 h, I was convinced that the chick was receiving essentially normal care and that all the behavior I had witnessed fell within the range of normal behavior. The next morning the chick was found to be in excellent condition, fully fluffed. Homer wasted little time in taking over its care--within 10 min of lights-on, nor was he seen to leave the nest even once during the day.

Care of the chick during the 2nd day was very attentive. It more or less duplicated that already described for Heloise, the 2nd and only survivor of the 2 chicks of the 2nd brood, except that the crop could be seen to be holding almost purely liquid food. The morning of the 3rd day was distinguished by the hatching of the 3rd egg between 10:00 and 11:00 h. Within a few min after hatching, this chick not only could sit up momentarily but it was vigorously kicking and crawling about on all fours.

The hatchling received very little attention in the 1st 10 min after I detected its presence, as the parents tended almost exclusively to the needs of the older chick. However, Homer shortly thereafter began to brood the hatchling, despite the fact that it still was quite moist. By 11:40 h, this hatchling, still far from dry, was able to sit up steadily and was allofed small amounts of liquid spontaneously by Homer, even without the preliminary of the chick's soliciting by cheeping. As usual, with hatchlings and very young chicks, when the parent relinquished its hold and withdrew its bill to prepare to deliver another portion of food, the chick usually fell over forward and had to regain its footing.

After the hatchling's very light 1st meal it was brooded again by Homer, with Helena sitting close by for much of the remainder of the day. At 12:40 h it received its 2nd very light meal from both parents, and its 3rd still-very-light meal at 13:00 h, when almost dry. At 14:00 h, I noticed it struggling to sit up at Homer's side, but not very successfully. Finally, at 14:20 h, it received its first good-sized meal, trickle-fed by Homer. When Helena, who was temporarily out of the nest, heard the chick cheeping as it was allofed, she descended hastily and contributed a small amount after Homer ceased allofeeding. After several small intervening allofeedings, the hatchling received its 2nd large meal, this time from Helena (at 16:58 h), mostly also by trickle-feeding. At the same time Homer allofed the 2-day-old chick. During subsequent days, Helena spent much less time in the nest with Homer and the chicks. On a number of occasions when she was perched outside and above, she hastened down to the nest and joined-in allofeeding the chicks when she heard Homer begin to allofeed them. She was less welcome to do so at other times.

Allofeeding of the chicks on the following day was by trickling and tongue-flicking in roughly equal amounts. It was during one of these allofeedings, in which both parents participated, that I first observed transfer of food, albeit for very brief periods, between Helena and Homer. The precise exchanges could not be ascertained with certainty, except for one instance, when Helena removed a glob of food adhering to the surface of Homer's bill. As I often had noted before, the act of allofeeding a chick by one parent in the presence of the other, seemed to be taken by the other as an invitation to participate also, and even to displace the one. Consequently, whenever both parents were present and only one chick was being allofed, feeding often took the form of a competitive participation in which both parents pressed forward continually. It is during such interactions that one is most likely to observe the simultaneous allofeeding of a single chick by both parents.

CHICKS 5-7 DAYS OLD ALLOFED IN ALTERNATION. With only 2 chicks present, Homer customarily alternated in allofeeding them with single regurgitations, first allofeeding one and then turning to the other. I once saw him alternate 5 times (i.e., 5 feedings of each) before a repetition of 2 successive regurgitations with the same chick. During the course of these alternations the chick that was not being allofed at the time usually waited its turn, with its head close by, without trying to push in prematurely. In fact, it sometimes even shied away from the vigorous movement. Occasionally a waiting chick reached upward as it explored with its bill. Upon penetrating the gap between the parent's mandibles, the regurgitation to another chick usually was interrupted. The youngest of the 2 chicks of this brood had an anomalous voice at the time and sometimes scarcely made a sound while being allofed by vigorous pumping.

CHICKS 1-3 DAYS OLD ALLOFED IN SEPARATE BOUTS. I first took note of Homer's habit of allofeeding the 2 chicks in alternation when they were 5 and 7 days old, and became quite familiar with it thereafter. Accordingly, his behavior contrasted all the more sharply 2 months later, when he was allofeeding the 2 chicks of the next brood on the morning when they were only 1 and 3 days old. During that bout of tongue-flick allofeeding, both chicks stood before him in the soliciting posture but he allofed only the 3-day-old chick, in a total of about 8 successive regurgitations. About midway between these feedings, after withdrawing from the older chick and mandibulating, he grasped the young chick's bill as if also to allofeed it. But he withdrew immediately, as if in error, and resumed allofeeding the older chick.

Inasmuch as the younger chick also was sitting up and soliciting to be allofed (by reaching upward with its bill) the interpretation of Homer's behavior seems fairly clear. It would appear that the food that Homer was delivering to the older chick was insufficiently digested, liquified, or merely filtered, to be suitable for the younger chick. Rather than "shift gears" at the time, Homer (or perhaps Helena) allofed the younger chick later. That same evening I twice more witnessed bouts of tongue-flick allofeeding of the chicks by Homer. In both bouts he allofed the older chick 5 or 6 regurgitations but allofed the younger one only once, briefly, or not at all. In a 3rd, following, bout, he allofed the younger chick 5 regurgitations. By the following day, Homer (and Helena) had resumed tongue-flick allofeeding the chicks in brief alternating regurgitations, but the young also were being trickle-fed--particularly by Helena--in individual bouts that usually lasted over 30 sec.

ONCE INITIATED, ALLOFEEDING CONTINUES IN TOTAL DARKNESS. Inasmuch as Homer often began to "load up" the chicks for the night not much later than 22:00 h, a full 4½ hours before the lights were to be extinguished, I took advantage of his concerted allofeeding bouts to ascertain whether allofeeding of the chicks would proceed in total darkness. The answer was an unequivocal "yes," provided only that Homer was in the process of allofeeding them at the time the lights were extinguished, with the chicks in very close proximity. Regurgitation after regurgitation continued in total darkness. It seems somewhat unlikely, however, that the chicks would be allofed so expeditiously, if at all, in total darkness if they were not close by and Homer had to seek them out.

CONCERTED FEATHER-PICKING BY HOMER. No sooner were feather quills of appreciable size present (at age 10-12 days) than Homer began feather-picking the wings of both chicks. Thereupon, I housed him separately during nights, for most of the day, and during all of my absences. At first, I returned him to the family enclosure for a few min roughly every 2 h during the day to assist in the allofeeding of the chicks. Inasmuch as allofeeding them usually took precedence over feather-picking them, this could be done at a cost of 2 or 3 feathers per chick per allofeeding bout, whereas had he been permitted to remain with them at all times, he might have denuded them within 1 or 2 days. Gradually, however, he allofed less and feather-picked with increasing tenacity.

At 16-18 days of age, I restricted Homer's visits with the chicks to mornings and late afternoons or evenings. Nor was either Helena or Heloise immune to his attentions. On one occasion he plucked a bill full of feathers from the back of Helena's neck (in time, he denuded a small area of her back at the base of the neck), and on several occasions he picked feathers from Heloise. It was evident, however, that he derived little sustenance from these feathers, and he confined almost all his attentions to picking the rapidly-growing feathers of the chicks. It is noteworthy, however, that nest preparation took priority over feather-picking. Thus, as Helena and Homer approached the next breeding cycle, Homer tended to alternate between allofeeding the chicks and nest preparation. But if a chick approached too closely as he "fussed about" in the nest, it was bound to lose feathers.

ANOTHER FEATHER-PICKING TECHNIQUE. Once the chicks were well-feathered but prior to fledging, I restored Homer to the enclosure more or less continuously. His feather-picking then was confined, at first, to awkwardly snatching feathers from the chicks forebreast, abdominal, vent, or ventral uropygial areas, for it was only these late-appearing coverts that could be grasped easily by their still exposed shafts and extracted with their bases attached. However, as these bases became covered and inaccessible, Homer quickly learned to nuzzle his bill down into the chick's dorsal coverts and spread them enough to see (or feel) and grasp the bases of feathers there, with resulting continued losses.

One of the definitive results that emerged from housing the 2nd (Heloise) and 3rd (Julian and Marcus) broods of Helena and Homer together throughout the period of incubating, brooding, and fledging of the 3rd brood occurred in the period 7 days prior to and during the period of fledging of the chicks. Homer had begun to "brood the nest" and spent hours "fussing about" in it, and he also had copulated at least once with Helena. During this period, Heloise (the sole chick of the 2nd brood) was repelled vigorously from the nest and nest area whenever she attempted to enter it or even to come near while Homer occupied it. Julian and Marcus, on the other hand, were tolerated completely. During the earlier period, in the days before the chicks had left the nest, Heloise never was seen to try to enter it.

The Fourth Brood of Helena and Homer

The rearing of a 4th brood of 2 chicks (the first of 3 eggs was infertile) was begun by Helena and Homer precisely 8 weeks later, whereupon all their chick-care behavior and feather-picking by Homer, described above, were repeated, except as otherwise noted. Again, I observed that a hatchling would not be allofed until, as, and when it was able to sit up and solicit food. At first, I gave Homer access to the feathering chicks, whereupon he denuded their backs, shoulders, and breasts by feather-picking. Subsequently, I began isolating him again to give them relief. Another device to spare the young from Homer's attentions was to place them in a 2nd nestbowl, as Homer eventually began to "brood" the main nest frequently. He also continued occasionally to feather-pick Helena.

PARENTAL RECOGNITION OF CHICK VOCALIZATIONS. Inasmuch as the chicks of the 6th brood of Carmen and Cosimo were being reared in the upper portion of enclosure A, directly above, and were only 6 days younger than the 2 chicks of the 4th brood, many opportunities were afforded to confirm that Helena and Homer could recognize the distress calls and appearance of their own chicks, as opposed to those of Carmen and Cosimo, and vice versa. However, the parents became agitated on hearing the calls or seeing the young being flighted only during the 2 weeks or so spanning the fledging period. For example, when the 2 chicks of Helena and Homer were housed out of sight in enclosure N, just above enclosure A, they, particularly Homer, became greatly agitated when the chicks cried out in distress when I handled them or when they were harassed by Budgerigars or lovebirds, but not when the chicks of Carmen and Cosimo cried out in similar circumstances.

On another occasion, I flighted Helena and the 5 offspring of her 2nd, 3rd, and 4th broods. All through the noise and excitement of their flighting, including panics, as Cockatiels cried out on being harassed by lovebirds on whose enclosures they had alighted, Carmen and Cosimo showed no more than normal interest, but the moment I added a separately-housed juvenile from their 6th brood to the group and it gave a distress call, Carmen and Cosimo became greatly agitated, vocalized, and climbed about on the front face of their enclosure. When the juvenile quieted down, so too did they. [For the care of the 5th brood of Helena and Homer, see pp. 497-510, **The Fifth Clutch and Brood of Helena and Homer.**]

Unassisted Care of a Fresh Hatchling

On January 22, 1987, I had the unusual opportunity to observe Carmen's unassisted care of the 1st hatchling of her 10th brood and her 1st undisputed allofeedings of it. During the previous 24 h I was alerted to an imminent hatching by the parents' great excitement and attentiveness to the eggs. At noon on the 22nd, I opened the door to enclosure A (lower section) with the intention of flighting Carmen and Cosimo and examining the eggs. Although Cosimo was competing with Carmen for the eggs at the time, he accepted the invitation but Carmen remained steadfast on the eggs.

At 12:55 h I was alerted to the hatching by the sight of a shell cap off to Carmen's side. Although the chick had hatched sometime after 12:30 h, and was not yet thoroughly dry, it was sufficiently coordinated to receive a first very light trickle-fed meal at 13:35, a 2nd more substantial one at 14:15 h, a 3rd one at 15:06 h, and a 4th at 15:32 h. Meanwhile, amidst the colony noise and excitement, Cosimo was unaware of the events occurring in enclosure A and showed no inclination to return.

When Cosimo eventually did enter the enclosure at 16:20 h, he received a most unwelcome reception, including hisses, very vigorous threats, and very sharp pecks, amidst a great deal of mutual Mandible-fluttering. After about 3 min of contesting for the chick and eggs, he succeeded in acquiring them from Carmen, and she went off to eat. Cosimo trickle-fed the hatchling briefly at 16:45 h. This was the only time I had the opportunity to witness the unassisted and uncontested care of a hatchling by a solitary parent or had seen such a relatively prompt series of 1st allofeedings, albeit only relatively light and brief ones. Often the parents are busily occupied competing for a fresh hatchling and the eggs, and the 1st allofeeding may not occur until after several hours.

PART 2. PEACH-FACED LOVEBIRDS

CARE OF EGGS BY PEACH-FACED LOVEBIRDS

The female lovebird of all species is the sole incubator of the eggs, and this is thought to be true of all members of the subfamily psittaculinae, to which lovebirds belong (27). Accordingly, the treatment of Peach-faced Lovebird egg-care is much simplified compared to that for Cockatiels, since there is no nest exchange between one parent and the other or consequent competition for the eggs. Males are not known to incubate the eggs or care for them actively in any way (except for eating and/or discarding the shells).

For example, in the care of the 2nd clutch of Cassandra and Cyrus, which was incubated in a NB with a Plexiglas sidepane, when Cyrus was alone in the NB guarding the eggs, he usually gave them a wide berth; he stood or sat off to the side or rear of the IA. In the case of pairs breeding in an open nestbowl, however, I found it not to be unusual for the male, Cyrus included, to stand over the eggs in the female's absence. Although lovebirds were not tested as extensively as Cockatiels for relict egg-care responses, they too have retained a number of those that are found in Cockatiels. [Only the crippled, and therefore clumsy, Titus, sat on eggs, unintentionally, as he crowded into the small nestbowl at the side of his mate, Flavia.]

Literature Accounts

NEST SITE AND ITS DEFENSE. Dominance in parrots is known to be correlated with nest-site selection and defense. Adult lovebirds show an interest in possible nesting sites soon after they form pair bonds; juvenile pairs do so soon after attaining their adult plumage. The female--the dominant sex--investigates entrance holes and chooses a suitable cavity within which to build a cup-like nest. She alone prepares and brings in the nesting material (see p. 259). The male remains close to her through these proceeedings, but his interest seems to focus on her, rather than on matters pertaining to the nest site. The resident pair defends a NB but often allows others to sit on top of it. Members of both sexes attack intruders, but most of the defense of the entrance hole falls to the male, presumably because the female usually is occupied with incubating and brooding (3).

OVIPOSITION AND CLUTCH SIZE. The eggs normally are laid at roughly 2-day intervals, but this is subject to variation with season, temperature, and quality of food (27). Occasionally, 2 eggs are laid on successive days, and, rarely, 2 days may elapse between ovipositions. The size of the clutch is 3-8 eggs, depending largely on the age of the hen and the quality of her nourishment. [It is said that some breeding pairs do not sample greens and other supplements (27); my birds took avidly to celery and corn.] Young birds not uncommonly lay only 3 eggs in their 1st clutch. It is well known that, in the absence of a NB, females may oviposit and attempt to nest on the enclosure floor (787).

CLUTCH-SIZE REGULATION---DETERMINATE LAYERS. Laparotomies (ovarian scannings) have been performed on birds that had just completed their clutches. From the existence of regressing (atretic) ovarian follicles (the forerunners of the eggs) of graded sizes, it appears that, unlike the situation in Budgerigars, clutch size may not be determined by a certain predetermined number of follicles becoming active. Rather, it would appear that some physiological mechanism cuts off the supply of hormones to the active ovary, and so terminates an otherwise continuous progression of follicular ripening and oviposition (3). [The normal progress of an "egg" down the oviduct seemingly can be checked, and even "reversed," at any stage of maturation (135).] As with all parrots, lovebirds are determinate layers, that is, they cannot be induced to continue to oviposit by removing the eggs as they are laid (see pp. 165, 166, **The Distinction between Determinate and Indeterminate Layers**).

COMMENCEMENT OF INCUBATION---INCUBATORY PERIOD. Some observers find that Peach-faced Lovebird hens begin to incubate immediately on laying the 1st egg, others find that incubation does not begin until after the laying of the 2nd or 3rd egg (834). The incubatory period generally ranges from 21 to 24 days. As is usually the case, the period is lengthened in cold weather. Some Maked Lovebird hens (A. p. personata) are said to begin incubating the 1st egg, others do not begin to incubate until the clutch is nearly complete (27). Fischer's Lovebird hens are said to begin incubating after laying the 2nd or 3rd egg (834). Moreau was of the impression that incubation by lovebirds generally began with the 1st or 2nd egg (12).

However, the fact that a bird sits over eggs is not necessarily an indication that the eggs are being incubated. It is known that some doves, for example [and at times, male Goshawks, even though lacking an incubatory patch], may sit over their eggs without heating them (28). Moreover, the present studies have shown that, unless the posture and elevation of the sitting bird are known, conclusions as to whether the eggs are being incubated are mere guesswork. Often birds sitting within nestboxes merely shield or guard the eggs--the equivalent of the 2nd phylogenetic stage of egg care (see p. 511).

INCUBATING EGGS---ABSENCES FROM THE NESTBOX. Though only the hen incubates the eggs, the male often sits in the NB with her, close against her side and facing in the same direction, but not encroaching upon the eggs (3). He often allofeeds her in this position--providing most, perhaps sometimes all, of her food during the early portion of the incubatory period. He not infrequently spends the entire night with her.

When the hen occasionally--perhaps 3 or 4 times per day--exits the NB briefly to eat, drink, or void (the egesta being especially voluminous at that time), she ordinarily also engages in an intense session of comfort movements. Then she takes a few moments to strip and tuck nesting material for one or more trips to the nest. When disturbed in the NB, the parents often either merely cower, with their heads lying flat on the bottom, or they flee through the entrance (3).

PRE-HATCHING SOUNDS, PIPPING, HATCHING. The developing chick can be heard cheeping, beginning about 2 days before it is due to hatch (3, 27). One also can hear very faint ticking or clicking sounds produced by bill clapping or respiratory movements (see pp. 172, 191). The eggs may pip as early as 48 h before hatching, as the egg tooth cuts through the shell. The egg becomes fractured in a circle running around its blunt end. As soon as the end is free, the chick's head falls out and moves about freely. The chick then frees itself completely by kicking vigorously with its legs (3). The inside of the smaller end of the shell is found to contain a bit of dry feces. The natal down, which is much less abundant than on Cockatielian hatchlings, dries rapidly, and the chick is said to be allofed within about 60 min.

MAINTAINING PROPER HUMIDITY. There is not complete accord on either the need for, nor the best way of providing, moisture to prevent the eggs from desiccating (see discussion in 27). Since inspection of the NB is common practice, and generally has no ill effect, breeders commonly spray the eggs. Silva and Kotlar recommend a heavy spraying of the sides of the NB and of the nesting material (7).

After one of the chicks kicked through a shell that was too soft, I ceased spraying the eggs. Rather, I adopted the practice of injecting water (with a dropper), either down the side-corners of the NB into the shavings, or directly into the shavings (to keep the humidity high), with occasional very light misting of the eggs (for Cockatiels and Budgerigars, as well). I used a similar procedure with eggs being incubated in open nestbowls. However, I also found that roughly 50% of the fertile eggs of 5 lovebird clutches hatched when incubated in the open on enclosure floors at a relative humidity of 35-50%, even without supplemental moistening (see Table 4, clutches labelled "unfacilitated").

The Present Findings

SYNOPSIS OF PARENTAL BEHAVIOR PRECEDING AND DURING INCUBATION

PRELIMINARIES. Coitus often takes place several times per day, may consume as many as 5-6 min per session, may occur daily during the period of oviposition, may precede oviposition by many days, and may be preceded (most frequently) or followed (least frequently) by courtship activity, such as courtship feeding (in which the male feeds the female). [In the 3 primitive lovebird species, the Madagascar, Abyssinian, and Red-faced Lovebirds, the female sometimes courtship-feeds the male (3, 4, 27).] These long and frequent sexual unions apparently serve several functions: maintenance of the pair bond, arousal and synchronization of the reproductive physiologies of the pair, and bringing together of the sex cells (4).

If nest-building materials are available (I provided paper, wood shavings, and the exterior cloth coverings of the enclosures), a great deal of time usually is spent by the female in the acts of stripping, tucking, and transporting such material to the nest area or NB, and building or lining a nest.

PREPARING AND SITTING IN THE NEST. The male usually follows the female around during these activities and copies her actions, with varying degrees of success. Some of my males eventually became proficient at all 3 activities, stripping, tucking, and transporting, through observation and practice. However, their strips never were uniform like those prepared by a female, as uniformity is a detail that either cannot be reproduced by, or escapes the notice or ‘concern’ of, the males. The hen usually spends long periods sitting in the nest, with or without eggs, chewing and softening the nesting materials, whether they require further processing or not.

The male does not sit alone in an empty nest (i.e., in the absence of either the female or a clutch) and engage in such activity, but he may sit beside the hen and allogroom and allofeed her, particularly after incubation has begun. Except during the first few nights, males infrequently spent the night in the nest with their mates during the incubatory period. They usually entered early in the morning (sometimes after lights-on and sometimes before) and allogroomed and allofed them. During the day, though, they sometimes spent long periods in the NB. When the hens nested in the open on the enclosure floor or in nestbowls, the male not infrequently spent the night in the nest with the female. Titus, the crippled male, invariably did so.

SITTING ON THE EGGS. When the hen can be watched as she incubates in open nestbowls and "transparent" NBs, one finds reason to question beliefs based only on observations of presence in the NB. I refer specifically to the assumption that the hen always, or even usually, sits tightly on the eggs (i.e., incubates) beginning with the 1st or 2nd egg. Nor is it likely that the practice is uniform among different hens, among hens of different ages, or for the same hen with different clutches (recall the variation among Masked Lovebird hens mentioned above). Although the practice is not as marked as that of Cockatiels (see p. 416, **Loose Sitting for First Few Days**), there is a tendency to sit on the 1st few eggs less tightly than on later ones. Inexperienced hens are least attentive.

In cases where I was removing the eggs as they were laid, in usually unsuccessful attempts to discourage continued oviposition, I always could tell that a 3rd, 4th, 5th, etc., egg had been laid. In that event, the hen's body was tightly pressed into the nest, whereas the 1st and 2nd eggs sometimes even were found unattended.

DISCARDING DEFECTIVE EGGS. Light (dried out) eggs, damaged eggs, and plastic balls sometimes were discarded by the hen, usually by vigorous backward kicks that "sent them flying". This usually occurred after a fresh egg was laid, suggesting that the hens were able to detect faulty eggs and egg substitutes most readily when a fresh bona fide egg was present and provided a basis for comparison. [Such comparisons of eggs would not be unprecedented. A case even is known of a Garden Warbler (*Sylvia borin*) female that discarded her own 4th egg after her first 3 eggs had been replaced with dissimilar ones, presumably because it appeared to be abnormal in the presence of the other 3 (see B. Rensch, 1925, in 28).]

Previously discarded eggs were accepted again by lovebird hens after a freshly laid egg was removed. But if one of the substitute eggs was of normal weight, any accompanying eggs that were light were at risk to be discarded. Empty, but complete shells (having had their contents blown out) were almost certain to be cast out of the nest.

CONTRASTING EGG CARE IN OPEN AND ENCLOSED NESTS. Two observations of parental behavior during incubation were very impressive--one of a female, the other of males. Cassandra (and, to lesser degree, Petra) was responsible for the first of these. By way of introduction, half or more of the lovebird clutches were oviposited despite my failure to facilitate the breeding of paired birds. On such occasions, no NB was provided, and there was no supplemental nutritional allowance, not even cuttlebone or a mineral block. The latter items were provided only to safeguard the health of the hens after preventive measures had failed and oviposition had begun.

MARKED CHANGE IN EGG CARE. One aspect of Cassandra's behavior that impressed me was the marked change in her egg-care behavior in open nests. Whereas she was inattentive with the eggs of her 1st 2 clutches, both as to covering them properly and as to keeping them covered, the 3rd and 4th clutches were covered most attentively in both respects. With the latter 2 clutches, Cassandra could not be tempted from the eggs, even by the otherwise irresistible opportunity to be flighted. Nor could she be frightened from them by my presence, whereas she left the 1st 2 clutches if I even came near the enclosure. On the only two noted occasions when she left the eggs, it was for brief moments to bring nearby twigs of spray millet into the NB. Such highly attentive covering of the eggs by experienced hens in open nests takes on great significance when compared with the comparatively nonchalant treatment accorded to clutches in opaque NBs (see below).

GENTLE, THOROUGH, ATTENTIVE ALLOGROOMING BY THE MALE. The other impressive aspect was provided by the mates of incubating and brooding females. All observers have noted that the male allofeeds the sitting hen and even may provide her sole food during the early period of incubation. When one can observe the breeding pair continually in the NB or an open nest, one sees another function that males perform during their long sojourns in the nest. The males allogroom the females most gently, most attentively, and most thoroughly, and sometimes interminably; they do so without solicitation. Every exposed part of the hen's body is attended to, reminiscent of a masseur's attentions. Unlike the situation with Cockatiels, where unwelcome, excessive grooming is employed (carried out almost exclusively by the male) to drive the mate from the eggs or NB, the female lovebird appears always to welcome the male's grooming attentions. [I would suggest that the lengthy allogrooming of the sitting lovebird hen by her mate had its origin, in past times, in the allogrooming of the sitting bird by the mate as a tactic to displace the hen from the eggs, at a time when the eggs were incubated by members of both sexes.]

RELICT EGG-CARE RESPONSES

RELUCTANCE TO LEAVE EXPOSED, BUT NOT UNEXPOSED, EGGS. A comparison of the incubatory practices of Peach-faced Lovebirds in open nests and "transparent" NBs, with those in opaque NBs, disclosed striking differences. In closed NBs, a hen easily was coaxed from the NB, say, by the offer of flighting or spray millet, and might leave it for short periods many times per diem (see p. 735). On the contrary, in open nests and "transparent" NBs, an experienced, incubating hen was extremely reluctant to leave the eggs. For example, as mentioned above, Cassandra would leave an open nest-bowl only momentarily to obtain a nearby twig of spray millet. She would leave a "transparent" NB readily only after constructing an effective shield for the eggs. This latter behavior appears to harken back to times when avian ancestors nested on the ground, where eggs exposed during the day would be at risk to predation and, at certain times, to overheating.

SEARCH FOR, RECOVER MISSING EGGS---ROUTINELY SEARCH INCUBATIVE AREA. If all the eggs of a clutch are removed, the lovebird hen takes note of their absence even before entering the NB, performs visual searches for them (both from a fixed position and on foot), searches for them by nuzzling and plowing in the IA, resurfaces any eggs that are found, and returns them to the established IA. The sitting hen routinely searches the substratum of the IA and its near vicinity. When buried eggs are found, they are resurfaced and gathered in. It may take many hours to find eggs that are buried at a considerable depth or "far out" on the periphery of the IA. These responses appear to be relics of former adaptations of ancestors of birds for nesting in surface scrapes on a flat, level, yielding substratum, in which eggs easily could become displaced or buried.

The First and Second Clutches of Petra and Ramses

COPULATIONS AND EARLY ACTIVITY IN THE NESTBOX. For the 1st clutch of Petra and Ramses, laid in the summer of 1982, the NB was located on the enclosure floor. Three eggs were laid in it but these were poorly cared for and soon abandoned (Petra was barely 7 months old at the time). In the case of the 2nd clutch, the NB opened into the enclosure from the outside at the upper-right rear (Fig. 1a). Sexual unions were noted on the 3 days before and after the laying of the 1st 2 eggs (Oct. 22 and 24, 1982). The pair copulated at least twice on the 1st 2 of these days but Petra was receptive to Ramses on only one of 3 observed attempts on the 3rd day.

The birds often stirred up a great ruckus together in the NB during the 1st few days of incubation. The dominant female may still be feeding herself at this time. She often is very possessive over the NB and eggs, and reluctant to let the male enter or remain in the NB. She is even more domineering and exclusive in the NB before oviposition begins, when the NB is being explored and readied for use.

MALE GUARDS EGGS--SPENDS EARLY MORNING HOURS IN NESTBOX. By the 12th day of incubation, Petra had resumed partly feeding herself and spending a moderate amount of time out of the NB stripping paper. Ramses often occupied the NB at these times but, of course, I had no way of telling what he was doing inside. [From later observations of Cassandra and Cyrus in a NB with a Plexiglas sidepane and of clutches incubated in the open on enclosure floors, it was found that the male often guards the eggs at such times.] Although Ramses sometimes tried to mount Petra at that time, she repelled his advances. During this period, and after the eggs had begun to hatch, Ramses always entered the NB early in the morning. Perhaps this occurred around sunrise, but, at any rate, it was long before lights-on. He and Petra made a great deal of noise on these occasions, and Ramses often did not emerge for 1 or 2 h after lights-on.

HATCHING. Since the fertile eggs hatched on an essentially every-other-day schedule, it would appear that Petra had incubated the eggs beginning with the 1st one. The shells disappeared rapidly, generally having been eaten rather than broken up. The 2nd egg proved to be infertile and the 5th produced a chick that kicked a hole in the shell and needed aid to complete hatching (the egg shell was too soft from being excessively humidified). Neither this hatchling nor its youngest broodmate survived, leaving only the 2 males, Jagatai and Ogadai.

The Third Clutch of Petra and Ramses

UNUSUAL SITES FOR COITUS. The brood of the 3rd clutch of this pair may have been conceived on my shoulder and/or in my hair. I was flighting

Petra and Ramses daily, and they had adopted the habit of climbing about on me while I was servicing the enclosures. Apparently there was something very attractive about a cloth or hairy underfooting for sexual union, because the birds copulated on my shoulder (against my neck) on 2 occasions and in my hair on 2 others (as I watched in a mirror). On one of these occasions, they copulated in my hair in 3 discrete sessions lasting 3-4 min each, with courtship activity occurring in between and preceding copulations, consuming a total time in my hair of almost 20 min. They copulated at least another 4 times in the enclosure after the 1st egg was laid (on Dec. 27, 1982). [Mock copulatory movements of male Budgerigars on the finger or in the hair of an owner also are known (134).]

COURTSHIP TRICKLE-FEEDING. At about this time, and many times thereafter, I first noted a type of courtship feeding that appears not to have been described previously in lovebirds. After courtship-feeding Petra by the usual head-bobbing procedure, Ramses sometimes was seen to have "locked" his mandibles with hers. Both birds then began to vibrate their mandibles and heads rapidly, perhaps at 10-20 Hz. Sessions of these vibrations lasted as long as several min, during the course of which seeds occasionally were seen to be carried between the birds' mouths on saliva strings.

This was not noted in another pair until Flavia and Titus engaged in it while incubating their 1st clutch (which was infertile). Thereafter I noticed its occurrence frequently during both courtship and brooding by all breeding pairs. On several occasions I was able to see a head-bobbing allofeeding session transform gradually to one of trickle-feeding. Only after I saw nestlings being allofed in an almost identical manner, but with generally slower vibrations, did I realize that this was a method of courtship-feeding predominantly liquid food. [See p. 677 for observations of related behavior in other species.]

Feeding liquid, as opposed to semi-liquid or soft, food to adults is quite superfluous. It is only hatchlings and young nestlings that require liquid food. Accordingly, this behavior strongly suggests that one of the functions of courtship feeding is preparation and practice for the impending care of young chicks.

OVIPOSITION AND INCUBATION. Five eggs were laid, one every other day. The 1st 3 of these were replaced with 1¼-cm-diameter polyethylene balls, in an effort to synchronize the clutch. With the laying of the 4th egg, the 1st 3 were restored and incubation of the clutch began. To follow the orientation of the eggs, I marked them with dots opposite their identification numbers. To my surprise, egg orientation was altered very frequently, dozens of times per diem, even in the absence of competition for them. As noted above, lovebird hens also routinely search the neighborhood of the IA, just as do Cockatiels. They even will find and resurface eggs buried directly under the eggs of the clutch.

HATCHING. Of the 5 eggs of this clutch, the last 4 were fertile and produced 4 chicks, one of which was lost through an allofeeding mishap (see p. 749, **Suffocation of a Chick**). The first 2 hatchings (eggs #2 and #3) occurred on the same day, and the last 2, 1 and 2 days later. The members of this brood were the principal objects of the study described in Chapter 3, namely, Cassandra, Cyrus, and Cyrano. Cassandra and Cyrus also became the 2nd lovebird pair to breed (see pp. 732, 757).

The Fourth Clutch of Petra and Ramses

NEST BUILDING. Breeding by Petra and Ramses was not facilitated after they reared the 2nd brood. However, I flighted them almost daily in the presence of ample nesting material. Apparently an experienced, habituated mated pair in these circumstances, and in otherwise favorable surroundings, will breed regardless of unsupplemented nutrition and the absence of a NB. Petra began to oviposit again in early March but ceased after I removed 3 eggs.

By July 1, 1983, Petra had begun to build a nest on the floor in the right-rear corner of the enclosure, using paper that I had provided as raw material. She did this by stuffing and weaving the paper strips into the 1¼- x 2½-cm-mesh hardware cloth walls. [Unsuccessful attempts to weave strips of paper into the wire mesh of an enclosure have been noted in lovebird hybrids, but were regarded as anomalous behavior (1,156; see also pp. 528, 529).] Although I sought to deter breeding by removing the paper stock from the enclosure, it was too late; egg maturation already had begun. When I returned the paper, both Petra and Ramses pounced upon it immediately and resumed shredding and stripping it. Having decided to allow them to breed, I gave them appropriate nutritional supplements and snuggly covered the outside corner of the enclosure by their nest site.

"BROODING" THE OPEN NEST. By July 5, 1983, Petra was "brooding" the empty nest most of the day, incessantly chewing paper; Ramses stood guard over its environs, preventing intrusions by Cassandra, Cyrus, or Cyrano, then 6 months old. The juveniles quickly learned to give the area a wide berth. [Members of other lovebird species may be much more tolerant of essentially mature offspring while caring for another brood. In one case, a male Abyssinian Lovebird and his two 9-month old sons shared the NB with the brooding hen, and all 3 males participated in the allofeeding of the chicks (27).] During those days, Petra rushed out to attack me whenever I renewed supplies, and she was not averse to giving me a good nip.

OVIPOSITION---SUBSTITUTING PLASTIC BALLS FOR EGGS. I replaced each of the 1st 4 eggs with a plastic ball, as it was laid (every other day, beginning on the morning of July 8). At that time, it was impossible to coax Petra off of the open nest with the usual temptations, whereas this was achieved readily earlier, when she was incubating in an opaque NB. At most, she would leave the eggs momentarily to stretch. Ramses, of course, was allogrooming her in the very attentive manner described above and supplying most or all of her food. Even with the remainder of the colony in turmoil, Petra and Ramses remained close to the nest and nesting area.

PETRA TAKES BRIEF FLIGHTS---EGGS RESTORED TO NEST. On the day that the 3rd egg was laid, Petra and Ramses joined their 5 offspring when I flighted them, but both parents voluntarily returned to the nest and eggs in less than 8 min. When I flighted the entire family again the day after the 4th egg was laid, I placed the 4 plastic balls in a 3-cm deep bowl lined with paper and shavings. When Petra returned, she backed down onto the "clutch" along the enclosure wall from an upper perch, without seeming to notice the change. She nudged the 4 plastic balls into position with her bill and the side of her head. When I flighted the family during the evening of the next day, I returned Petra's eggs to allow incubation to commence. She took over their care routinely and adjusted their positions with her bill. The 5th (last) egg was laid during the next morning.

HATCHING---ALLOFEEDING HATCHLINGS. The 1st egg proved to be infertile but the 4th egg hatched on the evening of the 21st day (Aug. 6, 1983). Whereas Ramses previously had spent time in the nest only to allogroom and allofeed Petra, he then spent much additional time at her side. As will be seen below (p. 747 *et seq.*), the male plays a vital role during the 1st feedings of hatchlings. The 1st hatchling usually could be seen as it lay prone. By 23:30 h, the 5th egg also had hatched, but the unhatched eggs seemed to be getting most of the attention, rather than the hatchlings.

ALLOFEEDING THE FIRST HATCHLING---THE MALE ALSO VERY ACTIVE. I witnessed the 1st allofeeding of the youngest hatchling 75 min later, as it lay flat on its back under Petra's breast. Although Ramses was very busy at some activity at her side throughout this allofeeding, I could not ascertain, at that time, what his precise role was. [The prevailing, but erroneous, view is that the male does not allofeed the young during the 1st few days, and the similar view regarding Budgerigars also has proved to be erroneous; see 843 and, e.g., pp. 200-203, 752, 766, 767]

TWO EGGS FAIL TO HATCH---FURTHER BREEDING NOT FACILITATED. The 2nd and 3rd eggs contained fully-developed embryos but failed to hatch. [In retrospect, the failures probably traced to the fact that the eggs were stored at room temperature and were not turned.] By August 23, Petra was preparing a 2nd nest in the left-rear corner but, again, I did not facilitate further breeding at that time and removed the nestbowl. The 2 members of this brood were the sisters, Flavia and Zenobia, bringing the total number in the family to 9.

The Fifth Clutch of Petra and Ramses

A PREFERENCE FOR PRIVACY DURING COITUS. Since I wished to make further observations on parental care in an open nest, I facilitated breeding again in January, 1984 (I had aborted another clutch the month before by removing 2 eggs). It was then that I first observed the preference of lovebirds for privacy when copulating. This was on an occasion when Petra and Ramses stayed behind and copulated while Flavia and Zenobia were being flighted (ordinarily, being flighted was preferred over other activities).

OVIPOSITION COMMENCES---INFERTILE EGGS SUBSTITUTED. After I replaced the 1st egg with a infertile lovebird egg and provided a 3-cm deep bowl at the nest site, Petra oviposited again and began to sit on her 2nd egg outside the nestbowl. I also substitued an infertile egg for the 2nd one and placed both eggs in the nestbowl. Petra accepted these and sat them loosely during the day, but seemingly did not sit on them at night (although I did not check periodically during the night).

DEFECTIVE EGGS DISCARDED OR IGNORED---INCUBATION BEGINS. I substituted a light, dried-out lovebird egg for Petra's 3rd egg. Sixty min later, I found this egg discarded in a location that could have been reached only if the egg had been airborne, suggesting that it had received a vigorous kick from the nestbowl. I replaced the discard with another light egg, but found that Petra often left it uncovered while sitting on the other 2 eggs. This did not appear to be an oversight, as she was an experienced hen and could be seen adjusting the positions of the other 2 eggs while ignoring the light one. On the day that the 4th egg was laid, I found her incubating it alone, with all 3 substituted eggs lying unattended at her side. Presumably, Petra could recognize defective eggs when a freshly laid egg was on hand for comparison (see also pp. 733, 734).

After Petra laid the 4th egg, I returned the first 3 eggs, to allow incubation of the clutch to commence. A 5th egg was laid on schedule. Petra was soon seen not to be strictly attentive, even to her fresh eggs, sometimes leaving them partly exposed, or even totally exposed, though only for a few min. [On the other hand, Cassandra, who was incubating her 4th clutch at the same time (also in an open nest), covered her 6 eggs most attentively, shielding any extending portions with her wings.] To humidify this clutch (and Cassandra's), I placed 4 layers of paper toweling on the bottoms of the nestbowls, under the shavings, and moistened the toweling from time to time. The sitting hens did not manipulate the toweling.

FOSTERED HATCHLING NOT ALLOFED. By the 22nd day of incubation, no chick had hatched. The first and 2nd eggs were infertile; the 3rd and 4th developed but failed to hatch (again, probably because of storage at room temperature and lack of turning). At any rate, the 22nd day was a time when Petra and Ramses should have been in condition to care for a hatchling.

At the same time, an egg of Cassandra and Cyrus had just hatched but the parents seemed unable to give the hatchling proper care. When I fostered this already-weak hatchling and its empty shell into Petra's clutch, both parents were attentive to it and also began to eat the shell. But the chick did not cheep for food and they did not allofeed it. When they continued to ignore it, I placed it among Petra's eggs to keep it warm. After 60 min, since they were not attentive to it, I returned it to Cassandra and Cyrus (see pp. 734, 735, **Hatched Chick Cared for Improperly**). This was my first experience of the fact that a lovebird hatchling that did not cheep for food usually would not be allofed.

TITUS HATCHES---SOME PROBLEMS RESOLVED. The 5th egg hatched around 16:30 h the next day. This egg had been examined at 13:30 h and had not yet been pipped. Accordingly, the hatching process had taken less than 3 h (not the day or more, as some assert). Since this chick cheeped, it was cared for normally (in this case, lying flat on its back). Since the brood consisted of but this single chick, Titus (whose social interactions were the topics of Chap. 5), I was able to resolve some of the ambiguities of the care of the previous clutch.

I kept very close watch of the care of this chick. As a result, I was able to perceive, for the 1st time, one of the roles of lovebird parents during the allofeeding of hatchlings and very young nestlings, why this role is vital to the welfare of the young, and how the food probably is apportioned, as regards liquids and solids (see p. 747 *et seq.*, **Tongue-Flick Feeding, Wayward Food, and Clogged Nostrils**).

UNFACILITATED CARE OF CLUTCHES

Habituated, mated lovebird pairs with breeding experience typically continue to attempt to breed when housed together alone, even without NBs, nestbowls, nesting material, or flightings. This was true of all of 6 breeding pairs in the colony (Aspasia and Jagatai, Cassandra and Cyrus, Flavia and Titus, Zenobia and Cyrano, Juliana and Nero, and Petra and Ramses). Eggs typically were laid on the smooth plastic or metal enclosure floor pans in a shallow layer of wood shavings and, if I did not remove them, were incubated to varying degrees. Under these conditions the hens often were unable to cope with their clutches, in the sense that eggs continually were rolling out to the front, sides, and rear, and were subject to long periods of chilling (ambient temperature of 24-27°C; relative humidity 35-50%).

THE FIRST UNFACILITATED CLUTCH of Petra's was her 7th, oviposited during the period of December, 1985 to January, 1986. I removed the 1st 2 eggs but not the last 4. I provided the eggs no care, not even moistening, but Petra was fully attentive to them, except for the fact that she usually could manage them but poorly, as they frequently rolled out from under her. It was during this period that I first noted scratching movements on Petra's part in an apparent effort to prepare a depression for the eggs (see pp. 819, 820, **Scratching on Smooth Surfaces, A Relict Response to Freely-Rolling Eggs**). Petra also frequently mandibulated involuntarily as she rested or slept over the eggs (with eyes closed) just as she often did while chewing on paper or wood in the same posture while awake. The difference was that, with her bill and head resting on the enclosure floor when asleep, her mandibulating led to periodic thumping sounds as one of her mandibles struck the floor.

HATCHLING SUCCUMBS. The hatching deadline for the 3rd egg had come and gone and I had no expectation of seeing a chick, when, on the 26th day, a hatching occurred, 2 days beyond the usual maximum period of 24 days. The hatching occurred normally to all outward appearances, despite the lengthy incubatory period. At first, I made no change in the physical arrangements but, as Petra seemed to show very little interest in the chick, often leaving it to the side uncovered, I supplied a nestbowl on the next day so that it would, at least, be kept warm. Nevertheless, I found it dead the next morning and no further hatching occurred.

SECOND UNFACILITATED CLUTCH---UNUSUAL TIMING OF OVIPOSITION. Only 14 days later, Petra began to lay her 8th clutch on the enclosure floor. This was a most unusual case of egg production, as laying occurred at intervals of 2, 3, and 4 days (Feb. 15, 18, 22, 25, 27). I was not as surprised as before when the 1st egg hatched after 25 days, again despite many lengthy chillings and no moistening. As Petra again appeared to show no interest in the chick (Cleomenes), I supplied a nestbowl during the day of hatching. Inasmuch as Cleomenes was fledged successfully, it is apparent that what sometimes appears to be no parental interest can be deceiving.

The next morning, 2 of the remaining 4 eggs had been displaced somehow from the NB and I did not restore them. Ramses subsequently spent almost every night in the nestbowl with Petra and Cleomenes. Eight days later, I planned to replace the remaining 2 eggs with plastic balls, but heard clicks of bill clapping within one of them. In the late afternoon of the next day, the 24th day of incubation, the clicking seemed to be much fainter and perhaps less frequent. Suspecting that the shell was too hard and that the chick would succumb within it, I moistened the shell thoroughly with warm water, blotted it, and returned it to the nest (on all such occasions, Petra, sometimes joined by Ramses, attacked my gloved hand). On checking 40 min later, empty shells were to be seen and a healthy hatchling was being brooded. Inasmuch as Cleomenes already was 9 days old, I held little hope for the survival of the tiny hatchling (Theocritus, barely larger than Cleomenes' head), although Cassandra and Cyrus had successfully fledged a chick in the presence of a single sibling 7 days older. Again, I was unduly pessimistic as both chicks were cared for most attentively and fledged succesfully, though very heavily feather-picked.

UNFACILITATED CLUTCH IN THE PRESENCE OF FLEDGLINGS. Desiring to explore the possibilities of incubating and brooding in the presence of as-yet-unfledged young of a previous brood in a small enclosure (enclosure M of Fig. 1b), I did not remove Cleomenes and Theocritus (in the previous instances of incubating and brooding young in the presence of the preceding brood, the larger enclosure, B, was used, and the chicks of the preceding broods were much older). On April 28, 1986 Petra laid the 1st egg of another clutch of 5 eggs, at a time when Cleomenes and Theocritus were only about 5-6 weeks old and still were being allofed. After she laid the 4th egg, a nestbowl was provided as the eggs were more than usually unmanageable in the disrupting presence of the 2 juveniles. The latter very frequently sat in the IA with Petra, between her and one or more of the eggs. Inasmuch as the young were tolerated completely by Petra, there was total disorder in the nestbowl despite Petra's persistent efforts to maintain contact with the eggs. As a result all 5 eggs of this clutch eventually became "dimpled" or crushed and none hatched.

UNFACILITATED CLUTCH IN THE PRESENCE OF JUVENILES. On May 29, Petra laid the 1st egg of yet another clutch of 6 eggs. With the appearance of the 3rd egg, 4 days later, I provided a nestbowl again. Being a month older, Cleomenes and Theocritus were spending more time on perches. However, Cleomenes still spent every night in the nestbowl with Petra. Cleomenes also frequently fled in panic to the nestbowl every time I serviced the enclosure. Petra no longer tolerated the juveniles readily, though, but usually sought to bar their entrance or expel them from the nestbowl by biting them on the rump, back, legs, or toes. Ramses also frequently attacked the young when they were on the perches. However, neither parent ever bit hard enough to draw blood. Inasmuch as Cleomenes was very persistent, the enclosure was the scene of very frequent squealing and disorder, and the eggs again were subject to much bumping and jostling.

THREE HATCHINGS. Unlike the situation with the previous clutch, in which all of the eggs were damaged by accidental rough treatment, only 3 of the 6 eggs of the present clutch became crushed or "dimpled." Of the undamaged eggs, hatchings occurred on June 21, 22, and 26. In the case of the 3rd chick, I again noted that the parents seemed to be ignoring it on the day of hatching, despite its cheeps. As long as 7½ h after hatching (at 17:45 h), it had only a trace of food in its crop. Again, as usually was the case in the past with Cockatielian and lovebird hatchlings, appearances were deceiving, as the hatchling eventually was cared for normally.

The presence of the chicks of this brood in no way altered Cleomenes' habit of fleeing to the nest whenever I serviced the enclosure, which I did 5 or 6 times per diem, or of sleeping in the nest with Petra every night. Nor did it alter Petra's practice of attempting vigorously to expel him by pecking and biting him on almost every occasion. At a time when the nestlings were feathering, Cleomenes often sought to mingle closely with them in the morning as the parents sought to feed the chicks. At such times, the most vigorous attacks by Petra were required to dislodge and evict him. As a consequence of the intrusions of the juveniles, all 3 chicks frequently were being stepped on, sat on heavily, displaced and shoved about, and otherwise very much more than usually disturbed. Despite this rough handling, all 3 chicks were fledged successfully.

CLEOMENES TRICKLE-FEEDS PETRA. On the 3rd day after the 1st chick hatched, as Petra began to allofeed the chicks, Cleomenes joined in just as if he were her mate, but I was unable to ascertain whether it was mock participation or whether he actually contributed food. Cleomenes' brother, Theocritus, did not participate but kept well aloof from the nestbowl. Shortly after Petra finished a session of allofeeding, a quite unexpected event occurred, as Cleomenes began to trickle-feed Petra in bouts that lasted many minutes. He also trickle-fed her in lengthy bouts every morning for the next 5 days within tens of sec after lights-on. Ramses sometimes reached into their mouths with his bill and tongue and either contributed or removed liquid, I knew not which, or else he allofed the chicks or waited for Petra and Cleomenes to cease, whereupon he allofed Petra gobs of semi-liquid food. On subsequent days, only Ramses trickle-fed Petra.

One noteable implication of the fact that these 3 healthy chicks were able to survive under the highly adverse conditions described above is the following. Whenever lovebird chicks in a brood no larger than 3 succumb for inapparent reasons in the course of their early nestling days with experienced parents, the problem is more likely to lie in congenital deficiencies in the health of the chicks, rather than in inadequate parental care.

[During allofeeding bouts of Petra by Cleomenes, the latter's upper mandible usually was locked over Petra's lower mandible. On the 6th day, their jaws were widely agape and Cleomenes was seen to be flicking his tongue. There was no constant relationship between the relative levels of their heads, although that of Cleomenes usually was above Petra's. Many months later, as I continued to house the family of 7 together, Cleomenes continued to allofeed, or sometimes merely sought to allofeed, Petra on many occasions, without interference by Ramses. As juveniles, 2 males of this last brood of 3 also occasionally allofed Petra, making a total of 4 males in the family of 7 that sometimes allofed her.]

BASIS FOR JUVENILE PERSISTENCE. It will be recalled that in the previous instances in which Petra incubated eggs and brooded young in the presence of the offspring of previous broods, the offspring (Cassandra, Cyrus, and Cyrano, on the 1st occasion, and Flavia and Zenobia on the 2nd occasion) gave the nest area a wide berth and also were kept away actively or expelled by both Petra and Ramses. In the present case, however, the young frequently were tolerated and usually could be expelled only with the greatest of difficulty. Although in the present circumstance the floor space of the enclosure was only half that on the earlier occasions, the differences in behavior depended rather on the different ages of the offspring. In the 1st 2 cases the offspring were essentually mature, being 6-7 months old, and never were allowed in or near the IA. Consequently, they reacted in a normal manner and fled when they intruded into their parents' breeding area and were attacked.

In the present instance the 2 offspring were only 5-6 weeks old when the 1st clutch was oviposited and 9-10 weeks old at the time the 2nd was laid. Consequently, they were, at first, still using the nest as Petra laid eggs in it, and were tolerated completely by the parents. Thus, having become accustomed to using the nestbowl when it contained the eggs of the 1st clutch, and being tolerated, they were conditioned to doing so at the time the 2nd clutch was oviposited. As a result, when attacked by Petra, in her efforts to drive them (mostly Cleomenes) from the nestbowl, they were unable to perceive her intent, and could be driven from the nest only under the severe pressure of her attacks. An additional possibly pertinent factor is the fact that both Cleomenes and Theocritus had been very extensively feather-picked by Petra and Ramses and thus also were conditioned to the infliction of pain by their parents, which was without objective insofar as actions on their parts were concerned. In other words, they apparently could be driven from the nest only with great difficulty because they were handicapped in their ability to perceive the object of parental attacks.

[Recall, in this connection, that Cosimo experienced similar difficulties in rousting the 2 female juveniles of the 6th brood from the nestbowl while incubating eggs of the next clutch. In that situation grooming of the crissum was to no avail and relatively violent means had to be employed to expel them (see pp. 701, 702, **Cosimo Rousts Young Forcefully from the Nest**).]

OVIPOSITION-SITE FIDELITY

Having observed the remarkable oviposition-site fidelity of a Cockatielian hen in the care of eggs of the 5th brood of Helena and Homer, I investigated the same type of behavior in lovebirds. The opportunity presented itself in October-November, 1985, not long after fledging of the 5th brood of Petra and Ramses in the laboratory, shortly after the related observations with Helena and Homer. Petra and Ramses were being housed in enclosure H (base dimensions, 24 x 30 cm; height, 46 cm). I had previously inverted their 13½-cm-diameter nestbowl in the left-rear corner, so as not to facilitate further breeding. On the morning of October 28, the 1st egg of the next clutch was found in the front-right corner just in front of a food tray which projected 5 cm into the enclosure. Upon detecting it, I righted the nestbowl in the left-rear corner, bedded it with shavings, and placed the egg within it.

The effective area of the enclosure base was only 19 x 30 cm, because of the projecting food and water trays, and the center of the nestbowl was only 21 cm from the oviposition site, referred to hereafter as the IA (incubative area). In essence, the nestbowl was only one diameter from the opposite corner, where the egg had been oviposited, and it occupied over one quarter of the entire floor space. Despite these close quarters and the nearness of the egg in the nestbowl to the IA, Petra ignored the egg totally and, instead, "brooded the IA" on and off for the next 3 days, almost as attentively as if there had been an egg in it. At about 13:30 h on October 31, essentially one day late, she oviposited again in the IA. I allowed her to incubate the egg for approximately 1 h and then placed the egg in the nestbowl. Again she ignored the nestbowl and eggs and sat, instead, in the IA for another 20 min before ascending to a perch.

At this time I simply slid the nestbowl over one diameter's distance to the IA, that is, from the left-rear to the right-front corner, whereupon Petra descended and, after due cautious inspection, adopted it as a nest and began to incubate the eggs. Four h later, after she (with Ramses at her side) had ample time to accommodate to the new circumstances, I slid the nestbowl back to its original position in the left-rear corner. At first, both birds returned to the empty IA and sat on the bare floor. Then Ramses ascended to a perch and, a few min later, Petra investigated the nestbowl briefly from its rim and then also ascended to a perch.

After 2 h of desultory activity, including visits to and sitting in the IA but avoiding the nestbowl and eggs, I again slid the nestbowl back over to the IA, whereupon they adopted it again as the nest, this time without hesitation. Sixty min later, I returned the nestbowl to the right-rear corner and again they abandoned it, though Ramses did make a brief inspection. After another hour (at 22:50 h), I again slid the nestbowl over to the IA and again they took over the care of the eggs immediately and for the night.

It was quite obvious that Petra's fidelity to the IA was so great that she would not accept eggs at any other location, at least not when the change was made abruptly. But what if I allowed her to lay the 3rd egg in the nestbowl, lying over the IA, and then moved the nestbowl to the left-rear corner? Would her oviposition-site fidelity then continue to be directed to the IA, or would it shift to the nestbowl. In other words, it was a question of whether she identified the oviposition site from landmarks that were not in the immediate vicinity of the eggs or from landmarks in their very close vicinity, that is, from the nestbowl.

Although I resolved to seek an answer to this question, it was desirable to continue shifting the nestbowl back and forth to confirm that Petra continued to reject the nestbowl unless it was situated over the IA. Accordingly, after allowing Petra to incubate the eggs in the nestbowl until 11:00 h, usually with Ramses at her side allofeeding and allogrooming her, I shifted the nestbowl back and forth to and from the left-rear corner 3 times during the day, once for 40 min and twice for 15 min in the left-rear corner. Each time both Petra and Ramses abandoned it immediately upon the move to the left-rear corner and Petra returned to it promptly when it was replaced in the IA, with Ramses following.

A pattern also was evident upon nestbowl abandonment, which was that Petra first ate for a time at the food trays, with Ramses accompanying her. Afterwards, Petra usually squatted in the IA or perched above chewing on the towel covering the outside of the enclosure. Perching on the rim of the nestbowl and facing away from it, Ramses sometimes inspected the nestbowl and even hopped into it once but Petra was seen to inspect it only once. The following day I shifted the position of the nestbowl twice more, once for 15 min and once for 100 min, with the same result.

The following morning a 3rd egg was detected in the nestbowl and the question posed above could be answered. Accordingly, at 11:32 h I shifted the nestbowl to the left-rear corner once more, and again the pair abandoned it. Petra simply ignored it, sat in the IA for 20 sec, ate and drank, chewed on the towel, and returned to sitting in the IA. Then, after an absence of 7 min, she suddenly, without preliminary indication of interest, jumped abruptly into the nestbowl and onto the eggs for about 20 sec, and then resumed her other activities. After 15 min it was evident that the nestbowl would not be accepted in the left-rear corner, so I shifted it again to the IA, and again, as always before, Petra jumped into it immediately. After repeating the shift once more, with the same result of abandonment and reacceptance, I began the experiment of a gradual, rather than an abrupt, shift to the left-rear corner to see if she would accommodate gradually to a changed location.

Accordingly, 4 times, at 90-min intervals, I slid the nestbowl over toward the left-rear corner in 2-cm steps, without disturbing Petra as she sat within (by pushing it very slowly with the eraser-end of a pencil inserted through the enclosure bars). After the 4th shift, Petra arose from the eggs and investigated the then-exposed IA before settling on the eggs again. However, she shortly arose and perched on the nestbowl rim facing the IA for over 6 min, breathing so heavily that I feared she was ill. But then she settled in on the eggs again. After 2 more 2-cm shifts at 90-min intervals, the nestbowl had been returned to the left-rear corner but continued to be accepted as the nest. Twice during the following day I shifted the nestbowl back to the IA but neither time did she abandon the eggs. The nestbowl then had become the accepted site of incubation, regardless of its location on the enclosure floor.

As the significance and implications of oviposition-site fidelity already have been discussed above (p. 501), in the treatment of the similar behavior of the Cockatielian hen, Helena, they are not repeated here. The results of the present experiment are more remarkable in illustrating how sharply attentiveness to the eggs can be "turned on and off" repeatedly merely by relatively small shifts in their location. They also confirm that landmarks play a very strong role in the acceptance of an incubative area. This, of course, is adaptive, since the position of an incubative area (or nest) would be a more reliable guide for its identification than the configuration and properties of the incubative area itself. The latter would differ little from nest to nest. In this connection, Red-winged Blackbirds are known to respond to the nest site rather than to the nest or its contents until the young are 7 days old, when the calls of the chicks are used as individual identifiers (see 1,150).

The First Clutch of Cassandra and Cyrus

AN OPEN NEST IS BUILT. Cassandra worked so assiduously trying to gather nesting material from the cover of enclosure C, that I felt compelled to reward her efforts with some paper as nesting material (on Aug. 21, 1983). This soon occupied her undivided attention. She could not yet strip or tuck strips between her rump feathers (she was only 7 months old). But she was able to practice tucking Petra's strips of paper that fell from enclosure B, above. She also tried to tuck anything else that was long and narrow, such as sprigs of spray millet, from which she had first trimmed all the side twigs.

She built a very primitive nest structure in the rear-left corner of the enclosure, consisting of a bedding of pieces of toweling heaped up as a sort of partition between the corner and the rest of the enclosure. She spent much of her time sitting there 'contentedly' chewing paper, with Cyrus always in the near vicinity ready to repel any transgression by Cyrano (see Chap. 3).

OVIPOSITION---INSTALLATION OF A NESTBOX. Cassandra and Cyrus were seen to engage in coitus several times in the 10 days preceding the laying of the first egg (on Sept. 7). This egg fell through the $2\frac{1}{2}$-cm mesh of the enclosure floor, whereupon I provided Cassandra with a 2.9-cm-deep plastic bowl with shavings and a $1\frac{1}{2}$-cm-diameter plastic ball, as a substitute for the egg. When the shavings became scattered, I replaced them with paper strips. The 2nd egg was laid on schedule, and I also replaced it with a plastic ball, which Cassandra accepted without hesitation.

Though she spent a good deal of time in the nest covering the eggs and chewing pieces of paper, Cassandra also often was absent from it. On the day that she laid her 3rd egg, I removed Cyrano from the enclosure, because of fear for his safety (see p. 321). Since the inexperienced Cassandra was so easily frightened that she left the eggs whenever I came near, I installed a NB that same day.

ADOPTING THE NESTBOX. It was hours before either member of the pair ventured to enter the NB, but Cassandra finally did so at 15:00 h the next day. Though she herself only dared to "test" it from the inside perch, she would not permit the possibly-more-daring Cyrus to enter it. It was not until the morning of the next day that she spent some time exploring inside. After adopting the NB, she spent much of the next day perching in its entrance-hole surveying the outside scene. The plastic balls, of course, were largely unattended outside in the nestbowl. Cassandra laid her 4th egg on schedule, in the NB, but did not incubate it that day, not even after I supplemented it with her other 3 eggs. Instead, she guarded the entrance. She spent that night in the NB and also did so intermittently the next day, exiting at the sound of any excitement in the colony.

CLUTCH ABANDONED. During all this time, Cassandra excluded Cyrus from the NB, which meant that if she were going to incubate, she would either have had to alter her behavior or feed herself. On the next day (Sept. 15), however, she showed no further interest in the NB or eggs. Nor did she become interested in the eggs when I placed them in the outside nestbowl. Since she clearly was no longer in breeding condition, I removed the eggs and bowl and closed off the NB (I also returned Cyrano to the enclosure; see p. 321).

The Second and Third Clutches of Cassandra and Cyrus

DEEP NESTBOWL FOR THIRD CLUTCH. Oviposition of the 2nd clutch (of 4 eggs) of Cassandra and Cyrus commenced on the following October 16. By November 2, Cassandra had, to all intents, abandoned the clutch, so I removed the eggs at that time. Recall (pp. 321, 322) that I had removed Cyrano from the enclosure on October 15, the day before the 1st egg was laid, and returned him on November 2, after I removed the eggs. On November 28, again without facilitation of breeding, Cassandra laid the 1st egg of her 3rd clutch, which I replaced with a light, dried-out egg. For this clutch, I provided a 5-cm deep glass nestbowl, that would better retain nesting material, and from which light eggs could not be easily displaced.

A LIGHT EGG DISCARDED. Cassandra proved to be so attentive to the eggs of her 3rd clutch that, beginning with her 1st egg, she could not be tempted from the nestbowl by an invitation to be flighted (otherwise the most sought after activity). Two days later, she laid her 2nd egg and, shortly thereafter, discarded the light egg. This behavior confirmed the belief that a similar disposition of the light, substituted egg of the 2nd clutch was intentional, because there was no possibility of an egg being displaced accidentally from the glass nestbowl, as there was from the shallow plastic bowl (only 2.9 cm deep) that was provided for the 2nd clutch.

MORE LIGHT EGGS DISCARDED---ATTENTIVE INCUBATION. I then removed the fresh egg and substituted two new light ones, which Cassandra accepted and incubated. But after she laid her 3rd egg, 2 days later, she cast out both of the light eggs from the nestbowl and incubated only the fresh egg. After I removed the fresh egg and substituted an infertile egg and an empty eggshell, she incubated the egg but cast out the shell. After she laid her 4th egg, I restored her 1st 3 eggs.

Throughout this period, Cassandra incubated those eggs that she retained with the greatest of attentiveness, declining repeatedly to be flighted at any time. This behavior was all the more impressive because of the great care with which she also covered the eggs, with no egg ever being exposed inattentively as she incubated the clutch, compared to the desultory way in which she had both covered and incubated the eggs of the 1st and 2nd clutches.

EGGS INFERTILE OR TOO THIN-SHELLED. On the 11th day of incubation, I tempted her off the eggs momentarily, as she brought a twig of spray millet into the nest. Though she probably left the nestbowl to void at night, that was the only time I saw her leave the eggs during the day (i.e., while the lights were on). Throughout this period, Cyrus allofed and allogroomed her very attentively. However, despite Cassandra's incomparably attentive care of the eggs, no offspring was forthcoming. The eggs either were infertile or damaged, as a consequence of being too thin-shelled.

The Fourth Clutch of Cassandra and Cyrus

FIVE EGGS LAID---TIGHT SITTING AFTER THE THIRD. On January 29 and February 3, 1984, I observed Cassandra and Cyrus copulating. On the latter day, I also found that Cassandra already had laid 2 eggs, both of which had fallen through the mesh of the enclosure floor in the right-rear corner. One of these eggs had been damaged in the fall. Desirous of giving this persistent pair the opportunity to rear a brood, I restored the glass nestbowl and two plastic balls, and supplemented their diets appropriately. I also supplied paper for nesting material. This immediately received Cassandra's attention as she tried to strip it. Within 2 days, she was sitting on the plastic balls around the clock, but she was not sitting tightly on them, by any means. She laid her 3rd egg late that evening and 3 additional eggs thereafter, one every other day. She incubated these eggs very tightly, covering some portions with her wings.

HATCHED CHICK CARED FOR IMPROPERLY. On the 11th day of incubation, I added several layers of paper toweling to the bottom of the nestbowl and moistened them daily (as opportunity allowed). A chick hatched on the 22nd day of incubation. The parents were most attentive to it, and Cyrus stayed very close to Cassandra, but there was no sign of their having fed it after several hours. Accordingly, I tried to foster the hatchling with Petra and Ramses (see p. 726, **Fostered Hatchling Not Allofed**) and also gave them the shells (which Cassandra and Cyrus had discarded from the bowl).

Since Petra and Ramses would not allofeed the chick either, I returned it to Cassandra after 60 min. Apparently the chick was still vigorous enough to cheep for food, because Cassandra allofed it 4 h later, but this apparently was too little too late. The next morning at 08:00 h the chick was alive, but very weak, and at 09:00 h it was dead. The other 5 eggs were either damaged, infertile, or did not hatch. [In the light of subsequent experience, there need have been little concern over the welfare of the hatchling, since lovebird hatchlings sometimes are left unattended for hours, with the parents appearing to ignore them, yet seemingly without ill effect. On the other hand, nor should the temporary transfer of the hatchling to Petra's nest have had an ill effect.]

The Fifth Clutch of Cassandra and Cyrus

NESTBOX PROVIDED, OVIPOSITION COMMENCES. Determined to bring to fruition their persistent reproductive efforts, I supplied Cassandra and Cyrus with an opaque NB, which was adopted with little delay. As early as March 14, only 12 days later, a 1st egg was laid inside it. I removed the first 3 eggs as they were laid and replaced them with infertile or unhatched eggs from previous batches. I kept the removed eggs at room temperature and turned them several times daily.

CASSANDRA EASILY TEMPTED FROM EGGS. Although nothing would tempt Cassandra from the eggs of her 3rd and 4th clutches in open nestbowls, there was no difficulty in coaxing her briefly off her 5th clutch in the opaque NB. This was accomplished either by flighting Cyrus or feeding him spray millet. In the former case, Cassandra joined Cyrus for a short time as soon as she heard his excited calls and the sounds of flight. In the latter case, she joined him after 15-30 sec, when she heard him eating the millet, or within 1 or 2 sec, if he gave a characteristic "summons" chirp.

RELICT EGG-CARE RESPONSES TO LIGHT. These quite different responses of Cassandra in an opaque NB, as opposed to those in an open nestbowl, revealed the same influences of light (or exposure of the eggs) detected with Cockatiels, disclosing that lovebirds possess the same relict adaptive behavior. Thus, Cassandra was extremely reluctant to leave her eggs in an open nestbowl during the day, when they would have been exposed to view and to light in her absence. Only twice was she seen to do so, and then only momentarily, to bring in spray millet. By contrast, she had no hesitation to leave the eggs for short periods when the clutch was in the NB, where it was shielded from light and from view. The finding of a number of other clear-cut relict egg-care responses by Cassandra (see pp. 737-739) reinforces this conclusion. It also it pertinent, in this connection, that the hens of all lovebird species are known to bring in nest material at an increasing rate, when light enters the nest chamber through cracks (27).

INCUBATION COMMENCES---RELATIVELY NONCHALANT. With the laying of the 4th egg on March 19, I restored Cassandra's 1st 3 eggs and allowed incubation to commence. A following 5th egg was laid on schedule. I adopted the practice of spraying the NB daily, beginning on the 15th day, treating the walls and lid, but shielding the eggs while doing so; the latter were given only a light misting. As mentioned above, it was easy to coax Cassandra from the NB temporarily by making spray millet available or by flighting Cyrus. It was quite evident all through the period of incubation of this clutch that Cassandra was relatively nonchalant about the covering of the eggs, compared to her great attentiveness to them in an open nestbowl. She frequently entered the enclosure and stripped paper when the eggs were in the NB, whereas she never did so when they were in an open nestbowl.

CYCRUS JOINS CASSANDRA EVERY MORNING. Like his father Ramses in similar cirumstances, Cyrus always began the night sleeping in the enclosure, always joined Cassandra in the NB very early in the morning, and never exited the NB until 1 or 2 h after lights-on. On the 12th day of incubation (March 31, 17 days after the 1st egg was laid), I noted a great increase in the appetites of the birds. According to the birds' timetable, hatchings were imminent at this time. When I put some fresh paper in the enclosure the next day, Cyrus immediately began "fussing" clumsily with it. Within 30 sec, Cassandra exited the NB and was busy stripping it, showing again how exquisitely tuned the incubating hen is to sounds outside the NB (recall that she also could detect spray millet being eaten). By that time, Cassandra had become accomplished at both stripping and tucking paper, whereas Cyrus, as yet, could do neither.

HATCHINGS---CHICKS PROTECTED. By 17:30 h on the 21st day of incubation (April 9), faint clicks could be heard from the 2nd egg and vigorous cheeps from the 4th one. By 09:52 h the next morning, both eggs had hatched and the chicks appeared to be in excellent condition. No sound was to be heard from the other 3 eggs. When I tried to check the NB that evening, while Cassandra was out, she scurried in before I could get to it. In fact, she, even more than the Cockatiels, would rush back to the NB to protect the chicks as I approached. As a result, I had to make my inspections at times when she was quite occupied with other activities. This marked protective behavior proved to be typical behavior of brooding lovebird hens.

I succeeded in making another inspection 30 min later, and heard faint clicks from the 1st egg. The next morning the chick in the 5th egg also was clicking faintly. Early that evening, I heard some rapid cheeping from the NB, suggesting that the 1st egg had hatched. However, I was unable to coax Cassandra out of the NB with any temptation until 17:00 h the next day. In view of Cassandra's tenacity, it came as no surprise that both the 1st and 5th eggs had hatched (the 3rd egg proved to be infertile). One of the youngest chicks of this brood failed to survive, leaving the trio, Juliet, Romeo, and Zoltan, which are dealt with further on pages 757-762.

The Sixth Clutch of Cassandra and Cyrus

PRELIMINARY EXPERIMENTS WITH BURIED EGGS. Cassandra laid the 1st egg of her 6th clutch in the opaque NB on June 3, while still caring for the chicks of her 1st brood. I replaced this egg with an infertile one and buried the substitute egg 5/8-cm deep in the IA (Fig. 3b). Within 5 min, the egg was exposed but not resurfaced, suggesting, in the light of subsequent findings, that it lay unnoticed after being exposed accidentally.

After I reburied the 1st substitute egg, it still remained undetected at the time the 2nd egg was laid 2 days later. I removed the 2nd egg also, and buried a 2nd substitute egg in the IA near the 1st. Within 15 min, one of the eggs had been discovered and resurfaced. After burying it again and waiting another 15 min, I found one of the eggs about 10% exposed at the tip, whereupon I exposed the 2nd one a like amount. Within another 15 min, both eggs had been resurfaced. I then buried both eggs in the rear corner near the IA, about 10% exposed at one end, to see if they also would be resurfaced and returned to the IA. Thirty min later, I had my answer. Both eggs had been resurfaced and restored to the IA. These results warranted follow-up studies with a "transparent" NB.

FIRST OBSERVATIONS OF RESPONSES OVER A MISSING CLUTCH

At the outset of this experiment I was not confident that the lovebirds would accept a NB with a transparent sidepane and raise a brood in it. Not only are they widely studied birds, about which there is no report of such a breeding success, but parrots generally prefer dark nest cavities. Recall, in this connection, that if cracks allowing the entrance of light exist in their nest cavities, they cover these with nesting materials (see p. 260, **Constant Additions to the Nest**). The successful breeding of my Cockatiels under these conditions, and of Petra and Ramses in an open nestbowl, however, augered well for success.

"TRANSPARENT" NESTBOX INSTALLED---CAUTIOUSLY ACCEPTED. Early on the evening of June 5, I replaced the near sidewall of the NB with a pane of 5/32-cm-thick clear Plexiglas, leaving all else--shavings, eggs, positions, etc., unaltered. I also covered the sidepane temporarily with a white towel, so as not to have the change to the new conditions occur abruptly. Despite this precaution, Cassandra, at first, was very reluctant to enter the NB; she merely stood on the outside perch, looking in. She required 10 min to work her way in, bit by bit. When Cyrus tried to join her, she allowed him only a 3/4-way entry before repelling him with pecks. After another 5 min of squabbling, Cyrus was allowed to join her. Later that evening, the entire family of 5 were using the NB routinely, but Cyrus, as usual, spent the night outside.

PARTIALLY-EXPOSED EGGS RESURFACED AND RECOVERED. After servicing the enclosures the next morning, I uncovered the sidepane and again buried the 2 eggs in the corner, 10% exposed. When Cassandra entered, I then was able to observe that she went straight to the eggs matter-of-factly, wedged them out with her bill, nudged them back to the IA (a distance of about 9 cm), and sat over them. By mid-afternoon, she no longer was sitting on the eggs, but she and Cyrus often "popped" in and out of the NB together.

EGGS ABANDONED. When Juliet subsequently entered the NB, Cassandra followed her in and protected the eggs by covering them. Later, she came off of them momentarily to chase Cyrus out of the NB. Not long afterward, she was off the eggs again. Twenty min later, Cyrus was in the NB with her, trying without success to mount her. In the next few days, her attention to the eggs was very desultory. Since she did not lay a 3rd egg, it was evident that the combination of manipulating the eggs and the change in the NB--most likely the latter alone--had caused her to cease oviposition. By June 9, the eggs had been abandoned, so I removed them. Cassandra was, as yet, not habituated to the use of a "transparent" NB.

The Seventh Clutch of Cassandra and Cyrus

"TRANSPARENT" NESTBOX ACCEPTED. By June 16, Cassandra again was taking an interest in the NB and she began to exclude the young from it. By June 22nd, Cyrus was courtship-feeding her and both sometimes "fussed about" together in the NB--pecking, inspecting, testing, etc. By July 4, the pair had begun to copulate again. All through this period, Cassandra was stripping paper and forming a simple nest basin within the NB (July 8 was one of the days when Cassandra's broodmate brother, Cyrano, allofed her through the enclosure bars; see p. 329). By July 19, the 1st egg of the 7th clutch was laid. Meanwhile, the young had been removed and the parents had exclusive possession of the enclosure. The NB had been accepted, and the chances of a successful breeding in it seemed good.

SECOND OBSERVATIONS OF RESPONSES OVER A MISSING CLUTCH

INCUBATIVE AREA NUZZLED FOR MISSING EGG. When I detected the 1st egg on the morning of July 19 (laid the previous evening or night), I replaced it with an infertile egg of a previous clutch, which I buried in the far-rear corner (the corner nearest the IA; see Fig. 3b). Then I sat back and watched. As Cassandra was about to enter the NB, she paused on the outside perch facing inward. Apparently having already noted the absence of the egg, she scanned the entire NB floor, in an evident search for it. Then she entered and continued to look about on foot. Not seeing the egg, she then nuzzled around with her bill in the shavings in the IA, but her search did not extend to the corner where the egg was buried.

SLIGHTLY EXPOSED EGG RESURFACED AND RE-COVERED. After Cassandra left the NB, I exposed the top of the egg in the corner. When she re-entered, she wedged it out promptly, just as in the preceding experiment (with 2 eggs), nudged it back to the IA, and sat over it. During the remainder of the day, I noticed that Cassandra easily became frightened off the single egg when I passed nearby (but this skittishness quickly waned).

EGGS BURIED IN INCUBATIVE AREA RESURFACED PROMPTLY. After Cassandra laid her 2nd egg, I substituted for it, also, and buried both substitute eggs centrally in the IA, at a depth of 5/8 cm below the surface (Fig. 3b, position marked by the **X**). When Cassandra returned, she repeated her performance of the day before, first scanning the bottom of the NB from the outside perch, then walking around searching on foot, and then plowing up the IA with her bill. But this time, of course, she found the eggs immediately, wedged them out, and sat over them.

So far, I had showed that a lovebird hen takes note of the absence of missing eggs (when none remains), even before entering the NB, searches for them visually from the outside perch, searches for them visually on foot, searches for them by nuzzling and plowing in the IA with the bill, resurfaces any buried eggs that are discovered, and nudges them back to the IA. But do they also search routinely, as do Cockatiels?

TESTS FOR SYSTEMATIC, ROUTINE SEARCHING

ROUTINE SEARCHING DIRECTLY BENEATH THE CLUTCH? To answer the latter question, I set Cassandra a different test (at 12:05 h on July 20). I left the 2 substitute eggs in the IA but buried 2 more substitute eggs, 1¼ cm deep, directly beneath them, and a 3rd egg in the near-rear corner (the total depth of #3 shavings was 3 cm). The former 2 eggs were very unlikely to be found unless routine searching was systematic and at a depth, rather than merely haphazard peripheral surface pecking and nuzzling. The egg in the corner was even more unlikely to be found, since Cassandra did not dig there even during directed searching (unless she were to search there because it was a former burial site).

ROUTINE SEARCHING BENEATH CLUTCH VERIFIED. Within 26 h, Cassandra had found and resurfaced both of the eggs that had been buried in the IA and was sitting on a clutch of 4 eggs. Clearly, incubating Peach-faced Lovebird hens (at least, Cassandra) routinely search within the IA. I then reburied both eggs (at 12:30 h on July 21) in the same locations as before. [I easily could make these changes because Cassandra would leave the NB from time to time to strip more paper for the nest.] Within 5 h, she had recovered one of the eggs. She probably recovered the other one later that evening, because by 08:10 h the next morning she had recovered both eggs and also had a 5th egg (her 3rd) that she had laid during the night. The egg buried in the corner remained undetected.

SYSTEMATIC PERIPHERAL ROUTINE SEARCHING? I replaced Cassandra's 3rd egg with another infertile one on the evening of July 22 (17:15 h) and set up what I considered to be an even more stringent test for the existence of a routine search behavior. I left 2 substitute eggs in the surface clutch but buried another 3 eggs at a depth of 1¼ cm and a distance of 4 cm from the clutch. The 1st of these was buried directly to the front of the clutch, the 2nd directly to the rear, and the 3rd directly to the side (in the direction of the sidepane).

The 3 eggs thus lay roughly on the circumference of a 7½-cm-diameter semicircle (as shown by the solid black circles in Fig. 3b). A 4th egg remained buried in the corner (as before), about 5 cm from the egg buried to the rear. While finding the egg to the front would not be an impressive accomplishment, since Cassandra usually faced to the front, finding those to the side and rear would imply fairly systematic search routines. The one to the rear could be found fairly readily if the sitting hen faced about part of the time (which was infrequently observed in the NB), but the one to the side could not be found by the same routine, since there was no room for the hen to sit sideways, unless she pressed her underside up against the wall (as Cockatiels sometimes do).

SYSTEMATIC PERIPHERAL ROUTINE SEARCHING VERIFIED. To my amazement, Cassandra found the egg to the front within 100 min, and all 3 of them within 44 h--a very impressive performance, indeed. These results make a strong case for the thesis that incubating lovebird hens routinely search the IA and its periphery for possibly-buried eggs, and they suggest that no egg partially or totally hidden in the close neighborhood of the IA would go undetected for long. Although Cassandra required many hours to find some of the eggs that I had buried, all buried eggs were in unlikely locations and/or at quite unlikely depths. Closer, more superficially buried, eggs would have been found much sooner.

INCUBATION COMMENCES. On the morning of July 24, I found that Cassandra had laid her 4th egg, giving her a total of 6, counting the 5 substitutes. Accordingly, I restored her 3 *bona fide* eggs, allowing incubation of the clutch of 4 to commence. Once she had settled down to incubate--after her 3rd egg was laid--she no longer was frightened off the eggs by my being near or passing by, and she continued in this steadfast behavior throughout the incubatory period. As before, Cyrus spent a great deal of time in the NB with her, allofeeding and allogrooming her very attentively.

SHALLOW NESTBASIN PARTIALLY SHIELDS EGGS FROM VIEW. It was clear from observing Cassandra incubate the eggs, that a good fraction of her time was spent probing, and otherwise manipulating the shavings and debris in the IA. A 5th egg was laid on schedule (July 26) but I had seen no coitus for over 2 weeks. By that time, Cassandra had fashioned a shallow nestbasin in the shavings and had built up a rim of paper strips, feathers, and debris around it, blocking off much of the view of the clutch through the sidepane. This partial shielding presumably accounted for her willingness to leave the eggs unattended on the occasions when she left the NB to strip and accumulate additional nesting material.

CYRUS STANDS GUARD. Cassandra had adopted the habit of leaving the NB to attend to maintenance activities before lights-on in the morning, but whenever I found her outside, the eggs still were warm. Cyrus, meanwhile, continued to sleep outside the NB, but spend considerable time allofeeding, allogrooming, and sitting beside Cassandra in the NB during the day. On the 15th day of incubation (the 20th day after the 1st egg was laid), Cassandra left the clutch to eat and drink, leaving Cyrus in the NB. He just sat off to the rear of the IA, guarding the eggs until her return.

[On the other hand, when Zenobia and Cyrano were incubating their 1st clutch in an open nestbowl that provided very little space (at the laboratory), Cyrano customarily stood directly over the eggs when Zenobia was out stripping paper. When Flavia was out of the nestbowl in similar circumstances, the crippled Titus practically sat on the eggs.]

By the afternoon of the 18th day of incubation, when hatchings were imminent or overdue on Cassandra's timetable, she was spending very much more time away from the clutch, in marked contrast to her earlier habits. But Cyrus often stood guard while she was gone (the ambient temperature during her absences on that afternoon was 29°C).

A SOLE CHICK HATCHES. At 13:25 h on the 20th day of incubation, faint clicks were heard from the 4th egg, which was the only fertile egg in the clutch. These were much louder by 23:30 h, and the egg had hatched by 10:00 h the next day. By this time Cassandra was totally ignoring my near presence. On subsequent days, I replaced the infertile eggs, one by one, with three 2½-cm-diameter polyethylene balls to ease the weight of Cassandra on the nestling, Claudius. These were accepted routinely by Cassandra, and it was not until 2 weeks had passed that she ceased incubating them.

CARE AND BEHAVIOR OF PEACH-FACED LOVEBIRD YOUNG

Literature Accounts

CARE OF HATCHLINGS. It is thought that hatchlings need to be allofed with little delay. This is undertaken vigorously by the hen, who regurgitates food for them (7, 8). One readily can ascertain the times when the young are being allofed, since the feeding sounds can be heard distinctly from outside the NB. All workers agree (though erroneously; e.g., see, p. 752, **Male Allofeeds Hatchlings When Opportunity Affords**) that the male, at first, takes no direct part in their feeding. He is thought to allofeed the hen, who then allofeeds the chicks. While being allofed, nestlings up to 4-5 days old may lie on their sides, bellies, or backs, often with their limbs straight up in the air, or in other attitudes (3, 27).

Occasionally, inexperienced hens are inattentive. They either do not allofeed their hatchlings, or they do so improperly and the young die (8, 27). But the same hens often care for the next brood skillfully (8). On the other hand, if the chicks are hand fed for 2 or 3 days, it is said that the same inexperienced hens usually will begin to allofeed them. In Smith's view, such successes depend upon the much greater physical and sound stimuli provided by a larger chick as compared to those provided by a tiny hatchling. This view is supported by the fact that fostering a slightly older chick to an inattentive hen sometimes will stimulate her to allofeed the entire brood (27).

RECAPITULATION OF ANCESTRAL CHICK-CARE BEHAVIOR. These parental deficiencies in chick care can be interpreted within the same paradigm as those for egg care, including the proposed recapitulation of ancestral stages. I alluded to this briefly on p. 490 in connection with inadequate care of hatchlings by inexperienced Cockatiels. In this case, the parental-care behavior of the inattentive hens has not matured beyond the 3rd phylogenetic stage, corresponding to that for nidifugous young. Grooming, warmth, and escorting were provided for these, but they otherwise could fend more or less for themselves. After a few days, or in response to stronger evocative stimuli, the appropriate neural circuitry for the actions of allofeeding the young become available.

[The proposed phylogenetic stages in chick care are: (1st) no care; (2nd) grooming, protecting, and escorting the young; (3rd) grooming, protecting, escorting, and warming the young; and (4th) grooming, protecting, escorting, warming, and allofeeding the young (see Table 3, under "care of hatchlings and young nestlings").]

THE FOOD. The hatchlings and young nestlings are allofed a considerable amount of liquid nutrient, in addition to the husked seeds and other foods that have been partly softened and digested by the actions of water and mucus in the crops of the parents (3, 27, 442). Since the male allofeeds the female, who, in turn, allofeeds the chicks, it is suggested that the young receive more fully processed food than they would receive if the food passed only through the crop of one or the other parent (3). The tacit but apparently erroneous assumption is made that the female generally does not relay food directly from the male to the young, but first processes it further in her own crop.

DUAL, SEQUENTIAL PROCESSING OF FOOD? Certain of my observations support the thesis that such dual food processing may occur in Cockatiels but that it does not occur in lovebirds or Budgerigars (see below). For both species, though, many of the past assumptions concerning allofeeding habits seem to have been little more than guesswork. The evidence for dual sequential food processing for Cockatiels hinges on the observations that (a) Cosimo never relayed food directly from Carmen to hatchlings during their 1st day, but only to older nestlings; and (b) Carmen's allofeedings of Cosimo were almost always during the afternoon and evening. In other words, in both cases, time was allowed for pre-digestion, both before Cosimo relayed such food to hatchlings during their first day, and before Carmen relayed the processed food from her morning meals to Cosimo (see pp. 690, 691, **Carmen's Allofeeding of Cosimo**).

GLUTINOUS LIQUID FOOD AND ITS ORIGIN. As occurs with Budgerigars and Cockatiels, the proportion of regurgitated liquid food is diminished and that of solid food increased as the lovebird chicks grow. [According to Rutgers (104), Peach-faced lovebird young often have been fostered successfully with Budgerigars.] This is readily ascertained by inspecting the chicks' crops. The somewhat glutinous liquid food generally is accepted to be rich in animal proteins (proteins relatively rich in the basic amino acids). In part, it appears to be formed in the glandular stomach or proventriculus (27). There is no evidence that the crops of the parents contribute anything to the diet, as is the case with pigeons and doves (3).

"CROP MILK" is a holocrine secretion (consisting of dead and disintegrating cells) formed by a wholesale degeneration and conversion of the cell structure of the mucosal epithelium of the crops of both sexes of pigeons and doves that is indispensible for the rearing of the young (see 998). Through the production of such protein-rich secretions, the birds, in effect, bypass the common procedure of allofeeding the young an animal diet (1,150). Crop milk is secreted under the influence of the hormone prolactin, from the adenohypophysis (anterior pituitary gland; 442, 997, 998, 1,000, 1,225). It is a cheesy substance formed by cell proliferation in the deeper layers and desquamation (sloughing off) of superficial squamous (flattened) fat-laden cells and their fragments from the crop epithelium (14, 322). Because of the folding and pocketing of the crop mucosa, the secretion becomes compacted into coarse particles which, in due time, distend the crop sac of the squab. When the parents resume normal foraging, the crop milk becomes mixed with grain (1,000).

Rock Pigeon crop milk bears certain similarities to mammalian milks, in some respects to the milk of marine mammals, in others to the milk of dogs or rabbits (323, 998). By dry weight, it consists of 33.8% fat (in some cases, up to 51%, of which over 80% are triglycerides and 12% phospholipids), 58.6% protein, and 4.6% ash or minerals (443), and is rich in calcium (a lower content than has rabbit's milk) but differs from mammalian milk in being devoid of casein and lactose. It is low in vitamin A, thiamin, and ascorbic acid, but compares well in riboflavin content with cow's milk and with most mammalian milks as a source of fatty acids (see 28, 322, 998, 1,000).

Proliferation of the crop mucosa in the Rock Pigeon begins on about the 8th day of incubation; milk "secretion" begins on about the 14th to 18th day and generally lasts until 10-16 days after hatching (see 322, 998, 1,225). The adult crop returns to its normal undeveloped state by approximately 3 weeks after hatching. During its developmental cycle, the crop increases in weight from about 0.75 g to more than 3 g in the Rock Pigeon (1,225). One of the factors leading to regurgitation by Ring Doves is said to be tactile stimulation of the crop by the hatchling squab as it lifts its head unsteadily and brushes it against the parent in a soliciting posture (see 1,053).

In White Carneaux Pigeon squabs, the water in the crop contents decreased from 70% to 27% from the 1st to the 27th day, as the composition changed from mostly crop milk to mostly solid food. At the same time, the percentage of dry matter, and fat and protein, decreased from 27 and 46% to 3 and 17%, respectively, while carbohydrate increased from 21 to 74% (see 998). From the time of cessation of crop milk production to adulthood, the parents must procure food for the young without the benefit of a secretion product (998).

ALLOFEEDING YOUNG. Smith suggests that the soft, plaintive cheeps of the very young chicks have more allure to the hen than the harsher calls of the older ones (27). The hens would appear to search out the youngest chicks actively by "homing in" on these faint calls. This presumably ensures that the very youngest chicks get their share of food, even in the presence of broodmates so large that the youngest chicks are completely covered. Similar allofeeding priorities practiced by Budgerigar hens have been carefully documented (843; see pp. 200-203), and confirmed in the present studies (see p. 787, **Hen Tenaciously Feeds Youngest Chicks First**). Cockatiels also display allofeeding priorities but may not have recourse to the sounds of solicitations to differentiate between young of different sizes; see p. 686 *et seq.*, **Feeding and Competing for the Brood**, and p. 702, **The Seventh Brood of Carmen and Cosimo**).

The allofeeding lovebird parent apparently is able to find the bills of the young in the dim light of the nest, grasp the bills appropriately, and deliver food into them (27). This is essential with lovebird chicks, since the youngest ones do not have the strength to solicit food by any means other than calling. Contrary to Smith's view, where my own findings bear on the matter of priorities in the allofeeding of lovebird chicks, they suggest that the youngest chicks have the lowest priority.

IMPRINTING ON THE CALLS OF THE YOUNG. The importance of calls in soliciting food is shown by the fact that experienced lovebird hens will allofeed only the kinds of chicks upon whose calls they were first imprinted (whether of their own species or not). Later, after the chicks have opened their eyes, and their voices have changed, the hens apparently are unable to distinguish between the calls of chicks of different species and will nourish most fostered young indiscriminately. [Although these results first were attributed to differences in down color (3, 4), this explanation seems unlikely in view of the low illuminance in the NB by day, and it certainly is inadequate at night.]

DOWN---GROWTH---MATURATION---FEATHERING---BEHAVIOR. Hatchlings are said to have a dense, yellowish-orange coat of down, but all the hatchlings I observed had very much less down than do Cockatiels. Except for the 1st day, when the hatchling may lose weight (3), the growth of the nestling is continuous and very rapid (3, 27). After chicks are about 3 days old, both parents are said to allofeed them directly. The food then consists essentially of whole, hulled seeds. Although it had been thought that the male gradually took over the allofeeding, this was not seen to be the case with any of the broods of 6 breeding pairs whose allofeeding behavior I observed directly in open nestbowls or "transparent" nestboxes; rather, the male usually allofed chicks from the day of hatching, as the opportunity allowed--the more so, the larger the brood.

After 4 or 5 days, the chicks have gained enough strength to sit up and move about. When the hen leaves the nest, they then assume an unvarying attitude; they face inward toward one another in a warm huddle, with their heads interlinked, and with each chick hooking its bill over the nape (back of the neck) of another (3). Some tolerance to varying temperatures (poikilothermy) lasts until the chicks are about 10 days old; after that they can generate their own bodily heat and maintain constant body temperature (homeothermic endotherms). [Most chicks that die are said to succumb at about this time, from becoming too cold (27, 787).]

Until the young are fairly well developed, they make only restrained cheeping sounds while being allofed. After that, they clamour loudly during allofeeding. The eyes open at about 11 days after hatching. At that time, the chicks have attained about half their adult weight, and the hen stops brooding them during the day. After their eyes open, chicks no longer tend to assume any particular orientation toward each other, though they continue to huddle together closely. At some time between 9 and 11 days of age, the gray down begins to appear amidst, and obscure, the natal down. This immediately precedes the appearance of the pin feathers of the juvenal plumage (3, 27).

RESPONSES TO HANDLING. Virtually all workers recommend a daily handling and checking of chicks (either that or no handling at all) to confirm that they are warm, that the crops are full, that they are growing satisfactorily, etc. [Another very important reason for making such checks is mentioned on pp. 747-749, **Tongue-Flick Allofeeding, Wayward Food, and Clogged Nostrils.**] The chicks show no overt sign of fear until after their eyes have opened. Then they tend to avoid the intruder. The strengthening of the avoidance response with age probably reflects increased locomotor ability rather than increased fear (3).

Whether the young are handled or not, they tend to void when disturbed. It is rare for them to bite when handled gently, even at fledging. Once the eyes are open, handled chicks sometimes "scold" by making angry-sounding buzzing noises, but this never occurred in my experience. These sounds are very contagious to other young (even those with closed eyes) but do not deter the parents from entering the nest (27).

GROOMING AND SCRATCHING. While still in the nest, the young groom themselves and each other and are groomed by their parents. This may occur even before the feathers develop, when chicks have been seen to direct the grooming movements toward the non-existent primary feathers of the wing (3). The nestlings also will scratch their heads with their feet. Sometimes a foot is extended directly forward under the wing, rather than over the wing in the adult manner. The choice may hinge upon which maneuver is more convenient at the time, depending upon the position of the body (see also p. 261).

FLEDGING. Once the feathers of the juvenal plumage begin to break from their pins, and the chicks have achieved roughly their adult weight, their growth begins to slow (27). The weight gained afterwards makes them heavier than their parents (a common circumstance among young birds). Formerly, the excess weight was thought to be mostly fat that enabled the young to survive periods of food shortage and provided energy for feather growth and for exercising their muscles (28). Although this may be true in some species, the current view is that the excess weight more commonly is water, that is lost as plumage and, to lesser extent, other organs mature (245, 975). At any rate, excess weight of lovebird young is lost just before fledging, at about 42-43 days of age (3, 27). At this time, their food consumption also drops (7).

Fledging seems to occur gradually, in that the juveniles do not remain outside the NB for lengthy periods after first leaving it; ordinarily the slightest disturbance sends them scurrying back, not to be seen again until the following day. The gradual increase in the time that the young spend outside the nest may reflect their gradual accommodation to the unfamiliar new surroundings and bright light (3). But regardless of the amount of time spent outside during the day, the chicks return to the nest during the night for as long as the parents permit, which usually is at least for the 1st 2 or 3 nights. After that, they tend to spend their nights huddled together in the outside enclosure (3, 8, 27).

FLIGHT---FEATHER-PICKING---FEEDING---BITING. The young are fully feathered, including the tail, and capable of strong, sustained flight immediately upon leaving the nest. Within a short time, they learn to maneuver adroitly. Though the parents not infrequently feather-pick the chicks' heads, wings, and backs, the young soon feather out after being removed from the feather-picking parents (3, 7, 27).

The young begin trying to husk seeds as soon as they gain access to them, which usually is shortly after they leave the nest. For a period of about 2 weeks after fledging, they are decreasingly dependent upon the parents--almost entirely the male--for food, after which it is safe to relocate them into a nursery enclosure. During these weeks, they continue to solicit for food, making rather harsh, repetitive squeaks while proferring the open bill toward a parent or, occasionally, a broodmate (3). Sometimes one fledgling allofeeds another (very common in Budgerigars; see pp. 786, 793, 798, 807), the former bobbing its head in the adult manner.

Recently fledged young do not seem to be able to bite hard. This may be for lack of exercise of the powerful masseters (jaw muscles), or it may be an adaptation that prevents serious injury while the fledglings are learning to bill-fence with one another (3).

THE NEXT BREEDING CYCLE---SEXUAL MATURITY. The parents often will begin to breed again, even before the young are fledged, in which case both parents will engage in overlapping sexual and parental-care behavior (3). The degree to which fledglings and juveniles are tolerated depends upon the stage reached in the parents' next breeding cycle [see pp. 728-730, 750, which is representative also of the breeding behavior of Zenobia and Cyrano and Cassandra and Cyrus in the presence of prior broods]. The young become sexually mature at about 80 days of age, just over 5 weeks after fledging. However, most birds do not begin to exhibit sexual behavior until considerably later, usually after the post-juvenal molt is completed at about 4 months. Five-month old males have been known to fertilize eggs, but breeding by such young birds is inadvisable. Lovebirds can be bred successfully in their 2nd year. Their breeding life as individuals varies but males generally remain productive longer than females; best results from females are likely to be achieved up to the age of 4 yr (787).

The First Brood of Petra and Ramses

The 1st and 2nd broods of Petra and Ramses were incubated and reared in standard (opaque) NBs (Fig. 3b). No effort was made to follow their progress closely. Since my objectives did not include confirming or determining the timing of events, but rather studying behavior, no particular emphasis is placed on dates and elapsed times. These are not entirely overlooked, however, since they provide important reference points.

HATCHINGS---DISPOSAL OF EGGSHELLS--TWO CHICKS SUCCUMB. The first hatchling (egg #1), detected on November 12, 1982, at 12:44 h, was still moist from hatching. The 3rd egg did not hatch until 59 h later (the 2nd egg was infertile). In both cases, the shells already had been eaten at the times the hatchlings were detected. [In subsequent observations of brooding in open nestbowls, I often observed parents eat the eggshells after a hatching.] The 4th egg hatched 2 days later, and the 5th, after another 4 days; 10 days had elapsed between the 1st and last hatchings. The last chick to hatch was the one that kicked through its shell during hatching and had to be aided. It succumbed after 13 days.

Clamouring, food-solicitation sounds were noted first on the 18th day (Nov. 30). The youngest chick was so much smaller than the other two, and steadily losing ground, that I tried to facilitate its being allofed by removing the other two chicks for 60 min or more, until it had been allofed. However, being inexperienced, Petra and Ramses apparently were allofeeding it too great a proportion of solid food, leading to its death with an impacted crop after 4 weeks (its development was greatly retarded). This result probably was hastened by, if not actually the consequence of, Ramses' ceasing to eat soft food (fresh corn) in the preceding days.

HANDLING THE CHICKS---PARENTAL REACTIONS AND CARE. When I put the 2 surviving chicks (Jagatai and Ogadai) back into the enclosure after handling them at an age of roughly 1 month, the 'frantic' parents, especially Ramses, used all the methods at their disposal to herd them up into the NB, at the top, right-rear corner of the enclosure. Once they got them near the entrance, they forcefully guided and prodded them in. I routinely handled and examined the chicks at least twice per day at the age of 5 weeks, and flighted Ramses and Petra at the same time. Since the parents were habituated, they did not hesitate at that time to alight on, and walk over me--on my hands, knees, shoulders, in my hair, etc. All the while, they concernedly 'scolded' and pecked at me and the young. Ramses even remained with the chicks as I carried them back to the enclosure.

FIRST FLIGHTS---MUTUAL ALLOFEEDING BETWEEN THE YOUNG. By the end of the 5th week, Ramses still was herding the chicks back into the NB when they exited, but they doggedly persisted. Jagatai whirred his wings for the first time on December 19, and both young took their 1st flights 2 days later. The next day I saw Jagatai and Ogadai allofeed each other. In time, these two formed a homosexual pair bond, with the former playing the role of the female. By the end of the 6th week, one of the young, during their playful interactions, appeared to be trying to mount the other. [Jagatai eventually mated and bred with Aspasia (see pp. 834-838, **Lovebird Mating Between a Mature Male and a Juvenile Female**).]

While I have seen the topic of allofeeding between the young discussed and plausibly accounted for elsewhere, I have seen no mention or awareness of how this practice often begins among very young nestlings. I have witnessed these beginnings on several occasions. When a parent is allofeeding the young, the latter often are huddled together closely, proffering their bills for food. When the parent withdraws to regurgitate, in these circumstances, the young grasp each other's bills in the 'confusion,' and each seeks to obtain food from the other. These interactions set the stage for subsequent unilateral and mutual allofeedings.

[One of the chicks of the 3rd brood (Flavia or Zenobia) was in the habit of pressing her bill in so closely while her sister was being allofed, that Ramses sometimes unceremoniously slapped her head away vigorously with the side of his own.]

The Second Brood of Petra and Ramses

The 2nd brood of Petra and Ramses was the product of their 3rd clutch of 5 eggs, the 1st of which was laid on December 27, 1982 (see p. 723), and proved to be infertile. The brood consisted of Cassandra, Cyrus, and Cyrano, the main objects of the study detailed in Chapter 3. The 4th member of the brood succumbed when only a few days old, through a circumstance that arose because of the parents' inexperience. The circumstances not only underscored the importance of experience for the parents, but gave clues to the methods by which lovebirds, and doubtless many other avian parents, allofeed their chicks. This topic is taken up first.

TONGUE-FLICK ALLOFEEDING, WAYWARD FOOD, AND CLOGGED NOSTRILS.

ACCUMULATION OF WAYWARD FOOD. In my treatment of the literature accounts of the care of Cockatielian chicks, it was noted that the busy parents often regurgitate some food onto the chicks' backs, and that they re-eat this food. The literature accounts of chick care by lovebirds mention virtually nothing of food accumulating on the bills, heads (eyes, cheeks, nostrils, foreheads, etc.), and backs of the chicks. Yet this may prove to be a serious problem when inexperienced parents are involved. I noted it with almost all 1st broods, and with the 2nd and sometimes the 3rd broods of some pairs, including Petra and Ramses.

TONGUE-FLICK ALLOFEEDING AND DRIPPING FOOD. One may well ask why such an unusual problem should exist as a result of the allofeeding of very young lovebirds and Cockatiels (and probably many other parrots, but not Budgerigars, whose nostrils I never found to be soiled). My observations of the feeding of hatchlings and young nestlings in open nestbowls and nestboxes with Plexiglas sidepanes have revealed the basis for the wayward food.

As already described above for Cockatiels, I found that most of the food allofed to lovebird hatchlings and very young nestlings is tongue-flick allofed. In this process, liquid food is transferred from the tip of the tongue of the parent into the hatchling's mouth by being wiped off the tongue onto the inside edges of its upper mandible--in a series of rapid flicks, that I estimate at about 8-12/sec. This action is accompanied by a small amplitude vibration of the parent's head and usually of the head and body of the nestling when a few days old.

The lovebird chick's tongue also usually flicks at this time, probably in synchrony with swallowing of the liquid food. In fact, even in the allofeeding of older nestlings by massive tongue-flick allofeeding and vigorous head bobbing, the gobs of food often are transferred to the inner edges of the chick's upper mandible by tongue flicking. On the other hand, trickle-feeding (see p. 676) of lovebird hatchlings occurs much less frequently than tongue-flick allofeeding and sometimes is the mode of allofeeding older nestlings, perhaps then involving mostly a transfer of water.

The generalization emerges that all forms of allofeeding of lovebird chicks involve vibratory movements of the parent's head. In trickle-feeding there are very-small-amplitude vibrations of the head of the parent but the parent's tongue does not flick; rather, primarily liquid food trickles from it into the mouth of the chick. In tongue-flick and massive tongue-flick allofeeding, the head of the parent vibrates and its tongue flicks in synchrony. In allofeeding by head-bobbing or pumping, the head undergoes wide-amplitude movements and the tongue often flicks in synchrony. In all types of allofeeding, the chick's tongue evidently flicks in synchrony with swallowing.

The size of an adult's tongue is so large in comparison with that of a hatchling's bill, that some of the liquid comes into contact with the outside of the bill, adheres, and runs off onto the chick's head as it accumulates. At other times, when large gobs of semi-liquid food are delivered, much or most of it may run down the bill onto parts of the chick's head.

BILL-TO-BILL CONTACTS---POSITIONS OF THE YOUNG. The allofeeding parent employs various bill-to-bill means to facilitate delivering the food to the young, depending upon the positions that the young assume. Most frequently the hatchlings and very young nestlings are maneuvered onto their backs with their bills facing upward. The parent then inserts the tips of its upper and lower mandibles into the gape corners of the chick's bill, whereupon the chick usually gapes. As the parent grasps the chick's bill in this manner, it wipes the liquid intermittently from its tongue onto the inside edges of the chick's upper mandible in the manner described on p. 675. Sometimes only the lower mandible of the parent is inserted into the chick's bill, while the tip of the parent's upper mandible rests lightly on the chick's forehead (a method I also have observed in Cockatiels). The parent then tongue-flick allofeeds, as described above. I have seen both females and males use this technique.

GOBS OF WAYWARD FOOD. When chicks are only a day or two older--even as early as the 2nd day--the parent's tongue is flicked even more rapidly as the food is transferred. At this time, large gobs of semi-liquid (glutinous) food (of warm-butter consistency) often find their way onto the chicks' faces and heads and usually are recovered promptly by the allofeeding parent(s). Even large gobs delivered directly into the chick's mouth may be recovered by the allofeeding parent(s), to be allofed again thereafter in smaller portions. It is no exaggeration to say that the heads of chicks sometimes become thoroughly drenched with liquid or semi-liquid food during allofeedings by inexperienced parents.

CLEANING OF WAYWARD FOOD. In the cases of some birds, it apparently usually is the function of the female both to allofeed and to recover wayward food. In the cases of others, such as lovebirds and Budgerigars (see, e.g., pp. 751, 752, **Male Gives Cleaning First Priority**), the male parent may take over a large portion of the food recovery while the female is allofeeding the hatchlings and young nestlings. He also may recover food that drips, exudes, or otherwise finds its way onto the hen's bill while she is allofeeding the young, as well as while she herself is being allofed (all 6 of my breeding lovebird males performed these functions).

But the lovebird (and Budgerigar) hen also takes part in cleaning the heads of the young; her degree of participation depends upon the number of chicks to be cared for and whether the male is present or in position to reach the chicks' bills. The hen's upper mandible sometimes is seen to be heavily encrusted with an accumulation of dried food at one time, yet spotlessly clean and shiny at a later time. Presumably this latter cleaning is accomplished by the ministrations of the male.

CLEANING DRIED, CAKED FOOD---SUFFOCATION OF A CHICK. Frequent examinations of the young in the broods of inexperienced lovebirds are desirable to remove dried, caked food from their heads (and backs). Eyes, foreheads, and nares often are found to be heavily encrusted with thick films of dried food. These must be removed if growth is to proceed normally and serious problems are not to result. Keeping the external nares clear, of course, is crucial. If both become clogged, death of the chick is inevitable.

This was the accident that befell one member of this 2nd brood during the evening and night of January 28-29, 1983, either because of Ramses' inexperience or because of his absence together with Petra's inexperience. Perhaps the chick was unable to take the alternate course of breathing through its mouth, or if it could do this, it may have choked when being allofed at the same time. [Food passing from the oral cavity to the esophagus must cross the respiratory passageway from the choana(e) to the glottis. This region where the two streams, air and food, cross in the pharynx is known as the "pharyngeal chiasma" (431).]

POWDERED EXCRETA AND CLOGGED NARES. However, wayward food is not the only hazard facing the parrot nestling. Both lovebirds and Cockatiels, even those kept meticulously clean by their parents, inhale increasingly large quantities of dry powdered excreta as the NB becomes increasingly fouled. This material (primarily urates and derivatives thereof; 23, 157) accumulates within the nostrils and tends to occlude the internal passages. Solitary chicks often sleep in a prone position, sometimes with the bill stuck straight down in the bedding, in which the powder settles. However, this manner of clogging of the nares is not a potentially lethal problem. Not only does the rapid growth of the chick result in continuous enlargement of the nares, but older chicks can, and often do, overcome it by breathing through their mouths.

If one closely watches chicks whose nostrils are encumbered with powdered excreta, a time comes when a given occlusion breaks loose and flaps back and forth like a butterfly valve, with each inhalation and exhalation of the chick. One can free an occluded passage by delicately teasing apart the occluding material with a tiny, blunt object. It then may be expelled in a cloud of fine particles on the next exhalation. I do not recommend this procedure, though, as it is unnecessary and risks injury to the very delicate tissues of the chick. [All the tissues in small birds, even adults, are very fragile. Even the most careful manipulations with forceps or needles may tear them (135).]

CHICKS FLEDGE. Until the 38th day after hatching of the 1st chick, Petra and Ramses "rode herd" on them very closely to keep them in the NB, amidst a great deal of tumult. On that day, however, the chicks finally were out in force, though not yet able to fly. This was a period of great 'concern' on the part of the parents, who would come charging into the NB to protect the young whenever I peered under the lid to inspect them.

In this connection, the reactions of parent lovebirds when they already were in the NB, and I inspected it, depended on their degree of habituation. For example, the well-habituated birds, Petra and Ramses, stood their ground and attacked me if I reached in; the less well-habituated birds, Cassandra and Cyrus, fled at any inkling of my intrusion.

PREPARING TO BREED AGAIN. By the time of the first flights on the 41st day, Petra and Ramses were in breeding condition again and were copulating. Petra had begun intensive paper stripping 3 days earlier and laid the 1st egg of her next clutch 2 days later. By that same day, the young had become facile fliers and one of them also took its 1st bath, a very vigorous one. The typical situation within the enclosure at that time was to find all 5 resting birds in close contact, or to find Petra and Ramses together in one group, and the 3 young together in another, usually side by side. [When juveniles of the penultimate brood also are present with fledglings, they often are excluded from such a family cluster, as occurred when the 8th and 9th broods were present together (see pp. 728-730).]

A GREAT INQUISITIVENESS OF PETRA AND RAMSES, as regards new surroundings, was shown on March 11, 1983, when I flighted the family. Petra and Ramses had developed the habit of frequently landing on me and in my hair, ever since they first did so in their concern for Jagadai and Ogatai, when I handled the latter as fledglings. [Little by little Jagatai and Ogadai also took to doing so, but only if Petra and Ramses already were on me.] The day before, while Petra and Ramses were on me, I went to the bedroom to obtain something and they went with me. I tarried in the bedroom to give them time to take in the new vistas before returning to the living room.

On the day in question (Mar. 11), Petra and Ramses spent an inordinate amount of time on me when they were flighted, even though the welfare of the young ordinarily would have had first priority at the time. It was clear that they were tarrying on the chance that I would take them on another visit to the bedroom, and I eventually accommodated them.

EARLY FLIGHTS----PROTECTING THE YOUNG----FAMILY TIES. On these early flights, when Jagatai and Ogadai also were flighted, Petra and Ramses were very protective of the new brood, chasing off the older brothers at their slightest encroachment. Ramses almost always assumed the major role in protecting and otherwise looking after the young outside the enclosure; Petra, however, often gave greater priority to stripping and gathering paper. The same situation pertained during the flighting of the broods of my other breeding pairs (see below). The male always assumed the major role in escorting and overseeing the welfare of the fledged young.

During these flightings, and as late as 1 month later, at 11 weeks of age, the relative strengths of the family ties were evident. Usually the parents and the 3 fledglings stayed together as a close group, with the parents at first tagging after the fledglings, and the fledglings later tagging after the parents. But whenever the group split up, the parents almost always formed one group and the fledglings another. Otherwise, Ramses typically remained with the fledglings while Petra was occupied elsewhere.

During the latter part of this period, when the family of 5 were flighted, Cyrano began to show a preference for remaining on the home perch (near enclosure D, housing Jagatai and Ogadai). [Cassandra and Cyrus apparently were well on the way toward forming a pair bond.] At the end of the 12th week, I gave Cyrano to Bill Murphy (see pp. 315, 316). It also was at that time that the parents first began to tolerate the near presence of Jagatai and Ogadai with the 2nd brood while being flighted. All the birds then were landing on me, but only If Petra and Ramses led the way, and, even then, most of the offspring usually were hesitant to do so.

The Third Brood of Petra and Ramses

The 3rd and 4th broods of Petra and Ramses were reared in an open nestbowl, where I had my first opportunities to make close observations of all the proceedings. The following accounts of parental care are based on observations of these 2 broods and those of 5 additional breeding pairs, all of which also were raised in "transparent" nestboxes or open nestbowls and could be observed very closely.

CARING FOR THE HATCHLINGS. The 4th egg of the synchronized clutch was the first to hatch, early on the 21st day of incubation (Aug. 6, 1983). When I detected the presence of the hatchling at 07:30 h, it already was fully hatched, dry, and being cared for. Both parents were sitting side by side in the nestbowl, with the hatchling sheltered by the hen. I was aware of no allofeeding during the next 4 h, but I did hear some cheeping at 11:20 h. This could have been the 2nd chick hatching, since I was able to confirm its presence at 23:30 h that night. However, at that time the eggs seemed to be getting all the attention, not the chicks.

Finally, at 24:45 h, as I was about to turn off the lights for the night, I saw the allofeeding of the 2nd hatchling, as it lay flat on its back. After that, I saw Petra allofeed the 1st hatchling too, curled up in a quite different position. It appeared that when Petra's bill touched that of the chick, the latter opened reflexly to receive the food.

BOTH PARENTS FULLY OCCUPIED. Although I say that "I saw" these allofeedings, at first I had very little inkling of what was occurring. For one thing, I did not suspect that there might be anything unusual about how the allofeeding was accomplished, so I was not at pains to take careful note of it. For another, the nestbowl was 45 cm away and Ramses' head or bill often was positioned between me and the bills of Petra and the chicks. In addition, the parental manipulations occurred very rapidly.

My first impression was that the parents were competing to allofeed the chicks, because Ramses was fully as busy as Petra at whatever he was doing. Moreover, both birds seemed to be taking turns in rapid succession as they huddled in close over the chicks. In addition to the parental activity at the chicks' bills, and in the neighborhood of one another's bills, it could be seen clearly that the chicks were being touched elsewhere, even on their crops and bellies, a form of stimulation and grooming.

MALE GIVES CLEANING FIRST PRIORITY. From subsequent direct, very close observations of 6 breeding pairs (fully habituated to my presence) in open nestbowls, the transpiring events became clear, as well as why males may be even more busy than the hens. The male not only must prepare almost all the food and allofeed much of it to the hen, he usually is the major performer of the function of cleaning wayward food from the hen and chicks.

To accomplish this cleaning, a male must have his bill and tongue very close to the female's, in order to retrieve as much as possible of the food that drips from her and the chick's bills. Otherwise, much of this food would be lost when it fell to the nest bottom. In addition, he has to clean both sides of the hen's bill (the top of her bill usually has low priority) and the chicks' entire bills and heads. He also closely monitors the passage of food from a position at one side of the hen's mouth--often reaching into it once or twice per sec--as she allofeeds. Any large pieces of food that are brought forward in the process but held back (filtered) between the tongue and the palate are recovered by him and reswallowed. In accomplishing these activities, he insinuates himself very closely into all of the hen's allofeeding actions, not only following her leads but often aggressively initiating actions himself.

When the hen withdraws momentarily to regurgitate another portion of food, the male moves in close and licks clean the chick's bill and head. He also gives further attention to the sides of the female's bill and often transfers recovered and additional food to her tongue. Of course, the female also is attentive to dripping food, and cleans as the occasion demands. Nevertheless, when the male is careless in his attentions, the excess food sometimes runs all over the chicks' faces and heads, often including large pieces, which the hen usually recovers. As mentioned above, the male frequently removes large pieces of food (or errant tiny wood shavings) from the hen's mouth and tongue and the chick's mouth, even as she allofeeds, and he sometimes pushes or pulls her bill aside as he does so. The hen usually tolerates these very close attentions, but sometimes opposes his actions. The birds' tongues, of course, are the major instruments of these activities, but the bills also see very much use.

As I mentioned earlier, the whole process of allofeeding hatchlings and very young nestlings sometimes is suggestive of what it would look like if two surgeons were to operate together on a patient at 10 times normal speed. These actions were seen in the closest detail during the care of all subsequent lovebird broods. Almost all of the broods were raised in open nestbowls, and most pairs were so well habituated that I could watch them from a distance of only a few cm without disturbing them. When allofeeding the incubating hen, the male also cleans food from the side of her bill and recovers fallen particulate food, as well.

MALE ALLOFEEDS HATCHLINGS WHEN OPPORTUNITY AFFORDS. According to the literature, the male does not participate in the allofeeding of the chicks until after about the 3rd day. It is clear from my observations, however, that both parents allofeed hatchlings and very young nestlings, and that the process often is competitive from the very beginning. I frequently saw the parents allofeeding hatchlings and young nestlings in cooperative competition, each pushing the other's head aside every ½ sec or so and delivering portions of liquid food in a few tongue-flicks before being displaced in turn. Any failures of males to allofeed is more by default than disinclination. Since they do almost all of the food processing, allofeed the hen, and clean the hen and chicks--acts which take first priority --they simply have much less opportunity to allofeed the chicks.

However, whenever the opportunity affords, males allofeed chicks of any age, even fresh hatchlings. I often have seen experienced males allofeed chicks during the 1st 2 days, particularly the 2nd chick of a brood. Sometimes, the female does not even compete on such occasions but 'disinterestedly' incubates the eggs or tends to other chicks. However, the male does not always allofeed liquid food to hatchlings. On two occasions (see pp. 766, 767), Cyrus allofeed hatchlings their 1st meal, consisting of gobs of semiliquid food. One of these chicks succumbed the next day.

MALE TRANSFERS FOOD TO ALLOFEEDING HEN. Up until the time of allofeeding of the 1st chick of the 2nd brood of Zenobia and Cyrano (see pp. 770, 771), I was able to confirm only that the male cleans during the moments while the hen is engaged in allofeeding a chick. Of course, he also may allofeed the female or the chick when the hen withdraws her head momentarily, and he transfers recovered dripping food to the female's mouth. During the allofeeding of the chick referred to, however, I was able to make the observations whereby the last piece of the puzzle of the male's hectic activity fell into place.

Many times, I saw Cyrano holding Zenobia's bill within his own at the very times that she was tongue-flick allofeeding the chick. There was no possibility of his being engaged in cleaning at that time. Not only did he have no view of the food being transferred, but I could see precisely what was occurring. At last, I could comprehend why the allofeeding appeared to be intensely competitive, and why the male's intimately-near presence was essential. The answer was that the male often tongue-flick transfers liquid food to the female's tongue and to the inner surface of her upper mandible, even as she simultaneously tongue-flick allofeeds a hatchling or young nestling. In other words, some of the food is delivered in tandem from the male to the chick via the female's tongue as a momentary intermediary. When semi-liquid food is being transferred to chicks, the male also simultaneously transfers gobs of similar food directly onto the hen's tongue.

It is the occurrence of this latter method of feeding very young Peach-faced Lovebird (and Budgerigar; see p. 784, **Chick Allofeeding Indistinguishable from That of Lovebirds**) chicks that more or less rules out any essential role of doubly processed or doubly pre-digested food (i.e., food digested, in turn, by both the male and the female). [The evidence does, however, suggest the utilization of doubly-digested food in the allofeeding of Cockatiel hatchlings and very young nestlings (see pp. 690, 691, **Carmen's Allofeeding of Cosimo**).]

FEMALE MAIN ALLOFEEDER & PROTECTOR---COMPETITIVE COOPERATIVE FEEDING. I often saw Cyrus and Cyrano allofeed tiny hatchlings when the opportunity afforded. As chicks grow larger and need less cleaning--because more-solid food is being delivered with less dripping--the male is able to devote more time to allofeeding them. Nevertheless, the female remains the main allofeeder and protector during the nestling period. Sometimes the parents compete cooperatively in the allofeeding. Each crowds in impatiently to take his turn while the other is allofeeding, and often crowds away the other or even pulls away the other's bill to gain access to the chick.

In the case of the male, the impatience is both to deliver more food to the hen and to allofeed the chick. In fact, it is the higher priority afforded to allofeeding the hen and cleaning the hen and chick that usually diverts the male from allofeeding young chicks. Thus, after a "non-simultaneous" allofeeding of the hen, before the male can regurgitate another portion of food to allofeed the chick awaiting to be fed, the hen already is delivering the transferred food to it.

NESTLING PRIORITY FOR FOOD--NIGHT FEEDING? Insofar as priority in allofeeding the chicks is concerned, the older, larger chicks seem always to be allofed first. A tiny nestling cheeping continually during such allofeedings often seems to be 'ignored' totally until all the larger nestlings have been allofed. As a consequence, if circumstances are unfavorable in any way for raising young, the nestlings that represent the least investment of parental resources are the ones that fail to survive. Even in favorable circumstances, the younger chicks fall farther and farther behind the older ones in their development.

[The interpretation of the circumstance of allofeeding the older nestlings first and 'ignoring' a cheeping, tiny nestling or hatchling, is complicated by the uncertainty as to whether the allofeeding parent merely is delaying the allofeeding of the tiny nestling to allow time for more thorough processing of the food for it, as doubtless sometimes occurs]

In over 30 broods, the maximum number of young that survived in any brood was 3, with about 1 chick per brood lost as a consequence of parental inexperience or hatchling infirmity. Unhatched eggs beyond the 3rd or 4th have even lesser priority than the youngest chicks. They often get scattered by active chicks or are left uncovered by the hens. I have seen no indication that chicks are allofed at night (in total darkness). Typically they are "loaded up" in the evening and have but slight crops by morning, when they are "loaded up" again, paralleling the situation usually seen in Cockatiels.

YOUNG SIT UP, FLAP FORELIMBS. By 7-9 days of age the young were able to hold up their heads while being allofed (Cockatiels both sit up and hold up their heads within a few hours of hatching) and the next day one of them even could sit up to be allofed, sometimes with its forelimbs outstretched and flapping at the same time. This is known behavior that proved to be a common maneuver of lovebird and Cockatielian chicks while being allofed, as well as at other times. Ramses, alone, often was seen to be allofeeding the young at that age. The very high growth and metabolic rates of the chicks were evidenced by the volume of excreta that came to pack the nestbowl each day, necessitating a daily cleaning. In a NB, the egesta get plastered up the walls in the corners.

THE YOUNG GROOM, PANT, SCAMPER ABOUT. By the 20th day, the chicks were seen to groom themselves extensively for the first time. Before that, the parents had been allogrooming them frequently, usually accompanied by their cheeping. The largest chick was out of the nest 3 days later and could almost perch on a finger. Though both young could stand and scramble about in the nestbowl with ease, their tendency to remain within it was very strong. On the 25th day they were very much occupied chewing debris, and both were cooling themselves by panting (ambient air temperature, 30°C).

ADDITIONAL PERSPECTIVE ON FEATHER-PICKING. Meanwhile, Petra was very much occupied removing dried excreta that was adhering to their plumage, even as they 'complained' vigorously. It is very easy to see how this otherwise 'desirable' activity could become misdirected and result in feather-picking, and also to see why the cries of the young would not dissuade the attending parent from continuing, nor alarm the other parent.

VEHEMENTLY ATTACKED BY THE CHICKS. On the 27th day, both chicks were spending considerable amounts of time out of the nest. They occupied themselves chewing on paper, seeds, debris, and anything else within reach on the enclosure floor, but they were not yet climbing into the elevated food trays. For the first time, one of the chicks attacked me by lunging at my fingers, something no lovebird chick ever had done before. In the days to come, attacks by these chicks became more and more frequent. It was quite evident that they were learning to do this from their parents (primarily Petra), who at that time always attacked me with a fury when I serviced the enclosure. Chicks brooded in nestboxes never attacked me, as they never saw the parents do it (the parents always were outside the NB when I handled the young). [It is well known that chicks copy the maintenance activities of their parents.]

Within a week, the whole family was attacking me in unison, and the chicks were biting quite hard, though harmlessly. Of course, such attacks only occurred when the chicks were "at home" in the enclosure or nestbowl, never during handling or when outside the enclosure (and similarly for the parents). But these attacks soon were to cease, at least when the parents were absent; by the 38th day, chicks alone in the enclosure ran away and hid, rather than attack me.

CHICKS LESS FEARFUL. Another different behavior of sighted chicks reared in the open, that was noted with all subsequent broods reared in like circumstances, was that the chicks voided less frequently while being handled; chicks raised in closed NBs almost invariably did so. The difference traced to the fact that the former chicks were habituated to seeing me many times daily from within the nest, and came to lose much of their fear (also evidenced during the period when they attacked me rather than flee). On the other hand, chicks raised in closed surroundings saw me only infrequently, when I intruded on the privacy of the NB.

PROGRESS WITH SEED-EATING. On the 30th day, the chicks were well feathered (with tail feathers about 1½ cm long) and were starting to take note of the surroundings when I handled them. They also were chewing assiduously on seeds, though perhaps making but little progress. But by the next day, the largest chick was probably able to eat spray millet. They already could eat corn, and by the 34th day they were able to cope with the entire diet, though not with great facility.

It also was on the 30th day that Ramses first vigorously slapped away the head of one of the chicks when it pressed in too closely and determinedly while the other was being allofed. Partial blockage of the nostrils of the smaller of the 2 chicks was suggested by the fact that it panted at only 27°C, a temperature at which increased ventilation would not seem to have been necessary.

PARENTS ESCORT YOUNG. At about the time the chicks began to run away and hide rather than attack me (the 38th day), they were beginning to "gain their wings." On the 41st day, the parents stayed very close to me when I handled them, and their ‘concern’ was even greater the next day. Any wing-flapping by the young brought the parents promptly to their immediate vicinity, and they accompanied the young on all their short flights with the greatest of attentiveness. Within another 3 days, both chicks could fly with facility, and the parents no longer were "superprotective" of them. During these same days, the parents also ceased attacking me when I serviced the enclosures or otherwise reached toward the fledglings.

AGAIN IN BREEDING CONDITION----RAMSES LEARNS TO STRIP AND TUCK. By the beginning of the 11th week, Petra and Ramses were again in breeding condition and copulating. On October 18, I was surprised to find that Ramses had learned to tuck strips into his rump feathers, after many hours of watching and copying Petra do it. Within a few days it also was evident that the strips he was tucking were not always stolen from Petra. He had become so adept at stripping and tucking that I mistook him for Petra on one occasion. He still was far less skillful than was she (of course, his strips were not uniform), and he, at first, tucked strips into both his breast and rump feathers. Though he conveyed these tucked strips to the enclosure, he never was seen to employ them for any purpose other than to chew on them. On November 5, the entire family bathed together vigorously.

The Fourth Brood of Petra and Ramses

TITUS HATCHES. By this time my interest in the early care of the chicks was keen and I determined to make close observations on another brood in an open nestbowl (little did I suspect at the time that observations on many additional broods would be needed--including several fathered by the lone chick of this brood). The opportunity arose when the 5th egg of the 5th clutch of Petra and Ramses hatched, sometime shortly before 16:30 h on March 2, 1984, and the chick cheeped to be allofed. This was Titus, whose crippled right leg set the stage for many interesting observations, and about whose social interactions Chapter 5 is largely concerned. I repeat the events of his youth very briefly for the convenience of the reader.

ALLOFEEDINGS EASILY MONITORED---ONE CHICK EASILY CARED FOR. As Titus was the only chick in the brood, some of the ambiguities that obscured the early care of his older sisters, Flavia and Zenobia, were not encountered. I could easily monitor each of Titus' allofeedings by keeping alert for his periodic cheeping. The next day, for example, there were 7 allofeedings between 09:30 h and 15:00 h, and an 8th at 17:00 h, amounting to roughly 1 feeding/h. Petra typically allofed Titus as he lay on his back.

Although Petra was very attentive to Titus, caring for only 1 chick could not have been burdensome to her, as she never declined an opportunity to be flighted. Nor was it any problem to brood Titus in the presence of Flavia and Zenobia, as the sisters scarcely ever went near the nestbowl. Ramses always kept them on the alert to keep their distance when they were in the enclosure (as opposed to the tower). The family of 4 adults bathed together again on March 6.

TITUS CRIPPLED---HIS EARLY DEVELOPMENT. One of Titus' eyes was open on the 11th day but his right leg was splayed out to the side, the consequence of a congenital deformity. Titus continued to cheep quietly when being allofed, even on the 18th day, when his wing feathers were beginning to break from their sheaths. On the same day he 1st ventured from the nestbowl. He was seen to groom himself for the 1st time on the 23rd day. I was handling and examining Titus about 4 times per day at that time.

Although by the 27th day the parents were as yet 'unconcerned' over my handling of Titus, they attacked me, as was the case with the 3rd brood, whenever I serviced the enclosure. Ramses did this 'good-naturedly,' often merely feigning an attack and not biting hard, whereas Petra was not averse to giving me a painful nip. At that time, Titus typically snuggled his head against Petra's side when resting and sleeping, but sometimes he had his head under her. The next day (Mar. 30) was the day that Flavia siezed the opportunity to snuggle up against Titus in the nestbowl after the parents had left the enclosure on a flighting (see p. 643).

FEATHER-PICKING BEGINS. Being the sole member of the brood, the "unfortunate" Titus was destined to be feather-picked severely by his parents, most especially Petra, even though she had shown no tendency to treat any chick of her 1st 3 broods in that manner. The first signs of this were evident on the 28th day, when Titus squealed repeatedly as Petra incessantly groomed his rump, though it was not contaminated by droppings. This attention continued on and off into the late evening.

[It is interesting to note, in this connection, that all Nyasa Lovebirds are said to feather-pick their young, or to be most prone to do so (138). The habit is said to be "checked to some extent" by adding cod liver oil and calcium supplements to their diet (104). On the other hand, all species of parrots can become feather-pickers, though certain species have the reputation of being prime offenders, such as African Grays, Nanday Conures (*Nandayus nenday*), Cockatiels, macaws, and several species of cockatoos, particularly the Gang-Gang Cockatoo (138, 448).]

But this was just the beginning of Titus' misadventures in this regard. The time soon came when both parents were using him simultaneously as the hapless foil for their insufficiently requited urges to exercise parental care. I spare the reader further repetition of the prolonged feather-picking of Titus. These, incidentally, previewed a similar fate of the lone brood member, Claudius, at the hands of his parents, Cassandra and Cyrus. I end with the more felicitous note that he suffered no lasting injury. Perhaps I already have repeated more than necessary of the treatment recounted in Chapter 5, which also surveys the later interactions of Titus and his eventual mating and breeding with his older sister, Flavia.

The First Brood of Cassandra and Cyrus

The first brood of Cassandra and Cyrus was the product of their 5th clutch (a sole hatchling of the 4th clutch had succumbed and is not reckoned in Table 4; see p. 734), for which I provided a NB and facilitated breeding. I synchronized the eggs and allowed their incubation to begin on March 19, 1984. Since the eggs and young were brooded in an opaque NB, our focus with this brood is almost entirely on information obtained by observations in the enclosure, on periodic inspection within the NB, on handling of the young, and on flighting of the young and parents. I use this brood as the vehicle for a rather detailed accounting of parent-young interactions, fledging, and interactions with older relatives in the colony.

HATCHINGS---YOUNGEST CHICKS FALL BEHIND--HEAVILY CAKED WITH FOOD. The 2nd and 4th eggs hatched during the early morning of April 10, and the 1st and 5th at times unknown on April 12. Although Cyrus frequently entered the NB during the day, he was outside most of the time. He also usually was outside at the time of lights-off at night, but was almost always in the NB at the time of lights-on in the morning. Presumably he entered shortly after natural dawn.

The brood of 4 appeared to be healthy at midnight of April 13th, and 12 h later, but at 16:50 h on the 14th, it was evident that their heads were somewhat caked with dried food. On April 15, I peeled a big piece of dried food off of the smallest chick's bill, forehead, and one eye, and noticed that his crop was not full, like those of the other 3 chicks. That same day was the first since the 1st 2 chicks hatched that Cassandra spent an appreciable amount of time out of the NB eating. Late that night I noticed that the 2 youngest chicks were falling far behind in their development compared to the 2 oldest ones.

A SMALL CHICK SUCCUMBS. The next morning I found no food in the crop of one of the small chicks. I then removed the other 3 for 20 min to investigate the outcome of giving it the exclusive attention of the parents. During this time, I cleaned a considerable amount of caked food from the bills, heads, and wings of the other 3 chicks. It was quite evident that the inexperienced pair was doing poorly at keeping the young clean; Cyrus perhaps was largely responsible for this shortcoming.

When I returned the 3 chicks to the NB, the 4th chick was lying flat on its back with its crop half full of an orange-yellow liquid, which I took to be partly-digested corn. It seemed that the relatively tiny, retarded nestling was being given an appropriate diet of entirely liquid food, but, despite this, it was dead the next morning.

POOR PARENTAL MANAGEMENT---I CLEAN THE CHICKS. In the next 2 days the faces and foreheads of all 3 nestlings had to be cleaned repeatedly of dry, caked food that the inexperienced parents were allowing to run from their bills and accumulate upon them. The youngest chick was so much smaller than its 2 broodmates that its head usually was hidden under their bodies. They, on the other hand, could comfortably lean on each other. Moreover, Cassandra was spending an ever increasing amount of time out of the NB. Presumably Cyrus was taking over more of the allofeeding, or the intervals between feedings were lengthening, or both. When I flighted Cyrus on the 9th day, Cassandra left the NB and followed him after about 3 min, but she re-entered after about 2 min, ate spray millet for about 5 min, and returned to the chicks in the NB.

FURTHER DEVELOPMENT---INTERACTIONS WITH CYRANO. Both older chicks, Romeo and Juliet, had their eyes opened to slits by the 11th day, which also was the day of the surprising allofeeding of Cassandra by her broodmate, Cyrano, from outside of the enclosure (see p. 329). Cyrus not only did not interfere, he took turns with Cyrano allofeeding her. Cassandra had begun to spend many minutes at a time outside of the NB. Evidently she was tending very well to the needs of the young chick, Zoltan, and by the 14th day I was confident that he also would survive.

When Cyrano visited outside the enclosure on the 16th day (reckoning from the first hatchings), both Cassandra and Cyrus showed a great deal of interest in him but he did not allofeed Cassandra. His priorities apparently were altered drastically after his mating with Zenobia. At one time his sole objective seemed to be to courtship-feed Cassandra (see p. 318 *et seq.*).

ALTERED PARENTAL ATTENTION--CASSANDRA AGAIN ALLOFED BY CYRANO. By the 17th day, it could be said that Cassandra and Cyrus were allofeeding the young very competently, as the latter's crops always were full. The parents had become very partial to whole-grain bread, which had to be making up a fair part of the chicks' diet at the time. I was handling the young once or twice each day during this period, and the parents were becoming increasingly agitated when I did so. They tried ever more 'frantically' to get into the closed-off NB at such times.

It is of interest that Cyrus, like his father Ramses, sometimes bit my hand gently while I was servicing the enclosure, even though the chicks (and usually Cassandra) were in the NB and not being threatened directly. Cyrus had ceased entering the NB early in the morning before lights-on, evidently leaving the less urgent early morning allofeedings to Cassandra, alone. Cyrano paid another nonchalant visit to the outside vicinity of the enclosure on the 18th day (April 28). Four days later he allofed Cassandra through the bars about 12-15 regurgitations; Cyrus watched most of these feedings with no outward sign of 'concern.'

OCCLUDED NOSTRILS. In the early days of May, Zoltan (the youngest chick) was panting noticeably, with both of his nostrils partly occluded by powdered excreta. I partly cleared the left one with a blunt probe on May 3, but did not venture to work on the right one. The situation was much the same on the next day, but the material in the right nostril (under or within the cere) was beginning to come loose. A thorough cleaning of the NB more or less solved this problem.

"RIDING HERD" ON THE CHICKS. The following evening was one of those in which Cyrano, when flighted, had so little interest in Cassandra that he did not even visit outside the enclosure. Beginning on the 27th day, Cassandra and Cyrus began "riding herd" on the chicks on the inside of the NB entrance; they had very great difficulty restraining and containing the brood of 3, particularly in the morning. Once the chicks were settled, the parents spent much of the remainder of the day outside of the NB.

PARENTAL 'CONCERNS' DURING FLIGHTINGS. I began flighting the parents while I handled the chicks when the latter were 23 days old. On that day, the parents flew back and forth over me and the chicks several times and then gradually worked their way over from perch to perch onto my hand. But they stayed only for 10-15 sec before departing for the enclosures and visiting with Cyrano and the rest of the family. On the next 2 days they did not bother to visit the young but just flew back and forth over us several times. The following 2 days were repeats of the visit on the 1st flighting.

The next day (May 8), the parents flew by me so closely and rapidly that it was almost like dive bombing. Afterward, they worked closer, perch by perch, with the last stop for Cyrus being on my head for a few sec. It was not until 3 days later, when the chicks were 31 days old, that parental 'concerns' for them heightened to the point where both of them alighted on my head, perched on my knees, and came to the edge of the paper on which the chicks were supported. For the 1st time, the chicks pecked aggressively at each other's bills.

CONFINING THE CHICKS in the NB then was extremely difficult for the parents, and the tumult became ever greater. Cassandra undertook most of the guard duty but there were several times when she was not equal to the task and Cyrus had to come to her aid. By the 33rd day, the squeals of the young in the morning were almost endless as they crowded toward the entrance and repeatedly were thrown back bodily.

Thus, it came as a surprise to me on the next day to see Romeo and Juliet gain the entrance but not venture out. Though the parents still were keeping the young confined the next morning, Juliet somehow managed to elude their guard and exit to a position near the front of the NB, with the alarmed parents keeping close tab on her. She dared not venture very far, though, and it was not long before she had re-entered and Cassandra was guarding the entrance from the outside. Late that afternoon, Cassandra was "riding herd" on them from the inside again, amidst a tremendous uproar. Clearly, grown lovebird chicks are not easily restrained, and show somewhat the same tenacity of purpose as juveniles and adults.

MORE ON 'PARENTAL' CONCERNS. The 34th day was one on which the parents expressed very great 'concern' as I handled the chicks. Both perched on my hand, got down directly onto the paper with the chicks, and remained almost the entire time, all the while chattering alarmedly and moving about nervously. Cassandra led the way at that time. The following day was even more eventful. Although Cassandra led the way again, Cyrus was the more persistent of the 2 parents. They climbed about on my hands and arms and the paper, screeching all the while. The young also cheeped excitedly, and all the lovebirds in the colony joined in intermittently.

The parents essentially repeated their behavior the next day, with evidence of even greater 'concern,' including perching unhesitatingly on my hand. Cyrus stayed very close and almost allofed one of the chicks when it solicited. Virtually the same events were repeated on the next 3 days, with the exception that on the last of these days (May 18), I placed the young back on the enclosure floor, rather than in the NB. Usually, the parents did not return voluntarily to the enclosure, but had to be returned as they perched on the home perch. But on that day, as soon as the parents noticed the deviation, they went right into the enclosure after the young, with Cassandra leading the way. They soon had the young back in the NB.

OVERSEEING CHICKS. On the same day that Juliet managed to exit the NB in the morning, both she and Romeo managed to breach the parental guard in the early evening. The parents were quite burdened trying to oversee the movements and welfare of just these two oldest chicks. When they managed to get one chick back into the NB, Cassandra went in with it and kept it inside, while Cyrus stayed close to and and watched over the other one. But if I got up and approached the enclosure, the chick(s) dashed headlong for the NB entrance.

Again, on the next day, the parents tried to contain the chicks in the NB, but by early evening Romeo had made his way over to the night perch. On the following day (the 37th) both older chicks got out again and the excitement was great. Things finally settled down on the 38th day, as Romeo and Juliet were allowed to forage about on the enclosure floor. By midmorning, Cassandra and Cyrus had joined them, and I was witness to a tranquil family scene. Meanwhile, Zoltan, who had hatched 2 days after his broodmates, but had fallen at least 5 days behind in development, did not venture even to the NB entrance.

HANDLED CHICKS FLEE---BATHING. When I handled the young the next day, for the 1st time they jumped out of my hands and flew down 20-30 cm into my lap; they repeated this time and again without hesitation. The parents, of course, kept close by, greatly 'concerned' all the while. But the young could not yet gain altitude nor even sustain themselves in the air.

The parents again followed voluntarily when I returned the young to the enclosure floor. Zoltan made immediately for the cover of the NB, whereas Romeo and Juliet explored the entire enclosure, with Cassandra and Cyrus close by. Early that afternoon, all but Zoltan took head-ducking baths together from the edge of the water bowl. They then took to the perches to wing-whirr, preen, and dry out, the parents in one group and Romeo and Juliet in the other.

That evening I put Zoltan on the enclosure floor. After being allofed there by Cyrus, he immediately made for the NB. He could not enter at first, though, because of the congestion there, caused by the rest of the family in its near vicinity. Late that evening, Juliet engaged in a most vigorous session of wing-whirring. By this time Cassandra was spending her nights outside in the enclosure perched beside Cyrus, but she joined the chicks in the NB before lights-on in the morning.

FURTHER INTERACTIONS---JULIET SUSTAIN'S FLIGHT. The next day, the 40th, the events during handling were a repitition of those of the day before. When I returned the young to the enclosure floor, all of them made for the NB but none would enter, because the lid was open and it was not dark inside. Meanwhile Cassandra and Cyrus were eating cuttlefish bone from outside enclosure A, as they again were in breeding condition. But as soon as they were aware that the chicks were back in the enclosure, they also returned to it. Later that day, all 3 chicks were out in the enclosure together voluntarily for the 1st time, and likewise on all subsequent days.

During handling of the chicks on the next day, Juliet twice flew out of my hands to the enclosures. When I put the 3 young on the shelf perch (Fig. 2a), the parents joined them and looked after them, but did not encourage them to fly, by flying off. When the parents finally did fly off, no young followed. All 3 young spent much of that day in the enclosure. The next day's events were scarcely different in any respect, but I did see all 5 members of the family lined up together on the night perch for the 1st time. The following day, the 43rd, Juliet again was the only chick to take any flights, and the parents accompanied her. Cassandra resumed trying to strip the cloth covering of the enclosure, a sure sign that she was coming into breeding condition.

THE UNEXPECTED AFTERMATH---ROMEO ALSO FLIES---TITUS REJECTED. The 44th day (May 24) was the day of the unexpected aftermath in Cyrano's interactions with Cassandra when she solicited food from him through the enclosure bars, while repelling Cyrus, and Cyrano just watched 'unconcernedly' without allofeeding her (see p. 330). On that same day both Romeo and Juliet began to follow their parents in flight, but I still had to rescue them from the floor occasionally.

When I let the crippled Titus out with the young of this family, he tried repeatedly to associate with them, but Cassandra and Cyrus just as often protectively chased him away. Since I did not wish to facilitate immediate further breeding by this pair, I removed the NB that same day, with the result that the entire family was found perched together on the night perch the next morning.

SOCIAL INTERACTIONS DURING FAMILY FLIGHTINGS.

PROTECTIVE AND THREATENING INTERACTIONS. That day I flighted the family twice. Romeo and Juliet sometimes followed along with the parents but were not yet skilled fliers. Zoltan still had to be transferred from perch to perch by hand, as he would not venture from them. When I allowed Petra, Ramses, and Titus to join the family of 5, Cyrus pecked away his crippled, younger brother, Titus, twice. Each time, Ramses came to Titus' rescue and rousted Cyrus from his vicinity. Meanwhile, the 3 fledglings were temporarily forgotten on the side shelf, as they looked on intently; Cassandra and Cyrus then abandoned them temporarily and socialized with their own parents and Titus.

When Cassandra and Cyrus returned to the fledglings, Petra and Ramses followed along and tried to socialize with their grandoffspring. Not only did Cassandra and Cyrus guard the brood from the parents' solicitations, but, much to my surprise, the young also peck-threatened them. By late that evening, the rehoused family of 5 was creating such a din in the absence of a NB that I returned the NB, which quickly restored tranquility.

When I flighted the family the next morning, all but Zoltan emerged voluntarily, so I placed him on a perch by hand. Though Romeo and Juliet accompanied their parents about, neither of them was yet a facile flier. By the next day, Zoltan also tried to fly along, but often needed to be rescued from various landing points. I flighted Jagatai and Ogadai to let them socialize with the family, but they usually were chased away. Still the parents sometimes left the young and visited with these older brothers. During the times when the entire group did assemble, Cassandra and Cyrus kept a watchful and protective eye on the brood. When I flighted Titus too, they chased him off when he tried to join the group.

CHICK IN DISTRESS REJOINED---FAMILY FLIGHTS. On the 48th day, I still had to bring Zoltan out by hand to flight him. He could not, as yet, keep up with the family. On all of the many times that he was left behind and chirped in distress, the rest of the family hastily rejoined him. On occasion, Cyrus allofed him. Sometimes 2 of the young were left behind but quickly were rejoined by the 3rd and the parents.

Beginning on the next day there was no further crisis, as all of the young easily followed along with the parents. The family tended to keep to the paper-covered shelves, as all tried to copy Cassandra's paper stripping. Cyrus allofed the young from time to time. I removed the NB again to discourage breeding by the parents, but, again, the young raised such a great tumult with their squealing and bickering that I restored it again to bring tranquility to the colony.

TITUS STANDS FIRM----BREEDING RESUMED----EGG-BURIAL EXPERIMENTS. During those days, Cassandra often joined the young in the NB in the very early morning, but she spent the nights perched outside with Cyrus. On June 1, I tried the experiment of flighting Titus with just the 3 young. When they pecked at him under those conditions, he stood his ground and pecked back. Meanwhile, the parents were well into another cycle of breeding, with much courtship feeding and frequent copulations. When I flighted the family at that time (June 3), the parents and young tended to go their own ways, with the latter staying close to the home perch and the former visiting the various sites where nesting materials were to be found. The 1st egg of the 6th clutch was laid the next day. I substituted for this egg and the one that followed, and began the egg-burial experiments described above, including those with the use of a "transparent" NB (see p. 737 *et seq.*).

The Second Brood of Cassandra and Cyrus

The 2nd brood of Cassandra and Cyrus, consisting of the single male chick, Claudius, was reared in a NB with a Plexiglas sidepane that, again, allowed a fairly unimpeded view of the care and behavior of the occupants. The 4th egg of the clutch--the only one that was fertile--was laid on July 24 and incubation commenced immediately. When the hatchling was detected at 10:00 h on August 14, 1984, its down already was dry. Cassandra allofed it at 13:05 h, seemingly for the 1st time.

CHICK KEPT SPOTLESSLY CLEAN. If Cyrus was inattentive, careless, or overburdened in tending to the cleaning of the 1st brood, one would not suspect it from his performance with the 2nd one. He kept very close to Cassandra's bill as she allofed, cleaning thoroughly both Claudius' head and bill and Cassandra's bill. In fact, at no time during the brooding of Claudius was dry food found caked anywhere on his head or body.

PROTECTING LONE CHICK FROM BURDEN OF HEN'S WEIGHT. Cassandra kept the chick on its back under her breast, with its head just below her own, allowing convenient periodic allofeeding. This also made it very easy for Cyrus to tend to the cleaning. The next morning I exchanged the lovebird eggs for unhatched or infertile Cockatielian eggs, as the first step toward protecting Claudius from the burden of Cassandra's weight. Beginning on the next day, and on alternate subsequent days, I replaced one of these eggs with a 2½-cm-diameter plastic ball, each of which was accepted routinely by the hen.

HEN ALMOST EXCLUSIVELY ALLOFEEDS A SOLE CHICK. On the 6th day (Aug. 20), Cassandra still was doing almost all of the direct allofeeding of the chick, with Cyrus tending primarily to the cleaning, but he customarily allofed Cassandra first. When only 1 chick is present the male apparently participates very much less in its direct allofeeding than when 2 or more are present. And it would seem that the male does not take over most of the direct subsequent allofeeding of young in the nest, with only 1 chick present, anymore than it does with larger broods. The same circumstances applied during the brooding of the single chick, Titus, by Petra and Ramses.

Beginning on about the 9th day, Cassandra ceased to sit over the chick; thenceforth she kept it off to the side while she incubated the eggs. Even by the 11th day, Cassandra still was performing almost all of the direct allofeeding of the chick. She and Cyrus had been so thoroughly attentive to it, and the NB had so little excrement in it, that Claudius' nostrils were perfectly clear at that time. But with no sibling to lean against, he often lay prone in the shavings, and by the next day, the flaps over his nasal cavities were caked with a chalky layer.

On the 16th day I saw Claudius scratch his head over the wing while in the NB, and by the next day he was beginning to look about alertly while being handled; his nostrils still were caked with powder. Two days later he was very active and alert, squirming about and peering on high. Meanwhile, Cassandra had lost all interest in the balls that I had substituted for eggs, and they became scattered about in the NB.

CLAUDIUS HABITUATED TO ME---EXCESSIVE ALLOGROOMING BEGINS. Inasmuch as I was visible to Claudius through the sidepane, he was frightened very little by my handling of him. By the 21st day, even though I handled him frequently, he had voided only twice while being handled, whereas chicks reared in conventional NBs usually void on every disturbance. Inasmuch as his feathers had long since begun to break from their pins, the inevitable excessive allogrooming by the parents had begun. Like Titus before him, as the sole chick in the 4th brood of Petra and Ramses, Claudius squealed incessantly as they tended to him. By the 26th day it was clear that the top of his head and his neck were bearing the brunt of the excessive grooming. As in the case of Titus, these attentions, almost all by Cassandra, continued unabated for days, accompanied by loud vocalizations from Claudius.

CLAUDIUS ALLOFED IN MY HAND---HE CARESSES PARENTS' TOES. When I handled Claudius at 30 days of age, and flighted the parents, both of them perched next to him on my hands. Cyrus, who was least fearful of me, allofed him 3 times from his perch on my index finger. On this day and the next 2 days, Claudius nibbled at his parents toes, as he stood cupped in my hands, providing another example suggesting that nibbling or caressing the toes with the bill is a primitive mode of attention getting among lovebirds (see pp. 814, 815, **Attention Getting by Toe Caressing**).

CLAUDIUS NEARS FLEDGING---PARENTAL 'CONCERN' MOUNTS. Cyrus continued to be the one to show the most 'concern' when I handled Claudius, being the 1st to come over and perch near me. He allofed him in my hand again on the 33rd day. Claudius had begun to flap his wings from time to time, and if Cassandra had not joined him before then, she was sure to hasten over when the wing-flapping began. When I placed Claudius on the floor, both parents joined him and followed him closely as he moved about. Because he had one congenitally paralyzed toe, Claudius wing-flapped very much to maintain his balance as he climbed about in the enclosure. At such times the parents were greatly 'concerned' and followed him closely.

By the 37th day, Claudius was flying off to the enclosure when I handled him. Cyrus accompanied him on these flightings, but Cassandra was more occupied with eating cuttlefish bone by reaching in from outside the other enclosures. Two days later she laid the 1st egg of the next clutch, with Claudius not yet fledged. This was the day that I transferred the colony to the laboratory and gave Claudius to Linda York for further study (see pp. 833, 834, **Overcoming the Ultraconservative Feeding Habits of Lovebirds.**)

The Third Brood of Cassandra and Cyrus

NESTBOWL PROVIDED. Cassandra oviposited an 8th clutch of 5 eggs over the period just before and after I transferred the colony to the laboratory on Sept. 22, 1984. I removed these eggs one-by-one as they were laid. Without any facilitation, she began to oviposit a 9th clutch in a large food tray, laying her 1st egg on November 18 and her 8th one on December 5th. For a nest, I provided her with a 13-cm-diameter bowl, 5 cm deep, at the left-rear corner of the floor of the enclosure. I also shielded the bowl from above and along the two enclosure sides.

HATCHINGS---SMALLER CHICKS HAVE LOW PRIORITY. The 1st and 5th eggs were infertile, and the 7th did not hatch. The 2nd, 3rd, and 4th eggs hatched on roughly alternate days, and the chicks were cared for very attentively in the open nest, with very little notice being taken of me as I watched the proceedings closely from less than 30 cm away. The 6th egg hatched 4 days after the 4th and, though the chick was cared for, it consistently had the lowest priority.

Several times I watched the parents "load up" the 3 older chicks until their crops were bulging, all the while ignoring the hatchling, even though it usually cheeped for food continually during the proceedings. After 2 days of this low-priority attention, the tiny chick succumbed. Since it seemed quite likely that any additional hatchlings would fare even worse, I fostered the 7th and 8th eggs into the 1st clutch of Zenobia and Cyrano (see pp. 769, 770).

On several subsequent occasions with breeding lovebird pairs, I observed the loss of initially healthy cheeping latter-hatching chicks entirely through lack of sufficient parental care. Thus, as these doomed chicks cheeped repeatedly for food, the parents first "loaded up" their older broodmates. Since this also transpired with both the 3rd and 4th chicks to hatch in the 5th brood of Petra and Ramses, I fostered their 5th and 6th eggs with Aspasia and Jagatai, whose own 1st clutch yielded no chick (though 2 of 4 eggs were fertile). To my surprise, since 1st breeding attempts usually are unsuccessful, both eggs were hatched and the chicks were cared for skillfully and fledged without incident.

The several seemingly clear-cut cases of parental neglect that I witnessed among Peach-faced Lovebirds appear to support the "rule" of feeding proposed for passerines, namely, that the larger, most-aggressive nestlings are allofed preferentially (see 589), although one must bear in mind that the nesting circumstances in these studies departed considerably from those in the wild. Both of these findings and those with Cockatiels (e.g., see Part 1, Homer's habit of frequently allofeeding 2 nestlings in alternate bouts) appear to rule out a practice of random feeding of nestlings, such as appears to occur in Song Sparrows (589). Moreover, Budgerigar hens adhere to a fairly strict regimen of allofeeding chicks in the inverse order of their ages (see 843 and pp. 200- 203, 787).

NO FEATHER-PICKING IN A BROOD OF THREE. The 3 remaining chicks were brooded very attentively and developed and were fledged without notable incident. It may be significant, in connection with the genesis of parental feather-picking, that, although Claudius, the sole chick of the 2nd brood, had been feather-picked extensively on his head and neck, no chick of this brood of 3 showed any sign of parental feather-picking. On the other hand this pair heavily feather-picked all their subsequent 4 broods (see below).

INFLUENCES OF HABITUATION. It will be recalled that Petra and Ramses, and their 1st brood of Jagatai and Ogadai, were very well habituated, but that their 2nd brood, of Cassandra, Cyrus, and Cyrano received much less attention from me and were more wary. This difference between the 2 pairs of parents had interesting consequences. Thus, Petra and Ramses, but especially Petra, had no fear of me and usually attacked me vigorously when I serviced the enclosure and ventured too near the chicks or eggs in the nestbowl. In consequence, the chicks--mimicking their parents--also attacked me vehemently when they became sufficiently mobile.

On the contrary, being habituated to a much lesser degree, neither Cassandra nor Cyrus attacked me as I serviced their enclosure or sought to examine the chicks of their 3rd brood. Instead, they fled to the perches. In consequence of this, the chicks remained docile through the entire course of brooding (they saw me many times daily from the open nestbowl).

Cassandra, however, underwent a transformation of behavior in parallel with the approach of fledging time. The nearer the time of fledging, the bolder she became in attacking me and protecting the chicks (as noted also with the parents of all other broods of lovebirds and Cockatiels). At first, she merely approached docilely and nibbled at my hand, but the latter behavior gradually evolved into hard biting that drew blood. At the height of this behavior, she rushed to the attack at even a hint of my intrusion. During this period, it was necessary to flight the parents before exercising or otherwise tending to the young. With all subsequent clutches and broods of Cassandra and Cyrus, attacks were common when I serviced the enclosure, except when the brood had attained juvenile status.

The Fourth Brood of Cassandra and Cyrus

THIRTEEN-EGG CLUTCH---FIVE EGGS FOSTERED WITH BUDGERIGARS. Cassandra's 3rd brood had not yet been fledged when she began ovipositing another clutch, which was to be the most unusual of all lovebird clutches. Inasmuch as I did not wish to facilitate further breeding of the pair so soon, I removed the eggs, one by one, as they were laid, and fostered them with 2 breeding Budgerigar pairs, Cornelia and Cesare and Lucretia and Lysander, whose own eggs were infertile (see p. 780, **Attentive Incubation Begins**, p. 781, **Fostering Lovebird Eggs**).

However, this strategy did not deter Cassandra from continued oviposition. She behaved like an indeterminate layer, laying a total of 13 eggs on roughly the following days: January 27, 29, 31, February 2, 4, 7, 9, 12, 14, 17, 19, 21, and 23. This result gives one reason to question the validity of the prevailing view that Peach-faced Lovebirds, at least, are strictly determinate layers, and accords with Dilger's account of the continuous progression of follicular ripening and oviposition (see 3 and p. 718, **Clutch-Size Regulation**). Had I continued to remove Cassandra's eggs, she might have continued to oviposit. An alternative interpretation is that these eggs represented 2 successive clutches, but the timing of their laying does not support that view.

THREE FOSTERED EGGS RETURNED. By the time Cassandra laid her 9th egg, on February 14, both Budgerigar hens had abandoned their fostered clutches, although Cornelia had incubated hers attentively until then. Since the laying of 9 eggs is not unprecedented, I had no suspicion that additional eggs would be forthcoming. Accordingly, I allowed Cassandra to proceed with the incubation of the clutch. I gave her a nestbowl and restored eggs #1, #3, #5, and #6-8. The first 3 of these had been in Cornelia's care (#2 and #4, which had been fostered with Lucretia, were discarded), giving Cassandra a total of 7 eggs at the time.

UNPRECEDENTED HATCHING OF CHICKS WHILE HEN STILL OVIPOSITING. By the time Cassandra laid her 13th egg, 2 chicks already had hatched, and the 9 eggs and 2 chicks were quite unmanageable for her. Accordingly, I fostered 3 of the eggs with Zenobia and Flavia, both of whom also were ovipositing at the time, and discarded an infertile one. Eggs #1, #3, and #5, hatched on February 20, 22, and 27, several days overdue. These were the eggs that had been incubated by the Budgerigar, Cornelia, for roughly 2 weeks. The 1st chick, the male Bion, was cared for routinely. By this time, both Cassandra and Cyrus were so thoroughly habituated to my presence that they almost totally disregarded me when I serviced or approached their enclosure, particularly when they were allofeeding and allogrooming the chicks or each other. It seemed that I almost could have touched them without interrupting their activities.

HATCHLING ALLOFED FIRST BY MALE SUCCUMBS. Late on the morning of February 22, the newly hatched 2nd chick was lying on its back, off at Cassandra's right side, being allofed its 1st meal, not by Cassandra, but by Cyrus. Cassandra paid no heed as Cyrus delivered gobs of semi-liquid food by massive tongue-flick allofeeding rather than a liquid diet by trickle-feeding or tongue-flicking allofeeding. These proceedings were doubly surprising to me. It was the 1st time I had seen an uncontested 1st allofeeding of a hatchling by the male parent, and the 1st time I had seen a hatchling receive gobs of semi-liquid food, rather than small portions of more liquid food. The next morning this chick was dead, with very little food left in its crop. Did it die of being fed improperly, of insufficient food, of lack of brooding during the night, or of some abnormality? But for observations of the care of the 3rd chick of this brood and of the allofeeding of Budgerigar hatchlings and nestlings, I probably would have drawn a wrong conclusion.

ANOTHER HATCHLING ALLOFED FIRST BY CYRUS SURVIVES. Five days later (Feb. 27), the 5th egg hatched and, to my further surprise, a 1st-allofeeding episode essentially identical to the one described above was repeated. Cyrus, again, delivered gobs of semi-liquid food to the chick by massive tongue-flick allofeeding, as it lay off to Cassandra's side, and, again, Cassandra paid no heed to them. At the time, she was tongue-flick allofeeding the 1st chick, then 7 days old. In this connection, even older nestlings may receive a considerable fraction of their diet as tongue-flick allofed and trickle-fed liquid food. It is possible that the delivery of some liquid to older nestlings in this manner is primarily for its water content.

In view of the fate of the 2nd hatchling, it seemed unlikely that the 3rd hatchling would survive in these circumstances, especially in the presence of another chick--already 7 days old and very much larger than it. Yet the 3rd chick was brooded normally and fledged almost without incident. At the least, this result showed that a 1st meal consisting of gobs of semi-liquid, rather than more nearly liquid food, is not fatal to a hatchling. Subsequent observations of the allofeeding of hatchlings and young nestlings of Budgerigars revealed that all their food initially consists of semi-liquid gobs delivered by massive tongue-flick allofeeding.

PROCESSED FOOD REQUIRED FOR HATCHLINGS? Even though Cyrus allofed gobs of semi-solid food to 2 hatchlings as their 1st meal, this food very likely was processed more than the food customarily allofed to the hen. A circumstance suggestive of this occurred some time later (Aug. 10, 1985) when Cassandra and Cyrus were incubating the eggs of a subsequent clutch. On the evening of August 9, I had fostered an egg (#5) of a clutch of Flavia's (mated with Titus) into Cassandra's clutch.

This egg hatched sometime during the night and Cassandra and Cyrus both cared for the hatchling at the time of lights-on in the morning. They groomed it and grasped its bill several times as if to allofeed it, but no food was delivered, as judged from the hatchling's crop, and no tongue-flicking was observed. After this initial treatment neither foster parent showed any inclination to allofeed the hatchling during the next 2 h (I checked frequently while servicing the colony), though it was sheltered in normal fashion. This was most unusual behavior for a pair that often competed cooperatively to allofeed their nestlings. Accordingly, I gave the hatchling little chance of surviving. Yet the subsequent care of this chick (Bion) proceeded normally and it was fledged successfully.

A probable explanation for this behavior would appear to be that neither parent had sufficiently-well-processed food on hand for a fresh hatchling at the time of lights-on. One contributing factor, probably the major one, was the fact that the fostered egg had been laid and its incubation begun 5 days earlier than the 1st-laid egg of Cassandra's clutch. In essence, it hatched 5 days prematurely on the foster parents' timetable, so that sufficiently-well-processed food was not on hand. The other contributing factor may have been that the foster parents had insufficient advance notice of an imminent hatching, since the egg was fostered to them only about 6-10 h before it hatched. Normally the clicking sounds of a lovebird embryo associated with bill clapping may be heard as much as 24-48 h before hatching and probably stimulate the parents to begin the preparation and accumulation of properly processed food for hatchlings.

On several earlier occasions I observed similar behavior of a breeding pair upon receiving a fostered hatchling. The hatchling usually received attentive care from the foster parents but was not allofed. This happened, in fact, on August 9 with a hatchling from the same clutch of Flavia and Titus. Since the latter pair were unable to care for it properly, I fostered it unsuccessfully with the experienced pairs of Cassandra and Cyrus and Petra and Ramses. Both hens were incubating eggs at the time and both pairs groomed and tended the hatchling, but the latter was 6 days premature on their schedule and neither pair allofed it. But both pairs allofed their 1st hatchlings promptly, 6 and 7 days later, respectively.

UNUSUALLY SEVERE FEATHER-PICKING. The existence of a brood of 2 chicks differing in age by 7 days set the stage for unusual feather-picking episodes. In normal circumstances, that is, in a brood of 2 chicks differing in age by only 1 or 2 days, very severe feather-picking usually does not occur. In the present instance, the 1st chick was so far advanced in development in relation to the 2nd one, insofar as their feathering was concerned, that the brood of 2 received essentially the same excessive grooming attention that usually is accorded to solitary chicks.

Severe feather-picking of the oldest chick, Bion, began long before the youngest chick, Beatrix, had any feathers to be picked. By the time Beatrix was vulnerable to feather-picking, the excessive grooming habit had become so well established in Cassandra that it carried over in the treatment of Beatrix, and she also was severely feather-picked. As a result, both chicks received as severe a case of feather-picking on their heads, backs, napes, and breasts as I have seen among lovebirds. Because of this undesirable outcome, I weaned Beatrix and Bion 1 or 2 weeks earlier than was my custom, housing them with the Cockatielian pair, Kirsten and Rimski, and the youngest pair of Budgerigars. Within 2 weeks most of the evidence of feather-picking of their plumage was inapparent.

CYRUS ALLOFED AND ESCORTED SEPARATELY-HOUSED YOUNG. An interesting finding that emerged as a consequence of the early weaning was that Cyrus continued to allofeed the 2 juveniles through his enclosure bars when they visited while being flighted alone, and that he continued to escort them about and allofeed them when the family of 4 was flighted, even though the young were housed separately and he had no other contact with them. Cassandra also was friendly with them but her interests during flighting lay mostly in stripping nesting material, as she was well along with her next clutch.

One month later, while Cassandra and Cyrus were caring for the nestlings of their 5th brood, they had lost interest in the juveniles, Beatrix and Bion. When the family was flighted together, and the latter solicited food, the parents not only declined to allofeed them, they repelled them. On the other hand, the presence of Bion and Beatrix was tolerated outside of and atop the breeding enclosure containing the 3 nestlings of the 5th brood, i.e., the parents did not attack them through the bars, as they would have attacked any stranger.

The Fifth Brood of Cassandra and Cyrus

SIX OF EIGHT EGGS HATCH. The 1st egg of the clutch of the 5th brood of Cassandra and Cyrus was laid on April 9, 1985 and the 8th (and last) egg was laid on April 25. The 1st 2 of these eggs were fostered to a clutch of Zenobia and Cyrano (all of whose eggs had failed to hatch because of the disruptive influences of a fostered chick). Egg #3 hatched on May 6 and the hatchling received clear liquid nourishment in its 1st allofeeding at noon. Egg #4 hatched the next day but the nestling was dead on the following day with a residue of semi-solid food in its crop. Possibly it received its 1st meal from Cyrus and the food was insufficiently liquified.

Egg #5 hatched on May 10 and the hatchling was detected--almost dry--at 09:45 h. It was allofed by Cassandra, probably for the 2nd time at 14:15 h. Two days later, the 6th egg hatched, leading to a brood of 3 chicks. The hatchling was detected at 13:00 h but had not yet been allofed at 19:18 h. Semi-liquid white food was present in its crop at 23:32 h. This hatchling apparently was being neglected and was found dead on the afternoon of May 14, 2 days later. Egg #7 hatched on the evening of that same day, once again giving a brood of 3 chicks. To my surprise, the oldest chick, though large and well nourished, was found dead on the morning of May 16, at an age of 10 days. It appeared to be in excellent condition with its crop almost half full. Since it was off to the side of Cassandra in the morning, it appeared possible that it had been neglected accidentally and died of exposure, since even a dead chick usually is brooded.

TRICKLE-FEEDING OF OLDER CHICKS. The last egg hatched on the next day, again yielding a brood of 3 chicks, consisting of chicks from eggs #5, 7, and 8, which hatched on May 10, 14, and 17. Despite the great spread in the ages and the sizes of these chicks, and the ill-boding earlier loss of 3 of their broodmates, these chicks were fledged more or less routinely. During the care of this brood, I had the opportunity to observe several sessions of trickle-feeding of chicks even as old as 3 weeks, when fairly well feathered. This suggested again that the essentially fluid meals are delivered to older chicks primarily for their water content.

MORE FEATHER-PICKING. Again, with chicks spaced relatively far apart in age, the oldest feathered much earlier than the 2nd oldest, and Cassandra engaged in feather picking of its head, back, wings, and chest. The other 2 chicks were similarly treated as they feathered out, but not as badly as the 2 chicks of the 4th brood.

The First Clutch and Brood of Zenobia and Cyrano

TWO EGGS FOSTERED. On December 9, 1984, Zenobia and Cyrano returned to their enclosure voluntarily for the 1st time, while being flighted. The explanation was forthcoming later that afternoon, when Zenobia laid the 1st egg of her 1st clutch. Thereafter she laid 4 additional eggs on succeeding roughly alternate days, the last egg on December 18. To facilitate their breeding, I provided them with a nestbowl at the left-rear corner of their enclosure, together with the usual nutritional supplements (see pp. 288,

289). The floor of their enclosure pan provided a 5-cm height of shielding on its 2 sides, and I left the bowl unshielded from above. On December 20, I fostered Cassandra's 7th and 8th eggs into their clutch, as mentioned above, giving them a total of 7 eggs.

FOSTERED EGG HATCHES----CHICK RECEIVES CLOSE ATTENTION BUT SUCCUMBS. On December 28, 19 days after Zenobia laid her own 1st egg, Cassandra's 8th egg hatched. The parents groomed and cared for the chick at first, but did not allofeed it for several hours. When they finally attempted to allofeed it, Zenobia fed and Cyrano cleaned. Both appeared to perform these activities with great skill, providing me with additional opportunities for close observations. I saw Cyrano recover a large gob of semi-liquid food from the chick's head. Despite the foster parents' close attention, the chick received only a small amount of food during this 1st allofeeding.

Although both parents were very attentive to the hatchling, it did not appear to be receiving appreciable amounts of food into its crop, and the food that it did receive apparently was insufficiently liquified. It succumbed after 2 days, with whitish-colored food still in its crop. All the indications are that this apparently-perfectly-healthy chick died because of parental inexperience in food preparation, probably having been allofed too large a fraction of insufficiently processed food. In all other aspects of their care of the chick, despite this having been their 1st experience, the parents seemed to have performed skillfully.

TWO EGGS HATCH---A THIRD FOSTERED OUT. By January 5, the 27th day after the 1st egg was laid, there still was no sound from the eggs. At this time, hatching of the 1st egg was a week overdue and the 2nd egg proved to be infertile. Finally, On January 6, the 3rd egg hatched, already several days overdue; the 4th egg hatched that same evening. Both hatchlings received most attentive care and were fledged without difficulty and with no feather-picking by the parents (nor of subsequent broods). At the time of the hatchings, the 5th egg was in its 19th day of incubation, and I fostered it into the infertile 1st clutch of Flavia and Titus (see p. 772).

ZENOBIA ATTACKS BUT CHICKS FACE AWAY. Inasmuch as Zenobia had received much attention from me as a nestling, fledgling, and juvenile, she was well habituated. Lacking fear of me, she protected her chicks and eggs almost from the time of laying of the 1st egg. Only during the days of allofeeding the very young nestlings was she too busy to pay me much heed. Otherwise, she rushed over to attack me whenever I serviced or came near. Had her 2 chicks been witness to these attacks, they would have learned by example to attack me, just as had Zenobia herself as a chick. However, they adopted the habit of facing away into the left-rear corner of the enclosure and never were watching when I serviced it. As a consequence, they never went through a stage of attacking me.

The Second, Third, and Fourth Broods of Zenobia and Cyrano

NO EGG HATCHES. The 1st egg of the 2nd clutch of Zenobia and Cyrano was laid on February 9, 1985, and 2 additional eggs were laid on alternate days thereafter. In addition, I fostered 4 eggs of Cassandra's 13-egg clutch with them. Though mostly fertile, none of these eggs that Zenobia was incubating hatched. At any rate, on March 3, since her 1st egg already was overdue to hatch, she and Cyrano could be considered to have been in breeding condition to care for a hatchling.

WEAKENED HATCHLING FOSTERED INTO CLUTCH. It was on that day that the 3rd chick of the 2nd brood of Flavia and Titus hatched from a fostered egg and apparently was accidentally displaced from the nestbowl by the crippled Titus (see p. 773). Since this very much weakened and unfed hatchling would have had little chance to survive in the presence of its very much older foster broodmates, but could still cheep for food, I fostered it with Zenobia and Cyrano.

WEAKENED HATCHLING CARED FOR AS IF BY AN EMERGENCY FIRST-AID TEAM. The manner in which Zenonia and Cyrano cared for this "cold," hungry hatchling, left no doubt that they were in breeding condition to do so. Both took it over and hovered closely over it in the manner of an emergency first-aid team, with a burst of concentrated unwavering attention. In short order, it was being thoroughly groomed, allofed, and warmed. For many days the excellent progress of the chick gave hope that the fostering would have a successful outcome, and that it was possible for a fresh hatchling that had been left exposed and totally untended for several h, as had this one, to survive when given intensive care.

CHICK SUCCUMBS AFTER FIFTEEN DAYS. For 15 days, this chick received the most attentive care I have observed among lovebirds. After a slow start, in the 1st few days (possibly because of insufficiently pre-processed food), it appeared to be developing normally. Yet, on March 18, I found it dead in the nestbowl, with a plentiful quantity of food still in its crop. Both this result, and others experienced with lovebird chicks in the colony, strongly suggest that hatchlings, and even much older nestlings, are highly susceptible to the deleterious influences of prolonged periods of lack of food and proper warmth. Unlike the case with Cockatiels, the ultimate survival of such neglected chicks is highly unlikely, though they may appear to be thriving for many days after being given proper care.

A THIRD BROOD OF TWO CHICKS was reared by Zenobia and Cyrano in the period of July-September, 1985. Of a 6-egg clutch, 1 egg was infertile, 2 pipped but failed to hatch, and 3 hatched. However, the last of these hatched 4 days after the penultimate hatching, and the 3rd chick was neglected despite its initial vigor and its cheeping for food, as the parents favored its 2 older and much larger broodmates. Lack of attention to, and consequent demise of, latter-hatching chicks also was noted on the part of Cassandra and Cyrus and Petra and Ramses (see, for example, pp. 764, 765, **Smaller Chicks Have Low Priority**). As in the case of the 1st brood of Zenobia and Cyrano, there was no noticeable feather-picking of the 2 young despite very extensive grooming of them by both parents.

THE FOURTH BROOD consisted of 2 chicks, both fostered. One of these was fostered as a hatchling from the 6th brood of Petra and Ramses (see Table 4) when their own clutch proved to be infertile. Ten days later, I exchanged this chick for a 19-day-old crippled runt of the 6th brood of Flavia and Titus, in the hope that it would receive better care as the sole chick of a brood (see pp. 840, 841, **Pecking Open Eggs, Not an Irreversible Habit**). This chick was crippled congenitally in the same way as was Titus and, in addition, had developed a deformity in the lower mandible, which did not interface properly with the upper one. Whereas Zenobia usually brooded this chick at night, despite its advanced age, on the morning of the 10th day it was alone in the nest, weak and at about room temperature, with its crop only about 1/8th full. Though Zenobia and Cyrano gave it little attention during the day, both began to allofeed and care for it very attentively at about 22:00 h, as it could be heard cheeping faintly.

The care of the chick at that time is noteworthy. The chick had become so weak that its soliciting cheeps were plaintively faint and thin, like those of a tiny hatchling. At that time Zenobia and Cyrano allofed it an exclusively liquid diet, with its crop at least half filled. Although the chick was brooded that night it was dead (under Zenobia) the next morning, whereupon I restored the 1st fostered chick to the pair. The allofeeding of an entirely liquid diet to this faintly cheeping chick confirmed an earlier observation of the same nature with a chick of the 1st brood of Cassandra and Cyrus (see pp. 757, 758, **A Small Chick Succumbs**) and suggests that the food delivered to young chicks by lovebird parents tends to be tailored to the chicks' needs, as judged from the sounds of their cheeping. At the least it suggests that a weak, faintly cheeping older chick will be allofed food that is more than normally liquified for a chick of its age.

The First Clutch and Brood of Flavia and Titus

ATTEMPTS AT COPULATION---FOUR EGGS LAID. The 1st of many attempts of Titus to mount Flavia were seen on December 3, 1984. These occurred on the enclosure floor in 2 sessions that lasted a total of about 20 min. The reader will recall that Flavia previously had aggressively but unsuccessfully sought Titus' sexual attentions (see p. 658, **Unrequited Solicitations for Coitus**). Six days later, Flavia laid a very heavily bloodied egg, the 1st of her 1st clutch. This was followed by 3 additional eggs in the next 6 days, the last of these being much less bloodied than the 1st 3 eggs. At first, I did not facilitate continued laying by Flavia, nor allow her to retain the eggs, but removed them as they were laid.

INCUBATION COMMENCES---ADDITIONAL EGGS LAID. After heroic but still unsuccessful efforts by Titus to copulate with Flavia 4 days later, I gave her a nestbowl and returned her clutch, with the thought of fostering a fertile egg into it later. Flavia began to incubate the eggs almost immediately, though not very steadfastly, at first. The crippled Titus continued his attempts to copulate with her, sometimes even as she incubated the eggs. Three days later (7 days after she had laid her 4th egg), she commenced to oviposit again, laying an additional 4 eggs on alternate days, the last 3 of these being almost free of blood.

FOSTERED EGG HATCHES. I then removed the 1st 4 eggs, which, in any case, were infertile, but allowed Flavia to retain the last 4, which she brooded very attentively. Eight days after she had laid her last egg, I fostered the 5th egg of Zenobia's 1st clutch into her clutch. Two days later, this egg hatched. The time was 31 days after Flavia had laid her 1st egg, 20 days after I gave her back her clutch and a nestbowl, and 17 days after she resumed laying and produced her 5th egg.

HATCHLING RECEIVES VERY ATTENTIVE CARE. In view of this timetable, it seemed likely that Flavia was at an appropriate stage in the maturation of her reproductive capabilities to care for a hatchling, and she and Titus would have heard it clicking in much of the preceding 48 h. Indeed, both Flavia and Titus cared for the hatchling very attentively and, to all intents and purposes, quite skillfully. In this connection, Flavia and Zenobia were about 17 months old at the time, which was much older than either Petra or Cassandra and their mates at the times of their 1st breeding.

NESTLING SUCCUMBS AFTER TEN DAYS. The chick appeared to be developing normally for about one week, when, quite unaccountably, Titus ceased to eat fresh corn, his principal source of soft food. From that time onward the chick received less care and less food. Three days later the foster parents ceased to allofeed it, though Titus still allofed Flavia. Nonetheless, the chick was still very vigorous and could sit up and flop about. The next morning, at an age of 10 days, the chick was dead, but still with undigested food in its crop.

As this was the 1st clutch and chick of this pair, very little could be concluded from the outcome. On the one hand, there is the possibility of parental inexperience, on the other hand, that of an infirmity of the chick. Although the chick did not solicit for food on the last day--when it was not allofed--vocal utterances are not a prerequisite for the allofeeding of 10-day-old chicks.

The Second and Third Clutches and Broods of Flavia and Titus

SEXUAL UNION ACHIEVED---CHICKS CARED FOR VERY ATTENTIVELY. As a test of the resourcefulness of Flavia and the crippled Titus, I facilitated copulation for them. In Titus' clumsy attempts at mounting Flavia with only 1 fully useful leg, both birds had tried to steady themselves using their wings as "arms and hands." Accordingly, I provided two dowels in a V-pattern, 4 cm above their copulation perch. Both promptly adopted the use of this by draping their wings over it for support while copulating, which they carried out at the expense of considerable effort, but successfully, on many occasions thereafter.

Flavia laid the 1st egg of a clutch of 5 on January 28, 1985, and the last on February 6. The 1st of these hatched on February 20, and the 4th-laid on February 24. The 2nd egg had been damaged and dried out, while the 3rd was pecked open before completing development; the 5th was fertile but did not hatch. In addition to these eggs, Flavia also was incubating egg #6 of Cassandra's clutch of 13. The chicks were cared for expertly, and the prognosis for successful fledging appeared very good, indeed.

HATCHLING ACCIDENTALLY DISPLACED FROM NESTBOWL. The 3rd chick to hatch, on the early morning of March 3, was that from a fostered egg (Cassandra's 6th). It was more or less "lost" among the two older and very much larger nestlings, At 12:15 h that same day, I found this hatchling lying outside the nestbowl, unfed and cooled to room temperature (27°C). This occurrence brought to attention another obstacle to successful breeding by Flavia and Titus. Because Titus was crippled, yet spent much time at Flavia's side in the nestbowl, his clumsy movements were a threat to the safety of the chicks, and it appeared that he accidentally had displaced the hatchling from the nestbowl.

DISPLACED HATCHLING FOSTERED---ANOTHER CHICK OUTSIDE OF NESTBOWL. Although the displaced hatchling was weak and "cold," it still could cheep for food. It was clear that it would have had no chance to survive in the presence of the much older chicks, so I fostered it with Zenobia and Cyrano (as described on p. 771). Unfortunately, the chick that had hatched on February 24 stepped or fell out of the nestbowl twice and, each time, appeared to have received no parental care while outside.

On the 2nd of these occasions, on March 6, I found it to be "cold" and unfed. This chick appeared to be too weak to be allofed, and it was dead the next morning. At the time, I believed that Titus had accidentally displaced it from the NB. However, subsequent events were to show that, as they jockey about, chicks that are 10 days or more in age easily can step or fall from nestbowls that are only 2½-4 cm deep. After those experiences, I generally employed nestbowls that were 5-6¼ cm deep.

LAST CHICK ALSO A CASUALTY. On the following morning (March 7), I found that the oldest chick of Flavia and Titus also had an empty crop, even though it was warm and in the nestbowl, so I fostered it with Cassandra and Cyrus, one of whose chicks (the fosterling, Bion) was of the same age, and the other a week younger (see p. 766 et seq., **The Fourth Brood of Cassandra and Cyrus**). They accepted this chick into the clutch and cared for it along with the other 2 for 11 days. However, too long a period apparently had elapsed without food before I fostered this chick, since it steadily lost ground in development, compared to the other chick of the same age. On March 18 I found its crop empty again and it succumbed.

Accordingly, Flavia and Titus had failed with their 1st 2 broods. The 1st of these was a single fostered chick (from Zenobia) that they unaccountably ceased to allofeed after 10 days. The 2nd brood consisted of 2 of their own chicks together with 1 from a fostered egg (from Cassandra and Cyrus). Though the loss of 2 of the chicks from the 2nd brood appeared to have been accidental, there was no question but that they had ceased to allofeed the 3rd chick after about 2 weeks.

WHY DID PARENTS EXPERT AT ALLOFEEDING YOUNG CEASE TO FEED THEM? With these failures to continue the allofeeding of the chicks, one after 10 days and another after 14 days (and possibly a 3rd after 13 days), it seemed possible that a failure of the parents to achieve full brooding condition was the basis for the failures. On the other hand, these parents were quite skilled in the allofeeding of their chicks, as long as the urge to do so was present. [Recall, in this connection, that the most frequent cause of loss of nidicolous chicks is failure of the parents to allofeed them (27, 787).]

The only certain conclusion to be drawn from the care of the 2nd brood is that neither Flavia nor Titus would care for a chick displaced from the nestbowl, at least not if eggs or chicks remained within it. This also was found to be the case subsequently with a fostered chick brooded by Zenobia and Cyrano (see p. 775). Subsequent studies of this phenomenon with Cockatiels (see pp. 503-510, **Brood-Site Fidelity**) strongly suggest that Cockatielian chicks displaced from the nest are not cared for--usually ignored --until they are of sufficient age to be recognized by the parents.

THE THIRD CLUTCH AND BROOD

CHICKS AGAIN CARED FOR ATTENTIVELY. The fate of one of the 2 chicks of the 3rd brood of Flavia and Titus tends to confirm the answer to the question posed above. Out of a 3rd clutch of 6 eggs, 4 of them fertile, there were successful hatchings of the 2nd and 4th eggs, on April 15 and 18, 1985. I witnessed what appeared to be the 1st allofeeding of the 1st hatchling by both parents, thoughout which it cheeped. As before, Flavia and Titus were skillful in their allofeeding and cleaning, and there was never any sign of caked food. On several occasions I noted that Flavia had 1 chick under each wing as she incubated the remaining 4 eggs.

ONE CHICK SUCCUMBS, THE OTHER VIGOROUS BUT WITH A HALF-EMPTY CROP. Until the chicks were 8 and 11 days old, there was no evidence of abnormality, and the chicks always appeared to be well fed. Then on the morning of April 26, I found the youngest chick dead in the nest, with an empty crop. The oldest chick's crop was only half full but it was vigorous and healthy appearing, and sat up and moved about in normal fashion. Although Flavia and Titus were attentive to the chick, they did not allofeed it. Since I had 2 experienced lovebird hens incubating eggs at the time, I fostered the chick with Zenobia and Cyrano.

Zenobia's 3rd clutch already was overdue to hatch, so she and Cyrano were in breeding condition to care for a chick. In fact, the pair was very attentive to the fostered bird, including much grooming and moderate allofeeding. Since the chick continued to be very vigorous, the prospect that it would survive appeared to be very good. But, like its sibling of the 2nd brood, it stepped or fell out of the nestbowl 2 days later, and was totally neglected at the outside location. By the time I found it in the morning, it was "cold" and too weak to be allofed. Despite this, Zenobia and Cyrano cared for it lengthily and very attentively. It succumbed about 2 h after I restored it to the nestbowl.

It seems likely from these results, that the loss of the chicks that Flavia and Titus had ceased to feed was a result of a failure of the parents to achieve full breeding condition. [Recall that their 1st clutch was infertile and that their 1st brood consisted of a chick from a fostered egg.] This conclusion tends to be supported by the fact that Flavia abandoned the remaining eggs with alacrity after I removed the poorly fed chick of the 3rd brood, even though the last-laid egg was only 4 days overdue to hatch. [For an account of subsequent successful breeding by Flavia and Titus, see pp. 840, 841, **Pecking Open Eggs, Not an Irreversible Habit.**]

DEFENSE OF NEST SITE AND INCUBATIVE AREA

In late August, 1986, I transferred Petra and Ramses and their 8th brood (Cleomenes and Theocritus) and 9th brood (3 unnamed juveniles) from enclosure M to enclosure E to provide more space for them. At the same time I placed Margo and Sylvia in the vacated enclosure M (see also p. 846). On August 29, I exchanged Titian for Margot, as the latter was very aggressive toward Sylvia. [Titian was the sole survivor of the 6th brood of Flavia and Titus; see Table 4] Sylvia paired with Titian within a few days and she laid the 1st of 2 infertile eggs on October 28.

During the period after housing the family of 7 in enclosure E, I flighted the group every few days. So great was their attachment to their natal and breeding enclosure, M, in which Sylvia and Titian were housed, that on every such flighting, even as long as 4 months later, they made the outside of enclosure M the "home base" for their flights, clinging and sidling about outside it amidst great excitement and loud vocalizations. Petra often spent the entire time clinging to the back of enclosure M near her former IA. Unless I wore gloves to remove her and restore her to enclosure E, she bit me severely. Otherwise she bit me only when she was in breeding condition and I serviced her enclosure.

In early December, Sylvia and Titian were coming into breeding condition for the 2nd time and were being flighted daily. During their flighting on December 10, with their enclosure door fastened open, I concurrently flighted the family of 7. When the latter discovered that the door to enclosure M was open, they immediately entered the enclosure and took possession of it. Petra promptly re-occupied her former IA, defending it and vigorously repelling all intruders except Ramses, who frequently was at her side courtship-feeding her (Cleomenes also courtship-fed her from an overhead perch). The family spent virtually the entire 2-h flighting period in enclosure M, with the juveniles only exiting and flying about briefly or sidling about on the outside faces. Both Sylvia and Titian took up and maintained positions on an upper perch, from the time the family intruded. Being overwhelmed by sheer numbers, however, they did not defend the enclosure. Although I was able to restore the juveniles to enclosure E, one by one, as they temporarily left enclosure M, neither Petra nor Ramses would leave the IA; eventually I had to remove them by hand.

On the following morning, I noted that Sylvia had laid the 1st egg of another clutch in the same IA used by Petra. That set the stage for an experiment on defense of the IA by a laying hen. Since Petra was the matriarch of the colony, she was dominant over all other lovebirds and was accustomed to prevailing in all disputes. Accordingly, judging from her behavior on the previous day, she could be expected to occupy and defend her old IA vigorously, even against a breeding female that was not one of her direct offspring (Sylvia was a member of the 7th brood of Cassandra and Cyrus; see Table 4). On the other hand, Sylvia had just oviposited. Though she was not yet in the full incubatory condition, she was known to be a very tenacious fighter (see p. 845) who probably would strongly defend her nest and ovipositional site. Which hen would prevail?

When the flightings of the previous day were repeated and the family entered enclosure M, there ensued a great clamour and a vigorous struggle; Petra sought to occupy the IA but Sylvia would not yield it to her. Instead, the two hens grappled bodily, rolling about in the IA, "scolding," and biting at one another. Ramses and Titian merely looked on, keeping well out of range. Although no blood was drawn, as the struggle continued with no sign of abatement, I intervened after several min. Sylvia would have been no match for Petra in a lengthy fight, as she still was scrawny and thin from having been attacked incessantly earlier (see above and p. 845). [Regarding Petra's reproductive condition, she was seen to copulate 4 days later and laid the 1st egg of her next clutch 11 days after that.]

It seems clear from this result that, as might be expected, dominance relationships, no matter how strong, do not take precedence over the urges of a laying hen to defend her nest site and IA, though such relationships are known to take priority in other less vital circumstances (see, for example, p. 649, **Parent-Offspring Dominance is Pre-emptive**). The finding also illustrates the rapidity--essentially overnight--with which a hen's aggressive behavior becomes strengthened in response to the physiological changes accompanying the laying of the first egg.

PART 3. BUDGERIGARS: CARE OF EGGS AND YOUNG, AND BEHAVIOR OF YOUNG

BUDGERIGAR PAIRS HOUSED SEPARATELY IN PREPARATION FOR BREEDING. After transferring the colony to the laboratory on September 22, 1984, I housed the 2 pairs of Budgerigars separately. Cornelia (an albino) and Cesare (a blue mutant) were in enclosure E (see Fig. 2b) and Lucretia (a yellow mutant) and Lysander (green wild type) were in enclosure D. The enclosures were located 0.9 m apart in such a way that the birds were within sight of one another. In addition, a mirror (30 x 70 cm) was mounted about 1.2 m in front of the enclosures, allowing the birds to have a 2nd view of one another in it. All 4 birds were flighted together daily for up to 2 h. At such times, they socialized and interacted extensively in the friendly-to-competitive manners already described (67 and p. 119 *et seq.*).

BEHAVIOR IN RELATION TO THE NESTBOXES

COURTSHIP FEEDING BEGINS---A "TRANSPARENT" NESTBOX IS SUPPLIED. These Budgerigars had never been bred before. Within 5 days, Cesare was courtship-feeding Cornelia, and such feedings, and allofeeding (during incubation and brooding), continued during the periods described here. On October 3, I gave this pair a NB (see p. 282 and Fig. 3b) with a Plexiglas sidepane and a 2-cm layer of shavings on its floor. This was accepted only very cautiously (see also 67), but within 2 days Cornelia had excavated 2 hollows to "bedrock" in the layer of shavings.

SCATTERING SHAVINGS--OCCUPANCY PREFERRED OVER FLYING--CESARE EXCLUDED. There was a great deal of vigorous activity, taking the form primarily of pecking and scattering the shavings about. Unlike the typical practices of Cockatiels and lovebirds, the feet and legs were used extensively and very vigorously. Sometimes all the bedding layer of shavings was "turned over" and displaced during such activity. In the ensuing days, Cornelia spent more and more time pecking and otherwise "fussing about" in the NB, often even preferring to stay inside it, rather than be flighted with the others. At no time did she permit Cesare to join her in the NB.

DARKENING ENCLOSURES AND NESTBOXES---FIRST ATTEMPTS AT COITUS. On October 17, I also added a "transparent" NB to enclosure D, and covered the upper 1/3rds of both enclosures and the upper 2/3rds of both nestboxes with opaque black cloth (to faciliate breeding, in dimmer light; see 850). The cloths over the NBs gradually were raised to allow better observation of egg and chick care after oviposition began. [There is no other record of a Budgerigar pair breeding successfully in a "transparent" NB, although one of 8 pairs studied by Hinde and Putman oviposited under similar conditions (850).] Lucretia began to enter and explore her NB within 3 days, and, unlike Cornelia, she permitted her mate, Lysander, to enter at will, which he frequently did. On October 20, the first clumsy attempt of Cornelia and Cesare to copulate took place atop an enclosure housing Cockatiels (during a flighting period).

"BROODING NESTBOX"--ROUTINE USE OF, & RELUCTANCE TO LEAVE, NESTBOXES. By October 21, Lysander was courtship-feeding Lucretia within the NB, and the latter was actively pecking and scratching about in it. On this same day, Cornelia "brooded the NB" for the 1st time, that is, she sat in it for lengthy periods, as if incubating eggs or brooding young. By October 25, it was quite routine for the Budgerigars to enter and leave their NBs and to spend much of their time in them, pecking about, except that Cornelia did not allow Cesare to join her in the NB until after her 1st egg was laid.

Both females were reluctant to leave their NBs and enclosures for flighting, usually remaining within for 10-15 min, but sometimes for as long as 1 h after their mates had left the enclosures. On some occasions, neither Cornelia nor Lucretia left the enclosure. The birds were not noticed to make any effort to cover the Plexiglas sidepanes by heaping shavings against them, though shavings did temporarily build up against them from time to time.

PRELIMINARIES TO OVIPOSITION

COURTSHIP FEEDING---ATTEMPTS AT COITUS. By October 27, 1985, it was evident that, as is the practice of breeding lovebird pairs, the Budgerigar males usually were courtship-feeding their mates shortly after the lights were turned on each morning. The first attempts at coitus between Lysander and Lucretia occurred on November 2, as Lysander tried to mount her within the NB. Most subsequent attempted copulations of this pair occurred within the NB, even as Lucretia incubated eggs. All of these attempts within the NB were abortive.

FOSTERED EGG IGNORED. During a period when both females were reluctant to leave the NB or enclosure to be flighted, I placed a lovebird egg in Lucretia's NB. At first, its presence merely inhibited her from entering. Then, when she did enter, she ignored the egg. Meanwhile, she alone, or in cooperation with Lysander, had gradually been emptying the shavings from the NB, and these formed a heap below its entrance. By November 8, most of the shavings were outside. In flightings during this period, Cesare and Lysander, the two males, often exchanged seemingly friendly pecks on, or into, each other's bills, as if exchanging food.

FOSTERED EGGS AROUSE INTEREST---THIRD PAIR ACQUIRED. On November 8, I placed a lovebird egg in Cornelia's NB. At first, she did not notice it in its partly-buried position, as she stepped all over and around it. Then she became much interested in it and "mouthed" it, "fussed about" with it, and tucked it under her breast from time to time. But she soon lost interest in it and the ignored egg soon became almost completely buried as a result of movements in the NB. On the same day, I again placed an egg in Lucretia's NB. Lysander just mouthed it, but Lucretia pushed it around frantically, mouthing it all the while in great excitement. During those days neither female was likely to participate in flightings. On several occasions, I brought them out by hand, to ensure that they would receive adequate exercise to facilitate breeding.

On November 19, for only the 2nd time, Cesare tried unsuccessfully to copulate with Cornelia, this time atop a NB. On November 24, I brought in a pair of juvenile Budgerigars with wild-type plumage, in an effort to facilitate breeding in the exposed NBs (Budgerigars being obligatorily colonial).

COURTSHIP FEEDINGS---OTHER ADJUSTMENTS. In the following days, I flighted all 6 birds together daily, amid very much excitement and interactions. The frequent courtship feeding of their mates by Cesare and Lysander, at the time of lights-on in the morning, suggested that they continued to be in breeding condition, but no copulation was seen. On the other hand, the females again began to participate more promptly in flightings, often within 2 min of the opening of the enclosure doors.

On December 5, the juvenile Budgerigar pair engaged in courtship feeding for the 1st time, and the two adult pairs did so during flighting. On December 31, for the 1st time, Lucretia sometimes barred Lysander from the NB while she was inside. In a turnabout, Cornelia permitted Cesare to enter the NB while she was inside, also for the 1st time. Cesare was busy later that day picking at the cuttlefish bone.

OVIPOSITION BEGINS---INCUBATION NOT YET CONTINUOUS. Over 2 weeks later, on January 16, 1985, the 1st conclusive signs of success were noted, when both Cornelia and Lucretia laid their 1st eggs. Cornelia oviposited in the NB, whereas Lucretia did so in a food tray. Accordingly, the latter's egg was not discovered until the following morning. By then, it had been pecked open and partly dried out. [Ovipositing on an enclosure floor or in food trays has been noted by other workers, but only by birds exposed to less than 14 h of light per diem (850). In the present study the light regime was 17L:7D (see Chap. 2).]

Cornelia was not disturbed noticeably by my lifting the NB cover and looking inside (of course, I could see in through the sidepane, as well), but she did not incubate continuously. [According to Cayley and Lendon (1,056), "incubation..often commences with the laying of the 1st egg.."] Even on the 2nd day, she left the egg and NB in the late afternoon and stayed out until mid-evening. On the other hand, when she did incubate, she sat on the egg very tightly. She laid her 2nd egg at 16:30 h on the 2nd day (reckoning the day the 1st egg was laid as day 0). Though she would not be flighted that day, she left the NB several times. When she did incubate the eggs, they sometimes protruded in front of her or to her side.

FIRST OBSERVATIONS OF RESPONSES OVER A MISSING CLUTCH

EGGS BURIED NEAR INCUBATIVE AREA, FOUND AND RECOVERED. The stage now was set for investigating Cornelia's responses over a missing clutch. At 19:15 h that same day, I buried the two eggs next to each other by heaping shavings over them, to a depth of about 3/8 cm. They lay against the far wall, 5 cm from the IA and about $1\frac{1}{4}$ cm from the far-rear corner of the NB. I covered the entire floor of the NB with shavings to a depth of about $\frac{1}{2}$ cm. When Cornelia entered, she looked about the NB bottom briefly, but showed no sign of distress. After only a few sec, she left. In the light of subsequent findings, I would suggest that I had witnessed the reaction of a colonial hole-nesting hen, under the impression that she had entered the wrong nest hole.

After a few min, Cornelia re-entered the NB. This time, she conducted a visual search all about the NB floor, and pecked around gently in and near the IA. However, she just missed finding the eggs. She returned again 15 min later and searched about. This time she found both eggs, nudged them out and back into the IA, and incubated them. At this time, she was not incubating continuously, but would leave the NB for periods of 15-60 min or more.

ATTENTIVE INCUBATION BEGINS. At 23:09 h, after about a 30-min absence, Cornelia settled in on the eggs for the night. Although she was off the eggs but in the NB at lights-on the next morning, she returned to the eggs within a few min. She did not leave the NB during the next 4 h, and was allofed there by Cesare. From that time on, until February 14, almost a month later, Cornelia attentively incubated both her own infertile eggs and 3 fostered fertile lovebird eggs of Cassandra and Cyrus (see p. 766, **Five Eggs Fostered with Budgerigars**), both by day and by night. However, she abandoned the eggs about 6 days before a lovebird egg was due to hatch (all 3 eggs hatched, the 1st on February 20, after being returned to Cassandra).

SECOND OBSERVATIONS OF RESPONSES OVER A MISSING CLUTCH

EGG BURIED NEAR THE INCUBATIVE AREA---FOUND AND RESURFACED. Lucretia laid her 2nd egg in the early afternoon on January 19. At 19:45 h that evening, I buried it along the far side of the NB, 6 cm from the IA, under 3/8 cm of shavings. When Lucretia mounted the NB entrance, she missed the egg immediately, and paused there and scanned the entire inside floor of the NB. Then she entered and examined the floor thoroughly, in the same way that Cornelia had done on her 2nd visit after her eggs had been removed. After 18 sec she left, presumably also behaving in the manner of a colonial hole-nesting hen under the impression that she had entered the wrong nest hole.

Lucretia entered the NB 4 more times and made brief, but thorough, examinations. Her exploratory pecks into the shavings were very light and not very numerous. On the last of these 4 visits she found the buried egg and uncovered it. The next time she entered the NB she nudged the egg back to the IA and sat over it. All through the flightings of their mates that evening, both she and Cornelia remained on their eggs.

COITION AND/OR ALLOFEEDING IN EARLY MORNING. The next morning, Cornelia and Cesare engaged in activities that were to be repeated every morning for as long as oviposition continued. Within 5-20 sec after lights-on, Cornelia left the NB. Then she immediately took up a position perching on a natural branch in the enclosure. Thereupon, Cesare mounted her and attempted to copulate (for only the 3rd time that I had noted). These morning efforts at coitus became more and more skillful with each passing day. Though they appeared to be successful during the last few days of oviposition, success apparently came too late to produce fertile eggs. Allofeeding accompanied all these interactions, before, and/or during, and/or afterwards.

EARLY MORNING ACTIVITIES WITHIN NESTBOX. On the other hand, Lucretia seldom left the NB when the lights were turned on. Lysander usually joined her in the NB, instead, where he allofed her and sometimes tried to copulate with her even as she sat on the eggs, but with no notable success.

Once, when Lucretia left the NB after an attempted copulation, Lysander followed her about on the floor of the enclosure and on the perches, and tried to copulate with her again.

COMPLETING THE CLUTCHES, FOSTERING LOVEBIRD EGGS. Cornelia's 3rd egg was laid on January 20, just before 20:00 h. As she sat on the 3 eggs, they sometimes protruded to the front and/or side. Both hens remained on their eggs during the evening's flighting. Cornelia's 4th and 5th eggs were laid during the nights of January 23-24 and 25-26, while Lucretia's 3rd, 4th, and 5th eggs were laid on the night of January 21-22, the morning of the 24th, and the night of Jan. 25-26. None of the 3 eggs proved to be fertile and I eventually replaced them all with fertile lovebird eggs from a clutch of Cassandra's.

DIFFERING ATTENTIVENESS TO EGGS. Cornelia, who probably had experienced successful sexual unions with Cesare, cared for her eggs attentively night and day, until abandoning them on February 14. Lucretia, whose attempts at copulation with Lysander were clumsy, at best, eventually incubated her clutch or fostered clutch only during the day, just as do Cockatiels and lovebirds that have not progressed beyond the equivalent of the 2nd phylogenetic stage of egg care (see p. 511 and below).

THIRD OBSERVATIONS OF RESPONSES OVER A MISSING CLUTCH

QUESTIONS TO BE ASKED. The further experiments involving burying the eggs were designed to answer 3 questions:

(1) would the finding of but a single egg be enough to 'satisfy' a Budgerigar hen whose entire clutch had been removed or buried;

(2) do Budgerigar hens routinely search in the IA for possibly buried eggs; and

(3) do Budgerigar hens carry out directed or routine searches for buried eggs much beyond the confines of the IA?

The answer to the 1st question was an unequivocal "yes," and to the 2nd and 3rd, an unequivocal "no."

SEARCH MODES, NO ROUTINE SEARCH. To answer these questions, 3 or 4 eggs, comprising the entire clutches to the time of the experiment, were buried at separate locations, one near the IA, and the others 8-10 cm away from the IA. In all cases, the searches for the eggs were essentially as already described, both as regards visual searching and pecking. In the experiment with Lucretia, she again noted the absence of her eggs while still perched in the entrance on her way into the NB, whereupon she first paused there and looked about for them.

Only the nearest eggs were found by directed searches. After an egg was found, it was nudged into the IA and the hen sat on it 'contentedly' and searched no more. At no time was a hen sitting on an egg observed to peck about routinely in the neighborhood of the IA, as do Cockatiels and lovebirds as they incubate or sit lightly on their clutches, though Budgerigar hens did alter their sitting positions from time to time and face about 180°.

DISTANT EGGS RECOVERED ONLY ACCIDENTALLY. The only occasions on which buried eggs were recovered at a distance from the IA were when a male, milling about the sitting hen accidentally exposed one with his feet. When I partly exposed distant, unrecovered buried eggs, the hens soon spied and recovered them. In one case, Cornelia, at first, merely nudged such an egg under her breast, while still covering the other one at her rear, that is, before bringing the 2 eggs together into a common IA (reminiscent of Carmen's behavior; see p.452, **Displacement of Incubative Area Not Tolerated**).

LUCRETIA'S ATTENTIVENESS WANES---CLUTCH ABANDONED. By January 29, Lucretia's attentiveness to the eggs was waning, whereas Cornelia's was as strong as ever. Cornelia continued to exit the NB shortly after the time of lights-on in the morning to be allofed or to eat, and Lucretia continued to remain in the NB, usually to be allofed there by Lysander. On February 6, for the 1st time, Lucretia was on the outside NB perch at the time of lights-on in the morning, and from that time on her nighttime incubation of the eggs became irregular and eventually ceased. Within a week, she had altogether abandoned incubating them.

EXTRAORDINARY TREATMENT OF EGGS. On February 12, Lucretia engaged in most unusual behavior. At first she pushed all the eggs against the sidepane, as if trying to dispose of them. She continued to push them around, all about the NB, and otherwise manipulate them vigorously for much of the remainder of the day, doing this for over 8 h. She seemed to be quite restless during this activity, which even included kicking the eggs to the rear with her feet, and scattering sawdust about the NB.

Moreover, she would not allow Lysander to join her in the NB while engaged in these activities. She continued to engage in this unusual behavior, but with gradually diminishing intensity, for the next 2 days but incubated the eggs no further. Despite her very rough handling of them, the lovebird eggs were not damaged. I removed them on February 14, the same day that Cornelia abandoned incubating her fostered clutch. I returned the fostered eggs that Cornelia had been brooding to Cassandra since they had been incubated attentively; all 3 of them hatched subsequently (see p. 766). All of the eggs that Lucretia was incubating were discarded.

The Second Clutch of Lucretia and Lysander

All the Budgerigars were maintained as individual pairs in the ensuing months and were flighted periodically as a group. Lucretia and Lysander and Cornelia and Cesare continued to have access to "transparent" nestboxes. On September 26 and 28, 1985, Lucretia oviposited again but I had noted no copulation. The care of this 2-egg clutch was significant as it yielded results similar to those obtained repeatedly with both Cockatiels and Peach-faced Lovebirds in the early stages of clutch care or of clutch abandonment, with clutches that were incubated in open nestbowls or "transparent" NB's. Lucretia sat over and perhaps incubated the eggs almost continuously for the first 5 days, being allofed almost entirely by Lysander within the NB. She only occasionally emerged herself and ate very little on those occasions.

DAYTIME INCUBATION ONLY. Beginning on the 4th night, that is, the night of the day when the 3rd egg was due to be laid, Lucretia ceased nighttime incubation and spent the subsequent nights perched outside of the NB, usually near Lysander. It was evident that with the premature cessation of oviposition (a clutch of only 2 eggs being very unusual), she had not fully attained the 3rd phylogenetic stage of egg care. Each morning for the following 26 days, she returned to the NB and sat over the eggs within 15-30 sec of lights-on and spent the entire day on them with only infrequent brief absences.

On the evening of the last day, Lucretia began to push and manipulate the eggs vigorously in the same manner as with her 1st clutch. This time, however, there was no doubt as to her objective, as her manipulations included nudging an egg up the front face of the NB toward the entrance. After eventually puncturing one egg, she she lifted it on the tip of her penetrating bill and discarded it through the entrance. [I found that Cockatiels may peck open and discard damaged eggs in the same manner, usually under conditions in which the eggs cannot simply be rolled over the rim of a shallow nestbowl; e.g., see p. 699.] Lucretia did not return to the NB until 3 min after lights-on the next morning (Oct. 26) and she spent half that day nudging and manipulating the remaining egg before abandoning it. Not only did her practice of sitting over the eggs only during the day support the view of the existence of an ancestral stage in which the eggs were shielded and shaded only during the day, it also was evident that her treatment of long-overdue eggs was for the purpose of disposing of them. From subsequent behavior of Lucretia (see below), it was evident that she typically discarded defective or abandoned eggs from the NB.

An egg also was discarded from the NB during the brooding of Lucretia's 3rd brood. The egg was 10 days overdue to hatch and had dried to about half of its normal weight. The egg had a hairline crack but was not punctured or otherwise damaged. One can presume that Lucretia discarded it, as Lysander not only did not manipulate the eggs, he avoided making contact with them. A 5th egg, 3 days overdue to hatch, was retained.

CARE AND BEHAVIOR OF CHICKS

The Third Clutch and First Brood of Lucretia and Lysander

On November 11, 1985 Lucretia, who had spent much time within the NB in the preceding days, began to oviposit her 3rd clutch and laid a total of 5 eggs on alternate days. She began to incubate with the 1st egg and she spent most of the time in the NB; occasionally she exited briefly, particularly to eat celery. She received almost all of her sustenance from Lysander. The latter spent much time during the day allogrooming, allofeeding, and sitting beside her in the NB, but he slept outside at night. Several times during the day I found Lysander inexplicably sleeping on the floor of the enclosure with his head turned back and tucked under his scapulars. Inasmuch as I had witnessed no copulation, it came as a surprise on candling the eggs to discover that eggs #3-5 were fertile.

LUCRETIA LEAVES EGGS WITH LIGHTS-ON---FIRST HATCHING. Beginning on the 18th day of incubation, Lucretia left the eggs and took up a position on the inside perch of the NB within 5-30 sec after lights-on every morning but always resumed incubation after an absence of but 1 or 2 min. This behavior continued until the 10th day of brooding the chicks, after which she slept outside the NB at night. Egg #3 hatched not long before 18:00 h on the 20th day of incubation. When I first detected the hatchling, it was being allogroomed by Lucretia under her breast. I did not witness an allofeeding until 22:15 h the following day, because Lysander usually was in the NB participating in chick care and often blocked my view.

CHICK ALLOFEEDING INDISTINGUISHABLE FROM THAT OF LOVEBIRDS. The 1st witnessed allofeeding was very revealing, because the methods employed were virtually indistinguishable from those of the scores of joint lovebird allofeedings that I had witnessed closely. Both parents allofed the chick competitively as it lay on its back, each impatiently pushing the other's bill aside to take its own turn. In the brief intervals while one parent allofed before being displaced, the other cleaned excess food from the bills of both its mate and the chick. Frequently Lysander's pushing aside of Lucretia's bill was followed by allofeeding Lucretia rather than the chick, usually with his head below hers as the food was transferred. The hatchling cheeped very faintly as it was being allofed and this proved to be typical behavior of hatchlings and young nestlings. The older the chicks became, the more vigorous and loud their cheeping became, the higher became the rate of delivery of the individual notes of which each cheep consisted, and the longer the cheeps.

It seemed quite likely that Lysander also had been engaged in the same kinds of activities during the preceding allofeeding periods when he blocked my view, and this interpretation was strengthened by observations of the allofeedings of the subsequent 2 hatchlings and of the hatchlings of following broods. I witnessed many subsequent competitive parental allofeeding sessions of the chicks that were of precisely the same nature. Although Lysander usually cooperated with Lucretia in the allofeeding of a young chick, albeit competitively, it was she who selected the chick that was to be allofed.

Cockatielian parents also frequently compete to allofeed hatchings and nestlings and, but for the fact that the non-allofeeding Cockatielian parent engages much less in the cleaning of stray food and in the recovering of pieces too large for chicks to swallow, their behavior also is very similar to that of Budgerigars and lovebirds. Not only was the method of parental participation in the allofeeding of the chicks almost indistinguishable from that of lovebirds, but the subsequent degree of participation of Lysander in the allofeeding of the chicks through the time of fledging also was very similar. The main apparent difference was that Lucretia was somewhat more inclined to allow Lysander to allofeed a hatchling while she cleaned stray food than is the rule among lovebirds, where the hen is more likely to displace the male.

NO EVIDENCE OF "BUDGIE MILK." The great surprise in this first witnessed allofeeding was that there was no sign of budgie milk, no trickle-feeding, and no tongue-flick allofeeding, and this was true of all subsequent witnessed allofeedings of Budgerigar hatchlings and nestlings. All hatchlings and young nestlings received food delivered in semi-liquid gobs exclusively by massive tongue-flick allofeeding. This is precisely the form of food and manner of delivery by which lovebirds often allofeed young nestlings and the way the male, Cyrus, delivered the 1st meal to 2 lovebird hatchlings at a time when Cassandra was preferentially allofeeding older chicks (see pp. 766, 767). Cockatiels also allofeed older nestlings semi-liquid gobs of food of the same color and consistency.

ACTIVE ROLES OF NESTLINGS---SEED SELECTIVITY. At first the food delivered into the buccal cavity by the process of retroperistaltic pumping was filtered between the tongue and the palate (to remove whole seeds). But the degree of filtering gradually was reduced as a transition occurred to allofeeding older nestlings by a pumping action alone. All young chicks, even hatchlings and those only 1 day old, played a very active role in licking and swallowing food. This was unlike the behavior of very young lovebird or Cockatielian nestlings which sometimes partake passively when tongue-flick allofed. Parental consumption of bread, corn, and spray-millet was very heavy throughout the brooding and fledging periods, though relative consumption of corn and bread tended to decrease progressively as the chicks matured. It is noteworthy that the parents were very selective in the shape of the seeds fed to the young nestlings, choosing only round seeds and hulled oats, leaving spindle-shaped canary seeds essentially untouched, though the latter otherwise were favored.

Budgerigar nestlings also differ from those of lovebirds and Cockatiels in that, as they are allofed on their backs and their crops become full, they actively pull away and turn over on their bellies, even as hatchlings. Lovebird hatchlings are too uncoordinated for such movements and I never have witnessed this maneuver in lovebird chicks at any age. Cockatielian chicks almost always are allofed in a sitting position and they automatically droop lower and lower as the weight of a filling crop pulls them down. By the time a crop is full, a Cockatielian chick no longer pumps nor extends its head and neck upward to solicit.

The 2 other fertile eggs hatched at 2-day intervals. Lucretia, at first, continued to obtain most of the food for the chicks and herself from Lysander, and he also allofed the chicks frequently. As time passed, however, he less frequently allofed her and the chicks, and Lucretia began to leave the NB routinely to eat and be allofed outside by Lysander. I was able to confirm on many occasions the finding that the hen tends strongly to "load up" the youngest chick first, before allofeeding older chicks (843). Even as fledging time neared and the oldest chick solicited from the outside NB perch, Lucretia repeatedly reached past this chick to allofeed the youngest, who was soliciting from the inside perch of the NB.

THE SHELTERING OF THE CHICKS most resembled that of Cockatiels in that the young infrequently were "sat upon." They were preferentially sheltered under a wing or the breast. When only the 1st chick was present it usually was out of sight except when allofed, at which time it either was forward of the breast or to the side. With 2 chicks present, one often was under each wing, but sometimes both were under the right wing, on the side of the transparent side-pane (the hen's invariable brooding orientation was with her head facing the NB entrance). With all 3 chicks present, they most frequently were sheltered under the right wing, and were increasingly exposed as they increased in size. After the 10th day of brooding (youngest chick, 5 days old), when Lucretia began sleeping outside of the NB at night, she also frequently was absent from the NB during the day, at which times the chicks customarily huddled.

BRIEF CHRONOLOGY OF EVENTS. In terms of days of age, the eyes of the 1st chick opened at 9 days. The same nestling began to solicit food by warbling instead of cheeping at 16 days. The first instance of the oldest chick allofeeding its broodmates occurred at 22 days, while the first occasion on which Lucretia could be diverted temporarily from her allofeeding of the youngest chick occurred when the latter was 19 days old. The first perching of the oldest chick in the NB entrance hole was noted at 24 days, while the same chick left the NB and perched on the outside perch at 27 days. It entered the enclosure for a stay of 3 h on the same day. The oldest chick was observed eating corn and bread from the food tray at 28 days and all 3 chicks were out of the NB together for the first time when the oldest was 29 days of age. On that same night all 3 slept outside the NB on the enclosure floor. The youngest chick was observed eating corn and bread from a food tray for the 1st time at an age of 27 days. The 2 older chicks took their 1st tentative flights on the same day, when the eldest was 33 days old.

ENCRUSTED FOOD ON UPPER MANDIBLE----NARES SPOTLESSLY CLEAN. I began daily inspections of the chicks when the youngest was 4 days old. I found then, and for the next 9 days that almost every day, despite my daily cleaning, all of the chicks had food encrusted heavily along the leading outside edges of their upper mandible, and had semi-solid food caked solidly within its tip. These occurrences apparently trace to the facts that (a) food is delivered in relatively-large, semi-liquid gobs, with the occurrence of much overflow, as described above, (b) after the chicks were several days old the male ceased to participate as frequently in allofeeding them jointly with the female and, thus, one parent infrequently was cleaning while the other allofed, and/or (c) parental inexperience. Unlike the finding with lovebirds and Cockatiels, however, the external nares always were spotlessly clean. This tends to confirm that it is largely liquid (rather than semi-liquid) food, delivered by trickle-feeding or tongue-flick allofeeding, that runs down the upper mandible into the nares.

LACK OF NESTBOX SANITATION. Another dissimilarity from lovebird and Cockatielian behavior is that no evident nestbox sanitation was practiced by either the Budgerigar parents or the young. Voiding usually was indiscriminate and droppings were allowed to lie where they fell. As a result dry droppings were evenly distributed on the NB floor and and among the shavings, and the brooding area always was caked with undried excreta. As a consequence of these habits, the feet of the chicks always were caked heavily with dried excretory products, despite my cleaning them daily.

ALLOFED JOINTLY BY BOTH PARENTS EVERY MORNING. The most intense and regular participation of the male in the allofeeding of the chicks occurred within 10-30 min after the lights-on every morning. At that time both parents allofed the chicks, usually in the cooperatively competitive fashion described above. Although the details could not be observed on every occasion, because the male sometimes had his body blocking my view, both parents were busily engaged in the care of the chicks at that time every morning for the first 11 days. On 7 of those days I observed the allofeedings in detail.

NESTLINGS TEND TO ALLOFEED EACH OTHER. Stamps and her coworkers noted that Budgerigar chicks occasionally allofed one another, usually with an older chick allofeeding a younger one (843). These observations were confirmed and extended in the present study. More or less continuous observation and some experimental manipulation, however, revealed that the tendency of the chicks to engage in such allofeedings is very strong, and that allofeedings by the nestlings are of common occurrence after a chick is about 3 weeks old. In the first noted instance the eldest chick allofed both of its broodmates when it was 22 days old. On the next day the same chick allofed the next oldest chick quite lengthily, with transfer of food confirmed by observing it being mandibulated by the recipient, and by observing the donor mandibulating afterwards to regather scattered remnants in its buccal cavity.

Sometimes all 3 chicks had their bills in close proximity as food was transferred between them. Once the chick of middle age allofed the youngest one for 2 min. Once the eldest chick allofed the youngest one lengthily after having been allofed itself while perched in the NB entrance. On one occasion the chick of middle age (25 days), after being allofed lengthily by the hen as the former perched in the NB entrance, in turn, allofed the eldest chick as it perched on the outside NB perch. Once the eldest chick, facing inward in the NB entrance, allofed the youngest chick as it perched on the inner perch. At another time the youngest chick (age 31 days) allofed the chick of middle age as both perched side by side on the outer NB perch. On one occasion, as I handled the chicks, one in each hand, and held the eldest (32 days old) above the one of middle age, the eldest allofed the other lengthily, and I could readily observe transferred food being mandibulated. Lastly, after Lucretia had begun to "brood the NB" again and was guarding it from the inside perch, she allofed the 31-day-old youngest chick as it perched on the outside NB perch; the latter, in turn, allofed the chick of middle age as it stood on the enclosure floor. In all cases allofeedings between chicks were preceded by vocal solicitations.

HEN TENACIOUSLY FEEDS YOUNGEST CHICKS FIRST. Although not all allofeedings were observed, on no prefledging occasion was the hen observed to initiate feedings by delivering food to a chick other than the youngest one (perhaps 20-25% of the total number of allofeedings were observed). However, it was not until the 24th day of brooding the chicks, as noted above, that another chick was seen to divert Lucretia briefly from her allofeeding of the youngest chick. A 2nd such brief diversion was noted 2 days later. That the tendency to allofeed the youngest chick first remained very strong was illustrated by events of the next 3 days. On the 1st occasion, Lucretia had to force her way past the eldest chick as it perched in the entrance hole, in order to allofeed the youngest chick within the NB. She then also had to force her way out to resume eating. On both of the following 2 days, Lucretia had to reach over and beyond the eldest chick, as it perched on the outer NB perch, in order to allofeed the youngest one as it perched in the entrance hole. Details of the order of feeding chicks in the morning are given for the 2nd brood (see p. 791).

LIQUIDITY OF OLDER CHICKS' FOOD DECREASES AUTOMATICALLY. Though the practice of allofeeding the youngest chicks first can be understood in terms of ensuring that they get adequate food and attention in the presence of much larger, competitive nestmates, it also could be based in large part on the need for a differential processing of the food. Thus, since the crop contents are filtered to varying degrees according to the age of the chick being allofed, and to the greatest degree for the smallest chick, the most efficient means of accomplishing the filtering would be to allofeed the youngest chick first while the crop contents are most liquid. Then, as crop liquid becomes progressively exhausted, the older chicks get progressively less liquid and more solid food. In other words, Budgerigar parents may tend to deliver all crop contents in a like manner, with the amount of liquid received by a given chick depending primarily upon the amount of liquid remaining in the crop at the time.

WANING OF PARENTAL ALLOFEEDING, WAXING OF WARBLING SOLICITATIONS. As the chicks matured they were allofed decreasingly frequently by the parents, mostly the hen, but such allofeedings continued even after the chicks were eating by themselves and after fledging (first flights). At an age of roughly 16 days, the warbling solicitations of the chicks became increasingly persistent, and the less frequently they were allofed as time went on, the more continuous their warbling became. Between the 3 chicks this often meant that warbling occurred continuously for up to 20 min, usually not ceasing until after the last chick had been allofed.

During these days, in which large quantities of food were being delivered to the young, I noted two deviations in feeding and allofeeding behavior among the parents. The 1st of these was characteristic of that period alone, the 2nd was merely greatly accentuated at that time. The 1st was that the allofeeding of Lucretia by Lorenzo was speeded up by Lucretia's uttering a brief, high-pitched warble of very rapidly repeated notes (a type of utterance heard on no other occasion) every time that she had completed the swallowing of the last portion of food that had been delivered to her and was ready to receive the next portion. Since Lysander responded immediately to this call by allofeeding her another portion, allofeeding was much more efficient than at other times.

The 2nd of these deviations was a rapid type of "production line" eating by Lysander. He perched between the water tray and adjacent tray of corn and whole-grained bread pieces and, in rapid succession, grasped and swallowed bread crumbs for 2-3 sec and then pivoted to the water and took a quick draught for $\frac{1}{2}$-1 sec, then pivoted back to the bread tray, then to the water tray, etc., for up to 20 repetitions.

NO EVIDENT PARENTAL 'CONCERN' DURING HANDLING OR FLIGHTING OF YOUNG. As I handled the chicks daily, beginning when the youngest was 4 days old, I never observed evidence of parental 'concern,' even though handling occurred within their view. It will be recalled that, as fledging time approaches in lovebirds and Cockatiels, parental 'concern' mounts as the chicks are handled, whether the parents remain confined or are flighted. During first flights or even merely during wing-flapping, parental 'concern' peaks and the parents remain in close attendance of the fledgling young. In the case of lovebirds, the male remains in close attendance even when the young are quiescent. It is of interest that until the Budgerigar young become experienced fliers, their wing flapping is silent and their forward progression tends to be relatively slow, almost as if they were "floating." Once they are experienced their progression tends to be rapid and noisy. Similar but less marked changes were noted in lovebird and Cockatielian fledglings and probably are typical of the fledglings of many species.

The situation in this Budgerigar family can be encapsulated by relating that I never noticed any evidence of 'concern' for the safety of the young by confined or unconfined parents. This was so during my handling of the chicks, during chick wing-flapping, during their 1st flights, or during subsequent flighting. Nor was any 'concern' evidenced in the presence of other Budgerigars or of lovebirds (in the case of other Budgerigars, there was no need for concern, as other Budgerigars flew off when young approached them and solicited). The only evidence even of acknowledging the presence or existence of the young by the parents occurred when the young were perched outside, in which case the parents sometimes perched briefly near them.

On such occasions the parents usually flew off when the young approached them and solicited for food. During these flightings the parents usually occupied themselves with interacting with other housed birds or exploring open, unused enclosures. On the other hand, once the young had been fledged and housed in isolation from their parents, they sometimes persistently flew in Lucretia's wake, soliciting vigorously at every perch stop. At these times, Lucretia never allofed them but repelled them with pecks. On one such occasion a fledgling solicited with long whining squeals, just as I occasionally have heard Cockatielian fledglings solicit.

The Fourth Clutch and Second Brood of Lucretia and Lysander

INCUBATORY BEHAVIOR

DAYTIME INCUBATION ONLY. On January 3, 1986, 3 days before I weaned her 1st brood of 3 chicks, Lucretia began to pick and scrape on the mineral block. By the next day, she had begun to occupy and scratch about in the NB, and the following day she was "brooding" it and guarding it from the inside perch. The 1st and 2nd ovipositions occurred on January 13 and 15. However, she incubated the eggs only during the day, returning to them each morning shortly after lights-on at 09:30 h. Since no egg was laid on the 4th day, reckoning January 13 as day 0, it appeared that this would be another undersized 2-egg clutch, like her 2nd one (see pp. 782, 783) which she had incubated only during the day from the 4th day on and had abandoned after incubating for 26 daytime periods.

NIGHTTIME INCUBATION BEGINS WITH LAST EGG. However, as oviposition commenced again on the 6th day and 3 more eggs were laid, it appeared that production of the scheduled 3rd egg merely had failed. But despite the resumption of oviposition, there was no nighttime incubation until the night of the 10th day, the day on which the 5th egg was laid. Instead, Lucretia left the eggs and NB each night shortly after lights-off and returned each morning within 30-45 sec after lights-on. Thus, it appeared likely that only the 5th egg would hatch, possible that the 4th one would hatch (it had been left to chill to 24½-25½°C for 2 nights, without turning), but rather unlikely that the 1st 3 eggs would hatch, having been left unattended for from 4 to 10 nights. These expectations were based on the fact that nighttime incubatory inattentiveness had never been reported for successfully hatched clutches of Budgerigars, although it is the typical behavior of the Mountain White-crowned Sparrow hens, who withhold nocturnal incubation until after the penultimate egg is laid (1,106).

UNUSUAL HATCHING SCHEDULE. These expectations proved to be unduly pessimistic, however, as all 5 eggs hatched, though on a very unusual schedule that reflected Lucretia's unusual incubatory behavior. Thus, the 1st egg hatched very late, as reckoned from the time of oviposition, sometime during the late night of the 22nd day (Feb. 4), after being incubated for 10 daylight periods and 12½ additional full 24-h periods. If one merely sums the incubatory times, it comes to about 18 24-h periods, which is only 1 day over the normal minimum and within the usual range of 17-20 days (see p. 186). The 2nd egg hatched a few sec after 10:45 h the following day. Just before 10:45 h Lucretia was pecking at the shell of this egg, the cap of which already had been almost completely severed by the chick. When I glanced back only 15 sec later, she was grooming or aiding the chick as it emerged from the shell. The 3rd egg hatched not more than 1 or 2 h before 14:50 h on the next day. The 4th egg, which lacked only 2 nights of incubation, hatched after a cumulative time of slightly over 18 24-h periods, and the 5th, which received normal attentiveness, after 17 days.

CARE OF HATCHLINGS AND YOUNG NESTLINGS

ALLOFEEDINGS. I got my first glimpse of the eggshells from the 1st hatching at 09:30 h, and of the vigorous chick itself at 10:05 h; Lucretia had been sitting squarely on top of it. There was no sign of food in the hatchling's crop. I did not witness an allofeeding until 21:00 h. As always, with hatchlings and young nestlings, it was allofed solely by massive tongue-flick allofeeding with vigorous cooperative participatory movements by the chick, accompanied by faint cheeping. I did not witness extensive participation in chick allofeeding by Lysander until the morning of the day the 1st two chicks were 1 and 2 days old. On the morning of that day, the chicks' crops appeared to be 1/3-½ full at the time of lights-on. At 13:48 h one of the chicks was allofed extensively and competitively as described above, with Lysander, as before, allofeeding both Lucretia and the chick in the course of the proceedings.

ALLOFEEDING JOINTLY. On the following day, Lucretia came off the 3 chicks to eat shortly after lights-on. The chicks cheeped briefly as she left and small amounts of food could be seen in their tiny crops. At 10:05 h, Lysander participated briefly in allofeeding a chick and Lucretia before exiting. At 13:45 h, both parents participated in a lengthy joint allofeeding of the largest chick, which was "loaded up" so fully that it pulled away and turned over on its belly in resting position. Since Lysander infrequently allofed a young chick other than the one being allofed by Lucretia during this early period--since the major portion of his allofeeding was of his mate rather than of the chicks--Lucretia almost always was the parent that selected the chick to be allofed. On the following day, with 4 chicks present, Lucretia exited briefly at lights-on and voided and ate. Then both parents entered the NB and allofed individual chicks jointly in the usual fashion for 20 min and then intermittently for another 80 min. From this time on, continuing for about 2 weeks, Lucretia often had her upper mandible heavily caked with dried food, just as I sometimes had noted with lovebird hens, particularly Cassandra.

ALLOFEEDING DIFFERENT CHICKS CONCURRENTLY. On the following morning, with 5 chicks present, Lucretia again came off the brood briefly within 10 sec of lights-on. Within 1 min, however, both parents had entered the NB and began to allofeed the chicks. On this occasion, though, they sometimes allofed different chicks concurrently, rather than always cooperatively allofeeding the same chick. Moreover, the youngest chicks did not get allofed until last on this occasion. Again, allofeeding of the chicks continued intermittently for over 1 h, and frequently Lucretia merely rested or mandibulated while Lysander allofed chicks alone. Even 4½ h later, Lysander still was participating intermittently in the allofeeding of the 5 young. Although Lucretia's upper mandible was heavily caked with dry food at 16:10 h, it was spotlessly clean at 23:05 h. By this time the oldest chick (5 days old) could sit up shakily. The same circumstances were repeated on the following morning. Both parents again sometimes allofed separate chicks independently, and whichever chicks were most accessible were allofed 1st. On the same day, the eyes of the oldest chick (6 days old) were opening.

LONGER ABSENCES----LYSANDER COMPLETES ALLOFEEDINGS. The following day (Feb. 11) was the 7th day after the oldest chick had hatched and the 1st day that Lucretia began to absent herself from the NB for relatively long periods, say 5-20 min. On both this day and the following one, the chicks began to cheep as Lucretia left them at the time of lights-on, but shortly both parents were in the NB allofeeding them. I estimate that the parents at that time were spending 40-50% of their time allofeeding the chicks and that Lysander accounted for about 30% of the total food delivered directly to the chicks. On neither day did the youngest chick appear to be given priority in allofeeding. At that time, the chicks customarily cheeped only while being allofed, and when Lucretia exposed them, as she left them briefly in the early morning. After a quick initial allofeeding, they usually became quiet and then were allofed at a more leisurely pace all through the morning. As Lysander allofed Lucretia and competed with her to allofeed a chick, she often switched to another chick, leaving him to complete the allofeeding of the previous one.

YOUNGEST CHICK ALLOFED FIRST WHEN ACCESSIBLE-----ONE CHICK SUCCUMBS. Beginning on the following day, Lucretia typically allofed the chicks alone in the first vigorous morning allofeeding bouts and I could keep close account of which chick was allofed 1st. On that morning and the following one, she persistently fed the youngest chick 1st. On the 2nd of these 2 days, I found chick #4 dead under the huddled chicks, with an empty crop and no sign of abnormality. The lost chick was roughly 3 times as large as the youngest one and possibly was neglected accidentally.

On the 3rd morning of keeping close account, Lucretia again allofed the youngest chick 1st, while Lysander allofed some of the others. On the 4th morning, the congestion was such that when Lucretia returned to the NB after her customary brief exit, she could not locate the youngest chick and, instead, allofed the 2nd-youngest one. Meanwhile, the youngest, which was on the periphery, out of Lucretia's view, kept stretching up against the sides of its standing siblings but kept losing its balance and toppling over as they jostled about, After only 2 regurgitations to the 2nd-youngest chick, however, Lucretia and the youngest one made contact and she allofed it solely. Even as it fell over after each regurgitation, as Budgerigar chicks often do until 7-9 days old, she sought it out and continued to allofeed it.

That night was the 1st one during which Lucretia slept on a perch outside the NB. Again on the following morning, the youngest chick, then 8 days old, could not be located immediately by Lucretia, for the same reason, and she regurgitated twice to chick #2 and once to chick #3 before locating the youngest one and concentrating on it. The following morning (Feb. 18), when the oldest chick was 14 days old, was the 1st morning that there were loud squawks from some of the chicks accompanied by cheeping before Lucretia entered the NB. Again, when she entered, she did not locate the youngest chick at first, and fed a sibling 2 regurgitations before concentration her attentions on the youngest one. After 20 minutes, Lysander entered the NB and mostly allofed Lucretia. On the following morning, Lucretia allofed chicks while perched on the inside perch. From there, she had no difficulty in locating the youngest chick and loaded it up first, with only a momentary diversion in which an older chick received a regurgitation. This was the 1st day when I noted persistent solicitations by the chicks for food at times when no parent was present in the NB.

The following day was most unusual, in that the youngest chick did not solicit for food, showed no inclination to be allofed, and appeared to be rather lethargic. Accordingly, the other chicks were allofed 1st that morning. The same morning, I saw the 1st instance of one chick reaching into the mouth of another that had just been allofed and snatching out a morsel of food. Those were days in which Lysander customarily was outside the NB much of the morning, eating intensively between brief visits within, in which he customarily allofed Lucretia almost exclusively. On the following morning the youngest chick again did not sit up and solicit but was asleep on its side under the others. But this time, after Lucretia had allofed 2 regurgitations to an older chick, she probed about in the pile, located the youngest chick, roused it, and allofed it after it sat up. For the next 8 days, without fail, Lucretia first sought out the youngest chick and allofed it thoroughly before allowing herself to be diverted to the allofeeding of any of the others.

LUCRETIA MORE READILY DIVERTED-----CHICKS BLOCK NESTBOX ENTRANCE. On the day following this sequence of 8 days, she delivered 4-5 regurgitations to chicks #2 and #1 before allofeeding the youngest one. That was the last day during which the youngest chick was given very strong preference, partly because the older chicks then were beginning to leave the NB and perch in the entrance hole and on the inside and outside perches. Thus, on the next day, during the 1st period of intensive allofeeding, the youngest chick was fed 2nd, and Lucretia easily was diverted from allofeeding one chick to feed another. During the 2nd period of intensive allofeeding, however, she gave preference to the youngest chick. During these days Lysander's eating of bread and water and his allofeeding of Lucretia were facilitated in the manners described during the care of the 1st brood (see p. 788).

The manner of care and allofeeding of the nestlings during those days is conveyed by a few examples. Two days later (Mar. 4), the #1 chick was perched in the NB entrance in the early morning and Lucretia allofed it many regurgitations in one bout. Then she ate for several min and allofed it in another bout of about 5 regurgitations. Then she ate yet again for several min and also was allofed many times by Lysander. Thereafter she forced her way past chick #1 into the NB, allofed the youngest chick 4 regurgitations, and exited and ate once more. About 5 min later, Lysander also allofed the #1 chick in the entrance hole. Then, for a 2nd time, Lucretia forced her way past the #1 chick and into the NB. She clearly intended to allofeed the youngest chick again, because she kept pecking away chick #3, who had not yet been fed, as it solicited and presented its bill. But when the youngest chick did not present itself, she ultimately allofed 3 regurgitations to chick #3 and exited.

When Lucretia returned several min later, she allofed all 3 chicks from the inside perch. Meanwhile, Lysander again allofed chick #1 as it perched in the NB entrance. The next morning, chick #1 was the 1st to be allofed, this time by Lysander, as the former perched in the entrance. When Lucretia began allofeeding at 10:45 h, she fed chick #1 one regurgitation as she entered the NB and then allofed the youngest chick inside. During subsequent days, both Lucretia and Lysander allofed all chicks, primarily outside the NB and amid the clamour of frequent vigorous solicitations.

The Fifth Clutch and Third Brood of Lucretia and Lysander

COPULATIONS---HATCHINGS---ALLOFEEDINGS. I confine my description only to the most salient points concerning the incubation, brooding, fledging, and interactions of this clutch and brood. The 1st egg was detected on the morning of March 25, and Lucretia began intensive incubation forthwith. She left the NB briefly at 09:29 h and I witnessed a very brief copulation on a perch, followed by Lysander's allofeeding her. This was the 1st time I had witnessed copulation by the experienced pair. The next morning Lucretia again left the NB early--only about 1 min after lights-on--and the pair copulated briefly followed again by allofeeding. After the pair entered the NB, both exited and copulated again on the floor of the enclosure. On the morning of the next day, they only courted after lights on, following a visit of Lysander to the NB.

The 1st hatching occurred on April 13 between noon and 14:00 h. At 22:20 h, I noted that the chick had been fed, as the typical whitish-yellow material could be seen in its crop. At 22:35 h, I witnessed the typical, joint, cooperatively-competitive, massive tongue-flick allofeeding of the hatchling. It could be seen clearly that on many of the occasions when the male reached in his head and bill and displaced the allofeeding female, it was for the purpose of allofeeding her, not to clean or allofeed the chick, though both of these actions occurred at other times. Many subsequent allofeedings of the chicks of this brood were witnessed. A 2nd chick hatched during the late afternoon of April 15, and a 3rd late on the following day.

NIGHTTIME ALLOFEEDING CONFIRMED. Either the youngest or the 2nd-youngest chick was allofed 1st on the next day (April 17), the youngest on the following day, but the oldest on the next day. The following morning was the first occasion on which I confirmed that the chicks sometimes are allofed at night; when I turned on the lights, I discovered Lucretia in the act of allofeeding the youngest chick, whose crop already was half full. On 6 of the next 7 mornings the youngest chick was allofed 1st, and the 2nd-youngest one once. Four of these 1st feedings were jointly by both parents. As late as May 2, I noted that Lysander still was participating very heavily in the allofeeding of the chicks.

OLDEST CHICK CRIPPLED, SICKLY---ALLOFED BY BROODMATES. The 3rd brood was noteworthy for the fact that the oldest chick was crippled and sickly, and eventually succumbed, and the youngest one, Agrippina, was very long delayed in attaining the vigor for full flight. The oldest chick had its right leg splayed out partly to the side and did not begin to eat unassistedly, though it actively pecked about in the debris on the enclosure floor. Inasmuch as the other 2 chicks were eating normally, I placed them in another enclosure, with the thought that the eldest chick might receive more parental care. However, the parents were making preparations for another cycle of breeding and gave the chick absolutely no care.

Since the chick was starving slowly and losing weight, and I found that both of its broodmates were inclined to allofeed it when they came into contact with it, I placed it in their enclosure. Immediately upon doing so there followed a remarkable series of allofeedings and/or mock allofeedings of the oldest chick by Agrippina, that lasted almost 5 min, throughout which the oldest chick solicited vocally and vigorously. However, I could not confirm that any food was being transferred. Later that evening, though, the #2 chick also allofed the oldest one, and I could see at least a small amount of food being transferred. For the next 5 days, the oldest chick was groomed and allofed to some extent by its two broodmates, and also slept next to one or the other of them, but it gradually lost weight and strength and expired on May 24 (my attempts to allofeed the chick met with no acceptance of food). Although the chick was not saved, the circumstance was remarkable for the care given to it by its broodmates; whether the care was stimulated primarily by a perception that the bird was ill, or merely that it was much younger (because of its smaller size) and in need of parental attention, I cannot say.

AGRIPPINA SIX WEEKS LATE IN ACHIEVING NORMAL FLIGHT. The youngest chick, Agrippina, appeared to be normal until its ability for flight was inordinately delayed. Although it could gain altitude and stay airborne, this was achieved only with great effort. Its flight could best be described as being similar to that of a bird with wings partially clipped --great exertion, much sound and wing-flapping, but little progess. Nor did the bird evidence any great inclination to be flighted, usually remaining in its enclosure when flight was permitted and its broodmate was out flying. Not until about 6 weeks after the normal fledging time did this juvenile attain the flight capabilities of a fledgling (on July 11).

The Sixth and Seventh Clutches of Lucretia and Lysander

I did not wish to facilitate further breeding on the part of Lucretia and Lysander after the fledging of their 3rd brood, when Lucretia began to prepare the NB for another clutch. Accordingly, on May 21, 1986, I removed them from enclosure F, in which they had bred, and housed them in enclosure B, together with the 4 offspring of their 2nd brood, then 3½-months old, without any nesting facility. Despite the distractions of these offspring and the inhibitory effects of being placed in a strange enclosure lacking a NB, Lucretia and Lysander continued to court, and the 1st egg of her 6th clutch was laid on June 30.

EGG LAID IN FOOD TRAY. The 1st egg was laid at a very exposed location in a food tray on the right side of the enclosure at the front, half way up the side. Upon detecting the egg, I placed it in a nestbowl on the floor at the right rear. However, as might have been expected from the oviposition-site fidelity noted in lovebirds and Cockatiels, Lucretia ignored it and, instead, "incubated" the empty food tray. The young, on the other hand, displayed great interest in the egg, nudging it about and pecking at it. Since it became evident that Lucretia would not adopt a nest at a new location, I restored the egg to the food tray, whereupon she spent most of the rest of the day in the tray with it, "preparing a nest" and defending the site vigorously from the 4 offspring, even expelling Lysander from its vicinity several times.

YOUNG OF SECOND BROOD COMPETE FOR AND DESTROY EGGS. The next morning I found the egg on the enclosure floor, unattended, and restored it to the nest. Lucretia took over its care again but when she exited the tray and ate or perched, the young competed for the egg, pecked a hole in it, and discarded it from the nest-tray. I substituted a lovebird egg for it, and that too drew the continuous attention of the young. Late that afternoon, Lucretia oviposited again and I found the egg on the enclosure floor beneath a perch at the rear. However, Lucretia apparently had oviposited while on the perch, as the egg appeared to have been damaged in a fall, having a small flattened concavity on its surface. The lovebird egg also was discarded twice more that day by the young and pecked open.

The next day (July 2), the young continued to peck open and discard lovebird eggs that I placed in the nest-tray. That afternoon I rehoused the 4 young of the 2nd brood in their natal enclosure (F of Fig. 1b), leaving Lucretia and Lysander as the sole occupants of enclosure B, to attempt breeding with the food tray as nest. I also placed a feather-light dried-out Budgerigar egg and a full-weight lovebird egg in the nest-tray to ascertain Lucretia's response to their presence; she discarded both of them but did not peck them open.

ATTENTIVENESS TO EGG WANES, BREEDING EPISODE TERMINATES. The following day Lucretia continued to occupy and "prepare" the nest-tray, to which I had added a sprinkling of wood shavings. The next morning I found that the 3rd egg of her clutch had been laid in the nest tray, though she was sleeping on a perch. However, she entered the tray within 2-3 min of lights-on and sat over the egg for most of the day, leaving several times and eating, perching, and courting with Lysander. Once again, she did not incubate the egg at night. Nor was she highly attentive on the following day, perhaps about 25% of the time, but in the evening she settled into the tray-nest almost continuously. Attentiveness also was at a level of about 25% on the following day, but on the day after that, despite fairly consistent morning attendance to the care of the 3rd egg (which was fertile), she discarded the egg from the nest tray. I replaced it twice and she promptly discarded it twice more, both times within 10 min of its having been replaced. On a 3rd occasion, I returned it together with 2 plastic balls, 1¼ cm in diamater, all of which she discarded, as well as pecking a hole in the egg. That marked the end of the breeding episode.

After an additional 2 months in enclosure B, when it seemed unlikely that Lucretia would come into breeding condition again in the absence of a NB, I transferred her and Lysander back to (sole occupancy of) enclosure F. She laid a 7th clutch of 3 infertile eggs beginning on October 20, 1986. The care of this clutch was noteworthy in that Lysander typically spent over half of every day in the NB at Lucretia's side, sometimes head to tail, i.e., in opposite orientation. An 8th clutch was begun on December 16, 1986.

PRIVACY PREFERRED FOR SEXUAL UNION

In preceding sections and chapters, I have described how both lovebird and Cockatielian pairs tend to be inhibited from copulating in the near presence of other birds, how they tend to remain behind in an enclosure during flighting and copulate in the absence of the other occupants, and how they choose a "remote" site to copulate, in the presence of other birds. For example, Cassandra and Cyrus copulated on the enclosure floor when the offspring of prior broods were present and on upper perches, and Carmen and Cosimo repeatedly stayed behind and copulated after their offspring left the enclosure for flightings. I also have described how the male lovebird, Cyrano, after pair bonding with Zenobia, became increasingly aggressive toward the Budgerigars with which he was housed, and even expelled them from the enclosure when Zenobia was visiting with him, and how both he and Zenobia sought repeatedly to bar Flavia from entering enclosure E when Cyrano was housed therein.

EVICTING RETURNING OCCUPANTS FROM BREEDING ENCLOSURE. It remained for Lysander to provide the most striking and convincing evidence of such behavior during the period when he and Lucretia were breeding but housed together with the 4 juveniles of their 2nd brood in enclosure B. During the period between May 21 and June 29, 1986, I had flighted the family about every 3rd day by opening the enclosure door and letting them fly out at will. I noticed that Lucretia and Lysander usually were the last to leave and sometimes did not leave at all, but spent the time socializing and courting.

On the afternoon of July 1, a day after Lucretia laid the 1st egg of her 6th clutch (which the young had destroyed), I flighted the family, as usual, by opening the enclosure door. As usual, Lucretia and Lysander stayed behind. Since they were known to be breeding at the time, I watched the family very closely. Within 3 min, Lysander mounted Lucretia and they began to copulate in the fashion already described (p. 120, **Copulation**), except that Lysander maintained almost continuous bill contact with Lucretia throughout the act. As they were in the act of copulating, one of the young alighted on the front face of the enclosure and began to sidle toward the entrance. To my astonishment, upon perceiving the presence of the young bird, and without hesitation, Lysander dismounted, crossed to the entrance, and expelled it from the vicinity. He then returned directly to Lucretia, remounted her, and resumed the sexual act. Subsequently, after completing coitus, he several times more expelled the young as they sought to re-enter the enclosure. [I also once saw the lovebird, Cyrano, dismount abruptly from Zenobia in the midst of copulating, in order to repel an intruding lovebird from a front face of the enclosure, at a time when the 2 near-fledging young of their 7th brood were present.]

On the following day, Lucretia and Lysander courted at the rear of the enclosure for most of the morning and probably copulated again, though I did not witness it. That afternoon, I opened the enclosure door again. Once more, the young flew out but Lucretia and Lysander remained behind courting. And once again, Lysander approached the entrance time and again and barred any returning young from entering. Subsequently, both parents also exited the enclosure and flew about. Often on such flightings they climbed about on or entered and perched within enclosure F, their former breeding site, which they were very reluctant to leave. That same afternoon, I isolated the young in enclosure F, leaving Lucretia and Lysander as the sole occupants of enclosure B.

Taken together with the findings with the lovebirds and Cockatiels, the fact that Lucretia and Lysander customarily remained behind in the enclosure during flightings, and copulated shortly after the young left on at least one occasion, indicates that they too preferred privacy when copulating. Lysander's other behavior described above leaves little doubt that the male Budgerigar, at least, seeks to establish the nest or breeding area as being "off grounds" to other birds--even offspring--either as a site for incubating and brooding or even merely as a site for courting and copulating. Guarding and defense of the nest by the female Budgerigar are well known (844, 859).

CAKED FOOD ON UPPER MANDIBLE

With the 1st brood, daily inspections revealed food heavily caked both outside and inside the upper mandibles of all chicks, beginning on the 1st day of inspection, when the youngest chick was 4 days old. This could have been either a consequence of parental inexperience or a characteristic accompaniment of allofeeding of Budgerigar chicks even by experienced parents. The observations of the parental care of the 2nd brood tend to favor the parental inexperience alternative.

Thus, as I began inspections of the 2nd brood, when the youngest chick was 4 days old (Feb. 13), I found no significant amount of food caked on or within any upper mandible, and the same was the case in the ensuing 5 days. On the 6th day, I found only a small quantity of food caked on the upper mandible of chick #3. On the following day, the outside upper mandibles of chicks #1 and #4 were heavily caked with food and that of #2 was lightly caked. On the following 2 days, only the outside upper mandible of #4 was heavily caked, with slight to moderate caking on #3 the 1st day and on #2 the 2nd day.

The next day was the one of most extensive caking. The #1 chick's bill was uncaked but the bills of chicks #2 and #3 were heavily caked inside and those of #2 and #4 outside. On the following 2 days, only the bills of chicks #3 and #4 were caked, that of #4 outside on both days, that of #3 outside and inside on the 1st day and inside alone on the 2nd day. The situation was reversed the next day, with #1's bill heavily caked inside and out and #2's lightly caked inside. On the following day, the upper mandible of #4 was caked on the outside but so also was the lower, and the latter was so heavily caked that it must have been the overlooked accumulation of several days. On the 1st of the next 2 days, the bills of #2 and #3 were caked on the inside, and on the 2nd that of #4 was caked on the outside. No significant caking was noted after this time. Although this detailed enumeration of the caking of the bills gives the impression of rather considerable amounts, the fact is that caking was much more extensive with the 1st brood, to the extent that virtually every chick's upper mandible was caked inside and out almost every day.

CAKED EXCRETA ON FEET AND TOES

Inasmuch as no NB sanitation was practiced by my Budgerigars, insofar as the excreta of the young was concerned, and this led to severe encumbering of the feet and toes of the 1st brood, I removed all excreta of the 2nd brood daily, beginning when the youngest chick was 4 days old, with the following results. On the 1st day of examination the feet were uncaked but the NB bottom in part of the IA and to its outside were covered with hundreds of small dry droppings. There was no significant caking of the feet during the next 8 days and only a very light caking on the following day. On the other hand, the NB floor was covered every day with scores to hundreds of large dry droppings and the IA began to accumulate a continuous, compacted, ½-cm-depth carpet of semi-moist excreta. On the following day, the feet of all of the chicks had small caked plaques of excreta, which apparently were becoming more liquid as well as more voluminous. In addition, the NB bottom was becoming ever more moist, whereupon I began to add a sprinkling of wood shavings after cleaning, with the result that very little caking of the feet occurred thereafter.

LACK OF PARENTAL 'CONCERN' DURING FLIGHTING

The pre-fledged feathered young of the 2nd brood were placed outside the NB (by hand) where they perched on a trellis, daily, and the parents were flighted at the same time or afterward, sometimes with the young of the 1st brood or other adult pairs. As with the 1st brood, the results were almost diametrically opposed to those observed with either Cockatiels or lovebirds. At no time was a parent protective of a young bird upon the approach of a non-brood member. Nor at any time did a parent evidence 'concern' over the wing-flapping, flight, or distress calls of a chick. They sometimes were stimulated to flight by the general disturbance in the colony occasioned when an offspring took off from its perch, but they did not fly in its direction nor accompanied it during flight or at a landing site, as lovebird and Cockatielian parents invariably do.

The parents did, however, frequently perch next to or very close to the young. On only one occasion did Lysander very briefly allofeed one of his offspring as it perched outside the enclosure, and he infrequently came close enough for one of the young to make contact with him. When an offspring did make contact, he pecked it away. Lucretia, on the other hand, sometimes perched very close to the young. She most frequently repelled her young with pecks as they solicited vigorously for food or made contact with her, even though they sometimes might be losing their balance and slipping from the perch. However, on a number of occasions she allofed them (at most a total of 8 regurgitations divided among 2 young). [Recall that it is the male parent among Cockatiels and lovebirds that is most attentive to the young.] As with the 1st brood, once fledged and housed in isolation from their parents, the young, at first, tended to follow Lucretia about tenaciously and solicit for food, though unsuccessfully. In this connection, Wyndham has reported that adults usually respond aggressively to food solicitation by free-flying juveniles (171).

ALLOFEEDING AMONG THE YOUNG

Most of the phenomena of allofeeding among the young have been treated in descriptions of the behavior of the 1st and 3rd broods, so the present account is very brief and touches primarily on first observations of previously unrecorded behavior of the 2nd brood. As already mentioned, an instance of one chick reaching into another's bill and snatching a piece of food was noted for the first time when the oldest 3 chicks were 14-16 days old, though that was not, strictly speaking, allofeeding.

Four days later, I saw the first instance of allofeeding, when the #3 chick allofed the #1 chick (2 days difference in age) several regurgitations, with clearly evident transfer of food. On the same day, chick #1 mock allofed in succession, 3 regurgitations each to chicks #3 and #4. Two days later, chicks #1 and #2 took turns allofeeding #4. Four days later, after the termination of a bout of allofeeding by Lucretia, all 4 chicks participated in a frenzy of allofeeding exchanges with each other in various combinations. Lastly, some of the chicks allofed one another on the next day as I was examining them and they sat in a deep tray.

SUMMARY AND DISCUSSION

Cockatiels

Since much of the reproductive biology of Cockatiels already has been treated and some of the present findings already have been summarized in Chapter 4, Part 2, the present treatment is limited to the most salient findings not already summarized, particularly those that are new or differ from previous information.

LOCATION OF EGGS. Eggs that are displaced to any position within a NB are recovered and returned to the site of oviposition and incubation by members of either sex. My attempt to relocate the IA within the NB was not tolerated; the eggs simply were restored to the original IA. A male in breeding condition (in the 3rd phylogenetic stage) apparently will incubate "newly appearing" eggs placed in a former IA, whether they were laid at that site or not, but a female generally will incubate eggs only if they are at the site of oviposition. Moreover, a female may remove newly laid eggs from a former IA and restore them to the site of oviposition, even if her mate is incubating them in the former IA and she has to "steal" them from him. Helena more than once moved an egg about 30 cm from a former IA to a location as near as possible to the site of oviposition.

In an appropriately created situation, the male and female of a pair will incubate a divided clutch independently, uncooperatively, and highly attentively, provided only that the female's portion of the clutch (even only 1 egg) is at the site of oviposition and the male's portion is in a former IA. In such a circumstance, the male abandons the eggs at night but the female incubates both by day and by night, each bird following essentially the same pattern as followed normally during cooperative incubation of a single clutch, even though this is to the detriment of the male's portion of the clutch. Insofar as the situations created artificially could conceivably occur accidentally in the wild--in tree holes or on flat, level ground, in the present reproductive mode--the responses of the birds are adaptive. Insofar as the situations are unlikely to occur accidentally in the wild (the clutch divided between 2 locations), the responses--aside from the male leaving his portion of the divided clutch at night--are adaptive, not for present reproductive practice, but for the postulated ancestral practice, in which members of each sex incubated a separate clutch in a rapid double-clutching reproductive mode.

HATCHLINGS AND THEIR CARE. Fresh hatchlings may be vigorously active immediately upon emerging from eggshells; in some cases they even can sit up momentarily. They usually begin to cheep shortly after hatching and sometimes continue to vocalize until they are sheltered and/or allofed. Parents may or may not shelter a fresh, cheeping hatchling, perhaps primarily depending upon their experience and the degree to which the hatchling's down is dry and fluffed. The behavior of parents toward a fresh hatchling can give the misleading impression that they are ignoring it.

Inexperienced parents will not initiate the allofeeding of a newly hatched chick unless it also sits up and extends its bill upward, nor a hatchling sitting up and extending its bill upward unless it also cheeps. Experienced parents apparently will respond to the extension of the bill of a hatchling by allofeeding it, regardless of whether cheeping occurs, but neither the extension nor the cheeping is a prerequisite for their allofeeding of older nestlings. On the other hand, an older nestling--perhaps even a hatchling--appears not to be allofed unless it responds by bobbing (or pumping) its head and neck when its bill is grasped by a parent.

BROODING AND ALLOFEEDING OF YOUNG NESTLINGS BY EXPERIENCED PARENTS are carried out in a highly systematic fashion in which the chicks usually are spaced apart and usually do not interact with one another in the presence of a parent. Chicks are brooded under the breast feathers, under the wings, and/or under the tail, often progressing in that order of location with age. When being allofed, unsighted nestlings do not push and crowd one another, though they often extend their necks and heads toward the allofeeding parent. There is definite parental management in the order of allofeeding, which may take several forms, including giving highest priority to the youngest nestlings, and alternating the bouts of allofeeding between chicks (doubtless dependent upon the distribution of chick size). If two or more chicks are present and both parents are in the nest, allofeeding often is cooperative, but it may become a highly competitive affair in the presence of only 1 or 2 chicks.

When reckoned over the course of the entire period of brooding, parents may share about equally in the allofeeding of the young. During the early period some females may be most heavily involved in husking seeds and allofeeding their mates, who relay the food to the nestlings; later, females may do most, or even all, of the allofeeding of the young. The precise distribution of allofeeding contributions between the parents can be quite variable, apparently dependent upon the number of chicks in the brood, pair idiosyncracies, and experience.

In a brood of 3 or more chicks, food preparation and allofeeding of nestlings may occupy the parents fully, without competition. In other aspects than allofeeding, however, the parents are very competitive over the care of eggs and young, to the extent that bodily "force" may be necessary to effect a nest exchange. This competitiveness also manifests itself when a parent leaves the nest temporarily and unilaterally and eats, drinks, or voids. If the other parent seeks to take over the care of the eggs or chicks at such a time, the first one usually postpones or cuts short its maintenance activities and races back to the nest before the other can gain access. Unilaterally departing parents often behaved in a similar manner when I approached the nest to examine the eggs or chicks.

There is no hard and fast rule concerning the type of allofeeding that is practiced with young, although, regardless of the type, the actions involved progress from being very gentle with hatchlings to being very vigorous with increasingly mature young. The food delivered to hatchlings and very young nestlings usually is of largely liquid consistency, generally delivered by tongue-flicking but also often delivered by trickling. Tongue-flick allofeeding usually is accompanied by more pronounced gentle bobbing of a chick's head than is trickle-feeding, with the bobbing of the head of a parent being more or less passive. The solid-to-liquid ratio of the food is adjusted by the allofeeding parent by filtering the regurgitate between the tongue and the palate. Competition to allofeed a chick may lead to such close following by the non-allofeeding parent that the latter begins to allofeed before the participating parent has ceased, whereupon both allofeed at opposite sides of the chick's bill.

CHICK RECOGNITION. Up until the time that chicks are appreciably feathered, the parents apparently do not recognize them individually. An unrecognized chick will not be cared for if displaced from a non-enclosed brood site, even if the displacement is only to the outside rim of the nest. Even a recognized chick outside the rim of a non-enclosed open nest may not be cared for if another chick is present and under care within the nest. Consistent with this behavior of the parents, young, mobile nestlings do not wander from an open, flat site at which they are placed; their movements are such that they merely rotate or trace a tight circle about the initial point, even though their eyes are open, and the nest or a parent is within view nearby. Within a NB, however, mobile nestlings often wander about. Numerous observations revealed that parents recognized the vocalizations of their own chicks, as opposed to those of other chicks, when the vocalizations were emitted by young that were out of sight.

'CONCERN' FOR CHICKS. The males of both brooding pairs usually spent much more time than the females in the NB or nestbowl with the chicks. On some days they were not seen to leave the company of the chicks after taking over their care in the morning. Females often spend time at the side of the male in the NB or nestbowl (or perched at the rim of a nest) as the male broods young nestlings or incubates eggs, but the male usually does not remain at the side of an incubating or brooding female, probably because he must eat and tend to other maintenance activities during his infrequent absences. As the nestlings mature, both parents may be absent from the nest concurrently.

Parental 'concern' for the welfare of the chicks increases progressively as the chicks mature, reaching a high pitch at the time they take their 1st flights. This can be assessed, at first, (1) by the degree of parental protection and aggressiveness as one seeks to examine the chicks visually and by touching and removing them, (2) by the degree of parental agitation as the chicks are being handled exterior to the enclosure within sight of the parents while the parents are confined, and (3) by the degree to which the parents approach and perch next to, and accompany, the chicks when the former are being flighted while the latter are being handled.

Another indication of parental 'concern' becomes evident as the chicks near the time of fledging and the parents tenaciously guard the entrance to the NB and prevent egress of the young--an action sometimes requiring vigorous physical measures. At the height of parental 'concern,' when the young are learning to fly outside the enclosure, one or both parents always accompanies, escorts, and, when necessary, seeks to rescue them. The evidence suggests that the male is the primary provider of this care; he will leave a clutch to provide the care, whereas a female generally will not, and confined males usually become more agitated than the females on hearing distress calls from their fledglings. In general, it can be stated that the degree of parental 'concern' is in proportion to the degree of perceived risk to which the young are exposed, which is at a maximum when the young are taking their 1st flights. Even wing-flapping by stationary fledglings brings the parents immediately to their sides.

A CLEAR-CUT ASPECT OF FEATHER-PICKING by some Cockatiels, that may be of more or less general significance, was evident from the behavior of Homer, Helena, and Cosimo. These parents picked feathers from the young for the purpose of consuming the nutritious, blood-saturated pulp at their bases or, in the case of very small emerging feathers, for consuming the entire feathers. Once acquired, the habit became fixed and pernicious.

Lovebirds

As in the preceding summary for Cockatiels, the present summary is limited to the most salient findings not already summarized on pp. 719-722 and in Chapters 3, 5, and 7, particularly those that are new or differ from previous information. Nor are the remarkable results for oviposition-site fidelity summarized or discussed further, as these studies for lovebirds are discussed on p. 732, and for Cockatiels on p. 501.

NESTING. The hen of a pair was found to be highly domineering as regards exploration and occupancy of a NB before the onset of oviposition, usually totally excluding her mate or allowing him only brief occupancy, even on occasions before she herself ventured to enter or explore it. This behavior often tends to persist after the 1st egg is laid but soon gives way to total tolerance, as the male frequently visits the NB and allogrooms and allofeeds the female and may spend long periods at her side. As the incubatory period progresses and the female begins to absent the nest and eat and gather and process nesting material, the male often remains in the NB and guards the eggs at their side or rear.

PRIVACY---INTOLERANCE FOR YOUNG. One of the most impressive findings was noted repeatedly and also applies to Cockatiels and Budgerigars, namely, that in the presence of fledglings or juveniles of prior broods, the parents either seek out a secluded location--most distant from the young--for copulation, or they remain behind in the enclosure when the family is flighted, and engage in coitus in the absence of the young. The most striking illustration of this was provided by the Budgerigar male, Lysander (see pp. 795-796, **Privacy Preferred for Sexual Union**). A related phenomenon, also observed with breeding pairs of all 3 species, was an ever increasing intolerance for the presence of the young of a preceding brood, both generally and near the nest, as the incubatory and brooding periods of a current brood progressed.

SELECTIVE INCUBATION---INTRUSIONS IGNORED WHEN ALLOFEEDING CHICKS. Yet another phenomenon was noted in all 3 species, in hens that had not attained fully the 3rd phylogenetic stage of egg care or had regressed from it for one reason or another. In exposed nests, these hens incubated their eggs very attentively during the day, but abandoned them at night, and returned to them promptly at the time of lights-on. This is believed to recapitulate the equivalent of the 2nd phylogenetic stage of egg care (pre-incubatory), when eggs were shielded and guarded during the day but buried and guarded from a distance at night. Another common phenomenon among all 3 species, most strikingly exhibited by the most habituated individuals, was that when parents were engaged in allofeeding or allogrooming of young, they tended to ignore my intrusions as I sought to view the proceedings closely. Care of the chicks had too high a priority for parents so engaged to be interrupted by an intrusion that, in other circumstances, would have been distracting or disturbing.

CONCURRENT HATCHING AND OVIPOSITION. One of the most striking occurrences--to my knowledge quite unprecedented--was Cassandra's laying of a clutch of 13 eggs. She still was ovipositing at times when the 1st-laid eggs of the clutch were hatching. Though this extraordinary occurrence doubtless was a consequence of my removing the eggs as thay were laid, it illustrates the possibilities for variations in ovulatory and ovipositional habits in response to experimental manipulations (or environmental variation), even in a species thought to be strictly determinate-laying.

CONDITION OF HATCHLINGS---FOOD PROCESSING. Among the 3 species studied, the hatchlings of lovebirds are the most helpless. They usually cannot even sit up in coordinated fashion and hold up their heads until they are about 7-9 days old, whereas Cockatiels can do so within hours of hatching, and Budgerigar hatchlings are sufficiently coordinated to turn themselves over to terminate allofeeding by the parents. Several observations suggested that lovebird hatchlings and young nestlings are not allofed unless they solicit food by cheeping. Unlike the situation with Cockatielian and Budgerigar hatchlings, they are allofed in any position in which a parent can deliver the food. Also, unlike the situation with Budgerigar and Cockatielian chicks, lovebird hatchlings and very young nestlings appear to have the lowest priority for being allofed by the parents.

The evidence suggests that preliminary processing of food for hatchlings is a prerequisite in lovebirds, and that the bill clapping and respiratory sounds of the near term embryo stimulate the parents to begin food processing for a hatchling. This would account for the many occasions on which lovebird hatchlings cheeping for food were ignored by the parents, often at the very times that the parents were occupied with the allofeeding of older chicks. It also would account for the delays of many hours before some hatchlings were allofed. On two such occasions, when Cassandra ignored a hatchling as she allofed older chicks--perhaps because she had no food that was processed sufficiently for a hatchling--her mate, Cyrus, allofed the hatchlings gobs of semi-liquid food by massive tongue-flick feeding. On one of these occasions, the food may have been insufficiently well processed, since the hatchling died, but on the other, 5 days later, the food must have been suitable, since the hatchling survived.

These results also suggest and imply that merely filtering normal crop contents between the tongue and palate to remove particulate matter does not provide food that is suitable for nourishing a hatchling, since otherwise the parents could provide suitable food at almost any time. Some allofeeding behavior of Cockatiels also suggested a need for food processing for hatchlings. Budgerigar hatchlings receive gobs of only semi-liquid food by massive tongue-flick allofeeding, with no direct indication of pre-processing of the food. It is likely, however, that pre-processing occurs and that the youngest chicks, being allofed first, receive the highest proportion of the pre-processed food.

TRICKLE-FEEDING---ROLE OF MALE IN ALLOFEEDING. Most courting lovebird pairs engage in lengthy sessions of trickle-feeding of the female by the male--often lasting many min each. This would appear to function in part as practice for the subsequent delivering of liquid food to the young. Food delivered to the young in this manner is not necessarily more lengthily pre-processed than food allofed by tongue-flick or massive tongue-flick feeding; material delivered in this way often may be given primarily for its water content.

The male plays a vital role in the allofeeding of young nestlings. He husks and further processes most of the food, allofeeds it to the female, cleans excess food from the bill of the female and the bills and heads of the chicks during food delivery, removes large pieces of food from the mouths of both the hen and the chicks, delivers additional food to the female via her tongue, even as she allofeeds chicks, and last, but not least, allofeeds hatchlings directly whenever the opportunity affords. In fact, the allofeeding of the chicks in the presence of both parents often, if not usually, is both competitive and cooperative, with each parent often brushing aside or pulling away the other's bill in an effort to gain access to the chick, either to allofeed or clean it. But the male always seems to give first priority to cleaning. These actions usually occur with such great speed that lengthy, close observation usually is required to discern them.

When only a single chick is present, competitive allofeeding interactions usually reach their highest pitch. In time, however, the female becomes the almost exclusive allofeeder of a 1-chick brood. Even with larger broods, though, the hen is the main direct allofeeder throughout brooding. Although the male's participation in allofeeding usually is most intense in the early morning, the female eventually assumes these duties almost exclusively. In almost all respects the actions of parent Budgerigars during the allofeeding of chicks, and the degree of participation in the course of brooding, are virtually indistinguishable from those of lovebird parents.

Several cases and many occurrences were observed when a lovebird male other than the hen's mate allofed an incubating or brooding female. In none of these cases did the hen's mate interfere with or contest the act. He was more likely to take turns with the other male in the allofeeding when the opportunity afforded, and he sometimes did so. [Both Jagatai and Cyrano allofed Cassandra, Cleomenes and 2 male juveniles of her 8th brood allofed Petra, and Titian allofed Flavia.]

PROTECTING EGGS AND CONFINED CHICKS. The hen was by far the principal guardian of the eggs and chicks within the NB and enclosure, but the male also was protective to greater or lesser degree at various times. In general, the vigor with which the eggs and chicks were protected increased progressively as incubation and brooding progressed. Although the most habituated birds were very much more aggressive in these acts, at first, by the time of mid-to-late incubation all parents were about equally protective. [The major exception was Juliana in a nest on the floor of enclosure E. She uncontestingly yielded the eggs or chick to me at any time.] Initial gentle nipping of my fingers as I serviced, soon became nips and painful bites. By the time chicks were present, it was typical of most parents to come charging back to the NB or nestbowl to protect the chicks and "stand me off" if I sought to examine the chicks. Moreover, when I closed a NB entrance (with cardboard or a cork) while I examined the chicks, both parents typically worked frantically to gain access.

As chicks approached fledging time within a NB, the parents forcibly confined them to the NB and promptly "herded" an escapee back to it. As the chicks became more persistent in their efforts to exit, considerable physical effort on the part of the parents--sometimes bodily hurling the chicks back--was required to keep them confined, and a great tumult of movements and sound was the characteristic accompaniment. When fledging young succeeded in leaving the NB and were not "herded" back to it immediately, they were followed closely and protected from mishap. Although the fledglings of prior broods largely were tolerated by incubating and brooding parents, juveniles and older birds of previous broods were excluded from the nest and its vicinity and attacked vigorously if they intruded upon it.

PROTECTING FLEDGLINGS AND NESTLINGS OUTSIDE ENCLOSURE. Just as the hen is the principal guardian of eggs and nestlings within the NB or enclosure, the male is the principal guardian of chicks nearing the time of fledging and of fledglings outside the enclosure. Before the chicks were individually recognizable, and sometimes even afterward, the parents took no apparent notice of my handling them in plain sight within 1 or 2 m of the enclosure. But after chicks were feathered, and particularly when they were approaching the time of fledging, the confined parents became highly agitated as the chicks were handled within their view; they then typically clambered about excitedly on the nearest face of the enclosure, all the while chattering and shrieking loudly and harshly. If the chicks flapped their wings or I merely raised them on high, parental excitement reached a high pitch.

If the parents were flighted as I handled individually recognizable chicks, the parents perched on my hand or arm near the chicks, excitedly 'scolding' and voicing their 'concerns.' The older the chicks, the closer the parents approached and guarded them. Before the hen began a new cycle of nesting and breeding, she might be more aggressive and persistent than the male, but as a new cycle began, she often would leave the guarding of the chicks to the male and go off gathering and stripping nesting material. But if a chick flapped its wings or took flight, she returned immediately and joined the male in the vicinity of the chick, either as I held it in my hands or by following or escorting it. Gradually a female parent's 'concerns' for fledglings waned but attentive care by a male parent continued; he guarded, followed, and escorted them at all times.

On family flightings or outings that included members of previous broods or other relatives, the degree of parental protectiveness was in proportion to the youth of the brood. After fledging, parental attention would wane gradually to the point where the parents might temporarily abandon the chicks to their own devices and socialize with other birds, but any threat to the young brought them back immediately to the rescue. Similarly, when a family was flighted alone, though a youngest bird, not fully fledged, might be left behind frequently, its slightest distress, as signalled vocally or by wing-flapping, brought all members of the family immediately to its rescue, not just the parents. Even young that were fledged early and housed separately from the parents for weeks--to spare them from feather-picking--were followed, escorted, and protected on joint flightings. Such separately housed young also were tolerated as they climbed about outside their parents' enclosure, in circumstances in which other birds would have been attacked.

Budgerigars

COURTSHIP AND CARE OF EGGS. Both of the breeding pairs that were studied were inexperienced, were caring initially for 1st clutches, and one or both of them had not even copulated successfully. Accordingly, one may draw only very limited conclusions from their early breeding behavior, at least as regards the normal breeding behavior of experienced birds. In fact, in some cases the pairs exhibited opposite behavior at the same stage of breeding (i.e., the same stage if one overlooks differences in their degrees of copulational success).

On the other hand, the responses of the hens to missing clutches were in complete agreement. It seems quite likely that the latter responses are characteristic of the species, particularly in view of the fact that most of them duplicate known behavior of Peach-faced Lovebirds and Cockatiels, as described on pages 428 *et seq.* and 737-739. Similarly, the first activities of members of both pairs in the morning were to copulate and/or courtship feed, depending upon the stage in the ovipositional phase. Accordingly, these activities also may be typical of the species, especially when one considers that the first morning activity of male Peach-faced Lovebirds also is to courtship-feed their mates.

"BUDGIE MILK." The gobs of glutinous (colostrum-like), semi-liquid, creamy-white food delivered to young Budgerigar chicks by massive tongue-flick allofeeding differed in no discernible way from the food similarly delivered to young lovebird and Cockatielian chicks. Accordingly, there would appear to be no more reason to give this material the specific designation "budgie milk" than to similarly designate the very similar food delivered to young lovebird and Cockatielian chicks. In all cases it would appear to be food that merely is partially digested, crop softened, and probably supplemented with a protein-rich material, apparently having its origin in the proventriculus, as suggested by some workers (see 127, 135).

I am aware of the existence of no primary study of the nutrient designated as "budgie milk." It has been suggested (447) but without documentation, that budgie milk is formed only by the hen. Yet much of the food delivered to hatchlings and young nestlings by Budgerigar and lovebird hens merely is relayed to them from the males and would appear to be of the same composition as that delivered directly to the chicks by the males before and/or after they allofeed their mates. Nor has any sexual difference been described in the crop or proventriculus.

Accordingly, in the absence of analytical studies it seems reasonable to assume that the material in question is of essentially the same composition in all 3 species discussed, and that it is produced by members of both sexes. The assumption that Budgerigars produce a nutrient for the chicks that differs in some essential manner from that produced by, say, Cockatiels and lovebirds, perhaps was made following the observations of crop contents of graded composition in Budgerigar nestlings of different sizes (reasoning by analogy with Pigeon's milk), at a time before lovebirds and Cockatiels were being bred and before there was an awareness that the same phenomenon occurs in other species.

[Cockatielian and lovebird chicks also are fed a liquid filtrate of crop contents that is colorless or light yellow or orange (on the diets provided). It is delivered by trickle-feeding or tongue-flick allofeeding, primarily to hatchlings and very young nestlings but sometimes to chicks as advanced as 2 weeks old.]

ALLOFEEDING OF CHICKS BY MALES. In the studies of Stamps and coworkers (843, 844) it was found that that there was but limited and sometimes no participation of the male in allofeeding the chicks, and that participation, when it occurred, was greatest during the latter part of the brooding period, when chicks were 22 days old and older. Though caution is dictated when dealing with quantitative results obtained with only one pair of breeding birds, the present results nonetheless suggest that the situation may be quite different from that concluded from the earlier study. Thus, the present study revealed that the most intense and regular participation of the male (Lysander) in feeding the nestlings occurred within minutes, never more than ½ h, of lights-on in the morning (and the same is true of lovebird males). This time probably would correspond roughly to the first ½ h or so after dawn.

Inasmuch as the earlier studies in outdoor enclosures (in the spring and summer) did not include observations prior to 07:00 h, about 90-150 min after dawn, one must consider the possibility that the most intense periods of male participation in allofeeding were not observed (such activity also may be overlooked in field studies). This suggestion is rendered more plausible by the additional observation, with all 3 pairs of Budgerigars, that courtship feeding and/or copulation occur within minutes of lights-on in the morning, and the same is true almost invariably of courtship feeding in lovebirds. In other words, the period of very early morning (after brief stretching and grooming) appears to be a time of intense activities related to reproduction in breeding Budgerigars (and lovebirds); the activities then probably would make a significant contribution to their reproductive behavior. [Although the average number of hours of daylight is greater in Australia than in the U.S.A., one nevertheless recalls in this connection the remark of Robinson (959) concerning Australian birds "....if one cannot watch birds between 5 a.m. and 7 a.m., little of result can be expected."]

ADAPTIVE SIGNIFICANCE OF ALLOFEEDING BETWEEN NESTLINGS. The strong tendency of the nestlings to allofeed one another correlates with their equally strong tendency to perch in the NB entrance and on the inner and outer perches, often blocking the access of the parents to the interior. Neither lovebird nor Cockatielian nestlings habitually engage in either act, though both acts occasionally occur. Since the oldest nestlings are the first to perch in the entrance, are likely to be allofed there by the parents as they block access to the interior, and usually are the ones who allofeed the other nestlings, it seems very likely that the behavior is a device for relaying food from the parents to the young nestlings.

Though Lucretia was observed to force her way past the eldest nestling, as it blocked the entrance, in order to allofeed the youngest nestling inside, this may well not be a constant practice in the wild, where time is at a premium. In fact, the practice of allofeeding between nestlings probably evolved as a means of increasing the efficiency of allofeeding the nestlings toward the end of the brooding period, when absolute growth rates are greatest. Following this interpretation, one would expect to find it a common practice for older nestlings to perch in and be allofed at nest-hole entrances in the wild, though I am aware of no study relating to this matter. The behavior also qualifies as another form of cooperative breeding (see p. 332) and might well have been the earliest stage in the evolution of cooperative breeding behavior in some species (though "helpers at the nest" from prior broods have not been reported in Budgerigars).

THE SELECTIVE ALLOFEEDING OF YOUNGER, SMALLER NESTLINGS, as practiced by Budgerigar hens, also occurs in Cockatiels, though perhaps less rigidly (see p. 702, **The Seventh Brood of Carmen and Cosimo**). It has not been documented in any other avian species. A number of observations suggest that it occurs, though, for example, in the Fieldfare (*Turdus pilaris*), other parrots, Great Tits, and European Blackbirds. Its occurrence may, however, be partly or largely a consequence of differential behavior on the part of the nestlings (see 843 for a discussion and refs.).

Although the differential feeding of younger nestlings may, at first sight, appear to be inconsistent with the classical interpretation of hatching asynchrony as a mechanism for achieving brood reduction (see pp. 260, 261, **Asynchronous Hatching**), Stamps *et al.* suggest that, rather, it may allow better control over whether and when brood reduction occurs (843). Additionally, several alternative hypothesis for the adpatedness of hatching asynchrony have been advanced (see 843 and pp. 260, 261). A most remarkable observation concerning the allofeeding of Budgerigar nestlings that emerged from the present study was the finding that fledgling broodmates will allofeed a sickly member of a brood, though not with an efficiency sufficient for it to maintain weight or survive for more than a few days.

LACK OF CARE OF FLEDGING AND FLEDGED YOUNG. The most striking departure in parental care by Budgerigars as compared to that of lovebirds and Cockatiels is its virtually total absence during and after fledging. This behavioral departure is perhaps the more impressive in view of the strongly selective allofeeding of the youngest chicks by the hen. This disregard for the welfare of fledglings strongly suggests that Budgerigar nestlings in the wild do not leave the nest until they are entirely independent of parental care, and also would seem to imply that the post-fledging family ties (see p. 211, **Family Groups**) are relatively weak. The sharpness of the contrast suggests that comparatively strong post-fledging family ties may exist in lovebirds and Cockatiels in the wild.

ADDENDUM: LIGHTLY BURIED NESTLINGS BECOME SILENT AND STILL. In tests carried out in February, 1987, with the 1st brood of Lysistrata (member of 2nd brood of Lucretia and Lysander) and Hepheistus (member of 3rd acquired pair; see p. 778), consisting of 5 chicks, the nestlings were examined daily in an open container upon a bedding of #3 shavings. When fully mobile, they usually congregated in a heap, cheeping and squawking agitatedly and jockeying for a position in or under the heap. If they were covered by heaping the large surface shavings over them, they tended to cease vocalizing and jockeying about and to remain buried for some time, typically merely poking their heads out or about to facilitate breathing, usually with their eyes open.

This behavior would appear to be a relic of times when the ancestors of Budgerigars covered chicks in a surface nest with a layer of substrate or surface debris when absenting the nest or in times of danger, in which case it would have been adaptive for the chicks to be silent and still. As already noted (see pp. 580, 581), some extant birds cover their nestlings with sand or surface debris in these circumstances. The response probably had its origin in an early period of surface nesting.

CHAPTER 7. BEHAVIOR AND SOCIAL INTERACTIONS

THE TOWER COMPLEX, INFLUENCES OF PARTITIONED LIVING QUARTERS

JAGATAI AND OGADAI HOUSED TOGETHER. Jagatai and Ogadai were the two brothers of 1st brood of Petra and Ramses. Not long after being fledged, they were housed in enclosure E, atop enclosure A (Fig. 1a). Since enclosure E was set back about 10 cm from the front faces of enclosures A and B, Jagatai and Ogadai and their parents remained within sight of one another. This led to a great deal of excited screeching and attempts by the brothers to leave of the enclosure, since recently fledged lovebirds that are parted from their parents frantically attempt to return to them if they are housed within sight or sound of one another. The parents also maintained a keen interest in the whereabouts and activity of their sons, frequently looking at them through the top of the enclosure by sticking their heads through the 2½-cm-square mesh. These actions continued even after the 2nd brood of Petra and Ramses was fledged, though the latter continued to be housed with their parents.

VERTICAL TOWER ANNEXED TO ENCLOSURE B

CONSEQUENCES IMMEDIATE. These circumstances provided an ideal opportunity to study social interactions engendered by providing a significantly-located additional living annex to enclosure B, and observing the responses of parents and offspring to its availability. The additional space was provided in the form of a 10-cm-square tower extending upward 25 cm from the front-right top corner of enclosure B (Fig. 1a) in front of the right-front corner of enclosure D (which housed 2 Budgerigars at that time). Any occupants of this tower would have been in clear view of Jagatai and Ogadai in enclosure E, and vice versa. The tower was installed on May 5, 1982, about 2 weeks after Cyrano was given to Bill Murphy (see p. 315), leaving only his broodmates, Cassandra and Cyrus, housed in enclosure B, in the company of their parents, Petra and Ramses.

The presence of the tower precipitated immediate and dramatic interactions that were so disruptive that I had to ration the tower's accessibility to preserve harmony within the lovebird colony. No sooner did Petra and Ramses discover the tower and venture to enter it--after the customary conservativeness and cautious inspection--than it became the constant focal point of their attentions. Once within it, they climbed to its highest point and clung there, usually facing the location of Jagatai and Ogadai in enclosure E. There they stayed for over 1 h.

CASSANDRA AND CYRUS EXCLUDED. At first, Cassandra and Cyrus ignored the tower, their interests seemingly being monopolized by the novelty of having the entire enclosure to themselves and being free to roam it at will. As soon as they took note of the tower and ventured to enter it, however, they were expelled immediately by their parents. The latter would not tolerate their presence in it, not even the slightest penetration. After being expelled time and again, Cassandra and Cyrus began, instead, to spend a considerable amount of time at the nearest location at which their presence was tolerated, namely, on the nest perch just beneath the tower (Fig. 3b), not infrequently jockeying among themselves for the most favorable location. Were the parents merely being possessive of the desirable new and novel space, which allowed a clear view of Jagatai and Ogadai? Or, were they being protective of Cassandra and Cyrus in not letting them enter?

JAGATAI AND OGADAI QUARREL. These behaviors were interesting and provocative, but the responses of Jagatai and Ogadai were most surprising. It was their behavior that led me to close the tower and ration access to it for limited periods from time to time. No sooner was it possible to perch and vocalize within clear view of their parents, than Jagatai began attacking Ogadai relentlessly (the latter played the male role in the homosexual pair-bond). This occurred whenever Ogadai also sought to perch high up near the front of the enclosure at a position nearest his parents. Jagatai even followed the intruding and retreating Ogadai down to the enclosure floor and continued to attack him there. Only infrequently would he tolerate Ogadai's presence on a front perch in clear view of their parents.

TOWER ACCESS RATIONED. This interaction between Jagatai and Ogadai was less equivocal than that between the parents and Cassandra and Cyrus. It was evident that Jagatai was being possessive of the new, novel, and favored location with respect to his parents. As one might guess from this conclusion, the passage of time and further experiments were to show that possessiveness with respect to the new and novel location also was the main factor that governed the parents' exclusion of Cassandra and Cyrus.

The parents behaved in the same manner even when Jagatai and Ogadai were removed from the room; the tower location, itself, was the main attraction for them. Because of the unfavorable situation engendered for Ogadai, and the fact that access to the tower was so disruptive of the normal state of affairs in enclosure B, I closed off access to the tower after 3 h. The interactions described above were repeated day after day for the next 7 days, every time I allowed access to the tower.

ANOTHER EXAMPLE OF POSSESSIVENESS. Before continuing with the description of further events relating to the tower complex, I relate another pertinent series of incidents. These firmly establish the fact that dominant lovebirds become highly possessive over new and novel places to which they gain access. And the incidents are not complicated by the presence of young or the ability to view relatives in a nearby location. In the further treatments of events relating to the tower complex, the motive of maintaining exclusive possession then can be assumed, and one can concentrate on interpreting the accompanying social interactions.

The colony was transferred to the laboratory on September 22, 1984, and housed in the same and additional enclosures in a room measuring 2.1 x 4.62 m and 2.6 m high (Fig. 2b). To prevent excess exposure of the birds to drafts, I reduced the airflow from the 2 ceiling inlets and kept the room at 27°C. I also directed the incoming air away from the enclosures with shallow hoods made of sheets of epoxy-fiberglass. These hoods could be entered readily from the sides and ends by a flying bird. Since flighted lovebirds quickly discover and explore all regions of a flight area, the birds soon discovered these "cavernous" ceiling hoods and typically spent a good fraction of their flighted time excitedly exploring within them. The hood nearest the enclosures became the favorite visiting site.

Since the parents, Petra and Ramses, were dominant over their offspring, in the interests of simplicity I describe only those interactions that occurred when the parents were flighted with any of the offspring. On these occasions, Petra and Ramses spent about half their flighted time in the company of each other in the near air-hood. But they would not tolerate the simultaneous presence of any one of their offspring. Any other lovebird alighting or seeking to alight on the edge, to enter, was repelled with alacrity. Since the other birds were accustomed to visiting the hood in the absence of their parents, they were not easily discouraged (in fact, in my experience, lovebirds seem never to be easily discouraged) and they repeatedly had to be driven off forcefully. Petra and Ramses also usually behaved in this way when they perched on my head; it then became "off limits" for their mature offspring.

[The possibility that the tower and hood were defended as possible nesting sites can be ruled out by the facts that no effort ever was made to build a nest in them, and that, in time, after the novelty of visiting them was lost, they no longer were defended (see p. 813).]

INSTALLATION OF THE HORIZONTAL SECTION---NEW INTERACTIONS

MORE TENACIOUS QUARRELING. On May 13, I added an overlapping, horizontal, 38-cm annex to the tower. This extended along the front face of enclosure D (housing the 2 Budgerigars) and reached to within $2\frac{1}{2}$ cm of enclosure E (housing Jagatai and Ogadai). The new addition caused a good deal more excitement than the vertical section alone, making it even more imperative to limit periods of access to it. Almost immediately upon inspection of the new horizontal section, Petra and Ramses took to spending all their time in it, usually side by side. Most frequently they occupied the end closest to Jagatai and Ogadai.

With this development, Jagatai and Ogadai began to contest even more vigorously over perching close to their parents. Previously, Ogadai had been relatively submissive in yielding to Jagatai's proscriptions; but at this time he became much more tenacious in seeking access to positions near his parents. The outcome was an almost continuous state of fraternal squabbling.

CASSANDRA EXCLUDES CYRUS. The situation regarding Cassandra and Cyrus then became much more complicated. Since it had become possible for them to occupy the vertical section of the tower without Petra and Ramses necessarily taking notice of them, Cassandra's dominance over Cyrus began to be evidenced in the creation of a subplot within the main interactive theme. Cassandra then began to occupy the upper region of the vertical tower and altogether exclude Cyrus from it, chasing him out whenever he sought to join her. Cyrus had to be content with perching at its base or just within its entrance, where escape was easy.

CASSANDRA CONTINUALLY ENCROACHES AND GETS EXPELLED. But Cassandra was not content merely to occupy a position near the top of the vertical section. She repeatedly tried to creep over close to her parents in the horizontal section. Cyrus, in turn, crept up further into the vertical section as she advanced out of it. But every time Cassandra crept closer, as soon as Petra or Ramses--usually Ramses--detected her presence, one of them chased her completely out of the tower. They pursued her to its very base and, on some occasions, even followed after her when she exited. Cassandra sometimes fled in such haste that she caught Cyrus unawares and passed him on the way out, as he clung to the vertical sides. However, on such occasions, he quickly followed her out.

The foregoing gives an adequate representation of the new dynamic situation created by the addition of the horizontal annex. Again, it suffices to mention that the above-described events occurred several times during each session of accessibility. They were so disruptive of the normal routines in enclosures B and E that I limited tower access to only 1 or 2 h every few days. It is interesting and noteworthy that, in their prolonged stays in the horizontal section--with no opportunity to eat there--Ramses courtship-fed Petra from time to time.

SECOND VERTICAL SECTION INSTALLED

MORE ELABORATE INTERACTIONS. Approximately 1 month after installing the horizontal section, I added a 2nd vertical section at its end, rising 25 cm along the face of the right side of enclosure E, only 2½ cm distant from it. Its presence, of course, introduced further interactive complications. Petra and Ramses frequently perched along the side of the new annex, near its top, facing Jagatai and Ogadai in enclosure E, but they also frequently occupied the horizontal section.

When Petra and Ramses were in the new vertical section, it became possible for Cassandra to occupy the horizontal section with impunity, and for Cyrus to occupy the initial vertical annex, also without risk of expulsion. Sometimes Cassandra even tolerated Cyrus' presence at the entrance to the horizontal section. But, again, expulsions by active chases or mere intimidations were frequent, since Cassandra continued to try to creep over closer to Petra and Ramses, and Cyrus, in turn, and usually with little delay, kept trying to approach closer to Cassandra. In both cases, expulsions followed as soon as the encroachments were detected, and their vigor continued unabatedly.

JAGATAI TOLERATES OGADAI'S PRESENCE. But the situation concerning Jagatai and Ogadai was changing. While the brothers continued to have some vigorous competitive exchanges over favorable positions, Jagatai sometimes tolerated Ogadai's near presence with him across from their parents. This resulted in some periods of relatively peaceful coexistence within the family. However, I still found it desirable to limit access to the tower complex to only 1-3 h every few days.

PETRA BUILDS NEST---FREER TOWER ACCESS FOR JUVENILES. The 1st notable change in behavior in relation to the tower came about 2 weeks after installation of the 2nd vertical section. It was this change that drew my attention to the fact that Petra had begun to build a nest on the enclosure floor in the right-rear corner.

With the nest competing for her attention, Petra sometimes left Ramses alone in the 2nd vertical section of the tower, and sometimes both parents exited the tower, leaving it in the possession of Cassandra and Cyrus. On such occasions, Cassandra sometimes tolerated Cyrus but at other times forbade him a near approach. This made for a very amusing situation, because whenever a parent entered the tower--already occupied by Cassandra and Cyrus--both young came dashing hastily out past the entering parent, thereby avoiding the otherwise inevitable 'scolding' or physical "punishment."

PARENTS BREEDING---CYRANO RETURNED. Within a few days, Petra and Ramses had begun to copulate and Petra was spending much time in her crude nest of paper strips, with Ramses frequently standing guard, leaving the tower to the devices of the young. On July 7, I returned Cyrano to the colony (see p. 316) and placed him, Cassandra, and Cyrus in enclosure C, setting the stage for the events described in Chapter 3. The tower, of course, figures very prominently in the events of that Chapter. It was the locale at which Zenobia maintained a very close position to her mate, Cyrano, it was the locale from which she often excluded Flavia, and it was the locale to which both Zenobia and Flavia were restricted much of the time by Petra and Ramses while Titus, the sole chick of their 4th brood, was being brooded.

FAMILY OCCUPANCY. To complete the account of the tower, the 1st egg of the next clutch of Petra and Ramses was laid during the day after I removed Cassandra and Cyrus. On the morning of July 10, I tried to coax Petra off the nest by opening the tower, so that I could exchange her 2nd egg for a plastic ball. She did not oblige, however, only coming off the nest for a few moments to stretch.

The next time I gave the occupants access to the tower was on October 2, when Flavia and Zenobia were almost 2 months old. As is typical, Petra and Ramses tolerated the presence of the fledglings, although Ramses' first impulse was to evict the 1st chick that entered. Not only were the young then allowed to climb to the very top of the tower, the family of 4 sometimes spent hours together there. Although it might appear that possessiveness over occupation of the tower had abated for Petra and Ramses, it is more likely that their different behavior depended on the youthfulness of their offspring. Thus, lovebird parents even tolerate the presence of recently fledged young in a nest while incubating a clutch, whereas they tend strongly to exclude older juveniles (see pp. 728-730 for the care of clutches by Petra and Ramses in the presence of recently fledged young, as opposed to the presence of older juveniles).

Furthermore, since Flavia and Zenobia were not yet possessive of the tower amongst themselves, as was Cassandra with Cyrus, it appears possible that Cassandra's possessiveness was learned by example from her parents. In other words, she may have been copying the behavior of her parents toward her and Cyrus when she behaved herself in the same way toward Cyrus. [It is more likely, though, that the accord between Flavia and Zenobia in the tower merely was a manifestation of the tolerance of fledglings toward one another, or their immaturity.] On the other hand, the presence of the family in the tower again provoked aggressive interactions between Jagatai and Ogadai, as the former sought to occupy but exclude the latter from a prominent location and to restrict him to the enclosure floor.

LOVEBIRD POSSESSIVENESS OVER OBJECTS

MINERAL MIX AND GRIT. Lovebirds are not merely possessive over desirable locations. They can be equally possessive, at first, over new and/or novel objects. Since this facet of their behavior doubtless is not unfamiliar to bird fanciers, I confine my treatment to two examples. The 1st concerns the treatment accorded to a new supply of mineral mix and grit by Jagatai and Ogadai. Whenever a new supply was given it precipitated a great amount of excitement, because Jagatai monopolized the supply for a long period. No amount of vocal 'complaints' or trying to push in to get a share availed Ogadai in the least. Similar behavior was observed with other lovebirds and with Budgerigars.

POSSESSIVENESS OVER AN OWNER. Petra and Ramses both were habituated to being handled when I acquired them. As they were my 1st pair, they received a great deal of attention. After they had matured and bred, I handled them only when it was necessary to catch them for one reason or another. Of the pair, Ramses remained the most tractable. One mark of this was that he remained for many months the only lovebird in the colony that often would accept an invitation to perch on my finger, even while in his enclosure, rather than always fly off when I brought my hand near.

When servicing the enclosure of Patra and Ramses, the latter frequently remained perched together close to its front, and I often offered them a finger or thumb (either from within or through the bars, as a way of maintaining familiarity with them. When I did this, Ramses typically grasped it playfully in his bill, but Petra was not averse to giving me a nip. Ramses always pecked her away when she did this and he was nearby. Was he being protective, or possessive, or both?

Though I am not yet able to give a definitive answer to this question, I have a partial answer. Possessiveness definitely plays a role. I arrived at this conclusion from Ramses' behavior on two occasions when I flighted him and Petra while I was handling their pre-fledged, feathered son, Titus. They both customarily landed and perched on my fingers, wrist, or arm to guard him. During the times in question, when Petra perched on me close to Ramses, he pecked her away and made her fly off to another spot.

These actions of Ramses leave little doubt about his possessiveness, since it is otherwise unusual for a male lovebird to peck away his mate when she approaches him (but not vice versa). Also weighing against the interpretation of protectiveness is the fact that Ramses was not protective of me when he or Petra had eggs or young in the enclosure. Though Petra would give me a good nip on these occasions, if I let her, Ramses never interfered, as he did when no egg or young was present.

ATTENTION GETTING BY TOE-CARESSING

PETRA PROVIDES FIRST CLUE. All lovebirds are known to spend much time tending to the care of their feet, carefully removing flakes of dry skin or debris (835). On August 15, 1984, I gained a new perspective on the caressing of Cassandra's toes by Cyrano, which I long had thought to be a device which he had improvised to court Cassandra in safety from a lower perch in the presence of her mate, Cyrus. On that date, I saw Petra caress a toe of Titus, her son, in her bill as an act of attention-getting.

Petra had just bathed and was perched next to Titus on the night perch (Fig. 3b) as she dried. Titus, as usual, was grasping the side of the enclosure with the foot of his crippled right leg. Several times Petra solicited head allogrooming from him by the usual method of presenting the top of her sideways-tilted head below his. On two occasions, after Titus had taken no heed of her solicitations, she caressed one of his toes in her bill in successful maneuvers to gain his attention. Subsequently I saw Ramses employ the same act to gain the attention of Titus for head allogrooming.

[In the typical lovebird soliciting posture for head allogrooming, the soliciting bird tips its head sidewards toward and below the head of the other bird, ruffles its head feathers (which were wet in Petra's case), particularly on the face and throat, shuts or partially shuts its eyes, and remains quite still (3). I also have seen my lovebirds gain attention for allogrooming with a peck-like grooming action of the bill in the head feathers of the bird being solicited.]

In similar situations, a Cockatiel usually gets the attention of a bird being solicited with a gentle nudge or peck on the side of the head or neck. Following this, it presents the lowered head with the crest held tightly to the scalp (indicating submission) and the eyes partially closed. The head, of course, is at the appropriate angle and position for grooming at the desired location (127). Once one Cockatiel starts to groom another, it usually will continue to do so for 1 min or more. During this attention, the bird being groomed moves its head appropriately to direct the allogrooming bird's bill into untreated areas. But I was soon to learn that Cockatiels also sometimes caress toes to get attention when soliciting allogrooming.

THE COCKATIELS, CASIMIR AND IVAN. The 1st occasion on which I saw Cockatiels toe-caress was on the following September 28. The 4 young of the 4th brood of Carmen and Cosimo--Kirsten (the fostered granddaughter), Ivan, Rimski, and Casimir--were housed together in enclosure B. In the evening, Casimir presented his head to Ivan for allogrooming, without a prior attention-getting peck. Since Ivan's attention was directed elsewhere, he did not accede. Casimir then caressed one of Ivan's toes in his bill in a successful effort to get his attention to be allogroomed. Two days later, I saw the same act repeated successfully time and again by Casimir to get Ivan's attention for the same purpose.

A relatively inexperienced young lovebird, Titus, was the object of toe caressing in the one case, and inexperienced young Cockatiels were both object and perpetrator in the other case. Since, aside from Cyrano's solicitations to Cassandra, I never have seen adult birds toe-caress one another, this method of attention-getting may be a primitive one, now rarely or never employed between adults.

TYPES OF BILL-TOE CONTACTS FORM A CONTINUUM. The caressing or gentle grasping of toes by either lovebirds or Cockatiels has not been reported previously as an attention-getting act for allogrooming, as opposed to a mild act of aggression. The present observations reveal that bill-to-toe contacts form a continuum. There are the above-described very gentle contacts to gain attention for allogrooming, and there are firm, but not painful, contacts for emphasizing desires without any aggressive component. [Both Flavia and Ramses also sometimes also grasped Titus' crippled leg for this purpose.] These unaggressive contacts grade over to mildly painful, aggressive pinches to make a bird move over or relinquish a position, and thence to vigorous contact or biting to get attention when conveying a message with great force in an aggressive manner. In the limit, there is all-out aggression, with its unmistakable message, as when Jaws snipped off the tip of one of Cyrano's toes (see p. 316).

INDIVIDUAL RECOGNITION

FACIAL FEATURES SUFFICE FOR LOVEBIRDS. A finding that has emerged from the flighting studies of families that include several broods is that lovebirds can identify one another from facial features alone, just as we recognize one another. This also is believed to be true of some other birds, for example, Darwin's (Galápagos) finches, Mallards, and Mute Swans (*Cygnus olor*). In the case of the sexually monomorphic Egyptian Plovers, individual recognition of mates occurs at distances of many meters, but the mechanism by which it is achieved is unknown (230). For many birds, it may be idiosyncrasies of behavior and movement that supply the main cues (13, 29, 41, 101), while there are numerous cases of mate recognition by distinctive properties of voice and calls (28, 109; see also p. 275, **Some Examples**).

The identity of a lovebird arriving on the wing appears to be known to a standing or perched bird even before the former alights, when only its face would appear to be distinguishable. I suggest this because the perched bird's response seems to be determined beforehand. The alighting bird either is accepted or a peck is directed at it even as it alights. Indeed, the shape and markings of the cere, alone, would appear to provide more than ample means of identification.

Similarly, lovebirds in flight recognize a perched bird from at least 30 cm away. I noted this on several occasions. For example, I once flighted Jagatai and Flavia (Titus' mate) together to observe their interactions. Titus, whose right leg is crippled, declined to leave the enclosure. On previous occasions when he exited with Flavia he usually stayed close by her, following her on every change of location. When I took Titus out of the enclosure by hand, he spied Jagatai on an enclosure top. Mistaking him for Flavia, he flew up directly toward him. He recognized Jagatai from about 30-cm distance and veered off sharply, joining Flavia as soon as he detected her location. During these same flights, Flavia caught her foot between pieces of wire while Titus was 2 m away on the other side of the room. When she cried out in distress, Titus flew over to her immediately. Some simple disguising studies could yield interesting insights about individual recognition. Merely painting blue a female Budgerigar's cere leads males to mis-identify her as a male and attack her (18), even though a male can recognize his mate when she is so altered, by her voice (109).

HOLDING FOOD IN THE FOOT, AN INFREQUENT MANIPULATION BY COCKATIELS

COCKATIELIAN HABITS ARE OF PARTICULAR INTEREST. Whether or not the members of an avian species hold food in their feet, is one of the characteristics that has been used to assess taxonomic position. The smaller ground-feeding parrots are said generally to lack this ability, although it may occur atavistically in occasional individuals (819). The habits of Cockatiels have drawn much attention, since they are a key Australian bird of uncertain relationship, (30, 31). Courtney has itemized 13 features in which Cockatiels resemble cockatoos, and 18 in which they do not (30). Since it is unlikely that the features shared by these birds are results of convergent evolution (31), he favors the view of a common phylogeny of Cockatiels and cockatoos (i.e., that they are evolutionarily closely related; see p. 231).

One of the dissimilarities between Cockatiels and cockatoos is that the former are not known to hold food in the foot, whereas the latter do so. It was suggested that, as a result of having become adapted to foraging on the ground, Cockatiels lost the habit of holding food in the foot. Smith points out that Cockatiels pick up small seeds from the ground and shell them at such an extraordinarily great rate that use of the foot would slow their eating rate considerably (127).

NEGATIVE OBSERVATIONAL RESULTS UNRELIABLE. Abundant examples given in Chapter 4, Parts 1 and 2, illustrate the fact that the failure of Cockatiels to perform given acts in the normal course of events is a poor guide to whether they have lost or possess the ability to do so. No matter how closely or detailedly a bird may be observed in an effort to ascertain whether it can carry out a certain act, unless occasions arise in which the act is stimulated to occur, or becomes highly desirable or essential, the results of the study will be inconclusive. Thus, the fact that only one Cockatiel previously was seen to hold food in the foot, "although many Cockatiels have been studied" (127), is not conclusive.

My attention was called to this problem by the behavior of Cockatiels when they had access to small chains. It became evident very quickly that both Cockatiels and lovebirds find it exceedingly rewarding to "mouth" and otherwise manipulate all manner of hanging chains, but most especially those of the type formerly much used on lamp sockets and to secure pens. In the course of the birds' manipulations, I often saw them hold the chains up to their mouths with their feet, to facilitate chewing on them.

Since this act differs in no way from holding food up to the mouth in the foot, I planned to investigate the matter at another time under conditions in which grasping food in the foot would be necessary in order to eat. I never performed such an experiment, though, because several Cockatiels held food up to their mouths in their feet in the normal course of events, before I could provide the planned experimental conditions.

HELENA AND HOMER WITH SPRAY MILLET. As mentioned in Chapter 2, I customarily supplied spray millet as a treat for all of my birds. This was provided either in hanging plastic holders or trays, or on the floors of the enclosures. On one occasion I gave Helena and Homer a sprig of spray millet in a large seed tray that was suspended high on a side of their enclosure. Homer promptly perched on the edge of the tray and began to pick and eat seeds from the sprig.

Helena approached and perched on a branch in front of the tray and also sought to eat from it, while Homer was bent down eating. Since Cockatiels, in general, are intolerant of near approaches of another bird and the sharing of resources in such situations, Homer straightened up and pecked Helena's head sharply as she was reaching in to eat. She quickly withdrew but tried again a moment later, while Homer was bent down again, but with the same result.

As mentioned earlier (see p. 411), Homer's dominance over Helena was not strong (and she did not courtship-feed him). Instead of retreating as a more submissive female might have done, she quite matter-of-factly, as if she had been doing it routinely, reached into the tray with her left leg, picked up the sprig in her foot, conveyed it to her mouth, and fed on it. Homer then fed on it also as she held it. Eventually she released it and it fell to the enclosure floor.

NEED TO LOOK INTO THE LARGER ARENA OF "WHAT CAN HAPPEN." This observation alone eliminated the need to perform my previously planned experiment. Together with those on manipulations of hanging chains, it left little doubt that, when necessary, Cockatiels easily can and will convey food to their mouths with their feet, though they rarely do so in the normal course of events. Together with the findings on relict egg-care responses of Chapter 4, this finding reinforced the view that it is not enough simply to observe **what does happen**, either in the field or the laboratory. To complete the picture available to us, one also must look into the larger arena of **what can happen**. And to do this the experimental approach often is essential. This observation and those that are described in the following not only show that Cockatiels will use their feet to hold foods while feeding, when the occasion requires it, but that they will lift foods directly with the foot, an act that is regarded as being "most exceptional" even among parrots that customarily employ the feet to hold food items in (819).

COSIMO AND CARMEN, FEATHERS AND BREAD. At a later time, I observed Cosimo climb the enclosure side with a feather in his bill. On reaching and perching on the side of a food tray, he held up the feather with one foot while he chewed it and ran it through his bill. When the feather fell into the tray, he picked it up with his other foot and continued to "mouth" it while holding it with his foot. A few days later, much to my amazement, he gave the first of the most convincing demonstrations of all. While perched on a food tray, he reached into it with his right leg and grasped a 3-cm length of whole-grain bread (1-cm sq. in cross-section) with his foot and brought it to his bill. He then fed on it for a full 75 sec. Twice he held it clamped in his bill while he regripped it with his foot. The entire manipulation was done with ease, and matter-of-factly.

On 3 subsequent occasions I observed him doing essentially the same thing. The 1st time (Jan. 8, 1985) he held a bread crust in his left foot and chewed on it for over 60 sec. The 2nd time (Jan. 22, following) he held and regripped the crust repeatedly in his right foot as he chewed it to pieces. On this latter occasion, he picked up the crust with his bill several times after losing hold of it, and then transferred it to his right foot. On a 3rd occasion (May 12, 1986) I did not see him pick up the bread but only witnessed his eating it while holding it in his right foot. On another occasion, he held a large wood shaving up to his bill in his right foot as he chewed on it. Cosimo repeated this behavior on several subsequent occasions.

On one occasion, only, I observed Carmen perched on the rim of a food tray with her left foot and holding a feather up to her bill in her right foot while she chewed it and ran it through her bill. Each time the feather fell into the food tray she recovered it with her bill and then grasped it again with her right foot and continued to "mouth" it. As with the other birds, her foot was used expertly in these manipulations.

KIRSTEN, RIMSKI, CUTTLEFISH BONE. On the morning of July 11, during a period when Kirsten and Rimski were courting, I supplemented their mineral block with a loose, irregularly-shaped fragment of cuttlefish bone, about

3 x 4 x ½ cm in dimensions. Rimski spent the better part of the next 2 h chewing, scraping, and nibbling on this fragment. Repeatedly he carried the fragment in his bill up to a food tray or perch. Then he used one or both feet to hold it against the side of the tray, the enclosure side, or the perch while he chewed and scraped it ("tether-footed" feeding; 819). On subsequent days he repeated this behavior with other fragments of cuttlefish bone. Kirsten was observed on several occasions to hold fragments of cuttlefish bone against the enclosure floor with one foot while chewing on them. On one occasion Rimski carried a sprig of spray millet up to a food tray and held it against the tray rim with one foot while consuming it.

SCRATCHING ON SMOOTH SURFACES, A RELICT RESPONSE TO FREELY-ROLLING EGGS

Many birds excavate litter to uncover hidden food: unilateral scratchers use one leg at a time, e.g., many gallinaceous birds and Caracaras (*Polyborus*); bilateral scratchers displace the litter in a backward jump, using both feet simultaneously, e.g., many American emberizines; some thrushes (*Turdus* spp.) combine bill-sweeping with synchronous bilateral scratching (229); Egyptian Plovers use bilateral scratching and bill-sweeping at different times (230). Scraping or kneading with the feet, in fact, is found in many orders (101) and is one of the most widespread and persistent of all the movements of birds that build nests. It very likely is an inheritance from from the distant reptilian ancestors of birds.

Scraping with the feet by Cockatiels has not been reported previously, although it could well be employed during their ground foraging, if the occasion were to demand it. I never have observed it in birds foraging on enclosure floors. On the other hand, I observed it 8 times in birds during egg care, in all instances by hens (ancestral hens presumably would have been the first of the sexes to prepare nest scrapes).

EGG ROLLING FREELY ON SMOOTH METAL SURFACE. The first occasion occurred after Homer had discovered a buried egg on July 6, 1984, 24 days before Helena laid the 1st egg of her 1st clutch. At this time, the birds were coming into breeding condition, with nest-preparation activities and frequent sexual unions. Homer had wedged out a buried egg from the nest area and Helena had acquired it from him competitively. When she attemped to sit on it on a smooth metal surface denuded of wood shavings, the egg rolled about freely. Thereupon, Helena unleashed a flurry of rapid, vigorous, alternating scratching with both feet.

EGGS ROLLING FREELY ON PLYWOOD. The other 7 observations were during egg care by Carmen on August 28, 1984. Ten weeks earlier, she had laid the 1st egg leading to her 4th brood, and 2 days earlier she and Cosimo had retreated in alarm when I tried to foster a hatchling with them (see p. 497). During this period, Carmen was courtship-feeding Cosimo frequently and they were copulating from time to time as they came into breeding condition again. The first egg of Carmen's next clutch was laid 10 days later.

At any rate, on that day (Aug. 28), I placed 3 eggs on the clean plywood floor of the top portion of enclosure A. Both Carmen and Cosimo descended from their perches and tried to gather the eggs together and cover them. However, since the eggs rolled about freely this could not be achieved readily. Thereupon, on 7 different occasions Carmen, but not Cosimo, scratched at the plywood floor in brief vigorous flurries, seemingly seeking to prepare a depression for the eggs. On at least 2 of these occasions the scratching was unilateral and none of the bilateral scratchings appeared to occur simultanously with both feet.

As already mentioned in Chapter 4, this behavior, which seems to be superfluous to the needs of hole-nesters, strongly suggests that the ancestors of Cockatiels once nested in the primitive fashion on flat, level ground, sufficiently smooth and firm that eggs might roll about in the absence of a shallow scrape. It also suggests that such ground was sufficiently yielding, that vigorous scratching could prepare such a scrape.

Similar experiments were carried out with the lovebird pair, Petra and Ramses, who were allowed to nest on the smooth, flat plastic pan comprising the floor of their enclosure. Petra was quite unable to manage a clutch of 4 eggs on a continual basis under these conditions. Eggs were forever slipping out from under her in all directions. As she nudged these eggs back under herself, without rising off the others, she often simultaneously scratched unilaterally with her feet (see p. 727). She used much the same movements that the Budgerigar hens employed to scratch the crissum (see p. 63) while incubating eggs, i.e., the movements did not involve a downward extension, which would have necessitated rising from the eggs.

ACTS OF MANIPULATION

Some of the feats of manipulation performed by the parrots of this study are very impressive. Often I have felt certain that an item was suspended securely, with no possibility for the birds to disengage it, only to find it back on the enclosure floor a few days later. They untwist firmly twisted wire, they pry open metal rings, they unclip clips, and they lift and unhook long hairpin-like hooks. Many of the plastic and wood "toys" available for birds in pet stores get disassembled and chewed to pieces in a matter of days.

The most impressive feat that I have noted is the ability of lovebirds to open large (4-cm-long) safety pins. I still do not know precisely how they accomplish it. In the following, I describe some of the acts of manipulation that I have observed--including those that are difficult, unexpected, revealing, paradoxical, etc.

DISASSEMBLING AND UNFASTENING SPRAY-MILLET HOLDERS. Most fanciers of bird will be familiar with the plastic, large-meshed, conical spray-millet holders available at pet-supply stores. These are hung in the enclosure by a plastic hook and have a cross-rod at the bottom, with a round bell suspended on a ring at each end. The plastic hook snaps into two holes on the cage-like main body. Cockatiels, for example, easily wedge the snap fastenings open with their bills, allowing all but the harness-like hook to fall. And they seem find it highly rewarding to do so. As often as I kept re-attaching the body to the hook, they usually unhooked it again within a few min, sometimes in less than 1 min.

Eventually I abandoned the use of hooks and suspended the holders with wire yokes. Even so, unless the wire is well secured in the holes in the plastic, the birds will soon disengage it. Once the assembly is permanently hung, the birds will soon have the bells off the rings, after that, the rings off the rod, and, ultimately, the rod off the conical body. Though I have refastened the bells time and again, the only ones remaining in my entire collection are those in the Budgerigar enclosures.

Furthermore, these bells are a hazard for lovebirds, as the birds tend to get their bills wedged into the acoustical gaps. And the harder they bite, as they try to free themselves, the more securely they get wedged in. Twice I have had to rescue lovebirds that were hanging helplessly in mid air from such bells. Absences from lovebird colonies for more than a few hours at a time would not be well-advised unless all seamed bells were removed from their enclosures.

CYRANO AND PLATFORMS

One will recall that on February 8, 1984, I transferred Cyrano and 4 Budgerigars to enclosure E, to provide them with more space, since Cyrano was beginning to behave very aggressively in the smaller enclosure, D. [Of course, none of the birds ate very much for several days after this transfer, as birds usually are very conservative in their adoption of new quarters and food trays in new locations (see p. 291 et seq.).]

STUFFING PAPER INTO FOOD TRAYS. Several times in the following weeks I placed a new sheet of soft paper toweling, about 30-cm square, on the enclosure floor. This was to be renewed periodically in lieu of changing the wood shavings. To my surprise, I usually found the toweling crumpled and stuffed thoroughly into the food tray at the right-front bottom of the enclosure. On March 29, I watched the proceedings closely; each of the 5 times I supplied a new sheet of toweling, Cyrano perched on the edge of the food cup, crumpling it and stomping it into the tray with his feet as he reeled it in. I am unable to account for this behavior, and Cyrano never made any use of the paper in its changed location.

TRANSPORTING PAPER TO PERCHES. Next Cyrano began another manipulation of the toweling. He held an edge of the sheet of toweling in his bill and sought to carry the toweling up to his customary perch site on the ladder near Zenobia (see p. 325 *et seq.*). But inasmuch as the paper was very large, he kept stepping on it as he ascended. He then would lose his grip on it with his bill, the paper would fall to the floor, and he would descend and repeat the effort. This routine continued unabatedly and unsuccessfully until the paper was quite dilapidated. Late that same evening I provided a fresh piece of toweling and Cyrano spent about 55 min attempting to carry it up the vertical ladder to the perch site on the 30° ladder. Repeatedly failing in this, he stuffed the paper into the food tray.

On April 1, I provided Cyrano with a piece of cardboard, instead of toweling. He manipulated this repeatedly, but it proved to be quite unmanageable for him. After I exchanged it for a sheet of toweling, he crumpled the latter and stuffed it into the food tray. Then, over and over again, for more than 30 min, he kept pulling the paper out of the tray and stuffing it back in. [This was reminiscent of an observation in my studies of White-footed Mice, in which an animal repeatedly pulled cotton out of a nest through a crack at the rear and then stuffed it back through the front entrance (1,381).]

SEEKING TO PREPARE NEST OR REST AREA? Finally, I provided smaller pieces of toweling, that Cyrano could manage more easily. He lost little time in transporting these to his ladder-perch and manipulating them there. From the way he sought to weave the pieces around the rungs, it appeared that he might be endeavoring to prepare a soft, continuous rest area--or was he trying to entice Zenobia to his enclosure by providing a nest area? In any case, the paper toweling kept slipping from the rungs and he kept retrieving and reweaving the pieces.

PLATFORM ARRANGED---ACCEPTED, SOON DEMOLISHED. To test the hypothesis that Cyrano sought to prepare a soft bedding or continuous surface, I arranged such a surface for him. His purpose might be perceived by observing whether he would accept the surface, try to alter it, or tear it apart. With his known propensity to manipulate (but not strip) paper--as with all lovebirds--any degree of "acceptance" of the soft bedding would be a good indication that the construction met his needs, in part. Accordingly, I wrapped several layers of toweling about a 7½-cm length of the ladder at the perch site, and fastened it in place with 3 rubber bands.

After a cautious approach, Cyrano let out a loud chirp and readily accepted the prepared surface, by mounting it. After eyeing the rubber bands for some time (these were new to him) but making no effort to manipulate the paper, he descended to the bottom-right tray and ate sunflower seeds. When he returned, he first perched beside the ladder, rather than on it. Later, he mounted it and spent the night on it, at his usual location.

The next day was uneventful, in the sense that Cyrano engaged in his usual activities. Although he did not chew the toweling to pieces, he did "fuss" with it. By the next day, the toweling was still intact but becoming rather ragged; before the day was over, it was in a shambles. Much of the damage, however, was done, not by Cyrano, but by the Budgerigars. They usually appropriated Cyrano's perching area (in Zenobia's proxity) whenever Cyrano was being flighted or was at the food trays.

SECOND PLATFORM ACCEPTED. Those were days of great reproductive activity in the colony, and it was not until 2 months later that I provided Cyrano with another half-piece of toweling. Just as before, he brought this up to his perching area on the ladder and attempted to arrange it as a platform or bedding, with the same mishaps as before. I then fashioned a 2nd platform identical with the 1st, and again he accepted it, but only after about 25 min of hesitation. He also spent some time trying to augment it with the remaining half-piece of toweling, suggesting that he saw room for improvement. Eventually, he stuffed this half-piece into the food tray.

As far as I could ascertain, Cyrano did not sleep on the platform during the next 3 nights of its existence, though he used it routinely for perching during the days. Within 75 h, which is a rather long time for a fragile construction of paper to survive in the presence of 5 parrots, the platform was in tatters. Again, the Budgerigars were largely responsible for its destruction. I conclude from these observations that Cyrano sought to elaborate somehow on the structure or texture of his favorite perching area, but to what precise purpose remains uncertain. [Had I been less occupied with studying more pressing activities in the colony, I would have removed the Budgerigars and continued the study in their absence. Additional perspective is provided by the fact that a female lovebird (Margot), when given 10 x 25-cm sheets of paper, hauled them repeatedly to an upper perch and merely stripped and tucked them there, rather than at the enclosure floor, but no other female was observed to do so.]

LIFTING SLIDING DOORS. People who maintain small parrots in enclosures with sliding doors over food trays, will be familiar with the birds' manipulations of these doors. Usually they lift them by grasping the bottom bar in their bills and raising their heads and bodies, or they push them up using the top of the upper mandible. There can be no doubt that the birds performing these manipulations often are seeking egress from the enclosures, but successes are rare. This could be either because, with their heads raised to hold up the door, they cannot see that the way is clear to exit, or because the combination of movements in which the head is held on high while taking a step forward, is not employed in such circumstances. [Except during various kinds of social interactions, it probably is unusual for a bird to take steps without seeing where it is going.]

In any event, I am aware of but few instances in which lovebirds gained egress from enclosures by lifting sliding doors. Ogadai, at just over 7 weeks of age, exited once after I had separated him and Jagatai from their parents. In my experience, lovebirds usually learn such acts after only a single success. Accordingly, since the act was not repeated, it is very likely that Ogadai exited while Jagatai was lifting the door. Some other escapes took place when Petra and Ramses and the offspring of their 8th and 9th broods (see Table 4) were housed together in enclosure E; Cleomenes, one of the juveniles of the 9th brood, managed to escape 4 times while other lovebirds were being flighted. However, at first, he managed this alone only with difficulty, as I observed him attempting to exit unsuccessfully on several occasions. In time, the birds were escaping with such facility that I had to place weights on the doors.

In another instance, Claudius, the sole chick of the 2nd brood of Cassandra and Cyrus, escaped from a relatively small enclosure after I gave him to Linda York. Claudius was accustomed to being flighted and handled very frequently, and he tried repeatedly to leave the enclosure. After his 1st escape, he could not be kept confined unless the sliding door was fastened down with an alligator clip. In gaining exit, he first lifted the door with his bill and then threw his head back and chest out to hold the door up as he pressed forward under it. Lovebirds readily force their way past spring-loaded tilting doors; two birds accomplished this.

FLAVIA'S FORCED ENTRY INTO AN ENCLOSURE

However, feats of trying to get out of enclosures, whether successful or not, are neither as impressive nor as interesting as feats of trying to get into enclosures. I already mentioned that, when I flighted Cyrano from enclosure C (which he shared with Cassandra and Cyrus), he sought to enter enclosure D, in which he formerly had been housed, by manipulating the sliding door (there was no convenient perch site from which it might have been more readily lifted). Much more interesting and impressive, however, were Flavia's efforts and success in gaining access to the same enclosure sometime later, when it housed Jagatai and Ogadai.

INTERACTIONS WITH OLDER BROTHERS. At that time, Flavia was unmated and housed in enclosure B with her parents and her sister, Zenobia, who was mated to Cyrano. Jagatai and Ogadai were the only unmated males in the colony, and it was Flavia's habit to spend a great deal of time trying to strip paper in front of their enclosure and trying to court them, as best she could, whenever she was flighted. This always resulted in a great deal of excitement within the enclosure. Sometimes both Jagatai and Ogadai descended to the enclosure floor and challenged Flavia through the bars as she was occupied outside. At other times, Jagatai excluded Ogadai from the floor and challenged Flavia himself.

THE ENCLOSURE-D ARRANGEMENT---ENTRY ACHIEVED---STANDOFF WITH BROTHERS. Enclosure D is of the type designed to have food and water cups hanging inside at base-level that are installed from the outside, after which a transparent plastic sidepane (9 x 21 cm) is inserted by sliding it down into slots. These cups were not being used, and the sidepane merely closed off the gaps between the bars, into which the food cups otherwise were inserted. The sidepanes were left in place permanently, and no similar arrangement existed on any other enclosure.

One day during the flighting of Flavia, I investigated a great din of excited screeching and was astonished to find Flavia inside enclosure D with Jagatai and Ogadai, "holding them at bay." She was standing just inside the entrance, from which the sidepane had been removed, and they were standing on the other side. They were 'scolding' excitedly at her while she 'defiantly' screeched back at them. My astonishment was not merely over the fact of her being in their enclosure, but also because of the way she was holding her ground and they were holding back, not venturing to attack or expel her. This, I feel, is a very telling example of the female lovebird's dominance, even under the most unfavorable circumstances--in the enclosure of other birds, outside of the pair bond, and challenging a pair bond--and of the aggressiveness of a female lovebird in courting males. [At the time, Jagatai and Ogadai were a mated homosexual pair.]

SECOND CHANCE, SECOND ENTRY. I removed Flavia from the enclosure, replaced the sidepane, and went back to my paperwork. In retrospect, I should have watched, instead. I assumed that the sidepane had been dislodged accidentally, and that it was unlikely to happen again, so I did not watch the subsequent proceedings. Accordingly, I was shocked a few min later to find precisely the same situation occurring. Flavia apparently had learned how to remove the sidepane after only a single success. After restoring order again, I blocked access to the sidepane.

Regretting that I had not taken closer note of the proceedings, I offered Flavia the opportunity to repeat the performance on each subsequent day, but it was not until 8 days later that I learned how she had removed the sidepane. [In another example of learning after only one success, Flavia and Titus once found their way into enclosure A with the Cockatiels by working their way along under the enclosure cover to the gap for the NB entrance. When being flighted together again the next day, they almost immediately gained access again by the same route.]

ADDITIONAL ATTEMPTS WITNESSED. On the day in question, Flavia was "fussing about" at the side of enclosure D, and Jagatai and Ogadai were milling about excitedly on the other side of the sidepane. Then Flavia took the upper lip of the sidepane in her bill and lifted it several times. She also sometimes pushed it up under the upper side of her upper mandible. However, her upward thrusts only travelled about 4 cm on those occasions, whereas a displacement of 6 cm was necessary to dislodge the sidepane.

It was not until a month after her 1st success that I saw Flavia remove the sidepane again. She did this with a vigorous upward thrust, but, inasmuch the sidepane then fell back into a position in which it was tilted against the side of the enclosure, and space was cramped, she did not gain access to the inside. [Flavia ultimately mated with Titus (see p. 652

et seq.) but, because he was crippled, it required some assistance on my part for him to copulate with her.

ZENOBIA EXTINGUISHES LIGHT. The fluorescent light illuminating the enclosures was of the type where a small, red button on the back of the reflector frame had to be pushed down hard and held in until after ignition to turn it on, whereas a black button of the same size needed merely to be depressed by a light touch to turn it off. The birds often perched on the stem of this lamp, from which the buttons were within easy reach. One day, I was surprised to have the light go off while the lovebirds were being flighted.

A few days later it happened again, and I could narrow down the perpetrator to either Zenobia or Flavia. From then on, I watched closely while the sisters were flighted; not many days later I saw Zenobia "fussing around" with the black button until the light went off. Since I saw only her pecking at the button, it seems likely that she, like her sister Flavia with the sidepane, had learned the act after only 1 or 2 successes. On subsequent days and weeks, Zenobia's time during flights was very much taken up with her recently acquired mate, Cyrano, and the food and water in his enclosure (see p. 323 *et seq.*). She never again turned off the light.

DEPOSITING OBJECTS IN WATER CONTAINERS

I have noted only one mention in the literature that parrots of all kinds habitually deposit food in their water containers, and it is suggested that placing the water a short distance from the food discourages such behavior (see 834 and K. Flammer in 141). When I had large, glass water bowls on the floors of the enclosures of the Cockatiels and lovebirds, but particularly the latter, I often found that most of the movable objects in the enclosures, not just food, eventually came to lie in the water bowls--small food trays, paper, spray millet, detached pieces of toys, etc. One possible explanation was that the birds manipulated these objects extensively, during the course of which they sooner or later fell into the water. One need only assume, then, that the birds were reluctant to retrieve objects from the water, and that would account for the accumulations.

INTENTIONAL DEPOSITION. While this may happen occasionally, the explanation doubtlessly lies in another direction. Thus, in watching the activities of the lovebirds, I have seen them work hard and tirelessly to manipulate quite sizable objects, even food trays, into the water bowl, sometimes after repeated failures, and there can be no doubt of their objective. Furthermore, food also ends up in water trays hung high on the sides of the enclosures. One might explain the latter by assuming that food falls into the water accidentally during drinking and is not recovered, but other observations rule this out.

In their accommodations at the laboratory, Cassandra and Cyrus were housed together in enclosure M. I draped a plain white hand towel over the top, sides, and rear of this enclosure to shield them from drafts. To hold this in place, I fastened it at the top center, near the front of the enclosure, with a 2½-cm safety pin, with the clip above the towel. Within a few days they usually chewed the towel sufficiently to reach the clasp of the safety pin. Subsequently I would find the pin in their water tray, high on the side of the enclosure, far from the pin's previous location. Refastening the towel with a 4-cm safety pin did not thwart them; they managed to open it as well, and deposit it in the water container. After repeating the performance twice more, they began to be occupied with breeding. At a later date, they repeated the feat once more.

RENDERING CONSPICUOUS OBJECTS INCONSPICUOUS. The most consistent performances of Cassandra and Cyrus (apparently almost exclusively Cyrus) involved pieces of bread, cuttlefish bone, and sometimes kernels of corn. Day after day, these were carried from the floor of the enclosure up to near the top and deposited in the water tray, intentionally hung on high. When I put the pieces of bread in a tray with sunflower seeds and corn, hung high on the opposite side of the enclosure, each and every piece of bread usually was carried across and deposited in the water tray. This occurred invariably during incubation and brooding, even though I might supply 10 or more pieces of bread each day.

The precise mechanism was that Cyrus carried the bread or corn to the water tray, piece after piece, and began to consume it over the water surface, sometimes bracing it agaist the side of the tray. When the piece inevitably fell into the water on his losing his hold, he finished swallowing the food in his mouth, plucked the soaking bread or corn from the surface and repeated the process for as long as the food floated--usually only on the 1st soaking. As soon as the food no longer was retrievable from the water surface he returned to the food tray and then returned with another piece and repeated the process.

These results seem to establish beyond a doubt that confined lovebirds, at least, intentionally deposit food and other objects in their water containers. One reasonable explanation for this behavior is that the birds are rendering inconspicuous those objects in their surroundings that are likely to attract attention to their quarters by depositing them in a location that is itself usually the greatest object of attention. This interpretation is supported by the fact that Cassandra and Cyrus twice deposited the eggshell of a freshly hatched egg in their water tray, high on the side of the enclosure.

SOFTENING EDIBLES TOO HARD TO EAT. However, an observation that suggests an explanation that may strike closest to the origin of the behavior was called to my attention by Dr. M.P. Lipson. His Yellow-headed Amazon (*Amazona ochrocephala oratrix*) was in the habit of soaking in water all edible objects that were too hard to eat directly, until they were softened enough to be consumed. Thus, the habit in some parrots may have persisted from times when this was common practice with hard nuts and fruits that could not be consumed directly; it still may be of adaptive value.

FERDINAND AND PLASTIC BALLS. During the period when the Cockatielian pair, Isabella and Ferdinand, were housed in the lower section of enclosure A, partitioned off from their parents above (Carmen and Cosimo), I observed some skillful manipulations by Ferdinand. I had placed my supply of 1¼-cm and 2-cm plastic balls that I used as egg substitutes in a tray (4 cm deep) on the table top immediately adjacent to the left side of the enclosure. In subsequent days, Ferdinand extended his head into the tray through the $2\frac{1}{2}$ x 5-cm-mesh hardware cloth and rolled the balls out of the tray into the enclosure, where they fell through the $2\frac{1}{2}$-cm-square mesh of the enclosure floor. He accomplished this by nudging the balls up along the vertical back side of the tray, with the side of his head under them, until he maneuvered them up above the side and through the mesh.

LEARNING TO STRIP AND TUCK PAPER BY LOVEBIRDS

According to Dilger, neither stripping, tucking, nor carrying of nest materials is performed by males of heterosexual lovebird pairs. Males of homosexual pairs show no interest in nest material. He suggests that the cutting and carrying of nest material by males is learned through copying the activities of their mates (3). My findings are consistent with Dilger's conclusions in all respects. At no time did Jagatai or Ogadai, as a homosexual pair, show more than a passing interest in nest material or sheets of paper, even though, as fledglings, they had accompanied Petra on nest-material-collecting flights.

On the other hand, the males of heterosexual pairs in the colony tended to copy the paper stripping and tucking activities of their mates (see pp. 259, 260, **Handling and Preparing Nesting Material**). Members of both sexes may require a more or less long period of time to become proficient at these acts; it is true also of nest building by the females. However, an example to copy is not essential for the females, as it is for the males. In fact, implanted steroidal sex-hormones (estrogens) induce immature females to strip nest materials at least several weeks earlier than they normally begin this activity (134). While confined male Blue-crowned Hanging Parrots seemed to strip paper as much as did the females, it is not known whether they did this normally or only after learning it from the females (79).

SLOW LEARNERS, BECOME QUITE PROFICIENT. In the cases of both Ramses and his daughter, Cassandra, I was able to follow the progress of their learning quite closely, as I was following their activities for other reasons. Although Cassandra's progress was quite slow, she ultimately became quite skilled. Ramses accomplished his learning during flights with Petra, on which he frequently followed her from one paper-stripping site to the next. His interest in the paper seemed no less than hers, and he usually kept very close to her on those occasions.

Ramses often appropriated strips from Petra's rump feathers or contested directly for them as they came off her "production line," or while she ran them back and forth through her bill. As mentioned earlier (p. 755), he never learned to cut uniform strips, nor did he employ his strips for any purpose after carrying them back to the enclosure. But he otherwise became so proficient at stripping, tucking, and carrying, as to be mistaken easily for Petra at a distance. One difference, though, was that he occasionally tucked some pieces among his chest feathers.

Without the continuing example of Petra to copy, Cassandra proved to be a very slow learner at all nest-building-associated activities--stripping, tucking, carrying, as well as nest-building itself. Even as she laid clutch after clutch of eggs, she remained very clumsy at these activities. It was not until she was caring for her 7th clutch (in a NB with a Plexiglas side) that she constructed a recognizable nest. It should be kept in mind, though (see p. 319 *et seq*), that she had worked previously under unfavorable conditions, and more with cloth than with paper.

TINY STRIPS CUT FROM SUNFLOWER SEEDS SHELLS. The strength of the urge to strip and tuck is illustrated by Zenobia's behavior. During a period when she and Cyrano were copulating every day, she made and tucked tiny strips from the only raw material at hand, the shells of sunflower seeds. Of course, she could fashion no nest from these. Within 3 days, she laid the 1st egg of her 1st clutch (see p. 769).

LOVEBIRD PARENT-JUVENILE RELATIONSHIPS

THE MALE TAKES THE MAJOR RESPONSIBILITY FOR FLEDGLINGS. One of the most clear-cut facts to emerge from the lovebird studies was that the male of a breeding pair takes the major, and often sole, responsibility for the young outside of the enclosure and to large extent outside of the nest or NB (which would be the situation in the wild). The hen, except for grooming the young and staying very close to them outside the nest at fledging time, tends to occupy herself more with matters pertaining to the next brood. Paper-stripping then almost always takes priority over anything else during flighting. On the other hand, the male's top priority almost always is the care of the young, and the more vulnerable they appear to be, the greater his concern and the closer his attentions.

VISITING CONFINED JUVENILES DURING FLIGHTINGS. This situation received additional emphasis in the first days after I removed Jagatai and Ogadai from the company of their parents in enclosure B and housed them together in enclosure E. Whenever I flighted Petra and Ramses in the immediately following days, Petra went off to strip paper, but Ramses always went first to visit with Jagatai and Ogadai and remained in their company, just as he would have if the family had been flighted together.

YOUNG ESCORTED AND ALLOFED FOR WEEKS AFTER FLEDGING. Long before I normally would have removed the young of Cassandra's 4th brood, she began to lay her next clutch. Inasmuch as her tolerance for the two young was waning noticeably, I removed them to the company of Cockatielian and Budgerigar pairs in enclosure C. Whenever I flighted them they returned to the vicinity of their natal enclosure (enclosure M in the position of enclosure N in Fig. 2b) and were allofed through the bars by Cyrus. And, whenever I flighted Cyrus with them, he allofed them and escorted them about for weeks after their initial separation. Cassandra would leave the clutch for brief periods during these flightings, but she spent almost all her flighted time stripping paper.

While I have never seen parent lovebirds do bodily injury to their young when attacking them, tolerance of the hen for the young decreases considerably after they are fledged. At that time, both parents may become aggressive toward the young within the enclosure, particularly when they are breeding again. Even in these cases, though, there may be uncertainty over the basis for the interactions. In some cases, the male parent may be attempting to mount a daughter or to groom the young on the back. In other cases, the hen may may be trying to groom them or she may feel 'threatened' by the presence of an almost-full-grown female. [It is uncertain at what age the parents are able to distinguish between the sexes of the young but this presumably occurs at an age of about 4 months, when the young begin to exhibit sexual behavior (787).]

SAFETY AT INACCESSIBLE LOCATION. A particularly effective strategy on the part of the young was adopted by Cassandra and Cyrus (at 4 months of age) and Juliet, Romeo, and Zoltan (at 2 months of age, when eggs of the next clutch were present). As long as the young were perched at a place where the parents could reach them easily, they were in jeopardy of being harassed. But if they were in a location at which a special effort on the part of a parent was required to reach them, they were comparatively safe.

In both cases, the enclosures contained 12½-cm-diameter wooden rings suspended near their centers. These were the only perches in either enclosure (enclosures B and C, respectively) at which a young bird could not be reached by a parent merely by stretching from another perching or clinging location. Accordingly, the young not only fled to these perches when pursued (though not always with impunity) and generally favored them for perching, they also usually spent the night on them. Such a ring provided a close, comfortable, fit for Juliet, Romeo, and Zoltan.

INFECTIOUS BEHAVIOR

YOUNG FOLLOW PARENTAL LEADS, BUT NOT VICE VERSA. Juveniles of both lovebird and Cockatielian families housed together show a strong inclination to begin to engage in maintenance activities (bathing, grooming, eating) already initiated by another juvenile or, particularly, by their parents. [It is, of course, well known that young birds learn certain activities by mimesis, i.e., they copy their parents or other adult birds. I refer here, rather, to their engaging in an already-learned activity that has been initiated by another bird.]

On the other hand, parents only very infrequently follow the lead of their young in any activity. This was most assuredly true of the Cockatielian parents, Carmen and Cosimo and Helena and Homer, who were practically guaranteed not to engage in any activity initiated by their young, except vocalization or fright. I already have given an example of the strong tendency of Cockatiels to follow one another to the enclosure floor to forage (see p. 674). For the present example, I consider bathing.

BATHING

MATES STIMULATING EACH OTHER. I consider a 13-month period, from August, 1983, to August, 1984, inclusive, during which a total of 48 instances of bathing were noted, 29 of them in the 3-month period of April to June. There were 10 occasions when both birds of a mated pair were together and available (i.e., not engaged in incubating or brooding) and they bathed together, or one followed the other. These observations accord with the known strong tendencies of members of mated lovebird pairs to follow each other's leads in maintenance activities (3).

In 2 of the 10 cases, Cockatiels may have been stimulated to bathe by seeing a pair of lovebirds do so. In one case, Titus did not copy his parents, but this may have been because of his being hampered by his crippled leg, as he still was not completely mobile (Flavia and Zenobia were in the tower at the time). In another case, Titus was being flighted while Petra and Ramses bathed, and Flavia and Zenobia were in the tower, so none of them had an opportunity to copy the parents. Although Ramses visited Flavia and Zenobia afterward, while he still was very wet, that did not stimulate them to descend and bathe. On still another occasion, Cyrano entered his enclosure and bathed while being flighted, whereupon Zenobia followed him in and also bathed.

MATES NOT STIMULATING EACH OTHER. There were only 5 instances when one bird of a mated pair bathed and the other was available but did not follow suit. On one of these occasions, neither his mate, Petra, nor his juvenile son, Titus, joined the lovebird, Ramses. On another, Titus tried to join Ramses but Petra chased him away and, possibly as a result, Ramses did not bathe either. There were 14 instances when one bird of a mated pair bathed but the other was occupied incubating or brooding and did not follow suit. On 9 of these 14 occasions, the bather was within sight of the other bird, the latter being in an open nest. In fact, no incubating or brooding bird ever came off or away from eggs or young to follow its mate in the act of bathing.

SUBORDINATES AND DOMINANTS. No dominant bird ever followed the lead of a subordinate in bathing. There were 4 opportunities for this to occur during the period in question: Cassandra and Cyrus failed to follow their brother Cyrano's lead nor, on another occasion, that of their 3 offspring, Juliet, Romeo, and Zoltan; Carmen and Cosimo failed to follow the leads of 3 of their 4 offspring; and Petra and Ramses failed to follow Titus' lead (Flavia and Zenobia were in the tower). There were 5 cases when young followed the leads of their parents, all involving lovebirds. This exclusive distribution was largely because the Cockatielian young were housed separately from their parents from April to August, a period that accounts for 40 of the 48 examples. Lastly, there were 3 instances (one already mentioned in the above paragraph) when dominants bathed but temporarily excluded subordinates. In 2 of these cases, the subordinates bathed afterward.

BIRDS OF EQUAL RANK MAY NOT STIMULATE ONE ANOTHER. Once Flavia and Zenobia bathed together while visiting in enclosure A with the Cockatiels. Flavia and Cyrano each separately entered an empty enclosure while being flighted, and bathed. During the time that the two pairs, Isabella and Ferdinand, and Helena and Homer, were housed together in the lower portion of enclosure A, all 4 once bathed in succession. On another occasion, Helena and Homer bathed but Isabella and Ferdinand did not follow their example. In summary, excluding instances of dominants failing to follow subordinates, and those where one member of a pair was incubating or brooding, there were only 6 cases when one family member bathed and the others did not follow suit.

INTERSPECIFIC STIMULATION. During the period of several months that the male lovebird, Jagatai, was housed with the Cockatielian pair, Carmen and Cosimo (at the laboratory), there were two noted occasions when Jagatai took vigorous baths. On the 1st occasion, Carmen pressed in close to bathe also but was repelled by Jagatai. Cosimo, however, stood very close with wings outstretched and with various aspects of his body presented to catch the water in the shower being created by Jagatai. On the 2nd occasion, both Cockatiels pressed in close and were repelled, but then Carmen stayed close and went through antics similar to those described above for Cosimo, in order to benefit from the shower.

REDIRECTED COPULATION AND SELF-STIMULATION BY A LOVEBIRD

REDIRECTED COPULATION IN VARIOUS SPECIES. Several cases are known of males who, being stimulated to precopulatory activity by the presence of females but thwarted sexually because of the latters' unavailability for one reason or another, engaged in "redirected copulation" with substitute inanimate objects (183). A Fischer's Lovebird behaved in this way on several occasions, a Wood Thrush (*Hylocichla mustelina*) did so many times over a period of days, and an American Redstart (*Setophaga ruticilla*) did so over a period of 1 month. In all cases the females were present at the time of the redirected activity.

REDIRECTED COPULATION AND SELF-STIMULATION BY CYRANO. When Cyrano was housed with the Budgerigars in enclosure E (see Fig. 1a), adjacent to the tower, he spent a great deal of his time on the 30° ladder by the tower, frequently just across from Zenobia. He was able to allogroom her head and courtship-feed her through a 2½-cm-square aperture. Just as in the above cited cases, this proximitiy to an inaccessible female led to redirected copulation by Cyrano. In this activity, he clung to 2 rungs of the ladder, one held by each foot, and rubbed his vent region against the side of the ladder for 5-15 min. He did this at least once almost every day over a period of 10 weeks, before being moved to the laboratory, regardless of whether Zenobia was nearby in the tower.

This activity of Cyrano doubtless began as redirected copulation, as a result of sexual thwarting. But the fact that he subsequently engaged in it regularly in such long sessions over so lengthy a period, often in Zenobia's absence, suggests that it has to be regarded largely as sexual self-stimulation. Since lovebirds possess no intromittent organ, this would imply either that the region of the lovebird vent is erogenous, or that the proctodeum was everted during the process.

SELF-STIMULATION CEASES WHEN HOUSED WITH ZENOBIA. Once Cyrano was housed with Zenobia (in the same enclosure, E) at the laboratory, his self-stimulation ceased. His first sexual unions with her occurred at least daily during the week of November 19-26, 1984, during which period she was very domineering and aggressive toward him. She laid the 1st egg of a 1st clutch of 5 eggs on December 9.

EARLY MORNING COURTSHIP FEEDING BY LOVEBIRDS

FOUR SEPARATELY-HOUSED PAIRS. When the colony was transferred to the laboratory, each of the 4 pairs of mated lovebirds (Petra and Ramses, Cassandra and Cyrus, Zenobia and Cyrano, and Flavia and Titus) was housed separately. They engaged in all the activities typical of mated lovebird pairs --courtship feeding, mutual allogrooming, sleeping side by side, copulation, etc. [But copulation by Flavia and the crippled Titus had to be facilitated.] Then an additional characteristic behavior came to my attention that had almost entirely escaped my notice when the birds were maintained at my living quarters.

ALL PAIRS ENGAGE IN SAME ACTIVITY SIMULTANEOUSLY. Each morning each breeding pair engaged in precisely the same activity at the same time. Within a matter of seconds of the time of lights-on, after arousing themselves and stretching and/or grooming very briefly, each male courtship-fed his mate. This tended to occur regardless of the phase of the breeding cycle, that is, irrespective of whether the pair was copulating prior to or during laying, was incubating, was brooding, was in the immediate post-brooding phase, or even had not yet copulated (in the case of Flavia and Titus). [The illumination cycle at that time was 17L:7D.]

EARLY MORNING COURTSHIP FEEDING HAD ESCAPED NOTICE at my living quarters because I had only 2 pairs housed separately there, and because there was no abrupt change from conditions of night light to conditions of day light. Though there was an abrupt change to bright light when I turned the lights on in the morning, dawn usually had begun and been perceived several hours earlier, and the pairs were by no means always inactive before I turned the lights on. In short, with a more or less natural dawn, an abrupt change to brighter light in the morning, and only 2 pairs under observation at my domicile, very early morning activity was not necessarily synchronized, and courtship feeding did not stand out as a characteristic activity.

On the other hand, with a single very marked light change, and with 4 mated pairs under observation, activity became synchronized and the simultaneous courtship feeding was conspicuous. Accordingly, it would appear that the first activity engaged in by mated breeding lovebird pairs (and Budgerigars; see p. 778, **Courtship Feeding**) after being aroused from inactivity in the very early morning, is that the male courtship-feeds the female. [The only time that early morning courtship feeding took on any special significance at my living quarters was when Cyrano courtship-fed his sister Cassandra, while her mate, Cyrus, looked on (see p. 319).]

WELFARE OF A CRIPPLED LOVEBIRD

It will be recalled that Chapter 5 dealt principally with the social interactions of the male, Titus, with his parents and two older sisters, including his mating with one of these sister, Flavia. It also will be recalled that Titus was congenitally malformed. I describe here the course of Titus' subsequent actions and social interactions under the handicap of having his right leg splayed out to the side.

LEG USE UNCOORDINATED BY SIGHT. The type of crippling that Titus sustained is not uncommon, but I have seen no account of the welfare of an afflicted bird. It also is well known that parrots, using, as they do, the bill as a 3rd "leg," are able to survive when handicapped by the loss of one leg, and other birds doubtless also survive in this condition. In Titus' case, the crippled leg never was seen to be used in an eye-directed manner, that is, there never was any coordination of its movement based upon sight. Its grip on objects always was achieved blindly, through trial and error.

Titus always slept and perched, for any period of time, in a location where he could grip an object to the side or above with his crippled leg while perching with the other. Usually this object was the enclosure side, sometimes it was the side of a hanging perch, at other times the bars of the enclosure top. When he had no choice, he perched with the left leg and rested part of his weight on the long bones of the right leg or the knee.

SCRATCHING HEAD AND NEGOTIATING TOWER. In the matter of scratching the head with the right leg, Titus had no difficulty in bringing the leg over the wing, but the control of the leg parts, at first, was just as if they were directed normally. The result was that, for months, Titus only scratched straight up into the air. Despite this very lengthy, unpromising beginning, Titus eventually learned to redirect partially the right leg to achieve some degree of scratching of the head. Although Titus definitely was handicapped in all other situations, as far as locomotion with his legs was concerned, he was highly adept in the tower. There, it actually was advantageous to be able to grip one side sideways. In fact, it is my impression that Titus could negotiate the tower with greater speed and facility than could a normal bird.

UNABLE TO MAINTAIN MOUNT ON FLAVIA'S BACK. At the age of 23 weeks, Flavia and Titus formed a pair bond, as already described in Chapter 5. It was in this relationship that his crippled condition proved to be the greatest handicap. Perhaps the main difficulty stemmed from the fact that he was unable, at first, to maintain a mount on Flavia's back for sexual union. As a consequence of not being able to respond to her normal solicitations for copulation, Flavia became very aggressive. She often sought to mount him instead, as if he were the female and she the male. She also pursued him to the enclosure floor and stood over and harassed him there, as he assumed a position lying on his back. This situation eventually changed dramatically, however, as described on pages 658 and 773.

EXCESSIVE HARASSMENT---NORMAL RELATIONS FOLLOW SUCCESSFUL BREEDING. In addition to Flavia's harassment of Titus, apparently prompted by his sexual inadequacies, she also generally seemed to harass him much more than is normal in a lovebird-pair relationship. This surely was a natural outcome of his lesser ability to avoid her aggressive attentions. A lovebird female often engages in a considerable amount of aggressive attention toward her mate. This is largely thwarted by the abilities of her mate to avoid it. Since Titus was not adept at this, Flavia became excessively domineering.

I often flighted the pair merely to give Titus some respite. An early sign of Flavia's excessive attentions was that Titus lost so many feathers from his nape that large bare areas resulted. Another solution to giving Titus relief was to allow Flavia to incubate the 6 infertile eggs of her 1st clutch. Entirely normal relations followed upon my facilitating copulation by providing supports for Titus to grip with his wings. Once sexual unions were achieved and Flavia engaged in incubation and the brooding of young, her interactions with Titus were indistinguishable from those between other pairs.

OVERCOMING THE ULTRACONSERVATIVE FEEDING HABITS OF LOVEBIRDS

I gave Romeo and Juliet, two young from the 1st brood of Cassandra and Cyrus, to Linda York, who sought to train them to accept new food as a matter of routine. The generally accepted view is that, in the first few days after they leave the nest, parrots can be taught to sample new foods readily, but that once this brief period is over, further changes in diet become increasingly difficult. The results obtained with Romeo and Juliet show that by persistent effort, even older Peach-faced Lovebirds, at least, can be trained, not only to accept strange new foods, but to await them 'eagerly,' and even to compete for the opportunity to obtain them.

STRANGE FOODS CONSUMED WITH LITTLE HESITATION. Linda York did not acquire the birds until they were over 3 months old, 5 weeks after they were fledged. From the time of their acquisition, in addition to their having access to the foods to which they were accustomed (see pp. 288, 289, **Foods and Feeding**), they were offered daily samples of all foods making up the household fare. Within a few days, they were 'eagerly' anticipating receiving such supplements, fighting over access to them, and consuming them with little hesitation.

LOVEBIRD MATING BETWEEN A MATURE MALE AND A JUVENILE FEMALE

Petra and Ramses, the colony founders, were housed together from the time they were acquired, and the details of their mating (pairing) were not recorded. Nor were details of the matings of the broodmates, Jagatai and Ogadai (both males), or Cassandra and Cyrus recorded. Mating between the mature Zenobia and her older brother, Cyrano, was an ancillary topic of Chapter 3, while that between the mature Flavia and the juvenile Titus was the main topic of Chapter 5. It remained to investigate mating between a mature male and a juvenile female. To set the stage therefor, I broke the homosexual pair bond between Jagatai and Ogadai by giving away the latter.

GREAT INTEREST OF JAGATAI IN ALLOFEEDING. By coincidence, Jagatai was housed together with the Cockatiels, Carmen and Cosimo, in the top section of enclosure A, at the time that Cassandra and Cyrus were rearing their 3rd brood in enclosure M, atop enclosure A. One of the chicks (Aspasia) of this brood was the mate I intended for Jagatai (though at that time I could not be sure that the brood included a female). The great interest Jagatai evidenced in the family, while appearing, at first, to have its basis in the presence of the chicks, ultimately was found to be based in the very strong urge to allofeed the brooding female, Cassandra. These interactions are described on p. 333.

Shortly after she was fledged, I housed Aspasia with the 2 Cockatiels, Kirsten and Rimski in enclosure B, about 50 cm from enclosure A. Recall that Aspasia and her 2 broodmates and parents had been flighted periodically with Jagatai in the preceeding weeks. On all of these flightings, Jagatai allofed Cassandra repeatedly, followed her about everywhere, repelled her mate, Cyrus, when the latter came near, and mildly attacked the 3 chicks without provocation, by nipping their toes. On February 10, 1985, at an age of almost 2 months (she hatched the preceding year on Dec. 16), I flighted Aspasia alone with Jagatai for 20 min, for the 1st time, to observe their interactions preceding and during the planned mating.

FIRST AND SECOND FLIGHTINGS: Jagatai took immediate note of Aspasia but did not approach her. She, on the other hand, behaved toward Jagatai as a young juvenile would toward a parent (being only 2 months old, she was roughly 2 months shy of the age at which sexual behavior is believed to be first evidenced; 787). She "tailed after" him everywhere, and approached him time and again, often soliciting food. In return, Jagatai repelled her on every occasion, either by pecking at her bill or nipping her toes (on no occasion, at this time or later, did Jagatai injure her). At the time of this flighting, Jagatai showed no interest in allofeeding Cassandra, who was incubating another clutch. Roughly the same scenario was repeated during a 20 min flighting the next day, except that Aspasia had become more wary. She no longer solicited food, approached as closely, or followed consistently. Jagatai, on the other hand, was inclined to follow Aspasia when the latter left his vicinity, but he still nipped her toes without provocation.

THIRD AND FOURTH FLIGHTINGS: During a ½-h flighting on the 3rd day, Aspasia still initially followed Jagatai and was gently repelled with bill pecks and toe nips, but the birds often perched only a few cm apart. They clearly were becoming habituated to one another. Then Jagatai began sidling up to Aspasia more freqently but, as if uncertain of himself or her, he usually hesitated and ultimately nipped her toes. When Aspasia flew off, he usually followed her. Once Aspasia weakly solicited to be allofed but Jagatai did not respond.

During another ½-h flighting the next day (the 4th), Jagatai courtship-fed Aspasia once, for the 1st time, as she perched beneath him. Emboldened by this success, Aspasia pressed forward more assertively about 20 times, but Jagatai repeatedly repelled her, in the usual way, and did not allofeed her again that day. They stayed in each other's vicinity for the rest of the flighting, either one following the other, as necessary, with Jagatai still inclined to nip Aspasia's toes without provocation.

FIFTH AND SIXTH FLIGHTINGS: On the 5th day, they again kept company with each other during the flighting. Jagatai continued to nip Aspasia's toes, either when the latter approached him too closely or failed to yield to him when he approached. She solicited weakly 3 or 4 times to be allofed but Jagatai showed no inclination to accommodate her. After about 22 min, Jagatai flew off and visited Cassandra and Cyrus at their enclosure. Aspasia did not follow Jagatai but, instead, interacted aggressively with the Budgerigars, who also were being flighted. Following this, Jagatai mock courtship-fed Aspasia at the same positions they held during the courtship feeding of the day before, that is, he bobbed his head while inserting his bill in Aspasia's, but he had not regurgitated food beforehand, nor did he mandibulate afterward. Although Aspasia repeatedly sought to perch in contact with him, Jagatai would not accede.

On the next flighting (7th day), Aspasia continued to solicit food and try to approach closely to Jagatai, but was repelled repeatedly. I then flighted the two fledglings (unnamed) from the 1st brood of Zenobia and Cyrano with them, and Jagatai uniformly repelled all 3 of the young and nipped their toes. When I housed Jagatai, the 3 fledglings interacted closely, just as if they were broodmates; they were often in close contact.

SEVENTH FLIGHTING: On the 8th day, I first flighted Jagatai alone, whereupon he flew directly to Aspasia's enclosure and courtship-fed her. For the next 10 min they kept very close to each other on opposite sides of the enclosure front face, but Jagatai nipped Aspasia's toes repeatedly every time she exposed them through the mesh. Aspasia, however, never attempted to nip Jagatai's toes, even though they were at risk the entire time. When Jagatai temporarily moved down to enclosure C, below, Aspasia frantically paced the enclosure front face, peering down after him.

After I flighted Aspasia too, she and Jagatai went through their usual routines, at first, but then Jagatai courtship-fed Aspasia another 4 times. Again, the allofeeding took place at the same location as on the previous occasions (one courtship feeding and one mock feeding on the 4th and 5th days). Again, Aspasia was perched beneath him. During the rest of the flighting, Jagatai continued to maintain his distance and repel Aspasia with pecks and nips when she approached too closely to him.

EIGHTH FLIGHTING. On the next day, Aspasia tried 5 times to join Jagatai as the latter perched on a vertical bar, but she had not yet learned how to grasp the bar, and had to give up the effort. With that, Jagatai joined her. For the next 15 min they kept company with one another more or less matter of factly, without the occurrence of any courtship feeding and with Jagatai nipping Aspasia's toes only once.

After that, Jagatai flew over to Cassandra's enclosure and courtship-fed her 3 times. However, Cassandra was busily occupied chewing nesting material from the outside cloth. Furthermore, Cyrus actively repelled Jagatai, and even bit his toes once through the bars. Thereupon, Jagatai flew off and tried 3 times to rejoin Aspasia. The latter, however, flew away each time. After that, they resumed keeping company more or less nonchalantly, almost as if a mated pair.

NINTH FLIGHTING: The next day, Jagatai flew over to Aspasia's enclosure the moment I flighted him. Then the two of them perched next to one another across the bars for 3 min. Jagatai regurgitated food once, but did not courtship-feed Aspasia, perhaps because the latter was not close enough or did not cooperate. Jagatai either bit or tried to bite Aspasia's toes twice before flying off. [This seemingly was a good indication that they could not as yet be regarded as being pair bonded, as I had never seen a lovebird male bite his mate's toes through the bars of an enclosure.]

When I then flighted Aspasia too, she followed Jagatai about until the latter flew off and tried to allofeed Cassandra again. Jagatai succeeded once, but Cyrus kept driving him off through the bars of the enclosure. Recall, in this connection, that Jagatai was dominant to Cyrus when both were outside the enclosures, even in interactions involving Cassandra. Jagatai then rejoined Aspasia. At that time, when Jagatai sidled over to her on a perch, he no longer unprovokedly nipped at her toes or showed any intention to do so., but he still would nip her if she approached him too closely. Sometimes they perched next to each other in a friendly manner, with heads only 2-3 cm apart. After Jagatai flew off on his own for several min and Aspasia did not follow, I re-housed her, whereupon Jagatai flew over to the enclosure and kept her company. But he tried twice more to bite Aspasia's toes through the bars.

To test the status of their relationship, I housed Jagatai with Aspasia (in Aspasia's home enclosure with Kirsten and Rimski, where Jagatai was already "at home," as a result of previous visits). He "pestered" Aspasia repeatedly by nipping her toes, and also tried repeatedly to mount her and grasp her by her back feathers with his bill while doing so. Aspasia, of course, fled from his toe nips and tried to flee from his mounting advances. Aspasia became so "sensitized" to Jagatai's advances that she even fled from him repeatedly as Jagatai sought to perch next to her for the night. Jagatai finally did succeed in perching fairly close to her at the time of lights-off, but 10 min later Aspasia was alone, clinging to the enclosure side, and they also were apart the next morning at lights-on.

TENTH FLIGHTING: I then (February 20, 1985) began to flight the birds every other day. On the next flighting, Jagatai again flew directly to Aspasia's enclosure and they perched across the bars from each other in a very "chummy" way. As Jagatai moved about on the enclosure front face, Aspasia followed him closely, with only token attempts by Jagatai to nip her toes. He regurgitated once, as during the previous flighting, but again did not allofeed Aspasia. When I flighted Aspasia too, she approached closely to Jagatai and solicited to be allofed 4 times, but unsuccessfully. When they subsequently kept company, Jagatai no longer nipped at Aspasia's toes, though he twice pecked her away lightly. For the first time, Aspasia followed Jagatai when the latter flew down and perched on my head.

Again, I housed Jagatai and Aspasia for the night with Kirsten and Rimski. They interacted within the enclosure in much the same manner as 2 days before, except that Aspasia was somewhat less panicked by Jagatai's advances, though she continued to squeal as Jagatai tried to mount her. Jagatai was more successful in perching close to Aspasia, but, again, they were not perched side by side in the morning at the time of lights-on.

ELEVENTH FLIGHTING: If they were not to be regarded as already mated on the last flighting, they doubtless could be so regarded on the next one, 2 days later. Jagatai flew directly to Aspasia's enclosure and courtship-fed her twice on the last 2 of 4 regurgitations. When I flighted Aspasia, the two of them kept very friendly company, but with no further courtship feeding, despite some solicitations by Aspasia. Nor was there any hint of toe-nipping, though Jagatai still would discourage too close approaches with gentle head-peck threats. Again, Jagatai visited Cassandra's enclosure and was driven off by Cyrus. When I put the pair into Aspasia's enclosure, they ate together at the same seed tray, after which Jagatai courtship-fed Aspasia lengthily and repeatedly. Afterward, they interacted very "chummily" and Jagatai tried repeatedly to copulate with her. Although pairing may occur at an age of only 2 months, Aspasia probably still was well over a month too young to be in readiness for copulation. Though she did not flee, she emitted frequent squeals of distress.

The next morning the pair were perched side by side at the time of lights-on, and Jagatai courtship-fed Aspasia in the typical early morning fashion of mated lovebirds. In the following weeks, their interactions were those of pair-bonded lovebirds, including courtship feeding, mutual allogrooming, perching side by side, bathing together, etc. It took another month (indubitably by Mar. 26, at an age of 3 months and 10 days) for Aspasia to mature enough to assert female dominance over Jagatai. Two months later, Aspasia's sex was confirmed. Although she had not yet learned to strip paper, she tried to tuck the strips that I provided between her rump feathers and she built a primitive nest with them. When, in April, I observed Aspasia with a mouthful of the Cockatiel Kirsten's feathers, after a scuffle, I housed her and Jagatai separately in enclosure D.

DOES THE MALE COMMONLY TAKE INITIATIVE IN LOVEBIRD MATING? In the described instances of heterosexual pair bonding, the female took the initiative in all 3 cases. In the case of Zenobia and Cyrano, one probably can attribute the female initiative to Cyrano's "outcast" social position and consequent skittishness. In the case of Flavia and Titus, the result was to be expected, because Titus had been injured severely in an earlier attack by Flavia and feared her.

The present mating sheds very little light on this matter. No great significance can be attributed to Aspasia's taking the initiative in her early interactions with Jagatai, since her early behavior probably typifies the responses and solicitations of juveniles to parents, rather than the courting of another bird. The fact that Jagatai sometimes gave priority to courtship-feeding Cassandra, rather than keeping company with Aspasia, may merely have been because Aspasia was, at first, immature--not yet worthy of being considered as a possible mate (as in the case of the early interactions between Flavia and Titus). It was only in the very latest stages of the formation of the pair bond that Jagatai could be said to have aggressively pursued mating activities.

In order to answer the above query with confined birds it would be necessary to bring together adult, unmated birds of opposite sexes in neutral circumstances. The present results merely emphasize that females may take the initiative in courting and may pursue this activity with vigor and tenacity. The results presented in Chapter 3 show how very tenacious and unwavering a courting male can be. But Cyrano was not courting an unmated female in that example. Rather, he was courting one broodmate who already was mated to another one. Quite possibly, these special circumstances elicit quite different behavior than that seen when an unmated female is courted.

PERSISTING RECOGNITION OF PARENTS BY OFFSPRING BY EITHER SIGHT OR SOUNDS

In Chapter 4, in the treatment of Coition Sounds, I described how the other Cockatiels in the colony were stimulated to chirp and whistle when they heard Carmen uttering loud Coition Sounds during copulation, and also when they heard Cosimo uttering the same sounds after copulation or during courtship (see p. 414). At first, I thought that it was the sounds alone that stimulated the vocalizing of the other birds. Subsequently, I discovered that the sight, alone, of Carmen and Cosimo copulating was sufficient to stimulate the vocalizing of the other birds, before any sound was uttered by Carmen. On the other hand, the production of the same sounds by the other breeding pairs, Isabella and Ferdinand, and Helena and Homer, generally did not stimulate the other Cockatiels to vocalize more than normally, although they usually took note of the sounds and sometimes behaved excitedly. It appeared, at first, that the explanation for this failure was that Isabella and Helena were relatively quiet during copulation, so that they and their Coition Sounds tended to pass unnoticed. In this connection, various paired birds almost always were housed within sight of one another during these periods.

The matter might have rested there had it not been for the fact that the breeding of Helena and Homer--producing 7 young in 4 successive broods --yielded a 2nd family of Cockatiels. Prior to that time, I did not suspect that the vocalizing described above is not of general occurrence among unrelated Cockatiels as a response to the sight or sounds of copulation, but rather is an almost strictly familial response stimulated in Cockatielian offspring solely by parental behavior. Thus, the observations described above all were carried out when the adult birds in the colony consisted only of Carmen and Cosimo and various members of their first 5 broods.

At a later time (Nov.-Dec., 1985), Carmen and Cosimo were rearing their 7th brood in the upper section of enclosure A, and Helena and Homer were almost fledging their 5th brood in the lower section (their 1st brood had no survivor; see pp. 496, 497). Across from their enclosure in unobstructed view were Kirsten and Rimski (of the 4th brood of Carmen and Cosimo) in enclosure B, and Heloise, Julian, and Marcus (of the 2nd and 3rd broods of Helena and Homer) in enclosure C. Helena and Homer already had begun a 6th cycle of breeding and began to copulate one afternoon, whereupon their offspring in enclosure C began to chirp and whistle excitedly, but not the offspring of Carmen and Cosimo in enclosure B. It was then that it became evident that the response might be strictly a familial one.

To confirm and extend the observations several days later, approximately 1 day after Helena laid the 1st egg of her next clutch, I transferred Heloise, Julian, and Marcus to enclosure N, on top of enclosure A and out of sight of Helena and Homer. That afternoon, Helena and Homer copulated again, and again their 3 offspring in the enclosure above became excited and began to vocalize, whereas Kirsten and Rimski, who could both see and hear them did not respond vocally. Precisely the same behavior, in the same circumstances, was confirmed on several subsequent occasions.

Still later (Jan., 1986) Carmen and Cosimo copulated on 3 occasions for several min in the presence (in the same enclosure) of the young of their 7th brood (5 juveniles). Thereupon Kirsten and/or Rimski whistled, as also did a sole adult male of their 6th brood in the lower portion of enclosure A and Helena and Homer in enclosure N, above, but not one of the 5 offspring of Helena and Homer, who also were in the enclosures below and above, did so (nor did any of the young of the 7th brood).

The most impressive examples occurred on several occasions when I was flighting 2 members of the 7th brood of Carmen and Cosimo and had a 3rd member housed in the lower part of enclosure A (the other 2 juveniles no longer were in the colony). Carmen and Cosimo were in the upper part of enclosure A and began to copulate, as was their habit when the young were being flighted. As Carmen emitted the Coition Sounds over a period of 4-5 min, all 7 of her offspring, present at 4 different locations, began to chirp and whistle, but only infrequently did one of the 5 offspring of Helena and Homer join in, even though they were housed together with the offspring of Carmen and Cosimo that were responding. Instead, they usually just listened intently, sometimes cocking their heads in the direction of the copulating birds.

Thus, there is a very strong indication that either the sight or the sounds of parents copulating, but not of other Cockatiels doing so, will stimulate juvenile or mature offspring at other locations to vocalize months and even years after fledging. On the other hand, there generally was little or no vocalizing by another bird in response to Coition Sounds uttered by Kirsten and Heloise, as they copulated with Rimski and Julian, respectively; nor did these pairs have offspring. On one occasion, though, Cosimo was stimulated to utter Coition Sounds upon hearing them uttered by Julian in the enclosure below; neither bird was copulating at the time.

One can understand the above phenomenon partly in terms of the fact that breeding Cockatielian pairs typically begin their next breeding cycle before they have fledged the preceding brood. The young at this time are learning to eat, climb, wing-flap, etc., and are very alert to all occurrences in their surroundings (and still hoarse-rasping when intruded upon). The very specific sight and sounds of their parents copulating evidently leave a very long-lasting impression upon them, to the extent that these stimuli elicit great excitement on all future occurrences. It is, after all, essentially the only activity of the parents that the young cannot mimic at the time.

In the cases of all the broods of Helena and Homer, incubation and rearing occurred in open nests, so the parents always were within sight of the maturing young. In the cases of the first 4 broods of Carmen and Cosimo, however, the young were reared in NBs (both opaque and "transparent"). Although they had less opportunity to see, if not also to hear, their parents during those copulations that took place preceding the time of fledging, they had ample opportunities to observe it subsequently, as they were not housed separately until long after fledging (see Chap. 4, Part 2 and Chap. 6, Part 1).

It seems unlikely that this response to Coition Sounds would play any role in the behavior and breeding of Cockatiels in the wild, where ample opportunities for the privacy of copulating birds exist (it already has been noted at several points that pairs of all 3 of the species studied preferred to copulate in private; e.g., see pp. 725, 795, 796). The occurrence of the phenomenon in confinement would seem to emphasize the high degree to which pre-fledged and fledged young are alert to and affected by parental behavior. [In connection with vocal recognition of parents by chicks and young, members of several species of gulls are known to have such capabilities within several days of hatching, even on the 1st or 2nd day, while Guillemots acquire the ability while still in the egg (see 1,150).]

PECKING OPEN EGGS, NOT AN IRREVERSIBLE HABIT

It is well known that breeding birds occasionally acquire the habit, doubtlessly accidentally, of pecking open otherwise undamaged eggs; sometimes they consume the contents. It is generally believed that this habit, once acquired, is irreversible, and workers whose main interest is in breeding recommend that one dispose of birds that acquire it.

In the course of this study, the opportunity arose to study the breeding behavior of an egg-pecking hen. The 2nd clutch of Flavia and Titus consisted of 5 fertile eggs and produced 2 chicks, both of which failed to survive (see p. 773). One of the eggs of this clutch (perhaps even 2 of them), however, appeared to have been pecked open. The 3rd clutch consisted of 6 fertile eggs (oviposited Mar. 22-31, 1985) and also produced 2 chicks. The latter apparently were given inadequate care and succumbed after 9 and 11 days. The 4th and 5th clutches of 6 eggs (oviposited on May 16-25 and July 10-20, following) each produced 1 chick from 4 and 3 fertile eggs, respectively; these succumbed after only 1 day from inadequate care.

Two of the eggs of the 3rd clutch had been damaged by small holes before they were due to hatch and may have been the first 2 eggs pecked open by Flavia, but I was not alert to the possibility at the time and paid no special attention to the matter. However, I was suspicious when the same type of damage was noted with egg #5 of the 5th clutch after only 15 days of incubation. I repaired this egg but found it to be damaged again in the same manner 4 days later, but not pipped. This is reckoned as the 1st egg pecked open for certain by Flavia.

In the next 3 months Flavia oviposited several clutches with a total of 19 eggs. Sometimes I provided a nestbowl for her, in which to incubate the eggs, sometimes I removed the eggs as they were laid, sometimes I gave her substitute eggs. At any rate, she pecked open a total of 16 eggs on the following dates: Aug. 6, 15, 16(2), 18, 19, 21, 31, Sept. 4, 6, 15, 17, 19, 23(2), Oct. 4. I fostered 2 eggs from these clutches to Cassandra and Cyrus and they were hatched by them and fledged routinely (the males, Bion and Nero), except for being very severely feather-picked.

On October 22, 1985, Flavia began to oviposit another clutch but abandoned the 1st egg, which I had placed in a restored nestbowl (possibly because of oviposition-site fidelity). I then removed the egg and inverted the nestbowl. She oviposited again on October 27, but the egg was damaged in a fall. I then restored the nestbowl and she laid 5 additional eggs in it over the period of October 30-November 9, only 1 of which was pecked open (on Nov. 6, the day after it was laid). Two of the 4 remaining eggs were fertile and hatched on November 22 and 24th and the chicks were cared for attentively. Accordingly, it is evident that the habit of pecking open eggs is not irreversible, or, at least, not invariable, since Flavia incubated the 4 eggs over a period of weeks without damaging them (see also below, when only 1 egg of another clutch of 5 was pecked open).

[One of these chicks, Titian, was fledged successfully and housed thereafter with Flavia and Titus, leading to attentive paternal care on Titus' part that was reminiscent of the care that he himself had received from his father, Ramses (see also next section, **A Helper in the Boudoir**). The other chick was displaced accidentally, or fell out of, the nestbowl when it was 9 days old, but I restored it, still warm and seemingly none the worse for the exposure. However, this chick, like its father Titus (and a subsequent offspring of the 7th brood of Zenobia and Cyrano) had its right leg splayed out to the right and, in addition, had its lower mandible malformed. Since it progressively was lagging behind its broodmate, Titian, I fostered it to Zenobia and Cyrano, exchanging it for a fostered nestling of the 6th brood of Petra and Ramses that they already had been brooding for 10 days. They gave the crippled chick most attentive care. Notwithstanding this highly attentive care, however, the chick succumbed after another 11 days as a partially-feathered 29-day-old midget (see p. 771, **The Fourth Brood**). Titian eventually mated with Sylvia (see p. 846).]

A "HELPER IN THE BOUDOIR"

"Helpers at the nest" occur in many species and are well known (see p. 332, **Cooperative Breeding Among Non-Parrots**), the designation referring to birds, usually the offspring of previous broods--sometimes bachelor males--that aid a breeding pair in the allofeeding of nestlings and even in the incubation of eggs. However, I am unaware of any instance in which an avian helper substituted for his father as his mother's partner in coitus, an occurrence that appears all the more incongruous among birds that have a reputation for pairing for as long as both birds survive.

As stated above, I housed Titian, the only surviving offspring of Flavia's clutch of October 30-November 9, 1985, with his parents in enclosure H (Fig. 1b) in which a nestbowl was present. Titian was very well tolerated by both parents, grooming and being groomed by them and sometimes sleeping beside them. In the next few months, Flavia continued to oviposit eggs but incubated only irregularly. An occasional egg was pecked open, but in one case an egg was left undamaged and unattended in the nestbowl for over 4 weeks, up to the time of the occurrences being described here. I only very infrequently observed sexual union between the parents, the last occasion being on April 26.

FLAVIA SOLICITS TITIAN'S SEXUAL ATTENTIONS. Just 3 days after witnessing the last of these infrequent copulations with Titus, I was amazed to see Flavia on the floor of the enclosure soliciting copulation from her son Titian, then just over 5 months old. There followed 4 lengthy, vigorous sessions of coitus with Titian, after all but the last of which she solicited anew. During these proceedings Titus perched a mere 12 cm away on a side food tray, from which he was driven off twice by Flavia. After the last copulation Flavia joined Titus on an upper perch, where he allogroomed her. I witnessed two additional copulations between Flavia and Titian, 5 and 7 days later, both times upon a rear upper perch (but not the same one she used in sexual union with Titus). On both occasions Titus also was on an upper perch and he did not seek to interfere with their activity. As became evident later, the basis for the changed circumstances appeared to be that Titus either no longer used his wings to steady himself when mounting Flavia, or did so much less effectively, so that he was greatly handicapped in achieving sexual union.

In view of the unusual and apparently unprecedented nature of the interactions that occurred between these 3 lovebirds, I present them in some detail. In the course of the week following the 1st noted copulation between Titian and Flavia, Titus and Flavia continued to sleep side by side on an upper perch, apart from Titian. On the 7th day, the 1st egg of a new clutch was laid but a small piece of its shell was chipped off, apparently in falling. I placed the egg in the nestbowl and removed the egg remaining from the previous clutch; it essentially had been ignored for over a month.

TITIAN SLEEPS NEXT TO FLAVIA AND ALLOFEEDS HER. Flavia did not attend the egg that night but, for the first time in many weeks, she slept next to Titian, and apart from Titus. The next night she slept alone in the nestbowl incubating a 2nd egg, while Titus and Titian slept apart on the upper perches. Titian joined Flavia in the nest within 1 min of lights-on, and they also spent some time together in the nest later that day "fussing" about in it, as is customarily done in preparing a nest. Titian also had begun to allofeed Flavia, the 4th instance noted in the colony of a LB hen being allofed by a male other than her mate. Since I found that the chipped egg had become somewhat crushed and that the 2nd egg also was damaged, I removed them both. The damage to these eggs and most of those that were laid subsequently probably traced to the fact that they had very thin shells, as I had not been trying to facilitate breeding --rather the opposite--and had not, at first, supplied supplemental cuttlefish bone.

On the following night, with no egg in the nest, Flavia slept next to Titian on a perch, apart from her mate, Titus. The significance of this change in sleeping arrangements appears to be that Flavia had become more tolerant of Titian and less receptive to Titus. The latter, being crippled, could only perch next to Flavia if she had her right side facing the side of the enclosure, as he needed to grip the side with his splayed out right (leg and) foot. If Titian were already on Flavia's right side and against or facing the enclosure wall, and was tolerated, Titus did not displace him but perched elsewhere. Or, if Flavia had her left side adjacent to the enclosure side, and would not face around to accommodate Titus, he perched elsewhere.

TITIAN ACHIEVES FULL SURROGATE-MATE STATUS BUT DEFERS TO TITUS. On the following day, I noted that Titian also was trickle-feeding Flavia lengthily, which is behavior typical of the male mate. Titian then was performing or had performed all the mutual activities of a mate--copulating, allofeeding, allogrooming, and sleeping at Flavia's side, and also had become the object of all the less-than-affectionate attentions that Peach-faced Lovebird hens often bestow on their mates. The sleeping arrangement was the same on the following night, when a 3rd egg was laid. As the latter had been pecked open, I removed it. A 4th egg was laid 2 days later but, as it was cracked, I also removed it. In the 6 nights following the laying of the 3rd egg, Titus slept alone 4 nights and perched next to Flavia, with Titian on her other side the other 2 nights.

On the night of May 16, Flavia laid the 1st of a new clutch of 5 eggs and, beginning on that night, she slept in the nestbowl and incubated the eggs very attentively. On that night and the following night, Titian slept at her side in the nest, thereafter both he and Titus always slept on perches and always apart. Every morning for the next 25 days, namely, as long as incubation continued, the typical morning occurrences at the time of lights-on were that Titus would join Flavia in the nest, displacing Titian on the 2 occasions that the latter preceded him, and allofed her and engaged in mutual allogrooming with her. Whenever Titian approached at such times, Titus chased him away. However, after Titus had left, either later in the morning or at any time thereafter, Titian was welcome in the nest and also allofed Flavia and engaged in mutual allogrooming with her. Titus might displace him at any time, though. In other words, both father and son were accepted as mates but the son always deferred to the father.

TITIAN'S SURROGATE-MATE STATUS WANES. As incubation progressed, however, Titian's attentions appeared to become increasingly less welcome until, finally, by June 6, even Flavia usually repelled him if he approached the nest, although there were occasions when she accepted his presence briefly and socialized with him, just as with Titus. Thus, by then, almost all of Titian's status as a surrogate mate appeared to have been lost and Titus resumed the full role of mate.

Two of the 5 eggs of this clutch were fertile and presumably fertilized by spermatozoa from the son, Titian. On the 17th day of incubation, I removed 1 crushed egg, on the 22nd day another, on the 26th day another plus an egg that had been pecked open, leaving only a single fertile egg, which Flavia ceased to incubate 2 days later.

INTERRUPTED ATTEMPS TO COPULATE. On the morning of the same day that I removed 2 of the 3 remaining eggs, Titus mounted Flavia 4 times at their customary perch position but failed to copulate successfully. As they continued the effort again and again, they were interrupted each time by

Titian, who tried to try to climb up next to them but was pecked away each time by one of the parents. I then turned off the lights and removed Titian in the darkness, placing him above in the small enclosure K (Fig. 1b). When I turned the lights back on, both Flavia and Titus eyed the lower portion of the enclosure for 1 min or more, quite evidently missing Titian. For the next 20 min, however, one or the other parent exchanged chirps with Titian, one clearly responding to the other as judged from the timing, even though other lovebirds in the colony also were vocalizing excitedly. About 20 min later, Flavia and Titus copulated for about 45 sec. When I returned Titian 8 h later, both parents attacked him briefly but mildly (usually it is only the breeding female who briefly attacks an entering bird, whether it be her mate or an offspring).

FLAVIA AGAIN SOLICITS TITIAN'S SEXUAL ATTENTIONS. It might appear from this turn of events that Titian's sexual advances toward Flavia no longer would be accepted by her and that Titus had regained his full status as her mate. This proved not to be the case, however, for on June 16th, on two occasions 10 min apart, Flavia solicited copulations from Titian on a back perch. But each time that Titian mounted her, Titus, who was perched nearby, turned to face them, approached, and repelled Titian with pecks. After the 2nd occasion, Titus also courtship-fed Flavia. As long as Titian did not attempt to copulate with Flavia, his interactions with Titus were harmonious.

FURTHER COPULATION ATTEMPTS WITH TITUS, ULTIMATELY SUCCESSFUL. Thirty min later, Flavia and Titus attempted to copulate twice while Titian was at the food trays, but Titus was unable to obtain a secure mount. Four days later I witnessed 4 additional brief attempts, 2 of them lasting about 10 and 20 sec each. Titus no longer was employing his wings for support as he had done previously on successful occasions. It seemed quite evident that these failures must have been long-standing, and that they were the probable basis for Flavia's solicitations to, and acceptance of, sexual union with Titian. It was not until over 3 weeks later, when another breeding cycle began, that I witnessed a lengthy (4-5 min), successful copulation between Flavia and Titus, on which occasion Titus employed his wings to maintain his mount. Titian was at the food trays during the entire proceedings.

One would have to conclude from these events that at the time in question Flavia would accept either male as a sexual partner, but that Titus no longer would tolerate his son's copulating with her. More generally, it is quite evident that even so strong and otherwise exclusive a sexual relationship as between lovebird mates can become polyandrous in circumstances in which the male of the pair is handicapped and male offspring are present in a relatively confined breeding area.

A COLONY OF FOUR LOVEBIRDS

FOUR JUVENILES HOUSED TOGETHER. In March, 1986, I housed together (in enclosure E) 3 juveniles (Margot, Juliana, and Silvius, about 14 weeks old) from the 7th brood of Cassandra and Cyrus (2 of them from eggs fostered from Zenobia and Cyrano) with one juvenile (Nero, about 19 weeks old) of their 6th brood (a chick fostered from Flavia and Titus; see Table 4). The enclosure still contained the 30° ladder on which Cyrano had perched in proximity to Zenobia, and, in time, it was supplemented with 6 stout natural-branch perches, as agonistic interactions called for more dense structuring (to facilitate Silvius' escapes from attacks).

Almost from the beginning, Silvius adopted the ladder as a perch for resting and sleeping, and became a loner or outcast. This was an early sign that he probably was a male, who was being repelled and excluded by the older male, Nero. On the other hand, Nero, Margot, and Juliana slept side by side on a rear perch and socialized extensively with each other but never with Silvius.

NERO AND JULIANA MATE AND COPULATE, ATTACK SILVIUS, ACCEPT MARGOT. During the month of May, Nero and Juliana formed a pair bond and copulated on a lower perch on several occasions. Despite Nero's being mated to Juliana (as indicated by the facts that they copulated, mutually allogroomed, slept side by side, and that Nero courtship-fed her), Nero, Juliana, and Margot continued to sleep side by side on the same perch, and all 3 allogroomed one another. From the very first, Nero and Juliana attacked Sylvius by biting his toes and pursued him lengthily about the enclosure.

OVIPOSITION--ATTACKS ON SYLVIUS INCREASE IN FEROCITY. When Juliana oviposited the 1st of 5 fertile eggs on the enclosure floor on May 19, the attacks increased in ferocity and frequency, whereupon I added perches and a platform in the upper left corner of the enclosure, so that Sylvius could escape more readily and would have an alternate perch. Inasmuch as Juliana had a depth of at least 1-cm of shavings beneath her eggs and did not clear the shavings away, she had no difficulty keeping the eggs grouped beneath her. On the other hand, Zenobia, who also was incubating 5 eggs in similar circumstances at the same time, tended to scatter the shavings from the IA, so that her eggs rolled about freely.

Frequently Juliana came off her eggs to pursue and grapple with Sylvius. Despite the fact that Sylvius was bitten many times and that both Juliana and Nero grappled with him in seemingly ferocious combat amidst much squealing and squawking, I never detected blood being drawn. In part, if not largely, Sylvius' survival depended upon the fact that he defended himself vigorously and with the greatest of tenacity, and usually stood his ground after being pursued and cornered. Sylvius, himself, was not seen to initiate or provoke aggression nor to be attacked by Margot.

THOUGH MATED WITH JULIANA, NERO SLEEPS BESIDE MARGOT. The most remarkable occurrence was that when Juliana began incubating on May 19, Nero and Margot continued to sleep side by side, allogroom one another, and otherwise socialize, just as if they were a mated but non-breeding pair, at times when Nero was not occupied with allofeeding and allogrooming Juliana in the nest. On the other hand, Juliana was extremely aggressive toward Margot, just as toward Sylvius, attacking and pursuing her vigorously about the enclosure whenever she came near the nest, even though the pursuit sometimes led over the nest and eggs.

CHICK FLEDGED, ALL THREE ADULTS "ATTACK" SYLVIUS. Only 1 of the 5 fertile eggs hatched (on June 17) but insufficient moisture may not have been responsible for the failure of the other 4, as there was no sign of internal pipping of at least 3 of them. During the brooding of the chick, which was fledged without incident, there was no noticeable intensification or slackening of aggression of Nero toward Sylvius or of Juliana toward Margo and Sylvius.

After the chick was fledged but still housed in the same enclosure, agonistic interactions, at first, continued unabatedly. Nero and Juliana frequently perched with the fledgling but did not allow either Margot or Sylvius to approach it. Instead of slackening, "attacks" on Sylvius, then by all 3 adults, intensified. These attacks became so frequent and tenacious, with grappling on the enclosure floor and feathers flying, that I changed the housing arrangements. Otherwise, I felt that it would have been only a matter of time before Sylvius, who had lost much weight, would be seriously injured or killed.

HOUSED SEPARATELY, MARGOT SEEKS TO COURT SYLVIUS. I removed both Sylvius and Margot (who were broodmates) and housed them together in enclosure M. It then became clear that Margot's changed behavior toward Sylvius (after the chick of Nero and Juliana reached fledging age), was of the nature of attempts to socialize and court, rather than to attack him. But inasmuch as Sylvius had been under attack concurrently by both Nero and Juliana, he had fled or fought back tenaciously at the approach of any adult. By the time that he was housed separately with Margot, he was so skittish at the direct approach of any lovebird that he fled in panic on each of Margot's approaches.

SYLVIUS' PLUMAGE PLUCKED AND IN DISARRAY. Sylvius' breast plumage already was in great disorder from having been severely feather-picked by his parents and from its not having refeathered normally. Inasmuch as Margot pursued Sylvius relentlessly and sought to stay his flight by grasping him by primaries, chest, back, rump, or tail feathers, after only 2 or 3 days his plumage was partly plucked and totally disheveled, but no drop of blood was drawn (had Margot sought to injure him, he would have had countless wounds). In essence, the situation seemed to be almost a duplicate of Flavia's early courtship of Titus, except that Sylvius' situation was more 'desperate,' inasmuch as he did not have the benefit of parental protection or a relatively large enclosure within which to escape.

HOUSED HARMONIOUSLY WITH TITIAN, SYLVIUS REVEALED TO BE A FEMALE. In order to make enclosure M available to Margot and Sylvius, I had removed Petra and Ramses and the 5 offspring of her 7th and 8th broods and placed them in enclosure E. When I flighted the family of 7 during subsequent days, they sought to return to their natal and breeding enclosure, M, in which Sylvius and Margot were housed; they crowded about on its top and all of its faces and acted aggressively toward the occupants inside. Sidling about on the inside of its front face on one occasion, Sylvius received a bleeding wound on a toe from Petra. Thereupon, I decided to give him some relief and, at the same time, attempt a further experiment.

Accordingly, I removed Margot and transferred Titian to enclosure M with Sylvius, in the expectation that, being in a strange enclosure, Titian would be subordinate, at least temporarily, and not attack Sylvius, and that Sylvius was unlikely to attack any lovebird. That proved to be correct and, after a day's period of adjustment, the new companions coexisted harmoniously, often perching side by side, sleeping side by side, and even mutually allogrooming during mornings. Quite unexpectedly, early on the morning of the 4th day, Titian began to courtship-feed Sylvius and he did so on every morning thereafter. The suspicion then became very strong that, despite the many indications from social interactions that Sylvius was a male, the bird was a female. When Sylvius began to oviposit several weeks later, any doubt was resolved, Sylvius became Sylvia, and another breeding pair was at hand.

VOCALIZING IN THE DARK

It is well known that confined diurnal birds usually cease vocalizing when their enclosure is darkened, and generally cease activities also and retire. On most occasions, the small parrots of the colony were not exceptional in this regard. However, it is noteworthy that whenever the birds were agitated for one reason or another, their vocalizations usually continued unabatedly. Thus, whenever Carmen was flighted alone and Cosimo was not in a NB or nestbowl caring for eggs or chicks, he began to whistle excitedly and climb about on faces of the enclosure. His excited whistling usually continued, even if the lights were turned off, and did not cease until Carmen was returned to the enclosure.

Similarly, the other Cockatiels in the colony also usually began to whistle excitedly when some members were flighted and such whistling did not abate until the released birds ceased flying about and perched or foraged. Nor did this whistling cease abruptly if the lights were turned off shortly after the birds were flighted but had temporarily perched, though it did not last indefinitely as usually did Cosimo's whistling. [Recall, in connection with activity in the dark, that a Cockatielian parent allo-feeding a nestling in the dark would continue to do so immediately after the lights were turned off, with the chick still in position, and that I had confirmed that Budgerigar hens will feed young nestlings in the darkness of the night period (see p. 793, **Nighttime Allofeeding Confirmed**).]

Another example of vocalization in the dark concerns the juvenile Budgerigar, Agrippina, of the 3rd brood of Lucretia and Lysander (which had achieved flight 6 weeks late). Many of the Budgerigars of the colony were in the habit of squawking loudly when I caught them in the dark to rehouse them after flighting. Usually they began squawking as soon as I touched them, even if I did not take hold of them. On the other hand, Agrippina, who was flighted daily, began squawking in the dark as soon as I turned off the lights. This provided an aid to finding her, as she frequently was not in sight and always fled to difficultly accessible locations when I approached. Lastly, it will be recalled that, as a nestling, the Cockatielian female, Heloise, began to hoarse-rasp upon my morning intrusions as soon as she heard me enter the room, even before lights-on (see p. 709, **Eyes Open, Hoarse-Rasping and Hissing Begin**).

ADDENDUM ON INTERSPECIFIC FOSTERING

Care of a Lovebird Hatchling by Budgerigars

As noted above (p. 742), it is asserted that Peach-faced Lovebird young often have been fostered succesfully with Budgerigars, but the fostering age was not specified. A single example achieved at the end of this study, in which Budgerigars hatched a lovebird egg and cared for the hatchling, suggests that fostering of lovebird hatchlings with Budgerigars involves formidable obstacles, though these would not exist with nestlings of a few days of age. The impediments to successful fostering have to do with differences in allofeeding behavior. In the case of Budgerigars, it was noted (see p. 785, **Active Role of Nestlings**) that the hatchlings and nestlings play a very active role in licking and swallowing food, and that they are sufficiently well coordinated to turn over onto their bellies when sated. The parents allofeed them, at first, strictly by massive tongue flicking of gobs of semi-liquid food.

Lovebirds, on the other hand, are essentially helpless upon hatching and almost always are allofed liquid food by tongue flicking or trickling. They generally play a much less active role during allofeeding and often (when tongue-flick allofed) are passive. In one of the few cases observed in which a lovebird hatchling received its first meal by massive tongue-flick allofeeding, it succumbed during the night (see p. 766, **Hatchling Allofed First by Male Succumbs**). Accordingly, *a priori*, it can be suggested that lovebird hatchlings generally would be insufficiently active to deal with food delivered in semi-liquid gobs, which is the practice of Budgerigar parents. My single example is consistent with this assessment. Fostering Budgerigar hatchlings with lovebirds might be more successful.

In mid-January, 1987, the Budgerigar hen, Lucretia, was incubating a clutch of 4 eggs, only 2 of them fertile, at the same time that the lovebird hen, Petra, was incubating a clutch of 4 fertile eggs. On January 14, I fostered 2 of Petra's eggs to Lucretia's clutch and removed the 2 infertile eggs. One of Lucretia's fertile eggs was pipped on the same day but the chick was unable to hatch (the only such instance observed with a Budgerigar egg). On January 23, one of Lucretia's lovebird eggs hatched. Though Lucretia cared for and allofed the chick, I was unable to observe the proceedings closely, and am unaware of the extent of Lysander's participation. On checking the chick the next morning, I found it to be vigorous, but its crop was empty and its bill and the sides of its face were embedded in a solid mass of caked, dry food.

Upon removing the mask of food, I also found the chick's buccal cavity to be filled with almost-dry food. In addition, hulled round seeds were embedded in the down of its forehead, behind its eyes, and in other areas about its head. Four h after cleaning and restoring it, I checked the chick again and found a similar but much less extreme situation, but then the chick had about 1/3rd of a crop full of clear liquid food. After cleaning and restoring the chick, I checked it again 5 h later and found a similar situation, but with only about half as much clear liquid food in its crop. The next morning its crop was empty again and its face (and buccal cavity) again was embedded in a mask of dry food. I cleaned the chick 3 more times that day, finding only 1/10th or less of a crop of clear liquid food each time. The next morning the chick was dead.

It is clear from this result that the hatchling was unable to swallow the gobs of semi-liquid food delivered by Lucretia and that Lucretia, with or without Lysander's assistance, was unable to adjust sufficiently to the situation. The food simply exuded over the chick's bill and face and dried there, making a subsequent allofeeding impossible. The presence of the clear liquid food in the chick's crop suggests that the chick was taking only liquid into its esophagus, and that it was primarily the residue of the delivered semi-liquid food that was accumulating in its buccal cavity and caking its bill and face. Had Lucretia been delivering only liquid food (or Lysander been cleaning after her), there would have been no residue to accumulate. These results suggest that only exceptionally, perhaps with extensive cleaning by the male, would lovebird hatchlings survive when fostered with Budgerigars.

REFERENCES

1. Forshaw, J.M. 1978. *Parrots of the World.* TFH Publs., Neptune, N.J.
2. Bates, H.J. and R.I. Busenbark. 1978. *Parrots and Related Birds.* TFH Publs., Neptune, N.J.
3. Dilger, W.C. 1960. The comparative ethology of the African parrot genus *Agapornis. Z. Tierpsychol.*, 17:649-685.
4. Dilger, W.C. 1962. Evolution in the African parrot genus *Agapornis. Living Bird*, **1962**:135-148.
5. Bennett, R.B. 1961. *Care and Breeding of Budgerigars, Canaries, and Foreign Finches.* Arco Publishing, New York.
   Feyerabend, C. and M.M. Vriends. 1978. *Breeding Budgerigars.* TFH Publs., Neptune, N.J.
   Rutgers, A. 1958. *The Care and Breeding of Budgerigars.* Blandford Press, London.
6. Curtis, N. 1963. *Cockatiels.* TFH Publs., Neptune, N.J.
7. Silva, T. and B. Kotlar. 1981. *Breeding Lovebirds.* TFH Publs., Neptune, N.J.
8. Teitler, R. 1979. *Taming and Training Lovebirds.* TFH Publs., Nep-Neptune, N.J.
9. Sturman, J. and D. Schults. 1980. *Breeding Cockatiels.* TFH Publs.
10. Gordon, M.A., Bartholomew, G.A., Grinnell, A.D. and F. White. 1982. *Animal Physiology*, Macmillan, New York.
11. Reed, N.A., Squyres, T., Barrett, T., Squyres, D.D. and J. Hall, 1978. The Cockatiel, breeding, genetics, show standards, hand feeding, and colony breeding. *AFA Watchbird*, **V(5)**:6-26.
12. Moreau, R. 1948. Aspects of evolution in the parrot genus *Agapornis. Ibis*, **90**:206-239, 449-460.
13. Wing, L.W. 1956. *Natural History of Birds.* Ronald Press, New York.
14. Wallace, G.J. and H.D. Mahan. 1975. *An Introduction to Ornithology.* Macmillan New York.
15. Cade, T.J. and J.A, Dybas. 1962. Water economy of the Budgerygah. *Auk*, **79**:345-364.
16. Dilger, W.C. 1962. Methods and objectives of ethology. *Living Bird*, **1962**:83-92.
17. Dacke, C.G. 1979. *Calcium Regulation in Sub-Mammalian Vertebrates.* Academic Press, New York.
18. Cinat-Tomson, H. 1926. Die geschlechtiche Zuchtwahl beim Wellensittich (*Melopsittacus undulatus* Shaw). *Biol. Zbl.*, **46**:543-552.
19. Lack, D. 1966. Interrelationships in breeding adaptation as shown by marine birds. *Proc. Int. Ornithol. Congr.* **XIV**:3-42.
20. Berrill, N.J. 1953. *Sex and the Nature of Things.* Dodd, Mead & Co., New York.
21. Skutch, A.F. 1957. The incubation patterns of birds. *Ibis*, **99**:69-93.
22. Kendeigh, S.C. 1952. Parental care and its evolution in birds. *Illinois Biol. Mono.*, **22**:1-356.
23. Van Tyne, J. and A.J. Berger. 1976. *Fundamentals of Ornithology*, Wiley and Sons, New York.
24. Austin, O.L. 1961. *Birds of the World.* Golden Press, New York.
25. Lack, D. 1947. *Darwin's Finches.* Cambridge U. Press, Cambridge.
26. Howard, L. 1952. *Birds as Individuals*; 1956. *Living with Birds.* Collins, London.
27. Smith, G.A. 1979. *Lovebirds and Related Parrots.* Inkata Press, Melbourne.

28. Welty, J. 1982. The Life of Birds. Saunders College Pubs., New York.
29. Armstrong, E.A. 1947. Bird Display and Behavior. Lindsay Drummond Ltd., London.
30. Courtney, J. 1974. Comments on the taxonomic position of the Cockatiel. Emu, **75**:97-102.
31. Holyoak, D.T. 1972. The relation of Nymphicus to the Cacatuinae. Emu, **72**:77-78; 1973. Comments on taxonomy and relationships in the parrot subfamilies Nestorinae, Loriinae, and Platycercinae. Emu, **73**:157-176.
32. Allen, G.R. and C. Allen. 1981. Cockatiel Handbook. TFH Publs., Neptune, N.J.
33. Forshaw, J.M. 1969. Australian Parrots. Livingston Publ. Co., Wynnewood, Pa.
34. Lack, D. 1968. Ecological Adaptations for Breeding in Birds. Methuen & Co., Ltd., London.
35. Bartholomew, G.A. and W.R. Dawson. 1952. Body temperatures in nestling Western Gulls. Condor, **54**:58-60.
36. Lorenz, K. 1935. Der Kumpan in der Umwelt des Vogels. J. Ornithol., **83**:137-213, 289-413.
37. Dawson, W.R. and J.W. Hudson. 1970. Birds. In Comparative Physiology of Thermoregulation, Whittow, G.C., ed., pp. 223-310, Academic Press, New York.
38. Delacour, J. and E. Mayr. 1945. The family Anatidae. Wilson Bull., **57**: 3-55.
39. Thorpe, W.H. 1951. The learning abilities of birds. Ibis, **93**:1-52, 252-296.
40. Barnes, D.M. 1986. How cells respond to signals. Science, **234**:286-288.
41. Heinroth, O. and K. Heinroth. 1959. The Birds. Faber & Faber, London.
42. Wenzel, B.M. 1971. Olfaction in Birds. In Handbook of Sensory Physiology, vol. 4, part 1, L.M. Beidler, ed., pp. 432-448. Springer-Verlag, New York.
43. Bock, W.J. 1969. The origin and radiation of birds. In Comparative and Evolutionary Aspects of the Vertebrate CNS. Ann. N.Y. Acad. Sci., **167**:147-155; 1976. Recent advances and the future of avian classification. Proc. Int. Ornithol. Congr., **XVI**:176-184.
44. Heilmann, G. 1926. The Origin of Birds. Witherby, London.
45. Pearson, R. 1972. The Avian Brain. Academic Press, New York.
46. Tinbergen, N. 1950. Recent advances in the study of bird behavior. Proc. Int. Ornithol. Congr., **X**:360-374.
47. Zeier, H. 1970. Lack of eye to eye transfer of an early response modification in birds. Nature, **225**:708-709.
48. Knowlton, V.Y. 1964. Abnormal differentiation of embryonic avian brain centres associated with unilateral anophthalmia. Acta Anat., **58**:222-251.
49. Stresemann, E. 1959. The status of avian systematics and its unsolved problems. Auk, **76**:269-280.
50. Davis, D.E. 1942. The phylogeny of social nesting habits in the Crotophaginae. Quart. Rev. Biol., **17**:115-134.
51. Lack, D. 1940. Courtship feeding in birds. Auk, **57**:169-178.
52. Karten, H.J. 1969. The organization of the avian telencephalon and some speculations on the phylogeny of the amniote telencephalon. Ann. N.Y. Acad. Sci., **167**:164-179.
53. Skutch, A.F. 1935. Helpers at the Nest. Auk, **52**:257-273.
54. Bartholomew, G.A., Lasiewski, R.C. and E.C. Crawford. 1968. Patterns of panting and gular flutter in cormorants, pelicans, owls, and doves. Condor, **70**:31-34.

55. Swinton, W.E. 1965. *Fossil Birds.* Trustees British Museum, London.
56. Thomson, A.L. 1950. Breeding Seasons of Birds. *Ibis*, **92**:173-184.
57. Polyak, S. 1968. *The Vertebrate Visual System.* U. Chicago Press.
58. Ariëns Kappers, C.U., Huber, G.C. and E.C. Crosby. 1960. *The Comparative Anatomy of the Nervous Systems of Vertebrates, Including Man.* Hafner, New York.
59. Jerison, H.J. 1973. *Evolution of the Brain and Intelligence.* Academic Press, New York.
60. Drent, R.H. 1972. Adaptive aspects of the physiology of incubation. *Proc. Int. Ornithol. Congr.*, **XV**:255-280.
61. Knowlton, F.H. 1909. *Birds of the World.* Henry Holt & Co., New York.
62. Brereton, J. Le Gay. 1962. Evolution within the Psittaciformes. *Proc. Int. Ornithol. Congr.*, **XIII**:499-517.
63. Immelmann, K. 1962. Drought adaptations in Australian desert birds. *ibid.*, **XIII**:649-657.
64. Miller, A. H. 1962. Desert adaptations in birds. *ibid.*, **XIII**:666-674.
65. McLachlan, B. 1932. The Budgerygah or Shell-Parrot. *S. Australian Ornithol.*, **11**:158.
66. Finlayson, H.H. *et al.* 1932. Heat in the interior of South Australia and in Central Australia--holocaust of bird-life. *ibid.*, **11**::158-163.
67. Brockway, B.F. 1962. The effects of nest-entrance positions and male vocalizations on reproduction in Budgerigars. *Living Bird*, **1962**:93-101.
____. 1964. Ethological studies of the Budgerigar (*Melopsittacus undulatus*): Non-reproductive behavior. *Behaviour*, **22**:193-222.
____. 1964. Ethological studies of the Budgerigar: Reproductive behavior. *ibid.*, **23**:294-324.
____. 1964. Social influences on reproductive physiology and ethology of Budgerigars (*Melopsittacus undulatus*). *Anim. Behav.*, **12**:493-501.
____. 1965. Stimulation of ovarian development and egg laying by male courtship vocalization in Budgerigars (*Melopsittacus undulatus*). *ibid.*, **13**:575-578.
____. 1967. Social and experiential influences of nestbox-oriented behavior and gonadal activity of female Budgerigars (*Melopsittacus undulatus* Shaw). *Behaviour*, **29**:63-82.
____. 1967. The influence of vocal behavior on the performer's testicular activity in Budgerigars (*Melopsittacus undulatus*). *Wilson Bull.*, **79**:328-334.
____. 1969. Hormonal and experiential factors influencing the nestbox oriented behavior of Budgerigars (*Melopsittacus undulatus*). *Behaviour*, **35**:1-26.
____. 1974. The influence of some experiential and genetic factors including hormones, on the visible courtship behavior of Budgerigars (*Melopsittacus*). *ibid.*, **51**:1-18.
68. Keast, A., Crocker, R.L. and C.S. Christian. 1959. *Biogeography and Ecology in Australia*, Junk, The Hague.
69. Ostrom, J.H. 1976. Some hypothetical anatomical stages in the evolution of avian flight. *Smithson. Contrib. Paleobiol.*, **27**:1-21.
70. ____. 1974. *Archaeopteryx* and the origin of flight. *Quart. Rev. Biol.*, **49**:27-47.
71. Keast, A. 1950. Bird adaptations to aridity on the Australian continent. *Proc. Int. Ornithol. Congr.*, **X**:373-375.
72. Verheyen, R. 1948. Aspects et evolution du comportement maternel chez les oiseaux. *Gerfaut*, **38**:21-33.

73. Keast, A. 1961. Bird speciation on the Australian continent. *Bull. Museum Comp. Zool. (Harvard)*, **123(8)**:305-495.
74. Brereton, J. Le Gay and K. Immelman. 1962. Head-scratching in the Psittaciformes. *Ibis*, **104**:169-175.
75. Ostrom, J.H. 1976. *Archaeopteryx* and the origin of birds. *Biol. J.* Linn. Soc., **8**:91-182.
76. Thorpe, W.H. 1961. *Bird Song*. Cambridge U. Press, New York.
77. Yalden, D.W. 1971. The flying ability of *Archaeopteryx*. *Ibis*, **113**: 349-356.
78. Carpenter, F.M. 1953. The geological history and evolution of insects. *Amer. Sci.*, **41(2)**:256-270.
79. Buckley, F.G. 1968. Behavior of the Blue-crowned Hanging Parrot *Loriculus galgulus* with comparative notes on the Vernal Hanging Parrot *L. vernalis*. *Ibis*, **110**:145-164.
80. Collias, N.E. 1952. The development of social behavior in birds. *Auk*, **69**:127-159.
81. Davis, D.E. 1952. Social behavior and reproduction. *ibid.*, **69**:171-182.
82. Axelrod, D.I. and H.P. Bailey. 1968. Cretaceous dinosaur extinction. *Evol.*, **22**:595-611.
83. Grinnell, A.D. 1970. Comparative auditory neurophysiology of neotropical bats employing different echolocation signals. *Z. Vergl. Physiol.*, **68**:117-153.
84. Schodde, R. 1979. The mysterious origins of Australian birds. In *Reader's Digest Complete Book of Australian Birds.*, Reader's Digest Services Pty. Ltd., Sydney.
85. Seward, A.C. 1959. *Plant Life Through the Ages*. Hafner, New York.
86. Simpson, G.G. 1952. *The Meaning of Evolution*. Yale U. Press.
87. Colbert, E.H. 1961. *Evolution of the Vertebrates*. Wiley & Sons, New York.
88. Mayr, E. 1970. *Populations, Species, and Evolution*. Harvard U. Press.
89. Vaughn, T. A. 1972. *Mammalogy*. W. B. Saunders, Philadelphia.
90. Bellairs, A. 1968. *Reptiles*. Hutchinson U. Library.
____. 1970. *The Life of Reptiles*. University Books, New York.
91. Goin, C.J., Goin, O.B. and G.R. Zug. 1978. *Introduction to Herpetology*. Freeman & Co., San Francisco.
92. Augusta, J. and Z. Burian. 1963. *Prehistoric Reptiles and Birds*. Paul Hamlyn, London.
93. Porter, K.R. 1972. *Herpetology*. W.B. Saunders, Philadelphia.
94. Pope, C.H. 1955. *The Reptile World*. A.A. Knopf, New York.
95. Hensley, M.M. and J.B. Cope. 1951. Further data on removal and repopulation of the breeding birds in a spruce-fir forest community. *Auk*, **68**:483-493.
96. Klopfer, P.H. and J.P. Hailman. 1965. Habitat selection in birds. In *Advances in the Study of Behavior*, vol. 1, Lehrmann, D.S., Hinde, R.A. and E. Shaw, eds., pp. 279-303. Academic Press, New York.
97. Yapp, W.B. 1970. *The Life and Organization of Birds*. E. Arnold, London.
98. Griffin, D.R. 1981. *The Question of Animal Awareness. Evolutionary Continuity of Mental Experience*. Rockefeller U. Press, New York.
____. 1984. Animal Thinking. *Amer. Sci.*, **72**:456-464.
99. Griffin, D.R., ed. 1981. *Animal Mind-Human Mind*. Springer-Verlag, New York.
100. Harnad, S. and R.W. Doty. 1977. Introductory overview. In *Lateralization in the Nervous System*, S. Harnad *et al.*, eds., pp. xvii-xlviii, Academic Press, New York.
101. Skutch, A.E. 1976. *Parent Birds and Their Young*. U. Texas, Austin.

102. Thorpe, W.H. 1956. *Learning and Instinct in Animals*. Methuen & Co., London.
103. Farner, D.S. and J.R. King. 1971. Preface of *Avian Biology*, vol. 1, Farner, D.S. and J.R. King, eds., pp. xiii-xvi. Academic Press, New York.
104. Rutgers, A. 1965. *The Handbook of Foreign Birds*, vol. 2. Blandford Press, London.
105. Haartman, L. von. 1957. Adaptation in hole-nesting birds. *Evol.*, **11**:339-347.
106. Cracraft, J. 1973. Continental drift, paleoclimatology, and the evolution and biogeography of birds. *J. Zool.*, **169**:455-545.
107. Darwin, C. 1871. *The Descent of Man and Selection in Relation to Sex*. John Murray, London.
108. Stebbins, G.L. 1969. *The Basis of Progressive Evolution*. U. North Carolina Press, Chapel Hill.
109. Armstrong, E.A. 1973. *A Study of Birdsong*. Dover Publs. Inc., New York.
110. Mason, J.R., Aret, A.H. and R.F. Reidinger. 1984. Comparative assessment of food preferences and aversions via observational learning. *Auk*, **101**:796-803.
111. Mayr, E. 1980. Problems of Classification of Birds. *Proc. Int. Ornithol. Congr.*, **XVII**:95-112.
112. Keeton, W.T. 1980. Avian orientation and navigation: New developments in an old mystery. *ibid.*, **XVII**:137-157.
113. Leisler, B. 1980. Ökomorphologische Freiland- und Laboratoriumsuntersuchungen. *ibid.*, **XVII**:202-208.
114. Walsberg, G.E. 1980. Energy expenditure in free-living birds: Patterns and diversity. *ibid.*, **XVII**:300-305.
115. O'Connor, R.J. 1980. Energetics of reproduction in birds. *ibid.*, **XVII**:306-311.
116. Wyndham, E. 1980. Aspects of biorhythms in the Budgerigar *Melopsittacus undulatus* (Shaw), a parrot of inland Australia. *ibid.*, **XVII**:485-492.
117. Papi, F. et al. 1980. Olfactory and magnetic cues in pigeon navigation. *ibid.*, **XVII**: 569-573.
118. Kreithen, M.L. 1980. New sensory cues for bird navigation. *ibid.*, **XVII**:582-587.
119. Saunders, J.C. 1980. Frequency selectivity in parakeet hearing: Behavioral and physiological evidence. *ibid.*, **XVII**:615-619.
120. Feduccia, A. 1980. Morphology of the bony stapes (columella) in birds: Evolutionary implications. *ibid.*, **XVII**:620-624.
121. Marler, P. 1980. Song learning, dialects, and auditory templates: An ethological viewpoint. *ibid.*, **XVII**:637-641.
122. Rogers, L.J. 1980. Functional lateralization in the chicken forebrain revealed by cycloheximide treatment. *ibid.*, **XVII**:653-659.
123. King, W.B. 1980. Ecological basis of extinction in birds. *ibid.*, **XVII**:905-911.
124. Ripley, S.D. 1980. The potential of captive breeding to save endangered bird species. *ibid.*, **XVII**:923-926.
125. Liversidge, R. 1980. Seasonal changes in the use of avian habitat in Southern Africa. *ibid.*, **XVII**:1019-1024.
126. Snow, D.W. 1980. Regional differences between tropical floras and the evolution of frugivory. *ibid.*, **XVII**:1192-1198.
127. Smith, G.A. 1978. *Encyclopedia of Cockatiels*. TFH Publs., Neptune, N.J.
128. Vane, E.N. 1957. Rearing the Yellow-cheeked Amazon. *Avicult. Mag.*, **63**:183-188.

129. Eisner, E. 1961. The behavior of the Bengalese Finch in the nest. *Ardea*, **49**:51-69.
130. ____. 1960. The biology of the Bengalese Finch. *Auk*, **77**:271-287.
131. Feduccia, A. and H.B. Tordoff. 1979. Feathers of *Archaeopteryx*: asymmetrical vanes indicate aerodynamic function. *Science*, **203**:1021-1022.
132. Provine, R.R. 1984. Wing-flapping during development and evolution. *Amer. Sci.*, **72**:448-455.
133. Hamburger, V. and R.W. Oppenheim. 1982. Naturally occurring neuronal death in vertebrates. *Neurosci. Com.*, **1**:39-55.
134. Skadhauge, E. 1975. Renal and cloacal transport of salt and water. *Symp. Zool. Soc, London*, **35**:97-106.
____. 1978. Hormonal regulation of salt and water balance in seed-eating birds. In *Environmental Endocrinology*, pp. 222-229. Springer Verlag, New York.
135. Arnall, L. and I.F. Keymer. 1975. *Bird Diseases*. TFH Publs., Neptune, N.J.
136. Rogers, C.H. 1975. *Encyclopedia of Cage and Aviary Birds*. Pelham Books, Ltd., London.
137. Keymer, I.F. 1972. The Budgerigar. In *The UFAW Handbook of the Care and Management of Laboratory Animals*, ed. UFAW. Churchill Livingston, London.
138. Boosey, E.J. 1962. *Foreign Bird Keeping*. Iliffe Books Ltd., London.
139. Frith, H.J. 1969. *Birds in the Australian High Country*. A.H. & A.W. Reed, Sydney.
140. Brown, J.L. 1975. *The Evolution of Behavior*. Norton, New York.
141. Harrison, G.J., guest ed. 1984. *The Veterin. Clinics of N.A. Small Anim. Prac.*, vol. 14(2). W.B. Saunders, Philadelphia.
142. Rosskopf, W.J., Woerpel, R.W., Yanoff, S.R., Howard, E.B. and J.O. Britt. 1981. Dietary-induced parathyroid hyperplasia in a macaw. *Avian Practice*, Oct., pp. 778-779.
____, ____, and ____. 1981. Preservation responses in a dying Military Macaw. *ibid.*, pp. 1458-1459.
____, ____, Rosskopf, G. and D. Van De Water. 1982. Hematologic and blood chemistry values for common pet avian species. *ibid.*, Aug., pp.1233-1239.
____ and ____. 1983-84. Avian Axioms. *AFA Watchbird*, **X(6)**:5-6.
____ and ____. 1984. Symptomatology. *ibid.*, **XI(1)**:8-9.
____ and ____. 1984. Egg binding in cage and aviary birds. *ibid.*, **XI(2)**:5.
143. Pastore, N. 1954. Discrimination learning in the Canary. *J. Comp. Physiol. Psychol.*, **47**:288-289, 389-390.
____. 1961. Number sense and "counting" ability in the Canary. *Z. Tierpsychol.*, **18**:561-573.
144. Thomson, A.L., ed. 1964. *A New Dictionary of Birds*. McGraw-Hill, New York.
145. Swaiman, K.F. and F.S. Wright. 1975. *The Practice of Pediatric Neurology*. C.V. Mosby Co., St. Louis.
146. Luhan, J.A. 1968. *Neurology*., Williams & Wilkins Co., Baltimore.
147. Matthews, W.B. 1982. *Diseases of the Nervous System*. Blackwell Scientific Publics., Boston.
148. Fulton, J.F. and A.D. Keller. 1932. *The Sign of Babinski*. C.C. Thomas, Boston.
149. Innes, J.R.M. and L.Z. Saunders. 1962. *Comparative Neuropathology*. Academic Press, New York.
150. Steegmann, A.T. 1970. *Examination of the Nervous System*. Year Book Medical Publishers, Inc., Chicago.

151. Serventy, D.L. 1976. Introduction: Origins of Australasian avifauna. *Proc. Int. Ornithol. Congr.*, **XVI**:39.

152. Cracraft, J. 1976. Avian evolution in southern continents: Influences of paleogeography and paleoclimatology. *ibid.*, **XVI**:40-52.

153. Keast, A. 1976. The origins of adaptive zone utilizations and adaptive radiations, as illustrated by the Australian Meliphagidae. *ibid.*, **XVI**:71-81; Biological attributes and continental characteristics. *ibid.*, **XVI**:103-108.

154. Kirkpatrick, M. 1982. Sexual selection in the evolution of female choice. *Evol.*, **36**:1-12.

155. Dorst, J. 1974. *The Life of Birds.* Weidenfeld & Nicolson, London.

156. Ziswiler, V. 1976. Special Morphological Characters. *Proc. Int. Ornithol. Congr.*, **XVI**:201-205.

157. Dawson, W.R. 1976. Physiological and behavioral adjustments of birds to heat and aridity. *ibid.*, **XVI**:455-467.

158. Maclean, G.L. 1976. Arid-zone Ornithology in Africa and South America. *ibid.*, **XVI**:468-480.

159. Bergstrom, P.W. 1981. Male incubation in Wilson's Plover (*Charadrius wilsonia*). *Auk*, **98**:835-838.

160. Davies, S.J. 1976. Environmental variables and the biology of Australian and arid zone birds. *Proc. Int. Ornithol. Congr.*, **XVI**:481-488.

161. Bartholomew, G.A. 1972. The water economy of seed-eating birds that survive without drinking. *ibid.*, **XV**:237-254.

162. Vince, M.A. 1972. Communication between quail embryos and the synchronization of hatching. *ibid.*, **XV**:357-362.

163. Nelson, J.B. 1972. Evolution of the pair bond in the Sulidae. *ibid.*, **XV**:371-388.

164. Serventy, D.L. 1972. Causal Ornithogeography of Australia. *ibid.*, **XV**:371-388.

____. 1973. Origin and structure of Australian bird fauna. In *Birds of Australia*, by J.D. Macdonald, pp. 21-28, Reed Pty. Ltd., Sydney.

165. Hall, B.P. and R.E. Moreau. 1970. *An Atlas of Speciation in African Passerine Birds.*, British Museum, London

166 Keast, A. 1972. Faunal elements and evolutionary patterns:Some comparisons between the continental avifaunas of Africa, South America, and Australia. *Proc. Int. Ornithol. Congr.*, **XV**:594-622.

167. Safriel, U.N. 1972. The significance of clutch size in nidifugous birds. *ibid.*, **XV**:684.

168. Horner, J.R. and R. Makela. 1979. Nest of juveniles provides evidence of family structure among dinosaurs. *Nature*, **282**:296-298.

169. Feduccia, A. 1980. *The Age of Birds.* Harvard U. Press, Cambridge.

170. Regal, P.J. 1975. The evolutionary origin of feathers. *Quart. Rev. Biol.*, **50**:35-66.

171. Wyndham, E. 1980. Diurnal cycle, behavior and social organization of the Budgerigar *Melopsittacus undulatus*. *Emu*, **80**:25-33.

____. 1981. Breeding and mortality of the Budgerigar *Melopsittacus undulatus*. *ibid.*, **81**:240-242.

____. 1982. Movements and breeding seasons of the Budgerigar. *ibid.*, **82**:276-282.

172. Raven, P.H. and D.I. Axelrod. 1975. History of the flora and fauna of Latin America. *Amer. Sci.*, **63**:420-429.

173. Rich, P.V. 1975. Changing continental arrangements and the origin of Australia's non-passeriform continental avifauna. *Emu*, **75**:97-112.

174. Gilliard, E.T. 1958. *Living Birds of the World.* Doubledy & Co., Garden City, New York.

175. Olson, S.L . 1976. Alexander Wetmore and the study of fossil birds. *Smithson. Contrib. Paleobiol.*, **27**:xi-xvi.
176. Saunders, D.A., Smith, G.T. and N.A. Campbell. 1984. Egg shape within the Australian Psittaciformes with comments on the egg of *Nymphicus hollandicus*. *Emu*, **84**:36-37.
177. Carter, G.S. 1967. *Structure and Habit in Vertebrate Evolution*. U. Wash. Press, Seattle.
178. Meier, A.H. 1981. In review of *Biological Rhythms in Birds*. *Auk*, **98**:852.
179. Whetstone, K.N. and L.D. Martin. 1979. New Look at the origin of birds and crocodiles. *Nature*, **279**:234-236.
180. Sharov, A.G. 1970. An unusual reptile from the Lower Triassic of Fergana (in Russian). *Paleont. Zh.*, **1**:127-130.
181. Lack, D. 1954. *The Natural Regulation of Animal Numbers*. Oxford U. Press, London.
182. Olson, E.C. 1971. *Vertebrate Paleozoology*. Wiley-Interscience, New York.
183. Ficken, M.S. and W.C. Dilger. 1960. Comments on redirection with examples of avian copulations with substitute objects. *Behaviour*, **8**:219-222.
184. Raven, P.H. and D.I. Axelrod. 1974. Angiosperm biogeography and past continental movements. *Ann. Missouri Bot. Garden*, **61**:539-673.
185. Hart. E.H. 1978. *Budgerigar Handbook*. TFH Publs., Neptune, N.J.
186. Lewin, R. 1984. The paleoclimatic magic numbers game. *Science*, **226**:154-156.
____. 1985. Paleoclimates in Southern Africa. *Science*, **227**:1325-327.
187. Stevens, T.S. 1888. Notes on an intelligent parrot. *J. Trenton Nat. Hist. Soc.*, **3**:347-356.
188. Gould, S.J. 1985. A clock of evolution. *Nat. Hist.*, **92(4)**:12-25.
189. Mayr, E. 1983. The joy of birds. *ibid.*, **92(9)**:1
190. James, H.F. and S.L. Olson. 1983. Flightless birds. *ibid.*, **92(9)**: 30-40.
191. Able, K.P. 1983. A migratory bird's Baedeker. *ibid.*, **92(9)**:22-27.
192. Gould, S.J. 1983. Darwin at sea. *ibid.*, **92(9)**:14-20.
193. Martin, L.D. 1983. The origin of birds and of avian flight. *Curr. Ornithol.*, **1**:105-129.
194. Sibley, C.G. and J. E. Ahlquist. 1983. Phylogeny and classification of birds based on the DNA data of DNA-DNA hybridization. *ibid.*, **1**:245-292.
195. Abbott, I. 1980. Theories dealing with the ecology of landbirds on islands. *Adv. Ecol. Res.*, **11**:329-371.
196. Sibley, C.G. and J.E. Ahlquist. 1984. The relationships of the starlings (Sturnidae: Sturninae) and the mockingbirds (Sturnidae: Mimini). *Auk*, **101**:230-243.
197. Flint, E.N. and K.A. Nagy. 1984. Flight energetics in free-living Sooty Terns. *ibid.*, **101**:288-294.
198. Ingels, J.I., Ribot, J.-H. and B.H.J. de Jong. 1984. Vulnerability of eggs and young of the Blackish Nightjar (*Caprimulgus nigrescens*) in Suriname. *ibid.*, **101**:388-391.
199. Farabaugh, S.M. 1982. The ecological and social significance of duetting. In *Acoustical Communication in Birds*, vol. 2, Kroodsma, D.E. and E.H. Miller, eds., pp. 85-124. Academic Press, New York.
200. Parrish, J.W., Ptacek, J.A. and K.L. Will. 1984. The detection of near-ultraviolet light by nonmigratory and migratory birds. *Auk*, **101**:53-58.
201. Morse, D.H. and S.W. Kress. 1984. The effect of burrow loss on mate choice in the Leach's Storm-Petrel. *ibid.*, **101**:158-160.

202. Roby, D.D. and R.E. Ricklefs. 1984. Observations of the cooling tolerance of embryos of the Diving Petrel (*Pelecanoides georgi cus*). *ibid.*, **101**:160-161.

203. Gould, S.J. and R.C. Lewontin. 1979. The spandrels of San Marco and the panglossian paradigm: A critique of the adaptationist program. *Proc. Roy. Soc. London, Ser. B*, **205**:581-598.

204. Peters, R.H. 1976. Tautology in evolution and ecology, *Amer. Natur.*, **110**:1-7.

____. 1978. Predictable problems with tautology in evolution and ecology, *ibid.*, **112**:759-762.

205. James, F.C. and C.E. McCulloch. 1985. Data analysis and the design of experiments in ornithology. *Curr. Ornithol.*, **2**:1-63.

206. Olson, S.L. 1981. The museum tradition in ornithology--A response to Ricklefs. *Auk*, **98**:193-195.

207. Gaunt, A.S. and S.L.L. Gaunt. 1985. Syringeal structure and avian phonation. *Curr. Ornithol.*, **2**:213-245.

208. Goldstein, G.B. and M.C. Baker. 1984. Seed selection by juncos. *Wilson Bull.*, **96**:458-463.

209. Raitt, R.J., Winterstein, S.R. and J.W. Hardy. 1984. Structure and dynamics of communal groups in the Beechey Jay. *ibid.*, **96**: 206-227.

210. Sauer, G.C. 1982. *John Gould--The Bird Man: A Chronology and Bibliography.* U. Press of Kansas, Lawrence.

211. West, M.J. and A.N. Stroud. 1983. Mimicry of the human voice by European Starlings: the role of social interaction. *Wilson Bull.*, **95**:635-640.

212. Todt, D. 1975. Social learning of vocal patterns and modes of their application in Grey Parrots (*Psittacus erithacus*). *Z. Tierpsychol.*, **39**:178-188.

213. Hepp, G.R. and J.D. Hair. 1983. Reproductive behavior and pairing chronology in wintering Dabbling Ducks. *Wilson Bull.*, **95**:675-682.

214. Grant, G.G. 1982. Avian incubation: Egg temperature, nest humidity, and behavioral thermoregulation in a hot environment. *Ornithol. Mono.* **No. 30**, The Amer. Ornithol. Union, Washington, D.C.

215. Brunswig, N.L. and S.G. Winton. 1983. A dietary overlap of Evening Grosbeaks and Carolina Parakeets. *Wilson Bull.*, **96**:452.

216. Walkinshaw, L.H. 1940. Summer life of the Sora Rail. *Auk*, **57**:153-168.

217. Curtis, P.D. and C.E. Braun. 1983. Radiotelemetry location of nesting Band-tailed Pigeons in Colorado. *Wilson Bull.*, **95**:233-242.

218. Bechard, M.J. 1983. Food supply and the occurrence of brood reduction in Swainson's Hawk. *ibid.*, **95**:233-242.

219. Winterstein, S.R. and R.J. Raitt. 1983. Nestling growth and development and the breeding ecology of the Beechey Jay. *ibid.*, **95**: 256-268.

220. Ricklefs, R.E. 1983. Comparative avian demography. *Curr. Ornithol.*, **1**:1-32.

221. Nice, M.M. 1962. Development of Behavior in Precocial birds. *Trans. Linn. Soc. N.Y.*, **8**:1-211.

222. Winkler, D.W. and J.R. Walters. 1983. The determination of clutch size in precocial birds. *Curr. Ornithol.*, **1**:33-68.

223. Heagy, P.A. and L.B. Best. 1983. Factors affecting feeding and brooding of Brown Thrasher nestlings. *Wilson Bull.*, **95**:297-303.

224. Kridelbaugh, A. 1983. Nesting ecology of the Loggerhead Shrike in central Missouri. *ibid.*, **95**:303-308.

225. Kushlan, J.A. 1983. Pair formation behavior of the Galapagos Lava Heron. *ibid.* **95**:118-121.

226. Carey, C. 1983. Structure and function of avian eggs. *Curr. Ornithol.*, **1**:69-103.
227. Ford, N.L. 1983. Variation in mate fidelity in monogamous birds. *ibid.*, **1**:329-356.
228. Kroodsma, D.E., Meservey, W.R. and R. Pickert. 1983. Vocal learning in the Parulinae. *Wilson Bull.*, **95**:138-140.
229. Clark, G.A., Jr. 1983. An additional method of foraging in litter by species of *Turdus* thrushes. *ibid.*, **95**:155-157.
230. Howell, T.R. 1979. Brooding biology of the Egyptian Plover, *Pluvianus aegyptius. Univ. Calif. Publ. Zool.*, **113**, 93 pp.
231. Burtt, E.H., Jr. 1983. Head-scratching method of Galapagos Finches unaffected by variation in cranial morphology. *Wilson Bull.*, **95**:158-160.
232. Perrins, C.M. 1979. *British Tits.* William Collins Sons Co., London.
233. Immelmann, K. 1965. *Australian Finches.* Angus & Robertson, Sydney.
234. Rahn, H., Ar, A. and C.V. Paganelli. 1979. How bird eggs breath. *Sci. Amer.*, **240**:38-47.
235. Vanderstoep, J. and J.F. Richards. 1970. The changes in egg shell strength during incubation. *Poult. Sci.*, **49**:276-285.
236. Simkiss, K. 1961. Calcium metabolism and avian reproduction. *Biol. Rev. Cambr. Philos. Soc.*, **36**:321-367.
237. Zusi, R.L. 1984. A functional and evolutionary analysis of rhynchokinesis in birds. *Smithson. Contrib. Zool.*, **No. 395**, Smithson- Instn. Press, Washington, D.C.
238. Buitron, D. and G.L. Neuchterlein. 1985. Experiments on olfactory detection of food caches by Black-billed Magpies. *Condor.*, **87**: 92-95.
239. Ricklefs, R.E. 1977. Composition of eggs of several bird species. *Auk*, **94**:350-356.
240. Brawn, J.D. 1984. Defense of nest boxes by Western Bluebirds during the post-breeding period. *Condor*, **86**:494-495.
241. Nottebohm, F. 1984. Birdsong as a model in which to study brain processes related to learning. *ibid.*, **86**:227-236.
242. Breitwisch, R. and P.G. Merritt. 1984. Why do Northern Mockingbirds feed fruit to their nestlings? *ibid.*, **86**:281-287.
243. Gavrilov, V.M. and V.R. Dol'nik. 1984. [Bioenergetics and regulation of the postnuptial and postjuvenal molt in Chaffinches *Fringilla c. coelebs.*] *Tr. Zool. Nauk. SSSR*, **55**:14-61 (In Russian).
244. Murphy, M.E. and J.R. King. 1984. Sulfur amino acid nutrition during molt in the White-crowned Sparrow. *Condor*, **86**:314-332.
245. Ricklefs, R.E. 1983. Avian postnatal development. In *Avian Biology*, vol. VII, Farner, D.S., King, J.R. and K.C. Parkes, eds., pp. 1-83, Academic Press, New York.
246. Portmann, A. 1950. Le developpement postembyonaire, vol. 15, In *Traité de Zoologie*, P.-P. Grasse, ed., Masson, Paris.
247. Smith, S.M. 1983. The ontogeny of avian behavior. In *Avian Biology*, vol. VII, Farner, D.S., King, J.R. and K.C. Parkes, eds., pp. 85-160, Academic Press, New York.
248. Mundinger, P.C. 1970. Vocal imitation and individual recognition of finch calls. *Science*, **168**:480-482.
249. Diamond, J.M. 1972. Further examples of dual singing by southwest Pacific birds. *Auk*, **89**:180-183.
250. Thorpe, W.H. and M.E.W. North. 1965. Origin and Significance of the power of vocal imitation: with special reference to the antiphonal singing of birds. *Nature*, **208**:219-222.
251. Payne, R.B. 1973. Behavior, mimetic songs and song dielects, and the relationships of the parasitic Indigobirds (*Vidua*) of Africa. *Ornithol. Monogr.*, **11**:1-133.

Payne, R.B. and K. Payne. 1977. Social organization and mating success in local song populations of Village Indigobirds, *Vidua chalybeata*. *Z. Tierpsychol.*, **45**:113-173.

252. Stokes, A.W. 1971. Parental and courtship feeding in Red Jungle Fowl. *Auk*, **88**:21-29.
253. Kear, J. 1962. Food selection in finches with special reference to interspecific differences. *Proc. Zool. Soc. London*, **138**:163-204.
254. Ligon, J.D. and D.J. Martin. 1974. Piñon seed assessment by the Piñon Jay, *Gymnorhinus cyanocephalus*. *Anim. Behav.*, **22**:421-429.
255. Mueller, H.C. 1974. The development of prey recognition and predatory behaviour in the American Kestrel *Falco sparverius*. *Behaviour*, **49**:313-324.
256. Smith, S.M. 1973. A study of prey-attack behaviour in young Loggerhead Shrikes (*Lanius ludovicianus*) *Behaviour*, **44**:113-141.
257. Walsberg, G.E. 1983. Avian ecological energetics. In *Avian Biology*, vol. VII, Farner, D.S., King, J.R. and K.C. Parkes, eds., pp. 161-220.
258. Gaunt, A.S. 1983. An hypothesis concerning the relationship of syringeal structure to vocal abilities. *Auk*, **100**:853-862.
259. Brown, L.H., Urban, E.K. and K. Newman. 1982. *The Birds of Africa*, vol. 1, Academic Press, New York.
260. Balthazart, J. 1983. Hormonal correlates of behavior. In *Avian Biology*, vol. VII, Farner, D.S., King, J.R. and K.C. Parkes, eds., pp. 221-365.
261. Collias, N.E. 1944. Aggressive behavior among vertebrate animals. *Physiol. Zool.*, **17**:83-123.
262. Barfield, R.J. 1965. Induction of aggressive and courtship behavior by intracerebral implants of androgen in capons. *Amer. Zool.*, **5**:203.

____.1969. Activation of copulatory behavior by androgen implanted into the preoptic area of the male fowl. *Horm. Behav.*, **1**:37-52.

____. 1971. Activation of sexual and aggressive behavior by androgen implanted into the male Ring Dove brain. *Endocrin.*,**3**:709-712.

263. Gardner, J.A. and A.E. Fisher 1968. Induction of mating in male chicks following preoptic implantation of androgen. *Physiol. Behav.*, 3:709-712.
264. Crawford, W.C. and B.Glick. 1975. The function of preoptic mammilaris lateralis and ruber nuclei in normal and sexually inactive male chickens. *ibid.*, **15**:171-175.
265. Gibson, M.J. and M.F. Cheng. 1979. Neural mediation of estrogen-dependent courtship behavior in female Ring Doves. *J. Comp. Physiol. Psychol.*, **93**:855-867.

____ and ____ . 1981. The role of the midbrain in courtship behavior of the female Ring Dove (*Streptopelia risoria*): evidence from radio frequency lesion and hormone implant studies. *Brain Res.*, **207**:279-301.

266. Erickson, C.J. and J.B. Hutchison. 1977. Induction of nest-material collecting in male Barbary Doves by intracerebral androgen. *J. Reprod. Fertil.*, **50**:9-16.
267. Ball, G.H. 1983. Functional incubation in male Barn Swallows. *Auk*, **100**:998-1000.
268. Peterson, J. 1955. The breeding cycle of the Bank Swallow. *Wilson Bull.*, **67**:235-286.
269. Bailey, R.E. 1952. The incubation patch of passerine birds. *Condor*, **54**:121-136.

270. Hatch, S.A. 1983. Mechanism and ecological significance of sperm storage in the Northern Fulmar with reference to its occurrence in other birds. *Auk*, **100**:593-600.
271. Walsberg, G.E. 1983. In review of *Avian Incubation: Egg Temperature, Nest Humidity, and Behavioral Thermoregulation in a Hot Environment*. (ref. 214), by G.S. Grant. *Auk*, **100**:776-778.
272. Gratto, C.L., Morrison, R.I.G. and F. Cooke. 1985. Philopatry, site tenacity, and mate fidelity in the Semipalmated Sandpiper. *Auk*, **102**:16-24.
273. Komeda, S. 1983. Nest attendance of parent birds in the Painted Snipe (*Rostratula benghalensis*). *Auk*, **100**:48-55.
274. Ar, A. and H. Rahn. 1980. Water in the avian egg: overall budget of incubation. *Amer. Zool*., **20**:373-384.
275. Simpson, S.F. and J. Cracraft. 1981. The phylogenetic relationships of the Piciformes (Class Aves). *Auk*, **98**:481-494.
276. Olson, S.L. 1983. Evidence for a polyphyletic origin of the Piciformes. *Auk*, **100**:126-133.
277. Morton, M.L. and M.E. Pereyra. 1985. The regulation of egg temperatures and attentiveness patterns in the Dusky Flycatcher (*Empidonax oberholseri*). *Auk*, **102**:25-37.
278. Pettit, T.N., Grant, G.S. and G.C. Whittow. 1982. Body Temperature and growth of Bonin Petrel chicks. *Wilson Bull*., **94**:358-361.
279. Martin, P.G. 1977. Marsupial biogeography and plate tectonics. In *The Biology of Marsupials*, Stonehouse, B. and D. Gilmore, eds., Macmillan Press Ltd., London
280. Archer, M. and B. Fox. 1984. Background to vertebrate zoogeography in Australia. In *Vertebrate Zoogeography and Evolution in Australia*, Archer, M. and G. Clayton, eds., pp. 1-15, Hesperian Press, New S. Wales, Australia.
281. Martin, H.A. 1978. Evolution of the Australian flora and vegetation through the Tertiary: evidence from pollen. *Alcheringa*, **2**: 181-202.
282. Martin, H.A. 1984. Australian phytogeography. In *Vertebrate Zoogeography and Evolution in Australia*, Archer, M. and G. Clayton, eds., pp. 17-30, Hesperian Press, New S. Wales, Australia.
283. Fox, B. 1984. Ecological principles of zoogeography. *ibid*., pp. 31-43.
284. Archer, M. 1984. Earth-shattering concepts for historical zoogeography. *ibid*., pp. 45-59.
285. Kemp, E.M. 1984. Tertiary palaeogeography and the evolution of Australian climate. *ibid*., pp. 61-67.
286. Hope, J. 1984. The Australian Quaternary. *ibid*., pp. 69-81.
287. Galloway, R. and E.M. Kemp. 1984. Late Cainozoic environments in Australia. *ibid*., pp. 83-95.
288. Archer, M. 1984. Evolution of arid Australia and its consequences for vertebrates. *ibid*., pp. 98-108.
289. Molnar, R. and M. Archer. 1984. Feeble and not so feeble flapping fliers: A consideration of early birds and bird-like reptiles. *ibid*., pp. 409-419.
290. Rich, P. and G. van Tets. 1984. What fossil birds contribute towards an understanding of origin and development of the Australian avifauna. *ibid*., pp. 421-446.
291. Rich, P. and J. Balouet. 1984. The waifs and strays of the bird world or the ratite problem revisited, one more time. *ibid*., pp. 447-455.
292. Keast, A. 1984. Contemporary ornithogeography: the Australian avifauna, its relationships and evolution. *ibid*., pp. 457-468.

293. Harrison, C.J.O. 1982. The earliest parrot: A new species from the British Eocene. *Ibis*, **124**:203-210.
294. Brodkorb, P. 1971. Catalogue of fossil birds. Part 4 (Columbiformes through Piciformes). *Bull. Fla. St. Mus. Biol. Sci.*, **15**:163-266.
295. Beach, F.A. 1958. Evolutionary aspects of psychoendocrinology. In *Behavior and Evolution*, Roe, A. and G.G. Simpson, eds., pp. 81-102, Yale U. Press, New Haven.
296. Hinde, R.A. and N. Tinbergen. 1958. A comparative study of species-specific behavior. *ibid*., pp. 251-268.
297. Mayr, E. 1958. Behavior and systematics. *ibid*., pp. 341-362.
298. Simpson, G.G. 1958. The study of evolution: methods and present status of the theory. *ibid*. pp. 7-26.
299. Sperry, R.W. 1958. Developmental basis of behavior. *ibid*., pp. 128-139.
300. Macdonald, J.D. 1973. *Birds of Australia*. Reed Pty. Ltd., Sydney.
301. Peters, J.L. 1937. *Check-List of Birds of the World*, vol. 3, Harvard U. Press, Cambridge.
302. Chaplin, S.B. 1982. The energetic significance of huddling behavior in Common Bushtits (*Psaltriparus minimus*). *Auk*, **99**:424-430.
303. Mason, J.R. and R.F. Reidinger. 1981. Effects of social facilitation and observational learning on feeding behavior of the Red-winged Blackbird (*Agelaius phoeniceus*). *ibid*., **98**:778-784.
____ and ____. 1982. Observational learning of food aversions in Red-winged Blackbirds (*Agelaius phoeniceus*). *ibid*., **99**:548-554.
304. Kollar, E.J. and C. Fisher. 1980. Tooth induction in chick epithelium: expression of quiescent genes for enamel synthesis. *Science*, **207**:993-995.
305. Slijper, E.S. 1946. Comparative biologic-anatomical investigations on the vertebral column and spinal musculation of mammals. *Verh. koninkl. Nederland. Akad. Wetenschap., afd. naturkunde*., tweede sectie, deel XVII, **No. 5**:1-128.
306. Schreiber, R.W. 1983. In review of *Avian Biology*, vol. VI, Farner, D.S., King, J.R. and K.C. Parkes, eds., *Auk*, **100**:509-511.
307. MacArthur, R.H. 1971. Patterns of terrestrial bird communities. In *Avian Biology*, vol. 1, Farner, D.S. and J.R. King eds., pp. 189-221, Academic Press, New York.
308. Brodkorb, P. 1971. Origin and evolution of birds. *ibid*., pp. 19-55.
309. Storer, R.W. 1971. Classification of birds. *ibid*., pp. 1-18; Adaptive radiation in birds. *ibid*., pp. 150-188.
310. Selander, R.K. 1971. Systematics and speciation in birds. *ibid*., pp. 57-147.
311. Serventy, D.L. 1971. Biology of desert birds. *ibid*., pp. 287-339.
312. Immelmann, K. 1971. Ecological aspects of periodic reproduction. *ibid*., pp. 342-389.
313. Haartman, L. von. 1971. Population dynamics. *ibid*., pp. 392-459.
314. Cody, M.L. 1971. Ecological aspects of reproduction. *ibid*., pp. 462-512.
315. Orians, G. 1971. Ecological aspects of behavior. *ibid*., pp. 513-546
316. Ashmole, N.P. 1971. Sea bird ecology and the marine environment. *ibid*., pp. 224-286.
317. Gould, J. 1865. *Handbook of the Birds of Australia*, vol. 1. the author, London.
318. Stettenheim, P. 1972. The integument of birds. In *Avian Biology*, vol. II, Farner, D.S. and J.R. King, eds., pp. 1-63, Academic Press, New York.
319. Payne, R.B. 1972. Mechanisms and control of molt. *ibid*., pp. 103-155.

320. Jones, D.R. and K. Johansen. 1972. The blood vascular system of birds. *ibid.*, pp. 157-285.
321. Lasiewsky, R.C. 1972. Respiratory function in birds. *ibid.*, pp. 287-342.
322. Ziswiler, V. and D.S. Farner. 1972. Digestion and the digestive system. *ibid.*, pp. 343-430.
323. Fisher, H. 1972. The nutrition of birds. *ibid.*, pp.431-469.
324. Hazelwood, R.L. 1972. The intermediate metabolism of birds. *ibid.*, pp. 471-526.
325. Shoemaker, V.H. 1972. Osmoregulation and excretion in birds. *ibid.*, pp. 527-574.
326. Howell, T.R. and G.A. Bartholomew. 1959. Further experiments on torpidity in the Poor-will. *Condor*, **61**:180-185.
327. Tinbergen, N. 1953. *The Herring Gull's World*, Collins, London.
328. Maclean, G.L. 1974. Egg-covering in the Charadrii. *Ostrich*, **45**: 167-174.
329. Ar, A. and Y. Yom-Tov. 1978. The evolution of parental care in birds. *Evolution*, **32**:655-669.
330. Tucker, V.A. 1968. Respiratory physiology of House Sparrows in relation to high-altitude flight. *J. Exp. Biol.*, **48**:55-56; Respiratory exchange and evaporative water loss in the flying Budgerigar. *ibid.*, **48**:67-87.
331. Bartholomew, G.A. and T.J. Cade. 1963. The water economy of land birds. *Auk*, **80**:504-539.
332. Mickelsen, O. and M.G. Yang. 1966. Naturally occurring toxicants in foods. *Fed. Proc.*, **25**:104-123.
333. Swinton, W.E. 1960. The origin of birds. In *Biology and Comparative Physiology of Birds*, vol. 1, A.J. Marshall, ed., pp. 1-14, Academic Press, New York.
334. Storer, R.W. 1960. Adaptive radiation in birds. *ibid.*, pp. 15-55.
335. Serventy, D.L. 1960. Geographical distribution of living birds. *ibid.*, pp. 95-126.
336. Bellairs, R. 1960. Development of birds *ibid.*, pp. 127-188.
337. Rawls, M.E. 1960. The integumentary system. *ibid.*, pp. 189-240.
338. Bellairs, A. d'A. and C.R. Jenkin. 1960. The skeleton of birds. *ibid.*, pp.241-300.
339. Simon, J.R. 1960. The blood-vascular system. *ibid.*, pp. 345-362.
340. Salt, G.W. and E. Zeuthen. 1960. The respiratory system. *ibid.*, pp. 363-409.
341. Farner, D.S. 1960. Digestion and the digestive system. *ibid.*, pp. 411-467.
342. Portmann, A. and W. Stingelin. 1960. The central nervous system. In *Biology and Comparative Physiology of Birds*, vol. 2, A.J. Marshall, ed., pp.1-36. Academic Press, New York.
343. Portmann, A. 1960. Sensory organs: Skin, taste, olfaction. *ibid.* pp. 37-68.
344. Pumphrey, R.J. 1960. Sensory organs: Vision. *ibid.*, pp. 55-68.
345. ____ 1960. Sensory organs: Hearing. *ibid.*, pp. 69-86.
346. Höhn, E.O. 1960. Endocrine glands, thymus and pineal body. *ibid.*, pp. 87-114.
347. Witschi, E. 1960. Sex and secondary sex characters. *ibid.*, pp. 115-168.
348. Marshall, A.J. 1960. Reproduction. *ibid.*, pp. 169-213.
349. King, J.R. and D.S. Farner. 1960. Energy metabolism, thermoregulation and body temperature. *ibid.*, pp. 215-288.
350. Marshall, A.J. 1960. Breeding seasons and migration. *ibid.*, pp. 307-339.
351. Hinde, R.A. 1960. Behavior. *ibid.*, pp. 373-411.

352. Gibb, J.A. 1960. Bird populations. *ibid.*, pp. 413-446.
353. Lack, D. 1956. Variations in the reproductive rate of birds. *Proc. Royal Soc.* **B145**:329-333.
354. Nice, M.M. 1957. Nesting success in altricial birds. *Auk*, **74**:305-321.
355. McDiarmid, A. 1956. Some diseases of free-living wild birds in Britain. *Bull. Brit. Ornithol. Club*, **76**:145-150.
356. Pianka, E.R. 1977. Reptilian species diversity. In *Biology of the Reptilia*, vol. 7, Gans, C. and D.W. Tinkle, eds., pp. 1-34, Academic Press, New York.
357. Schoener, T.W. 1977. Competition and the niche. *ibid.*, pp. 35-136.
358. Burghardt, G.M. 1977. Learning processes in reptiles. *ibid.*, pp. 555-681.
359. Herrick, C.J. 1948. *The Brain of the Tiger Salamander, Ambistoma tigrinum.* U. Chicago Press, Chicago.
360. Minnich, J.E. 1982. The use of water. In *Biology of the Reptilia*, vol. 12, Gans, C. and F.H. Pough, eds. pp. 325-395. Academic Press, New York.
361. Bartholomew, G.A. 1982. Physiological control of body temperature. *ibid.*, pp. 167-211.
362. Gans, C. and F.H. Pough. 1982. Physiological ecology: Its debt to reptilian studies, its value to students of reptiles. *ibid.*, pp. 1-13.
363. Huey, R.B. 1982. Temperature, physiology, and the ecology of reptiles. *ibid.*, pp. 25-91.
364. Tracy, C.R. 1982. Biophysical modeling in reptilian physiology and ecology. *ibid.*, pp. 275-321.
365. Bancroft, G.T. 1985. Nutrient content of eggs and the energetics of clutch formation in the Boat-tailed Grackle. *Auk*, **102**:43-48.
366. Braun, H. 1952. Über das Unterscheidungsvermögen unbenannter Anzahlen bei Papageien. *Z. Tierpsychol.*, **9**:40-91.
367. Karten, H.J. 1979. Visual lemniscal pathways in birds. In *Neural Mechanisms of Behavior in the Pigeon*, Granda, A.M. and J.H. Maxwell, eds. pp. 409-430, Plenum Press, New York.
368. Jassik-Gerschenfeld, D., Teulon, J. and O. Hardy. 1979. Spatial Interactions in the visual receptive fields of the nucleus dorsolateralis anterior of the pigeon thalamus. *ibid.*, pp. 145-164.
369. Delius, J.D. and J. Emmerton. 1979. Visual performance of pigeons. *ibid.*, pp. 51-70.
370. Revzin, A.M. 1979. Functional localization of the nucleus rotundus. *ibid.*, pp. 165-175.
371. Maxwell, J.H. and A.M. Granda. 1979. Receptive fields of movement-sensitive cells in the pigeon thalamus. *ibid.*, pp. 177-197.
372. Miceli, D., Gioanni, H. Repérant, J. and J. Peyrichoux. 1979. The avian visual Wulst: I. An anatomical study of afferent and efferent pathways. II. An electrophysiological study of the functional properties of single neurons. *ibid.*, pp. 223-254.
373. Herrnstein, R.J., Loveland, D.H. and C. Cable. 1976. Natural concepts in pigeons. *J. Exp. Psychol. Anim. Behav. Proc.*, **2**:285-311.
374. Pettigrew, J.D. and M. Konishi. 1976. Neurons selective for orientation and bidocular disparity in the visual Wulst of the Barn Owl (*Tyto alba*). *Science*, **193**:675-678.
375. Delius, J.D. 1963. Das Verhalten der Feldlerche. *Z. Tierpsychol.*, **20**:297-348.
376. Hodos, W. 1976. Vision and the visual system: A bird's-eye view. *Prog. Psychobiol. Physiol. Psychol.*, **6**:29-62.
377. Richardson, W.J. 1971. Spring migration and weather in eastern Canada: A radar study. *Amer. Birds*, **25**:684-690.

378. Arey, L.B. 1947. *Developmental Anatomy*, Saunders, Philadelphia.

379. Glick, B. 1982. Bursa of Fabricius. In *Avian Biology*, vol. VII, Farner, D.S., King, J.R. and K.C. Parkes, eds., pp. 169-197, Academic Press, New York.

380. Mebs, T. 1972. Family: Falcons. In *Grzimek'a Animal Life Encyclopedia*, vol. 7, B. Grzimek, ed., Van Nostrand Reinhold, New York.

381. Vleck, C.M. and J. Priedkalns. 1985. Reproduction in Zebra Finches: Hormone levels and effect of dehydration. *Condor*, 87:37-46

382. Jenkins, D., Watson, A. and G.R. Miller. 1963. Population studies on Red Grouse (*Lagopus lagopus scotius*) (Lath), in North-East Scotland. *J. Anim. Ecol*., 32:317-376.

383. Stettner, L.J. 1974. The Neural basis of avian discrimination and reversal learning. In *Birds: Brain and Behavior*, Goodman, I.J. and M.W. Schein, eds., pp. 165-201, Academic Press, New York.

384. Schleidt, W.M. 1974. The comparative study of behavior. *ibid*., pp. 3-13.

385. Hodos, W. 1974. The comparative study of brain-behavior relationships. *ibid*., pp. 15-25.

386. Cohen, D.H. and H.J. Karten. 1974. The structural organization of avian brain: An overview. *ibid*., pp. 29-73.

387. Konishi, M. 1974. Hearing and vocalization in songbirds. *ibid*., pp. 77-86.

388. Zeigler, H.P. 1974. Feeding-behavior in the pigeon: A neurobehavioral analysis. *ibid*., pp. 101-132.

389. Freeman, B.M. 1971. Non-shivering thermogenesis in birds. In *Non-shivering Thermogenesis*, Proc. of symposium in Prague, L. Jansky, ed., pp. 83-96. Academia, Prague.

390. Murton, R.K. and N.J. Westwood. 1975. Integration of gonadotrophin and steroid secretion, spermatogenesis and behaviour in the reroductive cycle of male pigeon species. In *Neural and Endocrine Aspects of Behaviour in Birds*, Wright, P., Caryl, P.G. and D.M. Vowles, eds., pp. 52-89. Elsevier, New York.

391. Hutchinson, J.B. 1975. Target cells for gonadal steroids in the brain; Studies in steroid-sensitive mechanisms of behaviour. *ibid*., pp. 123-137.

392. Macphail, E.M. 1975. The role of the avian hyperstriatal complex in learning. *ibid*., pp. 140-162.

393. Zeier, H. 1975. Interhemispheric interactions. *ibid*., pp. 163-180.

394. Friedman, M. 1975. How birds use their eyes. *ibid*., pp. 140-162.

395. Salzen, E.A. and D.M. Parker. 1975. Arousal and orientation functions of the avian telencephalon. *ibid*., pp. 205-242.

396. Phillips, R.E. and F.W. Peek. 1975. Brain organization and neuromuscular control of vocalization in birds. *ibid*., pp. 243-274.

397. Gentle, M.J. 1975. Gustatory behavior of the chicken and other birds *ibid*., pp 305-318.

398. Tucker, D. and J.C. Smith. 1976. Vertebrate olfaction. In *Evolution of Brain and Behavior in Vertebrates*, Masterton, R.B., Bitterman, M.E., Campbell, C.B.G., and N. Hotton, eds., pp. 25-52. Wiley & Sons, New York.

399. Ebner, F.F. 1976. The forebrain of reptiles and mammals. *ibid*., pp. 147-163.

400. Webster, D.B. 1976. On the comparative method of investigation. In *Evolution, Brain, and Behavior: Persistent Problems*, Masterton, R.B., Hodos, W. and H.J. Jerison, eds., pp. 1-11, Wiley & Sons, New York.

401. Jerison, H.J. 1976. Principles of evolution of the brain and behavior *ibid*., pp. 23-45.

402. Olson, E.C. 1976. Rates of evolution of the nervous system and behavior. *ibid.*, pp. 47-77.
403. Whitney, G. 1976. Genetic considerations in studies of the evolution of the nervous system and behavior. *ibid.*, pp. 79-106.
404. Bennett, A.F. and W.R. Dawson. 1976. Metabolism. In *Biology of the Reptilia*, vol. 5, Gans, C. and W.R. Dawson, eds., pp. 127-223. Academic Press, New York.
405. Walls, G. 1942. *The Vertebrate Eye and Its Adaptive Radiation.* Cranbrook, Bloomfield Hills, Michigan.
406. Hinde, R.A. 1970. *Animal Behaviour.* McGraw-Hill, New York.
407. Hopson, J.A. 1980. Relative brain size in dinosaurs: Implications for dinosaurian endothermy. In *A Cold Look at the Warm-Blooded Dinosaurs*, Thomas, D.K. and E.C. Olson, eds., pp. 287-310. Westview Press, Boulder, Colorado.
408. Bakker, R.T. 1980. Dinosaur heresy-dinosaur renaissance. *ibid.*, pp. 351-462.
409. Hotton, N. 1980. An alternative to dinosaur endothermy. *ibid.*, pp. 311-350.
410. Ostrom, J.H. 1980. The evidence for endothermy in dinosaurs. *ibid.*, pp. 15-54.
411. Greenberg, N. 1980. Physiological and behavioral thermoregulation in living reptiles. *ibid.*, pp. 141-166.
412. Regal, P.J. and C. Gans. 1980. The revolution in thermal physiology. *ibid.*, pp. 167-188.
413. Roth, J.J. and E.C. Roth. 1980 The parietal-pineal complex among paleovertebrates. *ibid.*, pp. 189-231.
414. Lofts, B. and R.K. Murton. 1973. Reproduction in birds. In *Avian Biology*, vol. III, Farner, D.S. and J.R. King, eds., pp. 1-107. Academic Press, New York.
415. Kobayashi, H. and M. Wada. 1973. Neuroendocrinology in birds. *ibid.*, pp. 287-347.
416. Sillman, A.J. 1973. Avian vision. *ibid.*, pp. 349-387.
417. Wenzel, B. 1973. Chemoreception. *ibid.*, pp. 389-415.
418. Schwartzkopff, J. 1973. Mechanoreception. *ibid.*, pp. 417-477.
419. Hinde, R.A. 1973. Behavior. *ibid.*, pp. 479-535.
420. Menaker, M. and A. Oksche. 1974. The avian pineal organ. In *Avian Biology*, vol. IV, Farner, D.S. and J. R. King, eds., pp. 79-118. Academic Press, New York.
421. Bock, W.J. 1974. The avian skeletomuscular system. *ibid.*, pp. 119-257.
422. Calder, W.A. and J.R. King. 1974. Thermal and caloric relations of birds. *ibid.*, 259-413.
423. Berger, M. and J.S. Hart. 1974. Physiology and energetics of flight. *ibid.*, pp. 415-477.
424. Lack, D. 1965. Evolutionary ecology. *J. Ecol.*, **53**:237-245.
425. Pennycuick, C.J. 1975. Mechanics of flight. In *Avian Biology*, vol. V, Farner, D.S. and J.R. King, eds., pp. 1-75. Academic Press, New York.
426. Nottebohm, F. 1975. Vocal behavior in birds. *ibid.*, pp. 287-332.
427. Drent, R. 1975. Incubation. *ibid.*, pp. 333-420.
428. Vuilleumier, F. 1975. Zoogeography. *ibid.*, 421-496.
429. Marler, P. 1955. Characteristics of some animal calls. *Nature*, **176**: 6-7.
____ 1956. The voice of the Chaffinch and its function as a language. *ibis*, **98**:231-261.
430. Heinroth, O. 1922. Die Bezehiungen zwischen Vogelgewicht, Eigewicht, Gelegewicht und Brutdauer. *J. Ornithol.*, **70**:172-285.

431. Oring, L.W. 1982. Avian mating systems. In *Avian Biology*, vol. VI, Farner, D.S., King, J.R. and K.C. Parkes, eds., pp. 1-92. Academic Press, New York.
432. Pulliam, H.R. and G.C. Millikan. 1982. Social organization in the nonreproductive season. *ibid.*, pp.169-197.
433. Jacob, J. and V. Ziswiler. 1982. The uropygial gland. *ibid.*, pp. 199-324.
434. Sossinka, R. 1982. Domestication in birds. *ibid.*, pp. 373-403.
435. Scheid, P. 1982. Respiration and control of breathing. *ibid.*, pp. 405-453.
436. Rausch, R.L. 1983. The biology of avian parasites: Helminths. In *Avian Biology*, vol. VII, Farner, D.S., King, J.R. and K.C. Parkes, eds., pp. 367-442. Academic Press, New York.
437. Williams, J.B. and K.A. Nagy. 1985. Daily energy expenditure by female Savannah Sparrows feeding nestlings. *Auk*, **120**:187-190.
438. Moreau, R.E. 1966. *The Bird Faunas of Africa and Its Islands*. Academic Press, New York.
439. Dilger, W.C. 1982. Common types of cage birds. Revised by J. Bell, In *Diseases of Cage and Aviary Birds*, M.L. Petrak, ed., pp. 3-10, Lea & Febiger, Philadelphia; Cage and environment. *ibid.*, pp. 11-17; Behavioral aspects, *ibid.*, pp. 18-20.
440. Buckley, P.A. 1982. Avian genetics. *ibid.*, pp. 21-110.
441. Evans, H.E. 1982. Anatomy of the Budgerigar. *ibid.*, pp. 111-187.
442. Farner, D.S. 1982. Some physiological attributes of small birds. *ibid.*, pp. 188-219.
443. Tollefson, C.I. 1982. Nutrition. *ibid.*, pp. 220-249.
444. Tottenham, K. 1982. Orphan birds. *ibid.*, pp. 250-255.
445. Stone, R.M. 1982. Clinical examination and methods of treatment. *ibid.*, pp. 258-268.
446. Gandal, C.P. 1982. Anesthetic and surgical techniques. Revised by W. B. Amand. *ibid.*, pp. 304-328.
447. Taylor, T.G. 1982. French molt. *ibid.*, pp. 361-367.
448. Altman, R.B. 1982. Conditions involving the integumentary system. *ibid.*, pp. 368-381.
449. Arnall, L. and M.L. Petrak. 1982. Diseases of the respiratory system. *ibid.*, pp. 395-421.
450. T-W-Fiennes, R.N. 1982. Diseases of the cardiovascular system, blood, and lymphatic system. *ibid.*, pp. 422-431.
451. Minski, L. and M.L. Petrak. 1982. Diseases of the digestive system. *ibid.*, pp. 432-448.
452. Hasholt, J. and M.L. Petrak. 1982. Diseases of the urinary system. *ibid.*, pp. 449-457.
453. Blackmore, D.K. 1982. Diseases of the reproductive system, Revised by J.E. Cooper. *ibid.*, pp.
454. Hasholt, J. and M.L. Petrak. 1982. Diseases of the nervous system. *ibid.*, pp. 468-477.
455. Blackmore, D.K. 1982. Diseases of the endocrine system. Revised by J. E. Cooper. *ibid.*, pp. 478-490.
456. Small, E. and T.J. Burke. 1982. Diseases of the organs of special sense. *ibid.* pp. 491-496.
457. T-W-Fiennes, R.N. 1982. Infectious diseases. *ibid.*, pp. 497-515.
458. Cavill, J.P. 1982. Viral diseases. *ibid.*, pp. 515-527.
459. Arnstein, P. and K.F. Meyer. 1982. Psittacosis and ornithosis. Revised by J. Schachter. *ibid.*, pp. 528-534.
460. Keymer, I.F. 1982. Parasitic diseases. *ibid.*, pp. 535-598.
461. ____. 1982. Mycoses. *ibid.*, pp. 599-605.
462. Petrak, M.L. and C.E. Gilmore. 1982. Neoplasms. *ibid.*, pp. 606-637.
463. Minski, L. and M.L. Petrak. 1982. Obesity. *ibid.*, p. 638.

464. ____ and ____. 1982. Senility. *ibid.*, p.639.
465. Hasholt, J. and M.L. Petrak. 1982. Gout. *ibid.*, p. 639-644.
466. Rahn, H., Carey, C., Balmas, K., Bhathia, B. and C. Paganelli. 1977. Reduction of pore area of the avian eggshell as an adaptation to altitude. *Proc. Natl. Acad. Sci.*, **74**:3095-3098.
467. Tinbergen, N. 1959. Comparative studies of the behavior of gulls. *Behaviour*, **15**:1-70.
468. Von Holst, E. and Von St. Paul, U. 1963. On the functional organization of drives. *Anim. Behav.*, **11**:1-20.
469. Welty, J.C. 1980. Birds as flying machines. In *Birds*, Readings from Scientific American, with introductions by B. Wilson, pp. 14-22. W.H. Freeman, San Francisco.
470. Storer, J.H. 1980. Bird aerodynamics. *ibid.*, pp. 32-37.
471. Tucker, V.A. 1980. The energetics of bird flight. *ibid.*, pp. 46-53.
472. Smith, N.G. 1980. Visual isolation in gulls. *ibid.*, pp. 103-111.
473. Hailman, J.P. 1980. How an instinct is learned. *ibid.*, pp. 126-134.
474. Hess, E.H. 1980. "Imprinting" in a natural laboratory. *ibid.*, pp. 149-157.
475. Schmidt-Nielsen, K. 1980. Salt glands. *ibid.*, pp. 186-191.
476. Stettner, L.J. and K.A. Mattniak. 1980. The brain of birds. *ibid.*, pp. 192-199.
477. Taylor, T.G. 1980. How an eggshell is made. *ibid.*, pp. 201-207.
478. Rahn, H., Ar, A. and C.V. Paganelli. 1980. How bird eggs breathe. *ibid.*, pp. 208-217.
479. Thorpe, W.H. 1980. Duet-singing birds. *ibid.*, pp. 219-227.
480. Greenewalt, C.H. 1980. How birds sing. *ibid.*, pp. 228-239.
481. Wilson, W.O. 1980. Poultry production. *ibid.*, pp. 247-254.
482. Zerba, E. and M.L Morton. 1983. Dynamics of incubation in Mountain White-crowned Sparrows. *Condor*, **85**:1-11.
483. McNicholl, M. 1983. Hatching of Forster's Tern. *ibid.*, **85**:50-52.
484. Lanning, D.V. and J.T. Shiflett. 1983. Nesting ecology of Thick-billed Parrots. *ibid.*, **85**:66-73.
485. Miller, A.H. 1955. Concepts and problems of avian systematics in relation to evolutionary processes. In *Recent Studies in Avian Biology*, A. Wolfson, ed., pp. 1-22, U. Illinois Press, Urbana.
486. Friedmann, H. 1955. Recent revisions in classification and their biological significance. *ibid.*, pp. 23-43.
487. Fisher, H.I. 1955. Avian anatomy, 1932-1950, and some suggested problems. *ibid.*, pp. 57-104.
488. Emlen, J.T., Jr. 1955. The study of behavior in birds. *ibid.*, pp. 105-153.
489. Davis, D.E. 1955. Breeding biology in birds. *ibid.*, pp. 264-308.
490. Domm, L.V. 1955. Recent advances in knowledge concerning the role of hormones in the sex differentiation of birds. *ibid.*, pp. 309-325.
491. Herman. C.M. 1955. Diseases of birds. *ibid.*, pp. 450-467.
492. Wangensteen, O.D., Wilson, D. and H. Rahn. 1970-1971. Diffusion of gases across the shell of the hen's egg. *Respiratory Physiol.*, **11**:16-30.
Rahn, H., Paganelli, C.V. and A. Ar. 1974. The avian egg: Air-cell gas tension, metabolism and incubation time. *ibid.*, **22**:297-309.
493. Williams, H. and F. Nottebohm. 1985. Auditory responses in avian vocal motor neurons: A motor theory of song perception in birds. *Science*, **229**:279-282.
494. Konishi, M. 1965. The role of auditory feedback in the control of vocalization in the White-crowned Sparrow. *Z. Tierpsychol.* 22: 770-783.

495. Tanaka, T.G. and S. Nakajo. 1962. Participation of neurohypophyseal hormones on oviposition with hen. *Endocrinol.*, **70**:453-458.
496. Baerends, G.P. and R.H. Drent, eds. 1982. The Herring Gull and its egg. Part II. The responsiveness to egg features. *Behaviour*, **82(1-4)**:xiii + 416pp.
497. Howell, T.R. and G.A. Bartholomew. 1962. Temperature regulation in the Red-tailed Tropic Bird and the Red-footed Booby. *Condor*, **64**:6-18.
498. Greenewalt, C.H. 1968. *Bird Song: Acoustics and Physiology.*, Smithsonian Institution Press, Washington, D.C.
499. Ricklefs, R.E. 1969. Preliminary models for growth rates of altricial birds. *Ecology*, **50**:1031-1040.
500. Taylor, T.G. and D.A. Stringer. 1965. Eggshell formation and skeletal metabolism. In *Avian Physiology*, 2nd. ed., P.D. Sturkie, ed., pp. 485-514. Comstock Publishing Associates, Ithaca, New York.
501. Mayr, E. and D. Amadon. 1951. A classification of recent birds. *Amer. Mus. Novit.*, **No. 1496**:42pp.
502. Mayr, E. and C. Vaurie. 1948. Evolution in the family Dicruridae (birds). *Evol.*, 2:238-265.
503. Vaurie, C. 1949. A review of the bird family Dicruridae. *Bull. Amer. Mus. Nat. Hist.*, **97**:437-526.
504. McDowell, S. 1948. The bony palate of birds. Part I. The Paleognathae. *Auk*, **65**:520-549.
505. Kortlandt, A. 1940. Eine Uebersicht der angeborenen Verhaltensweisen des mittel-europäischen Kormorans (*Phalacrocorax carbo sinensis* Shaw und nodd.); ihre Function, ontogenetische Entwicklung und Phylogenetische Herkunft. *Arch. Neerl. Zool.*, **4**:401-442.
506. Udvardy, M.D.F. 1983. The role of feet in behavioral thermoregulation of hummingbirds. *Condor*, **85**:281-285.
507. Oliphant, L.W. 1983. First observations of brown fat in birds. *ibid.*, **85**:350-354,
508. Warham, J. 1983. The composition of petrel eggs. *ibid.*, **85**:194-199.
509. Ritchison, G. 1983. Possible "deceptive" use of song by female Black-headed Grosbeaks. *ibid.*, **85**:250-251.
510. Sturkie, P.D. and W.J. Mueller. 1976. Reproduction in the female and egg production. In *Avian Physiology*, 3rd. ed., P.D. Sturkie, ed., pp. 302-330, Springer-Verlag, New York.
511. ____. and H. Opel. 1976. Reproduction in the male, fertilization, and early embryonic development. *ibid.*, pp. 331-347.
512. Bolton, T.B. 1976. Nervous system. *ibid.*, pp. 1-28.
513. Kare, M.R. and J.G. Rogers, Jr. 1976. Sense organs. *ibid.*, pp. 29-52.
514. Sturkie, P.D. and P. Griminger. 1976. Blood: Physical characteristics, formed elements, hemoglobin, and coagulation. *ibid.*, pp. 53-75.
515. Sturkie, P.D. 1976. Heart and circulation: Anatomy, hemodynamics, blood pressure, blood flow, and body fluids. *ibid.*, pp. 76-101.
516. ____. 1976. Heart: Contraction, conduction, and electrocardiography. *ibid.*, pp. 102-121.
517. Fedde, M.R. 1976. Respiration. *ibid.*, pp. 122-145.
518. Whittow, G.C. 1976. Regulation of body temperature. *ibid.*, pp. 146-173.
519. ____. 1976. Energy metabolism. *ibid.*, pp. 174-185.
520. Sturkie, P.D. 1976. Alimentary canal: Anatomy, prehension, deglutition, feeding, drinking, passage of ingesta, and motility. *ibid.*, pp. 185-195.

521. ____. 1976. Secretion of gastric and pancreatic juice, pH of tract, digestion in the alimentary canal, liver and bile, and absorption. *ibid*., pp. 196-209.
522. ____. 1976. Kidneys, extrarenal salt excretion, and urine. *ibid*., pp. 196-209.
523. ____. 1976. Hypophysis. *ibid*., pp. 286-301.
524. Pettit, T.N. and G.C. Whittow. 1983. Water loss from pipped Wedge-tailed Shearwater eggs. *Condor*, **85**:107-109.
525. Mader, W.J. 1982. Ecology and breeding habits of the Savanna Hawk in the llanos of Venezuela. *ibid*., **84**:261-271.
526. Davis, L.D. 1982. Timing of nest relief and its effect on breeding success in Adélie Penguins (*Pygoscelis adéliae*). *ibid*., **84**: 178-183.
527. White, F.N. and J.L. Kinney. 1974. Avian incubation. *Science*, **186**:107-115.
528. Ringelman, J.K., Longcore, J.R. and R.B. Owen. 1982. Nest and brood attentiveness in female Black Ducks. *Condor*, **84**:110-116.
529. Ferrell, R. and L.F. Baptista. 1982. Diurnal rhythms in the vocalizations of Budgerigars. *ibid*., **84**:123-124.
530. Patterson, C.B., Erckmann, W.J. and G.H. Orians. 1980. An experimental study of parental investment and polygyny in male blackbirds. *Amer. Nat*., **116**:757-769.
531. Immelmann, K. 1972. *Die Australischen Plattschweifsittiche*. Ziemsen Verlag, Wittenberg Lutherstadt.
532. Grant, G.S., Pettit, T.N., Rahn, H., Whittow, G.C., and C.V. Paganelli. 1982. Regulation of water loss from Bonin Petrel (*Pterodroma hypoleuca*) eggs. *Auk*, **99**:236-242.
533. Homberger, D.G. 1980. Review of *"Nomina Anatomica Avium." ibid*., **97**:912-914.
534. Dufty, A.M., Jr. 1982. Movements and activities of radio-tracked Brown-headed Cowbirds. *ibid*., **99**:316-327.
535. Ricklefs, R.E. 1982. Some considerations on sibling competition and avian growth rates. *ibid*., **99**:141-147.
536. Tomback, D.F. 1980. How nutcrackers find their seeds. *Condor*, **82**: 10-19.
537. Hunter, M.H., Jr. 1980. Vocalization during inhalation in a nightjar. *ibid*., **82**:101-103.
538. Dawson, W.R. and A.F. Bennett. 1980. Metabolism and thermoregulation in hatchling Western Gulls. *ibid*., **82**:103-105.
539. Pinshow, B. and W.R. Welch. 1980. Winter breeding in Emperor Penguins: A consequence of the summer heat? *ibid*., **82**:159-163.
540. Smith, S.M. 1980. Demand behavior: A new interpretation of courtship feeding. *ibid*., **82**:291-295.
541. Hutchison, L.V. and B.M. Wenzel. 1980. Olfactory guidance in foraging by procellariiforms. *ibid*., **82**:314-319.
542. Kern, M.D. and A. Bushra. 1980. Is the incubation path required for the construction of a normal nest? *ibid*., **82**:328-334.
543. Carey, C., Rahn, H. and P. Parisi. 1980. Calories, water, lipid, and yolk in avian eggs. *ibid*., **82**:335-343.
544. Kroodsma, D.E. 1980. Winter Wren singing behavior: A pinnacle of song complexity. *ibid*., **82**:357-365.
545. Birchaard, G.F. and D.L. Kilgore, Jr. 1980. Ontogeny of oxygen consumption by embryos of two species of swallows (Hirudinidae). *ibid*., **82**:402-405.
546. Marsh, R.L. 1980. Development of temperature regulation in nestling Tree Swallows. *ibid*., **82**:461-463.
547. Vleck, C.M. 1981. Energetic cost of incubation in the Zebra Finch. *ibid*., **83**:229-237.

548. Dunn, E.H. 1980. On the variability in energy allocation of nestling birds. *Auk*, **97**:19-27.
549. Ricklefs, R.E. 1980. Geographical variation in clutch size among passerine birds: Ashmole's hypothesis. *ibid.*, 97:38-49.
550. Dol'nik, V.R. and V.M. Gavrilov. 1980. Photoperiodic control of the molt cycle in the Chaffinch (*Fringilla coelobs*). *ibid.*, **97**: 50-62.
551. Farner, D.S., Donham, R.S., Moore, M.C. and R.A. Lewis. 1980. The temporal relationship between the cycle of testicular development and molt in the White-crowned Sparrow, *Zonotrichia leucophrys gambelii*. *ibid.*, **97**:63-75.
552. Boersma, P.D., Wheelwright, N.T., Nerini, N.K. and E.S. Wheelwright. 1980. The breeding biology of the Fork-tailed Storm-Petrel (*Oceanodroma furcata*). *ibid.*, **97**:268-282.
553. Wiens, J.A. 1980. Theory and observation in modern ornithology: A forum. *ibid.*, **97**:409.
554. Emlen, J.T. 1980. Welcome mathematicians. *ibid.*, **97**:412-413.
555. Pulliam, H.R. 1980. On digesting a theory. *ibid.*, **97**:418-420.
556. Fretwell, S.D. 1980. On the philosophical basis of ornithology. *ibid.*, **97**:420-422.
557. Ettinger, A.O. and J.R. King. 1980. Time and energy budgets of the Willow Flycatcher (*Empidonax traillii*) during the breeding season. *ibid.*, **97**:533-546.
558. Ross, H.A. 1980. Growth of nestling Ipswich Sparrows in relation to season, habitat, brood size, and parental age. *ibid.*, **97**:721-732.
559. Ricklefs, R.E., White, S. and J. Cullen. 1980. Postnatal development of Leach's Storm-Petrel. *ibid.*, **97**:768-781.
560. Kear, J. and A.J. Berger. 1980. *The Hawaiian Goose/An Experiment in conservation.* Buteo Books, Vermillion, South Dakota.
561. Kern, M.D. and L. Coruzzi. 1979. The structure of the Canary's Incubation patch. *J. Morphol.*, **162**:425-452.
562. Ricklefs, R.E. and F.R. Hainsworth. 1968. Temperature dependent behavior of the Cactus Wren. *Ecology*, **49**:227-233.
563. Grau, C.R. 1976. Ring structure of avian egg yolk. *Poult. Sci.*, **55**:1418-1422.
564. Nolan, V., Jr. 1978. The ecology and behavior of the Prairie Warbler *Dendroica discolor*. *Ornithol. Monogr.*, **26**.
565. Dawson, W.R. and F.C. Evans. 1960. Relation of growth and development to temperature regulation in nestling Vesper Sparrows. *Condor*, **62**:329-340.
566. Temple, S.A. 1977. Preface of *Endangered Birds: Management Techniques for Preserving Threatened Species*, S.A. Temple, ed., U. Wisconsin Press, Madison.
567. Prothero, D.R. 1985. Mid-Oligocene extinction event in North American land mammals. *Science*, **229**:550-551.
568. Wiens, J.A. 1977. On competition and variable environments. *Amer. Sci.*, **65**:590-597.
569. Franck, D. 1974. The genetic basis of evolutionary changes in behaviour patterns. In *The Genetics of Behaviour*, J.H.F. van Abeelen, ed., pp. 119-140., North-Holland Publ. Co., Amsterdam.
570. Karli, P., Eclancher, F., Vergnes, M., Chaurand, J.P. and P. Schmitt. 1974. Emotional responsiveness and interspecific aggressiveness in the rat: Interactions between genetic and experiential determinants. *ibid.*, 291-319.
571. Parkes, K.C. 1966. Speculations on the origin of feathers. *Living Bird*, **5**:77-86.

572. Lind, H. and H. Poulsen. 1963. On the morphology and behaviour of a hybrid between Goosander and Shelduck (*Mergus merganser x T. tadorna*). *Z. Tierpsychol.*, **28**:558-564.

573. Wittenberger, J.F. and G.L. Hunt, Jr. 1985. The adaptive significance of coloniality in birds. In *Avian Biology*, vol. VIII, Farner, D.S., King, J.R. and K.C. Parkes, eds., pp. 1-78, Academic Press, New York.

574. Olson, S.L. 1985. The fossil record of birds. *ibid.*, pp. 79-238.

575. De Beer, G. 1956. The evolution of ratites. *Bull. Br. Mus.*, (*Nat. Hist.*) *Zool.* **4**:57-70.

576. Skowron, C. and M. Kern. 1980. The insulation in nests of selected North American songbirds. *Auk*, **97**:816-824.

577. Müller-Schwarze, D. and C. Müller-Schwarze. 1980. Display rate and speed of nest relief in Antarctic pygocelid penguins. *ibid.*, **97**:825-831.

578. Ricklefs, R.E. and S. Peters. 1981. Parental components of variance in growth rate and body size of nestling European Starlings (*Sternus vulgaris*) in eastern Pennsylvania. *ibid.*, **98**:39-48.

579. Simons, T.R. 1981. Behavior and attendance patterns of the Fork-tailed Storm-Petrel. *ibid.*, **98**:145-158.

580. Yang, S.H. and J.L. Patton. 1981. Genic variability and differentiation in the Galapagos finches. *ibid.*, **98**:230-242.

581. Phillips, R.E. and O.M. Youngren. 1981. Effects of denervation of the tracheo-syringeal muscles on frequency control in vocalizations in chicks. *ibid.*, **98**:299-306.

582. Power, H.W., Litovich, E. and M.P. Lombardo. 1981. Male Starlings delay incubation to avoid being cuckolded. *ibid.*, **98**:386-389.

583. Fitzpatrick, J.W. and G. E. Woolfenden. 1981. Demography is a cornerstone of sociobiology. *ibid.*, **98**:406-407.

584. Brown, J.L. 1981. On socio-ornithology. *ibid.*, **98**:417-418.

585. Clark, L. and R.P. Balda. 1981. The development of effective endothermy and homeothermy by nestling Piñon Jays. *ibid.*, **98**:615-619.

586. Kovacs, K.M. and J.P. Ryder. 1981. Nest-site tenacity and mate fidelity in female-female pairs of Ring-billed Gulls. *ibid.*, **98**: 625-627.

587. Cracraft, J. 1981. Toward a phylogenetic classification of the recent birds of the world (Class Aves). *ibid.*, **98**:681-714.

588. Janzen, D.H. 1981. *Ficus ovalis* seed predation by an Orange-chinned Parakeet (*Brotogeris jugularis*) in Costa Rica. *ibid.*, **98**: 841-844.

589. Reed, J.R. 1981. Song Sparrow "rules" for feeding nestlings. *ibid.*, **98**:828-831.

590. Mayr, E. 1983. Introduction to *Perspectives in Ornithology*, Brush, A.H. and G.A. Clark, Jr., eds., pp. 1-21, Cambridge U. Press, Cambridge.

591. White, F.N., Bartholomew, G.A. and T.R. Howell. 1975. The thermal significance of the nest of the Sociable Weaver *Philotairus socius*: Winter observations. *Ibis*, **117**:171-179.

Bartholomew, G.A., White, F.N. and T.R. Howell. 1976. The thermal significance of the nest of the Sociable Weaver *Philetairus socius*: Summer observations. *ibid.*, **118**:402-410.

592. Scott, J.P. and J. L. Fuller. 1965. *Genetics and the Social Behavior of the Dog*. U. Chicago Press, Chicago.

593. Manning, A. 1961. The effects of artificial selection for mating speed in *Drosophila Melanogaster*. *Anim. Behav.* **9**:82-92.

Manning, A. 1963. Evolutionary changes and behaviour genetics. *Proc. XIth Int. Congr. Genetics*, **3**:807-815.

____. 1968. The effects of artificial selection for slow mating in *Drosophila simulans*. I. The behavioral changes. *Anim. Behav.*, **16**:108-113.

594. Wiens, J.A. 1981. Single-sample surveys of communities: Are the revealed patterns real? *Amer. Nat.*, **117**:90-98.

595. Barlow, G.W. 1977. Modal action patterns. In *How Animals Communicate*, T.A. Sebeok, ed., pp. 94-125, U. Indiana Press, Bloomington.

596. Bentley, D.R. and R.R. Hoy. 1970. Postembryonic development of adult motor patterns in crickets: A neural analysis. *Science*, **170**: 1409-1411.

597. De Beer, G. 1954. *Archaeopteryx lithographica: A Study Based Upon the British Museum Specimen*. British Museum, London.

598. Moreau, R.E. 1950. The breeding seasons of African birds. 1. Land birds; 2. Sea birds. *Ibis*, **92**:223-267, 419-433.

599. Gould, S.J. 1980. Is a new and general theory of evolution emerging? *Paleobiology*, **6**:119-130.

600. Bekoff, A. 1978. A neuroethological approach to the study of the ontogeny of coordinated behavior. In *The Development of Behavior: Comparative and Evolutionary Aspects*, Burghardt, G.M. and M. Bekoff, eds., pp. 19-41, Garland Publ., New York.

601. McDiarmid, R.W. 1978. Evolution of parental care in frogs. *ibid.*, pp. 127-147.

602. Burghardt, G.M. 1978. Behavioral ontogeny in reptiles: Whence, whither, and why? *ibid.*, pp. 149-174.

603. Kroodsma, D.E. 1978. Aspects of learning in the ontogeny of bird song: Where, from whom, when, how many, which, and how accurately? *ibid.*, pp. 215-230.

604. Payne, R.B. 1981. Population structure and social behavior: Models for testing the ecological significance of song dialects in birds. In *Natural Selection and Social Behavior*, Alexander, R. D. and D.W. Tinkle, eds., pp. 108-120, Chiron Press, New York.

605. Burley, N. 1981. The evolution of sexual indistinguishability. *ibid.*, pp. 121-137.

606. Wells, K.D. 1981. Parental behavior of male and female frogs. *ibid.*, 184-197.

607. Emlen, S.T. 1981. Altruism, kinship, and reciprocity in the White-fronted Bee-eater. *ibid.*, pp. 217-230.

608. Ligon, J.D. 1981. Demographic patterns and communal breeding in the Green Woodhoopoe, *Phoeniculus purpureus*. *ibid.*, pp. 231-243.

609. Brown, J.L. and E.R. Brown. 1981. Kin selection and individual selection in babblers. *ibid.*, pp. 244-256.

610. Wilson, A.C. 1976. Gene regulation in evolution. In *Molecular Evolution*, F.J. Ayala, ed., pp. 225-234, Sinauer Assoc. Inc., Sunderland, Massachusetts.

611. Wingfield, J.C. 1985. In Review of Hormones and Behavior in Higher Vertebrates. *Auk*, **102**:219-220.

612. Roseberry, J.L. and W.D. Klimstra. 1984. *Population Ecology of the Bobwhite*. Southern Illinois Univ. Press, Carbondale.

613. Payne, R.B. 1984. Sexual selection, lek and arena behavior, and sexual size dimorphism in birds. *Ornithol. Mono.* **No. 33**, The Amer. Ornithol. Union, Washington, D.C.

614. Quinney, T.E. and C.D. Ankney. 1985. Prey size selection by Tree Swallows. *Auk*, **102**:245-250.

615. Arendt, W.J. 1985. *Philornis* ectoparasitism of Pearly-eyed Thrashers. II. Effects of adults and reproduction. *ibid.*, **102**:281-292.
616. Simpson, G.G. 1980. Fossil birds in evolution. In Papers in avian Paleontology. *Contrib. Sci. Nat. Hist. Mus. Los Angeles County*, **330**:3-8.
617. Rich, P.V. 1980. The Australian Dromornithidae: A group of extinct large ratites. *ibid.*, **330**:93-103.
618. King, A.S and D.Z. King. 1979. Avian morphology: General principles. In *Form and Function in Birds*, vol. 1, King, A.S. and J. McLelland, eds., pp. 1-38, Academic Press, London.
619. Duncker, H.-R. 1979. Coelomic cavities. *ibid.*, pp. 39-67.
620. McLelland, J. 1979. Digestive system. *ibid.*, pp. 69-181.
621. Johnson, O.W. 1979. Urinary organs. *ibid.*, pp. 183-235.
622. Gilbert, A.B. 1979. Female genital organs. *ibid.*, pp. 237-360.
623. Hodges, R.D. 1979. The blood cells. *ibid.*, pp. 361-379.
624. Akester, A.R. 1979. The autonomic nervous system. *ibid.*, pp. 381-441.
625. Lake, P.E. 1981. Male genital organs. In *Form and Function in Birds*, vol. 2, King, A.S. and J. McLelland, eds., pp. 1-61, Academic Press, London.
626. King, A.S. 1981. Cloaca. *ibid.*, pp. 63-105.
627. Bühler, P. 1981. Functional anatomy of the avian jaw apparatus. *ibid.*, pp. 439-468.
628. King, A.S. 1981. Phallus. *ibid.*, pp. 107-147.
629. Hodges, R.D. 1981. Endocrine glands. *ibid.*, pp. 149-234.
630. West, N.H., Langille, B.L. and D.R. Jones. 1981. Cardiovascular system. *ibid.*, pp. 235-339.
631. Rose, M.E. 1981. Lymphatic system. *ibid.*, pp. 341-384.
632. Bubien-Waluszewska, A. 1981. The cranial nerves. *ibid.*, pp. 385-438.
633. Cowles, R.B. 1946. Fur and feathers: A response to falling temperatures? *Science*, **103**:74-75.
634. Bucher, T.L. 1983. Parrot eggs, embryos, and nestlings: Patterns and energetics of growth and development. *Physiol. Zool.*, **56**:465-483.
635. Bilo, D. and W. Nachtigall. 1977. Biophysics of bird flight: Questions and results. In *Physiology of Movement--Biomechanics*, W. Nachtigall, ed., pp. 217-234, Gustav Fischer Verlag, Stuttgart.
636. Oehme, H., Dathe, H.H. and U. Kitzler. 1977. Flight energetics in birds. *ibid.*, pp. 257-273.
637. Csicsáky, M.J. 1977. Body-gliding in the Zebra Finch. *ibid.*, pp. 274-286.
638. Rowley, I. 1976. Co-operative breeding in Australian birds. *Proc. Int. Ornithol. Congr.*, **XVI**:657-666.
639. Cott, H.B. 1971. Parental care in the Crocodilia, with special reference to *Crocodylus niloticus*. *IUCN Publications New Series, Supp. Paper No. 32* (*Crocodiles*), **1**:166-180.
640. Romer, A.S. 1966. *Vertebrate Paleontology*, 3rd ed., U. Chicago Press, Chicago.
641. Cody, M.L. 1985. Personal communication.
642. Thomas, S.P. and R.A. Suthers. 1972. The physiology and energetics of bat flight. *J. Exp. Biol.*, **57**:317-335.
643. Humphreys, P.N. 1975. Ultrastructure of the Budgerigar testis during a photoperiodically induced cycle. *Cell Tiss. Res.*, **159**:541-550.

644. Conway, W. 1983. Captive birds and conservation. In *Perspectives in Ornithology*, Brush, A.H. and G.A. Clark, Jr., eds., pp. 23-36, Cambridge U. Press, Cambridge.
645. Barlow, J.C. and N.J. Flood. 1983. Research collections in ornithology--A reaffirmation. *ibid.*, pp. 37-54.
646. Mock, D.W. 1983. On the study of avian mating systems. *ibid.*, pp. 55-84.
647. Emlen, S.T. and S.L. Vehrencamp. 1983. Cooperative breeding strategies among birds. *ibid.*, pp. 93-120.
648. Walsberg, G.E. 1983. Ecological energetics: What are the questions? *ibid.*, pp. 93-120.
649. Krebs, J.R. Stephens, D.W. and W.J. Sutherland. 1983. Perspectives in optimal foraging. *ibid.*, pp. 165-216.
650. Avise, J.C. 1983. Commentary. *ibid.*, pp. 262-270.
651. Shields, G.F. 1983. Organization of the avian genome. *ibid.*, pp. 271-290.
652. Martin, L.D. 1983. The origin and early radiation of birds. *ibid.*, pp. 291-338.
653. Steadman, D.W. 1983. Commentary. *ibid.*, pp. 338-344.
654. Wiens, J.A. 1983. Avian community ecology: an iconoclastic view. *ibid.*, pp. 355-403.
655. Slater, P.J.B. 1983. Bird song learning: theme and variations. *ibid.*, pp. 475-499.
656. Baptista, L.F. 1983. Commentary. *ibid.*, pp. 500-506.
657. Walcott, C. and A.J. Lednor. 1983. Bird navigation. *ibid.*, pp. 513-542.
658. Reese, A.M. 1915. *The Alligator and Its Allies.* G.P. Putnam's Sons, New York.
659. Neill, W.T. 1971. *The Last of the Ruling Reptiles--Alligators, Crocodiles, and Their Kin.* Columbia U. Press, New York.
660. Carey, F.G. 1973. Fishes with warm bodies. *Sci. Amer.*, **228**:36-44.
661. Astheimer, L.B. 1985. Long laying intervals: A possible mechanism and its implications. *Auk*, **102**:401-409.
662. Trivers, R.L. 1972. Parental investment and sexual selection. In *Sexual Selection and the Descent of Man. 1871-1971*, B. Campbell, ed., pp. 136-179, Aldine, Chicago.
663. Barclay, J.H. and T.J. Cade. 1983. Restoration of Peregrine Falcon in eastern United States. In *Bird Conservation. 1*, S.A. Temple, ed., pp. 9-40. U. Wisconsin Press, Madison.
664. Haftorn, S. and R.E. Reinertsen. 1985. The effect of temperature and clutch on the energetic cost of incubation in a free-living Blue Tit (*Parus caeruleus*). *Auk*, **102**:470-478.
665. Cox, C. 1984. Crocodile nesting ecology in Papua New Guinea. *Field Document No. 5, Livestock Div., Dept. Primary Industry*, Food and Agricultural Organization United Nations, Port Moresby.
666. Ferguson, M.W.J. 1982. The structure and composition of the eggshell and embryonic membranes of *Alligator mississippiensis*. *Trans. Zool. Soc. Lond.*, **36**:99-152.
667. Poole, A. 1985. Courtship feeding and Osprey reproduction. *Auk*, **102**:479-492.
668. Collias, N.E. and E.C. Collias. 1984. *Nest Building and Bird Behavior*, Princeton U. Press, Princeton.
669. Tarsitano, S. and M.K. Hecht. 1980. A reconsideration of the reptilian relationships of *Archaeopteryx*. *Zool. J. Linn. Soc.*, **69**: 149-182.
670. Marler, P. 1981. Birdsong: The acquisition of a learned motor skill. *Trends Neurol. Sci.*, **3**:88-94.

671. Richardson, W.J. 1978. Timing and amount of bird migration in relation to weather: A review. *Oikos*, **30**:224-272.
672. Packard, G.C. and M.J. Packard. 1980. Evolution of the cleidoic egg among reptilian antecedents of birds. In *Physiology of the avian Egg. Amer. Zool.*, **20**:351-362.
673. Packard, G.C., Tracy, C.R. and J.J. Roth. 1977. The physiological ecology of reptilian eggs and embryos, and the evolution of viviparity within the Class Reptilia. *Biol. Rev. Cambr. Phil. Soc.*, **52**:71-105.
674. Packard, M.J., Packard, G.C. and T.J. Boardman. 1982. Structure of eggshells and water relations of reptilian eggs. *Herpetologica*, **38**:136-155.
675. Rand, A.S. 1972. The temperatures of iguana nests and their relation to incubation optima and to nesting sites and season. *ibid.*, **28**:252-253.
676. Chabreck, R.H. 1973. Temperature variation in nests of the American Alligator. *ibid.*, **29**:48-51.
677. Bartholomew, G.A. 1966. A field study of temperature relations in the Galapagos Marine Iguana. *Copeia*, **1966**:241-258.
678. Licht, P. and W.R. Moberly. 1965. Thermal requirements for embryonic development in the tropical lizard *Iguana iguana*. *ibid.*, **1965**:515-517.
679. Pooley, A.C. 1974. How does a baby crocodile get to water? *African Wildlife*, **28(4)**:8-11.
680. ____. and C.Gans. 1976. The Nile Crocodile. *Sci. Amer.*, **234**:114-124.
681. Ewert, M.A. 1979. The embryo and its egg: Development and natural history. In *Turtles--Perspectives and Research*, Harless, M. and H. Morlock, eds., pp. 333-413, John Wiley & Sons, New York.
682. Moll, E.O. 1979. Reproductive cycles and adaptations. *ibid.*, pp. 305-331.
683. Ehrenfeld, D.W. 1979. Behavior associated with nesting. *ibid.*, pp. 417-434.
684. Pooley, A.C. 1975. Maternal behavior in the Morelet's Crocodile, *Crocodylus moreleti*. *Copeia*, **1975**:763-764.
685. Guggisberg, C.A.W. 1972. *Crocodiles*. Stackpole Books, Harrisburg, Pennsylvania.
686. Werner, Y.L. 1972. Observations on the eggs of eublepharid lizards, with comments on the evolution of the Gekkonoidea. *Zool. Meded. Rijksmus. Nat. Hist. Leiden*, **47**:211-224.
687. Duncker, H.-R. 1972. Structure of avian lungs. *Respir. Physiol.*, **14**:44-63.
688. Hodsdon, L.A. and J.F.W. Pearson. 1943. Notes on the discovery and biology of two Bahamian freshwater turtles of the genus *Pseudemys*. *Proc. Florida Acad. Sci.*, **6(2)**:17-23.
689. Bennett, A.F. and K. Nagy. 1977. Energy Expenditure in free-living lizards. *Ecology*, **58**:697-703.
690. Schnell, G.D. and J.J. Hellack. 1979. Bird flight speeds in nature: Optimized or a compromise? *Amer. Nat.*, **113**:53-66.
691. Prange, H.D., Anderson, J.F. and H. Rahn. 1979. Scaling of Skeletal mass to body mass in birds and mammals. *ibid.*, **113**:103-122.
692. Duncker, H.-R., 1978. General morphological principles of amniotic lungs. In *Respiratory Function in Birds, Adult and Embryonic*, J. Piiper, ed., pp. 2-22, Springer-Verlag, Berlin.
693. Fedde, M.R. and W.D. Kuhlmann. 1978. Intrapulmonary carbon dioxide sensitive receptors: Amphibians to mammals. *ibid.*, pp. 33-50.
694. Torre-Bueno, J.R. 1978. Respiration during flight in birds. *ibid.*, pp. 89-94.

695. Scheid, P. and J.P. Holle. 1978. Adjustment of the regional pulmonary circulation to the profile of oxygen pressure along the parabronchus in the duck. *ibid.*, pp. 105-110.
696. Brackenbury, J. and A.R. Akester. 1978. A model of the capillary zone of the avian tertiary bronchus. *ibid.*, pp. 125-128.
697. Burns, B., James, A.E., Hutchins, G., Novak, G. and R.R. Price. 1978. Ventilatory ^{133}Xenon distribution studies in the Duck (*Anas platyrhynchos*). *ibid.*, pp. 129-135.
698. Molony, V. 1978. Airway resistance. *ibid.*, pp. 142-147.
699. Piiper, J. 1978. Origin of carbon dioxide in caudal airsacs. *ibid.*, pp. 148-153.
700. Rautenberg, W., May, B., Necker, R. and G. Rosner. 1978. Control of panting by thermosensitive spinal neurons in birds. *ibid.*, pp. 205-210.
701. Tullet, S.G. 1978. Pore size versus pore number in avian eggshells. *ibid.*, pp. 219-226.
702. Duncker, H.-R. 1978. Development of the avian respiratory and circulatory systems. *ibid.*, pp. 260-273.
703. Tazawa, H. 1978. Gas transfer in the chorioallantois. *ibid.*, pp. 274-291.
704. Baumann, R. and F.H. Baumann. 1978. Respiratory function of embryonic chicken hemoglobin. *ibid.*, pp. 293-297.
705. Laughlin, K.F. 1978. The effects of restricted gas exchange on embryonic heart rate. *ibid.*, pp. 299-303.
706. Zerba, E. and L.F. Baptista. 1980. Courtship feeding in some emberizine finches. *Wilson Bull.*, **92**:245-246.
707. Caccamise, D.F. 1980. Growth and development of major body components in the Monk Parakeet. *ibid.*, **92**:376-381.
708. Brown, C.R. and E.J. Bitterbaum. 1980. Implications of juvenile harassment in Purple Martins. *ibid.*, **92**:452-457.
709. Stone, W.B. and P.E. Nye. 1981. Trichomoniasis in Bald Eagles. *ibid.*, **93**:109.
710. Crocoll, S. and J.W. Parker. 1981. *Protocalliphora* infestation in Broad-winged Hawks. *ibid.*, **93**:110.
711. Bellrose, F.C. and R.C. Crompton. 1981. Migration speeds of three waterfowl species. *ibid.*, **93**:121-124.
712. Baptista, L.F., Morton, M.L. and M.E. Pereyra. 1981. Interspecific song mimesis by a Lincoln Sparrow. *ibid.*, **93**:265-267.
713. Morse, D.H. 1981. Foraging speeds of warblers in large populations and in isolation. *ibid.*, **93**:334-339.
714. Lehrman, D.S. 1958. Induction of broodiness by participation in courtship and nest-building in the Ring Dove (*Streptopelia risoria*). *J. Comp. Physiol. Psychol.*, **51**:32-36.
____. 1958. Effect of female sex hormones on incubation behavior in the Ring Dove (*Streptopelia risoria*). *ibid.*, **51**:142-145.
____. 1965. Interaction between internal and external environments in the regulation of the reproductive cycle of the Ring Dove. In *Sex and Behavior*, F.A. Beach, ed., pp. 355-380, Wiley,New York.
715. Beach, F.A. 1974. Behavioral endocrinology and the study of reproduction. *Biol. Reprod.*, **10**:2-18.
716. Gurney, M.E. and M. Konishi. 1980. Hormone-induced sexual differentiation of brain and behavior in Zebra Finches. *Science*, **208**: 1380-1383.
717. Kushlan, J.A. 1973. Observations on maternal behavior in the American Alligator, *Alligator mississippiensis*. *Herpetologica*, **29**:256-257.
718. Romanoff, A.L. and A.J. Romanoff. 1949. *The Avian Egg*. Wiley, New York.

Romanoff, A.L. 1960. *The Avian Embryo*. Macmillan, New York.
____. and A. Romanoff. 1967. *Biochemistry of the Avian Embryo: A Quantitative Analysis of Prenatal Development*. Wiley, New York.

719. Benson, L. 1957. *Plant Classification*. D.C. Heath & Co., Boston.
720. Burghardt, G.M. 1977. Of iguanas and dinosaurs: social behavior and communication in neonate reptiles. In *Social Behavior in Reptiles*. *Amer. Zool*., 17:177-190.
721. Garrick, L.D. and J.W. Lang. 1977. Social signals and behavior of adult alligators and crocodiles. *ibid*., 17:225-239.
722. Breitenbach, R.P., Nagra, C.L. and R.K. Meyer. 1963. Effects of limited food intake on cyclic annual changes in Ring-necked Pheasant hens. *J. Wildlife Mgmt*., 27:24-36.
723. Kendeigh, S.C. 1963. Regulation of nesting time and distribution in the House Wren. *Wilson Bull*., 75:418-427.
724. Hamner, W.M. 1963. Diurnal rhythm and photoperiodism in testicular recrudescence of the House Finch. *Science*, 142:1294-1295.
____. 1966. Photoperiodic control of the annual testicular cycle in the House Finch, *Carpodacus mexicanus*. *Gen. Comp. Endocrinol*., 7:224-233.
725. McKinney, F. 1973. Ecoethological aspects of reproduction. In *Breeding Biology of Birds*, D.S. Farner, ed., pp. 6-21, Nat. Acad. Sci., Washington, D.C.
726. Scott, M.L. 1973. Nutrition in reproduction--direct effects and predictive functions. *ibid*., pp. 46-59.
727. Watson, A. 1973. Discussion of paper of ref. 726. *ibid*., pp. 59-68.
728. Assenmacher, I. 1973. Discussion of paper of ref. 726. *ibid*., pp. 68-73.
729. King, J.R. 1973. Energetics of reproduction in birds. *ibid*., pp. 78-107.
730. Immelmann, K. 1973. Role of the environment in reproduction as a source of "predictive" information. *ibid*., pp. 121-147.
731. Frith, H.J. 1973. Discussion of paper of ref. 730. *ibid*., pp. 147-154.
732. Gee, G.F. 1973. Informal discussion of paper of ref. 730. *ibid*., pp. 155-156.
733. Assenmacher, I. 1973. Reproductive endocrinology: The hypothalamo-hypophysial axis. *ibid*., pp. 158-198.
734. Lofts, B. 1973. Discussion of paper of ref. 733. *ibid*., pp.198-206.
735. Follett, B.K. 1973. The neuroendocrine regulation of gonadotropin secretion in avian reproduction. *ibid*., pp. 209-243.
736. Oksche, A. 1973. Informal discussion of paper of ref. 735. *ibid*., pp. 261.
737. Drent, R. 1973. The natural history of incubation. *ibid*., pp. 262-311.
738. Kendeigh, S.C. 1973. Discussion of paper of ref. 737. *ibid*., pp. 311-320.
739. Beer, C.G. 1973. Behavioral components in the reproductive biology of birds. *ibid*., pp. 323-345.
740. Ricklefs, R.E. 1973. Fecundity, mortality, and avian demography. *ibid*., pp. 366-435.
741. Adkins-Regan, E. 1983. Sex steroids and the differentiation and activation of avian reproductive behavior. In *Hormones and Behaviour in Higher Vertebrates*, Balthazart, J., Pröve, E, and R. Gilles, eds., pp. 218-228, Springer-Verlag, Berlin.
742. Massa, R, Bottoni, L., and V. Lucini. 1983. Brain testosterone metabolism and sexual behaviour in birds. *ibid*., pp. 230-236.
743. Balthazart, J. and M. Schumacher. 1983. Testosterone metabolism and sexual differentiation in quail. *ibid*., pp. 237-260.

744. Hutchison, J.B. and Th. Steimer. 1983. Hormone-mediated behavioural transitions: A role for brain aromatase. *ibid.*, pp. 261-274.
745. Harding, C.F. 1983. Hormonal specificity and activation of social behaviour in the male Zebra Finch. *ibid.*, pp. 275-289.
746. Ottinger, M.A. 1983. Sexual behaviour and endocrinological changes during reproductive maturation and aging in the avian male. *ibid.*, pp. 350-367.
747. Pröve, E. 1983. Hormonal correlates of behavioural development in male Zebra Finches. *ibid.*, pp. 368-374.
748. Goldsmith, A.R. 1983. Prolactin in avian reproductive cycles. *ibid.*, pp. 375-387.
749. Silverin, B. 1983. Population endocrinology of the female Pied Flycatcher, *Ficedula hypoleuca*. *ibid.*, pp. 389-397.
750. Cheng, M.-F. 1983. Behavioural "self-feedback" control of endocrine states. *ibid.*, pp. 409-421.
751. Cohen, J. 1983. Hormones and brain mechanisms of vocal behaviour in non-vocal learning birds. *ibid.*, pp. 422-436.
752. Silver, R. 1983. Biparental care in birds: mechanisms controlling incubation bout duration. *ibid.*, pp. 451-462.
753. Wood-Gush, D.G.M. 1983. Reproductive behaviour in hens. *ibid.*, pp. 474-480.
754. Billet, F., Gans, C. and P.F.A. Maderson. 1985. Why study reptilian development? In *Biology of the Reptiles*, vol. 14, Gans, C., Billet, F. and P.F.A. Maderson, eds., pp. 1-39, Wiley, New York.
755. Moffat, L.A. 1985. Embryonic development and aspects of reproductive biology in the Tuatara, *Sphenodon punctatus*. *ibid.*, pp.493-521.
756. Hubert, J. 1985. Origin and development of oocytes. *ibid.*, pp. 41-74.
757. Ewert, M.A. 1985. Embryology of turtles. *ibid.*, pp. 75-267.
758. Miller, J.D. 1985. Embryology of marine turtles. *ibid.*, pp.269-328.
759. Ferguson, M.W.J. 1985. Reproductive biology and embryology of the crocodilians. *ibid.*, pp. 329-491.
760. Maderson, P.F.A. 1985. Some developmental problems of the reptilian integument. *ibid.*, pp. 523-598.
761. Cooper, E.L., Klempau, A.E. and A.G. Zapata. 1985. Reptilian immunity. *ibid.*, pp. 599-678.
762. Pearson, A.K. 1985. Development of the pituitary in reptiles. *ibid.*, pp. 679-719.
763. Hubert, J. 1985. Embryology of the Squamata. In *Biology of the Reptilia*, vol. 15, Gans, C. and F. Billet, eds., pp. 1-34, Wiley, New York.
764. Saint Girons, H. 1985. Comparative data on Lepidosaurian reproduction and some time tables. *ibid.*, pp. 35-58.
765. Shine, R. 1985. The evolution of viviparity in reptiles: An ecological analysis. *ibid.*, pp. 605-694.
766. Regal, P.J. 1978. Behavioral differences between reptiles and mammals: An analysis of activity and mental capabilities. In. *Behavior and Neurology of Lizards*, Greenberg, N. and P.D. MacLean, eds., pp. 183-202, NIMH, Rockville, Maryland.
767. Wright, S.J. 1981. Extinction mediated competition: The *Anolis* lizards and insectivorous birds of the West Indies. *Amer. Nat.*, **117**:181-192.
768. Smart, J.D. and N.F. Hughes. 1973. The insects and the plant: progressive paleoecological integration. In *Insect/Plant Relationships*, H.F. van Emden, ed., pp. 143-155, *R. Entomol. Soc.* Lond., **6**.
769. Vaughn, T.A. 1959. Functional morphology of three bats: *Eumops, Myotis, and Macrotus. U. Kansas Publ. Mus. Nat. Hist.*, **12**:1-153.

770. Aitken, R.N.C., Solomon, S.E. and E.C. Amoroso. 1976. Obervations on histology of the ovary of the Costa Rican Green Turtle, *Chelonia mydas* L. *J. Exp. Mar. Biol. Ecol.*, **24**:189-204.

Solomon, S.E. and T. Baird. 1976. Studies on the egg shell (oviductal and oviposited) of *Chelonia mydas* L. *ibid.*, **22**:145-160.

____ and ____. 1977. Studies of the soft shell membranes of the eggshell of *Chelonia mydas* L. *ibid.*, **27**:83-92.

____ and ____. 1979. Aspects of the biology of *Chelonia mydas* L. *Oceanogr. Mar. Biol. Ann. Rev.*, **17**:347-361.

771. Owen, D.Wm. 1980. The comparative reproductive physiology of sea turtles. In *Behavioral and Reproductive Biology of Sea Turtles. Amer. Zool.*, **20**:549-563.

772. Seymour, R.S. and R.A. Ackerman. 1980. Adaptations to underground nesting in birds and reptiles. *ibid.*, **20**:437-47.

773. Mrosovsky, N. 1980. Thermal biology of sea turtles. *ibid.*, **20**: 531-547.

774. Ackerman, R.A. 1980. Physiological and ecological aspects of gas exchange by sea turtle eggs. *ibid.*, **20**:575-583.

775. Seymour, R.S. 1979. Dinosaur eggs: Gas conductance through the shell, water loss during incubation and clutch size. *Paleobiol.*, **5**: 1-11.

776. Bennett, A.F. and J.A. Ruben. 1979. Endothermy and activity in vertebrates. *Science*, **206**:649-654.

777. Gowaty, P.A. 1983. Male parental care and apparent monogamy among Eastern Bluebirds (*Siala sialis*). *Amer. Nat.*, **117**:181-192.

778. Weatherhead, P.J. 1983. Two principal strategies in avian communal roosts. *ibid.*, **121**:237-243.

779. Mayr, E. 1983. How to carry out the adaptationist program? *ibid.*, **121**:324-334.

780. Ligon, J.D. 1983. Cooperation and reciprocity in avian social systems. *ibid.*, **121**:366-384.

781. Caple, G., Balda, R.P. and W.R. Willis. 1983. The physics of leaping animals and the evolution of preflight. *ibid.*, **121**:455-467.

782. Jepsen, G.L. 1970. Bat origins and evolution. In *Biology of Bats*, vol. 1, W.A. Wimsatt, ed., pp. 1-64, Academic Press, New York.

783. Moody, P.A. 1962. *Introduction to Evolution*, 2nd ed., Harper, New York.

784. Keast, A. 1977. Zoogeography and phylogeny: The theoretical background and methodology to the analysis of mammal and bird fauna. In *Major Patterns in Vertebrate Evolution*, Hecht, M.K., Goody, P.C. and B.M. Hecht, eds., pp. 249-312,

785. Pirlot, P. 1977. Wing design and the origin of bats. *ibid.*, pp. 375-418.

786. Luckett, W.P. 1977. Ontogeny of amniote fetal membranes and their application to phylogeny. *ibid.*, pp. 439-516.

787. Low, R. 1980. *Parrots, Their Care and Breeding*. Blandford Press, Dorset.

788. Greenewalt, C.H. 1960. The wings of insects and birds as mechanical oscillators. *Proc. Amer. Phil. Soc.*, **104**:605-611.

789. McLean, D.M. 1978. A terminal Mesozoic "greenhouse:" Lessons from the past. *Science*, **201**:401-406.

790. Romer, A.S. 1967. Major steps in vertebrate evolution. *ibid.*, **158**:1629-1637.

791. Emmons, L.H. and A.H. Gentry 1983. Tropical forest structure and the distribution of gliding and prehensile-tailed vertebrates. *Amer. Nat.*, **121**:513-524.

792. Mittwoch, U. 1983. Heterogametic sex chromosomes and the development of the dominant gonad in vertebrates. *ibid.*, **122**:159-180.

793. Ward, P. and A. Zahavi. 1973. The importance of certain assemblages of birds as "information-centers" for food finding. *Ibis*, **115**:517-534.
794. Cabana, G, Frewin, A., Peters, R.H. and L. Randall. 1982. The effect of sexual size dimorphism on variations in reproductive effort of birds and mammals. *Amer. Nat.*, **120**:17-25.
795. Spearman, R.I.C. and J.A. Hardy. 1985. Integument. In *Form and Function in Birds*, vol. 3, King, A.S. and J. McLelland, eds., pp. 1-56, Academic Press, New York.
796. Raikow, R.J. 1985. Locomotor system. *ibid.*, pp. 57-147.
797. Bang, B.G. and B.M. Wenzel. 1985. Nasal cavity and olfactory system *ibid.*, pp. 195-225.
798. Kühne, R. and B. Lewis. 1985. External and middle ears. *ibid.*, pp. 227-271.
799. Smith, C.A. 1985. Inner ear. *ibid.*, pp. 273-310.
800. Martin, G.R. 1985. Eye. *ibid.*, pp. 311-373.
801. Gottschaldt, K.-M. 1985. Structure and function of avian somatosensory receptors. *ibid.*, pp. 375-461.
802. Berkhoudt, H. 1985. Structure and function of avian taste receptors. *ibid.*, pp. 463-496.
803. Sibley, C.G. and J. E. Alquist. 1985. The phylogeny and classification of the Australo-Papuan passerine birds. *Emu*, **85**:1-14.
804. Bock, W.J. and J. Farrand, Jr. 1980. The number of species and genera of recent birds: A contribution to comparative systematics. *Amer. Mus. Novit.*, **2703**:1-29.
805. Mackowski, C.M. 1983. Eucalypts, wildlife and timber--A complex interaction. *Forest and Timber*, **19**:14-17.
806. Smith, P. 1985. Effects of intensive logging on birds in eucalypt forest near Bega, New South Wales. *Emu*, **85**:15-21.
807. Edwards, P.J. 1985. Brood division and transition to independence in blackbirds *Turdus merula*. *Ibis*, **127**:42-59.
808. Bourne, W.R.P. 1985. Comment: Reviews in Ibis. *ibid.*, **127**:123.
809. Zann, R. 1985. Slow continuous wing-moult of Zebra Finches *Poephila guttata* from southeastern Australia. *ibid.*, **127**:184-196.
810. Perrins, C.M. and R.H. McCleery. 1985. The effect of age and pair bond on the breeding success of Great Tits *Parus major*. *ibid.*, **127**:306-315.
811. Evans, S.M., Collins, J.A., Evans, R. and S. Miller. 1985. Patterns of drinking behaviour of some estrildine finches. *ibid.*, **127**:348-354.
812. Clark, A.B. and D.S. Wilson. 1981. Avian breeding adaptations: hatching, asynchrony, brood reduction, and nest failure. *Quart. Rev. Biol.*, **56**:253-277.
813. Richter, W. 1982. Hatching asynchrony: the nest failure hypothesis and brood reduction. *Amer. Nat.*, **120**:828-832.
814. Gustafsson, L. and S.G. Nilsson. 1985. Clutch size and breeding success of Pied and Collared Flycatchers *Ficedula* spp. in nest-boxes of different sizes. *Ibis*, **127**:380-385.
815. Keast, A. 1983. The biogeography of African non-passerine birds: some comparisons with Australia. Review of An atlas of speciation in African non-passerine birds, D.W. Snow, ed., *Emu*, **83**:46-48.
816. Longmore, N.W. and W.E. Boles. 1983. Description and systematics of the Eungella Honeyeater (*Meliphaga hindwoodi*), a new species of honeyeater from central eastern Queensland, Australia. *ibid.*, **83**:59-65.
817. Draffan, R.D.W., Garnett, S.T., and G.J. Malone. 1983. Birds of the Torres Strait: an annotated list and biogeographical analysis. *ibid.*, **83**:207-234.

818. Wyndham, E. 1981. Moult of the Budgerigar *Melopsittacus undulatus*. *Ibis*, **123**:145-147.
819. Smith, G.A. 1975. Systematics of Parrots. *ibid.*, **117**:18-68.
820. Marler, P. and P.C. Mundinger. 1975. Vocalizations, social organization and breeding biology of the Twite *Acanthus flavirostris*. *ibid.*, **117**:1-17.
821. Hespenheide, H.A. 1975. Selective predation by two swifts and a swallow in Central America. *ibid.*, **117**:82-96.
822. Becking, J.H. 1975. The ultrastructure of avian eggshell. *ibid.*, **117**:143-151.
823. Dow, D.D. 1980. Communally breeding Australian birds with an analysis of distributional and environmental factors. *Emu*, **80**:121-140.
824. Pidgeod, R. 1981. Calls of the Galah *Cacatua roseicapilla* and some comparisons with four other species of Australian parrots. *ibid.*, **81**:158-168.
825. Green, R.E. 1984. Double nesting of the Red-legged Partridge *Alectoris rufa*. *Ibis*, **126**:332-346.
826. Croxall, J.P. and C. Ricketts. 1983. Energy costs of incubation in the Wandering Albatross *Diomedea exulans*. *ibid.*, **125**:33-39.
827. Curio, E. 1983. Why do young birds reproduce less well? *ibid.*, **125**:400-404.
828. Moermond, T.C. 1983. Suction-drinking in tanagers Thraupidae and its relation to frugivory. *ibid.*, **125**:545-549.
829. Dawson, W.R. 1984. Physiological studies of desert birds. *J. Arid Envirs.*, **7**:133-155.
830. Thomas, D.H. 1984. Adaptations of desert birds: Sandgrouse (Pteroclididae) as highly successful inhabitants of Afro-Asian arid lands. *ibid.*, **7**:157-181.
831. Davies, S.J. 1984. Nomadism as a response to desert conditions in Australia. *ibid.*, **7**:183-195.
832. Skadhauge, E. 1981. *Osmoregulation in Birds*. Springer, Berlin.
833. Hughes, A. 1977. The topography of vision in mammals of contrasting life styles: comparative optics and retinal organization. In *Handbook of Sensory Physiology*, vol. 7/5, F. Crescitelli, ed., pp. 613-756, Springer, New York.
834. Hayward, J. 1979. *Lovebirds and Their Colour Mutations*, Blandford Press, Poole, Dorset.
835. Rowan, M.K. 1983. *The Doves, Parrots, Lories and Cuckoos of Southern Africa*. David Philip, Johannesburg.
836. Krebs, J.R. and N.B. Davies, eds. 1981. *An Introduction to Behavioural Ecology*. Blackwell, Oxford.
837. Perrins, C.M. and T.R. Birkhead. 1983. *Avian Ecology*. Blackwell, Oxford.
838. Williams, A.J., Siegfried, W.R. and J. Cooper. 1982. Egg composition and hatchling precocity in seabirds. *Ibis*, **124**:456-470.
839. Withers, P.C. 1981. The aerodynamic performance of the wing in Red-shouldered Hawk *Buteolinearis* and a possible aeroelastic role of wing-tip slots. *ibid.*, **123**:239-247.
840. Norberg, R.A. 1981. Why foraging birds in trees should climb and hop upwards rather than downwards. *ibid.*, **123**:477-484.
841. Faaborg, J. and C.B. Patterson. 1981. The characteristics and occurrence of cooperative polyandry. *ibid.*, **123**:477-484.
842. Wyndham, E., Hutchison, R.E. and B.F. Brockway-Fuller. 1981. Gonadal condition of non-breeding wild and domesticated Budgerigars *Melopsittacus undulatus*. *ibid.*, **123**:511-518.
843. Stamps, J., Clark, A., Arrowood, P. and B. Kus. 1985. Parent-offspring conflict in Budgerigars. *Behaviour*, **94**:1-40.

844. ____, ____, Kus, B. and P. Arrowood. 1985. Parent and offspring gender effects on food allocation in Budgerigars (submitted for publication).
845. Hutchison, R.E., Hinde, R.A. and B. Bendon. 1968. Oviduct development and its relation to other aspects of reproduction in domesticated canaries. *J. Zool. Lond.*, **155**:87-103.
846. Shellswell, G.B., Gosney, S. and R.A. Hinde. 1975. Photoperiodic control of Budgerigar reproduction: circadian changes in sensitivity. *ibid.*, **175**:53-60.
847. Hutchison, R.E. 1975. Influence of oestrogen on the initiation of nesting behaviour in female Budgerigars. *J. Endocrinol.*, **64**: 417-428;
Effects of ovarian steroids and prolactin on the sequential development of nesting behaviour in female Budgerigars. *ibid.*, **67**:29-39.
848. Cheng, M.-F. 1974. Ovarian development in the female Ring Dove in respect to stimulation by intact and castrated male Ring Doves. *ibid.*, **63**:43-53.
849. Hutchison, R.E. 1974. Temporal patterning of external stimuli and reproductive behaviour in female Budgerigars. *Anim. Behav.*, **22**:150-157.
850. Putman, R.J. and R.A. Hinde. 1973. Effects of light regime and breeding experience on Budgerigar reproduction. *J. Zool. Lond.*, **170**:475-484.
Hinde, R.A. and R. J. Putman. 1973. Why Budgerigars breed in continuous darkness. *ibid.*, **170**:485-491.
851. van Tienhoven, A. 1961. Endocrinology of reproduction in birds. In *Sex and Internal Secretions*, vol. II, W.C. Young, ed., pp. 1088-1169, Williams and Wilkens, Baltimore.
852. Franchi, L.L., Mandl, A.M. and Sir S. Zuckerman. 1962. The development of the ovary and the process of oogenesis. In *The Ovary*, vol. 1., Sir S. Zuckerman, ed., pp. 1-88. Academic Press, New York.
853. Franchii, L.L. 1962. The structure of the ovary. B. Vertebrates. *ibid.*, pp. 121-187.
854. Perry, J.S. and I.W. Rowlands. 1962. The ovarian cycle in vertebrates. *ibid.*, pp. 275-309.
855. Eckstein, P. 1962. Ovarian physiology in the non-pregnant female. *ibid.*, pp. 311-359.
856. Asdell, S.A. 1962. The mechanism of ovulation. *ibid.*, 435-449.
857. Miller, M.R. 1948. The seasonal histological changes occurring in the ovary, corpus luteum, and testis of the viviparous lizard, *Xantusia vigilis*. *U. Calif. Publ. Zool.*, **47**:197-223.
858. Stamps, J.A. 1976. Egg retention, rainfall and egg laying in a tropical lizard *Anolis aneus*. *Copeia*, **1976**:759-764.
859. Masure, R.H. and W.C. Allee. 1934. Flock organization of the Shell Parakeet *Melopsittacus undulatus*. *Ecology*, **15**:388-398.
860. Hutchison, R.E. 1977. Temporal relationships between nesting behaviour, ovary and oviduct development during the reproductive cycle of female Budgerigars. *Behaviour*, **60**:278-303.
861. Stanley, A.J. and E. Witschi. 1940. Germ cell migration in relation to asymmetry in the sex glands of Hawks. *Anat. Rec.*, **76**:329-342.
862. Van Ness, J., Maxwell, I.H. and W.E. Hahn. 1979. Complex population nonpolyadenylate m-RNA in mouse brain. *Cell*, **18**:1341-1349.
863. Hoar, W.S. 1969. Reproduction. In *Fish Physiology*, vol. 3, Hoar, W.S. and D.J. Randall, eds., pp. 1-72, Academic Press, New York.

864. Gorbman, A. 1983. Reproduction in cyclostome fishes and its regulation. *ibid.*, vol. 9, Part A, Hoar, W.S., Randall, D.J. and E.M. Donaldson, eds., pp. 1-29.
865. Dodd, J.M. 1983. Reproduction in cartilaginous fishes (Chrondrichthyes). *ibid.*, pp. 31-95.
866. Nagahama, Y. 1983. The functional morphology of teleost gonads. *ibid.*, pp. 223-275.
867. Licht, P. and G.C. Gorman. 1979. Reproductive and fat cycles in Caribbean *Anolis* lizards. *U. Calif. Publ. Zool.*, **95**:1-52.
868. Smith, H.M. 1979. *Handbook of Lizards*. Cornell U. Press, Ithaca.
869. Bennett, A.F. 1983. Ecological consequences of activity metabolism. In *Lizard Ecology*, Huey, R.B., Pianka, E.R. and T.W. Schoener, eds., pp. 11-23, Harvard U. Press, Cambridge.
870. Nagy, K.A. 1983. Ecological energetics. *ibid.*, pp 24-54.
871. Porter, W.P. and C.R. Tracy. 1983. Biophysical analyses of energetics, time-space utilization, and distributional limits. *ibid.*, pp. 55-83.
872. Regal, P.J. 1983. The adaptive zone and behavior of lizards. *ibid.*, pp. 105-118.
873. Ferguson, G.W., Hughes, J.L. and K.L. Brown. 1983. Food availability and territorial establishment of juvenile *Sceloporus undulatus*. *ibid.*, pp. 134-148.
874. Ballinger, R.E. 1983. Life-history variations. *ibid.*, pp. 241-260.
875. Mertens, R. 1960. *The World of Amphibians and Reptiles*. Harrap, London.
876. Skoczylas, R. 1978. Physiology of the digestive tract. In *Biology of the Reptilia*, vol. 8, Gans, C. and K.A. Gans, eds.,pp. 589-717.
877. Hopson, J.A. 1979. Paleoneurology. *ibid.*, vol. 9, Gans, C., Northcutt, R.G. and P. Ulinski, eds., pp. 39-146.
878. Platel, R. 1979. Brain weight--body weight relationships. *ibid.*, pp. 147-171.
879. Quay, W.B. 1979. The parietal eye--pineal complex. *ibid.*, pp. 245-406.
880. Von Düring, M. and M.R. Miller. 1979. Sensory nerve endings of the skin and deeper structures. *ibid.*, pp. 407-441.
881. Peterson, J.A. 1983. The evolution of the subdigital pad in *Anolis*. I. Comparisons among the anoline genera. In *Advances in Herpetology and Evolutionary Biology*, Rhodin, A.G.J. and K. Miyata, eds., pp. 245-283, Museum of Comparative Zoology, Cambridge.
882. Estes, R. 1983. The fossil record and early distribution of lizards. *ibid.*, pp. 365-398.
883. Medem, F. 1983. Reproductive data on *Platemys platycephala* (Testudines: Chelidae) in Colombia. *ibid.*, pp. 429-434.
884. Moermond. T.C. 1983. Competition between *Anolis* and birds: a reassessment. *ibid.*, pp. 507-520.
885. Auffenberg, W. 1983. Courtship behavior in *Varanus bengalensis* (Sauria: Varanidae). *ibid.*, pp. 535-551.
886. Vitt, L.J. and J.D. Congdon. 1978. Body shape, reproductive effort, and relative clutch mass in lizards: resolution of a paradox. *Amer. Nat.*, **112**:595-608.
887. Berger, P.J. and G. Burnstock. 1979. Autonomic nervous system. In *Biology of the Reptilia*, vol. 9, Gans, C., Northcutt, R.G. and P. Ulinski, eds., pp. 1-57, Academic Press, New York.
888. Kusuma, A., ten Donkelaar, H.J. and R. Nieuwenhuys. 1979. Intrinsic organization of the spinal cord. *ibid.*, pp. 59-109.
889. ten Donkelaar, H.J. and R. Nieuwenhuys. 1979. The brainstem. *ibid.*, pp. 133-200.

890. Schwab, M.E. 1979. Variation in the rhombencephalon. *ibid.*, pp. 201-246.
891. Parent, A. 1979. Monoaminergic systems of the brain. *ibid.*, pp. 247-285.
892. Belekhova, M.G. 1979. Neurophysiology of the forebrain. *ibid.*, pp. 287-359.
893. Wyndham, E. 1978. Ecology of the Budgerigar *Melopsittacus undulatus* (Shaw) (Psittaciformes: Platycercidae). Ph.D. Thesis, U. New England, Armingdale, Australia 2351.
894. Saidapur, S.K. 1978. Follicular Atresia in the ovaries of nonmammalian vertebrates. *Int. Rev. Cytol.*, **54**:225-244.
895. Crews, D. and M.C. Morse. 1986. Evolution of mechanisms controlling mating behavior. *Science*, **231**:121-125.
896. Blackburn, D.G., Vitt, L.J. and C.A. Beuchat. 1984. Eutherian-like specializations in a viviparous reptile. *Proc. Natl. Acad. Sci.*, **81**:4860-4863.
897. Andrews, R. and A.S. Rand. 1974. Reproductive effort in anoline lizards. *Ecology*, **55**:1317-1327.
898. Jones, R.E., Fitzgerald, K.T., Duvall, D. and D. Banker. 1979. On the mechanisms of alternating and simultaneous ovulation in lizards. *Herpetol.*, **35**:132-139.
899. Sibley, C.G. and J.E. Ahlquist. 1986. Reconstructing bird phylogeny by comparing DNA's. *Sci. Amer.*, **254(2)**:82-92.
900. Jones, R.E. 1978. Ovarian cycles in nonmammalian vertebrates. In *The Vertebrate Ovary*, R.E. Jones, ed., pp. 731-762, Plenum, London.
901. Hardisty, M.W. 1978. Primordial germ cells and the vertebrate germ line. *ibid.*, pp. 1-45.
902. Merchant-Larios, H. 1978. Ovarian differentiation. *ibid.*, 47-81.
903. Tokarz, R.R. 1978. Oogonial proliferation, oogenesis, and folliculogenesis in nonmammalian vertebrates. *ibid.*, pp. 145-179.
904. Guraya, S.S. 1978. Maturation of the follicular wall of nonmammalian vertebrates. *ibid.*, pp. 261-329.
905. Lance, V. I.P. Callard. 1978. Hormone control of ovarian steroidogenesis in nonmammalian vertebrates. *ibid.*, pp. 469-502.
906. Wallace, R.A. 1978. Oocyte growth in nonmammalian vertebrates. *ibid.*, pp. 469-502.
907. Espey, L.L. 1978. Ovulation. *ibid.*, pp. 503-532.
908. Byskov, A.G. 1978. Follicular atresia. *ibid.*, pp. 533-562.
909. Ellinwood, W.E., Nett, T.M. and G.D. Niswender. 1978. Ovarian vasculature: structure and function. *ibid.*, pp. 583-614.
910. Burden, H.W. 1978. Ovarian innervation. *ibid.*, pp. 615-638.
911. Jones, R.E. 1978. Control of follicular selection. *ibid.*, pp. 763-788.
912. Ballinger, R.E. 1978. Variation in and evolution of clutch and litter size. *ibid.*, pp. 789-825.
913. Jones, R.E. 1978. Evolution of the vertebrate ovary: an overview. *ibid.*, pp. 827-840.
914. Smith, H.M., Sinelnik, G., Fawcett, J.D. and R.E. Jones. 1972. A unique reproductive cycle in *Anolis* and its relatives. *Bull. Philadelphia Herpetol. Soc.*, **20**:28-30.
915. Ishii, S. 1980. Hormone-receptor interactions I: peptide hormones. In *Avian Endocrinology*, Epple, A. and M.H. Stetson, eds., pp. 1-15, Academic Press, New York.
916. Tanaka, K. 1980. Hormone-receptor interactions II: steroid hormones. *ibid.*, pp. 17-31.
917. Hartwig, H.-G. 1980. The structure of the pineal gland. *ibid.*, pp. 33-51.

918. Binkley, S. 1980. Functions of the pineal gland. *ibid.*, pp. 53-74.
919. Oksche, A. and H.-G. Hartwig. 1980. Structural principles of central neurendocrine systems. *ibid.*, pp. 75-84.
920. George, J.C. 1980. Structure and physiology of posterior lobe hormones. *ibid.*, pp. 8-115.
921. Baylé. J.-D. 1980. The adenohypophysiotropic mechanisms. *ibid.*, pp. 117-145.
922. Goldsmith, A.R. and B.K. Follett. 1980. Anterior pituitary hormones. *ibid.*, pp. 147-165.
923. Clark, N.B. and K. Simkiss. 1980. Time, targets and triggers: a study of calcium regulation in the bird. *ibid.*, pp. 191-208.
924. Glick, B. 1980. The thymus and bursa of fabricius: endocrine organs? *ibid.*, pp. 209-229.
925. Hazelwood, R.L. 1980. The avian gastro-enteric-pancreatic system: structure and function. *ibid.*, pp. 231-250.
926. Kobayashi, H., Uemura, H. and Y. Takei. 1980. Physiological role of the renin-angiotensin system during hydration. *ibid.*, pp. 319-330.
927. Farner, D.S. and E. Gwinner. 1980. Photoperiodicity, circannual and reproductive cycles. *ibid.*, pp. 331-366.
928. Wingfield, J.C. 1980. Fine temporal adjustment of reproductive functions. *ibid.*, pp. 367-389.
929. Assenmacher, I. and M. Jallageas. 1980. Circadian and circannual hormone rhythms. *ibid.*, pp. 391-411.
930. Lofts, B. and R. Massa. 1980. Male reproduction. *ibid.*, pp.413-434.
931. Sharp, P.G. 1980. Female reproduction. *ibid.*, pp. 435-454.
932. Hertelendy, F. 1980. Prostaglandins in avian endocrinology. *ibid.*, pp. 455-479.
933. Braun, E.J. 1980. Renal osmoregulation. *ibid.*, pp. 499-516.
934. Phillips, J.G. and S. Harvey. 1980. Salt glands in birds. *ibid.*, pp. 517-532.
935. Sossinka, R., Pröve, E. and K. Immelmann. 1980. Hormone mechanisms in avian behavior. *ibid.*, pp. 533-547.
936. Haase, E. and R.S. Donham. 1980. Hormones and domestication. *ibid.*, pp. 549-565.
937. Jones, R.E. 1975. Endocrine control of clutch size in reptiles. IV. Estrogen-induced hyperemia and growth of ovarian follicles in the lizard *Anolis carolinensis*. *Gen. Comp. Endocrinol.*, **25**: 211-222.
938. Tokarz, R.R. and R.E. Jones. 1979. A study of egg-related maternal behavior in *Anolis carolinensis* (Reptilia, Lacertilia, Iguanidae). *J. Herpetol.*, **13**:283-288.
939. Bahr, J., Kao, L. and A.V. Nalbandov. 1974. The role of catecholamines and nerves in ovulation. *Biol. Reprod.*, **10**:273-290.
940. Hoar, W.S. 1965. Comparative physiology: hormones and reproduction in fishes. *Ann. Rev. Physiol.*, **27**:51-70.
941. Gilbert, A.B. 1971. The ovary. In *Physiology and Biochemistry and the Domestic Fowl*, Bell, D.J. and B.M. Freeman, eds., pp. 1163-1208, Academic Press, New York.
942. McIndoe, W.M. 1971. Yolk synthesis. *ibid.*, pp. 1209-1223.
943. Gilbert, A.B. 1971. Control of ovulation. *ibid.*, pp. 1225-1235.
944. Aitken, R.N.C. 1971. The oviduct. *ibid.*, pp. 1237-1289.
945. Gilbert, A.B. 1971. Egg albumen and its formation. *ibid.*, pp. 1291-1329.
946. Simkiss, K. and T.G. Taylor. 1971. Shell formation. *ibid.*, pp.1331-1343.
947. Gilbert, A.B. 1971. Transport of the egg through the oviduct and oviposition. *ibid.*, pp. 1345-1352.

948. ____ and D.G.M. Wood-Gush. 1971. Ovulatory and ovipository cycles. *ibid.*, pp. 1353-1378.

949. Gilbert, A.B. 1971. The egg: its physical and chemical aspects. *ibid.*, pp. 1379-1399.

950. ____. 1971. The egg in reproduction. *ibid.*, pp. 1401-1409.

951. ____. 1971. The endocrine ovary in reproduction. *ibid.*, pp. 1449-1468.952.

952. Schall, J.J. 1983. Small clutch size in a tropical whiptail lizard (*Cnemidophorus arubensis*). *J. Herpetol.*, **17**:406-408.

953. Smith, H.M., Sinelnik, G., Fawcett, J.D. and R.E. Jones. 1972. A survey of the chronology of ovulation in anoline lizard genera. *Trans. Kansas Acad. Sci.*, **75**:107-120.

954. Martin, S.G. 1974. Adaptations for polygynous breeding in the Bobolink, *Dolichonyx oryzivorus. Amer. Zool.*, **14**:109-119.

955. Vitt, L.J. and H.J. Price. 1982. Ecological and evolutionary determinants of relative clutch mass in lizards. *Herpetol.*, **38**:237-255.

956. Bickford, A.A. 1965. A fully formed and functional right oviduct in a single comb White Leghorn Pullet. *Avian. Dis.*, **9**:464-470.

957. Ficken, M.S. and R.W. Ficken. 1962. The comparative ethology of the wood warblers: *a review. Living Bird*, **1**:102-121.

958. Marler, P. 1957. Specific distinctiveness in the communication signals of birds. *Behaviour*, **11**:13-39.

959. Robinson, A. 1945. The application of 'territory and the breeding cycle' to some Australian birds. *Emu*, **45**:100-108.

960. ____. 1949. The biological significance of bird song in Australia *ibid.*, **49**:291-315.

961. Ames, P.L. 1975. The application of syringeal morphology to the classification of the Old World insect eaters (Muscicapidae). *Bonn. zool. Beitr.*, **26**:107-134.

962. Hildén, O. 1975. Breeding system of Temminck's Stint *Calidris temminckii. Ornis Fennica*, **52**:117-144.

963. Pitelka, F.A., Holmes, R.T. and S.F. MacLean, Jr. 1974. Ecology and the evolution of social organization in Arctic Sandpipers. In *Ecology and Evolution of Social Organization. Amer. Zool.*, **14**:185-204.

964. Jenni, D.A. 1974. Evolution of polyandry in birds. *ibid.*, 14:129-144.

965. Jones, P.J. and P. Ward. 1976. The level of reserve protein as the proximate factor controlling the timing of breeding and clutch size in the Red-billed Quela *Quela quela. Ibis*, **118**:547-574.

966. Bartholomew, G.A. and V.A. Tucker. 1963. Control of changes in body temperature, metabolism, and circulation by the agamid lizard, *Amphibolurus barbatus. Physiol. Zool.*, **36**:199-218.

967. Kendeigh, S.C., Dol'nik, V.R. and V.M. Gavrilov. 1977. Avian Energetics. In *Granivorous Birds in Ecosystems*, Pinowski, J. and S.C. Kendeigh, eds., pp. 127-204, Cambridge U. Press, Cambridge.

968. Wiens, J.A. and R.F. Johnston. 1977. Adaptive correlates of granivory in birds. *ibid.*, pp. 301-340.

969. Kendeigh, S.C., Wiens, J.A. and J. Pinowski. 1977. Epilogue. *ibid.*, pp. 341-344.

970. Cody, M.L. 1971. Finch flocks in the Mohave Desert. *Theor. Popul. Biol.*, **2**:142-158.

971. Korf, H.-W., Oksche, A., Ekström, P., Gery, I., Zigler, J.S., Jr., and D.C. Klein. 1986. Pinealocyte projections into the mammalian brain revealed with s-antigen antiserum. *Science*, **231**:735-737.

972. Crowley, T.J., Short, D.A., Mengel, J.G. and G.R. North. 1986. Role of seasonality in the evolution of climate during the last hundred million years. *ibid.*, **231**:579-584.
973. King, J.R. 1974. Seasonal allocation of time and energy resources in birds. In *Avian Energetics*, R.A. Paynter, Jr., ed., pp. 4-85, Nuttall Ornithol. Club, Cambridge, Mass.
974. Calder, W.A. 1974. Consequences of body size for avian energetics. *ibid.*, pp. 86-151.
975. Ricklefs, R.E. 1974. Energetics of reproduction in birds. *ibid.*, pp. 152-297.
976. Tucker, V.A. 1974. Energetics of natural avian flight. *ibid.*, pp. 298-333.
977. Norberg, U. 1985. Evolution of vertebrate flight: an aerodynamic model for the transition from gliding to active flight. *Amer. Nat.*, **126**:303-327.
978. Ball, G.F. and R. Silver. 1983. Timing of incubation bouts by Ring Doves. *J. Comp. Psychol.*, **97**:213-225.
979. Ridley, M. 1978. Paternal care. *Anim. Behav.*, **26**:904-932.
980. Gerhart, J.C. *et al.* 1982. The cellular basis of morphogenetic change. In *Evolution and Development*, J.T. Bonner, ed., pp. 87-114, Springer-Verlag, Berlin.
981. Katz, M.J. 1982. Ontogenetic mechanisms: the middle ground of evolution. *ibid.*, pp. 207-212.
982. Maderson, P.F.A. *et al.* 1982. The role of development in macroevolutionary change. *ibid.*, pp. 279-312.
983. Gould, S.J. 1982. Change in developmental timing as a mechanism of macroevolution. *ibid.*, pp. 333-346.
984. Tiffney, B.H. 1985. Geological factors in the evolution of plants. In *Geological Factors in the Evolution of Plants*, B.H. Tiffney, ed., pp. 1-10, Yale U. Press, New Haven.
985. Awramik, S.M. and J.W. Valentine. 1985. Adaptive aspects of the ori-origin of autotrophic eukaryotes. *ibid.*, pp. 11-21.
986. Chapman, D.J. 1985. Geological factors and biochemical aspects of the origin of land plants. *ibid.*, pp. 23-45.
987. Barrett, S.F. 1985. Early Devonian continental positions and climate: a framework for paleophytogeography. *ibid.*, pp. 93-127.
988. Cope, M.J. and W.G. Chaloner. 1985. Wildfire: an interaction of biological and physical processes. *ibid.*, pp. 257-277.
989. van Tienhoven, A. 1983. *Reproductive Physiology of Vertebrates*. Cornell U. Press, Ithaca.
990. Bock, W.J. 1983. On extended wings: another view of flight. *The Sciences*, **23**:16-20.
991. Lorenz, K. 1970. *Studies in Animal Behavior*, vol. 1 (originally published in 1937), Harvard U. Press, Cambridge.
992. Maynard Smith, J. and G.R. Price. 1973. The logic of animal conflict. *Nature*, **246**:15-18.
993. Stent, G.S. 1981. Strength and weakness of the genetic approach to the development of the nervous system. *Ann. Rev. Neurosci.*, **4**:163-194.
994. Case, T.J. 1978. On the evolution and adaptive significance of postnatal growth rates in the terrestrial vertebrates. *Q. Rev. Biol.*, **53**:243-282.
995. Bull, J.J. 1980. Sex determination in reptiles. *ibid.*, **55**:3-21.
996. Weaver, J.C. 1983. The improbable endotherm: the energetics of sauropod dinosaur *Brachiosaurus*. *Paleobiol.*, **9**:173-182.
997. Abs, M. 1983. Ontogeny and juvenile development. In *Physiology and Behaviour of the Pigeon*, M. Abs, ed., pp. 1-18, Academic Press, New York.

998. Griminger, P. 1983. Digestive system and nutrition. *ibid.*, pp. 19-38.
999. McNabb, F.M.A. 1983. Excretion. *ibid.*, pp.41-53.
1,000. Chadwick, A. 1983. Endocrinology of reproduction. *ibid.*, pp. 55-72.
1,001. Powell, F.L. 1983. Respiration. *ibid.*, pp. 73-95.
1,002. ____. 1983. Circulation. *ibid.*, pp. 97-116.
1,003. Aulie, A. 1983. The fore-limb musculature and flight. *ibid.*, pp. 117-129.
1,004. Rautenberg, W. 1983. Thermoregulation. *ibid.*, pp. 131-148.
1,005. Wenzel, B.M. 1983. Chemical senses. *ibid.*, pp. 149-167.
1,006. Necker, R. 1983. Somatosensory system. *ibid.*, pp. 169-192.
1,007. Necker, R. 1983. Hearing. *ibid.*, pp. 193-219.
1,008. Emmerton, J. 1983. Functional morphology of the visual system. *ibid.*, pp. 221-244.
1,009. ____ 1983. Vision. *ibid.*, pp. 245-266.
1,010. Schmidt-Koenig, K. 1983. Orientation. *ibid.*, pp. 267-283.
1,011. Goodwin, D. 1983. Behavior. *ibid.*, pp. 285-308.
1,012. Baptista, L. and M. Abs. 1983. Vocalizations. *ibid.*, pp. 309-325.
1,013. Delius, J. D. 1983. Learning. *ibid.*, pp. 327-355.
1,014. Tanabe, Y. and T. Nakamura. 1980. Endocrine mechanism of ovulation in chickens (*Gallus domesticus*), Quail (*Coturnix coturnix japonica*), and duck (*Anas platyrhynchos domestica*). In *Biological Rhythms in Birds: Neural and Endocrine Aspects*, Tanabe, Y., Tanaka, K. and T. Ookawa, eds., pp. 179-188, Springer, New York.
1,015. Rayner, J.M.V. 1979. A new approach to animal flight mechanics. *J. Exp. Biol.*, **80**:17-54.
1,016. Cott, H.B. 1975. *Looking at Animals: A Zoologist in Africa.* Scribner's Sons, New York.
1,017. Cody, M.L. 1973. Coexistence, coevolution and convergent evolution in seabird communities. *Ecology*, **54**:31-44.
1,018. Green, L., Brecha, N. and M.S. Gazzaniga. 1978. Interocular transfer of simultaneous but not successive discriminations in the Pigeon. *Anim. Learn. Behav.*, **6**:261-264.
1,019. Ostrom, J.H. 1979. Bird flight: how did it begin? *Amer. Sci.*, **67**:46-56.
1,020. Wenzel, B.M. and L.J. Rausch. 1977. Does the olfactory system modulate affective behavior in the Pigeon? In *Tonic Functions of Sensory Systems. Ann. N.Y. Acad. Sci.*, **290**:314-330.
Wenzel, B.M. 1974. The olfactory system and behavior. In *Limbic and Autonomic Nervous Systems Research*, L.V. DiCara, ed., pp. 1-40.
1,021. Jacobson, M. 1970. *Developmental Neurobiology.* Holt, Rinehart and Winston, New York.
1,022. Greene, G.L., Gilna, P. Waterfield, M. Baker, A., Hort, Y. and J. Shine. 1986. Sequence and expression of human estrogen receptor complementary DNA. *Science*, **231**:1150-1154.
1,023. Goldman, B.D. 1981. Structure of protein and peptide hormones. In *Neuroendocrinology of Reproduction*, N.T. Adler, ed., pp. 3-12, Plenum Press, New York.
1,024. ____. 1981. Histology of the pituitary. *ibid.*, pp. 13-17.
1,025. Feder, H.H. 1981. Essentials of steroid structure, nomenclature, reactions, biosynthesis, and measurements. *ibid.*, pp. 19-63.
1,026. ____. 1981. Perinatal hormones and their role in the development of sexual dimorphic behaviors. *ibid.*, pp. 127-157.
1,027. Adkins-Regan. 1981. Early organizational effects of hormones. *ibid.*, pp. 159-228.

1,028. Elliot, J.A. and B.D. Goldman. 1981. Seasonal reproduction. *ibid.*, pp. 377-423.
1,029. McCann, S. 1981. Central nervous system control of the pituitary. *ibid.*, pp. 427-445.
1,030. McEwen, B.S. 1981. Cellular biochemistry of hormone action in brain and pituitary. *ibid.*, pp. 485-518.
1,031. Scharrer, B. 1977. Evolutionary aspects of neuroendocrine control process. In *Reproductive Behavior and Evolution*, Rosenblatt, J.S. and B.R. Komisaruk, eds., pp. 111-124, Plenum, New York.
1,032. Gadgil, M. and W.H. Bossert. 1970. Life Historical consequences of natural selection. *Amer. Sci.*, **104**:1-24.
1,033. Cohen, J. 1971. The comparative physiology of gamete populations. *Adv. Comp. Physiol.*, **4**:267-380.
1,034. Barnes, D.M. 1986. Lessons from snails and other models. *Science*, **231**:1246-1249.
1,035. Huston, T.M. and A.V. Nalbandov. 1953. Neurohumoral control of the pituitary in the fowl. *Endocrinol.*, **52**:149-156.
1,036. Quinn, W.G. and J.L. Gould. 1979. Nerves and genes. *Nature*, **278**:19-23.
1,037. Hairston, N.G., Smith, F.E. and L.B. Slobodkin. 1960. Community structure, population control and competition. *Amer. Nat.*, **94**:421-425.
1,038. Donovan, B.T. 1977. The hypothalamo-pituitary axis. In *Control of Ovulation*, Crighton, D.B., Haynes, N.B., Foxcroft, G.R. and G.E. Flemming, eds., pp. 3-4, Butterworths, London.
1,039. Ellendorff, F. 1977. Extra-hypothalamic centres involved in the control of ovulation. *ibid.*, pp. 7-19.
1,040. Kordon, C. 1977. The role of neurotransmitters in the secretion of pituitary gonadotropins and prolactin. *ibid.*, pp. 21-28.
1,041. Hartree, A. 1977. Structure of gonadotropins as related to function. *ibid.*, pp. 91-99.
1,042. Hay, F.H. and R.M. Moor. 1977. Changes in the Graafian follicle population during the follicular phase of the oestrous cycle. *ibid.*, pp. 177-196.
1,043. Richards, J.S., Rao, M.C. and J.J. Ireland. 1977. Actions of pituitary gonadotropins on the ovary. *ibid.*, pp. 197-216.
1,044. Hansel, W. and J.E. Fortune. 1977. The applications of ovulation control. *ibid.*, pp. 237-263.
1,045. Follett, B.K. 1977. Photoperiodism and seasonal breeding in birds and mammals. *ibid.*, pp. 267-293.
1,046. McNabb, B.K. 1978. The evolution of endothermy in the phylogeny of mammals. *Amer. Nat.*, **112**:1-21.
1,047. Gosney, S. and R.A. Hinde. 1976. Changes in sensitivity of female Budgerigars to male vocalizations. *J. Zool.*, **179**:407-410.
1,048. Ulinski, P.S. 1983. *Dorsal Ventricular Ridge*. John Wiley & Sons, New York.
1,049. Komisaruk, B.R., Terasawa, E. and J.F. Rodriguez-Sierra. 1981. In *Neuroendocrinology of Reproduction*, N.T. Adler, ed., pp. 349-376, Plenum Press, New York.
1,050. Savile, D.B.O. 1957. Adaptive evolution in the avian wing. *Evol.*, **11**:212-224.
____. 1962. Gliding and flight in vertebrates. *Amer. Zool.*, **2**:161-166.
1,051. Cody, M.L. 1966. A general theory of clutch size. *Evol.*, **20**:174-184.
1,052. Moreau, R.E. 1972. *The Palaearctic-African Bird Migration Systems*. Academic Press, New York.

1,053. Freeman, B.M. and M.A. Vince. 1974. *Development of the Avian Embryo*. Chapman and Hall, London.

1,054. Smith, G.A. 1976. Notes on some species of parrot in captivity. *Avicult. Mag.*, 82:22-32.

1,055. Eastman, W.R., Jr. and A.C. Hunt. 1966. *The Parrots of Australia*, Angus and Robertson, Sydney.

1,056. Cayley, N.W. and A.H. Lendon. 1973. *Australian Parrots in Field and Aviary*, Angus and Robertson, Sydney.

1,057. Crook, K.A.W. 1981. The break-up of the Australian-Antarctic segment of Gondwanaland. In *Ecological Biogeography of Australia*, vol. 1, A. Keast, ed., pp. 1-14. Junk, The Hague.

1,058. Powell, C. McA., Johnson, B.D. and J.J. Veevers. 1981. The early Cretaceous break-up of eastern Gondwanaland, the separation of Australia and India, and their interaction with southeast Asia. *ibid.*, pp. 15-29.

1,059. Kemp, E.M. 1981. Tertiary palaeogeography and the evolution of the Australian climate. *ibid.*, pp. 31-49.

1,060. Galloway, R.W. and E.M. Kemp. 1981. Late Cainozoic environments in Australia. *ibid.*, pp. 51-80.

1,061. Nix, H.A. 1981. The environment of *Terra Australis*. *ibid.*, pp. 103-133.

1,062. Recher, H.F. and P.E. Christensen. 1981. Fire and the evolution of the Australian biota. *ibid.*, pp. 133-162.

1,063. Specht, R.L. 1981. Major vegetation formations in Australia. *ibid.*, pp. 163-297.

1,064. ____. 1981. Ecophysical principles determining the biogeography of major vegetation formations in Australia. *ibid.*, pp. 299-333.

1,065. Dettmann, M.E. 1981. The Cretaceous flora. *ibid.*, pp. 355-375.

1,066. Christophel, D.C. 1981. Tertiary megafossil floras of Australia as indicators of floristic associations and palaeoclimate. *ibid.*, pp. 377-390.

1,067. Martin, H.A. 1981. The Tertiary flora. *ibid.*, pp. 391-406.

1,068. Beadle, N.C.W. 1981. Origins of the Australian angiosperm flora. *ibid.*, pp. 407-426.

1,069. Pryor, L.D. and L.A.S. Johnson. 1981. Eucalypts, the universal Australian. *ibid.*, pp. 499-536.

1,070. Clifford, H.T. and B.K. Simon. 1981. The biogeography of Australian grasses. *ibid.*, pp. 537-554.

1,071. Webb, L.J. and J.G. Tracey. 1981. Australian rainforests: patterns and change. *ibid.*, pp. 605-694.

1,072. Beadle, N.C.W. 1981. The vegetation of the arid zone. *ibid.*, pp. 695-715.

1,073. Costin, A.B. 1981. Vegetation of high mountains in Australia. *ibid.*, pp. 717-731.

1,074. Nelson, E.C. 1981. Phytogeography of southern Australia. *ibid.*, pp. 733-759.

1,075. James, S.H. 1981. Cytoevolutionary patterns, genetic systems and the phytogeography of Australia. *ibid.*, pp. 761-782.

1,076. Specht, R.L. 1981. Evolution of Australian flora: some generalities. *ibid.*, pp. 783-805.

1,077. Main, B.L. 1981. Australian spiders diversity, distribution and ecology. *ibid.*, vol. 2, pp. 807-852.

1,078. Bishop, M.J. 1981. The biogeography and evolution of Australian land snails. *ibid.*, pp. 923-954.

1,079. Tindale, N.B. 1981. The origin of the Lepidoptera relative to Australia. *ibid.*, pp. 955-976.

1,080. Howden, H.F. 1981. Zoogeography of some Australian Coleoptera as exemplified by the Scarabaeoidea. *ibid.*, pp. 1,007-1,035.

1,081. Williams, W.D. 1981. Inland aquatic systems: an overview. *ibid.*, pp. 1,079-1,099.

1,082. Watson, J.A.L. 1981. Odonata (dragonflies and damselflies). *ibid.*, pp. 1,139-1,167.

1,083. Zwick, P. 1981. Plecoptera. *ibid.*, pp. 1,169-1,182.

1,084. Lansbury, I. 1981. Aquatic and semi-aquatic bugs (Hemiptera) of Australia. *ibid.*, pp. 1,195-1,211.

1,085. Pianka, E.R. 1981. Diversity and adaptive radiations of Australian desert lizards. *ibid.*, pp. 1,375-1,393.

1,086. Keast, A. 1981. The evolutionary biogeography of Australian birds *ibid.*, vol. 3, pp. 1,587-1,635.

1,087. Dawson, W.R. 1981. Adjustments of Australian birds to thermal conditions and water scarcity in arid zones. *ibid.*, pp. 1,649-1,674.

1,088. Kikkawa, J., Monteith, G.B. and G. Ingram. 1981. Cape York Peninsula: major region of faunal interchange. *ibid.*, pp. 1,695-1,742.

1,089. Keast, A. 1981. Distributional patterns, regional biotas, and adaptations in the Australian biota: a synthesis. *ibid.*, pp. 1,893-1,997.

1,090. ____. 1981. Origins and relationships of the Australian biota. *ibid.*, pp. 1,999-2,050.

1,091. Macphail, E.M. 1982. *Brain and Intelligence in Vertebrates*, Clarendon Press, Oxford.

1,092. Rieke, G.K. 1978. Forebrain projections of the Pigeon olfactory bulb. *J. Morph.*, **158**:41-56.

1,093. Repérant, J. 1973. Nouvelles données sur les projections visuelles chez le Pigeon (*Columba livia*). *J. Hirnforsch.*,**14**:151-188.

1,094. Cracraft, J. 1984. Conceptual and methodological aspects of the study of evolutionary rates, with some comments on bradytely in birds. In *Living Fossils*, Eldredge, N. and S.M. Stanley, eds., pp. 95-104, Springer-Verlag, New York.

1,095. Meyer, E.R. 1984. Crocodilians as living fossils. *ibid.*, pp. 105-131.

1,096. Maisey, J.G. and K.E. Wolfram. 1984. *"Notidanus." ibid.*, pp. 170-180.

1,097. Schram, F.R. and R.R. Hessler. 1984. Anaspidid Syncarida. *ibid.*, pp. 192-195.

1,098. Cracraft, J. 1974. Continental drift and vertebrate distribution. *Ann. Rev. Ecol. System.*, **5**:215-261.

1,099. Whittow, G.C. 1973. Evolution of thermoregulation. In *Comparative Physiology of Thermoregulation*, G.C. Whittow, ed., pp. 201-258, Academic Press, New York.

1,100. Marler, P., Dufty, A. and R. Pickert. 1986. Vocal communication in the domestic chicken. I. Does a sender communicate information about the quality of food referent to a receiver? *Anim. Behav.*, **34**:188-193.

1,101. Marriott, D.G. 1970. Cockatiels--their versatility as foster parents. *Avic. Mag.*, **76**:212.

1,102. Jerison, H.J. 1979. The evolution of diversity in brain size. In *Development and Evolution of Brain Size: Behavioral Implications*. Hahn, M.E., Jensen, C., and B.C. Dudek, eds., pp. 29-57, Academic Press, New York.

1,103. Zamenhof, S. and E van Marthens. 1979. Brain weight, brain chemical content, and their early manipulation. *ibid.*, pp. 163-185.

1,104. McLaughlin, R.L. and R.D. Montgomeries. 1985. Brood division by Lapland Longspurs. *Auk*, **102**:687-695.

1,105. Miller, R.S. 1985. Why hummingbirds hover. *ibid.*, **102**:722-726.
1,106. Mead, P.S. and M.L. Morton. 1985. Hatching asynchrony in the Mountain White-crowned Sparrow (*Zonotrichia leucophrys oriantha*): a selected or incidental trait. *ibid.*, **102**:781-792.
1,107. Marchant, S. 1986. Long laying interval. *ibid.*, **103**:247.
1,108. Zerba, E. and M.L. Morton. 1983. The rhythm of incubation from egg laying to hatching in Mountain White-crowned Sparrows. *Ornis., Scand.*, **14**:188-197.
1,109. Heath, J.E. 1968. T origins of thermoregulation. In *Evolution and Environment.*, E.T. Drake, ed., pp. 259-278, Yale U. Press, New Haven.
1,110. Oksche, A. 1983. Reflections on the structural basis of avian neuroendocrine systems. In *Avian Endocrinology*, Mikami, S., Homma, K. and M. Wada, eds., pp. 3-10, Springer-Verlag, Berlin.
1,111. Blähser, S. 1983. Topography, ontogeny, and functional aspects of immunoreactive neuropeptide systems in the domestic fowl. *ibid.*, pp. 11-24.
1,112. Mikami, S.-I. 1983. Avian adenohypophysis: recent progress in immunocytochemical studies. *ibid.*, pp. 39-56.
1,113. Sato, T. and K. Wake. 1983. Nervous organization of the pineal organ in birds. *ibid.*, 59-65.
1,114. Yamada, J., Kitamura, N. and T. Yamashita. 1983. Avian gastrointestinal endocrine cells. *ibid.*, pp. 67-79.
1,115. Yoshimura, Y. and O. Koga. 1983. Ultrastructural changes in follicular stigma during the ovulation process in the hen. *ibid.*, pp. 107-115.
1,116. Imai, K. 1983. Characteristics of rapid growth of the ovarian follicles in the chicken. *ibid.*, pp. 117-124.
1,117. Kamiyoshi, M. and K. Tanaka. 1983. Endocrine control of ovulatory sequence in domestic fowl. *ibid.* pp. 167-177.
1,118. Konishi, H. and K. Homma. 1983. Role of the eyes in external coincidence and modulation of steroidal feedback in male Japanese Quail. *ibid.*, pp. 179-190.
1,119. Ueck, M. and H. Umar. 1983. Environmental, neural, and endocrine influences on the parenchyma of the avian pineal organ and its various responses. *ibid.*, pp. 201-215.
1,120. Tanabe, Y., Doi, O. and T. Nakamura. 1983. Ontogenesis and photoperiodic regulation of the pineal hormone synthesis in the chicken (*Gallus domesticus*). *ibid.*, pp. 217-227.
1,121. Deviche, P. 1983. Interactions between adrenal function and reproduction in male birds. *ibid.*, pp. 243-254.
1,122. Uemura, H., Kobayashi, H., Okawara, Y. and K. Yamaguchi. 1983. Neuropeptides and drinking in birds. *ibid.*, pp. 255-262.
1,123. Wingfield, J. C. 1983. Environmental and endocrine control of avian reproduction: an ecological approach. *ibid.*, pp. 265-288.
1,124. Silverin, B. 1983. Population endocrinology and gonadal activities of the male Pied Flycatcher (*Ficedula hypoleuca*). *ibid.*, pp. 289-305.
1,125. Scanes, C.G., Lauterio, T.J. and F.C. Buonomo. 1983. Annual, developmental, and diurnal cycles of pituitary hormone secretion. *ibid.*, pp. 307-326.
1,126. Johnston, S. and H.R. Carter. 1985. Cavity-nesting in Marbled Murrelets. *Wilson Bull.*, **97**:1-3.
1,127. Howes-Jones, D. 1985. Relationships among song activity, context, and social behavior in the Warbling Virea. *ibid.*, **97**:4-20.
1,128. Kroodsma, D.E. 1985. Development and use of two song forms by the Eastern Phoebe. *ibid.*, **97**:21-29.

1,129. Byrkjedal, I. 1985. Time-activity budget for breeding Greater Golden-Plovers in Norwegian mountains. *ibid.*, 97:486-501.
1,130. Warriner, J.S., Warriner, J.C., Page, G.W., and L.E. Stenzel. 1986. Mating system and reproductive success of a small population of polygamous Snowy Plovers. *ibid.*, 98:15-37.
1,131. Bons, N. 1981. Immunocytochemical localization of neurohormones in bird hypothalamus. In *Recent Advances in Avian Endocrinology*, Pethes, G., Péczely, P. and P. Rudas, eds., pp. 15-24, Pergamon Press, Budapest.
1,132. Rabii, J. Buonomo, F., and C.G. Scanes. 1981. Studies on the hypothalamic regulation of luteinizing hormone secretion in the domestic fowl. *ibid.*, pp. 25-34.
1,133. Kawashima, M., Kamiyoshi, M. and K. Tanaka. 1981. Progesterone receptors in hypothalamus and pituitary of the hen during the ovulatory cycle. *ibid.*, pp. 35-42.
1,134. Massa, P., Sharp, P.J. and L. Bottoni. 1981. The metabolism of sex steroids in the bird central nervous system and pituitary. *ibid.*, pp. 53-60.
1,135. Scanes, C.G. 1981. Adenohypophysial hormones: their chemistry, physiology, and control. *ibid.*, pp. 61-71.
1,136. Kühn, E. R., Decuypere, E., Chadwick, A., Van Itterbeeck, P., and H. Michaels. 1981. Plasma prolactin and thyroid hormone concentration after hatching following different incubation temperatures in the chicken. *ibid.*, pp. 73-85.
1,137. Etches, R.J., Croze, F. and C.E. Duke. 1981. Plasma concentrations of lueinizing hormone, progesterone, testosterone and estradiol in follicular and peripheral venous plasma during the ovulation cycle of the hen. *ibid.*, pp. 89-107.
1,138. Johnson, A.L. and A. van Tienhoven. 1981. Hypothalamo-hypophyseal sensitivity to central injections of progesterone and LH-RH in the laying and molting hen. *ibid.*, pp. 99-107.
1,139. Burke, W. H., Dennison, P. T., Silsby, J. L. and M. E. El Halawani. 1981. Serum prolactin levels of turkey hens in relation to reproductive function. *ibid.*, pp. 109-116.
1,140. Cunningham, F.J. and S.C. Wilson. 1981. Adenocortical function and the ovulation cycle of the hen. *ibid.*, pp. 133-142.
1,141. Daniel, J.Y. 1981. Characterization and regulation of androgen receptors in the preen gland of adult male ducks. *ibid.*, pp. 153-161.
1,142. Rzasa, J. 1981. Prostaglandin production by the hen oviduct in vivo and in vitro. *ibid.*, pp. 177-183.
1,143. Olson, D.M., Bellier, H.V. and F. Hertelendy. 1981. The role of prostaglandins in oviposition. *ibid.*, pp. 197-202.
1,144. Shimada, K. 1981. The role of the ovarian follicles in uterine contraction associated with ovulation and oviposition. *ibid.*, pp. 197-202.
1,145. Hammond, R.W., Todd, H. and F. Hertelendy. 1981. Are prostaglandins involved in ovarian function of the domestic hen? *ibid.*, pp. 203-213.
1,146. Tóth, M., Asbóth, G., Olson, D.M. and F. Hertelendy. 1981. Nature of PGF-2-alpha binding to uterine membranes in laying hens. *ibid.*, pp. 215-222.
1,147. Hertelendy, F. 1981. Current and future trends in prostaglandin research. *ibid.*, pp. 223-229.
1,148. Taylor, T.G. 1981. The regulation of calcium metabolism in birds. *ibid.*, pp. 311-320.
1,149. Farner, D.S. 1981. Recent progress in avian endocrinology--closing remarks. *ibid.*, pp. 459-465.

1,150. O'Connor, R.J. 1984. *The Growth and Development of Birds*. John Wiley & Sons, New York.
1,151. Bartholomew, G.A. and T.R. Howell. 1964. Experiments with nesting behavior of Laysan and Black-footed Albatrosses. *Anim. Behav.*, 12:549-559.
1,152. Vleck, C.M. and G.J. Kenagy. 1980. Embryonic metabolism of the Forktailed Storm Petrel: physiological patterns during prolonged and interrupted incubation. *Physiol. Zool.*, **53**:32-42.
1,153. Jansen, J.H.F., Kuijpers, A. and S.R. Troelstra. 1986. A Mid-Brunhes climatic event: long-term changes in global atmosphere and ocean circulation. *Science*, **232**:619-622.
1,154. Sloan, R.E., Rigby, J.K.,Jr., Van Valen, L.M. and D. Gabriel. 1986. Gradual dinosaur extinction and simultaneous ungulate radiation in the Hell Creek Formation. *ibid.*, **232**:629-633.
1,155. Curry-Lindahl, K. 1969. The influence of man on the African Avifauna: introduction to symposium. *Ostrich Suppl.*, **8**:429-444.
1,156. Buckley, P.A. 1969. Disruption of species-typical behavior patterns in F_1 hybrid *Agapornis* parents. *Z. Tierpsychol.*, **26**:737-743.
1,157. Conner, E.F. and D. Simberloff. 1986. Competition, scientific method, and null models in ecology. *Amer. Sci.*, **74**:155-162.
1,158. Hails, C.J. and D.M. Bryant. 1979. Reproductive energetics of a free living bird. *J. Anim. Ecol.*, **48**:471-482.
1,159. Oppenheim, R.W. 1972. Prehatching and hatching behaviour in birds: a comparative study of altricial and precocial species. *Anim. Behav.*, **20**: 644-655.
____. 1973. Prehatching and hatching behavior: comparative and physiological considerations. In *Behavioral Embryology*, G. Gottlieb, ed., pp. 163-224, Academic Press, New York.
1,160. Kurz, E.M., Sengelaub, D.R. and A.P. Arnold. 1986. Androgens regulate the dendritic length of mammalian motoneurons in adulthood. *Science*, **232**:395-398.
1,161. McGowan, C. 1984. Evolutionary relationships of ratites and carinates: evidence from ontogeny of the tarsus. *Nature*, **307**: 733-735.
1,162. Barrington, E.J.W. 1980. Hormones and evolution: after 15 years. In *Hormones, Adaptations and Evolution*, Ishii, S., Hirano, T. and M. Wada, eds., pp. 3-13, Springer-Verlag, Berlin.
1,163. Bern, H.A. 1980. Primitive control of endocrine systems. *ibid.*, pp. 25-33.
1,164. Fujita, T., Kobayashi, S., Yui, R. and T. Iwanaga. 1980. Evolution of neurons and paraneurons. *ibid.*, pp. 35-43.
1,165. Ball, J.N., Batten, T.F.C., and G. Young. 1980. Evolution of hypothalamo-hypophysial systems in higher vertebrates. *ibid.*, pp. 57-70.
1,166. Mikami, S.-I. 1980. Comparative anatomy and evolution of the hypothalamo-hypophysial systems in higher vertebrates. *ibid.*, pp. 57-70.
1,167. Lederis, K., Fisher, A. W., Geonzon, R. M., Gill, V., Ko, D. and S. Raghavan. 1980. Arginine vasotocin in fetal, newborn and adult mammals: evolution in progress. *ibid.*, pp. 71-77.
1,168. Gorbman, A. 1980. Endocrine regulation in Agnatha: primitive or degenerate? *ibid.*, pp. 81-92.
1,169. Assenmacher, I. and M. Jallageas. 1980. Adaptive aspects of endocrine relations in birds. *ibid.*, pp. 93-102.
1,170. Pang, P.K.T. and J.A. Yee. 1980. Evolution of the endocrine control of vertebrate hypercalcemic regulation. *ibid.*, pp. 103-111.

1,171. Oksche, A. 1980. The pineal organ--a component of photoneuroendocrine systems: evolution, structure, function. *ibid.* pp. 123-134.
1,172. Wingfield, J.C. 1980. Sex steroid-binding proteins in vertebrate blood. *ibid.*, pp. 135-144.
1,173. Nandi, S., Yang, J., Richards, J., Guzman, R., Rodriguez, R. and W. Imagawa. 1980. Role of growth factors and classical hormones in the control of growth and function of mammary tissues. *ibid.*, pp. 145-155.
1,174. Licht, P. 1980. Relationship between receptor binding and biological actions of gonadotropins. *ibid.*, pp. 167-174.
1,175. Farner, D.S. 1980. Evolution of the control of reproductive cycles in birds. *ibid.*, pp. 185-191.
1,176. Tanabe, Y. 1980. Evolutionary significance of domestication of animals with special reference to reproductive traits. *ibid.*, pp. 193-201.
1,177. Fujita, H. 1980. Evolution of the thyroid gland. *ibid.*, pp. 231-239.
1,178. Fontaine, Y.-A. 1980. Evolution of pituitary gonadotropins and thyrotropins. *ibid.*, pp. 261-270.
1,179. Ostrom, J.H. 1985. Introduction to *Archaeopteryx*. In *The Beginnings of Birds*, Hecht, M.K., Ostrom, J.H., Viohl, G. and P. Wellnhofer, eds., pp.9-20, Freunde des Jura-Mus. Eichstätt, Willibaldsburg; The meaning of *Archaeopteryx*. *ibid.*, pp. 161-176.
1,180. Viohl, G. 1985. Geology of the Solnhofen lithographic limestone and the habitat of *Archaeopteryx*. *ibid.*, pp. 31-44.
1,181. Buisonjé. P.H. de. 1985. Climatological conditions during deposition of the Solnhofen limestones. *ibid.*, pp. 45-66.
1,182. Regal, P.J. 1985. Common sense and reconstructions of the biology of fossils: *Archaeopteryx* and feathers. *ibid.*, pp. 67-74.
1,183. Feduccia, A. 1985. On why the dinosaur lacked feathers. *ibid.*, pp. 75-79.
1,184. Thulborn, R.A. and T.L. Hamley. 1985. A new palaeoecological role for *Archaeopteryx*. *ibid.*, pp. 81-89.
1,185. Yalden, D.W. 1985. Forelimb function in *Archaeopteryx*. *ibid.*, pp. 91-97.
1,186. Peterson, A. 1985. The locomotor adaptations of *Archaeopteryx*: glider or cursor? *ibid.*, pp. 99-103.
1,187. Wellnhofer, P. 1985. Remarks on the digit and pubis problems of *Archaeopteryx*. *ibid.*, pp. 123-134.
1,188. Walker, A. 1985. The braincase of *Archaeopteryx*. *ibid.*, pp. 123-134.
1,189. Hinchliffe, J.R. 1985. 'One, two, three' or 'two, three, four:' an embryologists view of the homologies of the digits and carpus of modern birds. *ibid.*, pp. 141-147.
1,190. Hecht, M.K. 1985. The biological significance of *Archaeopteryx*. *ibid.*, pp. 149-160.
1,191. Martin, L.D. 1985. The relationship of *Archaeopteryx* to other birds. *ibid.*, pp.177-183.
1,192. Gauthier, J. and K. Padian. 1985. Phylogenetic, functional, and aerodynamic analyses of the origin of birds and their flight. *ibid.*, pp. 185-197.
1,193. Bock, W.J. 1985. The arboreal theory for the origin of birds. *ibid.*, pp. 199-207.
1,194. Molnar, R.E. 1985. Alternatives to *Archaeopteryx*: a survey of proposed early or ancestral birds. *ibid.*, pp. 209-217.
1,195. Raath, M.A. 1985. The theropod *Syntarsus* and its bearing on the origin of birds. *ibid.*, pp. 219-227.

1,196. Peters, D.S. and W. Fr. Gutmann. 1985. Constructional and functional preconditions for the transition to powered flight in vertebrates. *ibid.*, pp. 233-242.

1,197. Peters, D.S. 1985. Functional and constructive limitations in the early evolution of birds. *ibid.*, pp. 243-249.

1,198. Rietschel, S. 1985. Feathers and wings of *Archaeopteryx*, and the question of her flight ability. *ibid.*, pp. 251-260.

1,199. Balda, R.P., Caple, G. and W.R. Willis. 1985. Comparison of the gliding to flapping sequence with the flapping to gliding sequence. *ibid.*, pp. 267-277.

1,200. Rayner, J.M.V. 1985. Mechanical and ecological constraints on flight evolution. *ibid.*, pp. 279-288.

____. 1985. Cursorial gliding in proto-birds. *ibid.*, pp. 289-291.

1,201. Norberg, U.M. 1985. Evolution of flight in birds: aerodynamic, mechanical, and ecological aspects. *ibid.*, pp. 293-302.

1,202. Norberg, R.A. 1985. Function of vane asymmetry and shaft curvature in bird flight feathers; inferences on flight ability of *Archaeopteryx*. *ibid.*, pp. 303-318.

1,203. Tarsitano, S.F. 1985. The morphological and aerodynamic constraints on the origin of avian flight. *ibid.*, pp. 319-332.

1,204. Schaller, D. 1985. Wing evolution. *ibid.*, pp. 333-348.

1,205. Scheich, H. 1985. Auditory brain organization of birds and its constraints for the design of vocal repertoires. In *Experimental Behavioral Ecology and Sociobiology*, Hölldobler, B. and M. Landauer, eds., pp. 195-209, Gustav Fisher Verlag, Stuttgart.

1,206. Maclean, G.L. 1968. Field studies on the sandgrouse of the Kalahari Desert. *Living Bird*, **1968**:209-235.

1,207. Rakic, P. Bourgeois, J.-P., Eckenhoff, M.F., Zecevic, N. and P.S. Goldman-Rakic. 1986. Concurrent overproduction of synapses in diverse regions of the primate cerebral cortex. *Science*, **232**:232-235.

1,208. Howgate, M.E. 1984. The teeth of *Archaeopteryx* and a reinterpretation of the Eichstätt speciment. *Zool. J. Linn. Soc.*, **82**: 159-175.

1,209. Yalden, D.W. 1984. What size was *Archaeopteryx?* *ibid.*, pp. 177-188.

1,210. Pettigrew, J.D. 1986. Flying primates? megabats have the advanced pathway from eye to midbrain. *Science*, **231**:1304-1306.

1,211. Nowicki, S. and R.C. Capranica. 1986. Bilateral syringeal interaction in vocal production of oscine bird sound. *ibid.*, **231**: 1297-1299.

1,212. Tucker, B.W. 1938. Functional evolutionary morphology: the origin of birds. In *Evolution*, G.R. de Beer, ed., pp. 321-336, Clarendon Press, Oxford.

1,213. Veevers, J.J. et al. 1984. *Phanerozoic Earth History of Australia*, J.J. Veevers, ed., Clarendon Press, Oxford.

1,214. Knudsen, E.I. and M. Konishi. 1978. Space and frequency are represented separately in auditory midbrain of the owl. *J. Neurophysiol.*, **41**:870-884.

1,215. Nachtigall, W. 1977. Zur Bedeutung der Reynoldszahl in der Schwimmphysiologie und Flugbiophysik.--Physiology of movement-biophysics. *Fortschr. Zool.*, **24(213)**:13-56.

1,216. Pirlot, P. 1977. Wing design and the origin of bats. In *Major Patterns in Vertebrate Evolution.*, Hecht, M.K., Goody, P.C. and B.M. Hecht, pp. 375-410, Plenum Press, New York.

1,217. Smith, J.D. 1977. Comments on flight and evolution of bats. *ibid.*, pp. 427-437.

1,218. Hill, B.G. and M.R. Lein. 1985. The non-song vocal repertoire of the White-crowned Sparrow. *Condor*, **87**:327-335.
1,219. Marder, J., Idit, G.-L., and P. Raber. 1986. Cutaneous evaporation in heat-stressed Spotted Sandgrouse. *ibid.*, **88**:99-100.
1,220. Robertson, R.J., Gibbs, H.L. and B.J. Stutchbury. 1986. Spitefullness, altruism, and the cost of aggression: evidence against superterritoriality in Tree Swallows. *ibid.*, **88**:104-105.
1,221. Emlen, J.T. 1986. Responses of brooding Cliff Swallows to nidicolous parasite infestations. *ibid.*, **88**:110-111.
1,222. Bergstrom, P.W. 1986. Daylight incubation sex roles in Wilson's Plover. *ibid.*, **88**:113-115.
1,223. Alatalo, R.V., Carlson, A., Lundberg, A. and S. Ulfstrand. 1981. The conflict between male polygamy and female monogamy: the case of the Pied Flycatcher *Ficedula hypoleuca*. *Amer. Nat.*, **117**: 738-753.
1,224. Suga, N. and W.E. O'Neill. 1979. Neural axis representing target range in the auditory cortex of the Mustache Bat. *Science*, **206**:351-353.
1,225. Friedman, M. and D.S. Lehrman. 1968. Physiological conditions for stimulation of prolactin secretion by external stimuli in the male Ring Dove. *Anim. Behav.*, **16**:233-237.
1,226. Huxley, J. 1938. Darwin's theory of sexual selection and data subsumed by it, in the light of recent research. *Amer. Nat.*, **72**:410-433.
1,227. Ghiselin, M.T. 1969. *The Triumph of the Darwinian Method*. U. Calif. Press, Berkeley.
1,228. Pohl-Apel, G. 1980. Sexuelle Ontogenese bei Männlichen Wellensittichen *Melopsittacus undulatus*. *J. Ornithol.*, **121**:271-279.
1,229. Trillmich, F. 1976. Spatial proximity and mate-specific behaviour in a flock of Budgerigars (*Melopsittacus undulatus*: Aves, Psittacidae). *Z. Tierpsychol.*, **41**:307-331; The influence of separation on the pair bond in Budgerigars (*Melopsittacus undulatus*: Aves, Psittacidae). *ibid.*, **41**:396-408.
1,230. Mayr, E. 1972. Sexual selection and natural selection. In *Sexual Selection and the Descent of Man*, B.J. Campbell, ed., pp. 87-104, Aldine Publ. Co., Chicago.
1,231. Selander, R.K. 1972. Sexual selection and dimorphism in birds. *ibid.*, pp. 180-230.
1,232. Quarton, G.C. 1970. Prefatory comments on evolution of brain and behavior. In *The Neurosciences*, F.O. Schmitt, ed., pp. 5-7, Rockefeller U. Press, New York.
1,233. Nauta, W.J.H. and H.J. Karten. 1970. A General profile of the vertebrate brain, with sidelights on the ancestry of the cerebral cortex. *ibid.*, pp. 7-26.
1,234. Kingsolver, J.G. and M.A.R. Koehl. 1985. Aerodynamics, thermoregulation, and the evolution of insect wings: differential scaling and evolutionary change. *Evol.*, **39**:488-504.
1,235. Winkler, D.W. 1985. Factors determining a clutch size reduction in California Gulls (*Larus californicus*): a multi-hypothesis approach. *ibid.*, **39**:667-677.
1,236. Northcutt, R.G. 1981. Evolution of the telencephalon in nonmammals. *Ann. Rev. Neurosci.*, **4**:301-350.
1,237. Nieuwkoop, P.D. and L.A. Sutasurya. 1983. Some problems in the development and evolution of the chordates. In *Development and Evolution*, Goodwin, B.C., Holder, N. and C.C. Wylie, eds., pp. 123-135, Cambridge U. Press, Cambridge.
1,238. Horder, T.J. 1983. Embryological bases of evolution. *ibid.*, pp. 315-352.

1,239. Hall, B.K. 1983. Epigenetic control in development and evolution. *ibid.*, 353-379.
1,240. Meldrum, D.R. 1986. Personal communication.
1,241. Hayssen, V. and D.G. Blackburn. 1985. Alpha-lactalbumin and the origins of lactation. *Evol.*, **39**:1147-1149.
1,242. Riedl, R. and R.P.S. Jefferies. 1978. *Order in Living Organisms.* Wiley & Sons, New York.
1,243. Weathers, W.W. and D.F. Caccamise. 1975. Temperature regulation and water requirements of the Monk Parakeet, *Myiopsitta monachus. Oecologia*, **18**:329-342.
1,244. ____ and D.C. Schoenbaechler. 1976. Regulation of body temperature in the Budgerygah, *Melopsittacus undulatus. Aust. J. Zool.*, **24**:39-49.
1,245. Crane, P.R., Friis, E.M. and K.R. Pedersen. 1986. Lower Cretaceous angiosperm flowers: fossil evidence on early radiation of dicotyledons. *Science*, **232**:852-854.
1,246. Horder, T.J. 1981. On not throwing out the baby with the bath water. In *Evolution Today*, Scudder, G.G.E. and J.L. Reveal, eds., pp. 163-180, Carnegie-Mellon U., Pittsburgh.
1,247. Sibley, C.G. and J.E. Ahlquist. 1981. The phylogeny and relationships of the ratite birds, as indicated by DNA-DNA hybridization. *ibid.*, pp. 301-335.
1,248. Langston, W., Jr. 1981. Pterosaurs. *Sci. Amer.*, **244(2)**:122-136.
1,249. Galaburda, A., Sherman, G. and N. Geschwind. 1985. Cerebral lateralization: historical note on animal studies. In *Cerebral Lateralization in Nonhuman Species*, S.D. Glick, ed., pp.1-10, Academic Press, New York.
1,250. Arnold, A.P. and S.W. Bottjer. 1985. Cerebral lateralization in birds. *ibid.*, pp. 11-39.
1,251. Geschwind, N. 1985. Implications for evolution, genetics, and clinical syndromes. *ibid.*, pp. 247-278.
1,252. McCasland, J.S. 1983. Neuronal control of bird song production. *Ph.D. Thesis*, California Institute of Technology, Pasadena.
1,253. Bock, W.J. 1972. Species interactions and macroevolution. *Evol. Biol.*, **5**:1-24.
1,254. Leppik, E.E. 1972. Origin and Evolution of bilateral symmetry in flowers. *ibid.*, **5**:49-85.
1,255. Keast, A. 1972. Ecological opportunities and dominant families, as illustrated by the neotropical Tyrannidae (Aves). *ibid.*, **5**: 229-277.
1,256. Mayfield, H.F. 1979. The Amateur in Ornithology. *Auk*, **96**:168-171.
1,257. Marcgant, S. 1972. Evolution of the genus *Chrysococcyx, Ibis*, **114**:219-233.
1,258. Wittenberger, J.F. and R.L. Tilson. 1980. The evolution of monogamy: hypotheses and evidence. *Ann. Rev. Ecol. Syst.*, **11**: 197-232.
1,259. Tavistock, Marquess of and J. Delacour. 1926. Cockatoos. *Avic. Mag.*, **4**:148-155.
1,260. Tavistock, Marquess of. 1931. The nesting of Worchester's Hanging Parrot. *ibid.*, **9**:299-301.
1,261. Prestwich, A.A. 1947. On the nesting habits in captivity and freedom of *Agapornis* and *Coryllis. ibid.*, **53**:22-30.
1,262. ____. 1954. Breeding of the Lineolated Parrakeet. *ibid.*, **60**: 1-3.
1,263. Henry, G.M. 1962. The Ceylon lorikeet *Loriculus beryllinus* (Forster). *ibid.*, **68**:81-83.

1,264. Forshaw, J.M. 1962. The parrots of Australia. *ibid.*, **68**:98-106; 2. The Eastern Rosella. *ibid.*, **68**:129-136; 3. The Red-rumped Parrot. *ibid.*, **68**:199-207.

1,265. Buckley, F.G. 1965. The occurrence and treatment of candidiasis in the Blue-crowned Hanging Parrot (*Loriculus galgulus*). *ibid.*, **71**:143-145.

1,266. Wittenberger, J.F. 1979. The evolution of mating systems in birds and mammals. In *Handbook of Behav. Neurobiol.*, **3**:271-349.

1,267. Oppenheim, R.W. and L. Haverkamp. 1986. Early development of behavior and the nervous system. *ibid.*, **8**:1-33.

1,268. Fentress, J.C. and P.J. McLeod. 1986. Motor patterns in development. *ibid.*, **8**:35-97.

1,269. Bottjer, S.W. and A. P. Arnold. 1986. The ontogeny of social learning in songbirds. *ibid.*, **8**:129-161.

1,270. Aronson, L.R. 1970. Functional evolution of the forebrain in lower vertebrates. In *Development and Evolution of Behavior*, Aronson, L.R., Tobach, E., Lehrman, D. and J.S. Rosenblatt, eds., pp. 75-107, W.H. Freeman & Co., San Francisco.

1,271. Gottlieb, G. 1970. Conceptions of prenatal behavior. *ibid.*, pp. 111-137.

1,272. Kuo, Z.-Y. 1970. The need for coordinated efforts in developmental studies. *ibid.*, pp. 181-193.

1,273. Hinde, R.A. and J.G. Stevenson. 1970. Goal and response control. *ibid.*, pp. 216-237.

1,274. Gottlieb, G. 1971. *Development of Species Identification in birds.* U. Chicago Press, Chicago.

1,275. Bucher, T.L. and G.A. Bartholomew. 1984. Analysis of variation in gas exchange, growth patterns, and energy utilization in a parrot and other avian embryos. In *Respiration and Metabolism of Embryonic Vertebrates*, R.S. Seymour, ed., pp. 359-372, Dr. W. Junk Publ., Dordrecht.

1,276. Sperry, R.W. 1971. How a developing brain gets inself properly wired for adaptive function. In *The Biopsychology of Development*, Tobach, E., Aronson, L.R. and E. Shaw, eds., pp. 27-44, Academic Press, New York.

1,277. Hamburger, V. 1971. Development of embryonic motility. *ibid.*, pp. 45-66.

1,278. Gottlieb, G. 1971. Ontogenesis of sensory function in birds and mammals. *ibid.*, pp. 67-128.

1,279. Lehrman, D.S. 1971. Experiential background for the induction of reproductive behavior patterns by hormones. *ibid.*,pp. 297-302.

1,280. Brown, C.R. 1986. Cliff swallow colonies as information centers. *Science*, **234**:83-85.

1,281. Crompton, A.W., Taylor, C.R. and J.A. Jagger. 1978. Evolution of homeothermy in mammals. *Nature*, **272**:333-336.

1,282. Rothenbuhler, W. 1964. Behavior genetics of nest cleaning in Honey Bees. IV. Response in F_1 and backcross generations to disease-killed brood. *Amer. Zool.*, **4**:111-123.

1,283. Phillips, R.E. 1968. Approach-withdrawal behavior of Peach-faced Lovebirds, *Agapornis roseicollis*, and its modification by brain lesions. *Behaviour*, **31**:163-184.

1,284. Nottebohm, F. 1976. Phonation in the Orange-winged Amazon Parrot, *Amazona amazonica*. *J. Comp. Physiol.*, **108A**:157-170.

1,285. Sibley, C.G. and J.E. Ahlquist. 1972. A comparative study of the egg white proteins of non-passerine birds. *Bull. Peabody Mus. Nat. Hist.*, **39**:1-276.

1,286. Clancey, C.L. 1980. *S.A.O.S. Checklist of Southern African Birds*, Southern African Ornithological Society.

1,287. Serventy, D.L. 1972. A historical background of ornithology with special reference to Australia. *Emu*, **72**:41-50.
1,288. Horton, D.R. 1972. Speciation of birds in Australia, New Guinea and the southwestern Pacific islands. *ibid.*, **72**:91-109.
1,289. Bucher, T.L. 1985. Ventilation and oxygen consumption in *Amazona viridigenalis*. *J. Comp. Physiol.*, **155B**:269-276.
1,290. Impekoven, M. 1976. Prenatal parent-young interactions in birds and their long term effects. *Adv. Study Behav.*, **7**:210-253.
1,291. Marler, P. and S. Peters. 1982. Developmental overproduction and selective attrition: new processes in the epigenesis of bird-song. *Devel. Psychobiol.*, **15**:369-378.
1,292. Keast, A. 1968. Evolution of mammals on southern continents. *Quart. Rev. Biol.*, **43**:225-233.
1,293. Cooke, H.B.S. 1968. Evolution of mammals on southern continents. II. The fossil mammal fauna of Africa. *ibid.*, **43**:234-264.
1,294. Turner, F.B. 1970. The ecological efficiency of consumer populations. *Ecology*, **51**:741-742.
1,295. Sperry, R.W. 1965. Embryogenesis of behavioral nerve nets. In *Organogenesis*, De Hann, R.L. and H. Ursprung, eds., pp. 161-186, Holt, New York.
1,296. Perry, D. 1986. *Life above the Jungle Floor*. Simon & Schuster, New York.
1,297. Debenham, F. 1954. The geography of deserts. In *Biology of Deserts*, J.L. Cloudsley-Thompson, ed., pp. 1-6, Institute of Biology, London.
1,298. Boyko, H. 1954. Plant ecological problems in increasing the productivity of arid areas. *ibid.*, pp. 28-34.
1,299. Bodenheimer, F.S. 1954. Problems of physiology and ecology of desert animals. *ibid.*, pp. 162-167.
1,300. Regal, P.J. 1977. Ecology and evolution of flowering plant dominance. *Science*, **196**:622-629.
1,301. Lillegraven, J.A. 1972. Ordinal and familial diversity of Cenozoic mammals. *Taxon*, **21**:261-274.
1,302. Colbert, E.H. 1965. *The Age of Reptiles*, Weidenfeld and Nicolson, London.
1,303. Clemens, L.G. 1973. Development of Behavior. In *Comparative Psychology*, Dewsbury, D.A. and D.A. Rethlingshafer, eds., pp. 238-268, Ronald Press, New York.
1,304. Barnes, D.M. 1986. Steroids may influence changes in mood. *Science*, **232**:1344-1345.
1,305. Lang, D.A., Smith, G.D., Stezowski, J.J. and R.E. Hughes. 1986. Structure of pressinoic acid: the cyclic moiety of vasopressin. *ibid.*, **232**:1240-1242.
1,306. Burger, W.C. 1981. Heresy revived: the monocotyledon theory of angiosperm origin. *Evol. Theory*, **5**:189-225.
1,307. McGinnies, W.R., Goldman, B.J. and P. Paylore. 1968. The Major Deserts. In *Deserts of the World*, McGinnies, W.R., Goldman, B.J. and P. Paylore, eds., pp. 8-17, U. of Arizona Press.
1,308. Griffiths, M. 1978. *The Biology of Monotremes*, Academic Press, New York.
1,309. Teitelbaum, P. 1967. *Physiological Psychology*, Prentice-Hall, Englewood Cliffs, New Jersey.
1,310. Stebbins, G.L. 1974. Flowering Plants: Evolution above the Species Level, Harvard U. Press, Cambridge.
1,311. Dahlgren, R. and F.N. Rasmussen. 1983. Monocotyledon evolution. *Evol. Biol.*, **16**:255-395.
1,312. Densmore, L.D., III. 1983. Biochemical and Immunological Systematics of the order Crocodilia. *ibid.*, **16**:397-465.

1,313. Thorne, R.F. 1976. A phylogenetic classification of the Angiospermae. *ibid.*, **9**:35-106.
1,314. Szarski, H. 1980. A functional and evolutionary interpretation of brain size in vertebrates. *ibid.*, **13**:149-174.
1,315. Hinchliffe, J.R. and M.K. Hecht. 1984. Homology of the Bird Wing Skeleton. *ibid.*, **18**:21-39.
1,316. Murray, B.G., Jr. 1984. A demographic theory of the evolution of mating systems as exemplified by birds. ibid., **18**:71-140.
1,317. Hughes, R.L. 1977. Egg membranes and ovarian function during pregnancy in monotremes and marsupials. In *Reproduction and Evolution*, Calaby, J.H. and C.H. Tyndale-Biscoe, eds., pp. 281-291, Australian Acad. Science, Canberra.
1,318. Callard, I.P. and V. Lance. 1977. The control of reptilian follicular cycles. *ibid.*, pp. 199-209.
1,319. Jehl, J.R., Jr. and B.J. Murray, Jr. 1986. The evolution of normal and reversible sexual size dimorphism in shorebirds and other birds. In *Current Ornithology*, vol. 3, R.F. Johnston, ed., pp. 1-86, Plenum Press, New York.
1,320. Payne, R.B. 1986. Birdsongs and avian systematics. *ibid.*, pp. 87-126.
1,321. Lawton, M.F. and R.O. Lawton. 1986. Heterochrony, deferred breeding and sociality. *ibid.*, pp. 187-222.
1,322. Willson, M.F. 1986. Avian frugivory in seed dispersal in eastern North America. *ibid.*, pp. 223-279.
1,323. Oring, L.W. 1986. Avian polyandry. *ibid.*, pp. 309-351.
1,324. Morrison, M.L. 1986. Bird populations as indicators of environmental change. *ibid.*, pp. 429-451.
1,325. Temple, S.A. 1986. The problem of avian extinctions. *ibid.*, pp. 453-485.
1,326. Flohn, H. 1984. Climate evolution in the Southern Hemisphere and the equatorial region during the late Cenozoic. In *Late Cainozoic Palaeoclimates of the Southern Hemisphere*, J.C. Vogel, ed., pp. 5-20, A.A. Balkema, Boston.
1,327. Salinger, M.J. 1984. New Zealand climate: the last five million years. *ibid.*, pp. 131-150.
1,328. Bowler, J.M. and R.J. Wasson. 1984. Glacial age environments of inland Australia. *ibid.*, pp. 183-208.
1,329. Thomas, D.S.G. and A.S. Goudie. 1984. Ancient ergs of the Southern Hemisphere. *ibid.*, pp. 407-418.
1,330. Wasson, R.J. 1984. Late Quaternary palaeoenvironments in the desert dunefields of Australia. *ibid.*, pp. 419-432.
1,331. Lancaster, N. 1984. Aridity in southern Africa: age, origins and expression in land forms and sediments. *ibid.*, pp. 433-444.
1,332. Besler, H. 1984. The development of the Namib dunefield according to sedimentological and geomorphological evidence. *ibid.*, pp. 445-453.
1,333. Ward, J.D. 1984. A reappraisal of the Cenozoic stratigraphy in the Kuiseb valley of central Namib Desert. *ibid.*, pp. 455-463.
1,334. Brain, C.K. 1984. The terminal Miocene event: a critical environmental and evolutionary episode? *ibid.*, pp. 491-498.
1,335. Tobias, P.V. 1984. Climatic change and evolution--evidence from the African faunal and hominid sites. *ibid.*, pp. 515-520.
1,336. Oppenheim, R.W. 1981. Neuronal cell death and some related regressive phenomena during neurogenesis: a selective historical review and progress report. In *Studies in Developmental Neurobiology*, W.M. Cowan, ed., pp. 74-133, Oxford U. Press, New York.
1,337. Bekoff, A. 1981. Embryological development of the neural circuitry underlying motor coordination. *ibid.*, pp. 134-170.

1,338. Pough, F.H. 1973. Lizard energetics and diet. *Ecology*, **54**:837-844
1,339. Sussman, R.W. and P.H. Raven. 1978. Pollination by lemurs and marsupials: an archaic coevolutionary system. *Science*, **200**:731-736.
1,340. Lillegraven, J.A. 1979. Introduction to Mesozoic mammals. In *Mesozoic mammals*, Lillegraven, J.A., Kielen-Jaworowska, Z. and W. A. Clemens, eds., pp. 1-6, U. Calif. Press, Berkeley.
1,341. Crompton, A.W. and F.A. Jenkins, Jr. 1979. Origin of mammals. *ibid.*, pp. 59-90.
1,342. Lillegraven, J.A. 1979. Reproduction in Mesozoic mammals. *ibid.*, pp. 259-276.
1,343. ____, Kraus, M.J. and T.M. Brown. 1979. Paleogeography of the world of the Mesozoic. *ibid.*, pp. 277-308.
1,344. Diamond, I.T. and W.C. Hall. 1969. Evolution of neocortex. *Science*, **164**:251-262.
1,345. Krassilov, V.A. 1973. Mesozoic plants and the problem of angiosperm ancestry. *Lethaia*, **6**:163-178.
1,346. Raven, P.H. 1977. A suggestion concerning the Cretaceous rise to dominance of the angiosperms. *Evolution*, **31**:451-452.
1,347. Vitt, L.J. and W.E. Cooper, Jr. 1985. The relationship between reproductive and lipid cycling in the skink *Eumeces laticeps* with comments on breeding ecology. *Herpetol.*, **41**:419-432.
____ and ____. 1986. Skink reproduction and sexual dimorphism: *Eumeces fasciatus* in the southwestern United States, with notes on *Eumeces inexpectatus*. *J. Herpetol.*, **20**:65-76.
1,348. Tinkle, D.W., Wilber, H.M. and S.G. Tilley. 1970. Evolutionary strategies in lizard reproduction. *Evolution*, **24**:55-74.
1,349. Tinkle, D.W. and J.W. Gibbons. 1979. The distribuiton and evolution of viviparity in reptiles. *Misc. Publ. Mus. Zool. U. Mich.*, **No. 54**.
1,350. Sawyer, J.B. and J.C. Hozier. 1986. High resolution of mouse chromosomes: banding conservation between man and mouse. *Science*, **232**:1632-1635.
1,351. Simmons, K.E.L. 1957. The taxonomic significance of the head-scratching methods of birds. *Ibis*, **99**:178-181.
1,352. Krementz, D.G. and C.D. Ankney. 1986. Bioenergetics of egg production by female House Sparrows. *Auk*, **103**:299-305.
1,353. Riska, D. 1986. An analysis of vocal communication in the adult Brown Noddy (*Anous stolidus*). *ibid.*, **103**:359-369.
1,354. Nilsson, S.G. 1986. Evolution of hole-nesting in birds: on balancing selection pressures. *ibid.*, **103**:432-435.
1,355. Purves, D. and J.W. Lichtman. 1985. Geometrical differences among homologous neurons in mammals. *Science*, **228**:298-300.
1,356. Scott, D.M. and C.D. Ankney. 1983. The laying cycle of Brown-Headed Cowbirds: passerine chickens? *Auk*, **100**:583-592.
1,357. Zach, R. 1982. Hatching asynchrony, egg size, growth, and fledging in Tree Swallows. *ibid.*, **99**:695-700.
1,358. Wingfield, J.C. 1984. Androgens and mating systems: testosterone-induced polygyny in normally monogamous birds. *ibid.*, **101**: 665-671.
1,359. Feare, C.J., Spencer, P.L. and D.A.T. Constantine. 1982. Time of egg laying of Starlings *Sturnus vulgaris*. *Ibis*, **124**:174-178,
1,360. Goldberger, M.E. 1982. Introductory remarks. In *Changing Concepts of the Nervous System*, Morrison, A.R. and P.L. Strick, eds., pp. 17-19, Academic Press, New York.

1,361. Hand, P.J. 1982. Plasticity of the rat cortical barrel system. *ibid.*, pp. 49-68.
1,362. Diamond, I.T. 1982. Changing views of the organization and evolution of the visual pathways. *ibid.*, pp. 201-233.
1,363. Berkley, M.A. 1982. The geniculocortical system and visual perception. *ibid.*, pp. 295-319.
1,364. Berlucchi, G. 1982. Interaction of visual cortical areas and superior colliculus in visual interhemispheric transfer in the cat. *ibid.*, pp. 321-336.
1,365. Sherman, S.M. 1982. Parallel pathways in the cat's geniculocortical system: W-, X-, and Y-cells. *ibid.*, pp. 337-359.
1,366. Tusa, R.J. 1982. Visual cortex: multiple areas and multiple functions. *ibid.*, pp. 235-259.
1,367. Hoffman, P. *et al.* 1982. Influences of neurohypophyseal hormones and related peptides on adiabatic phenomena in the central nervous system. *ibid.*, pp. 743-755.
1,368. Bailey, W. H. 1982. Mnemonic significance of neurohypophyseal peptides. *ibid.*, pp. 787-804.
1,369. Ricklefs, R.E. 1975. The evolution of cooperative breeding in birds. *Ibis*, **117**:531-534.
1,370. Emlen, S.T. 1982. The evolution of helping. I. An ecological constraints model. *Amer. Nat.*, **119**:29-39.
1,371. Berman, N. and P. Sterling. 1976. Cortical suppression of the retino-collicular pathway in the monocularly-deprived cat. *J. Physiol.*, **255**:263-273.
1,372. Wall, P.D. 1977. The presence of ineffective synapses and the circumstances which unmask them. *Phil. Trans. Roy. Soc. Lond.*, **B278**:361-372.
1,373. Dodt, E. and K.H. Jessen. 1961. The duplex nature of the retina of the nocturnal gecko as reflected in the electroretinogram. *J. Gen. Physiol.*, **44**:1143-1158
1,374. Tinbergen, N. *et al.* 1962. Egg shell removal by the Black-headed Gull *Larus ridibundus* L.; a behavior component of camouflage. *Z. Tierpsycol.*, **19**:74-117.
1,375. Nethersole-Thompson, C. and D. Nethersole-Thompson. 1942. Egg-shell disposal by birds. *British Birds*, **35**:162-169, 190-200, 214-224, 241-250.
1,376. Heywood, V.H. 1985. *Flowering Plants of the World*. Prentice Hall, Englewood Cliffs, New Jersey.
1,377. Cronquist, A. 1981. *An Integrated System of Classification of Flowering Plants*. Columbia Univ. Press, New York.
1,378. Pepperberg, I.M. 1981. Functional vocalizations by an African Grey Parrot (*Psittacus erithacus*). *Z. Tierpsychol.*, **55**:139-160.
____. 1983. Cognition in the African Grey Parrot: preliminary evidence for auditory/vocal comprehension of the class concept. *Anim. Learning Behav.*, **11**:179-185.
1,379. Barnes, D.M. 1986. Brain architecture: beyond genes. *Science*, **233**:155-156.
1,380. Campbell, B. and E. Lack. 1985. *A Dictionary of Birds*. Buteo Books, Vermillion, South Dakota.
1,381. Majerus, M.E.N. 1986. The genetics of evolution of female choice. *Trends Ecol. Evol.*, **1**:1-7.
1,382. Dingle, R.V., Siesser, W.G. and A.R. Newton. 1983. *Mesozoic and Tertiary Geology of Southern Africa*. A.A. Balkema, Rotterdam.
1,383. Waldman, M. 1970. A third specimen of lower Cretaceous feather from Victoria Australia. *Condor*, **72**:377.
1,384. Dumont, J.P.C. and R.M. Robertson. 1986. Neuronal circuits: an evolutionary perspective. *Science*, **233**:849-853.

1,385. Arbas, E.A. 1983. Neural correlates of flight loss in a Mexican Grasshopper, *Barytettix psolus*. I. motor and sensory cells. *J. Comp. Neurol.*, **216**:369-378.
1,386. Graziadei, P.P.C. and G.A.M. Graziadei. 1985. Neurogenesis and Plasticity of the olfactory sensory neurons. *Ann. N.Y. Acad. Sci.*, **457**:127-142.
1,387. Stewart, A.J., Blake, D.H. and C.D. Ollier. 1986. Cambrian river terraces and ridgetops in central Australia: oldest persisting landforms? *Science*, **233**:758-761.
1,388. Brown, J.H. and A.C. Gibson. 1983. *Biogeography*. C.V. Moseby Co., St. Louis.
1,389. Thompson, R.F. 1986. The neurobiology of learning and memory. *Science*, **233**:941-947.
1,390. Kerr, R.A. 1986. Ancient river system across Africa proposed. *ibid.*, **233**:940.
1,391. Kavanau, J.L. 1967. Behavior of captive White-Footed Mice. *ibid.*, **155**:1623-1639.
1,392. Greene, H.W. 1986. Natural history and evolutionary biology. In *Predator-Prey Relationships*, Martin, E.F. and G.V. Lauder, eds., pp. 99-108. U. Chicago Press.
1,393. Basinger, J.F. and D.L. Dilcher. 1984. Ancient bisexual flowers. *Science*, **224**:511-513.
1,394. Dilcher, D.L. and W.L. Kovach. 1986. Early angiosperm reproduction: *Caloda delevoryana* gen. et sp. nov., a new fructification from the Dakota Formation of Kansas. *Amer. J. Bot.*, **73**:1230-1237.
1,395. Mutter, J.C. 1986. Seismic images of plate boundaries. *Sci. Amer.*, **254(2)**:66-75.
1,396. Nickell, W.P. 1943. Observations on the nesting of a Killdeer. *Wilson Bull.*, **55**:23-28.
1,397. Walters, J. 1956. Eirückgewinnung und Nistplatzorientierung bei See- und Flussregenpfeifer (*Charadrius alexandrinus*). *Limosa*, **29**:103-129.
1,398. Olson, S.L. and D.T. Rasmussen. 1986. Paleoenvironment of the earliest hominoids: new evidence from the Oligocene avifauna of Egypt. *Science*, **233**:1202-1204.
1,399. Johnson, W.C. and C.S. Adkisson. 1986. Airlifting the oaks. *Nat. Hist.*, **95(10)**:40-47.
1,400. Kerr, R.A., 1986. Mapping orbital effects on climate. *Science*, **234**:283-284
1,401. Rivier, C., Rivier, J. and W. Vale. 1986. Inhibin-mediated feedback control of follicle-stimulating hormone secretion in the female rat. *Science*, **234**:205-208.
1,402. Blackburn, D.G., and H.E. Evans. 1986. Why are there no viviparous birds? *Amer. Nat.*, **128**:164-190
1,403. Gould, S.J., 1986. Of kiwi eggs and the Liberty Bell. *Nat. Hist.*, **95(11)**:20-29.
1,404. Bakker, R.T. 1986. How dinosaurs invented flowers. *Nat. Hist.*, **95(11)**:30-38.
1,405. Hallam, A. 1985. A review of Mesozoic climates. *J. Geol. Soc. Lond.*, **142**:433-445.
1,406. Reid, B. and G.R. Williams. 1975. The kiwi. In *Biogeography and Ecology in New Zealand*, G. Kuschel, ed., pp. 301-330, D.W. Junk, The Hague.
1,407. Kinski, F.C. 1971. The consistent presence of paired ovaries in the kiwi (Apteryx) with some discussion of this condition in other birds. *J. Ornithol.*, **112**:334-357
1,408. Calder. W.A. 1979. The kiwi and egg design: evolution as a package deal. *Bioscience*, **29(8)**:461-467.

Multiauthored Treatises and Symposia Volumes Consulted

Acoustical Communication in Birds, vol. 2 (199*)
Advances in Herpetology and Evolutionary Biology (881)
Advances in the study of Behavior, vol. 1 (96)
Animal Mind-Human Mind (99)
Avian Biology, vols. I(103), II(318), III(414), IV(420) V(425), VI(431), VII(245) VIII(573)
Avian Endocrinology (Mikami, Homma, and Wada; 1,110)
Avian Endocrinology (Epple and Stetson; 915)
Avian Energetics (973)
Avian Physiology, 2nd ed. (500), 3rd ed. (510)

The Beginnings of Birds (1,179)
Behavior and Evolution (295)
Behavior and Neurology of Lizards (766)
Behavior and Reproductive Biology of Sea Turtles (771)
Behavioral Embryology (1,159)
Biogeography and Ecology in Australia (68)
Biological Rhythms in Birds: Neural and Endocrine Aspects (1,014)
Biology of Bats (782)
Biology and Comparative Physiology of Birds, vols. 1(333), 2(342)
Biology of Deserts (1,297)
The Biology of Marsupials (279)
Biology of the Reptilia, vols. 5(404), 7(356), 8(876), 9(877) 12(360), 14(754), 15(763)
The Biopsychology of Development (1,276)
Bird Conservation, vol. 1 (663)
Birds: Brain and Behavior (383)

Cerebral Lateralization in Non-Human Species (1,249)
Changing Concepts of the Nervous System (1,360)
A Cold Look at the Warm-Blooded Dinosuars (407)
The Comparative Anatomy of the Nervous System of Vertebrates, Including Man (58)
Comparative and Evolutionary Aspects of the Vertebrate Central Nervous System (43)
Comparative Physiology of Thermoregulation (37)
Comparative Psychology (1,303)
Control of Ovulation (1,038)
Current Ornithology, vols. 1(193), 2(205), 3(1,319)

The Development of Behavior: Comparative and Evolutionary Aspects (600)
Development and Evolution (1,237)
Development and Evolution of Behavior (1,270)
Development and Evolution of Brain Size (1,102)
Deserts of the World (1,307)
Diseases of Cage and Aviary Birds (439)

Ecological Biogeography of Australia (1,057)
Ecology and Evolution of Social Organization (963)
Endangered Birds: Management Techniques for Preserving Threatened Species (566)
Environmental Endocrinology (134)
Evolution (1,212)
Evolution of Brain and Behavior: Persistent Problems (400)
Evolution of Brain and Behavior in Vertebrates (398)
Evolution and Development (980)
Evolution and Environment (1,109)
Evolution Today (1,246)
Experimental Behavioral Ecology and Sociobiology (1,205)

Fish Physiology, vol. 3 (863)
Form and Function in Birds, vols. 1(618), 2(625), 3(795)

The Genetics of Behavior (569)

*Reference number of the first citation of the work.

AUTHOR INDEX

Authors and pages

C

N

REFERENCE NUMBER INDEX

Reference numbers and page numbers

SCIENTIFIC NAME INDEX

COMMON NAME INDEX

GENERAL INDEX